Germ

THE ROUGH GUIDE

The Rough Guide to Germany Credits

Text Editor: Jack Holland
Proofreading: Pat Yale
Typesetting: Andy Hilliard, Gail Jammy
Production: Susanne Hillen, Vivien Antwi

Rough Guide Series Editor: Mark Ellingham

Special thanks are due to Jack Holland, who kept faith with this book to the end, supervising it through all its long and complicated processes with unfailing dedication and good humour; also to John Gawthrop, for filling many gaps and for so much last-minute assistance in getting everything completed.

For their hospitality, help, encouragement and advice, thanks to Helen McLachlan, Claire Sharp, the Woizick family, Beta Korsak for endless patience and second opinions, Marianne Sauter, Tony Leicester, Janet Barrie, Peter Bork for providing bar facilities in Berlin, Stefan and Renate Loose, Klaus Schindler, Catherine Charley, Annekathrin Gordos, Birgit Lang, the Stechow family, Claudia Zahn, Andreas Schlegel and Bernd Oppermann; to all the tourist offices in Germany who provided so much useful source material; to Agatha Suess and the staff of the German National Tourist Office in London for consistently speedy responses to requests for information; to the many East German families who shared their experiences of life under totalitarian rule; and to all the dozens of readers – and in particular Dale Langford for an exceptionally useful letter – who wrote in with comments about the previous guide to West Germany. Please keep writing!

This edition published 1992 by Rough Guides Ltd, 1 Mercer Street, London WC2H 9QJ.
Reprinted 1992 and 1993.

Distributed by the Penguin Group:
Penguin Books Ltd, 27 Wrights Lane, London W8 5TZ
Penguin Books USA Inc., 375 Hudson Street, New York 10014, USA
Penguin Books Australia Ltd, 487 Maroondah Highway, PO Box 257, Ringwood, Victoria 3134, Australia
Penguin Books Canada Ltd, 10 Alcorn Avenue, Toronto, Ontario, Canada M4V 1E4
Penguin Books (NZ) Ltd, 182–190 Wairau Road, Auckland 10, New Zealand

Parts of this book were originally published in the UK as *West Germany: the Rough Guide* by Harrap Columbus.
Previous edition published in the US and Canada as *The Real Guide Germany*.

Typeset in Linotron Univers and Century Old Style to an original design by Andrew Oliver.
Printed in the United Kingdom by Cox and Wyman Ltd (Reading).
Illustrations in Part One and Part Three by Edward Briant.
Basics illustration by Simon Fell; Contexts illustration by David Loftus.

1024p. Includes index.

A catalogue record for this book is available from the British Library.

ISBN 1-85828-025-7

Germany

THE ROUGH GUIDE

Written and researched by
Gordon McLachlan

With additional accounts by
John Gawthrop, Jack Holland, Jackie Jones, Phil Lee,
Natascha Norton, Claire Sharp and Claire Terry

THE ROUGH GUIDES

CONTENTS

Introduction viii

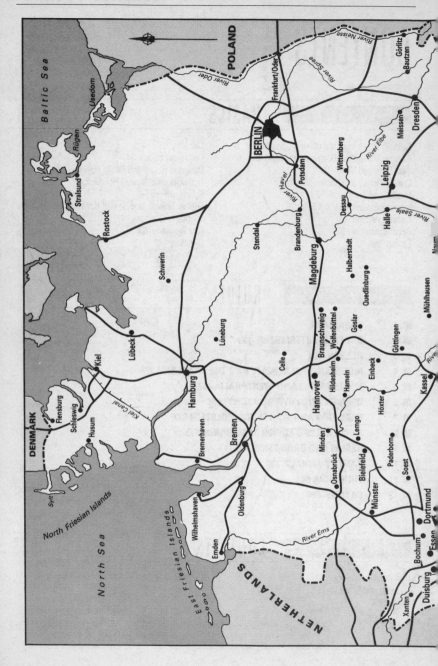

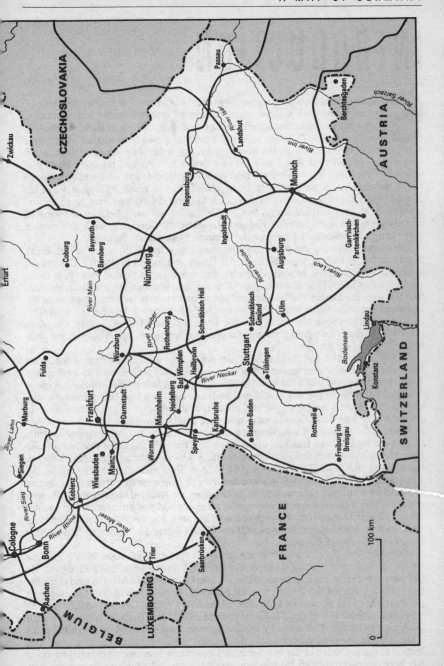

INTRODUCTION

Germany has always been the problem child of Europe. For over a millennium it was no more than a loose confederation of separate states and territories, whose number at times topped the thousand mark. When unification belatedly came about in 1871, it was achieved almost exclusively by military might; as a direct result of this, the new nation was consumed by a thirst for power and expansion abroad. Defeat in World War I only led to a desire for revenge, the consequence of which was the Third Reich, a regime bent on mass genocide and on European, indeed world, domination. It took another tragic global war to crush this system and its people. When the victors quarrelled over how to prevent Germany ever again becoming dominant, they divided it into two hostile states; the parts held by the western powers were developed into the **Federal Republic of Germany**, while the eastern zone occupied by the Soviets became the **German Democratic Republic**.

The contest between the two was an unequal one – the GDR, never able to break free from being a client state of the Soviet Union and forced to adopt a Communist system at odds with the national character, had fallen so far behind its rival in living standards that in 1961 the authorities constructed the notorious electrified barbed wire frontier, with the **Berlin Wall** as its lynchpin, to halt emigration – the first time in the history of the world that a fortification system had been erected by a regime against its own people. Thereafter, the society settled down, but the GDR was a grey, cheerless place whose much trumpted economic success was a mirage, and bought at the price of terrible pollution problems.

On the other hand, the Federal Republic– which was seen as the natural successor to the old Reich, if only on account of its size – had not only picked itself up by the bootstraps, but developed into what many outsiders regarded as a **model modern society**. A nation with little in the way of a liberal tradition, and even less of a democratic one, quickly developed a degree of political maturity that put other countries to shame. In atonement for past sins, the new state committed itself to providing a haven for foreign refugees and dissidents. It also became a multiracial and multicultural society – even if the reason for this was less one of penance than the self-interested need to acquire extra cheap labour to fuel the economic boom. A delicate balançe was struck between the old and the new. Historic town centres were immaculately restored, while the corporate skyscrapers and well-stocked department stores represented a commitment to a modern consumer society. Vast sums of money are lavished on preserving the best of the country's cultural legacy, yet equally generous budgets are allocated to encouraging all kinds of contemporary expression in the arts. The uncanny mix of European tradition and American vitality was as if the United States had managed to acquire a few thousand years of history.

Officially, the Federal Republic was always a "provisional" state, biding its time before national re-unification occured. Yet there was a realisation that nobody outside Germany was really much in favour of this. "I love Germany so much I'm glad there are two of them", scoffed the French novelist François Mauriac, articulating the unspoken gut reactions of the powers on both sides of the Iron Curtain. German division may be cruel, but at least it had provided a lasting solution to the German "problem". Such thinking was rendered obsolete by the unstoppable momentum of events in the wake of the **Wende**, the peaceful revolution that toppled the Communist regime in the GDR, leading to the full union of the two Germanys less than a year later. Yet initial euphoria has been quickly replaced by concern about the myriad problems facing the new nation as it attempts to integrate the bankrupt social and economic system of the GDR into the successful framework of the Federal Republic. While Germany may officially be one again, it will certainly continue to look and feel like two separate countries until the end of the century – and probably well beyond. Moreover, international pressure has ensured that, far from being a re-creation of the old Reich, it can be no more than the nineteenth-century concept of a *Kleines Deutschland* ("little Germany"), excluding not only Austria but also the "lost" Eastern Territories, which are now part of Poland, Czechoslovakia and Russia.

In total contrast to Germany's intrinsic fascination as the country which has played such a determining role in the history of the twentieth century, is its otherwise predominantly **romantic image**. This is the land of fairy-tale castles, of thick dark forests, of the legends collected by the Brothers Grimm, of perfectly preserved timber-framed medieval towns, and of jovial locals swilling from huge foaming mugs of beer. As always, there *is* some truth in these stereotypes, though most of them are conditioned by the southern part of the country, particularly **Bavaria**, which, as a predominantly rural and Catholic area, stands apart from the urbanised Protestant northern part of the country which engineered the unity of the nation last century and thereafter dominated its affairs.

Regional characteristics, indeed, are a strong feature of German life, and there are many hangovers from the days when the country was a political patchwork, even though some historical provinces have vanished from the map and others have merged. More detail on each of the current Länder, as the constituent states are now known, can be found in the chapter introductions. **Hamburg** and **Bremen**, for example, retain their age-old status as free cities. The Imperial capital, **Berlin**, also stands apart, as an island in the midst of the erstwhile GDR where the rich liberalism of the West was pushed to its extreme, sometimes decadent, always exciting. In polar opposition to it, and as a corrective to the normal view of the Germans as an essentially serious race, is the **Rhineland**, where the great river's majestic sweep has spawned a particularly rich fund of legends and folklore, and where the locals are imbued with a Mediterranean-type sense of fun. The five **new Länder** which have supplanted the GDR, and in particular the small towns and rural areas, are in many ways the ones which best encapsulate the feel and appearance of Germany as it was before the war and the onset of foreign influences which were an inevitable consequence of defeat.

Where and when to go

There's enough variety within all but the smallest Länder to fill several weeks of travel, and you may prefer to confine your trip to just one or two regions. Among the **scenic highlights** are the Bavarian Alps, the Bodensee, the Black Forest, the valleys of the Rhine and Mosel, the Baltic island of Rügen, the Harz, and Saxon Switzerland. However, you may prefer one of the many less spectacular areas of natural beauty, which can be found in every province – these are the places the Germans themselves love the most, and where they spend their holidays and weekends. Several of the cities have the air of capitals, though **Bonn** has lost the role it "temporarily" carried for fifty years. Nearby **Cologne**, on the other hand, is one of the most characterful cities in the country, and the richest in historic monuments. Bavaria's capital, **Munich**, is another obvious star and boasts of having the best the country has to offer – whether in museums, beer, fashion or sport. **Nürnberg** reflects on its bygone years of glory, while **Frankfurt** looks on itself as the "real" capital of the country; and **Stuttgart** and **Düsseldorf** compete for the title of champion of German postwar success. In the east, **Dresden** is making a comeback as one of the world's great cultural centres, while **Leipzig** is getting ready to return to its role as one of the continent's main trading centres. However, as all these cities have suffered to a considerable extent from bomb damage and ugly postwar redevelopment, the smaller places in many respects offer a richer experience. Chief among such places is the university city of **Heidelberg**, star and guiding light of the Romantic movement. Trier, Bamberg, Regensburg, Rothenburg and Marburg in the west, and Potsdam, Meissen and Quedlinburg in the east, are among the many towns which deserve to be regarded among the most outstanding in Europe.

The best **times to go** are between April and October. Germany has a fairly volatile climate, not so very different from Britain's. Summers are usually warm, but not over-poweringly so; good weather may come at an unexpected time, while it's not uncommon to have several abrupt changes in temperature within a single day. Rain occurs fairly regularly throughout the year. Unless you're intending to go skiing, winter travel can't really be recommended, other than for seeing the cities stripped of tourist hordes. Otherwise, there's a chance of snow at any time from November onwards. In the really popular areas, the claustrophobic effect of masses of organised tour groups is a factor to be taken into account between mid-June and mid-September: best avoid such places altogether then, and head for the many less spoiled alternatives. All things considered, however, the ideal times for visiting Germany are late spring and early autumn.

AVERAGE TEMPERATURES (°F)		Berlin	Frankfurt	Hamburg	Munich
January	Max	48	50	36	35
	Min	10	14	28	23
February	Max	52	54	37	38
	Min	10	16	28	23
March	Max	63	66	44	48
	Min	19	25	31	30
April	Max	72	75	55	56
	Min	28	32	38	38
May	Max	82	84	64	64
	Min	36	37	46	45
June	Max	86	88	69	70
	Min	43	45	51	51
July	Max	90	91	73	74
	Min	48	50	55	36
August	Max	88	90	72	73
	Min	46	48	54	55
September	Max	82	82	66	67
	Min	39	41	49	54
October	Max	70	70	55	62
	Min	30	32	43	48
November	Max	55	59	45	56
	Min	25	27	37	40
December	Max	50	52	39	44
	Min	16	19	31	33

To convert °Fahrenheit to °Centigrade subtract 32 and multiply by 5/9
Rainfall is consistent throughout the year for all the above cities, at 2–3 inches per month; only Munich exceeds this, with an average 4–6 inches per month in summer

PART ONE

THE
BASICS

GETTING THERE FROM THE USA AND CANADA

Partly as a result of the presence of US military forces, German cities, especially those in the west, are well-served by US airlines. Fares between North America and Germany are among the cheapest transatlantic crossings, and there's rarely any financial advantage to stopping off in another country en route. Frankfurt, Germany's largest airport, handles most international flights, followed by Munich, Hamburg, Berlin, Stuttgart and Dusseldorf. Lufthansa, the German national airline, currently has the only direct flights from the US or Canada to what used to be East Germany, serving Dresden and Leipzig via Frankfurt.

FLIGHTS FROM THE USA

While certain airlines offer regular non-stop services to Germany from a few US cities, it usually works out less expensive to change at New York or other major airports. Discounters advertising in the travel sections of the Sunday papers have the most competitive fares, often for consolidated seats on major airlines rather than on charter flights. These, however, can be costly to change. If you meet their conditions, student/youth and independent travel agencies like *Council Travel* or *STA Travel* are also worth contacting.

Given the wealth of budget options available, the APEX offerings of the major carriers like *TWA* and *Lufthansa* are rarely good value, but sometimes offer perks like a week's free car rental or discount rail travel. All prices are subject to US airport taxes and surcharges, currently $28.

FROM THE EAST COAST

No matter what season, fares on the **New York–Frankfurt route** are among the best travel bargains going, with seat consolidator prices through *TFI Tours*, 34 W. 32nd Street (☎212/736 1140 or ☎1-800/825 3834) beginning at around $210 one-way, $350 round-trip in winter, rising to around $250 one-way, $500 round-trip during the peak summer season. Often as not these are for non-stop flights on major carriers, though such cheap fares are rarely available directly through the airlines.

Fares to **other German cities** are only slightly higher but somewhat harder to come by, though in the off-season especially you can pick up some great deals. For example, *Delta* has offered $478 round-trip fares to anywhere they fly in Germany – Frankfurt, Munich, Berlin or Hamburg – from any major US city. However, during the peak summer season this rises to a whopping $1056.

Among the **agencies**, *STA Travel* offers one-way fares from New York for between $220 and $350 depending on the season; it costs roughly the same no matter where you fly to in Germany, but count on an additional $50 to $100 if you start your journey from anywhere other than New York. One-ways usually cost half the round-trip fare, plus $20.

TOLL-FREE AIRLINE NUMBERS

American Airlines ☎ 1-800/433-7300
Air Canada ☎ 1-800/776-3000
British Airways ☎ 1-800/247-9297
Delta ☎1-800/241 4141
KLM ☎ 1-800/777-5553

LTU ☎ ☎1-800/888-0200
Lufthansa ☎ 1-800/645-3880
Sabena ☎ 1-800/955-2000
TWA ☎ 1-800/221-2000
United Airlines ☎ 1-800/241-6522

AIRLINES IN THE US AND CANADA

Air Canada, 26th Floor, Place Air Canada, 500 Dorchester Blvd W, Montréal, PQ H2Z 1X5 (☎514/879 7000).

Air France, 888 Seventh Ave, New York, NY 10106 (☎212/830-4000 or 800/237-2747); 875 N Michigan Ave, Chicago, IL 60611 (☎312/440-7922); 2000 rue Mansfield, Montréal, PQ H3A 3A3 (☎514/284-2825); 151 Bloor St W, Suite 600, Toronto, ON M5S 1S4 (☎416/922-5024).

American Airlines, PO Box 619616, Dallas/Fort Worth International Airport, Dallas, TX 75261 (☎817/267-1151 or 800/433-7300).

British Airways, 530 Fifth Ave, New York, NY 10017 (☎800/2479297); 1001 bd de Maisonneuve Ouest, Montréal, PQ H3C8 (☎800/668-1059); 112 Kent St, Ottawa, ON K1P 5P2 (☎613/236-0881); 1 Dundas St West, Toronto, ON M5G 2B2 (☎416/250-0880).

Canadian Airlines, 2500 Four Bentall Center, 1055 Dunsmuir St, Box 49370, Vancouver, BC V7X 1R9 (☎604/270 5211)

Continental Airlines, 2929 Allen Parkway, Houston, TX 77019 (☎713/821-2100 or 800/231-0856).

Delta Airlines, Hartsfield Atlanta International Airport, Atlanta, GA 30320 (☎404/765-5000).

Icelandair, 360 W 31st St, New York, NY 10001 (☎212/967-8888 or 800/223-5500).

KLM, 565 Taxter Rd, Elmsford, NY 10523 (☎212/759-3600 or 800/777-5553); 225 N Michigan Ave, Chicago, IL 60601 (☎212/861-9292); 1255 Green Ave, West Mount, Montréal PQ H3Z 2A4 (☎514/933-1314 or 800/361-5073).

Northwest Airlines, Minneapolis-St Paul International Airport, St Paul, MN 55111 (☎612/726-1234 or 800/225-2525).

Sabena, 720 Fifth Ave, New York, NY 100022 (☎800/955-2000); 5959 W. Century Blvd, Los Angeles, CA 90045 (☎213/642-7735); 1001 bd de Maisonneuve Ouest, Montréal, PQ H3A 3C8 (☎514/845-0215).

Swissair, 608 Fifth Ave, New York, NY 10020 (☎718/995-8400 or 800/221-7370); 2 Bloor St W, Suite 502, Toronto, ON M5S 2V1 (☎416/960-4270).

TWA, 100 South Bedford Rd, Mount Kisco, NY 10549 (☎212/290-2141 or 800/892-4141).

United Airlines, PO Box 66100, Chicago, IL 60666 (☎708/952-4000 or 800/241-6522).

US Air, Crystal Park Four, 2345 Crystal Drive, Arlington, VA 22227 (☎703/418-7000 or 800/622-1015).

UTA, 323 Geary St, Suite 401, San Francisco, CA 94102 (☎415/397 84 00)

Virgin Atlantic Airways, 96 Horton St, New York, NY 10014 (☎212/206-6612 or 800/862-8621).

Besides Lufthansa, another airline to try is *LTU*, which bills itself as "Germany's other airline" and has flights out of New York and Miami to Frankfurt, Munich or Dusseldorf for $399 in winter, $599 during the summer peak season.

FROM THE WEST COAST

Flying from the **West Coast** isn't that much more expensive than flying out of New York; in fact, especially in the off-season, you can pick up round-trip flights from LA, San Francisco or Seattle to Frankfurt for around $450 – which means you can travel to Europe for not much more than it costs to fly across the country. During shoulder and peak seasons prices are still very low, starting around $600 round-trip. As usual, the best fares are available through the seat consolidators advertising in the travel sections of the Sunday *LA Times* or the *San Francisco Examiner/Chronicle*. APEX fares on Lufthansa and other major carriers start at around $700 round-trip in low season, rising to well over $1000 in summer.

DIRECT FROM CANADA

Canadians have fewer budget options than Americans, and you'll probably do best travelling to New York and buying a flight from there. One budget possibility that's more of an option for Canadians is to fly to London and make your way from there. Also, many of the budget flights offered through the student/youth travel agency *Travel Cuts* involve a mandatory change in London, and you can stop over for a week or so at little or no extra charge. The best selection is out of **Toronto**, with one-way flights to Frankfurt starting at CDN$400, CDN$750 round-trip. From Montreal, count on spending CDN$650–850 depending on the season. APEX fares from Vancouver to Frankfurt on Air Canada cost from CDN$788 in winter, CDN$1404 in summer.

DISCOUNT FLIGHT AGENTS AND CONSOLIDATORS IN THE US AND CANADA

Access International, 101 W 31st St, Suite 104, New York, NY 10001 (☎800/TAKE-OFF). *Consolidator with good East Coast and central US deals.*

Airkit, 1125 W 6th St, Los Angeles, CA 90017 (☎213/957-9304). *West Coast consolidator with seats from San Francisco and LA.*

Council Travel, 205 E 42nd St, New York, NY 10017 (☎212/661-1450). 312 Sutter St, Suite 407, San Francisco, CA 94108; (☎415/421-3473); 14515 Ventura Blvd, Suite 250, Sherman Oaks, CA 91403 (☎818/905-5777); 1138 13th St, Boulder, CO 80302 (☎818/905-5777); 1210 Potomac St NW, Washington, DC 20007(☎202/337-6464); 1153 N Dearborn St, Chicago, IL 60610 (☎312/951-0585); 729 Boylston St, Suite 201, Boston, MA 02116 (☎617/266-1926) 1501 University Ave SE, Room 300, Minneapolis, MN 55414 (☎612/379-2323); 2000 Guadalupe St, Suite 6, Austin, TX 78705 (☎512/472-4931); 1314 Northeast 43rd St, Suite 210, Seattle, WA 98105; ☎206/632-2448. *Nationwide US student travel organisation.*

Discount Club of America, 61-33 Woodhaven Blvd, Rego Park, NY 11374 (☎718/335-9612). *East Coast discount travel club.*

Discount Travel International, Ives Bldg, 114 Forrest Ave, Suite 205, Narbeth, PA 19072 (☎215/668-2182 or 800/221-8139). *Good deals from the East Coast*

Encore Short Notice, 4501 Forbes Blvd, Lanham, MD 20706 (☎301/459-8020 or 800/638-0830). *East Coast travel club.*

Interworld, 3400 Coral Way, Miami, FL 33145 (☎305/443-4929). *Southeastern US consolidator.*

Moment's Notice, 425 Madison Ave, New York, NY 10017 (☎212/486-0503). *Travel club that's good for last-minute deals.*

Nouvelles Frontières, 12 E 33rd St, New York, NY 10016 (☎212/779-2600); 800 bd de Maisonneuve Est, Montréal, PQ H2L 4L8 (☎514/288-9942). *French discount travel firm. Other branches in LA, San Francisco and Quebec City.*

STA Travel, ☎800-777-0112 (nationwide); 48 E 11th St, Suite 805, New York, NY 10003 (tele-sales ☎212/986 9470); 7202 Melrose Ave, Los Angeles, CA 90046 (tele-sales ☎213/937 5781); 82 Shattuck Sq, Berkeley, CA 94704 (☎510/841 1037); 166 Geary St, Suite 702, San Francisco, CA 94108 (☎415/391 8407); 273 Newbury St, Boston, MA 02116; (☎617/266-6014). *Worldwide specialist in independent travel.*

Stand Buys, 311 W Superior St, Chicago, IL 60610 (☎800/331-0257). *Good Midwestern travel club.*

Travel Cuts, Head Office: 187 College St, Toronto, ON M5T 1P7 (☎416/979-2406). Others include: MacEwan Hall Student Centre, University of Calgary, Calgary, AL T2N 1N4 (☎403/282-7687); 12304 Jasper Av, Edmonton, AL T5N 3K5 (☎403/488 8487); 6139 South St, Halifax, NS B3H 4J2 (☎902/494-7027); 1613 rue St Denis, Montréal, PQ H2X 3K3; (☎514/843-8511); 1 Stewart St, Ottawa, ON K1N 6H7 (☎613/238 8222); 100–2383 CH St Foy, St Foy, G1V 1T1 (☎418/654 0224); Place Riel Campus Centre, University of Saskatchewan, Saskatoon S7N 0W0 (☎306/975-3722); 501–602 W Hastings, Vancouver V6B 1P2 (☎604/681 9136); University Centre, University of Manitoba, Winnipeg R3T 2N2 (☎204/269-9530). *Canadian student travel organisation.*

Travelers Advantage, 49 Music Sq, Nashville, TN 37203 (☎800/548-1116). *Reliable travel club.*

Travac, 1177 N Warson Rd, St Louis, MO 63132 (☎800/872-8800). *Good central US consolidator.*

Travel Avenue, 130 S Jefferson, Chicago, IL 60606 (☎312/876-1116 or 800/333-3335). *Discount travel agent.*

Unitravel, 1177 N Warson Rd, St Louis, MO 63132 (☎800/325-2222). *Good, reliable consolidator.*

Worldwide Discount Travel Club, 1674 Meridian Ave, Miami Beach, FL 33139 (☎305/534-2082).

TRANSITING VIA EUROPE

Though it may be more interesting, it's not usually cheaper to stop over in **another European country** and make your way to Germany from there. You may occasionally find cheap flights to **Paris** (on *UTA*) or **Amsterdam** (on *KLM*, which recently joined forces with *Northwest*), but the most common deals available through the seat consolidators are on scheduled airlines plying long-haul routes to the Gulf States, almost all of which stop in **London**. From mainland Europe, **trains** are the cheapest and easiest way to make the final leg to Germany; from England, flying is sometimes as cheap as ground travel and can save a day or two — see the following pages for details.

GETTING THERE FROM BRITAIN AND IRELAND

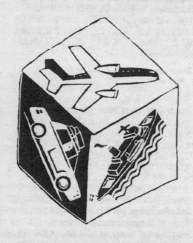

BY PLANE

It's easy and quick to **fly** to Germany from the UK: every major west German city has numerous daily links with London (Heathrow and Gatwick), as well as with several regional UK airports. Flight times are around 1hr to 1hr 30min hours. Often you'll find that the lowest fares and the most frequent flights are to Frankfurt, very much at the centre of German air routes — so if you're planning a lot of travelling within Germany, it can be worth your while beginning your explorations there. To fly to other German cities costs slightly more, and Berlin is most expensive of all to reach, as much as twice the lowest fare to Frankfurt. However, it's well worth the cost if you're planning on travelling in the former GDR, which has as yet few direct air links with Britain.

In general, seasonal variations are slight and there are few short-term **special deals**, although it's always a good idea to check the latest offers by scanning the travel pages of the Sunday newspapers and, if you're in London, *Time Out* or the many giveaway magazines. Details of cut-rate flights from other UK cities will, of course, be advertised in local newspapers.

Of the companies who specialise in cheap flights to Germany, the **German Travel Centre** (see box for address) consistently has the most attractive prices — like most discounted plane fares, their tickets carry restrictions regarding minimum and maximum stays and the ability to change the return date, but if you're visiting for at least a weekend and staying for not more than a month or two you'll be able to take up some extremely good return flight options: specimen fares are Düsseldorf £84, Frankfurt £78, Hamburg £105, Munich £126 and Berlin £121. Usually these flights will be short hops with airlines on long-haul routes to the Gulf states or the USA, and they all leave from London.

Also worth investigating are the flights offered by **GTF Tours**. This is particularly true in the low season (between October and Easter), when their rates, except to Frankfurt, are generally cheaper than those of their competitors.

From regional UK airports the best offers (besides any charter flight you may be able to pick up; see below) are the *British Airways' Poundstretcher* deals: from Manchester (to Düsseldorf £97, Frankfurt £114, Hamburg £121, Munich £112, Berlin £149); Birmingham (to Frankfurt £104, Hamburg £111, Munich £129, Düsseldorf £86); and Glasgow (to Frankfurt £125, Düsseldorf £107, Berlin £160). Any high street travel agent will have the full details.

Booking a regular ticket with *British Airways* or the German national carrier *Lufthansa* is out of the question for anybody on any kind of budget, since they charge two or even three times as much as what you'll find elsewhere, even for the so-called "Eurobudget" and "Youth fares" – both around £200 return.

If you can find one, **charter flights** – whereby you fill the vacant seats on a plane booked by a major holiday company – may save you a few pounds over the cheapest discounted fares, but you're limited in flexibility, and such flights are few and far between. It's no better news for **students** or anyone **under 26**, since student fares are rarely lower than can be found

AIRLINES AND AGENTS

British Airways, 156 Regent St, London W1R 5TA (☎081/897 4000).

Campus Travel, 52 Grosvenor Gardens, London SW1W 0AG (☎071/730 3402).

Council Travel, 28a Poland St, London W1 (☎071/287 3337).

Dan Air, 21 Cockspur St, London SW1 (Charter ☎071/839 1192; scheduled ☎0345/100 200).

German Travel Centre, 8 Earlham St, London WC2 (☎071/836 4444).

GTF Tours, 182–186 Kensington Church St, London W8 4DP (☎071/792 1260).

Lufthansa, 23–26 Piccadilly, London W1V 0EJ (☎071/408 0322).

STA Travel, 86 Old Brompton Rd, London SW7 3LQ and 117 Euston Rd, London NW1 2SX

elsewhere, although independent travel specialists like **STA Travel** and **USIT/Campus Travel** are certainly worth contacting for cheap fares.

FROM EIRE

Prices between Ireland and Germany are pretty high, and even the youth and student fares offered by the independent experts **USIT** (19/21 Austin Quay, Dublin 2 ☎01/778117) are steep: from Dublin, typical *one-way* fares are: to Düsseldorf IR£82, Frankfurt IR£87, Hamburg IR£92, Munich IR£102; flying to Berlin requires booking a flight to London and a separate one onward, costing IR£168 in total.

FROM AUSTRALIA AND NEW ZEALAND

Unfortunately, there's no financial short cut other than buying a ticket to London and then another on to Germany from there. The lowest current one-way fares from Australia to London are around A$1200, and from New Zealand, NZ$1220.

BY TRAIN

Unless you qualify for one of the discounts listed below, there are no savings to be made travelling to Germany **by train**: in fact you'll usually be paying more than travelling by plane or coach. The only exceptions to this are the **European Saver** fares offered to Hamburg (£54), Bonn, Cologne and Düsseldorf (£59 each), and Dortmund (£65), and these limit you to just four days at your destination. Otherwise, **regular return tickets** are valid for two months and you're permitted to stopover en route. Prices from London to the main cities are: Düsseldorf £73, Frankfurt £95, Hamburg £118, Munich £120, Berlin £137, Leipzig £139 and Dresden £150.

Rail travel is more economically feasible if you're a **student** or **under 26**, or aged **60 or over**. Those in the first two categories qualify for the discounted fares offered by **Eurotrain** (52 Grosvenor Gardens, London SW1W 0AG ☎071/730 3402), whose return fares from London are: to Düsseldorf £57.80, Frankfurt £79.60, Hamburg £65.80, Munich £111.80, Berlin £99.60, Leipzig £123, and Dresden £132.

Another cash-saving possibility for those resident in Europe for the preceding six months is the **InterRail pass**. For those **under 26** this currently costs £175 for one month's travel (or £145 for 15 days) on all European (and Moroccan) railways and gives half-priced discounts on British trains and some cross-Channel ferries. Alternatively, the **over 26 card** gives the same benefits to older travellers, minus the concessions on British trains and the ferries. This is available for £235 for a month, or £175 for 15 days. Obviously these passes can be used on Germany's extensive rail network (see *Getting Around*) and could cut costs significantly if well used.

If you're 60 or over, the **Rail Europ Senior Card** brings you 30% discounts on rail and sea travel in most of Western Europe, including Germany. To obtain this card, you must first have a *Senior Citizen Railcard* (details from any railway station) and pay an extra £7.50 at any British Rail Travel Centre or travel agent specialising in European rail.

Most **routings** from London are daily and cross the Channel from Victoria via Dover to Ostend (taking 1hr 40min) or from Liverpool Street via Harwich to the Hook of Holland (6hr 30min). Some trips between Dover and Ostend use the *Jetfoil* service but, though this saves time, it also lands you with a £6.50 surcharge. The only other crossing is with the *Scandinavian Seaways* boat from Harwich to Hamburg (see *By*

Boat, below). Once you have crossed the Channel, connections are simple and speedy – getting you to Frankfurt in six hours and to Berlin in ten, for example.

BY COACH

Travelling to Germany by **coach** won't bring any major savings over the cheapest air fares, and the journey will be long and uncomfortable, interrupted every 3–4 hours by stops at motorway services. There are, however, plenty of options, all run by **Eurolines** (52 Grosvenor Gardens, London SW1W 0AG ☎071/730 0202) from London (Victoria), and bookable through travel agents.

Summer frequencies, timings and return fares to the major cities are: to Cologne (daily, 13hrs) £56; Frankfurt (three a week, 18hrs) £65; Hamburg (five a week, 22hr 30min) £70; Munich (three a week, 23hrs 30min)) £82; Berlin (four a week, 26hr) £90. Winter departures are only slightly fewer and fares are the same as during the summer.

If you're **outside London**, *Eurolines* will book you a *National Express* coach to London but with no reduction over the usual domestic fare. Another option from elsewhere in the country is the *Transline* service, also run by *Eurolines* and aimed at British military personnel stationed in Germany. These services travel directly (ie you don't have to change coaches in London) to Germany from all over the UK, including Cardiff, Bristol, Glasgow, Edinburgh and the major cities in northern England. The disadvantage is that the coaches travel to military bases, often some distance from the big German cities. From London, *Transline* fares are £59–66.

There are **student** and under 26 **youth fares** on offer but they only shave a few pounds off the adult fares and are not available on the *Transline* service. Some **discount agents**, who you'll see advertised in newspapers and listings magazines, may also be able to reduce prices but, again, not by more than a few pounds.

BY BOAT

There's only one **ferry** which plies directly from the UK to Germany, run by *Scandinavian Seaways* between Harwich and Hamburg from mid-March to the end of September. The trip lasts 20½ hours and passengers are required to book at least a couchette berth, which makes the lowest single fare £70 during the peak period (mid-June to the start of September) and £55 at other times, provided both outward and inward journeys are made on a Monday, Tuesday or Wednesday (**students** qualify for a 50% reduction on these fares). Travelling at the weekend costs about half as much again.

On this boat you can also take your car, £40 each way for an average-sized one, although obviously this is only a good idea if you're planning to spend your time in northern Germany or are driving on to Berlin or the former GDR. If you're aiming instead for the Rhineland and the south, it's a far better bet to take one of the main **shorter Channel crossings** by boat or hovercraft from Dover, Folkestone or Ramsgate (operated by *P&O*, *Sealink* and *Sally Lines*) to Boulogne, Calais or Dunkerque in France, or to Ostend or Zeebrugge in Belgium, or from Harwich to the Hook of Holland – any of which will leave a drive of no more than 2–3 hours to the German border (for more details on these ferries and driving to Germany, see *By Car* below). From the **north of England**, there's a routing from Hull to Zeebrugge or Rotterdam with *North Sea Ferries*, whose summer passenger fares are £41 each way, with a 50% **student reduction** on midweek fares.

Any travel agent in the UK should be able to provide details and make ferry bookings for you, which should be done well in advance especially if you're travelling during the summer or over holiday periods.

BY CAR AND HITCHING

By car to Germany, the hardest choice you'll have to make is where to cross the Channel (see *By Boat*, above), a decision dependent simply on which part of Germany you're heading for. For northern Germany or Berlin and the former GDR, you'll save time by taking a boat to Holland (or, of course, directly to Hamburg), but for anywhere else you're best off landing either in Belgium or France. The complicated algebra of fuel costs against ferry tariffs to determine which is the cheapest route is, frankly, not worth the bother of calculating for the small savings which you might make. That said, it's an idea to check with travel agents for any special cross-Channel deals on offer, although in general there's little to choose between the main operators in south-east

---

CROSS-CHANNEL FERRY LINES

From Britain

Scandinavian Seaways Parkeston Quay, Harwich, Essex CO2 4QG (☎0255/241234, in London 15 Hanover St, London W1 ☎071/4936696).

Sealink/Stena Lines Charter House, Park St, Ashford, Kent TN24 8EX (☎0233/647047).

Hoverspeed Maybrook House, Queens Gardens, Dover, Kent, CT17 9UQ (☎0304/240241).

North Sea Ferries King George Dock, Hedon Rd., Hull, N. Humberside HU9 5QA (☎0482/795141).

P&O European Ferries Channel House, Channel View Rd, Dover, Kent, CT17 9TJ (☎0304 203388).

Sally Lines 81 Piccadilly, London, W1V 0JH (☎071/409 2240)

From Ireland

Irish Ferries 2–4 Merrion Row, Dublin 2 (☎01/610511).

England. You'll spend about £13 for each person and £53 for a vehicle in summer (or around £170 for two people and a car using the hovercraft crossing).

From Hull, *North Sea Ferries* (see above) will take your car to Zeebrugge or Rotterdam for a further £52 each way. You can also put your motor on the *Scandinavian Seaways* sailing directly from Harwich to Hamburg (see above) for £40 each way.

Once across, particularly if you drive through Holland or Belgium – less so in France – you'll rarely be travelling on anything but motorways all the way to any German city (and international border formalities are virtually non-existent – you'll be waved straight through unless you or your vehicle look highly suspicious). From the Channel ports allow about 3 hours to Cologne or Düsseldorf, 6–7 to Hamburg or Frankfurt, and 12 to Munich or Berlin. For practical details on driving in Germany see *Getting Around*. Both the *AA* and *RAC* publish **route maps** of the areas you'll be passing through, and it's worth getting hold of these; they're free to members.

Most **hitch-hikers** who start thumbing in the UK will be expected to pay for their ferry passage, and should aim for either Ostend or the Hook of Holland, which are the most strategic hitching routes towards Germany. For all but the absolutely penniless, it's a smarter idea to buy a coach or boat ticket to one of these ports and start hitching from there. One innovative alternative is the German *Mitfahrzentralen* organisation, whose bureaux put drivers and hikers in touch for a small fee and a contribution towards petrol (for example Munich–London DM90). They have offices throughout Germany: see *Getting Around* for more details.

PACKAGE HOLIDAYS

Most travel agents have brochures detailing the many **package holidays** to Germany. For the most part, however, you'll pay far more than would be the case if you arrange everything yourself. But if you're in a rush or just can't be bothered with the donkey work, they do represent a reliable and normally well-organised alternative.

The most common type of package, and also the best value, are **motoring holidays**, whereby you drive your own car to Germany and have pre-arranged accommodation (and sometimes meals) in hotels or guest houses in several locations. The pick of these are operated by *DER Travel Service* (18 Conduit St, London W1R 9TD ☎071/408 0111), who have a wide selection of packages all over Germany and whose prices include ferry travel from a choice of five UK ports. Typical charges are around £200 for a week for two people in the Rhineland or Black Forest, roughly £20 more for Bavaria, although prices vary and it's worth booking as early as you can before the best deals are snapped up.

The same company offers **fly-drive packages,** whereby you fly to a German city and pick up a hired car there; a much wider selection of this type of deal is offered by *GTF Tours* (address above). A particularly imaginative example is their "go-as-you-please" tour, which includes vouchers which can be redeemed at any of 96 hotels all over Germany (except, as yet, in the former GDR). Prices, based on four people travelling together, begin at £295 per person for 5 nights. A separate fly-drive package, this time with a fixed itinerary, is also offered to eastern Germany, costing from £452 for 7 nights.

Similar, and also fairly common, are **self-catering packages**, such as those run by **Hoverspeed** (Maybrook House, Queens Gardens, Dover CT17 9UQ ☎0304/240241, or in London ☎071/554 7061), who have holiday bungalows and chalets scattered around some scenic but fairly isolated parts of the German countryside. If this appeals, these holidays can be money savers for largish groups (ie four–eight people), since prices are based on a car and two adults sharing, and each extra adult pays just £25 per week (although taking a second car costs £80–100 depending on season). For two people, costs work out at around £300 for a week and include the hovercraft crossing from Dover.

Less worthwhile are the short **city breaks** offered by most major travel agents, which provide you with a flight and hotel accommodation in a German city for three to seven nights. Without exception you'll be spending as much as £100 more over a week than you would if you booked a flight and found the accommodation yourself. If you're still interested, however, expect to spend £240 for three nights in Berlin, slightly less for other cities.

There are also a number of German organisations who run **cycling tours** which include accommodation: full details from the German National Tourist Office in London (see *Information and Maps*).

RED TAPE AND VISAS

British and other EC nationals can all enter Germany on a valid passport. British subjects can also enter the country on a UK Visitors' Passport, available from post offices for £7.50. The official time limit for stays in the country is 90 days, but enforcement of this is fairly lax: it's unlikely, for example, that your passport will be date-stamped on arrival.

US, Canadian, Australian and New Zealand passport holders can also enter the country for 90 days (in any one year) for a touristic visit without a visa: however you're strongly advised, if you know your stay will be longer than this, to apply for an extension visa from the local German embassy *before* you go. In order to extend a stay once in the country, all visitors should contact the *Ausländeramt* (Alien Authorities) in the nearest large town: addresses are in the phone books.

EC nationals are also entitled to **work in Germany**, but anyone else has to have secured a job **before** arrival in order to get a work permit, for which they should apply to their local German consulate or embassy. For casual labour jobs during harvests or in the hotel and catering trades, nobody is going to ask too many questions, but wages are accordingly low and the work tough.

GERMAN EMBASSIES

Great Britain 23 Belgrave Square, London SW1X 8PZ (☎071/235 5033).

Eire 31 Trimelston Ave, Booterstown, Blackrock, Co. Dublin (☎1/693011).

USA 4645 Reservoir Rd NW, Washington 20007 (☎202/298 4000).

Canada PO Box 379, Post Station A, Ottawa, Ont. K1N 8V4 (☎613/232-1101).

Australia 119 Empire Circuit, Yarralumia A.C., Canberra 2600 (☎62/701911).

New Zealand 90–92 Hobson St., Wellington (☎4/736063).

COSTS, MONEY AND BANKS

Despite the cost of unification, Germany is still one of the world's most industrialised and wealthiest consumer societies, and its currency, the Deutschmark, is one by which international financial standards are set. It's also a cash society: people carry money with them, rather than rely on credit cards. In the face of these facts, it's surprising that this is a country that's affordable to travel in, with the reasonable price of food and accommodation helping keep costs down.

At the time of writing the exchange rate was DM2.8 to the pound sterling, DM1.67 to the US dollar.

COSTS

If you're prepared to cut every corner by staying in youth hostels or campsites, and never eating out, you could get by on upwards of DM40–50 (£14–17) per day, though DM60–80 is a more realistic budget on which to enjoy yourself properly. If you have the means to spend a bit more than that, you should be able to live really well. Bear in mind that visiting cities will cost far more than staying in the countryside, (with a trip to Berlin guaranteed to knock a large hole in any budget), and that travel in the former GDR (which was previously a rip-off) is now markedly cheaper in almost every respect than in west Germany. If you intend to base yourself mainly in the east, you should be able to reduce the above figures by a quarter.

But wherever you travel, it's essential to beware of a number of possible pitfalls, as it's all too easy to end up spending two or three times as much as these figures.

Accommodation costs per person can be confined to an average of about DM15 per day for youth hostels, around DM20–25 for rooms in private houses, and around DM30–40 for basic guest houses and hotels: there's rarely anything saved by taking double rooms, which cost roughly twice the above rates. **Food** prices in shops are slightly lower than in Britain, and eating out is markedly cheaper at every level – except for the scarcity of bargain lunches. Snack bars abound, and for around DM8 you can put together a very filling meal. DM20 should buy a hearty German meal plus drink in a pub-restaurant, while a decent dinner in a classy restaurant can often be had for DM30, or not much more. **Drink** is marginally more expensive than in Britain, but the quality, especially of the beer, is significantly higher.

Public transport is the one area where prices are likely to present a problem. A single fare within a city, for example, is often as high as DM3, while a sample single train fare from Munich to Frankfurt would be DM95. The only ways in which you can soften these costs are to utilise rail and other passes, confine your travel to a limited area, or make use of the organised alternative, the *Mitfahrzentralen* (see "Getting Around").

MONEY

German currency is the *Deutschmark*, which comes in **notes** of DM5, DM10, DM20, DM50, DM100, DM200, DM500 and DM1000; and **coins** of DM0.01 (one *Pfennig*), DM0.05, DM0.10, DM0.20, DM0.50, DM1, DM2 and DM5. You can bring as much currency as you wish into Germany.

TRAVELLERS' CHEQUES AND CREDIT CARDS

Travellers' cheques are the safest way of carrying the majority of your money. They can be cashed in any bank or exchange office, and used in flashier shops in larger cities. **Eurocheques** (issued by most British banks with a Eurocheque card) can be used without any problems everywhere, both in banks and shops or restaurants. If you're using them to get cash you pay a 1.6% fee to the bank, plus a small handling fee chargeable to your UK bank account.

Unusually, for such a consumer-orientated society, **credit cards** are little used in Germany: only the major cards will be known and accepted, and then only in large department stores or upscale restaurants in the larger cities.

Should you need **cash** on your plastic, the *Deutsches Verkehrsbank* (see below) will give a cash advance against *Visa* and *Master Card* (*Access*) cards, subject to a DM150–200 minimum. Various other banks offer cash advance facilities – look for stickers in their windows to find out which credit card they're associated with. *American Express* card holders can use that company's facilities in the major cities.

BANKS

Banking hours are Monday to Friday 9am–noon and 1.30–3.30pm, with late opening on Thursday until 6pm, though these are often extended. If you're on a tight budget, it may be worth shopping around several banks (including the savings banks or *Sparkasse*), as the rates of exchange offered can vary, as can the amount of commission deducted. The latter tends to be a flat rate, meaning that small-scale transactions should be avoided whenever possible.

Exchange facilities for cash and travellers' cheques can be found in virtually all banks (except in the former GDR, where this service is still fairly underdeveloped) as well as in commercial exchange shops called *Wechselstuben*, usually located near stations and airports, though often also in city centres, on the main shopping street. The *Deutsches Verkehrsbank* has branches in railway stations of most main cities; these are generally (but not invariably) open seven days a week, and until quite late in the evening.

HEALTH AND INSURANCE

British and other EC nationals are entitled to free medical care in Germany on production of a form E111, available from main post offices or the DSS Leaflets Unit, PO Box 21, Stanmore, Middlesex HA7 1AY. Officially, you need to apply for your E111 at least two weeks before you leave. Without this form you'll have to pay in full for all medical treatment, which is expensive – currently a minimum of DM40 for a visit to the doctor.

Whether or not you get an E111, it's sensible to take out some form of **travel insurance**, since this not only covers medical expenses, but also insures your money and belongings against loss or theft. But before you purchase any insurance, check what you may have already. North Americans, in particular, may find themselves covered for medical expenses and loss of or damage to valuables while abroad, as part of a family or student policy.

Travel insurance schemes, from around £20 (US$32) per month, are sold by all travel agents: *ISIS* polices, from *STA Travel* or branches of *Endsleigh Insurance* (London office: 97–107 Southampton Row, WC1 4AG; ☎071/580 4311), are usually good value. Remember that you have to keep all receipts of medical services if you want to make an insurance claim back home, and that any claims for theft need to be registered at the local police station.

APOTHEKEN

To get a prescription made up you need to go to an *Apotheke*: pharmacists here are well-trained and often speak English. *Apotheken* serving **international prescriptions** can be found in most large cities, and a rota of **late-opening** or **24-hour Apotheken** in larger towns is posted on all Apotheken doors. German doctors usually speak English, but if you want to be certain, your consulate can provide a list of English-speaking doctors in the major cities. In the event of an **emergency** anywhere in the country, phone ☎110 for the police, who will get you an ambulance.

INFORMATION AND MAPS

Before you leave, it's worth contacting the German National Tourist Office, who have extensive information on campsites, youth hostels, hotels, train timetables and many glossy brochures besides. In London their office is at 65 Curzon Street, W1Y 7PE (☎071/495 3990).

ON THE SPOT INFORMATION

This is rarely a problem in Germany. You'll find **tourist offices** everywhere, even in tiny villages – addresses are listed in the guide. In western Germany they're almost universally friendly and very efficient, providing large amounts of free and often useful literature, maps and glossy bumph in a selection of languages. A few places charge for these, but the majority provide them free. The German word for a tourist office is *Fremdenverkehrsamt* (or just *Verkehrsamt*) though many sport a sign saying *Tourist Information*. Another useful facility is that they can book a room for you, for which there's normally a small fee (though not inevitably) a small fee (see "Accommodation").

Many **tourist offices in the former GDR** have been quick to grasp the potential of an increased number of visitors, and are already as well geared-up as their counterparts in the west. Others, however, are still stuck in a Communist time-warp, with a hostility to the very notion of public service. Be particularly wary of being asked to buy overpriced and shoddy-looking overstocks of leaflets made under the old regime: not only is the propaganda they espouse tiresome, they're of limited practical use as they will still show now-suppressed street names. Note that east German tourist offices will book rooms in private houses (though usually not in hotels) for a DM1–5 fee.

The **German National Travel Agency** is universally represented by the *DER* offices, generally to be found near train stations or next to tourist offices. They'll book your national and international train tickets, as well as provide general information about travel onwards from Germany. It's worth knowing that there's a *DER* office in London at 18 Conduit St, W1R 9TD (☎071/499 0577).

MAPS

German **maps** set international standards, and there's no shortage of excellent regional, motor-

GERMAN NATIONAL TOURIST OFFICES

Australia
Lufthansa House, 12th floor, 143 Macquarie Street, Sydney (☎02/221 1008).

Belgium
Rue du Luxembourg 23, Brussels (☎02/512 7744).

Denmark
Vesterbrogade 6 D III, Copenhagen (☎01/1207095).

Holland
Hoogoorddreef 76, Amsterdam (☎020/978066).

Norway
Klingenberggt 7, Oslo (☎02/422380).

Sweden
Birger Jarlsgatan 11, Stockholm (☎08/145095).

USA
747 Third Avenue West, New York, NY 10017; ☎212/308 3300.

44 S. Flower St., Suite 220, Los Angeles, CA 90017; ☎213/668 7332.

Place Bonaventure, Montréal, Québec H5A 1B8; ☎514/8778 9885.

ing and hiking maps in most bookshops, newsagents and tourist offices. The best general maps are those printed by *RV* or *Kümmerly and Frey*, whose 1:500,000 map is the most detailed single sheet of the country available.

Specialist maps marking cycling routes or alpine hikes can be bought in the relevant regions, and addresses for written or personal enquiries are listed in the Guide. Information on German **alpine climbs and hikes** can be obtained from the *Deutscher Alpenverein*, Prater Insel 5, 8000 München 22. Other useful reference guides available are: *Fahrrad-Atlas* (DM14.95),

the best for cycle routes in Germany; and *Mitfahrzentralen in Europa* (DM6), which is in three languages and lists all hiking agencies, their fees and regional accommodation options. If you'd like to order these books before starting your journey write to *DJH-Hauptverband*, Postfach 220, 4930 Detmold. In Britain, the best selections of maps are at *Stanfords* (12-14 Long Acre, London WC2 9LP; ☎071/836 1321). In the USA, try the *Complete Traveller*, 199 Madison Ave, New York NY10016 (☎212/685 9007) or the *Rand McNally Mapstore*, 150 East 52nd St, New York NY10022 ☎212/758 7488.

GETTING AROUND

While it may not be cheap, getting around Germany is spectacularly quick and easy. Barely a square inch of the country is untouched by an unfailingly reliable public transport system and driving, too, at least in the west, is a painless, straightforward affair (once you've adapted to the high speeds) on what's probably the best road network on the continent. Other forms of travel are equally well-organised and it's a simple matter to jump from train to bus on the integrated network. Costs can be offset by various discounts available to visitors, and it's worth studying all the options outlined below before committing yourself.

TRAINS

THE WEST

By far the best means of public transport in western Germany are trains: the **rail network**, operated by the national company *Deutsche Bundesbahn (DB)*, covers most of the country, and where natural obstacles or a sparse population make rail routes unrealistic, *DB*s buses

(*Bahnbusse*, see below) take over. North–south travel is particularly straightforward, while east–west journeys are likely to be less direct and require a change of train (or bus) along the way. Everywhere services are fairly punctual (except on Sundays, when slight delays are commonplace) and very efficient, although generally more expensive than their equivalents in the UK, averaging about DM23 per 100km.

There are several **types of train**: most luxurious is the new 250km per hour **InterCityExpress (ICE)**, which – as yet – only operates on the Hamburg–Frankfurt–Munich route; the supplement to be paid increases with the distance travelled. Otherwise, the fastest and most comfortable trains, and the best option between major cities, are the **InterCity (IC)** and **EuroCity (EC)** trains (identical except that the *EC*s cross international borders). With these you can travel from one end of the country to the other – Hamburg to Munich, for example, takes 6½ hours. The only drawback is the supplement (*Zuschlag*) of DM7 (or DM6 if you buy it at the station before boarding the train), which is compulsory unless you've already invested in a *German Rail Pass*: see below).

Slightly downscale from the *IC*s and *EC*s are the new *InterRegio (IR)* trains offering a swift service between smaller centres – and charging a DM4 supplement for journeys of under 50km. You may still find yourself travelling on the rolling stock they're designed to replace – the relatively cumbersome *D-Zug*, or – slowest of the lot – the ambling *E-Zug* trains. Around major cities, the S-Bahn is a commuter network on which **InterRail** cards and the *German Rail Pass* are valid; though neither can be used on the underground U-Bahn system, or on municipally-owned trams and buses.

The colossal national **timetable** (*Kursbuch*) can be bought from stations for DM10, though it's too bulky to be easily portable. A condensed version of it (*Städteverbindungen*), concentrating on routes between cities, can be obtained from Thomas Cook offices or the DER Travel Service; it comes free with the German Rail Pass. Otherwise, you can easily plan your route by picking up the many free leaflets detailing inter-city services, available at any main railway station.

TICKET TYPES

Regular tickets (*Fahrkarten*) are valid for two months and permit you to break the journey as often as you wish. Prices are based on distance travelled and therefore a return will cost the same as two singles. If you're making a lot of rail journeys and don't have an InterRail pass, it's extremely sensible to buy one of the **discount passes** exclusively for foreigners, available from the DER Travel Service in London, and a number of agents around the country. Officially, these are not on sale in Germany itself, other than at frontier posts such as Aachen or Konstanz. However, provided you can prove you are not resident in Germany, you should be able to buy them at main stations in the major cities.

The broadest-ranging pass is the **German Rail Pass**, which entitles the holder to unlimited travel on all trains and *Bahnbusse* in the former West Germany, on DR trains in the former East Germany, on the buses which ply the tourist-orientated "scenic routes" such as *Burgenstrasse* ("Castle Road"), *Rhein-Mosel*, *Romantische Strasse* ("Romantic Road") and *Schwarzwald Hochstrasse* ("Black Forest Highway"), and the *K-D Line* steamers on the Mosel and on the Rhine between Cologne and Mainz (see "By Boat", below).

Valid for five, ten or fifteen days (not necessarily consecutive) within the period of a month,

the German Rail Pass can be excellent value. There's a slightly cheaper version for those **under 26**, known as the **Junior Tourist Card** (*Juniortouristenkarte*), which offers the same benefits at reduced prices.

More localised but still temptingly priced, the **DB Regional Rail Rover** (*Regionaltourenkarte*) gives unlimited travel on trains and *Bahnbusse* for any 10 days out of 21 in a specific area of West Germany – 30 different regions in all, including all the main holiday spots. The pass costs £33 for one person, £45 for two people or £55 for a family group (one or both parents or grandparents accompanied by any number of unmarried children under 18). It's best bought before you leave, as to qualify for one when in Germany you'll need a return rail ticket into your chosen area that totals over 250km in *each* direction.

GROUP TRAVEL, KIDS AND COUCHETTES

There are various other possibilities for **several people travelling together**. The *Sparpreis* and *Supersparpreis* fares for return journeys of over 200km entail one person paying the full fare, while those accompanying (up to four adults and one child) pay half-price. *Supersparpreis* tickets (which are around twenty percent cheaper) cannot be used on Fridays or Sundays after 10am. Lesser reductions are also available for families and small groups making return journeys of between 50km and 200km, and (on singles as well as returns) for six or more adults travelling in a group.

If travelling with **kids**, note that those under 4 travel free, while those between 4 and 11 travel for half the adult price. On long journeys, such as from the North Sea coast to Bavaria, it's worth considering travelling **overnight**. Couchettes (which are not segregated by sex) are a reasonable bargain at DM25 in a 6-berth cabin, DM35 in a 4-berth, but sleepers are very expensive at upwards of DM65. If aiming to sit up, avoid Fridays and Sundays, when conditions can be very cramped; on other nights you should manage to find an empty or near-empty compartment.

RAIL PASSES			
	5 days	10 days	15 days
German Rail Pass (Over 26)	£99	£149	£179
Junior Tourist Card (Under 26)	£69	£ 89	£109

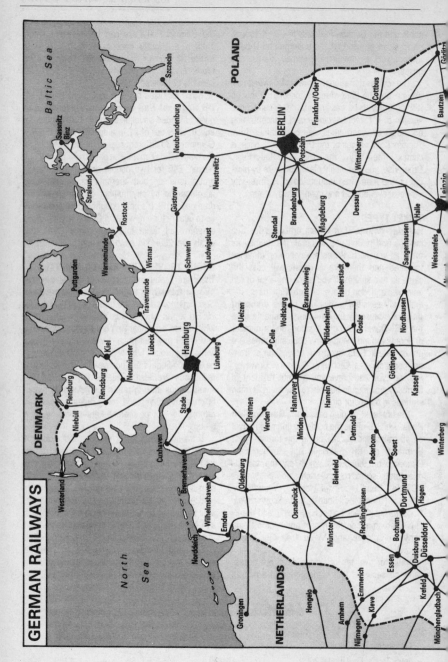

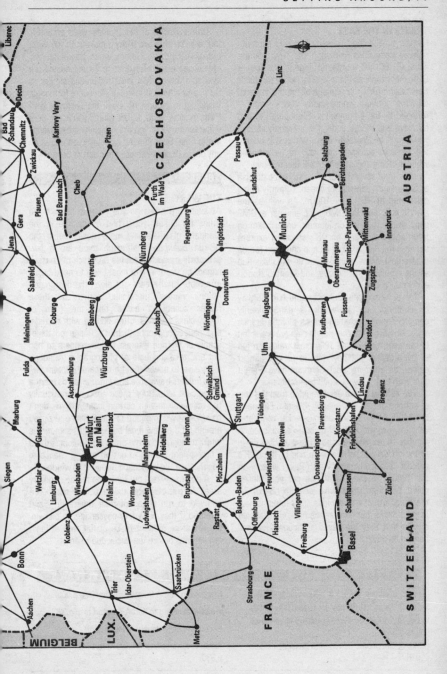

TRAINS IN THE EAST

For the time being, Germany has two separate railway companies: although DB now operate some IC, EC and InterRegio lines in the former GDR, most services there are still run by *Deutsche Reichsbahn (DR)*, the remains of the old imperial railways network whose name was – oddly – retained by the Communists. Eventually the two railways will merge under the cunningly-chosen new name of *Deutsche Bahn*, which will enable the western acronym and logo to be retained while avoiding accusations of another takeover.

In spite of several price hikes since the demise of Communism, **fares** are cheap, currently being calculated at DM12 for 100km. As well as the standard IC and EC DM6 supplements, a DM3 supplement is levied on journeys under 50km on InterRegio trains and on DR's so-called express services (marked as D or Ex and shown in red on timetables). Most trains, however, are classified as the dreaded *Personenzug*, and seem to stop at every milk churn.

Never having been subject to much in the way of cutbacks, the **network** is extraordinarily comprehensive, including scores of little branch lines. However, Beeching-style cuts are predicted in the near future: until 1990 most trains ran full to overflowing, but now they're usually almost empty, as so many east Germans have bought cars with their newly-earned Deutschmarks.

The **rolling stock** used, ranging from the sort of antique diesels last seen in Western Europe in the 1960s to lumbering double-decker commuter vehicles, can make travel quite an experience. A number of **narrow-gauge steam railways** in active passenger service were one of the GDR's biggest tourist magnets with foreign visitors. In the 1980s, an average of one per year closed down, but eight still survive (see box below). As these operate at a heavy loss, their future is now in the balance, but popular nostalgia alone should ensure that they are saved – though they may have to be privatised.

One downside of the unmodernised system is that **most trains are filthy** – make sure you wear old or discardable clothes when travelling. The low prices also mean that few concessions are available, other than child reductions similar to DB's, and a limited range of discounts for people travelling in groups. Although the **German Rail Pass** is now valid on DR trains, you'll get poor value for money if you use it mainly or exclusively in the east. Bear in mind too that it isn't valid on any buses or cruise ships in this part of Germany.

BUSES

THE WEST

At such rare times as you *have* to forsake the trains for buses, you'll find no decline in the standard of efficiency, many buses being the DB-run *Bahnbusse*, although there are a few **privately operated routes** on which rail passes cannot be used. You're most likely to need buses in remote rural areas – or along the designated "scenic routes" mentioned earlier. On these routes scheduled buses take the form of luxury-class coaches, often packed with tourists, and pause long enough by the major points of scenic or historic interest for passengers to hop out and take a couple of photographs. Although expensive to use without a railcard (*German Rail Pass* holders travel free and *InterRail* cards merit a 50 percent reduction), these coaches are usually the only way to visit certain locales if you don't have your own transport or the patience to zigzag around on the slow local buses (trains sometimes whizz through the same areas but seldom is there a convenient station to get off at or a chance to see much of the landscape through the windows).

A point to watch out for in the remoter country areas is **punctuality**: unlike trains, buses are allowed to run ahead of their timetable – and often do if they have few passengers to pick up. It's therefore prudent to be at the stop at least ten minutes before the bus is due to arrive.

EASTERN GERMANY'S NARROW-GAUGE STEAM RAILWAYS

Island of Rügen: Putbus to Göhren (see p.696)

Bad Doberan to Kühlungsborn West (see p.682)

The *Harzquerbahn*: Wernigerode to Nordhausen (see p.823)

The *Selketalbahn*: Gernrode to Hasselfelde (see p.817)

Cranzahl to Kurort Oberwiesenthal (see p.906)

Freital-Hainsberg to Kurort Kipsdorf (see p.920)

Radebeul Ost to Radeburg (see p.920)

Zittau to Kurort Jonsdorf and Kurort Oybin (see p.930)

Finally, note that Germany, unlike Britain, does not have **long-distance** bus companies undercutting the railways. Indeed, the only – and very limited – opportunities for inter-city bus travel are on stretches of the long-haul international routes.

THE EAST

Given the extensiveness of the rail network, there's even less need to resort to buses in the former GDR than in west Germany, although in rural areas you'll often find that they offer more direct routes and thus major savings in terms of time. Fares are broadly similar to those of the trains. Buses are operated by municipal transport authorities rather than by DR, so rail passes are *not* valid. A few luxury coaches have been introduced on the longer routes; conditions on shorter journeys – which generally use the "accordion bus" with its sparse provision of seats – can still be rather cramped despite the fall-off in custom since the demise of Communism.

BOATS

Travelling by **boat** is another option, though more for relaxation than covering large distances. All along the **Rhine** and **Mosel** rivers, and on various Bavarian lakes, there are innumerable local boats waiting to ferry you across or around the waters for a small sum. For a longer trip, *K-D Line* steamers sail on the Rhine between Cologne and Mainz, and on the Mosel between Koblenz and Cochem, every day from April to October inclusive. On this vessel, possession of a German Rail Pass will get you free passage – although with any other railcard you'll need to pay the full fare.

The steamers call at many riverside hamlets and you can get on or off wherever you want. The fare, as you'd expect, depends on how far you travel; Cologne to Koblenz, for example, costs DM69, although you can make savings by taking a return journey along a shortish section, such as Koblenz to Lorelei and back for DM27.40. Several smaller companies also operate short-haul services along both the Rhine and Mosel, and along most other main navigable rivers as well. The best bargains are to be found in the former GDR, where there are particularly beautiful cruises to be had on the Elbe, particularly the stretch from Dresden south into Czechoslovakia.

Germany's biggest lake, an enormous bulge in the Rhine called the **Bodensee**, is also a prime spot for water-borne travel, either for a lazy cruise or to explore the nooks and crannies of its shoreline, which spans Austria and Switzerland as well as Germany; full details are in Chapter One, *Baden-Württemberg*.

TRAMS

THE WEST

Municipal transport in most western German cities is still centred on **trams**. More often than not, these are sleek modern numbers capable of moving at a fair speed between stops; nowadays, they also often have an underground stretch in the city centre, where they're known as the **U-Bahn**. This is often a source of confusion; it's important to remember that cities such as Berlin and Munich have a much more extensive U-Bahn system using tube trains as distinct from trams, while in cities with trams only you may have to look both above and below ground in the central area to find the stop for the service you want. **Buses** are also much in use, particularly in servicing suburbs and outlying areas.

Tickets, which can be bought from automatic vending machines or the driver, are valid on all the different forms of transport (which include the S-Bahn and mainline trains as well in conurbations such as Frankfurt, Stuttgart, Cologne-Bonn and the Ruhrgebiet) and you can change from one to another, with no supplement for transfers. **Single** fares are expensive – DM3 is the minimum rate in many cities. It's therefore advisable either to buy in **blocks** (usually offering a total saving of around 30%), or invest in a **fixed time period** (generally 24 hours) ticket. The latter can be a tremendous bargain – in some cities, up to two adults and two children are covered by the ticket, for an outlay of around DM9.

THE EAST

Old boneshaker **trams** are the mainstay of the public transport system in east German cities, and should serve most of your requirements, although you may have to take the occasional **bus**. The same **tickets** are valid in both, and, if several times the price they were only a couple of years ago, are still a bargain, with DM0.50 having been established as the standard price in the vast majority of cities since 1991. **Buying** them, however, can be a problem, as they are seldom available from drivers, and the first automatic vending machines have only just begun to appear. Instead, they have to be purchased from ticket offices (there's usually one outside main stations) or from agents (the tourist office is a good bet, otherwise try shops and kiosks at random). Two points to watch out for are that in some cities you can only buy tickets in blocks, and that it can be very difficult or even impossible to buy them on Saturday afternoons and Sundays – a legacy from the old Communist system. This won't be an acceptable excuse if you're confronted by an inspector, so if you find yourself caught out, try to buy one from a fellow-passenger.

PLANES

While **domestic flights** are numerous and quick between the major cities, they are also expensive; Frankfurt–Hamburg costs DM260, Frankfurt–Berlin DM209, both one-way, for example – clearly only worthwhile if you're in a desperate rush. (If you are, it's worth looking out for any special reductions on return flights since it may save money just to use the return ticket for one-way travel.) There are a few **student fares** although these are only applicable to those living and studying in Germany. Any tourist office or *Lufthansa* agent will be able to provide full details of the current offers. If you definitely want to fly between German cities and are starting and finishing your journey in the UK, it's cheaper to book all the flights together, although this usually means that dates of travel cannot be changed.

CARS

DRIVING IN THE WEST

As well as using the **right-hand side** of the road, west German traffic moves *fast*, and if you're used to doddering along on sedate English country lanes you'll soon be reduced to a bundle of nerves. Once you get used to it, though, driving on west Germany's excellent road system is an unadulterated pleasure. Most of the Gerhard Berger impersonating is done on the motorways, or *Autobahnen* – the most extensive and efficient such network in Europe, though the *Autobahnen* in the north can sometimes be of two lanes only. Petrol stations, roadside restaurants and motels are located every 30–40km, and every city and virtually all the towns are within simple striking distance, using equally high quality secondary roads to link them to the *Autobahnen*. Four-star unleaded petrol currently costs around DM1.25 per litre.

There are no legally enforced **speed limits** on the *Autobahnen* although there is a *recommended* limit of 100–130kmph. There is an official speed limit on country roads of 80–100kmph, and in built-up areas of 50kmph.

After you've remembered which side of the road you should be on, the main **driving rules** to bear in mind are quite simple: traffic coming from the right normally has **right of way**; **seatbelts** are compulsory for those riding in the front seats; and **children under 12 years** must sit at the back. There are **on the spot fines** for speeding and other offences: for speeding these are charged on a sliding scale from about DM20–DM50; after a cut-off point of roughly 25km above the limit, you're charged and taken to court.

Foreigners may drive for one year with a national or international driving licence (for more than a year you must have a German licence). As in the UK, at least third party **insurance** is mandatory (normal third party insurance in the UK doesn't cover foreign travel, although more extensive polices do – check with your insurers to be sure). It's not necessary to carry a Green Card, but some other form of proof of insurance is essential.

If you **break down**, the *ADAC* (*Allgemmeiner Deutscher Automobileclub*) will fix your car free of charge if you are a member of the AA or RAC, if it's a minor problem, but for jobs taking over half an hour you'll have to pay for labour and parts in full (so make sure your insurance covers this). On an *Autobahn*, the *ADAC* can be contacted with one of the **orange emergency telephones**, indicated by yellow luminous markers along the verge. On the phone, ask specifically for "*Stassenwachthilfe*" ('road patrol assistance').

DRIVING IN THE EAST

Driving in the east presents a few minor problems, which it would be wise to bear in mind. The most obvious one is the appalling state of the **roads**. Where the road does have a tarmac covering there are often frighteningly deep **potholes** to contend with. Be ready for flat tyres.

Only the former **transit motorways**, financed in the past by the West German government, are in a reasonable state of repair. Otherwise roads tend to be narrow two-lane stretches of alternating cobblestones and pitted tarmac, with what appear on maps as respectable-looking tertiary roads often turning out to be little more than tracks.

Other on-road **hazards** include eastern boy-racers of all ages (and both sexes) showing off their new (and not-so-new) western cars, drivers of older eastern models who eschew headlamps after dark, and mammoth Soviet trucks lumbering unexpectedly out of forest side roads. Another problem is a scarcity of petrol stations; if you're driving out from Berlin into the hinterland always make sure you fill up before departing. Former *Intertank* (hard-currency) petrol stations are marked on most maps and the ex-transit stretches are usually quite well served, but smaller towns that in the west would probably boast a couple of filling stations often have nothing.

In cities (especially Berlin) be aware also that **trams** always have the right of way. Unfamiliarity with the traffic system means that unwary visiting drivers are prone to cutting in front of turning trams at junctions – a frightening and potentially lethal error. Also, when trams halt at their designated stops it's forbidden to over-take until the tram starts moving, to allow passengers time to cross the road and board.

Speed limits in the east, which will probably change, are 100kmph on motorways, 80kmph on main roads and 50kmph in built-up areas and on railway level-crossings. Another surviving GDR traffic regulation is the "*Grüner Pfeil*", or green arrow attached to traffic lights at the right-hand turning lane at junctions: it means if the light is at red, but no traffic is appoaching from the left, you may proceed. This idiosyncrasy may be done away with, much to the chagrin of most east Germans.

If you **break down**, the reciprocal cover for RAC and AA members provided by *ADAC* (see above) is also available in the east; don't, however, expect the same level of service as in the west, or assume that garages will have anything more than the most obvious spares for the most common of cars.

CAR HIRE
Car hire (*Autovermietung*) is available at most airports and major train stations, and regional tourist offices will always be able to inform you of the nearest car rental firm – although the major companies like *Avis*, *Budget* or *Hertz* are easy to find, smaller local companies often offer better rates. Rates tend to be higher than in the UK (around DM350 for a small hatchback for a week), but you can save quite a bit by booking a week or more in advance through a UK office and picking up (and paying for) the car when you arrive.

The car hire agency *Holiday Autos* (☎081/ 491 1111) guarantees to provide the cheapest rates around. You must pay for everything in England before you leave, and weekly rates for a small car in Germany (including the collision damage waiver and unlimited mileage) start at £138. With the major firms there are no **drop-off charges** (ie you can collect a car, say, from Hamburg, drive it to Munich and return it to the car hire company's office there for no additional fee) although you'll be expected to leave a deposit.

TAXIS
In western cities and towns, taking into account the high cost of local public transport, several people sharing a cab may actually save money over using a local bus or train. Taxis have a sign on the roof which is illuminated if they are free. Hail one from the street, or wait at the taxi stands – alternatively there are always plenty hovering around railway stations and big hotels.

HITCHING

Hitching is common practice all over Germany and with the excellent *Autobahn* network it's usually quite easy to cover long distances in a short time – provided you get a lift *before* you reach the motorway, since hitching (like walking and cycling) on them, or their access roads, is illegal. You're likely to have just as much luck using the secondary roads, or *Bundestrassen*, anyway. The criss-crossing nature of the road system means the drivers will have no idea where you're going unless you remember to make a **sign** stating your destination.

If you don't want to face the uncertainty of traditional hitching, the Germans have developed an institutionalised form called **Mitfahrzentralen**, located in most large cities (including many recently-opened branches in the east) and listed in the *Guide* where applicable. These are agencies that put drivers and hitchers in touch with each other for a nominal fee, and then it's up to the participants to work out an agreeable petrol contribution, usually a simple two-way split, although the agency does suggest a reason-able sum. There's a valuable safety factor in this system, since all drivers have to notify the agen-cies of their addresses and car registration numbers. There are also a few **women-only** hitching agencies, known as *Frauenmitfahr-zentralen* – again, these are listed in the *Guide*.

CYCLING

Cyclists are well catered for in Germany: though (sensibly) they're banned from the *Autobahnen*, many smaller roads have marked cycle-paths, and bike-only lanes are a common sight in cities and towns. Fairly hassle-free **long distance cycling** is possible all over the country, but obviously you'll need a strong pair of legs and a sturdy, reliable machine to get much joy out of the Bavarian Alps (a good map is essential too – see "Information and Maps"). To take your own **bike on a train** (not permitted on *ICs*, *ECs* or small local trains), you need to purchase a "bicycle ticket" or **Fahrrad-Karte** which costs DM8 (reduced to DM4.60 if covering a distance of less than 100km) – and you have to take the bike to the luggage van yourself.

Between April and October, the best place to **hire a bike** is from a railway station participating in the **Fahrrad am Bahnhof** scheme (most of them, in fact), whereby a bike costs just DM10 per day. You can return it to any other participating station and *German Rail Pass* or *InterRail* card holders get a 50% discount. This is obviously perfect for splitting train travel with pedalling as and when the mood, terrain or weather takes you. During the rest of the year, or in an area where there's no suitable station, simply look in the phone book under *Fahrradverleih* to find the address of a local bike rental outlet. Hiring this way, however, means you'll have to leave a deposit, usually around DM50.

WALKING AND HIKING

The German countryside is laced with colour-coded **hiking trails**, most of which are no more arduous than a Sunday afternoon stroll (for a large number of locals, in fact, they *are* Sunday afternoon strolls), though many trails are actually sections of much longer hikes. Very few hikes pass through remote or isolated areas and there's always a village, campsite or youth hostel fairly close by (or even on the route) so you can make a trek of just a few hours or of several days' duration without much trouble. The best of the trails are listed in the *Guide* and the local tourist offices have masses of **information and maps** (*Wanderkarten*) relating to the walks in their area.

Because the hikes are so easy, you won't need any specialist equipment, but make sure you're wearing well-worn-in shoes and have a comfortable day-pack for carrying picnic provisions.

If you're used to hiking in the Scottish Highlands or the English Lake District, you should be aware of **potential frustrations**: the prevalence of trees in all the scenic areas (with the exception of the Bavarian Alps and Swabian Jura) not only means that you're only occasionally rewarded with long-range views, but also ensures that there's seldom much chance to deviate from the regimentation of the marked paths. However, don't let this rigidity fool you into skimping on proper maps: at times the trails can peter out or become confused, particularly when signs have become weather-worn or have been vandalised.

ACCOMMODATION

Be it highrise city hotels or half-timbered guest houses in the country, accommodation of all types is easy to find in Germany and can often be good value – especially in the growing number of rooms available in private houses. For those on a really tight budget, the youth hostels and campsites which proliferate over the entire country are a sound, cost-cutting alternative.

HOTELS

THE WEST

An immensely complicated grading system applies to German **hotels**, with no fewer than 80 classifications according to price and services provided. Despite this, and perhaps ironically, they're all more or less the same: clean, comfortable and functional with conveniences like TV, phone and *en suite* bathroom usually taken for granted in the medium range establishments upwards. The listings in the *Guide* concentrate on the best options from the points of view of convenience and economy. However, you should always call into the nearest tourist office to check any special deals which they may have with local establishments; this can result in you spending less than the figures quoted on the official **hotel lists** which every tourist office provides. Many tourist offices charge around DM3 for finding you a room, but others perform the service gratis. You should take care *not* to turn up in a large town or city when there's a trade fair, or *Messe*, taking place — at such time hotels often double their rates and still manage to get booked solid.

Rarely is there any great saving to be made by two people sharing as opposed to one person travelling alone. In country areas, the least you'll have to spend is about DM30 for a single, DM50 for a double – at least DM10–15 extra for something similar in a city. Remember that any accommodation costs cut by staying on the outskirts of a city will be offset by the high cost of public transport into the centre.

THE EAST

Under Communism, only about sixty **hotels** – most of them in the super-luxury class – were open to foreigners visiting East Germany. While the situation has improved since then, there's likely to be a desperate shortage of hotel rooms for some years to come. This is particularly the case **in cities**, where the demand from visiting businesspeople, mostly from west Germany, means it can be impossible to get a hotel room on weekdays without a reservation months in advance. Grossly inflated prices are another consequence of this failure of supply to meet demand. In **holiday areas**, the situation is much better, thanks to the privatisation of many hotels and homes formerly reserved for trade unions; indeed, there are many remarkable bargains on offer at the moment. The position in medium-sized **towns** is a bit more complex: new owners taking over state-owned hotels generally aim to upgrade them (notably by the provision of seldom-encountered *en suite* facilities). This means that closures can be expected, and that **prices** in the next few years are certain to be volatile. Although the summer 1991 prices have been given in the text, they need to be treated with caution, as within a year many will have doubled.

PENSIONS AND PRIVATE ROOMS

THE WEST

To escape the formality of a hotel, look for one of the plentiful **pensions**, which may be rooms above a bar or restaurant or simply space in a private house; in urban areas these cost about the same as a hotel but in the countryside are usually a bit cheaper. An increasingly prevalent budget option (especially in busy holiday areas) is **bed and breakfast** accommodation in a private house (look for signs saying *Fremdenzimmer* or *Zimmer frei*). These are seldom other than a really good deal: prices vary but are usually around DM25 for a single, DM40 for a double. However, very few west German **cities** have private rooms on offer other than to relieve congestion when there's a trade fair on. Rates are comparable with those of hotels. Also in the more rural areas, and particularly plentiful along the main touring routes, are **country inns** or **guest houses** (*Gasthäuser*). These charge around DM45 per night for a double (much more in really popular areas) in what's usually an atmospheric old building, and the cost includes a wholesome country breakfast.

Farmhouse holidays are increasingly popular in Germany, and in many ways are the best bargains of all, with full board rates from as little as DM30 per day. Full lists are available from local tourist offices; the major snag is that this option is really only feasible if you have your own transport.

THE EAST

To the traveller's advantage, thousands of rooms in **private houses** have become available in what was formerly East Germany since the *Wende*. Starved of contact with westerners for decades, and welcoming the extra cash (a pressing necessity for many as unemployment has soared), many east Germans have done what was forbidden for years, and opened up their houses to guests. Provided you can speak some German, this is an interesting experience in itself, as most people offering this service are extremely friendly and eager to tell you all about life under Communism, and their hopes and fears for the future. Furthermore, **prices** are remarkably low – often even less than a youth hostel or campsite. They begin at as little as DM10 for bed and breakfast, and seldom rise – even in Berlin, Leipzig and Dresden – above DM30. Often you'll be offered a substantial evening snack at no extra charge.

The only snag is finding the houses: this is easy enough in country areas where you only have to look for the *Zimmer frei* signs, but completely impossible in the cities, where many rooms are in highrise flats and thus not advertisable from the street. Nearly all **tourist offices** will book you a room for a fee ranging from DM1–5. There are also a number of privately-run **agencies** competing with them, and these are well worth investigating, as they sometimes have better deals; they're also usually open until late in the evening. However, some charge outrageous mark-ups (sometimes taking as much in commission as they give the family renting the room). Beware in particular of tourist offices or agencies who want to levy a daily fee: in that case, book for one night and then try to negotiate with your hosts. If you're intending to do a lot of travelling in east Germany, it would be a good idea to cut out the middlemen and invest in one of the **directories** of private rooms for rent, of which the most comprehensive is *Herzlich Willkommen – 27,500 Privatquartiere in der DDR* (Mair, DM19.50). In and around Berlin, the London-based company *Berlin Homestays* offers accommodation that can be booked before you leave: see p.720.

YOUTH HOSTELS

In Germany, you're never far away from a **youth hostel** (*Jugendherberge*) – the YH movement was born here, in fact, in 1909 – and these are likely to form the backbone of genuine budget travelling. Note, however, that at any time of the year they're liable to be block-booked by school groups – this is particularly likely on weekdays during the summer, and at weekends out of season. It's therefore advisable to make a reservation by phoning or writing to the hostel as far in advance as possible to be sure of a place – and be prepared to put up with the marauding adolescents. Though most **wardens** and their staff are courteous and helpful, there's an unfortunate minority who seem to be leftovers from the leadership of the Hitler Youth, insisting on rigid regimentation and pedantic enforcement of the rules. You should be wary, too, of **age restrictions** (see below) and the fact that prices are slightly cheaper if you're under 27 years of age.

With the merger of the formerly separate East and West associations in 1991, all hostels are now run by the German Youth Hostel Association

(*Deutschejugendherberge*) and indicated by signs reading "DJH". The hostels divide into a number of **categories** according to facilities and size of room, which determines their price per night: **Grade I** hostels (charging DM12) are basic affairs with large dormitories, sometimes even lacking heating and hot water; **Grade II** (DM14) hostels are slightly better-equipped and usually have eight-bedded rooms; **Grade III** (DM14.50) hostels have four- and six-bedded rooms, more communal leisure rooms and washing facilities; **Grade IV** (DM15.50) hostels are another step up and generally in busier regions, with leisure and sports facilities; while **Grade V** hostels (DM17.50) are essentially the same as those in Grade IV but located in cities. **Grade VI** (DM26.20) hostels are also known as **youth guest houses**, and contain two- and four-bedded rooms; the fee includes full bedlinen.

These prices, which are inclusive bed and breakfast rates, are for IYHA members under 27; those over 27 pay DM2–3 more per night (except in the Grade VI hostel); non-members will be charged an extra DM4 per night. If you're not a member and intend to use hostels for more than a couple of nights, it's wise to buy a year's *IYHF* **membership** for £8 from the *YHA* shop/office at 14 Southampton St, London WC2 (☎071/836 1036), or from your own national association, before leaving. You can buy the same thing at larger hostels in Germany but it's slightly more expensive.

Only **sheet sleeping bags** or sheets are permitted (you may be asked to show them to the warden): and if you don't have either, you can **hire a sleeping bag** for up to 10 days for DM2.

German youth hostels do carry a number of other **rules and restrictions**. **Reservations** will only be held until 6pm unless you've informed the warden that you'll be arriving late. When things are busy, **priority** is given to people under 18, or hiking families travelling with children. Those **over 27**, if they've not made a reservation, are only supposed to get a place if the hostel is not fully booked at 6pm – though this is by no means strictly applied. A more serious restriction for this age group is that they can't use the hostels in **Bavaria** at all, unless accompanying children. All hostels have a **curfew**, which can be as early as 10pm (and usually is in rural areas) but may be later, as is the case in all the big cities. 10pm is usually the latest time you are able to check in. **Length of stay** is officially limited to three days unless a longer period has been booked in advance. You can, however, stay longer – provided you're not going to deprive new arrivals from getting in. In **winter** many hostels close altogether; many more shut every other weekend.

The location of many of the country's youth hostels, plus directions for reaching them by public transport, can be found in the *Guide*. If you need a complete list (there are over 750 in all), it can be found in the German Youth Hostel Association's handbook, called *Deutsches Jugendherbergsverzeichnis*, available at most German hostels and tourist offices for DM8.

The **Naturfreundehaus** association offers a variant on the hostel theme. Its establishments, often located in rural countryside close to towns and cities, are designed more for older people, with accommodation in singles, doubles or very small dorms.

CAMPING

Big, well-managed **campsites** are a feature of Germany, and they're located almost anywhere anybody could even think about wanting to camp. It's significant that sites are officially graded on a scale beginning at "good" and working up to "excellent". Even the lowest grade have toilet and washing facilities and a shop nearby on the site, while the grandest are virtually open-air hotels with swimming pools, supermarkets and various other comforts – though it must be said that camping purists find German sites rather too regi-

mented. **Prices** are based on facilities and location, comprising a fee per person (DM3–5) and per tent (DM3–4). There are extra fees for cars, caravans, etc, so you could easily spend quite a bit more than you might in other countries if there are several of you travelling in a car.

Bear in mind, too, that many sites, especially those in popular holiday areas, are nearly always full from June to September, and you should arrive early in the afternoon for a good chance of getting in. Most campsites close down in the winter, but those in popular skiing areas remain open all year.

We've listed the most useful sites in the *Guide*, and you can also pick up the highly condensed **list** of west German sites which is available free from the German National Tourist Office and other German travel specialists in the UK. For DM21.80, you can can get the complete official guide from the German Camping Club, the *DDC*, directly from them at Mandlestr. 28 D 8000, Munich 23. The motoring organisation, *ADAC*, also produces a similarly priced guide which includes Germany and much of northern and central Europe. A complete list of sites in the former East Germany can be found in *DDR Privatplätze für Camping and Wohnmobile* (Alexandra Verlag, DM19.80).

Rough camping has recently been made illegal in the interests of protecting the environment, though a blind eye seems to be turned to camper vans: indeed stays ranging from 24 hours to 3 days are sometimes officially sanctioned.

EATING

German food is, as a rule, both good value and of high quality. However, it does help if you share the national penchant for solid, fatty food accompanied by compensatingly healthy fresh vegetables and salad. The pig is the staple element of the German menu – it's prepared in umpteen different ways, and just about every part of it is eaten. It also forms the main ingredient for sausages, which are not only the most popular snack, but are regarded as serious culinary fare – in Bavaria, there are even specialised *Wurstkuchen* ("Sausage Kitchens") which have gained Michelin ratings.

BREAKFAST

The vast majority of German hotels and guest houses include breakfast in the price of the room; in youth hostels you also have to pay for this meal on top of the regular accommodation charges. Although some places go in for the spartan French affair of rolls, jam and coffee, the normal German breakfast lies midway betweeen this and the elaborate Scandinavian cold table. Typically, you'll be offered a small platter of **cold meats** (usually sausage-based) and **cheeses**, along with a selection of marmalades, jams and honey. Muesli or another cereal is sometimes included as well, or as an alternative to the meats and cheeses. You're generally given a variety of **breads**, one of the most distinctive features of German cuisine. Both brown and white rolls are popular; these are often given a bit of zap by the addition of a condiment, such as caraway, coriander, poppy or sesame seeds. The rich-tasting black rye bread, known as *Pumpernickel*, is a particular national favourite, as is the salted *Bretzel*, which tastes nothing like any foreign imitation. Coffee (which is normally freshly brewed) is the usual accompaniment, but tea – whether plain or herbal – is now far more popular in Germany than was the case even a few years ago, while drinking chocolate is another common alternative. A glass of fruit juice – almost invariably orange – is sometimes included as well.

If breakfast isn't included in your accommodation costs, you can usually do quite well by going to a local **baker's shop**, which generally open from 7am, if not before. Most chain bakeries have an area set aside for breakfast, a practice taken up by some family establishments as well. The coffee and chocolate on offer tend to be of high quality, and there's the added bonus of being able to choose from the freshly-made bakery on display; DM2–3 should cover an adequate breakfast. More filling fare can be obtained from cafés and snack bars.

SNACKS AND FAST FOOD

Just as the English have their morning and afternoon tea, so the Germans have *Kaffee und Kuchen* (coffee and cakes). Though the elegant type of **café** serving a choice of espresso, capuccino and mocha to the accompaniment of cream cakes, pastries or handmade chocolates is indelibly associated with Austria, it's every bit as popular an institution in Germany. This hardly constitutes a cheap snack but is unlikely to be a rip-off – except in the most obvious tourist traps.

More substantial food is available from **butcher's shops**; even in rural areas, you can generally choose from a variety of freshly roasted meats to make up a hot sandwich. It's also worth going to the open-air **markets** which are held anything from once to six times a week in the central square of most towns. With a bit of judicious shopping round the stalls, you should be able to make up an irresistible picnic for an outlay of a few Deutschmarks. Larger cities tend to have a daily indoor version of this, known as the *Markthalle*.

The easiest option for a quick snack, however, is to head for the ubiquitous **Imbiss** stands and shops. In the latter you have the option of eating in or taking away; the price is the same. These indigenous types of snack bar tends to serve a range of sausages, plus meat-balls, hamburgers and chips; the better ones have soups, schnitzels, chops and salads as well. Spit-roasted chicken is usually recommendable, and has long been something of an east German speciality; it's usually very cheap, at around DM3.50 for half a bird. Mustard is usually available at no extra cost with all dishes, whereas small supplements are levied for mayonnaise or ketchup. Most Imbiss places sell beer, but as many are unlicensed you may be forbidden from consuming it on the premises.

Among the fast food **chains**, *Kochlöffel* stands out for cleanliness and good food. The speciality here is spit-roast chicken; prices compare very favourably with the American-owned hamburger joints, whose popularity is wholly undeserved. Another chain with acceptable food is *Weinerwald*, but its menu, set-up and price structure are more comparable to a restaurant than a snack bar. The butcher's chain *Vincent Murr* sells full main courses to be eaten on your feet, costing DM5–10. Virtually the only places outside northern Germany where you can eat salt-water fish are in the shops of the *Nordsee* chain. These vary a lot in quality, but unfortunately the standard of the fish prepared for consumption on the premises is seldom equal to that sold for home cooking.

Ethnic snack bars (which have still to make an impact on eastern Germany) are predominantly Italian or Greek/Turkish. The **pizzerias** are a major boon if you're on a tight budget. Either taking away or eating standing up, prices start at around DM3.50 for a simple tomato and cheese pizza, rising sharply according to the topping chosen. Look out for the ones using a coal-fire oven; these are likely to produce a tastier (and not necessarily more expensive) product than those tied to electricity. Most pizzerias also serve pasta dishes, though these are usually less of a bargain. As always, the **kebab** houses adapt their technique to suit the national taste. What in Britain would be called a "Döner kebab" is known as *Gyros*, and is based much more on real lamb meat and fat. It's also served in a puffier type of bread, generally with *tsatziki* as a sauce, and costs DM4–5.

MAIN MEALS

All **restaurants** display their menus and prices by the door, as well as which day is their *Ruhetag*, when they're closed. Hot meals are usually served throughout the day, but certainly where it says *durchgehend warme Küche*. The *Gaststätte*, *Gasthaus*, *Gasthof*, *Brauhaus* or *Wirtschaft* establishments, which are the nearest equivalents to old-fashioned English inns, mostly belong to a brewery and function as social meeting points, drinking havens and cheap restaurants combined. Their style of cuisine is known as **Gutbürgerliche Küche**; this resembles hearty German home cooking (hence the comparatively low prices), and portions are almost invariably generous. Most of these places have a hard core of regular customers who sit at tables marked *Stammtisch*; unless invited to do so, it's not the done thing to sit there. The bulk of the menu is the same all day long, though some establishments offer two- or three-course lunches at a bargain price. **Standards** in west German restaurants are amazingly high: you're far less likely to be served a dud meal than in almost any other country. Don't expect the same in east Germany, where erratic restaurant performances are likely to continue for a few years to come.

Choice for **soup** is fairly restricted, and tends to be based on an adaptation of foreign fare; prices are usually in the range of DM3–6. Among the most popular are *Gulaschsuppe*, a liquidised version of the staple Magyar dish (despite often being dignified as *Ungarische*, it's not something a Hungarian would recognise); *Bohnensuppe*, which is often quite spicy, and derived from the Serbian model; and *Zwiebelsuppe*, which is a direct copy of the famous French brown onion soup, usually with floating cheese and croutons. In east Germany, *Soljanka* is a spicy Ukrainian soup with sliced sausages. More authentically German are the clear soups with dumplings, of which the Bavarian *Leberknödelsuppe* is the best known. Other **starters** tend to be fairly unsophisticated – either a salad, paté or cold meat dish; prices are similar to those for soups.

Main courses in all German restaurants are overwhelmingly based on **pork**. As a rule, this is of noticeably higher quality than in Britain, and the variety in taste wrought by using different sauces (it's quite common to find a choice of up to twenty different types) and unexpected parts of the animal means that the predominance of the pig is far less tedious than might be supposed. As an alternative to the ubiquitous *Schnitzel*, try *Schweinehaxe* (knuckle) or *Eisbein* (trotters), both particularly delicious when roasted. **Sausages** regularly feature on the menu, and can be surprisingly tasty, with distinct regional varieties.

Whereas a main course pork-based dish is likely to cost DM15 or less, one with **beef** will cost a fair bit more. As is the case with snack bars, **chicken** dishes are comparatively cheap. Many restaurants have a **game** menu, with more exotic poultry such as duck or goose, along with venison, rabbit and hare; prices then tend to be DM20 or more.

Outside northern Germany, where a wide variety of newly caught salt-water **fish** is readily available, you'll probably have to be content with fresh-water varieties; trout is by far the most popular, though there's obviously a greater choice in places close to lakes and rivers. Where salt-water fish is available, the unfamiliar (to British palates, at least) rosefish (*Rotbarsch*) is generally the most reliable. Oddly enough, you're far more likely to encounter a choice of fresh fish in east Germany, where there is the long-established *Gastmahl des Meeres* chain.

The main course price invariably includes **vegetables**. Potatoes are usually roasted, chipped, fried in slices or made into a cold salad; boiled spuds are becoming increasingly popular, but they are rarely baked or mashed. Dumplings made from potatoes and flour are a common alternative. Cabbage is the other popular accompaniment – the green variety is pickled as *Sauerkraut*, whereas the red is normally cooked with apple as *Apfelrotkohl*. Salads of lettuce, cucumber, beetroot, carrots and gherkins are often included as a side-dish. The noodles known

A LIST OF FOODS AND DISHES

Basics

Frühstück	breakfast	Brot	bread	Joghurt	yoghurt
Mittagessen	lunch	Brötchen	bread roll	Zucker	sugar
Abendessen	supper, dinner	Butter	butter	Pfeffer	pepper
Messer	knife	Butterbrot	sandwich	Salz	salt
Gabel	fork	Belegtes Brot	open sandwich	Öl	oil
Löffel	spoon	Marmelade	jam	Essig	vinegar
Speisekarte	menu	Honig	honey	Senf	mustard
Teller	plate	Käse	cheese	Sosse	sauce
Tasse	cup	Fleisch	meat	Reis	rice
Glas	glass	Fisch	fish	Spätzle	shredded pasta
Vorspeise	starter	Ei	egg	Maultaschen	form of ravioli
Hauptgericht	main course	Gemüse	vegetables	Rechnung	bill
Nachspeise	dessert	Obst	fruit	Trinkgeld	tip

Soups and Starters

Suppe	soup	Flädlesuppe,	clear soup with pancake
Erbsensuppe	pea soup	Pfannkuchensuppe	strips
Linsensuppe	lentil soup	Leberpastete	liver paté
Bohnensuppe	bean soup	Lachsbrot	smoked salmon on bread
Zwiebelsuppe	onion soup	Melone mit Schinken	melon and ham
Hühnersuppe	chicken soup	Grüner Salat	mixed green salad
Gulaschsuppe	thick soup in imitation of	Gurkensalat	cucumber salad
	goulash	Fleischsalat	sausage salad with onions
Leberknödelsuppe	clear soup and liver dumplings	Schnittlauchbrot	chives on bread
Fleischsuppe	clear soup and meat dumplings	Sülze	jellied meat loaf
Ochsenschwanzsuppe	oxtail soup	Würzfleisch	supreme of pork

Meat and Poultry

Aufschnitt	mixed slices of cold sausage	Huhn, Hähnchen	chicken
Bockwurst	chunky boiled sausage	Innereien	innards
Bratwurst	grilled sausage	Jägerschnitzel	cutlet in wine and mushroom sauce
Broiler	chicken	Kanninchen	rabbit
Currywurst	sausage served with piquant sauce	Kassler Rippen	smoked and pickled pork chops
Eisbein	pig's trotters	Kotelett	cutlet (cheapest cut)
Ente	duck	Krautwickerl	cabbage leaves filled with mincemeat
Fasan	pheasant	Lamm	lamb
Fleischpflanzerl	meatball (in Bavaria)	Leber	liver
Frikadelle	meatball	Leberkäse	baked meatloaf served hot or cold
Froschschenkel	frogs' legs	Lunge	lungs
Gans	goose	Nieren	kidneys
Geschnetzeltes	shredded meat, usually served with rice	Ochsenschwanz	oxtail
Gyros	kebab	Rahmschnitzel	cutlet in cream sauce
Hackbraten	mincemeat roast	Rindfleisch	beef
Hackfleisch	mincemeat	Sauerbraten	braised pickled beef
Hammelfleisch	mutton	Saure Lunge	pickled lungs
Hase	hare	Schaschlik	diced meat with piquant sauce
Herz	heart	Schinken	ham
Hirn	brains	Schlachtplatte	mix of cured meats, including blood sausage, liver sausage and boiled meat
Hirsch, Reh	venison		

Meat and Poultry (continued)

Schnecke	snail	Wiener Schnitzel	thin cutlet in breadcumbs
Schnitzel Natur	uncoated cutlet (usually pork)	Wienerwurst	standard boiled pork sausage
Schweinebraten	roast pork		
Schweinefleisch	pork	Wild	wild game
Schweinehaxe	pig's knuckle	Wildschwein	wild boar
Speck	bacon	Wurst	sausage
Truthahn	turkey	Zigeunerschnitzel	cutlet in paprika sauce
Weisswurst	white herb sausage made with veal and pork	Zunge	tongue

Fish

Aal	eel	Krabben	crab	Schwertfish	swordfish
Forelle	trout	Lachs	salmon	Seezunge	sole
Hecht	pike	Makrele	mackerel	Skampi	scampi
Hering, Matjes	herring	Muscheln	mussels	Thunfisch	tuna
Hummer	lobster	Rotbarsch	rosefish	Tintenfisch	squid
Kabeljau	cod	Sardinen	sardines	Zander	pike-perch
Karpfen	carp	Schellfisch	haddock		
Kaviar	caviar	Scholle	plaice		

Vegetables

Blumenkohl	cauliflower	Paprika	green or red peppers
Bohnen	beans	Pellkartoffeln	jacket potatoes
Bratkartoffeln	fried potatoes	Pilze	mushrooms
Champignons	button mushrooms	Pommes frites	chips
Erbsen	peas	Salzkartoffeln	boiled potatoes
Grüne Bohnen	green beans	Reibekuchen	potato cake
Gurke	cucumber	Rosenkohnl	brussels sprouts
Karotten, Möhren	carrots	Rote Rübe	beetroot
Kartoffelbrei	mashed potatoes	Rotkohl	red cabbage
Kartoffelpuree	creamed potatoes	Rübe	turnip
Kartoffelsalat	potato salad	Salat	salad
Knoblauch	garlic	Sauerkraut	pickled cabbage
Knödel, Kloss	dumpling	Spargel	asparagus
Kopfsalat	lettuce	Tomaten	tomatoes
Lauch	leeks	Weisskohl	white cabbage
Maiskolben	corn on the cob	Zwiebeln	onions

Fruits

Ananas	pineapple	Mandarine	tangerine
Apfel	apple	Melone	melon
Aprikose	apricot	Obstsalat	fruit salad
Banane	banana	Orange	orange
Birne	pear	Pampelmuse	grapefruit
Brombeeren	blackberries	Pfirsich	peach
Datteln	dates	Pflaumen	plums
Erdbeeren	strawberries	Rosinen	raisins
Feigen	figs	Schwarze	
Himbeeren	raspberries	Johannisbeeren	blackcurrants
Johannisbeeren	redcurrants	Trauben	grapes
Kirschen	cherries	Zitrone	lemon
Kompott	stewed fruit or mousse		

Cheeses and Desserts

Emmentaler	Swiss Emmental	Kaiserschmarrn	shredded pancake served with powdered sugar, jam and raisins
Käseplatte	mixed selection of cheeses		
Schafskäse	sheep's cheese		
Weichkäse	cream cheese		
Ziegenkäse	goat's cheese	Käsekuchen	cheesecake
Apfelstrudel mit Sahne	apple strudel with fresh cream	Keks	biscuit
		Krapfen	doughnut
Berliner	jam doughnut	Nüsse	nuts
Dampfnudeln	large yeast dumplings served hot with vanilla sauce	Nusskuchen	nut cake
		Obstkuchen	fruitcake
		Pfannkuchen	pancake
Eis	ice cream	Schokolade	chocolate
Gebäck	pastries	Schwarzwälder Kirschtorte	Black Forest gateau
		Torte	gateau, tart

Common Terms

Art	style of	Geräuchert	smoked
Blau	rare	Gutbürgerliche Küche	traditional German cooking
Eingelegte	pickled		
Frisch	fresh	Hausgemacht	home-made
Gebacken	baked	Heiss	hot
Gebraten	fried, roasted	Kalt	cold
Gedämpft	steamed	Spiess	skewered
Gefüllt	stuffed	Topf (Eintopf)	stew, casserole
Gegrillt	grilled	Vom heissen Stein	raw meats you cook yourself on a red hot stone
Gekocht	cooked		

as *Spätzle* and *Maultaschen* are a distinctive component of Swabian cuisine, occasionally adopted elsewhere.

Desserts in restaurants are an anti-climax, where they exist at all. The Bavarian *Dampfnudel* is one of the few distinctive dishes; otherwise there's just the usual selection of fresh and stewed fruits, cheeses and ice creams. Sweet tooths are obviously far better catered for in cafés.

Germany now being a multicultural society, there's a wide variety of **ethnic** eateries. The density of these is very much in line with the general *Gastarbeiter* influx, and there's a heavy southern European bias. Of these, the Italian are generally the safest recommendations; there are also plenty offering Balkan and Graeco-Turkish cuisines. All of these are worth heading for if you're on a tight budget. As with the snack bars, these have still to make much of a splash in **the east**. However, some compensation is offered here by the continued survival of restaurants offering the cuisines of Russia, the Ukraine, and such erstwhile Communist countries as Hungary and Czechoslovakia.

Vegetarians will find east Germany extremely difficult – menus are almost exclusively for carnivores, and even an innocent-sounding item like tomato soup will have small chunks of meat floating around in it. In the west too you'll need to go out of your way to find anything other than salads, omelettes and pancakes, though major cities and towns do tend to have innovative specialist restaurants (listed in the guide whenever possible); even small communities often have a simple wholefood place.

DRINKING

The division between eating and drinking in Germany is less demarcated than is the case in Britain. Despite their inevitable connotations with beer and wine, the *Brauhäuser* and *Weinstuben* inevitably double as restaurants, though there are some purely drinking dens, generally known as *Kneipen*. Apart from beer and wine, there's nothing very distinctive about German beverages, save for *Apfelwein*, a variant of cider. The most popular **spirits** are the fiery *Korn* and after-dinner liqueurs, which are mostly fruit-based. Both **hot** and **soft** drinks are broadly the same as in Britain.

BEER

For serious beer drinkers, Germany is the ultimate paradise. Wherever you go, you can be sure of getting a product made locally, often brewed in a distinctive style. The country has around 40% of the world's breweries, with some 800 (about half the total) in Bavaria alone. It was in this province in 1516 that the *Reinheitsgebot* ("Purity Law") was formulated, laying down stringent standards of production, including a ban on chemical substitutes. This has been rigorously adhered to ever since (even in products made for export), and was also taken up by the rest of the country, but only for beers made for the domestic market. It was not so scrupulously adhered to by the Communists, but has since been re-introduced in those east German breweries which have survived closure.

Unfortunately, it has fallen foul of the EC bureaucrats, who deem it a restriction on trade (very few foreign beers meet the criteria laid down, and therefore could not be imported). The Germans are therefore no longer able to enforce what has been deemed a restriction on trade, but this thankfully hasn't forced them into lowering their own standards, the entire brewing industry having re-affirmed its commitment to the *Reinheitsgebot*. All in all, the current outlook is very rosy: although the odd brewery bites the dust each year, there has been a revival of long-forgotten techniques, often put into practice in new small *Hausbrauereien*.

More generally, there's an encouraging continuation of old-fashioned **top-fermented** brewing styles. Until last century, all beers were made this way, but the interaction of the yeasts with a hot atmosphere meant that brewing had to be suspended during the summer. It was the Germans who discovered that the yeast sank to the foot of the container when stored under icy conditions; thereafter, brewing took on a more scientific nature, and yeast strains were bred so that beer could be **bottom-fermented**, thus allowing its production all year round. While the *Reinheitsgebot* has ensured that bottom-fermented German brews are of a high standard, the technique has been a major factor in the insipidity of so much beer in other countries, including Britain. The top-fermentation process, on the other hand, allows for a far greater individuality in the taste (often characterised by a distinct fruitiness), and can, of course, now be used throughout the year, thanks to modern temperature controls. All wheat beers use this process.

DRINKS GLOSSARY

Wasser	water	*Tomatensaft*	tomato juice
Sprudel, Selters	sparkling mineral water	*Zitronenlimonade*	lemonade
Milch	milk	*Bier*	beer
Milchshake	milk shake	*Weisswein*	white wine
Kaffee	coffee	*Rotwein*	red wine
Kaffee mit milch	coffee with milk	*Roséwein*	rosé wine
Tee	tea	*Sekt*	sparkling wine
Zitronentee	lemon tea	*Glühwein*	hot mulled wine
Kräutertee, Pflanzentee	herbal tea	*Apfelwein*	apple wine
Kakao	cocoa	*Herrengedeckt*	cocktail of beer and Sekt
Trinkschokolade	drinking chocolate	*Weinbrand*	brandy
Apfelsaft	apple juice	*Korn*	rye spirit
Traubensaft	grape juice	*Likör*	liqueur
Orangensaft	orange juice	*Grog*	hot rum

BEER GLOSSARY

Alt Literally, any beer made according to an old formula; particularly associated with the dark brown top-fermented barley malt beer of Düsseldorf (also made in Mönchengladbach and Münster).

Altbierbowl Glass of *Alt* with addition of a fresh fruit punch.

Berliner Weisse Wheat beer from Berlin, usually served in a bowl-shaped glass, and with addition of woodruff (*mit Grün*) or raspberry essence (*mit Schuss*).

Bock Light or dark strong beer, originally from Einbeck, but particularly popular in Bavaria, containing at least 6.25% alcohol.

Dampfbier 'Steam beer' from Bayreuth, a fruity brew top-fermented in its own yeast.

Doppelbock Extra-strong *Bock*, usually made specially for festivals.

Dunkel Generic name for any dark beer.

Eisbock 'Ice beer', particularly associated with Kulmbach; the freezing process increases and concentrates the alcohol.

Export Originally, beers made to be exported. Now used to describe a premium beer, or in association with the brewing style of Dortmund, stronger than a Pils and lying midway between dry and sweet in taste.

Hausbrauerei 'House brewery', or pub where beer is brewed on the premises.

Hefe-Weizen Wheat beer given strong yeast boost.

Hell, Helles Generic names for light beers.

Hofbräu Brewery formerly belonging to a court; that in Munich is the most famous.

Klosterbräu Brewery attached to a monastery.

Kölsch Top-fermented pale coloured beer peculiar to Cologne, invariably served in small glasses.

Kristall-Weizen Sparkling brew made from wheat: the beer answer to champagne.

Maibock Pale, high premium *Bock*, specially made to celebrate spring.

Malz Unfermented black malt beer, similar to sweet stout.

Märzenbier Strong beer made in March, but stored for later consumption; particularly associated with Munich's *Oktoberfest*.

Münchener Brown coloured lager, a style pioneered in Munich.

Pils Bottom-fermented golden coloured beer; very high hop content.

Radler Shandy.

Rauchbier Aromatic beer from Bamberg made from smoked malt.

Spezial Name given by breweries to their premium product, or to that made for special events.

Starkbier Generic name for strong beers.

Steinbier Beer made with the help of hot stones, an old technique recently revived in Coburg.

Urquell Name used to identify the original of a particular brewing style.

Vollbier Standard (as opposed to premium) type of beer.

Weihnachtsbier Special strong beer made for Christmas.

Weisse Pale coloured wheat beer.

Weizen Light or dark wheat beer.

Zwickelbier Unfiltered beer.

A quick beer tour of Germany would inevitably begin in **Munich**, which occupies third place in the world production league table. The city's beer gardens and beer halls are the most famous drinking dens in the country, offering a wide variety of premier products, from dark lagers through tart *Weizens* to powerful *Bocks*. Nearby **Freising** boasts the oldest brewery in the world, dating back to the eleventh century. In Franconia, distinctive traditions are found in **Bamberg** (national champion for beer consumption per resident), **Kulmbach**, **Coburg** and **Bayreuth**.

In Baden-Württemberg, the local brews are sweeter and softer, in order to appeal to palates accustomed to wine; **Stuttgart** and **Mannheim** are the main production centres. Central Germany is even more strongly wedded to wine, though there are odd pockets of resistance. Indeed, **Frankfurt**, the German cider metropolis, also has the largest brewery in the country, *Binding*.

Further north, where it's too cold to grow grapes, the beer tradition returns with a vengeance. **Cologne** holds the world record for the number of city breweries, all of which produce the jealously-guarded *Kölsch*. **Düsseldorf** again has its own distinctive brew, the dark *Alt*. **Dortmund** even manages to beat Munich for the title of European capital of beer production, and is particularly associated with *Export*. Less well known, but equally good, are the delicate brews of the **Sauerland** and **Siegerland**, made using the soft local spring water.

Hannover, **Bremen** and **Hamburg** all have long brewing pedigrees, with many of their products widely available abroad. The most distinctive beers of the northernmost Länder, however, are those of **Einbeck** (the original home of *Bock*) and **Jever**. In contrast to these heady brews is the acidic *Weisse* of **Berlin**, which is completely transformed into a refreshing summer thirst-quencher by the addition of a dash of syrup.

East German brews are far less exciting: **Magdeburg** has a long and varied tradition, but elsewhere there's seldom anything other than the standard fare of light beers and local variations of Pils, of which the best are from **Radeburg** near Dresden and those made from the soft water of the **Vogtland**.

WINE

Most people's knowledge of German wine starts and ends with *Liebfraumilch*, the medium sweet easy-drinking wine that for the last few years has been the best selling wine in the UK. Sadly, its success has obscured the quality of other German wines, especially those made from the *Riesling* grape, which many consider one of the world's great white varieties; and it's worth noting that the *Liebfraumilch* drunk in Germany tastes nothing like the bilge swilled back in Britain.

The vast majority of German wine is white since the northern climate doesn't ripen red grapes regularly. If after a week or so you're pining for a glass of red, try a *Spätburgunder* (the *Pinot Noir* of Burgundy).

First step in any exploration of German wine should be to understand what's on the label: the predilection for Gothic script and gloomy martial crests make this an uninviting prospect, but the division of categories is intelligent and helpful – if at first a little complex.

Like most EC wine, German wine is divided into two broad categories: *Tafelwein* ("table wine", for which read "cheap plonk") and *Qualitätswein* ("quality wine"), equivalent to the French *Apellation Controllée*.

TAFELWEIN

Tafelwein can be a blend of wines from any EC country; *Deutscher Tafelwein* must be 100% German. *Landwein* is a superior *Tafelwein*,

equivalent to the French *Vin de Pays* and medium dry. Like all German wines, *Tafelwein* can be *trocken* (dry) or *halb-trocken* (medium dry).

QUALITÄTSWEIN

There are two basic subdivisions of *Qualitätswein*: **Qba** (*Qualitätswein eines bestimmten Anbaugebietes*) and **Qmp** (*Qualitätswein mit Prädikat*). "Qba" wines come from eleven delimited regions and must pass an official tasting and analysis. "Qmp" wines are further divided into six grades:

Kabinett The first and lightest style.

Spätlese Must come from late-picked grapes, which results in riper flavours.

Auslese Made from a selected bunch of grapes, making a concentrated medium-sweet wine. If labelled as a *Trocken*, the wine will have lots of body and weight.

Beerenauslese Wine made from late-harvested, individually picked grapes. A rare wine, made only in the very best years, and extremely sweet.

Trockenbeerenauslese Trocken here means dry in the sense that the grapes have been left on the vine until some of the water content has evaporated. As with *Beerenauslese*, each grape will be individually picked. This is a very rare wine which is intensely sweet and concentrated.

Eiswein Literally "ice wine", this is made from *Beerenauslese* grapes – a hard frost freezes the water content of the grape, concentrating the juice. The flavour of an *Eiswein* is remarkably fresh tasting, due to its high acidity.

GRAPE VARIETIES

These often appear on wine labels and are a handy guide to judging a wine's flavour.

Riesling Germany's best grape variety. It can have a floral aroma when young, is often "honeyed" when ripe, and develops interesting bouquets after 5–7 years in the bottle.

Gewürztraminer Gewürz means spicy, and the wine has an intense aromatic nose, likened by some people to lychees and by others to Turkish delight.

Müller-Thurgau The most widely planted grape in Germany. Its flavour is less distinguished than *Riesling* but is generally fruity, has less acidity and a grapey, Muscat taste.

Silvaner A fairly neutral wine, quite full-bodied and often blended with more aromatic varieties.

WINE REGIONS

Particularly at the *Qualitätswein* level, regional variations in climate produce markedly differing styles of wine.

Mosel-Saar-Ruhr The steep banks of the river Mosel and two of its tributaries enable the vines to catch long hours of sun, thus allowing grapes to ripen in one of the world's most northerly plantations. Much Riesling is grown in the slatey soil, producing elegant wines in the best years.

Rheingau On the sloping northern bank of the Rhine as it flows between Hochheim and Assmanshausen, this is a small, prestigious region that produces wines slightly fuller than those from the Mosel region. They're considered to be among the country's finest.

Nahe Both geographically and stylistically between the Mosel-Saar-Ruhr and the Rheingau, this is a relatively small region whose wines are often underrated.

Rhein-Hessen Germany's main producer of *Liebfraumilch* from large plantations of Müller-Thurgau and Silvaner grapes.

Rheinpfalz A southern wine region that produces full-bodied, ripe wines, chiefly *Liebfraumilch* and *Riesling*.

Baden The most southerly wine-growing region, extending as far as the Bodensee. The warm climate allows French grape varieties to be grown here, and the majority of the wines are dry in flavour.

COMMUNICATIONS

POST OFFICES

Post offices (*Postamt*) are normally open Monday–Saturday 8am–6pm. Outbound mail should reach the UK within a few days. In the major cities, there's a separate **parcels office** (marked *Pakete*), usually a block or so away, where you have to go to send bulky items.

Poste Restante services are available at the main post offices in any given town (see listings in the *Guide* for addresses in the major cities): collect it from the counter marked *Postlagernde Sendungen* (always remember to take your passport). It's worth asking anyone writing to you to use this designation as well as, or instead of,

Poste Restante. Incredible as it may seem in view of the country's reputation for super-efficiency, many German post offices don't understand the international term and are likely to return a letter to the sender marked "address unknown". Bear in mind also that mail is usually only held for a couple of weeks. **Telegrams** can be sent either by ringing ☎1131, or from any post office.

The old **East German postal service** has already been fully amalgamated with that of the west, but as yet doesn't function as well: expect long delays on letters.

TELEPHONES

THE WEST

Telephoning is simple in west Germany, and most kiosks are equipped with basic instructions in several languages, including English. You can **call abroad** from all but those clearly marked "National". Coins of DM0.10, DM1 and DM5 are accepted; only wholly unused ones are returned. Calling rates are slightly cheaper after 8pm and at weekends. Some boxes are equipped with a ringing symbol to indicate that you can be called back on that phone. The major international codes are given in the box below; remember then to omit the initial zero from the subscriber's number.

For **local calls**, you need to insert a minimum of DM0.30, which will last for up to eight minutes. In the guide, local codes are included

INTERNATIONAL DIALLING CODES FROM WESTERN GERMANY

Britain ☎00 44	USA ☎00 1	New Zealand ☎00 64
Irish Republic ☎00 353	Canada☎ 00 1	Australia ☎00 61

USEFUL NUMBERS IN THE WEST

Operator ☎03	Operator Wake-up call ☎1141
Directory enquiries ☎1188 (for Western Berlin and Germany)	Ambulance ☎112
	Fire ☎112
International directory enquiries ☎00118	Police ☎110

USEFUL NUMBERS IN THE EAST

Operator ☎180	Ambulance ☎115
International operator ☎181	Fire ☎112
Directory enquiries ☎180	Police ☎110

with each telephone number, except in major cities, where they're given in a box towards the start of each account.

The number of **card phones** is on the increase. A card, available from post offices for DM12 or DM50, is worth buying, especially if you're intending to call home. However, an easier option is to use the **direct phone service** facility of the main post office (*Hauptpost*): a phone booth will be allocated to you from the counter marked *Fremdgespräche*, which is also where you pay once you've finished.

THE EAST

Notwithstanding the heroic efforts which are being made to improve the situation, the telephone system in what used to be East Germany – in common with all other former Communist states – is a disaster. The complicated networks, which have still to be properly rationalised, existed in large part for the benefit of the secret police and as yet, relatively few households have a phone, as the waiting list used to be upwards of fifteen years long.

Provision of **public phones** is also woefully inadequate. A few western-style kiosks have now been established in the main cities, but for the most part booths have the old phones which seldom give anything in the way of dialling information. As in the west, DM0.30 is the minimum charge for a call; generally only DM0.10 and DM1 coins are accepted.

Unless you're calling within a city, the major snag is that **codes** – within the former GDR itself

as well as to west Germany and abroad – change according to the place from where you're dialling. It therefore hasn't been possible in the guide to list any eastern German codes: local numbers only are given. You're thus pretty well forced to use the **direct phone service** facilities to be found in main post offices and railway stations, or at least to go there to find out the precise code you require. Actually, once you've found this out, it's easy enough to call abroad from any booth – something which was completely impossible before mid-1991.

MEDIA

Germany is well supplied with **British newspapers**; in the larger cities it's relatively easy to pick up most of the London-printed editions on the same day.

With a few exceptions, **German newspapers** tend to be highly regionalised, mixing local and international news. Only the liberal *Frankfurter Rundschau* and Munich's *Süddeutsche Zeitung* are distributed much outside their own areas. Berlin produces two reputable organs: the *Tagespiegel*, a good left-wing read, and the Greenish/alternative *Tageszeitung*, universally known as the *Taz*. Of the national daily papers, the two best sellers come from the presses of the late and unlamented Axel Springer: *Die Welt* is a right-wing heavyweight, and the tabloid *Bild* a reactionary, sleazy and sensationalist rag that even Rupert Murdoch would be ashamed to publish. The *Frankfurter Allgemeine* is again conservative, appealing particularly to the business community, but unusual in following a politically independent line.

Germany has more **magazines** than any other country in Europe. The leftish weekly news and current affairs magazine *Der Spiegel* is the most in-depth magazine for political analysis and investigative journalism. Unless your German is fluent, though, it's a heavy and often difficult read. Though further to the right, *Die Zeit*, the weekly magazine of the newspaper of the same name, is a wider-ranging (and to learners of the language, easier-to-read) alternative. *Stern* is the most popular current affairs magazine, though no longer in the same league as *Die Zeit* or *Der Spiegel* since its prestige took a tumble following its publication of the forged Hitler diaries a few years ago. In order to bolster a flagging circulation it has resorted to a broader-based, populist low-brow content. Of the style magazines, *Tempo* is a rip-off of *The Face* but less fashion obsessed and more likely to come up with interesting articles on a wide range of issues. *Wiener* is similar, but more iconoclastic and acerbic.

German **television** can't hold a candle to British TV, its ads and presentation style generally still stuck in the modes used in the 1960s and early 70s. But satellite TV is bringing a new impetus to the industry, and it being a very rich enterprise, a great deal of change is undoubtedly on the horizon. Whether it will improve quality is another story. There are two main national channels, *ARD* and *ZDF*, and then there's the *Drittes Programm*, which features separate regional and educational programmes. Other channels sometimes available are the Austrian and Swiss ones, and each state also has its local channels. The only **English-speaking radio** channels are the *BBC World Service*, the British Forces station *BFBS* (99FM) and the dire American Armed Forces radio station *AFN* (88FM), which combines American music charts with military news. These should continue broadcasting for at least as long as the troops remain.

BUSINESS HOURS AND PUBLIC HOLIDAYS

Shopping hours in western Germany were strictly curtailed by a law passed in the 1950s in a bid to counter national workaholic tendencies, a measure which has defied numerous attempts at reform. All shops must close at 6.30pm on weekdays, at 2pm on Saturdays (or at 4pm on the first Saturday of the month, known as *Langer Samstag*, and in the four weeks before Christmas), and all day Sunday (except for bakers, who may open between 11am and 3pm). Late opening is allowed till 8.30pm on Thursdays. Pharmacists can extend their opening hours on a strict basis of rotation. The only other exceptions are shops in and around railway stations, which generally do stay open late and at weekends. These are for *bona fide* travellers only, and you could theoretically be asked to show a ticket, though in practice you're most unlikely to find this absurd restriction applied.

In east Germany, in order to encourage the growth of fledgling new businesses, this law is not yet rigidly enforced. However, few shops take advantage of the opportunity for extended opening hours.

Museums and **historic monuments** such as castles and palaces are, with very few exceptions, closed all day Monday. Otherwise, opening times (which are detailed in the guide) are noticeably more generous in western Germany than in other countries, with lunchtime closures rare. Most major civic museums are additionally open on at least one evening per week. The situation in the former GDR is less satisfactory: many museums and monuments still close two days a week, and evening openings are unheard of.

In range and diversity, German museums far surpass those of most other European countries, a legacy of the nation's long division into a plethora of separate states, and of the Romantic movement, which led to a passion for collecting. **Admission charges** for the museums vary enormously, and tend to reflect whether the relevant authority regards them as a social service or an exploitable asset, rather than their intrinsic quality. All the museums in Stuttgart, for example, are free, whereas those in comparably wealthy Düsseldorf (which arguably are not as good) average DM5 each. Historic monuments tend to charge around DM2–3, comparing favourably with similar places in Britain. In east Germany, however, admission prices can be high – a result of the shortage of municipal funds. Wherever you

PUBLIC HOLIDAYS

New Year's Day (1 Jan)
Epiphany (6 Jan)
Good Friday (changes annually)
Easter Monday (changes annually)
May Day (1 May)
Ascension Day (changes annually)
Whit Monday (changes annually)
Corpus Christi (changes annually, and is honoured only in Baden-Württemberg, Bavaria, Hessen, Rhineland-Palatinate, North Rhineland–Westphalia and Saarland)

Feast of the Assumption (15 Aug, honoured only in Bavaria and Saarland)
Day of German Unity (3 Oct)
All Saints Day (1 Nov, honoured only in Bavaria, Baden-Württemberg, Rhineland-Palatinate, North Rhineland–Westphalia and Saarland)
Day of Prayer and National Repentance (variable date in Nov)
Christmas Day (25 Dec)
Boxing Day (26 Dec).

go, a **student card** nearly always brings a reduction in admission costs.

In the west, there's rarely any difficulty gaining access to **churches**; hence opening times are only listed in the guide for ancillary attractions such as treasuries or towers, or when set times are rigidly enforced. Bear in mind that churches used for Protestant worship (predominantly in Swabia, Hessen and northern Germany) tend to keep office hours, whereas those in Catholic areas usually open earlier and close later.

All but a handful of historic **churches in the former GDR** are Protestant; access to them was decidedly ungenerous in the Communist period and, although much improved, is still far from ideal. The opening of many important churches is dependent on volunteers; they're generally open for reasonable periods in high summer, but are often shut altogether out of season. Where possible, current opening times have been given in the guide, though there are hopeful signs that access will become easier in the future.

FESTIVALS AND ANNUAL HOLIDAYS

Germany probably has more annual festivals than any other European country, with almost every village having its own summer fair, as well as a rich mixture of religious and pagan festivals that have merged over the ages to fill the whole calendar.

These tend to flourish most in Bavaria, Baden-Württemberg and the Rhineland. In the former GDR, there are far fewer festivals, other than those devoted to high culture. Communism is by no means entirely to blame for this, the roots lying in the puritanism which has long characterised this area's history.

The most famous German festival is undoubtedly the **Oktoberfest** in Munich, but **Carnival** and the **Christmas fairs** are other annual highlights, and take place all over the country. There's also a wealth of **music festivals**, ranging from opera seasons to open-air jazz and rock concerts. Main events are listed in the guide (with the most important described in detail), but here's a general overview.

JANUARY is a quiet month, though there are various events associated with the **Carnival season**, particularly the proclamation of the "Carnival King". Climax of the season comes in FEBRUARY or MARCH, seven weeks before the date nominated for Easter. The Rhenish *Karneval*

GERMANY'S MUSEUMS — A TOP TWENTY

Berlin *Dahlem Museum* (p.738). One of the most comprehensive collections of old masters in the world; particular strengths are the early Netherlandish, German, Dutch and Italian schools. Fabulous displays of sculpture and ethnology are also featured.

Berlin *Pergamon Museum* (p.750). Archaeology museum full of blockbuster exhibits from all the great classical civilisations.

Braunschweig *Herzog-Anton-Ulrich-Museum* (p.603). Choice display of old master paintings (especially Flemish, Dutch and German) and decorative arts.

Cologne *Römisch-Germanisches Museum* (p.465). Wide-ranging archaeology museum specially constructed around a giant Roman mosaic.

Cologne *Wallraf-Richartz/Ludwig Museum* (p.465). Works by the most distinctive school of German fifteenth century painters rub shoulders with a staggering cross-section of international twentieth century art.

Darmstadt *Landesmuseum* (p.348). An absorbing and eclectic mix of German Primitives, old masters, Jugendstil decorative art, avant-garde sculpture, archaeology and natural history.

Dresden *Albertinum* (p.918). The dazzling 'Green Vault' treasury takes pride of place in a museum which also contains important collections of modern paintings and antique sculptures.

Dresden *Gemädegalerie* (p.918). A collection of old masters which, if not among the largest in the world, is nonetheless unsurpassed for the sheer overall quality of its exhibits.

Düsseldorf *Kunstsammlung Nordrhein-Westfalen* (p.483). Has to be the ritziest and most extravagantly funded gallery of modern art in the country.

Frankfurt *Städel* (p.335). One of Europe's most comprehensive art galleries, where the whole course of German painting can be compared to trends elsewhere in Europe.

Hamburg *Kunsthalle* (p.642). Wide-ranging art gallery – the best place to find out about the diversity of nineteenth century German painting.

Hannover *Landesmuseum* (p.553). Varied mix of European art down the centuries, plus archaeological and natural history departments.

Karlsruhe *Kunsthalle* (p.289). Nineteenth-century period-piece art gallery, with the most offbeat collection of old master paintings in the country.

Kassel *Gemäldegalerie* (p.373). A collection of seventeenth century Dutch and Flemish paintings equal to any in the Low Countries, along with classical sculptures and a range of other old masters.

Munich *Alte Pinakothek* (p.65). One of the greatest art galleries in the world. Along with by far the best collection of old German masters in existence, there's outstanding representation of the early Netherlandish, Flemish, Dutch, Italian, French and Spanish schools.

Munich *Deutsches Museum* (p.71). Compendious and spectacular celebration of technology in every imaginable form; its hands-on displays are equally fascinating for kids and graduate engineers.

Nürnberg *Germanisches Nationalmuseum* (p.135). A monument to the best of German civilisation down the centuries – medieval statuary, Renaissance globes, historic musical instruments and paintings from all periods.

Stuttgart *Daimler-Benz Museum* (p.199). A glittering and diverse array of historic vehicles, all designed and manufactured by this merged company or its two predecessors.

Stuttgart *Staatsgalerie* (p.197). Excellent collection of (particularly German) old master paintings, plus the country's own answer to the Pompidou Centre.

Trier *Landesmuseum* (p.401). Startlingly fresh interpretation of classical civilisations that's a world away from the usual dry-as-dust style of presentation.

---

tends to have rather more gusto than its Bavarian counterpart, known as *Fasching*. Cologne has the most spectacular celebrations (detailed in the *Guide* on p.474), followed by those of Mainz and Düsseldorf; the *Rosenmontag* parades are the highlight. Baden-Württemberg's *Fastnet* is a distinctive, very pagan, Carnival tradition, best experienced in Rottweil. Another old pagan rite is the *Schäfertanz* held in Rothenburg in March. This time of year sees things hotting up for **Easter**,

and colourful church services are held throughout the country, particularly in rural Catholic areas. Another important APRIL festival is the witches' sabbath of *Walpurgisnacht*, celebrated throughout the Harz region on the 30th of the month.

MAY marks the start of many **summer festivals**. Costume plays such as the *Rattenfänger Spiele* in Hameln begin regular weekend performances, while there are classical concerts in historic buildings, notably the Schlosstheater in

Schwetzingen. Every ten years (next in 2000), the famous *Passionspiele* in Oberammergau begins its run. On a lighter note, there's the *Stabenfest* in Nördlingen. **Whitsun**, which usually falls towards the end of the month, sees distinctive religious festivals in the small Bavarian towns of Kötzting and Bogen. On the same weekend, there are two celebrated reconstructions of historic events – the *Meistertrunk* drama in Rothenburg and the *Kuchen und Bunnen Fest* in Schwäbisch Hall. Shortly afterwards, *Corpus Christi* is celebrated in Catholic areas, and is best experienced in Cologne. JUNE sees important **classical music** festivals, with the *Bach-Woche* during the second weekend of the month in Lüneburg, the *Händel-Festspiele* in Göttingen and Halle, the *Schumann-Woche* in Zwickau and the *Europäische Wochen* in Passau, while there's a big festival of all kinds of music held under canvas in Freiburg. Throughout northern Germany, the shooting season is marked by *Schützenfeste*, the largest being Hannover's. Bad Wimpfen's *Talmarkt*, which begins at the end of the month, is a fair which can trace its history back a thousand years.

JULY is a particularly busy festival month, with summer fairs and both **wine** and **beer** festivals opening up every week; pick of the latter is that in Kulmbach. Dinkelsbühl's *Kinderzeche* and Ulm's *Schwörmontag* are the most famous folklore events at this time. The Bayreuth *Opernfest*, exclusively devoted to Wagner, is held during late July, but note that all tickets are put on sale a year in advance and immediately snapped up. AUGUST is the main month for colourful displays of fireworks and illuminations, such as the *Schlossfest* in Heidelberg and *Der Rhein in Flammen* in Koblenz. There are a host of *Weinfeste* during the month in the Rhine-Mosel area, notably those in Rüdesheim and Mainz, while Straubing's *Gäubodenfest* is one of the country's largest beer festivals. Other important events at this time are the *Plärrer* city fair in Augsburg, the *Mainfest* in Frankfurt and the *Zissel* folk festival in Kassel.

Paradoxically, Munich's renowned *Oktoberfest* actually begins on the last Saturday in SEPTEMBER. This month sees many of the most bacchanalian festivals, such as Heilbronn's *Weindorf* and Bad Cannstatt's *Volksfest*. OCTOBER sees things quietening down, though there's still the odd *Weinfest* in the Rhineland, along with the *Freimarkt* folk festival in Bremen. In NOVEMBER, there's the month-long *Hamburger Dom* fair in Hamburg, while the *Martinsfest* on the 10th/11th of the month is celebrated in Northern Baden and the Rhineland, most notably in Düsseldorf. Finally, DECEMBER is the month of Christmas markets (variably known as *Christkindelsmarkt* or *Weihnachtsmarkt*), and, if you were to choose just one, it should be Nürnberg's, which swells with traditional stalls selling everything from toys and trinkets to delicious sweets and biscuits.

SPORTS

Sports occupy a central position in German life: indeed it was the Germans who were chiefly responsible for developing sport towards its present key role in modern international society. This began with the introduction of gymnastics into schools as a means of pre-military training during the Napoleonic Wars; it continued in an overtly political way with Hitler's exploitation of the 1936 Olympic Games and the GDR's nurturing – at great cost and by dubious means – of a sporting elite as a means of gaining international prestige. Facilities for both spectators and participators remain excellent in both parts of the united Germany, which seems likely to maintain its current leading tion in football, tennis, athletics and other sports, while doing its utmost to shed sinister undertones of the past.

FOOTBALL

Football is the nearest Germany comes to having a national sport. The West German team's victory in the 1990 World Cup equalled the record of three wins in the competition while marking the end of separate representation for the two German states. Failure to produce a successful national team was always recognised as the biggest failure of the GDR's sports policy, though on the one occasion the two German states met in a tournament – in the 1974 World Cup – the East Germans scored what proved to be a hollow victory, as their victims subsequently went on to lift the trophy.

The ***Bundesliga*** elite division is as fiercely competitive as the English First Division, and even the best-known clubs are likely to find themselves in relegation difficulties if they are in indifferent form. With the admission of the top two east German clubs, it has 20 teams for the 1991-2 season, but the aim is to reduce this to just 16 in a couple of years. The German style of play, mirroring the national character, tends to be based on well-organised, methodical teamwork, rather than on the individual brilliance favoured in Latin countries. League matches are held on Saturday afternoons; European cup games are usually on Wednesday evenings.

By far the most famous **team** is *Bayern München*, whose record down the years entitles it to be ranked among the world's top clubs. Given the game's working class roots, it's not surprising that many of the other leading clubs – *Borussia Mönchengladbach*, *Borussia Dortmund* and *Kaiserslautern* – are based in industrial towns. Others which have enjoyed recent success are *Werder Bremen*, *Hamburger SV*, *FC Köln* and *VfB Stuttgart*. Only eight erstwhile GDR teams – among whom *Dynamo Dresden* has the best record – have survived as going professional concerns. Those which have been reduced to amateur status include *Dynamo Berlin* (now *FC Berlin*), the Stasi-sponsored team whose connections were a significant factor in their ten consecutive championship triumphs.

TENNIS

Tennis has been a real German obsession ever since 1985, when the 17 year-old Boris Becker blasted all his opponents off the court to become the first unseeded and youngest ever men's singles champion at Wimbledon. Equally significant has been the steamrolling success of Steffi Graf, who won all four Grand Slam tournaments at the age of 19; although the "invincible" tag she once had has been shed in the last couple of years, starts any tournament she enters as odds-on favourite to reach the semis at least.

Despite Germany's leading position in the game, the **tournaments** staged in the country are only second-string events on the international circuit, although the presence at them of these two established stars, plus the latest sensation, Michael Stich, is pretty well guaranteed. In early May, the Citizens' Cup for women is held in

Hamburg; the German Open for men is held in the same city the next week, with the women's version following later that month in Berlin. The German Mästers for women takes place at a variable venue in late September, while Stuttgart hosts a men's event towards the end of the season, usually in October.

ATHLETICS

In just one area of sport the old GDR has strengthened the winning potential of the new country – **athletics**. Though West Germany did once in a while produce an outstanding individual athlete – like hurdler Harald Schmidt – it could never match the consistency of the East, which reaped a massive crop of golds at every Olympics. This consistency was always dogged by allegations of drug-taking, a complaint that was often justified. However, East German training methods were at least as legitimate as those in the West – witness the Ben Johnson doping scandal and the mysterious sudden improvement in form shown by certain US athletes. Since unification, athletes from the former GDR have continued their winning ways, albeit with a touch more glitz than before.

The main annual grand prix **events**, however, are all in the former West, with successive meets in early September in Cologne, Berlin and Koblenz.

OTHER SPORTS

Main venues for **motor sports** are Hockenheim near Heidelberg (where the Formula 1 Grand Prix is held each July) and the venerable Nürburgring. The leading **equestrian** events are held consecutively in Hamburg and Aachen in June, while the celebrated dressage displays in Celle take place in September and October. Germany's **horse racing** calendar is dominated by the spring and autumn season at Iffezheim near Baden-Baden, and by the Derby week in Hamburg in late June.

WINTER SPORTS

From December to February, **winter sports** competitions, many associated with the skiing World Cup, are held in the southern part of the country. The main venues are Garmisch-Partenkirchen and Oberstdorf in Bavaria, and the Black Forest resorts of Todtmoos, Todtnau, Furtwangen and Schonach.

AVERAGE PRICES FOR SIX-DAY SKI PASSES	
Garmisch-Partenkirchen DM176, DM117 kids, (50 lifts)	**Bayrischzell** DM131, DM98 kids, (25 lifts)
Oberstdorf DM172, DM129 kids, (35 lifts)	**Mittenwald** DM115, DM75 kids, (7 lifts)
Reit im Winkel DM137, DM90 kids, (13 lifts)	**Berchtesgaden** DM115, DM75 kids, (10 lifts)
	Schliersee DM120, DM75 kids, (20 lifts)

The German Alps offer some very attractive **ski resorts**, often overlooked in the rush to get to Austria, Switzerland and France. Everyone has heard of **Garmisch-Partenkirchen** (720m–2966m), if only because of the 1936 Olympic runs still used by many professionals. Unfortunately it's an expensive – though well equipped – resort. For equally excellent facilities, plenty of runs and lifts, affordable prices and a beautiful setting, **Oberstdorf** (700m–2224m) is undoubtedly the all-round winner. Other, smaller resorts, which are high on picturesque views and ideally suited to novice and medium skiers, are **Reit im Winkel** (700m–1850m), **Bayrischzell** (800m–1724m), **Mittenwald** (750m–2385m), **Berchtesgaden** (550m–1800m) and **Schliersee** (800m–1693m). These are all traditional resorts, each with quite a few runs, good accommodation and plenty of activities other than skiing available. Families are especially well catered for, with resident ski schools to take care of the kids. **Travel** to the German resorts is normally by plane to Munich, where trains connect with most skiing areas, the journey taking less than two hours in all cases. If you go on a package tour, a coach will normally pick you up from the airport, but check with your travel agent. The largest expense apart from your flight ticket will be the ski pass, and above is a guide to the kind of prices to be expected.

POLICE, TROUBLE AND SEXUAL HARASSMENT

The German police (*Polizei*) are not renowned for their friendliness, but they usually treat foreigners with courtesy. It's important to remember that you are expected to carry **ID** (your passport, or at least a student card or driving licence) at all times. Failure to do so could turn a routine police check into a drawn out and unpleasant process. **Traffic offences** or any other misdemeanours will result in a rigorous checking of documentation, and on-the-spot fines are best paid without argument. The police are generally very correct, and shouldn't subject you to any unnecessary chicanery.

Reporting thefts at local police stations is straightforward, but inevitably there'll be a great deal of bureaucratic bumpf to wade through. All **drugs** are illegal in Germany, and anyone caught with them will face either prison or deportation: consulates will not be sympathetic towards those on drug charges.

The level of **sexual harassment** is fortunately very low in Germany, and single women in restaurants, bars and cafés are nothing unusual and don't generally get bothered. People will come and sit at your table if there's limited space, but that doesn't automatically mean you're about to get chatted up. Even hitch-hiking is relatively safe here, and although men in Germany can be just as macho as anywhere else, they don't often show it in public. Large cities increase the likelihood of problems, as do long train journeys, but common sense and a firm manner should be enough to evade most unpleasant encounters (see also the following section).

The GDR's claim that it was a crime-free state was a myth: there were always unsafe areas in the main cities, and particular problems with skinheads and football hooligans; these have, if anything, increased since unification. Bear in mind that the level of **theft** in this part of Germany has – inevitably – increased dramatically in line with unemployment and the dashed hopes of the many who have found their dreams of quick riches unfulfilled. However, provided you take the normal precautions, there's certainly no particular cause for alarm.

Throughout Germany the number to ring for the police is ☎**110**.

WOMEN'S GERMANY

Women have traditionally been confined to a very subordinate role in German society, and this improved only relatively amid the postwar prosperity of the Federal Republic. Few women reach senior positions in the main **political parties**; indeed, Chancellor Kohl has been chauvinistic enough to woo the female vote by referring to "our pretty women" as "one of Germany's natural resources". To some extent, the situation has changed with the arrival of the Greens as a credible political force, with the formidable Petra Kelly the best-known of several women in its corporate leadership. Many commentators, however, see this merely as a natural extension of the tendency for women to be at the forefront of German radicalism, continuing the tradition established by the early Communist leader Rosa Luxemburg, and continuing via the terrorist groups of the 1970s.

There are no effective laws against sex discrimination. Few women manage to get to the top in the **professions** and civil service, even though they now account for nearly half the total of university undergraduates. The situation has improved somewhat in medicine, with 20% of doctors being women, and in the Protestant churches, which now allow women to become pastors. It's similarly difficult for a woman to climb the corporate ladder, though it's now quite normal for a daughter to succeed her father as head of a **business** – a far cry from the days when the Kaiser had to intervene personally to find a suitable husband for Bertha Krupp, in order to ensure the continuing credibility of the famous armaments conglomerate.

Officially, **the GDR** claimed to have established sexual equality, and it earned extravagant praise from many western feminists who accepted this at face value. The reality was very different. Honecker's (often estranged) wife was the only woman who reached a senior governmental position, and, in spite of the obligation placed on women to work, they fared little better elsewhere. In addition, because of the declining population, women were encouraged to have as large a family as possible; they were also expected to take the brunt of the shopping (involving much patient queuing) and household chores. This added up to a well-nigh intolerable burden on many, and it was small wonder that two out of every three marriages – the highest percentage in the world – ended in divorce.

If you want to find out about grass roots feminism, the best bet is to contact the local **women's centre** (*Frauenzentrum*). These are found in most cities, and are listed in the *Guide* whenever known. They're run with the usual German sense of organisation and efficiency; they usually have a café and discussion groups and workshops. Another distinctive feature of the feminist scene is the provision of **women's houses** (*Frauenhäuser*) to cater for rape victims and battered wives. There's at least one in every major city: addresses obviously have to be kept secret, but the telephone numbers can be found in the appropriate local directory. To end on a brighter note, there are plenty of **women's bookshops** (the best of which are listed in the *Guide*), as well as women-only *Mitfahrzentralen* (see "Getting Around"). The *Frauen Adressbuch* (Berlin: Courage) gives full feminist listings.

GAY GERMANY

Germany is one of the best countries in Europe in which to be gay (in German, *schwul*). The only real legal restriction is that the male age of consent is 18, and on the whole it's a tolerant place as far as attitudes go.

However to this rosy picture it's necessary to add a serious **caveat**. In rural areas people are often hostile towards gays and this intensifies in the Catholic southern part of the country, particularly in ultra-conservative **Bavaria**. Here small-town prejudice was given a judicial edge by the local parliament which, in 1987 under the late and fairly unlamented Franz-Josef Strauss, introduced mandatory AIDS testing for people who were suspected of being HIV positive. Not content with this draconian measure they also formulated a law whereby HIV positive people who don't follow official guidelines on "proper behaviour" can be arrested and held indefinitely. Both these measures remain firmly in force

Fortunately saner attitudes prevail in the rest of Germany, particularly in the **big cities**, all of which have thriving gay scenes, as do many medium-sized and even relatively small towns. The listings sections in this book usually give a run-down of the gay scene in the larger cities and towns, giving some kind of gay group contact address and telephone number wherever possible.

The main gay targets are Berlin, Hamburg, Cologne, Munich and Frankfurt. Berlin in particular has, despite the horrors of the past, a good record for tolerating an open and energetic gay and lesbian scene; as far back as the 1920s Christopher Isherwood and W.H. Auden both came here, drawn to a city where, in sharp contrast with oppressive London, there was a gay community which did not live in fear of harassment and legal persecution.

The national gay organisation is the *Bundesverband Homosexualität*, PO Box 120 630, 5300 Bonn 12 and there's a also a national AIDS help organisation; the *Deutsche AIDS-Hilfe e.V (D.A.H.)* at Nestorstrasse 8–9, 1000 Berlin 31 (☎030/896 9060). The most widely-read gay magazine is *Männer* which comes out bi-monthly and costs DM16.80.

Many of the attitudes described above apply equally to **lesbians**. Outside of major cities, Germany's lesbian community is perforce more muted; being openly out in rural areas is impossible. Most of the women's centres listed in the *Guide* have details of local bars and meeting places. Alternatively, *GAIA's Guide*, available from bookstores in Britain and Germany, lists lesbian bars and contact addresses throughout the country. Worth scanning while you're in Germany is *UKZ-Unsere Zeitung*, the monthly lesbian magazine

DIRECTORY

ADDRESSES The street name is always written before the number. *Strasse* (street) is commonly abbreviated as *Str.*, and often joined on to the end of the previous word. Other terms include *Gasse* (alley), *Ufer* (quay), *Platz* (square), *Allee* (avenue) and *Ring* (ring road).

AIRPORT TAX does not apply in Germany.

BOOKS The Germans are voracious readers and all large cities have a superb choice of bookshops, many of which also stock a range of English-language publications.

CONTRACEPTIVES A glowing spectrum of **condoms** is available from vending machines installed in just about every toilet throughout

Germany; they can also be bought in supermarkets and pharmacies. If you're into bizarre varieties, you're well catered for; if not, best bring your own. To get a prescription for **the pill** you'll need to see a doctor, so again it's worth stocking up before leaving.

DISABLED TRAVELLERS The **Touristik Union International** (TUI), Postfach 610280, 3000 Hannover 61, (☎0511/5670) has a centralised information bank on many German hotels, pensions and resorts that cater to the needs of disabled travellers or those with specific dietary requirements – not in specially designed and separate establishments, but within the mainstream of German tourist facilities. The TUI can book you on to a package tour or organise rooms according to individual itineraries, taking into account each customer's needs, which are gauged from a questionnaire filled out before booking arrangements commence. Their services also include such details as providing suitable wheelchairs for train travel, the transportation of travellers' own wheelchairs, and the provision of transport at airports and stations.

ELECTRIC CURRENT The supply is 220 volts, and anything requiring 240 volts (all UK appliances) will work. Sockets are of the two-pin variety, so a travel plug is useful.

EMBASSIES AND CONSULATES are listed under the relevant cities. Bear in mind that the level of help, other than in Berlin or Bonn, is likely to be variable – some cities keep up a fantasy diplomatic life, in which the honorary consul is a local businessman who has bought the title for the kudos it confers on him.

JAYWALKING is illegal in Germany and you can be fined if caught. Even in the irreverent atmosphere of west Berlin, locals stand rigidly to attention until the green light comes on – even when there isn't a vehicle in sight.

KIDS Travelling with youngsters shouldn't be a problem. Kids under 4 travel free on the railways; those between 4 and 11 qualify for half-fare. On many municipal public transport tickets, kids travel free if accompanied by an adult. Similarly reduced rates are offered by hotels and guest houses. Most towns and cities have creche facilities: contact tourist offices for details. The most suitable entertainments for kids are listed in the *Guide*.

LAUNDRY Launderettes are not a very common sight in Germany west or east, but they do exist – look under *Wäscherei* in the local Yellow pages to find the nearest. Dry cleaners (*Reinigung*) are more frequent, but also quite expensive. Many youth hostels have washing machines in their basements; otherwise you'll have to make do with a sink.

LEFT LUGGAGE All main stations have a vast number of left luggage lockers. The smallest and cheapest are large enough to hold all but the bulkiest rucksack or suitcase, and at DM2 for 24 hours they make humping heavy luggage around town a false economy. The overwhelming majority of lockers in the former GDR have been converted to accept DM2 coins only, whereas most of those in west Germany also take DM0.50 and DM1 pieces. Leaving bags with the station attendants costs DM2 per item, but this is often the only option in small towns, where the hours of service are often very restricted.

RACISM Thanks to the massive influx of *Gastarbeiter*, mainly from southern Europe, Germany is now firmly multicultural. However, there's no effective law against racial discrimination, and it's far from unknown for crankish pub landlords or nightclub proprietors to refuse entry on simple colour grounds.

STREET NAMES Streets in the former GDR are gradually being stripped of their Communist names, though progress on this is variable: some towns have already changed all maps and nameplates; others are, in different ways, using the two names in tandem; while a few are lagging behind, not intending to make any changes until 1992. The most ubiquitous names which are set to disappear include Karl Marx, Friedrich Engels, Lenin, Rosa Luxemburg, Karl Liebknecht, Ernst Thälmann, Wilhelm Pieck, Otto Grotewohl and Klement Gottwald; there are also many other lesser lights similarly honoured who are about to vanish into well-deserved oblivion.

STUDENT CARDS are worth carrying for the substantial reductions on entry fees they bring.

TIME GMT plus one hour. Clocks are turned an hour forward at the end of March, and an hour back at the end of September.

TIPPING This is seldom necessary in west German restaurants, as prices are almost invariably inclusive, but rounding up to at least the next mark is still expected in the former GDR – and even if you omit to say so, this will often be taken as read when change is proffered. In taxis, add a mark or two to the total.

CHAPTER ONE

BAVARIA

Bavaria (*Bayern*) is the original home of many of Germany's best-known clichés: beer-swilling *Lederhosen*-clad men, sausage dogs, cowbells and Alpine villages, *Sauerkraut* and *Wurst* and the fairy-tale castle of Neuschwanstein. Yet all this is only a small part of the Bavarian picture, and one that's restricted to the Alpine areas of the south.

Historically and **politically**, Bavaria has always occupied a special position within Germany. Although a wealthy duchy within the Holy Roman Empire, its rulers preferred artistic patronage to the territorial expansionism and dynastic feuding characteristic of the rest of the nation. A fundamental change in status occurred at the beginning of the nineteenth century, when it profited from Napoleon's decision to re-order the map of Germany: Bavaria was doubled in size, and promoted to the rank of a kingdom. Thereafter, it retained much of its independence and its own monarch, even after the union of Germany in 1871. Following the abdication of the monarchy after World War I, Bavaria briefly became a free state, but quickly became a hotbed of right-wing extremism: Hitler had his first successes there, and for several years the Nazi Party was regarded elsewhere in Germany as a provincial Bavarian joke. This reputation for reactionary politics continues to the present day: Bavaria has long been ruled by the ultra-conservative CSU, the often uneasy sister party and coalition partner of Germany's ruling CDU. Until his death in 1988, local politics had been dominated for three decades by Franz Josef Strauss, state Minister-President – and general bogeyman to non-right-wing Germans. In the rest of Germany Bavarian stereotypes abound; the typical *Bayer* is seen as a loud bully intent on getting his or her own way. Bavarians see themselves as warm, humorous lovers of a good time. Take your pick, though the chances are you'll find elements of truth in each view.

Bavaria is made up of four distinct regions, each with its own identity and culture, and its cities are equally varied in character. In **Munich** Bavaria has a cosmopolitan, if conservative, capital, that ranks as one of Germany's star attractions. The city lies at the centre of **Upper Bavaria**, the state's heartland, a region that ranges from the snow-capped peaks of the **Alps** to gentle hop-growing farmland. It's a traditional, deeply Catholic area whose rural traditions continue in spite of the inroads of mass tourism. Architectural tastes are marked by a preference for extremes, from extravagant late Gothic via decadent Mannerism and the most grandiose Baroque to the effervescent Rococo style – seen at its best in the pilgrimage churches – for which the province is famous.

West of here is **Bavarian Swabia**, detached by Napoleon from the rest of its traditional province, which was thereafter officially know as Württemberg. Nonetheless, it remains subbornly tied to its former province in cultural outlook – seen most obviously in the distinctive pasta-based cuisine – even though it is also the home of the most famous of the outrageous Romantic castles which form such a crucial part of the Bavarian stereotype. Outside of the mountainous **Allgäu** area in the south, this is a region of undulating agricultural country, ideal for walking and cycling holidays, dotted with medieval towns along the route of the **Romantic Road** – one of Germany's major tourist routes – and the upper reaches of the **River Danube**. The pristine local capital of **Augsburg** has been a place of importance since the days of the Romans, and has a

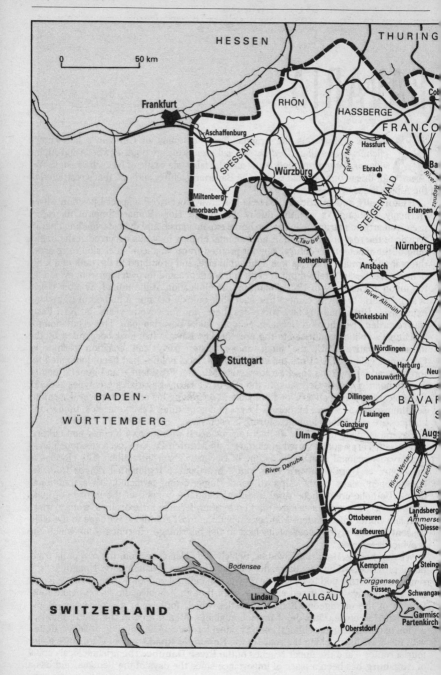

highly distinctive appearance, thanks to the resplendent Renaissance buildings from the time when it was the banking capital of Europe.

To the north lies **Franconia**, which was likewise not absorbed into Bavaria until 1803, and which remains an area apart: most Franconians prefer to cultivate their own heritage, considering it more refined than that of their southern cousins. The most obvious evidence of Franconia's separateness can be seen in the wine-growing area around **Würzburg** in the northwest, where a culture quite at odds with the beer-loving rest of Bavaria exists. In the northeast of Franconia the difference can be seen most obviously in the elegantly plain Baroque architecture of the Lutheran strongholds of **Ansbach** and **Bayreuth** – the Reformation left Franconia more or less split down the middle along religious lines. The capital **Nürnberg**, a city risen from the rubble of wartime destruction and restored to the splendour of its Middle Ages heyday, was another city which quickly embraced Protestantism. Yet nearby **Bamberg**, whose magnificently varied architectural legacy is unsurpassed in all of Germany, remained staunchly Catholic.

Eastern Bavaria, incorporating the old provinces of Lower Bavaria and the Upper Palatinate, is the state's backwater; a rustic, relatively poor region where life in the highlands revolves around logging and workshop industries like traditional glass production. However, the region also has a number of urban attractions, most notably the wonderfully well-preserved medieval cities of **Regensburg** and **Landshut** – each of which was once capital of Bavaria – and the border town of **Passau**, notable for its harmonious Baroque layout.

Travel is made easy by a generally good network of trains and regional buses, though public transport is sometimes a little thin on the ground in Bavarian Swabia and Eastern Bavaria – having a car makes life easier here. Cycling is an excellent and very popular way to get around, and is facilitated by a great many marked cycling paths throughout the state. **Accommodation** is uniformly good, and it's normally not too difficult to find a bed, though problems may be experienced in the mountain resorts and some of the more popular tourist towns. An unfortunate **restriction for travellers over 27** is that they're barred from using youth hostels, though reasonably priced private rooms in most places should compensate.

MUNICH (MÜNCHEN)

Pending Berlin's full recovery from its long period of division, **MUNICH** is the German city which most has the air of a capital about it. Even though it has never ruled over a territory any larger than the present-day Land, the grandiose palaces from Bavaria's era as an independent kingdom give it the appearance of a metropolis of great importance. When this is added to a remarkable postwar economic record (courtesy of such hi-tech giants as the car manufacturer BMW, the aerospace company MBB, and the electronics group Siemens), and to its hard-won status as the national trendsetter in fashion matters, it's easy to see why Munich is often presented as a German Paris. This is the place most Germans want to come to if they are forced to leave their own beloved *Heimat*: students flock here to study; the rich and jet-set like to live here, as do writers, painters, musicians and film-makers, creating one of Europe's most vibrant cultural scenes. It's all the more ironic, therefore, that Munich's other, more familiar face is of a homely city of provincially-minded locals whose zest for drinking, seen at an extreme during the annual **Oktoberfest**, is kept up all year round in cavernous beer halls and spacious gardens. Another paradox is that, while the city has gained notoriety as a hotbed of right-wing extremism ever since Hitler established his first political foothold there, it's actually very liberal by Bavarian standards: it was a noted centre of resistance to Nazism, and has generally been governed by the SPD, currently in alliance with the Greens.

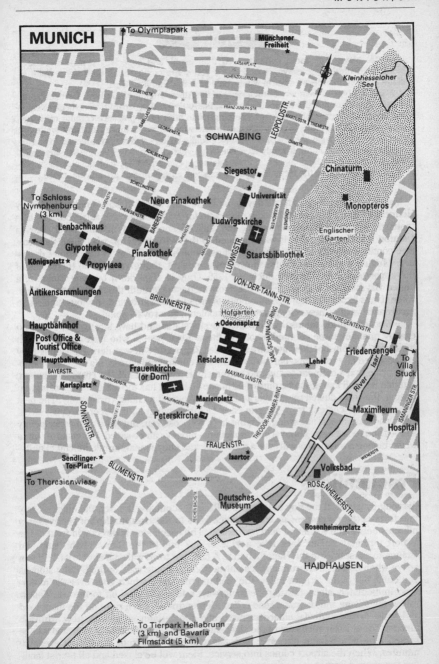

MUNICH

To Olympiapark

Münchener
Freiheit ★

KAISERPLATZ

HOHENZOLLERNSTR.

Kleinhesseloher
See

ELISABETHSTR.

FRANZ-JOSEPH STR

SCHWABING

Siegestor ★

Chinaturm

Neue Pinakothek

Universität ★

Monopteros

To Schloss
Nymphenburg
(3 km)

Lenbachhaus

Ludwigskirche

Glyptothek

Alte
Pinakothek

Englischer
Garten

Königsplatz ★

Propylaea

Staatsbibliothek

Antikensammlungen

BRIENNERSTR.

VON-DER-TANN-STR.

PRINZREGENTENSTR.

Hofgarten

Hauptbahnhof

Odeonsplatz ★

Post Office &
Tourist Office

Friedensengel ★

★ Hauptbahnhof

Residenz

Lehel ★

To
Villa
Stuck

BAYERSTR.

MAXIMILIANSTR.

Karlsplatz ★

Frauenkirche
(or Dom) ★

Maximileum

Marienplatz ★

Hospital

Peterskirche ★

FRAUENSTR.

Sendlinger- ★
Tor-Platz

Isartor ★

BLUMENSTR.

Volksbad

To Theresienwiese

ROSENHEIMERSTR.

Deutsches
Museum

Rosenheimerplatz ★

HAIDHAUSEN

To Tierpark Hellabrunn
(3 km) and Bavaria
Filmstadt (5 km)

FÖHN

If people seem even more bad-tempered than usual, and especially if car-drivers are being particularly aggressive, look up . . . if you see a picture-book blue sky without a cloud in sight and there's a warm wind, you'll probably find it's **Föhn**.

Föhn is a type of weather characteristic of the Alpine region of southern Germany, but it's also found around the Rocky Mountains, the Andes and in Japan. No-one is quite sure exactly why it occurs, but it has something to do with high pressure coming over the mountains which results in clear skies and warm weather in southern Germany, while on the Italian side it's cloudy and often raining. Usually visitors and new residents don't have any problems with Föhn. It's only after five to ten years that people become sensitive and suffer various combinations of migraine, fainting spells, irritability and sleeplessness. So while you're enjoying the views, don't be surprised if all around you are in a foul mood.

Munich is something of a late developer in German terms. It was founded in 1158 by Henry the Lion, the powerful Saxon duke who for a short time also ruled Bavaria, as a monastic village (*Mönchen*=monks) and toll-collection point on the River Isar, a Danube tributary. In 1180, it was allocated to the **Wittelsbachs**, who ruled the province continuously until 1918 – the longest period achieved by any of the nation's dynasties. Munich was initially overshadowed by Landshut, though it became the capital of the upper part of the divided duchy in 1255. Only in 1503 did it become capital of a united Bavaria, and it remained of relatively modest size until the nineteenth century, when it was expanded into a planned city of broad boulevards and spacious squares in accordance with its new role, granted by Napoleon, as a royal capital.

Münchener pride themselves on their special status and have strong views on who exactly qualifies to be counted as one of them. Even people who have made Munich their home for most of their lives are still called *Zugereiste* ("newcomers"), meaning they are accepted city residents, but are by no means considered equals. It's the sort of stubborn pride that's both endearing and extremely irritating. Despite its cosmopolitanism, Munich is small enough to be digestible in one visit, and has the added bonus of a great setting, the snow-dusted mountains and Alpine lakes just an hour's drive away. The best time of year to come is from June to early October, when all the beer gardens, street cafés and bars are in full swing. Staying here will cost you, but it's worth every penny and – if you're not fussy about accommodation – money can be saved. For visits of over a week, buying a travel pass will save a great deal, and cheap meals aren't difficult to find.

Practicalities

Arriving by **plane** at the tiny old airport of **Riem** just outside the city, the quickest way into town is the *Flughafen-City* coach, which goes to the **Hauptbahnhof** every twenty minutes between 6.40am and 9pm for DM5.50. The coach stop is directly in front of the airport terminal. Failing this, take a #139 or #37 bus to the Riem S-Bahn stop and change to a fast train to the Hauptbahnhof. A taxi into town will cost about DM25. If you arrive when no buses are running, it's only a twenty-minute walk to the S-Bahn stop: as you come out of the airport, follow the road to your right, which goes over the motorway. Immediately after crossing the motorway, a footpath goes off to the left. Follow this to the village and the main road called Riemerstrasse. Turn right off the main road and walk to the end of Leibergerstrasse and the S-Bahn stop. The **new Munich airport**, some 30km northeast of the city centre, is due to open in May 1992 and will be served by a new S-Bahn line, #S8, with departures to and from the airport every 20 minutes. When the airport comes into service, Riem will be closed and all tourist facilities transferred from there to the new terminal.

There's a **tourist information desk** in the arrivals area of the airport for general information, free maps and lists of hotels, but they can't book rooms. At the Hauptbahnhof, the **main tourist office** (Mon–Sat 8am–11pm, Sun 1–9.30pm; ☎239 1256) is opposite platform 11. Other useful items in the vicinity are a **bank** (daily 6am–11.30pm) and a **24-hour post office**, just across the street from the tourist office. The inter-city **bus station** is also just a stone's throw away.

Public transport

Munich's public transport system is good, though the fare and ticketing system is complicated. Best bet is to buy a **travel pass** on arrival, from the Hauptbahnhof ticket office – to reach it go down to the U-Bahn level and follow signs to the Starnberger Bahnhof and then to the *Zeitkartenstelle*. Prices vary according to how many zones are required. Your best bet is to buy a pass for zones 0000 and 1200 which cover the city centre and most of Schwabing. This currently costs DM11.40 for a week or DM44.50 for a month. One drawback is that passes are only valid from Monday to Monday, so buying mid-week means losing out. A weekly pass for the entire city transport system, including places like the Ammersee or Dachau, costs DM46.20. A pass for just the city without the regional S-Bahn routes costs DM29.70 per week or DM115.50 per month. There are also *Zeitkarten* offices at the Ostbahnhof and at the Poccistrasse U-Bahn station. You'll need your passport and two photos to buy any of these passes – and be prepared to queue.

Tickets

Otherwise, tickets for city transport are available from ticket machines in all U-Bahn stations, at some bus and tram stops, and inside trams. This is where it gets particularly complicated: if you're going longer distances across the city you will need to buy a **blue ticket** (DM10), and then stamp two strips for every zone crossed. To find out how many strips you need to delete, either ask the conductor or at a ticket office. Alternatively, look at the transport maps at any station, tram or bus stop, which show the number of zones between any two points. **Red tickets** (DM8) are only for children aged 4-15 or short trips for adults. **Twenty-four-hour tickets** for the entire city cost DM8, or DM16 for the city and S-Bahn region. Tickets must be stamped before any journey, though it's not necessary to stamp every strip; it's just the last that needs to be deleted. Those freeloading without a ticket face an on-the-spot DM60 fine, which is frequently enforced. Plain-clothed ticket controllers turn up regularly, and anyone without immediate cash or ID is taken to the nearest police station.

Finding a place to stay

Cheap **accommodation** can be hard to find, especially during the high season in the summer, though prices are usually constant throughout the year. It is virtually impossible to find accommodation during the Oktoberfest beer festival/fair that runs from the last Saturday in September to the first Sunday in October. Turn up very early in the day to be in with a chance, and be prepared to queue for hours at the tourist office. The least expensive option for those under 23 is the *Kapuzinerhölzl* mega-tent, run by the city council during the summer, where up to 500 people sleep *en masse*. Those under 27 can use one of the city's three **hostels**, while for those over 27 the cheapest option is the very central *Haus International*. For just a little more money, considerably greater comfort can be found among the city's **pensions** and **hotels**. The tourist office at the Hauptbahnhof will book rooms for you for a fee of DM4, and, whatever your choice, it would be sensible to phone first. There are also four main **campsites** in and around the city.

Hostels

If you're under 27 or a parent travelling with children under 18, there's a choice of three **youth hostels**. Most central is at *Wendl-Dietrich-Strasse 20* (☎131156): U-Bahn to Rotkreuzplatz, then walk down the Wendl-Dietrich-Strasse. This is the largest and most basic hostel, with 535 beds in assorted dormitories. Prices start at DM14.80 for bed and breakfast, plus DM3 extra for sheets if you don't have a sleeping bag. Warm meals from DM5.50, check-in time noon–1am. Smaller, though more upmarket, is the *Youth Guesthouse Thalkirchen* at Miesingstr. 4 (☎723 6550): U-Bahn to Harras, then tram #16 to Boschetsriederstrasse. Prices (including breakfast) range from DM21 for a bed in a large dormitory to DM29 for a single room. Check-in time 7am–11pm. Not very central, but in an old castle right next to the Isar, is *Burg Schwaneck*, Burgweg 4-6, 8023 Pullach (☎793 0643): S-Bahn #7 to Pullach and then follow the signs to the *Jugendherberge*. Prices range from DM11.80 in six- to eight-bed rooms to DM13.80 in four-bed rooms, all including breakfast. Check-in time 5pm–1am.

A further choice for which you don't need a hostel card, and for which there's no age limit, is the *Haus International*, Elisabethstr. 87 (☎185081): U-Bahn to Hohenzollernplatz, then bus #33 or tram #12, and get off two stops later at Barbarastrasse. Centrally located in Schwabing, room sizes range from five beds (DM31 per person) to singles (DM44). Phone first. There's a youth hostel for **women only**, with an age limit of 25, very near the Hauptbahnhof at Goethestr. 9 (☎555891). Prices are around DM27–31, and again it's advisable to phone ahead.

Camping

Among the **camping** options, the cheapest for under-23s is the *Kapuzinerhölzl* youth camp, open from the end of June to the end of August: take the U-Bahn to Rotkreuzplatz, then tram #12 to the Botanischer Garten, walk down Franz-Schrank-Strasse and turn left at the end of the road. Apart from the sleeping tent, there are showers, a canteen and an information bureau. Price per person is DM6, which includes blankets, an air mattress and tea in the morning. Check-in time 5pm–9am. If you don't mind the lack of privacy and the imperfect security for personal belongings, this is a cheap and fun place to be, and although its officially for travellers under 23 and for a maximum of three nights, the people in charge are very flexible and older girl-friends or boyfriends won't usually be turned away. For more information, phone ☎141 43000.

The best conventional campsite is *Thalkirchen* at Zentralländerstr. 49 (15 March–31 Oct; ☎723 1707): U-Bahn to Implerstrasse, then bus #57 to its final stop. (Once the new U-Bahn route is finished, take it to Thalkirchen.) It's the most central site for the city and in an attractive part of the Isar river valley. Be warned that it's very popular during the Oktoberfest period because it's very close to the fairground. Second choice is the *Obermenzing* site, at Lochhausenerstr. 59 (15 March–31 Oct; ☎811 2235): S-Bahn to Obermenzing, then bus #75 to Lochhausenerstrasse about five stops later. This site is in a posh suburb and close to the magnificent Nymphenburg palace and parks. The campsite at *Dachauerstr. 571* (☎150 6936) is open all year, but awkward to reach: S-Bahn to Moosach, then bus #709 or #710 to the site.

Hotels and pensions

Reckon on an absolute minimum of about DM40 for a single room; most often you'll pay around DM60. Usually the shower will be shared and breakfast is always included in the price. Many pensions offer rooms with three to six beds, and these are a very good way to cut costs if you're travelling in a group and much more pleasant than hostel-type accommodation. Almost all the places listed here are in Schwabing and all are within close range of where you'll want to be.

SINGLES FROM DM40–60, DOUBLES DM65–110

Am Kaiserplatz, Kaiserplatz 12 (☎349190). Singles DM39, doubles DM67–75. Very friendly, good location and big rooms. Wacky decor, with each room done in a different style – ranging from red satin to Bavarian rustic.

Clara, Wilhelmstr. 25 (☎348374). Singles DM55, doubles at DM80–98. Close to the Leopoldstrasse.

Excelsior, Kaulbachstr. 85 (☎348213). Only has doubles at DM90–95. Opposite the *Irish Pub* and close to the Leopoldstrasse.

Frank, Schellingstr. 24 (☎281451). Singles DM55, doubles DM70–85, 3–4 bed rooms for DM40 per person. Best place in town in terms of prices and atmosphere. Mainly frequented by young travellers. Lovely big rooms, and there's a fridge available to keep food in.

Isabella, Isabellastr. 35 (☎271 3503). Singles DM26–36, doubles DM62–68. Only has 12 beds with one bathroom on the landing. Run by a quirky old lady.

Steinberg, Ohmstr. 9 (☎331011). Singles DM45–69, doubles DM85–120. Friendly and good location.

Strigl, Elisabethstr. 11 (☎271 3444). Singles DM50–55, doubles DM75–85. Rather gruff management, but good location and reasonable prices.

Wilhelmy, Amalienstr. 71. Singles DM45–55, doubles DM75–88, 3–4 bed rooms at DM40 per person. Very quiet and well-situated.

SINGLES FROM DM60–95, DM100–160

Adria, Liebigstr. 8a (☎293081/83). Singles DM80–185, doubles DM140–210. Quiet residential area, but close to Schwabing. Hotel standard rather than pension.

Blauer Bock, Sebastiansplatz 9 (☎231780). A recommended central hotel. Singles DM60–100, doubles DM85–140.

Hauser, Schellingstr. 11 (☎281006). Singles DM85–100, doubles DM110–160. Nothing special, but good location.

Hotel Eder, Zweigstr. 8 (☎554560). Singles DM55–70, doubles DM85–130, 3-bed rooms DM165–185. Quiet road, but very central between the Hauptbahnhof and the Marienplatz.

Lettl, Amalienstr. 53 (☎283026). Singles DM94–140, doubles DM150–190. Friendly hotel.

Münchener Kindl, Damenstiftstr. 16 (☎264349). Singles DM70–85, doubles DM110–150. Close to the Marienplatz and yet the road is very peaceful, out of the maelstrom of busy shoppers.

Stephanie, Türkenstr. 35 (☎284031). Singles DM 60–95, doubles DM100–140. Useful only if everywhere else is full.

The city

Heart of the city and its Altstadt is the **Marienplatz**; the pedestrian centre fans out from here in an approximate circle of one square kilometre. This is tourist and shopping land, with all the city's major department stores, the central market, the royal palace and the most important churches. North of Marienplatz, Ludwigstrasse and Leopoldstrasse run straight through the heart of **Schwabing**, Munich's entertainment quarter, full of *Schickies* (German yuppies) who frequent the many bars and pose in the street cafés. It's also close to the city's main park, known as the **Englischer Garten**, with one of the city's most famous beer gardens, the *Chinesischer Turm*. West of the Marienplatz–Schwabing axis is the main **museum quarter**, with the superb Alte Pinakothek and the most important of Munich's 36 museums. Running the length of the eastern part of town is the River Isar, and under the heading *Along the Isar*, you'll find a description of a side of Munich not usually seen by visitors. **Nymphenburg**, with its palace and gardens, is the most enticing of the outer districts.

> The telephone code for Munich is ☎089

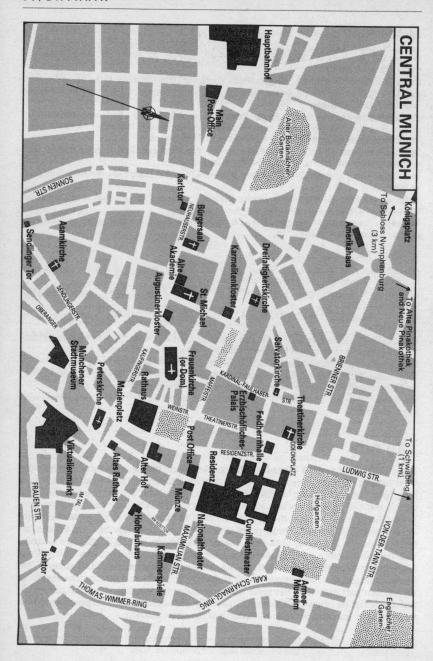

CENTRAL MUNICH

Hauptbahnhof

Main Post Office

Alter Botanischer Garten

Königsplatz

To Schloss Nymphenburg (3 km)

To Alte Pinakothek and Neue Pinakothek

Amerikahaus

SONNEN STR.

Karlstor

NEUHAUSERSTR.

Bürgersaal

Asamkirche

Sendlinger Tor

SENDLINGERSTR.

OBERANGER

Alte Akademie

St. Michael

Augustinerkloster

Karmelitenkloster

Dreifaltigkeitskirche

Salvatorkirche

BRIENNER STR.

KARDINAL-FAULHABER-STR.

Erzbischöfliches Palais

Theatinerkirche

ODEONSPLATZ

To Schwabing (1 km)

LUDWIG STR.

Münchener Stadtmuseum

Peterskirche

Rathaus

KAUFINGERSTR.

Frauenkirche (or Dom)

MAXFESTR.

WEINSTR.

THEATINERSTR.

Post Office

Feldherrnhalle

RESIDENZSTR.

Hofgarten

VON-DER-TANN STR.

Viktualienmarkt

FRAUEN STR.

Marienplatz

Altes Rathaus

IM TAL

Alter Hof

Hofbräuhaus

AM KOSTTOR

Residenz

Münze

MAXIMILIAN STR.

Nationaltheater

Cuvilliéstheater

Isartor

THOMAS-WIMMER-RING

Kammerspiele

KARL-SCHARNAGL-RING

Armee-Museum

Englischer Garten

The Altstadt

Relatively little is left of medieval Munich, but three of the **gateways** remain to mark today's city centre. Bounded by the **Odeonsplatz** and the **Sendlinger Tor** to the north and south, and the **Isartor** and **Karlstor** to the east and west, it's only a fifteen-minute walk from one end to the other. This doesn't mean you can see everything in one day: the place is tightly packed and realistically needs two or three days to explore thoroughly.

Marienplatz and around

Marienplatz marks the most central spot in the city and the heart of the U-Bahn system below. About a quarter of the size of London's Trafalgar Square, there's something almost cosy about it: street musicians and artists entertain the crowds and local youths lounge around the central fountain. At 11am and noon, the square fills with gawping tourists and the noise of clicking shutters as the carillon in the **Rathaus** jingles into action, displaying two events that happened on this spot: the marriage of Wilhelm V to Renata von Lothringen in 1568, and the first *Schäfflertanz* ("coopers' dance") of 1517, intended to cheer people up during the plague. This dance is still held every seven years, next in 1998.

The Rathaus itself is an ugly neo-Gothic monstrosity built in the late nineteenth century; the only redeeming features are the view from the **tower** (May–Oct Mon–Fri 9am–4pm, Sat & Sun 10am–7pm; DM2) and the open-air **café** in the cool and breezy courtyard, perfect for having a drink away from the crowds. To the right is the plain Gothic tower of the **Altes Rathaus**, which was rebuilt in its original fifteenth-century style after being destroyed by lightning. Today it houses the **Spielzeug Museum** (Mon–Sat 10am–5.30pm, Sun 10am–6pm; DM4, DM1 kids), a fascinating collection of toys, including many long out of fashion.

Just to the south is the slightly elevated **Peterskirche** (popularly known as *Alter Peter*), the oldest church within the bounds of the old city walls. Its distinctive **tower** (Mon–Fri 9am–8/5pm, Sun 10am–5/7pm according to season; DM2) offers an even higher and better view than that from the Rathaus, and is far less touristed. Originally a pillared Romanesque basilica, the church owes its present form to a fourteenth-century Gothic rebuilding following a fire. The **high altar** is a collaboration between Erasmus Grasser and Jan Polack, respectively Munich's leading sculptor and painter in the fertile late Gothic period; there are also many embellishments by the city's leading Baroque and Rococo artists. However, your attention is most likely to be caught by the grizzly **shrine to Saint Munditia**, the patron saint of single women. Her skeletal relics are poised in a glass box on a side altar, including the skull wrapped in netting with two glass eyes gazing out from a deathly face.

Following Burgstrasse or Sparkassenstrasse from the Altes Rathaus, you soon come to the **Alter Hof**, a shady medieval courtyard which was the original palace of the Wittelsbachs. To the north lie the **Postamt**, a Baroque palace transformed last century to serve as the post office, and the Renaissance **Münze** (Mint). However, the prime attraction in this area is the **Hofbräuhaus** just to the east. This describes itself, without fear of contradiction, as "the most famous pub in the world", and is the epitome of the Munich beer hall, with its spacious chambers, hard benches, well-worn tables, crowds of revellers and traditional oompah music. Originally the court brewery, it boasts an uninterrupted tradition dating back to 1589, though the present building is some three centuries younger. A favourite haunt of Hitler in the days when he was struggling to establish the Nazi Party, it still has a hard-core local clientele, though these days it's mainly patronised by tourists, who are charged rip-off prices for an admittedly excellent *Mass* (measure) of beer.

The Frauenkirche

The other great symbol of Munich is the **Frauenkirche** (or **Dom**), whose copper onion-domed towers – one a little shorter than the other – dominate the skyline. It stands in its own small square, just to the west of the Rathaus. Close up, the building, built as a parish church but now the seat of an archbishop, isn't really seen to its best advantage: its redbrick Gothic architecture is unrelievedly spare. The lofty white-washed interior, however, has inspired the **legend of the Devil's Footprint**. Apparently the architect Jerg Ganghofer (who also built most of the other surviving medieval monuments in the city) made a pact with the Devil: in order to get enough money to complete this church, he had to construct it without a single visible window. When the Devil came to inspect the completed church, he saw the high Gothic windows from a distance and thought he'd get the builder's soul. Once inside, he was led to a certain point from which not one window was visible, since all were hidden by pillars. Stamping his foot in rage the Devil stormed off, leaving his black footprint in the pavement by the entrance hall. Rebuilding following war damage has meant the trick no longer quite works from this particular point, but the footprint is still there.

In the first nave chapel to the south is the huge Mannerist **tomb of Ludwig IV**, a belated tribute, made over a hundred years after his death, to the first of only two Wittelsbachs who managed to get elected as Holy Roman Emperor. Many of the figures are by Hubert Gerhard, a Dutch-born sculptor whose work is still a ubiquitous feature of the city. Many of the church's other artistic treasures have been destroyed, among them Erasmus Grasser's **choir stalls**, though the arresting wooden statues were saved and placed on the modern replacements. There also remain beautiful stained glass windows in the ambulatory chapels, notably the central Sakramentskapelle, which also has a notable painted **altar**, *The Virgin of the Protecting Cloak*, by Jan Polack.

West of Marienplatz

The almost straight line between Marienplatz and the Hauptbahnhof is the hub of the city's commercial activity; alongside the numerous department stores, many of the city's most famous beer halls are to be found, as well as a series of contrasting churches. At the point where the pedestrianised Kaufingerstrasse changes its name to Neuhauser Strasse, you'll find the deconsecrated **Augustinerkloster**, now housing the **Deutsches Jagd- und Fischerei Museum** (daily 9.30am–5pm, Mon also 7–9pm; DM4), an array of hunting and fishing trophies which is hardly in line with today's atti-tudes to blood sports.

A little further down the street, the Mannerist facade of **St Michael** stands unassum-ingly in line with the street's other buildings. Built between 1583 and 1597 under the auspices of Wilhelm V, this Jesuit church – the first in northern Europe – was intended to symbolise the local victory of Catholicism over Lutherism. Hubert Gerhard's large bronze statue between the two entrances shows the Archangel Michael fighting for the Faith and killing Evil in the shape of a satyr. The interior, with a barrel vault second only in size to St Peter's in Rome, is decorated in elegant white stucco. In the crypt below (Mon–Fri 10am–1pm and 2–4pm, Sat 10am–3pm; DM1) you'll find the tombs of the Wittelsbach dynasty, among them the famous castle-builder Ludwig II, whose coffin is permanently draped with flowers, a candle burning at its foot.

Alongside the church, forming a continuous architectural unit with it, is the **Alte Akademie**, the college where the Jesuits instilled their burning missionary ideals in the hearts and minds of their pupils. In front is the **Richard-Strauss-Brunnen**, a foun-tain in honour of the Munich-born composer whose lushly orchestrated works continue to polarise opinion among music lovers to an extent rivalled only by his own great idol, Wagner. The reliefs show scenes from his highly erotic opera *Salomé*, based on Oscar Wilde's play of the same name.

Continuing westwards, you soon arrive at the **Bürgersaal**, which was built for a Marian student congregation in the early eighteenth century but later transferred to the Jesuits. Pride of the upstairs **oratory** (Mon–Fri 11am–3pm) is a set of guardian angels under the organ gallery, carved by Ignaz Günther, Bavaria's greatest Rococo sculptor. However, it's the crypt at entrance level that is most visited, since **Rupert Mayer**, one of the city's main Nazi opponents, is buried here and his grave has become something of a pilgrims' centre, particularly since his recent beatification. Father Mayer was the parish priest during the war and became such a nuisance to the authorities that he was shipped off to Sachsenhausen concentration camp. Because of his immense popularity and the bad press his death would have caused, he was transferred to house arrest in the Alpine Ettal monastery. He survived to return to the Bürgersaal after the war, but died later the same year.

South of Marienplatz

Immediately south of Peterskirche is the **Viktualienmarkt**, the city's main market-place for the last 200 years. Bossy women sell delicious-looking fruit and veg, as well as all kinds of cheeses, meats and delicatessen; if you get talked into buying, be warned it's not cheap, though the quality is excellent. Right in the middle of all the bustle is a small beer garden, a good place to have a snack.

On St Jakobsplatz to the rear is the **Münchener Stadtmuseum** (Tues–Sat 9am–4.30pm, Sun 10am–6pm; DM5, DM2.50 students). This has fascinating permanent displays about the history of the city, supplemented by changing special exhibitions. Look out in particular for the magnificently contorted set of *Morris Dancers*, carved as adornments for the ballroom of the Altes Rathaus by Erasmus Grasser. Also here are a number of specialist collections – on photos and films, brewing, and puppets. The last-named is one of the largest in the world, ranging from Indian and Chinese paper dolls to the large mechanical European variety.

To the west is Sendlinger Strasse, where at no. 62 you can see the small **Asamkirche** (officially known as **St-Johann-Nepomuk**), one of the most enchanting examples of a Rococo church in Bavaria. Built between 1733 and 1746, it's the crowning effort of the partnership of the two Asam brothers, who here successfully achieved their goal of a building whose architecture was completely integrated with all aspects of its interior decoration. The younger brother, Egid Quirin Asam (who was the sculptor and stuccoist), bought the land and underwrote the cost of the whole enterprise, which was intended to serve as his private family church, and therefore one where he had the rare luxury of being able to put his artistic ideals into effect without the intervention of a patron. If you're not used to the wild use of colour and gold and countless plaster curls, the interior will seem completely over the top – but it's a perfect example of its kind. Asam added a Rococo facade to the sixteenth-century house next door and lived there for the rest of his life.

North of Marienplatz

The poshest part of the city centre lies north of Marienplatz, where ritzy shops and expensive cafés line Theatinerstrasse, Maffeistrasse and Kardinal-Faulhaber-Strasse. The last-named has the most ostentatious buildings of the lot, mostly palaces of the earlier rich which have been turned into banks and insurance houses. One which is still lived in is François Cuvilliés' **Erzbischöfliches-Palais**, the residence of the local archbishop. At the end of the street is the tall six-storey Gothic tower of the **Salvatorkirche**, the former cemetery chapel of the Frauenkirche, but designated as the church of the local Greek Orthodox community three years before Prince Otto of Bavaria became King of Greece in 1832.

East of here, on Parcellistrasse, is the former **Karmelitenkloster**, which, when it was built in the 1650s, marked the belated German debut of the Baroque style, building activity having been effectively suspended during the Thirty Years' War. It was all but destroyed in an air raid, though the church has been reconstructed to serve as a library. In contrast, another Carmelite church further along the street, the **Dreifaltigkeitskirche**, was one of the few historic buildings in Munich to come through the last war unscathed. It's a copybook example of Italianate Baroque by the Swiss architect Giovanni Antonio Viscardi (who was also responsible for the design of the Bürgersaal), with a vivacious dome fresco of *The Adoration of the Trinity*.

The Residenz

In the late fourteenth century, the Wittelsbachs moved their seat from the Alter Hof in the heart of the Altstadt to a new site at what was then the northeastern periphery of the town. Between 1570 and 1620, this fortress was replaced by a splendid Mannerist **Residenz**, constructed by a team of mostly Netherlandish architects and designers led by **Friedrich Sustris**. It was modified and expanded in the Baroque and Rococo periods, though the most significant additions were made, in accordance with its new function as a royal palace, by **Leo von Klenze**, the architect primarily responsible for giving Munich its nineteenth-century face: he added the rusticated Königsbau facing Max-Joseph-Platz to the south and the Festsaalbau on the garden side to the north. Extensively destroyed in the last war, the Residenz was almost totally rebuilt in the 1950s and 1960s – and is still the subject of restoration work.

The Residenzmuseum

About half the palace, including all the most significant historical apartments, is open to the public as the **Residenzmuseum** (Tues–Sat 10am–4.30pm, Sun 10am–1pm; DM3.50), entered from Max-Joseph-Platz. To see it all you have to go round twice, as part of it is open mornings only, with a different section open in the afternoons.

On both tours, you see the **Ahnengalerie** (Ancestors' Gallery), decorated in the richest Rococo style, which looks for all the world like a Hall of Mirrors, except that the glass is replaced by 121 (mostly imaginary) portraits of the Wittelsbachs, who tried to give their line the most prestigious roots possible by including tenuously linked predecessors like Charlemagne. The morning tour then procedes to the Mannerist **Grottenhof** (Grotto Court), whose centrepiece is a fountain with a statue of Perseus. Under the loggia is the grotto of tufa, crystal and coloured shells, framing a statue of Mercury. Alongside is the **Antiquarium**, the oldest and most original part of the palace. This long, cavernous chamber was built in 1571 to house the family's famous collection of antiquities. A generation later, its austere architecture was sharply modified in accordance with the new Mannerist craze to serve as a festive hall, and its tunnel vault covered with humanist-inspired frescos. In the **Kurfürstenzimmer** (Rooms of the Elector), look out for three paintings by Bernardo Bellotto, who here applied to Munich the technique his uncle Canaletto had used so successfully to immortalise the Venice of his day. Other highlights of the morning circuit are a passageway hung with a cycle of 25 views of Italy by the Munich Romantic painter Carl Rottmann, and a suite of rooms containing extensive collections of fourteenth- to nineteenth-century Chinese, Japanese and European porcelain.

The last stage of the morning tour can also be seen in the afternoon. This includes the eight appropriately named **Reiche Zimmer** (Rich Rooms) in the sumptuous Rococo style of François Cuvilliés, and the five **Nibelungen Säle** (Halls of the Nibelungs), in which medieval Germany's most famous epic is depicted in a series of paintings by Julius Schnorr von Carolsfeld. Other rooms can be seen in the afternoon only, and include further displays of ceramics, along with the silverware collection and the Baroque **Goldener Saal** (Golden Hall). You can also see the two chapels, which were both built in the early years of the seventeenth century. The larger **Hofkapelle**, which is closely modelled on the town church of St Michael, was for general use, while the more lavish **Reichekapelle** was built for the private meditations of one of the most famous of the Wittelsbachs, Maximilian I. Another memento of Maximilian comes with the **Steinzimmer**, a suite of profusely furnished rooms with a complicated set of allegories illustrating the Elector's personal vision of the world and the after-life.

The Schatzkammer

Sharing the same entrance but requiring a separate ticket is the **Schatzkammer** (same times; DM3.50), which houses a really fabulous collection of treasures. Among the early items, look out for the late ninth-century **miniature ciborium** that belonged to King Arnulf of Carinthia, and the **cross** of Queen Gisela of Hungary. There's a spectacular array of **crowns** too, but the star piece of the whole display, kept in a room of its own, is the **statuette of St George**, made in Munich around 1590 for Wilhelm V. This has a base of gold, silver and enamel, and is encrusted with diamonds, rubies, sapphires, emeralds and rock crystal to create a truly dazzling effect. The outstanding German Renaissance tradition in the decorative arts can be seen in a host of chalices, tankards, caskets, pendants, clocks and portable altars. Faced with such competition, the Bavarian **crown jewels**, made in the early nineteenth century soon after the duchy was promoted to a kingdom, seem rather tame.

The rest of the complex

From the entrance on Residenzstrasse, you pass through the Kapellenhof into the elongated **Brunnenhof**, in the middle of which stands a large fountain in honour of the Wittelsbachs, replete with allegorical figures of the Elements, river gods, tritons and dragons. At the far end is the entrance to the **Cuvilliéstheater** (Mon–Sat 2–5pm, Sun 10am–5pm; DM2), a perfectly intact Rococo gem, dripping in gold and bristling with intricate carvings and delicate stucco. Formerly the Wittelsbachs' private theatre, it's now the jewel in the crown of the city's performing arts venues, being ideal for Mozartean opera productions. It's deservedly named after the man who built it, **François Cuvilliés**, a tenacious little Walloon who began his career in the debilitating role of court dwarf to the Elector Max Emanuel, but proved that he was capable of greater things by designing defensive systems for the army he was precluded from joining. As a result, he was sent to Paris to study the latest architectural theories, and on his return developed the new Rococo style to its most extravagant limits in a series of stunningly original buildings, of which this is one of the finest.

The northwestern part of the Residenz, entered from Hofgartenstrasse, houses the **Staatliche Sammlung Ägyptischer Kunst** (Tues–Sun 9.30am–4pm, Tues also 7–9pm; DM3). As well as objects from all periods of Egyptian antiquity, this features displays of Coptic art and monumental reliefs from Assyria. Highlights include the gold treasure of the Queen of Meroë and Egyptian statues from the palace of Emperor Hadrian. The **Hofgarten** to the north, formerly the royal park, is an ideal place for a quiet stroll. At the far end, the bombed-out **Armeemuseum** was until recently left as an anti-war memorial: its contents have been transferred to Ingolstadt. Now it's being rebuilt to house the new Bavarian State Chancellery, but it's already known as the "Straussoleum", after Franz Joseph Strauss, whose pet project it was.

The nineteenth-century city

The additions to the Residenz were merely one aspect of the changing face of Munich in line with its new royal status; the city was greatly expanded, particularly to the north, with a series of broad boulevards and spacious squares lined by grandiosely self-confident Neoclassical buildings.

Odeonsplatz

In 1817, Leo von Klenze began the project to link Munich with the outlying village of Schwabing to the north by constructing the **Odeonsplatz** at the far end of the Residenz. The southwest corner of this square, however, was already occupied by the Baroque **Theatinerkirche** (or **St Catejan**), which ranks as one of Munich's most regal churches, its golden-yellow towers and green copper dome adding a welcome splash of colour to the city skyline. It was designed in the 1660s by the Bolognese Agostino Barelli, on the model of St Andrea della Valle in Rome, though many alterations to the original plan were made by Enrico Zuccalli, his successor as court architect, and it was only completed by Cuvilliés over a century later – hence the Rococo bravura of the facade.

Although other buildings in the square, including the **Odeon** itself (originally a music college, now a government office), are by Klenze, the building which finished it off, the **Feldherrnhalle** on the southern side, is by his rival **Friedrich von Gärtner**, who replaced him in royal favour after he fell out with King Ludwig I over the latter's overly exotic architectural tastes. The hall, closely modelled on the Loggia dei Lanzi in Florence, shelters statues of Bavaria's two greatest military heroes: Johann Tilly, the Imperial Field Marshal in the Thirty Years' War, and Karl Philipp von Wrede, the commander of the Bavarian corps originally allied with Napoleon, which changed sides in time to help defeat the French at the Battle of the Nations. Between the two is a memorial to the Bavarian dead of the Franco-Prussian War. It was here on 9 November 1923 that armed police stopped Hitler's "Beer Hall Putsch" (see below) in its tracks,

---

THE BEER HALL PUTSCH

During the early 1920s **Adolf Hitler** had taken over a fringe right-wing nationalist party in Munich, the **National Socialist German Worker's Party** (NSDAP), and turned it into a militant and vocal political unit. With astonishing rapidity the party, and Hitler himself, became a significant force on the Bavarian political scene, attracting support from the multitudes of Germans who blamed the political establishment for the country's recent defeat in World War I. The NSDAP formed its own private army, the *Sturmabteilung* or SA, whose members were drawn mainly from the ranks of disaffected war veterans and which was used to break up the meetings of rival political groups. From the very beginning the avowed aim of the Nazis was the overthrow of the German Republican government and a reversal of Germany's postwar humiliation. On September 2, 1923 Hitler, spurred on by the recent French occupation of the Ruhr region and the economic chaos caused by hyper-inflation, went public with his vision for the future in a speech at Nürnberg. Enlisting the support of General Erich von Ludendorff, the former wartime dictator, he began laying plans for the overthrow of the government.

Hitler and his fellow conspirators chose a patriotic meeting in the *Bürgerbräukeller*, a large beer hall on the southeastern edge of the city centre, on November 8, as the moment to strike their blow. As the Bavarian state commissioner Gustav von Kahr addressed a large crowd, the SA surrounded the hall and Hitler, brandishing a pistol, made a dramatic entrance. He claimed that both the Bavarian and Reich governments had been overthrown and that the army was with him. Kahr and the assembled crowd proved unwilling to back the coup, and it was only with the arrival of Ludendorff that opinion began to swing in the putschists' favour. The advantage was soon lost, however, when Hitler was briefly summoned away. Kahr, who had been forced to declare his support for Hitler, took the opportunity to leave the building, and Hitler, on his return to the *Bürgerbräukeller*, was dismayed to find that his revolutionary government had collapsed.

The following morning, Hitler, Ludendorff and 3000 of their supporters (including Hermann Göring and Rudolf Hess) began their march on central Munich. They soon encountered the first obstacle, a unit of armed policemen blocking the Ludwigsbrücke and

opening fire on the future dictator's band of would-be revolutionaries as they stood at the head of the narrow Residenzstrasse, in the shadow of the Feldherrnhalle.

Ludwigstrasse

From Odeonsplatz, the dead straight **Ludwigstrasse** leads to Schwabing. Its name comes from King Ludwig I, who commissioned it; though it remained unfinished when he was forced to abdicate as a result of a scandal caused by his affair with a dancer, he continued to fund it from his private resources – a decision which later proved to have been a shrewd business investment, as he was able to let the buildings at enormous rates. The most southerly palaces, up to and including the **Staatsarchiv**, are in a style imitating the Italian Renaissance. Immediately to the north, and in a broadly similar style, is **Staatsbibliothek**: it houses one of Europe's richest libraries, the most famous treasure being the original of the great monastic collection of medieval songs and poems, *Carmina Burana* (see box on p.100*)*.

Beyond stands one of the country's most significant nineteenth-century churches, the inevitably-named **Ludwigskirche**. It's an example of the peculiarly German architectural style known as *Rundbogenstil*, which took its cue from any previous form of building – whether Classical, early Christian, Romanesque or Renaissance – using rounded arches; this appears to have been the invention of Ludwig as much as Gärtner. The chancel fresco of *The Last Judgment* by the Nazarene painter Peter Cornelius is one of the largest paintings in the world, and is a self-conscious (if ultimately unsuccessful) attempt to rival Michelangelo.

with it their route into the city. At this point Göring stepped forward, declaring that his men would shoot a number of hostages if the police opened fire, and the putschists were allowed through. They continued to Marienplatz, where they were joined by the Nürnberg Jew-baiter, Julius Streicher, who had been haranguing the crowds.

From here Hitler and his supporters headed down Residenzstrasse, making for the War Ministry where a group of the SA under the command of Ernst Röhm were surrounded by government soldiers. As they moved past the Feldherrnhalle towards Odeonsplatz they found the end of the narrow street blocked by police. This time the police wouldn't budge, despite the exhortations of the plotters. Suddenly a shot was fired, allegedly by Hitler or Streicher, followed by a fusillade of gunfire from both sides. When the smoke began to clear a minute later, sixteen Nazis and three policemen were dead or dying, and many more seriously injured, Göring among them, though Hitler himself escaped with only a dislocated shoulder caused as he was pulled down when the man next to him fell fatally wounded. Only Ludendorff and his adjutant were left standing, and these two marched out onto Odeonsplatz. The general was arrested, while Hitler made his escape by car. Göring and Hess fled to Austria, and a few hours later Röhm surrendered. The putsch was over.

Hitler was arrested two days later at the country home of a rich supporter. However, he was able to use his subsequent trial for high treason as an opportunity to make the most of this apparently irreversible defeat. Reporters from all over Germany and members of the foreign press flocked to Munich, where a sympathetic judiciary allowed Hitler to turn the courtroom into a platform from which to demonstrate his oratorical skills and promote his cause to a wider public, far beyond the boundaries of Bavaria. Although the German Penal Code stipulated life imprisonment for anyone attempting to subvert the Constitution by force, Hitler's sentence was a mere five years. He served less than nine months in far from harsh conditions in the fortress at Landsberg. Once again Hitler was able to turn an apparent setback to his advantage. He used his time in prison to receive a stream of important visitors and to dictate *Mein Kampf* (or "My Struggle for Four and a Half Years against Lies, Stupidity and Cowardice", to translate the book's full original title), a rambling exposition of his ideas and philosophy that was to form a blueprint for Nazi inhumanities over the next two decades.

Further north is the main building of the **Ludwig-Maximilian-Universität**, which is now the biggest university in Germany. Although it's relatively young – for centuries the University of Bavaria was in Ingolstadt, transferring to Landshut before establishing itself in Munich in 1826 – it has a distinguished academic record. The philosopher Friedrich Wilhelm von Schelling was an early luminary, while later professors have included such celebrated scientists as Georg Simon Ohm (discoverer of the law of magnetic resistance which bears his name), Justus von Liebig (father of scientific agriculture) and Wilhelm Conrad Röntgen (inventor of the X-ray). Linking the university with the **Priesterseminar** (Seminary) opposite is a circular plaza known as Geschwister-Scholl-Platz. This is one of a large number of places in Germany dedicated to the memory of Hans Scholl and his sister Sophie, the Munich students who launched the *Weisse Rose* resistance movement to Hitler – an act of defiance which cost them their lives.

The final building on Ludwigstrasse, before it passes into Schwabing and becomes known as Leopoldstrasse, is the **Siegestor**, a triumphal arch balancing the Feldherrnhalle, this time exclusively dedicated to commemorating the Bavarian army's part in the wars against Napoleon between 1813 and 1815.

Königsplatz

West of Ludwigstrasse, a planned town was laid out on a strict geometrical pattern of huge squares. The focus of this is **Königsplatz**, which was intended as a sort of Bavarian Acropolis, with a grassy middle surrounded by showpiece public buildings. In the Nazi period, it was paved over to serve as a parade ground, and it has only recently been returned to its original form.

On the north side of the square is the **Glypothek** (Tues, Wed and Fri–Sun 10am–4.30pm, Thurs noon–8.30pm; DM3.50), built by Klenze to house Ludwig I's collection of Greek and Roman sculptures. These include the magnificent carvings from the Aphaia temple of Aegina, which rank among the supreme masterpieces of Hellenistic art. As they were acquired under decidedly dubious circumstances, the Greeks would like them back: indeed they rank alongside the British Museum's Elgin Marbles at the top of Greece's shopping list in appeals for the return of its country's looted heritage. Across the square, a later building contains the **Staatliche Antikensammlungen** (Tues and Thurs–Sun 10am–4.30pm, Wed noon-8.30pm; DM3.50, DM6 for joint ticket with the Glypothek), whose displays include Greek vases from the fifth and sixth centuries BC, as well as beautiful jewellery and small statues from Greek, Etruscan and Roman antiquity.

On the west side of the square is the **Propylaeum**, a severe twin-towered structure in an unashamedly derivative Grecian style. The reliefs show the Greek War of Independence against the Turks, whose successful conclusion led to the western powers forcing Prince Otto of Bavaria on the victors as their king. This didn't prove to be a happy match: Otto's authoritarian methods went down badly with his subjects, and he was eventually forced to abdicate. Before that had happened, however, this Propylaeum had already been built in his honour.

Just off Königsplatz, facing the Glypothek in a picturesquely manicured garden, is the **Lenbachhaus** (Tues–Sun 10am–6pm; DM5), the villa of the nineteenth-century Bavarian painter **Franz von Lenbach**, an enormously successful high society portraitist. Many of his paintings are displayed inside, in rooms furnished as he knew them. Works by other Munich painters down the centuries are also featured, with the highlight being those by the *Blaue Reiter* group (see *Contexts*), whose members included **Kandinsky**, **Klee**, **Marc** and **Macke**; the collection here of the first of these is particularly outstanding. In recent years the museum has also concentrated on important contemporary German art, and it's always worth checking for special exhibitions.

On Arcisstrasse, opposite the Glypothek, is the most sinister building in Munich. Now serving as a music academy known as the Musikhochschule, it was formerly the **Braunhaus**, the local Nazi headquarters, and the place where Neville Chamberlain made the infamous agreement to force Czechoslovakia to cede Hitler the Sudetenland.

The Alte Pinakothek

The **Alte Pinakothek** (Tues–Sun 9am–4.30pm, Tues and Thurs also 7–9pm; DM4), a Florentine-style palazzo at Bärer Str. 27 to the north, is one of the largest art galleries in Europe, housing an outstanding collection of paintings spanning the period from the fourteenth to eighteenth centuries, including the finest representation of the German School to be found anywhere in the world (for more information on these artists, see *Contexts*). The ground floor covers fifteenth-century German painting in the left wing, and sixteenth- to seventeenth-century German and Dutch painting in the right, while the first floor begins with fifteenth-century Netherlandish painting in the left wing, and then proceeds to German, Italian, Flemish, Dutch, French and Spanish art.

THE GERMAN SCHOOL

German painting of the fifteenth century has predominantly religious themes, and, in keeping with an age that believed art was for the greater glory of God, the names of many of the artists have not survived. Look out for the beautifully observed narrative cycle which has provided the nickname of **Master of the Life of the Virgin** for an unknown Cologne painter, and the idiosyncratic *trompe l'oeil* scenes of a Bavarian contemporary, **Master of the Tegernsee Altar**, whose panels are executed as if in imitation of a carved retable. From the following generation, the works of the Tyrolean **Michael Pacher** stand out. Though better known as a sculptor, his luxuriant *Altarpiece of the Four Fathers of the Church*, an early attempt at fusing the rich late Gothic style of southern Germany with the new approach of the Italian Renaissance, shows he was no less talented with the brush than the chisel.

Under the impact of the Renaissance, portraiture became increasingly popular, and **Dürer's** *Self-Portrait* is one of the most famous paintings from this time, the artist looking out with a self-assured poise, his face framed by shoulder-length golden locks and his torso clad in a regal fur coat. The inscription on the painting reads: "Thus I, Albrecht Dürer from Nürnberg, painted myself in imperishable colours at the age of 28". He certainly achieved everlasting fame, but his self-portrait as a Christ-like figure, together with the inscription, is just a touch Dorian Gray. The famous panels of *The Four Apostles* come from the very end of Dürer's career and are generally held to be his greatest achievement. Originally, they were meant as wings of an altarpiece dedicated to the Virgin, but the project was scrapped when the city of Nürnberg – with the artist himself an enthusiastic supporter – went over to Protestantism.

Another painting with a Reformation connection is **Grünewald's** *Disputation of SS Erasmus and Maurice*. This was commissioned by the leading member of the conciliatory Catholic party, Cardinal Albrecht von Brandenburg. The gorgeously attired Saint Erasmus, who is shown arguing for the peaceful conversion of the world against the armed struggle favoured by the Negro warrior Saint Maurice, represents a double allusion to the contemporary approach favoured by the Cardinal and his great friend, Erasmus of Rotterdam. Grünewald himself was of a far more impassioned nature – as can be seen in his early *Mocking of Christ* – and he shortly afterwards became a supporter of the extreme wing of Protestantism. Strange as it seems, Cardinal Albrecht also patronised Luther's very own propagandist, **Lucas Cranach the Elder**, who took advantage of the new liberties of the age to introduce sensually explicit nudes – such as the full-lengths of *Lucretia* and *Venus and Cupid* – into German art for the first time. This approach was soon taken up and developed by **Hans Baldung**, as in the pair of allegorical female figures, perhaps representing *Prudence* and *Music*.

Albrecht Altdorfer's *Battle of Alexander*, depicting the victory of Alexander the Great over the Persian king Darius III in 333 BC, is a masterpiece of another new genre, that of history painting. It's a large painting, packed with action. Literally hundreds of soldiers are individually painted in minute detail, but at the same time represented as a heaving mass, dramatically giving the sense of a momentous battle.

THE FLEMISH AND DUTCH SCHOOLS

Among the fifteenth-century Flemish works, **Rogier van der Weyden's** *Adoration of the Magi*, which was commissioned for St Kolumba in Cologne, is regarded as one of the greatest portrayals of this classic, Christmas-card subject. It makes a fascinating contrast with the tiny house altar of the same scene (known as *The Pearl of Brabant* because of its highly polished sheen), which seems to be the only surviving painting by **Dieric Bouts the Younger**. Equally outstanding is **Memling's** lyrical *Seven Joys of the Virgin*, which integrates all the scenes into a single dream-like fantasy of architecture and landscape. From the following century comes **Pieter Bruegel the Elder's** *Land of Cockaigne*, depicting a seemingly utopian scene of plenty, where food cooks itself and pigs come ready-roasted. It's full of entertaining details, but, for all its humour, the real purpose of the work was actually to condemn gluttony and idleness.

Centrepiece of the entire museum, and the main consideration in its architectural design, is the collection of works by the seventeeth-century Flemish painter **Rubens**. Sixty-two paintings display a wide range of the artist's prodigious output, including everything from the *modellos* the master made for the guidance of his large workshop to such massive finished altarpieces as *The Fall of the Rebel Angels* and *The Last Judgment*; from intimate portraits such as *Rubens and Isabella Brandt in the Honeysuckle Bower* (painted to celebrate his first marriage) to such boisterous mythological scenes as *Drunken Silenus*, and from the quiet beauty of *Landscape with a Rainbow* to the horrors of *The Massacre of the Innocents*.

Van Dyck, Rubens' most distinguished pupil, is also extensively represented, with portraits and religious scenes drawn from the main phases of his career. The small cabinet rooms beyond contain the largest collection of works in existence by **Adriaen Brouwer**, the most trenchant observer of the seamier side of life in seventeenth-century Flanders. There's also a haunting *Passion Cycle* by **Rembrandt**, commissioned by the House of Orange as Reformed Protestant visions of Holy Week. In both *The Raising of the Cross* and *The Deposition*, the familiar figure of Rembrandt himself appears as a leading witness to the events.

THE ITALIAN, FRENCH AND SPANISH SCHOOLS

The Italian section begins with three little panels from a dispersed altarpiece by **Giotto**; other highlights include **Fra Filippo Lippi's** classically inspired *The Annunciation*, **Botticelli's** theatrical *Pietá*, **Raphael's** tender *Holy Family*, and a rare authenticated example of the young **Leonardo da Vinci**, *Madonna of the Carnation*. However, works by **Titian** steal the show here, notably the *Seated Portrait of Charles V*, which perfectly captures the self-confident poise of a man of destiny, and *Christ Crowned with Thorns*, dating from the end of the artist's very long life and executed with an amazingly Impressionistic sense of freedom. The French display includes **Poussin's** *Lamentation over the Dead Christ* and several classical landscapes by **Claude**. There's also a room of seventeenth-century Spanish painting, including a *Portrait of a Young Man* by **Velázquez**, and genre pictures by **Murillo**; the latter were to have an enormous influence on French and English art of the following century.

The Neue Pinakothek

The **Neue Pinakothek** (Tues–Sun 9am–4.30pm, Tues also 7–9pm; DM4) immediately to the north houses collections of eighteenth- and nineteenth-century painting and sculpture. After the wealth and variety of its neighbour, it can't help but seem a little thin on the ground, but it does have good examples of Neoclassical, Romantic and Realist art.

Sober and clear, the portrait of the *Marquise de Sourcy de Thélusson* by the French painter **David** is a beautiful example of the Neoclassical style of shiny white skins and glossy canvases. Of all the works from the mid-nineteenth century Romantic period, those by the Munich painter **Carl Spitzweg** are among the best. He painted scenes from everyday life, depicting human emotions and frailties with a wry sense of humour and cartoon-like style. *The Poor Poet, The Bookworm* and *The Childhood Friend* cover just some of his themes, which are always subtly observed and with a dig against pretension.

Of the works by French Impressionists, **Manet's** *Breakfast in the Studio* is probably the most famous, but other than that, there's not much to choose from in this section. Turn-of-the-century art is represented by a few paintings by **Cézanne**, **van Gogh** and **Gauguin**, highlights of which are one of van Gogh's *Sunflowers* and Gauguin's *Breton Farmwomen*. The main German exponent of this phase is **Liebermann**, whose *Boys by the Beach* beautifully captures a scene from turn-of-the-century life. The museum rounds off with a small selection of Art Nouveau. **Franz von Stuck's** *Sin* is the most striking piece, the vice represented as a lascivious woman exposing herself. Much more romantic and stylised is **Klimt's** portrait of *Margarethe Stonborough-Wittgenstein*.

Maximilianstrasse

Maximilian II, who succeeded his disgraced father in 1848, also wanted to have a show-piece boulevard named in his own honour; indeed, he had begun planning for it long before he came to the throne. The resultant **Maximilianstrasse** runs east from Max-Joseph-Platz in front of the Residenz, forming Munich's answer to the Champs-Elysées.

As with Odeonsplatz, there was already an extant building at the beginning of the street, this time Klenze's **Nationaltheater**, which maintains its reputation as one of Europe's most prestigious opera houses; almost completely destroyed by bombs in World War II, it was re-created for a little matter of DM63 million. In many ways, it sets the tone for the rest of the street, which is a real theatre quarter, an almost equally prestigious venue being the Jugendstil **Münchener Kammerspiele** at no.26. Across the road is the city's most exclusive address, the *Hotel Vierjahreszeiten*, while elswhere are some two dozen commercial galleries and a seemingly endless number of luxury shops selling the latest fashions and trendiest designer goods as proof of Munich's status as the nation's style-setter.

Over the hideous ring road, at no.42 on the street, is the **Staatliches Museum für Völkerkunde** (Tues–Sun 9.30am–4.30pm; DM3), illustrating the art and history of non-European cultures in a series of excellently-presented changing exhibitions. Further east is a huge bronze monument to Maximilian II. To the north, St-Anna-Strasse leads to the Franciscan church of **St Anna im Lehel**, which was designed by Johann Michael Fischer and decorated by the Asam brothers.

Prinzregentenstrasse

The last of Munich's three great boulevards is **Prinzregentenstrasse**, which runs east from the Prinz-Carl-Palais at the far end of the Hofgarten. Laid out at the end of the nineteenth century and the beginning of the twentieth, its name comes from Prince Luitpold, who ruled as regent after the deposition of his nephew Ludwig II. Nowadays, it's the city's second main museum quarter.

The **Haus der Kunst**, the first building on the northern side, was built by the Nazis as a showcase for the sort of art they favoured. By a pleasing irony, the building now houses the **Staatsgalerie Moderner Kunst** (Tues–Sun 9am–4.30pm, Thurs also 7–9pm; DM3.50), which in large part is devoted to the "degenerate" Expressionist and abstract art they ridiculed and destroyed. Alongside examples of all the main German artists of the century are works by foreign big names such as Picasso, Braque, Matisse, Dalí, Magritte, Mondrian and de Chirico; it's also worth checking on the regular special exhibitions.

Further along the street is the rambling pile of the **Bayerisches Nationalmuseum** (Tues–Sun 9.30am–5pm; DM3). On the first floor are arms and armour, ivories and sacred objects plus a superb display of German wood sculpture at its fifteenth- and sixteenth-century peak. In particular, there are examples of **Tilman Riemenschneider's** art drawn from all phases of his career, ranging from the early *St Mary Magdalene Surrounded by Angels*, via a magnificently characterised set of Apostles made to adorn the Marienkapelle in Würzburg, to the serene late *St Barbara*. Many of his most talented contemporaries – Hans Multscher, Michel and Gregor Erhart, Hans Leinberger and Erasmus Grasser – are also well represented. From the following generation is a statuette of *Judith with the Head of Holofernes* by **Conrad Meit**, the only major German sculptor to work in an Italianate style. There's also a miniature *Portrait of Harry Meynert* by **Hans Holbein the Younger**; this depicts a painter-colleague at the English court of Henry VIII and is one of only a handful of miniatures by Holbein to have survived. Despite the focus on Bavarian art, there's a decent Italian Renaissance section, which includes six magnificent bronze reliefs of *The Passion* by **Giambologna**, plus sculptures by Luca della Robbia and Antonio Rossellino. The museum's entrance level features Bavarian folk art and a collection of Christmas cribs, while the second floor has stained glass, crystal, ceramics, clocks and models of Bavarian towns as they appeared in the sixteenth century.

Next in line is the former Prussian embassy, now housing the **Schackgalerie** (Wed–Mon 9am–4.30pm; DM2.50). Count Schack was Munich's most important art patron during the nineteenth century, supporting struggling painters such as Franz von Lenbach, Marées, Böcklin and others until they achieved public acclaim. The museum, which preserves his collection intact, contains important examples of all those artists, plus other Romantic painters such as Feuerbach and Spitzweg.

Just behind the Bayerisches Nationalmuseum at Lerchenfeldstr. 2 is the **Prähistorische Staatssammlung** (Tues–Sun 9am–4pm, Thurs until 8pm; DM2.50). This makes a good attempt at bringing alive Bavarian prehistory, the Roman occupation and early medieval life. Lots of models, drawings and artefacts are presented in an accessible and interesting manner.

Schwabing

Munich must be one of the cliquiest cities around, and there's nowhere better to observe its different tribes than in the district of **Schwabing**, just north of the city centre. Best place for people-watching is along **Leopoldstrasse**, the northern continuation of Ludwigstrasse, which forms the district's main axis. A much larger area than the city centre, Schwabing spreads untidily to the left and right of this central line, the **Englischer Garten** making up one pleasant border. The rest of the quarter reaches as far north as Studentenstadt, and to the **Olympiapark** and Josephsplatz in the west. If you intend to venture any further than the bars and cafés of the Leopoldstrasse, hiring a bicycle is the best solution (see *Listings*, below).

Schwabing actually divides into three distinct areas. West of Leopoldstrasse, residential streets mix with wacky shops, student bars and restaurants. Along the centre line and to its right, trendy shops and café-bars ensure permanent crowds, day and night. Nightclubs are thick on the ground here too, especially around the Wedekindplatz near Münchener Freiheit. The far north of Schwabing is a tidily bourgeois residential area, uninteresting for visitors apart from the Olympiapark, which is way out, at the end of the U-Bahn line.

It was during the Second Reich and the Weimar Republic (though by then its reputation was eclipsed by Berlin) that Schwabing gained its reputation as a leading German centre for radical bohemian chic. Its inhabitants and habitués included outcast revolutionary politicians, the young Lenin and Hitler among them, the artists of the *Blaue Reiter* group, and writers such as Ibsen, the Mann brothers, Rilke, Brecht and Wedekind. Today, in contrast, Munich's real Latin Quarter has moved to Haidhausen, leaving Schwabing as the favourite haunt of the city's *Schickies*. For information on the trendiest places to be seen, see *Eating and drinking*, p.73.

The Englischer Garten

The **Englischer Garten** takes its name from the eighteenth-century landscaping fashion which tried to create parks resembling untouched nature. Occupying what was formerly marshland, it was created at the instigation of Bavaria's most unlikely statesman, the American-born Benjamin Thompson, who was a leading minister under the garden-loving Elector Carl Theodor (see Schwetzingen in Chapter Two).

When you've had enough of the city, the Eisbach meadow opposite the **Monopteros** (a Neoclassical temple by Klenze) is a good place to relax. The city's main playground, people come here to sunbathe, picnic, swim in the aptly named *Eisbach* ("ice-stream") or ride horses. Visitors often find the large-scale nudity a little unnerving – and it certainly wouldn't be acceptable in any other German city. Even "respectable" businessmen will pop over in the lunch hour, fold their suits in a neat pile and read the paper stark naked. There are rules on where exactly nude sunbathing is allowed, but the police have given up trying to face the inevitable protest and bare bottoms.

A diversion uniting everyone in Munich is beer-drinking, which seemingly takes place all the time, especially in the summer when all the beer gardens are open. One of the most famous is around the **Chinesischer Turm** (known locally as the **Chinaturm**) just to the north of the Monopteros, though its days as the best in town are long gone. What used to be *the* place to meet in Munich has become sadly over-commercialised, with expensive food and uniformed guards to watch over propriety, though it's still worth seeing and remains one of the city's most famous landmarks. It's at its best (or worst) on Sunday afternoons, when a Bavarian band blares across the crowd from the heights of the Chinaturm itself. Two, more peaceful, beer gardens are not far off by the **Kleinhesseloher See**. The lakeside one is the more attractive and good for mellow summer evenings, while the *Hirschau* beer garden tends to have a local crowd rather than tourists, and is found by following the small road turning right out of the car park.

Heading north from the Kleinhesseloher See, you get the feeling of being in the countryside rather than in a city park. Paths criss-cross over the flat wooded valley, and the *Aumeister* beer garden by the Föhringer Ring flyover is just the place to have a leisurely drink and some good food. Not much further, along Sondermeierstrasse, you come to an outdoor swimming pool known as the *Floriansmühle*. Set in fields, it's a little on the dilapidated side, but its small scale makes it preferable to its teeming counterparts elsewhere in the city.

The Olympiapark

During the summer months of July and August the **Olympiapark** is the setting for open-air rock and pop concerts every weekend. Usually it's local bands of varying standards, but it doesn't cost anything and is worth checking out; the venue is a modern-day version of a Greek theatre, known as the **Theatron**, right next to the park's lake. The stadia all around were built for the 1972 Olympics (see overleaf) and still have a somewhat futuristic look about them. In particular, the main **Olympiastadion** is a strange construction of steel poles and plexiglass expanses, looking rather like an overgrown tent. From the 190 metres-high **tower** (daily 9am–midnight; DM4), there's a wonderful view over Munich and the Alps.

THE 1972 OLYMPICS

The sporting stories of the 1972 Olympics were completely overshadowed by an horrific terrorist attack mounted by the Arab *Black September* group. On the morning of September 5, the guerillas stormed the Israeli quarters, killing two athletes and taking nine hostages with demands that 200 Palestinians in Israeli jails should be released. The Olympic Games were suspended while 12,000 police moved into action around the Israeli quarter, and the Chancellor, Willy Brandt, flew in to conduct negotiations with the terrorists. It was agreed that they would be flown with their hostages to a friendly Arab country, but, as the guerillas and their captives crossed the tarmac to board a waiting jet, the police cut the airport lights and began shooting. The result was a bloodbath: all nine hostages were killed along with four Arabs and one policeman; three Arabs survived. This severely tarnished the ideal of the "Olympic spirit", and the subsequent games in Montreal – the first of three successive Olympiads to be the subject of major political boycotts – took place under a shadow of fear and massive security.

Just to the west rises another of Munich's most arresting modern buildings, the **BMW-Gebäude**, symbolically shaped as four tightly clustered cyclindrical towers. The separate structure alongside houses the **BMW-Museum** (daily 9am–5pm; DM4.50). Disappointingly, there are hardly any vintage models, the museum being more an advert for the company – concentrating on its flash modern cars and motorbikes – than a source of illumination on its development.

Along the River Isar

If the Marienplatz and Schwabing are the stuff of tourist brochures, the environs of the **River Isar** are the private face of Munich. There are S-Bahns and buses heading back to the city centre from both ends of the river, but hiring a bike (see p.82) is really the best way to explore since the valley widens out to about a kilometre in places, and, nearest the city centre, the east bank is on a steep hill.

North of the Englischer Garten

For swimming in natural surroundings, head for the **Unterföhringer See**. To get there, cross over to the eastern side of the river by the Aumeister at Leinthaler Brücke and follow the main road through the village of UNTERFÖHRING, then left down Am Poschinger Weiher. The little lake itself is almost obscured by trees, providing plenty of shade on hot summer days. Try to avoid weekends when space gets very tight.

Back towards town, there's a cycling path on the east side of the Isar from the Leinthaler Brücke, and only a short way along, the *St Emmeransmühle* up on St Emmeranstrasse is a rather posh little beer garden with prices to match. It's pretty and worth stopping off for a quick drink, if not to eat. The quarter along this part of the river is known as the **Herzogpark**, and some of the city's more exclusive villas line its leafy streets. Cross back over the river at Max-Joseph-Brücke, and the road leads straight on to the Englischer Garten.

South of the Englischer Garten

Following Prinzregentenstrasse across the Isar over the Luitpoldbrücke, you come to the **Friedensengel**, a nineteenth-century monument to peace shining in its newly restored gold splendour. There's a good view of Munich from up here, and on New Year's Eve people come up to watch the fireworks across the city. Past the Europaplatz at Prinzregentenstr. 60 is Munich's most eccentric nineteenth-century building, the **Villa Stuck** (Tues–Sun 10am–5pm; DM3.50). This was the house of Franz von Stuck, the leader of the Munich Secession, and was designed by him – using a decidedly eclectic mix of styles, though showing distinct echoes of the city's Neoclassical palaces built earlier in the century – in his only attempt at architecture. Inside is a large collection of his paintings, plus other examples of turn-of-the-century art, with Jugendstil predominating. South of the Friedensengel, the **Maximileum**, a grandiose palace by the Dresden architect Gottfried Semper, finishes off Maximilianstrasse; intended as a cultural establishment, it's now home to the Bavarian parliament.

Just to the east, Wienerplatz marks the beginning of **Haidhausen**. Around here it's still more or less the working-class quarter that it always was, with its own market and the large and shady beer garden of the *Hofbräukeller*. Until the early 1980s, Haidhausen was a run-down part of town that had become something of a Turkish ghetto. The peeling squares and prewar houses have since been rediscovered, and now trendy little health-food stores, alternative craftshops and hip bars have sprouted like mushrooms. It's become *the* place to live, and, as you might expect, spiralling rents have forced out most of the original inhabitants.

Down towards the Isar on the Rosenheimer Strasse is hidden one of Munich's real gems, the **Volksbad** (Tues–Thurs 8am–7.30pm, Fri 8am–8.45pm, Sat 8am–5pm, Sun 7.30am–12.30pm; DM6), a beautifully restored Jugendstil indoor swimming hall. High stuccoed ceilings arch over two pools, with mahogany changing cubicles surrounding each, and the sound of splashing water issuing from sculptured fountains makes the atmosphere perfect. There are a couple of saunas and a traditional Turkish bath.

On an island spanned by Ludwigsbrücke is the **Deutsches Museum** (daily 9am–5pm; DM8). Covering every conceivable aspect of technical endeavour, from the first flint tools to the research labs of modern industry, this is the most compendious collection of its type in Europe. The sheer scale of the place is in itself impressive and some of the examples of innovative engineering – biplanes, cars, boats and so forth – are ranged in rooms the size of hangars. However, this is more than a conventional science and technology museum writ large – it's the consistent clarity and imagination of its presentations that make a visit so enjoyable. One part of the building has been converted into a replica of the Lascaux caves while elsewhere there's a convincingly gloomy mock-up of a coalmine. Meticulously constructed large-scale models are featured, and the use of interactive displays makes them as absorbing for kids as adults. It's best to go there in the morning – come later on and you'll regret leaving too little time.

From the Reichenbachbrücke onwards, paths follow the course of the Isar all the way to the city's zoo, **Tierpark Hellabrunn**, and the suburb of Menterschwaige. The east bank rises steeply here and the river and canals are completely hidden by thick woodland. Finally, if you want to see Bavaria's equivalent of Hollywood, and Europe's largest film-making centre, there are guided tours through **Bavaria Filmstadt** (April–Oct daily 9am–4pm; DM11). It's two kilometres further south from the zoo, by Bavariafilmplatz.

The Theresienwiese

Southwest of the Hauptbahnhof, reached by U-Bahn #4 or #5, lies the inevitable trade fair quarter. In addition to the functional exhibition halls, Munich also has a large egg-shaped fairground, known as the **Theresienwiese**. For most of the year, this is an unremarkable meadow, but for sixteen days it's home to Germany's biggest and most famous annual event, the world-famous beer festival-cum-fair, the **Oktoberfest.**

At other times, the only points of note are those overlooking the field to the west. The colonnaded **Ruhmeshalle** (Hall of Fame) is a Bavarian counterpart to the earlier Walhalla near Regensburg, and was likewise paid for by Ludwig I and built by Leo von Klenze. In front stands the colossal bronze **Bavaria statue**, a very Germanicised derivative of the art of Classical Greece, which was designed by Ludwig von Schwanthaler, and took a little matter of six years to cast.

THE OKTOBERFEST

Munich's **Oktoberfest** has its origins in the marriage between the Bavarian Crown Prince Ludwig (the future King Ludwig I) and Princess Thérèse of Saxe-Hildburghausen on 17 October 1810. A massive fair was held on the fields now named after the Princess, and it was such a popular event that it has been repeated annually ever since, growing larger each year. Nowadays, it's quite simply an orgy of beer-drinking: each Munich brewery has its own huge **tent**, where in addition to beer, pretzels and chicken halves are sold. Visitors sit ten to a bench with acquaintances and strangers alike, and after a few litres of beer half the hall is dancing and belting out numbers on the tables. The accompanying **fair** offers some great rides to churn your guts, some so hairy that they're banned in countries like the US.

Despite its name, the Oktoberfest actually begins in September – on either the last or penultimate Saturday of the month. The traditional **opening ceremonies** revolve around the great horse-drawn brewery wagons arriving at the fairground at 11am to the sound of brass bands and much pomp and speech-making. That evening, a **folklore concert** is held in the *Circus Krone*, Marsstr. 43, involving a selection of those taking part in the big **procession** the following day. It leaves from the centre of town at 10am, this time made up of hundreds of traditional folklore groups, marching bands, musicians, jesters, commercial floats and decorated horsemen that slowly converge on the fairground. A week later, a concert of all the Oktoberfest bands is held on the steps of the Bavaria statue at 11am, though this is postponed for a week if the weather is poor.

The proportions of the fair are so massive that the grounds are divided along four main **avenues**, creating a boisterous city of its own, heaving with revellers from morning till night for sixteen consecutive days. Ostensibly a family affair, with rides and stalls of every description jostling for customers, it's also a time for serious drinking attracting visitors from all over the world, with Australians, New Zealanders and Italians forming the largest foreign contingents. Things are fairly relaxed during daylight hours, but get increasingly wild as the evening wears on. If you're looking for excitment head for the *Hofbräuhaus* beer tent at closing time (about 11pm), when things start hotting up as staff try to eject hundreds of fighting drunk beer fans.

For **information** on the opening ceremonies and pageants, read the *Monatsmagazin* or contact the tourist office; advance **tickets** for the folklore concert are available from the organisers, *Münchener Verkehrsverein-Festring*, Pestalozzistr. 3a (☎260 8134). Even though entrance to the grounds is free, expect to spend lots of money. Accommodation during this time is not usually hiked up price-wise, but you'll have trouble finding anything at all if you haven't booked in advance. Many Munich women choose to avoid the Oktoberfest altogether, and it's probably wise for unaccompanied women to proceed with caution after dark, avoiding the more raucous tents.

Nymphenburg

Schloss Nymphenburg (Tues–Sun 10am–12.30pm and 1.30–4pm; DM2.50, or DM6 including the pavilions; take the U-Bahn to Rotkreuzplatz and then tram #12) was the summer residence of the Wittelsbachs. Its kernel is a small Italianate palace begun in 1664 by Agostino Barelli for the frivolous Electress Adelaide, who dedicated it to the pastoral pleasures of the goddess Flora and her nymphs – hence the name. Her son Max Emmanuel commissioned an ingenious extension, whereby four pavilions were built to the side of the palace and connected to it by arcaded passages. Later, the palace itself was modified and further buildings added, resulting in a remarkably unified whole, despite having been nearly a century in the making. By this time, an extensive French-style park had been laid out as an appropriate backdrop. In 1761 the famous porcelain factory was transferred to the site, but plans to establish a planned town on the model of Ludwigsburg in Württemberg came to nothing.

The approach to the palace is either side of a tree-lined canal stretching nearly a kilometre, and when it freezes over in winter it makes a favourite spot for ice-skaters. Through the palace gates, the first hundred metres continue the schloss's strict symmetry with manicured lawns and straight paths lined with marble statues. The park then opens up into a country landscape, with two lakes and a number of small royal lodges. As you'd expect, the interior of the palace is high Baroque, with rich gold-plated stucco ornamentation and ceiling frescos. The most famous room is the *Schönheitsgallerie* – a collection of 36 portraits of Munich beauties who caught King Ludwig I's eye between 1827 and 1850. In the south wing you can visit the **Marstallmuseum** (same times; DM2.50) which houses the incredibly elaborate coaches and sleighs of the Wittelsbachs, including several made for the ill-fated Ludwig II.

The Park

More enticing than the palace itself are the walks in the wonderful **Park**. Three of the four pavilions, which are all of a markedly different character, were designed by Joseph Effner, the innovative court architect who was also responsible for the harmonisation of the palace. Immediately behind the northern wing is the **Magdalenenklause**, deliberately built to resemble a ruined hermitage, with a grotto and four simple cell-like rooms within. It's a very early example of the historicism which was later to become a German obsession, borrowing elements from Roman, Gothic and even Moorish architecture. The Elector would come here when he wished to meditate – and he hadn't far to go if he tired of its peace and asceticism. Westwards through the park is the **Pagodenburg**, which was used for the most exclusive parties thrown by the court. Effner's third building, the **Badenburg**, lies on the opposite side of the canal. It reflects contemporary interest in chinoiserie, though both the bathing room and the two-storey banqueting hall are in the richest Baroque tradition.

For all their charm, Effner's pavilions are overshadowed by the stunning **Amalienburg**, the hunting lodge built behind the south wing of the Schloss by his successor as court architect, **François Cuvilliés**. This is arguably the supreme expression of the Rococo style, marrying a cunningly thought-out design – which makes the little building seem like a full-scale palace – with the most extravagant decoration imaginable. The entrance chamber, with its niches for the hunting dogs, must be the most tasteful kennel ever built. However, the showpiece is the circular *Spiegelsaal* (Hall of Mirrors), best seen on a bright day when the shimmering light casts magical reflections on the silvery-blue walls, the rocaille console tables, the panelled garlands and the rich stucco nymphs and putti.

To the north of the Schloss, the **Botanical Gardens** (daily 9am–7pm, hothouses closed 11.45am–1pm; DM3) hide all manner of plants in their steamy hothouses, the landscaped herbarium and other plant collections making up a very fragrant whole.

Eating and drinking

Mensas are the cheapest places to get a good basic meal: you're supposed to have a valid student card to eat in them, but no-one seems to check. Standard opening times are Mon–Thurs 9am–4.45pm, Fri 9am–3.30pm; the most central mensa is at Leopoldstr. 15, in the back courtyard. Two more are in the main building at Schellingstrasse, and at the Technical University, Arcisstr. 17. If you're really hard up, most **butchers' shops** sell bread rolls with various hot and cold fillings from as little as DM1.80. Excellent places for this type of snack are the *Vinzenz Murr* butchers, which usually have an area within the shop to eat snacks and serve larger meals too. In Schwabing, there are branches at Münchener Freiheit and Schellingstr. 21. Otherwise it's not difficult to eat well for little money in Munich. **Italian restaurants** are especially cheap and do excellent pasta dishes for around DM8.50, and in the Bavarian **Gaststätten**, filling soups, salads and sandwich-type dishes can be found for around DM5. Even more substantial Bavarian meals like *Weisswürste, Leberkäse, Schweinebraten* and *Knödel* or *Hacksteak* (see "Eating" in *Basics* for descriptions) normally cost between DM8 and DM12. Not surprisingly, drinking is never a problem in this city and beverages of any kind are available all day and almost all night. Apart from the *Gaststätten* and beer gardens, Munich also has a very lively café-bar culture, which carries on well into the early hours.

Restaurants

Munich has a wide selection of **restaurants**, and plenty of places offer good food at reasonable prices. Oddly, given Munich's large Turkish population, the city only has a few decent Turkish restaurants, though most other types of cuisine are readily available.

Balkan

Dalmatiner Grill, Geibelstr. 10. Haidhausen's best bet for affordable Balkan specialities. DM15–25.

Isabellahof, Isabellastr. 4. Very popular and cheap Schwabing restaurant, with superb cooking. DM9–25.

Makarska Grill, Schleissheimerstr. 182. An established favourite with good service and an excellent menu.

Zadar Grill, Theresienstr. 54. Good food and service at medium prices. DM15 and up.

French

Alter Ego, Artilleriestr. 5. Slightly pseudo-French in flavour, but sensible prices make it a better bet than some of the more genuine, but expensive, gourmet havens. DM13–20.

Bernard & Bernard, Innere Wienerstr. 32. Right next to the Wienerplatz in Haidhausen. Great for crêpes. Closed Saturday.

Le Fleuron de Isar, Erhardstr. 27. Small, welcoming place, with realistic prices. DM10–20.

Rue des Halles, Steinstr. 18. In the heart of Haidhausen with an excellent, if slightly pricey menu. DM20 plus.

Stengelhof, Stengelstr. 2. The students' favourite. Try the *mousse au chocolat*.

Werneckhof, Werneckstr. 11. Schwabing place which manages to combine decent prices with a touch of exclusivity. DM15–30.

Le Zig Zag, Andreestr. 10. Popular brasserie, dishing up French fare in truly Bavarian-sized portions. DM25 and up.

Greek

Anti, Jahnstr. 36. Good food and good prices, with pleasant surroundings and service. DM10–25.

Entaxi, Bergmannstr. 4. Among the best Greek places in town and usually full. DM8–25.

Kyklos, Wilderich-Lang-Str. 10. One of the oldest Greek places in the city; better than average, with excellent *gyros*. DM12–30.

Lyra, Bazeillestr. 5. Intermittently fashionable and always packed. DM7–25.

Rembetiko, Dreimühlenstr. 2. Pleasant surroundings and not too expensive. An enthusiastic and capable live band plays here most evenings.

Symposium, Ligsalzstr. 38. Cheapish and good, despite the tacky decor.

Italian

Adria, Leopoldstr. 19. A popular late-night joint in Schwabing, with excellent pizzas at reasonable prices.

Bella Italia, Weissenburgerstr. 2. Part of a chain of about twelve restaurants, this is the long-standing favourite. DM8–14.

Taverna Ischitana, Pündterplatz 2. A little classier than some of the others, but you pay for it. DM30 and up.

Turkish

Istanbul, Landwehrstr. 42. Splendid range of kebab possibilities and handy central location. DM10–30.

Marmara, Goethestr. 7a. Another central option with a menu that explores some of the more unfamiliar aspects of Turkish cuisine. DM10–25.

Bei Sülö, Rosenheimerstr. 82. Haidhausen's best Turkish place. DM8–25.

Vegetarian

Gollier, Gollierstr. 83. Excellent food with organically-produced drinks available. DM10–25.

Kornkammer, Haimhauserstr. 8. A vegetarian *Imbiss* in Schwabing.

Kornstadl, Frauenstr. 18. Another *Imbiss*-type place with a broad range of vegetarian meals. DM7–20.

La Cantina, Weissenburgerstr. 39. Haidhausen's most popular vegetarian restaurant. DM8–27.

Vierjahreszeiten, Sebastianplatz 9. Light and airy restaurant with reasonable prices. DM10–25.

Vitamin-Büffet, Herzog-Wilhelmstr. 25. Popular with city-centre yuppies and hippy types alike. DM10–27.

Gaststätten

For traditional **Bavarian cooking**, the following places are cheap and friendly, often with music, providing meals to a mainly student-type clientele. Food prices range from about DM10–25; other possibilities can be found in the beer halls section below.

Alter Ofen, Zieblandstr. 41. A little worn about the edges but still immensely popular with its student crowd.

Atzinger, Schellingstr. 98. One of the best places to pop in for a cheap lunch.

Baal, Kreittmayrstr. 26. Good for relaxed socialising in the evening.

Braunauer Hof, Frauenstr. 40. Slightly more formal atmosphere than most places but still offering local cuisine at middle-of-the-range prices.

Burg Pappenheim, Baaderstr. 46. Fine old bar, that's hugely popular with just about everyone.

Frauenhofer, Frauenhoferstr. 9. For a bit of theatre with your beer – usually gets packed early in the evening.

Kaiser Friedrich, Friedrichstr. 27. A little smarter than some, but still good value for money.

Schelling Salon, Schellingstr. 54. Excellent place for large cheap breakfasts and playing pool.

Weinbauer at Fendstr. 5. Cheap and unpretentious place, despite its Schwabing location.

Drinking

The **beer garden** (*Biergarten*) and **beer cellar** (*Bierkeller*) are Munich's most characteristic institutions. Generally speaking the terms apply to roomy halls (rather than cellars) standing in leafy gardens, serving strong, heady beer brewed either on the premises or in a nearby brewery. Although many have become tainted by excessive tourism, they remain an essential and unmissable feature of the city. For more information on them – and the products they serve – see below.

Beer halls

Augustinerbräu, Neuhauser Str. 16. One of several beer halls and gardens on this central street, with an unusually long menu.

Augustiner Keller, Arnulfstr. 52. Near the S-Bahn stop Hackerbrücke, in one of Munich's grottier quarters, with a large, shady garden and hardly a tourist in sight.

Aumeister, Sondermeierstr. 1. At the far northern end of the Englisher Garten, this one is a good place for daytime breaks.

MUNICH'S BEER CULTURE

Munich's **beer halls** have their origins in the Middle Ages, when brewers stored barrels indoors, planting chestnut trees around their premises to shade them from the heat of the sun. These days beer gardens remain popular with natives and visitors alike, really coming into their own in summer when tables and chairs are set up in the open. Beer is served in litre *Maas* measures (often incorrectly called *Steins* by tourists), and the enduring image is that of the traditionally-clad waitress sailing from table to table clutching several enormous, foaming glasses in each hand. Many beer gardens serve up roasted half chickens (always well-salted to ensure a healthy customer thirst) with side orders of potato salad, while some have more extensive menus, and others allow you to bring your own food.

Beer garden **etiquette** can be a little hard to grasp for outsiders: don't sit at a *Stammtisch* (regular's table) as you won't be served and the staff won't bother to tell you, preferring to let you figure it out for yourself.

Munich ranks as the third largest producer of beer in the world, and it can legitimately claim to be both the most influential and the most varied in output: it pioneered *Weizen* and brown-coloured beers, and adapted the original *Bock* of Einbeck to the form in which it's generally known today. Nowadays five major breweries operate in the city. Largest is *Paulaner*, which produces a full range of styles, generally with a drier flavour than those of its competitors; the dark and extremely powerful *Salvator-Doppelbock* is its star product. It also owns two formerly independent breweries, *Hacker* and *Pschorr*, though these are run separately. *Löwenbräu*, better-known abroad through being a bigger exporter, produces a similarly wide variety of generally maltier beers. *Hofbräu*, the oldest of the breweries, still makes the classic *Maibock* plus some of the best Weizens, though its standard line is an *Export*. The main strength of *Augustiner* is its pale (*Hell*) beer, though it produces several prestigious dark brews as well. *Spaten* has the best amber beer, known as *Ur-Märzen*, though it's best known for its *Franziskaner* Weizens and Bocks.

Biergarten am Flaucher, in the Flaucherpark (U-Bahn Thalkirchen). Hiding amid the tall trees of the park, it does excellent fish dishes in summer.

Bräustübl der Forschungsbrauerei, Unterhachinger Str. 76. Small *Hausbrauerei* with garden in a southeastern suburban setting. Reached by U-Bahn #8 or S-Bahn #2; closed Mon.

Chinesischer Turm, in the Englischer Garten. Though worth a passing visit, this famous beer garden has become a real tourist trap.

Franziskaner Fuchs'n Stuben, Perusastr. 5. A good choice for either a full meal or a snack: it's said to serve Munich's best *Weisswurst*, the essential accompaniment to a pre-lunch drink.

Hirschau, Gysslingstr. 7. Reasonable, but the oompah bands are a little off-putting.

Hirschgarten, Hirschgartenallee 1. Near the Nymphenburg palace, this one, notwithstanding its seating capacity of over 2000, is rather civilised – which is not necessarily a recommendation in a beer garden.

Hofbräuhaus, Platzl 9. The unmissable one – though nowadays it's by far the least authentic of any on this list.

Hofbräukeller, Innere Wienerstr. 19. Nestling under ancient chestnut trees in Haidhausen, this is a very popular evening destination.

Löwenbräukeller, Nymphenburger Str. 2. Serves excellent food – and offers the rare chance to order beer by the half-litre.

Mathäser, Bayerstr. 5. Calling itself a *Bierstadt* (beer city), this is reputedly the largest pub in the world, with a capacity for over 5000 drinkers in its 15 halls.

Menterschwaige, Harthauserstr. 7. One of Munich's best beer gardens. On the edge of the Isar valley, out in the southern suburbs, it's the place to bring a picnic to go with your beer.

Platzl, Munzstr. 8. Facing the Hofbräuhaus, this is the Munich outpost of the rural *Ayinger* brewery, a worthy rival to its city counterparts in terms of variety of products. Features folk music and cabaret as well.

Salvatorkeller, Hochstr. 77. High up on the Nockherberg, and venue for the spring *Starkbierfest*, this is one of the oldest havens for serious beer drinkers.

Seehaus, in the Englischer Garten. An excellent setting on the shores of the Kleinhesseloher See – feed the swans while you drink.

Spatenhofkeller, Neuhauser Str. 26. Features hearty Bavarian cooking at lower than average prices.

Zum Pschorrbräu, Neuhauser Str. 11. One of the best choices for a full meal; also something of a novelty, as it incorporates a wine cellar.

Bars

The city's social life revolves around its bars. Beer, coffee and snacks are served in most places, and while the list of "in" and "out" bars is ever-changing, these are top of the pile for the moment. *Schickies* hang out in **Schwabing** and hipsters head for **Haidhausen**, though things are pretty provincial in both areas. The city's bars suffer from licensing laws almost as ridiculous as those in the UK (midnight closing at most places).

Baadercafé, Baaderstr. 47. A popular pre-club bar open until 1am.

Café an der Uni, Ludwigstr. 24. Very popular with students from the nearby University, and nearly always packed to the gills.

Café Giesing, Bergstr. 5. Friendly place, often with live music.

Cairo, Breisacherstr. 30, Haidhausen. A little off the beaten track, but worth it for the relaxed atmosphere and good breakfasts.

Casino, Kellerstr. 21, Haidhausen. Barn-like place that's one of *the* Haidhausen hang-outs, though it's sometimes hard to see why.

Drugstore, Feilitzschstr. 12, Schwabing. Lively place that manages to avoid the usual Schwabing excess.

Extrablatt, Leopoldstr. 7, Schwabing. Ritzy café-bar that's worth visiting at least once.

Franci's, Franziskanerstr. 2a, Haidhausen. Always well-patronised by a mixed crowd who are drawn here by cheapish prices.

Grössenwahn, Lothringerstr. 11, Haidhausen. Well-known bar that's considered quite cool by the Munich in-crowd.

Harry's New York Bar, Falkenturmstr. 9. A central cocktail bar where you can listen to the pianist tinkling away until 3am.

Hinterhof Caféhaus, Sedanstr. 29, Haidhausen. A health food café for times when the beer and schnapps become too much.

Julep's, Breisacherstr. 18, Haidhausen. Recommended cocktail bar with a popular happy hour.

Nachtcafé, Maximiliansplatz 5 (7pm–5am). Haunt of the true night owls, this is the place to see and be seen in the early hours of the morning.

Oase, Amalienpassage, Schwabing. A mixed, slightly studenty crowd in this excellent bar. The terrace is a great place for summer lounging.

Palmengarten, Herzogstr. 93, Schwabing. Though not too bad in the early evening, this place fills with an obnoxiously affluent crowd as the night wears on.

Reitschule, Königinstr. 34, Schwabing. Place to be seen if you aspire to Munich high life, but it's expensive and the service is off-hand.

Roxy, Leopoldstr. 48, Schwabing. Smart café-bar with a good range of cocktails.

Ruffini, Orffstr. 22. Friendly bar with a good roof terrace.

Schumanns, Maximilianstr. 36. Munich's movers and shakers congregate here, so this is the place to head for if you're looking to make contacts.

Sedan, Gravelottestr. 7, Haidhausen. Another much-touted Haidhausen haunt.

Stöpsel, Preysingstr. 18, Haidhausen. Health food place; no danger of having a good time here, amid the woolly jumpers and Birkenstocks.

Wunderbar, Hochbrückenstr. 3. A central cellar-bar so hip that the owner asked not to be included in this guide (open until 3am).

Traditional cafés

These are the traditional *Kaffeee und Kuchen* places, seemingly favoured mainly by ladies with lapdogs. They're great places to load up on cakes, cream and strong coffee. All these cafés are only open during normal shopping hours, which usually means from 8.30am to 6pm.

Café Feldherrnhalle, Theatinerstr. 38. Break your city-centre wanderings here. Well placed for the Residenz and around.

Café Frischhut, Blumenstr. 7–11. Near the Viktualienmarkt, and a good place to sample a *Schmalznudel.*, a kind of large deep-fried doughnut, eaten either plain or sprinkled with sugar. Baking starts at 5am here, so it's also a popular place for hungry nightclubbers on their way home.

Café Kreuzkamm, Maffeistr. 4. A delicious array of cakes and sweets makes this one of the best in town.

Café Luitpold, Briennerstr. 11. More basic kind of café with a plainer clientele.

Café Schneller, Amalienstr. 59, Schwabing. A University location makes this popular with students rather than the antique lady contingent.

Wine bars

Not a great deal of choice in this beer haven, but the following are all worth a visit:

Le Bordeaux, Erich-Kästner-Strasse 14, Schwabing. A friendly venue for an evening's relaxed wine drinking.

Clochemerle, Rablstr. 37, Haidhausen. Popular (and usually full) wine bar with a wide selection of French wines.

Pfälzer Weinprobierstuben, Residenzstr. 1. Wines and food from the Rhineland served in a pleasant atmosphere in this central wine bar.

St Georg Weinstuben, Lamontstr. 11, Haidhausen. Recommended cellar wine bar.

Südtiroler Weinstadl, Amalienstr. 53. Near the Hauptbahnhof, this wine bar has an amazing selection, mainly from the southern Tyrol region. You can taste most of them before committing yourself to buying a bottle.

Weinstadl, Burgstr. 6. This unpretentious place, serving excellent wines, is housed in one of the city's oldest buildings. There's a terrace in summer.

Weintrödler, Briennerstr. 10 (5pm–6am). Open after everywhere else has closed, and consequently always full.

Music and nightlife

Munich has a great deal to offer **musically**, whether you're into classical concerts or more modern stuff. There's everything you'd expect to find in a cosmopolitan capital, and during the summer a glut of open-air music festivals takes place in or around the city. Three orchestras of international repute are based here, and the annual opera festival in July ranks with the Salzburg and Bayreuth festivals. Not that it's all highbrow: there's plenty of trash and tinsel as well, though perhaps the bars are more interesting than the discos. Best sources for listings are the *Münchener Stadtmagazin* or *In München*, available at any kiosk.

Rock and pop

During the summer the **free rock concerts** by the lake in the Olympiapark, at the purpose-built stage known as the *Theatron*, usually get going around 2pm. Several **venues** have regular music programmes throughout the year:

Café Giesing, Bergstr. 5. Run by the singer Konstantin Wecker, and usually featuring small bands or solo artists.

Domicile, Leopoldstr. 19, Schwabing. Mostly jazz bands with some rock.

Theaterfabrik Unterföhring, Föhringer Allee 23 (S3 to Unterföhring, then follow the crowds). For biggish name-group concerts. Admission from about DM30.

Wirtshaus im Schlachthof, Zenettistr. 9. A central venue for just about everything from rock to jazz, with theatrical happenings too. Admission from about DM30.

Jazz

Munich has a monthly jazz magazine called *Münchener Jazz-Zeitung*, available in music shops and jazz venues. The city is corporate headquarters of *ECM*, an avant-garde jazz record label, and club dates are accordingly more exciting than the German norm, attracting many big names on tour. The following venues play predominantly jazz, but check programmes:

Allotria, Türkenstr. 33, Schwabing. This traditional Bavarian bar has a lively jazz programme that attracts the beard and woolly jumper brigade.

Domicile, Leopoldstr. 19, Schwabing. The hip jazzer's favourite hangout.

Jam, Rosenheimer Str. 4, Haidhausen. A good bet for solid, reliable jazz, though don't expect any musical surprises.

Max-Emanuel, Adalbertstr. 33, Schwabing. The clientele takes its music just a little bit too seriously here, though the place is open until 1am.

Schwabinger Podium, Wagnerstr. 1, Schwabing. If watching earnest German jazzers sweating their way through Dixieland tunes is your idea of a good time then this is the place you should head for.

Unterfahrt, Kirchenstr. 96, Haidhausen. Munich's modern jazz venue. Big names and unknowns play here, and the music is nearly always excellent. Closed Monday.

Discos and nightclubs

Munich has a thriving nightclub scene, though in this city where money and appearances are everything, the snooty attitudes of many places can be rather off-putting. Most places are open 10pm–4am and entrance is about DM10.

Babalu, Leopoldstr. 19, Schwabing. Excellent funk, soul and salsa one-nighters.

Cadillac, Theklastr. 1. Funk and soul sounds attract black US servicemen and locals alike (9pm–4am).

Crash, Lindwurmstr. 88. Heavy metal mecca and headbanger's delight (8pm–1am, Fri–Sat 8pm–3am).

Far Out, Am Kosttor. Central venue where chart stuff, hip-hop and techno are the order of the evening.

Jackie O, Rosenkavalierplatz 12. Just about the strictest door policy in town, so unless you're loaded and look it, forget it (10pm–4am).

Liberty, Rosenheimerstr. 30, Haidhausen. Funk and black dance sounds.

Nachtwerk, Landsbergerstr. 189. One of the city's best and most affordable nightlife possibilities. They put on occasional indie gigs here too. Saturday and Sunday.

Park Café, Sophienstr. 7. Ranks among Munich's most popular and stylish nightclubs (10pm–3am).

P1, Prinzregentenstr. 1 (10pm–4am). This is the coolest place in town to be – if you can get past the door. Dress up in your best rags and bring loadsamoney.

Rollpalast, Aubingerstr. 48. A roller-disco (skate hire available) where you can skate to hip-hop and chart sounds (8pm–1am).

Sugar Shack, Herzogspitalstr. 6. Standard disco in the centre of town but fun nevertheless (11pm–4am).

Sunsplash, Rosenheimerstr. 46, Haidhausen. Munich's only reggae disco.

Tanzlokal Grössenwahn, Klenzestr. 43. Top twenty sounds draw a conservative crowd. (9pm–1am).

Wolkenkratzer, in the *Hertie* tower, Leopoldstrasse, Schwabing. The views are better than the music, and this place lives on its novelty value.

Classical

A number of resident orchestras and two opera houses cater to a very spoilt audience. The *Münchener Philharmonie* is conducted by Sergiu Celibidache, one of the great conductors of the century, a man who has developed an aura by his stubborn refusal to make records. The *Bayrisches-Rundfunk-Sinfonie-Orchester* is conducted by the Englishman Sir Colin Davis, and the *Staatsorchester* plays for the opera under the direction of Wolfgang Sawallisch. Of the subsidised orchestras, the *Münchener Kammerorchester* and the *Kurt-Graunke-Orchester* are perfectly respectable, but their subsidies mean that they have to play to their sponsors' tastes, which aren't always sensational. Main venues for concerts are the spanking new *Gasteig Kulturzentrum* on Kellerstrasse (☎418614) and the plush *Herkulessaal* in the Residenz. The *Nationaltheater* (☎221316) on Max-Joseph-Platz is Munich's answer to Covent Garden, with grand opera and ballet, whereas the *Staatstheater* on Gärtnerplatz (☎201 6767) has a mixed programme of operetta, musicals and the more popular operas.

Best way to find out what's on and for how much is to buy the city's **official monthly programme** (*Monatsmagazin*) from the tourist office. Advance tickets for concerts can be bought at the relevant box offices or commercial ticket shops, such as the one located in the Marienplatz U-Bahn station. Opera tickets can be bought at the advance sales office at Maximilianstr. 11 (Mon–Fri 10am–12.30pm and 3.30–5.30pm, Sat 10am–12.30pm). On the night of a show, you could try the box office in the Nationaltheater, which opens one hour before performances begin.

The **Münchener Opernfest**, which takes place from the middle of July to the beginning of August, has a very high reputation. Classical concerts are also held at Schloss Nymphenburg, Schloss Schleissheim and in the courtyard of the Residenz at this time of year.

Theatre and cinema

Munich has eleven major **theatres** and around 28 fringe theatres, plus eight cabaret venues, all of which are listed in the official programmes and the local press. Almost all productions are exclusively in German, though with a smattering of the language things aren't too incomprehensible. Check the *Münchener Stadtmagazin* or the *Monatsmagazin* for what's currently showing.

Venues

Cuvilliéstheater, Residenzstr. 1 (☎296836). Munich's star venue for drama, this Rococo building was venue for the premiere of Mozart's *Idomeneo*.

Marionettentheater, Blumenstr. 29a (☎265 1712). A puppet theatre – mainly for kids, though once a week the marionettes are put to more serious use in the performance of an opera or drama classic.

Münchener Kammerspiele, Maximilianstr. 26 (☎237210). An excellent venue, offering a wide variety of productions.

Residenztheater, Max-Joseph-Platz 1 (☎225754). Traditional dramatic fare in high quality productions.

Theaterfabrik Unterföhring, Föhringer Allee 23 (☎950 5666). Always worth checking out, this venue is used for pop concerts as well as cabaret shows.

Cinemas

Non-German **films** are usually dubbed into German, but if you're in need of hearing some English check out the following places, which specialise in showing films with the original soundtrack. Entrance prices vary according to where you sit, but range between DM10 and DM14.

Cinema, Nymphenburger Str. 31 (☎555255);
Europa im Atlantik, Schwanthalerstr. 2-6 (☎555670);
Türkendolch, Türkenstr. 74 (☎271 8844).

Festivals

Inevitably, all local **festivals** stand in the shadow of the Oktoberfest (see box above), but there are plenty of other annual events. **Fasching**, Munich's Carnival, begins in earnest immediately after Epiphany with a week-long series of costume parades. Fancy-dress balls are held regularly up to and including Carnival Week, whose festivities come to a climax on Ash Wednesday with a ceremony of washing money bags at the Fischerbrunnen in Marienplatz. A couple of weeks later begins **Starkbierzeit**, the period when strong beer is served in the taverns to help make the stringencies of Lent bearable. More specially-brewed strong beer can be sampled at the **Maibock-Anstich** in May.

The **Auer Dult** is a traditional market that takes place on the Mariahilfplatz during the last weeks of April, July and October each year. It has a combination of hardware, crafts and antiques, as well as a fairground for the kids. An annual **Christmas market**, known as the *Christkindlmarkt*, is held on the Marienplatz during the month of December, though the ones at the Münchener Freiheit, and around the Pariser Platz in Haidhausen are less commercialised with more hand-made crafts.

The gay scene

Deeply conservative Bavaria is not the best part of Germany in which to be **gay**. There are ultra-extreme elements who would be quite happy to see a return to the pink triangles and persecution of the Nazi era, though fortunately their views have yet to be given legislative back-up. Munich doesn't have a gay quarter, though there are a couple of gay bars around the Gärtnerplatz. For information your best bet is probably to contact the *Schwulkulturzentrum* (Gay Cultural Centre), Auenstr. 31 (☎725 4533), where meetings are held every fourth Thursday of the month at 8pm.

Women

The Women's Centre, *Frauenzentrum*, Güllstr. 3 (Mon–Fri 6–11pm; ☎725 4271) runs a series of workshops and a café for all women, not just lesbians. On Tuesday between 1pm and 8pm, women from 13 to 20 years meet in the café, with Friday evenings specifically for lesbians. Cafés that cater predominantly for lesbians are *Café am Gift*, St. Martinstr. 1; *Frauencafé im Kofra*, Baldestr. 8; and *Mädchenpower-Café*, Baldestr. 16. The only nightclub is *Mylord*, Ickstättstr. 2a (daily 6–9pm, 6pm–3am weekends), which gets mixed reviews.

Men

The male gay scene has a number of recognised meeting points though most places tend to keep a fairly low profile: the following bars, however, are well known: *Bolt*, Blumenstr. 15; *Cock*, Augsberger Str. 21; *Colibri*, Utzschneiderstr. 8; *Die Spinne*, Ringseissestr. 1; *Juice*, Baaderstr. 13; and *Klimperkasten*, Maistr. 28; *Nil*, Hans-Sachs-Str. 2 and *Teddybar*, Hans-Sachs-Str. 3. *New York*, Sonnenstr. 25 (10pm–4am), is a gay disco offering chart and dance sounds. The *Ochsengarten*, Müllerstr. 47, is a leather bar, and the *Deutsche Eiche*, Reichenbachstr. 13 was Fassbinder's favourite *Gasthaus*, with a mainly (though by no means exclusively) gay clientele.

Listings

Airlines *British Airways*, Promenadeplatz 10 (☎292121); *Lufthansa*, Lenbachplatz 1 (☎51130); *TWA*, Landwehrstr. 31 (☎597643).

Airport information (☎921 12127).

American Express Promenadeplatz 6 (Mon–Fri 9am–5.30pm, Sat 9am–noon; ☎21990).

Babysitter service (☎229291 or ☎394507).

Bike hire Cheapest is *Aktiv-Rad*, Hans-Sachs-Str. 7. DM10 per day; DM50 per week. The bike stand by the entrance to the Englischer Garten on the corner of Königinstrasse and Veterinärstrasse charges DM15 per day, DM50 per week, but is only open in summer. *Bayern Bike Tours*, Hauptbahnhof, exit Arnulfstrasse (daily 9am–6.30pm), hires out bikes complete with maps and commentary to guide you around the sights via the city's cycle-paths. DM22 per day, DM30 overnight: DM150 or passport as deposit. You can also hire bikes at many of the outlying *S-Bahn stations*, such as Aying, Dachau, Freising, Herrsching, Holzkirchen, Starnberg and Tutzing – useful when exploring the city's environs.

Books *Anglia English Bookshop*, Schellingstr. 3, has a good selection of paperbacks and English-language newspapers.

Car hire *Europcar*, Schwanthalerstr. 10a (☎594723). Also has offices at the airport.

Car repairs Phone the *ADAC* on (☎767676) any time.

Consulates *British*, Amalienstr. 62 (☎394015); *Irish*, Mauerkircherstr. 1a (☎985723); *American*, Königinstr. 5 (☎23011); *Canadian*, Maximiliansplatz 9 (☎558531); *Dutch*, Nymphenburger Str. 1 (☎594103).

Cultural institutes The following have film shows and run various social functions advertised in the local press: *Amerika-Haus*, Karolinenplatz 3 (☎595367), which has a useful library and recent newspapers; *British Council*, Bruderstr. 7/III (☎223326), offers similar services; *Deutsch-Englische Gesellschaft*, 8 München 33, Postfach 328 (☎362815); *Deutsch-Kanadische Gesellschaft*, Lohensteinstr. 33 (☎566843); *Munich Scottish Association*, Waldsaumstr. 19 (☎714 6990).

Emergencies *Police* (☎110); *Doctor* (☎558661); *Dentist* (☎723 3093); *Dispensing chemist* (☎594475); *Gynaecological* (☎218 02611). At the *Internationale Apotheke* (Neuhauserstr. 8), you can get your prescription no matter which country it comes from.

Hospital Ismaningerstr. 22 (☎11401).

Launderettes Pestalozzistr. 16; Lilienstr. 73; Lindwurmstr. 38; Amalienstr. 61; Münchener Freiheit 26; Belgradstr. 11a; Herzogstr. 32 and 67; Kurfürstenstr. 10, 14 and 37; Wendl-Dietrich-Str. 23; Schleissheimer Str. 117.

Mitfahrzentrale Amalienstr. 87 (☎280124); also a women-only branch at Güllstr. 3 (☎725 1700).

Peace movement *Deutsche Friedens-Union* (*DFU*), Hess Str. 51, 10am–5pm.

Police Ettstr. 2 (☎2141).

Poste Restante Bahnhofsplatz 1 (☎538 82732). Open 24 hours a day: take your passport.

Sports *FC Bayern München*, Germany's most consistent football club, winner of many European trophies down the years, play at the *Olympiastadion* in the Olympiapark, which is also the venue for major athletics meetings.

Taxis (☎21611).

Travel agents *Studiosus Reisen*, Luisenstr. 43 and Amalienstr. 73.

Women's bookshop Arccistr. 57 (☎272 1205).

Women's centre Güllstr. 3 (☎725 4271).

UPPER BAVARIA

The name of **Upper Bavaria** (*Oberbayern*), Munich's own traditional province, is associated above all with the **Alps**. Quite simply, this is the most spectacular scenery Germany has to offer, a wonderfully contrasting array of glacial lakes and peaks commanding stunning panoramic views, with many dramatic castles and churches thrown in for good measure. In contrast, other parts of the province are relatively little known, yet offer plenty of varied attractions. Between the Alps and the capital lie some equally enticing lakes and monasteries; to the east are the valleys of the **Inn** and **Salzach** rivers; while north of Munich are several wonderful old towns, most notable of which are the former university and ducal seat of **Ingolstadt** and the cathedral city of **Eichstätt**.

Heading north from Munich

North of Munich, making easy day trips by the city's excellent S-Bahn network, are several varied excursion possibilities. **Dachau** concentration camp is a harrowing but valuable experience, while **Oberschleissheim** has three more palaces, and **Freising** is one of Bavaria's most venerable towns; in addition, there are the villages of the **Holledau** region, the world's largest hop-producing area, which is ideal for unhurried exporation by bike.

Dachau

Situated on the S-Bahn #2 line, 17km north of Munich, **DACHAU** is a picturesque provincial town. But whatever its charms may be, the place, the word itself, has associations with horrors that have been indelibly stamped on the consciousness of twentieth-century Europe. Dachau was Germany's first **concentration camp**, built in 1933, and the model for all others. Though not itself an extermination camp, many thousands were murdered here, and the motto that greeted new arrivals at the gates has taken its own chilling place in the history of Third Reich brutality: *Arbeit Macht Frei* – "Work Brings Freedom". The camp was mainly for political prisoners, and numbered among its inmates Pastor Martin Niemöller, the former French Premier Léon Blum, and Johann Elser, who tried to assassinate Hitler in 1939.

To reach the camp or **Konzentrationslager** (Tues–Sun 9am–5pm; free), take bus #722 from Dachau's Bahnhof, or follow the "KZ" signs. The rows of huts where prisoners lived were all torched by the Allies after the war, and neat windswept patches of rectangular gravel mark their former outlines. A replica of one of these huts gives some idea of the cramped conditions prisoners were cooped up in, but the only original buildings still standing are the gas chambers, never used, since the war ended before they could be set to work. Open ovens gape at the shuddering visitor, and bright whitewashed walls almost distract from the ominous gas outlets set in the ceilings of the shower rooms. The stark wire perimeter fencing and watchtowers also remain. A permanent **exhibition**, with photographs and accompanying text in several languages including English, speaks for itself. Turn up at 11.30am or 3.30pm and you can also view the short, deeply disturbing, documentary *KZ-Dachau* in English. In recent years there have been repeated arguments about whether or not to open a centre for visitors to attend discussion forums on the issues raised by visiting the camp. In 1987 an international youth centre was to be opened for German and foreign schoolchildren to meet, but it was blocked by the right-wing town council – an important opportunity lost.

Oberschleissheim

Outside the satellite town of **OBERSCHLEISSHEIM**, 14km from Munich by S-Bahn #1, is the third major palace complex of the Wittelsbach rulers of Bavaria; each palace is in a park a few minutes' walk from the Bahnhof. The original, very modest **Altes Schloss** (Tues–Sun 10am–5pm; DM2) was built at the beginning of the seventeenth century as a spiritual retreat for the pious Duke Wilhelm V, who used only two of its forty-four rooms, going out every day to pray in the hermitages in the nearby woods.

Suitably, therefore, the building, which was almost completely destroyed in the war, has been rebuilt to house a museum of religious folk art.

Far more significant is the **Neues Schloss** (Tues–Sun 10am–12.30pm and 1.30–5pm; DM2) commissioned by the Elector Max Emmanuel almost exactly a century later. This project was initially riddled with bad luck: architect Enrico Zuccali failed to establish sufficiently secure foundations for such an enormous building; as a result, it had to be propped up with mounds of earth, spoiling the proportions and leaving the impression that it is built on quicksand. Work then had to be halted for ten years when the Elector was forced into exile for ten years as a result of his defeat in the War of the Spanish Succession. However, building eventually resumed under the direction of Joseph Effner; aided by such outstanding decorators as Ignaz Günther, Cosmos Damian Asam and Johann Baptist Zimmermann, he turned a potential disaster into one of Germany's finest Baroque palaces. An added attraction is a display of 300 Renaissance and Baroque paintings: although an overspill from the Alte Pinakothek, it still includes examples of Tintoretto, Veronese, Rubens and van Dyck, among others.

Prior to deciding on this extravaganza, Max Emmanuel had asked Zuccali to build the **Schlösschen Lustheim** (same times; DM2) at the opposite end of the park; the two are linked by a finely landscaped canal. On this occasion, the architect created an Italianate masterpiece, which now contains an impressive collection of Meissen porcelain.

Freising

FREISING, the terminus of S-Bahn #1, some 35km north of Munich, is one of Bavaria's oldest towns. As an important episcopal see from 739 to 1803, it used to be the spiritual capital of Bavaria; its title is still retained by the archbishop, who now resides solely in Munich. The **Dom**, situated on a hill above the picturesque town centre, retains its Romanesque shell, but the interior was transformed into the grand Baroque style by the Asam brothers. They didn't, however, tamper with the crypt, whose vault is supported by the amazing *Bestiensäule*, a column covered with carvings of fantastic animals. A secular claim to fame here is the **Weihenstephan-Brauerei** to the west of the Dom, which has been operating since 1040 and reckons to be the oldest brewery in the world. Today it's all very modern and part of Munich's Technical University, but its traditional beers are still served in the adjoining beer garden.

Ingolstadt

Even by German standards, **INGOLSTADT**, 60km due north of Munich, reeks of prosperity, courtesy of its four oil refineries, fed by pipelines from France and Italy, and the Audi car factory which migrated from Zwickau when the Iron Curtain went up. At least some of the wealth generated is used wisely, for the town spends more money on the upkeep of its historic monuments than anywhere else in Bavaria – even Munich, which has fifteen times the population. Compact enough to be seen in a day, and unspoiled by mass tourism, Ingolstadt, for centuries one of Germany's most redoubtable fortresses, is also of special note as the most intriguing example of the country's many university towns which lost their *raison d'être* when academic life was suspended during the Napoleonic Wars, never to be revived.

The fortifications

The old city snuggles within its medieval horseshoe-shaped **walls** on the north bank of the Danube, safely away from the industrial quarters. In the nineteenth century, an additional set of fortifications in a stern Neoclassical style was designed by Leo von Klenze to encase them, and to protect both sides of the bridgehead. Those on the south bank, centred on the **Reduit Tilly**, have been converted into a grandiose park which will feature an important garden show throughout 1992; from here there's a marvellous view of the whole skyline.

Crossing over Konrad-Adenauer-Brücke, the most impressive stretch of the medieval walls lies just to the left; it's made yet more picturesque by the houses which were built directly on to it. This section is pierced by the **Taschenturm** ("Pocket Tower"), whose tall, whitewashed and gabled silhouette has a fairty-tale look about it, for all that it's perfectly genuine. Even it is eclipsed, however, by the **Kreuztor** which now stands like a pint-sized castle in splendid isolation further north. Nowadays, it seems hard to believe that such a lovingly-crafted masterpiece of brickwork was built for purely military purposes.

Beyond, a green belt has been laid out round the huge polygonal fragments of the Neoclassical fortifications. One of these, the **Kavalier Hepp** (Tues–Sat 9am–noon and 1–5pm, Sun 10am–noon and 2–5pm; DM2) to the northwest now contains an historical museum whose exhibits range from a Celtic silver hoard via sculptures from the medieval city gates and Johannes Eck's teaching stool to a stuffed horse said to have been King Gustavus Adolphus' mount during the Swedish siege in the Thirty Years' War.

The Neues Schloss

From here, you can continue all the way round the walls to the strongest point of the defences, the **Neues Schloss**, which sits in gleaming white spendour at the far end of the waterfront. The original structure with its distinctive angular towers was built in the fifteenth century during the short period when Ingolstadt was capital of an independent duchy; the imposing battlements were added a hundred years later. Both in architecture and situation it looks completely un-German, resembling instead a French château; this is explained by the fact that Duke Ludwig the Bearded, who endowed Ingolstadt with many of its finest buildings, became a convinced Francophile during his youth at the court of his brother-in-law, King Charles VI of France. Part of the Schloss now houses the **Bayrisches Armeemuseum** (Tues–Sun 8.45am–4.30pm; DM3.50), the most comprehensive collection of arms and armour in Germany. On the ground floor, the *Dürnitz*, the great banqueting hall, forms an appropriately grand setting for an outstanding section on the Thirty Years' War. Highlight of the displays upstairs is the booty, including a magnificent golden helmet, captured from the Turks in 1682; here also is the finest room in the building, the *Schönen Saal*, whose vault springs from a graceful central pillar.

The town centre

The pedestrianised shopping streets lie west of the Neues Schloss. Along Hallstrasse, and now very much in the shadow of the huge modern Stadttheater, is the modestly-sized **Altes Schloss**, built in the thirteenth century as a second residence for the Landshut dukes. Later prettified by the addition of ornate gables, it was demoted to serving as a granary when the new Schloss was built, but has found a new lease of life as the public library. Further along is the **Altes Rathaus**, created at the end of last century by knocking several old burghers' houses together. Behind rise the massively severe towers of the Gothic **Stadtkirche St Moritz**, whose interior was tarted up in the eighteenth century with extravagant stucco. On Ludwigstrasse, a block to the north, is the **Ickstatthaus**, the most ornate of the town's many Rococo mansions.

From the Stadtkirche, Dollstrasse and Hoher Schulstrasse lead westwards to the **Hohe Schule**, built as a prebendary, but from 1472 until 1800 the main building of the

University of Bavaria, one of the most famous in Germany and a leading centre of Counter-Reformation theology. Ingolstadt's academic tradition lay dormant until 1989, when an economics faculty was opened, but several reminders of its pre-eminence survive in this quarter. One of these is the **Alte Anatomie** at the end of Griesbadgasse to the southeast, a dignified, classically-inspired Baroque building whose courtyard once again serves as a herb garden. The interior contains the **Deutsches Medizinhistorisches Museum** (Tues–Sun 10am–noon and 2–5pm; DM2), which shows the evolution of medical instruments from the ancient Egyptians to the present day.

The Liebfrauenmünster

To the north, and just east of the Kreuztor, is the huge **Liebfrauenmünster**, begun by Duke Ludwig as a sacred counterbalance to the Neues Schloss at the opposite end of town. The unfinished towers, set at startlingly oblique angles, are reminiscent of those of the castle, but otherwise this is a copybook German hall church, the plain brickwork outside brilliantly offset by the sweeping elevation of the whitewashed interior. As work neared completion in the early sixteenth century, the masons created for the six nave chapels the most spectacularly ornate **vaults** in the entire history of European architecture. Here the delicately coloured filigree stonework has been twisted into such shapes as a crown of thorns, a giant insect and great flowering plants, which seem to sprout from the ceiling like huge jewels. The church served as the parish of the University, whose centenary was commemorated by the commissioning of Hans Mielich's **high altar**: look out for the scenes on the reverse, showing cameos of the different faculties at work. On the north side of the ambulatory is the bronze epitaph to **Johannes Eck**, the Ingolstadt theologian who provided the (none too successful) frontline Catholic defence against Luther. Also of special note are the brilliantly coloured **stained glass windows** of the east end, made from designs by Dürer and his followers.

The Maria-de-Victoria-Kirche

A very different but equally dazzling church is the **Maria-de-Victoria-Kirche** (Tues–Sun 9am–noon and 1–5pm; DM1) immediately to the north on Konviktstrasse, an oratory built by the Asam brothers for the Jesuit-run Marian student congregation. Egid Qurin's simple little hall is little more than a stage-set for Cosmos Damian's colossal **ceiling fresco**, which was executed in just eight weeks. Its subject – a complicated allegory on the mystery of the Incarnation – hardly seems to matter, as you're likely to be completely mesmerised by its illusionistic tricks, in which everything appears to be in correct perspective, no matter what your vantage point. Ask the caretaker to let you see the **monstrance** depicting the Battle of Lepanto, another display of Rococo pyrotechnics, this time by an Augsburg goldsmith.

The Tillyhaus

Directly opposite, at the corner of Johannesstrasse, stands the **Tillyhaus**, where Field Marshal Johann Tilly, the Catholic hero of the Thirty Years' War, died in 1632. By then his awesome military reputation was in tatters, his once-invincible troops having been unequal to the challenge posed by the new fighting techniques adopted by the Swedish army. The wounds of which he died were sustained in a vain attempt at preventing the Swedes crossing the Lech in their sweeping advance on Munich, though at least there was the compensation that Ingolstadt's fortifications proved strong enough to withstand the enemy siege. At the end of the street is a square dominated by the **Franziskanerkirche**, whose plain architecture is enlivened by a magnificent set of Renaissance and Baroque epitaphs.

Practicalities

Ingolstadt's **Hauptbahnof**, a junction of the Munich–Nürnberg and Ulm–Regensburg lines, lies 2km south of the old city, to which it's connected by regular buses. The **tourist office** (Mon–Fri 8am–noon and 1–5pm; ☎0841/305415) is in the old riding school right beside the Altes Schloss at Hallstr. 5. There's a **youth hostel** close to the Kreuztr at Friedhofstr. 4½ (☎0841/34177). **Camping** facilities are available at Auwaldsee on the outskirts (☎0841/68911). Cheapest **hotels** with a decent location are *Zum Anker*, Tränktorstr. 1 (☎0841/32091), *Riedenburger Hof*, Am Nordbahnhof (☎0841/81740) and *Schutterhof*, Brodmühlweg 5 (☎0841 34621), all charging from DM30 per person. The first of these has one of the best **restaurants** in town; other good choices are the one in the Stadttheater and *Tafelmeier*, Theresienstr. 31. Main local **festival** is the *Bürgenfest* on the first weekend of July.

Neuburg an der Donau

NEUBURG AN DER DONAU, 22km upstream from Ingolstadt on the railway line to Ulm, makes for an enjoyable afternoon's outing. It doesn't seem to be on any tourist trail, yet is a rarity for Bavaria: medieval towns are two a penny, but Neuburg is characterised by Renaissance architecture and dreamy cobbled streets that give it the feeling of a forgotten town. Perched on a chalk promontory overlooking the Danube, the town was a strategic trading post in Roman times, but its real moment of glory was in 1505, when it became the capital of the House of Pfalz-Neuburg, a junior branch of the Counts Palatine of Heidelberg. During the next hundred years it was redesigned and built up into an elegant town with an imposing castle and beautiful Renaissance and Baroque buildings on leafy squares. The **Karlsplatz** in particular is a perfect picture of stylish sixteenth-century design, and the facade of the **Hofkirche** forms a fine base to the square's symmetry. This church was intended as a Protestant answer to the Jesuits' St Michael in Munich, but the ruling family converted back to Catholicism during its construction, so it was finished off in a rather more elaborate manner than originally intended. The interior has wonderfully plain white stucco, with just a lick of gold and sparing use of black veined marble-effect to create a light and harmonious whole.

The Residenzschloss

Neuburg's most significant and dominant building is the **Residenzschloss** (Tues–Sun 10am–5pm; DM3), built between 1530 and 1545 by order of Ottheinrich, the future Elector of the Palatinate, who was later to transform the great Schloss in Heidelberg. The displays concentrate on presenting the history of the duchy of Pfalz-Neuburg, the region's palaeolithic origins, and its religious art and garments – a strange combination, but interesting nevertheless. A highlight of the collection are the embroidered altar cloths and ceremonial vestments, each delicately embroidered in a particular range of colours depending on the ceremony for which they were used. Also of note is the **Schlosskapelle**, one of the earliest custom-built Protestant churches, adorned with a cycle of frescos illustrating the Bible in line with the tenets of the new faith.

Eichstätt and the Altmühl valley

EICHSTÄTT, 27km northwest of Ingolstadt, can be reached via a short branch railway from the main lines to Nürnberg and Würzburg. Nowadays, it's best known as the gateway to Germany's largest *Naturpark*, the **Altmühl valley**, a Jurassic region first inhabited by humans 100,000 years ago, whose soils have produced many yields of prehistoric fossils and minerals in a quite remarkable state of preservation. The town itself deserves to be far better known: for centuries it was a prince-bishopric at the junction of the three historic provinces of Bavaria, Franconia and Swabia, and was sufficiently prestigious for one its rulers to gain election as Pope Victor II. Having been almost completely destroyed in the Thirty Years' War, it was rebuilt by Italian Baroque architects, giving it an incongruously Mediterranean appearance. Since it was incorporated into Bavaria in the Napoleonic reforms, it seems to have gone to sleep, though in 1980 it became the seat of a new Catholic University – the only one in the German-speaking world.

The town

The main part of Eichstätt lies on the right bank of the Altmühl, on the opposite side of the river from the Stadtbahnhof, which is connected by diesels to the mainline Bahnhof. As you'd expect, the **Dom** is the focal point of this part of town. Essentially, it's a fourteenth-century Gothic structure with a number of Baroque accretions, of which the facade is the most jarring – for all that it's a fine design in its own right. The Dom is especially notable for a number of outstanding works of art. Prominent among these is the *Pappenheimer altar* in the north transept, a virtuoso carving by an unknown late Gothic master of the Crucifixion, in which each of the myriad figures is carefully characterised. In the chancel, look out for the extraordinarily realistic *seated statue of St Willibald*; a memorial to the first Eichstätt bishop. Though dating from just a couple of decades after the altar, it is fully Renaissance in style and is by one of the few German sculptors to master this idiom, **Loy Hering**, who also carved *Wolfsteinaltar* on the west wall and the *Crucifix* in the Sakramentskapelle. Off the west side of the cloisters is the **Mortuarium**, which is anything but the grim chamber its name suggests: it's a superb Gothic hall divided by a row of differently shaped columns, one of which is known as the Schöne Säule ("Beautiful Pillar") from its profuse carvings. There's also a brilliantly coloured stained glass window of *The Last Judgment*, designed by Holbein the Elder, and a *Crucifixion* group by Hering.

South of the Dom

South of the Dom is **Residenzplatz**, one of Germany's most harmonious squares, lined with magnificent Baroque and Rococo palaces of the local knights and canons, and with the cheerful Marienbrunnen in the centre. The **Residenz** (guided tours Mon-Thurs at 9am, 10am, 11am, 2pm and 3.30pm, Fri at 9am, 10am and 2pm, Sat and Sun 10–11.30am and 2–3.30pm; DM2), formerly the home of the prince-bishops, is now occupied by offices, which seems a rather unworthy use of a building with such decorous features as the monumental staircase and the second-floor *Spiegelsaal*. At no. 7 on the same square is the **Diözesanmuseum** (April–Oct Tues–Sun 9.30am–1pm and 2-5pm, Sun 11am–5pm; DM1), containing the Dom's treasury and a varied collection of sacred art: worth a quick browse if that's your cup of tea.

Continuing south, you pass the handsome Jesuit **Schutzengelkirche** en route to the stately Hofgarten, one of whose borders is taken up by the long frontage of the **Sommerresidenz**, formerly the second residence of the bishops, now the administrative headquarters of the Catholic University. Just beyond is the **Kapuzinerkirche**, which houses a twelfth-century Holy Sepulchre, one of the earliest and most accurate reproductions of the Jerusalem original, constructed with the help of descriptions supplied by Crusaders who had been there.

The Marktplatz and Willibaldsburg

On the opposite side of the Dom, the commercial life of the city is centred on **Marktplatz**, another Baroque square whose central fountain bears another statue of Saint Willibald. Further north is the convent of **St Walburg**, a popular pilgrimage place, as it contains the tomb of the eponymous saint, Willibald's sister. There's the bonus of the best view of the town and the valley from the balcony in front of the church.

Occuping a dominant position high above the left bank of the Altmühl, and reached via Burgstrasse from the rear of the Bahnhof, is the **Willibaldsburg**. The earliest parts of this huge fortress date back to the mid-fourteenth century, but the most prominent part is the sumptuous palatial wing designed in the early seventeenth century by the great Ausburg architect Elias Holl. This section now houses the **Jura Museum** and the **Historisches Museum** (both April–Sept Tues–Sun 9am–noon and 1–5pm; Oct–March Tues–Sun 10am–noon and 1–4pm; DM2). Here you can see some of the many finds made in the region; don't be put off by the subject matter, as hi-tech display techniques make this a fascinating experience. The rarest object is the skeleton (one of only five in the world) of a prehistoric bird known as the archaeopteryx, while the most imposing is the four-metres-high, 60,000-years-old mammoth.

Practicalities

The **tourist office** (May–Oct Mon–Fri 9am–noon and 1–6pm, Sat 10am–noon and 1–5pm, Sun 10am–noon; Nov–April Mon–Fri 8am–noon and 1–4pm only; ☎08421/7977) is at Kardinal-Preysing-Platz 14. In addition, there's a separate information centre for the Altmühl valley at Notre Dame 1 (☎08421/6733). The **youth hostel** lies to the west of town at Reichenaustr. 15 (☎08421/4427), but the only **campsites** in the region are much further down the Altmühl. However, plenty of **private houses** offer rooms at DM25 per person or less: the tourist office will supply you with a list. Reasonably-priced **hotels** with a central loction include *Gasthof Goldener Alder*, Westenstr. 76 (☎08421/4488), with singles from DM30, doubles from DM54; *Gaststätte Frey*, Bahnhofplatz 15 (☎08421/2850), at DM30 per person; and *Gasthof Ratskeller*, Kardinal-Preysing-Platz 8 (☎08421/1258), singles from DM35, doubles from DM60. A good choice for a full **meal** is *Krone*, Domplatz 3, which also has a beer garden.

The Altmühl valley

The **River Altmühl** winds its way on either side of Eichstätt, forming a boundary with the Franconian Jura immediately to the north. You can follow it along cycle paths and small roads all the way to the confluence with the Danube at Kehlheim, about 80km to the east. However, it's not really worth going past the fortified town of BEILNGRIES (about halfway along this stretch), as the river's meandering, picturesque route has thereafter been spoiled by being turned into a straight shipping lane for the canal linking the Rhine, Main and Danube. Heading northwest along the river is a better idea if you plan to make your way back to Munich or to move on to Nürnberg or Würzburg: the railway line more or less follows the valley to the junction of TREUCHTLINGEN, and continues along it for a while on the way to Würzburg.

From Munich to the Alps

Most people will probably want to go straight from Munich to the Alps, but between the two lie several enticing destinations. The city's playground area includes five out-of-town lakes, of which the **Starnberger See** and **Ammersee** make an unmissable prelude to exploration of their Alpine counterparts. Just to the west of the latter is the old city of **Landsberg**, a stop on the famous tourist route known as the Romantic Road. Further south, the district of **Pfaffenwinkel** forms the forelands of the Alps; here are **Wessobrunn**, one of the country's oldest and most influential monasteries, and the **Wieskirche**, its most celebrated pilgrimage church.

The Five Lakes

The **Five Lakes** (*Fünf-Seen-Land*) – of which two are major and three very small – can easily be explored in day trips from Munich by S-Bahn.

The Starnberger See

Lying just to the southwest of the city and reached by S-Bahn #6, the largest lake of the group, the **Starnberger See**, is predominantly the domain of the city's rich and their weekend villas. The main resort on the lake is **STARNBERG** at the northernmost tip; here you'll find the local **tourist office** at Kirchplatz 6 (☎08151/13274), which will be able to help out with accommodation should you want to stay. Undoubtedly the most bracing way to explore the lake is by **boat**; *Schiffhart auf dem Starnberger See* is based at Dampfschiffstr. 5 (☎08151/12023) and charges DM17.50 for a round trip, while journeys from one stop to the next cost DM5.50.

The S-Bahn continues down the west coast as far as its terminus at TUTZING. This is the more commercialised side, developed for public use with cafés and restaurants

---

KING LUDWIG II (1846-86)

Alternatively known as "Mad" Ludwig or "The Dream King", **Ludwig II** was a man born out of his time. The most lavish of artistic patrons, he tried to create an escapist world of fantasy at a time when Europe was irreversibly set on a whole new path of international power politics, industrialisation and empire-building. Before he came to the throne at the age of eighteen, Ludwig had experienced the two great formative influences in his life – the revolutionary new music dramas of Richard Wagner and the architecture of the court of the long-dead French king, Louis XIV. In Wagner he found a true soul-mate, a man with visions as grandiose as his own; he rescued the bankrupt composer from financial ruin and created one of the most extraordinary partnerships between patron and artist ever known. Wagner's evocations of Germany's mythical heroic past were also to inspire Ludwig's greatest passion, the creation of castles fit to rival those of the Sun King. He authorised a flurry of building activity, with no regard to the expense: the castles of **Linderhof** (p.96) and **Neuschwanstein** (p.185) between them cost 15 million gulden, while the attempt to build a full-scale copy of Versailles on Herrenchiemsee accounted for an even larger sum.

An irony of all this is that these expressions of a deluded grandeur were partly paid for by Bismarck's Prussia, which made massive payments to both Ludwig and the Bavarian state in return for the surrender of full independence, and absorption into the Second Reich under the rule of the Prussian Kaisers. Even this was insufficient to prevent Ludwig's debts mounting ever higher, yet he refused to curtail his building schemes. In 1886, his ministers, fearing the state's financial collapse, persuaded a group of doctors to declare him insane, a label already attached to his younger brother and heir. Accordingly, he was placed under house arrest in Schloss Berg, and his uncle Luitpold was installed as regent.

A few days later, he and his personal psychiatrist went out for a walk; their bodies were later dragged up from the lake. Ludwig's lungs had no water in them, suggesting that he could not have drowned; in any case, he was a strong swimmer unlikely to have got into difficulties so near the shore. Marks on the doctor's body suggest he had been involved in a violent struggle, though whether he had attacked the king or vice versa, or whether both were victims of a third party, has never been resolved. Perhaps Ludwig had suffered a genuine attack of madness: on the other hand, he might well have been murdered, as he had become a major political embarrassment. That the mystery remains seems a fitting end to the sad melodrama of Ludwig's life; the final irony is that his fantasy castles have become Bavaria's biggest tourist draw – and thus a significant and continuing contributor to the state coffers

vying for your money; the main public beach is at POSSENHOFEN. On the eastern shores, the lake is mainly lined with private properties and it's not always possible to get at the water, though there are some small public stretches between the villages of BERG, LEONI and AMMERLAND. The **Schloss** of the first-named (which is still a private residence of the Wittelsbachs –now demoted back to their old title of Dukes of Bavaria – and not open for visits) was where the ill-starred King Ludwig II (see opposite) was staying at the time of his mysterious death. A small chapel, modelled on the Church of the Holy Sepulchre in Jerusalem, has been erected nearby in his memory.

Another tribute comes in the form of Germany's most popular long-distance footpath, the **King Ludwig Way** (*König-Ludwig-Weg*), covering the 120km between Starnberg and Füssen. It's easy to follow, being marked by signposts showing a blue K with a crown; although the scenery is magnificent, the terrain is undemanding and is easily covered in a four- or five-day hike.

The Ammersee

The S-Bahn #5 line goes from Munich to the resort of **HERRSCHING** on the **Ammersee**; its three previous stops cover the remaining lakes of the group – WESSLING is by the minute lake of the same name; STEINEBACH is on the west side of the deep blue Wörthsee; while SEEFELD lies on the peaceful Pilsensee. Herrsching is a favourite place to go swimming and sailing and can get very crowded, particularly on summer weekends. There's a footpath along the water's edge to the west, where a few public beaches are slotted in between stretches of private property. **Boat trips** are run by *Schiffahrt auf dem Ammersee* (☎08143/229 for information).

Andechs, Bavaria's "Holy Mountain", is a beautifully-sited Benedictine monastery and pilgrimage centre. The walk up from Herrsching winds through attractive woodland paths, but be warned that it's quite strenuous towards the end: the lazy alternatives are buses #951 and #956 that go from outside the S-Bahn stop. In the late fourteenth century, the relics brought here from Jerusalem by the local count in 952 were rediscovered. To celebrate this, a Gothic church was built, and this is the one you see today, albeit with an interior remodelled in Rococo style. An additional enticement for the modern pilgrim is the delicious strong **beer** brewed by the monks, which they serve in the *Gasthaus* attached to the monastery.

Across the lake lies **DIESSEN**, a village whose population includes a sizeable artistic colony, with potters pre-eminent. Here you'll find the area **tourist office** at Mühlstr. 4a (☎08807/1048), plus a **campsite** (☎08807/7305). On the hill above is an Augustinian **Kloster**, which boasts one of Bavaria's finest Rococo churches: the design is by J.M. Fischer, the high altar by Cuvilliés, while among the side altars is a superb *Martyrdom of St Sebastian* by Tiepolo.

Landsberg

The historic town of **LANDSBERG** lies west of the Ammersee, some 55km from Munich. Its full name is Landsberg am Lech, as it stands on the banks of the River Lech, and its emblem is the fifteenth-century Gothic **Bayertor**, one of the town's medieval defensive gates. During the Middle Ages Landsberg was a fortified border town between Swabia and Bavaria, and made its money from levies on trade passing on the salt road from Salzburg to Memmingen. From these rich pickings, Landsberg's burghers built themselves a flashy **Rathaus**, which today forms the showpiece of the main square. Its fancy stuccoed Rococo facade was added by the great church-builder Dominikus Zimmerman, who did a stint as burgomaster of the town; he also built **St Johannes** on Vorderanger. Another famous resident, if only for nine months, was Adolf Hitler, who was banged up in the local fortress for trying to mount the Munich *Putsch* in 1923; he used the time to write his infamous treatise *Mein Kampf*.

There's no youth hostel here, but an excellent **campsite** (☎08191/47505) is just a few minutes' walk from the centre of town, at the far end of the Pössingerstrasse, which turns into the Pössinger Weg; it's right next to a forest and near the Lech. The cheapest **hotel**, at about DM30 per person, is *Zederbräu*, Hauptplatz 155, (☎08191/2241), and there are also rooms in private houses in the region of DM25 per person. Try *Ferienhaus Kander*, Aggensteinstr. 14, (☎08191/2517) or *Erna Rabe*, Johann-Festl-Str. 4 (☎08191/46931). The **tourist office** (☎08191/128246) is in the Rathaus.

The Pfaffenwinkel

The pre-Alpine countryside south of the Five Lakes is known as the **Pfaffenwinkel** (literally, "Clerics' Corner"). It has no major towns, but – as the name suggests – is dotted with religious foundations of various kinds, including two of the most famous in the country. Walking is by far the best way to explore this area, and the King Ludwig Way (see above) cuts all the way through it.

Wessobrunn

The tiny village of **WESSOBRUNN**, some 10km southwest of the Ammersee, holds an honoured place in German culture as the place where the earliest-known text in the language, the ninth-century *Wessobrunn Prayer*, was discovered in the monastery library in the nineteenth century. A century earlier, the village had assumed national leadership of a different kind, as the craftsmen and stuccoists based there took the lead in disseminating the Rococo style throughout southern Germany; three leading artistic dynasties – the Schmuzers, the Feuchtmayers and the Zimmermanns – were all originally from Wessobrunn.

The former monastic church of **St Johannes** preserves the belfry and a *Crucifix* from its Romanesque predecessor, but is otherwise a typical example of the Wessobrunn style, its interior richly draped in stucco. To the northeast stands the **Wezzobrunnen**, a well-house built over a miraculous spring which inspired the monastery's foundation. However, the most impressive part of the complex is the **Kloster** itself (guided tours Mon–Sat at 10am, 3pm and 4pm, Sun 3pm and 4pm), particularly the ornate *Fürstengang* (Princes' Gallery).

Steingaden and the Wieskirche

STEINGADEN, some 20km southwest, boasts another **Kloster**, whose natural sandstone architecture is a welcome contrast to the plethora of colour characteristic of the region. However, only the church's exterior and the cloisters preserve their romantically dilapidated Romanesque aspect: the interior was remodelled in the familiar manner.

A further 20km south of Steingaden are two of the famous Bavarian royal castles (see p.185), Closer at hand, unassumingly tucked away in the countryside 5km southeast, is the **Wieskirche** ("Meadow Church"), the best-known pilgrimage church in Germany and the finest achievement of the Wessobrunn School – one important enough to be listed by UNESCO as a World Heritage Site. It owes its existence to a decision by the Steingaden monks to discard a statue of the suffering Christ which they formerly carried in their Holy Week processions. It was acquired by a farmer's wife, who found the figure crying when she prayed before it: so many pilgrims flocked to the simple shrine her husband built that the monks asked **Dominikus Zimmermann** to erect a suitably worthy temple for the image. His carefully thought-out design, based on his earlier pilgrimage church in Steinhausen (see *Chapter Two*), has an almost umbilical relationship with the mountains in the background.

The plain exterior belies the almost indecent extravagance inside. Light streams in from the high windows of the oval nave, creating an inviting and joyful atmosphere;

plain white pillars sparkle like snow-capped mountains, but at the same time form a modest contrast to the stuccoed and gold-plated ornamentation of the arches above, and the vast fresco by Johann Baptist Zimmermann (Dominikus' elder brother) in the cupola. The contrast is intended to symbolise earth below and the glorious heavens above, with the blue base of the central fresco representing God's pity and forgiveness spreading over mankind.

The Alps

The **Upper Bavarian Alps**, stretching about 180km along the Austrian border, form some of the most gloriously beautiful countryside to be found in Europe. It's here amid classic picture-book scenery that you'll find the Bavarian folklore and customs that are the subject of so many tourist brochures: men still wear leather *Lederhosen* and checked shirts, and women the traditional *Dirndl* dresses with frilly blouses and embroidered aprons. On a superficial level it can all seem very kitschy, but look beyond the packaged culture and you'll find life here steeped in a fascinating mixture of Catholic and pagan rites that dominate the annual calendar – events usually accompanied by large amounts of eating and drinking.

Running from the border with Bavarian Swabia in the west to the Austrian frontier near Berchtesgaden in the east, the Upper Bavarian Alps offer a landscape of gentle slopes and rich mixed forests at their western end. Head for **Oberammergau** where the world-famous Passion Play is staged every ten years, or **Ettal** with its historic Benedictine monastery and nearby **Schloss Linderhof**. From here it's only a few kilometres to the international ski-resort of **Garmisch-Partenkirchen**, above which towers the **Zugspitze**, Germany's highest and most famous peak. Virtually next door to Garmisch is **Mittenwald**, which often unfairly gets missed due to its prestigious neighbour.

The eastern part of the Alps, from **Tegernsee** to **Berchtesgaden**, is heavily geared to the tourist trade. If you're looking to get away from it all, the **Sudelfeld** hills are usually quiet as they are not served by public transport. There are no dramatic heights until the Berchtesgadener Land, an area that includes the town of **Berchtesgaden** itself as well as the marvellous peak of the **Watzmann** and the high ridges forming the border with Austria.

Also serving as tourist magnets are the **Upper Bavarian lakes**, most of which lie in the glacial valleys of the Alpine foothills, though some, like the **Walchensee** and the **Königssee**, are actually in the mountains. The largest foothill lakes, in order of size, are the **Chiemsee**, **Tegernsee** and **Staffelsee**, and there are innumerable smaller ones. Among these, the **Schliersee** is scenically one of the most rewarding.

As if the scenery weren't enough, manifold culinary delights are available in the wonderful old *Gaststätten*, often with beer gardens, where traditional Bavarian menus and innumerable regional beers go down a treat. **Regional transport** in the Alpine areas is reasonably good: coming from München there are rail links to many destinations, while there's a good network of connecting bus services between the Alpine towns, the only snag being that some of these only operate once or twice a day. **Accommodation** shouldn't be a major problem, except during July and August in the most sought-after destinations, and can be surprisingly inexpensive. There's a huge choice of rooms in private houses (identified by the *Zimmer frei* signs; contact the local tourist office if you want to make an advance booking); prices range from DM15–25 per person, except in major resorts such as Garmisch, where you can expect to pay a bit more. Youth hostels (for the under 27s) and campsites are also plentiful, and have been listed in the text below.

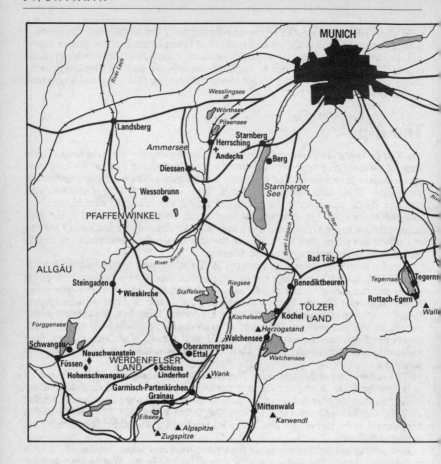

Oberammergau and around

OBERAMMERGAU, the terminus of a branch railway line at the western end of the Upper Bavarian Alps, is world-famous for the **Passion Play** (see over page) that the local villagers have been performing since 1634. The next performances won't take place until the year 2000, so the huge **Passionspielhaus**, custom-built in the 1930s to ensure every member of the audience has a good view of the performance, will be echoingly empty until then.

Without the tradition of the play, it's likely that Oberammergau would be stuck in total obscurity, instead of being the tourist trap it has become, crammed with souvenir shops selling examples of the local woodcarving to the choking busloads of organised tour parties who roll up every summer. Nonetheless, it does preserve features genuinely characteristic of small Alpine communities. In particular, many of the houses have the traditional **frescos**, which you can see as either quaint or kitsch. This style of decoration, known as *Lüftlmalerei*, is a uniquely Catholic art, dating from the period of the Counter-Reformation, which successfully fostered an increased religious zeal. Thus the

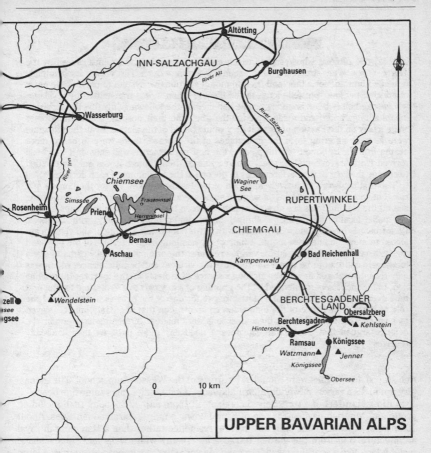

UPPER BAVARIAN ALPS

scenes depicted are usually based on biblical stories, making a highly distinctive transfer of a sacred art form to secular buildings. The modest **Pfarrkirche** is a typical example of the Wessobrunn School of church building, with a fine set of frescos by the Augsburg artist Matthäus Günther.

If you want to stay here (and without advance booking it will only really be an option out of season) the **tourist office**, at Eugen-Papst-Str. 9a (☎08822/1021) will help you find a private room. One of the cheaper local **pensions** is the *Hotel-Pension Wenger*, Ludwig-Lang-Str. 20 (☎08822/4788), a little way east of the centre of town. There's also a **youth hostel** at the southwestern edge of town at Mahlensteinweg 10 (☎08822/4114).

Ettal and Schloss Linderhof

ETTAL, 4km down the road, is a little less touristy. It's a small health resort, but is mainly notable for the Benedictine **Kloster**, whose church has a twelve-cornered nave design, based on the Church of the Holy Sepulchre in Jerusalem. The original fourteenth-century structure was rebuilt in the Baroque style by Enrico Zuccalli, and the

THE PASSION PLAY

In 1632, **the plague**, whose spread was greatly facilitated by the famines caused by the Thirty Years' War, struck the area around Oberammergau. The village itself initially remained immune for a time and tried to mount a protective system to prevent the entry of infected persons, but fell victim to the disease when it was transmitted by a villager who worked elsewhere. So many people had died by the following July that the surviving inhabitants gathered and made a pledge that they and their descendants would forever stage a play on the Passion of Jesus if they would be rid of the plague. Even though some were already suffering from the first stages of the disease, there were to be no more deaths from it. In honour of the pledge, the first performance was staged; it has been revived (with few exceptions) every ten years since then, though it was quickly decided to change the year of the performances to the one at the beginning of each decade.

The cast is always exclusively made up of local villagers, who vie for the honour of a role, but with up to 200 players on stage in some scenes, most get a chance to participate, and all the leading roles are now alternated between two actors. Even the props have to be made locally, displaying a shrewd sense for combining piety with business. Performances last five and a half hours, with a two hour break for lunch, and visitors are forced to move on after two nights. Controversy has long been a feature of the play, and the text has had to be revised for various reasons: the original gradually came to seem too bawdy and had to be toned down, while the virulent anti-Semitic stance, which was only recently watered down, was for long a source of protests. In the most recent production, traditionalists were offended by the granting of a key part to a Protestant for the first time ever, and by the choice of a mother-of-two for one of the actresses who shared the role of Mary, in defiance of the long-enforced convention that she could only be played by a virgin. Cynics scoffed that these decisions were made to attract media attention; the defence argued that Oberammergau doesn't need any more publicity than it already receives.

rich stucco decorations were moulded by artists of the Wessobrunn school. The monastery produces a variety of wonderful fruit liqueurs and brandies, plus some fine beers.

Schloss Linderhof (April–Sept daily 9am–12.15pm and 12.45–5pm; DM6 including grotto and Moorish pavilion) is one of King Ludwig's more restrained fantasies. About 10km west of Ettal, it was built as a private residence rather than a statement in royal architecture, and from the garden terraces its creamy white walls and square shape make it look like a sparkling wedding cake. As you enter, it's impossible to miss a large bronze statue of one of Ludwig's heroes, Louis XIV, the French Sun King, and, in spite of this being a private retreat, Ludwig still had a royal reception room built with intricate gold-painted carvings, stucco ornamentation and a throne canopy draped in ermine curtains, said to be from the coronation gown of King Otto of Greece. The bedroom is also daftly luxurious: the large bed is cordoned off by a richly carved balustrade, and royal-blue velvet extends to a great canopy overhead, no doubt creating the reassuring feeling of sleeping on the throne.

However, the top attraction is the delightful **park**. The palace forms the axis of a cross design, which is built on the Italian Renaissance model of terraces, cascades and pools rising up in front and behind, while the shorter gardens to the right and left have strictly manicured lawns, hedges and flowerbeds. Initially, it's hard to tell that the surrounding "wild" scenery is actually a clever English garden design that gradually blends into the forests of the mountain beyond. A number of romantic little buildings are dotted around the park, the most remarkable of which is the **Venus Grotto**. It's supposed to be based on the set from the first act of Wagner's opera *Tannhäuser* and has an illuminated lake with an enormous golden conch floating on it in which the king would sometimes take rides.

The Staffelsee and Riegsee

Within easy striking distance of Oberammergau are a brace of lakes. The **Staffelsee**, near the village of MURNAU, 8km northeast of Oberammergau at the point where the branch railway joins with the main Munich–Garmisch line, is a large reedy moor lake. This means that its dark waters get agreeably warm in the summer and make it ideal for swimming. **Cruises**, run between June and mid-September by *Motorschiffahrt Staffelsee* (☎08841/8794), are another possible diversion. On the western shore, only accessible by boat, there's a nudist beach, though you'll find that topless sunbathing is pretty much standard practice in most places. The countryside around the lake is flat marshland – don't forget the mosquito repellent. If you want a quieter but colder experience, the **Riegsee** is not far to the east of the Staffelsee.

For accommodation lists, contact the local **tourist office**, Kohlgruberstr. 1, Murnau (☎08841/2074). Both lakes have **campsites** (☎08841/9870 and ☎08841/5992 respectively).

Garmisch-Partenkirchen

GARMISCH-PARTENKIRCHEN, some 19km south of Oberammergau by road, is the most famous resort in the German Alps, partly because it's at the foot of the highest mountain – the Zugspitze – and also because it hosted the Winter Olympics over fifty years ago. The location is marvellous, placed between the gentle Ammer mountains and the imposing peaks of the Wetterstein chain which form the frontier with Austria. During the winter months Garmisch is one of the foremost skiing bases, and it has excellent facilities for skating and other winter sports too; in summer, mountaineers and hiking enthusiasts come to explore the craggy heights, while the less energetic take advantage of the painfree ascents possible by cable car.

What were two separate villages have merged over the years to form one town, but there are still distinct identities, with Garmisch aspiring to ritzy shops and trendy brasseries, while Partenkirchen retains its Alpine village feel. The attractive Ludwigstrasse in Partenkirchen, lined with traditional painted houses, also has some friendly inns and cafés that aren't over-expensive. In the Garmisch end of town, on the other hand, you're likely to be asked to make room for someone else if you don't spend enough money.

Practicalities

Garmisch-Partenkirchen's **Bahnhof** is handily placed between the two constituent villages; immediately to its rear is the **Zugspitzbahnhof**, terminus of the mountain railway. At the latter you can buy a special seven-day pass allowing the use of most cable cars, something well worth considering if you're planning on doing a lot of hiking here. These are available between June and October inclusive, at DM65 or DM40 for kids under 16. Three-day winter ski passes for the region cost DM112 (DM78 for under-16s), while a weekly pass will set you back DM225 (DM161 for under-16s). Nearby, at Bahnhofstr. 34 is the **tourist office** (Mon–Sat 8am–6pm, Sun 10am–noon; ☎08821/ 1800).

The **youth hostel**, Jochstr. 10 (☎08821/2980; bus #6 or #7 from the Bahnhof) isn't very central, and insists on 11pm lights-out. A much friendlier place in the same price range and without an age restriction is the *Naturfreundehaus*, Schalmeiweg 21 (☎08821/4322). Otherwise the *Ohlsenhof*, Von-Brug-Str. 18 (☎08821/2168) comes highly recommended by other travellers, and has singles around DM30 and doubles around DM60. The *Mirabell*, Hindenburg Strasse 20 (☎08821/4826) is good too, and charges around DM28 for singles and DM56 for doubles. There's a **campsite** (☎08821/ 3180), ideally placed for the peaks, by the village of GRAINAU to the west.

The peaks

From Garmisch, there are two possibilities for ascending the **Zugspitze** (2966m) by public transport; each costs DM30 single, DM50 return in summer, DM29 single, DM43 return in winter. The electric train, the *Zugspitzbahn*, travels westwards to a forest lake, the **Eibsee**. Here you can either continue by the rack railway, which goes up a winding tunnel carved through the interior of the mountain, or transfer to the *Eibseebahn* cable car. Whereas the latter goes straight to the summit, the former deposits you at the *Hotel Schneefernhaus* (2645m), which commands a huge skiing area. There's then the possibility of ascent to the summit by the *Gipfelbahn* cable car, or of walking via the tunnel to the customs point, the *Zugspitzkamm* (2805m), from where yet another cable car, the *Tiroler Zugspitzbahn*, runs to EHRWALD in Austria. The **views** from the top are all you'd expect, stretching from the Tyrolean High Alps to the Allgäu and the Bavarian lowlands.

Closer to Garmisch, the **Alpspitze** (2628m) is the highest peak in a range popular with serious hikers. In this case, there's no cable car to the summit, though one runs to the nearby **Osterfelderkopf** (2050m) for DM19 single, DM27 return. Three more summits further north, **Kreuzeck** (1652m), **Eckbauer** (1236m) and **Hausberg** (1350m) also have their own (correspondingly less expensive) cable cars, so it's easy enough to devise your own itinerary according to how much walking you want to do. Close to the last-named is the magnificent gorge known as **Partnachklamm**, which can be traversed by a circular path hewn out of the rock.

East of Garmisch, the unfortunately named **Wank** (1780m) offers the best view of the basin in which the town is set, as well as a complete panorama of the Wetterstein chain. A cable car goes to the summit for DM13 single, DM19 return.

Mittenwald

It's absurd that Garmisch gets the lion's share of tourism when, just 20km southeast by road or rail, **MITTENWALD** has the best of everything only on a smaller and friendlier scale. Goethe said in 1786 that Mittenwald was like a "living picture book", and so it remains. A large village with traditional frescos on many houses, Mittenwald still feels like a community and not just a resort. This is reflected in the **Pfarrkirche SS-Peter-und-Paul**, which has beautifully carved seats and each family's nameplate attached to their special section on the benches. The statue outside honours **Mathias Klotz**, who brought the highly specialised craft of violin-making to Mittenwald in the seventeenth century and saved the village from being an impoverished backwater. In the preceding two centuries, Venetian merchants had located their main market here for trading Italian and German goods, making Mittenwald rich in the process, but that source of wealth was destroyed when the merchants returned their market to its original location in Italy, and the village went into decline until the new industry was founded. Since then local violin-makers have achieved international fame, with musicians paying DM15,000 for a violin that will last for generations. Examples from some of the finest violin-makers can be seen in the little doll's house of a museum, the **Geigenbaumuseum** (May–Oct Mon–Fri 10–11.45am and 2–4.45pm; DM3) in the Ballenhausgasse. Not far away, in the road called Im Gries, stand the oldest Mittenwald houses, with frescos decorating their frontages, the kitsch effect pleasantly diminished by faded colours.

Towering above Mittenwald is the **Karwendl** (2244m), one of the most popular climbing destinations in Germany, and the local **mountaineering school** (Dekan-Karl-Platz 29) runs tours and courses throughout the summer, as well as supplying guides for small groups. The view from the top is one of the most exhilarating and dramatic to be found, and a cable car goes there for DM14 single, DM23 return.

Practicalities

The **tourist office** is located at Dammkarstr. 3 (Mon–Sat 9am–5pm ☎08823/1051). Being an hour's walk from the Bahnhof, the **youth hostel** at Buckelwiesen 7 (☎08823/1701) isn't a very practical accommodation option. However, there are plenty of good places to stay in the village, such as *Haus Alpenruh*, Schillerweg 2 (☎08823/1375), *Gästehaus Bergfrühling*, Dammkarstr. 12 (☎08823/8089), or *Haus Berghof*, Grobelweg 37 (☎08823/1556): all charge around DM25 per person. The nearest **campsite** (☎08823/5216) is 3km north, on the road to Garmisch and open all year. For **eating** and **drinking**, there are many good traditional inns, notably on Innsbrücker Strasse.

The Tölzer Land

To the north of Mittenwald, the **Tölzer Land** offers altogether gentler scenery, but has a rich folklore tradition of riflemen's festivals and costumed parades. The one town, BAD TÖLZ, is a plush spa catering mainly for the elderly brigade, but the area also embraces two lakes plus one of the oldest and most celebrated monasteries in Germany.

The Walchensee

Of the two lakes, the **Walchensee**, 19km from Mittenwald, is by far the more dramatic. Nobody knows just how deep it is. The water is so cold in the lower reaches that the many trees fallen from the mountainous shores haven't been able to sink completely; instead they've formed a sort of false bottom to the lake, which is quite impenetrable. The mysteries surrounding the lake aren't just about its physical nature either – many people believe that it was here that the Nazis dumped their hoarded treasures in the last few days of the war, because truck after truck is said to have driven up here and emptied its contents into the lake. Plenty of divers have tried their luck and some have died, tangled up in the branches or with their lifelines ripped; it can be a sinister place up here when the sun has gone

On a sunny day, though, the lake is beautiful and boats cut through the green waves, their sails full with the mountain breeze. If you're into boats and windsurfing, this is a good place to come, especially since it's never as crowded as the lowland lakes and is cheaper too. Rowing boats can be rented for the day from the *Hotel Schwaigerhof* for DM10–DM16 per hour. Surfboards cost from about DM15 per hour to DM50 per day. A very popular tour around here is the two-hour walk from URFELD at the northern tip of the lake to the summit of the **Herzogstand** (1731m). From here you can see both the region's lakes plus the snow-capped Austrian peaks to the south and the Bavarian plateau to the north. Alternatively, take the cable car from the village of WALCHENSEE on the western shore (DM6.50 single, DM10 return).

Among the accommodation possibilities are a **campsite** in Walchensee (☎08858/237) and a **youth hostel** at Mittenwalder Str. 17 (☎08851/230) in Urfeld.

The Kochelsee

A wonderful twisting 9km-long road links Urfeld with the **Kochelsee**. This lake combines lowland and highland attractions: to the north lies marshland while the Benediktenwand, the first slopes in the Alpine chain, rise immediately from its southern shore. The shoreline has an agreeably empty feel to it compared with many others, with hardly any private property around the edges. Having said that, the lake and immediate surrounding area are a bit boring in themselves, being completely flat and without memorable views. The village of **KOCHEL** on the northeastern side is the largest settlement; it's the terminus of a branch rail line which links up with the

Munich S-Bahn network at the Starnberger See.. Here you"ll find the local **tourist office** at Kalmbachstr. 11 (☎08851/338), while **cruises** are run between June and September by *Motorschiffahrt Kochelsee* (☎08851/416 for information). Accommodation possibilities include a **youth hostel** at Badstr. 2 (☎08851/5296) and the **campsites** *Kesselberg* (☎08851/464) and *Renken* (☎08851/5776).

Kochel is interesting mainly for two of its former inhabitants. First of these was Balthasar Mayer, the celebrated **Blacksmith of Kochel**, who led the 1705 rebellion of Upper Bavarian farmers against the Austrian occupation. Bavaria had fought against the Austrian Habsburg rulers in the War of the Spanish Succession and lost, so Austrian troops had occupied the region. Their brutal rule led to the farmers' rebellion, which has since become a symbol of Bavarian *Heimatliebe* or patriotism. The plotters of the uprising, mostly farmers, were betrayed, and they and their leader died in the battle at Sendling near Munich; their graves are still to be found in Sendling church-yard, now a part of the capital.

Another local resident was **Franz Marc**, a member of the *Blaue Reiter* group of abstract Expressionist painters that included Kandinsky, Macke and Klee. Marc lived around here from 1908 until 1916, when he died in World War I at the age of 36. Unlike his friends, he preferred country life, and his pictures of horses and other animals are his most famous works. The **Franz-Marc-Museum** at Herzogstandweg 43 (Tues–Sun 2–6pm; DM3.50) contains a highly representative collection of his work, comprising about a hundred paintings, as well as examples of other members of the *Blaue Reiter* group.

Benediktbeuern

BENEDIKTBEUERN, 8km north of Kochel on the road to Bad Tölz, is a small village with its back to the Benediktenwand. The **Kloster** dates back to 789 and is thus the oldest in Upper Bavaria, though the present buildings are Baroque. Its church boasts a **fresco cycle** of the life of Christ painted by Hans Georg Asam (father of the famous brothers), but is rather eclipsed by the **Anastasiakapelle**, a separate structure to the north, which is a miniature Baroque masterpiece by Johann Michael Fischer. In 1930, the buildings were re-occupied by a congregation of Salesian monks, who have established it as a school and cultural centre. Concerts and important exhibitions are often held; there are a restaurant and beer garden, plus a **youth hostel** (☎08857/88350). A second, women-only, hostel can be found at Bahnhofstr. 58 (☎08857/260).

CARMINA BURANA

Benediktbeuern is chiefly famous for the manuscript known as *Carmina Burana*, which was compiled and illuminated here in the late thirteenth century, remaining in the monastery library until the Napoleonic secularisation, when it was carted off to Munich. Although this anthology of eleventh- to thirteenth-century (mostly Latin) lyrics by itiner-ant scholars and monks contains some religious pieces, its primary concerns are decid-edly earthly, with moral and satirical verses, ribald love laments, and bucolic drinking and gaming songs all featured. In 1935 the Munich composer Carl Orff was inspired to write a technicolour choral and orchestral showpiece on some of the texts; this has become probably the single most popular piece of "serious" music composed this century, and one championed by nearly all leading conductors, though it has become the pet hate of all "progressive" critics, who loathe its unmodernistic tunefulness and the eclectic range of styles imitated. At the time this cantata was written, the musical notation in the manuscript itself was thought to be indecipherable, but painstaking detective work by musicologists has enabled these hauntingly pure and simple songs to become one of the mainstays of the repertoire of early music groups.

The Tegernsee and around

The **Tegernsee**, some 15km east of Bad Tölz, is perhaps the most beautiful lake in Bavaria. For this reason it's long been a favourite with the rich, who built their weekend homes along its privately owned sections, and in the southern village of **ROTTACH-EGERN** you'll find one of the most expensive hotels in Bavaria complete with high-fashion boutique and piano-bar. The *haute couture* in Rottach-Egern is pretty incongruous in this country setting, and the neo-locals take themselves ever so seriously. For a wonderful view of the area, however, go up the **Wallberg** (1722m); the cable car costs DM10 single, DM18 return.

On the east bank of the lake is the village of **TEGERNSEE**, terminus of a branch railway to Munich. As a perfect antidote to the designer Bavarians, visit the *Bräustüberl*, where the local farmers go to drink each other under the table and play cards. Things get quite rowdy sometimes when fists start thundering down onto the tables, but there's also a large beer garden, so you needn't upset the regulars sitting around the *Stammtisch* inside. The *Bräustüberl* is in the north wing of the **Kloster**, which is one of the oldest in Bavaria and was a major cultural centre for many centuries. In 1500 its library was more extensive than the Vatican's, but the valuable archives and books were largely destroyed during secularisation, and the rest were taken to Munich. The village is also the best place from which to take **boat trips** on the lake; these are run by *Motorschiffahrt Tegernsee*, Seestr. 70 (☎08022/4760). The nearest **youth hostel** (☎08029/552) is only a few kilometres by bus from here, in the village of SCHARLING at Nördliche Hauptstr. 91.

The Schliersee

Surrounded by wooded mountains and lush farmland, the **Schliersee** has more of an Alpine feel about it. Set at the northeastern corner on a branch rail line from Munich which then loops round the west side of the lake, the pretty town of **SCHLIERSEE** at the northeastern end of the lake hasn't yet been annexed by the Porsche-driving set. Traditional life is still strong here, and one of those traditions is poaching game. Of course it's illegal and the foresters don't hesitate to shoot poachers on sight – even nowadays. One of the most famous poachers ever to have lived in the Alps is buried just outside Schliersee; his name was **Jennerwein**, and just to prove a point, the local poachers yearly put a freshly killed mountain buck on his grave on the anniversary of his death.

There's a sailing school in Schliersee where you can hire boats and surfboards, while **cruises** are run from May until early October by *Motorschiffahrt Schliersee* (☎08026/4640). For swimming you're better off at the southern end of the lake, past the village of FISCHHAUSEN. The most obvious excursion is to ascend the **Schliersberg** (1061m) to the east; the trip by cable car costs DM4 single, DM7 return. There are two **campsites**: *Alpenblick* (☎08026/4644) and *Lido* (☎08026/6624); information about other accommodation can be had from the **tourist office** in the Kurwerwaltung (☎08026/4069),

The Spitzingsee

The **Spitzingsee** up above the Josefsthal valley (just to the south of the Schliersee) is a little lake mostly associated with winter sports. During the summer there's nothing particularly attractive about the lake or village, and it wouldn't be worth a special trip to see it, but snow and ice transform the place into a magical winter scene, and the surrounding slopes form one of the busiest and best skiing resorts in Bavaria, though it gets hopelessly crowded at weekends. There's a **youth hostel** in the Josefsthal valley (Josefstalerstr. 19; ☎08026/71068); the nearest Bahnhof is FISCHHAUSEN-NEUHAUS.

Bayrischzell

BAYRISCHZELL, terminus of the branch railway, is a small resort in the enclosed setting of the upper valley of the River Leitzach. Coming from the Schliersee, stop off at the *Winkelstüberl Café* on the road between FISCHBACHAU and ELBACH, which is open until late in the evening: the size of the cake portions is famous throughout the area. The **Sudelfeld** hills above Bayrischzell are one of the most isolated parts of the Bavarian Alps and a great area to go walking away from the crowds, though hang-gliding from the bare hilltops has become popular. There's a **youth hostel** (☎08023/675) which can be reached by walking from Bayrischzell's Bahnhof to the chair lift on the other side of the village and then taking a ride to the top: best phone first.

Behind the Sudelfeld rises the rocky peak of the **Wendelstein** (1838m). A spanking new cable car, costing DM13.50 single, DM22 return, ascends from Bayrischzell. However, a more atmospheric approach is up the eastern side of the mountain: from DEGERNDORF, on the main Munich–Innsbruck line, a rack railway runs to within 100m of the chapel-crowned summit, which is reached by means of a steep path carved out of the rock.

The Chiemsee

The **Chiemsee**, some 35km east of the Wendelstein, is Bavaria's largest lake. Its principal resort, conveniently placed for visiting all the local beauty spots, is **PRIEN** on the western shore, which lies on the main Munich–Salzburg railway. Here you're also at the hub of the watersports activities and of the **ferry** connections run by the *Chiemseeschiffahrt* (☎08051/6090). There are also two of the lake's many **campsites** – *Hofbauer* (☎08051/4136) and *Harras* (☎08051/2515). At Carl-Braun-Str. 46 (☎08051/2972) is one of the local **youth hostels**; the other, reachable by bus, is by the moor lakes in the nature reserve to the north, in the hamlet of HEMHOF (Haus 84; ☎08053/509). Information about other sorts of accommodation can be had from the **tourist office** at Alte Rathausstr. 11 (☎08051/69050).

Reachable from Prien in just a few minutes by boat, the Chiemsee's largest island, the **Herreninsel**, is the site of King Ludwig II's final monument to glorious absolutism and isolation: **Schloss Herrenchiemsee** (daily 9am–5pm; DM4). After saving the island – which was previously occupied by a monastery – from deforestation, Ludwig II set about building a complete replica of Versailles, but funds ran out in 1885 with only the central body of the palace built. For all the money squandered on it, the king only ever lived there one week. The island is a great place to go for walks, and you can just imagine Ludwig galloping through the mists on his morning ride. By the landing stage there's a beer garden with a good view of the lake.

The **Fraueninsel** alongside is a much smaller island, built up with holiday homes, restaurants, cafés and an ancient, still-functioning Benedictine nunnery – hence the name. Its **Klosterkirche** is one of the few in Upper Bavaria to have escaped the clutches of Rococo interior designers, and still preserves its original Romanesque form save for the picturesque extensions to the tower and the fancy late Gothic vault. An even rarer survival is the Carolingian gatehouse or **Torhalle** (May–Oct daily 11am–6pm), which features an upstairs chapel with ninth-century frescos; accurate reproductions of the church's now-concealed Romanesque ceiling paintings are also on view.

The environs of the lake

If you want to get to know the glorious countryside around the Chiemsee's quieter northern coastline, hire a bicycle at Prien Bahnhof and visit places like **STEIN**, with its legendary cave hideout and castle brewery, or **Kloster Seeon**, set on an island in the tiny Klostersee. To the south of the lake rises the **Kampenwand** (1669m), one of the most popular hiking areas in the Alps; the lazy way up is the cable car, costing DM11.50 single, DM18 return, from the inland village of ASCHAU.

The **Simssee**, a little to the west of the Chiemsee, is less touristy, though by no means quiet, because it's so close to the industrial town of ROSENHEIM, where the railway lines from Munich to Innsbruck and Salzburg split. There's an adequate beer garden by the water's edge in PIETZING, where there's also a public beach; alternatively KROTTENMÜHL on the other side of the lake is a good place for swimming.

Bad Reichenhall

East of the Chiemsee, there are no more dramatic peaks until you come to the most spectacular part of the entire Bavarian section of the Alps, in the extreme southeast corner of Germany, hard by the Austrian border. The gateway to this is **BAD REICHENHALL**, an old salt-producing town on the River Saalach just 19km from Salzburg. Its saline springs are the most concentrated in Europe, with a salt content of 24 percent; the curative properties of this led to its nineteenth-century development into one of the country's classiest spas, a status it still holds.

At the southern end of town is the **Alte Saline** (guided tours April–Oct daily 10–11.30am and 2–4pm; DM6), a saltworks established in the sixteenth century, but remodelled in the 1830s by King Ludwig I according to the mock-medieval tastes then in vogue. All the equipment is in good working order, but production has long since moved to larger and more practical premises a few blocks away. Just to the north begins the elegant Ludwigstrasse, the town's main street, at the far end of which is the **Kurpark**, complete with the inevitable Kurhaus, casino and carefully-tended gardens, complete with many exotic flowering plants. Still further north, beyond Karlspark, is the basilica of **St Zeno**, built in the early thirteenth century in the Lombard Romanesque style. Although remodelled down the centuries, it preserves some of its original features, including the peaceful cloisters and the magnificent, very Italianate coloured marble entrance portal complete with crouching lions and a tympanum showing the Madonna and Child adored by the church's patron and Saint Rupert, the first Bishop of Salzburg.

The **Hauptbahnhof** lies west of here on the main outer axis. Just to the south, at Wittelsbacherstr. 15 (☎08651/3003), is the **tourist office**. Ask here for an **accommodation** list: Bad Reichenall is one of the most expensive places in the Alps, with no hostel or campsite, though there are a fair number of rooms available from upwards of DM25 per person in private houses. A second station, **Bahnhof Kirchberg**, is at the extreme southern end of town, and is the more convenient for visiting the Alte Saline. Immediately across the river is the terminus of the cable car to the principal local vantage point, the **Predigtstuhl** (1613m); the trip costs DM14 single, DM21 return.

The Rupertiwinkel

The area to the north of Bad Reichenall is known by the rather comical name of the **Rupertiwinkel**, in honour of Saint Rupert. Here you'll find a couple more lakes – the **Abtsdorfer See** and the **Waginger See**; although both can be reached by train, they're still out of the way and off the main tourist trail. These are shallow moor lakes favoured by campers, who use them as a cheap base for day trips to Salzburg. Other places worth visiting in the region are TEISENDORF, which has excellent beer at the *Weininger* brewery in the Poststrasse and the monastery brewery in HÖGLWÖRTH, a few kilometres south, which has a charming lakeside setting – actually it's more of a fishpond than a lake, but it's very picturesque.

The Berchtesgadener Land

Almost entirely surrounded by mountains, the area south of Bad Reichenhall, the **Berchtesgadener Land**, gives the impression of being a separate little country. In fact this is exactly what it used to be: for centuries it was one of the smallest constituent states of the Holy Roman Empire, ruled by an Augustinian prior. There's a magical atmosphere here, especially in the mornings, when mists rise from the lakes and swirl around lush valleys and rocky mountainsides. Not surprisingly the area is steeped in legends, often featuring the spiky peaks of the **Watzmann** (2713m), Germany's second highest mountain. A popular one has it that they're really the family of a tyrant king who ruled the area so mercilessly that God punished its members by turning them to stone.

Berchtesgaden

The town of **BERCHTESGADEN** itself is 18km from Bad Reichenhall via a magnificent scenic road. Its heart is an attractive triangular square dominated by the **Schloss** (May–Sept Sun–Fri 10am–1pm and 2–5pm; Oct–April Mon–Fri 10am–1pm and 2–5pm; DM4.50), the seat of the priors, who latterly tended to be members of the Wittelsbach dynasty. Following the Napoleonic secularisation, when Berchtesgaden was at last incorporated into Bavaria, the Schloss was transformed into a sumptuous royal residence. After World War II, the deposed King Ludwig III fled there, and it remains the private property of the family. Inside you can see the art treasures collected by his son, Crown Prince Ruprecht – medieval religious wood carvings, sixteenth- and seventeenth-century Italian furniture, and a fearsome collection of weaponry. Some parts of the medieval architecture still survive as well, notably the Romanesque cloister with its beautiful columns, and the graceful Gothic dormitory. Alongside the Schloss is the **Stiftskirche**, another Romanesque and Gothic mix, which contains the tombs of the priors plus an elaborate set of choir stalls.

Apart from these sights, the main pleasure in Berchtesgaden is to wander the winding streets and enjoy the lovely views of the valley and mountains. However, despite the long queues and the hefty entrance fee, an experience you certainly shouldn't miss is going down the salt mine or **Salzbergwerk** (May 1–Oct 15 daily 8.30am–5pm; Oct 16–April 30 Mon–Fri 12.30–3.30pm; DM12.50), which has been the region's source of wealth since 1515. Donning the traditional protective clothing (don't wear a skirt), you're taken deep into the mountain astride a wooden train, rather like those that kids ride on, only bigger. Once underground the one-hour tour passes all the machinery and processes of salt-mining in disused shafts connected by wooden shoots, which everyone descends in groups of three, rather like at the fairground. It's great fun, so don't let the commercial trappings of the tour spoil it for you.

The Königssee

Star attraction of the town's surroundings is the **Königssee**, Germany's highest lake, which lies 5km south and can be reached by bus. This bends around the foot of the Watzmann, rather like a Norwegian fjord, but it's anything but a lonely place, and the stunning beauty can be hard to appreciate underneath the hordes of tourists: it really is worth getting up early to catch the atmosphere of the place before everyone else arrives. From the village of KÖNIGSSEE at the northern tip, you can get a great view of the lake and the surrounding peaks by taking the cable car up the **Jenner** (1874m); this costs DM18 single, DM23 return. **Ferries**, run by *Motorschiffahrt Königssee*, Seestr. 55 (☎08652/4026), make round trips to the far end of the lake and back. Although likewise rather expensive at DM15 return, it's money well spent; the boats have been electric-powered since 1909, so the deep green waters are refreshingly clean and healthy.

There are some great mountain trails to follow from **ST BARTHOLOMÄ**, a hamlet at the foot of the Watzmann on the western shore, whose Baroque chapel, with its three projecting apses, features in all the tourist brochures. Another good starting point is SALET at the far end of the Königssee, just a few minutes' walk from another lake, the **Obersee**.

Obersalzberg

High above Berchtesgaden to the east is the village of **OBERSALZBERG**, which can be reached from the town by cable car (DM7 single, DM10 return), or by a steep winding road. Hitler rented a home here which was later enlarged into the **Berghof**, a stately retreat where he could meet foreign dignitaries. With a final dramatic sweep of steps, its setting was expressly designed to awe visitors. Here, in 1938, British Prime Minister Neville Chamberlain journeyed to dissuade Hitler from attacking Czechoslovakia, the first in a series of meetings that ended with Chamberlain returning from Munich clutching the infamous piece of paper that would ensure "peace in our time" at the expense of Czechoslovakia. "He seemed a nice old man," smirked Hitler of the agreement, "so I thought I would give him my autograph". Today the remains of the Berghof are almost entirely overgrown; what was left after wartime bombing was blown up by US troops in 1952 to avoid it becoming an object of pilgrimage for future Nazi generations.

THE TREACHERY OF MUNICH

The actions of the British and French governments in failing to support the Czechs against the forces of the Reich remains one of the most infamous sell-outs in history; it has destroyed the reputation of Neville Chamberlain, and given the policy of appeasement – seen at the time by many as the only pragmatic response possible to Hitler's territorial demands – a bad name.

The crisis arose over the **Sudetenland**, part of Czechoslovakia that had a sizeable German-speaking minority, and which had always resented having been included in the new Czechoslovak republic of 1918. Encouraged by the rise of Nazism, and aided by rocketing Sudeten German unemployment, the Sudetenlanders were increasingly attracted to Hitler's Germany. With the Nazi annexation of Austria (the Anschluss) on March 11, 1938, Hitler was free to focus his attention on the Sudetenland, calling for outright autonomy for the region. By August he had massed his troops on the border, with the intention of invading Czechoslovakia.

On September 15, Chamberlain flew to Berchtesgaden on his own ill-conceived initiative, to "appease" the Führer. A week later, Chamberlain flew again to Germany, this time to Bad Godesberg, vowing to the British public that the country would not go to war (in his famous words) "because of a quarrel in a far-away country between people of whom we know nothing". Nevertheless, the French issued draft papers, the Royal Navy was mobilised, and the whole of Europe fully expected war. Then in the early hours of September 30, in one of the most treacherous and self-interested acts of modern European diplomacy, prime ministers Chamberlain and Daladier (for France) signed the **Munich Diktat** with Mussolini and Hitler – without consulting the Czechoslovak government – agreeing to all of Hitler's demands. The British and French public were genuinely relieved, and Chamberlain flew back to cheering crowds, waving his piece of paper and guaranteeing "peace in our time".

Betrayed by his only Western allies and fearing bloodshed, Czech leader Beneš capitulated, against the wishes of most Czechs. Had Beneš not given in, however, it's doubtful anything would have come of Czech armed resistance, surrounded as they were by vastly superior hostile powers. On October 15, German troops occupied the Sudetenland, and in March 1939 marched into the rest of the Czech lands without opposition.

One of the very few legacies of the Third Reich still looked upon with a large amount of pride is the 6.5km-long **Kehlsteinstrasse**, which rises from Obersalzberg in a series of curves before making a bold ascent up the northwest side of the **Kehlstein** (1834m). The road – generally considered the most spectacular in the country – is impassable because of snow for most of the year and permanently closed to normal traffic, but regular local buses make the ascent from early May until mid-October. From the bus terminus, there's a long tunnel through the mountain to a lift, which covers the final 124m to the summit. Here is a restaurant, originally intended as Hitler's tea house, which became known as the "Eagle's Nest". The views across the Alps – as far as Salzburg on a clear day – are stunning.

Another magnificent road from Obersalzberg, this time one on which you can take your own transport, is the 21km-long **Rossfeld-Höhen-Ringstrasse**. This circular route passes through glacier country, then for a time hugs the Austrian frontier, allowing for an easy ascent to the top of the Hennenkopf (1551m), before making a return loop to Obersalzberg through the wooded Oberau valley.

Ramsau

Just off the main road from Bad Reichenall, about 9km from Berchtesgaden, is the small resort of **RAMSAU**, which makes an excellent jump-off point for some of the finest walks in the area. The main **trail up the Watzmann**, for example, begins at the Wimbachbrücke just east of the village; at 1930m, after 3–4 hours of walking, there's the *Watzmannhaus* refuge (☎08652/1310), where you can break the journey for the night. To the west of Ramsau is another beautiful lake, the **Hintersee**, framed by the enchanted forest of the Zauberwald, the rugged precipices of the Reiteralpe and the icy blue Hochkalter (2608m), the most northerly glacier in the Alps.

Practicalities

The regional **tourist office** is at the extreme southern end of Berchtesgaden, just opposite the Bahnhof at Königsseer Str. 2 (Mon–Fri 8.30am–5.30pm; ☎08652/5011). There are also many smaller branches, including in Königssee (☎08652/61161) and Ramsau (☎ 08657/1213). The only official **youth hostel** is in the village of STRUB, 2.5km west of Berchtesgaden on the road to Ramsau, at Gebirgsjägerstr. 52 (☎08652/2190); a privately-run hostel can be found in Königssee at Seestr. 29 (☎08652/5046). In addition to the aforementioned *Watzmannhaus*, there are nearly a score of **mountain refuges**, which are ideal for serious walkers; most of the accommodation space is on mattresses for which you'll need your own sleeping bag, but a limited number of beds are always available. Nearest **campsite** to Berchtesgaden is *Allweglehen* (☎08652/2396) in UNTERSALZBERG; there are also two by the Königssee – *Grafenlehen* (☎08652/4140) and *Mühlleiten* (☎08652/4584) – and one by the lily-strewn Taubensee just north of Ramsau (☎08657/284). There's the usual range of accommodation in private homes; apart from those, the cheapest **guest houses** in Berchtesgaden itself, charging DM25–DM30 per person, are *Hansererhäusl*, Hansererweg 8 (☎08652/2523); *Haus Bergwald*, Duftbachweg 3–5 (☎08652/2586); and *Berlerlehen*, Rennweg 19 (☎08652/1590).

The Inn-Salzachgau

The **Inn-Salzachgau** is the name given to the triangular area north of the Alps whose western and eastern boundaries are defined respectively by the mighty River Inn and its tributary, the Salzach. Inevitably, the landscapes of this rich farming country can't compete with those further south, but it's an unspoiled area preserving several fine old towns which well merit a detour from the established tourist circuits.

Wasserburg

The region's gateway is **WASSERBURG**, superbly set on a promontory on a loop of the River Inn, 55km east of Munich and 30km north of the Alpine railway junction of ROSENHEIM. In the fifteenth and sixteenth centuries, the town became prosperous through shipping and its position on key salt trade routes, but it fell into decay, never to recover. Today, it's a sleepy little place of narrow streets and crooked medieval houses whose vaguely Italianate appearance is a direct consequence of the old trading links. The best **views**, showing the buildings rising abruptly from the Inn, are obtained by crossing over the river and turning left.

Heart of the town is Marienplatz, dominated by the tall step gables of the **Rathaus**, whose first-floor *Ratssaal* (guided tours Tues–Fri 10am, 11am, 2pm, 3pm and 4pm, Sat and Sun 10am and 11am; DM1) is decorated with richly carved woodwork and painted panels. The disparate assortment of houses which complete the square make a picturesque group, with arcades and oriels prominent; they range from the old toll-house, the **Altes Mauthaus**, which is Gothic with a Renaissance facade, to the fripperies of the **Kernhaus**, a Rococo patrician mansion designed by Johann Baptist Zimmermann. On the nearby Kirchplatz rises the parish church of **St Jakob**, whose nave is a masterpiece by Hans von Burghausen, an inspired Gothic architect who left a profound mark on the eastern regions of Bavaria; the chancel and tower were added later in the fifteenth century and show a somewhat abrupt change in building materials from brick to stone. Inside, the highlight of the furnishings is the elaborate late Renaissance pulpit.

Altötting

From Wasserburg, the railway closely follows the course of the Inn as far as the junction of MÜLDORF, where it splits, with one branch line continuing eastwards to **ALTÖTTING**. This little town of spires and domes is one of the most venerable in Germany, having been a favourite residence of both the Carolingian emperors and the early Bavarian dukes, but for the past five hundred years it has chiefly been famous as a **place of pilgrimage**, being one of the claimants to the title of the most visited shrine in the country.

The centre

An immaculately tended square lined by dignified buildings, **Kapellplatz** forms the centre of the town. Its outsized dimensions really come into play at the time of the big pilgrimages: the most important is to celebrate the Feast of the Assumption (15 Aug); Corpus Christi (variable date in May/June) is next in order of rank, but there are many others throughout the year. The goal of the believers is the **Gnadenkapelle** (or **Heilige-Kapelle**) in the centre of the square, a tiny octagonal chapel which offers a tantalising reminder of Altötting's distinguished early history as it dates back to Carolingian times and may once have served as the baptistery of the imperial palace. In 1489, a three-year-old local child who had drowned in the Inn was cured when her grief-stricken mother placed her in front of the **wooden statue** of the *Black Madonna* at the high altar. News of the miracle quickly spread, and the chapel was immediately extended by the erection of a chancel and covered walkway. The sculpture seems to have been working cures relentlessly ever since, to judge from the thousands of **ex-votos** – many of them outstanding examples of folk art – which now completely cover the walls. Since the seventeenth century, it has been housed in an elaborate silver shrine and is now generally to be seen draped in gorgeous robes which stand in stark contrast to the simplicity of the original carving. Opposite the altar are appropriately-shaped **urns** containing the hearts of many of the Bavarian dukes, who thereby commended the most precious part of themselves to the special care of the Virgin.

Across from the Gnadenkapelle is the twin-towered **Stiftskirche**, a fine late Gothic church erected in the early years of the sixteenth century in order to cater for the ever-growing influx of pilgrims. Its **Schatzkammer** (Easter–Nov Mon–Sat 10am–noon and 2–4pm, Sun 10am–noon and 1–4pm; DM1) contains an excellent collection of treasury items. Particularly outstanding is the *Goldene Rössl*, a masterpiece by a French gold-smith of the turn of the fifteenth century From the church's cloisters you can descend to the **Tilly-Gruft** where you can peer into the coffin containing the gruesome skeleton of Field Marshal Johann Tilly, the chief Catholic hero of the Thirty Years' War.

On the opposite side of Kapellplatz is the **Wallfahrt- und Heimatmuseum** (April–Oct Tues–Fri 2–4pm, Sat 10am–noon & 2–4pm, Sun 10am–noon & 1–3pm; DM1), which documents the history of the pilgrimage. As the Stiftskirche eventually proved insufficiently large for the number of people who flocked here, a monstrous neo-Baroque **Basilika**, capable of accommodating 6000 worshippers at a time, was erected just off the square at the beginning of the present century.

Practicalities

Altötting's **tourist office** (Mon–Sat 8am–noon and 2–5pm; ☎08671/8068) is in the Rathaus, Kapellplatz 2a. Here you can book to stay in one of the many **private houses** with rooms to let: rates are DM18–28 per person, making the town the most obvious base for exploring the whole region, unless you insist on staying in a hostel or camp-site, both of which it lacks. There are also plenty of **hotels**; the cheapest, charging from DM26 per person, is *Bahnhofsgaststätte*, Bahnhofplatz 6 (☎08671/6137) right beside the Bahnhof and just a few minutes' walk south of Kapellplatz. It's also possible to pay DM40 or less in the classy hotels in and around the main square: all have excellent **restaurants**, with prices lower than you might expect. For **drinking**, however, the top choice is *Hell-Bräu*, the *Gasthaus* – complete with beer garden – of the local brewery, situated just to the north at Herrenmühlstr. 15.

Burghausen

At the terminus of the branch railway 15km southeast of Altötting lies **BURGHAUSEN**, which for centuries ranked alongside Munich, Landshut and Ingolstadt as one of the four residential cities of the Bavarian dukes. Nowadays, it's a modest-sized border town – the Salzach forms a natural frontier between Germany and Austria before this function is usurped by the Inn at the confluence of the two rivers – and a centre for computer-based industries, which account for its affluent feel.

A tightly-packed Altstadt nestles along the bank of the river. Most of the buildings of note are found on the elongated **Stadtplatz**: on the eastern side are the colourful former ducal administrative buildings and the Rathaus; the south side is closed by the Gothic parish church of St Jakob, while at the opposite end stands the Gymnasium established by the Jesuits, now serving once more as a school. An alley leads from the middle of the east side of the square to the finest local vantage point, the bridge over the Salzach to Austria.

From here, you get a great view of the **Burg**, which stands on a ridge high above the old town and between two stretches of water, the Salzach and the Wohrsee. Measuring 1030m from end to end, it ranks as the longest castle in Europe; having no fewer than six courtyards, it has the appearance of a complete upper town, rather than simply a fortress. The oldest surviving section of the fortifications dates back to the mid-thirteenth century, but much of what can be seen today is due to the expansion carried out at the end of the fifteenth century when there was fear of a Turkish invasion. Steps lead up from Stadtplatz to the main residential part of the palace, set in the last of the courtyards, but it's more fun to circle round and go up from the Wohrsee side, entering via the massive double gateway known as the **Georgstor**. Alternatively, you can walk through the whole complex by approaching it from its vulnerable northern side: that way, you can readily appreciate the successive obstacles facing would-be attackers.

The former ducal apartments now house the **Staatliche Sammlungen** (April–Sept daily 9am–5pm; Oct–March Tues–Sun 9am–4pm; DM1.50), a collection of German paintings and furniture contemporary with the Burg itself. In addition, the inner of the castle's two chapels, notable for its elegant vaulting, can be seen. The *Kemenate*, the chambers of the duchess, now house the **Historisches Stadtmuseum** (daily March, April, Sept and Oct 8am–4.30pm; May–Sept 9.30am–6pm; DM1.50), featuring the usual local history displays, but well worth visiting for the sake of the late Gothic interiors, the finest part of the entire Burg.

Practicalities

Burghausen's **Bahnhof** is situated just over 1km north of the town centre, which is reached by following Marktler Strasse straight ahead. The **tourist office** (Mon–Fri 9am–noon and 2–5pm; ☎08677/2435) is at Stadtplatz 112. **Hotels** are generally much pricier than you'd expect, with rates of over DM60 the norm, though *Hofbauer*, with a very central location at In den Grüben 119 (☎08677/2517), is an exception, charging from DM35 per person. There's also a **youth hostel**, enticingly set in the third court-yard of the Burg (☎08677/4187). The town centre has plenty of traditional **wine bars** and **restaurants**; those attached to hotels all have beer gardens. Hottest nightspot is the *Jazzkeller* in the Mautnerschloss on Mautnerstrasse at the southern edge of the old town, which attracts the big names for periodic **jazz festivals**.

EASTERN BAVARIA

Eastern Bavaria (*Ostbayern*), which incorporates **Lower Bavaria** and the **Upper Palatinate** (two of the three provinces into which the medieval duchy was divided), is the least well-known region of the whole state, among Germans as well as visitors. Part of the reason for this is that its eastern boundary is the Czechoslovakian border, which was effectively a dead-end until a few years ago. Misconceptions about remote forests populated by bumpkin inhabitants have kept almost everyone except hiking enthu-siasts away, so while tourists crowd each other out in the south and Alpine regions, the east remains an insider's tip even during the busy months of July and August.

Curiously enough, the region includes both of the cities that preceded Munich as capital of Bavaria. **Regensburg**, the main seat of power in the tribal days of the Dark Ages and nowadays capital of the Upper Palatinate, managed to escape almost unscathed in the last war, and stands today as the most complete and one of the most beautiful medieval cities in Germany. In the region's southwestern corner is the wonderfully preserved city of **Landshut**, capital of Lower Bavaria and, during the fifteenth and sixteenth centuries, rival to Munich in terms of wealth and status. Heading downstream along the Danube are ancient towns like **Straubing**, **Deggendorf** and **Passau**, the last being a particularly enticing destination. The stretch south of the river tends to be flat and uninspiring agricultural land, but on the northern side, hills, castle ruins and forests liven up the landscape.

Most of the southeastern part of the region is taken up by the **Bavarian Forest**, the largest forested area in Central Europe and one that still retains much of its primeval character, especially in the **National Park** between Frauenau and Mauth. Traditionally a poor and remote region, a couple of train routes make it relatively accessible, and campsites, hostels and private rooms abound. It's more mountainous here than further north, though the highest peaks barely reach the 1500m mark. In addition to the obvi-ous hiking attractions, the Bavarian Forest has an unexpectedly vibrant cultural life, especially during summer, when **festivals** and rituals take place throughout the region. Further north lies the **Upper Palatinate Forest**, an agricultural backwater with a few surprises.

Landshut

Picturesquely set below wooded hills on the banks of the Isar 70km northeast of Munich lies **LANDSHUT**. The Wittelsbachs established it as their capital at the beginning of the thirteenth century, and the town consistently outshone Munich, even when the latter became capital of the separate duchy of Upper Bavaria. However, when the local dukes died out in 1503 and Bavaria became a united province again, it lost its status as a capital; following a brief flowering as the second residence, it went into decline, never to recover. As a result, its showpiece centre was subject to few later alterations and remains wonderfully evocative of its fifteenth- and early sixteenth-century heyday. Nowadays, it's put to good use as the perfect backdrop for Germany's largest costumed festival.

Altstadt

The magnificence of Landshut's main street is immediately suggested by its name: it's designated **Altstadt**, the term normally used for the entire central part of a German city. Starting from the banks of the Isar, it ascends towards the old feudal fortress dominating the town by means of a majestically sweeping curve. Of an unusual width and spaciousness, it's lined with a resplendent series of colourful high-gabled mansions of widely varying design.

Two very different hall churches stand at either end of the street; both were designed by **Hans von Burghausen**, one of the most brilliant late Gothic architects. Overlooking the river is the **Heiliggeistkirche** (or **Spitalkirche**), which uses the same architectural methods as its earlier counterpart at the opposite end, but with each detail cleverly modified: the tower, for example, stands over the transept and manages

---

THE LANDSHUT WEDDING

The original **Landshut Wedding** (*Landshuter Hochzeit*) was a spectacular society affair: the Archbishop of Salzburg conducted the ceremony, while all the leading nobles of Germany and Poland were present, including the Holy Roman Emperor Friedrich III and his son, the future Maximilian I. Afterwards, the people of Landshut celebrated for a week at the expense of the bridegroom's father, Duke Ludwig the Rich, and it is recorded that 40,000 chickens, 11,500 geese, 2700 lambs and sheep, nearly 700 pigs, 400 calves and over 300 oxen were consumed.

Needless to say, there is no such munificence in the modern recreations of the event, which, with eyes firmly on the tourist market, have been moved from the original November date to high summer and go on for four weeks. **Weekends** are the best times to come: each Saturday at 9pm, the gathering of the guests is re-enacted, while at 2.30pm on Sundays, the **wedding procession** makes its way through the streets of the town, with a medieval-style **tournament** following at 4.30pm. Some 2000 participants are involved, each decked out in authentic reproductions of the costumes of the period. In addition to various impromptu events, there are also concerts of fifteenth-century music in the Stadtresidenz and Burg Trausnitz, while entertainments are held in the Rathaus; the latter are repeated on the evenings of Wednesay, Thursday and Friday.

The next **performances** will occur in June and July 1993. **Tickets** for the tournament and indoor events, and grandstand seats for the procession are available in advance from Landshut's tourist office

a highly idiosyncratic effect in spite of its stumpiness. The hospital buildings it served are across the road, but these were rebuilt in the Baroque period. About halfway down Altstadt is the **Rathaus**, an assemblage of several burghers' mansions. Under the patronage of King Ludwig II, this was given a neo-Gothic facelift last century, starting with a new facade. A team of Romantic artists was then asked to decorate the main reception hall, the **Prunksaal** (Mon–Fri 2–3pm; free). They painted it with colourful scenes showing the 1475 wedding between the last Duke of Lower Bavaria and Princess Jadwiga of Poland. Such a stir was caused by this work that the people of Landshut decided they would re-enact the event – and have done so every four years throughout this century (see box opposite). Whether consciously or not, this seems to signify the locals' satisfaction with their present provincial lot: it was the couple's fail-ure to produce a male heir which led to the end of the Lower Bavarian duchy and Landshut's present status as a modest-sized market town, rather than the huge metrop-olis it might otherwise have become.

Across from the Rathaus is the **Stadtresidenz** (April–Sept daily 9am–noon and 1–5pm; Oct–March Tues–Sun 9am–noon and 1–4pm; DM2). Modelled on the *Palazzo Tè* in Mantua, this was begun in 1537 as the first palace in the Italian Renaissance style to be built north of the Alps. Though the wing facing the street was later given a somewhat Germanic Neoclassical facade, the rest of the building – and in particular the magnificent courtyard – immediately evokes a sunny Mediterranean atmosphere. The local museum is housed inside, but it's completely eclipsed by the apartments themselves. Most notable is the *Italienischer Saal*, with its carved medallions of the Labours of Hercules and ceiling frescos which juxtapose biblical and mythological scenes.

Dominating Altstadt from the far end is Landshut's proudest adornment, the tower of **St Martin**. In design alone, it's extraordinarily ingenious, beginning as a square shape, then narrowing and changing into an octagon. With a height of 133 metres, it's also the tallest brick structure in the world. The walls of the main body of the church are pierced by five portals bearing rich terracotta sculptures. The interior, with slender pillars sweeping up to the lofty network vault, is hardly less impressive than the tower, the spareness of effect enhanced by the relative lack of furnishings. Nonetheless there are some fine works, such as Michel Erhart's impassioned *Triumphal Cross*, the elaborate choir stalls and the high altar. Best of all is the larger-than-life polychrome wood *Madonna and Child* in the south aisle, carved around 1520 by the local sculptor Hans Leinberger. Deliberately made to be admired from different angles (and thus not seen to effect in photographs), it's a work which attracts golden reviews from artistic cognoscenti.

The rest of the town

From St Martin, you can climb up to the romantically dilapidated **Burg Trausnitz** (same times as the Stadtresidenz; DM2); the long haul up hundreds of steep steps is worth the effort for the view alone, stretching over Landshut's red-tiled roofs and church steeples and along the Isar valley. Parts of the old fortress (which predated the town) remain, including a double Romanesque chapel and a Gothic hall, but the bulk of the surviving complex results from the Renaissance rebuilding, which is a generation later than the Stadtresidenz. A highlight is the *Narrentreppe* ("Buffoons' Staircase"), deco-rated with vivacious portrayals of characters from the *commedia dell'arte*. To the east lies the expansive **Hofgarten**,which offers more belvederes with fine panoramic views.

Practicalities

Landshut's **Hauptbahnhof** is well to the northwest of the centre beyond the Abtei Seligenthal; it's a junction on the main Munich–Regensburg line, with services east to the Bavarian Forest and south to the Inn valley. The **tourist ofice** at Altstadt 315

(☎0871/23031) has a private room booking service and is the best contact concerning the *Landshuter Hochzeit*. Cheapest **hotel** is *Gasthof Bayerwald*, Bayerwaldstr. 43 (☎0871/71423) with singles from DM25 and doubles from DM48; a more central possibility is *Pension Sandner*, Freyung 627 (☎0871/22379), charging DM35 per person. The **youth hostel** is just south of Burg Trausnitz at Richard-Schirmann-Weg 6 (☎0871/23449), while the **campsite** (☎0871/53366) is on the banks of the Isar in the northeastern district of Mitterwöhr. For cheapish **eats** try the *Bernlocher Pizzeria*, Ländtorplatz 2-5, while the *Hoferbräu*, Neustadt 444 offers more Germanic fare in traditional *Gaststätte* surroundings. A good local beer garden is the *Hofreiter*, Neustadt 505.

Regensburg (Ratisbon)

"Regensburg surpasses every German city with its outstanding and vast buildings," drooled Emperor Maximilian I in 1517. The centre of **REGENSBURG** has changed remarkably little since then; its undisturbed medieval panorama still beats all other cities in the country hands down, while its *Gaststätten* and beer gardens – the favoured haunts of the large student population – along with its stunning location on the banks of the Danube make it a great place to spend a couple of days.

Founded as the military camp *Castra Regina* by the Romans, the city remained of importance during the subsequent Frankish period and was capital of the earliest Bavarian duchy. Most of the surviving architecture originates from the glory days between the thirteenth and sixteenth centuries. Regensburg was then a Free Imperial City (the only place in what was then Bavaria to be independent of the Wittelsbachs) and rich from trade with Europe, the Balkan states and the Orient. Goods sailed into town on the Danube and ships still ply the route to the Black Sea today. Although other cities may have a more spectacular cathedral or town hall as a focal point, none can match the satisfyingly integrated nature of the Regensburg townscape, which gives a unique insight into the size, shape and feel of a prosperous community of the Middle Ages.

A city whose penchant for jokiness has been given many visible expressions, Regensburg is nowadays a prosperous centre for hi-tech industries. It's also an excellent base from which to discover the idyllic countryside along the northern reaches of the Danube and the valleys of the two tributaries which join it at this point, the Naab and the Regen. Train connections into the Bavarian Forest and south to Passau are fast and efficient from here.

> The telephone code for Regensburg is ☎0941

Getting around and finding somewhere to stay

The **Bahnhof** is at the southern end of the city. From there, follow Maximilianstrasse straight ahead to reach the centre. The **tourist office** is in the Altes Rathaus (Mon–Fri 8.30am–6pm, Sat 9am–4pm, Sun 9am–noon; ☎507 2141). Everything of interest is within easy walking distance around the centre of town, and the **youth hostel**, Wöhrdstr. 60 (☎26839) is about five minutes' walk from the heart of things, on an island in the Danube. Cheapest **hotel** in the town centre is the *Weisse Lilie*, Fröhliche-Türkenstr. 4 (☎57515), which charges from DM32 for singles and DM55 for doubles. Other reasonably priced options include *Weidenhof*, Maximilianstr. 23 (☎53031), with singles from DM33, doubles from DM58; *Peterhof*, Fröhliche-Türkenstr. 12 (☎57514 or 58874), with singles from DM35, doubles from DM60; and *Roter Hahn*, Rote-Hahnen-Gasse 10 (☎560907 or 52599), with singles from DM38, doubles from DM68. Two cheaper places, both on an

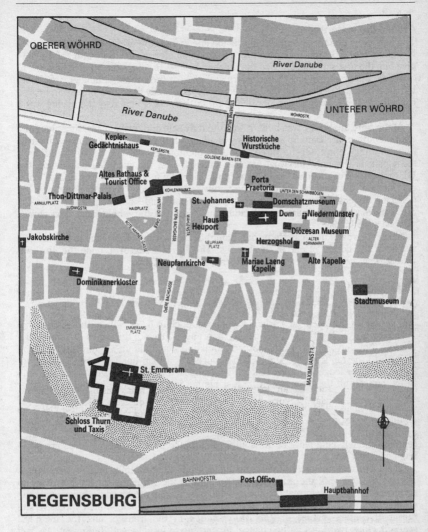

REGENSBURG

island in the Danube, are *Stadlerbräu*, Stadtamhof 15 (☎85682), at DM27 per person, and *Spitalgarten*, St-Katharinen-Platz 1 (☎84774) at DM30 per person. The **campsite** (March–mid-Nov only) is about twenty minutes' walk from the centre of town, pleasantly situated next to the Danube by Weinweg 40 (☎26839).

The city

Most of what you're likely to want to see in Regensburg is crowded within a relatively small area; the medieval centre is only about twice the size of the original Roman fort, so exploration on foot is an easy business. However, it's a place which rewards serendipity – there are no fewer than 1300 buildings listed as being of historical interest.

Around the waterfront

The best view of Regensburg's medieval skyline is from the twelfth-century **Steinerne Brücke** ("Stone Bridge"). Legend has it that the builder made a pact with the Devil to give him the first soul that crossed the finished bridge. In return the builder was able to complete his project in just eleven years and so beat the cathedral builder, who'd bet him he'd be finished first. But the bridge builder didn't only trick his competitor, he also tricked the Devil, because the first living thing that was sent across the bridge was a donkey.

At the time the bridge was built, it was the only safe and fortified crossing along the entire length of the Danube and had tremendous value for the city as a major international trading centre. Of the three original watchtowers, the one above the bridge's town gate is the only survivor. On the left, just past the medieval salt depot, the **Historische Wurstküche** (daily 8am–7pm) originally functioned as the bridge workers' kitchen. It's been run by the same family for generations and serves nothing but delicious Regensburger sausages with sweet mustard and sauerkraut. Have a look at the watermark on the outside wall and you'll see that the whole place was almost washed away in 1988.

Along the road known as Unter den Schibbögen, remains of the Roman fort are still visible at the corner of one of the houses. The **Porta Praetoria**, once the northern watchtower, was discovered during restoration work in 1887.

The Domstadt

Immediately to the south lies a dense complex of ecclesiastical buildings, known as the **Domstadt**. The **Dom** itself is Bavaria's most magnificent example of the Gothic building period. It replaced an earlier Romanesque church, of which the **Eselsturm** ("Donkey Tower") is the only remaining part above ground; this takes its name from the fact that donkeys were used to carry building materials up a ramp inside. If you look up to the top from the Dom's back courtyard, a man holding a jug sticking out from the upper ledge becomes visible: he's supposed to be the original architect who threw himself off the tower when he lost his bet with the bridge builder. Two other examples of humour on the exterior relate to the medieval Jewish community. A relief on the left main pillar of the facade shows small figures dancing around a calf – an architectural expression of an old prejudice that Jews are only interested in money, symbolised by the golden calf. Pure malice, on the other hand, prompted the little relief on the left-hand pillar of the southern entrance, where Jewish figures are suckling on a great sow.

The Dom took almost 300 years to build, from 1250 to 1525, and the two spires weren't erected until the mid-nineteenth century; the main reason for the delay in completion was the Reformation, during which the bishop remained Catholic, while the secular leadership went Lutheran. Highlights of the interior include the expressive late thirteenth-century statues of *The Annunciation* in the transept and the medieval **stained glass windows** in the chancel. According to local legend, Judgment Day will be heralded when the real human hair on the late sixteenth-century wooden *Crucifix* on south transept wall grows to knee-length! Another quirky feature is the pair of fourteenth-century figures in the niches either side of the western nave entrance: on the left is the **Devil's grandmother** and on the right the **Devil** himself who were to remind the congregation that as soon as they left the safety of the church evil and temptation awaited.

The **cloisters**, which are only accessible during **guided tours** (May–Oct Mon–Sat 10am, 11am and 2pm, Sun noon and 2pm; Nov–April Mon–Sat at 11am, Sun at noon; DM2.50), have two interesting chapels, of which the **Allerheiligenkapelle** is a Romanesque gem, with many of the original twelfth-century frescos surviving. Nearby, the eleventh-century **Stephanskapelle** was the bishop's private chapel, and though the frescos have been lost, the altar is from the original building period. The hollowed-out section of the altar indicates that it used to contain the relics of a martyr, generally believed to have been Saint Florian, and the openings at the base were for the faithful to insert intercessory notes to him.

Housed in the former bishop's palace on the north side of the Dom is the **Domschatzmuseum** (April–Oct Tues–Sat 10am–5pm, Sun 11.45am–5pm; Dec–March Fri and Sat 10am–4pm, Sun 11.45am–4pm; DM2), a collection of ecclesiastical vestments and gold and silver ceremonial ware ranging from the eleventh century to the present day. Further treasures, including paintings and sculptures, are contained in the **Diözesanmuseum** (April–Oct Tues–Sun 10am–5pm; DM2, DM3 for joint ticket) occupying the church of **St Ulrich** at the rear of the Dom. Constructed in the Transitional style between Romanesque and Gothic, the building itself is one of the most remarkable in the city, featuring an unusual vaulted gallery at the west end.

Previously, St Ulrich was the Dom's parish church, but this function has passed to the **Niedermünster** further east, a Romanesque collegiate foundation given a decorous Baroque interior. Underneath, important excavations have revealed remains of various previous churches on the site, plus Roman buildings; enquire at the tourist office for details of the guided tours which periodically go round them. The church itself is the place where you can normally hear the *Domspatzen* ("Cathedral Sparrows"), the most famous choir in western Germany. At the opposite end of the Domstadt, adjoining the northwestern end of the Dom, is the Gothic church of **St Johannes**, the former baptistery; it contains an altarpiece of *The Fair Virgin* by Altdorfer.

South of the Dom

On the corner of the Pfauengasse leading off the Domplatz, there's a very nondescript door just past the corner shop which leads to an interesting place of folkloric worship. Dedicated to the Virgin Mary, it's the town's smallest chapel, known as the **Mariae-Laeng-Kapelle** after the seventeenth-century belief that the best way to get one's prayers heard was to write out prayer notes the same length (*laeng*) as Mary herself. The Church never accepted this idea, but people have come here ever since to pray to Mary and leave notes and gifts. Occasions when help has appeared are recorded by the faithful in little framed cards or pictures, crowding the back of the chapel.

At the far end of the Domstadt lies the Alter Kornmarkt, whose northwestern corner is defined by the so-called **Römerturm**, though its earliest masonry is Carolingian rather than Roman. A covered passageway links it to the Romanesque ducal palace, the **Herzogshof**, now a cultural centre. On the south side of the square stands the **Alte Kapelle**, whose sober medieval exterior hardly prepares you for the riotous fricassee of Rococo decoration inside.

The **Stadtmuseum** (Tues–Sat 10am–4pm, Sun 10am–1pm; DM2.50) lies just to the southeast, on Dachauplatz. This encompasses over 100 rooms spread out on four floors of the former Minorite monastery, and charts the town's cultural and artistic history over the past 2000 years. Not surprisingly the wealth of exhibits and information is rather overwhelming, but the layout is clear, with each floor related to a different subject or era. Of particular interest is the section on **Albrecht Altdorfer**, who, apart from being one of Germany's greatest artists, was also a leading local politician, being involved in the decisions which saw the expulsion of the Jews and the introduction of the Reformation. Among his etchings shown here are two of the beautiful Romanesque–Gothic synagogue he helped destroy, which make a fascinating documentary record. The remains of the frescos he painted for the *Kaiserbad* are also here, along with a panel showing *The Two St. Johns*, which is set in a typically luxuriant Danube landscape.

A few minutes' walk to the east, the **Neupfarrkirche** stands rather forlorn in the middle of a car park, occupying the site of the old synagogue. Originally, it was intended to be a vast pilgrimage church dedicated to the Virgin as thanksgiving for deliverance from the Jewish "peril"; the model for this ambitious design can be seen in the Stadtmuseum. However, the city council's cynical attempts to foster the bogus cult met with such apathy from the faithful that it was hastily dropped. When the council decided to adopt the Reformation a few years later, the church was completed in a much reduced form to serve as the city's Protestant flagship. Notwithstanding its unfortunate history and situation, the interior is very dapper, with an unusual little hexagonal nave. In the entrance of Neupfarrplatz 7 you'll see a pilfered Jewish tombstone – the ultimate status symbol for medieval Christians – set into the wall.

The merchant quarter

The streets west of the Dom were where the merchants who made Regensburg so prosperous in the Middle Ages had their homes. Unique for a German medieval town are the many **towers** built in the style of Italian fortified palaces; about twenty of these survive. Unlike their southern counterparts, however, they had no real defensive function; instead they were a statement of the competitive ethos that ruled their owners' lives: the higher the tower, the richer and more prestigious the occupier.

Directly facing the Dom is the **Haus Heuport**, which boasts another of the city's jokey sculptures in the form of a stone relief at the left-hand corner of the courtyard staircase representing the seduction of a careless virgin. One of the most beautiful of the fortified towers with high balconies is the **Baumburgerturm** in Watmarkt, just west of here. The **Goldener Turm** in the Wahlenstrasse is the town's highest remaining tower, and on its top floor there's a very cosy wine bar.

Apart from the Dom, the town's most important Gothic structure is the **Altes Rathaus** on the Kohlenmarkt. From the outside it's difficult to get an idea of its grand scale. To appreciate this you need to take a guided tour of the **Reichstagsmuseum** within (Mon–Sat 9.30am, 10.30am, 11.30am, 2pm, 3pm and 4pm, Sun 10am, 11am and noon; May-Sept tours in English Mon–Sat 3.15pm; DM3), which is worth it to see, among other things, the beautiful Renaissance panelling and fittings in the *Kurfürstliches Nebenzimmer* (Electors' ante-chamber) and the *Blauer Saal* (Blue Hall) with its glittering star-studded ceiling. All the original furnishings remain, including the torture chamber in the basement with some pretty gruesome instruments. The largest and most significant room is the **Beratungszimmer der Reichsstände**, where the Perpetual Imperial Diet met from 1663 to 1806. A kind of parliamentary forum for the Empire, it was where representatives from the ruling orders came together to debate the country's imperial policies. The seating order was stricly defined by status, and the different colouring of the benches indicates individual groups – red for Electors, green for lesser princes.

Outside, on the right-hand side of the Rathaus entrance, a little alleyway twists around the back, known as **Zum Roten Herzfleck** ("Red Heart Patch"), a polite name that barely admits its origin, since for many years the house in the corner here was the town's brothel. Meanwhile, on the left-hand side of the Rathaus steps, the town's official measurements, cast in iron and mounted on the wall, were used in medieval times to sort out rows between merchants and customers if someone thought they'd been cheated. People would take their cloth or shoe, for example, and compare it to the fixed measures on the Rathaus. The public nature of these settlements functioned as a good deterrent to would-be crooks, since everyone could witness the proceedings.

To the west lies **Haidplatz**, a square which was built to be seen. Its largest building is the **Haus zum Goldenen Kreuz** which was the town's main hotel between the sixteenth and nineteenth centuries and the site of one of Regensburg's biggest scandals, when Emperor Charles V fell in love with a local girl called Barbara Blomberg. They used to meet in this house, and their son Juan de Austria was born here in 1547.

In the grand tradition of royal illegitimates, he became a great naval commander, winning the Battle of Lepanto against the Turks, and died Governor of the Netherlands in 1578. Less scandalous, but fun in passing, is the little stone mouse hidden in the right-hand corner outside the shop window on the ground floor. The locals say that if you rub it your purse will never be empty. Also on the square is the **Thon-Dittmer-Palais**, nowadays one of the main cultural venues; during the summer concerts and plays are held in its courtyard.

On Keplerstrasse to the north, the **Kepler-Gedächtnishaus** (guided tours Tues–Sat 10am, 11am, 2pm and 3pm, Sun 10am and 11am; DM2.50) is dedicated to the famous astronomer who lived and worked in Regensburg during the early seventeenth century – on the occasions when he was not wasting his talents dabbling in astrology in order to earn his keep from the superstitious monarchs of the day. Compiler of the *Rudolphine Tables* and author of *The Mystery of the Universe*, Kepler achieved major advances in the study of both astronomy (proving the elliptical path of planetary movements) and optics (being the first to understand how the eye works). His family actually lived in no. 2 Keplerstrasse, but he died at no. 5 while visiting a merchant friend, and it's this house that's been turned into a museum of his life and times.

The southwestern quarter

The southwestern part of Regensburg was formerly something of a monastic quarter, and although the monks have long gone, their buildings survive. Particularly intriguing is **St Jacob** just off Bismarckplatz. It was first settled by Irish Benedictines, but is still generally known as the *Schottenkirche* in honour of the Scottish community which lived there from the sixteenth century until its dissolution in 1878, when the monks returned to Fort Augustus on Loch Ness. Pollution from the busy road in front of the church has blackened the exterior, and the profusion of sandstone figures is badly eroded, but the main **portal** is still as eye-catching as ever, with its mixture of pagan and Christian images and delicate patterns carved on the pillars.

On Beraiterweg to the east stands the **Dominikanerkirche**, one of the first Gothic buildings in Germany; it likewise has a fine portal, adorned with a statue of its patron, Saint Blasius. One of the priors during the period the monastery was under construction in the thirteenth century was Saint Albertus Magnus, later the city's bishop. Among the most highly regarded scholars and philosophers of medieval Europe, he was a man of unusually broad sympathies, being steeped in the works of his Jewish and Arab contemporaries.

At the extreme southern end of the old city is the former Benedictine monastery of **St Emmeram,** another great centre of learning in days gone by. The Romanesque architecture of the church is smothered inside by the exuberant decorative sheme created by the Asam brothers, but the grandiose double portal with its eleventh-century figures of Christ between Saints Emmeram and Dionysius survives, while under the apse is a crypt dating back to the eighth century. More superb sculptures can be seen among the pantheon of monuments to leading figures in early Bavarian history: most notable are the grief-stricken Gothic tombstone to the executed Queen Hemma and its idealised counterpart to the legendary Blessed Aurelia.

Following the Napoleonic secularisation, the monastic buildings were acquired by the Thurn and Taxis family (see box overleaf) and converted into the most modern residence of the day, with hot and cold running water, flushing toilets, central heating, and most luxurious of all, electricity. The resultant **Schloss Thurn und Taxis** (guided tours Mon–Fri 2pm and 3.15pm, Sun 10am and 11.15am; DM2) isn't open to the public when the family is in residence, but at all other times a guide will show you the state rooms, still regularly in use, with some wonderful Brussels tapestries on the walls recording the family's illustrious history.

THE THURN AND TAXIS DYNASTY

The Thurn and Taxis family is generally accepted as being the richest in Germany, with a fortune estimated at five billion Deutschmarks. Originally known as Daxis and based in the Dolomite region between Austria and northern Italy, they came to prominence in the sixteenth century by developing a European-wide postal system, of which they held a monopoly within Germany itself for some 250 years. In the process, they were raised to the highest rank of the nobility with the title of Prince, moving their base to Regensburg in 1748 when they became the Holy Roman Emperor's personal representatives at the Perpetual Imperial Diet. When this ratified Napoleon's dissolution of the empire, including the secularisation of the monasteries and an end to the independence of nearly all the city states, the family seized the opportunity to acquire a new home for themselves and to build up control over the local economy. Currently they're reckoned to own nearly a fifth of Regensburg – a real irony, given the city's long independence from any kind of aristocratic control – as well as extensive tracts of land in the Bavarian Forest. The most visible sign of their varied business interests is the eponymous brewery, the largest one in Bavaria still in private hands, though locally its beer is known as *Tod und Teufel* ("Death and the Devil"). Much of the wealth is currently being held in trust for the heir to the title, who inherited his fortune at the age of seven.

In the former **cloisters** (same times; DM1) you get a fascinating visual record of the stylistic development of the Gothic style from the twelfth to the fourteenth century. It's easy to tell how far each abbot progressed with the building programme by the number of arches along the ceiling before his portrait is hewn into the stone at the crossover. Highlight of this section is the *Normannisches Portal*, its zigzag patterns around the arch indicating the Norman origins of the first monks to settle here. The **Marstallmuseum** (guided tours Mon–Fri 2.40pm and 3.15pm, Sun 10.40am and 11.15am; DM3) holds an enormous collection of Thurn and Taxis coaches down the ages, ranging from those used during the centuries when they held the imperial postal franchise to ceremonial carriages, travelling coaches and winter sleighs.

Eating and drinking

You're spoilt for places to eat and drink in Regensburg, with a bewildering variety of restaurants (including not a few of real curiosity value), bars, beer gardens and cafés, both traditional and modern.

Restaurants

Alte Münz, Fischmarkt 8. Top class traditional restaurant with a special line in small delicacies of the Upper Palatinate known as *Schmankerlküche*.

Antagon, Rote Hahnengasse 2. Best choice in town for vegetarian food.

Dampfnudel-Uli, Watmarkt 4. Eccentric little restaurant serving mainly dumplings, housed in the Bamburger Turm.

Fischerhaus, Untere Regenstr. 7 . Speciality fish restaurant.

Historische Wurstküche, An der Steinernen Brücke. The famous sausage restaurant which has become one of the essential sights of Regensburg.

Kneitinger, Arnulfsplatz 3. Excellent traditional *Gastätte* of one of the local breweries.

Prösslbrau, Adlersberg. Out in the suburbs and reached by bus #12, this is how a country *Gasthaus* should be, with a large shady beer garden serving the products of a small private brewery and good, sensibly priced food. You can also go for very peaceful walks around here.

Zur Goldenen Krone, Kepplerstr. 3. Offers a huge choice of reasonably-priced schnitzels with temptingly varied fillings; as an added attraction there's a beer garden in a quaint medieval courtyard, overgrown with vines.

Bars

Alt-Regensburger Weinkeller, Fischgässel 4. One of a group of wine bars clustered around Fischmarkt, which are particularly recommendable in summer when tables are set up outside.

Goldene Ente, Badstr. 32. One of the leading student hangouts.

Namenlos, Rote Löwengasse 10. Atmospheric bar with good music.

Schwedenkugel, Haaggasse 15. Another student favourite.

Türmchen, Wahlenstr. 14. The cosiest wine bar in town, at the top of the highest medieval tower.

Beer gardens

Bischofshof, Am Dom. Has the best location of all right in the shadow of the Dom; its restaurant in the adjacent episcopal palace has one of the most adventurous menus in the city, yet is surprisingly affordable.

Kneitinger Garten, Müllerstr. 1. Has a great location on the Danube island of Unterer Wöhrd.

Kneitinger Keller, Galgenbergstr. 18. With 1200 seats, this is Regensburg's largest beer garden; it's up by the University and is accordingly popular with students.

Spitalgarten, Stadtamhof, Katharinenplatz 1. On the island of Stadtamhof, right by the river at the far side of the Steinerne Brücke, this is a great local favourite.

Cafés and café-bars

Altstadt Café, Hinter der Grieb 8. Good unpretentious place in one of medieval Regensburg's most characteristic streets.

Ambrosius, Brückstr. 5. Best choice for breakfast; open till 1am.

Orphée, Untere Bachgasse 8. Self-consciously trendy; open evenings only.

Palletti, Pustet Passage, Gesandtenstr. 9. Currently the favourite haunt of the in-crowd.

Prinzess, Rathausplatz 2. The oldest coffee house in Germany, founded in 1686, and still the best choice for hand-made chocolate and cakes.

Nightlife and festivals

Regensburg's main **theatre**, featuring a varied programme of drama, opera and musicals, is the *Städtische Bühnen*, Bismarckplatz 7. Other venues include the open-air courtyard of the Thon–Dittmer-Palais; the *Turmtheater* in one of the medieval towers, the Goliathhaus at Watmarkt 5; and the marionette *Figurentheater* in the Stadtpark. For **discos**, the most enduringly popular place is the *Sudhaus*, Untere Bachgasse (9pm–2am). Try also *Scala*, Gesandtenstr. 6, Pustet Passage (9pm–3am) and *Why Not*, Obermünsterstr. 14 (8pm–4am), which are pretty provincial musically.

Two big beer **festivals**, each lasting two weeks, take place annually – the *Frühjahrsdult* at Whit, and the *Herbstdult* at the end of August and beginning of September. Held on alternate years are a couple more folk events – the *Altstadtfest* in June and the *Oberpfalzwoche* in September. There is also a contrasting pair of music festivals each summer: the *Bach-Woche* in June and the *Bayerisches Jazz-Weekend* in July.

Listings

Bike hire from the tourist office.

Car hire *Avis*, Friedenstr. 6 (☎97001); *Inter-Rent*, Hermann-Geib-Str. 5 (☎75094).

City river trips May–Sept hourly 10am–4pm; Oct–April 11am and hourly 1–4pm; DM7.50, including going through the rapids under the Steinerne Brücke. Tickets can be bought at the landing stage beside the Historische Wurstküche.

Danube cruises to Walhalla Easter-Oct daily at 10.30am and 1.30pm, returning at 12.15pm and 3.30pm; to Geisling via Walhalla June–Aug Tues and Thurs at noon, Sept Thurs at noon; to Straubing July and Aug Wed at 9am; to Passau June–Sept Sun at 7.30am; to the Altmühl valley May–Sept Sun at 9am; along Rhine-Main-Danube Canal May–Sept daily at 11am and 2pm. All departures are from Werftstrasse on the island of Unterer Wöhrd.

Launderettes *Martin*, Malergasse 9; *Potempka*, Heiliggeistgasse 1; and *Self-Service*, Ostengasse, near the Donaumarkt.

Medical emergencies (☎73073 or ☎560066).

Mitfahrzentrale Jakobstr. 12 (☎57400 or 58267); also functions as a normal travel office.

Poste Restante on Bahnhofstrasse immediately to the left on leaving the Bahnhof.

Women's centre *Frauenzentrum* (☎57404).

Around Regensburg

At the confluence of the Altmuhl and the Danube about 20km southwest of Regensburg by bus or rail is **KELHEIM**, a little medieval town unusual for its time in having been laid out as a planned grid. Crowning the Michelsberg above is the **Befreiungshalle** ("Liberation Hall"; April–Sept daily 8am–6pm; Oct–March 9am–noon and 1–4pm; DM1.50), one of two grandiose constructions on either side of Regensburg funded by King Ludwig I and built by Leo von Klenze. Designed in the manner of an early Christian rotunda, it commemorates the Bavarian dead in the wars against Napoleon.

From Kelheim boat trips (16 May–13 Sept daily at 9.15am, 10am, then every 30 min until 5.10pm; DM5 single, DM7 return; bicycles carried for DM4) pass through the famous **Donaudurchbruch** gorge. Here the Danube washes past some very attractive wooded hillsides, and then dramatically cuts through white cliffs, becoming a fast current only 80m wide. The river took an estimated 4000 years to force its way through these rocks; once past the obstacle, it widens out into a generous sweep. Situated here on a bend of the river is **Kloster Weltenburg**, Bavaria's oldest monastery, founded in the seventh century by Benedictine monks. Its church, an early example of the collaborative skills of the Asam brothers, has as its focal point an illusionistic high altar depicting the fight between Saint George and the dragon. These days the monastery is best known for its dark beer, brewed on the premises and served in its own *Gaststätte*.

Ludwig I's **Walhalla** monument (April–Sept daily 9am–6pm; Oct 9am–5pm; Nov–March 10am–noon and 1–4pm; DM1.50) stands high above the Danube 11km east of Regensburg; by far the most atmospheric approach is by boat (see *Listings* above). Self-consciously modelled on the Parthenon in Athens, the building takes its name from the Nordic mythological resting place for warriors' souls, and contains busts of 118 famous Germans, along with 64 plaques for older celebrities whose likenesses are unknown. The qualification adopted for being a German is decidedly generous, as Swiss and Austrians are included, as well as men such as Erasmus and Copernicus who would definitely have considered themselves outsiders; yet there are several unfathomable omissions along with others whose claim to fame is decidedly dubious. If the whole idea behind this project now seems slightly sinister, the view across the Danube valley is magnificent, and the surrounding park and forests are good places for picnics.

South along the Danube

Between Regensburg and Passau, the Danube flows through some of the most fertile land in Bavaria. Lined by the highlands of the Bavarian Forest to the north and the Bavarian Lowlands to the south, the **Gäuboden**, as it's known, is one of the country's main granaries. Its flatlands have been cultivated for centuries, and archaeological finds go back as far as the Neolithic Age. For the visitor, the agricultural land south of the Danube holds little interest, though the larger towns along the river itself, such as **Straubing**, **Deggendorf** and **Passau**, are certainly worth a visit. The first two are small market towns, with enough together to fill a day trip, while the latter is a rarely visited beauty perched on a peninsula at the confluence of the Danube, Inn and Ilz.

Although excellent road and train connections exist along the Danube's course, travelling this stretch without exploring the **highlands** north of the river would mean missing out on the first glorious reaches of the Bavarian Forest region. Heading north the wooded countryside soon rises up, quickly becoming a landscape of hillside villages and dozens of medieval castles. Probably too hilly for all but the fittest cyclists, motorbikes or cars are the only solution for country day tours. Any of the aforementioned towns would make a good touring base.

Straubing

About 30km downstream from Regensburg, **STRAUBING** is the main market town of the Gäuboden, and each year in August, Bavaria's second largest **fair** takes place here. It began in the early nineteenth century as an occasion for the farmers of the region to meet, do business and celebrate. These days it has expanded into a scaled-down Oktoberfest – though one that still attracts over a million visitors. Check ahead with the tourist office (see below) for exact dates of the festival, and don't expect to find cheap accommodation available during this time.

The pedestrian heart of Straubing is dominated by the town's symbol, the five-pointed Gothic tower next to the **Rathaus**, and lined by the medieval and Baroque facades characteristic of Bavaria's rural towns. Visually Straubing is nothing out of the ordinary, but its wide central market on the high street makes for a pleasant stroll. Following Fraunhoferstrasse away from the main thoroughfare, you'll find the **Gäubodenmuseum** (Tues–Sun 10am–4pm; DM2), which holds a famous Roman treasure (*Römerschatz*), discovered in the region in 1950. An extensive collection, it includes everything from iron and bronze tools and domestic ware to beautifully crafted armour and masks.

The **St-Jakob-Münster** on Jakobsgasse was built by the great late Gothic architect Hans von Burghausen, though the profusion of Baroque altars and chapels from a later age mask the puritanical aspect of the original. There's an almost indecent profusion of side chapels, each sponsored by different wealthy families and all trying to outshine each other: the **Schusterkapelle**, boasting an altarpiece by Holbein the Elder, is the most prestigious.

Every four years (next in 1993) a **theatrical festival** relates the death of a local girl called Agnes Bernauer. In the best tradition of tragedy, the story revolves around the love between two people from separate worlds destroyed by bigotry and self-interest. In the fifteenth century, the heir to the local duchy fell in love with the beautiful commoner Agnes and they got married in secret. When the old duke found out about this, he tricked his son into leaving town for a while, then had Agnes tried for witchcraft and drowned in the Danube. She's been a favourite character in local songs and storytelling ever since, and the play about her life and death is taken from a ballad written last century. The guilty duke erected a chapel to Agnes' memory in the cemetery of the church of **St Peter**, just east of the town centre; nearby stands an ossuary painted with the Dance of Death.

Practicalities

The **tourist office** is in the Rathaus (Mon–Fri 8.30am–noon and 2–5pm; ☎09421/16307). Cheapest hotels in town are *Weisses Rössl*, Landshuter Str. 65 (☎09421/32581) at DM25 per person, and *Landshuter Hof*, Landshuter Str. 36 (☎09421/30366) at DM30 per person: both are south of the station. Otherwise the choice is between the **youth hostel** at Friedhofstr. 12 (☎09421/80436), just east of the station and the **campsite** at Dammweg 17, near the Gstütt bridge (1 May–15 Oct; ☎09421/12912). For **eating and drinking**, a decent local *Gaststätte* is the centrally-located *Röhrl*, Theresienplatz 7.

Bogen and St Englmar

A few kilometres further along the Danube, **BOGEN** is an old pilgrimage centre at the foot of the steep Bogenberg. An uneventful place for most of the year, it bursts into life on Whit Sunday with a great pilgrimage and fair, when a twelve and a half-metre candle is carried up the Bogenberg and into the church at the top. The origins of this vaguely bizarre event lie in the fifteenth century, when a beetle plague around Holzkirchen near Passau ruined much of the forest. The people vowed that if the plague would end, they'd carry a pine pole wrapped in wax to the Bogenberg church as thanks: one of the dafter examples of faith on record. The plague did disappear, and the annual 75-kilometre pilgrimage from Holzkirchen to Bogen has taken place ever since.

Up in the hills 10km to the north of Bogen, **ST ENGLMAR** is the venue for another religiously based festival each Whit Monday. Legend has it that a hermit named Englmar came to live here around the year 1086 and was murdered by a jealous companion, who hid the body under snow in the forest. But at Whitsun the next year, the local priest found Englmar's perfectly preserved body and brought it to the village chapel to be buried. Ever since, the spot has been a pilgrimage centre, and on Whit Monday the villagers re-enact the search for Englmar, riding festively decorated horses and wearing medieval-style clothes.

Deggendorf and around

Some 25km kilometres downriver from Straubing, **DEGGENDORF** doesn't merit an overnight stay in itself, but the nearby forests and countryside of the northern hills are great areas for hiking. If you're into beer festivals, try to time your visit for the end of July and first week of August, which is when the local *Volksfest* is on. The **tourist office** in the *Stadt-Café* building on Oberer Stadtplatz (Mon–Fri 8am–noon and 2–6pm; ☎0991/380169) can advise you on the best hiking routes.

Around Deggendorf, villages like BERNRIED, KALTECK, BISCHOFSMAIS and RUSEL are good bases for walks, with plenty of clearly marked paths through the forests and connecting the peaks. Dedicated hikers tend to stay in **OBERBREITNAU** near Bischofsmais, which has a few simple guest houses as well as a **youth hostel** (☎09920/265), only accessible on foot or via the **Geisskopfbahn** chair lift service. Many of the local farmers rent out parts of their farms for self-catering holidays, which are becoming increasingly popular, especially for people with young children.

Passau

"In all of Germany I never saw a town more beautiful" is how the marauding Napoleon Bonaparte is said to have reacted to **PASSAU**. Tucked away in the far southeast on the Austrian border, most people pass by en route to Austria and thus miss a place that the tourist brochures hail as the "Bavarian Venice". While that's the standard exaggeration, the town does have a certain magic, and its character is indeed very much defined by water: tightly packed on to a peninsula between the confluence of the Danube and Inn,* the Ilz joins here as well, coming down from the hills of the Czech border. For centuries, Passau was the seat of a powerful prince-bishopric, and it was probably for

---

* The great merged river which flows from here via three European capitals to the Black Sea has been known as the Danube since the days of antiquity. However, as was first noticed a couple of centuries ago, the Inn has not only travelled further to reach this point, but is also both deeper and broader. As the subsequent course of the river from the point of convergence favours neither the one nor the other conclusively, the Inn has a far better case to be considered the main river, with the Danube as its tributary – though it's unlikely that this will ever be officially recognised.

this court that Germany's national epic, the *Nibelungenlied* (see Worms, *Chapter Four*), was written at the turn of the thirteenth century. Nowadays, it's a bustling town given a youthful edge by a University founded in 1978.

Around town

Virtually the whole of Passau burnt down in the seventeenth century, so the architectural picture features predominantly Baroque, Rococo and Neoclassical facades, which give the town a pleasingly elegant feel in spite of the unceremoniously tight squeeze of buildings. Space is at a premium on the peninsula, which is only a few metres wide at its tip and still only 300m wide by the time you come to the enormous **Dom**, which is suitably enthroned at the highest point, about a kilometre inland. The original Gothic structure was almost completely destroyed by fire, to be replaced by a Baroque building designed by the Italian masters Lurago, Carlone and Tencalla. Inside, white stucco ornamentation crowds into almost every available space, creating a heavy and overloaded impression. The most notable piece is the **organ**, which is the largest in the world with no fewer than 17,300 pipes and 231 separate registers. Turn up between noon and 12.30pm on a weekday and you can hear it being played during the lunchtime organ recitals (May–Oct; DM3; also Thurs at 7.30pm until Dec 3; DM6).

The **Residenzplatz** is one of the very few open spaces in this tightly packed town; it offers a fine view of the Dom's resplendent east end, the only significant section remaining from the Gothic period. Lined by the airy, pastel-coloured eighteenth-century homes of former wealthy families as well as the bishop's residence, the small cobbled square still holds something of the atmosphere of a once-salubrious past. One of the buildings contains the **Spielzeugmusem** (daily 9am-6pm; DM3, DM1 kids), a small collection of nineteenth-century European and American toys, which also has a few reproductions of wooden toys and games on sale.

Down towards the Danube, the Gothic **Rathaus** is an imposing nobleman's home taken over for civic purposes after one of the local rebellions in the thirteenth century. Look just under the tower and you'll see the marks from the alarmingly high floods that have plagued the town across the centuries. For those interested in the art of handmade glass, the **Glasmuseum** (daily 9am–5pm; DM3) in the *Hotel Wilder Mann* on the square has a collection ranging from Biedermeier to Jugendstil, with an awful lot of kitsch in between. Between here and the tip of the peninsula, alleys and lumpy streets intertwine in picturesque disorder, the original medieval townscape being at its most visible.

Not surprisingly, Passau spilt across the two main rivers to form suburbs on the banks of the Danube and Inn. On the north side, across the Danube, the land rises up sharply to the former palace of the local prince-bishops, the **Veste Oberhaus** (15 March–31 Oct Tues–Sun 9am–5pm; DM3). If you don't fancy the steep walk up the hill, take a bus from the Rathausplatz, which leaves every thirty minutes from 10.30am to 11.30am and from 12.30pm to 4.30pm. Contrary to what you might expect, the palace wasn't fortified to protect Passau's citizens in times of war but to protect the bishop from the independently-minded townspeople who resented his rule. They attacked the Veste on a number of occasions but never succeeded in breaking through; the bishop, on the other hand, had an excellent vantage point from which to bombard the town. Inside, the local and regional history from Roman times to the present is exhibited; outside, you get a wonderful picture-postcard view of the town from up here.

Practicalities

The **tourist office** (Mon–Fri 9am–6pm, Sat 9am–noon; ☎0851 33421) is near the Bahnhof, in the Nibelungenhalle just off Neuburgerstrasse. Within the Veste Oberhaus is the **youth hostel** (☎0851/41351), while there's a **campsite** next to the River Ilz at

Halserstr. 34 (☎0851/41457). Two affordable **hotels** in Passau's Altstadt, pleasantly located at the tip of the peninsula, are *Gasthof zum Hirschen*, Im Ort 6 (☎0851/36238) with singles for DM30 and doubles from DM55, and *Pension Rössner*, Bräugasse 19 (☎0851/35218) with singles for DM50 and doubles from DM75.

Nightlife in Passau is a livelier prospect than you might imagine in such a small place, since the University has spawned the *Scharfrichterhaus* at Milchgasse 2, a venue for live music and cabaret with a cinema and relaxed bar. Another youthful watering hole is the *Stadtschreiber* on the corner of Schustergasse and Schrottgasse. The *Altstadt Café* in the Schustergasse is best for a snack and coffee in the daytime, and at *Zum Passauer Tölpel*, Fritz-Schäffer Promenade, Höllgasse 22, you'll find a vegetarian restaurant. In the same area, the *Innstadt Bräustüberl* at the corner of Schmiedgasse and Löwengrube serves good cheap meals. Further west, at Heiliggeistgasse 4, is the *Heiliggeiststüberl*, a superb cellar restaurant.

Passau is ideally placed for a sortie into **Czechoslovakia**, and Prague is just 190km away. Other European capitals are also within easy reach: **cruises** down the Danube to Vienna and Budapest are run between May and September by *DDSG-Agentie Passau* (☎0851/33035). On a more modest scale, *Donauschiffahrtgesellschaft Wurm & Köck*, Höllgasse 26 (☎0851/2066) have regular daily one-hour sails around Passau, leaving from Rathausplatz. The *Maidult* in May is a large and colourful market and beer **festival**, while during the *Europäische Wochen* in June, July and August concerts are played by internationally renowned orchestras and musicians, and there's also ballet and opera. Passau's star **venue**, worth checking on throughout the year, is the eighteenth-century *Hoftheater*, Innstr. 4.

The Bavarian Forest

Rather uncharitably known as the "Bavarian Congo" because it's poor, provincial and a bit out of the way, the **Bavarian Forest** (*Bayerischer Wald*) is not only one of the last wildernesses in Europe, it's also a region that's retained much of its traditional culture in an unpackaged form, by virtue of being less well-known and visited than the more obvious target of the Black Forest. The craggy earth is full of rocks and barely fertile, and the people of the region had to develop means of survival other than farming. Easy availability of firewood made **glass-blowing** a natural industry, and workers still tend to be employed in the traditional huts, working by hand and mouth in the heat of the furnaces. Except for one or two large factories, glass production is still more of a craft than an industry here, and going on a tour of one of the traditional glass-blowing huts is a treat you shouldn't miss.

Generally, **prices** are relatively low, and even during the height of summer finding accommodation is never a problem. Transport to the area is provided by train services from Regensburg, Straubing and Deggendorf; there's also a good regional bus service, but don't expect a frequency of service of more than once or twice a day. If you want to go on some of the longer hikes and take in the sights and scenery, reckon on staying around a week.

The forest

The actual *Bayerischer Wald* (the forest, as opposed to the general area) is part of a much larger whole spreading across the Czech border into Bohemia to form Central Europe's largest forest region. On the German side, it's approximately defined by the Czechoslovakian border to the north and the Danube to the south, the Austrian border to the southeast and the town of **Kötzting** to the northeast. It's superb hiking country, with well-marked paths of varying length and difficulty throughout the region. Specialised maps pointing out routes are on sale in almost every village tourist office.

The most ancient part of the forest has been declared a **National Park**, which is about 130 square kilometres roughly bounded by the Czech border and the villages of **Mauth, Grafenau, Spiegelau** and **Frauenau**. The two highest peaks are the **Rachel** (1453m) and the **Lusen** (1373m), but the region isn't all mountainous and stretches of moorland open up the forest, while the **Rachelsee** is an isolated splash of blue at the foot of the Rachel. An excellent **information centre** about the park and its facilities is located in NEUSCHÖNAU in the *Hans-Eisenmann Haus*, Böhmstr. 35 (Mon–Sat 9am–5pm; ☎08558/1300). They also run slide-shows and tours of the National Park, and although they're all in German, you will undoubtedly find someone who can explain things in English if necessary. This would also be the right place to find out a bit more about *Waldsterben*, the death of Europe's forests due to acid rain. The statistics are grim and seem to be worsening at an alarming rate: for example in 1983 forty per cent of Germany's forests were diseased. By 1985 the number had risen to 78 per cent, and the problem shows little sign of abating.

Outside the National Park, the **Grosser Arber** (1456m) is the highest mountain of the region, and together with the **Arbersee**, this is the most touristy area, and the only place where you're likely to encounter coach-loads of people touring the "sights". Much quieter, and with great views across to Bohemia, is the **Grosser Osser** (1293m) near LAM and the Czech border. For easy hiking, head for the central highlands and the **Kaitersberg** hills near Kötzting, which has what's considered the best hiking route of the whole area.

There's a **youth hostel**, Waldhäuser, Herbergsweg 2 (☎08553/300; bus from Grafenau Bahnhof) right in the middle of the National Park, which makes an ideal base for hiking. Other hostels are spread around the region generally, in Mauth, Frauenau, Zwiesel, on the Arber, and in Lam. **Guest house** prices are generally in the region of DM15–25 per person, and if you stay in a farmhouse, prices can be as low as DM11–18 each.

Frauenau

The best place to see the living crafts of glass-blowing and cutting is in the village of FRAUENAU, to the northeast of the National Park. Here you'll find the **Freiherr von Poschinger Kristallglasfabrik** (guided tours Mon–Sat 9.45–11.30am and 12.45–1.30pm; DM1.50), the oldest glass-making factory in the world and an excellent place to watch workers transform red molten lumps into glasses, plates and ornaments.

For a technical history of glass production and representative work of each age, the **Glasmuseum**, Am Museumspark (daily 9am–5pm; DM3) gives a very comprehensive illustration. Highlights of the collection are exquisite seventeenth- and eighteenth-century Venetian pieces, and some anarchic Jugendstil vases. Local specialities, such as heavy cut crystal and delicate snuff bottles, are also included.

The **tourist office** is in the Rathaus (Mon–Fri 8am–noon and 1–5pm, Sat 9–11.30am; ☎09926/710). Here you can pick up a list of guest house addresses and prices: most charge about DM15–25 per person. If you want to stay in a farm, you'll have to go a couple of kilometres up the road to the village of FLANITZ. The very basic **youth hostel** (☎09926/543) is in *Haus St Hermann* opposite the police station on the main road.

Bodenmais

BODENMAIS is typical of small towns of the region, surrounded by picturesque countryside and alive with colourful fairs during the summer, and religious festivals throughout the year. The most interesting **hiking route** up the Arber goes from here, passing the waterfalls of the **Risslochschlucht** gorge on the way. For this reason Bodenmais is one of the most popular places to base a holiday, and during summer it gets very busy, though nothing like as crowded as the Alpine region.

Iron and silver were once mined in this region, and tours are guided through Bodenmais' *Erzbergwerk* mine on the **Silberberg** (bus from Bodenmais), about two kilometres outside the village. The whole mountain is riddled with horizontal mine-shafts, among them the **Barbara-Stollen** (daily 10am–5pm; DM5) halfway up. Unless your German is very good, however, you won't understand the guides, who speak a strong local dialect, and, apart from the original fifteenth-century part of the shaft, it's not a particularly interesting tour.

Kötzting

A better use of time would be to keep your feet firmly above ground and head for **KÖTZTING**, at the foot of the Kaitersberg, right on the edge of the Bavarian Forest region. The most interesting time to come here is around the *Pfingstritt* festival on Whit Monday. This is a religious festival, probably founded in an ancient Germanic fertility rite, which involves the menfolk riding their richly adorned horses to a nearby pilgrimage church, and a symbolic wedding of a young couple elected as Whit bride and groom. For the rest of the year, the surrounding hiking opportunities form the main pull to this place. It's not wildly picturesque in itself, more a handy base for excursions, with plenty of inns and *Gasthäuser* to fill the evenings.

The Upper Palatinate

The very name of the **Upper Palatinate** (*Oberpfalz*) is rather confusing, as the term "Palatinate" is so closely associated with the Rhineland. There are historical reasons for this: the Wittelsbachs who ruled Upper and Lower Bavaria were actually the junior members of the dynasty, the most senior branch of which had the title of Electors Palatine of the Rhine. The southerly parts of their territories – consisting of a northerly continuation of the Bavarian Forest, plus a Jurassic landscape to the west – therefore became known as the "Upper Palatinate" to distinguish them from their main holdings. This name has been retained as one of the modern administrative units into which Bavaria is divided, although it has been expanded to include places which had no historical connection with the province, notably the erstwhile Free Imperial City of Regensburg, which now serves as its capital.

The Upper Palatinate Forest

The **Upper Palatinate Forest** (*Oberpfälzer Wald*) is shaped like a tall triangle with the baseline running between **Schwandorf**, **Furth im Wald** and **Cham**, and the apex at **Waldsassen**. It's a lonely region, with few towns and a scant population, but it's also beautiful, especially between the hilly forested border and the B22 road connecting Weiden to Cham. The landscape is less dramatic than further southeast, so the area has had little tourism and continues to be a sleepy backwater of farms and villages, punctuated with the occasional dilapidated castle. As you might expect, public transport is a problem here. North–south travel is only practicable on the mainline train route that heads north from Regensburg via Schwandorf and thereafter closely follows the course of the River Naab, but subsidiary lines make inroads to the east at various points along the way.

Cham and Furth im Wald

The small fortified town of **CHAM**, where the railway line from Schwandorf connects with the main route through the Bavarian Forest, makes a good springboard into the region. There's a **tourist office** here at Propsteistr. 46 (☎09971/4933); as well as providing the usual services, they also offer a special facility of transporting your rucksack for you on certain hiking routes, an innovation called *Wandern ohne Gepäck*. Cham is best-known for the **beers** made by the *Hofmark* brewery, which has been in existence since the sixteenth century; it employs traditional techniques, with the malty *Würzig-Mild* and the dry *Würzig-Herb* being its main products.

Another possible base is **FURTH IM WALD** on the Czech border, just under 20km to the northeast by road or rail. If you time your visit for the second and third Sundays in August, you'll witness one of Bavaria's largest traditional **festivals**, the *Drachenstich*. Best time to arrive is on the second Sunday, when the festivities kick off with a great procession of some 200 horses and hundreds of people in traditional costume. The festival, which goes back as far as 1431, is based on the legend of Saint George and the dragon, and the story is re-enacted in a show that's performed several times over the festival period. The whole spectacle lasts for about 75 minutes, ending in the grand and gory finale of the dragon's death, where the skewered monster spews blood over the street during its death throes. Tickets for the show start at DM4 for a standing position and then rise steadily to DM22; they can be ordered from *Drachenstichfestausschuss*, Stadtplatz 4 (☎09973/9308.) If you don't fancy the dragon spectacle, the beer tents and fair offer a lively alternative.

Furth im Wald has a **youth hostel** at Daberger Str. 50 (☎09973/9254). Cheap accommodation alternatives are easy to find throughout the whole region.

Trausnitz and Weiden

Heading north on the B22 road, you pass through a landscape of rolling hills, forests and little river valleys. About 25km north of Cham, a small road goes off to **TRAUSNITZ**, a village set in a bend of the River Preimd, with a **youth hostel** (☎09655/344) in the local medieval **Burg**. It's pretty basic, but then staying in a castle isn't something you do every day, and if you wake early enough, you might see the forest deer out in the valley for their morning grazing.

WEIDEN, another 10km north, is a busy market town with nothing in particular worth staying over for; from here on the best option is to take the smallest roads you can find, preferably near the border region if you enjoy remote empty landscapes.

Waldsassen

WALDSASSEN, right on the northern edges of the Upper Palatinate in the so-called **Steinwald** ("Stone Forest"), is best known for its huge **Stift** (collegiate church), built by Georg Dientzenhofer in the late seventeenth century, and ranking as one of the masterpieces of German Baroque. The most impressive part of the complex is the **Stiftsbibliothek** (summer Tues–Sun 10–11.30am and 2–5pm; winter Tues–Sun 10–11am and 2–4pm), whose wooden bookcases are embraced by idiosyncratic statues representing all the trades that go into the making and selling of books. Carved by local artists Karl Stilp and Andreas Witt, they include everyone who is even remotely connected with books, such as the shepherd (whose sheepskins are turned into bookbinding), the pulp-maker and more obvious ones like the bookseller and the reader.

Although it actually lies in Franconia, the **Kappel** pilgrimage church is so close to Waldsassen that the two should be mentioned together. Also by Dientzenhofer, this church is set in tranquil countryside a few kilometres up the road, and built in a rare circular design. It's made up of three apses and three little onion-domed towers, which neatly symbolise the Holy Trinity to which it's dedicated.

Amberg

AMBERG, which lies 20km northwest of Schwandorf on the rail line to Nürnberg, was the capital of the Upper Palatinate until supplanted when Regensburg was incorporated into the province. No more than a medium-sized county town these days, it was for centuries the centre of a prosperous ore-mining industry, which finally came to an end a few years back. The other traditional speciality of beer-making, in contrast, continues to thrive, and the town still has nine separate breweries.

Considerable sections of the once-formidable **Stadtmauer**, which is regularly punctuated by austere square watchtowers with steeply sloping tiled roofs, remain intact. Four of the original five gateways remain, of which the most impressive is the **Nabburger Tor** at the southeastern entrance to the town, one of only a handful of twin-towered municipal fortifications to have survived in Germany. However, the most eye-catching part of the defences is the so-called **Stadtbrille** ("Town's Spectacles") a short walk to the west. Spanning the River Vils, which cuts right through the middle of the Altstadt, this fortified bridge gets its nickname from the perfect pair of circles its paired arches reflect in the water; the best view of this is from the Ringbrücke immediately to the south.

One of the two parish churches, **St Georg**, doubled as the southeastern part of the fortifications. Its counterpart, **St Martin**, which dominates the central Marktplatz, has preserved its majestic fifteenth-century hall church architecture intact. Also on the square is the decidedly eclectic **Rathaus**, while on Schrannenplatz to the west is the town's most distinctive church, the oval **Schulkirche**, whose extravagant Rococo decoration includes a shell-shaped choir gallery.

Practicalities

The **Hauptbahnhof** lies hard by the inner ring road on the eastern side of the centre, just a few minutes' walk from Marktplatz. On the block immediately south of the square, at Zeughausstr. 1a is the **tourist office** (Mon–Fri 9am–noon and 2–4.30pm, Sat 10am–noon; ☎09621/10233). The **youth hostel** is ideally placed right by the river north of Marktplatz at Fronfestgasse 22 (☎09621/10369). Otherwise, the cheapest **hotels** with a central location are *Goldene Krone*, Waisenhausgasse 2 (☎09621/22994), with singles from DM25 and doubles from DM48, and *Wagner*, Obere Nabburger Str. 31 (☎09621/12755), charging DM30 per person. Best **restaurant** is *Altdeutschstube* on Schrannenplatz. Main **festivals** – offering good opportunities for sampling the diverse products of the local breweries – are the *Altstadtfest* in June and the *Bergfest* in July.

FRANCONIA

Geographically the largest part of Bavaria, **Franconia** (*Franken*) makes up the north of the state, with Thuringia, Hessen and Baden-Württemberg forming its borders. About half of it is covered by highland forest ranges, which span the entire width of the province, but the chief attractions are urban. **Nürnberg**, Bavaria's second city, is a particularly evocative place, with its heady reminders of the very best and the very worst of German culture. Within easy reach are **Erlangen**, with its famous University, and the courtly town of **Ansbach**, while to the north lie Wagner's **Bayreuth**, **Coburg**, the town from which the British royal family originally descended, and the artistic treasure chest of **Bamberg**. Further west are the old episcopal residential cities of **Aschaffenburg** and **Würzburg**. The latter is the starting point of Germany's most popular tourist route, the **Romantic Road**, whose highlights include the magnificently well-preserved medieval towns of **Rothenburg ob der Tauber** and **Dinkelsbühl**.

Franconia's **history** goes back a long way: it takes its name from the Frankish tribes of whose territory it formed a major part. In the tenth century it was made into a duchy which stretched all the way to the Rhine, but this was later split into two and the name retained only for the eastern half. Somehow the region never established itself as a coherent entity like Bavaria; even the mighty Bishop of Würzburg's secular title of Duke of Franconia did little to unite the area, which was splintered into many different power bases. Emperor Maximilian I's decision to restructure the Empire into ten confederate regions in the sixteenth century did at least establish Franconia as a distinctive cultural entity. This lasted until 1803, when most of Franconia was absorbed into the new Bavarian kingdom.

Today, even after nearly 200 years of being part of Bavaria, the people still cling to their **regional heritage** and often only grudgingly see themselves as Bavarian. Certainly their dress, food and dialect are quite different. No-one wears *Lederhosen* here and Nürnberg is one of a very few cities to have a Socialist mayor in this conservative state. On the other hand, the regions along the border with Thuringia (formerly the virtually impermeable border with the GDR) harbour some of the most fanatically nationalist and right-wing people in the country. This **political divide** has been closely linked to a religious one, created by the adoption of the Reformation in the margraviates of Ansbach and Bayreuth. It is also reflected in architecture, where the plain lines and more sombre colours of Lutheran Baroque make a potent contrast to the sometimes overrich Catholic style. Even drinking habits are different, with central and western Franconia a staunch beer zone, while the district around Würzburg is very much a wine area.

Nürnberg (Nuremberg)

Nothing more magnificent or splendid is to be found in the whole of Europe. When one perceives this glorious city from afar, its splendour is truly dazzling. When one enters it, one's original impression is confirmed by the beauty of the streets and the comeliness of the houses. The burghers' dwellings seem to have been built for princes. In truth, the kings of Scotland would be glad to be housed so luxuriously as the ordinary citizen of Nürnberg.

This mid-fifteenth century eulogy, written by the future Pope Pius II, shows the esteem in which medieval **NÜRNBERG** was held. As the favourite royal residence and seat of the first Diet called by each new emperor, the city then functioned as the unofficial capital of Germany. It was a status which had been achieved with remarkable speed, as Nürnberg was only founded in the eleventh century; thereafter, its position at the intersection of the north–south and east–west trading routes led to economic prosperity, and, as a corollary, political power. The arts flourished, too, though the most brilliant period was not to come until the late fifteenth and early sixteenth centuries, when the roll-call of citizens was led by **Albrecht Dürer**, Germany's most complete personification of Renaissance Man.

Like other wealthy European cities, Nürnberg went into gradual economic and social decline once the maritime trading routes to the Americas and Far East had been established; moreover, the official civic adoption of the Reformation cost the city the patronage of the Catholic emperors. It made a comeback in the nineteenth century, when it became the focus for the Pan-German movement, and the **Germanisches Nationalmuseum** – the most important and extensive collection of the country's arts and crafts – was founded at this time. In 1835, the first German railway was built there, linking the city to the neighbouring town of Fürth. Nürnberg's symbolic status for the German nation was given a horrifying twist during the Third Reich. Even today the city's image as the home of quaint markets and dreaming spires, and as the world's leading centre for the production of children's toys, is marred by its indelible association with the Nazi regime and the war-crime trials after the war. The site of the old mass rallies still stands, and in spite of all the picturesque views the medieval city centre offers, the weather-beaten **Nazi architecture** outside town creates an equally telling impression.

The telephone code for Nürnberg is ☎0911

Even though the Altstadt is quite small there's so much to see in Nürnberg that two or three days are probably the minimum amount of time necessary to get to know the place. It's especially enticing in the summer, when the Altstadt is alive with street theatre and music, and there are open-air pop concerts in the parks and stadiums; but there's always a wide and varied range of nightlife.

Getting around and accommodation

Arriving at the **Hauptbahnhof**, you're just outside the medieval fortifications of the Altstadt. **Exchange facilities** (Mon–Sat 7.45am–7.45pm, Sun 9.15am–12.30pm) are available in the main hall. Across from this is the main **tourist office** (Mon–Sat 9am–8pm; ☎233632); another branch (Mon–Sat 9am–1pm and 2–6pm, Sun 9am–1pm and 2–4pm; ☎233634) is at Hauptmarkt 18 in the Altstadt. **Public transport**, though hardly neccessary for the compact city centre, is provided by trams, U-Bahns and buses, and the same tickets are valid on all three. Tickets can be bought at almost any station and the price of a journey is dependent on how many zones you cross. Maps next to ticket machines explain the zone system.

A top-class **youth hostel** (☎241352; U-Bahn to Plärrer and then tram #4 to the Vestnertor) is located in part of the city's castle overlooking the Altstadt. There's another **youth hotel** – without age restrictions, and charging from DM19 – to the north of the city at Rathsbergstr. 300 (☎529092); the journey from the Hauptbahnhof by tram #2 and then bus #41 takes 20 minutes. Reasonably priced **hotels** in the Altstadt include: *Alt-Nürnberg*, Breite Gasse 40 (☎224129), with singles from DM30 and doubles from DM50; *Maar*, Breite Gasse 31 (☎224535), at DM32 per person; *Schwänlein*, Hintere Sterngasse 11 (☎225162), singles from DM34 and doubles from DM60; and *Fischer*, Brunnengasse 11 (☎226189), singles DM35 and doubles from DM65. There are also a number of alternatives not too far from the rear of the Hauptbahnhof; among them are *Vater Jahn*, Jahnstr. 13 (☎444507), with singles from DM32 and doubles from DM60; *Humboldtklause*, Humboldtstr. 41 (☎413801), singles from DM33 and doubles from DM64; and *Melanchthon*, Melanchthonplatz 1 (☎412626), DM36 for singles and DM68 for doubles. The **campsite** (May–Sept only) is in the Volkspark near the Dutzendteich lakes (☎408416; tram #12 from the Marientunnel near the Hauptbahnhof).

The Altstadt

On 2 January 1945 a storm of bombs reduced ninety percent of Nürnberg's city centre to ash and rubble. Yet walking through the **Altstadt** today, you'd never guess this had ever happened, so loving and effective was the postwar rebuilding. Covering about four square kilometres, the reconstructed medieval core is neatly spliced by the River Pegnitz and surrounded by the ancient **Stadtbefestigung** (city ramparts), which are guarded by eighty towers and pierced by four massive gateways. To walk from one end to the other takes about twenty minutes, but much of the centre, especially the area around the castle (known as the **Burgviertel**), is on a steep hill, and speedy walking is impractical. This makes wandering around all the more pleasurable, the rise and fall of the streets creating lopsided views and houses squeezing together as if for comfort. The atmosphere is pleasantly relaxed as well; most of the area is pedestrianised, and there's little in the way of city rush within the fortifications. It's not all medieval pictures, however. Significant areas of modern architecture and open spaces are also prominent, thus ensuring a refreshing (and deliberate) mix of old and new.

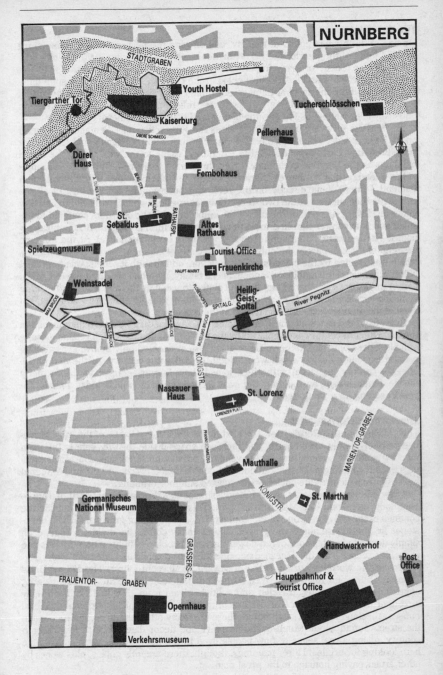

The Kaiserburg

On one of the highest points of the city, and offering the best views, the **Kaiserburg** (guided tours of the interior daily 9.30am–noon and 12.45–4/5pm; DM3) sits chunkily above all else. Scene of many imperial meetings from the eleventh to the sixteenth century, this castle was the "treasure chest of the German Empire", and, despite innumerable modifications and war damage down the centuries, it remains a key feature of the city's silhouette. In fact, it's two fortresses rolled into one, and as such offers an unusually illuminating insight into the history and politics of medieval Germany.

The earliest surviving part of the castle is the **Fünfeckturm** ("Pentagonal Tower") on the eastern side, which dates back to the eleventh century Salian epoch. A century later, Frederick Barbarossa decided to extend the castle to the west, using the Salian buildings as the first line of defence. From this period there remain several examples of the smooth ashlar structures characteristic of the Hohenstaufens. The **Sinwellturm** ("Round Tower"), built directly on the rock, can be ascended for the best of all the views. Another survivor is the two-storey **Kaiserkapelle**, a chapel whose high and airy upper level was reserved for the use of the emperor, with the courtiers confined to the squat and heavy lower tier. In a most unusual architectural arrangement, the bizarrely named **Heidenturm** ("Heathens' Tower") was built over its chancel. At the extreme east end of the complex is the only fourteenth-century addition, the **Luginslandturm**, which was erected by the city council. Its function, odd though it seems, was to protect Nürnberg against the ambitious Hohenzollern family, who had acquired the old Salian part of the fortress as a hereditary fief and aimed to use it as their base for establishing control over local affairs. After a long war of attrition, the city emerged victorious, but most of the original castle was destroyed in the process.

Apart from the east wall, the Hohenstaufen residential quarters were demolished in the mid-fifteenth century and replaced by the late Gothic **Palais**, which retains its suite of halls. These now look rather plain and soulless, redeemed only by two eye-catching painted wooden ceilings, which were added the following century. At the end of the fifteenth century, the local authorities joined their Luginslandturm to the formerly hostile Fünfeckturm by building the vast **Kaiserstallung**, which today makes the perfect setting for a youth hostel.

The northwestern quarter

The area around the **Tiergärtner Tor** next to the Kaiserburg is one of the most attractive parts of the old town centre, and the open space inside the city gate is the main meeting point for summertime street vendors, artists and musicians. On warm evenings the surrounding pubs spill out onto the cobblestoned piazza and the half-timbered houses form a picturesque backdrop for relaxed summer drinking.

A few minutes' walk away along Johannisstrasse lies the **Johannisfriedhof** (April–Sept daily 7am–7pm; Oct–March 8am–5pm). This medieval cemetery, set outside the confines of the old city, is one of the country's most fascinating graveyards. The tombstones lie lengthwise above the graves, like so many coffins lined side by side, each simply decorated with a bowl of red-flowering plants. Look carefully on the "lids" – some show little scenes from the deceased person's life or trade chiselled into the stone.

Among the worthies buried in the graveyard is Albrecht Dürer. The **Dürer-Haus** (Tues & Thurs–Sun 10am–5pm, Wed 10am–9pm; DM3.50), where the versatile painter, engraver, scientist, writer, traveller and politician lived from 1509 to 1528, is virtually next door to the Tiergärtner Tor. It's one of the very few completely original medieval houses still standing in the city, though there are many other skilful reconstructions in the streets round about. Much of the furniture and decor dates back to the fifteenth century, giving a real sense of how people lived in the late Middle Ages. Don't come here looking for original Dürer paintings, though: there are only copies, plus works by other artists paying homage to the great man.

Southeast from here runs Bergstrasse, where at no.19 you'll find the **Altstadthof**, a late sixteenth-century courtyard. Here you can visit the **Hausbrauerei** (guided tours hourly Mon–Fri 2–7pm, Sat & Sun 11–7pm; DM4.50), a museum-piece brewery put back into production a few years ago. Its main line is a wonderful unfiltered dark beer; this can be bought in bottles at the end of the tour, or sampled on draught in either of the adjoining restaurants. Proceeding southwards past the Weinmarkt, you come to the **Spielzeugmuseum** (Toy Museum; Tues and Thurs–Sun 10am–5pm, Wed 10am–9pm; DM2) at Karlstr. 15. This celebrates Nürnberg's continuing role as the world metropolis of toy production by means of a thorough historical presentation of the craft. It's a must for kids – but is just as enjoyable for adults, who can enjoy a sentimental wallow in nostalgia. Further south, the huge half-timbered **Weinstadel**, a medieval wine depot, overlooks a particularly picturesque stretch of the Pegnitz, lined with weeping willows and spanned by the covered wooden walkway known as **Henkersteg** ("Hangman's Bridge").

St Sebaldus

Nürnberg's oldest and most important church, the twin-towered **St Sebaldus**, lies just to the east of the Speilzeugmuseum via the quaint Weissgerbergasse. The exterior positively drips with sculpture: on the south side are early fourteenth-century portals dedicated to the Last Judgment and to the Virgin Mary, while to the north is the slightly later Bridal Doorway, with its carvings of the Wise and Foolish Virgins.

An even more astonishing array of works of art can be found inside the church. Particularly striking is the bronze **shrine of St Sebald**, an early sixteenth-century masterpiece which combines late Gothic and Renaissance decoration and is heavy with religious symbols. **Peter Vischer the Elder**, aided by his two sons, took eleven years to complete this project; look out for the self-portrait of the master founder at work, dressed in skullcap and apron. On the pillar behind is an expressive *Crucifixion* scene (whose figures are taken from two separate groups, made two decades apart) by Nürnberg's most famous sculptor, **Veit Stoss**. The same artist also made the *St Andrew* and the three stone *Passion* reliefs on the end walls of the chancel.

The northeastern quarter

Immediately to the east of St Sebaldus is the **Altes Rathaus**, a self-confident late Renaissance building in the style of a Venetian *palazzo* which incorporates two older houses. If you're into the gorier side of medieval times, visit the torture chambers in the **Lochgefängnisse** underneath (May–Sept Mon–Fri 10am–4pm, Sat and Sun 10am–1pm; DM3). On a lighter note, go through to Rathausgasse to see one of the finest of the city's many fountains, the Renaissance **Gänsemännchen Brunnen**, which shows a farmer carrying two water-spouting geese to market.

Up the road at Burgstr. 15 is the **Fembohaus** (Tues & Thurs–Sun 10am–5pm, Wed 10am–9pm; DM3), now containing the municipal museum. Originally built for a rich merchant, the interior decor is truly startling, featuring lurid colour schemes of pastel pink, yellow and green, with riotously ornate white stuccoed ceilings forming the icing on top. Of the exhibits, the most entertaining are in room 22, frivolous pictures of human passion, dreams and bodily functions: for some reason bees and wasps crop up a lot.

East of here is Egidienplatz, on the north side of which stands the **Pellerhaus**. Originally the finest patrician house in the city, it was almost totally destroyed in the war, but the stately arcaded late Renaissance courtyard has been painstakingly reconstructed. Further along, in the shadow of the modern University buildings, is the earlier **Tucherschlösschen** (guided tours Mon–Thurs 2pm, 3pm and 4pm, Fri 9am, 10am and 11am, Sun 10am and 11am; DM2). This home of another (and, thanks to their beer, still prominent) Nürnberg dynasty survived in better shape, enabling it to be fully restored to serve as an illuminating illustration of the lifestyle enjoyed by its former owners.

The Hauptmarkt and around

Commercial heart of the city and main venue for the normal daily markets and the famous Christmas market, the **Hauptmarkt** lies just south of the Altes Rathaus, occupying the site of the Jewish quarter, which was razed to make way for it in a fourteenth-century pogrom. In the centre of the square stands a brightly-coloured replica of the celebrated Gothic **Schöner Brunnen** ("Beautiful Fountain"). A tall stone pyramid chiselled out in filigree style and adorned with statues of the Electors accompanied by pagan, Jewish and Christian heroes, prophets, evangelists and church fathers, it has the dimensions of a great church spire rather than a mere fountain.

The Hauptmarkt's east side is bounded by the **Frauenkirche**. This little jewel of a church, commissioned by Emperor Charles IV as his court chapel, was one of the first buildings by the celebrated Parler family. Its facade, sheltering a porch with a delicately carved doorway dedicated to the Nativity, was enlivened in the early sixteenth century by the addition of a gable, an oriel and a clockwork mechanism known as the *Männleinlaufen*, which tinkles away each day at noon. The rather recondite story it tells is of the **Golden Bull** of 1356, whereby the church's founder established the identites of the seven Electors (here shown honouring him) on a permanent basis, as well as designating Nürnberg as the city in which every new emperor had to hold his first Imperial Diet. Among the works of art inside, pride of place goes to the *Tucher Altar* in the chancel, a late Gothic *Crucifixion* **triptych** painted by an unknown but highly expressive artist – now dubbed the Master of the Tucher Altar as a result – who was Nürnberg's finest painter of the period prior to Dürer.

Walking southwards from Hauptmarkt, you cross the River Pegnitz by Museumsbrücke, which gives you a good view of the **Fleischbrücke** to the right (modelled on the Rialto Bridge in Venice) and the **Heilig-Geist-Spital** on the left. The latter – one of the largest hospitals built in the Middle Ages – stands on an islet, with two graceful arches spanning the water. Now a restaurant, it has an old-world inner courtyard with wooden galleries.

The southern quarter

Following Königstrasse south from the river, you shortly come to the parish church of **St Lorenz**. At first sight, it's remarkably similar in appearance to St Sebaldus; the reason for this is that Nürnberg grew out of two separate settlements either side of the Pegnitz, which competed with each other for the most imposing church. In fact it soon becomes apparent that, notwithstanding the near-identical shape and ground plan, the churches are actually quite different, with the constituent parts of St Lorenz built about fifty years after those of its counterpart. Thus the nave, complete with a majestic main portal and a resplendent rose window, is modelled on the High Gothic cathedrals in France, while the hall chancel, lit by a gleaming set of stained glass windows, is in the Flamboyant style. Look out for the graceful late fifteenth-century **tabernacle** some 20m high, worked out of local sandstone by **Adam Kraft**, who depicted himself as a fiery, pensive figure crouching at the base. Equally spectacular is the larger-than-life polychrome wood *Annunciation* by **Veit Stoss** which is suspended from the ceiling above the high altar.

Outside the church is another wonderful fountain, the Mannerist **Tugendbrunnen**, in which water gushes from the breasts of the Seven Virtues and from the trumpets of the putti. Diagonally opposite is the oldest house in the city, the thirteenth-century **Nassauer Haus**. If you follow Karolinenstrasse west from here, you can see two notable modern additions to the city's tally of fountains. The **Peter-Henlein-Brunnen** on Hefnersplatz honours the local inventor who produced the first-ever pocket watch in the early sixteenth century. On Ludwigsplatz further east is the **Ehekarussell Brunnen**; illustrating a poem by the cobbler Hans Sachs (see opposite), it displays six scenes from marriage, humorously alternating between bliss and nightmare.

THE MASTERSINGERS OF NÜRNBERG

Nürnberg was only one of many homes of the distinctive form of lyric poetry known as *Meistergesäng*, which flourished from the fourteenth century onwards, practised mainly by members of the skilled artisan class. The rules were highly pedantic, with words having to be fitted to *Töne* composed by thirteenth-century minstrels, and by the sixteenth century it had become a rather moribund art, despite a relaxation of the restrictions placed on the introduction of new *Töne*.

Nonetheless, it had a glorious final fling in Nürnberg, thanks above all to **Hans Sachs**. For a man who had to fit his literary activities into his spare time away from his trade of shoemaking, Sachs was unbelievably prolific, producing some 6000 works, including well over 100 full-length plays which do not, however, show him at his best. Apart from some of the most accomplished *Meistergesänge*, Sachs wrote *Schwänke* (humorous stories told in doggerel verse) and *Fastnachtspiele* (dramatic interludes performed at Shrovetide). He was also a propagandist for the Reformation, coining Luther's proudly borne nickname of "the Nightingale of Wittenberg". That grandest of grand operas, Wagner's *The Mastersingers of Nürnberg*, is a celebration of the art of Sachs and his cronies; though historically rather wayward, it ranks as the most spectacular of the many tributes paid to the city by the Romantic movement.

Returning to the Nassauer Haus and continuing down Konigstrasse in the direction of the Hauptbahnhof you come to the massive and austere Renaissance **Mauthalle**, whose sloping roof is pierced by six tiers of windows. Formerly a granary and later a customs house, it now houses various stores. Beyond is the Gothic church of **St Martha**, whose main claim to fame is that it served as the hall of the Mastersingers or *Meistersingers*.

If you've time or inclination there's the **Handwerkerhof** (20 March–23 Dec Mon–Sat 10am–6.30pm; restaurants open till 10pm) by the Königstor, an enclosed "medieval" village that brings to life historic Nürnberg trades such as handmade tin soldiers, dolls, brass objects and the famed *Lebkuchen* spice-cakes. Hot *Apfelstrudel* or the local delicacy of *Nürnberger Bratwürste* for sale in old-style taverns are very tasty. Just outside the Altstadt to the west of here, at Lessingstr. 6, is the **Verkehrsmuseum** (Transport Museum; April–Sept daily 9am–5pm, Oct–March Mon–Fri 10am–4pm, Sat and Sun 10am–5pm; DM4). This concentrates on German railways and has many ancient locomotives, including the country's first train (named the *Adler* after Germany's eagle symbol), parked in its showrooms. An instructive section on the role of the railways during the Third Reich is also featured, as well as an impressive stamp display.

The Germanisches Nationalmuseum

The **Germanisches Nationalmuseum** on Kornmarkt (Tues–Fri 9am–5pm, Sat and Sun 10am–5pm, Thurs also 8–9.30pm; DM4; free on Sun and Thurs evening), which concentrates almost exclusively on the German cultural tradition, is one of the largest and most varied collections in the country. It occupies the late fourteenth-century **Karthaus** (Charterhouse) which is itself of considerable interest as the most complete example of this type of monastery in Germany, though the modern galleries which have been added to provide badly needed extra display space seriously mar the effect.

THE GROUND FLOOR

On the **ground floor**, the first rooms contain the earliest items, ranging from a golden cone from the Bronze Age to the tenth-century *Echternach Gospels*. Immediately following is the section devoted to medieval **stone sculptures** from some of Nürnberg's most famous buildings, brought here for conservation, and replaced *in situ* with copies. You next enter the **Karthauskirche**, which still preserves the simple Gothic form favoured by the silent Carthusian monks.

In the adjoining cloister are carvings by **Veit Stoss**, including an anguished *Crucifixion*, a light-hearted pair of *Tobias and the Archangel Raphael*, and the *Rosenkranztafel*, a large wooden panel graphically portraying the drama of Judgment Day. A few sculptures by the other great woodcarver of the period, **Tilman Riemenschneider** – notably a noble figure of *St Elizabeth* – can be seen in the gallery beyond, which is chiefly devoted to fifteenth-century painting. The most important work here is *The Annunciation*, one of the best of the few surviving works of **Conrad Witz**, who played a crucial role in moving German painting towards a greater sense of realism: the perspective attempted in this panel is a world away from the flat backgrounds found in most of the other paintings here. Next comes an outstanding collection of historical **musical instruments**, which occupies the whole of the south wing.

THE FIRST FLOOR

German painting at its Renaissance peak dominates the **first floor**, where you can see some **Dürer** originals. *Hercules Slaying the Stymphalian Birds* is a fairly early work, and the only mythological painting by the artist to have survived. The pair of imaginary portraits of *The Emperor Charlemagne* and *The Emperor Sigismund* were commissioned to adorn the room in which the imperial treasury (now in Vienna) was kept during the years it was displayed in Nürnberg; the actual crown, orb and sceptre are accurately depicted in the paintings. In contrast, *Emperor Maximilian I* and *Michael Wolgemut* are portraits made from life; the latter is a touching yet unsentimental portrayal of the artist's former teacher, by then a wrinkled old man of 82. Three panels from a dispersed series of *The Life of St Florian* by **Altdorfer** use the landscapes of the Danube valley to impressive effect; this same backdrop also occurs in **Baldung**'s *Rest on the Flight into Egypt*. Most interesting of several works by **Cranach** is *King Christian II of Denmark*; the monarch had by then been deposed and had fled to Wittenberg, where he stayed as the artist's house guest.

The following rooms focus on the diversity of Nürnberg's achievements during the Renaissance. There was a strong **goldsmith** tradition, shown to best effect in the superbly fashioned model of a three-masted ship. The city also played a leading role in the fast-developing science of geography, and you can see the first globe of the earth, made by **Martin Behaim** in 1491 – just before the discovery of America. From three-quarters of a century later is a globe of the heavens by another local man, Wenzel Jamnitzer. This floor's south wing is entirely devoted to German **folklore** and in particular religious traditions which show the roots of customs still very much alive in rural areas.

Luitpoldhain

In virtually everyone's mind the word Nürnberg conjures up thoughts of Nazi rallies and the war-crime trials: in most peoples' memories are the scratchy black-and-white newsreels of fanatical crowds roaring *Sieg Heil*, and of Göring, Ribbentrop and other leaders standing in the dock a few years later. Nürnberg has the unenviable task of facing up to its historical role (see box) more closely and openly than other cities, and the authorities, to their credit, have made a positive move towards helping visitors get to grips with the events of that time. The park known as the **Luitpoldhain** in the southeastern suburbs of the city, where many of the Nazi buildings still stand, has been dedicated to the memory of their victims, though it is also used for commercial and recreational purposes. If this seems a somewhat incongruous mix, it is in reality a case of history turning full circle, as the Luitpoldhain was originally laid out for the Bavarian Jubilee Exhibition of 1906, and was later a memorial for the dead of World War I before being commandeered by the Nazis.

NÜRNBERG UNDER THE NAZIS

As the present city council is eager to point out, the Nazis' choice of Nürnberg as the backdrop for their *Reichsparteitage* had little to do with local support of the "brown" ideology. Indeed, in marked contrast to Munich, the votes cast for them here in each of the elections before their assumption of power were derisory. The crucial factor was what the medieval city represented in German history: not only had it been the *de facto* capital, its rapid rise to prominence was seen as showing the nation's dynamism at its very peak. Also, the local police made it very easy for the NSDAP to gain the upper hand here, since they resented centralised Bavarian control and hoped to gain more independence if the Nazis took over.

The first of the **Nürnberg rallies** was held in 1927; between 1933 and 1938 they were an annual event, Hitler using the 1938 rally to raise world tension during the Munich crisis. As the most important display of Nazi power for home and foreign consumption, they were highly organised and ritualised mass demonstrations. Hitler's speeches formed the climax of the show, the intention being to show his own unquestioned status as *Führer* and the total unity of purpose existing between the leadership and the led. Up to 250,000 people took part in these events, which were expertly stage-managed and totally hypnotic for the mass of participants. The sheer organisational skills which had to be brought to bear were themselves a form of preparation for war – and intended as a further warning to potential enemies. Leni Riefenstahl's film *Triumph of the Will*, a lyrical, often poetic hymn to Nazism, is the best record of the week-long rallies.

There was no more fanatical proponent of the Nazis' anti-Semitic policies than the Franconian party chief, **Julius Streicher**, who strode around the city administering instant "justice" with his whip, and whose depravities reached such depths that even fellow party members felt sickened. His odious anti-Semitic newspaper *Der Stürmer* was specifically designed to stir up hysteria against the Jews, with its stories of their alleged child sacrifices and sexual perversities. The highlight of his career came with the passing of the so-called **Nürnberg Laws** in 1935, which deprived Jews of their citizenship and forbade relations between Jews and Gentiles. It was through these laws that the Nazis justified their extermination of six million Jews, 10,000 of whom came from Nürnberg – where the Jewish population was reduced to single figures by the end of the war.

So great was Nürnberg's identification with the proudest demonstrations of power of the Third Reich that it was deliberately chosen by the victorious Allies as the place for the **war-crime trials**, which are graphically recounted in Rebecca West's book *A Train of Powder*. The surviving leading players of the "Thousand Year Reich", before whom an entire nation had trembled for twelve years, now mostly appeared as broken men – and were publicly shown up as the ragbag of fanatics and misfits they had in reality always been. Ten of the most important Nazis – Ribbentrop, Keitel, Kaltenbrunner, Rosenberg, Frank, Frick, Streicher, Seyss-Inquart, Sauckel and Jodl – were successively hanged here at short intervals in the early hours of 16 October 1946. Ex-Field Marshall Hermann Göring committed suicide by swallowing a concealed cyanide pill two hours before his appointed execution. Of the rest, Hess, Funk and Raeder were confined to prison for life, while Speer, Schirach, Dönitz and Neurath were all given long-term sentences. Three men were acquitted: the propaganda officer Hans Fritzsche; Franz von Papen, the bungling ex-Chancellor who was more responsible than anyone else for Hitler's initial assumption of power; and Hjalmar Schacht, the financial guru who had managed the economic affairs of the Third Reich with the same enthusiasm, shrewdness and lack of political concern as he had shown when running the national economy in the days of the Weimar Republic.

At the northern entrance to the park is the **Luitpoldarena**, where parades of Nazi groups such as the SA and SS were held. Its grounds contained the former exhibition hall where the party conferences were held, but this was completely destroyed by bombing in 1945. The custom-built but unfinished **Kongressbau** behind, however, remains standing, and is the most chilling surviving visual reminder of the pretensions of the Third Reich. Built in the debased Neoclassical style beloved of modern totalitarian dictators, it self-consciously tries to present an updated, upstaging version of Rome's Colosseum. Appropriately enough, all attempts to find a suitable use for this monstrosity have come to nought; part of it is used as a store, while it's pressed into occasional service for crowd-pulling pop concerts.

To the rear, the **Grosse Strasse** leads over the artificial lake down to another parade ground, the **Märzfeld**. The dimensions of this road – 2km long and 60m wide – are awesome; the vista it opens up includes a distant view of the Kaiserburg, thus creating a visual reference to the symbolic union the Nazis wished to have with the medieval city. Nowadays, part of it is used as a car park by visitors to the modern trade fair buildings nearby. You can then return to the Kongressbau by taking the path to the east. This passes firstly the **Stadion**, used for meetings of the Hitler Youth but now returned to its original purpose as a sports venue as home of the football club *FC Nürnberg*. Further north is the **Zeppelinfeld**, which was transformed by Albert Speer (Hitler's favourite architect, and subsequently armaments minister) into a stadium for the most important parades. The colonnaded tribunes, so familiar from old films, had to be dismantled for safety reasons, but the towers and terraces remain. Nowadays, the complex is used as a sports centre for American troops, and for the celebrated **Norisring car races** in late June. (Information and tickets are available from *MCN Motorsport-Club Nürnberg*, Spittlertorgraben 47, ☎267990.) Between May and October, *Fascination and Force*, a multi-media presentation on the city's Nazi legacy, is staged here; for exact times and dates, contact the tourist office, who also produce the useful leaflet *Nürnberg 1933-1945*.

Eating, drinking and nightlife

Nürnberg is the liveliest Bavarian city next to Munich, with a wealth of watering-holes and nightspots to suit all tastes and pockets. If the Bavarian's favourite snack is a *Weisswurst*, the Franconian's is the *Bratwurst*. These are slim pork sausages, roasted over wood fires and served with a choice of accompaniments: *sauerkraut*, potato salad, onions or radishes. The most curious culinary feature of Nürnberg is that these sausages have been turned into an item of serious cuisine, best sampled in the highly-rated speciality restaurants to the accompaniment of a glass of one of the wide variety of beers produced by the local *Tucher* or *Patrizier* breweries. Equally ubiquitous are Nürnberger *Lebkuchen*, delicious spice-cakes made from flour, nuts, honey, eggs and spices. Usually they're only eaten around Christmas: this is the only place you can buy them all year round.

The relevant public transport services are listed for all places mentioned here other than those in the Altstadt.

Sausage Restaurants

Bratwurst-Friedl, Hallplatz 21. Offers a full, moderately-priced menu in addition to the sausage specialities.

Bratwurst-Glöcklein, Im Handwerkerhof. Despite its commercialised position in the crafts market, the food here can rival that of any of its competitors.

Bratwurst-Häusle, Rathausplatz 1. With its huge chimney for grilling the sausages smoking over the main square, this is the most famous of the group: in spite of the restricted menu and frequent tourist hordes, it really shouldn't be missed.

Bratwurst-Röslein, Obstmarkt 1. Has a full, fairly upmarket menu in addition to the traditional sausage fare.

Other Restaurants

Böhms Herrenkeller, Theatergasse 19. Popular old wine bar-cum-restaurant.

Frankens U-Bahn, Pilotystr. 73 (tram #4 to Juvenellstrasse). Combines reasonably priced food with a good atmosphere.

Heilig-Geist-Spital, Spitalgasse 12. Occupying the medieval hospital, this is arguably the city's most atmospheric restaurant; the food is outstanding too.

Kettensteg, Kettensteg (bus #36 to Hallertor). Traditional *Gasthaus* with picturesque beer garden by the River Pegnitz.

Nassauer Keller, Karolinenstr. 2. Highly-rated restaurant in the cellars of Nürnberg's oldest house.

Palais Schaumburg, Kernstr. 46 (U-Bahn to Gostenhof). Offers excellent meals – including an extensive and inexpensive vegetarian menu – plus a beer garden.

Pele-Mele, Grossweidenmühlstr. 17 (bus #34 to Grossweidenmühlstrasse). Presents a choice of riverside beer garden or cool vaulted cellar in which to have your meal.

Zig-Zag, Rohledererstr. 6 (tram #6 to Hallerstrasse). Excellent Spanish meals in a bar-type setting.

Zum Peter, Regensburger Str. 51 (tram #4 to Peterskirche). Varied menu, including good vegetarian dishes, as well as a beer garden.

Bars

Cosmopolitan, Johannisstr. 40 (tram #6 to Hallerstrasse; Tues–Sun 6pm–1am). Serves excellent cocktails and a few snacks.

Freudenpark, Kilianstr. 125 (bus #46 to Langer Steig). Has a thirty-page drinks list that should keep you busy,

Landwehr, Schlotfegergasse 36 (U-Bahn to Weisser Turm). Good choice for late-night drinking (and eating); also has occasional live music.

O'Neill's, Bärenschanzstr. 121 (U-Bahn to Bärenschanze). The local Irish pub, situated well off the beaten track.

Vogel-Bar, Pirkheimerstr. 7 (tram #9 to Friedrich-Ebert-Platz). Set in a superb Art Deco interior, serving a choice of 160 cocktails to a very yuppie clientele.

Werkstatt, Adam-Klein-Str. 87 (U-Bahn to Maximilianstrasse). A real oddity: features spare car parts for interior design, and beer served out of a petrol pump.

Cafés and café-bars

Balazzo Brozzi, Hochstr. 2 (tram #4 to Obere Turnstrasse). Good place to start the day if you want a choice of cheap and decent breakfast dishes.

Meisengeige, Innerer-Laufer-Gasse 37 (bus #36 to Innerer-Laufer-Platz). Tiny café-bar catering for a mixed and unpretentious crowd; there's also a small cinema attached that runs an off-beat selection of films you won't find in the commercial venues.

Mohr, Färberstr. 3 (U-Bahn to Weisser Turm). Traditional (if far from cheap) café which serves excellent crêpes.

Ruhestörung, Tetzelgasse 21 (bus #47 to Rathaus). One of the main young and trendy watering-holes, always worth looking into.

Music bars

Rock-Café Brown Sugar, Marientorgraben 3 (tram #13 to Marientor). Best of the city's seemingly endless number of heavy metal bars, with pinball machines and videos amongst the heady attractions.

Schmelztiegel, Bergstr. 21 (tram #4 to Tiergärtnertor). Jazz bar which plays predominantly Dixieland.

Starclub, Maxtorgraben 33 (bus #47 to Maxtor). Combination of a music bar and traditional beer haven, complete with garden.

Steps, Johannisstr. 83 (bus #34 to Brückenstrasse). Jazz bar which plays anything but Dixieland.

Zabo-Linde, Zerzabelshofer Hauptstr. 28 (bus #43 or #44 to Zerzabelshof/Mitte). Both a traditional *Gaststätte* with beer garden and a regular venue for live music, ranging from rock to disco. Worth making the trip out for, if the evening's music programme appeals. Check in the *Plärrer*, Nürnberg's listings magazine (see *Listings*).

Nightclubs

Amico, Köhnstr. 53 (tram #13 to Widhalmstrasse; Sun–Wed 9pm–2am, Fri–Sat 9pm–3am). Gay disco-bar with a tiny dance floor.

Comeback, Engelhardgasse 2/Ottostrasse (U-Bahn to Weisser Turm; daily 8pm–4am; DM5). Another gay hangout, this is a disco during the summer, a very expensive *Pilsbar* at other times.

Das Boot, Hafenstr. 500 (bus #67 to Rotterdamer Strasse; Sun–Thurs 8pm–4am, Fri 8pm–8am, Sat 8pm–9am; DM3 weekdays, DM10 weekends). Nürnberg's most unusual venue: as the name suggests, this was a ship whose three decks have been converted into a disco. In compensation for the weekend prices, your ticket entitles you to DM6 off your first drink.

Dröhnland, Humboldtstr. 116 (U-Bahn to Aufsessplatz; daily 7pm–1am; DM5). Cosy place offering TV, video games and pinball machines, which is popular with people who like going to nightclubs without having to make too much of an effort. Also serves food.

Lonestar, Felsenstr. 5 (bus #67 to Grosskraftwerk; daily 7pm-3am; charge for live gigs only). Plays country and western fare, catering mainly for the American GIs from the nearby base in Fürth.

Mach 1, Kaiserstr. 1–9 (U-Bahn to Lorenzkirche; Wed–Sun 9pm–4am; reckon on about DM10 to get in). Currently the city's trendiest venue; the four different bars ensure variety, and there are some good lighting effects.

Culture and festivals

The main **theatre** venue, with the *Opernhaus* and the *Schauspielhaus*, is at Richard-Wagner-Platz, just a few minutes' walk to the west of the Hauptbahnhof. **Concerts**, notably those by the *Nürnberger Symphoniker*, are held at the *Meistersingerhalle*, some 2km southeast of the centre. Nürnberg really comes alive in the summer when **open-air music festivals and concerts** abound. A special calendar entitled *Sommer in Nürnberg* is available from the tourist board, and tickets are available from *AZ-Kartenvorverkauf*, Winklerstr. 15, *Karstadt-Kartenvorverkauf*, An der Lorenzkirche 2, and *Kartenvorverkauf Werner*, Bretie Gasse 47.

The season starts off in late May with **Musica Franconia**, a week-long series of concerts of old music played on period instruments. For a fortnight in June, the **Kulturzirkus**, an international theatre festival, is held. Towards the end of the same month begins the three-week-long **Internationale Orgelwoche**, featuring organ recitals in the city's churches and in the *Meistersingerhalle*; the office for information and tickets is at Bismarkstr. 46 (☎163528). The **Bardentreffen** in the last week of July or first week of August is a popular annual event where singers and songwriters from Europe come together in free open-air concerts all over the city. An equally high status is enjoyed by the **Ost-West Jazzfestival** in the last week of October, which encompasses every jazz style and brings together musicians from around the world.

Prominent among folklore festivals is the **Altstadtfest** at the end of September, a local fair celebrating Franconian culture, with lots of food and drink, as well as river tournaments and a procession in traditional costumes. Finally, with a 400-year tradition, the Nürnberg **Christkindlesmarkt** (Christmas market) held on the Hauptmarkt from 25 November until 24 December, is the largest and most popular in Germany, as well as being the founder of what has become very much a national institution, with derivatives found in every town of any size. It stands apart from its imitators by the wealth of handmade quality goods on sale, such as toys, brass utensils and tin soldiers, glass objects of all kinds, and, of course, the delicious *Lebkuchen*.

Listings

Airport ☎3506 200 for flight information.

Car hire *Avis Rent-a-Car* (airport, ☎49696 or ☎528966); *Hertz* (airport, Untere Grasergasse 25, ☎209086 or ☎527719); *ES Europa-Service*, Fürther Str. 31 (☎260308).

Hospital Flurstr. 17 (☎3980; U-Bahn to Ostenhof, then bus #34 heading towards Rathenauerplatz).

Laundry On the corner of Obstmarkt and Bindergasse.

Mitfahrzentrale Allersbergerstr. 31a (☎446 9666).

Medical emergencies Kesslerplatz (☎533771).

Post Restante Bahnhofsplatz 1.

Taxis (☎20555).

What's on Consult either the *Monatsmagazin* (DM2), available from the tourist office, or the *Plärrer* magazine (DM3), on sale at any kiosk.

Women's bookshop Innerer Kleinreuther Weg 28 (Mon–Fri 10am–6pm, Sat 10am–1pm).

Women's centre Saldorferstr. 6 (☎263309; U-Bahn to Gostenhof). Runs an evening bar on Tuesday, Friday and Saturday.

Erlangen

Just 20km north of Nürnberg, and regarded as an integral part of its conurbation, **ERLANGEN** is nevertheless itself a major city, with its own distinctive history, traditions and appearance. On the revocation of the Edict of Nantes in 1683, ending religious toleration in France, a large number of Huguenots settled here at the invitation of Margrave Christian Ernst of Bayreuth. A **planned town** of regular streets and squares in the sober Baroque style then current in Protestant circles was built to accommodate them; this was extended to cover the whole of the city when the medieval Altstadt was destroyed by fire twenty years later. The Huguenots, skilled in textiles and leather crafts, established Erlangen's reputation as a major industrial centre, a tradition maintained today by electro-technics and power engineering. Indeed, Erlangen might be regarded almost as a company town of Siemens, were it not for the presence of the University, founded in 1743 and now shared with Nürnberg. The presence of so many students ensures an almost continuously lively atmosphere, and makes what might otherwise seem a place of specialist appeal into one seriously worth considering as an alternative base to its famous and more expensive neighbour.

Around town

Arriving at the **Bahnhof**, at the western side of town, you're immediately confronted with the quarter of the original refugees. Across Bahnhofplatz stand the parish administration buildings of the **Hugenottenkirche**, which fronts the eponymous square on the far side. Outside, it appears as a plain box, enlivened only by the tower which was added a generation after the main body of the building. Inside, the wooden galleries have been arranged to give the illusion that the church is round in shape; otherwise, the pulpit provides the only decorative touch. Across Hugenottenplatz is the **Universitätskirche**, which has a similar tower but is otherwise less austere, its double-galleried hall interior being enlivened with rich stucco work. A fine group of eighteenth-century houses, including the old pharmacy, stand around the church.

A couple of blocks to the north, divided by the pedestrian section of the central Hauptstrasse, are two more important squares. To the west is Marktplatz, on whose southern side is the **Stutterheimsches Palais**, formerly the Rathaus, now the public library and main local cultural centre. Across the road is Schlossplatz, in the centre of which is a statue to Margrave Friedrich, the founder of the University. The **Schloss** itself, which takes up the entire eastern side of the square, is now the University's administrative headquarters. Despite Erlangen's association with technology, its academic tradition has been strongest in the humanities. Three of Germany's best-known nineteenth-century philosophers – Fichte, Schelling and Feuerbach – taught there. However, the most famous professor was the Orientalist **Friedrich Rückert**, who introduced poetry based on Persian, Sanskrit and Chinese models into the

German language. Schubert and Brahms were among the composers who set his texts, while Mahler's kaleidoscopic song cycles *Rückert-Lieder* and *Kindertotenlieder* have raised his artistic standing to a level far beyond its purely literary merit.

Some compensation for the fact that the Schloss' original interiors were lost in a fire last century is the **Schlosspark** to the rear. The first part of this is a formal French garden, closed off by the horseshoe-shaped **Orangerie** to the north, and with the **Hugenottenbrunnen** – a large allegorical fountain which is the town's one example of the extravagance of forms normally associated with the Baroque style – as centrepiece. Further reaches of the park are laid out in the English manner; tucked away in the middle is an equestrian memorial to Margrave Christian Ernst.

Immediately north of the Schloss is the **Wasserturm**, which served as the student prison for most of last century (see p.308). Northeast of here is Theaterplatz, whose south side is lined by the three buildings primarily responsible for Erlangen's continued high standing in the dramatic field. The **Markgrafentheater**, indeed, is the town's finest feature, a Rococo jewel worthy of Bayreuth itself and still put to regular use. Alongside it stand the **Redoutensaal**, built as the main festival hall of the local Margraves, and the **Marstall** (stables), now the home of the experimental *Theater in der Garage*. North of here, at the top end of Haupstrasse, is the **Dreifaltigkeitskirche**, originally the parish church of the Altstadt, but rebuilt in the Lutheran Baroque style of its two counterparts in the new town. Its most distinctive feature is the way the pulpit and altar are combined into a single unit.

Beyond the built-up area are the ample open spaces of the **Burgberg**, the main public park. For eleven days up to and including Pentecost (variable date in May/June) each year, this is the site of the **Bergkirchweih**, one of Bavaria's leading folk festivals. It's rather like a smaller version of Munich's Oktoberfest, with orgies of beer drinking in massive tents, hairy funfair rides, and performances of traditional and rock music. However, it has the advantage of being less blatantly commercialised and thus more authentically German, and of having all the attractions concentrated in a manageable area.

Practicalities

The **tourist office** (☎09131/25074) is beyond the southern end of Hauptstrasse at Rathausplatz 1. Erlangen really scores in its range of accommodation options. There's a **youth hostel** right in the heart of town at Südliche Stadtmauerstr. 35 (☎09131/862255 or 862274), while the **campsite**, which is open all year round, is only a short walk to the rear of the Bahnhof at Wöhrmühle 6 (☎09131/28499). At the same address is a hotel, *Regnitz-Stuben* (☎09131/25303), charging DM35 for singles, DM55 for doubles. Broadly similar rates are available at a couple of places with an even more central location: *Drei Könige*, Dreikönigstr. 2 (☎09131/25159), and *Oppelei*, Halbmondstr. 4 (☎09131/21562). The latter has a well-regarded **restaurant**; another good choice is *Grüner Markt*, just off Marktplatz at Einhornstr. 9. Plenty of **student bars** and **discos** can also be found dotted all over the town centre.

Ansbach

ANSBACH, 50km southwest of Nürnberg, wears a grand air which is quite disproportionate to its small size: having chosen the town as their home, the local margraves were keen to have a seat of suitable splendour, and over the centuries Ansbach became quite polished, its streets characterised by Renaissance and Baroque buildings. Alongside its architecture, Ansbach has gone down in the annals of German history as the site of the unsolved murder of enigmatic **Kaspar Hauser** (see box), Europe's most notorious foundling.

THE MYSTERY OF KASPAR HAUSER

One day in 1828, a plainly dressed, bewildered-looking youth turned up in the streets of Nürnberg, carrying two letters addressed to the authorities. One was from a labourer who claimed to have guarded him for the past sixteen years, albeit in conditions of close confinement; the other purported to be from his natural mother, stating that his deceased father had been a cavalry officer. The boy gave his name as **Kaspar Hauser**, but he was unable to tell anyone where he came from, shunned all nourishment except for bread and water, and seemed to lack all knowledge of external objects. His appearance caused an immediate sensation in the local press; this soon spread across Germany and beyond, fuelled by the burgeoning interest in psychology and the abnormal. There were all kinds of wild speculations as to his origins: one theory that was particularly popular was that he was the eldest son of Grand Duke Carl Ludwig of Baden, who had been kidnapped by order of his step-mother, though this seemed to be disproved by evidence that the child in question had died in infancy. In due course Kaspar was educated and proved to be highly intelligent and creative. He moved to Ansbach in 1831, becoming clerk to the president of the court of appeal. Just as he seemed to be falling out of the limelight, he met his violent death there two years later. His murderer was never found, adding a final unsettling mystery to his life story: many suspected that he had died by his own hand. Much has been written about him since, little of it conclusive.

The centre

The **Residenzschloss** (daily 9am–noon and 2–5pm; DM3) is situated just on the edge of the old town centre, and is best-known for its Rococo interior. Highlights are the high-ceilinged ballroom, the *Spiegelkabinett* (Cabinet of Mirrors), and the *Fayencenzimmer* (Porcelain Gallery), which displays thousands of delicately designed tiles made in the local factory. Just across the road the **Hofgarten** and **Orangerie** form a pleasant setting for walks along paths lined by centuries-old trees. It was in this park in 1833 that poor Kaspar Hauser received fatal stab wounds, and just next to the Orangerie is a stone memorial with the inscription: "Here died a man unknown by means unknown". The local **Markgrafenmuseum** on Schaitbergerstrasse (Tues–Sun 10am–noon and 2–5pm; DM1) documents the story of his life and times in a comprehensive fashion, though you'll need to have some German to get the most from the exhibition.

Right in the middle of the old town centre is the church of St **Gumbertus**. Originally it was part of a Romanesque Benedictine monastery, but the only remainder from that period is the **crypt** (Fri–Sun 11am–noon and 3–5pm). Just off the Gothic chancel is the **Schwanenritterordenkapelle**, containing the elaborate tombs of members of the Order of the Swan, a lay foundation of the local margraves. The **nave** was remodelled in the eighteenth century into a vast preaching hall according to the restrained Lutheran tastes of the day. It's a classic among German Protestant churches – all slate grey and cream, without paintings or side altars, it presents a cool clarity. The focus is the small marble altar, and above it the pulpit marks the only splash of gold in the whole interior. Encircling the church on three sides is a gallery, which is the best vantage-point from which to get an impression of the complete effect.

Festivals and practicalities

A number of **festivals** take place in Ansbach, of which the best-known is the *Bach-Woche*, which occurs every two years at the end of July. Concerts are held in St Gumbertus, which has excellent acoustics. The *Ansbacher Rokokospiele* are period plays performed in the Residenzschloss and the local parks at the beginning of July each year. Held every four years (next in 1994), the *Heimatfest* is a grand occasion where eighteenth-century music and dance play the most important part, but there's also a fair with plenty of regional delicacies.

For enquiries about these, visit the **tourist office** in the Rathaus on Martin-Luther-Platz (Mon–Fri 8.30am–12.30pm and 2–5pm; ☎0981/51243). A couple of reasonably-priced central **hotels**, both just a few streets north of the Hofgarten, are *Schwarzes Ross*, Schlossstr. 21 (☎0981/86507) with singles at DM27 and doubles at DM45, and *Birnbaum*, Nürnberger Str. 35 (☎0981/94379), with singles at DM40 and doubles starting at DM65. For **eating and drinking** try *Der Platengarten*, Promenade 30, (in the town centre), which does good Franconian specialities.

Bayreuth

Situated about 80km northeast of Nürnberg within easy reach of several of Franconia's most scenic areas, polished and respectable **BAYREUTH** enjoys its reputation as one of the great cultural centres of Europe. Except for the festival period during late July and the first three weeks in August, it's a quiet provincial town, whose fame is due to a series of imported creative spirits. First of these was the eighteenth-century **Margravine Wilhelmine**. One of Frederick the Great's sisters, she was intended for the English royal throne, but her father was diplomatically inept and messed up her chances, so she got stuck with the notoriously boring Margrave Friedrich. Instead of settling down to obscurity, however, Wilhelmine set about creating a lively court, hiring Europe's best architects, artists and musicians to transform her surroundings into something more elegant and sophisticated. A century later, **Richard Wagner** decided to settle in Bayreuth because the town offered to build him a stage large enough to put on his grand-scale opera productions. The impetus generated by him was tremendous, and Bayreuth's opera festival has been rightly famous ever since. Although the festival – like everything else to do with Wagner – was tarnished by association with Hitler's patronage and exploitation for propaganda purposes, it continues to flourish as one of the great annual events of the music world.

The town centre

Margravine Wilhelmine's proudest legacy is the **Markgräfliches Opernhaus** (guided tours Tues–Sun 9–11.30am and 1.30–4.30pm; DM2) on Opernstrasse in the heart of town. Erected in the 1740s by Guiseppe and Carlo Galli da Bibiena of the great Bolognese dynasty of theatre-designers, it's unobtrusively built to blend in with the general contours of the street, keeping its glamour for the interior, which is entirely of wood and painted in dusky greens, blues, browns and gold. This subdued elegance makes for a fascinating contrast with the gaudy glitter of its Munich counterpart, the Cuvilliéstheater. Equally rich in shape and form, the very different execution of the Baroque style here is not just a mark of Wilhelmine's influence, but also of the prevailing Lutheran taste which had established itself in Bayreuth in the sixteenth century. Although Wagner found it too small for his purposes, it makes an ideal venue for eighteenth-century opera, of which there's a separate annual **festival** at the end of May.

Immediately to the west stands the **Schlosskirche**, a Baroque hall church erected in the following decade. Painted in a delicate pink and adorned with tasteful stucco-work, it contains, in an oratory beneath the organ, the tombs of Wilhelmine and her husband. Alongside, dominated by its octagonal Renaissance tower, is the **Altes Schloss**. Much of this palace was accidentally burnt down in 1753 by the unfortunate Margrave Friedrich with a misplaced candle.

Just to the south, at Kanzleistr. 1, is the **Stadtmuseum** (July and Aug Mon–Fri 10am–5pm; rest of year Tues–Fri 10am–5pm; DM2). Its displays concentrate mainly on the eighteenth century, with collections of fine local porcelain and glazed beer mugs, rustic furniture and weapons, as well as exhibits relating to the Bayreuth margraves.

From here, a short detour can be made to the **Maisel-Brauerei** (guided tours daily at 10am) at Kulmbacher Str. 40, a steam-powered brewery of 1887 still in perfect working order. Although production has been moved to a modern plant next door, its highly individual steam beer (*Dampfbier*) is its main line. This, along with all the other beers made here, can be sampled at the adjoining bar.

The Hofgarten

At the northwestern end of the Hofgarten, which lies south of the Altes Schloss, is the replacement **Neues Schloss** (guided tours Tues–Sun 10–11.30am and 1.30–4.30pm; DM3). Wilhelmine succeeded here in creating something all her own and each room is different, ranging from the ballroom in white, gold and blue, to the *Japanisches Zimmer* (Japanese Room), grottoes and a striking wood-panelled dining-room. Best of all is the *Spiegelzimmer* (Mirror Room), lined from top to bottom with broken and uneven shapes, as if put together from several broken mirrors. Based on a personal design by Wilhelmine, it's thought to be her comment on the false glamour of her age, too concerned with appearances. Her other personal stamp is the split-tailed dragon motif, which was her favourite emblem and appears throughout the palace in different sizes and materials.

The Richard-Wagner-Museum

To the east stands the sternly Neoclassical **Villa Wahnfried**, now the **Richard-Wagner-Museum** (daily 9am–5pm; DM2.50, DM3.50 in July and Aug). Wagner had this built to his own designs as his Bayreuth home: its enigmatic name literally means "peace from delusion". The interior was well tuned to cosy middle-class life, centred around a large sitting-room-cum-concert-room for the composer. This was the setting

---

RICHARD WAGNER (1813–83)

As the annual crowds to Bayreuth testify, no composer – with the possible exception of Mozart – has a more loyal, not to say adoring, following than **Richard Wagner**. His influence on musical history is also unsurpassed: his operas were revolutionary in their approach, using a recurring theme, or *leitmotiv*, for programmatic purposes, and varying it to depict psychoanalytical developments; he expanded the orchestral palette (including the invention of the Wagner tuba) to create a more sumptuous sound than had ever previously been heard; and he developed a new harmonic language in which rich chromaticism predominates. Apart from a few early works and occasional pieces, Wagner's output consists of lengthy "music dramas", all but one of them based on heroic love themes drawn from Germanic mythology. In these, he attempted to fuse all the arts: not only did he compose the music, he chose the plots and the associated symbolism, wrote the libretti, and took an active role in staging and presentation.

Representing the Romantic approach to the arts at its most extreme, Wagner was a dreamer whose ambitions were only realised courtesy of the patronage of his equally unworldly soul-mate, King Ludwig II of Bavaria. For all his accomplishments, he was always a controversial figure, and even today he remains a composer whose stature is disputed far more than any other: despite the legions of adulators, many music lovers of otherwise catholic tastes listen only to fragments of his works, if they listen to them at all. This is not simply a question of Wagner's excessive nationalism and virulent anti-Semitism, which made the appropriation of his music by the Nazis inevitable. To all but the most initiated, his texts are mere doggerel, while his music is long-winded and repetitive, a point encapsulated in one of the famous asides made by the conductor Sir Thomas Beecham: "We've been playing for two solid hours and we're playing this bloody tune still!"

for Wagner's famed soirées, attended by intellectuals, musicians and royalty alike. His wife Cosima was the daughter of another famous composer, Franz Liszt, and the combination of the couple's backgrounds and interests made the household an important focus of German cultural life. Theirs was also one of the most famous love stories of the nineteenth century (he lured her from her first husband, the conductor Hans von Bülow, who was sufficiently stoic about the affair to maintain his role as the leading contemporary interpreter of Wagner's music), and they lie buried together in the villa's garden.

The Deutsches-Freimaurer-Museum

Likewise in the Hofgarten is the **Deutsches-Freimaurer-Museum** (Tues–Fri 10am–noon and 2–4pm, Sat 10am–noon; DM2), an intriguing museum dedicated to the Freemasons. They're represented here as a sort of collective peace movement rather than anything sinister, and the library of some 12,000 volumes is an important centre for research. It's revealing to see just how many well-known people were Freemasons, including Harry S. Truman, Churchill, Frederick the Great, Dickens, Goethe, Haydn and Mozart. The movement has its origins in seventeenth-century England and Scotland, where it was originally a society for stonemasons. Hence the grades of membership still relate to that trade, and a new member is called a "rough stone", who is to live by the motto of "introspection".

The Festspielhaus

Set on a little hill at the far northern end of town (from the Hauptbahnhof, go along Bürgerreuther Strasse in the opposite direction from the town centre) is the **Festspielhaus** (guided tours Tues–Sun 10–11.30am and 1.30–3pm; closed Oct; DM3), the custom-built theatre for the performance of Wagner's music dramas. Although designed by Gottfried Semper, the leading German architect of the day, it's remarkable far less for its merits as a building than for its unique acoustics – one reason people are prepared to pay silly prices to attend the annual summer festival. The theatre was inaugurated in 1876, when the *Ring Cycle* was performed in its entirety for the first time; ever since, nothing but Wagner's operas have been performed. After the composer's death in 1882, his widow Cosima ensured that the annual festival continued, and various family members have been in charge ever since. It was during his English daughter-in-law Winifred's "reign" from 1931 to 1944 that the festival had the unfortunate honour of Hitler's patronage, and he stayed as her house-guest whenever he came to Bayreuth. Wagner buffs still argue over the extent to which she should be blamed for the misappropriation of Wagner's music during the Nazi era, but the arguments have now lost much of their relevance and the focus is back on the musical productions, now run by Wolfgang Wagner.

Such is the demand for **tickets** that you need to write the year before you wish to visit to: *Kartenbüro, Festspeilleitung Bayreuth*, Postfach 10062, 8580 Bayreuth. Otherwise, the only realistic chance of getting to see a performance is by being part of a special festival package tour from abroad.

The Eremitage

Lying 4km east of town, and reached by bus #2 from Marktplatz, is the curious **Eremitage** (guided tours Tues–Sun 9–11.30am and 1–4.30pm; DM2). The place has its origins in the eighteenth-century fad of the nobility for playing at asceticism by occasionally staying in sparse monks' cells and eating nothing but soup. But when the original hermitage was given to Wilhelmine as a birthday present, she proceeded to build a glamorous retreat set in landscaped gardens decorated by fountains and pools, with live peacocks adding the final touches to her quirky vision of retreat as perfect indulgence. The old hermitage still stands, and some of the excessively bare cells remain. Wilhelmine's **Sonnentempel** is built at a small distance at the highest point of its romantic park. Designed in a horseshoe shape and fronted by arcades lined with pillars, the whole thing is completely encrusted with glass mosaics that sparkle madly in the sun. It seems horribly gaudy by modern standards, and the only way to appreciate it at all is to stand back slightly so that the multitude of glittery colours doesn't overwhelm. In accordance with the fashion of the times, there's also a small artificial ruin which was used as an open-air theatre, where even Wilhelmine took to the stage, often with her friend Voltaire.

Practical details

Bayreuth's **tourist office** is just to the north of the Altes Schloss at Luitpoldplatz 9 (Mon–Sat 9am–6pm; ☎0921/22015). The **youth hostel**, Universitätsstr. 28 (☎0921/25262) isn't particularly central, but the bus service (#4 from the Bahnhof) is regular since it's almost next door to the University. Otherwise the cheapest **hotels** charge in the region of DM25–45 for singles and DM50–80 for doubles. Most convenient is *Schindler*, Bahnhofstr. 9 (☎0921/26249), while not far away is *Zum Herzog*, Kulmbacherstr. 2 (☎0921/41334). In a quiet quarter near the centre of town, the *Gasthof Goldener Löwe*, Kulmbacherstr. 30 (☎0921/41046) is very cosy and serves great food and local beers.

Around Bayreuth

Not the least of Bayreuth's attractions is its proximity to three of Franconia's most scenic areas. At least parts of each of these are relatively little known, and make a refreshing alternative to the province's more obvious tourist attractions, particularly if you fancy a spot of hiking.

Franconian Switzerland

The pear-shaped area bounded by the rivers Regnitz, Pegnitz and Main is popularly known as **Franconian Switzerland** (*Frankische Schweiz*): as well as Bayreuth, Erlangen and Bamberg are possible jumping-off points for its exploration. More sparsely forested than the ranges surrounding it because of the infertile Jurassic ground, Franconian Switzerland has an abundance of varied natural attractions such as strange rock formations, lonely high plateaux and stalactite caves. While poor quality soil also accounts for the low population, the region nevertheless has a plethora of castles, usually perched on conical hills above tightly packed villages or overlooking picturesque valleys.

From Bayreuth, the easiest approach by public transport is to take a train south to PEGNITZ, then continue westwards by bus. A good base base for exploring the region is castle-crowned **POTTENSTEIN**, some 20km away, where there's a **youth hostel** at Jugendherbergsstr. 20 (☎09243/1224), along with a **campsite** (☎09243/206). This is the nearest village to the most impressive of the caves, the **Teufelshöhle** (guided tours April–Oct daily 8am–6pm; Nov–March Tues and Wed 10am–noon, Sun 1.30–3.30pm; DM3), which lie a couple of kilometres to the southeast.

The star of the region is the little market town of **GÖSSWEINSTEIN**, perched high above the valley of the River Wiesent 9km to the west. It's also a pilgrimage centre, and the **Wallfahrtskirche** is a masterly creation by Balthasar Neumann, given a distinctive note by the pyramidal high altar. The Burg provides a second focus to the town; from here you can follw the paths to the **Marienfelsen**, a series of cliffs punctuated by belvederes offering wonderful views over the valley and beyond. At the western edge of Gössweinstein, at Etzdorfer Str. 142 (☎09242/259), is another **youth hostel**.

From here, you can follow the Wiesent towards its confluence with the Regnitz at **FORCHHEIM**, some 20km north of Erlangen on the main rail line to Bamberg. The town itself is attractive: the Pfarrkirche and the moated Pfalz both date back to the fourteenth century, while there are many half-timbered houses. A few kilometres east is the **Walberla**, a flat-topped hill which is the region's main "peak". It's traditionally dedicated to Saint Walpurgis, and, on the first Sunday of May, is the site of one of Franconia's best festivals, when thousands gather for the annual *Volksfest* and an orgy of beer and food. The villages around here, such as KIRCHEHRENBERG, LEUTENBERG and HUNDSHAUPTEN, are well-known in their own right for having some of the best country *Gaststätten* in the region.

The Fichtelgebirge

The **Fichtelgebirge** ("Spruce Mountains") just east of Bayreuth are not really as mountainous as their name would imply, but rather a craggy landscape of crumbling granite hills, wildly romantic and full of bubbling streams and large areas of forest interspersed with highland moors. Three trains run daily from Bayreuth to WARMENSTEINACH. The **youth hostel** at Haus no. 42 (☎09277/249) in the adjacent village of OBERWARMENSTEINACH would be a good base for hiking. Other accommodation in local farms and guesthouses in the region can be arranged at the regional **tourist office** at Bayreuthestr. 4 (☎09272/6255) in FICHTELBERG, a further 6km west, while just to the north of this village, on the banks of the Fichtelsee, is the **campsite** (☎09272/270). All these places offer easy access to the most popular of the "mountains", the **Ochsenkopf** (1024m). Unfortunately, this is marred by a huge television tower on top, along with a cable car and the attendant commercial trappings.

To see the best of the Fichtelgebirge, you really have to head further west. The strangest landscape the range has to offer is what's known as the **Luisenburg** near WUNSIEDEL, 12km from Fichtelberg. Again the name is misleading, as there's no castle here but instead a kind of rocky sea of granite blocks, eroded over the years to look like some giant child's pebbles left strewn untidily across the countryside. Its natural drama makes it a perfect open-air theatre, whose possibilities are put to full use in an annual summer season of plays.

The Franconian Forest

Until 1989, the **Franconian Forest** (*Frankenwald*), the extreme northeastern corner of the province, was one of the least-known corners of western Germany. Hemmed in on three sides by the GDR and deprived of access to neighbouring communities, it wore an air of neglect and consequently saw few tourists. Now that the border has reopened, the area is being regenerated and will profit from its proximity to the well developed Thuringian Forest.

Kulmbach

Situated on the extreme western fringe of the forest, **KULMBACH** was sufficiently far from the border to escape the blight from which the rest of the region suffered. It predated Bayreuth, which is only 25km distant, as the seat of the local margraves, and their vast fortified castle, the **Plassenburg** (April–Sept Tues–Sun 10am–4.30pm; Oct–March 10am–3.30pm; DM2.50) still rises high above the town. Given the feudal austerity of its outline, the main courtyard, known as the **Schöner Hof**, comes as a complete surprise. One of the richest creations of the German Renaissance, it bristles with intricate carvings, including medallion portraits of the Hohenzollerns. Because the Plassenburg was used as a prison throughout the nineteenth century, very little of the original interior remains. Some state rooms have been restored, but its main function nowadays is to house the **Zinnfigurenmuseum**, thought to be the world's largest collection of tin figurines, comprising some 300,000 individual pieces.

Back down in the town, the main attraction is the **beer**: in medieval times, everyone who became a citizen of Kulmbach automatically received the right to brew their own beer, and the town remains a major brewery centre, with an astonishing variety of products. The *Eisbock* of the *Reichelbräu* is a powerful ice beer; the *Schwarzbier* of the old monastic *Klosterbräu* is one of Germany's best dark beers; while *EKU*'s *Kulminator 28* claims to be the strongest brew in the world. A major **festival** is held annually in late July/early August, but the beers can be sampled all year round at the *Gaststätten* of the breweries, of which *Stadtschänke*, Holzmarkt 3 and *EKU-Inn*, Klostergasse 7 are in the town centre.

Coburg

COBURG, which lies about 50km northwest of Kulmbach, was one of the towns most affected by the postwar division of Germany. Capital of an independent duchy for nearly four centuries, the ruling house of Saxe-Coburg had been masterly at self-promotion: in the nineteenth century its clever dynastic marriage policy had resulted in family ties with ruling royal families in Belgium, Bulgaria and Portugal as well as with the star prize of Britain. This was achieved when **Albert of Saxe-Coburg-Gotha** married his first cousin, Queen Victoria, thus establishing the present ruling dynasty of Britain, tactfully renamed as the House of Windsor during World War I. When the last duke abdicated in 1920, the locals voted for union with Bavaria, despite the lack of any previous political connections. This proved to be a fortuitous choice, as it saved Coburg from the fate of all the other old Saxon-Thuringian principalities, which were incorporated into the GDR after World War II. However, refugees flocked over the border to the town which, almost inevitably, became one of the main rallying points of neo-Nazism and a place noted for its disquieting atmsophere and backward economy. With a bit of luck, the re-opening of access to its traditional hinterland and markets will help end this unsavoury situation, as Coburg is a handsome town which deserves to attract more visitors.

Around town

The **Veste Coburg**, the great castle that gives the town its name, is one of the largest remaining medieval fortresses in Germany. Towering high above the valley, it dates back in part at least as far as the twelfth century, though most of the present massive structure of twin walls and inner courts was built when the independent duchy was created in the sixteenth century. The inner court is made up of four main buildings and the part known as the **Hohes Haus** (April–Oct Tues–Sun 9.30am–1pm and 2–5pm; Nov–March Tues–Sun 2–5pm; DM2.50) is home to a very extensive collection of art, glassware, weapons and an historical exhibition. Most famous is the 300,000-strong collection of graphics, which can only ever be partially displayed and includes work by Rembrandt, Dürer and Cranach. In 1530, the year of his heresy trial, Martin Luther took refuge in the Veste for a while and found time to write no fewer than sixteen works on the issues arising from the Reformation. He stayed in the building known as the **Fürstenbau** (guided tours April–Oct Tues–Sun 9.30am–noon and 2–4pm; Nov–March Tues–Sun at 2pm, 2.45pm and 3.30pm; DM3.50), where his room is preserved. Look out too for the portrait gallery of the illustrious Saxe-Coburgs.

The Schloss Ehrenburg

The dukes didn't actually live in the Veste: they chose, in common with the fashion of the time, to live nearer their subjects in **Schloss Ehrenburg** (guided tours Tues–Sun at 10am, 11am, 1.30pm, 2.30pm & 3.30pm; also at 4.30pm in summer; DM2.50) in the town centre. Considering that this wasn't a royal household itself, the palace is incredibly rich and sumptuous in its interior design, with precious tapestries lining walls and intricate parquet floors made to different designs in each room. The furnishings too are priceless pieces collected from all over Europe, and there are even modern gadgets such as Germany's first flushing toilet in the room in which Queen Victoria used to stay. Also of special note is the chapel attached to the palace, a fine example of Lutheran Baroque whose no-frills interior has been beautifully restored.

Around the Marktplatz

Just to the west of here is the central **Marktplatz**, lined with handsome Renaissance buildings erected in the early years of the duchy, and with a statue of Prince Albert, paid for by his widow, in the middle. The **Rathaus** on the southern side was extensively rebuilt in Rococo style, but retains the characteristic two-storey oriel, plus the main hall on the second floor. Opposite stands the **Stadthaus**, the former government building, still in all its original splendour. Leading off the square are several streets of half-timbered houses: look out for the grandiose **Münzmeisterhaus** on Ketschengasse. Further down the same street is what's arguably the most imposing of the town's Renaissance buildings, the **Gymnasium Casimirianum**, founded with the intention of developing into a university, but which never rose beyond the status of a school.

St Moritz and Schloss Rosenau

Across from the Gymnasium is the Gothic church of **St Moritz**, which is given a distinctive appearance by its two very dissimilar towers, both capped by Baroque helmets. The chancel houses superb funerary monuments to the local sixteenth- and early seventeenth-century dukes, notably the huge alabaster memorial to Johann Friedrich II and his wife. In contrast, there's the quiet dignity of the fifteenth-century tombstone to the knight Albrecht von Bach, situated under the southern tower.

Prince Albert was born outside the town at tiny **Schloss Rosenau** (Tues–Sun 10am–noon and 1.30–4.30pm; DM2) in 1819, and spent much of his youth playing around this romantic little castle set in a wonderful park designed in the English fashion to imitate nature. There's an attractive 14km-long path leading from the Veste to the park of Rosenau and back to Coburg, which is well worth following if you've got the time to spare.

Practicalities

Coburg's **Bahnhof** is situated on the northwestern side of town; the quickest way to the centre is by going sharp left along Lossaustrasse. The **tourist office** is just off the Marktplatz at Herrngasse 4 (April–Oct Mon–Fri 9am–12.30pm and 2–7pm, Sat 9am–12.30pm; Nov–March Mon–Fri 9am–12.30pm and 2–5pm; ☎09561/95071). For a slightly more alternative view of Coburg, head for the nearby **Bürgerhaus**, which runs a daily café-bar and also functions as a general meeting point for young people and local activists. The **youth hostel**, Schloss Ketschendorf, Parkstr. 2 (☎09561/15330) is unfortunately one of the most draconian you're likely to encounter, so if at all possible you'd be better off staying in a **private house**; the tourist office can book this. Reasonable and fairly cheap **hotel** possibilities include *Gasthof Juliusturm*, Pilgramsroth 45 (☎09561/29968), with singles from DM25 and doubles from DM50; and *Gasthof Frankenbräu*, Mauer 4 (☎09561/95231), with singles DM35 and doubles DM65. Good places to **eat** and **drink** include the *Ratskeller* in the Rathaus, *Goldener Traube*, Am Viktoriabrunnen 2, and *Goldener Anker*, Rosengasse 14. In spite of its relatively small size, Coburg keeps up the strong **theatre** tradition of the court in the renamed *Landestheater* on Schlossplatz.

Banz and Vierzehnheiligen

Some 20km south of Coburg, **Kloster Banz** is perched high above the valley of the River Main. This former Benedictine monastery was begun by Leonhard Dientzenhofer in 1695. After his death, his brother Johann took over, designing the elongated church, which is richly decorated with frescos, altars and fancy woodwork. The monastic buildings now belong to the CSU who've turned the place into a grand venue for conferences and training courses for their party faithful; unless you number yourself among them, you won't be going inside.

Much more rewarding to visit is the pilgrimage church known as **Vierzehnheiligen** ("Fourteen Saints"), which faces Banz from the opposite bank. One of the most important and original Baroque churches in the country, it's generally considered to be Balthasar Neumann's supreme accomplishment. It takes its name from the legend that a shepherd had recurring visions here of Christ with the fourteen Saints of Intercession. The centrepiece of the basilica is an altar dedicated to the fourteen saints, known as the *Gnadenaltar*, around which the entire interior is designed. This gives it the unusual shape of an oval nave and short transept, with the altar taking up the central point of the transept crossing. The marble and stucco altar is built to a pyramid design, rich in Rococo curls and cherubs as well as the white marble figures of the the fourteen saints.

Bamberg

There can be no doubt about the status of **BAMBERG** as one of the most beautiful small towns not just in Germany but in the world. Its relative geographical isolation, some 60km north of Nürnberg, was a key factor in preserving its magnificent **artistic heritage** from the ravages of war. More can be learned about architectural history in a couple of days here than from weeks of studying textbooks: every single European style from the Romanesque onwards has left its mark on Bamberg, each bequeathing at least one outstanding building. For art lovers, there's the added bonus of the most marvellous array of sculpture to be found in the country.

Not the least of Bamberg's attractions is that, in contrast to Franconia's other picturesque old cities, it hasn't been mothballed into a museum-piece. It's an animated city of modern industries which profits from the youthful presence of a university. It's also one of the country's great **beer** centres: Bambergers knock back proportionately more booze than the inhabitants of any other town, being served by no fewer than ten breweries which together produce thirty different kinds of beer. Most notable is the appropriately named *Rauchbier* ("smoky beer"): made from smoked malt according to a formula developed in the sixteenth century, it's as distinctive a local brew as you'll find in Germany, leaving its own very special lingering aftertaste.

Bamberg was brought to prominence by the saintly eleventh-century **Emperor Heinrich II**, who wanted to turn it into a German metropolis on a scale and of an importance to rival Rome. Though the city has in fact never grown particularly big, it nonetheless has a sense of spacious grandeur which belies its actual size. Like the Italian capital, Bamberg is built on seven hills, pocked with belvederes which each offer a different perspective on the city. The Dom and related structures take up the entire crown of the main hill, towering high above the town to form the **Domstadt**. Unique in Germany, it was headquarters of the prince-bishopric which ruled until the Napoleonic suppression, whereupon it gave way to the purely spiritual archbishopric still based here. Clinging to the lower slopes of the valley of the River Regnitz are the residential districts which constitute an unusually complete Baroque townscape of picturesque corners, with the play of light on the river lending an extra sense of magic to the scene.

Arriving and finding somewhere to stay

Bamberg's **Bahnhof** is about fifteen minutes' walk to the northeast of the historic centre. From there, follow Luitpoldstrasse straight ahead, before turning into the third street on the right, Obere Königstrasse. Then cross the bridge over the *Rhein-Main-Donau-Kanal* and you're right in the heart of the lower town. The **tourist office** (Mon–Fri 8am–5/6pm, Sat 8am–12.30pm; ☎0951/21040) is on an island in the River Pegnitz at Geyerswörthstr. 6; it's worth noting that no charge is made for finding accommodation.

Two **youth hostels** serve Bamberg: the *Stadion*, Pödeldorferstr. 178 (☎0951/12377 or 56002; bus #2 from the Bahnhof), which is rather plain but with a handy situation, and the *Wolfsschlucht*, Oberer Leinritt 70 (☎0951/56002 or 54552; bus #1, #7 or #11 from the Bahnhof to ZOB Promenade, then change to bus #18 to Regnitzufer), which is a top-class youth hostel, pleasantly situated on the banks of the Regnitz, 2km south of the city centre. Another 2km further down the river is the local **campsite** (☎0951/56320).

Cheapest **hotels** in town are the *Wilder Mann*, Untere Sandstr. 9 (☎0951/56462) and *Zum Gabelmann*, Kesslerstr. 14, (☎0951/26676), which charge around DM25 per person, excluding breakfast. Of the more expensive alternatives, *Anita*, Kleberstr. 39, (☎0951/23533), with singles DM40 and doubles DM70, is conveniently central, while there are a couple of recommendable brewery-owned establishments on Obere Konigstrasse: *Spezial* at no.10 (☎0951/24304) charges upwards of DM35 per person, *Zum Fässla* at no.21 (☎0951/22998) from DM42. If you're thinking of staying here for longer periods, it's worth consulting the **Studentenwerk**, Austr. 37 (☎0951/203283) for advice on renting rooms in student halls over the summer.

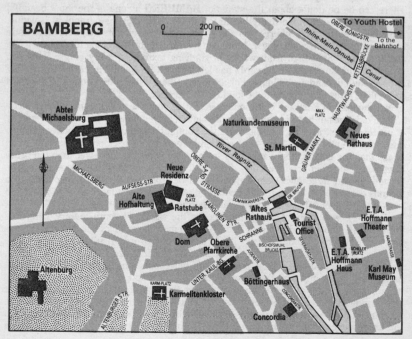

The lower city

Heart of the lower town is the **Maxplatz**, dominated by Balthasar Neumann's **Neues Rathaus**, which was originally built as a seminary. Your best bet is to use this square as a focal point for wandering around the centre and gradually head towards the Domstadt across the river. A market is held every day on Maxplatz, and the adjoining Grüner Markt stands in the shadow of **St Martin**, a huge Jesuit church designed by the Dientzenhofer brothers, who were responsible for many of the best Baroque buildings in the city. Just off the square, at Fleischstr. 2, the **Naturkundemuseum** (Mon–Fri 8am–noon and 1–5pm; DM1) is of rather specialised appeal, though an added attraction is that the collections of rare and exotic birds and other animals are displayed in beautiful Neoclassical exhibition rooms.

On an islet anchoring the Obere Brücke and Untere Brücke together is the **Altes Rathaus**, which is almost too picturesque for its own good. Except for the half-timbered section overhanging the rapids, the original Gothic building was transformed into Rococo, and its walls are busily tattooed with exuberant frescos. The famous **Klein-Venedig** ("Little Venice") of fishermen's houses is best seen from the Untere Brücke and presents one of the very few medieval scenes you'll find in the lower parts of town.

Elsewhere, the architectural character is almost completely Baroque. Walking around town the facades glow in rich ochre and russet tones, their elaborate stucco and intricate frescos unashamedly exuding the wealth of their former residents. Grandest, but perhaps a little vulgar too, is the **Böttingerhaus** at no. 14 in the Judengasse, on the western side of the Regnitz. Built by the Franconian chargé d'affaires in the early eighteenth century, it now houses a very posh restaurant and hotel. The nearby **Concordia** water-palace on the banks of the river belonged to the same man: the best time to see it is in the evenings from the opposite river bank, when the effect is heightened by its glittering reflection in the water.

Further east, at Schillerplatz 26, is the tiny **E.T.A. Hoffmann-Haus** (May–Oct Tues–Fri 4–6pm, Sat–Sun 10am–noon; DM1), which was the home of one of the foremost figures of the Romantic movement (see below). Of more slender literary interest is the **Karl May Museum** (Wed 2–5pm, Thurs–Sat 9am–noon and 2–5pm, Sun 9am–1pm; DM2), round the corner at Hainstr. 11. This houses the works of the much-translated author of countless cowboy and Indian stories along with a collection of native North American Indian weapons and tools.

ERNST THEODOR AMADEUS HOFFMANN (1776–1822)

A native of the Prussian university city of Königsberg (today called Kaliningrad), **Theodor Hoffmann** was a man of extraordinarily varied talents. For most of his life, he was employed by the civil service, but for the years he lived in Bamberg (1808–13) he tried to establish himself as a composer, conductor and theatre director, having previously failed as a painter. Music was his greatest interest, but, notwithstanding the fact that he was arguably the first truly Romantic composer, he came to realise that his genius lay with words. He developed into an unusually perspicacious music critic, then increasingly devoted himself to his real forte as an author of weird short stories that reflected his own rather schizophrenic nature. Appropriately enough, he was a constant source of inspiration to later composers: Offenbach portrayed his bizarre personality in the opera *The Tales of Hoffmann*, while his stories formed the basis for two of the great Romantic ballets, Delibes' *Coppelia* and Tchaikovsky's *The Nutcracker*. His finest works are the chillingly supernatural *The Golden Pot* from the very end of his Bamberg years, and the later *Mademoiselle de Scudéry*, which is now generally regarded as the first detective story ever written.

The Domplatz

The spacious, sloping **Domplatz** is lined with such a superb variety of buildings that it has no possible rival for the title of Germany's finest square. It unfolds like a great picture-book of architecture: with no more than a turn of the head you can see how Romanesque evolved into Gothic; and how the latter developed through various phases before giving way to the Renaissance, which in turn was supplanted by Baroque.

The Dom

Consecrated in 1012, the **Dom** (often dignified as the **Kaiserdom**) was burnt down twice in the following two centuries, and the present structure of golden sandstone is the result of a slow rebuilding process that continued throughout the thirteenth century. During this period architectural tastes were beginning to change, but the ground plan follows the precedent of the imperial cathedrals of the Rhineland in having a choir at both ends of the building, each of which is flanked by twin towers. The east chancel is dedicated to the warrior Saint George, symbolising the Empire, while its western counterpart bears a dedication to Saint Peter, representing the Papacy. These were the first and last parts of the Dom to be completed, and you can see that the rounded Romanesque arches and heavy vaults of the eastern choir had given way to the tall pointed windows and graceful ribs characteristic of early Gothic by the west end. In between, the nave was erected in the so-called Transitional style, offering a fascinating insight into the way the original masons were experimenting with the new techniques. Notwithstanding the addition of identical lead steeples during the Baroque period, the **towers** are also very different. The eastern pair are massive and heavy, whereas those to the west have a lighter, almost ethereal feel.

Inside the Dom

What makes the Kaiserdom one of Europe's greatest cathedrals is the astonishing array of **sculptural decoration**. As with the architecture, this was initially executed in an orthodox Romanesque style, the best example being the *Fürstenportal* on the nave's north side, facing the main slope of the square. Its tympanum warns of *The Last Judgment*, while the progressively receding arches are each adorned with the figure of an Apostle standing on the shoulders of an Old Testament prophet. Carvings in a similar style can be found on the *Marienportal* on the right-hand door to the east chancel, which shows the Madonna and Child adored by the Kaiserdom's patrons, founders and builders, and on the choir screen panels, also placing Apostles and prophets in juxtaposition.

THE BAMBERG RIDER

Created by an unknown French-trained artist, the most famous of all this sculpture is the enigmatic **Bamberg Rider** (*Bamberger Reiter*), one of the few equestrian statues which had been made since the days of classical antiquity. Nobody knows for sure who this noble figure is; the Romantics imagined it was an idealised portrait of a German emperor of the Hohenstaufen line. This was eagerly seized on by the Nazis, and during the Third Reich the statue was the national symbol of Germanic perfection, adorning every public hall and classroom. Two other statues to look out for are *Ecclesia* and *Synagogue*, the female personifications of the Christian and Jewish faiths, now placed at the south-east end of the nave. The victory of Christianity over Judaism is highlighted by the women's contrasting countenances: the Christian is a beautiful woman clad in rich cloth, while the Jewess stands blindfolded holding a broken rod and wearing a plain tunic that emphasises the outline of her fallen breasts. Even finer are the two figures of *The Visitation* directly opposite. The Virgin Mary is young and bright, draped in a swirling dress; Saint Elizabeth is an ancient, haggard old crone whose expression speaks of an overwhelming sense of pathos.

OTHER SCULPTURE

As a perfect complement to the carvings associated with its construction, the Dom also contains a masterpiece by the each of the two most famous sculptors of another great period for German art, the early sixteenth century. Focus of the nave is the white lime-stone **tomb** of the canonised imperial couple Heinrich II and Kunigunde, which stands slightly elevated as a result of the crypt built below. **Tilman Riemenschneider** laboured away for fourteen years on this sarcophagus, whose reliefs depict scenes taken from the life and times of the couple. The south transept contains **Veit Stoss'** dark limewood *Nativity Altar*, made when the artist was about eighty years old, as a result of a commission from his son, who was a Carmelite prior in Nürnberg. It was meant as a sort of artistic testament, executed without the usual studio assistance. Unfortunately, it's unfinished – the younger Stoss, a virulent anti-Protestant, was kicked out of Nürnberg when the city council adopted the Reformation, and the sculptor received no payment for his retable, which was soon afterwards moved to Bamberg.

Although it's not accessible to the public, it's worth knowing that the western choir holds the only **papal grave** in Germany, namely that of Pope Clement II. He was the local bishop before becoming Pope, but died in 1047 after having ruled for a mere twelve months. **Tomb slabs** to the Dom's other bishops can be found scattered throughout the church. The most impressive, artistically speaking, is the *Monument to Friedrich von Hohenlohe* in the south aisle, just before the transept. Dating from the latter half of the fourteenth century, it conveniently represents the period midway between the Bamberg Rider and the works of Riemenschneider and Stoss.

The Diözesanmuseum

The **Diözesanmuseum** (Easter–Oct Tues–Sun 10am–5pm; DM2) is in the chapter-house off the cloisters on the south side of the Dom, and is entered from the square. Highlight is the collection of **ecclesiastical vestments**, the vibrant colours and intricate designs amazingly well-preserved. Also kept here are the six original statues from the *Adamportal*, the dogtooth doorway to the left of the east choir. Here the ubiquitous Emperor and his wife turn up in the company of the Dom's two patrons, plus Adam and Eve. The last two are unashamedly sensual; covered only by fig-leaves, they come as near to erotic art as was ever dared in the Middle Ages.

The rest of the square

The **Ratstube** opposite the Dom is a Renaissance gem, with elegantly tapering gables and an ornate oriel window. It now contains the **Historisches Museum** (May–Oct Tues–Sat 9am–noon and 2–5pm, Sun 10am–1pm; DM2), which covers local and regional history from the Stone Age to the twentieth century, as well as Bamberg's rich art history. Adjoining it is the **Reiche Tor**, in which Heinrich and Kunigunde appear once more; the model they carry is recognisably the Kaiserdom. This gate leads into the huge fifteenth-century courtyard of the **Alte Hofhaltung**, the former episcopal palace, which incorporates the remains of the eleventh-century hall of the Imperial Diet. The overhanging eaves of the huge sloping roof shelter two tiers of wooden galleries, and there's an unusual perspective on the towers of the Dom.

Across the street is the building which supplanted it in the eighteenth century, the **Neue Residenz** (daily 9am–noon and 1.30–5pm; DM2.50). It's an early example of the passion for building huge new palaces in the Baroque style that was to sweep across the German principalities, built in a massive L-shape and standing in sumptuous splendour overlooking the town below. Inside, the richly decorated state rooms culminate in the grandiloquent imperial ballroom. Also housed in the palace is the **Staatsgalerie Bamberg**, with medieval and Baroque paintings by German masters. Look out for *The Great Flood*, a typically idiosyncratic work by **Hans Baldung Grien**, who here tackled with relish a subject most painters shied away from; there are also several examples of

Lucas Cranach the Elder. While you're here, have a look into the reading room of the **Staatsbibliothek** too, for a glimpse of a delicate white and pink stucco ceiling in the best tradition of Baroque interior design.

The hills

From the rose garden at the back of the Neue Residenz there's a view of the **Michaelsburg**, which is crowned by a huge **Abtei** (abbey). Much of the original Romanesque shell of the church remains, though it was modified in the Gothic and Baroque periods. The interior is an amazing hotchpotch, its ceiling depicting over 600 medicinal herbs. Housed in the cellars of the monastic buildings is the **Fränkisches Brauereimuseum** (Mon–Fri 1–4pm; DM3), which shows just how those famous local brews are made, and displays all the old gear that used to be necessary for traditional brewing. Even if you're not interested in this, it's worth coming up here for the wonderful panorama of Bamberg's skyline and surrounding hills.

Yet another place for a great view is the **Altenburg**, a ruined castle at the end of the very steep Altenburger Strasse. Walk up to it via the Untere Kaulberg and past Karmelitenplatz, and you'll find the **Karmelitenkloster**. The Romanesque **cloister** (daily 8–11am and 2–5.30pm), the largest in Germany, has been preserved, and its sculptured thirteenth-century columns each have their own individual patterns, revealing just how rich the imagination of early medieval craftsmen could be. Along with the depiction of biblical scenes on the capitals, there's a fabulous bestiary, ranging from fearsome dragons to weird creepy-crawlies.

Eating and drinking

Bamberg's main strength in the food and drink field is, inevitably, the beer halls of its breweries, though it also has a few wine bars and its fair share of good cafés. Unfortunately, many of the best restaurants charge exorbitant prices, but you can get solid, good-value food in most of the brewery-owned establishments.

Restaurants, beer halls and wine bars

Bürgerbräu-Stübla, Urbanstr. 18. Good value *Gaststätte* which features plenty of vegetarian fare.

Greifenklau, Laurenziplatz 20. Beer cellar and garden with bonus of fine view over the city.

Hofbräu-Schänke, Dominikanerstr. 10. Restaurant combining traditional beer hall atmosphere with wholefood dishes.

Mahrsbräu-Stübla, Wunderburg 10. Cosy little pub which is a genuine "local". The same brewery also has a beer garden at Oberer Stephansberg 36.

Schlenkerla, Dominikanerstr. 6. Not to be missed: a seventeenth-century tavern serving what's generally regarded as the best Bamberg *Rauchbier*. Also does light meals.

Spezial, Sternwartstrasse. Known locally as *Zinser* after the ebullient character who runs it, this beer cellar-cum-garden is one of the most popular in town.

Weierich, Lugbank 5. The most reasonably-priced of the city's top-notch restaurants, serving Franconian specialities in a rustic setting.

Würzburger, Zinkenwörth 6. Classy wine restaurant in a half-timbered building.

Zum Zwiebeltreter, Promenadestr. 6a. Hugely popular cellar bar.

Zur Drehorgel, Oberer Sandstr.18. Traditional *Weinstube*, serving good value meals.

Cafés and café-bars

Café Abseits, Pödeldorfer Strasse. Music bar frequented by a young clientele.

Café am Dom, Ringleinsgasse 2. An ideal place to adjourn for *Kaffee und Kuchen* when exploring the Domplatz.

Michaelsberg, Michaelsberg 10e. Has the benefit of a wonderful view over Bamberg.

Rosengarten, Neue Residenz. Another good terrace café; open May to Oct only.
Strandcafé, Memmelsdorfer Str. 82. Popular rendezvous point for "alternative" types.

Nightlife and Culture

The best **nightclub** is *Downstairs*, Langestr. 16 (daily 10pm–3am; DM10 Fri and Sat, of which DM5 goes towards the first drink). If this closes too early for you, head for the *Weinstadl*, Dominikanerstr. 5, which stays open till 4am. For its size, Bamberg is an amazingly vibrant cultural centre, especially for **classical music**. Indeed, it's probably the smallest city in the world with a top-class symphony orchestra. The *Bamberger Symphoniker* was actually the old *Deutsches Orchester* of Prague, who fled over the border at the time the Iron Curtain was going up. They're especially known for their candle-lit concerts in the Neues Residenz. The main **theatre**, not surprisingly, is the *E.T.A. Hoffmann-Theater* on Schillerplatz; the resident company also holds an open-air season in June and July in the Alte Hofhaltung. Tickets for all musical and theatrical events are available from the *Bamberger Veranstaltungsdienst* at Langestr. 24; you can also book there for **river cruises**. Main **festivals** are *Corpus Christi* (variable date in May/June) and the *Sandfest* in August, which features colourful church processions and fishermen's jousts. The **Women's centre** is at Untere Sandstr. 9 (☎0951/55440).

Around Bamberg

Within easy reach of Bamberg are three popular hiking regions: to the east is the previously-described Franconian Switzerland, while westwards lie the **Steigerwald** and the equally heavily forested range of the **Hassberge**. Even if you're not into long walks, there are places in each well worth making the target of a day trip.

The Steigerwald

In **POMMERSFELDEN**, about 20km south of Bamberg, stands **Schloss Weissenstein** (guided tours April–Oct daily 9am–noon and 2–5pm; DM4), the jewel in the crown of the enormous building programme Prince-Bishop Lothar Franz von Schönborn funded from the sizeable fortune he assured himself by masterminding the election of Emperor Charles VI in 1711. Built around the same time as Germany's other great Baroque palaces such as Nymphenburg, Würzburg and the Neue Residenz in Bamberg itself, Weissenstein was designed by Johann Dientzenhofer in equally ostentatious proportions. The entrance hall of the central pavilion takes up the full height of the three-storey palace, and the showpiece **double staircase** swings up to upper galleries that encase the hall rather like great Italian courtyards. The ceiling fresco uses clever perspective and elegantly rounds off a perfect whole. Elsewhere, you'll find richly decorated mirror cabinets, state rooms and the obligatory ballroom, known as the *Marmorsaal* because of the stuccoed marble pillars that line its walls. From mid-July to mid-August each year, it's used for the classical concerts of the *Collegium Musicum*, an international festival of young musicians. For information and tickets, contact the *Schlossverwaltung* (☎09548/203).

Also recommendable, particularly if you've got your own transport, is a trip through the heart of the forest along the *Steigerwald Höhenstrasse* from SCHLÜSSELFELD, 15km west of Pommersfelden, to ELTMANN, set on the south bank of the Main 19km northwest of Bamberg. En route you pass through **EBRACH**, whose Rathaus houses the regional **tourist office** (☎09553/217). This town grew out of a twelfth-century Cistercian **Abtei**, of which large parts remain today. The church's exterior is one of the finest German examples of the order's distinctive early Gothic building style, but the inside was radically changed in the eighteenth century, with pink stuccoed marble pillars and golden yellow ornamentations.

The Hassberge

Star attraction of the Hassberge is the small town of **HASSFURT**, which stands on the northern bank of the Main on the looping main railway between Bamberg and Würzburg. Its fifteenth-century **Ritterkapelle** is a late Gothic chapel with a stone tympanum depicting the journey of the three Magi to the newborn Christ. Apart from Hassfurt, many other little towns and villages still retain much of their old Franconian character, and more often than not there's a small castle nearby as well. A good example is half-timbered **KÖNIGSBERG**, about 10km northeast.

Aschaffenburg

King Ludwig I called **ASCHAFFENBURG**, which is situated on the River Main at the extreme northwestern corner of the state, his "Bavarian Nice". Although the city has lost some of its charm since those days, the well-preserved historic centre and pleasant parks make it an agreeable place to spend a day or two, and it's also the obvious jumping-off point for exploring the unspoiled highland countryside which surrounds it. Once the second residence of the Archbishop-Electors of Mainz, Aschaffenburg is now mainly a dormitory town for Frankfurt and home to 8000 American soldiers – who, if nothing else, have done a lot for local fast food outlets and used car dealerships.

Around town

Aschaffenburg's centre is compact and can easily be covered in a few hours. From the Hauptbahnhof walk down Frohsinnstrasse, turn right into Erthalstrasse and you come to **Schloss Johannisburg**, the town's main attraction. This very French-looking late Renaissance red sandstone pile served the archbishops as a palace rather than filling any defensive role. Today the first and second floors are home to the **Schlossmuseum** (April–Sept daily 9am–noon and 1–5pm; Oct–March daily 10am–noon and 1–4pm; DM3), which houses over 400 paintings from the fifteenth to the eighteenth century, with the emphasis on devotional works by Lucas Cranach the Elder and his contemporaries, along with Dutch and Flemish landscapes. Also of note is the **Schlosskirche** which contains fine alabaster reliefs and a magnificent doorway.

A few minutes' walk along the Main, downstream from Schloss Johannisburg, is **Das Pompejanum**, a replica of the house of Castor and Pollux in Pompeii, built in the nineteenth century for King Ludwig I. Unfortunately only the exterior of this Roman-looking villa has been restored following extensive war damage, but its gardens of Mediterranean trees and plants and its vineyard sloping down to the River Main make for an enjoyable stroll.

A walk down Pfaffengstrasse from Schloss Johannisburg takes you through the heart of the Altstadt, with its narrow streets of half-timbered houses, and leads to Stiftsplatz and Aschaffenburg's other main sight, the **Stiftskirche**. Founded in 957, the church combines Romanesque, Gothic and Baroque styles and it's this architectural identity crisis that gives it real visual impact. The church boasts late Romanesque cloisters, a crucifix dating from 1120 and a small panel of *The Lamentation* by Grünewald.

Also worth visiting is **Schöntal Park**, on the eastern edge of the old city centre, with a lake, a ruined monastery and the **Fasanerie** (Pheasantery). It's reached by walking up Lindenallee, crossing the railway bridge and going up Bismarckallee, which is itself a recreational hotspot in summer with restaurants and beer gardens. **Schönbusch Park**, on the western bank of the Main (best reached by bus #3 from Freihofplatz) is an "English" style landscape garden, designed by eighteenth-century Germany's premier landscape gardener, Friedrich Ludwig von Sckell, and featuring a labyrinth of paths leading through woods and gardens past miniature temples and mazes.

Finally, on the southern edge of town at Obernnauer Str. 125 (reached by bus #1 from Schweinheimer Strasse), the **Rosso Bianco Collection** (Tue–Fri 10am–4pm, Sat and Sun 10am–6pm; DM10) has the biggest collection of racing cars in the world – some 200 gleaming Porsches, Ferraris, Alfa-Romeos and the like which even non-enthusiasts will find themselves drooling over.

Practicalities

The **tourist office** is at Dalbergstrasse 6 (☎06021/30426). **Camping** is possible at Mainpark See (☎06021/278222) and in the suburb of Mainaschaff (☎06021/278222), fifteen minutes away by a #44 bus from the Hauptbahnhof. The **youth hostel** is at Beckerstrasse 47 (☎06021/92763) and is best reached by #22 bus from Platanenallee, getting off at the third stop on Würzburger Strasse. Cheap **hotels** include *Central*, which is in the pedestrian zone in the middle of town at Steingasse 5 (☎06021/23392) and offers singles at DM34 and doubles at DM70; the equally central *Goldenes Fass*, Sandgasse 26 (☎06021/22801), with four singles at between DM22 and DM50 and one double at DM55; and *Syndikus*, a few minutes' walk from the Stiftskirche at Loeher Str. 40, with singles at DM40.

The best **restaurants**, **cafés** and **bars** in the Altstadt are on Rossmarkt and Dalbergstrasse. *Klimperkasten* at Rossmarkt 21 is a lively, friendly pub with regular live music, and *Café Blech* at Rossmarkt 43 is trendy café-bar. *Engelsberg* at Dalbergstr. 66 is a traditional but arty pub and a good starting point for exploring the surrounding streets which are full of of reasonable *Gaststätten* and *Weinstuben*. There's also a cluster of reasonably priced bars and eateries in Würzburger Strasse, not far from the town's youth hostel. Worth checking out in the summer are the *Hofgut Fasanerie*, Bismarckalle 1, whose beer garden is part of the Fasanerie, and the *Zeughaus*, Bismarckallee 5, where you can drink locally produced ciders in the shade of chestnut trees.

The Spessart and Rhön

Aschaffenburg lies at the foot of the **Spessart**, one of Germany's largest and least spoiled forests, which stretches northwards from the slalom course of the River Main. It contains some of Germany's oldest oaks, many dating back well over 500 years; delicious wild mushrooms grow in abundance; and there's a rich wildlife. The **Rhön**, as the highlands are known after the River Sinn, continue the northeasterly direction of the range and are likewise shared with Hessen, but have a somewhat different character. Here the landscape is made up by the remains of ancient volcanoes; the vegetation is more sparse, the forest tending to stay in the valleys, leaving the hilltops to windy moorlands which are very popular with hang-gliders. Both these upland areas are ideal for hiking, and have well-marked trails for both walkers and cyclists.

The Odenwald

A rather more obviously enticing destination is the **Odenwald**, a forest facing the Spessart across the Main which straddles across into both Baden-Württemberg and Hessen. The Bavarian section includes two small towns well worth making the object of a day trip: they are easily combined, as both lie on a railway line from Aschaffenburg.

MILTENBERG, which lies 45km upstream in a due southerly direction, is a particularly good example of the half-timbered towns so characteristic of central Germany. Its picturesque triangular **Marktplatz** features many of the finest houses, along with the Gothic church of St Jakob and a Renaissance fountain. The square slopes up to the **Mildenburg**, a restored medieval castle in whose courtyard stands an enigmatic five-metre-high monolith dating back to Roman times, if not before; there's also a good view of the town from up here. On Hauptstrasse are several notable buildings: *Zum Riesen* at no. 97 is an inn with an uninterrupted tradition since the fifteenth century; the **Altes Rathaus** at no. 137 is a likeable example of fifteenth-century architecture; while behind the *Kalt-Loch-Bräuerei* at no. 199 is the **Alte Synagoge**, one of the few medieval Jewish temples left in Germany.

A further 10km south is **AMORBACH**, like Aschaffenburg a former possession of the Archbishops of Mainz. In the mid-seventeenth century the court architect Maximilian von Welsch was commissioned to transform its Romanesque **Abtei** into something more in keeping with the times. He responded with a design which is restrained by Bavarian standards – he went as far as preserving the original towers – yet which is none the worse for that, being a masterly exercise in late Baroque grandeur. Outstanding features of the church are the ceiling frescos, the wrought-iron screen dividing the nave from the transept and the sweet-toned organ. **Guided tours** (Mon–Sat 9am–noon and 1–5/6pm, Sun noon–5/6pm; DM2.50) are run through the slightly later monastic buildings, which give a foretaste of the emergent Neoclassical style in such lovely interiors as the *Bibliotheksaal* and the *Grüner Saal*.

Würzburg

Capital of Franconian wine and northern starting point of the **Romantic Road** (see box on p.166), Germany's most famous tourist route, **WÜRZBURG** spans the River Main some 110km northwest of Nürnberg. During the night of 16 March 1945 it got the same treatment from Allied bombers that Nürnberg had received two months earlier. The 1200-year-old city had no important war industries but the presence of a busy railway junction provided a tenuous rationale for its destruction. Unfortunately, Würzburg has been less successful in rebuilding itself: gone is the Altstadt, and instead there are individual surprises of Baroque and Gothic beauty sandwiched between modern supermarkets and the new town. For all that, the city's location on the banks of the river Main, a number of really outstanding sights and a superb range of places to eat and drink easily justify a visit of several days.

Würzburg has been one of Germany's most influential episcopal cities for many centuries, and some of the greatest architects and artists were hired by the prince-bishops, bequeathing an exceptionally rich legacy. Prominent among them was the sculptor **Tilman Riemenschneider**, whose hauntingly characterised carvings, executed in the heady years leading up to the Reformation, decorate so many churches throughout Franconia. A later period saw the patronage of **Balthasar Neumann** who was then totally unknown and untried, but who duly developed here into the most inventive and accomplished architect of eighteenth-century Europe.

The telephone code for Würzburg is ☎0931

Getting around and finding somewhere to stay

Just outside the **Hauptbahnhof** at the northern end of the city centre there's a **tourist office** (Mon–Sat 8am–8pm; ☎37436) which can book rooms for DM4. Two other branches are near the centre of town, at the *Haus zum Falken* in the Eichhornstrasse (Mon–Fri 9am–6pm, Sat 9am–2pm; ☎37398), and in the *Würtzburg-Palais am Congress Centrum* near the Friedensbrücke (Mon–Thurs 8am–5pm, Fri 8am–noon; ☎37335). The **youth hostel**, Burkardcrstr. 44 (☎42590) is situated on the left bank of the Main

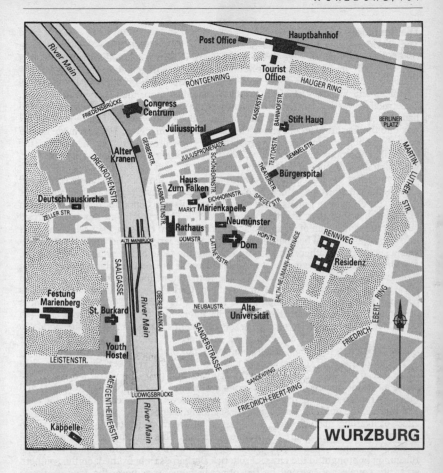

below the Marienberg fortress; take tram #3 to Ludwigsbrücke from the Hauptbahnhof). Nearest **campsite** is on Winterhäuserstrasse (☎705598) in the suburb of HEIDINGSFELD, about 4km south of Würzburg and best reached by taking the #16 bus from Barbarossaplatz. There are plenty of reasonably-priced **hotels** between the Hauptbahnhof and the city centre, including *Weinhaus Schnabel*, Haugerpfargasse 10 (☎53314) at DM30 per person; *Gasthof Kirchlein*, Textorstr. 17 (☎53014), with singles from DM35 and doubles from DM55; and *Pension Siegel*, Reisgrubengasse 7 (☎52941), with singles DM35 and doubles DM68.

The city

The heart of the old city lies between the Main and the Residenz, roughly encom-passed by the Juliuspromenade to the north and Neubaustrasse to the south. Most of the sights lie within this compact area, though you need to cross over to the right bank for a couple of major attractions – and the best views.

The Residenz

The **Residenz** (April–Sept Tues–Sun 9am–5pm, Oct–March Tues–Sun 10am–4pm; DM4.50) on the eastern edge of the town centre is a truly marvellous palace set in a park to match. It was intended to symbolise all the wealth and status of the Würzburg bishops, and to show they could hold their own with such great European courts as Versailles and Vienna – which, in artistic terms, they more than succeeded in doing. Construction was left largely in the hands of the prolific **Balthasar Neumann**, who had started off as a humble craftsman of churchbells and weapons before working his way into the fine art of architecture. The palace is built in a great U-shape made up of a central pavilion and four equally proportioned two-storey courts. In themselves, the external proportions are impressive, but they're rather overshadowed by the overwhelming magnificence of the interior.

As you enter the palace via the central wing, you're almost immediately confronted with the famed **staircase** which is covered by a single unsupported vault of audacious design. In response to jealous rivals who claimed this was bound to collapse, Neumann offered to have a battery of artillery fired under it. This experiment was never carried out, but full vindication of Neumann's faith in his design came in 1945, when the vault held firm against aerial bombardment. Its **fresco**, the largest in the world, thus miraculously survived unscathed. An allegory extolling the fame of the prince-bishops in the most immodest way imaginable, it was painted by the greatest decorator of the age, the Venetian **Giovanni Battista Tiepolo**. The four continents then known are depicted paying their respects to the ruler of Würzburg, Carl Philipp von Greiffenklau, who is transported to Heaven in triumph in the centre of the composition. Each continent is personified as a representative female character, Europe being a Greek goddess enthroned above a globe to symbolise this continent's status as ruler of the world. To her right, sitting on an old cannon, a reference to his original trade, Balthasar Neumann surveys the scene; behind him are Tiepolo and his fellow-decorators.

The guided tour of the palace will take you on to the **Weisser Saal**, whose plain white stucco is a tasteful contrast to the staircase and gives the visitor a break before being hit by the opulence of the **Kaisersaal**, which is the centrepiece of the palace and the room reserved for the use of the emperor whenever he happened to be in the area. The marble, the gold-leaf stucco and the sparkling chandeliers combine to produce an effect of dazzling magnificence, but finest of all are more frescos by Tiepolo, which dovetail with the architecture to absolute perfection. This time they glorify the concept of the Holy Roman Empire and Würzburg's part within it. On the ceiling, Beatrix of Burgundy is brought to the city as Frederick Barbarossa's betrothed: on the southern wall, the couple are married by the prince-bishop. From here, the tour continues through an array of **state rooms**, painstakingly recreated from the ashes with the help of photographs and old etchings.

Built discreetly into the southwest corner of the palace in order not to spoil the symmetry, the **Hofkirche** (which you visit independently) is a brilliant early example of the spatial illusionism that was to become a Neumann speciality – the interior, based on a series of ovals, appears to be much larger than is actually the case.

The episcopal and academic quarters

From the Residenz, it's only a short walk along Hofstrasse to the city's episcopal centre, in which the two main churches nestle side-by-side. The more northerly is the **Neumünster**, a Romanesque basilica partly rebuilt in the Baroque period, whose perfect symmetry is highlighted by a twin set of steps leading up to the elevated entrance from either side. Inside the church are a number of sculptures by Riemenschneider and frescos by Johann Zimmermann, of Wieskirche fame. However, the most precious element is the **crypt**, the burial place of Saints Kilian, Kolonat and

Totnan, Irish missionaries martyred in 689 for trying to Christianise Franconia. The busts of the three martyrs on the thirteenth- century altar are copies of the originals by Riemenschneider, which were destroyed in 1945.

If you leave the Neumünster by its northern exit, you'll come to the tiny **Lusamgärtchen** and the remains of the twelfth century cloister. These days it's a romantically overgrown square, and at its centre is a commemorative block to the famous medieval minstrel **Walther von der Vogelheide**. He was the most popular poet and singer of the early thirteenth century, but also a valued political commentator of the Staufen rulers, which is why he was given a pension from the estate of this church and is assumed to have been buried in the cloister in 1230. His popularity still holds, and local residents always ensure that fresh flowers decorate his memorial stone, over 750 years after his death. To the northeast stand several fine old mansions, including the Renaissance **Hof Conti**, the present-day home of Würzburg's bishop.

The **Dom**, again consecrated to Saint Kilian, was one of the largest Romanesque churches in Germany, but was completely burnt out in 1945, and only the exterior is true to the original. Inside, the rich stucco embellishments of the eighteenth century have only been restored in the transept and chancel, and for the rest the walls are left plain white, with surviving **tombstones** of canons and prince-bishops lining the pillars: look out for those on the seventh and eighth bays of the north side, which are both by Riemenschneider. At the end of the northern transept, Balthasar Neumann's **Schönbornkapelle** holds the remains of four bishops from the House of Schönborn, the dynasty which specialised in collecting episcopal appointments and then building great palaces as spin-offs – Bamberg, Pommersfelden, Bruchsal and Würzburg itself being among their legacies.

A couple of blocks south of here, the eastern end of Neubaustrasse is dominated by the huge Renaissance frontage of the **Alte Universität**, built in the late sixteenth century by order of one of the city's most elightened prince-bishops, Julius Echter. The attached church also dates from this period, but the tower was added by Antonio Petrini, the seventeenth-century Italian architect who was responsible for transforming Würzburg into one of Germany's first Baroque cities. Neubaustrasse and the streets further south still function as the epicentre of the city's still-flourishing academic tradition (see also *Eating and Drinking* below).

Marktplatz, the hospitals and the waterfront

To the west of the episcopal quarter is the city's commercial heart, centred on **Marktplatz**, whose daily food market ensures that there's always a lively bustle. Just off the northeast side is the **Haus zum Falken**, the city's prize example of a Rococo mansion, bristling with white stucco decorations and perfectly restored to the very last curl. It now houses one of the city's tourist offices and the municipal library.

Overlooking Marktplatz is the **Marienkapelle**, an exceptionally graceful Gothic church of the fourteenth century, whose most interesting feature is the arch above the northern portal. The scene represented is *The Annunciation*, and if you look closely, you'll see that the artist has chosen to be very literal in his interpretation. There's the usual Archangel with his scripted band indicating his speech to Mary, but another band leads from God the Father above to Mary's ear, and tucked away in the folds of this band, a little baby is sliding down towards her. Originally the Marienkapelle was adorned by some of Riemenschneider's most famous statues, such as *Adam and Eve*, but they were already so badly eroded by the nineteenth century that they were replaced by copies. Inside, the burial place of Balthasar Neumann is marked on the first pillar to the right from the market portal, and another famous local artist, the fifteenth-century painter Mathis Grünewald, is commemorated by a copy of his *Isenheim Altar*.

Eichhornstrasse leads eastwards from the Markt to Theaterstrasse, where you'll find the **Bürgerspital**, a charitable institution for the poor, old and sick established in the early fourteenth century by the wealthier citizens of the city. Its good works were funded from its vineyards, still among the largest in Germany; in accordance with the wishes of the founders, residents get a quarter of a litre of wine each day and double on Sundays. The Gothic chapel remains from the initial complex, though other parts were rebuilt in the Baroque period. A short walk away on Juliuspromenade is the **Juliusspital**, a second and much larger institution of the same kind. It takes its name from its benefactor, Bishop Julius Echter, but again it was rebuilt in the Baroque period, partly by Petrini, who added the beautiful little pharmacy, which survives as an intact period-piece. It's best to visit the hospitals when you're in the mood for something to eat and drink, as they each incorporate a *Weinstube* (see below) where the products of their vineyards can be sampled. While walking between the two, it's worth making a short detour down Hauger Pfarrgasse to see Petrini's strikingly Roman-looking **Stift Haug**, which contains a large painting of *The Crucifixion* by Tintoretto.

At the western end of Juliuspromenade, the eighteenth-century **Alter Kranen** (old cranes), used to unload shipping, stand guard over the Main. Further south stands the **Alte Mainbrücke**, the oldest bridge spanning this river. Built in 1133, it was often damaged over the centuries, most recently in 1945 when the Allies toppled the eighteenth-century statues of the town's bishops and saints into the river. However, some of the originals have been reinstated, joining with a number of copies to oversee the traffic once again.

The Marienberg

Towering high above the left bank of the Main, the **Festung Marienberg** (April–Sept Tues–Sun 9am–noon and 1–5pm; Oct–March 10am–noon & 1–4pm; DM3) was home to the ruling bishops from the thirteenth century until 1750, when they moved to the Residenz. What you see today is therefore the result of 500 years of building that was usually concerned with improving fortifications against possible attack from the mob across the river. Clashes between the bishops and the people weren't uncommon, especially since the town's loyalty tended to be with the emperor and not the bishop. Two of the most momentous attacks on the fortress were during the Peasants' Revolt of 1525 and the Swedish occupation in 1631. The failure of the former was unfortunate for Tilman Riemenschneider, the local mayor as well as the star artist: having backed the peasants, he was locked up in the Marienberg dungeons for his stance, where he was held and tortured for eight weeks before being sent off into obscurity. The sacking by the Swedes led to the loss of many treasures, including the valuable court library which can now be found in the Swedish town of Uppsala. Two more devastations were those by the Prussian army in 1866 and during the 1945 air raid, so although much of the original structure has been restored, the interiors are largely missing.

The fortress consists of a central medieval core, but the courtyard also contains the round **Marienkirche**, which dates back to the eighth century and is thus probably the oldest intact church in Germany. Another structure of special note is the **Brunnenhaus**, whose unbelievable 105-metre well was chiselled through rock around the year 1200 to ensure self-sufficiency in water. Surrounding this are a number of buildings erected during the rule of Julius Echter, who aimed to convert the old castle into a residential palace. The massive fortifications encasing the Marienberg were added under Philip von Schönborn, with the aim of returning the complex to the status of a fortress following the disaster of the Swedish occupation. He also built the **Zeughaus** which now houses the large **Mainfränkisches Museum** (daily April–Oct 10am–5pm, Nov–March 10am–4pm; DM3). Pride of place among the collections is taken by a magnificent array of **Riemenschneider sculptures**, including the original stone carvings from the Marienkapelle.

Elsewhere on the left bank

On your way up to or down from the Marienberg, it's worth pausing to see the **Deutschhauskirche**, a very early Gothic church with fine carvings built by the Teutonic Knights. Returning to the waterfront and continuing south along Dreikronenstrasse, you pass **St Burkhard**, whose late Gothic choir picturesquely straddles the street, forming a sort of covered walkway. It's also worth a quick look inside, to see a tender *Madonna and Child* by Riemenschneider.

Finally, during work on the Residenz, Balthasar Neumann took time off to build the **Käppele**, a pilgrimage church imperiously perched on the heights at the southwestern end of the city. Its twin towers, crowned with onion domes, seem to beckon the faithful to make the ascent. Apart from the opportunity to see the interior, lavishly covered with frescos and stucco, it's well worth visiting for the **view** from the terrace – the finest in Würzburg – which offers a frontal view of the Marienberg surrounded by its vineyards, with the city nestling snugly in the valley below.

Eating and drinking

Würzburg is a place for gourmets, or even for those who simply enjoy good food, for although meals here aren't necessarily cheap, they're certainly worth it. The best places to sample the local wines and traditional Franconian cooking are in the famous *Weinstuben*, but the city is amply endowed with restaurants and bars to suit all tastes.

Weinstuben

Bürgerspital, Theaterstr. 19. The obvious place to sample the wines from the vineyards of the famous old hospital. Produces very dry *Riesling*, *Silvaner* and *Müller-Thurgau* in roughly equal numbers; the food is almost equally excellent and surprisingly reasonably priced. Closed Tues.

Hofkeller, Residenzplatz 1. The former court vineyards maintain a modern rivalry to those of the two hospitals; their wide variety of wines can be enjoyed here in the splendid cellars of the Residenz itself. Closed Mon.

Juliusspital, Juliuspromenade 19. Full-bodied wines, with *Silvaner* being the most common type, are characteristic of this hospital's vineyards; they're matured in old oak casks to give a particularly strong flavour. Meals are also very good value here. Closed Wed.

Stachel, Gressengasse 1. The city's oldest wine-drinking inn, it has a particularly picturesque courtyard for *al fresco* meals, but is pricier than its rivals. Closed Sun.

Other restaurants

Backöfele, Ursulinergasse 2. Top-class traditional *Gaststätte* right in the heart of the city.

Burggaststätten, Festung Marienberg. The restaurant complex in the Marienberg includes a *Weinstube* (featuring wines from the *Hofkeller*), a beer garden (selling the local *Hofbräu* beers) and a traditional café; any of these is well worth splashing out on when you're visiting the fortress.

Hofbräukeller, Höchberger Str. 28. In this wine stronghold, it's appropriate that the leading *Bierkeller*, whose garden can seat 1000 people, is way out of the centre on the western side of the city. An adventurous menu includes many vegetarian options as well as the expected Franconian dishes.

Mal was anderes, Bahnhofstr. 22. Würzburg's main vegetarian and wholefood specialist.

Russ, Wolfhartsgasse 1. Small, medium-priced restaurant with a high gastronomic reputation.

Schiffbäuerin, Katzengasse 7. Top choice for local fish specialities; also has a fine selection of wines.

Stadt Mainz, Semmelstr. 39. Although excellent, note that this historic inn is *the* tourist spot in town, so keen to cater for everybody that it not only prints its menu in five languages, but also in Braille.

Bars and café-bars

Erste Würzburger Hausbrauerei, Burkarder Str. 2–4. The only house brewery in town, producing an unfiltered beer; also serves Franconian dishes.

Gehrings, Neubaustr. 24. Café-bistro right by the Alte Universität.

Sanders, Sanderstr. 7. The place to come for cocktails; stays open till 2am every night.
Till Eulenspiegel, Sanderstr. 1a. Student *Kneipe* with a good range of wines, beers and snacks.
Wirtshaus Met, Sanderstr. 15. Music pub which does a side-line in raclettes and fondues.

Listings

Bike hire At the Hauptbahnhof.

Car hire *Avis*, Schürerstr. 2 (☎50661).

Festivals Each June, the Kaisersaal in the Residenz is the opulent setting for the *Mozartfest*. At the beginning of July is the *Kilianifest*, Franconia's most important religious festival, during which time thousands of Catholic pilgrims come here – both to worship and celebrate.

Main cruises Information and tickets by the *Alter Kranen* on the riverbank at the bottom of Juliuspromenade; two different firms operate cruises in summer. Downstream, the destination is VEITSHÖCHHEIM, with its Rococo Schloss and gardens (April–Sept Tues–Sun 9am–1pm and 2-5pm; DM2). Upstream, you can sail to the fortified towns of OCHSENFURT and SULZFELD.

Mitfahrzentrale Bahnhofsvorplatz-Ost (☎12904).

Post Restante Bahnhofsvorplatz-West.

THE ROMANTIC ROAD

Glibly named, but with many beautiful spots along it, the **Romantic Road** (*Romantische Strasse*) runs for 350km between Würzburg and Füssen in the Allgäu. The road gets its name from the fact that it passes gently rolling countryside, which is never very dramatic but instead pleasantly unspoilt and tranquil: the kind of region where nature lovers and romantics feel most at home – according to the tourist board.

If pushed for time, taking the *Europabus* along the whole or part of the route is a good way to get a quick impression; both Eurail and the German Rail Pass are valid, but note that services run just once a day in each direction, and only during the summer. One snag is that this only covers the well-trodden tourist trail of medieval showpiece towns. Furthermore, stops are very short, which means that you only get a superficial impression unless you break your journey for a day or trust to the infrequent local buses. (Many places on the route are not served by rail.) It's essential to detour from the main drag to get a full impression of the area and to escape the tourists: exploring the regions alongside becomes much more rewarding with your own transport and presents an ideally peaceful holiday tour.

For the first section of the Road after Würzburg – Tauberbischofsheim, Bad Mergentheim, Weikersheim and Creglingen – see *Chapter Two*. The stage after that, including Rothenburg and Dinkelsbühl, is described below, followed immediately by the first part of the Bavarian Swabia section, that between Nördlingen and Augsburg. For the next stretch, along the Lech valley via Landberg and Steingaden, see p.91–93. The southern terminus at Füssen is described on p.184.

Rothenburg ob der Tauber

ROTHENBURG OB DER TAUBER, which is some 60km south of Würzburg, is the most famous and most visited medieval town in Germany, and although it's very beautiful and completely preserved in its original form, it has been reduced to the ultimate museum-piece with little life of its own except that which revolves around the tourist trade. Nonetheless, it should still merit at least one overnight stop: the only way to get this place to yourself is to stay the night and go out, either early in the morning or in the evening, when the crowds have gone. Perched high above the River Tauber in its deep furrow of a valley, Rothenburg's location is a good reason to use it as a base, especially if you're in the mood for country walks.

Rothenburg's status as the only walled medieval town in Germany without a single modern building is due to a fortuitous series of circumstances. Its prosperous medieval period was followed by a spectacular slump in its fortunes as it found itself cut off from the new trading routes and reduced to the status of a very provincial market town. Without money to expand or erect new buildings, it vegetated until the nineteenth century, when its self-evident attraction for the Romantic movement led to the enforcement of strict preservation orders. Having already had a narrow escape from total destruction in the Thirty Years' War (see below), it was similarly fortunate to survive World War II, when it lay directly in the path of the American advance. Thankfully, a civilian working for the US army, J.J. McCloy (later the High Commissioner to Germany), knew and loved Rothenburg, and persuaded the generals to spare it from saturation shelling.

It takes about an hour to walk around the town via the sentry walk on the four-teenth-century **Stadtmauer**, and this is the best way to get your bearings and a first impression. Tightly packed within the walls, the town's houses get larger towards the middle where the local patricians and merchants lived. Nearer the wall, tradesfolk and peasants lived in crooked little dolls' houses, half-timbered and with steeply pointed roofs. The plan of the town is also highly distinctive, having a shape like a question-mark, with an elongated southern stalk.

Marktplatz

The sloping central **Marktplatz** is dominated by the arcaded front of the **Renaissance Rathaus**, which supplanted the Gothic building which stands behind it. Its 60-metre **tower** (April–Oct daily 9.30am–12.30pm and 1–5pm; Nov–March Sun noon–3pm only; DM2) is the highest point in Rothenburg and provides the best view of the town and surrounding countryside. The original **Gothic Rathaus** (daily 8am–6pm; free) is separated from the newer one by a covered courtyard, which is where you'll find the crumbly old entrance, unchanged for centuries. Inside are sixteenth-century furnishings and the stark thirteenth-century *Kaisersaal*, often used as the main law court. Prisoners were kept in the dungeons or **Historiengewölbe** (mid-March–Oct 9am–5pm; DM2) below, which were said to be more dreadful than any others of the day.

The other main tourist attraction on the Marktplatz is the pair of figures looking out from the windows on either side of the three clocks on the gable of the **Ratsherrntrinkstube** ("Councillors' Tavern"). Every day at 11am, noon, 1pm, 2pm, 3pm, 9pm and 10pm, they re-enact the most famous moment in Rothenburg's history. In 1631, during the Thirty Years' War, the imperial army, led by the fearsome Johann Tilly, captured the town and intended to destroy it as a punishment for its support of the Protestant cause. In a gesture of peace, the general was brought the huge civic tankard known as the *Meistertrunk*, which was filled with wine to its capacity of 3.25 litres, and was persuaded to accept the wager that Rothenburg should be spared if one of the councillors could down the contents in a oner. The former burgomaster Georg Nusch duly obliged: it's supposed to have taken him ten minutes, after which he needed three days to sleep off the effects.

To the opposite side of the Marktplatz is Rothenburg's largest building, the Gothic parish church of **St Jakob** (daily Easter–Oct 9am–5.30pm; rest of year 10am–noon and 2-4pm; DM2), whose main body and two towers rise above the sea of red roofs like a great ship, visible for miles around. The entrance fee is worth paying to see the works of art inside. Finest is **Riemenschneider**'s *Holy Blood Altar*, exquisitely carved in lime-wood, with a centrepiece showing the Last Supper Also of note is the church's high altar, the *Zwölfbotenaltar*, by the Nördlingen artist Friedrich Herlin. The outer wings illustrate *The Legend of St James*; the scene where the saint's dead body is carried to a medieval town features a depiction of fifteenth-century Rothenburg.

North of Marktplatz

Just to the northwest of St Jakob is the **Reichstadtmuseum** (daily April–Oct 10am–5pm; Nov–March 1–4pm; DM2.50) on Klosterhof. This occupies the former Dominican convent and is most interesting for the building's original medieval workrooms, such as the kitchen complete with its former utensils. Displays relate mainly to Rothenburg's history, art and culture, and include a selection of furniture, sculpture, paintings and arms; the original *Meistertrunk* is a star feature. Also of note is the collection on Jewish local history. In the thirteenth century Rothenburg had a large settlement of Jews, but their synagogue and ghetto were destroyed in the fifteenth-century pogroms. You can see one surviving feature of their heritage, however, by going eastwards from here along Judengasse. At the end, built up against the twelfth-century **Weisser Turm** (White Tower), is the former Jewish dance hall, whose walls are embedded with gravestones.

At the extreme northwestern end of town stands the late Gothic church of **St Wolfgang** (March–Oct daily 10am–noon and 2–6pm). Traditionally the parish of the local shepherds, it forms a unit with the **Klingentor** as a key part of the fortifications of the town.

West of Marktplatz

Herrngasse, which leads west from Marktplatz, is the widest street in Rothenburg, being where the local nobs lived. It's well worth taking time to look into the courtyards of these mansions, particularly that of the *Staudtsches Haus*, with its wrought-iron gratings, galleries, oriel window and staircase tower. Also on this street is the severe early Gothic **Franziskanerkirche**, which still preserves the rood screen which divided the monks from the laity. Its walls and floor are covered with funerary monuments to local families, and there's a startlingly realistic fifteenth-century retable showing *The Stigmatisation of St Francis*.

At the end of the street, a small bulge sticks out on to a promontory formed by a twist in the River Tauber below. In the early Middle Ages there used to be a castle belonging to the Hohenstaufen emperors here, but it was destroyed by a violent earthquake in 1356. The only parts remaining from that period are the **Burgtor**, a watchtower which is the oldest of all the 24 towers, and the **Blasiuskapelle**, with murals dating from the fourteenth century. You get the best view of the Tauber valley from here too.

South of Marktplatz

At no. 13 on Hofbronnengasse, which leads off the southern side of Marktplatz, is the **Puppen- und Spielzeugmuseum** (daily Jan and Feb 11am–5pm; March–Dec 9.30am–6pm; DM3.50), Germany's largest private collection of toys and dolls. The exhibits date from 1780 to 1940 and are all beautifully displayed in spacious surroundings. Facing you across Burggasse at the end of the street is the fascinating **Kriminalmuseum** (daily April–Oct 9.30am–6pm; Nov–Feb 2–4pm; March 10am–4pm; DM3), which contains extensive collections attesting to medieval inhumanity in the shape of torture instruments and related objects – for example the beer barrels that drunks were forced to walk around in. An added attraction is that all exhibits are fully labelled and explained in English.

Schmiedgasse, which leads off the southeastern corner of Marktplatz, is lined with the most prestigious of all the mansions in town. One of Rothenburg's most famous mayors, Heinrich Toppler, lived at no. 5, now the *Gasthof zum Greifen*. He was council leader at the time of the town's greatest prosperity, but fell into disgrace and was imprisoned in the Rathaus dungeons, dying there after two months of starvation and torture. Next door is the *Bauermeisterhaus*, the finest house in town, built by the same architect who designed the Rathaus, Leonhard Weidmann. The first floor is adorned with statues of the Seven Virtues; on the next level, the Seven Deadly Sins sound their warning notes. Burgomaster Nusch of *Meistertrunk* fame lived at no. 21, now an inn called *Roter Hahn*. Today, all three of these houses are top-class **restaurants**, and the first two both have bargain menus. For an insight into how the medieval tradesfolk lived, it's worth making a short detour east along Alter Stadtgarten to see the **Handwerkerhaus** (April–Oct daily 9am–6pm and 8–9pm; Nov–March Sat & Sun 2–4pm; DM3), a workman's house with all the original furnishings and tools.

At the far end of Schmiedgasse is the **Plönlein**, an outrageously picturesque little triangular square. Beyond lies the narrow southern stem of the town, which functioned as the hospital quarter. The **Spital** itself is a complex of various dates: the chapel is Gothic, the main building is by Weidmann. One of the town's two youth hostels occupies the former bakery; another is in the nearby **Rossmühle**, a sixteenth-century mill formerly powered by sixteen horses. To the east is the **Spitalbastei**, the strongest as well as most modern part of the fortification system, dating from the turn of the seventeenth century.

Outside the walls

From either Plönlein or the Spitalbastei, you can descend to the **Doppelbrücke**, a Gothic viaduct faithfully reconstructed following destruction in the war. From here, there's a superb long-range view of Rothenburg. A quite different but equally good panorama can be had by following the S-bend in the Tauber downstream to the **Engelsburg**, a hill formerly covered with vineyards; an alternative approach to this is via the path from the Burggarten. Below stands the **Topplerschlösschen** (Fri–Sun 1–4pm; DM3), a summer and weekend retreat for Burgomaster Heinrich Toppler. This late fourteenth-century tower house has a bizarre top-heavy effect, with the upper storeys jutting out well over the stumpy base.

From here it's a 2km walk down the Tauber to DETWANG, a handsome village usually designated as the stop on the Romantic Road immediately prior to Rothenburg, though it has now officially been swallowed up by the larger town. The Romanesque **Pfarrkirche** (April–Oct daily 8.30am–noon & 1.30–5/6pm, Nov–March Tues–Sun 10am–noon & 2–4pm) contains another masterpiece by Riemenschneider, the *Kreuzaltar*, featuring a central *Crucifixion* by the master, with wing reliefs of *The Agony in the Garden* and *The Resurrection* by his assistants.

ROTHENBURG'S FESTIVALS

If you can stand the crowds and a certain sense of tweeness, it's worth trying to make your visit coincide with one of Rothenburg's many **festivals**. Each Whit Monday, the **Meistertrunk drama** is re-enacted – albeit with no more than a pretence at matching Nusch's feat. The preceding day sees one of the renditions of the historic **Schäfertanz** ("Shepherds' Dance") in front of the Rathaus; this is repeated on selected Sundays in spring and summer. According to one tradition, the dance began as a thanksgiving for Rothenburg's deliverance from the plague; another theory asserts that it derives from the celebration of a discovery of hidden treasure by one of the shepherds. Also at Whit, and throughout July and August, there are costume performances of **plays by Hans Sachs**. The second weekend in September sees the **Freiereichstadtfest**, featuring pageants and a fireworks display.

Practicalities

The highly efficient **tourist office** is in the Ratsherrntrinkstube on Marktplatz (Mon–Fri 9am–noon and 2–6pm, Sat 9am–noon; ☎09861/40492). They can help with accommodation, which may be hard to find on your own during the high season but which can still be affordable. As mentioned earlier, the two **youth hostels** are in beautifully restored half-timbered houses off the bottom of the Spitalgasse. One is the *Rossmühle* (☎09861/4510), the other the *Spitalhof* (☎09861/7889), and there's little to choose between them. The **campsite** is in Detwang (☎09861/3177 or 6463). **Private homes** renting out rooms charge around DM25 per person. Enquire at the *Blasi* family residence, Alter Stadtgraben 12 (☎09861/5198), or *Frau Angermeier* at Schrannenplatz 12 (☎09861/3456). **Pensions** offering singles for DM30–38 and doubles for DM55–75 are: *Schmölzer*, Rosengasse 21 (☎09861/3371), and *Hofmann*, Stollengasse 29, (☎09861/3371). For the best places to **eat** and **drink,** try the previously-mentioned inns on Schmiedgasse. Finally, note that Rothenburg isn't on a passenger railway line: the nearest station is at STEINACH on the stretch between Würzburg and Ansbach; **buses** provide regular connections to and from the trains which ply this route.

Dinkelsbühl

Heading south from Rothenburg, the Romantic Road passes through SCHILLINGFÜRST, with its Baroque Schloss, and medieval FURTWANGEN. Both are worth a quick look if you've got time to spare, but the next major way station is **DINKELSBÜHL,** which lies 13km south of the latter, and about 40km from Rothenburg. Although it presents another immaculately preserved townscape from the Middle Ages, it has so far managed to avoid being completely overrun by tourists and thus has an authentically soporific air.

The **Stadtmauer** survives almost intact, except for the sentry walk, of which only a small section remains. It's therefore best to begin your tour by walking round the outside of the walls via the pathway known as the Alte Promenade. Of the four gateways, the eastern **Wörnitz Tor** is part of the original thirteenth-century fortification system, though it was later prettified by the addition of a clock gable and a coating of orange paint. Proceeding southwards, you pass the most photogenic of the towers, the **Bäuerlinsturm**, whose projecting half-timbered upper storey was added when it passed into residential use. Beyond stands the late fourteenth-century **Nördlinger Tor** which was again embellished with a Renaissance gable. Alongside it is the **Stadtmühle**, perhaps the most formidable-looking mill ever built; because it lay outside the walls, it had to be fortified with corner towers and gun loops. The western section of the Stadtmauer is pierced by a series of round towers, but its gateway, the **Segringer Tor**, is a decorative Baroque replacement for the one destroyed in the Thirty Years' War. However, the northern **Rothenburger Tor** still preserves most of its medieval form, including a sturdy gatehouse.

Within the walls, the dominant monument is the church of **St Georg** on Weinmarkt. This preserves the tower of its Romanesque predecessor, but is otherwise a textbook Gothic hall church from the second half of the fifteenth century, with an airily light interior of slender pillars and elaborate network vaults. Look out for the didactic *Panel of the Ten Commandments*, which pairs each scene with a warning of the consequences of failure to obey. Another feature of special note is the unusual sculpted depiction of *The Last Supper* on the exterior of one of the choir chapels.

Facing the church are five magnificent mansions, of which the most notable are the half-timbered **Deutsches Haus**, now the leading local hotel-restaurant, and the resplendently-gabled **Schranne**, which contains the town's main festive hall. More fine

---

DINKELSBÜHL FOLKLORE

The oddest tradition in Dinkelsbühl is that it is one of the last places in Europe still guarded by a paid **nightwatchman**: decked out in anachronistic gear, he sets out on his rounds from St Georg at 9pm each evening, 9.30pm in June and July. However, the most famous piece of local folklore is the **Kinderzeche**, a ten-day-long festival held each July, the pivotal date being the third Monday of the month. This commemorates an event in the Thirty Years' War which has obvious parallels with Rothenburg's *Meistertrunk*. This time it was the Swedes who were bent on destruction. Although Dinkelsbühl had a predominantly Protestant population, the town council was, as the result of an imperial decree following defeat in the Schmalkaldic Wars, entirely made up of Catholics. According to legend, when the town finally capitulated after a long siege, the Swedish commander was dissuaded from ransacking it by a deputation of local kids. The events are re-enacted in plays performed in the Schranne, while on the Monday and each of the two Saturdays and Sundays there are costumed pageants through the streets. Music is provided by the *Knabenkapelle*; perhaps the best-known boys' band in Germany, its members are kitted out (ominously or charmingly, depending on your point of view) like little soldiers in red and white eighteenth-century uniform. In line with Bavarian taste, there are side-shows of open-air theatre, fireworks and the inevitable beer tents.

---

houses can be seen down Segringer Strasse to the west: nos. 3 and 5 share a single gable, while no. 7 has a lovely arcaded, flower-strewn courtyard. In the opposite direction, the Altrathausplatz in the shadow of the Wörnitz Tor is another of the most picturesque corners, with the **Löwenbrunnen** (Lion Fountain) as its focal point.

Practicalities

The **tourist office** is on Marktplatz (Mon–Fri 9am–noon and 2–6pm, Sat and Sun 10am–noon and 2–4pm; ☎09851/90240). Ask here if you're interested in staying in either a **private house** or a neighbouring **farm**; provided you've got your own transport, the latter can be a tremendous bargain, particularly for stays of four days or more. Otherwise, there are plenty of **hotels**; it should be possible to get a room for around DM30 at *Roter Hahn*, Lange Gasse 16 (☎09851/2225); *Goldenes Lamm*, Lange Gasse 26-28 (☎09851/2267); *Sonne und Palmengarten*, Weinmarkt 11 (☎09851/2330 or 6044); *Zum Nördlinger Tor*, Nördlinger Str. 46 (☎09851/456); or *Pension Lutz*, Schäfergässlein 4 (☎09851/454). Note, however, that prices at most of these vary unusually widely according to the size and quality of the room. All the hotels in the town centre have good **restaurants**, which are generally surprisingly good value: even *Deutsches Haus* serves affordable meals. The **youth hostel** is housed in an old granary at Koppengasse 10 (☎09851/509 or 825), while there's a **campsite** (☎09851/7817) to the northeast of the old town, just off the road from Rothenburg. Dinkelsbühl lies on a railway line which used to provide a useful link with Nördlingen, the next stop on the Romantic Road some 30km south, but this has been superceded, probably permanently, by a **bus** service.

BAVARIAN SWABIA

Approximately bordered by the Rivers Iller and Lech, the southwestern part of Bavaria has a small-scale landscape of rolling farmland dotted with quiet villages and medieval towns. The region is called **Bavarian Swabia** (*Bayerisch-Schwaben*) and used to form part of the medieval Duchy of Swabia, the rest of which became the separate state of Württemberg. Its capital is **Augsburg**, an elegant city with fine Renaissance architecture, largely unspoilt by later building.

North of here is the stretch of the **Romantic Road** immediately following the initial Franconian section; its main draw is **Nördlingen**, a well-preserved walled town in a truly extraordinary setting. There's also a relatively little-known part of the **Danube valley**, including towns such as **Donauwörth**, **Dillingen** and **Günzburg** which were once major medieval trading posts but are now picturesquely provincial. South of Augsburg is the **Allgäu** region. The hilly pre-Alpine section includes the pretty town of **Kaufbeuren** and the health resort of **Ottobeuren**, whose Benediectine abbey should stun even the most jaded visitor of Baroque churches. Beyond here, everything is played against the dramatic backdrop of snow-capped mountains and sparkling lakes: highlights are the pair of fantasy castles near **Füssen**; **Oberstdorf**, a top-class resort set amid challenging peaks; and the island town of **Lindau** on the Bodensee.

An added pleasure of travelling through this region is the distinctive and excellent **food**: delicate handmade pasta and rich sauces quite different from the Italian kind, followed by sweets with irreverent names like *Nonnenfürzle* ("Nun's Fart") and *Versoffene Jungfern* ("Drunken Virgins").

Nördlingen

NÖRDLINGEN, together with ninety-nine villages, lies in an enormous crater, known as the **Ries**, which was formed by a meteor about 15 million years ago. The crater, which has a diameter of about 25km, is among the largest on earth, and presents one of the main locations for scientists to study stone formations similar to those on the moon. It also provided ideal terrain for the Apollo 14 team to prepare for their lunar mission.

The town centre

Along with Rothenburg and Dinkelsbühl, Nördlingen makes up the trio of towns on the Romantic Road which have almost completely retained their fortified medieval character. Of the three, it's probably the least intact, the historic sense diluted by a couple of modern eyesores; but the illusion remains clear. The fourteenth-century **Stadtmauer** forms an almost perfect circle, guarded by five gates, eleven towers and one bastion. As at Rothenburg, you can traverse the covered sentry walk all the way round the 3km circuit. There are also limited opportunities for ascending the eastern gateway, the **Löpsinger Tor** (May–mid-Oct Fri, Sat and Sun 10am–noon and 1.30–4.30pm; DM2).

The Danielturm and St Georg

However, the best view is from the 90-metre **Danielturm** (daily 9am–sundown; DM3), the town's symbol, its highest building – and also the bull's-eye of the circular urban plan. Crafted out of volcanic stone from the Ries crater, the tower illustrates a gradual shift in architectural tastes from the late Gothic of its lower storeys to the full-blooded Renaissance of its cupola. Halfway up the stairs is what looks like a huge wooden hamster wheel: built for convicts, whose job it was to keep the wheel that operated the lift turning, it was used until the last century. The Danielturm actually forms part of the hall church of **St Georg**, which closely resembles its contemporaneous namesake in Dinkelsbühl. Pride of the furnishings is the emotional polychrome wood *Crucifixion* group at the high altar, recently recognised as the work of the Dutchman Nicolaus Gerhaert von Leyden, one of the greatest sculptors of the fifteenth century.

Around the Rathaus

On the opposite side of the spacious Marktplatz lies the **Rathaus** which has an entertaining little detail beside its ritzy outdoor stairway. The space underneath the steps used to hold the town's prisoners, and just by the wooden entrance is a medieval fool carved into the wall with an inscription saying *Nun sind unser zwey* – "Now there are two of us". (Him, and you looking at him.) Directly across is the half-timbered **Tanzhaus** (Dance Hall), bearing a statue of Emperor Maximilian I who had a special affinity with the town; he's depicted in the guise by which he most wanted to be remembered, that of a chivalrous knight. Walking northwards from Marktplatz, you reach the curious building known as the **Klösterle** ("Little Monastery"), which has had a decidedly chequered history. Once the church of the bare-footed Franciscan friars, it was converted into a grain store after the Reformation, and is now the town's main festive hall.

The Stadtmuseum

Beyond, on Vordere Gerbergasse, is the **Spital**, an extensive medieval hospital complex complete with its own church, mill and stores. It now houses the **Stadtmuseum** (March–Nov Tues–Sun 10am–noon and 1.30–4.30pm; DM4), whose main treasure is a colourful cycle of paintings of *The Legend of St George* by the fifteenth-century local master Friedrich Herlin; originally this formed the reverse of Gerhaert's high altar in the eponymous church. The local history section features terrible exhibits from the torture chambers that were used throughout the Middle Ages, but especially during the sixteenth-century witch-hunts: in Nördlingen alone 35 women were put to death. There's also a diorama of the Battle of Nördlingen of 1634, the worst Protestant reverse in the Thirty Years' War, when the Swedes were at last defeated by the numerically superior combined forces of the Imperial army and Spain. On nearby Hintere Gerbergasse, a brand new **Reiskrater-Museum** (mid-Jan to mid-Dec Tues–Sun 10am–noon and 1.30–4.30pm; DM3) has been established to give detailed information on the Ries crater's formation and geological history.

Practicalities

Nördlingen's **Bahnhof**, which lies on the slow route between Augsburg and Stuttgart via Schwäbisch Gmünd, is just to the southwest of the old town. The **tourist office** is at Marktplatz 2 (April–Sept Mon–Fri 8am–6pm, Sat and Sun 9.30am–12.30pm; Oct–March Mon–Fri 8am–5pm ☎09081/4380 or 84116). Of the **hotels**, the following are the cheapest, with rates beginning at DM25: *Auktor*, Salvatorgasse 4 (☎09081/3240); *Walfisch*, Hallgasse 15 (☎09081/3107); and *Zum Goldenen Lamm*, Schäfflesmarkt 3 (☎09081/4206). The last-named has one of the best **restaurants** in town; another good choice is the brewery-owned *Zum Engel*, Wemdinger Str. 4 (☎09081/3167 or 6373), whose rooms are more expensive, beginning at DM38 for singles, DM72 for doubles. There's also a **youth hostel**, outside the old town walls at Kaiserwiese 1 (☎09081/84109).

If you're around town in mid-May, look out for the *Stabenfest*, an annual **festival** that celebrates the arrival of spring with a children's procession. On the appointed day (a Monday), trumpets sound the festival's beginning from the heights of the Danielturm and boys gather holding flags and poles decorated with flowers, the girls wearing costumes and crowns of flowers around their heads. At around 9am, the procession moves off accompanied by music and song until it reaches the Kaiserwiese, where the usual trappings of a Bavarian fair are set up around the beer tent. Another popular yearly event is the *Scharlachrennen* in September, whose origins lie in a horse race first held in 1438, with a piece of red cloth as a prize. Today, carriage events are also featured.

Harburg

From Nördlingen, it's only about 15km by road or rail to the next stop on the Romantic Road, the small town of **HARBURG**. High above, dominating the valley of the River Wörnitz, is a huge **Schloss** (guided tours mid-March–Oct daily 9–11.30am and 1.30–4.30pm; DM5), which was founded in the twelfth century by the Hohenstaufen emperors, before passing to the Counts of Oettingen, whose descendants still own it. Never taken in battle, its fortifications and residential buildings – which date from a variety of periods – survive in pretty good condition. The Fürstenbau has been fitted out as a **museum**, whose valuable art treasures include one of the most extensive collections of work by the great woodcarver Tilman Riemenschneider outside Würzburg.

The Danube valley

About 10km south of Harburg, the Wörnitz flows into the **Danube**. From here, there's a choice of routes: the Romantic Road continues south to the regional capital of Augsburg, but it would be a pity not to follow the Danube for a bit, either downstream to Neuburg and Ingolstadt (see *Upper Bavaria*), or upstream towards the boundary with Baden-Württemberg at Ulm. The landscape of the latter route, with its wide river bed and flat moorland interspersed by chalky promontories, makes for good **walking** and **cycling** country. There's a well-marked, 240km-long cycling route all the way from Ulm to Regensburg in Eastern Bavaria; bikes can be hired at most train stations and returned to another station almost anywhere in western Germany. Dotted along the river bank are a number of small historic towns which make welcome stopping-off points.

Donauwörth

Itself a staging post on the Romantic Road, **DONAUWÖRTH** is a busy, workaday market town at the confluence of the Danube and Wörnitz. Until last century, it was the last navigable point on the Danube, and this situation has helped give it an illustrious history out of all proportion to its present size. Once a prosperous city-state on the key trade route between Nürnberg and Augsburg, its attempted capture by the Imperial party in 1608 directly led to the division of Germany into hostile Protestant and Catholic military alliances, which in turn resulted in the devastations of the Thirty Years' War.

Although badly destroyed in 1945, Donauwörth has been carefully restored. The central **Reichsstrasse**, named after the old trade route, once more gives testimony to that time. Its most prominent monument is one of the fifteenth-century hall churches so typical of the region, **St Mariae Himmelfahrt**, which boasts a notable set of stained glass windows and a delicately tapering tabernacle. Two other Gothic public buildings on the street are the **Rathaus** and the **Tanzhaus**; these now house the tourist office (☎0906/789145) and the top local restaurant respectively. However, they're rather upstaged by a private residence, the magnificent Renaissance **Fuggerhaus**, built for the famous Augsburg banking dynasty (see box on p.178). Also of special note is the Baroque monastery and pilgrimage church of **Heiliges-Kreuz** on the street of the same name, which is an outstanding example of the distinctive churches built and decorated by the craftsmen of Wessobrunn. Finally, parts of the town's fortifications survive, including two gateways – the **Riedertor** and the **Färbertor** – on the Danube side.

Dillingen

About 40km upstream from Donauwörth lies **DILLINGEN**, a good example of that very German phenomenon, the ex-university town. A property of the Augsburg prince-bishopric from the mid-thirteenth century, it lay in obscurity until the Reformation. Because of the key role Augsburg played in the momentous events of the time, the bishops moved their main residence to Dillingen, establishing a college of Catholic theology in 1549 which was granted university status five years later. Along with Ingolstadt – ironically another city deprived of its university in the Napoleonic period – it became a leading theoretical centre of the Counter-Reformation.

Nowadays demoted to serving as a teacher training college, the academic buildings are concentrated on Kardinal-von-Waldburg-Strasse, the street named in honour of their founder. The **Alte Universität** itself boasts a resplendent main hall, the *Goldener Saal*, though this was closed for restoration at the time of writing. Even more intriguing is the **Studienkirche**, which was built in the early seventeenth century as a simplified version of the revolutionary Jesuit church of St Michael in Munich and given an unlikely but highly successful Rococo interior transformation a century and a half later. It's reckoned to be one of the most imitated buildings in the country, inspiring hundreds of other churches. The reason for this is that, during the eighteenth-century craze for building new churches in southern Germany, a large percentage of the priests had spent their formative years worshipping here and thus regarded it as something of a model design.

Günzburg

GÜNZBURG, the last significant stop before the Land border is reached, is a likeable market town, with gabled houses characteristic of the late Middle Ages. Its history is every bit as illustrious as Donauwörth's: at the beginning of the fourteenth century it came into the possession of the Habsburgs, who built the Renaissance **Schloss** as one of their residences, earning the town the nickname of "Little Vienna". Marie-Antoinette stayed there en route to her wedding in Paris, a journey along the self-same route between the capitals whose trading importance gave Günzburg its prosperity. However, the town's outstanding monument is Dominikus Zimmerman's **Liebfrauenkirche**, a Rococo masterpiece which rings the changes on the oval design he favoured in both the earlier Steinhausen and the later Wieskirche, adopting instead a rectangular format.

Two annual **festivals** liven up the place in the summer: the two-day *Guntia-Fest* at the end of June, and the *Sommerfest* in August. For information on exact dates, contact the **tourist office**, in the Rathaus on Schlossplatz (☎08221/903111). Cheapest **hotel** is the *Gasthof Rose*, Augsburger Str. 23 (☎08221/5802), which charges between DM20 and DM25 per person. There's also a **youth hostel** right in the heart of town at Schillerstr. 12 (☎08221/95525).

Augsburg

Only 60km northwest of Munich, and a quarter of the size, **AUGSBURG** certainly doesn't suffer from any inferiority complexes. Founded in 15BC as *Augusta Vindelicorum* by two stepsons of Augustus Caesar, the city is one of the oldest in Germany, with a name which still means exactly what it did in Roman times: "Fortress of Augustus". A Free Imperial City from 1276 and a frequent choice for meetings of the Diet, Augsburg had its heyday between the fifteenth and seventeenth centuries, when the **Fugger** and **Welser** dynasties made it Europe's most important centre of high finance; as a result it grew into one of the largest cities on the continent. It was the one place in Germany to take the Renaissance style to its heart, and the stylish buildings of **Elias Holl** still dominate the cityscape today.

Local people seem genuinely proud of the town, and they've gone to vast expense to restore the numerous palaces and civic buildings to their original splendour. In fact civilian municipal life is the key to Augsburg's history. Trade and banking riches spawned a social conscience – in 1514 Augsburg built the world's first housing estate for the poor, the **Fuggerei**, an institution still in use today. Here too the revolutionary reforms of Martin Luther found their earliest support, as the city played a pivotal role in the Reformation and its aftermath. It became the model example of how different faiths could co-exist, making this visible by the curious practice of building new Protestant churches alongside existing Catholic ones.

Despite these associations, Augsburg isn't just a museum-piece. It has long been a leading centre for **new technologies**: here, for example, Rudolf Diesel invented the engine which has put his name into languages all round the world. There's also a lively cultural scene ranging from Mozart festivals to jazz and cabaret, and the local University means that plenty of student bars and a thriving "alternative" culture keep the place on its toes.

The telephone code for Augsburg is ☎0821.

Getting around and accommodation

The **Hauptbahnhof** lies just to the west of the Altstadt. **Exchange facilities** are available within the station (Mon–Fri 9.45am–noon and 2.30–5.45pm, Sat 9.30am–1.30pm, Sun 10am–1.30pm), while the **tourist office** (Mon–Fri 9am–6pm, Sat 9am–1pm; ☎36026) is just outside at Bahnhofstr. 7. The **youth hostel** is centrally located, three minutes' walk from the Dom, at Beim Pfaffenkeller 3 (☎33909); if you're coming from the Bahnhof, take tram #2 to *Stadtwerke*. **Hotels** in the region of DM30 for singles and DM60 for doubles are to be found in the suburb of LECHHAUSEN, 1.5 km from the city centre and well connected by three bus routes. Try the following for good value: *Bayerische Löwe*, Linke Brandstr. 2 (☎702870); *Linderhof*, Aspernstr. 38 (☎73216); and *Märkl*, Schillerstr. 20 (☎791499). The nearest **campsite** is at motorway exit *Augsburg-Ost*, next to the Autobahnsee (☎714121).

The city

Augsburg is a remarkably easy city to get to grips with, and everything you're likely to want to see is within walking distance of the centre. The Altstadt is defined by the old fortifications, substantial parts of which still survive; the central Maximilianstrasse makes a ready reference point for exploring the various quarters.

Rathausplatz

Heart of the city is the spacious cobbled **Rathausplatz**, which turns into a massive open-air café during the summer and a glittering Christmas market in December. At the baseline of this great semi-circle stands the massive **Rathaus** (daily 10am–6pm; free), built by Elias Holl, and generally regarded as Germany's finest example of a secular Renaissance building. The proportions and style of the elegantly plain exterior topped by two octagonal towers recall a Florentine palace rather than a town hall, a likeably overstated symbol of Augsburg's wealth and influence. What stands today is a painstaking reconstruction of the original, whose shell was all that survived the 1944 air raid which targeted the city's Messerschmidt aircraft factories. Not that you'd guess this from looking at the showpiece **Goldener Saal**, which is once more resplendent with its gold-leaf pillars, marble floor and painted cedarwood ceiling .

Next to the Rathaus stands the **Perlachturm** (daily April, May and Sept 10am–6pm; June–Aug 10am–9pm; Oct 10am–4pm; DM2): originally the town's watchtower, it was remodelled by Holl to its present height of just over 70m. A climb to the top gives a good vantage point from which to take in the whole town and get your bearings on Augsburg's main axis, neatly formed between the Dom to the north and the church of SS-Ulrich-und-Afra at the far end of Maximilianstrasse to the south. Back at ground level stands the Mannerist **Augustusbrunnen**, one of many grandiose fountains dotting the centre of the city, bearing symbolic figures representing Augsburg's four rivers.

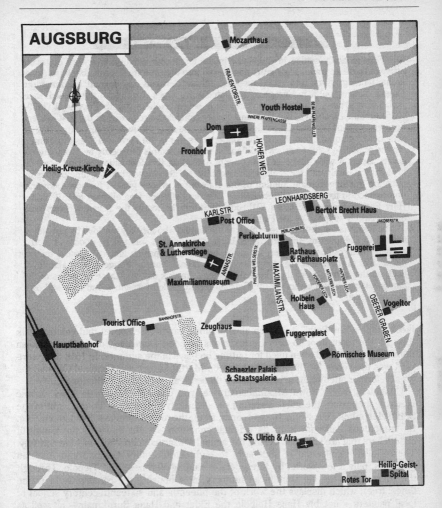

AUGSBURG

Mozarthaus

FRAUENTORSTR.

Youth Hostel

BEI ST PFAFFENKELLER

INNERE PFAFFENGASSE

Dom

Fronhof

Heilig-Kreuz-Kirche

HOHER WEG

LEONHARDSBERG

KARLSTR.

Bertolt Brecht Haus

Post Office

JAKOBERSTR.

Perlachturm

PERLACHBERG

St. Annakirche
& Lutherstiege

Rathaus
& Rathausplatz

Fuggerei

ANNASTR.

PHILIPPINE WELSERSTR.

MAXIMILIANSTR.

Maximilianmuseum

VORDERER LECH

HINTERER LECH

MITTLERER LECH

Holbein
Haus

Vogeltor

OBERER GRABEN

Tourist Office

BAHNHOFSTR.

Zeughaus

Fuggerpalast

Hauptbahnhof

Römisches Museum

Schaezler Palais
& Staatsgalerie

SS. Ulrich & Afra

Heilig-Geist-
Spital

Rotes Tor

Maximilianstrasse

Maximilianstrasse is a true showpiece thoroughfare, lined with the headquarters of the leading corporate and municipal bodies, and the palatial residences of the richest merchant families who dominated their affairs. It's named in honour of the Habsburg Maximilian I, the last Holy Roman Emperor to preside over a unified empire and the man who set in motion his family's ambitious plans for European-wide domination. Augsburg was his favourite residence – no doubt partly because his political scheming was dependent on the backing of the city's bankers.

The first building of note is the fourteenth-century **Weberzunfthaus**, the guild hall of the linen weavers. Beyond, in the centre of the street, is the resplendent **Merkurbrunnen** by Dutch-born Mannerist, Adrian de Vries, court sculptor to the Habsburgs. Soon after, the **Fuggerpalast** stands proudly to the right. Built in 1515 by

> ### THE FUGGER DYNASTY
>
> The Fugger family settled in Augsburg in the fourteenth century, and were originally active in the linen trade. They gradually moved into the even more profitable business of money-lending, which they established throughout Germany and beyond, becoming the biggest banking outfit in Europe and reputedly five times richer than the Medici, their Italian counterparts. Although the youngest of seven brothers, **Jacob Fugger II** (1459–1525) became the head of the firm, and can legitimately be regarded as the first modern business tycoon. He established the family interests as a public company, expanding its activities by gaining mining rights for copper and silver in the Tyrol and Silesia and entering the profitable spice trade. In addition, he safeguarded his prosperity by spreading his assets across a wide range of investments, including the acquisition of land – which brought the family into the ranks of the nobility. He also moved into big-time politics by initiating the long-running funding of the Habsburgs, whose goal of European domination seemed to have been achieved when Charles I of Spain won election in 1519 as the Holy Roman Emperor Charles V through outright bribes to the seven Electors with money largely supplied by the Fuggers.
>
> The Reformation dealt a severe blow to the family, who lost key markets by remaining faithful to Catholicism, though the Habsburg connection was put to good use in the establishment of business interests in the burgeoning Spanish empire. Some 4 million ducats lent to the Habsburgs have never been repaid, but the Fuggers were able to sit back on the income from their landed holdings. To this day, the three branches of the family retain a high position in the German league table of wealth – and they still own their own bank.

Jacob Fugger "the Rich", it still remains in family hands (see above), but you can walk through the main door to see the luxurious arcaded *Damenhof*, designed in Italian Renaissance style and often used for putting on plays in the summer. In 1518 this courtyard was the venue for the meeting between Martin Luther and Cardinal Cajetan, the great reformer attempting to justify his 95 theses against Catholic orthodoxy.

Continuing south down Maximilianstrasse, you come to Adrian de Vries' heroic **Herkulesbrunnen**, the most arresting of all the city's fountains. To the right is the **Schaezlerpalais** (Tues–Sun 10am–4/5pm; free), the town's foremost Rococo building. Its sumptuous ballroom is in its original condition – right down to the candle-lit chandeliers that are still used during the annual Mozart concerts held in June and July. There's also a collection of sixteenth- to eighteenth-century German and Austrian paintings, plus a few works by foreigners, including Veronese and Tiepolo. Through the courtyard is the old Dominican nunnery, now housing the **Staatsgalerie** (same times; free), which displays the work of the fifteenth- and sixteenth-century school of local painters – notably Hans Holbein the Elder and Hans Burgkmair – as well as Dürer's portrait of Jacob Fugger "the Rich", looking every bit the king-maker that he was.

Towards its end, Maximilianstrasse widens and sweeps up to the late Gothic basilica of **SS-Ulrich-und-Afra**, whose onion-domed tower is the earliest example of what came to be a distinctive architectural trademark, particularly in southern Germany. In the airily light interior are the tombs of the city's two patrons. Saint Afra, a Roman virgin martyr, is interred in a simple Romanesque sarcophagus, whereas Saint Ulrich, the local prince-bishop whose army helped save the empire by turning back the rampaging Magyars at the Battle of Lechfeld in 955, is honoured by an ornate Rococo shrine. The monumental gilded altars by Hans Degler are early masterpieces of Baroque. In the early eighteenth century, the tiny Lutheran church of **St Ulrich** was built up against the basilica as a sign of religious tolerance, its gabled front creating a cheerful contrast to its sober neighbour.

East of Maximilianstrasse

Just to the southeast of SS-Ulrich-und-Afra is another distinctive landmark, the **Rotes Tor**, a fortified tower strengthened by Holl at the time of the Thirty Years' War, whose courtyard is now put to effective use as an open-air theatre. The same architect's **Heilig-Geist-Spital** alongside is likewise a cultural centre, featuring displays of handicrafts and the celebrated *Puppenkiste* marionette theatre.

Following Bäckergasse and then Dominikanergasse back towards the city centre, you come to the former Dominican monastery, which now houses the **Römisches Museum** (Tues–Sun 10am–4/5pm; free), the city's collection of prehistoric and Roman remains. The whitewashed interior of the church makes an excellent setting for the artefacts, and the uncluttered layout is in pleasant contrast to the warehouse-like approach of so many museums. One of the highlights is a life-sized second-century bronze horse's head, which was probably part of a statue honouring Emperor Marcus Aurelius.

East of here is the most impressive surviving part of the medieval **Stadtmauer**, dominated by the fifteenth-century **Vogeltor**; several other gateways and fragments of walls can be found scattered around the eastern and northern boundaries of the old city. Beyond lies the picturesque old artisans' quarter, laid out along the narrow canals of the Vorderer, Mittlerer and Unterer Lech. These back streets must have looked very similar a few hundred years ago, when they were populated with the tradesfolk and craftspeople who serviced the grand houses on Maximilianstrasse. At Vorderer Lech 20 the **Holbeinhaus** (Tues–Sun 10am–4/5pm; free) stands on the site of the original, which was destroyed in 1944. Here Hans the Younger, portraitist of the brilliant English court of Henry VIII, spent his childhood, his father having established himself as the city's leading painter. Changing exhibitions complement documents on the artists' lives.

The city's relationship with another of its famous sons, **Bertolt Brecht**, is a little more clouded: the embarrassing fact is that the people of Augsburg couldn't stand Brecht while he was alive – but then neither could he stomach his bourgeois home city. Today, however, all is forgotten, and his birthplace at Auf dem Rain 7 has been turned into a memorial **museum** (Tues–Sun 10am–4/5pm). Not surprisingly this concentrates on the artist's Augsburg period, using mainly photographic material of the playwright and his contemporaries, as well as of early theatrical productions of his works.

BERTOLT BRECHT AND AUGSBURG

Bertolt Brecht was born in 1898, the son of a sales assistant, and seemed set for a conventional middle-class life. He went to the local grammar school, was confirmed in the Lutheran church, and was just trying his hand in the school paper when World War I broke out in 1914. He remained in Augsburg for the duration of the war, emerging as a staunch pacifist and becoming a porter in the local hospital. When he left the town in 1919, it was to sign on as a medical student in Munich, though it was soon apparent where his ambitions really lay, and he became a regular contributor to the literary and theatrical events at the University. More than two decades later, he used the backdrop of the city during the Thirty Years' War, when the tensions caused by its religious duality boiled over into terrible bloodshed, as the setting for a short story, *The Augsburg Chalk Circle*. This was subsequently re-worked, using the same plot but with a completely different location, into one of his most famous plays, *The Caucasian Chalk Circle*.

The Függerei

One "Our Father", one "Hail Mary" and one "Credo" daily, plus DM1.72 per annum, and good Catholic paupers can retire to the **Fuggerei** at the age of 55. It's the world's oldest housing estate for the poor and must be one of the cleverest ploys ever devised for a place in Heaven – even if it now seems that Jacob Fugger's seeming generosity was at least partly inspired by the opportunities it offered for laundering part of his fortune. Entered via a gate which, in accordance with the still-enforced original regulations, is kept locked between 10pm and 5am, it's a town within a town, and, compared with modern housing estates, is a real idyll: two-storey ivy-covered houses line six carless streets, the cloister-like atmosphere disturbed only by the odd ringing doorbell. Admittedly it all seems a bit like walking through a giant doll's house, and the inhabitants are used to having hoards of tourists peering through their windows. However, for the price and the odd prayer it still seems like a pretty good deal: in fact the rent, the equivalent of one Rhenish guilder, has been frozen since the scheme started in 1514, though the 300 residents who live there now have to pay a modest supplement to the local authority for such modern conveniences as running water and street cleaning.

The **Fuggereimuseum** (March–Oct daily 9am–6pm; Nov Sat and Sun 9am-6pm; DM1) has been set up in one of the original houses, no. 13 in the Mittlere Gasse; its furnishings vividly illustrate the lifestyle of the community's inhabitants of the seventeenth and eighteenth centuries. Another house from the time of the first settlement is no. 14 in the same street, which is where Mozart's great-grandfather lived in the late seventeenth century.

West of Maximilianstrasse

Exactly the other side of town, in the Annastrasse, stands the unassuming **church of St Anna**; judging from its outside appearance, you'd never guess that it's one of the most important monuments in Augsburg. In 1509, Ulrich and Jacob Fugger endowed a memorial chapel here for themselves and their deceased brother Georg. The clout they wielded is shown by the fact that, against all convention, this formed an extension of the nave, instead of taking the humbler normal position off an aisle. It seems there was a certain amount of skulduggery on both sides of this agreement – the prior thereby hoped to increase the capacity of his church without having to dip into the funds, while the brothers did their utmost to seal off public access from the word go.

AUGSBURG AND THE REFORMATION

Luther's summons before Cajetan was the first of four meetings in Augsburg which were crucial to the subsequent history of the entire Christian world. The rebellious monk was given no opportunity to explain his position: instead, he was ordered to make an unconditional repentance. His refusal to do this led him to fear for his life, and he escaped from the city forthwith under cover of darkness. Twelve years later, with the Reformation already established in many parts of Germany, Charles V called a Diet in an attempt to enforce conformity, with Luther banned from attendance. However, the rulers of the Protestant parts of the Empire, including the Elector of Saxony and the Landgrave of Hessen, refused to acquiesce, an action which effectively meant the end of the Holy Roman Empire in all but name. Luther's lieutenant Philipp Melanchton drew up the **Augsburg Confession** on behalf of the Protestant princes. This document, which remains the basic creed of all Lutheran churches, stated there was no difference of faith with Catholicism, but there were seven abuses of practice to which they objected.

When wars failed to re-unite the Empire, Charles V tried again in 1547 by means of the **Augsburg Interim** to enforce conformity. This gave way to the Reformers on two points – the right of priests to marry, and of the laity to receive wine as well as bread at Communion. However, this was insufficient to placate the Protestant parts of the realm, and Charles finally had to concede defeat by the compromise **Peace of Augsburg** seven years later, which recognised that Germany was now divided into a host of separate states. From then on, the ruler of each territory was free to choose his own religion – and to force his subjects to follow suit or go elsewhere; the Catholic position was safeguarded by forcing ecclesiastical princes to cede their lands and territory if they wished to convert. Only in the Free Imperial Cities (such as Augsburg itself) were the two faiths supposed to be allowed to co-exist.

The sumptuous **Fuggerkapelle** which resulted marks the belated German debut of the full-blooded Italian Renaissance style, a spin-off of the family's extensive business interests in Italy. An integrated, no-expenses-spared decorative scheme – marble pavement, stained glass, choir stalls, balustrade with putti, a monumental sculptural group of *The Lamentation over the Dead Christ*, and memorial relief tablets made after woodcuts designed by Dürer – creates an effect of overwhelming richness, now sadly somewhat diminished as a result of wartime destruction. No-one knows for sure whether the chapel was created by German or Italian craftsmen, but its influence on Augsburg was profound, inspiring all subsequent building activity there for over a century.

The architectural innovations aren't the only reason for St Anna's importance; it's also celebrated because of its historical role during the Reformation, in which Augsburg played such a prominent part (see opposite). Luther found refuge with its Carmelite monks when he was summoned to meet the Pope's legate Cardinal Cajetan, and today part of the monastery has been turned into the **Lutherstiege** (Tues–Sun 10am–noon and 3–5pm; free), a museum of the reformer's life and times. Along with extensive documentation on the events, you can see the *Luther Kammer*, the actual room where he stayed in 1518; the *Empore*, the old gallery for the Carmelite monks, shows the excommunication bull which resulted from his refusal to retract his views.

Across from the monastery, at Philippine-Welser-Str. 24, is the **Maximiliansmuseum** (Tues–Sun 10am-4/5pm; free), whose displays illustrate the city's historic and cultural development. Here you can see Elias Holl's building plans, exquisite book illustrations, and exhibits on the artisan and trade guilds from the tenth to the eighteenth century. The sixteenth-century mansion is itself of note as the home of the Welsers, Augsburg's second most powerful family, who once owned all of Venezuela. A couple of blocks further south, dominating the square named after it, is the **Zeughaus**, the first structure designed by Holl in his capacity as municipal architect. It's a brilliantly original composition whose facade is uncannily anticipatory of the Baroque style to come. Above its doorway is a striking monumental bronze group of *St Michael overcoming Satan*, the masterpiece of Hans Reichle, one of the few native German Mannerists.

North of Maximilianstrasse

Dominating the northern part of the old city is the **Dom**. Architecturally, it's a bit of a hotchpotch: in the fourteenth century, Gothic aisles were added to the original eleventh-century structure; a hundred years later, a lofty hall choir replaced its predecessor altogether. Nonetheless, it contains many outstanding features. The southwestern entrance has enormous Romanesque **bronze doors**, decorated with 32 endearingly simple panels portraying the story of Adam and Eve. In contrast, the **portals** on the north and south sides of the chancel are dedicated to the Virgin Mary, and are crowded with richly decorative Gothic sculptures. On the southern side of the nave's clerestory are five **stained glass windows** showing the Old Testament figures of Moses, David, Hosea, Daniel and Jonah. The freshness of colour and the vibrancy of the design make it hard to believe they were made in the eleventh century: they're the oldest windows to be found in any church in the world. Another Romanesque survivor is the **bishop's throne** in the west choir, imperiously perched on crouching lions. Look out also for the four fine **altarpieces** by Hans Holbein the Elder, fixed to the pillars at the end of the nave, of scenes from the life of the Virgin.

Facing the Dom's facade is the **Fronhof**, the former episcopal residence and the place where the Confession of Augsburg was first presented. Nowadays, it's the seat of the regional government; the Catholic bishop now lives in the palace at Hohen Weg 18 on the other side of the Dom. Further west is the **Heilig-Kreuz-Kirche**, another of the groups of paired Catholic and Protestant churches. Both contain fine religious paintings, with the star being the former's high altar of *The Assumption* by Rubens.

North of the Dom, at Frauentorstr. 30, is the **Mozarthaus** (Mon, Wed and Thurs 10am–noon and 2–5pm, Fri 10am–noon and 2–4pm, Sat and Sun 10am–noon; free), which documents the lives of Leopold and Wolfgang Amadeus and contains a number of bits and pieces of the original furnishings. Actually, this modest little house was the birthplace of Leopold, who moved to Salzburg long before his famous son was born; nonetheless, you can't really blame Augsburg for wanting to claim a place in the Mozart biography. In any case, Leopold himself, best-known as a Svengali figure, is now recognised as a highly competent composer in his own right, whose works include one of the best trumpet concertos ever written and the comical *Toy Symphony*.

Eating and drinking

In the food and drink field, Augsburg's main strengths are a wide range of restaurants offering hearty traditional fare, plus a surprisingly large number of student pubs. In addition to the places listed below, it's worth knowing about the market and meat halls off Annastrasse, where you'll find several *Imbiss* stands which are the best bet for on-your-feet snacks.

Restaurants

Don Giovanni, Schmiedberg 15a. Good cheap Italian restaurant.

Drei-Rosen, Blücherstr. 27. Augsburg's only vegetarian restaurant; closes on Wednesdays.

Fuggerei-Stube, Jakoberstr. 26. The "local" of the Fuggerei, serving some of the best food in town.

Fuggerkeller, Maximilianstr. 38. Typically hearty German fare at reasonable prices is served up in the cellar of the Fuggerpalast.

Sieben-Schwaben-Stuben, Bürgermeister-Fischer-Str. 12. Offers really excellent traditional Swabian cooking: read up on "Drunken Virgins" and "Stone Men" in the newspaper-type menu.

Zeughaus-Stuben, Zeughausplatz 4. Another good choice for local cuisine, in the historic setting of the Zeughaus itself.

Bars and cafés

Alte Münz, Mittlerer Lech. Augsburg's only gay bar.

Alternativ-Kneipe, Kappeneck 30. Friendly, youthful café-bar with a wide range of drinks and snacks.

Café Stadler, Bahnhofstr. 30. Elegant choice for *Kaffee und Kuchen* – and conveniently placed to while away the time waiting for a train.

Grauer Adler, Mittlerer Lech 7. Student pub cum cabaret venue.

Riegele, Herman-Köhl-Str. 5. Spacious student bar which also serves small meals.

Sputnik, Steffenstr. 32. The leading late-nighter; open 9pm till 3am, 4pm at weekends.

Striese, Kirchgasse 1. Another student favourite, sometimes featuring theatre and live music.

Thing, Vorderer Lech 45. Popular rendezvous point with the younger brigade.

Underground, Kapuzinergasse 1. Jazz bar with good atmosphere and late opening hours though rather unimaginative music.

Nightlife and festivals

Augsburg's most famous **theatre** is the *Puppenkiste*; even with the language barrier, kids will love the marionette shows, but tickets are hard to come by: contact the box office at Spitalgasse 15 (☎324 4976) well in advance. The *Freilichtbühne* in the adjoining Rotes Tor mounts its open-air season of plays – with Brecht now featuring regularly – in June and July. Another attractive venue is the little Baroque *Schauspielhaus Komödie*, Vorderer Lech 8, though the much larger and functional *Stadttheater*, Kennedyplatz 1 and the *Kongresshalle*, Göppinger Str. 10 are where most highbrow dramatic and musical events are held.

There's a surprising dearth of **discos** and nightclubs, but try *Alexis*, Ulmerstr. 121 (Sun–Thurs 9pm–2am, Fri and Sat 9pm–3am). Heavy rock fans should check out the *Rockfabrik*, Riedinger Str. 24 (Mon–Thurs 8pm–3am, Fri and Sat 8pm–4am), north of the city centre on tram route #26 from Königsplatz.

The main local **festival** is *Plärrer*, which is rather like a smaller version of Munich's Oktoberfest, except that it takes place twice annually, lasting for a fortnight on each occasion. Under the name of *Georgi-Dult*, the spring version of this begins on the Sunday after Easter; its autumn counterpart is called the *Michaeli-Dult* and takes place on the last week in August and the first in September. Other annual events are the *Mozartfest* in June and July; the *Jakober Kirchweih* at the end of July; the *Friedensfest* (Peace Festival) on 8 August; the *Herbstfestat* at the end of September; and the *Christkindlesmarkt*, whose opening on 23 November is marked by a colourful pageant, and which features live Christmas music each subsequent weekend.

Listings

Bike hire available at the Hauptbahnhof.

Bookshop *Probuch*, Göggingerstr. 34, specialises in contemporary German literature and alternative books.

Community Arts Centre *Kresslesmühle*, Barfüsserstr. 4 (☎37170). A meeting place for many action groups, with live music and cabaret in the evenings.

Launderettes *Karkosch*, Vorderer Lech 27; *Kraus*, Bismarckstr. 11; *Poloczek*, Katharinengasse 22; *Steidle*, Ulmer Str. 143.

Student cultural centre *Asta Kulturzentrum*, Reitmayrgasse 4 (☎519610). Basically offers the same services as a British student union.

Women's centre Mauerbergstr. 31 (Mon–Tues 10.15am–12.15pm, Thurs 1–6pm; ☎153307). Runs a café and advice centre at these times.

The Allgäu

The southwesternmost part of Bavaria is known as the **Allgäu**, and is as famed for its cheeses – which are the finest produced in Germany – as for its magnificent scenery. There are four constituent parts to the region. Closest to Augsburg is the **Lower Allgäu** (*Unter-Allgäu* or *Allgäuer Voralpenland*), a rolling pre-Alpine landscape punctuated by a few towns, among which **Kaufbeuren** and **Ottobeuren** are particularly worth visiting. Prime attractions of the **Eastern Allgäu** (*Ost-Allgäu*) are the frivolous and extravagant but irresistible castles of **Hohenschwangau** and **Neuschwanstein**, which rather overshadow the neighbouring town of **Füssen**. Jutting into Austria is the **Upper Allgäu** (*Ober-Allgäu*), a classic Alpine area dominated by the resort of **Oberstdorf**. Finally, there's the **Western Allgäu** (*West-Allgäu*), part of which lies in Baden-Württemberg, though the Bavarian section includes the island town of **Lindau** on the shores of the **Bodensee**.

Kaufbeuren

Just south of Augsburg, the Romantic Road passes out of Bavarian Swabia, only re-entering it just before the terminus at Füssen. As an alternative to following the established route, which here enters its least interesting stretch, follow instead the Wertach valley 50km southwest by road or rail to **KAUFBEUREN**, which is in many ways reminiscent of the better-known and more heavily touristed medieval towns further north. Its sweet cobblestoned centre with picturesque houses is surrounded by an intact **Stadtmauer**, part of whose sentry walk survives. At the northwestern corner is the impressive fortified church of **St Blasius**, whose round tower has a decidedly military and unecclesiastical appearance. Ironically, the interior is a graceful Gothic hall, with an outstanding high altar featuring carvings by Jörg Lederer. The best time to visit the town is on the third Sunday of July when the highpoint of the main local **festival**, the *Tänzelfest*, occurs. This features a costumed procession performed by 1600 children, re-enacting a visit to the town by Emperor Maximilian I in 1497.

Northeast of the old part of Kaufbeuren is the suburb of **NEUGABLONZ**. This has a unique status in Germany, as it's the only community set up after World War II by refugees from a single area of the many in Eastern Europe from which German-speakers were forcibly displaced. The original Gablonz district, which had had a large German community since the sixteenth century, lay in the infamous Sudetenland, which was ceded to Hitler in 1938, but returned to Czechoslovakia after the war. (For information on how it is today, see *Czechoslovakia: The Rough Guide*.) Nearly a fifth of the 100,000 German inhabitants re-settled here, bringing with them their traditional glass and jewellery industries, which continue to be the mainstay of their economy today.

Ottobeuren

Some 25km west of Kaufbeuren is the small health resort of **OTTOBEUREN**. Situated on a gentle incline, the **Reichsabtei** stands alone above the village. This Benedictine abbey founded in 764 is one of the most imposing and grandiose monasteries north of the Alps. Its patron Charlemagne gave the abbot important rights, elevating him to the status of a prince who could make levies on the locals.

Architecturally the abbey has undergone many changes since its foundation, but its present Baroque **Abteikirche** was created, after several false starts by other architects, by the Munich master J.M. Fischer in the eighteenth century. It's huge: physical details such as the 90-metre nave and 60-metre transept hardly convey the bombastic impression you get on entering. The wealth of altars, frescos, paintings and stuccoed embellishments needs time to be appreciated fully, and yet there's nothing busy about the whole effect. Among the many treasures, a twelfth-century Romanesque *Crucifixion* is the most precious, but also special are the elaborate choir stalls and the three **organs**, considered among the most beautiful instruments in the world.

Apart from the church, there's also a **museum** (Mon–Sat 10am–noon and 2–5pm; Sun 10am–noon and 1–5pm; DM3), which is housed in a part of the abbot's palace. Highlights are the amazingly delicate seventeenth- and eighteenth-century inlaid furniture pieces and the beautiful Baroque library, which looks more like a ballroom than a place for contemplation, so rich is the decor of marble pillars and frescoed ceiling. Note also the theatre, which was an important element of arts teaching in any eighteenth-century Benedictine monastery.

Should you want to stay, there's a **youth hostel** at the southern edge of the village at Faichtmayrstr. 38 (☎08332/368), along with plenty of other budget accommodation. For a full list, contact the **tourist office** in the *Kurverwaltung* on Marktplatz (Mon–Fri 8am–noon and 2–5pm, May–Oct Sat 9am–noon).

Füssen and around

Füssen, which lies in a beautiful setting close to the Austrian border between the **Forggensee** reservoir and the **Ammer** mountains, is used by most visitors as a jumping-off point for the two royal castles situated some 5km to the southeast. However, the town itself is not without interest. If you're in the mood for a less famous but rather more aesthetically pleasing castle, visit the **Hohes Schloss** (April–Nov Mon–Sat

10am–noon and 2–4pm; DM3), which dominates the Lech valley from a position high above the town centre. Formerly a residence of the Bishops of Augsburg, it contains a number of Gothic apartments, the most notable being the *Rittersaal*. Below it stands the church of **St Mang**, named in honour of the eighth-century "Apostle of the Allgäu"; although mostly Baroque, it incorporates an earlier chapel painted with a representation of *The Dance of Death*. Now the local parish, the church was previously part of a Benedictine monastery whose handsome interiors now house the local history collections of the **Museum der Stadt Füssen** (April–Oct Tues–Sun 11am–4pm, Wed also 6–8pm; Nov–March Tues–Sat 2–4pm; DM3).

Hohenschwangau and Neuschwanstein

Highly commercialised and very expensive, the Bavarian royal castles are nonetheless worth the trip, if only for the surrounding scenery. **Hohenschwangau** (April–Sept daily 9am–5.30pm; Oct–May daily 10am–4pm; DM7) is, by origin, a genuine medieval fortress. The twelfth-century building was heavily damaged by Napoleon in 1800 and 1806, and was restored in an over-the-top Romantic style a few decades later when Crown Prince Maximilian bought it. **King Ludwig II** spent his youth here: a mark of his individualism is left in the bedroom, where he had the ceiling painted with stars that were spotlit in the evenings. The music room testifies to one of Ludwig's main passions, and in particular to his special friendship with the composer Richard Wagner who used to come and stay. Below the castle is the quiet **Alpsee**, great for quiet walks and very cold swims.

Neuschwanstein (same times; DM8) was built by Ludwig II between 1869 and 1886. A little higher up the mountain, it has since become famous in countless posters, cards and Disney films as the ultimate story-book castle, all fairy-tale pinnacles, swirling in a dream-like mist. It really looks far better from a distance than close up or inside: the architecture is a hotchpotch of styles, ranging from the Byzantine throne-hall to the Romanesque study, to an artificial grotto next to the living-room. Appropriately enough, it wasn't designed by a professional architect but by a team of theatre designers who were practiced at creating stage sets for Wagner's operas. The castle was never completed because King Ludwig was dethroned while work was still in progress. It's a bizarre monument to a very sad and lonely man.

A path behind Neuschwanstein leads to the **Marienbrücke**, a steel bridge regarded as quite a feat of engineering when it was constructed last century; it traverses the dramatic **Poellat gorge**, with its rushing waterfall. Continue steeply past the bridge for about another three hours and you reach the top of the **Tegelberg** (1720m), which commands views stretching as far as Munich on a good day. Another way to get up here is to take the cable car (daily 8.30am–5pm, DM12 ascent, DM19 return). The *Gasthaus* just below the castle serves **meals** at prices lower than you might expect.

Practicalities

Füssen's **Bahnhof**, the terminus of a line from Kaufbeuren, is at the northern end of town. From outside, **buses** marked *Königschlösser* leave at regular intervals for the castles. A couple of minutes' walk to the east, at Augsburger Torplatz 1, is the **tourist office** (July and Aug Mon–Fri 8am–noon and 1–7pm, Sat 10am–noon and 4–6pm, Sun 10am–noon; Sept–June Mon–Fri 8am–noon and 2–6pm, Sat 10am–noon; ☎08362/7077). Ask here about **private rooms**, which can be surprisingly good value at around DM20 per person, though a stay of three nights may be required. There are plenty of **hotels** in town, or, if you fancy staying near the castles, try *Haus Schwansee*, Parkstr. 9 (☎08362/8353), or *Pension Weiher*, Hofwiesenweg 11 (☎08362/81161): rates begin at DM25. The **youth hostel** is at the western edge of town at Mariahilferstr. 5 (☎08362/7754), while there are **campsites** by the Bannwaldsee and the Forggensee.

If you happen to be in the area on October 13, you can see the unique **Colomansfest** at the Colomanskirche near the village of SCHWANGAU, on the other side of the castles from Füssen. So many people come for this event that the service is held in the fields outside: it's to give thanks for the cows' safe return from the Alpine pastures, and to bless the horses – who are ridden round the church three times for good luck – used for the dangerous work of bringing logs from the mountain forests. The priest and honoured guests lead the procession in beautifully decorated horse-drawn carriages and a hundred or so riders follow behind. After the blessing, the whole procession, to the sound of a brass band, slowly makes its way to the village for the beer and food which are obligatory accompaniments to any Bavarian festival.

Oberstdorf

Imagine your ideal mountain resort and **OBERSTDORF** will almost certainly fit the picture. Tucked away amid mountains and valleys that are classic chocolate-box countryside, the old village has grown discreetly, without the high-rise aberrations found elsewhere, but with equally excellent sports facilities, including swimming pools, a skating rink and an Olympic ski-jump. There are lots of friendly bars in the streets around the Marktplatz, yet if you walk a little further the roads soon lead to open fields. The agricultural life of the place makes itself felt too, especially in summer, when the clanking of cowbells wakes you at daybreak. In the countryside around, villages are ablaze with geraniums on every balcony and window ledge; the air is exhilaratingly fresh and clean, the aromatic pine forests are still alive with deer, and on the mountain crags you might even catch a glimpse of chamois bucks.

The valleys and peaks

The higher mountain valleys beyond Oberstdorf take you to lonely Alpine huts and the sort of views that give a surge of energy. Serious mountaineers will find the **Nebelhorn** (2224m) to the east of town the most challenging, while for less strenuous Alpine walking the **Fellhorn** (2039m) and **Söllereck** (1706m) to the south make good alternatives – the latter is especially gentle. All three peaks are also accessible by cable car, and in winter form the heart of an excellent skiing range. Another highly recommendable excursion is to the **Breitachklamm** gorges, some 6km southwest of Oberstdorf; these are best seen in late winter, when draped with ice.

Finally, a bit further south, the valley known as **Kleinwalsertal** is a real novelty. Once one of the most isolated corners of the Alps, it was settled by a hardy people known as the Walsers who gave their allegiance to the House of Habsburg. Today, it remains officially part of Austria, although it uses the Deutschmark as its currency, and is only accessible by the road from Oberstdorf, which is serviced by regular buses.

Practical details

What makes Oberstdorf just about perfect is that it has plentiful cheap accommodation. At Haus no. 8 in the neighbouring village of KORNAU (bus connection from Oberstdorf Bahnhof), you'll find the nearest **youth hostel** (☎08322/2225). Alternatively, there are a number of reasonably priced **guest houses** near the centre of Oberstdorf, all charging from DM20 to DM38 per person. These include *Alpenglühn*, Wittelsbacherstr. 4 (☎08322/4692); *Amman*, Weststr. 23 (☎08322/2961); and *Buchenberg*, Lorettostr. 6 (☎08322/2315). The **campsite**, at Rublingerstr. 10 (☎0832/4022), is open all year. If you find you need help with finding somewhere to stay, contact the **tourist office** (Mon–Sat 8am–noon and 2–6pm; ☎08322/7000) on the Marktplatz. For **bars and restaurants** your best bet is the area around Pfarrstrasse. Try *Intermezzo* on the corner with Oststrasse, or *Ungewitter* on Freiherr-von-Brutscherstrasse, but walk past anywhere with a band playing "traditional" music – a sure sign it's a tourist trap.

Lindau

At their most westerly point the Alps descend to the waters of the **Bodensee** and the tiny island town of **LINDAU**, which is nowadays linked to the mainland by a road bridge and rail causeway. It's the starting point of the **German Alpine Road**, (*Deutsche-Alpenstrasse*), a tourist route that runs the length of the German Alps, terminating 250km away in Berchtesgaden. In the Middle Ages, Lindau was a bustling trading post, and rich merchants built grand gabled houses on town squares that have a distinct Italian flavour. The half-timbered buildings lean over like stacks of dominoes, and narrow streets like Zitronengasse lead to quiet nooks and crannies.

At the southern end of the island is the **harbour**, which, with its hazy views across the lake to the Alps, is the most popular spot in town. Its narrow entrance is guarded by two tall pillars, one a lighthouse, the other bearing the defiant Lion of Bavaria. The previous lighthouse, the **Mangturm**, stands in the middle of the sheltered port and was originally part of the medieval fortifications. Around it stand large hotels from an age when nineteenth-century travellers resided here in splendour. As soon as the summer sun comes out, the harbour promenade fills with coffee tables, giving a Mediterranean feeling to the bustling waterfront. Several **ferries** operate on the lake (for full information, see p.248); if you prefer a bit more independence, all sorts of boats, canoes and windsurfers can be hired from the yacht marina east of the harbour.

On Reichsplatz in the centre of the island, stands the Gothic **Altes Rathaus**; unfortunately the elaborate murals added to it make it seem rather overdressed in comparison with the buildings around it. From here, you can walk west along the axial Maximilianstrasse, before turning north to see the **Diebsturm** ("Brigands' Tower"), the other surviving part of the fortifications. Alongside is Romanesque **St Peter**, now a war memorial, and the sole church in Lindau still in its medieval state. Hans Holbein the Elder's *Passion Cycle* in the chancel is his only surviving fresco composition.

The most stylish building in Lindau is the **Haus zum Cavazzen** (Tues–Sat 9am–noon and 2–5pm, Sun 10am–noon; DM3) on Marktplatz towards the eastern end of the island, whose three-storey Baroque facade is painted in subtle sandy-red tones, and which contains one of the most attractive local history museums of any town in Bavaria. There's an intriguing collection of seventeenth-century family trees painted on wooden panels that open up like a photo-album, to reveal little portraits and dates for each member. A particular rarity among the other items are the seventeenth- and eighteenth-century paintings mocking Luther, known as *Spottbilder*. On the second and third floors are fine displays of furniture, ranging from items from the workshops of Lindau's former artisan guilds to the beautifully inlaid *Biedermeier* furniture of "polite society".

Should you only have time for one trip outside the island, take bus #7 to the suburb of HOYREN and walk up the **Hoyrenberg** for a stunning view of the lake and the Austrian and Swiss Alps. The villages and apple orchards around here seem very quiet after Lindau: OBERREITNAU, UNTERREITNAU and BODOLZ are especially pretty.

Practicalities

The **Hauptbahnhof** is at the southwestern corner of the island, right beside the harbour. Just across from the entrance is the **tourist office** (Mon–Fri 8am–noon and 2–6pm, Sat 9am–12.30pm; ☎08382/26000). The **youth hostel**, Herbergsweg 11 (☎08382/5813; buses #1, #3 and #6 from the Hauptbahnhof) on mainland Lindau is likely to be closed for refurbishment until 1993. Best bargains among the **hotels** on the island, costing in the region of DM30–DM45 per person, are *Inselgraben*, Hintere Metzgergasse 4–6 (☎08382/5481); *Gästehaus Ladine*, In der Grub 25 (☎08382/5326); and *Gästehaus Limmer*, In der Grub 16 (☎08382/5877). The **campsite** *Lindau-Zech* (☎08382/72236) is by the lakeside to the east of the island and open from April to September.

You'll find that the cheapest **restaurants** are in the road suitably named In der Grub, where there's also a friendly bar called the *Schalldämpfer*. Don't expect too much in the way of nightlife, though it's just about worth checking out the purpose-built entertainments area of bars and discos on Von-Behring-Strasse in the mainland suburb of REUTIN (follow Bregenzer Strasse for about a kilometre east from Herbergsweg). The main annual **festival** around here is the *Bregenz Opern- und Musikfest*, which takes place from mid-July to mid-August, and although Bregenz is in Austria, many people stay in Lindau because it's cheaper. Performances are held on an enormous stage on the water, with the audience watching from an open-air amphitheatre on shore.

travel details

From Munich to Augsburg (3 an hour; 30min); Regensburg (1; 2hr); Nürnberg (1; 1hr); Würzburg (1; 2hr 20min); Rosenheim (1; 40min); Ulm (1; 2hr 15min); Stuttgart (10 daily; 2hr 15min); Frankfurt (frequent; 4hr); Strasbourg (6 daily; 5hrs); Zurich (5 daily; 4hrs 20min); Cologne (12 daily 5hrs 20min); Hamburg (2 daily; 8hrs); Ingolstadt 3 daily; 45min); Garmisch-Partenkirchen frequent; 1hr 15min); Innsbruck (16 daily; 2hr 25min); Salzburg (frequent; 1hr 30min); Düsseldorf (6 daily; 6hr 30min).

From Nürnberg to Coburg (1 an hour; 1hr 35min); Bamberg (2; 45min); Passau (1; 2hr 20min); Ansbach (2; 45min); Bayreuth (2; 1hr 10min); Passau (10, 2hr 30min); Augsberg (10; 1hr) Frankfurt (1; 2hrs).

From Würzburg to Frankfurt (frequent; 1hr 20min); Cologne (frequent; 3hr 40min); Stuttgart (10 daily; 2hrs).

CHAPTER TWO

BADEN-WÜRTTEMBERG

Baden-Württemberg only came into existence in 1952 as a result of the merger, approved by plebiscite, of three relatively small provinces established by the American and French occupying forces. Theodor Heuss, the first Federal President, saw it as "the model of German possibilities", and it hasn't disappointed, maintaining its ranking as the most prosperous part of the country, as well as one of the few to go against the national trend of a diminishing population. Being weak in natural resources, the area has had to rely on ingenuity to provide a spur to its industrial development, and ever since the motor car was invented here last century, it has been at the forefront of the world technology scene.

Ethnically, culturally and historically, the Land has two separate roots. The people of **Baden**, the western part of the province, are predominantly Catholic, and are generally seen as being of a relaxed, almost carefree disposition. Their neighbours in **Württemberg** (or Swabia, as the locals still prefer to call it), on the other hand, are renowned for being hard-working, thrifty and house-proud, values instilled in them since the Reformation they embraced so openly. This stark division, however, has been much modified by the extensive influx of refugees from the Eastern Territories after World War II: along with their descendants, they now account for about a quarter of the total population.

For variety of scenery, Baden-Württemberg is rivalled only by Bavaria. The western and southern boundaries of the province are defined by the River Rhine and its bulge into Germany's largest lake, the **Bodensee**. Immediately beyond lies the **Black Forest**, one of Europe's main holiday areas. Here rises another of the continent's principal waterways, the **Danube**, which later forms a grandly impressive gorge at the foot of the **Swabian Jura**, the range in which the Neckar begins its increasingly sedate northerly course. At the eastern end of the province there's an even gentler valley, that of the **Tauber**.

Each of Baden-Württemberg's three largest cities – **Stuttgart**, **Mannheim** and **Karlsruhe** – was formerly a state capital (of Württemberg, the Palatinate and Baden respectively). All were extensively damaged in World War II and none could be called beautiful, though each has plenty of good points. Unfortunately, the historical centres of **Freiburg im Breisgau** and **Ulm** were also bombed, but both their Münsters, which rank among Germany's greatest buildings, were spared. Other than this, Baden-Württemberg's lack of a heavy industrial base meant that it escaped the war relatively lightly. Germany's two most famous university cities, **Heidelberg** and **Tübingen**, were hardly touched, enabling the former to maintain its cherished role as the most romantic and swooned-over place in the entire country.

Almost equally enticing is the wealth of towns which stand as period pieces of different epochs. **Bad Wimpfen** and **Schwäbisch Hall** each preserve the form and appearance of the Middle Ages, whereas **Rottweil** has medieval survivals amid streets which bridge the gap between Renaissance and Baroque, and **Haigerloch** is a varied confection enhanced by a superb natural setting. **Bruchsal**, **Ludwigsburg** and **Rastatt** are proud courtly towns in the full-blown Baroque manner, while **Schwetzingen** is a creation of pure Rococo fantasy and **Baden-Baden** remains wonderfully evocative of its

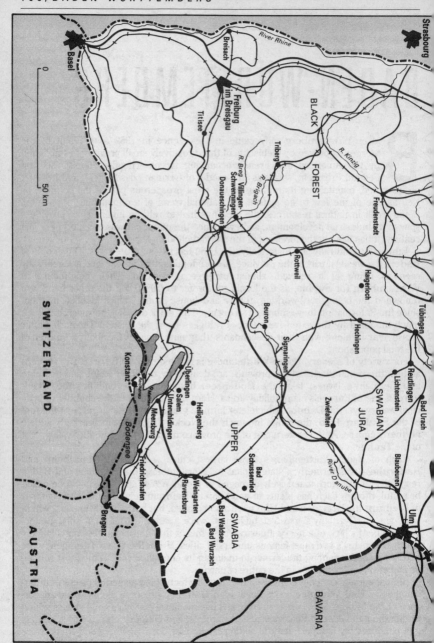

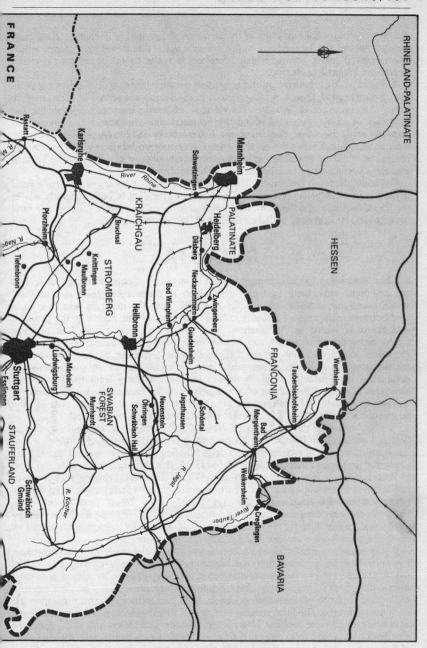

nineteenth-century halcyon years as the favourite playground of European aristocracy. Another special historical feature of the province is the number of monasteries which have survived intact, among which **Maulbronn** ranks as the most complete and impressive in northern Europe.

A typically comprehensive **public transport** network means there's never any problem moving around, though waiting periods in rural areas not served by trains may be longer than is normal in Germany. Travelling is rendered particularly enjoyable by the profusion of scenic routes, of which the *Schwarzwalder-Hochstrasse* and the railway lines known as the *Schwarzwaldbahn*, the *Höllentalbahn* and the *Donautalbahn* are the most outstanding. There's the usual provision of **accommodation** in youth hostels and campsites, while the availability of lodgings in private houses is well above the national average. Only in Stuttgart are prices a possible problem.

Politically, Baden-Württemberg leans well to the right, a legacy of its strong rural heritage and small urban proletariat. The Minister-President is **Lothar Späth**, star of the liberal faction within the CDU, who was widely tipped as a future Chancellor – until his arch-rival Helmut Kohl pulled off the feat of German unification.

SWABIA

Swabia (*Schwaben*) has long ceased to exist as any form of political entity, yet such is the emotional attachment to the name (which at times takes on a near-mystical significance) that it stubbornly refuses to vanish from the map, far less from local consciousness. The rugged plateaux cutting right through the middle of the province continue to be known as the **Swabian Jura**, and two of many former Free Imperial Cities, **Schwäbisch Gmünd** and **Schwäbisch Hall**, have adopted their present forenames in order to show where their loyalties lie. Certainly, the name is far more popular than that of Württemberg, taken from the aristocratic family who established dominance over most of rural Swabia in the Middle Ages from their capital of **Stuttgart**. It remains something of a sore point that the Land of Baden-Württemberg was not designated as Swabia, on the grounds that to do so would have offended the people of Baden, with their very different ethnic and historical background.

In many respects, the position of Swabia within Germany is analogous to that of Scotland within Great Britain, and it's the butt of broadly similar jokes: indeed one of these maintains that the *Schwobs* were originally Scots, but were booted out of their homeland for taking thriftiness just a bit too far. At the Reformation, the extreme wing of Protestantism – here known as **Pietism** – took firm root, bringing with it a firm commitment to the work ethic and a burning sense of individualism, tempered only by communal loyalties. Even today, the jingle *Schaffe, spare, Häusle baue* ("work, save, build a house") remains something of a Swabian motto. There's also no doubt that the intellectual rigour fostered in the province has led to its nurturing a gallery of inventors, philosophers and poets out of all proportion to its size.

If you despair of mastering the horrendous complexities of the German language, it's worth bearing in mind that the ingenious Swabians have developed a partial solution to the problem, put to everyday use in their own **dialect**. By adding *-le* to most nouns, they don't have to worry about genders (which immediately become neuter), while they omit the cumbersome *ge-* prefix from past participles, and regularise the declension of verbs. The local **cuisine** is no less distinctive, with noodles as ubiquitous as in Italian or Chinese cooking. Nearly every savoury dish comes with either *Spätzle*, a shredded pasta made from eggs and flour, or *Maultaschen*, which, with the exception of the sauces used to cover it, is broadly similar to ravioli. Equally popular are *Flädle* (pancakes) which turn up in both soups and desserts.

Swabia's exact boundaries are a matter of controversy. The *echt Schwob* lives in an area bounded by **Heilbronn**, **Tübingen** and the two towns with *Schwäbisch* as their prefixes. However, the term has historically been used to describe all of southwestern Germany, other than the bulk of the Black Forest, as far east as **Ulm** and Augsburg which were allocated by Napoleon to Swabia's long-time rival Bavaria, although the former soon managed to escape from its clutches.

Stuttgart

STUTTGART breathes modern-day success. Düsseldorf and Hamburg may have more millionaires, but Baden-Württemberg's capital has the highest general standard of prosperity of any city in Germany, or, indeed, in Europe. Beaming out imperiously from its lofty station above the city centre is the local trademark, the three-pointed white star of Daimler-Benz. The famous Mercedes vehicles produced by this company are cherished status symbols to which executives the world over aspire, while those of the rival Porsche factory are the high-performance playthings which have become an essential acquisition for those who feel the need to flaunt their wealth. Together they have made Stuttgart into a car production centre to rival Detroit; along with the almost equally celebrated electronics giant Robert Bosch they have given the city a place at the world forefront of the high-tech industrial scene.

These days, Stuttgart is the one German city which is a sure-fire Christian Democratic stronghold; since 1974, it's been ruled by the country's most high-profile mayor, **Manfred Rommel** (son of the wartime general). Yet, for all the present self-confidence, it was initially slow to develop. Founded around 950 as a stud farm (*Stutengarten* – hence the city's name), it only became a town in the fourteenth century, and lay in the shadow of its more venerable neighbours right up to the early nineteenth century, when Napoleon raised Württemberg to the status of a kingdom and placed the former Free Imperial Cities under its control. Though Stuttgart's standing as a royal capital was only to last for a century, the city has never looked back.

From the point of view of conventional sights, Stuttgart has relatively little to offer. On the other hand, it has a range of superb **museums** to appeal to all tastes, and a varied cultural and nightlife scene. It also has the advantage of an enviable **setting** in a hollow surrounded by hills, which enables the cultivation of vineyards within a stone's throw of the centre and means that unsightly industrial pockets can be tucked away out of sight. This is complimented by a liberal endowment of parks and gardens, which successfully soften what would otherwise be a drab and unappealing cityscape.

Arrival and practicalities

The **Hauptbahnhof** – an impressive example of railway architecture, built during the Weimar Republic – is plumb in the centre of the city. Immediately behind is the **bus station**. Line #A departs every 20 minutes between 5am and midnight to the **airport** (☎790 1388 for flight information); the journey costs DM6. In front of the Hauptbahnhof is the underground Klett-Passage, whose shops stay open until late at night. Here also is the **tourist office** (*i-Punkt*; Mon–Sat 8.30am–10pm, Sun 11am–6pm or 1–6pm according to season; ☎2228 240/1). The integrated **public transport** network, which covers nearby towns as well as the Stuttgart metropolitan area, enables you to switch among buses, trams, the U-Bahn, and mainline and S-Bahn trains. Given that the sights are very scattered, it's worth investing in a DM8 24-hour ticket.

> The telephone code for Stuttgart is ☎0711

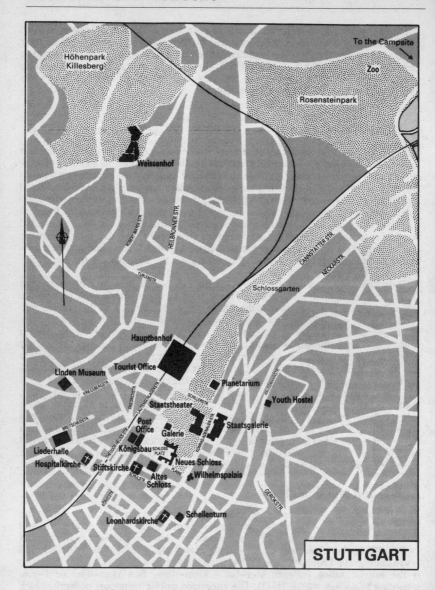

Accommodation

To some extent, the astronomical cost of rented accommodation in Stuttgart – even London prices are in an altogether lower league – is reflected in **hotel** rates. However, there are bargains going, often with a decent location to boot. Cheapest in the centre is *Pension Märklin*, Friedrichstr. 39 (☎291315), with singles from DM28, doubles from DM55. Other budget options are *Florian*, Florianstr. 7 (☎265962), from DM30 per person; *Pension Schilling*, Kernerstr. 63 (☎240860), which charges DM35 for singles, DM58 for doubles; *Eckel*, Vorsteigstr. 10 (☎290995), with singles from DM35, doubles from DM65; and *Schwarzwaldheim*, Fritz-Elsar-Str. 20 (☎296988), at DM35 per person. Alternatively, ask the tourist office to book you a room; there's no charge for this service.

The **youth hostel** is only about fifteen minutes' walk east of the Bahnhof at Haussmannstr. 27 (☎241583). Check the rates carefully before paying, as prices are sometimes mysteriously inflated. There's also an unofficial hostel, the *Jugendwohnheim*, at Richard-Wagner-Str. 2-4a (☎241132), which is a bit more expensive at around DM30 per night. The **campsite** is at Cannstatter Wasen (☎558696) on the banks of the River Neckar in Bad Cannstatt.

The city centre

One consequence of having been a late developer is that Stuttgart has one of the most manageable centres of any large German city, and one which has a spacious feel in spite of its compact size.

Schlossplatz

From the Hauptbahnhof, follow Königstrasse straight ahead past the modern Dom (a strong contender for the title of the dullest cathedral in Europe), and you arrive at **Schlossplatz**. The vast open space here comes as a welcome relief after the hectic bustle of the neighbouring streets, but it does mean that it's the favourite spot of the tramps and alcoholics who form a noticeable sub-class amid the prosperity. On the eastern side of the square is the colossal Baroque **Neues Schloss**, now used for various state purposes by the government of Baden-Württemberg, and otherwise out of bounds to visitors. Opposite is the **Königsbau**, lined with shops all along its 135-metres-long facade. It's in the late Neoclassical style much favoured in the city; another example of this is the **Jubileumssäule**, erected in the centre of Schlossplatz to commemorate the 25th anniversary of the accession of King Wilhelm I of Württemberg.

On the north side of the square is the Kunstgebäude, containing the **Galerie der Stadt Stuttgart** (Tues–Fri 10am–6pm, Sat and Sun 11am–5pm; free). This contains some superb works by **Otto Dix**: the luridly-coloured *Grosstadt* triptych, indeed, is one of his finest canvases, perfectly conjuring up the Weimar Republic's false sense of values and its smoky, decadent nightclub scene. In *Unlikely Lovers* and *The Triumph of Death*, Dix returned to two subjects popular with painters of the German Renaissance, giving them a vicious modern twist; he also gave visual vent to the horrors of World War I in *Trench Warfare*. After this, the rest of the gallery is an anti-climax, but there are a number of small works by the three leading Stuttgart painters of this century – Adolf Hölzel, Oskar Schlemmer and Willi Baumeister.

The Altes Schloss

At the southern end of Schlossplatz is the **Altes Schloss**. A fortress was first built on this site in the tenth century to protect the stud farm; one wing survives of the fourteenth-century moated castle which succeeded it. In the 1550s, the rest of the building was replaced by a resplendent Renaissance palace with a majestic triple-tiered courtyard, designed by Aberlin Tresch. This forms the perfect setting for nominally-priced concerts of classical music throughout the summer. Ask at the porter's desk for the key to the **Schlosskapelle**, which disputes with its counterpart in Torgau the right to be regarded as the earliest example of Protestant religious architecture. The interior was specially designed in accordance with the tenets of the new faith, with its emphasis on preaching rather than the sacraments: it's a simple rectangular hall with galleries on three sides, and the elevated pulpit is given the same prominence as the altar.

Badly damaged in the war, much of the Schloss is given over to the **Landesmuseum** (Tues & Thurs–Sun 10am–5pm, Wed 10am–7pm; free). Highlight of this richly varied museum is the **Kunstkammer** of the House of Württemberg, displayed in one of the corner towers. The first floor has small bronze sculptures of predominantly Italian origin, while the second is laid out in the manner of a Renaissance curio cabinet, with the star exhibit being a beautiful set of Gothic playing cards. On the top storey are the nineteenth-century crown jewels, the most notable being a necklace with the 22-carat *Harlequin* diamond.

The Baroque sleighs of the dukes can be seen on the ground floor of the main part of the building, along with a sparkling array of glass. Upstairs is a large and important collection of Swabian devotional wood sculptures, arranged thematically rather than chronologically, thus offering inviting comparisons. Many of these are in a folk idiom, others show a profound sense of artistic pathos, as in **Multscher's** *Muttergottes*, **Riemenschneider's** *Holy Women* and *St. James*, **Syrlin the Younger's** *Passion* cycle (made for the original Münster in Zwiefalten) and the graceful *Talheim Altar*, with carvings by an anonymous Ulm craftsman and paintings by the **Master of Messkirch**. Displayed alongside are fine examples of stained glass. On the same floor, the **archaeology** section includes finds from the excavations at Troy, varied Roman antiquities (notably a stunning third-century cameo of Jupiter), the intact grave of a Celtic prince, and jewellery from the Frankish period. The top floor features historical musical instruments, predominantly of the keyboard variety, and a wonderful array of **clocks.**

Schillerplatz and the Stiftskirche

To the west, the Altes Schloss overlooks **Schillerplatz**, Stuttgart's sole example of an old-world square. A pensive statue of Schiller himself by Bertel Thorwaldsen presides in the middle. Also here are three more Renaissance buildings – the **Prinzenbau,** the **Alte Kanzlei** (Old Chancellery) and the gabled **Fruchkasten** (Granary). Behind its facade, the last-named preserves its original fourteenth-century core; this has now been converted to house the **Lapidarium** (Tues & Thurs–Sun 10am–5pm, Wed 10am–7pm; free). It's well worth popping in to see its collection of stone fragments from Roman times; particularly impressive are the surviving parts from a massive Jupitersäule, erected around 200 AD in a settlement near Heilbronn.

At the back of Schillerplatz is the **Stiftskirche**. Its present form is due to the prolific late fifteenth-century Stuttgart architect Aberlin Jerg, whose special skill, shown here to good effect, lay in welding old and new parts of buildings into a coherent whole. The western tower, an octagon on a square base, is Jerg's own work; unfortunately, the planned openwork steeple was never built. Inside the church, the choir is lined with one of the most important pieces of German Renaissance sculpture, an **ancestral gallery** of the Counts and Dukes of Württemberg. Each of the eleven swarthy figures is brilliantly characterised – a considerable feat of imagination on the part of the sculptor, Sem Schlör. Look out also for the gilded late Gothic pulpit, and the relief of *Christ Sheltering Humanity*.

The eastern boundary

A large modern boulevard, Konrad-Adenauer-Strasse, forms the eastern boundary of the city centre. At the southern end is the **Leonhardskirche**, another church reworked by Aberlin Jerg, containing the funerary monument to the celebrated Renaissance humanist and Hebrew scholar, Johannes Reuchlin. To the north is the Neoclassical **Wilhelmspalais**, used by the last Kings of Württemberg as their main residence; it's now the main municipal archive and library.

Across the road, at the back of the Neues Schloss, lies the **Akadamiegarten** This forms a southerly extension of the **Schlossgarten**, which stretches for 4km all the way to the banks of the Neckar. On the right is the straggling complex of the **Staatstheater**, a mecca for the performing arts (see below). Further on, close to the Hauptbahnhof, is the **Planetarium** (sessions Tues & Thurs 10am & 3pm, Wed & Fri 10am, 3pm & 8pm, Sat & Sun 2pm, 4pm & 6pm; DM5), whose projection equipment, made by Carl Zeiss, the famous Stuttgart optics company, ranks among the most modern in Europe.

The Staatsgalerie

Facing the Staatstheater from the other side of Konrad-Adenauer-Strasse is the **Staatsgalerie** (Tues & Thurs 10am–8pm, Wed & Fri–Sun 10am–5pm; free). It's not often that an art gallery ranks as one of the most imposing buildings in a major city, but this is an exception. James Stirling – internationally regarded as Britain's most accomplished postwar architect – was commissioned to build an extension to the solid Neoclassical home of the city's magnificent collection of paintings, which was no longer big enough to accommodate the ever-growing acquisition of modern works. The result, completed in 1984, has been much praised as an original masterpiece. In some ways it resembles another British design on foreign soil, the much larger Pompidou Centre in Paris, but is wholly lacking in the deliberate perversities of that structure, while varying the surface textures to far better effect.

The displays begin upstairs in the old building. Of the medieval works, the earliest and most important is a **Bohemian School** altarpiece made in 1385 for a chapel on the outskirts of Stuttgart. You'll either see the inner part, in which Good King Wenceslas is flanked by Saint Vitus and Emperor Sigismund, or else the Biblical scenes on the wings; the position is changed every fortnight. Among many examples of the fifteenth-century Swabian School, those by the Ulm painters **Bartolomäus Zeitblom** and the **Master of the Sterzing Altar** stand out, particularly the latter's courtly *Journey of the Magi*. The most startling work in the gallery is the huge, violently expressive *Herrenberg Altar* by **Jerg Ratgeb**, a man who knew all about violence himself in his other calling as a radical political leader. His reputation rests almost entirely on this single work, which cleverly compresses the Passion scenes into four panels and has an unusual reverse side, showing the Apostles going out to preach the Word to all the corners of the earth. By another idiosyncratic artist, **Hans Baldung**, are *Man of Sorrows* and *Portrait of Hans Jacob*.

The Italian section begins with two wonderfully stylised panels of *The Apocalypse* by a mid-fourteenth-century **Neapolitan** master, and continues with some excellent examples of the Venetian Renaissance, including works by Bellini, Carpaccio and Tintoretto. However, the gems of the display are several sketches by **Tiepolo**, notably a superbly compressed study for the central section of the great staircase fresco in Würzburg's Residenz. **Memling's** sensual *Bathsheba at her Toilet* kicks off the Low Countries section. The brilliant but rare Mannerist **Joachim Wtewael** is represented by an animated cycle of portraits of *The Four Evangelists* and by an enamel-like *Adoration of the Shepherds*. There are two masterpieces by **Michael Sweerts**, another long-forgotten artist who has recently come to the fore: the pendants *Taste* and *Sight*, each characterised by an allegorical figure of a child. **Rembrandt** also treated the theme of sight – a subject particularly close to an artist's heart – in the tender *Tobit Healing his Father's Blindness*. It forms a sort of unofficial counterpart to the horrific *Blinding of Samson* in Frankfurt, which was painted the same year. One of his earliest works, *St Paul in Prison*, is also on show, along with important examples of Hals, Rubens and Terbrugghen.

Biggest surprise of the gallery is a whole room devoted to **Edward Burne-Jones's** cycle of *The Legend of Perseus*. Commissioned by Arthur Balfour, the future British Prime Minister, this constitutes one of the finest achievements of the Pre-Raphaelite movement. Three of the eight scenes were never completed, but the full-scale cartoons shown here make ample substitutes. Other nineteenth-century highpoints are *Bohemian Landscape* and *The Cross in the Woods* by **Friedrich**, an impressive group of works by a local Neoclassical sculptor, **Johann Heinrich Dannecker**, and a decent cross-section of French Impressionism.

The modern extension begins with the seven vibrant figures **Oskar Schlemmer** made for the kaleidoscopic *Triadschen Ballett* in 1922. Displayed high up on pedestals, they're arguably his most original creations. Alongside are monumental bronzes by **Matisse**, while examples of many of the century's leading sculptors can be found in the sculpture court downstairs or scattered throughout the galleries. A wooden group entitled *The Bathers* constitutes one of the main items in what's regarded as the finest **Picasso** collection in Germany. **Modigliani** is represented by *Portrait of Chaim Soutine* (the Russian-born painter) and *Reclining Nude*. The entire progress of German art this century is copiously traced: particular outstanding are **Kirchner's** *Friedrichstrasse, Berlin*; **Dix's** *Matchstick Seller*; and **Beckmann's** *Self-Portrait with Red Scarf*. Avant-garde works occupy the end halls, while important temporary exhibitions are regularly featured downstairs.

The western quarters

The streets in the grid-plan western half of the city centre are given over almost entirely to shopping. Almost the only building of note is the **Hospitalkirche,** which is a rare example of Aberlin Jerg being allowed to design his own building from scratch. Unfortunately only the chancel has survived intact; it houses a monumental *Crucifixion* by the Heilbronn sculptor Hans Syfer.

Further west, on Hegelplatz at the opposite end of the Stadtgarten, is the **Linden Museum** (Tues, Wed & Fri–Sun 10am–5pm, Thurs 10am–8pm; free). This well-presented ethnology museum has displays covering the full gamut of non-European cultures, with Peru, Melanesia, Benin and the Congo being particularly well-represented. A full-scale reproduction of an Islamic bazaar, using many original exhibits, is one of the most eye-catching features.

Outside the centre

If Stuttgart's centre is one of the easiest to come to terms with in all of Germany, the exact opposite is true of the city as a whole, several of the main attractions being dotted all over the suburbs. However, everything is readily accessible with a bit of forward planning and proper use of the excellent integrated municipal transport network.

The Weissenhofsiedlung and the Rosensteinpark

Below the Killesberg hill to the northwest of the centre, reached by bus #43, is the **Weissenhofsiedlung**. This settlement was laid out in 1927, in conjunction with an exhibition of the *Deutscher Werkbund*. Sixteen well-known architects contributed to this Bauhaus scheme, among them Le Corbusier, Gropius and Mies van der Rohe. Badly bombed in the war, the houses have been restored, but with variable success, and it's only worth making a special trip here if you're passionately keen on modern architecture. The **Höhenpark Killesberg** (May–Sept DM1.50, free at other times) immediately behind is a large, remarkably peaceful recreation area. It's equipped with scented gardens, a flamingo park, and fields with donkeys, rabbits and sheep, making it a good place to take kids.

More generally enticing is the **Rosensteinpark** at the far end of the Schlossgarten; take U-Bahn #1 or #2 to Mineralbader. At the bottom end of the park is an artificial lake; a little way up the hill is the ritzy **Schloss Rosenstein** (Tues, Thurs & Fri 9am–5pm, Wed 9am–8pm, Sat 9am–6pm, Sun 10am–6pm; free, but likely to be closed for repairs until 1993), the former country house of the Kings of Württemberg, complete with rose garden, fountains and heroic statues. The interior now houses a natural history museum; the fossil part of the collection is separately housed at the western end of the park in the **Museum am Löwentor** (same times; free). At the northern extremity is the superbly landscaped **Wilhelma** (daily 8am–4/5/6pm according to season; DM7, kids DM2.50), originally laid out as a Moorish garden for King Wilhelm I. Nowadays, it has a zoo with some 8000 animals, along with hothouses and other botanical arrangements.

Bad Cannstatt

From the Rosensteinpark, it's just a hop across the Neckar to the old spa town of **BAD CANNSTATT**, whose favourable situation at a bend in the river meant that it initially outstripped Stuttgart, only to lose importance down the centuries to the extent that it was incorporated into its erstwhile rival in 1905. If you're coming from the city centre, take either a mainline train, or S-Bahn #1, #2 or #3.

Nowadays, Cannstatt is best known as the home of a huge beer festival (see box on p.204), and as the main sports and recreation area of the Stuttgart conurbation. However, it also preserves some of the faded elegance of a once-fashionable spa, and a great deal of self-confident turn-of-the-century architecture remains. There are a few older buildings, too, such as the **Stadtkirche**, another Aberlin Jerg confection, retaining parts of earlier Romanesque and Gothic structures. The **Kurpark**, with its mineral water springs and shady willow paths, is the most restful spot in Stuttgart.

Overlooking the park at Taubenheimerstr. 13 is the **Gottlieb-Daimler-Memorial** (daily April–Oct 11am–4pm; free). In 1882, Daimler, who was consumed by the dream of developing a new means of mechanical propulsion, gave up his highly successful corporate career, acquired a villa in Cannstatt (destroyed during the war), and carried out his top-secret experiments in an expanded version of its greenhouse, which somehow managed to escape the bombs. This humble, unpromising setting was where Daimler toiled away in obscurity for four years, aided only by his protégé Wilhelm Maybach. In their quest to create a light, fast-moving internal combustion engine which could power a moving vehicle, Daimler and Maybach invented the motorbike by 1885; the following year, the motorboat and four-wheeled motor car had been added to their achievements. A further year on, they established a factory in the town.

The Daimler-Benz Museum

By an extraordinary coincidence, another German inventor, **Carl Benz**, invented a motor car in the same year as Daimler, though neither was aware of the other's work. Both went on to run highly successful factories producing their inventions; these were united in 1926 (long after Daimler's death and Benz's retirement) and are now based at UNTERTÜRKHEIM, immediately south of Bad Cannstatt. In 1986, the **Daimler-Benz Museum** (Tues–Sun 9am–5pm; free) was set up to celebrate the centenary of the inventions. Unless you positively rue the day the car was invented, this museum, the best of its kind in the world, is an absolute must. Even entering here is an experience – take S-Bahn #1 to Neckarstadion, then walk straight ahead at the exit to the works entrance, or else go by bus #56 to Stadion. In accordance with the company's megalomaniacal obsession about industrial espionage, you then have to wait for a special sealed minibus to take you through the factory complex to the museum doors which are opened only in conjunction with these arrivals.

Over seventy **historical vehicles** are on display, all with their bodywork restored to pristine condition and looking fully roadworthy. The earliest exhibit is the *Daimler Reitwagen* of 1885, the first-ever motorbike, which was capable of 12kmh. Benz's patent *Motorwagen* (a tricycle whose engine and bodywork are both his own design) from January the following year just beats the Daimler-Maybach *Motorkusche* (which was fitted into a four-wheeled horse-carriage) for the title of the world's first car. Both used one cylinder engines and had a maximum speed of 16kmh. The Daimler company's first *Mercedes* dates from 1902. This Spanish-sounding name was borrowed from the daughter of the firm's principal foreign agent, Emil Jellinek; it proved so successful a trademark that it replaced the recently-deceased founder's name on all products.

You'll doubtless find your own favourites among the exhibits, which include fire-engines, motor boats, aeroplanes and buses. However, the **luxury cars** steal the show – look out for the elite handmade *Grand Mercedes* models of the 1930s, including one used by the Japanese royal family, the official *300d* limousine of Konrad Adenauer, and the first of the "Popemobiles", the *Landaulet* of Paul VI. Equally impressive are the space-age vehicles specially designed for **world record attempts**; these look so futuristic it's hard to believe they were made more than half a century ago. In 1938, the *W125* achieved 437.7kmh on the Frankfurt–Heidelberg autobahn, still the fastest speed ever registered on a public road. The *T80* was designed for travel at 600kmh – but World War II killed off this project, which was never subsequently revived.

The southern suburbs

In the hills due south of the city centre, reached by tram #15, is the 217-metres-high **Fernsehturm** (daily 8am–10.30pm; DM4 including ascent by lift). Completed in 1956, this was the first such television tower ever built and has been much imitated round the world, most of all in Germany itself, where it often became a civic obsession to acquire such an amenity. The view from the observation platform is much the best Stuttgart can offer, stretching over the Swabian Jura to the Black Forest and the Odenwald, with the Alps visible on clear days.

In the former ice cellar of the *Schwabenbräu* brewery at Robert-Koch-Str. 12 in the southwestern suburb of VAIHINGEN (reached from the centre by S-Bahn #1, #2 or #3) is the **Schwäbisches Brauerei Museum** (Tues–Sun 10.30am–5.30pm; free). This charts the history of beer-making from the third century BC right up to the present day; exhibits include a complete experimental brewery from the 1930s, a collection of drinking vessels and pieces of old equipment. Not surprisingly, there's an enticing selection of beers on sale at the bar.

Schloss Solitude

On a ridge hill in the hills to the west of the city centre, reached by bus #92, is the appropriately named **Schloss Solitude** (April–Oct Tues–Sun 9am–noon & 1.30–5pm, Nov–March Tues–Sun 10am–noon & 1.30–4pm; DM2). This exquisite oval pleasure palace, built in the 1760s, was the main summer residence of the Württemberg court. It ranks as the masterpiece of Pierre Louis Philippe de la Guépière, one of the prime movers behind the introduction of the Louis XVI style (which marks the transition from Rococo to Neoclassicism) into Germany. A bonus here is that you're free to wander round its marbled and panelled apartments without being subject to the ubiquitous guided tour.

The Porschewerk

Based right beside the Bahnhof of the northern suburb of NEUWIRTSHAUS (served by S-Bahn line #6), Porsche, in accordance with its carefully cultivated flash image, is considerably more relaxed about prying visitors than Daimler-Benz. Not only can you wander at will around the factory site; there are free **guided tours of the production lines** every working day. These are generally booked solid weeks in advance, but a few extra visitors are allowed to tag on at short notice, though it's best to phone first (☎827 5685).

The Bohemian-born **Ferdinand Porsche** had already had a brilliant career when he set up in Stuttgart after World War II. As Austrian director of Daimler-Benz, he was responsible for the design of the handsome if underpowered *Pullman* saloons, and led the technical team involved with the world record attempts. His services had also been acquired by Hitler for the creation of the original *Volkswagen*. For his own enterprise, Porsche concentrated on the opposite end of the market. The fifty vehicles on show in the **Porsche Museum** (Mon–Fri 9am–noon & 1.30–4pm; free) at Porschestr. 42 illustrate all the company's models from the *356 Roadster* of 1948 to those currently in production. They show that the basic formula of a sleek aerodynamic design coupled to a high-performance rear engine has in fact altered remarkably little, even if the "duck's tail" spoiler, first introduced in 1973, has definitely helped boost the macho image even further.

Eating and drinking

Stuttgart's expensive reputation thankfully doesn't entirely extend to food and drink; though fancy restaurants abound, there are also any number of places offering traditional Swabian dishes at low cost, with plenty of ethnic eateries to stimulate the most jaded palate. Local **wines** are almost equally divided between *Riesling* (white) and *Trollinger* (red) varieties. Demand for these within Stuttgart itself is often so high that they can't be obtained elsewhere. The best and safest recommendations for sampling these vintages are the many **Weinstuben;** these cosy, homely establishments are archetypally German, and are as well known for their solid cooking as for wine, but note that they're open evenings only and are closed on Sundays. A wide variety of **beers** is produced in Stuttgart as well. The *Hofbräu*'s gentle, sweetish *Herren-Pils* is probably the most popular brew locally; the rival *Schwaben-Bräu*'s *Meister-Pils* has a far more bitter taste. Outside the city, *Dinkelacker*'s products are the best-known: these include the classic *CD-Pils*, plus both light and dark varieties of *Weizen*.

Weinstuben

Bäcka-Metzger, Aachener Str. 20, Bad Cannstatt. A genuine local, serving superb food.

Bäckerschmiede, Scurwaldstr. 42. Renowned for its *Gaisburger Marsch*, the apotheosis of Swabian cooking, a rich stew of beef, potatoes and *Spätzle*.

Kachelofen, Ebehardstr. 10. The preferred haunt of the local bigwigs.

Klösterle, Marktstr. 71, Bad Cannstatt. Another great favourite of the spa town, occupying a medieval beguinage.

Schellenturm, Weberstr. 72. Housed in an old prison tower, with an appropriately cosy atmosphere.

Weinhaus Stetter, Rosenstr. 32. Offers the largest choice of wines: over 300 in all.

Zur Kiste, Kanalstr. 2. The most famous and popular of Stuttgart's Weinstuben.

Other restaurants

Greiner-Stuben, Arnulf-Klett-Platz 1. This complex of five restaurants and cafés is conveniently located oppoiste the Hauptbahnhof; bargain daily menus are available in the *Bräustüble*.

Iden, Schwabenzentrum, Ebehardstr. 1. Has the widest range among the city's vegetarian restaurants.

Ketterer, Marienstr. 3b. Best of the restaurants in a traditional beer hall set-up.

L'Aleph, Ebehardstr. 22. Italian food in a lively atmosphere with occasional live bands and regular art exhibitions.

Max-und-Moritz, Geiss Str. 5. Pizzeria mainly patronised by students.

Movenpick Restaurant Marché, Königstr. 16. Much the best self-service restaurant, with salads particularly good value.

Olympic, Bohnenviertelstrasse. Greek taverna which is another student hangout.

Russische Datscha, Aachener Str. 23, Bad Cannstatt. A rare opportunity in western Germany to sample Russian cooking.

Schalom, Hospitalstr. 36. Kosher Israeli restaurant.

Stuttgarter Lokalbrauerei, Calwer Str. 31. *Hausbrauerei* serving good-value meals.

Zeppelin-Stüble, Lautenschlager Str. 2. Classy hotel restaurant directly facing the Hauptbahnhof.

Nightlife

Despite Stuttgart's status as a large university city, there's no single concentration of trendy **nightspots**. Instead, the action takes place in a variety of small pockets spread throughout the city. The following is a list of those currently "in":

Café Stella, Haptstätter Str. 57. One of the leading gay hangouts; less trendy than some, and never uncomfortably busy.

Casino, Mörikestr. 69. Crowded cellar bar with an underground, punkish feel to it.

Dixieland Hall, Marienstr. 3 (Tues–Sat 7.30pm–1am). Leading trad jazz venue, though modern styles are also featured. Entrance upwards of DM6, but drinks and food are reasonably priced.

Exil, Filderstr. 61. A former punk paradise taken over by arty types; jazz and blues are played in a laid-back atmosphere.

Jenseitz-Schwulencafé, Bebelstr. 25. Stuttgart's main gay café; predominantly male, and prone to become very crowded.

Laboratorium, Wagenburgerstr. 147. Crowded jazz café popular with the alternative set, including a large Green Party contingent; occasionally features cabaret.

Life, Bolzstr. 10. Café with live rock and occasional reggae; looks far more rough than it actually is. Serves huge cheap pizzas and excellent beer.

Longhorn, Heiligen Wiesen 6. The place to go to hear country and western music.

Merlin, Furtbachstr. 14. Alternative café and arts centre.

Oz, Büchenstr. 10. Lively but musically run-of-the-mill disco.

Rock Café Soho, Schwabstr. 16a. Small bar with modern decor and predominantly young clientele.

Röhre, Wagenburgtunnel, Neckarstr. 34 (daily 8pm–2am). The celebrated "tunnel" nightclub occupies what was originally designed as a new railway line. Live bands play everything from jazz to punk; it's also a disco patronised mainly by the most fashion-conscious locals.

Roxy, Königstr. 51. Popular if conventional disco.

Treff Fröhlich, Liederhalle, Berliner Platz 1. Best place for cocktails; expensive, but generally worth it.

Culture

Local prosperity helps fund a highbrow cultural scene which is arguably richer and more diverse than that of any other city of comparable size in Europe.

Theatres

Stuttgart's leading highbrow venue is the *Staatstheater*, Obere Schlossgarten 6 (☎221795), a complex of three separate houses. The resident **ballet** and **opera** companies alternate in the *Grosses Haus*; the former is one of the most famous in the world, with the great tradition established in the 1960s by the South African-born John Cranko (many of whose choreographies remain in the repertoire) ably carried on under his protégé, the Brazilian Marcia Haydée. **Drama** is featured in the *Kleines Haus*, while the James Stirling-designed *Kammertheater* is equipped with a moveable stage and seating, and puts on more experimental work. The *Theater im Depot*, Landhausstr. 188 is an even more way-out subsidiary venue.

Among the city's other **theatres**, the Jugendstil *Altes Schauspielhaus*, Kleine Königstr. 9 (☎225505), specialises in nineteenth- and twentieth-century classics, while contemporary plays and forgotten older works are performed at *Theater der Altstadt* on Charlottenplatz (☎244332). Comedies of all kinds are put on by *Kömodie in Marquardt*, Bolzstr. 4–6 (☎291484). *Renitenz-Theater*, Königstr. 17 (☎297075), is the place to go for satirical cabaret; good German is obviously needed for an appreciation. *Theaterhaus Stuttgart* (☎402070) Ulmerstr. 241 is the big venue for alternative events, including feminist work and visiting foreign groups. At Höhenpark Killesberg between May and

October, the *Varieté-Theater* presents circus-type shows between 4pm and 8pm daily. Other places suitable for taking **kids** are the *Puppen und Figuren Theater*, Eberhardstr. 61d (☎241541), home of several puppet companies, and the *Kruschteltunnel*, Möhringer Str. 56 (☎282543/473396), whose shows are meant for the under-12s. Mime is the predominant fare at the *Makai-City-Theater*, Marienstr. 12 (☎626208).

Classical music

The three halls of the *Liederhalle* on Schloss Strasse (☎221795) serve for concerts of all kinds. Pick of the city's five orchestras is Karl Münchinger's *Stuttgarter Kammerorchester*; their style may now be a little old-fashioned, but they played a crucial role in dusting the cobwebs off Baroque music, being primarily responsible for raising Vivaldi from the oblivion of two centuries to his present status as one of the most popular of all composers. The smaller halls often feature performances by the local *Melos-Quartett*, currently one of Europe's finest string quartets. Stuttgart is, after Leipzig, the main centre for research into Bach performance practice, so any concerts by Helmut Rilling's *Bach Collegium* are worth looking out for. The city has more top-class choirs than anywhere else in Germany, the most celebrated being the *Hymnus Chorknaben*. Free concerts are often held in the churches – the Stiftskirche has a series at 7pm during the winter months. Every three years (next in August/September 1994), Stuttgart is host to an international *Musikfest*, with orchestras from all round the world.

Cinemas

Leading cinema is the *Kommunales Kino*, Neckarstr. 47 (☎221320), which shows a lot of British and American films. These are sometimes in the original, sometimes dubbed – the programme always makes clear which. An even bigger, but more mainstream, selection of English-language films can be seen at *Corso*, Hauptstr. 6 (☎734916). Other worthwhile cinemas are *Atelier*, Kronprinzstr. 6 and *Lupe*, Kriegsbergstr. 11.

Listings

Airlines *British Airways* Kriegsbergstr. 28 (☎299471); *Lufthansa*, Lautenschlagerstr. 20 (☎20441); *American Airlines*, Charlottenstr. 44 (☎236 9412); *Pan-Am*, Flughafen (☎790 1314); *TWA*, Sophienstr. 38 (☎058183).

American Library Friedrichstr. 23a (☎2298317).

Bookshops *Weises Hofbuchhandlung* and *Wittwer*, both on Obere Königstrasse, are the main general shops. There's a women's bookshop (*Frauenbuchladen*) at Olgastr. 75.

Car hire *Autohansa*, Hegelstr. 25 (☎693322); *Avis*, 18 Katharinenstrasse (☎241441); *InterRent*, Friedrichstr. 28 (☎221749); *Hertz*, Hohenstaufenstr. 18 (☎643044).

Consulates *British*, Lenzhalde 65 (☎220359); *American*, Urbanstr. 7 (☎210221).

Duty Dentist (☎780 0266).

Duty Doctor (☎280211).

Markets The daily markets in the *Markthalle* on Schillerplatz are ideal for putting a picnic together. On Saturday mornings, a *flower market* is held on Schillerplatz itself, while there's also a *flea market* on Schlossplatz.

Mitfahrzentrale Lerchenstr. 68 (☎221453).

Neckar cruises *Neckar-Personnen-Schiffahrt*, Anlegestelle Wilhelma, Bad Cannstatt (☎5410473/4).

Pharmacies (☎224310) for information as to which one is open outside normal hours.

Post office Main office, with Poste Restante, is at the rear of the Königsbau on Schillerplatz. The branch in the Hauptbahnhof is open until 11pm.

Sports The *Neckarstadion* in Bad Cannstatt is the main stadium for outdoor events, including the matches of the leading local football team, *VfB Stuttgart*, one of the most consistent in Germany in recent seasons. Indoor events, including an international tennis tournament in November, are held at the Martin-Schleyer-Halle alongside it (☎561565).

The main annual event is the sixteen-day *Cannstatter Volksfest*, held on the last week in September and the first in October. Founded in 1818 by King Wilhelm I of Württemberg, it's the second biggest beer festival in the world. In fact, most of the features are direct imitations of the larger *Oktoberfest* in Munich, although the beers on tap are all Swabian. If wine is your tipple, the *Stuttgarter Weindorf*, held in the city centre from the last Friday in August until the first Sunday in September, has over 300 varieties available for tasting. Another big wine festival is the *Fellbacher Herbst*, held on the second weekend of October in FELLBACH, which adjoins Bad Cannstatt to the east. The *Weihnachtsmarkt*, beginning in late November, has existed since the seventeenth century and is thus one of the oldest in the country, but the harlequins and tightrope walkers have unfortunately long gone, to be replaced by the standard offerings. Other notable events are a *Lichtfest* on Killesberg in early July, and the *Frühlingsfest*, lasting for a fortnight in late April/early May.

What's on The tourist office's well-filled monthly programme of events, *Stuttgarter Monatsspiegel*, costs DM1.60. "Alternative" listings can be found in both *Stuttgart Live* and *Ketchup*, available from newsagents.

Women's centre Kernerstrasse 31 (☎296432).

Esslingen

If Stuttgart seems rather thin on historic monuments, ample compensation is provided by **ESSLINGEN**. Nowadays, this is virtually a southeastern suburb of the state capital, reached in 15 minutes by S-Bahn #1, but for centuries it was a Free Imperial City and jealously guards its municipal independence. Last century, it became an important centre of machine tool manufacturing and is still ringed by ugly factories which provide a sharp contrast to the vineyard-clad hills above. However, the old centre has been preserved almost intact. With its winding streets, narrow alleys, spacious squares and dramatic views, it's one of the most visually pleasing – and most unexpected – parts of this otherwise hi-tech dominated part of Baden-Württemberg.

Around town

From the Bahnhof, go straight up the street of the same name. To the left, the Neckar canal is crossed by an old footbridge. Two more bridges can be seen down to the right; the second of these, the fourteenth-century **Innere Brücke**, is outstanding, incorporating a graceful chapel which now serves as a memorial to the victims of the Third Reich.

The Marktplatz

Heart of the town is the **Marktplatz**, scene of markets on Wednesday and Saturday mornings. Dominating the square is the Romanesque-Gothic **Stadtkirche St Dionys**, whose two towers are linked by a covered passageway, which served as a defensive look-out post. The church preserves its late Gothic rood screen, along with a soaring tabernacle and a font from the same period. In the chancel are glittering stained glass windows, made in the late thirteenth and early fourteenth centuries. If you're keen on archaeology, it's well worth coming here on a Wednesday between 2pm and 5pm, when you can view the extensive underground **excavations** for DM1.50. These include Roman finds, plus the foundations of two previous churches on this spot, which date from periods when surviving buildings are extremely scarce – the first was erected around 720, the second throughout the first half of the following century.

On the south side of the Stadtkirche, next to the canal, is an old cemetery chapel of similar date which was converted in the Renaissance epoch to serve as the **Stadtarchiv**. Facing the back of the church is the **Speyrer Zehnthof**, a mid-sixteenth- century tithe barn. Since 1826, this has served as the headquarters of the oldest *Sekt* cellar in Germany; production of high-quality sparkling wines remains a local speciality. The **Spitalkelter**, a half-timbered structure on the north side of Marktplatz, is an earlier relic of the city's wine tradition, having been built as a wine-pressing factory, before later becoming a hospital.

Rathausplatz

Adjoining Marktplatz to the east is Rathausplatz. The **Altes Rathaus** began life in the early fifteenth century as a merchants' trading hall and tax collection point, but was taken over for municipal purposes at the end of the following century. It was then given a cheerful pink frontispiece, much influenced by Dutch buildings of the time, and adorned with an astronomical clock. Opposite is the Baroque **Neues Rathaus**, originally a patrician palace. Beyond are a number of picturesque old streets, along with the Hafenmarkt, where you'll find the thirteenth-century **Gelbes Haus** (Yellow House), probably Germany's oldest surviving and most architecturally distinguished brothel. However, it hasn't served its original purpose since a fire devastated the town in 1701.

West of Marktplatz

Just west of Marktplatz is **St Paul**, a Dominican monastery consecrated by Albertus Magnus in 1268. It's of particular significance in marking the debut on German soil of the sober, unadorned Gothic architecture characteristic of the mendicant religious orders. In total contrast is the **Frauenkirche** on the brow of the hill behind, which represents the Gothic style at its most elaborate. The marked resemblance, albeit on a reduced scale, to the great Münster in Ulm is no coincidence: it shared the same master masons, members of the Ensinger and Böblinger families. There are two exquisite portals, showing the *Life of the Virgin* and *The Last Judgment*, while the hall church interior has lovely stained glass windows made a generation after those in the Stadtkirche. However, as at Ulm, it's the highly decorated **tower**, crowned with an openwork spire, which provides the most memorable feature.

At the east end of the Frauenkirche is the **Blaubeurer Pfleghof**, the most impressive of about a dozen such institutions in Esslingen, which served as town headquarters and charitable institutions of rural monasteries. From here, you can ascend to the **Burg** along its own covered ramparts. What must once have been a mighty thirteenth-century defensive system, bolstered in the sixteenth century, has almost entirely disappeared, save for the walls themselves, the bulky *Hochwacht* (the corner tower where the fortifications stop climbing) and the *Dicker Turm* (Fat Tower) at the summit. This was restored last century in the Romantic manner, and is now an excellent, if pricey, restaurant. From here, there's a good **view** over the Neckar Valley towards the Swabian Jura.

Practicalities

The **tourist office** (Mon–Fri 8am–6pm, Sat 9am–noon; ☎0711/351 2553) is on Marktplatz. Esslingen makes an alternative base to Stuttgart, if you don't fancy paying the latter's prices. The **youth hostel**, however, is a long way to the north of town at Neuffenstr. 65 (☎0711/381848). A more viable commuting base would be *Gasthof Falken*, Bahnhofstr. 4 (☎0711/357288), with singles at DM30, doubles DM50. The town centre abounds with places to **eat** and **drink**. *Palmscher Bau* on Innere Brücke has a beer garden, while *Zum Schwanen* on Franziskanergasse has a tiny house brewery and specialises in *vom heissen Stein* dishes. If you fancy a **hike**, the *Höhenweg* is a 27km-long circular marked path round the hills; a leaflet on it is available from the tourist office.

Ludwigsburg and Marbach

The creation of **LUDWIGSBURG** began in 1697, when French troops destroyed an isolated hunting lodge of the House of Württemberg which lay some 15km north of Stuttgart and 35km south of Heilbronn. Although German petty princes often fought against France, they were ardent admirers of the absolutist form of government practised there, and when Duke Eberhard Ludwig decided to rebuild the lodge, he soon found himself desiring something rather grander. By 1704, he hit on the idea of a planned town (named, needless to say, in his own honour); five years later, he had decided to make this his main residence and the Duchy's new capital. To entice people to come to live there, he provided free land and building materials, plus exemption from taxes for fifteen years – an offer which duly found plenty of takers.

Ludwigsburg's palaces

The Baroque **Schloss** (guided tours April–Oct daily 9am–noon & 1–5pm, Nov–March Mon–Fri at 10.30am & 3pm, Sat & Sun at 10.30am, 2pm & 3.30pm; DM3.50) took thirty years to build under the direction of a whole team of architects, and was only completed in the year of the patron's death. By then, funds had completely dried up and much of the lavish interior decoration was only put in place by his successors, who actually prefered to live in Stuttgart. There are 432 rooms in all, grouped in eighteen separate buildings arranged round three courtyards; some sixty of these are included in the compulsory tour. Among the highlights are two chapels, one each for the Protestants and Catholics, and a theatre, the first in the world to be equipped with a revolving stage. The *Ordenshalle* serves as an opulent venue for the concerts which take place throughout the summer festival season. Also housed in the Schloss is a branch of the **Landesmuseum** (Tues–Sun 10am–5pm; free). Appropriately enough, this concentrates on the decorative arts produced in Baroque courts, including plenty of examples of the local porcelain.

The **gardens** (daily 7.30am–8.30pm) are the scene of a huge floral festival, *Blühendes Barock*, held between April and October each year. In front of the Schloss, the formal Baroque section has been re-created from old plans. To the east are various modern additions to the facilities, including a Japanese garden, an aviary and the *Märchengarten*. The last named is a kitsch folk-tale playground with huge model giants, witches and other fairy-tale figures, complete with sound effects. Kids will love it, but otherwise it's not worth paying the inclusive DM9 entrance fee.

A better destination for a stroll is **Schloss Favorite** (guided tours Tues–Sun 10am–noon & 1.30–4pm; DM2) in the grounds immediately to the north, which was built as a resting-place for Ludwig and his cronies on their hunting trips. Even if you don't want to see yet another Baroque interior, it's still worth coming to enjoy the grounds, to which there's free access. It's then a walk of about 30 minutes to the third and last of Ludwig's palaces, **Monrepos**. This has a tranquil lakeside setting which is perfect for a picnic, but the building itself is in private hands and there's no admission. Within the grounds is the town's top luxury hotel; surprisingly, this has a reasonably priced (and excellent) restaurant.

The town centre

In contrast to Mannheim and Karlsruhe, the Schloss is not the epicentre of the Ludwigsburg plan; that distinction belongs to the **Marktplatz**. As in the Schloss, there are churches for both the Catholic and Protestant faiths, facing each other across the square. One of Ludwigsburg's main claims to fame is that it has nurtured rather more than its fair share of literary celebrities, and an obelisk in **Holzmarkt** immediately to the north commemorates four nineteenth-century writers who were born in the town – the Romantic poets Eduard Mörike and Justinus Kerner, and the realist philosophers Friedrich Theodor Vischer and David Friedrich Strauss. **Mörike** was the most significant of this group; in spite of an uneventful life as a tutor and country pastor, he produced some of the greatest lyric poetry of the age, which was to be a major source of inspiration to all the leading song-writers in the German tradition, especially Hugo Wolf. Schiller went to school in the town, while the revolutionary writer Friedrich Schubart did a six-year stint as organist of the Protestant church.

Practicalities

Ludwigsburg's **Bahnhof** is just a short walk to the west of the town centre. As well as being on the main line between Stuttgart and Heilbronn, it's linked to the state capital by S-Bahn #4 and #5. The **tourist office** (Mon–Fri 8.30am–noon & 2–5.30pm, Sat 9–11.30am; ☎07141/910636) is at Wilhelmstr. 12. If you want to stay the night, rather than visit on a day trip, your best **hotel** bet is *Kugelberg*, Bottwalrtalstr. 86 (☎07141/550209), charging DM35 per person. The **youth hostel** is at Gemsenbergstr. 21 (☎07141/51564); take bus #423 from the Bahnhof to its terminus. Most young inhabitants of Ludwigsburg confine their nightlife to Stuttgart, but the town has several good, inexpensive **restaurants**. Among the obvious choices are *Roter Ochsen* and *Margherita* on Holzmarkt, along with the pricier *Weinhaus Schnepple* on Marktplatz. Even better is *Württemberger Hof* on Bismarckstrasse, which offers a comprehensive vegetarian menu, alongside standard Swabian fare. For cheap Italian food, try *Café Roma* in the Marstallcenter.

Marbach

A few kilometres northeast of Ludwigsburg, at the terminus of S-Bahn #4, is **MARBACH**. This small town of half-timbered houses is indelibly associated with **Friedrich Schiller**, who was born in the house at Niklastorstr. 20, which is now a small **museum** (daily 9am–5pm; DM1) in his memory. It's a modest building, entirely typical of Marbach – the writer's mother had also been born in the town, and the family moved back to this rented property when his father retired from the army. As space is obviously restricted here, a much grander memorial was created early this century in the shape of the **Schiller Nationalmuseum** (daily 9am–5pm; DM2), which is housed in a huge mock-Baroque castle perched high above the Neckar Valley. If you're at all into literary memorabilia, this is a must, with mementoes not only of Schiller, but of all the other leading Swabian writers as well.

FRIEDRICH SCHILLER (1759-1805)

Considered in Germany to be one of the great lions of world literature, Schiller's fame elsewhere chiefly rests on a single poem, known in English as *Ode to Joy*, part of which was used by Beethoven for the choral finale of his titanic Ninth Symphony – the first time ever that words had been used in a symphonic composition. The strong liberal sentiments of this work are wholly characteristic of the output of Schiller, who was very much a product of the Age of Enlightenment. After his early *Sturm und Drang* period, he began to concentrate increasingly on large-scale historical problems, and was himself a practising historian, holding a chair at the University of Jena and writing a mammoth, Protestant-inspired account of the Thirty Years' War. This research provided him with the raw material for his dramatic masterpiece, the *Wallenstein* trilogy. Like his other mature plays, which took Mary Stuart, Joan of Arc and William Tell as subjects, this addresses basic moral issues in the light of the vexed question of historical greatness.

The *Stadthalle* near the museum has one of the best **restaurants** in town, offering the bonus of fine panoramic views from its terrace; *Goldener Löwe*, on the same street as Schiller's birthplace, is another good choice. There's no hostel or campsite, but **rooms** at DM25 per head are available at *Krone*, Güntterstr. 2 (☎07144/5125) and *Pension Schmierer*, Marktstr. 7 (☎07144/15565).

Maulbronn and the Stromberg

MAULBRONN, whose famous Cistercian Kloster is the best-preserved medieval monastery north of the Alps, lies in the heart of the hilly **Stromberg** region, the north-westernmost part of Swabia. In 1557, just a couple of decades after the last monks had left, a Protestant school was established there under the protection of the Dukes of Württemberg; this meant that Maulbronn never suffered the normal fate of serving as a stone quarry, far less as a target for iconoclasts and revolutionaries, and stands today as a complete monastic complex giving a unique insight into a way of life which exercised such enormous power and influence throughout the medieval period. A wonderfully evocative description of the monastery (thinly disguised as Mariabronn) in its heyday can be found in the picaresque novel *Narziss and Goldmund* by Hermann Hesse, one of the school's most famous old boys.

The outbuildings

A characterless modern town has grown up on the slopes above the Kloster, but that is forgotten as soon as you enter the walled precincts of the monastery by the Romanesque **Klostertor**. Immediately to the right of the entrance is a ruined chapel, in which early masses were said; facing it is the priest's house, now converted into a **museum** (April–Oct daily 9.30–noon & 2–5pm; free). It's well worth popping in, if only to see the model explaining the whole layout.

Beyond here, you pass into the spacious main **Klosterhof**, the first part of which is taken up by a jumble of predominantly late Gothic half-timbered buildings. These served as the storerooms and workshops, which were the province of the lay-brothers of the monastery. They're now put to a variety of uses: the forge has been converted into a restaurant; the stables serve as the Rathaus and **tourist office** (Mon & Thurs 8am–noon & 1–5.30pm, Tues & Wed 8am–noon & 1–4.30pm, Fri 8am–1.30pm, Sat & Sun 11am–5pm; ☎07043/10317); while the stone-built mill, the oldest of the buildings, is now a **youth hostel** (☎07043/6535). This is linked to the passageway along the ramparts, at the end of which is the thirteenth-century **Haspelturm** ("Witches' Tower").

A tour of the outbuildings can be completed by walking round the outside of the main quarters. At the southeast corner is the **Faustturm**, so called from having been the residence of the original Dr Faust (see overleaf), whose claim to be able to manufacture gold gained him employment for a time by an unscrupulous abbot who was willing to try anything to bolster the monastery's sagging finances. Within the corresponding corner to the north the Dukes of Württemberg built a Renaissance **Jagdschloss** with fairy-tale corner turrets; it now forms the girls' section of the school they founded.

The Kloster

Facing the courtyard is the **Kloster** proper (April–Oct daily 8.30am–6.30pm, Nov–March Tues–Sun 9.30am–1pm & 2–5pm; DM3), founded in 1147 in what was then the isolated valley of the River Salzach. This was exactly the sort of location favoured by the reforming Cistercian order, whose rule stressed both spirituality and the importance of manual labour. Here they had access not only to water, but also to the wood and stone which were necessary for the extensive building works. According to legend, the site was chosen when the monks, who had established their monastery at an unsuitable place nearby a few years before, stopped to water their mules – hence the name Maulbronn, meaning "Mule Well".

The **church** was the first part to be built; it's in the severe, unadorned style laid down in the tenets of the order, with no tower and no decoration. Later generations were less enthusiastic about asceticism, whether in life or architecture; in order to enliven their church they replaced the wooden roof with a lofty net vault, added a row of chapels with elaborate traceried windows to the south side, and commissioned works of art. There's also a fascinating glimpse into the sense of worldly hierarchy practised by the monks right from the time of the church's construction. The fathers reserved the eastern part of the church for their own exclusive use, confining the lay-brothers to the nave by the erection of a stone screen; members of the public weren't allowed into the church at all.

Instead, a **porch** (or "Paradise"), enabling visitors to look in on the services, was built on to the facade of the church in 1220. This seems to be the earliest building in Germany to show awareness of the new Gothic style pioneered in France. The same anonymous mason then began building the cloister, completing the southern wing plus the **monk's refectory** on the opposite side. His style shows all the sense of discovery characteristic of the beginning of an era; still influenced by the Romanesque penchant for mass, he introduced the ribbed vault and the pointed arch not only for their constructional advantages, but also for the decorative effect which could be obtained by varying the forms they took. The refectory is a masterpiece, which is all the more appropriate in view of the Cistercian custom of making the dining hall particularly splendid and luminous, in order to draw thoughts away from the frugality of the meals. The rest of the cloister, including the graceful **chapter house** on the east side, dates from around a century later; the use of elaborate tracery is the first visible sign of the dilution of the early Cistercian ideal of austerity. As a culmination, a striking polygonal **well-house** was added to house the fountain where the monks washed before each meal. Buildings continued to be added periodically – the long, narrow **parlatorium** (the room where conversations were held) beside the chapter house was built by a lay-brother at the end of the fifteenth century, while the cloister was given a picturesque half-timbered upper storey soon after.

The frescos

In the early sixteenth century, as the original Cistercian ideal of plain and unadorned architecture held ever less appeal, the most violently expressive of German artists, **Jerg Ratgeb**, was commissioned to execute a series of fresco cycles. He made a series of preliminary red chalk drawings, which can still be seen; these include the depiction of the legend of the monastery's foundation in the well-house, and a number of allegorical subjects (incorporating a stern self-portrait) in the refectory. Completion of the project was interrupted by the Reformation when the painter abandoned art in favour of politics, serving as "War Councillor" and "Chancellor" of the Peasants' Revolt in 1525. The failure of this rebellion led to Ratgeb's arrest; he was quartered in the Markt in Pforzheim a decade before his erstwhile patrons became very different casualties of the Reformation.

Practicalities

Maulbronn is slightly tricky to reach by **public transport**. It's best to come by bus from MÜHLACKER, which is a regular stop for trains between Stuttgart and Karlsruhe; although there's a stop named "Maulbronn West" on the branch railway line to Bruchsal, it's some 3km from the Kloster. As an alternative to the excellent but expensive **restaurant** *Klosterkeller*, go just outside the gates to *Scheffelhof* which serves homely and hearty fare, including imaginative vegetarian dishes. A short walk to the east of the Kloster is the **Tiefer See**, an artificial lake created by the monks in order to give themselves a regular supply of fish; it's now a centre for swimming and water sports. As well as the hostel, there are a few **guest houses**; cheapest are *Undi*, Südmährer Str. 6 (☎07043/7225), at DM25 per head, and *Ochsen*, Stuttgarter Str. 54 (☎07043/7314), with singles DM26, doubles DM50.

The Stromberg

The **Naturpark Stromberg-Heuchelberg** stretches over an area of 330 square kilometres north and east of Maulbronn as far as the River Neckar. It's cut by two deep valleys, the Kirbach and the Metter, which provide fertile agricultural land. Grapes have been cultivated on the slopes since the eighth century, if not before. Red **wines** – *Trollinger*, *Lemberger*, *Schwarzriesling*, *Spätburgunder* and *Portugieser* – make up the bulk of the current output; white varieties include the well-known *Riesling*, as well as *Müller-Thurgau*, *Kerner* and *Ruhlander*. Much of the area, however, is taken up by the two separate mountain ranges after which the park is named. These are actually fairly gentle, with even the highest peaks being under 500 metres. A **footpath**, laid out in the seventeenth century for military use, crosses right through the middle of the park, linking Mühlacker with EPPINGEN directly to the north; it makes a good day's hike, offering a mixture of forest and upland scenery. There are also a couple of **bird sanctuaries** within easy reach of Maulbronn – *Rossweiher* is just beyond Tiefer See, while *Aalkistensee* is a couple of kilometres west of the town.

Knittlingen
KNITTLINGEN, 6km northwest of Maulbronn, is notable for only one reason – it was the birthplace of the notorious necromancer **Johannes Faust**. Inevitably, a **museum** charting his impact has been set up in the half-timbered house where he is believed to have been born (Tues–Fri 9.30am–noon & 1.30–5pm, Sat & Sun 10am–6pm; DM2).

JOHANNES FAUST AND THE FAUST LEGEND

Surprisingly little is known about the real-life Johannes Faust, though he seems to have been a celebrity in his day and the leading intellectuals of the time took him seriously, while regarding his practices as wholly evil. Unlike other leading practitioners of the occult, such as Nostradamus and Paracelsus, Faust left no tangible legacy, and his name would certainly have passed into oblivion had it not been for an unknown author who in 1587 published the *Faustbuch*, a pot-boiling collection of tales allegedly told by the magician, who had died nearly half a century before; this quickly became a bestseller, despite the crudity of the text. It was the English playwright Christopher Marlowe who, just a few years afterwards, first realised the dramatic possibilities of the story, endowing the hero with a tragic dignity.

Ever since, the Faust legend – with its themes of absolute knowledge, absolute power and the relationship between the two – has ranked as one of the great subjects of the European literary tradition, one capable of a vast variety of interpretations and a convenient backdrop for the discussion of all kinds of issues. Lessing provided a happy ending, a lead followed by Goethe, whose vast two-part drama is the unchallenged summit of all German literature. It took him the best part of sixty years to write; in it, he explored the entire European cultural heritage. In the present century, the Faust themes are equally relevant, and Thomas Mann provided an appropriately updated version of the story in his novel of 1950.

Heilbronn and around

HEILBRONN, which lies in the Neckar Valley just to the east of the Stromberg, is deemed to mark the boundary of the mystical concept of Swabia – no true *Schwob* would live any further north. Today, it still boasts one of the richest folklore traditions in Germany and is also a leading centre for **wine** production – some five million litres, mostly *Riesling* and *Trollinger* varieties, are produced each year by the surrounding vineyards. Sadly, however, the old streets were almost razed to the ground in an air raid at the end of 1944. The rebuilding programme was unusual in that it concentrated on providing housing in the town centre, with most commercial activity banished to the suburbs. Only a few first class monuments now remain, and it's best to time your visit to coincide with one of the many **festivals** (see box on next page) which dot the calendar.

Around town

The surviving monuments are conveniently grouped closely together in the town centre. By far the most imposing is the Gothic hall church of **St Kilian** – or rather, its amazing later adjunct, the sixteenth-century **belfry**. One of the few examples of ecclesiastical architecture in Northern Europe directly inspired by the Italian High Renaissance, its lower parts are richly decorated, much in the manner of the late Gothic style then still popular elsewhere in Germany, while the upper storeys are built in the manner of a miniature Classical temple. At the summit, the *Männle* (a statue of an infantryman bearing the municipal coat of arms) lords it over the town. Inside the church is a wonderful retable of *The Virgin and Child with Saints* by a local man, **Hans Syfer**, one of the seemingly endless number of virtuoso carvers active in late fifteenth-century Germany. Underneath the building is the *Heiliger Brunnen*, a well with supposedly miraculous properties, from which the town's name is derived.

Directly opposite St Kilian is the **Rathaus**, another amalgam of Gothic and Renaissance, whose facade is enlivened by a graceful balcony used for making public pronouncements and by an astronomical clock. The latter, which tells the day and the month as well as the time, was considered the ultimate municipal status symbol when it was installed in 1580. Its construction was entrusted to Isaak Habrecht, the finest horologist of the day, who had previously created what still ranks as one of Europe's most spectacular clocks, that inside Strasbourg Cathedral.

Also on Marktplatz is the **Käthchenhaus**, a Gothic patrician mansion embellished with a Renaissance oriel. It takes its name from the legend of Käthchen of Heilbronn, best known as a result of the play by Heinrich von Kleist. Käthchen was the product of a one-night stand between a German emperor and the wife of the blacksmith of Heilbronn. Her true identity was only revealed when, as a fifteen-year-old, she developed a mystical attraction to a count who had a premonition that he was going to marry an emperor's daughter. The town still gets a lot of mileage out of the story – every two years, a pretty local girl is designated as "Käthchen", to preside over all the festivals and to adorn the front cover of all the glossy promotional brochures.

In the pedestrian precinct south of Marktplatz is the **Deutschhof**, formerly belonging to the Teutonic Knights, which contains a Gothic church and Baroque administrative buildings. The **Städtisches Museum** (Tues 10am–7pm, Wed–Sun 10am–noon & 2–5pm; free) is now housed in the latter, though its natural history and archaeology departments are in the Renaissance **Gerichtshaus** (Law Courts) across the street. There's also a third section, devoted to shipping on the Neckar, in its own building on Frankfurter Strasse, not far from the river itself. Up Obere Neckarstrasse from the Gerichtshaus is one of the few surviving parts of the medieval fortifications, the tower known as the **Götzenturm**. It's so called as a result of the daring escape made from it by the great adventurer Götz von Berlichingen, who was held prisoner there in 1519.

Practicalities

The **Hauptbahnhof** is situated just to the west of the centre, which is reached by following Bahnhofstrasse straight ahead. Cheapest centrally-sited **hotel** is *Schlachthof*, Frankfurter Str. 83 (☎07131/ 81413), charging from DM30 per person. Otherwise, the **tourist office** (Mon–Fri 9am–5.30pm, Sat 9am–12.30pm; ☎07131/562270) on Marktplatz will find you a room at no extra cost. The **youth hostel** is at Schirrmannstr. 9 (☎07131/72961): take bus #1 to the Trappensee terminus.

Best **restaurant** for Swabian specialities is the *Ratskeller*; for something a bit cheaper, try *Kronprinz* on Bahnhofstrasse. *Sonnenstube* on Querschulgasse is a good vegetarian café, while *Rialto* on Innsbrucker Strasse is recommendable for Italian fare. *Dechpavilion*, on top of a row of shops on Kaiserstrasse, is the most enticing **bar** in Heilbronn, offering a fine view over the town by night. Youthful hangouts include *Freak* on Albert-Schaffler-Strasse (reached by bus #10), *Altstadt* on Happelstrasse (which runs musical theme nights), *Hard Rock Café* on Neckarsulmer Strasse and *Bukowskis* on Hafenstrasse (which, come the weekend, never seems to close).

Classical music can be heard at the *Harmonie* concert hall on Allee; look out for performances by the *Württemberger Kammerorchester*, one of the best chamber orchestras in Europe. On the same street, the spanking new *Stadttheater* presents all forms of **drama**. The booking office for **Neckar cruises** is beside Friedrich-Ebert-Brücke. There are generally at least a couple of sailings each day in summer to Gundelsheim; trips round the harbour are occasionally offered as an alternative.

HEILBRONN'S FESTIVALS

Foremost of the many local festivals is the *Heilbronner Herbst*, which begins with a procession through the streets on the first Saturday in September, and continues with a parade of lantern-bearing children and a fireworks display the next day. Later in the week, the *Weindorf* (Wine Village) is set up for nine days in the town centre, with the inevitable oompah bands to enliven the atmosphere. Nearly two hundred vintages are on offer at the various booths; in contrast to the inflated prices normally charged at German festivals, the rates are surprisingly reasonable – usually DM1 per glass. Heilbronn's other big event is the *Neckarfest*, featuring historical boat pageants, a flotilla of bizarre home-made "water transport" contraptions, aquatic tournaments and a serenade of lights. This takes place during June, but in even numbered years only, as it alternates with the more orthodox *Stadtfest*. Other festivals are the huge *Pferdemarkt* (Horse Fair) in February and the *Unterländer Volksfest* in late July/early August; the latter sees beer take a rare centre-stage role in this wine stronghold.

Around Heilbronn: Weinsberg and Neckarsulm

WEINSBERG, 6km east of Heilbronn, is, as its name suggests, a town surrounded by sloping vineyards. It's particularly associated with the nineteenth-century *Schwäbischer Dichterkreis* (Swabian School of Poets), which often held rendezvous in the home of one of their members, the Weinsberg doctor, Justinus Kerner. This is now a **museum** of memorabilia (Tues–Sun 10am–noon & 2–5pm; DM1.50). Kerner was fascinated by the supernatural, and the **Geisterturm** in his own grounds is so named after the spirits who haunted it. The part-Hungarian, part-German Nikolaus Lenau stayed there when writing his unfinished *Faust*; this was to inspire the celebrated, demoniac *Mephisto Waltz* by a man of similarly mixed nationality, Franz Liszt.

Above Weinsberg are the scanty remains of the **Weibertreu** (Faithful Wives) fortress, named in honour of the curious legend with which it's associated. In the twelfth century, the castle was besieged by the brother of its owner, who had taken the opposing side in one of the frequent disputes between the emperor and the Pope. Before moving in for the final massacre, the attackers decided to show clemency to the women of the castle, telling them they could go free, taking with them only what they were themselves able to carry. When the women came out, the besiegers were dumb-founded by what they saw – each had hoisted her husband on her shoulders, thus, by the terms of the agreement, saving his life.

Neckarsulm
NECKARSULM, a similar distance north of Heilbronn, has a heavily-restored castle formerly belonging to the Teutonic Knights, which now houses the **Deutsches Zweirad Museum** (daily 9am–noon & 1.30–5.30pm; DM2.50), with some 250 bikes and motorcycles from the early nineteenth century to the present day. This also incorporates the collection of NSU, Germany's leading manufacturer in the field. From here, it's only a short journey by train to Bad Wimpfen and the route of the Neckar castles (see p.311–15).

The Swabian Forest

The **Swabian Forest** (*Schwäbischer Wald*) stretches over a neat, almost square geographical area between Heilbronn and Stuttgart in the west, and Schwäbisch Gmünd and Schwäbisch Hall in the east. To the north, it enters Franconia where it gives way to the flat plain of Hohenlohe, while its southern extremity borders the Stauferland. Stretching over some 900 square kilometres, the whole area is designated a *Naturpark*. Thickly wooded, it consists of three separated forest areas, plus two ranges of hills. Though there's little that's tremendously dramatic, the region offers the opportunity of escaping from the crowds, on weekdays at least. The old Roman **Limes Wall**, some of whose towers have been restored to serve as vantage-points, traverses the forest from north to south; and there's a marked trail along the entire route.

At the heart of the forest is the town of **MURRHARDT**, which lies on the railway line between Ludwigsburg and Schwäbisch Hall, and makes the obvious base from which to plan your explorations. The only **youth hostel** in the region is at Karnsberger Str. 1 (☎07192/7501) at the northern end of town, while there's a **campsite**, *Am Waldsee*, in the neighbouring village of FORNSBACH (☎07192/6436). Murrhardt also boasts an outstanding monument in the **Walterichskapelle**, a tiny, highly ornamented late Romanesque chapel adjoining the fifteenth-century Stadtkirche. A number of half-timbered houses and a section of the town walls also survive.

Schwäbisch Hall

SCHWÄBISCH HALL, which lies just beyond the Swabian Forest and south of the Hohenlohe plain, was an important centre of minting, making the silver *Häller* (or *Heller*), the smallest unit of currency used in the Holy Roman Empire. Though now long out of circulation, the *Heller*'s name lives on as a simile for worthlessness in many idiomatic expressions in modern German. Ultimately, the coin's name derives from the industry on which the local economy was originally based: *Hall* means "Place of Salt". Excavations show that the salt springs attracted Celtic tribes to establish a permanent settlement here; following the medieval revival, they served as the keystone of local prosperity, only going into decline in the nineteenth century with discoveries of richer deposits elsewhere. Subsequent attempts to develop a more modern industrial base failed, as did a bid to make Hall a bathing and health resort on the lines of so many other German spas. Coupled with the fact that bombing in World War II caused little more than superficial grazing, this means that the town preserves an unusually intact reminder of its medieval self, complete with tantalising insights into the social and political preoccupations of the time.

Marktplatz

The central, steeply sloping **Marktplatz** is lined by a series of superb buildings which form an encyclopaedia of German architecture. Its present character was largely determined during the late medieval period, at a time when the rampantly successful bourgeoisie had ousted the aristocracy from control of the council, forcing many of the latter to leave town. As a symbol of the self-confident spirit, it was decided to build a spectacular new church, to be approached by a monumental flight of 42 (now 54) steps. The dramatic possibilities of this backdrop were immediately evident, and the space was used for jousting and tournaments.

Today, the Marktplatz is put to triumphant use as an **open-air theatre**. This is one of the most impressive you're ever likely to come across, with magical staging effects in a dense, rapt atmosphere. The season lasts from mid-June to early August, and usually features a play by Shakespeare, a European classic and a twentieth-century work. Performances start at 8.30pm, but the scramble for the best seats begins as early as 6pm. Tickets cost around DM15 and are available from the theatre headquarters at no. 8 on the square. Next door is the **tourist office** (April–Sept Mon–Fri 9am–noon & 2–6pm, Sat & Sun 10am–2pm; Nov–March Mon–Fri 9am–noon & 2–5pm; ☎0791/ 751246). If you want to make a detailed visit of the old streets, ask for their *Walking Tour* brochure, which has a good map and extensive historical information in English.

The Münster

The late Gothic **Münster** (mid-March–Oct Mon–Sat 9am–noon & 2–5pm, Sun 11am– noon & 2–5pm; DM1 including ascent of the tower) has a nave in the hall church style with slender pillars and wide vaults, that contrasts with the much higher choir, which was only completed in 1525, the year that the authorities of Hall decided to go over to Protestantism. Luther's youthful protégé **Johannes Brenz** – a far more tolerant figure than most of the leading lights of the time – came from Heidelberg to be the new preacher. His portrait can be seen on one of the epitaphs in the nave. Another particularly interesting memorial tablet is in the fourth chapel from the left in the ambulatory; this was made for his own tomb by the sixteenth-century artist and calligrapher Thomas Schweiker, who painted with his feet, having been born without hands or arms. The most striking work of art, however, is Michel Erhart's impassioned *Crucifixion*, placed above the Netherlandish *Retable of the Passion* at the high altar.

Elsewhere on Marktplatz

Another embellishment to the Square, erected at the same time as the Münster's chancel, is the **Marktbrunnen**, showing Saint Michael in the company of two other warriors against evil, Samson and Saint George. Rather bizarrely, the structure also incorporates the pillory, still preserving the manacles which bound the wrong-doers. The north side of the square is lined with a picturesque jumble of buildings, including what are now two of the best (and most expensive) hotel-restaurants in town, the graceful half-timbered *Goldener Adler*, an inn since the sixteenth century, and the gaunt stone *Ratskeller*. Opposite are a series of houses which traditionally belonged to various religious and charitable bodies. The west side of the square seems to be jinxed – the church which formerly stood there was destroyed by fire in the eighteenth century, to be replaced by the **Rathaus**, which was in turn a rare casualty of the last war. However, it's been successfully restored, its ritzy curved facade and stately belfry giving it the look of a sumptuous Baroque palace.

The rest of the town

South of Marktplatz run a series of alleys – Untere Herrngasse, Obere Herrngasse and Pfargasse – which are all lined with superb old buildings often linked to one another by stairways. They all lead to the **fortifications**, which survive in part all round the town, unfortunately shorn of most of the towers which were demolished when Hall became part of the Kingdom of Württemberg in the early nineteenth century. Rising high above the weakest part of the defensive system is the massive **Neubau**, which, in spite of its name, dates back to the time of the Reformation. It served as an arsenal and granary, and is now a concert hall. The other dominant building at this side of town is the eight-storey **Keckenburg**, a tower-house from the Staufer period. Along with a diverse series of historic buildings nearby, it houses the **Hällisch-Fränkisches Museum** (Tues & Thurs–Sun 10am–5pm, Wed 10am–8pm; free). Well above average for a regional collection, this has displays on local history and industry, archaeology, geology, crafts and sacred sculpture.

A short walk from here brings you to the banks of the sedate River Kocher, lined with weeping willows and with a picturesque group of stone and wooden bridges reaching out to three islets. From the quays on the opposite side, you have an outstanding **view** of the main part of the town, rising majestically in tiers. The left bank, which had its own set of walls and towers, was the artisans' district; it clusters around St **Katharina**, a Gothic church with gorgeous fourteenth-century stained glass windows. At the northern end is a reproduction of the oldest of the bridges, **Henkersbrücke** ("Hangman's Bridge"), named after the house on it, in which the holder of the least coveted municipal office was forced to live as the stigma of the position meant he was forbidden to reside in town.

The northern part of Hall presents another characterful old quarter, beginning at the **Säumarkt** (Pig Market), which features a sixteenth-century tower and weigh-house, behind which is the late seventeenth-century tannery, whose arcades were used for drying skins until 1972. As a contrast, there's the Neoclassical solemnity of the guard station of the Württemberg army. Leading off the square is Gelbinger Gasse, the longest and arguably the finest street in Hall, whose buildings cover the full gamut of styles from Gothic to Jugendstil. Look out in particular for no. 25, the **Engelhardbau**, the Baroque mansion of a town councillor; and for no. 47, the late Renaissance **Gräterhaus**, whose beam decoration includes the scraping tools of the tanners, an indication that the house was built by a prosperous member of that guild.

Practicalities

Schwäbisch Hall's **Bahnhof** is on the western bank of the Kocher; it's a fifteen minute walk to the centre straight ahead via Bahnhofstrasse, then over the river. The **bus station** is at the diametrically opposite end of town, by the bank of the Kocher just outside the northern quarter. There's a **youth hostel** at Langenfelderweg 5 (☎0791/2260); from the rear of Marktplatz, follow Crailsheimer Strasse (the ring road) in an easterly direction, then turn left into Blutsteige. The **campsite** is south of town at Steinbacher See (April–mid-Oct only; ☎0791/2984). For a central location, the best value **hotels** are *Krone*, Klosterstr. 1 (☎0791/6022), at upwards of DM29 per person; and *Dreikönig*, Neuestr. 25 (☎0791/7473), with singles DM34, doubles DM67.

Eating

Many of the best **restaurants** have their eyes on the well-heeled short-stay tourist, but homely Swabian cooking is available at low cost at *Zum Darle* on Blockgasse and *Salzsiedler* on Schulgasse. There's also a widely varied clutch of ethnic eateries along Gelbinger Gasse. The local *Haller Löwenbräu* **beer** (not to be confused with its Munich namesake) is available as both Pils and Weizen. Evening entertainment possibilities are headed by the open-air theatre, but **kids** will prefer the *Marionettentheater* near the left-bank quay at Im Lindbach 9, which has both historical and modern puppets.

Festivals

Schwäbisch Hall's salt heritage is celebrated each Whit weekend in one of Baden-Württemberg's most famous **festivals**, the *Kuchen und Brunnen Fest der Haller Salzsieder* (Cake and Fountain Festival of the Salt-Simmerers of Hall). This commemorates the occasion when the salt workers quenched a fire at the town mill. It features dancing and music on the Grasbödele (one of the islets) by the simmerers in their red, black and white historical costume. There's also a simulation of the blaze and a tattoo, both held on the Marktplatz.

Comburg

Perched magisterially on its hill a couple of kilometres south of Hall via the banks of the Kocher is one of the most outstanding sights of southern Germany, the awesome **Klosterburg Gross Comburg**. Fortress-monasteries are common enough in Spain and the Middle East, but such blatant expressions of the Church Militant are extremely rare in Western Europe. In 1079 this collegiate foundation was endowed by the Count of Comburg, Burkhard II, who, as a cripple, felt unable to perform the normal aristocratic duties and decided to retire to a monastic life. Much of the original Romanesque architecture survives intact, including the mighty ring wall with its defensive towers. The extensive additions to the complex made down the years included the progressive strengthening of the entrance, and you now pass through the Baroque *Bastion* and the Renaissance *Zwingertor* before arriving at the Romanesque **Michaelstor**, guarding a 12 metres-long tunnel which served as the last line of defence. As the Baroque monastic buildings are now used as a college, there's normally unrestricted entry to the courtyard. Here you can see another Romanesque survival, the hexagonal **Ebehardskapelle**, which is ornamented with a graceful dwarf gallery. Its function is disputed, but it probably served as an ossuary.

The **Klosterkirche** (mid-March–mid-Nov Tues–Sat 9am–noon & 1.30–5pm, Sun 1.30–5pm; DM1) retains the three imperious towers of the first church, but was otherwise rebuilt in the Würzburg Baroque style. Although the exterior retains much of the austerity of its predecessor, the interior, with its gleaming white stuccowork, comes in complete contrast. It still preserves, however, two stunning twelfth-century treasures made in the monastery's once-celebrated workshop: an enormous golden wheel-shaped **chandelier** (which is even larger and more impressive than those in Aachen and Hildesheim, the only others to have survived) and the gilded beaten-copper **antependium** (altar front), which has engravings of Christ surrounded by his disciples. A number of masterly tombs, including that of the founder, can be seen in the **chapter house**, which still preserves its Romanesque form.

It's also worth crossing over to the hill directly opposite, crowned by the **Klein Comburg**. This was founded as a convent about thirty years after its big brother and was also used for some time as a hospice. The church here was always very much the poor relation, but scores in the fact that it preserves its simple original form.

Wackershofen

Some 5km northwest of the centre of Hall is **WACKERSHOFEN**, where you'll find the **Freilichtmuseum** (April, May & Oct Tues–Sun 10am–5.30pm, June–Sept Tues–Sun 9am–6pm; DM3). This brings together redundant rural buildings from throughout the north of Baden-Württemberg, including the Tauber Valley and the eastern Jura but concentrating on the Hohenlohe region. Ceramics, furniture-making and textiles are among the crafts demonstrated, while there's a *Backofenfest* on the last weekend in September. A historic inn, *Roter Ochsen*, is among the reconstructed buildings, providing a handy stopping-off point for lunch.

Schwäbisch Gmünd and the Stauferland

SCHWÄBISCH GMÜND is 45km south of Schwäbish Hall through the dense tracts of the Swabian Forest, and a similar distance east of Stuttgart on an almost dead straight railway line. Known in the Middle Ages for the luxury goods produced by its goldsmiths, silversmiths, jewellers, glass-blowers and watchmakers, today it's a lively provincial town which has neither grown too big for its own good, nor got stuck in a time-warp. Not that the latter was much of an option as Gmünd had a large American military presence – which brought it a certain amount of notoriety (see box) – from the end of the war until its winding-down in 1991.

MUTLANGEN – GERMANY'S GREENHAM COMMON

The American base in Schwäbisch Gmünd's northern suburb of Mutlangen provided one of Germany's constant news stories of the last decade. Protests first erupted there in 1983, with the decision to allow Cruise and Pershing missiles to be installed on the site, an act which inflamed particular passions in Germany as the country is expressly forbidden under the postwar treaties from holding nuclear weapons of its own. Many prominent intellectuals, including the world-famous novelists Günter Grass and Heinrich Böll, were at the forefront of the peace campaign, while another well-known writer, Walter Jens, was arrested and fined for blocking the road to the base when the missiles arrived the following year. Protests continued with renewed vigour until the fall of the Berlin Wall and national unification enabled the Americans to make a swift withdrawal, leaving only a token force on the site.

The Heiligkreuzmünster

Gmünd was founded by the first of the emperors of the local Hohenstaufen dynasty (see below), Conrad III, but after the family died out, it became a Free Imperial City. Around 1310, the citizens began the construction of the **Heiligkreuzmünster** as the centrepiece of their town. Some time later, Heinrich Parler arrived from Cologne and took charge of operations; he was later aided by his son Peter, who was soon after called to Prague, where he developed into one of the most brilliant and imaginative architects Europe ever produced. The Parler style – of which this church is recognised as the prototype – soon usurped France's long-standing architectural leadership and made its mark on a host of cities throughout *Mitteleuropa;* the celebrity status of the family is confirmed by the fact that, in contrast to the general anonymity of most of the medieval masons who designed the great medieval cathedrals, they are relatively well-documented. In spite of the lack of a tower, the Münster, whose exterior bristles with highly elaborate pinnacles, gables and gargoyles, floats high above the town. Its five entrance **portals** introduce the characteristic Parler sculpture, which aimed at a far greater sense of realism than had hitherto been in vogue. The figures are short and stocky, and are often placed in dramatic relationships to each other; they have life-like facial expressions and wear contemporary dress, with heavy horizontal drapery folds.

The interior

However, there's no doubt that it's the **interior** which is the real show-stopper; it was the first hall church to be erected in southern Germany, and triumphantly gives the lie to the theory that this form of building is inherently dull and unvaried. Standing just inside the main western entrance, you're confronted by the majestic spectacle of 22 huge rounded pillars marching towards the choir. They support a coloured vault which grows ever richer, moving from a fanciful pattern of ribs in the nave to a rich tapestry of network and star shapes in the chancel which, contrary to normal practice, was the last part to be built. The ring of side-chapels, cleverly placed between the buttresses so that their presence can't be gauged from outside, contain a wealth of late Gothic altarpieces, notably a *Tree of Jesse* in the baptistery. There's a wonderful set of Renaissance **stalls** by the Augsburg carver Adolf Daucher, who also made the pulpit. Above the seats stand animated figures of the Apostles (on the left) and Old Testament prophets; a peculiarity is that each figure is carved twice and placed back-to-back, so that it faces the ambulatory as well as the choir. At the opposite end of the church, the flowery mid-seventeenth-century case of the organ presents a contrasting piece of virtuoso woodwork.

The rest of the town

The original parish church, the octagonal-towered **Johanniskirche** on the central Bocksgasse, is overshadowed by the Münster but is nevertheless a highly unusual building. It dates from the very end of the Romanesque period in the mid-thirteenth century and is extravagantly adorned all round its exterior with delicate reliefs of fantastic animals, fables, hunting scenes, flowers and foliage. The interior (May–Oct Sun–Fri 10am–noon & 2–4pm, Sat 2–4pm, Nov–April Sat 2–4pm, Sun 10am–noon & 2–4pm only) has nineteenth-century pastel murals and also serves as a repository for original lapidary fragments from the Münster and elsewhere.

Facing the west end of the Johanniskirche is the **Prediger**, a former Dominican monastery which has been converted into a cultural centre, along with a **museum** (Tues–Fri 2–5pm, Sat & Sun 10am–noon & 2–5pm; free) which contains good collections of medieval and Baroque sculpture, in addition to examples of the town's expertise in jewellery-making and the usual local history displays. On the opposite side of the Johanniskirche is the **Marktplatz**, now largely Baroque in character, with several cheerful mansions and a rather saccharine fountain bearing a double-sided statue of the *Madonna and Child*. However, there are also a number of half-timbered houses from earlier periods, notably the **Amtshaus Spital** at the far end. A bit further east are four of the five remaining towers of the fourteenth-century city wall, with the highest of the group, the **Königsturm**, a short walk to the south.

The **Hauptbahnhof** is just to the northwest of the centre, which is reached by following Uferstrasse straight ahead, before turning into Bocksgasse. Just behind, there's a wonderful wooded uphill walk along Taubentalstrasse, past shrines dating as far back as the fifteenth century, to the dark, secret **St-Salvator-Kapelle** at the top. This former hermit's cave and its adjoining stone-walled rooms are bedecked with candles, icons, statues and other religious paraphernalia.

Practicalities

The **tourist office** (Mon–Fri 9am–5.30pm, Sat 9am–12.30pm, May–Oct also Sun 10am–1pm; ☎07171/603415) is in the Prediger. There's a **youth hostel** at Taubentalstr. 45 (☎07171/2260), in a peaceful hilly location to the rear of the Hauptbahnhof. **Camping** is possible to the west of town at *Schurrenhof* (☎07165/8190). Among the centrally-placed **guest houses**, cheapest are *Weisser Ochsen*, Parlerstr. 47 (☎07171/2812), with singles at DM27, plus a double at DM46; and *Goldener Stern*, Vordere Schmiedgasse 41

(☎07171/66337), which charges DM30 per person. If you want your visit to coincide with a **festival**, come on the second Saturday in June, when *Schwabenalter* celebrates those who have passed their fortieth birthday – the watershed year for the acquisition of true wisdom, according to Swabian custom. Otherwise, *Fastnet* is the main event, reaching a climax on Shrove Tuesday.

There are plenty of good places to **eat** and **drink** in the centre; best for traditional Swabian fare is the historic *Fuggerei* on Münstergasse, though it's on the expensive side. Recommendable cafés include *Margrit* on Johannisplatz which has delicious cakes, the long-established *Zieher* on Marktgässle, the candle-lit *Eiscafé Piazetta* on Marktplatz, and *Spielplatz* on Münsterplatz, which often features exhibitions of contemporary international artists. Alternatively, try the restaurant in the *Stadtgarten* (between the Hauptbahnhof and the centre) which offers quality dishes at low cost, with the added bonus of views across the park; in the halls here **concerts** of all kinds take place. The local **beer** is *Aloisle*, made with the soft spring water of the Swabian Jura. For serious drinking, head for *Bierakademie* on Ledergasse which serves what it claims are the fifteen best brews in the world. *Taverne* on Kornhausstrasse is the main concession to the American community, fitted out to resemble a saloon bar of the Fifties.

The Stauferland

Schwäbisch Gmünd lies in the heart of the **Stauferland**, a countryside of gentle slopes, lush meadows and juniper heathland straddling the northern end of the Swabian Jura and the southern edge of the Swabian Forest, which is ideal for hiking if you prefer routes which aren't too strenuous. It's named after its former overlords, the **Hohenstaufen dynasty**, who were one of the dominant forces in the politics of early medieval Germany and Italy. Originally Counts of Swabia, they captured the office of Holy Roman Emperor in 1133 and held on to it until 1254. Their leading member was the great Crusader and champion of chivalry **Frederick Barbarossa**, later to become one of the heroes of the nineteenth-century Romantic movement.

Just south of Gmünd the landscape is characterised by three conical wooded hills, the **Kaiserberge**, each commanding an extensive view and each formerly crowned by a feudal castle; to walk around them makes for the best day trip in the region. Most westerly is **Hohenstaufen** (684m) itself, lying mid-way between Gmünd and GÖPPINGEN. Unfortunately, the ancestral home of the family was completely destroyed in the 1525 Peasants' Revolt, leaving little more than the foundations. A few kilometres on is the holiday resort of RECHBERG, nestling below **Hohenrechberg** (707m), whose Romanesque Burg survived largely intact until being burnt out last century. It's an impressive ruin nonetheless, and is definitely the one to visit if you haven't time to see all three. The area has been a place of pilgrimage since the fifteenth century; the present Baroque church is approached uphill via a set of Stations of the Cross. Further east is **Stuifen** (757m), the highest but least atmospheric of this group of hills.

Tübingen

"We have a town on our campus," runs a local saying in **TÜBINGEN**. No irony is intended – the **University** dominates the life of this city to an extent unparalleled even in Germany's other world-famous centres of learning, such as Heidelberg, Marburg and Göttingen. Over half the population of 70,000 is in some way connected with the University, and the current size of the town is due entirely to the twentieth-century boom in higher education – it was not until a hundred years ago that the number of inhabitants reached five figures, having remained static since the time of the University's foundation in 1477.

Tübingen's **setting**, on the gentle slopes above the willow-lined banks of the Neckar, some 30km south of Stuttgart, immediately sets the tone of the place. Upstream, the river follows a turbulent course, but here it's serene and placid, the perfect backdrop for the unhurried and unworldly groves of academe. For obvious reasons, the town is often described as a German counterpart of Oxford or Cambridge. Certainly, it's the nearest equivalent, and the sight of the students punting on the river on a balmy summer evening is strongly reminiscent of similar scenes on the Cam or Cherwell. However, there are important differences. Germany has a far more egalitarian higher education system than England or north America – most students attend their local institution, and there's no trace of the Anglo-Saxon conception of an intellectual, social and political elite being nurtured in a couple of historic universities. Tübingen even has one of the few left-wing councils in Baden-Württemberg, and the Greens have chalked up many successes, notably the dropping of plans for an urban ringway. Moreover, there's no collegiate system and little in the way of student societies, other than the small and discredited duelling *Verbindungen*. There are no impassioned Union debates, extravagant balls or nostalgic wallowings in ancient traditions, while carefree displays of high jinks are kept firmly in check. Study is treated as a serious business, and the prevailing atmosphere is of the peace and quiet that's necessary for scholarly contemplation.

The old town, having been spared the ravages of war, is a visual treat, a mixture of brightly painted half-timbered and gabled houses ranging from the fifteenth to the eighteenth century, grouped into twisting and plunging alleys. There are few truly outstanding buildings, but the whole ensemble is much more than the sum of its parts.

Holzmarkt

Two large squares provide a setting for communal activities, one of which, **Holzmarkt**, is built around a fountain dedicated to Saint George. Here also is the *Buchhandlung Heckenhauer*, where Hermann Hesse spent a four-year apprenticeship as a bookbinder and bookseller at the end of the last century, having dropped out of formal education.

The Stiftskirche St Georg

Dominating the square is the **Stiftskirche St Georg**, an outwardly gaunt late Gothic church erected at the end of the fifteenth century, with a contrastingly stunning interior. Under the extravagant stellar vault of the nave, there's a Flamboyant pulpit adorned with reliefs of the Madonna and the Four Doctors of the church, and crowned by a tapering canopy; more fine sculptured figures can be seen around the north windows. A triple-arched rood screen sheltering a painted retable by Hans Schäufelein, a pupil of Dürer, leads to the **chancel** (April–Sept Mon–Sat 10am–noon & 2–5pm, Sun noon–5pm, Oct–March Fri 2–4pm only; DM1). Here an outstanding series of stained glass lancet windows, dating from the same period as the church's construction, cast their reflections on the pantheon of the House of Württemberg. In 1342 this family bought Tübingen, then no more than a village, from the local grandee; on the promotion of their territory to a duchy in 1495, they made the town their second residence. The thirteen tombs show the development of Swabian sculpture in the Gothic and Renaissance periods; finest is that of Countess Mechthild, made in the workshop of Hans Multscher of Ulm. Look out also for the monument to Duke Eberhard the Bearded, founder of the University. The **tower** (same times, summer only; DM1) can be ascended for a view over the red roofs of Tübingen to the Neckar and the Swabian Jura.

Elsewhere on Holzmarkt

On the far corner of the square, which doubles as part of Munzgasse, is the original home of the University, the **Alte Aula**, rebuilt in Baroque style for celebrations marking the 300th anniversary of its foundation. Also here, at no. 15, is **Cottahaus**, the former headquarters of the famous company, now based in Stuttgart, which represented the high-point of Tübingen's publishing tradition, begun soon after the foundation of the University. **Johann Friedrich Cotta**, who took over an ailing family company set up five generations previously, was one of the most astute publishers of all time; through friendship with Schiller, he came to know and publish all the leading figures of the German Enlightenment, and also set up the *Allgemeine Zeitung*, whose independence and liberal views came as a blast of fresh air in the context of the censored and despotically controlled press of the time. The **Studentenkarzer** (Students' Prison) at no. 20 in the same street is older than the one in Heidelberg and has more varied graffiti, but unfortunately isn't so accessible (guided tours Sat at 2pm; DM1).

Above the Neckar

Overlooking the banks of the Neckar on Bursagasse, the street immediately below, is the **Hölderlinturm** (Tues–Fri 10am–noon & 3–5pm, Sat & Sun 2–5pm; DM2). Originally part of the medieval fortifications, it's now named after one of Tübingen's most famous alumni, **Friedrich Hölderlin**, who lived here in the care of a carpenter's family, hopelessly but harmlessly insane, from 1807 until his death 36 years later. There's a collection of memorabilia of the poet, largely ignored in his lifetime, but now regarded as one of the greatest Germany ever produced. Hölderlin's odes show complete mastery of the rhythms used by the bards of ancient Greece; he also saw their gods as symbolic of real forces whose presence was felt in everyday life alongside those of the Christian virtues. Just before the onset of his madness, he produced his most striking work, grandiose apocalyptic visions couched in complex language and original imagery, showing the anguished state of his own existence – "A son of earth I seem, born to love and suffer."

The Bursa

Further along the street is the **Bursa**, a former student residence and philosophy lecture hall from the earliest days of the University, rebuilt at the beginning of the nineteenth century in Neoclassical style. There's a memorial to Philipp Melanchton, who lectured here for a time after his graduation at the age of seventeen. At no. 4b is the house of his uncle, the humanist and Hebrew scholar **Johannes Reuchlin**, who was the star academic of the early years of the University. His research interests embroiled him in a major controversy when the Dominicans, backed by the Emperor, tried to suppress all Jewish books on the grounds of blasphemy; a posse of distinguished scholars immediately leapt to his defence.

The Evangelisches Stift

At the end of the street is the **Evangelisches Stift**, a Protestant seminary established in a former Augustinian monastery in 1547 as the theological faculty of the University. It has maintained a high academic reputation, but the nature of the courses, encouraging the questioning of traditional theology rather than its indoctrination, has led to the ironic if logical result that its most famous graduates have followed careers outside the church: it's been nicknamed the "Trojan Horse of intellectual giants". An early example of this trend was the great astronomer Johannes Kepler, who studied here at the end of the sixteenth century. Hölderlin, who never managed to find the sense of belief to accompany his essentially religious outlook was another; he was joined by his classmates, Hegel and Schelling, subsequently the dominant figures of German philosophy. From here you can continue down Neckarhalde to **Theodor-Haering-Haus** (Tues–Sun 2.30–5.30pm; free) which contains collections on the history of the town, and on publishing and the book trade. En route, at no. 24, is the birthplace of **Christoph Uhland**, the lyric poet and chronicler of old German legends who gave up his professorship in order to enter politics, serving as the local deputy in the German National Assembly of 1848–9.

The Markt, the Schloss and around

The **Markt**, heart of old Tübingen, is just a short walk uphill from the Stift. It preserves many of its Renaissance mansions, along with a fountain dedicated to Neptune, round which markets are held on Mondays, Wednesdays and Fridays. The **Rathaus**, originally fifteenth-century but much altered down the years, is covered with historical frescos, though these are hardly more than a hundred years old; other eye-catching features are the pulpit-like balcony for public announcements and the gabled pediment housing an astronomical clock made in 1511.

Burgsteige, one of the oldest and most handsome streets in town, climbs steeply from the corner of the Markt to **Schloss Hohentübingen**, the Renaissance successor to the original eleventh-century feudal castle. Entry is via a superb **gateway** in the form of a triumphal arch, made in 1604. It's adorned with the arms of the House of Württemberg and the riband of the Order of the Garter; the latter had recently been bestowed on Duke Friedrich by Queen Elizabeth I. What comes afterwards is an anti-climax – there's a second, less ornate doorway leading to a drastically restored courtyard – but it's worth going up for the sake of the view. You can wander around the complex freely, but only by taking a **guided tour** (April–Sept Sat 5pm, Sun 11am & 3pm; DM3) can you see the prison and the cellars with a vat capable of holding 18,700 gallons.

The northwestern part of town, immediately below the Schloss, has traditionally been reserved for the non-academic community. Here are some of the city's oldest and most spectacular half-timbered buildings, such as the municipal **Kornhaus** on the alley of the same name, and the **Fruchtschranne**, the storehouse for the yields of the ducal orchards, on Bachgasse.

THE GOGEN

The northwestern quarter is especially associated with the *Gogen*, or vine-growers, who often doubled as farmers or agricultural labourers. They're renowned for their rich fund of earthy **humour**, mainly dating from the turn of the century when there was a lucrative trade in the contents of cesspools, then used as fertilizers. The pomposity of the academic world offered a ready-made target for the wit of the *Gogen*, as in the following exchange:

Gog: Do you read the *Tübinger Chronik*?

Student: Certainly not; I read the *Frankfurter Allgemeine*. The *Tübinger Chronik* is so worthless that I only use it to wipe my behind.

Gog: In that case you'd better watch out that your arse doesn't get cleverer than your head.

The northeastern quarters

The corresponding quarter northeast of the Markt is once more dominated by the University. Down Collegiumsgasse is the **Wilhelmstift**, built in the late sixteenth century as the Collegium Illustre, an academy for members of the Protestant nobility, but since 1817 the site of the Catholic seminary. This building became the focus of worldwide media attention in the early 1970s when its leading theologian, the Swiss **Hans Küng**, published a series of articles and books attacking cherished doctrines, notably papal infallibility. The upshot was that he was stripped of his sacral offices, but he has remained in Tübingen as a professor, a celebrity, an ecumenical leader – and a Catholic. (Interestingly enough, the majority of priests on the staff here cohabit and consort openly with their "housekeepers", but they run no risk of being sacked – unless they should wish to regularise their relationships in line with Biblical teaching.) Küng is one of a few cult figures on whom the University depends for such vitality as it has; another is the left-wing novelist Walter Jens, who teaches classics.

Crossing Langegasse and continuing along Metgergasse, you come to the **Nonnenhaus**, most photogenic of the half-timbered houses, with its outside stairway and *Sprachhaus*. Two other buildings of particular note just off the Holzmarkt are the **Lateinschule** at Schulberg 10, and the enormous **Pfleghof** on the street named after it. The latter, now converted into student residences, was built in the fifteenth century as the tithe barn of the Bebenhausen monastery (see below).

Just outside the northeastern boundary of the old town are the former **Botanical Gardens**. These have been replaced by another complex (Mon–Fri 7.30am–4.45pm, Sat & Sun 10–11.45am & 1.30–4.30pm), complete with arboretum and hothouses, located, along with most of the modern buildings of the University, a kilometre or so north by the ring road. The gardens serve as a reminder that botany has long been one of Tübingen's strong subjects. One of the leading lights in the academic life of the sixteenth century, Leonhard Fuchs (after whom the fuchsia is named), published an exhaustive and practical encyclopaedia on plants and their medicinal properties.

Practicalities

The **Hauptbahnhof** and **bus station** are side by side just five minutes' walk from the old town – turn right and follow Karlstrasse straight ahead. At the edge of Eberhardsbrücke is the **tourist office** (Mon–Fri 8.30am–6.30pm, Sat 8.30am–12.30/5pm according to season; ☎07071/35011); this is the only place you can change money outside the standard banking hours.

Accommodation

The **youth hostel** is on the banks of the Neckar, a short walk to the right on the far side of the bridge at Gartenstr. 22/2 (☎07071/23002). To reach the **campsite**, also with a riverside setting at Rappenberghalde (☎07071/43145), it's quicker to turn left on leaving the Hauptbahnhof, and cross at Alleenbrücke. **Hotels** aren't thick on the ground and tend to be expensive, far out or both. *Zum Ritter*, just outside the old quarter at Am Stadtgraben 25 (☎07071/22502) is the best bet, with singles at DM42 and doubles from DM65; similar rates are available at *Binder*, Nonnengsasse 4 (☎07071/52643). *Am Schloss*, Burgsteige 18 (☎07071/21077) has an ideal location and rooms beginning at DM40, though the average price is much higher. *Kürner*, Weizsäckerstr. 1 (☎07071/22735) charges from DM38 for singles and DM69 for doubles, but involves a long commute. The tourist office also has details of private rooms from DM25.

Eating

The best **restaurant** in the centre of Tübingen is *Forelle*, an olde worlde wine bar at Kronenstr. 8; the town's other citadels of gourmet food are *Museum*, Wilhelmstr. 3, and *Landgasthof Rosenau* in the new Botanical Gardens. For cheaper eating, try *Café Pfuderer* on Marktplatz which serves Swabian specialities in a tea-room atmosphere. Also on this square is *Marktschenke*, a lively student bar with jukebox. Nearby on Haaggasse are *Deutsche Weinstube*, with a good basic menu, and *Jazzkeller*, which features live music in the evenings.

Etc. . .

For highbrow **culture**, there's a choice between the traditional fare of plays and concerts at *Landestheater*, Eberhardstr. 6, and the experimental productions of the tiny *Zimmertheater*, Bursagasse 16. Tübingen also boasts a number of good **bookshops**, notably on Munzgasse and Bursagasse. **Bikes** can be hired either at the Hauptbahnhof or the campsite, with tandems available at the latter. **Rowing boats** are available at Neckarbrücke; if you want to try **punting**, ask at the tourist office or take the DM6 piloted trip which leaves from the Hölderlinturm at 4pm on Saturdays.

Bebenhausen and Naturpark Schönbuch

Immediately to the north of Tübingen are the former hunting grounds of the Dukes and Kings of Württemberg, now re-stocked with deer and designated as the **Naturpark Schönbuch**. The main road to Stuttgart cuts right through this protected landscape, but its 150 square kilometres are virtually uninhabited – a welcome break from the urban area which encircles it. Several streams lace across the gently undulating countryside, which is largely covered with a coniferous forest of spruce, pine, larch and fir; as usual, there's a network of marked hiking trails.

Bebenhausen

Within the park is the village of **BEBENHAUSEN**, just 5km north of Tübingen, of which it's now officially a part. It can be reached by bus, but it's far more fun to sample the park's scenery on foot. There's a choice of trails – you can either follow the course of the Goldersbach, parallel to the main road, or else set out from the Botanical Gardens and continue via Heuberger Tor and the path beside the Bettelbach. In 1190, a group of Cistercian monks arrived in Bebenhausen, taking over from a Premonstratensian congregation who had settled there just a decade before. The **Abtei** (Tues–Fri 9am–noon & 2–5pm, Sat & Sun 10am–noon & 2–5pm; DM2) is set in a walled enclosure with many half-timbered outbuildings matching those in the village; the superb main complex presents a cross-section of medieval European architecture. That the buildings survive in remarkably complete condition is due to the fact that they were converted into a (now defunct) Protestant seminary after the Reformation.

The church and Jagdschloss

Best place to begin your tour is with the **church**, in the Transitional style between Romanesque and Gothic characteristic of the Cistercians; it was completed in 1228, but modernised a century later with the addition of the huge, airy east window, still with the original stained glass in between the tracery. At the beginning of the fifteenth century an eccentric crown-shaped tower topped with a miniature openwork steeple was built over the crossing. Unfortunately, the nave was truncated to a third of its original size after the suppression of the monastery, so the dimensions are now more those of a chapel. A suite of rooms – the chapter house, parlatorium and lay-brothers' hall – was built along the east walk of the present cloister in a pure early Gothic style after work had finished on the church.

In the middle of the fourteenth century, the **summer refectory** was added to the southern side. Not only is this Bebenhausen's great glory, it's one of the finest Gothic buildings in Germany, a dining room like no other. Three central pillars stand like palm trees sprouting out their branches to form a vault of consummate grace and precision, which is painted with motifs of plants and birds. Later, the outer walls of the cloister were built, including a pretty **well-house**. This isn't quite symmetrical, as the mason himself realised, playfully confessing his guilt by adding a corbel of a fool holding up a mirror to show him where he had gone wrong.

Also in the monastery grounds is the **Jagdschloss** of the Kings of Württemberg (guided tours, lasting 1 hr, Tues–Fri 9am, 10am, 11am, 2pm, 3pm, 4pm, Sat & Sun 10am, 11am, 2pm, 3pm, 4pm; DM2.50). This was adapted from the monastery's former guest house and is luxuriantly furnished in nineteenth-century style, with many souvenirs of the chase. The building later did improbable service as a parliament, being the headquarters of the Land of Südwürttemberg-Hohenzollern, which was set up by the French in 1945, but merged into the more viable province of Baden-Württemberg seven years later. Be warned that the tours are heavy on detail and that there's nothing very exciting to see – it certainly makes an anti-climax to a visit to the monastery.

The Swabian Jura

The **Swabian Jura** (*Schwäbische Alb*) is the name given to the series of limestone plateaux forming the watershed between the valleys of the Rivers Rhine, Neckar and Danube. It's a harsh, craggy landscape, with poor soils and a severe climate, though its appearance has mellowed thanks to the plantation of forests. Geological faults have meant that individual mountains have become detached from the main mass; these formed ideal natural defensive fortresses for feudal overlords, and many are still crowned by castles. The Jura has few towns and even less in the way of major sights; the area is primarily of note for its **hiking** possibilities. As normal in Germany, marked trails cross the countryside, and the views on offer have a majestic sweep, even if they're often rather monotonous. It's an area rich in **flora**, with thistles, daphnes, anemones and lady's slippers being particularly prominent.

The following section describes the western and central parts of the Jura. For the southern and eastern border (which has much the grandest scenery of all), see *The Upper Danube Valley*; to the north the Jura merges imperceptibly into the Stauferland (see p.219). **Public transport** in the area is slightly complicated. The railway lines tend to run parallel to each other, involving circuitous connections, while some of the bus companies are entirely in private hands, meaning that (most unusually) rail passes are not always valid.

Reutlingen

Just 10km east of Tübingen, reached in a few minutes by Stuttgart-bound trains, **REUTLINGEN** is generally considered to be the gateway to the Swabian Jura. Unfortunately, it isn't a very auspicious beginning, since it's now almost almost entirely given over to the hi-tech engineering industries which have made this part of Germany so prosperous. In total contrast to Tübingen, which it must once have resembled, it was devastated during World War II and only a few notable monuments remain.

Prominent among these is the Gothic **Marienkirche**, whose tall spire can be seen all over the town, making the sole challenge to the skyscrapers' monopoly. The church was begun as a thanksgiving for the successful defence of Reutlingen in 1247 against the forces of the royal pretender Heinrich Raspe, an action which preserved its status as a Free Imperial City; it was completed a century later with the erection of the main **tower** (Tues–Fri 4–5.30pm, Sat 10am–1pm, Sun 8–11.30am; DM1). Inside the church are some surprisingly well-preserved frescos, fifteenth-century stained glass windows, and an octagonal font and Holy Sepulchre from around the turn of the sixteenth century. In addition, there are some pretty **fountains** – the *Marktbrunnen* and the *Kirchbrunnen* are both sixteenth century in date, and each bears a statue of an emperor - and a couple of the medieval **gateways**.

Bad Urach

Some 20km east of Reutlingen is **BAD URACH**, which nowadays primarily devotes itself to serving as a health resort and has the standard, predictable spa facilities. Nevertheless, it also has many half-timbered houses (otherwise a rarity in the Jura), with the most impressive being the sixteenth-century group on **Marktplatz**, which also boasts a Renaissance fountain with a statue of Saint Christopher.

In 1442, when the county of Württemberg was partitioned, Urach was made joint capital with Stuttgart. A new **Residenzschloss** (guided tours April–Oct Tues–Sun 10am–noon & 2–5pm; Nov–March Tues–Sun at 11am, 2pm, 3pm & 4pm; DM2.50) was therefore begun, at around the time of the birth here of Ebehard the Bearded, the man who re-united Württemberg as a duchy and founded the University of Tübingen. The most impressive rooms are the Gothic *Türnitz* on the ground floor, and the upstairs *Goldenes Saal*, originally built by Ebehard, but sumptuously transformed at the end of the Renaissance epoch. Likewise associated with Ebehard is the **Stiftskirche** opposite, erected in late Gothic style by his court architect, Peter von Koblenz; the octagonal tower was, however, only completed last century. Inside are marvellous furnishings contemporary with the architecture – two pulpits, choir stalls, Ebehard's own praying desk, a font and stained glass.

Just to the west of town is the **Uracher Wasserfall**, which is notable for its wonderful secluded setting, rather than for the volume of water it produces. Nearby are the eerie **Güterstein** stables, originally built in the sixteenth century for the local dukes; further into the hills are more waterfalls, a nature reserve and the ruins of **Burg Hohenurach**. The countryside is also particularly beautiful around the nearby tiny village of GLEMS, further to the west in the foothills of the Jura. Here the scenery is luxuriant and verdant, brimming with wild flowers and foliage.

There's a **youth hostel** at Burgstr. 45 (☎07125/8025) on the southwestern side of town, and a **campsite**, *Pfahlhof*, (☎07125/8098), along with an abundant choice of **guest houses**, of which the cheapest is *Weberbleiche*, at no. 11 on the street of the same name (☎07125/7339). The town has many elegant **cafés**, while the **beers** of the local *Olpp* brewery are among the finest made in Swabia.

Lichtenstein

LICHTENSTEIN is the designation given to a federation of villages 12km south of Reutlingen. The name is taken from the **Schloss** (guided tours April–Oct daily 9am–noon & 1–5.30pm; Nov, Feb & March Sat, Sun & holidays 9am–noon & 1–5pm; DM4), set on a high, narrow peak, and familiar through its appearance on the covers of all the tourist brochures to the region. Like many other castles in the area, it's a Romantic fantasy, erected in the 1840s as a replacement for one demolished in 1802. In the rebuilding, the architects were strongly influenced by the imaginary descriptions of its predecessor contained in the historical novel *Lichtenstein*, which was published in 1826. This was written by a remarkable author, Wilhelm Hauff, who died at the age of 25 but bequeathed a very considerable output, including many fairy stories which are still popular in Germany today. Not that everything is a fake: there's an excellent collection of arms and armour, while the chapel has Gothic stained glass windows and a beautiful fifteenth-century altarpiece of *The Death of the Virgin* by an unknown Swabian painter. It's a good thirty minutes' walk from the village to the castle, but worth doing for the fantastic views across the Jura.

A similar distance further up, and reached by marked footpath, is the **Nebelhöhle** ("Misty Cave"; March–Nov daily 8.30am–5.30pm; DM3), an impressive stalactite grotto, some 380m in length. Although its full extent was only discovered this century, it had long been used as a refuge by the Württemberg dukes. Most unusually, you're allowed to wander around at leisure, instead of being subjected to the normal guided tour. A similar formation, the **Bärenhöhle** ("Bears' Cave"; same times and price) is 3km south of Lichtenstein near the village of ERPFINGEN.

Zwiefalten

The peaceful, recuperative health resort of **ZWIEFALTEN** lies in a valley at the edge of the Swabian Jura, just a few kilometres north of the Danube. Its name, meaning "duplicate waters", refers to the two streams which converge at this point. In the late eleventh century, a daughter church of Hirsau was established here. The huge Romanesque complex survived until 1738 when, in preparation for its change in status to an Imperial Abbey, subject only to the rule of the Emperor, and in accordance with the passion for all things Baroque, it was demolished to make way for an entirely new set of buildings. This arrangement lasted for only a few decades; after the Napoleonic suppression, the church was given to the local Catholic parish and the outbuildings were converted into an asylum – a situation which persists to this day.

The Münster

The **Münster** is a worthy rival to the great pilgrimage churches of Bavaria. Its highly original design, largely the work of **Johann Michael Fischer**, is already apparent from the outside, where the identical white towers with their green onion domes are placed over the transept, leaving room for a classically inspired facade whose alternate use of concave and convex shapes imparts a feeling of movement. However, this is no more than a prelude to the lavishness of the interior, in which Fischer was aided by the best decorators of the age.

Standing by the entrance grille, your eye is drawn down the enormous length of the church, yet is also diverted to the wavy lines of the side chapels; to the grey and rose marble columns with their gold-leaf capitals which shine like jewels against the pristine white walls; to the huge vault paintings glorifying the Virgin; and to the confessionals shaped like fantastic grottoes. At the end of the nave, a statue of the fiery prophet Ezekiel, set in an elaborate baldachin with depictions of the coming fall of Babylon, strikes a warning note; this theme is continued in the **pulpit** opposite, in which his visions of sin and death on the base are contrasted with the triumph of the Cross on the sounding-board. The monks' choir is the most extravagantly sumptuous part of all, featuring a virtuoso set of walnut **stalls**, adorned with gilded limewood reliefs illustrating the life of the Virgin. Be warned that the entrance grille is generally closed between 11am and 1pm during the summer and all day through the week in winter, leaving you only with the sweeping initial view.

Practicalities... and boats

If you want to use Zwiefalten as a base for exploring the Jura, **rooms** are available in five different pensions from around DM25–35 per head, or in private houses for a little less. *Gasthof Post*, Hauptstr. 44 (☎07373/302), has the largest capacity, as well as the best restaurant. The obvious place to sample the excellent varieties of **beer** made in the *Klosterbräu* is in its own *Gaststätte* next door.

Following the Ach, one of Zwiefalten's rivers, for a couple of kilometres northwards, brings you to the **Friedrichshöhle** (or **Wimsener Höhle**), where it disappears underground. This is the only subterranean river in Germany which is readily accessible to the public; it's possible to penetrate a short way along the crystal-clear waters into the cave by **boat** (April–Oct daily 9am–6pm; DM3) before the passage becomes too narrow.

Hechingen

The market town of **HECHINGEN** lies on and around a hill some 25km southwest of Reutlingen, with regular rail connections from both there and Tübingen. In the lower part of town, close to the Bahnhof, a pilgrims' route, complete with wayside shrines, leads to the **Franziskanerkirche St Luzen**. This late sixteenth-century church is advanced for its time (by German standards), showing the late Renaissance feeling its way towards Baroque. Rather plain-looking from outside, it's lusciously ornate within, containing richly decorated half-columns and pilasters, an elaborate vault with large polychrome keystones, and shell-shaped niches with statues of the Apostles.

The upper town, which preserves a number of quaint, twisting streets, is entered via the bulky **Unterer Turm**. Built at the same time as St Luzen, this is now the only surviving part of the fortifications. Crowning the highest point of the hill is the **Stiftskirche**, erected in the grandly sombre Neoclassical Louis XVI style by the French architect Michel d'Inxard. Look out for the grave slab of Count Eitelfriedrich von Zollern, made by the doyen of bronze-casters, Peter Vischer of Nürnberg. In the nearby Goldschmiedstrasse, which plunges back down the hill, is the Baroque **Synagoge**, recently immaculately restored to serve as a cultural centre.

There's no hostel or campsite in the vicinity, but **hotel** prices are invariably reasonable: try *Rapphof*, Niederhechinger Str. 57 (☎07471/2779), which charges DM20–25 per person, or *Haus Pleli*, Alte Rottenburger Str. 2 (☎077471/3776), with singles DM25, doubles DM38. Best **restaurants** are *Schwanen* on Bahnhofstrasse and *Klaiber* on Obertorplatz.

Burg Hohenzollern

Rearing high above Hechingen, some 4km south of town on the most prominent of all the isolated rocks of the Swabian Jura, is **Burg Hohenzollern** (daily April–Oct 9am–5.30pm, Nov–March 9am–4.30pm; DM4), the ancestral seat of what became the most powerful family in Germany. From afar, the fortress, girded with intact battlements and bristling with a varied assortment of soaring towers, looks like the perfect incarnation of a vast medieval castle. Close up, however, it's soon apparent that the present complex is almost entirely a Romantic dreamland – not inappropriately so, given the fantastical nature of the family saga (see box). It was commissioned by the most heritage-conscious of the clan, King Friedrich Wilhelm IV, and built by the military architect August Stüler, a pupil of the great Schinkel. Only the fifteenth-century **St-Michael-Kapelle** survives from the previous fortress; it has been retained for the use of the Roman Catholic branch of the family and preserves beautiful Gothic stained glass windows, along with Romanesque reliefs from its own predecessor.

THE HOHENZOLLERN DYNASTY

Even in a country whose entire history is dominated by the rise and fall of powerful dynasties, there's nothing quite comparable to the story of the **Hohenzollerns**. Their path to national leadership seems like a carefully hatched master-strategy which took centuries to achieve, yet which had a certain remorseless inevitability about it. The barren, windswept territories they ruled in their capacity as Counts of Zollern from the thirteenth century hardly seemed an auspicious beginning, while their first attempt at aggrandisement, in their capacity as Burgraves of Nürnberg – then the effective capital of the Holy Roman Empire – was soundly defeated by that city's independently minded council.

Frustrated in their quest for power at the heart of the empire, the Hohenzollerns turned to its periphery. In 1415, they were put in charge of the March of Brandenburg and were thus responsible for securing the country's eastern frontier; they also gained one of the seven seats on the imperial electoral college. The big breakthrough came in 1525, when Albrecht von Hohenzollern, Grand Master of the Teutonic Knights, converted to Protestantism and secularised the order's holdings as the secular Duchy of Prussia, which paid nominal homage to the Polish crown; this gave the family a power-base beyond the jurisdiction of the Emperor. By 1701, the Hohenzollerns had wrested Prussia from dependency on Poland; they conferred royal status on themselves and merged their territories. In time, they built up a centralised military state which, by skilful warfare and diplomacy, became one of the great powers of Europe. The nineteenth century saw the completion of the jigsaw – as the Habsburgs increasingly turned their attentions towards the Balkans, the Hohenzollerns ousted them from German leadership, eventually excluding them altogether from the unified nation they created by 1871. As if by a bitter irony, the family's reign was brief – Germany's defeat in World War I led to the collapse of the old aristocratic order and the abolition of the monarchy.

Between 1952 and 1991, the neo-Gothic **Schlosskapelle** contained the tombs of Friedrich Wilhelm I, the "Soldier King", and his son of the same name, Frederick the Great, but these were returned for internment to Potsdam in a theatrical and highly publicised ceremony which was criticised by many as an untimely sop to the nation's militaristic past, but which was defended, notably by Chancellor Kohl, as a necessary cathartric process (see p.774). The **Schatzkammer** contains valuable heirlooms, notably the crown of Prussia, reconstructed in 1889 after the original was destroyed. There's also the snuffbox that saved the life of Frederick the Great at the Battle of Kunersdorf by absorbing a bullet, which is still embedded in it.

Haigerloch

Unchallenged star of the western part of the Swabian Jura is **HAIGERLOCH**. Buses run from Hechingen, which is 17km east, and from Tübingen via Rottenburg, but the railway line is now used only for occasional steam train jaunts in the summer months. One of the most outstanding small towns in Germany, Haigerloch's isolation means it's considerably less self-conscious than most of its rivals. Here there's a perfect blend of landscape and architecture, with the unorthodox setting, on rocks high above an S-bend on the River Eyach, playing a crucial role. The surrounding countryside is at its most luxuriant in May, when the **lilac** is in full, riotous bloom, but the autumnal tints are almost equally beguiling and it's hard to be disappointed by the picture at whatever time of year you choose to come.

About town

The northern side of the river is dominated by the **Schloss**, a photogenic jumble of mostly Renaissance buildings which replaced a medieval fortress. Until a few years ago, it was in the possession of the Hohenzollern family, who were probably based in Haigerloch in the eleventh century – before they moved to what is considered their ancestral home. Nowadays, the Schloss serves as a hotel and arts centre, so there's nothing to see inside. You can, however, enter the **Schlosskirche** lower down the hill, which has an outwardly Gothic appearance, in spite of being built at the turn of the seventeenth century. The interior was given the full Rococo treatment 150 years later, with the addition of elaborate altars, frescos and stuccowork. It's also worth walking eastwards through the woods from the Schloss courtyard; after a few minutes, you come to the **Kapf**, a belvedere with a large cross which commands a superb view over both parts of Haigerloch.

Underneath the Schloss' rock is the **Atomkeller-Museum** (May–Sept daily 10am–noon & 2–5pm; March, April, Oct & Nov same times Sat & Sun only; DM1). Here, in March and April 1945, a distinguished group of German scientists carried out a series of experiments in nuclear fission. Throughout the war, the Allies had trembled at the prospect that Germany would be first to develop atomic weapons; thankfully, Hitler never took the project very seriously, while Himmler, who was nominally in charge of the scientists, constantly diverted the researchers into absurd pet projects of his own. When the Americans captured Haigerloch on 23 April, they made a point of rounding up the scientists; the reactor was dismantled and shipped to the USA in order to help with the successful testing of the atomic bomb just three months later.

Ironically, the American victory in this particular race owed a lot to Albert Einstein, who, as a Jew, had been forced to leave Germany in 1933. Haigerloch itself had been something of a Jewish stronghold until 1941. The **ghetto** can be seen at the western edge of the upper town; the synagogue and the rabbi's house still survive, though neither is used for its original purpose. There's also a Jewish cemetery, which (most unusually) is located well inside the municipal boundaries.

Further up is the pilgrimage church of **St Anna**, erected in the 1750s as an integrated ensemble with the monumental garden enclosure and the facing curate's house. The interior of the church has a sense of spaciousness out of all proportion to its small size. It's filled with examples of Rococo workmanship of the highest class – extravagant stucco work, vivacious sculptures, a ceiling fresco showing the dedication of the church and a silvery-toned organ. This miniature masterpiece has traditionally been assumed to be the work of Johann Michael Fischer, but is now thought to have been built by Tiberius Moosbrugger, a member of an inventive family of Swiss architects who worked extensively throughout Central Europe.

Outside the church is a belvedere offering the directly opposite panorama to that from the Kapf. Another fine view can be had from the **Römerturm** (April–Oct Sat & Sun 9am–6pm, variably on other days; DM1) which dominates the centre of town. In spite of its name, it's of Romanesque, not Roman origin, and formed part of the citadel of the Counts of Zollern. The nineteenth-century Protestant **Pfarrkirche** contains a meticulously made copy of Leonardo da Vinci's *Last Supper*. If you see a busload of excited Italian tourists in town, the reason is that they've come specially to see this painting, which is, needless to say, in far better condition than the original.

Practicalities

The **tourist office** (Mon–Wed & Fri 8am–noon, Thurs 8am–noon & 4–6pm; ☎07474/69727) is in the Rathaus at Oberstadtstr. 11. Haigerloch, like so many places in the Jura, has no hostel or campsite. There are, however, a couple of cheap **pensions** – *Nägele*, Hohenbergstr. 34 (☎07474/6162), charges DM25 for singles, DM44 for doubles, while *Krone*, Oberstadtstr. 47 (☎07474/411), has singles at DM32, doubles at DM60; the latter also has an excellent restaurant. The chimney of the *Schlossbräu* brewery on the banks of the Eyach is the only sign of industry for miles around. A surprisingly adventurous range of **beers** is made there – Pils, three varieties of Weizen, shandy, and *Spezial*. Best place to sample these is their own *Gastätte Schlössle* on Hechinger Strasse, which also does good meals at reasonable prices.

Rottweil

When the Romans came on a road-building mission to southwestern Germany around 73 AD, they brought with them dogs to drive the livestock and defend the camp; in time, these were successfully bred with local species. The resultant cross-breed has survived down the centuries, named after **ROTTWEIL**, the town which developed from the Roman settlement of *Arae Flaviae*, which stood at the intersection of the two main highways linking Strasbourg with Augsburg, and the Aargau region of Switzerland with the Middle Neckar. A familiar sight all over the world, the **Rottweiler**, with its characteristic mixture of black and tan markings, stocky frame and stubby tail, has built up a reputation as hard-working and (overly) loyal. Local butchers trained the Rottweiler to pull their carts – hence its alternative name of *Metzgerhund* ("butcher's dog") – but it's now used by the German police, army, customs and mountain rescue services, and as a guide for the blind.

In spite of the fact that the dog has put Rottweil's name into many foreign languages, this unhurried provincial market town is itself relatively little-known. Lying between the Black Forest and the Swabian Jura, it's way off the beaten tourist track, with nothing of interest nearby and no overwhelming set-piece of its own to draw the crowds. Yet, in further contrast with the Rottweiler (which, for all its intelligence, is rather an ugly brute), the town is a visual marvel. Its isolation spared it from the horrors of modern warfare, and it has changed very little since the seventeenth century. Add to this highly original townscape a dramatic **setting** (Rottweil is ready made for photography), a history as remarkable as that of any epic, one of the most impressive arrays of sculpture in Germany and a rich tradition of festivals, and you have what deserves to be considered one of the most enticing small towns in the country.

The Hochbrücke and Hochbrücktorstrasse

Rottweil is built on a strategically secure spur high above the still young River Neckar; this restricted area meant the buildings had to be packed tightly together, with no room for expansion. It's approached via the **Hochbrücke**, which spans a deep gully. The site of Arae Flaviae lies just over 1km to the left down Königstrasse; extensive **Roman baths** have been excavated at the corner of what is now the cemetery.

The Hochbrücktorstrasse
Immediately over the bridge, and named after the tower which once guarded it, is **Hochbrücktorstrasse**, the town's north–south axis. Here you immediately see the grouping of brilliantly colourful **old houses** characteristic of Rottweil. These are mostly late Renaissance or Baroque in style, and are adorned with three-sided oriel windows, sometimes reaching up several storeys. Each balcony tries to outdo its neighbour in the profusion of carvings. These often illustrate the coat of arms of the original family or the emblem of the guild to which they belonged; others bear the Imperial Eagle, proud symbol of a Free Imperial City (a status this little town held for nearly six centuries). At the end of Hochbrücktorstrasse is the slender red sandstone **Marktbrunnen**, the most elaborate of the town's four Renaissance fountains. Built in tiers like a wedding cake, it's decorated with delicate statuettes made after woodcuts by Hans Burgkmair, and is crowned by a figure of a Swiss soldier, in commemoration of the "perpetual bond" between Rottweil and the Confederation of Switzerland.

The Kapellenkirche
Standing in a cramped square just behind is the **Kapellenkirche**, Gothic successor to an old pilgrimage chapel. It was begun in the early fourteenth century as a miniature version of the Münster in Freiburg, but money ran out with only the square lower part of the tower completed. This is built in a manner reminiscent of the English Decorated style and was perhaps designed by one of the Parler family. Some 150 years later, the Duke of Württemberg's architect, Aberlin Jerg, added a double octagonal storey to the tower, which is a surprisingly effective foil to the older section, providing Rottweil with the dominant central monument it needed. The church's outstanding **sculptural decoration** is by several identifiable masters, with the mystical and gentle style of the so-called "Marienmeister" perfectly contrasting with the lively narrative approach of his successor, the "Christusmeister". These works have been replaced *in situ* by copies; the originals are now in the Lorenzkapelle (see below).

Hauptstrasse

From the northern side of the church, you pass into the resplendent main street, **Hauptstrasse**, which runs uphill by constantly changing gradients. It's lined by an even more impressive group of houses than those on the perpendicular Hochbrücktorstrasse. The oldest of these, no. 62, dates back to the thirteenth century, while the next two buildings, including the historic inn *Gasthaus Zum Stern*, are in late Gothic style. To see the backs of these houses, whose half-timbering is uncharacteristic of Rottweil, go down to the massive viaduct, a notable piece of nineteenth-century engineering which carries the road out of town high over the valley. From here, there's also a sweeping view over the Swabian Jura.

The Stadtmuseum and around

Among the houses in the upper half of Hauptstrasse is the home at no. 20 of the family of Bartholomäus Herder, founder of a publishing house whose interests include Europe's largest output of Catholic books. It now serves as the unusually absorbing **Stadtmuseum** (Mon–Thurs & Sat 9am–noon & 2–5pm, Fri 9am–noon, Sun 10am–noon; free). On the ground floor are the most important excavations from Arae Flaviae, dominated by the second century **Orpheus mosaic**. Made of some 570,000 coloured stones, this shows the god playing his lyre to the enchantment of the birds and beasts around him – among them a dog, who is doubtless an early Rottweiler. Upstairs, the extraordinary **Pürschgerichtskarte** of 1564 – a tour de force of detail – proves how little Rottweil's overall appearance has altered. An adjoining room is devoted to the town's **Fastnet** celebrations (see below), with wooden masks of the principal characters and a painstakingly executed cardboard cut-out of the *Narrensprung* – which makes an acceptable substitute if you don't manage to see the real thing.

Directly across the street, the **Apostelbrunnen**, with its figures of Saints Peter, James and John, has been re-erected in front of the **Altes Rathaus**, whose simple Gothic architecture gives the street a rare touch of sobriety. Entered from Rathausgasse is the **tourist office** (Mon–Fri 9.30am–12.30pm & 2–6pm, May–Sept Sat 9.30am–12.30pm; ☎0741/494280). Ask here to see the *Ratsaal*, the former council chamber of the city-state, which boasts a coffered ceiling, carved woodwork and stained glass windows.

The top of Hauptstrasse is closed by the formidable **Schwarzes Tor** (Black Tower). Its lower section, with its rough masonry, dates back to 1230; the upper storeys were added around 1600 as a prison. Continuing uphill, you come to the **Hochturm** via the alley of the same name. This also belongs to the Staufian period and is a watchtower guarding Rottweil's vulnerable western flank, the only one to lack a natural defensive barrier. In the late eighteenth century, an octagon was added to the top to serve as a look-out gallery; it commands a superb view of the town and surrounding countryside. A plaque on the door tells you which family currently holds the key; otherwise, ask for it at the tourist office.

North of Hauptstrasse

Rathausgasse leads from the Rathaus to Münsterplatz, with the **Heilig-Kreuz-Münster**, a late Gothic basilica with a tall tower. Its most important work of art is an anguished *Crucifixion* at the high altar which is attributed to Veit Stoss. Proceeding down Bruderschaftsgasse at the eastern side of the Münster, you pass the **Dominikanerkirche**, a Gothic church with a sumptuous Baroque interior, and the last of the Renaissance fountains, the **Christophorusbrunnen**, with a relief of the city's coat-of-arms as well as a statue of Saint Christopher carrying the Christ child.

The Lorenzkapelle

At the end of Lorenzgasse is the **Lorenzkapelle** (Tues–Sat 10am–noon & 2–5pm, Sun 2–5pm; DM1), a late Gothic funerary chapel which for over a century has housed a remarkable collection of Swabian **wood sculpture**. Among the early works, generally in a folk-art idiom, a refined early fourteenth-century series of Apostles stands out. By the fifteenth century, sculptors had gained a more prestigious position in society and showed a more definite artistic personality, as can be seen here in the work of the masters of Ulm, such as Hans Multscher, Michel Erhart, and Jörg Syrlin the Younger. Due to lack of space, it has only been possible to have a fraction of the collection on view, though that will change shortly with the opening of a new museum beside the Dominikanerkirche.

When this is ready, it's planned to give over the chapel to **stone sculpture**, which is now displayed in the modern annexe. Pride of place here is given to the original carvings from the Kapellenkirche. Look out for the two reliefs by the "Marienmeister", which rank among the most original and touching works of the Middle Ages: *The Opening of the Book* symbolises Knowledge, while the tender *Betrothal of the Knight* is an allegory of the marriage of Jesus to the Christian soul. From the same church is the *Weckenmännle*, a humorous figure who probably served as the basis of the pulpit: it's thought to be a self-portrait of Anton Pilgram, who later became master mason at the Dom in Vienna. Outside the Lorenzkapelle is the **Pulverturm** (Powder Tower), one of the remaining vestiges of the fortifications.

Practicalities

Rottweil lies on the main railway line between Stuttgart and Tuttlingen, with onward connections to Switzerland; even international trains stop here. It can also be reached from various points in the Black Forest via the junction of HORB, 35km north. Arriving at the **Bahnhof**, turn right and walk uphill as far as the Hochbrücke.

Accommodation and food
The **youth hostel** has an ideal location in the centre of town at Lorenzgasse 8 (☎0741/7664), but there's no campsite. Three cheap pensions lie on Hauptstrasse, all charging around DM30 per head. *Hasen* at no. 69 (☎0741/7798), at the foot of the street by the viaduct, has a friendly management who offer good-value meals in the style of their countries of origin – Mexico and Greece. Across the road at no. 66 is *Löwen* (☎0741/7640), while further up at no. 38 (☎0741/7412) is *Goldenes Rad*. Prices at the aforementioned *Gasthaus Zum Sternen* are way above the odds, but it's possible to enjoy the superb cuisine in its *Weinstube* without making too outrageous a dent in the budge; *Lamm* at no. 45 is another historic inn with a high reputation for food. There's also a wide choice of genteel cafés around the town centre.

Festivals
All **festivals** stand in the shadow of Fastnet (see below), but other folklore events include the week-long *Volksfest* in mid-August and the *Stadtfest* on the second weekend in September. On a more highbrow note, there's a series of **concerts** of Renaissance and Baroque music in late April/early May, and of chamber recitals later in the month, while for a fortnight in October a mixed programme of drama, cinema, exhibitions, jazz and classical music takes place.

THE ROTTWEIL FASTNET

Rottweil is at its most animated during the Carnival season, and its **Fastnet celebrations** – which are fifteenth-century in origin and very different from those in the Rhineland – are arguably Baden-Württemberg's top popular festival. The action begins on the evening of the Thursday before Carnival Sunday (variable date Feb/March) with the *Schmotzige*, in which groups perform satirical revues of the previous year's events. On the Sunday, the mayor hands over control of the town for the duration of the festival, and the afternoon features a children's procession. The highpoint comes at 8am sharp the following morning with the *Narrensprung* (Parade of Fools), which is repeated on Shrove Tuesday at both 8am and 2pm. This features a cast of colourfully dressed characters in wooden masks. Their names are untranslatable; among them are the friendly *Gschell*, who represents the promise of summer, the fiery *Biss* and the vampire-like *Federahannes*, who both appear to symbolise the winter months, and *Fransenkleid*, a haughty aristocratic woman.

The Upper Danube valley

For much of its course through Germany, the **Danube** gives little hint of the great river it is to become. Most of the famous landscapes with which it's associated lie in the Balkans, yet there's a short stretch early in its course which is fully equal to anything downstream. Known as the **Bergland Junge Donau** (Mountain country of the young Danube), this begins just beyond Donaueschingen and continues as far as Sigmaringen. The **railway** line to Ulm, the *Donautalbahn*, closely follows the mazy path of the river and ranks as one of the finest scenic routes in the country. There are services every couple of hours or so; the only snag is that there are relatively few stops.

The river valley forms the centrepiece of the **Naturpark Obere Donau**, which stretches northwards to the Heuberg, the highest range of the Swabian Jura; about half the area is forest, though a large amount is used for farming. It's superb country for **hiking**, particularly above the valley, where there are any number of belvederes offering wonderful views of the river's meandering course. If you've an interest in **flora**, note that springtime sees the countryside awash with snowdrops, narcissi and daphnes, while orchids and the tall Turk's Cap Lily blossom at the end of the season. Autumn is if anything even more beautiful; then the white limestone rocks of the valley are perfectly offset by the golden tones of the trees and shrubs lower down. Plenty of inexpensive accommodation makes the region ideal for a break away from the crowds.

Beuron

BEURON lies right in the heart of the *Junge Donau* at the point where the scenery is at its most dramatic, about quarter of an hour beyond TUTTLINGEN, where there's a junction with the railway between Stuttgart and Switzerland. It's immediately obvious that religion has loomed large in this place – one of the tall, seemingly impenetrable rocks on the opposite bank of the Danube is crowned by a large cross.

The village itself, laid out on a terrace above the river, clusters round the enormous **Kloster**. Completely rebuilt in the Baroque period, its size belies the fact that very few monks (sometimes no more than fifteen) ever actually lived there. Architecturally, the late seventeenth-century monastic buildings are superior to the church, which dates from forty years later. By south German standards, it's fairly restrained, though the nave vaults are decorated with colourful frescos; the legend of the monastery's foundation is sandwiched between scenes from the lives of its patrons saints, Martin and Augustine. Sixty years after the Napoleonic suppression, the Kloster was taken over by a Benedictine congregation who played a leading role in the revitalisation of European monastic life, an ideal that by then seemed to be a thing of the past. They pioneered a new, simple style of architecture based on early Christian and Romanesque models; an example of it is the Frauenkapelle which they added to the north side of their own church to house a fifteenth-century Swabian sculpture of the *Pietà* which is alleged to possess miraculous powers. Even more significant was the revival of the use of **Gregorian chant**, and the monks remain among the world's leading practitioners of the art. Try to catch one of the main services (High Mass Mon–Sat 11.15am, Sun 10am; Vespers Mon–Sat 6pm, Sun 3pm) to hear the stark, ethereal beauty of this, the most elemental of all forms of music.

Hikes and practicalities

Among the many superb **hikes** which can be made around Beuron, two stand out. Back in the direction of Tuttlingen (but reached via the Holzbrücke, at the opposite side of town from the Bahnhof), you come after 6km to **Knopfmacherfelsen**, reckoned to be the finest of all the belvederes overlooking this stretch of the Danube. To the east, a similar distance away, is **Burg Wildenstein**, a feudal castle-stronghold dating back to the eleventh century in a stunningly precarious situation overlooking the Danube; part of it now houses a **youth hostel** (☎07466/411).

Information on these walks, and on the *Naturpark* as a whole, is available during normal working hours from the **tourist office** in Beuron's Rathaus. Here you can also obtain a list of private houses with **rooms** to let from as little as DM20. Otherwise, the cheapest place to stay is the pilgrims' *St-Gregorius-Haus* (☎07466/202) opposite the Kloster, which charges DM33 for singles, DM64 doubles; *Pension Wasch* beside the Bahnhof (☎07466/423) is only marginally more expensive. The **campsite** (☎07579/559) is in HAUSEN IM TAL, the next village to the north.

Sigmaringen

Just beyond Hausen is the last stretch of high cliffs; between THIERGARTEN and GUTENSTEIN, these are replaced by jagged rock needles. Thereafter the landscape is tamer, though there are exceptions, notably at **SIGMARINGEN**, the train's next stop. This pint-sized princely capital came into the hands of the **Hohenzollern** dynasty in 1535, having at one time belonged to their rivals, the Habsburgs. The branch of the family who lived here remained Catholic and supplied the last ill-fated Kings of Romania. They were very much junior relations of their Berlin cousins, but provided a useful south German foothold for the Prussians during their predatory takeover of the country last century.

There's no doubting the photogenic quality of the **Schloss** (Feb–Nov daily 8.30am–noon & 1–5pm; DM5). However, it's essentially a product of the final phase of the Romantic movement, a sort of Swabian counterpart to "Mad" Ludwig's castles in Bavaria, which moves abruptly from one pastiche style to another. Only the towers remain from the medieval fortress, which was sacked in the Thirty Years' War, then ravaged by fire in 1893. The *Waffenhalle*, with over 3000 pieces of arms and armour, is reckoned the best private collection in Europe; it's also a reminder of just how much the Hohenzollerns' rise to national leadership owed to their espousal of the military solution to problems. A dream-like neo-Gothic hall contains a good collection of south German paintings and sculptures of the fifteenth and sixteenth centuries, including works by the so-called **Master of Sigmaringen**, who was actually two people: the brothers Hans and Jacob Strüb. The entry ticket also covers admission to the **Kutschenmuseum**, a collection of historic coaches housed in the former stables.

Beside the Schloss is the Rococo **Johanniskirche**, containing the shrine of Saint Fidelio, a local man who became the first Capuchin martyr when he was murdered in 1622 by the fiercely Calvinist inhabitants of the Grisons region of Switzerland. In the town itself, there's nothing much to see, other than the usual array of half-timbered houses, mostly dating from the Baroque period.

If you want to use Sigmaringen as a base, there's a **youth hostel** at Hohenzollernstr. 31 (☎07571/13277) at the northeastern side of town, a **campsite** (☎07571/5479) by the Danube, and a few hotels, the cheapest of which are in outlying villages. The **tourist office** (Mon–Fri 9am–12.30pm & 2–5.30pm, Sat 9am–noon; ☎07571/106233) is at Schwabstr. 1, between the Bahnhof and the Schloss. Main **festivals** are *Fastnet* and the *Donaufest*; the latter is held at the end of July and features a small-scale version of the fishermen's jousts made famous in Ulm. The local *Zoller* beer is widely available.

Blaubeuren

Between the next two train stops, MENGEN and RIEDLINGEN, there's an extensive stretch of marshland on the right bank of the Danube, frequented by many species of waterfowl. After EHINGEN, the *Donautalbahn* leaves the Danube and loops towards Ulm via **BLAUBEUREN**, which lies in a wonderful amphitheatre-like setting at the edge of the Swabian Jura. With its mix of natural and artistic attractions, this ranks as one of the most enticing places in the region and a good choice as a **hiking** base. The rocky hills above not only afford superb views over the red roofs of the spaciously laid-out little town and the wilder landscape beyond; they also offer constant surprises, such as labyrinths, caves, grottoes and ruined castles.

About town

At the opposite end of town from the Bahnhof is the **Blautopf**, a shady pool formed during the glacial period; it's the source of the River Blau, the Danube tributary from which the town derives its name. In spite of its small size, the Blautopf is all of 20 metres deep, while its waters have a constant temperature of 9°C. The best time to see it is on a sunny, showery day. In bright weather, the pool is a deep emerald blue, but the rain turns this successively to a lighter shade, then green, then a yellowish brown. Alongside is the **Hammerschmiede** (daily 9am–6pm; DM2), a remarkable piece of industrial archaeology. Built in the mid-eighteenth century as a water-mill, it was converted into a smithy at the beginning of the following century, before doing service as a mechanical workshop up to 1956, when it was finally retired – though the clanking machinery is still in full working order.

To the side of the Blautopf is the extensive complex of the former **Kloster**. Just 25 years after it had been completely rebuilt in late Gothic style, Württemberg went over to the Reformation; the monastery was disbanded and the buildings were put to use as a Protestant school. As in Maulbronn, with whose seminary Blaubeuren is now united, there's a remarkably complete picture of a monastic community, with a series of picturesque half-timbered workshops lining the courtyard. You can wander around here, and also in the cloister with its abutting lavabo and chapter house with tombs of the patrons.

The **church** (Palm Sunday–1 Nov daily 9am–6pm, rest of year Mon–Fri 2–4pm, Sat & Sun 10am–noon & 2–5pm; DM1.50) ingeniously preserves the tower of its Romanesque predecessor as a barrier separating the monks' choir from the nave. Only the former is kept open: it bristles with flamboyant works of art, among which the **high altar** – one of the finest in the country, and the only one of its kind to have escaped the iconoclasts – stands out. It's a co-operative work by at least two major Ulm studios – that of the sculptor **Michel Erhart** and his son **Gregor**, and of the painter **Bartholomäus Zeitblom**, who was assisted by **Bernhard Strigel** and at least one other pupil. When closed, it illustrates the Passion; the first opening shows scenes from the life of Saint John the Evangelist, patron of the Kloster. The carved heart of the retable has figures of the Virgin and Saints flanked by reliefs of *The Adoration of the Shepherds* and *The Adoration of the Magi*. Originally, this part was only shown on the major feast days of the church calendar. Nowadays, it can be seen any time a tour group is passing through, which means frequently during the summer months, though the only guaranteed times are Sundays at 2.30pm and 3.30pm.

Also within the monastery walls is another survivor which is unique of its kind, the **Badhaus**, which was added to the amenities in 1510. It now houses the local museum (daily 10am–5pm; DM1.50), but the main interest is in the building itself – on the ground floor, you can see the baths and heating system, while upstairs is a room decorated with hunting frescos. The archaeological part of the collection is housed in the **Spital** (April–Oct Tues–Sun 10am–5pm, closed Mon; DM1), the most imposing of the half-timbered houses in the town centre.

Practicalities

There's a **youth hostel** at Auf dem Rucken 69 (☎07344/6444) on a hill at the eastern side of town, between the Bahnhof and the Blautopf. Alternatively, there are two **hotels** on Marktstrasse; all except the more expensive *Zum Ochsen*, which has the best restaurant in town, have a going rate of around DM35 per head. **Tourist information** is available at the Rathaus during office hours.

Ulm

When Hermann Hesse returned to **ULM** – "this extraordinarily beautiful and unusual city" – several decades after his only previous visit, he wrote: "I had not forgotten the city walls or the Metzgerturm, nor the Münster's choir and the Rathaus; all these images encountered those in my memory, and hardly differed from them; however, there were countless new images, that I saw as if for the first time: ancient fishermen's homes tilted at an angle in the water, tiny houses on the city ramparts, stately burghers' residences in the alleys, an unusual gable here, a majestic doorway there."

This description shows how much more there is to Ulm than the two reasons its name is so familiar to school swots and TV quiz contestants – for having the highest church spire in the world, and for being the birthplace of one of the all-time giants of science, **Albert Einstein**. Regrettably, some tolerance is now necessary for enjoyment of Ulm; a single air raid at the end of 1944 caused one of the worst devastations suffered by any German city, wiping out the vast majority of the historic centre. Much of this had to be rebuilt quickly in a functional modern style. Try not to let this put you off; many of the finest streets escaped lightly and are still the subject of painstaking restoration projects. Moreover, only superficial damage was inflicted on Ulm's magnificent centrepiece, one of the greatest buildings in Germany.

The Münster

From miles away, the massive west tower of the **Münster** acts as a beacon to the city. Even seeing it for the first time from the unprepossessing surroundings of the bland shopping precinct which leads to town from the Hauptbahnhof, you can hardly fail to be impressed – the openwork **steeple** soars so high above everything else it seems to be a real-life fulfilment of those old master paintings which depict an imaginary Tower of Babel shooting through the clouds. In fact, the spire and upper storey of the tower were for centuries no more than a seemingly impossible dream and were only finished in 1890, faithfully following drawings made four hundred years before.

Some history

Work on the Münster began in the last quarter of the fourteenth century under the direction of the most famous master mason of the day, **Heinrich Parler**, and was continued by his descendants. Credit for its ultimate appearance, however, must go to the head of the succeeding dynasty, **Ulrich von Ensingen**, who altered the plans to make the church wider and loftier, and designed the lower part of the great tower. Despite the Münster's huge size, it was built as, and remains, no more than a parish church. For all that it stands as an act of humility before God, this church was also an expression of a vain civic pride: its capacity of 20,000 was more than twice the population of the city at the time, then one of the largest in Germany. At the end of the fifteenth century, when the structure was substantially complete, the architect **Matthäus Böblinger** made a drawing (which can be seen in the Ulmer Museum) for the completion of the tower, reaching to a height that had never previously been attempted. When he tried to build it, however, cracks appeared in the masonry and he fled in disgrace. As his successor's main problem was to repair the existing building, no more work was done on the tower, and the project was abandoned altogether when the city formally adopted the Reformation in 1530. It was only when the Romantic movement reawakened interest in the Middle Ages that steps were taken to finish it.

The exterior

Apart from offering the satisfaction of seeing the Münster completed exactly according to the wishes of those who planned and funded it, the tower now offers the bonus of the stupendous **view** that can be had by ascending to the platform (daily June–Aug 8am–6.45pm; times reduce seasonally to 9am–3.45pm; DM2). Most unusually, you're allowed to go the top of the spire, which is only eighteen metres short of the 161 metres-high summit. A fair amount of puff is needed to climb the 768 steps, but you're rewarded with a panorama which stretches over the city and the Danube to the Swabian Jura and Black Forest, with the Swiss Alps visible on a clear day. On the final stage, there's also the rare opportunity to see the filigree architecture of an openwork spire at close quarters.

In accordance with Ulm's great sculptural tradition, there are no fewer than five superb **portals** to the Münster; that under the tower is appropriately the grandest. Above the doorway are depictions of the *Book of Genesis*, while the pillars have masterly statues of saints in the "Soft Style" of **Master Hartmann**, the first Ulm sculptor known by name. The ensemble is completed by a poignant *Man of Sorrows* (now replaced by a copy; the original can be seen inside), an early work by **Hans Multscher**, the founding father of the remarkable group of late Gothic and early Renaissance German sculptors.

The interior

The sense of massive space in the **interior** is as overwhelming as the tower's great height; the impression is aided by the simplicity of the design, which comprises a wide nave of five aisles culminating in a single chancel, with no intervening transept. Best time to come here is on a bright morning, when the sun's rays filter through the stained glass windows on to what might legitimately claim to be the greatest set of **choir stalls** ever made: "a bold oaken outburst of three dimensional humanism" was how Patrick Leigh Fermor described them. Made between 1469 and 1474 under the direction of two local men, **Jörg Syrlin the Elder** and **Michel Erhart**, the sheer profusion and originality of their carvings – particularly the vibrant life-sized busts – immediately grab your attention. They're a hymn of praise to the achievements of the antique as well as to the Christian world, with women, for once, given the same recognition as men.

Ulm's obsession with the steeple motif can be seen in the huge canopy covering the **font**, and in the sounding board added to the **pulpit** which includes, high up above the column capitals, a second pulpit inaccessible to a human preacher – a symbol that the sermon was really delivered by the Holy Ghost. It's seen even more spectacularly in the slender, tapering **tabernacle**, a structure of gossamer delicacy for all its towering height. In spite of its figurines of popes and bishops, this somehow survived the iconoclasm which denuded the Münster following the introduction of the Reformation. Over the triumphal arch leading to the chancel is a colossal crowded **fresco** of *The Last Judgment*, placed in such a position in order that every member of the congregation could see it. As an antidote to the massiveness that is the dominant characteristic of the Münster, there's the **Besserer-Kapelle** to the right of the chancel, a private family chapel retaining its beautifully drawn and coloured fifteenth-century stained glass windows.

The rest of the city

Even if the rest of the city is dwarfed in every way by the Münster, there remain atmospheric quarters both to the the north and south, between the natural boundaries of the hills and the Danube

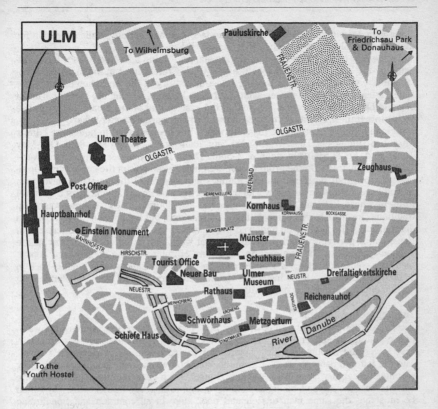

The Rathaus and Marktplatz

That other self-conscious symbol of civic pride, the **Rathaus**, is situated just a block away from the Münster across Neuestrasse, the central arterial road. Even in a country as rich in picturesque town halls as Germany, there's none quite so agressively photogenic as this disparate jumble of buildings, which has been restored to a pristine approximation of how it looked in 1540. That was when the northern front was rebuilt in the Renaissance style and equipped with an arcaded passageway; the local painter **Martin Schaffner** was then let loose on the exterior walls, covering them with a series of brilliantly coloured **frescos** of religious subjects, plus allegories of the Vices and Virtues. On the southern side of the building he painted battle scenes, along with a barge (symbolising Ulm's dependence on the Danube), plus the coats of arms of the city's trading partners. Between the windows here are polychrome statues of six of the Electors, carved the previous century by Master Harmann. Even more luxuriant is the eastern facade, with figures by Multscher of Charlemagne, the Kings of Hungary and Bohemia, and two pages; there's also an elaborate astronomical clock made in 1520. Inside the Rathaus, you can see a replica of the equipment used in 1811 by **Albrecht Berblinger**, "The Tailor of Ulm", in an ill-fated attempt to fly across the Danube; widely regarded in his own day as an eccentric fool, he's since been elevated to the status of a local hero. In 1944, the Rathaus formed an appropriately grand backdrop for the notorious state funeral of Field Marshal Erwin Rommel, who accepted this consolation prize, along with a draught of poison, rather than face trial and certain public execution for his alleged involvement in the July Plot against Hitler.

To the rear of the Rathaus is the Marktplatz, preserving a few old houses but dominated by the brightly-coloured **Fischkasten** (Fish Crate), finest of the many old fountains in the city. Made during the late fifteenth century in the workshop of Syrlin the Elder, it features statues of three saints attired as knights, bearing the coats of arms of city and Empire. In Taubenplätzle, just off the eastern end of the square, is the bronze **Delphinbrunnen**; a century younger, it was formerly part of a water-tower.

Behind stands a Renaissance mansion which has been adapted to house the **Ulmer Museum** (June–Sept Tues, Wed & Fri–Sun 10am–5pm, Thurs 10am–8pm, Oct–May Tues, Wed, Fri & Sat 10am–noon & 2–5pm, Thurs 10am–noon & 2–8pm, Sun 10am–1pm & 2–5pm; free). On the ground floor are choice examples of the city's artistic heritage; the **original figures** from the Rathaus and several of the fountains have been moved here. Alongside further works by Multscher and Erhart are carvings by **Daniel Mauch**, whose Italianate style represents the last flourish of Ulm's great sculptural tradition. The city's heritage in painting is far less rich, but Schaffner's *Eitel Besserer* (a descendant of the family who endowed the chapel in the Münster) is a masterpiece of Renaissance portraiture, and there are several works by an influential master of the previous generation, **Bartholomäus Zeitblom**. Highlight of the archaeology department is a weird *Statuette of a Woman with the Head of a Lioness*, which dates back to 30,000 BC. Upstairs, Ulm's history is extensively documented, with an illuminating section on the construction of the Münster.

The southern quarters

Westwards down Neuestrasse is the vast bulk of the **Neuer Bau**, a municipal warehouse built in the sixteenth century; its pentagonal courtyard contains a graceful staircase tower and a fountain with a statue of Hildegard, one of Charlemagne's wives. Turning left into Sattlergasse, you come to Weinhof, whose main building is the early seventeenth-century **Schwörhaus** (Oath House). Each year, the mayor addresses the citizens from the balcony, taking an oath according to the constitution of 1397 by which he must be "the same man to rich and poor alike in all common and honourable matters without discrimination or reservation". This was an advanced statement for its time, and is often taken as evidence that medieval Ulm was a democratic state. In fact, what the document signified was a passing of power from the patrician class to the guilds, who established an inbuilt majority for themselves on the council.

One of the most interesting features of Ulm is the way the old patterns of settlement can still be clearly discerned. Between here and the Danube is the celebrated **Fischerviertel** (Fishermen's Quarter), whose quaint scenes of half-timbered houses, waterways, courtyards and tiny bridges so delighted Hermann Hesse. This was actually the area where the artisan classes lived – the island on the Blau and the streets alongside were inhabited by tanners and millers, while on Fischergasse you can see a boatman's house at no. 18 and a baker's at no. 22, as well as a fisherman's at no. 23. Look out for the **Schiefe Haus** (Crooked House), a hefty half-timbered building from about 1500 standing beside a remnant of the twelfth-century fortifications; it takes its name from its pronounced tilt over the river, into whose bed it's fastened by stilts. Another picturesque vista is on Fischerplätzle, which looks towards Häuslesbrücke and boasts the late fifteenth- century **Zunfthaus** (the fishermen's guildhall) and the seventeenth-century **Schöne Haus**, adorned with a scene of shipping on the Danube.

From here, you can walk high above the Danube along the medieval ramparts, now laid out as a shady promenade with a view over the backs of the Fisherviertel. Parallel with the Rathaus is the most impressive surviving gate, the **Metzgerturm** (Butchers' Tower), locally dubbed "The Leaning Tower of Ulm" because it slants a good two metres from the vertical. Beyond Herdbrücke is the patrician **Reichenau Hof**, while

Grünen Hof just to the north has the oldest intact buildings in Ulm – the Romanesque **Nikolauskapelle** (whose interior has Gothic frescos), and a stone house of similar date. Nearby is the **Dreifaltigkeitskirche**, a plain Lutheran preaching house in the late Renaissance style, incorporating the Gothic chancel of the monastery which previously stood on the site. For a really superb **view** of Ulm, with the Münster rearing high up behind the houses of the Fishermen's Quarter, cross over to the quays of NEUE-ULM, which to all intents and purposes is the city's southern extension but which isn't even in the same province, the Danube marking the frontier with Bavaria.

The northern quarters

The merchants and craftsmen of medieval Ulm tended to live in the streets north of Neuestrasse. These aren't nearly so well preserved, but some fine buildings remain. Just behind the Münster's east end is the sixteenth-century **Schuhhaus**, the guildhall of the shoemakers; it's now used for art exhibitions. Beyond is the Judenhof, the former ghetto; no. 10 seems to pre-date the pogrom of 1499. The streets immediately north of the Münster contain rows of simple houses once inhabited by skilled craft workers, along with several stores, finest of which is the **Kornhaus**. In spite of its self-confident look and its current function as a concert hall, this was built as a panic measure at the end of the sixteenth century in the belief that there would soon be a famine. Look out also for Herrenkellergasse 12, whose turret served as a look-out post for fathers trying to keep an eye on the evening jaunts of their eligible daughters.

Further north on Frauengrabben and Seelengrabben are terraces of soldiers' houses from the early seventeenth century, beyond which is the **Zeughaus** with a monumental Renaissance gateway and other surviving parts of the medieval fortifications. Ulm's military role reached a peak in the mid-nineteenth century with its transformation into a fortress of the German Confederation. This citadel was seventeen years in the making, but never once had to withstand a siege; the crumbling buildings are dotted all round the outer perimeter of the city. Finest is the **Wilhelmsburg**, an intact fort crowning the commanding heights of the Michelsberg at the extreme north of the city; it's well worth climbing up for the superb **view** which provides a perfect counterpart to the one from the banks of the Danube. If you walk up via Frauenstrasse, you can see the **Pauluskirche**; built to serve the Protestant members of the garrison, it ranks as one of the finest Jugendstil churches in Germany.

Wiblingen

WIBLINGEN, 5km south of Ulm and reached by bus #3 or #8, is now a large dormitory suburb but for centuries was no more than a hamlet clustered round the Benedictine **Abtei**. The present extensive complex, which offers a rare opportunity to see the luxuriance of south German Baroque in close proximity to a bastion of the Reformation, was erected in a leisurely fashion throughout the eighteenth century. Only twenty years after completion, the abbey was secularised; the monastic quarters are now used by the University of Ulm.

Left of the entrance is the **Bibliothek** (April–Oct Tues–Sun 10am–noon & 2–5pm, Nov–March Tues–Fri 2–4pm, Sat & Sun 10am–noon & 2–4pm; DM2). One of the most opulent designs of its kind, it's lavishly adorned with stuccowork of shells, leaves and putti, columns painted pink and blue to resemble marble, large allegorical statues representing the Virtues (four secular, four monastic) and a colossal ceiling fresco glorifying wisdom, with subjects from the Bible and pagan mythology freely mixed together. The **Abteikirche**, which is later in date, shows a shift from Rococo self-indulgence towards the solemnity of Neoclassicism. On the flattened domes are masterly, highly theatrical *trompe l'oeil* frescos by **Januarius Zick**, with a foreshortened *Last Supper* and a cycle illustrating *The Legend of the Cross*. This latter subject was chosen to act as a stimulus to the meditations of the pilgrims who came here to see relics of the Crucifix; the powerful sculpture of the scene by Michel Erhart was acquired from the Münster for the same reason.

Practicalities

The **tourist office** (Mon–Fri 9am–6pm, Sat 9am–12.30pm; ☎0731/64161) is housed in an ugly modern pavilion in front of the Münster; be sure to pick up their free monthly programme of events, *Wohin in Ulm*. Several **hotels** are conveniently located; the cheapest is *Fischkasten*, Marktplatz 16 (☎0731/64910), which charges DM28 for singles, DM54 doubles. Alternatives include *Hirschmann*, Syrlinstr. 1 (☎0731/64671), at DM30 per person; and *Anker*, Rabengasse 2 (☎0731/63297), with singles at DM38 and doubles DM70. There's also a concentration of cheap pensions in the suburb of PFUHL to the east. The **youth hostel** is 4km southwest of the centre at Grimmelfinger Weg 45 (☎0731/384455); take tram #1 to Ehinger Tor, then bus #4 or #9 to Königstrasse. However, there are no camping facilities in the surrounding area. **Motor boat trips** on the Danube (May–Sept) depart from Metzgerturm.

Food and drink

Ulm has a wide range of places to **eat** and **drink**. The *Ratskeller* is a bit more adventurous than usual, with a good vegetarian supplement to the menu. Behind on Markplatz is *Kneipetrödler*, a lively tavern popular with local students which is a real mecca for lovers of the tart and refreshing *Weizen* beer – there are over twenty varieties to choose from. The Fischerviertel is ideal for a pub crawl. On Fischergasse are two traditional inns – *Allgäuer Hof*, the place to come for pancakes, and *Forelle*, arguably the city's best restaurant, especially for fish dishes. The old *Zunfthaus* on the same street has been converted into a beer hall serving Swabian dishes, while *Gerberhaus* on Weinhofberg is another good choice for this style of cuisine. For a wine bar atmosphere, try *Weinkrüger* on Weinhofberg. At the eastern end of Neuestrasse is the old-world *Café im Gindele*; there's also a good choice of cafés in and around Münsterplatz. Three more inns with a long heritage can be found north of the Münster – *Herrenkeller* on the alley of the same name, *Goldener Bock* on Bockgasse and *Drei Kannen* in a wonderful Renaissance building with a loggia front on Hafenbad. Local **beers** are *Münster* and *Gold Ochsen*; the *Braustüble* of the former is west of the centre at Magirusstr. 44, on the route of tram #1.

Culture and festivals

In 1641, Ulm became the first city in Germany to establish a permanent civic **theatre**; its modern successor, the *Ulmer Theater* on Olgastrasse, presents drama, opera and operetta; it also has a small cinema. For cabaret, there's *Theater im Fundus* on Deinselsgasse. **Concerts** (all kinds) and large-scale spectaculars are featured at the *Donauhalle* in Friedrichsau Park by the Danube; more intimate highbrow musical events are held in the *Kornhaus*. Choral music is performed in the Münster every other Saturday, while the five-manual organ can be heard daily between 11am and noon. There's jazz most evenings at *Sauschsdall*, Prittwitzstr. 36, while *Charivari*, Stuttgarter Str. 13, is a youth centre featuring live bands and adventurous film programmes.

The main annual **popular festival** is *Schwörmontag* on the penultimate Monday of July; this begins at 11am in the Weinhof with the mayor's taking of the oath, and continues in the afternoon with a barge procession down the Danube. On the preceding Saturday evening there's the *Lichterserenade*, with thousands of illuminations. Each June, the *Stadtfest* is held in Münsterplatz. However, the most spectacular local tradition, *Fischerstechen* ("Fishermen's Jousting"), a colourful tournament with boats in place of horses, is only held at four year intervals (next in July 1994). Prior to the competitions, there are processions and dances in the streets.

UPPER SWABIA AND THE BODENSEE

Upper Swabia (*Oberschwaben*) is a triangular-shaped area of rich farmland to the south of the Danube; this is one of the least urbanised parts of the country, with no major cities and only a few medium-sized towns. Although the spa resorts and magnificent Baroque and Rococo monasteries are well-known to the Germans themselves, they're little visited by foreigners. This is in marked contrast to the **Bodensee** (also know as Lake Constance, or the *Schwäbischer Meer* – the "Swabian Sea") on the southern border. In reality an enormous bulge in the River Rhine, which enters it from the Austrian side to the east and leaves it again on the Swiss border to the west, it's the largest lake in Germany and one of its most popular holiday destinations. Thanks to its balmy, dry climate it has developed into the nearest the country comes to having a Riviera, though thankfully the shorelines have been preserved from high-rise developments. **Meersburg** and **Überlingen** on the northern side are two of Germany's most picturesque towns; across the water are **Konstanz**, the most cosmopolitan centre in this whole region, and the contrasting islands of **Mainau** and **Reichenau**.

The Upper Swabian spas

In the heart of Upper Swabia is a group of health resorts, each specialising in mud bath (*Moorheilbad*) cures and lying on both of the area's two tourist routes, the **Baroque Road** (*Barockstrasse*) and the **Spa Road** (*Bäderstrasse*). Any one of these is a good choice for a relaxing break, or as a base for exploring the whole region.

Bad Schussenried

BAD SCHUSSENRIED lies some 60km southwest of Ulm on the railway line to the Bodensee; alternatively, it can be reached by bus from Riedlingen in the Danube valley via BAD BUCHAU, the least interesting of the four Upper Swabian spa towns. Ultra-modern clinics now form a large part of its overall appearance, but the Baroque buildings of the huge former Premonstratensian **Kloster** at the northeastern edge of town retain their pre-eminence.

The monastic church, now the **Pfarrkirche St Magnus**, was built by a whole team of architects, including several members of the prolific Beer and Thumb families. Save for the single tower with its distinctive onion dome, it's rather plain on the outside, but the interior, set beneath Januarius Zick's **ceiling frescos** of scenes from the life of Saint Norbert, the order's founder, is far more arresting. Highlight of the furnishings is the set of **choir stalls**, whose backs have limewood reliefs providing a complete illustrated Bible. However, the church is rather overshadowed by the **Bibliotheksaal** (April–Oct daily 10am–noon and 2–5pm; Nov–March Mon–Fri 2–4pm, Sat & Sun 10am–noon & 2–4pm; DM1.50) in the former conventual buildings. There's no library in all of Germany to compare with this luxuriant creation, designed by **Dominikus Zimmermann** at the same time as he was working on the famous Wieskirche in Bavaria. It's a masterly balance of colour, light and shade, with the white porcelain statues contrasting with the pink marble columns and the ethereally blue bookcases with their *trompe l'oeil* volumes. The ceiling fresco, appropriately enough, is a glorification of Wisdom in both heavenly and earthly guises.

Bad Schussenried's **Bahnhof** is in KÜRNBACH, an incorporated village 1.5km south. To the rear of the station is the **Freilichtmuseum** (April–Oct Tues–Sat 9am–6pm, Sun 11am–6pm; DM3), a collection of redundant rural buildings from the surrounding area, though the centrepiece, a large seventeeth-century farmhouse, is original to the spot.

Practicalities

There are about thirty houses with **rooms** to let, mostly at DM20–25 per person; the main concentrations are at the southern end of the main part of town, on Welfenstrasse, Blasius-Erler-Weg and Mozartstrasse. The **hotels** *Zur Linde*, Biberacher Str. 3 (☎07583/2234), and *Oefner*, Konradstr. 7 (☎07583/2506), are both centrally placed and cost only a little more. A full list of places to stay is available from the **tourist office**, Bahnhofstr. 10 (Mon–Fri 9am–noon & 2–5pm, Easter–Sept Sat 10am–noon; ☎07583/40134).

Steinhausen

STEINHAUSEN, 5km northeast of Bad Schussenried to which it's connected by bus, clusters round the **Wallfahrtskirche**, described in all the tourist brochures as "the most beautiful village church in the world". This designation is rather a cheat, as it was not intended as a church for parish worship; rather it was the goal of a pilgrimage sponsored by the monks of Schussenried, and Steinhausen itself remains an official part of that town. Nonetheless, it's a building of the highest artistic importance, being generally accepted as the earliest church in the full-blown Rococo style: that is to say one in which architecture, painting and decorations are all fused into an indivisible whole. This unity was made possible by the close collaboration between the **Zimmermann brothers**: Dominikus as architect, Johann Baptist as painter. The church consists of a large nave and a tiny chancel, both oval in shape; pristine white pillars, which look as if they're made of china, shoot up to the vault, whose **fresco**, an evocation of Heaven in limpid pastel colours, seems to be a continuation of the architecture. No less remarkable is the **stuccowork**, with its superbly crafted depictions of the animal, bird and plant kingdoms.

The main **pilgrimages** are on Good Friday and on the day of the patron saints, Peter and Paul (29 June). Across from the church is a **hotel**, *Zur Linde* (☎07583/2381), costing from DM28 per person and with an excellent restaurant.

Bad Waldsee

Some 15km southeast of Bad Schussenried, and reached either by bus or by a looping branch railway line, is **BAD WALDSEE**, which enjoys a pretty setting on an isthmus between two lakes, and which benefits from a rather more animated market town feel than its soporific neighbour.

From just outside the Bahnhof, you get a fine view of the town over the Stadtsee, the larger of the lakes and a popular boating centre. Rising above everything else is the Baroque **Stiftskirche**, whose twin facade towers are set at startling angles to one another. It's yet another church in which Dominikus Zimmermann had a hand, but this time only with the furnishings: he created the multicoloured high altar, plus the smaller ones to the side. However, the greatest treasure is a resplendent early Renaissance bronze epitaph in the northern aisle, nicknamed *Der eiserne Mann* ("The Iron Man"), to a local noble. In the medieval town centre, which lies between the Stiftskirche and the quiet spa quarters to the south, are a number of half-timbered houses and step-gabled public buildings. The most notable are the **Kornhaus** and the **Rathaus**, the latter being a spectacular example of the late Gothic penchant for picturesque effect. Further west is the Renaissance and Baroque **Schloss** of the local grandees, the House of Waldburg-Waldsee. It's closed to the public, but you get a good view of the exterior by walking round the rustic-looking Schloss See, the smaller of the town's lakes.

Practicalities

The **tourist office** (Mon–Fri 8am–noon & 2–5pm, May–Sept also Sat 10am–noon; ☎07524/101341) is at Ravensburger Str. 1 beside the Rathaus. Here you can get a complete list of all the rooms available in **private houses**, which generally cost DM25 or even less; the most convenient is *Ott*, Bahnhofstr. 24 (☎07524/8919). There are also several **hotels**; *Post*, Hauptstr. 1 (☎07524/1507) charges upwards of DM30 per person and has one of the best **restaurants** in a town which is noticeably better off for places to eat and drink than the other spas in the region. Main local **festival** is the *Altstadt- und Seenachtfest* in August, featuring a fireworks display over the Stadtsee.

Bad Wurzach

The last of the spas, **BAD WURZACH**, is very similar in feel to Bad Waldsee, from which it lies 12km southeast, There are regular bus services between the two; Bad Wurzach is no longer on a rail line. Dominating the main Markstrasse is the dignified white **Schloss**, now a school run by Jesuits. Although the castle is mostly closed to the public, the main entrance is generally kept open to enable visitors to see the resplendent **staircase**, one of the finest ever built in the Baroque period, and its gloriously profane ceiling fresco of *The Apotheosis of Hercules*. On Schulstrasse, the eastern continuation of the street, are the **Kloster Maria Rosengarten**, a still-inhabited convent whose ornate Rococo chapel can be visited, and the grandly Neoclassical parish church of **St Verena**. However, the most intriguing monument is the half-timbered **Leprosenhaus** (Easter–Oct Fri, Sun & hols 2–5pm) at the edge of town on the road southwest to Ravensburg; a leper colony existed there from the mid-fourteenth century until the end of the eighteenth century.

Practicalities and festivals

The **tourist office** (Mon–Fri 9am–noon & 2–5pm, Easter–Nov Sat 9am–noon; ☎07564/302150) is at Mühltorstr. 1. A generous number of **private rooms** are available as in the other spas; prices if anything are slightly cheaper, with DM20 the average. Bad Wurzach is also the only one of the towns with a **campsite**; it's by the outlying village of WIESEN (☎07564/3482) to the southeast. There are a couple of reasonably priced hotels in the centre: *Adler*, Schloss Str. 8 (☎07564/2802), and *Ochsen* on Herrenstrasse (☎07564/2826), both charging around DM30 per person. The best time to visit is on the second Friday in July, when Upper Swabia's most distinctive **festival**, the *Heilig-Blut-Fest*, takes place. Here this takes the form of a mounted pilgrimage to the Baroque church on the **Gottesberg**, the hill to the south; over 1500 horses take part, with their riders decked out in colourful costumes.

North of town is the **Wurzacher Ried**, 14 square kilometres of moorland punctuated by woods and tarns with an extraordinarily rich indigenous flora and fauna. The whole area is a nature reserve and is listed by the Council of Europe as a landscape of outstanding botanical and geological importance.

Weingarten and Ravensburg

Just over 30km south of Bad Schussenried on the main rail line to the Bodensee are two adjacent towns which are so close together as to be virtually one unit, yet which are very different in appearance and jealously guard their own municipal independence. Both are foundations of the Welf dynasty, one of the two most powerful families of early medieval Germany, and one which held sway in its later base in Lower Saxony right up to the present century.

Weingarten

The town of **WEINGARTEN**, nowadays quite a bustling place, was originally no more than an adjunct to the huge hilltop Benedictine **Kloster** of the same name, which remains the sole monument of note. At the end of the seventeenth century, plans were drawn up to transform this, one of Germany's most famous medieval monasteries, into the principal centre of monasticism north of the Alps. Such an ambitious project was never fully realised, but the Baroque complex which was built is nonetheless the largest monastery in the country and, since its re-settlement from Beuron in 1922 after over a century of closure, an active centre of Roman Catholic education.

The **Basilika** is strikingly reminiscent of St Peter's in Rome and is a colossal structure, even if, both in its length and the height of its central dome, it's only about half the size of its great model. Apart from the dome, the most striking feature of the exterior is the huge convex facade; inside, the massive white pillars convey an overpowering sense of massiveness. The vivacious **ceiling frescos** by Cosmas Damian Asam glorify Christ, the Virgin and Saint Benedict; no less eye-catching are the **choir stalls**, Josef Anton Feuchtmayer's first major commission. However, the most impressive feature of the furnishings is the **organ** by Josef Gabler. Not only is it one of the finest instruments in Europe, but the case is also a particularly ingenious design, with the pipes housed in a series of towers specially constructed so as not to obscure the facade windows.

As in Bad Wurzach, the *Heilig-Blut-Fest* is the main **festival**; the monastery's most treasured relic is the focus of the procession. If you want to stay, *Waldhorn*, Karlstr. 47 (☎0751/405125), is a recommendable **hotel** charging from DM33 per person; it also has a good restaurant. Liveliest **bar** in town is *Schenderhannes* on Abt-Holler-Strasse which has a beer garden.

Ravensburg

If most of Upper Swabia seems too provincial and too relentlessly Baroque, then the regional "metropolis" of **RAVENSBURG** offers a refreshing antidote. This former Free Imperial City became, courtesy of the linen trade, one of the richest towns in Germany in the fifteenth century; although it's modest in size by present-day standards, it feels much bigger than it actually is through its status as the market centre for a large area. Even if it lacks a spectacular centrepiece, its medieval core presents an unusually satisfying and well-preserved townscape, dominated by the towers and gates of the former fortifications, now laid out as a promenade encircling the heart of the old city.

About town

From the Bahnhof, Eisenbahnstrasse leads straight ahead to the centre, but the first group of monuments can be seen by turning left when you reach Untere Breite Strasse. On the corner with Charlottenstrasse is the **Vogthaus** (Tues–Sat 3–5pm, Sun 10am–noon & 3–5pm; free), a half-timbered patrician residence of the fifteenth century. It's now the local museum, but the house itself, which includes rooms in Gothic, Renaissance and Baroque styles, is the main attraction. Further down the street is the **Zehntscheuer**, a large timber-framed building of the previous century which looks for all the world like a farmhouse; previously part of the leper hospital, it's now an arts centre. Behind it is part of the Stadtmauer, including the round **Wehrturm** and the tall square **Gemalter Turm** (Painted Tower), which preserves the jazzy decoration which was once a feature of all of Ravensburg's towers.

A few minutes' walk east is another corner of the wall, with the round **Grüner Turm** (Green Tower) and the step-gabled **Frauentor**. Another tower here doubles as the belfry of the **Liebrauenkirche**, the town's parish church. From the original fourteenth-century building, there remains the beautiful portal tympanum with scenes from the life of the Virgin. The interior has often been remodelled but preserves some fine stained glass windows in the chancel. It formerly contained one of the masterpieces of fifteenth-century German sculpture, the *Ravensburg Madonna* (a haunting carving showing the Virgin sheltering humanity under her cloak), but this has been replaced by a copy, the original now being in the Dahlem Museum in Berlin.

Marienplatz, which is really a broad street rather than a square but which is used for outdoor markets, leads to the heart of the city, with a whole series of public buildings from the period when Ravensburg was at the height of its prosperity. An indication of the importance of commerce to the city is the fact that the **Rathaus** is overshadowed by the **Waaghaus** alongside; the latter had the weigh house and mint (Ravensburg was long a major centre for coin production) on the ground floor, with the trading hall upstairs. It was adorned in the mid-sixteenth century with the **Blaserturm**, a watch-tower crowned by a Renaissance octagon which has become the symbol of the town.

Bachstrasse leads southwest past more fine buildings to the **Untertor**, while Marktstrasse snakes up to the other main gateway, the **Obertor**. Continuing upwards, and therefore out of the boundaries of the old city, you come to the so-called **Mehlsack** (Sack of Flour), a cylindrical tower erected by the independently minded city council in the sixteenth-century as an extra line of defence against the expansionist designs of the aristocratic owners of the **Veitsburg**. A path climbs up steeply to this fortress, imperiously perched on the hill above; on the way you pass through the half-timbered **Burghaldentorkel**, the only surviving example of twenty buildings in the town where grapes were stored and pressed. The original Veitsburg was probably the birthplace of Henry the Lion, founder of Munich and one of the most powerful princes of the Middle Ages (for more information, see Braunschweig, *Chapter Six*), but this castle has completely disappeared, leaving only some later workshop buildings, now modernised as the youth hostel, and a small Baroque pavilion which houses a restaurant. However, it's well worth going up for the sake of the wonderful views of the town you get on the way.

Practicalities

The **tourist office** (Mon 8am–12.30pm, Tues–Fri 8am–12.30pm & 2.30–5.30pm, Sat 9am–noon; ☎0751/82324) is at Marienplatz 54. Several centrally-sited **hotels** charge around DM28–35 per head, including *Humpistube*, Marktstr. 46 (☎0751/21910), *Café Baur*, Marienplatz 1 (☎0751/25616) and *Weinstube Muke*, Herrenstr. 16 (☎0751/23006). The most atmospheric place to stay, however, has to be the **youth hostel** in the Veitsburg (☎0751/25363). Best choices for **food** and **drink** are *Räuberhöhle*, Burgstr. 14, *Ratstube*, Marienplatz 19, and the restaurant in the Veitsburg. *Fastnet* is the main festival.

The north shore of the Bodensee

Surpassed in size among the Alpine lakes only by the much lower-lying Lake Geneva, the **Bodensee** is 14km across at its widest point and about 65km long, offering a wealth of opportunity for watersports or relaxing breaks. Its main, eastern part is known as the Obersee, while the northern of the western forks is the Überlinger See, the southern the Untersee. Of the three countries bordering it, Germany has the lion's share of the shoreline, including the entire northern side. Although the warm climate means that the sweeping views across to the Alps are often lost in haze, this is never-theless one of the most beautiful parts of Germany, with a couple of the country's most outstanding small towns as added attractions. A **corniche road**, served by regular buses, runs all the way along the shore from the eastern end at Lindau (see *Chapter One*); this is far preferable to the railway, which deviates inland, though the ferries (see below) offer the best means of seeing the lake.

BOAT TRIPS ON THE BODENSEE

By far the largest operator of passenger ships on the lake is the DB-run *Bodensee-Verkehrsdienst*, whose main offices are: Seestr. 22, Friedrichshafen (☎07541/201389); Hafenstr. 6, Konstanz (☎07531/281398); and Am Hafen, Lindau (☎08382/6099). DB rail passes are valid; there's also a special *Bodenseepass*, costing DM70, which allows travel on all the ships on 7 days within a 15-day period, plus half-price travel by ship, train or bus on the remaining days. However, normal fares are very reasonable, being calculated at similar rates to other forms of public transport. Bikes can be taken on board without extra charge. Frequency of services is very seasonal, but free current timetables are available at all the harbours. Excursion cruises are run in summer, though these offer few advantages over the main scheduled routes, which are:

● Friedrichshafen–Romanshorn (Switzerland). The only car ferry operated by the company.

● Kreuzlingen (Switzerland)–Konstanz–Reichenau–Schaffhausen (Switzerland). The most scenic of the routes, continuing along the Rhine and terminating at the Rheinfall.

● Konstanz–Meersburg–Lindau–Bregenz (Austria).

● Konstanz–Meersburg–Mainau–Überlingen.

Perhaps the most useful crossing of all, however, is the car ferry across the very heart of the lake between Konstanz and Meersburg. Run by the *Stadtwerk Konstanz* (☎07531/803393), it operates throughout the day and night, with frequencies ranging from 15 minutes to one hour. In addition, various smaller companies offer excursions on the lake; check locally for the best deals.

Friedrichshafen

Situated at the widest part of the Bodensee, 22km west of Lindau and 19km south of Ravensburg, **FRIEDRICHSHAFEN** is best known for its distinguished place in aviation history (see opposite), Despite being the only industrial blot on the lake, it manages a decidedly curious double existence, taking full advantage of its setting to serve as a rather flashy resort.

The eastern part of the waterfront has been laid out as an attractive promenade with gardens. At the far end is the one historical monument of any note, the onion-towered **Schlosskirche**, built at the very end of the seventeenth century in a tastefully restrained Baroque style. Its monastic buildings were converted into a palace for the Kings of Württemberg last century and are still in private hands. Part of the Rathaus in the drab pedestrianised town centre houses the only other obvious draw, the **Zeppelin- und Bodensee-Museum** (May–Oct daily 10am–5pm, Wed till 7pm; Nov–April Tues–Sun 10am–noon & 2–5pm, Wed till 7pm; DM2.50). This contains a large collection of works by the folksy school of painters based in the Bodensee in the fifteenth century, but the main attraction is the aviation section on the top floor which contains a number of original aircraft, plus fascinating archive film (English soundtrack available) of the Zeppelins.

Practicalities

There are two railway stations: the **Stadtbahnhof** near the promenade and the **Hafenbahnhof** further east by the commercial harbour. In a pavilion facing the former is the **tourist office** (Mon–Fri 10am–5pm, Sat 10am–noon; ☎07541/203291). The

---

ZEPPELINS AND DORNIERS

Count Ferdinand von Zeppelin, a native of Konstanz, was intrigued by use of hot-air balloons in the American Civil War, which he witnessed as an official observer. He developed its lighter-than-air idea to build a rigid airship with a cigar-shaped trussed frame supported by gas cells; the first model, the *LZ-1*, was tested in Friedrichshafen (which thereafter became both the manufacturing and launch base) in 1900. These strange, silent machines, capable of going at no more than 35 kilometres per hour, were turned from their original peaceful purpose to undertake bombing missions in World War I. Afterwards, however, their potential for long-distance travel was realised, and in 1928 the new, specially-built *Graf Zeppelin* made the first transatlantic passenger flight, then a round-the-world trip the following year. By 1937 it had made 590 flights, including 114 ocean crossings. Disaster then struck when the huge new airship *Hindenburg* crashed while landing in New Jersey, killing 36 passengers. No more flights were undertaken, and production was not resumed after the factory's destruction in the war, although by then a safe, non-inflammable gas had been developed.

Claude Dornier, originally an employee of Zeppelin, used the Bodensee to test his "flying boats", but eventually moved into the production of fighter aircraft. His planes were extensively deployed in the Blitz, something which seems to have been a sore point with the French occupying forces in 1945, who systematically looted the factory. Unlike its counterpart, this was revived and is still in operation under the management of Daimler-Benz.

---

youth hostel is in the eastern part of town at Lindauer Str. 3 (☎07541/72404); the two **campsites** (☎07541/73421 and ☎07541/42059) are at the opposite end. Cheapest **hotels**, charging from DM30 per head, are *Wald-Café Maier*, Am Seewald 36 (☎07541/72440), *Pension Wurster*, Georgstr. 14 (☎07541/72694), and *Ailinger Hof*, Ailinger Str. 49 (☎07541/22788). Best place to **eat** is the classy *Kurgartenrestaurant* in the *Graf-Zeppelin-Haus* overlooking the lake.

Meersburg

MEERSBURG, which clings to a steeply sloping site 16km from Friedrichshafen, is one of those places which perfectly fits the tourist board image of Romantic Germany. It therefore usually swarms with an uncomfortably large numbers of day-trippers, but it's an atmospheric and picturesque little town well worth braving the hordes to see.

Arriving by the corniche road, which at this point passes high above the Bodensee, you enter the historic quarter via the dignified **Obertor**. It's then just a short walk down to the riotously picturesque **Marktplatz**, where three streets converge. Steigstrasse, lined on both sides with half-timbered houses, then plummets towards the lake; its west side, with a sloping ramp giving access to the houses, is particularly eye-catching.

All over town, you get tantalising glimpses of its great pride and joy, the **Altes Schloss** (March–Oct daily 9am–6pm, Nov–Feb 10am–5pm; DM6), whose round corner towers and gabled central block make for a distinctive silhouette. Founded by the Merovingian King Dagobert, it boasts of being the oldest surviving castle in Germany, a claim recently substantiated by the discovery that some sections of the masonry do actually appear to date back as far as the seventh century. For most of its history, it was a seat of the Prince-bishops of Konstanz, who extensively rebuilt it throughout the medieval period, making it their main residence when they were bundled out of their city at the Reformation; since secularisation, it has been in private ownership. Despite the fact that it's still lived in, much of the castle has the bleak, forbidding feel it must always have had: the kitchen has its medieval utensils, while the dungeons display a collection of arms and armour. Germany's greatest woman poet, **Annette von Droste-Hülshoff**, came to live here during the 1840s as guest of the then-owner, her brother-in-law, Baron von Lassberg. Her rooms, whose period furnishings are in stark contrast to the austerity of the medieval chambers, are still as they were in her day, and many of her most famous poems are exhibited on the walls.

The **Neues Schloss** above was built under the direction of Balthasar Neumann in the mid-eighteenth century, when the Prince-bishops decided they warranted a more comfortable and modern residence. It now houses a cultural centre and local **museum** (April–Oct daily 10am–1pm & 2–6pm; DM3), which includes displays on Claude Dornier and the fifteenth-century Cologne painter Stefan Lochner, who is thought to have been a native of the town. There's a wonderful view over the Bodensee from the gardens in front; an even better one can be had from the belvedere known as the **Känzele** a short walk to the east.

Practicalities

The Seepromenade below the Altes Schloss, lined with cafés and restaurants, many specialising in fresh fish from the lake, is the most popular rendezvous point. Here also is the **harbour** for the *Bodensee-Verkehrsdienst* ships; the terminal for the **car ferry** to Konstanz is some 700m west. **Buses** stop near the latter, as well as near the Obertor; Meersburg is not on the railway line. The **tourist office** (Mon–Fri 8am–noon & 1.30–5pm; April–Sept also Sat 10am–2pm; ☎07532/82383) is at Kirchstr. 4 at the top of the town.

If you want to base yourself in only one resort while touring the Bodensee, Meersburg is probably the best choice, as its central location means that everywhere is within easy reach. Unfortunately, it has no hostel or campsite, but otherwise there's ample accommodation. Cheapest options are in the **guest houses** clustered on Stettener Strasse near the eastern entrance to town, such as *Gästehaus Fahr*, at no. 25 (☎07532/6519), with singles from DM28, doubles from DM50, *Gästehaus Irmgard* at no. 23a (☎07532/9494), charging from DM33, and *Haus Sylvia* at no. 21c (☎07532/6307), whose rates begin at DM30. Another concentration can be found further west and uphill on Von-Lassberg-Strasse, the view compensating for the steep climb up. It usually costs far more to stay in the old part of town; an exception, with an excellent situation in the street behind the waterfront, is *Pension Klingenstein*, Unterstadtstr. 14 (☎07532/6630), whose cheapest rooms cost DM31 per person.

Unteruhldingen and Birnau

Next resort along the lake, 7km away, is UHLDINGEN-MÜHLHOFEN, a federation of several previously separate villages. Shoreside **UNTERUHLDINGEN** has the most unusual open-air museum in Germany, the **Pfahlbauten** (guided tours daily April–Oct 9am–7pm; DM3), containing conjectural re-creations of Stone Age dwellings, remains of which were found here, built on huge wooden stilts driven into the bed of the lake.

About twenty minutes' walk uphill is the Cistercian **Basilika Birnau** whose wonderful, isolated setting is unfortunately now marred by the uncomfortable proximity of the main road. Built in just four years, it's a collaboration by three of the finest Rococo artists – the architect Peter Thumb, the fresco painter Gottfried Bernard Götz and the sculptor Josef Anton Feuchtmayer. The dazzling interior, a paean of praise to the Virgin Mary, provides a fitting complement to the natural beauty of the surroundings; its illusionistic tricks reach a climax in the cupola which incorporates a mirror to enhance its effects. Look out for the famous statuette known as the *Honigschlecker* (a cherub sucking the finger that has just been inside a bee's nest); it's placed beside an altar dedicated to Saint Bernard of Clairvaux, in honour of the claim that his words were as sweet as honey.

Überlingen

A further 5km on, the former Free Imperial City of **ÜBERLINGEN**, nowadays a specialist *Kneipp* health resort, rises gently above the lake. For sheer good looks and polished appearance, it has few rivals in all of Germany: with its magnificent public buildings of a distinctive pale green stonework, picturesque alleys of half-timbered houses, glorious lakeward vistas and luxuriant gardens, it seems almost indecently favoured for a place whose population has never numbered more than a few thousand.

About town

Dominating the town is the **Münster**, a huge Gothic structure which was constructed over a period of two hundred years. Its two towers make a fascinating pairing. The tall square clock tower to the south, which provides a landmark visible from far off, was specially heightened to serve as a watchtower, and crowned with an octagonal Renaissance lantern. In contrast, its stumpy northern counterpart which houses the huge *Osanna* bell, nestles under a steeply pitched wooden roof which looks as though it should belong on a barn rather than a church. The sobriety of the rest of the exterior sharply contrasts with the majestic interior, whose intricately vaulted nave of five aisles, built in the second half of the sixteenth century, shows the by then archaic Gothic style bowing out with a bang. Also marking the end of an era is the tiered main **altarpiece**, carved by Jörg Zürn in the early seventeenth century, which was the last of the great series of wooden retables illustrating Biblical stories which adorn so many German churches; soon after, these were completely supplanted by more florid Baroque altars. Zürn also made the graceful tabernacle alongside, while he or members of his family carved four of the altars which adorn each of the fourteen nave chapels.

Across Münsterplatz, and backing on Hofstatt, the market square, is the **Rathaus** (Mon–Fri 9am–noon & 2.30–5pm, Sat 9am–noon; free). Its first-floor *Ratsaal*, complete with panelled walls, projecting arches and a ribbed ceiling, is a masterpiece of late fifteenth-century design: the sweetly carved statuettes and coats of arms represent the powers in the Holy Roman Empire and are a glorification of Überlingen's status as a city-state within it. At right-angles to the Rathaus, and with a stone relief of the town's own arms, is the Renaissance **Alte Kanzlei** which now houses the municipal archives.

Climbing up either Krummebergstrasse or Luitzengasse on the northern side of Münsterplatz brings you to the **Reichlin-von-Meldegg-Haus** (Tues–Sat 9am–12.30pm, Sun 10am–3pm; DM2), another late fifteenth-century building, this time in the rusticated style of the Florentine Renaissance, named after the wealthy doctor whose home it was. The interiors include a chapel and an ornate Rococo *Festsaal*, but most of the space is taken up by a surprisingly good *Heimatmuseum*, including the largest collection of dolls' houses in Germany, ranging from Renaissance to Jugendstil. From the balcony at the end of the gardens is the best **view** in Überlingen, showing the town etched out against the background of the Bodensee and Swiss Alps.

Above the northwest side of Münsterplatz is the **Franziskanerkirche**, with a spare, gaunt exterior typical of the mendicant orders. Its interior, however, was given the full Baroque treatment. More striking than the church is the resplendent late Gothic **Franziskanertor**, the northern entrance to the town. This is one of seven surviving gateways and towers of the **Stadtmauer**, which has now been laid out as a shady promenade. Its moated western and northern sections are particularly impressive.

The waterfront is dominated by the Neoclassical **Greth**, crowned with a huge slanting roof. Formerly a corn exchange, it's now a cultural centre and also houses the **tourist office** (Mon–Fri 8am–noon & 2–6pm, Sat 9am–noon, Sun 10am–noon; ☎07551/4041). Just to the west is is the gabled Gothic **Zeughaus** (Easter–Oct Mon–Sat 10am–noon; DM2), containing a private collection of arms and armour. At the end of the promenade are the *Kurpark* and spa quarters.

Practicalities

The **Bahnhof** lies at the extreme western end of town, but **buses** stop on the one-way streets immediately south of the Münster. There's a large modern **youth hostel** at the eastern end of the waterside at Alte Nussdorfer Str. 26 (☎07551/4204), and four separate **campsites** in the vicinity: one in the town itself (☎07551/64583), the others in NUSSDORF to the east. **Hotels** are plentiful, though mostly pricey for the Bodensee area, being geared to the lucrative spa market. Among the less expensive options, at DM25 upwards, are *Pension im Dorf*, Friedhofstr. 26 (☎07551/65625), *Haus Klemm*, Zum Hecht 66 (☎07551/63749), and *Pension Otterbeck*, Seehaldenweg 9 (☎07551/64982).

You don't have to look hard to find places to **eat** and **drink** in Überlingen – the town is full of elegant cafés, restaurants and wine bars. First choice for atmosphere is the *Spitalkeller im Steinhaus*, housed in a medieval building across from the Franziskanerkirche, though *Weinstube Reichert* on the promenade is probably the best bet for food. Among **festivals**, the most important is the *Schwedenprozession*, commemorating this Catholic town's successful defence of its independence against the Swedes in the Thirty Years' War. This is performed twice annually: on the Sunday after 16 May, and on the second Sunday in July. *Fasnacht* is also a big annual event and bizarrely features Bengali costumes.

Inland from the Bodensee

Just inland from Überlingen, and connected to it by regular buses, are two outstanding sights well worth the short detours.

Salem

SALEM, a grouping of villages 11km east, is centred on the great **Reichsabtei** of that name. Formerly a Cistercian monastery, and the mother house of Birnau, it was taken over on secularisation by the Grand Dukes of Baden and remains in the possession of their descendants. Part of the complex is now occupied by one of Germany's most exclusive schools, founded by Kurt Hahn who later emigrated to Britain and established Gordonstoun. There's also a hotel, *Schwanen* (☎07553/283), which has an excellent restaurant and rooms from DM40.

The **Münster** (guided tours April–Oct Mon–Sat 9am–noon & 1–5pm, Sun 11am–5pm; DM2) is rarely used for public worship and hence has an inevitable coldness about it. Nonetheless, it's an outstanding example of the grandly sober Gothic architecture of the Cistercians, with their favoured characteristics of a large chancel terminating in a flat east end. In the eighteenth century, the church was littered with a series of altars and monuments in a very early Neoclassical style; the marriage of two very different kinds of artistic austerity works surprisingly well. It's necessary to go on a separate tour to see the **Schloss** (same times; DM3). Although originally the conventual part of the monastery, this indeed seems more like a palace, having been built in a luxuriant Baroque style following the destruction of the medieval buildings in a fire. The *Kaisersaal*, a richly decorated reception hall to accommodate any visiting Imperial entourage, is particularly impressive.

Heiligenberg

Commanding a grandstand view over the whole Bodensee area on the heights above Salem and some 7km away by road, is the little *Kurort* of **HEILIGENBERG**; unfortunately, there's no bus directly linking the two. Its enormous **Schloss** (guided tours daily April–June & mid-Aug–Oct 9am–noon & 1–6pm; DM3) came into the possession of the House of Fürstenberg in the sixteenth century; they had the existing medieval castle radically rebuilt, creating in its place one of the largest and finest Renaissance palaces in Germany. The **Rittersaal** is outstanding, especially its intricately carved coffered ceiling (which is suspended from the vault on steel rods to support its weight), and the glass paintings of coats of arms. Only marginally less impressive is the brightly painted **Schlosskapelle**, which is arranged more like a theatre than a chapel and has beautiful stained glass windows brought from the former Dominican monastery in Konstanz. You're allowed up into the family oratory to inspect the vault, with its seemingly inexhaustible series of angels in different guises, at close range.

Between the Schloss and the village is the graceful **Glockenturm** (Bell Tower), built by Jerg Schwartzenberger, the principal architect of the Schloss. There are plenty of **hotels**, such as *Bayerischer Hof*, Röhrenbacher Str. 1 (☎07554/217), and *Haus Alpenblick*, Betenbrunner Str. 14 (☎07554/355), each charging from DM30 per person.

Konstanz (Constance)

By any standards, **KONSTANZ** has a remarkable geographical position. It's split in two by the Rhine, which re-emerges here from the Obersee (the main part of the Bodensee) as a channel for a brief stretch, before forming the Untersee, the arm from which it finally re-emerges as a river. The Altstadt is a tiny enclave on the otherwise Swiss side of the lake, a fact which was of inestimable benefit during the war when the Allies desisted from bombing it for fear of hitting neutral Switzerland. Curiously enough, the latter is one country to which Konstanz has never belonged: probably founded by the Romans, it has been a Prince-bishopric and a Swabian Free Imperial City, then Austrian, before finally being allocated to Baden. Between 1414 and 1418, when the conclave met here to resolve the Great Schism, the city was the nerve-centre of European power politics (see below). Nowadays, it contents itself with more modest roles as a resort town, frontier post and seat of a new university whose students help to give it a relaxed, carefree air all year round.

THE COUNCIL OF 1414–18

In 1409, the Council of Pisa elected Alexander V pope in an attempt to end the **Great Schism**, which had left rival claimants to the papacy in Rome and Avignon since 1378. Far from solving the problem, however, this left the world with three competing popes. Eventually, Emperor Sigismund forced Alexander's successor, John XXIII, to call an ecumenical council of ecclesiastical and secular rulers in Konstanz in 1414. This became one of the largest and most extraordinary gatherings in world history: the sittings lasted four years, during which time 72,000 visitors (more than seven times the number of the permanent population) flocked to the town. As well as re-uniting the Church, the intention was also to reform it, as its institutions and practices, notably the rite of confession, apostolic supremacy and the granting of indulgences, had come under attack from **Jan Hus**, the first Czech Rector of Prague University, who had gained a large popular following in the process. Hus was guaranteed a safe return passage in order to defend his views, but was imprisoned, tried and condemned as a heretic, and handed over to the secular authorities for burning at the stake.

John XXIII, who realised he was likely to lose his position as pope, attempted to sabotage the council by withdrawing from it, whereupon it issued the highly dubious *Sacrosancta*, affirming its own superiority over the papacy. In 1417, both John and Gregory XII, his Roman rival, agreed to step down in favour of a compromise candidate; although the Avignon pope, Benedict XIII, stubbornly refused to do likewise, he found himself deserted by his supporters and was deposed. The way was therefore cleared for the election of Cardinal Oddo Colonna as Pope Martin V and an end to the schism. Various reforms, primarily financial, were then enacted, but the failure to undertake anything more radical – symbolised by the treatment of Hus – eventually led to a far more serious and lasting split in the Church with the Reformation exactly a century later.

The Münster

The famous conclave met in the **Münster**, suitably set on the highest point of the Altstadt. Its subsequent history has been less glorious: once the Reformation had taken hold, the local bishop was driven out of town, and after the see (which dated back at least as far as the seventh century) was dissolved in 1821, the church sank into insignificance. Begun as a Romanesque pillared basilica – whose outline is still obvious – building continued for 600 years, so there are marked differences in style, particularly in the interior: the aisles and their chapels are Gothic, while the organ-case and gallery were built during the Renaissance, and the original ceiling was replaced by a vaulted Baroque one. The spot on which Hus is said to have stood during his trial is marked in the central aisle, by the 24th row.

Of the furnishings, the most remarkable are the vigorously carved fifteenth-century **choir stalls** designed by Nicolaus Gerhaert, and the broadly contemporary and equally ornate **Schnegg**, a staircase in the northern transept. From here you descend to the **Konradikapelle**, named in honour of Saint Konrad, a tenth-century Bishop of Konstanz, who is commemorated by a Gothic funerary slab and a golden shrine. The saint would probably still recognise the tiny **crypt** further on, the oldest surviving part of the building, whose walls are hung with remarkable gilded enamel medallions. From here, you pass out into the Gothic cloisters, off which are several imposing chambers, notably the rotunda known as the Mauritiuskapelle, which houses a magnificent late thirteenth-century **Holy Sepulchre**, inspired by the orginal in Jerusalem. Next door is the Sylvesterkapelle, with a complete cycle of fifteenth-century frescos of the life of Christ.

For a fine view of the town, climb up the **tower** (Mon–Sat 10am–5pm; Sun 1–5pm; DM1). The central lantern and openwork spire of this are nineteenth-century additions to the massive Gothic facade, whose three sections were, most unusually, all of similar height, giving it a decidedly forbidding and unecclesiastical look.

The rest of the town

On Münsterplatz are a number of fine old mansions, including the **Haus zur Katz**, a fifteenth-century guildhouse which is the earliest example of rusticated stonework in Germany, and the **Haus zur Kunkel**, formerly the residence of the sacristan. Behind the latter's Baroque exterior lurk some original thirteenth-century rooms, one of which features some beautiful early Gothic frescos showing linen weavers at work; a sign tells you at which door to ring in order to see them.

Between here and the Rhine is the best-preserved part of town, the *Niederburg*, a quarter of twisting little alleys lined by old houses. Overlooking the river are two fragments of the fortifications – the **Pulverturm** and the **Rheintorturm**. The latter, hard by the modern Rheinbrücke which carries the main road and railway into the heart of Konstanz, is particularly impressive; it dates back to the late twelfth century and preserves some scanty frescos. Across the bridge is **Seestrasse**, a promenade of grandiosely elegant villas, one of which contains the **casino** which acts as a particular magnet to the Swiss, who have no such facility in their own country.

At the southeast corner of the Rheinbrücke is the **Insel-Hotel**, one of the most exclusive in Germany, occupying the old Dominican monastery. Its cellars were used to imprison Hus, and it was also the birthplace of Ferdinand von Zeppelin, a statue to whom can be seen overlooking the main **harbour** – a bustle of colourful sails in the summer – just to the south. Behind it is the **Konzilgebäude**, a fourteenth-century storehouse with a prominent hipped roof. It owes its name to the disputed contention that it was the scene of the election of Pope Martin V; nowadays it has been restored to serve as a festival hall and is not, apart from the restaurant, normally open to the public.

Konstanz's two market squares, Fischmarkt and Marktstätte, are respectively west and southwest of the Konzilgebäude. South of the latter, along the street of the same name, is the **Rosgartenmuseum** (Tues–Sun 10am–5pm; free), which has a good collection of local archaeological finds, in particular from the palaeolithic period, and also art and craft exhibits from the Middle Ages. The museum was designed in 1871, and everything, including the original display cabinets, is as it was then, creating a pleasantly musty atmosphere. You might think from the name that the building must originally have had something to do with roses, but it's an old euphemism for the local horse abattoir: the German for horse was traditionally *Ross*, but by omitting one letter people could say *Rosgarten* and ignore its sorry purpose.

Worth a quick look is the adjacent **Dreifaltigkeitskirche**, the church of the old Augustinian monastery: it was frescoed during the time of the Council with scenes from the history of the order, plus portraits of various personalities, among them Emperor Sigismund. Returning to Marktstätte, Kanzleistrasse leads west past the Renaissance **Rathaus**, whose facade was jollied up by the addition of Romantic murals. At the end of the street is **Obermarkt**, which is lined with more colourful mansions; here, in 1417, the Hohenzollerns were invested with control over the March of Brandenburg, a crucial step in their drive, achieved four and a half centuries later, to unite the German nation under their control.

Hussenstrasse leads south from here to the **Schnetztor**, a fourteenth-century fortified gateway complete with outer courtyard. On the way you pass, at no. 64, the **Hus-Museum** (June–Sept Tues–Sat 10am–5pm, Sun 10am–noon; Oct–May Tues–Sat 10am–noon & 2–4, Sun 10am–noon; DM2). This half-timbered house, where the reformer stayed on his arrival in Konstanz, was bought by the Prague Museum Society in 1923 to turn it into a memorial to one of Czechoslovakia's most important national heroes. Apart from his importance as a religious thinker, Hus had a major influence on the Czech sense of nationhood and almost single-handedly established his country's national literature.

Practicalities

The DB **Bahnhof**, the terminus of the line from the Black Forest, is right beside the Konzilgebäude; immediately south is its Swiss counterpart, which is the departure point for most **bus** services beyond the urban area. In front of the former, at Konzilstr. 5, is the **tourist office** (Mon–Fri 8am–8pm, Sat 9.30am–1.30pm & 4–7pm, Sun 10am–1pm; ☎07531/284376). For information on **boat trips**, see the box on p.248. Note that the car ferry to Meersburg is in the suburb of STAAD; all other services leave from the harbour behind the Bahnhof.

Accommodation
The **youth hostel** is at Zur Allmannshöhe 18 (☎07531/32260; bus #4 from the Bahnhof to *Jugendherberge*, or bus #1 to *Post Allmannsdorf*). There's a **campsite** near the car ferry at Am Wasserwerk (☎07531/31388), and a couple more further north in the incorporated fishing village of DINGELSDORF: *Klausehorn* (☎07533/6372) and *Fliesshorn* (☎07533/5262); all three can be reached by bus #4. The latter suburb also has a couple of lakeside **hotels**, which are competitively priced at around DM30–35 per person: *Gasthaus Seeschau*, Zur Schiffslände 11 (☎07533/5190) and *Gasthaus Anker*, Zur Schiffslände 5 (☎07533/6220). Many of their more central counterparts are in historic buildings and hence somewhat more expensive than usual, though arguably worth it for the atmosphere. By far the cheapest option in the Altstadt is *Blauer Bock*, Husenstr. 36 (☎07531/22741), charging from DM30 per person. However, lower rates can be had in the many **private rooms** available all over town: the tourist office has a complete list and will make bookings.

Food, drink and festivals

Among places to **eat** and **drink**, the *Konzilgebäude* deserves a special mention for both quality and setting. Other choices are the historic (if pricey) wine bars, *Spitalkellerei*, Brückengasse 16, and *St Stephanskeller*, St-Stephans-Platz 43; and *Bürgerstuben*, Bahnhofplatz 7, which features Bodensee fish specialities. The local *Ruppaner* **beers** are good, especially the *Edel-Pils*. Main annual **festival** is the *Seenachtsfest* in August, with a spectacular display of fireworks over the Bodensee. Classical music concerts , the *Konstanzer Internationale Musiktage*, are held throughout the summer.

The Bodensee islands

There are only two islands of any size in the Bodensee, and, notwithstanding the fact that both put their rich soils to good use, they could hardly be more different: **Mainau** is an exotic, scented floral isle which seems to have been wafted up from the Mediterranean, while **Reichenau**, which is mostly given over to the cultivation of fruit and vegetables now, retains its three ancient monasteries as vivid reminders of its status as one of the cradles of German civilisation. Ironically enough, the easiest way to reach either of the islands is by bus (causeways having been constructed to link them to the mainland), though it's obviously far more atmospheric to arrive by boat.

Mainau

Just 45 hectares in area, **Mainau** (Easter–mid-Oct daily 6am–7pm; DM10, DM3 kids; rest of year daily 9am–5pm; DM5, kids free), which lies in the Überlinger See, nonetheless possesses an aura of immense grandeur, thanks to the riotous colours of the flowers and shrubs which bedeck it, and the exhilarating long-distance views over the lake across to the opposite shore, which are particularly spectacular at sunset. It's like a little tropical paradise – or it would be were it not for the relentless presence of thousands of visitors every day for at least six months of the year. With this in mind, try to come as early as possible: the crowds start to build up by mid-morning. Local bus #4 from the centre of Konstanz stops at the end of the causeway at the western approach to Mainau; ferries between Meersburg and Unteruhldingen call at the landing stage at the opposite side of the island.

For over 500 years Mainau belonged to the Teutonic Knights, and the **Schloss** at the highest point of the island is a typical example of the Baroque architecture they favoured during the time they were based in Bad Mergentheim. It's now the residence of the island's flamboyant Swedish owner, Count Bernadotte, a descendant of the Grand Dukes of Baden who took possession of Mainau last century. Only the chapel, with its frothy ceiling paintings and elaborate woodwork, can be visited, though that hardly seems to matter as the carefully manicured gardens, which occupy almost every available part of the island, are what everyone comes to see.

The gardens

A combination of the freak micro-climate and the utilisation of scientific techniques means that at least part of the garden is in bloom for half of the year; a unique feature is the presence of three-dimensional **floral sculptures**, which were specially created as diversions for the youngest visitors. **Spring** is the most delightful season here, with a big display of orchids in the Palmenhaus, along with an array of tulips, hyacinths, narcissuses and primroses outside; later azaleas and rhododendrons appear. **Summer** sees the rose walk at its best, while palm trees, bananas, lemons and oranges also ripen then. **Autumn** features a dahlia show, whereafter the colour disappears, leaving only the year-round greenery of the cedars, sequoias and cypresses until the cycle starts again.

As well as various snack bars, there are a couple of places where you can have a full **meal**: the *Comturey-Keller*, which has special lunchtime menus, and the classy *Schwedenschenke* uphill by the Schloss. Note that, although you can stay on until late in the evening, you have to be off the island by midnight.

Reichenau

Reichenau, set in the Untersee 8km west of Konstanz, has a history almost as venerable as the city itself. Monastic life was established here in 724, and three monasteries, which all survive, were in place by the end of the ninth century. Many of the early abbots also held high positions in the Holy Roman Empire, and the island was a famous centre of scholarship, literature and painting, with the two arts combined in the great local speciality of manuscript illumination: products of the Reichenau school are among the most prized possessions of some of the world's great libraries. However, by the twelfth century the monasteries were already in decline from their early peak of having well over a hundred monks, and there was no more than a token monastic presence for several hundred years before the dissolution in 1803. Nowadays, two-thirds of the island's area is devoted to market gardens, giving it a character not dissimilar to the tulip-growing regions of Holland. Very quiet and sedate, it's a popular holiday resort with pensioners and families, who rent apartments around its coast.

The monasteries

Just 4.5km long and 1.5km wide, the layout of Reichenau is easy to grasp. There are three villages, each centred on a monastery, which in no way disrupts its isolated setting.

First up is OBERZELL, with the church of **St Georg**, the only one of the trio not completely reconstructed at a later date. The dignified Romanesque entrance hall was the sole significant addition made to the original, one of the most complete examples of Carolingian architecture to have survived anywhere in Europe. Inside is a wonderful set of Ottonian **frescos**, which are about a century younger than the building and show the same style as the famed Reichenau miniatures, albeit on a monumental scale. The eight main scenes, whose colours have been vividly brought out in a recent restoration, illustrate the miracles of Christ – subjects which were mostly eschewed by later artists.

Just over a kilometre further on is MITTELZELL, whose large **Münster** is the mother-church of Reichenau. Its present form, apart from the Gothic chancel, dates from the very beginning of the eleventh century. By this time Reichenau had been ousted from German artistic leadership by Hildesheim, where the contemporary work was far more refined and developed than the design chosen here, which is reminiscent of an early Christian basilica. Nonetheless, it's an impressive sight, particularly when viewed from across the garden on its northern side. The **Schatzkammer** (May–Sept daily 11am–noon & 3–4pm; DM1) on the northern side of the chancel contains a carved fifth-century ivory pyx and a poignant Romanesque *Crucifix* from St Georg, along with the usual array of reliquaries.

Towards the far end of the island is NIEDERZELL, with the twin-towered twelfth-century Romanesque church of **SS Peter und Paul**. This is the least distinctive of the three and is further marred by a fair amount of frivolous Baroque interior decoration, but a fresco of *The Last Judgment*, the final expression of the Reichenau school of painting, can be seen in the apse.

Practicalities

Reichenau's **tourist office** (May–Sept Mon–Fri 8.30am–noon & 2–6pm, Sat 9am–noon; March, April & Oct Mon–Fri 8.30am–noon & 2–5pm; Nov–Feb Mon–Fri 9am–noon; ☎07534/276) is at Ergat 5 in Mittelzell. There's a **campsite** (☎07534/7384) on the shore in Niederzell, plus a score of **private houses** with rooms to let. Cheapest **hotel**, charging from DM30 per person, is *Kaiserpfalz*, Abt-Berno-Str. 1 (☎07534/275), in Mittelzell. If you want to treat yourself, the *Romantik-Hotel Seeschau*, An der Schiffslände 8 (☎07534/257), overlooking the harbour in Mittelzell, costs from DM70 per person, and has one of the best restaurants in the Bodensee area. Nearby, at Untere Rheinstr. 21, is *Reichenauer Salatstuben*, offering a huge self-service cold buffet.

Ferries between Konstanz and the Swiss city of Schaffhausen call at Reichenau. Otherwise, regular DB buses leave from outside the Bahnhof in Konstanz; less conveniently, there's also a stop near the island on the main railway line to the Black Forest. Between the two is the **Wollmatinger Ried**, a protected landscape of reedy marsh, islets and flowery meadows inhabited by a rich variety of birdlife which is recognised as being of exceptional importance. An **information centre** (April–Oct Mon–Fri 9am–noon & 2–5pm, Sat & Sun 10am–5pm; ☎07531/78870) has been set up in the Reichenau Bahnhof; **guided visits** (the only permitted method of entry) are usually made daily, except on Sundays and Mondays, throughout this period.

THE BLACK FOREST REGION

Even in a country where woodland is so widespread as to exert a grip over such varied aspects of national life as folklore, literature and leisure activities, the **Black Forest** or *Schwarzwald* stands out as a place with its own special mystique. Stretching 170km north to south, and up to 60km east to west, it's by far the largest German forest – and the most beautiful. Geographically speaking, it's a massif in its own right, but forms a pair with the broadly similar French Vosges on the opposite side of the Rhine valley, which demarcates the borders with both France and Switzerland. The name of the forest comes from the dark, densely packed fir trees on the upper slopes; oaks and beeches are characteristic of the lower ranges. With its houses sheltering beneath massive sloping straw roofs, its cuckoo clocks and its colourful, often outrageous trad dress, the Black Forest ranks second only to Bavaria as the font of stereotyped images of the country.

Even as late as the 1920s, much of this area was a rarely penetrated wilderness sunk in an eerie gloom, forming a refuge for everything from boars to bandits. Romantics were drawn here by the wild beauty of watery gorges, dank valleys and exhilarating mountain views. Nowadays, most of the villages have been opened up as spa and health resorts, full of shops selling tacky souvenirs, while the old trails have become manicured gravel paths smoothed down for pensioners and prams. Yet, for all that – and in spite of fears about the potentially disastrous effects of *Waldsterben*, which may have affected as many as half the trees – it remains a landscape of unique character, and by no means all the modernisations are drawbacks. **Accommodation** for example, is plentiful and generally excellent value. **Railway** fans will find several of the most spectacular lines in Europe, some of them brilliant feats of engineering. Note, though, that the trains tend to stick closely to the valleys, that **bus services** are much reduced outside the tourist season, and that **walking** is undoubtedly the most satisfying way to travel.

Most of the Black Forest is associated with the Margraviate (later Grand Duchy) of **Baden**, whose old capital of **Baden-Baden** – once the ultimate playground of the mega-rich – is at the northern fringe of the forest, in a fertile orchard and vineyard-growing area. This was later usurped by custom-built **Karlsruhe**, which is technically outside the Black Forest but best visited in conjunction with it. The only city actually surrounded by the forest is **Freiburg im Breisgau**, one of the most distinctive and enticing in the country.

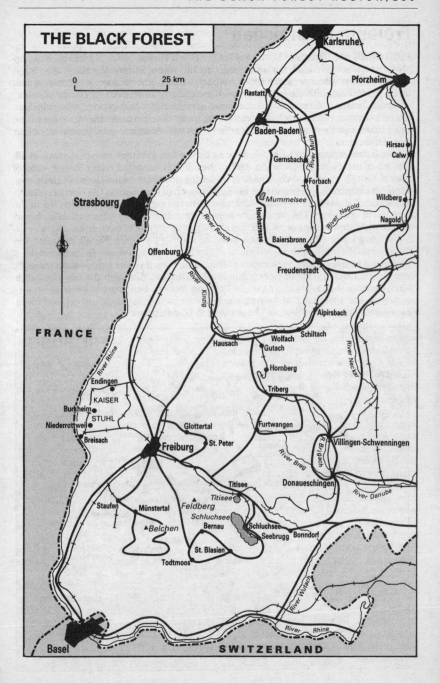

THE BLACK FOREST

0   25 km

Karlsruhe

Pforzheim

Rastatt

Baden-Baden

Hirsau
Calw

Gernsbach

Forbach

Mummelsee

Wildberg

Strasbourg

Hochstrasse

Nagold

Baiersbronn

River Rench

Offenburg

Freudenstadt

River Kinzig

River Murg

River Nagold

FRANCE

Alpirsbach

Schiltach

Wolfach

Hausach

Gutach

Hornberg

River Neckar

River Rhine

Triberg

Endingen

KAISER

Burkheim

STUHL

Niederrottweil

Furtwangen

Glottertal

Breisach

St. Peter

Freiburg

R. Brigach

Villingen-Schwenningen

River Breg

Titisee

Donaueschingen

Titisee

River Danube

Staufen

Münstertal

Feldberg

Schluchsee

Schluchsee

Bernau

Bonndorf

▲*Belchen*

Seebrugg

St. Blasien

Todtmoos

River Wutach

River Rhine

Basel

SWITZERLAND

Freiburg im Breisgau

FREIBURG IM BREISGAU, "capital" of the Black Forest, basks in a laid-back atmosphere which seems completely un-German. As the seat of a university since 1457, it has an animated, youthful presence which, unlike so many other academic centres, is kept up all year round, with the help of a varied programme of festivals. It's a city of music, of street theatre and buskers – and a haunt of colourfully clad gypsies, who find here the one German city in which they can feel at home. Furthermore, the sun shines here more often, and there are more vineyards within the municipal area, than in any other city in the country.

The locals explain Freiburg's singularity by the fact that they aren't Germans at all, but Austrians. Between 1368 and 1805, when it was allocated to the buffer state of Baden, the city was almost continuously under the protection of the House of Habsburg. It's often claimed that the Austrians brought a touch of humanity to the German character, and that it was their eventual exclusion from the country's affairs which led to the triumph of militarism. The persistence here of the relaxed multicultural climate characteristic of Austria is living proof that there's more than a grain of truth in this cliché.

Freiburg makes the most obvious base for visiting the Black Forest, with fast and frequent public transport connections to all the famous beauty spots. In its own right, it warrants a couple of days' exploration at least, and, even if you're only passing through, you should make a point of visiting the lovely **Münster**. Although the city was extensively destroyed in a single air raid in 1944, no modern building has been allowed to challenge the supremacy of its magisterial tower, which the doyen of art historians, Jacob Burckhardt, described as "the greatest in Christendom".

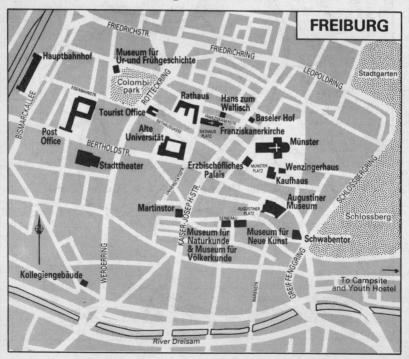

> The telephone code for Freiburg is ☎0761

Arrival and practicalities

The **Hauptbahnhof**, which has the **bus station** on its southern side, is about ten minutes' walk from the city centre. Following Eisenbahnstrasse straight ahead, you come to the **tourist office** at Rotteckring 14 (May–Oct Mon–Sat 9am–9.30pm, Sun & holidays 10am–noon; Nov–April Mon–Fri 9am–6pm, Sat 9am–3pm, Sun 10am–noon; ☎368 9090).

For DM3, the tourist office will find you a room; if you arrive after closing time, there's an electronic noticeboard equipped with a phone telling you which places have vacancies, though this is not an exhaustive service. Among **hotels** with a central location, the cheapest is *Schemmer*, Eschholzstr. 63 (☎272424), with singles upwards of DM34, doubles at DM60. Comparable options further out include *Pension Gisela*, Am Vogelbach 27 (☎82472), and *Hirschen*, Breisgauer Str. 47 (☎82118), at DM30 per person; *Löwen*, Breisgauer Str. 62 (☎84661), and *Gihring*, Eggstr. 10 (☎74963), both with singles DM35, doubles DM60. Among a clutch of pensions to the south of the city, halfway towards Schauinsland, are *Dionysos*, Hirschstr. 2 (☎29353), with singles DM34, doubles DM60; and the Yorkshire-run *Zum Kybfelsen*, Schauinslandstr, 49 (☎29440), with a single at DM50, doubles DM80. Prices start at around DM20 in **private houses**, but a stay of at least three nights may be required.

The luxurious **youth hostel** is at Karthäuserstr. 151 (☎67656; take tram #1 to Hasemannstrasse) at the extreme eastern end of the city, ideally placed for walks in the hills or along the banks of the River Dreisam. Nearby, but slightly nearer town, is one of five **campsites**, *Hirzberg* (April–mid-Oct; ☎35054); while *Möselpark* (mid-March–Oct; ☎72938) is south of the houses on the opposite side of the river. Southwest of the centre, and open all year, is *St Georg*, Basler Landstr. 62 (☎43183). Cheapest place to camp is the all-year *Breisgau* (☎07665 2346), way to the north in the village of HOCHDORF; also here is the huge *Tunisee* site (April–Oct; ☎07665 2249/1249).

If you're staying far out, it makes sense to invest in a **rover ticket** on the public transport system. Prices are DM6 for 24 hours, DM8 for 48 hours and DM11 for 72 hours; single journeys are DM2.50, or DM10 for strips of five.

The Münster and Münsterplatz

Crafted out of a dark red sandstone quarried in one of the surrounding hills, the **Münster** (or **Dom**) is so magnificent and overpowering that it puts the rest of the city in the shade. Not the least remarkable fact about it is that, though it rivals any of the great European cathedrals, it was built as a mere parish church. No funds from the well-lined coffers of the ecclesiastical top brass were forthcoming for its construction – the costs were met entirely from the pockets of local citizens, to whom it was the ultimate symbol of municipal pride. In 1827, on the suppression of the Prince-bishopric of Konstanz, the Münster's artistic standing was given due recognition when it became the seat of the Upper Rhenish archbishopric.

The exterior

Work on the Münster began in about 1200, to replace a much simpler church dating from the time of the town's foundation eighty years before. The **transepts** were built first, in the picturesque late Romanesque style then still popular in Germany. However, there was an abrupt change when the masons became aware of the structural advantages of Gothic, which the French had already mastered. At first, the same masons began building in this unfamiliar idiom; later, one of the architects of Strasbourg

Cathedral took over. He created a masterly **nave**, resplendent with flying buttresses, gargoyles and statues, yet already diverging from French models in its spatial unity.

Further originality is evident in the west **porch**, begun around 1270. Part of both the interior and exterior (it's fenced off these days, but you can enter it from inside), it had to accommodate the same sculptural programme that the French were able to spread all over the facade and transept. The figures, which still bear traces of colouring, are much the most important German works of their time. A sweetly carved *Madonna and Child* guards the door; above, the tympanum illustrates the entire New Testament. On the end walls, the Wise and Foolish Virgins confront each other, while deliberately shrouded on the west wall (at the point where the natural light is weakest) are the most striking figures: Satan as Prince of Darkness, beguilingly disguised as a youthful knight, and Sensuality, who has toads and serpents writhing on her back.

The single **tower** (March–Nov Mon–Sat 9.30am–5pm, Sun 1–5pm; DM1.50) above the porch was a unique design for its time, but was subsequently much imitated, most notably at Ulm. Though it seems to be an organic unity, it wasn't planned as a whole. The square plan of the lower storeys supports a soaring octagon, bearing animated statues of prophets and angels, which forms the stage above the bells. From the platform, you're rewarded with a fine panorama over the city and the Black Forest. However, the best view is of the lace-like tracery of the **openwork spire**, which rounds off the tower with a bravura flourish. The first of its kind, it was inspired by the mysticism of the time and symbolises the human soul stretching out to receive divine knowledge. Many similar spires were planned for subsequent German churches, though most remained unbuilt until the nineteenth century. Exceptions are the two miniature versions which were immediately placed on Freiburg's own **Hahnentürme** (Cock Towers).

For the **chancel**, begun in the mid-fourteenth century (about 25 years after the completion of the spire), the authorities again struck it lucky with their choice of architect, a man named Johannes of the famous Parler dynasty. His regular geometric layout marked a major advance on French models, and his two **portals**, particularly the northern one dedicated to the Creation, are adorned with superbly expressive sculptures – look out for the unusual depiction of God resting on the seventh day.

The interior

Inside, the transept is lit by luminous **stained glass** windows of the early thirteenth century. Most of those in the nave date from a hundred years later and were donated by the local trades and guilds, who incorporated their coats of arms. Other items to look out for are a delicate late thirteenth-century *Madonna* on the west wall, a poignant fourteenth-century *Holy Sepulchre* in the south aisle, and the pulpit, an archaic Gothic work of the mid-sixteenth century with depictions of Freiburg personalities of the day. At the entrance to the chancel is a fine *Adoration of the Magi* by the leading local woodcarver of the late Gothic period, Hans Wydyz. This artist sometimes collaborated with the mercurial **Hans Baldung**, Dürer's most talented follower, whose high altar triptych of *The Coronation of the Virgin* – arguably his masterpiece – can be glimpsed from this point.

To see the chancel, and to get a better view of the Baldung triptych including a look at the nocturnal *Crucifixion* on its reverse side, you have to take a **guided tour** (daily departure times posted at the south transept entrance; DM1.50). In the Universitätskapelle, there are two wings of a curious **Holbein** retable. The portraits of the donor family are by Hans the Elder, but the main scenes of *The Nativity* and *Epiphany* are youthful works by his son, whose superior gifts are already in evidence. A *Rest on the Flight into Egypt* in the Kaiserkapelle has sculptures by Wydyz and a painted background by Baldung, who also designed many of the stained glass windows in the chapels, though some of these have been replaced by copies. Hans Sixt von Staufen, another talented local sculptor of the time, carved the *Madonna of Mercy* in the Locherer Kapelle. In the Villinger Kapelle is a rare relic of the first Münster, a silver *Crucifix*.

Münsterplatz

Until the war, the spacious **Münsterplatz** formed a fitting setting for the great church in its midst. However, the north side was flattened by bombs (which miraculously hardly touched the Münster itself) and only the late fifteenth-century **Kornhaus**, the municipal granary, has been rebuilt. The rest of the square has survived in much better shape; the daily market is one of the most enticing in the country, with a mouth-watering selection of goodies on offer to make up a picnic. There are also a couple of pretty **fountains** directly in front of the Münster – the *Georgsbrunnen* and the *Fischbrunnen* – along with three tall columns that bear statues of the local patron saints.

The south side of the square is dominated by the blood-red **Kaufhaus**, a sixteenth-century merchants' hall; its arcaded facade bears four statues by Sixt von Staufen of members of the House of Habsburg. On either side of the Kaufhaus are handsome Baroque palaces – to the west is the **Erzbischöfliches Palais** while the **Wenzingerhaus** stands to the east. The latter was named after the artist Christian Wenzinger who built it as his own residence; an elaborate font designed by him can be seen in the Münster's Stürzelkapelle. Plans are afoot to convert the interior into a museum; this will be well worth visiting, if only to see the resplendent Rococo staircase, complete with frescoed ceiling. The square is closed on the far side by another Baroque building, the former **Hauptwache** (Guard House), and by the canons' residences.

Around the city

A peculiarity of Freiburg is the continuous visible presence throughout the old part of the city of its **sewage system**, known as the *Bächle*. These are rivulets, fed by the River Dreisam, which run in deep gulleys, serving as a trap for the unwary pedestrian or motorist. Formerly used for watering animals and as a sure precaution against the fire hazard which accounted for so many medieval towns, they have their purpose even today, helping to keep the city cool.

South of Münsterplatz

Following the main channel of the *Bächle* southwards, you come to the **Schwaben Tor**, one of two surviving towers of the medieval fortifications. On Oberlinden, just in front, is **Zum Roten Bären** which is said to be Germany's oldest inn – a function it has held since 1311, although the building itself is two centuries older. The parallel **Konviktstrasse** has won conservation prizes for the restoration of its old houses.

Just to the west is Salzstrasse, which is lined with Baroque and Neoclassical mansions. Also here is the **Augustiner Museum** (Tues–Fri 9.30am–5pm, Sat & Sun 10.30am–5pm; free), which takes its name from the former monastery whose buildings it occupies. One of the most pleasing smaller collections in Germany, it makes an essential supplement to a visit to the Münster, containing as it does many works of art, such as gargoyles, statues and stained glass which have been replaced *in situ* by copies to prevent further erosion. Also on show are examples of the religious art of the Upper Rhine, along with folklore displays on the Black Forest. There are also a few top class old masters. Three panels of a *Passion Altar*, including the central *Crucifixion*, constitute the most important surviving paintings by the great but mysterious draughtsman known as **Master of the Housebook**. *The Miracle of the Snow* by **Grünewald** is one of the wings of the altarpiece now in Stuppach: it depicts Pope Liberius laying the foundation-stone of Santa Maria Maggiore in Rome, following a miraculous fall of snow on Midsummer's Day. As well as his stained glass, **Baldung** is represented by three typically unorthodox paintings, notably a *Cupid in Flight*, while there's a brightly coloured *Risen Christ* by **Cranach**.

South of here, on Marienstrasse, is the **Museum für Neue Kunst** (same times; free). Though it can't rival the richness of the parent collection, it does have a good cross-section of twentieth-century German painting. Beside it stands the Baroque **Adelhauserkirche**, retaining important works of art from its predecessor, notably a fourteenth-century *Crucifix*. The former convent buildings now house the **Museum für Naturkunde**, which has a dazzling display of gems, and the **Museum für Völkerkunde,** with exhibits drawn from all non-European cultures (both same times as the other museums; free). From here, follow Fischerau, the former fishermen's street, and you come to the other surviving thirteenth-century tower, the **Martinstor**, which now stands in the middle of Freiburg's central axis, Kaiser-Joseph-Strasse.

The western quarters

Immediately west of here is the **University quarter**, the liveliest part of the city during term-time and the best place to check out Frieburg's nightlife. Alongside the inevitable modern buildings are several interesting older structures, including two Rococo mansions and a large Jugendstil lecture hall. On Bertoldstrasse, to the north, are the Universitätskirche, formerly a Jesuit college, and the Baroque Alte Universität.

The **Neues Rathaus**, formed out of two separate Renaissance houses, one of which has an oriel adorned with a noble relief of *The Lady and the Unicorn*, was an earlier home of the University. It forms part of a shady chestnut tree-lined square, whose other buildings include the **Altes Rathaus**, itself a fusion of several older buildings, and the plain Gothic Franciscan monastery church of **St Martin**. A few minutes' walk to the west, in the Columbipark opposite the tourist office, is the **Columbischlössle**, a nineteenth-century villa built for a Spanish countess, which served after the war as parliament for the short-lived Land of Südbaden. It now houses the **Museum für Ur- und Frühgeschichte** (daily 9am–7pm; free), which has important archaeological collections on the Black Forest region, particularly from the times of the Alemanni and the Franks; the treasury items in the basement are particularly worth catching.

In the alley behind St Martin is the cheerful late Gothic facade of the **Haus Zum Wallfisch**. For two years, this was the home of the great humanist **Desiderius Erasmus**, the most conciliatory and sympathetic of the leading figures of the Reformation period, who was forced to flee from his residence in Basel in the light of the turbulent religious struggles there. A late fifteenth-century palace nearby, on the main Kaiser-Joseph-Strasse, is known as the **Baseler Hof** as it served for nearly a century as the residence of the exiled cathedral chapter of the Swiss city.

Outside the centre

It's well worth climbing one of the hills surrounding the city for the sake of the wonderful views they offer. The **Schlossberg** immediately to the east of the city centre makes for an easy ascent by a path from the Schwabentor; there's no need to take the cable car. This summit also has the benefit of including close range views of the Münster. For photography, it's best to come in the morning. To the south, the **Lorettoburg** (where the stone for the Münster was quarried) makes a good afternoon or evening alternative. Far higher, and thus with more spectacular panoramas than either of these, is the **Schauinsland** (1284m), still within the city boundaries but a good 15km southeast, reached by tram #2 or #4 to Günterstal, then bus #21. A series of marked nature trails comb the area, which is still inhabited by chamois, or you can ascend by a 15 minute cable car ride.

Eating, drinking and nightlife

Freiburg is a superb place for food and drink, with **restaurants** and **bars** to cater for all tastes and pockets, the liveliest concentration, as you'd expect, clustered around the University quarter. The city has a similarly eclectic choice of other entertainments.

Restaurants

Greiffenegg-Schlössle, Schlossbergring 3. First choice for *al fresco* eating, with a terrace commanding a superb view over Freiburg and the Kaiserstuhl.

Grosser Meyerhof, Grünwälderstrasse 7. Top quality south German fare at eminently reasonable prices.

Kleiner Meyerhof, Rathausgasse 27. Smaller, more select and more expensive version of the above.

Markgräfler Hof, Gerberau 22. One for a splurge, particularly if you want to sample its astonishing wine list.

Milano, Schusterstr. 7. Bargain-priced trattoria.

Oberkirchs Weinstuben, Münsterplatz 22. Top-notch wine cellar with superb and not overly expensive food.

Ratskeller, Münsterplatz 11. Another excellent wine cellar, and better value than most of its counterparts.

Tessiner Stuben, Bertoldstr. 17. Vegetarian restaurant-cum-wine bar, complete with garden.

Wolfshöhle, Konviktstr. 8. One of the best Italian restaurants in the country.

Zum Roten Bären, Oberlinden 12. Germany's oldest inn is renowned for its food; very pricey, but worth the money.

Zur Traube, Schusterstr. 17. A quieter alternative to the wine bars on nearby Münsterplatz.

Bars and cafés

Café Atlantik, Schwabentorring. Run-down music pub serving very cheap food in the evenings.

Café Journal, Universitätstr. 3. Popular if fairly expensive student hangout, which is more of a disco-bar.

Café Windlicht, Filcherau. Drinks here are good value, and can be consumed at tables set out on the cobbled street outside

Dampfross, Löwenstr. 7. Another student favourite, serving inexpensive meals.

Hausbrauerei Feierling, Gerberau. In addition to the fruity *Inselhopf* beer brewed on the premises, imaginative meals are also served.

Uni-Café, Universitätsecke. The trendiest place with the Freiburg in-crowd; serves a wide selection of coffees and has good snacks.

Music and theatre

Freiburg now ranks as one of the leading German cities for **jazz**, thanks to the new *Jazzhaus* on Schwenlinstrasse which has concerts every evening at 8.30pm. The list of those who have appeared here already includes many of the world's leading artistes. **Classical music** can be heard in a variety of locations: orchestral concerts at the *Stadthalle* on Messplatz, chamber and instrumental recitals in the *Paulussaal* on Dreisamstrasse, the *Kaufhaus* on Münsterplatz, and the *Musikhochschule* on Schwarzwaldstrasse. All types of music are performed at the University's *Audimax*. At the moment the "in" **disco** is *Unverschämt* on Humboldstrasse.

Main **theatre** venue is the *Freiburger Theater* on Bertoldstrasse, which has three auditoria plus the *Theatercafé* where late-night cabaret and variety shows are held. The intimate *Wallgrabentheater* on Rathausgasse specialises in modern plays. Pick of the **cinemas** are *Cinemathek* on Bertoldstrasse and *Kommunales Kino*, Alter Wiehrebahnhof.

Listings

Bike hire *Radhaus*, Habsburgerstr. 128 (☎280832); *Zweirad Müller*, Klarastr. 80 (☎278320).

Car hire *InterRent*, Wilhelmstr. 1a (☎31066/7).

Consulate *British*, Buchenstr. 4 (☎583117).

Festivals The *Fastnet* celebrations are among the best in Baden-Württemberg; there are burning ceremonies on the evening of Shrove Tuesday, as well as parades of jesters the day before. Both the *Frühlingsfest* in May and the *Herbstsfest* in October last for ten days, and include spectacular fairground amusements. In June, the two-week *Internationales Zeltmusikfest* features all varieties of music, performed under canvas. Later in the month, five days are given over to a wine market known as the *Weintagen*. Mid-August has the nine days'-long *Weinkost*, a sampling session for wines produced in the Freiburg region.

Medical emergencies (☎85085)

Mitfahrzentrale Belfortstr. 55 (☎36749).

East of Freiburg

Some 20km east of Freiburg, and connected by regular bus services, is **ST PETER**, a tiny health resort clustering round a Benedictine **Kloster**. This was founded in the eleventh century, but the present complex belongs to a rebuilding begun in 1724. Peter Thumb built the striking twin-towered church, a classically-inspired Baroque design of unusual width and spaciousness. On the pillars are statues of members of the House of Zähringen by Josef Anton Feuchtmayer, in commemoration of the fact that this monastery was, like the city of Freiburg and the state of Baden, one of their foundations. The monastic buildings, now used as a seminary, are Rococo in style, dating from a generation later. Particularly eye-catching is the galleried **library**, gleaming with white stuccowork and frescos. Colourful costumed **festivals** are held in the village on Corpus Christi and on the Sunday after the feast day of Saints Peter and Paul (29 June).

A few kilometres northwest is **GLOTTERTAL**, reached via the gentle wine-growing valley of the same name. This has gained national fame as a result of the hospital perched above the village which forms the setting for the soap opera *Black Forest Clinic*, Germany's answer to *Coronation Street* and *Dallas*.

Breisach and the Kaiserstuhl

BREISACH, perched high above the Rhine on a promontory about 30km west of Freiburg, is an archteypal frontier post in what has been one of the most heavily-disputed parts of Europe. Even if the river is now firmly established as a natural border and the town regarded as being indisputably German, the turbulent legacy of its past is still clearly visible.

The ramparts

As has been the case since at least the early thirteenth century, the upper town is surrounded by **ramparts**. The ones visible today bear the unmistakable stamp of the greatest of all military engineers, the Frenchman Sébastien Vauban, who was also responsible for laying out the town of NEUF BREISACH on the opposite bank. Indeed, the monumental **Rheintor** at the northwest end of Breisach itself is as purely French a building as can be seen in Germany. Yet, just above it, the gabled medieval **Kapftor** could hardly be more German in feel, and the same applies to the earlier **Hagenbachtor** on the brow of the hill further south. Just beyond this is one of Breisach's many belvederes, offering grandstand views of France.

The Münster

Looming high above all else in the spacious, half-deserted upper part of town is the **Münster**. From outside, it's no beauty, fashioned out of rough, diffuse stonework, and truncated on the southern side in order to squeeze into an irregular, constricted space.

It was originally built in the late Romanesque period on the foundations of a Roman fortress; the nave, transept and the two "Cock" towers survive from this time. The upper parts of the southern tower were re-fashioned in Gothic style in the early fourteenth century, a period which also saw the construction of a new chancel (under which is an open crypt – apparently the only one of its kind in the world) and the stumpy facade, whose tympanum illustrates the life of the Münster's patron, Saint Stephen. At the end of the fifteenth century, it was decided to commission new decorations for the interior of the Münster rather than rebuild it; as a result, it came to acquire one of the most impressive arrays of **works of art** of any church in Germany, all created at the transitional point between Gothic and Renaissance.

Filling the three walls of the west end is a huge **fresco cycle** of *The Last Judgment* by **Martin Schongauer**, the father-figure of the golden age of German art. Sadly, it's in a very faded condition, but enough remains to suggest that it must have been nearly as remarkable as Michelangelo's famous depiction of the same subject in the Sistine Chapel. Contemporary with the frescos is the filigree **rood screen**. In the chapel beside it is a silver **shrine** containing the relics of the early martyr-Saints Gervase and Protase, which were swiped from Milan at the same time as those of the Three Magi (which were taken to Cologne), and allegedly arrived in Breisach by miraculous means, whereupon they became the joint patrons of the town. The reliefs on the lid include an illustration of this journey, complete with a depiction of fifteenth-century Breisach.

Saints Gervase and Protase turn up again on the right wing of the main **retable**, while on the opposite side of the central *Coronation of the Virgin* are the martyred deacons, Saints Stephen and Lawrence. This altarpiece is an astonishing piece of wholly eccentric yet hyper-skilled woodcarving. It may be late Gothic, but the entwined mass of cherubs, the swirling hair and drapery folds of the figures are uncannily anticipatory of the Baroque style of over a century later. Many attempts have been made to unmask the identity of the mysterious sculptor, known as **Master HL** after his cryptic signature, but to no conclusive effect. The sinuous upper part of the retable is by a more orthodox carver, but is still remarkable for the fact that it's actually higher than the ceiling, a trick achieved by means of a subtle slant.

Practicalities

Breisach's **Bahnhof** is at the southern end of town; from there follow Neutorplatz and Rheinstrasse and you come to Werd, where you'll find the **tourist office** (Mon–Fri 8.30am–12.30pm & 1.30–5.30pm, Sat 8.30am–noon; ☎07667/83227). Ask there about **Rhine cruises** and visits to **wine cellars** – the town is the headquarters of the largest winery in Europe, the *Zentralkellerei Badischer Winzergenossenschaften* (☎07667/82270). **Cafés** and **restaurants** are scattered all over the lower town, but are almost entirely absent in the upper part. The spanking new **youth hostel** is by the river at Rheinuferstr.

INTO FRANCE

Some 25km west of Breisach, and served by five buses per day, is the beautiful old Alsatian city of **COLMAR**. French since 1918, Colmar was German for much of its history, a fact abundantly clear from its general appearance, and from the fact that most inhabitants are bilingual. It was the home town of medieval artist Martin Schongauer, and a good deal of his work can be seen there; it also possesses Grünewald's titanic *Isenheim Altar*, generally regarded as the supreme masterpiece of German painting. A short train journey to the north is cosmopolitan **STRASBOURG**, specially chosen as home of the European Parliament in honour of its mixed Franco-German history. It was a free city of the Holy Roman Empire for three centuries and its magnificent Cathedral is mostly the work of German masons. For more details on these cities, see our guide to *France*.

12 (☎07667/7665). Cheapest **hotel**, at DM30 per person, is *Kaiserstühler Hof*, Richard-Müller-Str. 2 (☎07667/236). Alternatively, there's a **campsite**, *Münsterblick* (☎07667/285), in the village of HOCHSTETTEN 2km south.

The Kaiserstuhl

Breisach stands in the shadow of the **Kaiserstuhl**, an isolated volcanic mass which appears much higher than its 559 metres because of the flat landscape all around. Its name, meaning "Emperor's Seat", is tenuously associated with a legend similar to that of King Arthur and the Knights of the Round Table: it's said that Emperor Frederick Barabarossa, who died on his way to the Holy Land to fight the Infidel, is resting in this mountain, waiting for his second coming. Until recently, the Kaiserstuhl was a haunt of nature lovers, who came to admire its luxuriant orchids and butterflies. However, the 1970s saw a stepping-up of its status as a **wine** area, with the plantation of vineyards arranged in neat, regular terraces; this went so far that there have been worries that the ecological balance has been irretrievably spoiled. Whatever the case, the volcanic soils impart a sharp, distinctive taste to the local white wines, notably *Silvaner*, *Riesling*, *Gewürtstraminer* and *Ruländer*; there's also a much-praised rosé, *Weissherbst*.

The cemetery church of St Michael in **NIEDERROTTWEIL**, 8km north of Breisach, has another superb retable, again based on a *Coronation of the Virgin*, by Master HL. Just to the north is the old wine-growers' town of **BURKHEIM**, which preserves a number of seventeenth-century houses. Prettiest of all the towns in the area is **ENDINGEN** on the northern side of the mountain, built round a graceful Marktplatz, whose Rathaus and Kornhaus both date back to the sixteenth century.

Public transport in the area is sparse by German standards; the only rail service *Deutsche Bundesbahn* operates is between Breisach and Freiburg. However, a privately-owned line circles the Kaiserstuhl, with several trains per day; steam locomotives occasionally chug along this route in summer. Otherwise, it's ideal country for walking.

The Southern Black Forest

The southern part of the Black Forest is a mountainous region encompassed by the French border to the west and the Swiss border to the south, and gradually petering out towards the southeast, somewhat before the shores of the Bodensee. Its landscape of forested hills is especially wonderful around the high points of the **Belchen** and the **Feldberg**. At 1414m and 1493m respectively, they're hardly mountains in the Alpine sense, but on clear days you get vast panoramas from their summits, reaching as far as the Swiss Alps and the western Rhine valley. While there are only two main highways heading from west to east (one following the Swiss border on the southern side of the region, and the road connecting Freiburg to Konstanz on the northern side), **travel** along the fringes of this area is easy and efficient by train. The interior, on the other hand, involves circuitous connections by infrequent bus services.

Around Belchen

Belchen, surrounded by deep gorges some 20km south of Freiburg, is the most beautiful of the southern peaks, with wonderful views and quiet little villages in the valleys.

Münstertal

One of those valleys is the **Münstertal**, dotted with the characteristic low shingle roofs of traditional Black Forest farms, set among lush pastures clinging to the steep hillsides of the northern Belchen reaches. On the southwestern outskirts, near the village of

NEUENWEG, you'll find the **Nonnenmattweiher**, which is one of the oldest lakes of the region, formed during the receding Ice Age and an excellent place to combine hiking with fishing or simply picnicking. Be prepared for a lot of steep paths and deep furrows, and take some strong hiking shoes.

Some time in the seventh century, Irish missionaries came to Christianise this area: the most famous, Saint Trudpert, was murdered in 607 after only three years of missionary work. The **Kloster St Trudpert** in the upper Münstertal was founded about 250 years later, and the large Baroque complex you see today is the visual centre of the whole upper valley. It was a Benedictine monastery until secularisation in 1806, but now it's home to the *Josephschwestern* order of nuns. The refreshingly plain Baroque interior of the church is considered architect Peter Thumb's masterpiece: white stucco decorations predominate, with only the ceiling frescos and side altars adding discreet colour.

The Münstertal is awash with accommodation possibilities; look out for the *Zimmer frei* signs. There's a **youth hostel** at WIEDEN (☎07673/538; train from Freiburg to Münstertal, then bus).

Staufen

Following the Münstertal west, the foothills sink into the Rhine valley, the landscape quickly changing into gently rolling hills that make up some of Germany's most famous vineyards and provide a lucrative living to many small and ancient towns. Of these, **STAUFEN** is particularly attractive. Situated at the bottom of the Münstertal and surrounded by its vineyards, its idyllic location makes it a great base for relaxed hiking tours, while the cobbled streets and medieval houses mean it's worth a visit in its own right. The place also harbours a murky past in the shape of **Doktor Faustus** (Johannes Faust – see also p.210). He came here in 1539 at the behest of Count Anton von Staufen, who was in serious debt and hoped to extricate himself by using the great necromancer's alleged ability to manufacture gold. However, Faust accidentally blew himself into small pieces when an experiment exploded in his room in the *Gasthaus Zum Löwen*.

The **tourist office** is in the Rathaus (☎07633/80536). If you want to stay in the *Zum Löwen*, Hauptstr. 47, (☎07633/7078), prepare to pay upwards of DM145 for a double; Faust's room, no. 5 on the third floor, is available for rent. Much cheaper is *Kreuz-Post*, Hauptstr. 65 (☎07633/5240), with singles DM35, doubles from DM53; a few rooms in private houses are available for less than this. The annual *Sommerfest* is held during the last week in June, while the local *Weinfest* takes place on the first weekend in August. Star vineyards of the area are on the **Batzenberg** just north of town, and wine connoisseurs come from all over to go wine-tasting in the surrounding cellars. An even bigger *Weinfest* is held in nearby SCHÖNBERG in late April and early May.

Around Feldberg

Feldberg, the highest peak in the Black Forest, was, until last century, the heart of a remote and wild region, far away from human habitation. Nowadays, in contrast, the area is one of the most popular holiday destinations in Europe.

Höllental

The most atmospheric approach to Feldberg is by train from Freiburg. For the first leg of this, you pass through the narrow and formerly almost inaccessible **Höllental** (Hell Valley) gorge, which lies between HIMMELREICH and HINTERZARTEN. The track was first laid in 1887 by Robert Gerwig, who had earlier constructed the *Schwarzwaldbahn* (see p.274), and was an amazing technical achievement for the time, using a network of tunnels and viaducts. To appreciate both the scenery and the engineering, however, you really need to get out and walk along the footpath on the gorge's northern side; it takes about four hours to make a one-way trip.

Titisee and Schluchsee

TITISEE, the next stop after Hinterzarten, lies on the glacial lake of the same name. It's a highly commercialised and inordinately popular summer resort, particularly with spa holidaymakers around retirement age. If you want to stay, there's a **youth hostel** at Bruderhalde 27 (☎07652/238) on the way to Hunterzarten, four **campsites**, and plenty of other inexpensive accommodation in hotels and private houses.

Far preferable is **SCHLUCHSEE**, which lies on a larger glacial lake after which it's named directly to the south. From Titisee, trains crawl up the side of the Feldberg towards Germany's highest station, FELDBERG-BÄRENTAL, which is the place to alight if you want to walk all the way up the mountain. They then descend to Schluchsee, terminating a couple of kilometres further on at the hamlet of **SEEBRUGG**, which has a decent beach with sailing and windsurfing facilities. Motorised boats aren't allowed on the lake, a fact that makes for pleasant (and clean) swimming.

There's a **youth hostel** at Im Wolfsgrund 28 in Schluchsee (☎07656/329), plus a **campsite** (☎0765/7739). Another hostel is at Haus 9 in Seebrugg (☎07656/494); here also is *Pension Berger* (☎07656/238), which charges DM22 for singles, DM38 doubles.

Feldberg and the mountain resorts

In the eighteenth and nineteenth centuries, the rounded heights of the **Feldberg** itself (which can be reached more directly by bus from Freiburg than by the train connection) were denuded of forest and turned into highland pastures, so today the peak stands treeless above a sea of forest and isn't in itself particularly attractive. The TV tower and radio dishes plus the chairlift (DM3 one-way, DM4 return) and gravel path to the top don't do the place any favours either, and the hotel and souvenir shop just about ruin it. Nonetheless, the area roundabouts is still an excellent hiking region, with many beautiful trails through uninhabited forests and gorges laced with a couple of romantic waterfalls and streams along the way. Even near the Feldberg, you'll find unspoilt and quiet places like the **Feldbergsee**, only accessible on foot, and the **Windgfällweiher**, another lake near the village of ALTGLASSHÜTTEN a few kilometres southeast.

For keen hikers, **BERNAU,** 5km south of Feldberg, is a good place to stay. It's actually a collection of small villages and farms, ideal for groups looking for farmhouse accommodation or private holiday flats. Contact the **tourist office** in the *Kurverwaltung* (☎07675/896) for accommodation lists and brochures.

The picturesque village of **TODTMOOS** is another centre for walking enthusiasts, offering all the facilities of Alpine villages. Its **tourist office** in the *Kurpark* (Mon–Sat 8am–noon & 1–5pm; ☎07674/534) provides accommodation lists, local brochures and hiking maps. There's no official youth hostel here, but instead the *Europäisches Jugendgästehaus* (☎07674/410). Todtmoos is also an ideal base from which to explore the rarely-visited **Hotzenwald**, which seamlessly extends south from the Black Forest, until dropping sharply towards the Rhine valley that marks the Swiss border.

St Blasien

The most famous monastery of the Southern Black Forest is in **ST BLASIEN**, some 20km southeast of the Feldberg. Burnt down a number of times, the church was given its present shape in 1768, when the local prince-abbot hired the Frenchman Michel d'Ixnard to design one of Germany's grandest classically-inspired buildings. The great dome, carried by twenty Corinthian pillars, was modelled after St Peter's in Rome, and is one of the most notable pieces of Neoclassical architecture in the country. Inside, the great rotunda is a blaze of white marble, shining oppressively new and creating an atmosphere reminiscent of a cold, oversized bathroom. Perhaps an unfair description for an architectual masterpiece, but the overwhelming white everywhere distracts from appreciating the beautiful symmetry and uncluttered space.

For brochures and accommodation lists contact the **tourist office**, Am Kurgarten (Mon–Fri 9.30am–noon & 2.30–5pm, Sat 10am–noon; ☎07672/41430). The nearest **youth hostel** is in MENTZENSCHWAND, at Vorderdorferstr. 10 (☎07675/326; bus from Seebrugg). This is a particularly beautiful hostel, located in one of the all-wood traditional farmhouses, 8km up the road from St Blasien.

Bonndorf

BONNDORF, on the eastern edges of the Black Forest, is an excellent hiking base, set among rich orchards. It's very close to the so-called "Grand Canyon" of the Black Forest, the **Wutachschlucht**, which is a small riverine gorge, very narrow in places, with gushing white-water shooting over mossy rocks and lined by ancient forest. About 10km long, it has been declared a nature reserve; a map of it is available for DM6 from the **tourist office** (☎07703/7607) on Schloss Strasse. The local **youth hostel** is at Waldallee 19 (☎07703/359); the cheapest **hotel**, at DM25 per person, is *Haus Schüler*, Lindenstr. 9 (☎07703/7164).

The Central Black Forest

The central part of the Black Forest is the one most enshrined in popular imagination. This is the land of cuckoo clocks, of huge balconied farmsteads with hipped roofs, and of some of the world's most outrageous headgear: the *Schäppelkrone*, a "crown" made from hundreds of colour glass beads and ribbons, and the *Bollenhut*, the woollen pom-pom hat whose colour indicates the wearer's marital status (red for unmarried, black for married). As a result, it's hardly surprising that this is the part of the forest which has gone in most for the tourist hard-sell, and is consequently the most spoiled, with an abundance of accommodation, a highly developed network of trains and buses, and a surfeit of tacky souvenir shops. Nonetheless, it's easy enough to escape from the organised tour groups, while the good communications make travel by public transport a pain-free experience.

Donaueschingen

Gateway to the central Black Forest is the railway junction of **DONAUESCHINGEN**, which lies some 50km northwest of the Bodensee on the windswept Baar Plateau. Both its name and fame are due to its status as the official source (see overleaf) of one of the world's most celebrated rivers, the **Danube** (*Donau*), though it's also of note as a well-preserved example of a tinpot princely capital.

Initially, the harsh climate militated against its growth – it was no more than a hamlet until the 1720s when Prince Joseph Wilhelm Ernst of the **Fürstenberg** dynasty descended from his feudal castle in the hills above to begin the planning of a new courtly town. In spite of their meagre and unpromising holdings of land, the Fürstenbergs belonged to the first rank of German nobility, owing their promotion to having for a long time served as confidants and advisers of the hereditary emperors, the Habsburgs. They further built up their power base by earmarking certain sons for careers in the Church; by this means they gained the bishopric of Strasbourg and control of several monasteries.

About town

The **Schloss** (guided tours April–Sept Mon & Wed–Sun 9am–noon & 2–5pm; DM5) is actually a fairly unassuming Baroque building at the far end of its park; much of the interior was modernised at the end of the nineteenth century. Its trappings are typical: Brussels tapestries, assorted objets d'art and family portraits. Among the last-named,

THE SOURCE OF THE DANUBE

In the Donaueschingen's Schlosspark a grandiose early nineteenth-century fountain has been erected round the *Donauquelle*, a very unassuming spring. This flows eastwards through the grounds (at times invisibly below the surface), before joining the **Brigach**, a headstream which rises in the Black Forest and which has become a substantial river by the time it reaches this point. At the edge of town a couple of kilometres further on is the more substantial confluence with another and bigger Black Forest headstream, the **Breg**; from then on, the combined waters are known as the **Danube**. It's the longest river in Europe after the Volga, and the only important one to flow from west to east, following a course of some 2840 kilometres through seven different countries, eventually forming a labyrinth-like delta in Romania which feeds into the Black Sea. Whether or not the *Donauquelle* is really the ultimate source of this great river is a matter for dispute – the spring which feeds the Breg has a far better geological claim. However, given that the crucial merger occurs at Donaueschingen, it's easy to see why the town has managed to be blessed with official recognition.

there's one surprise – *Max Egon* was painted by the English artist Graham Sutherland. The sitter kept up the family tradition of musical patronage (Mozart and Liszt had both been guests) by establishing a **festival** now known as the *Donaueschinger Musiktage*. Held each October in the modern Donauhalle at the western end of town, this focuses on the work of contemporary composers. Many of the century's leading musicians – Stravinsky, Hindemith, Boulez and Stockhausen – have had works premiered there.

The main family treasures, known as the **Fürstenburg-Sammlungen** (March–Oct Tues–Sun 9am–noon & 1.30–5pm, Dec–Feb Tues–Sun 9am–noon & 1.30–4pm; DM5), are housed in a building on Karlsplatz, a Baroque square situated over the main road directly behind the Schloss. Here various zoological and mineralogical collections are set out in the old-fashioned manner of cabinets of curiosities. There's also a room devoted to the history of the Fürstenbergs, complete with their ceremonial coach and sleighs. However, the main attraction is the outstanding second floor display of South German and Swiss paintings and sculptures of the fifteenth and sixteenth centuries. Highlight is **Hans Holbein the Elder's** *Grey Passion*, an expressive cycle of twelve pictures formerly in SS Ulrich und Afra in Augsburg. It takes its name from the idiosyncratic device of showing all the participants dressed in grey – until half-way through, when they change into white. There's also an important array of works by the enigmatic **Master of Messkirch**, one of Dürer's most distinctive followers, including parts of his eponymous work, and the jewel-like *Wildensteiner Altar*.

On a terrace to the side of the Schloss is the twin-towered **Johanniskirche**, whose restrained Baroque style is reminiscent of the churches then being built in Bohemia, rather than elsewhere in southern Germany. In the nave there's a wooden *Madonna* by the eccentric **Master HL**; though pre-dating the building by over 200 years, it doesn't look at all out of place.

Other than these obvious attractions, all closely grouped together, Donaueschingen doesn't have much in the way of sights. However, several **streets** are good examples of period pieces. An example is Josefstrasse, linking the Bahnhof with the town centre, which is lined by stately Baroque and Neoclassical mansions. The outbuildings of the court are found on Haldenstrasse; the library here possesses one of the three original thirteenth-century manuscript versions of *The Nibelungenlied*. Though this street is now tucked away between the town centre and the Brigach, it's easily located by the chimneys of the *Fürstenberg* **brewery**, one of the most famous in Germany. In its present form it dates back to 1705, but the family's initial beer-making rights were granted in the thirteenth century.

Practicalities

The obvious place to sample the products of the brewery (the Pils is one of Germany's best) is the *Bräustüble*, housed in a pink Baroque palace on Postplatz. Plenty more places to **eat** and **drink**, including several classy cafés, can be found on Karlstrasse, the town's main shopping street, which runs west from the Johanniskirche. At no. 58 is the **tourist office** (Mon–Fri 8am–noon & 2–5/6, Sat 9am–noon; ☎0771/3834). They have a list of private houses with **rooms**, which cost from DM20 for singles, DM30 for doubles. Alternatively, *Pension Wölfle*, Mühlenstr. 25 (☎0771/2808), and *Bären*, Josefstr. 7-9 (☎0771 2518), both charge around DM25 per head. The **campsite** (☎0771/5511) is 8km away on the banks of the RIEDSEE.

Villingen-Schwenningen

Created as recently as 1972, the double town of **VILLINGEN-SCHWENNINGEN**, some 15km north of Donaueschingen, is a decidedly curious union, as its two constituent parts belonged for centuries to different countries: Villingen, on the very fringe of the Black Forest, was Austrian before being allocated by Napoleon to Baden, while Schwenningen, set on the Baar plateau, was part of Württemberg. Villingen, much the more attractive of the two, really comes to life during the Shrovetide celebrations of **Fastnet**, which rival Rottweil's as the best in southern Germany.

At other times, Villingen is a busy enough market town, its pristine houses set behind the medieval **Stadtmauer**, of which several sections, including three towers and three impressive gates, survive. The huge **Münster** provides a central focus, particularly the two tall flamboyant towers of the late Gothic chancel, which was tacked on to the Romanesque nave when its predecessor burned down. Unfortunately the interior was completely redecorated – none too successfully – in the eighteenth century, but compensation comes in the variety of colourful mansions which form the Münsterplatz. These include the Romanesque **Rabenscheuer** to the north and the gabled Gothic **Alte Rathaus** (Tues–Sun 10am–noon, Thurs also 3–5pm; DM2) to the west, where you can see both the main council chamber on the first floor and the former prison and torture room above, as well as a collection of fine medieval tapestries.

Also worth a visit is the **Franziskaner-Museum** (Tues, Thurs & Fri 3–5pm, Thurs 10am–noon & 3–5pm, Sat & Sun 10am–noon; DM2) at Rietstr. 39 on the western edge of the old town, which has comprehensive collections of material on the prehistory, folklore and crafts of the Black Forest. The adjoining buildings of the old monastery, the **Franziskaner-Klosteranlage** (Tues–Fri 10am–noon & 3–5pm, Sat & Sun 10am–noon; DM1), give a good idea of the severely functional Gothic architecture that was favoured by the mendicant friars, and contain displays of sacred art.

Practicalities

The **tourist office** (Mon–Fri 8.30am–12.30pm & 1.30–5.30pm, Sat 8.30am–1.30pm; ☎07721/82311) is at Rietstr. 8. There's an official **youth hostel** in the very north of Villingen at St Georgener Str. 36 (☎07721/54149), along with the YMCA's *CJVM-Hüttle* (☎07720/5315) in a secluded wooded setting on the road between Schwenningen and WEILERSBACH. In addition, there are **private rooms** aplenty, a list of which can be obtained from the tourist office. Among **hotels**, *Gasthof Bären*, Bickenstr. 19 (☎07721/55541), which has singles from DM36, doubles from DM65, is particularly recommendable; it also has one of the best **restaurants** in town, with an extensive vegetarian menu. Another good choice for eating is the *Ratskeller* in the Oberes Tor at the end of Obere Strasse, which also has a beer garden. For **live music**, try the *Jazzkeller*, Webergasse 6, or *Scheurer*, Kalkofenstr. 3.

THE SCHWARZWALDBAHN

Villingen is the terminus for one of the most spectacular railways in Europe, the *Schwarzwaldbahn* to OFFENBURG in the Rhine valley. Laid out between 1863 and 1873, this line successively follows the valleys of the Brigach, Gutach and Kinzig rivers, cutting through what had hitherto been impenetrable countryside, and was intended as a major prestige project by the Grand Duchy of Baden, which was always keen to present itself at the forefront of German progressiveness. It was built by the nation's most celebrated railway engineer, Robert Gerwig, who later went on to construct the St Gotthard route over the Alps, as well as another Black Forest line, the *Höllentalbahn*. The nature of the terrain posed technical problems which had never previously been tackled, notably the need to climb a gradient of 448m in the short distance of 11km. To achieve this, Gerwig built 36 tunnels through the mountains, plus a series of daring hairpin bends. Two of these – the narrow, deep and rocky stages between St Georgen and Triberg, and between Triberg and Hornberg – involve the railway virtually doubling back on itself to accomplish the ascent.

Triberg

Heart of the central part of the Black Forest is the little town of **TRIBERG**, which lies at an altitude of 1000 metres 25km northwest of Villingen. It's a spa and health resort, with the forest acting as a dust filter, ensuring particularly pure air. Some of the most imposing scenery in the region is nearby, and Triberg itself makes a good base for a day or two's relaxation. Arriving at the **Bahnhof** is a strange experience, as there's nothing but cliffs on either side of the narrow tracks it's easy to understand the derivation of the town's name, a corruption of "three mountains", after the peaks which surround it. From here, the centre is a fifteen minute walk uphill.

Prime attraction is the **Gutacher Wasserfall** at the top end of town. At 162 metres, it ranks as the highest waterfall in Germany and is undeniably impressive, even though it plunges in seven separate stages instead of a single dramatic dive. Unfortunately, in a reverse of the normal German penchant for unrestricted access to nature, it's sealed off, with a DM2 levy for admission.

Ample compensation, however, is provided by the **Schwarzwald Museum** (May–Sept 9am–6pm; Oct–April 10am–noon & 2–5pm; DM3) on Wallfahrtstrasse, which offers fascinating insights into the rural culture of the Black Forest as it was – and, to some extent, still is. There's a fine group of woodcarvings by the rustic local artist Karl Josef Fortwängler who depicted the thick-set country bumpkins of the area in an idiosyncratic yet highly sympathetic manner. In addition, there's a large model of the *Schwarzwaldbahn*, while music boxes, clocks and examples of the traditional dress for carnivals and everyday wear complete the display. Further up the hill is the Baroque **Wallfahrtskirche St Maria in den Tannen,** whose painting of *The Virgin of the Pines* draws pilgrims for its allegedly miraculous qualities.

Practicalities

The **youth hostel** is high in the hills at Rohrbacher Str. 35 (☎07722/4110); a bus will take you as far as the waterfall and then it's a very steep twenty minute climb. Otherwise, try one of the cheap **hotels**, such as *Krone*, Schulstr. 37 (☎07722/4524), which charges from DM28 per head and also serves excellent food, or *Gasthaus Schwarzwaldstüble*, Ober-Vogthuber-Str. 25a (☎07722/3324), which has singles at DM35, doubles DM60. A full accommodation list is available from the **tourist office** (Mon–Fri 8am–noon & 2–5pm, Sat 10am–noon; ☎07722/81230) in the *Kurverwaltung*, Luisenstr. 10. Most of the **cafés** here are reasonable, especially those along Hauptstrasse, where you'll also find several restaurants.

Furtwangen

FURTWANGEN, 15km south of Triberg, isn't one of the more appealing towns in the Black Forest but is of note as the leading centre of clock production. If you've a serious interest in the craft, the **Deutsches Uhrenmuseum** (April–Oct daily 9am–5pm, Nov–March Mon–Fri 9am–noon & 2–4pm; DM3) on Gerwigstrasse is the place to come: it has over 1000 timepieces of all weird and wonderful shapes and sizes on view, including many from overseas.

Among a number of recommendable excursions which can be made from Furtwangen, two stand out. The **Brend**, 6k to the northwest, is one of the best vantage-points in the central part of the Black Forest, standing at a height of 1148 metres. Another road leads in a roughly parallel direction just to the north along the side of the Breg to the river's source. This is known as the **Donauquelle**, as the Breg is one of the two Black Forest rivers which meet at Donaueschingen to form the Danube, and thus has a good (if contentious) geological claim to be regarded as the ultimate source of the great river itself.

The Gutach valley

The **Gutach valley** north of Triberg is best known as the home of the *Bollenhut*, which is often wrongly assumed to be a regional costume of the Black Forest. At **HORNBERG**, where it traverses a huge viaduct, the *Schwarzwaldbahn* emerges into a light and airy landscape again. There's a fine view of the ensemble of town and railway from the ruined Burg set high on a hill to the west.

A few kilometres north is is the town of **GUTACH** itself, outside which is the **Schwarzwälder Frelichtmuseum** (April–Oct daily 8.30am–6pm; DM4), a collection of buildings from the region. Centrepiece is what's probably the most famous house in the Black Forest, the late sixteenth-century *Vogtsbauernhof*. With its huge sloping roof and tiered facade, it's an outstanding example of the characteristic vernacular building style of the region. This was the original farmhouse on the site, whereas the various other exhibits have, of course, been removed from other locations. There are four more farmsteads, along with a wooden chapel and all kinds of workshops – smithies, granaries, a bakehouse, a distillery and various types of mills. Displays on the folklore and lifestyle of the region are also featured, and there are demonstrations of all the old crafts.

CLOCKMAKING IN THE BLACK FOREST

The first clocks to be seen in the Black Forest were mechanical contraptions brought by pedlars from Bohemia in the 1640s. Someone must have had the idea of reproducing them in wood, as a couple of decades later the first workshops had appeared. Originally, clockmaking was an adjunct to farming and forestry, and was normally a co-operative venture involving several families, each of whom specialised in a different part of the business, such as woodcarving, painting, or making the mechanism. The products were sold by itinerant hawkers, who gradually began to expand their operations abroad; by the end of the eighteenth century, demand was so great that clockmaking became a lucrative full-time trade for many families and the single largest local industry. It has remained of key importance to the local economy to this day.

Although the cuckoo clock (*Kuckucksuhr*) is what most tourists want to buy, the alternative *Schilderuhr*, which has a hand-painted clockface, has a far longer and more prestigious tradition. Beautiful models designed to the customer's specification can be ordered throughout the central Black Forest region; these contrast dramatically with the cheapjack junk sold in the tackier souvenir shops.

The Kinzig valley

At the next stop, HAUSACH, the Gutach merges with the **Kinzig**; similarly, there's the junction of the *Schwarzwaldbahn* with the *Kinzigtalbahn*. **HASLACH**, an old market town and health resort just 8km from Hausach, is the most striking place on the former line's stretch along the Kinzig towards the terminus at Offenburg. Its Rathaus is tweely painted with depictions of locals in trad dress, while the former **Kapuzinerkloster** (April–Oct Tues–Sat 9am–5pm, Sun 10am–5pm, Nov–March Tues–Fri 10am–5pm; DM2) has a huge collection of Black Forest costumes and folklore displays.

Following the *Kinzigtalbahn* eastwards from Hausach, the first stop is **WOLFACH**, situated at the point where the river after which the village is named joins the Kinzig. It also has a museum worth seeing if you've developed a taste for the customs of the region. Housed in **Schloss Furstenberg**, its main subject is mining, in honour of the fact that there were once 500 local pits in operation. The masks used at *Fastnet* are also on display, the celebrations here being rated among the best in Baden-Württemberg. **SCHILTACH**, a pretty, flower-lined place of half-timbered houses a further 10km east, is again set at the confluence of its river with the Kinzig.

Alpirsbach

ALPIRSBACH, 19km northeast of Schiltach, is grouped round the former **Kloster**, now a Protestant parish church. Begun in the late twelfth century, it preserves much of the simple, pure Romanesque form characteristic of the style of building championed at Hirsau (see p.280). The east end is especially notable – later Gothic masons ingeniously perched the chancel above the existing storey. Only one tower was built, however, and this was only finished in the Renaissance period, when it received an unusual gabled top. The late Gothic cloisters are often used for open-air concerts in summer.

A number of handsome half-timbered buildings decorate the centre of Alpirsbach, most notably the Rathaus; the town also makes a good centre for walks in the Kinzig valley. If you want to stay, there's a **youth hostel** high on the Sulzberg at Reinerzauersteige 80 (☎0744/2477); there are also two **campsites** and plenty of reasonably priced pensions. The *Klosterbräu* produces a wide variety of excellent **beers**.

The Northern Black Forest

To non-Germans, the northern stretch of the Black Forest, most of which belonged to Württemberg rather than Baden, is the least familiar part. Yet here are some of the most imposing of the landscapes – the forest really does look at its blackest and is cut by several deep, dark valleys which provide the strongest possible contrast to the long panoramic views obtained from the hills. There are three main **touring routes**, each offering a widely varying choice of scenery: the Black Forest Highway, the Black Forest Valley Road and the circuitous Black Forest Spa Road. Walking or cycling are the best ways for **getting around**, but superb scenic railway lines, closely hugging the river valleys, enable all of the second and part of the third of these routes to be followed by even the most sedentary. Buses fill in the gaps, though the frequency of these varies considerably according to season, often drying up altogether in the winter months.

Freudenstadt

The hub of the transport system of the Northern Black Forest is **FREUDENSTADT**, situated at high altitude on a plateau bordered by the Rivers Murg and Kinzig. There's no more polished, spick and span town in the country; coupled to its extreme climate and arcaded streets, it has a feel reminiscent more of Switzerland than Germany. Its regularly-built streets look gleamingly new, but it's new only in one sense, its history being dogged by ill luck in contradiction of its name, which means "town of joy".

Some (interesting) history

Freudenstadt was in fact founded in 1599 by **Duke Friedrich I of Württemberg**. He had three main aims in establishing the new community: to give a much-needed boost to his ever-empty state coffers by exploiting the silver mines in the nearby Christophstal; to provide a home, at a time of high religious rivalry, for Protestant refugees from Austria; and to have a new, "secret" capital for Württemberg, which he dreamed of building up as an effective counterweight to France on the one hand and the Habsburg-dominated Holy Roman Empire on the other.

A highly talented Italian-trained architect, **Heinrich Schickhardt**, was accordingly charged with designing the first planned town in the province. He laid it out in the manner of a vast Roman camp, centred on a spaciously grandiose central square. In the middle, there was meant to be an even bigger Schloss than the one in Stuttgart but it was never built – the silver mines proved to be a **mirage**, and the town was devastated by **epidemic and fire** within 35 years of its birth, whereupon it lost all sense of importance. Something of a comeback was made in the nineteenth century with its development into one of the leading spas in the Black Forest. Two weeks before the end of World War II, **disaster struck again** – French artillery bombarded the town, and when it fell, the victors ran amok; only two streets survived the blaze intact. Within five years, however, Freudenstadt had been completely **rebuilt** to the old plans. This was regarded as a stunning achievement, even by the miraculous standards of German postwar reconstruction, but the undeniable effect – avoided in more painstaking restoration projects – is that the historic buildings look anachronistically modern.

Marktplatz

Freudenstadt is still sufficiently singular to justify a look round, even if you aren't attracted to the leisure facilities or the excellent hiking opportunities in the neighbourhood. The **Marktplatz** must have seemed extraordinary when it was first built; it's an impressive sight even to the modern eye which is far more attuned to the large-scale, and it still ranks as much the biggest square in Germany. At diagonally opposite corners are the two main public buildings, the **Rathaus** and the **Stadtkirche**.

The Stadtkirche is particularly intriguing, built in an L-shape so that the men and women of the congregation could be segregated. Indeed, the arrangement meant they could not even see each other – the better to keep their minds off sex and on the sermon. The church houses a magnificent polychrome wooden **lectern** made around 1150, which bears large statues of the Four Evangelists and their symbols; it's unique of its kind and one of the most important pieces of Romanesque church furniture to have survived. Along with the **font**, made about half a century earlier and adorned with carvings of symbolical fantastic animals, it presumably came from one of the Black Forest monasteries.

Practicalities

There are two railway stations: the **Stadtbahnhof** is just a few minutes' walk from Marktplatz and has the **bus terminus** just outside, whereas the **Hauptbahnhof** is at the eastern edge of town, at a much lower altitude. The **tourist office** (April–Oct Mon–Fri 9am–6pm, Sat & Sun 9am–noon, Nov–Mar Mon–Fri only 9am–noon & 2.30–5pm; ☎07441/ 8640) is in the *Kurverwaltung* on Promenadeplatz. **Hotels** and **pensions** are scattered all over town; for the lowest rates, at DM25 per head or less, try the concentration on Lauterbadstrasse. Alternatively, there's a **youth hostel** at Eugen-Nägele-Str. 69 (☎07441/7720), not far from the Stadtbahnhof, and a **campsite**, *Langenwald* (☎07441/

2862), 3km to the west. Plenty of elegant **cafés** and **restaurants** line Marktplatz; best food is at no. 12, *Jägerstüble*. A good alternative is *Gasthof See* on Forststrasse, near the Stadtbahnhof.

The Black Forest Highway

The **Black Forest Highway** (*Schwarzwald-Hochstrasse*), linking Freudenstadt with Baden-Baden, is one of Germany's most famous roads. Up to five buses run daily in each direction in summer along this 60km stretch, which has no villages to speak of. However, there are plenty of **hotels**, many with spa facilities and nearly all on the expensive side. In addition, there's a single **youth hostel**, *Zuflucht* (☎07804/811), located at a particularly scenic part just off the main road 19km north of Freudenstadt. It makes an excellent base for hiking in summer and for skiing in winter. Hiking along the accompanying trail is really much the best way to see the area, which is pocked with belvederes offering vast panoramas towards the Rhine and the French Vosges.

Just beyond the hostel is the **Buhlbachsee**, the first of several tiny natural lakes along the highway. Before this, however, is a by-road leading west to OPPENAU which joins with another fine scenic road running north to the coomb of **Allerheiligen**, rejoining the *Hochstrasse* at RUHESTEIN. Allerheiligen has the ruins of a former Premonstratensian **Kloster**, the first Gothic building in southwest Germany, probably built by the same team of masons as Strasbourg Cathedral. An impressively curling stepped **waterfall** can also be seen, while there's also a good restaurant, the *Klosterhof*, which makes its own fruit wines and liqueurs.

East of Ruhestein is the **Wildsee**, but the most celebrated of the lakes is the **Mummelsee** a further 8km north. It stands at the foot of the Hornigsrinde (1164m), the highest point in the northern Black Forest, offering a particularly outstanding view. The Mummelsee itself, now a popular boating centre, is allegedly haunted by water-sprites and by the luckless King Ulmon, who was condemned by a sorceress to live for 1000 years, in spite of his continuous pleas to be released to join his friends in the after-life. This legend has proved a potent inspiration for many German writers and formed the subject of one of Eduard Mörike's most evocative poems. It's often necessary to change buses here, particularly out of season when there are no through services.

The Murg valley

The **Murg valley** north of Freudenstadt is the second stage of the Black Forest Valley Road (*Schwarzwald-Tälerstrasse*). This is the only one of the three scenic routes which doesn't officially begin at Freudenstadt, its first stretch being the Kinzig Valley from Alpirsbach.

What is arguably the most scenic of all the region's railways, the 60km *Murgtalbahn* line to Rastatt, follows a parallel course to the road. Though never more than a modest stretch of water, the River Murg cleaves an impressively grand valley in its downward journey towards its confluence with the Rhine. One of the recommendable hikes which can be made from **BAIERSBRONN** (the first stop, 6km north of Freudenstadt) is westwards along the course of the young river towards its source in the shadow of the 1055 metre-high **Schliffkopf**.

All the little towns along the Murg have impressive settings, and make good bases for exploring an underrated part of the Black Forest. Particularly worthy of mention is **FORBACH**, about half-way down the line, which has a wonderful sixteenth century single-span covered wooden bridge, the largest of its type in Europe. West of town is some fine countryside, with the artifical **Schwarzenbach Stausee**, a watersports centre, and the tiny **Herrenwieser See**. The latter lies below the **Badener Höhe**, whose TV tower commands an extensive view of the region. There's a **youth hostel** just to the north of Forbach at Birket 1 (☎07228/2427) and another out in the sticks at Haus no. 33 in HERRENWIES (☎07226/257). **Campsites** are also to be found in both locations, as well as a good number of cheap pensions.

GERNSBACH, 13km further north, is also very pretty, boasting a handsome gabled Renaissance Rathaus, along with historic ramparts, fountains and half-timbered houses. Though there's no hostel or campsite here, accommodation in private houses starts from as little as DM20 per head.

The Nagold valley

Much the most impressive stretch of the Black Forest Spa Road (*Schwarzwald-Bäderstrasse*) is the wonderfully dark, secret **Nagold valley**. The *Nagoldtalbahn*, which runs most of the way alongside it, begins at the railway junction of HORB, which has connections to Stuttgart, Tübingen and Rottweil, but there's also a branch line to Freudenstadt which links up 6km further north, at EUTINGEN.

Nagold and Wildberg

NAGOLD is one of only two towns of any size in the area. Shaped like an ellipse at the point where the River Waldach flows in from the west, it's surprisingly industrial, but also possesses plenty of handsome timber-framed houses. There's a fine panorama to be had from the ruined Burg perched high above the town. Further north on the eastern side of the valley are two gentle peaks also well worth climbing for their views – **Kühlen** and **Emmingen**.

WILDBERG, 13km downstream, preserves part of its walls, including two towers, along with a thirteenth-century Dominican monastery, a late fifteenth-century Rathaus, an old stone bridge and a Renaissance fountain. Neither of these towns has a hostel, though both have **campsites**. Plenty of cheap accommodation is also available in private houses and inns.

Calw

"The most beautiful town of all that I know," was how Hermann Hesse described **CALW**, the old textile centre which is the focal point of this valley. The eulogy needn't be taken too seriously – his judgment was more than a little bit coloured by the fact that he happened to have been born and bred there, though he eventually chose to reside in Switzerland, an act that probably says more about the place than his words. Fans of Hesse's novels – which have achieved a cult status far beyond the German-speaking world – will certainly want to come here to see his **birthplace** on Marktplatz, and the collection of memorabilia in the **Heimat Museum** (May–Oct Mon–Fri 2–4pm, Sun 10am–noon; free) on Bischofstrasse.

Other than this, Calw boasts an impressive array of half-timbered houses, mostly dating from the late seventeenth and early eighteenth centuries, just after a fire had destroyed the medieval town. One of the few older monuments is the **Nikolausbrücke** from around 1400, which incorporates a picturesque little votive chapel. Hesse, true to form, considered the bridge and the square on its west bank to form an assemblage superior to the Piazza del Duomo in Florence.

If you want to stay, there's a **youth hostel** right in the centre of town at Im Zwinger 4 (☎07051/12614). **Campsites** are found at Eiselstätt (☎07051/12131 or 13437) in the eastern part of town, and in the outlying villages of STAMMHEIM (☎07051/4844) and ALTBURG (☎07051/50788). Cheapest **hotels** are *Alte Post*, Bahnhofstr. 1 (☎07051/2196), charging from DM25 per person, and *Rössle*, Hermann-Hesse-Platz 2 (☎07051/30052), whose rates begin at DM28.

Hirsau

HIRSAU, 2km downstream, is now a small spa and officially part of Calw, but actually has a far longer history. Its Benedictine **Kloster**, indeed, was once the most powerful monastery in Germany, serving as mother-house to a host of dependent congregations and initiating a highly influential reform movement whose main effect was to free religious houses from the clutches of secular patrons, placing them instead under the direct control of the pope. The simple original monastic church is tucked away in among a number of much later buildings, not far from the bridge over the Nagold. A ninth-century Carolingian structure, it was re-built in the mid-eleventh century, and now serves as the Catholic parish church of **St Aurelius**.

The eleventh-century complex, built in warm red sandstone, was directly modelled on the most famous and powerful monastery of the day – that of Cluny in Burgundy – on sloping ground above the west bank of the Nagold. Almost completely destroyed by the French in the War of the Palatinate Succession, only the **Eulenturm** (Owl Tower), originally one of a pair, survives from this epoch: you have to go to Alpirsbach to get an impression of how it must once have looked. However, there are also fragments from later building periods, notably the late fifteenth-century **cloisters**, the early sixteenth-century **Marienkapelle** (now restored to serve as the Protestant church), and the Renaissance **Jagdschloss** of the Dukes of Württemberg, who expelled the monks after the Reformation, taking the land over as pleasure and hunting grounds.

Pforzheim

The end of the Black Forest proper, some 30km north of Calw, comes at the large industrial town of **PFORZHEIM**. Here the River Nagold joins the Enz, which thereafter follows an easterly course to its confluence with the Neckar. Pforzheim often christens itself *Goldstadt*, in recognition of its continuing role, held since the Middle Ages, as a leading centre of the jewellery trade. However, the town was devastated at the end of the war and its overall appearance is uncompromisingly modern.

There are a couple of fairly interesting Gothic churches in the town centre. The **Schlosskirche**, immediately opposite the Hauptbahnhof, has a lofty chancel containing the grandiose Renaissance wall tombs of the Margraves of Baden, who lived for a spell in the now-vanished castle. On Altstädterstrasse, **St Martin** retains a Romanesque portal and has mid-fifteenth-century wall-paintings in the choir. Otherwise, the only attraction is the **Reuchlinhaus** (Tues–Sun 10am–5pm; free) on Jahnstrasse south of the centre. Named in honour of the great humanist and Hebrew scholar who was a native of the town, this contains a museum illustrating the history of jewellery from Ancient Egypt to the present day.

The **tourist office** (Mon–Fri 9am–1pm & 2–6pm, Sat 9am–noon; ☎07231/392190) on Marktplatz is the main centre for information about the northern parts of the Black Forest. Pforzheim isn't the sort of place you're likely to want to hang around in for long, but the **youth hostel**, housed in the ruined Burg Rabeneck (☎07231/72604) in the village of DILLWEISSENSTEIN to the south, makes a good base for exploring the lower reaches of the Nagold Valley.

Tiefenbronn

TIEFENBRONN, an unassuming-looking village situated at the extreme edge of the Black Forest in the peaceful valley of the River Würm 12km south east of Pforzheim, has two claims to fame. Firstly, it's a renowned gastronomic centre; people come not only from Pforzheim, but also from Stuttgart and beyond, in order to eat at the *Ochsen-Post*, a hotel in a seventeenth-century timber-framed building. The main restaurant, one of the best in southern Germany, is incredibly expensive, but the *Bauernstuben*, open evenings only, is just about affordable.

From the outside, there's little to suggest that there's anything remarkable about the steep-roofed fourteenth-century Gothic church of **St Maria Magdalena**. Architecturally, it's very ordinary indeed, yet it contains a magnificent array of **works of art** which put to shame those in most cathedrals. Jewel-like stained glass windows, made in Strasbourg around 1370, illuminate the choir, and there are fifteenth-century wall-paintings throughout the church, including a depiction of *The Last Judgment*, a frieze of coats of arms, and portraits of the family who provided the endowments. The high altar tells the story of the Passion and has panels of the Nativity on the reverse.

However, this is outclassed by the altar dedicated to the local patron saint, which is housed in the southern aisle. One of the most beautiful of all European Gothic paintings, it bears a curious inscription: "Weep, Art, weep and lament loudly, nobody nowadays wants you, so alas, 1432. Lucas Moser, painter of Wyl, master of this work, pray God for him." Nothing is known about the embittered **Lucas Moser**, whose style seems oddly modern for its day. The first German painting to try a realistic approach, including a sense of perspective, it still has all the grace and delicacy characteristic of the earlier "Soft Style". It shows Mary Magdalene washing Christ's feet, her miraculous journey in a ship without sail or rudder to Marseille, her stay there and her last communion in the Cathedral of Aix-en-Provence.

Baden-Baden

> *It is an inane town, full of sham, and petty fraud, and snobbery, but the baths are good . . . I had had twinges of rheumatism unceasingly during three years, but the last one departed after a fortnight's bathing there, and I have never had one since. I fully believe I left my rheumatism in Baden-Baden. Baden-Baden is welcome to it. It was little, but it was all I had to give. I would have preferred to leave something that was catching, but it was not in my power.*
>
> Mark Twain, *A Tramp Abroad.*

Mark Twain's ambivalent reactions to **BADEN-BADEN** – he actually seems to have revelled in the snob aspect, delighting in the fact that the little old woman he sat behind in church and had decided to foster, turned out to be the Empress of Germany – mirrors the contrasting reactions of late nineteenth-century visitors to this town, then the glittering rendezvous of the wealthy and famous.

In the present century, the idle rich classes who made Baden-Baden the "summer capital of Europe" have been almost entirely wiped out. The Bolshevik Revolution accounted for the Russian landowners, while World War II took care of their counterparts in Prussia and the Balkans. Yet, if Baden-Baden isn't quite what it was, it has still maintained its image remarkably well; like Bath in the UK, it has a sense of style that no other spa in the country can quite match. This is in large measure thanks to the German infatuation with the concept of the spa cure, which is underpinned by an incredibly lenient health insurance system. Buoyed by the postwar economic prosperity, people flock here to enjoy a taste of a lifestyle their parents could only have dreamed about. It remains a place you're likely to either love or hate, but is somewhere which definitely should be experienced at first-hand: decide for yourself whether it deserves Henry Adams' description as "morally delicious" .

The Kurhaus and casino

The **Kurhaus** was built in the 1820s by Weinbrenner as the focal point of the new spa quarter on the west side of the Oos. Its solemn, stately facade of eight Corinthian columns is now approached via an elegant shopping arcade of expensive shops. Bénazet's son Edouard, *Le Duc de Zero*, added an opulent suite of gaming rooms to the

The discovery of hot springs in the Florintinerberg, on the east side of the River Oos, was due to the Romans, who found in them cures for arthritis and rheumatism. They established a settlement at this point, known simply as *Aquae* (Waters). The vernacular form of this was later used not only for the town, but also for the margraviate established by the **Zähringen** family, who moved here in the eleventh century to rule their combined territories at the western frontiers of the Holy Roman Empire. In the sixteenth century, the Swiss alchemist and doctor Paracelsus utilised the springs to save the life of Margrave Philipp I. However, Baden-Baden's rise to international fame only came about as a result of Napoleon's creation of the buffer state of Baden in 1806, 35 years after it had lost its role as ducal capital to Karlsruhe. The Grand Dukes promoted their ancestors' old seat as a resort and began embellishing it with handsome new buildings, many designed by the Neoclassical architect Friedrich Weinbrenner.

A casino formed an integral part of the facilities from the beginning, though it only took off with the arrival from Paris in 1836 of the flamboyant impresario **Jacques Bénazet**, *Le Roi de Bade*. With gambling outlawed in France, he devoted all his energies to building up Baden-Baden as the gambling capital of Europe. Among the famous visitors was Dostoyevsky, who became a compulsive addict, a theme he treated in his novella *The Gambler*. In 1872 Kaiser Wilhelm I – a faithful annual visitor to Baden-Baden over a period of forty years – abolished gambling throughout his newly-united Empire, forcing the town to concentrate on its spa facilities once more. However, the gaming tables were licensed again by Hitler in 1933, and have remained in operation ever since, save for the break caused by World War II.

Kurhaus, employing the same team of designers as had worked on the Paris Opéra; they married the contemporary style of *La Belle Epoque* to the extravagant type of decor found at Versailles. Highlight is the *Wintergarten*, with its glass cupola, Chinese vases and pure gold roulette table, which is used only on Saturdays or for special guests. Almost equally striking is the *Rotes Saal*, covered from top to bottom in red silk damask from Lyon, and with a glorious marbled fireplace and raised oval ceiling.

The easiest way to see these is to take a **guided tour** (daily April–Sept 9.30am–noon; Oct–March 10am–noon; DM3). However, it's far more fun to go when the action is on. A **day-ticket** costs DM5, with no obligation to participate. Formal dress (ie any kind of jacket and tie for men, skirt or dress for women) is a precondition of entry; access is officially forbidden to residents of Baden-Baden, anyone under 21 and students, though the last barrier isn't insurmountable. Roulette is played daily 2pm–2am (until 3am on Saturday), black jack from 5pm–1am Monday–Thursday, 4pm–1am Friday and Sunday, 4pm–2am Saturday, while baccarat is for the real night owls, running daily 3pm–6am. Minimum stake is DM5; maximum is DM50,000 though this limit is waived for baccarat.

Around Lichtentaler Allee

South of the Kurhaus runs Baden-Baden's most important thoroughfare, the **Lichtentaler Allee**. This was originally lined with oaks, but was transformed at the instigation of Edouard Bénazet into a landscape in the English style, with the addition of exotic trees and shrubs. It requires little effort of the imagination to visualise the procession of aristocratic carriages along this route; at Kettenbrücke, at the far end, an attempt was made on the life of Wilhelm I in 1861.

First of the buildings on Lichtentaler Allee is the Parisian-style **Theater**. This opened in 1862 with the premiere of Berlioz's opera *Béatrice et Bénédict*, and a high standard of both musical and theatrical performance is maintained there to this day. Next in line comes the **International Club**, built by Weinbrenner for a Swedish princess but now the headquarters of the big flat races which are held in IFFEZHEIM, 12km northwest of

Baden-Baden. There's a meeting in May, and a *Grosse Woche* in late August, which is the most important in the German calendar and now ranks as the high-point of the Baden-Baden season. Further along is the **Kunsthalle** (Tues & Thurs–Sun 10am–6pm, Wed 10am–8pm), which often hosts major loan exhibitions of twentieth-century art.

Immediately north of the Kurhaus is the **Trinkhalle** (Pump Room; daily 10am–5.30pm), built by a follower of Weinbrenner, Heinrich Hübsch. There are fourteen large frescos by the Romantic painter Jakob Götzenberger, illustrating legends about the town and the nearby countryside. Different varieties of spring water are dispensed from a modern mosaic fountain, with grape juice offered as an alternative.

The Michaelsberg, which rises behind the spa quarter, is named after the last Romanian Boyar of Moldavia, Michael Stourdza, who settled in Baden-Baden after he had been expelled from his homeland. In 1863, his teenage son was murdered in Paris; as a memorial, he commissioned the **Stourdza Mausoleum** to be built on the hill. Construction of this domed chapel, the most distinguished of the three nineteenth-century churches in Baden-Baden built for expatriate communities, was entrusted to the aged Leo von Klenze who had created so much of nineteenth-century Munich, but he died before it was complete.

The Altstadt

Little remains of the old town of Baden-Baden, which was almost completely destroyed in a single day in 1689, the result of a fire started by French troops. However, half-way up the Florintinerberg is the Marktplatz, where you'll find the **Rathaus**, formerly a Jesuit college but partially remodelled by Weinbrenner to serve as the original casino. Opposite is the **Stiftskirche**, a Gothic hall church whose tower is an amalgam of the Romanesque lower storeys of the first church, a Gothic octagon and a Baroque cap.

It may seem out of keeping that Baden-Baden possesses one of the all-time master-pieces of European sculpture, but the Stiftkirche's 5.4 metres-high sandstone *Crucifixion*, depicting Christ as a noble giant triumphant over his suffering, certainly warrants such a rating. Carved in 1467, it stood for nearly five centuries in the Altes Friedhof, before being moved inside for conservation reasons. The work is signed by **Nicolaus Gerhaert von Leyden**, a mysterious, peripatetic sculptor of Dutch origin who pioneered a realist approach to art which was to have a profound influence on the German carvers of the next generation. As with his few other remaining works, this shows complete technical mastery allied to a wholly original form of expression. The tabernacle was made about twenty years later by a mason who had clearly come under Gerhaert's spell, while there are also several impressive **tombs** of the Margraves of Baden lining the chancel; particularly eye-catching is the Rococo monument to "Türkenlouis" (see also p.286), replete with depictions of his trophies.

From Marktplatz you can climb the steep steps to the **Neues Schloss** whose terrace commands the best view over Baden-Baden, a dramatic mixture of roof-tops, church spires and the Black Forest surroundings. The site served as the seat of the Margraves of Baden from 1437, and of the Catholic line of Baden-Baden when the House divided in 1525.* Still the property of the Zähringen family, the main Renaissance and Baroque apartments can only be seen by **guided tour** (May–Oct

---

* This division into Catholic and Protestant lines is the source of the town's curious double-barrelled name. The Protestants moved to Durlach and founded the House of Baden-Durlach; the Catholic branch therefore became known as the House of Baden-Baden, following the usual practice, on the division of a state, of modifying the original name by adding that of its capital. Although this is also what the town itself has commonly been called ever since, the name was only officially adopted in 1931, more out of snobbery than anything else, in order to distinguish it from lesser spa towns named Baden in Austria and Switzerland.

Mon–Fri at 3pm; DM3). However, another wing now serves as part of the local **museum** (Tues–Sun 10am–12.30pm & 2–5pm; DM2).

The baths

Hidden underneath the Stiftskirche are the remains of the Roman Imperial Baths; the more modest **Römerbad** (Easter–Oct daily 10am–noon & 1.30–4pm; DM2.50) just to the east on Römerplatz was probably for the use of soldiers. If you don't fancy paying the entrance fee, you can still see the ruins through the glass-fronted windows.

The Friedrichsbad and the Caracalla Therme

Above the ruins is what must rank as one of the most magnificent bathing halls in the world, the **Friedrichsbad** (daily 10am–10pm). Begun in 1869, it's as grandly sumptuous as a Renaissance palace. This elaborateness is at least partly due to the fact that, as gambling was outlawed while the building was under construction, the medicinal springs became even more crucial to local prosperity than they had been before. The red and white sandstone facade is crowned with sea-green cupolas, while inside the pools are surrounded by pillars, arches and classical-style tiles, giving a truly exotic atmosphere. Speciality of the house is a "Roman-Irish Bath", which consists of a two hour programme of showers, hot air and steam baths, soap and brush massage, thermal bathing, and a half-hour snooze in a specially-designed rest room. The entire treatment is nude, with mixed bathing all day Wednesday and Friday. It will set you back all of DM32, though there are cheaper options – and the really broke need only fork out DM0.10 for an unlimited supply of thermal drinking water.

The **Caracalla Therme** (daily 8am–10pm) on the same square is a vast complex, completed in 1985, as a replacement for the former *Augustabad*. There are seven pools, both indoors and out, which are all at different temperatures, along with a sauna, solarium and massage facility. In reality, it's no more than an upmarket swimming hall with thermal water springs, though it makes an ideal complement to the Friedrichsbad. Its humbler status is reflected in the considerably cheaper prices: it costs DM15 for a two-hour swim and DM6 for each subsequent hour.

The Südstadt and Lichtental

The Südstadt, immediately south of the Florintinerberg, was traditionally the home of foreigners. Just off Bertholdsplatz is the onion-domed **Russische Kirche** (April–Oct Mon, Wed & Fri–Sun 2–5pm; DM1), while the neo-Gothic **Johanneskirche** on Bertholdstrasse was built as the Anglican parish of All Saints and was the place where Mark Twain had his encounter with the Empress. Beyond the church, which was given to German Lutherans in 1938, is the **Gönneranlagen**, a fine floral park with pergolas, fountains and a rose garden.

Lichtental

Still further south is the old village of **LICHTENTAL**, which can be reached directly from the town centre (or, indeed, the Bahnhof) by bus #1. The tranquil thirteenth-century **Kloster** (Mon–Sat 2–5pm. Sun 10am–noon, closed first Sun in month; DM1.50) is still occupied by Cistercian nuns, who keep up a long tradition of handicrafts, and also make several fiery liqueurs, which can be bought at their shop. There are two Gothic chapels: the larger one is used for services, while the other, the **Fürstenkapelle**, served as the pantheon of the Margraves of Baden prior to the Stiftskirche. Particularly outstanding is the tomb of the foundress Irmengard, carved by a Strasbourg mason in the mid-fourteenth century.

Just up the road from here, at Maximilianstr. 85, is the **Brahms-Haus** (Mon, Wed & Fri 3–5pm, Sun 10am–1pm; DM1), a tiny attic crammed with memorabilia, left exactly as when the great composer lived in it during the years 1865 to 1874. This was the period when Brahms, ever-conscious of his mantle as Beethoven's successor, was struggling to establish himself as a symphonist, only publishing his first, tormented essay in this form after he had passed his fortieth birthday. Its elegaic successor was largely written during a later visit to Lichtental, while part of the massive *Ein Deutsches Requiem*, his most important choral work, was also composed here.

Other suburbs

The original castle of the Margraves, **Hohenbaden** (Tues–Sun 10am–8pm; free), is situated on the wooded slopes of the Battert, some 3km from the Neues Schloss, from which it's reached via Alter Schlossweg. At one time, it boasted over a hundred rooms but is now very ruinous, albeit still very much worth visiting for the sake of the sweeping views; there's also a good and reasonably priced restaurant. To the east lies the wine-growing community of **EBERSTEINBURG**, likewise dominated by a ruined fortress of the local rulers. Further south is the **Merkur**, the highest hill in the Baden-Baden range. There's a choice of trails along it, or you can ascend to the summit by an unusually steep rack railway (daily 10am–6pm; DM6 return).

Practicalities

The **Bahnhof**, on the fast Freiburg to Karlsruhe line, is 4km northwest of the centre in the suburb of OOS. The branch-line has now closed, and the **Alter Bahnhof**, at the fringe of the spa quarter, is now a restaurant and arts centre. Take bus #1; walking is a false economy, and the elliptical valley of the River Oos isn't at all scenic at this point.

Accommodation

The **tourist office** in the *Kurverwaltung* on Augustaplatz (Mon–Sat 9am–10pm, Sun 10am–10pm; ☎07221/275200) has accommodation lists and will help you find a place. A few rooms are available in **private houses** for around DM25, though the tourist office is unlikely to help with these. Try, however, Dr Helena Reich (☎07221/24294), The main concentration of cheap **hotels** is within easy reach of the Bahnhof. *Zum Engel*, Ooser Hauptstr. 20 (☎07221/61610), charges from DM23 per head, while *Zur Linde*, Sinzheimer Str. 3 (☎07221/61519), has singles at DM24, doubles at DM47, and *Goldener Stern*, Ooser Hauptstr. 16 (☎07221/61509), charges DM40 for singles, DM74 for doubles. In Lichtental, *Deutscher Kaiser*, Hauptstr. 35 (☎07221/72152), has singles from DM30, doubles from DM50. The town centre is much more expensive, though *Zur Nest*, Rettigstr. 1 (☎07221/23076), has five rooms going for DM32 per head.

Baden-Baden's **youth hostel** is between the Bahnhof and the centre at Hardbergstr. 34 (☎07221/52223); take bus #1 to Grosse-Dollen-Strasse, from where the way is signposted. **Camping** presents more of a problem, with no sites in the immediate vicinity. Nearest is in a large pleasure park named Oberbruch (☎07223/23194) in the outskirts of BÜHL, three stops away by slow train.

Eating and drinking

Among places to **eat** and **drink**, the *Münchener Löwenbräu* on Gernsbacher Strasse is good; complete with beer garden, it's like a little corner of Bavaria and serves excellent meals. The aforementioned *Zur Nest* is another of the town's better restaurants, as is *Badener Stuben* across the street. For a trendy atmosphere, try *Leo's* on Luisenstrasse, while *Bratwurstglöckle* on Steinstrasse serves solid, low-cost German food.

Rastatt

In 1698, Margrave Ludwig, nicknamed "Türkenlouis" on account of his victories over the Turks, decided to shift his seat from Baden-Baden to **RASTATT**, then an insignificant village 15km to the north, just before the point where the River Murg flows into the Rhine. This move was partly precipitated by the dilapidated condition of the Neues Schloss after the War of the Palatinate Succession. However, it was also conditioned by the courtly culture of the time, which had decided that hilltop fortresses were redundant and should be replaced by planned palatial towns on the model of Versailles.

About town

The massive red sandstone **Schloss** was built in just ten years to plans by an Italian architect, Domenico Rossi. It's approached via a spacious U-shaped courtyard, guarded by a balustrade with writhing Baroque statues, while the central wing is topped by a glistening figure of Jupiter, dubbed the *Goldenen Mann*. The main reception rooms of the interior are under long-term restoration, but some are now accessible by **guided tour** (Tues–Sun 9.30am–5pm; DM2). In addition you can see the **Wehrgeschichtliches Museum** (Tues–Sun 9.30am–5pm; free) and the **Freiheitsmuseum** (Tues–Fri 9.30am–5pm, Sat & Sun 9am–noon & 2–5.30pm; free) on the ground floor. The former shows weapons, uniforms and other military memorabilia from medieval times to the present day. The latter traces the history of German liberalism – a slender theme. Rastatt was chosen as the venue for this museum because it was the last stronghold of the rebels in the Revolutions of 1848–49 – one of the few occasions when the authoritarian nature of German society was seriously challenged. In the north wing of the building, entered from Lyzeumstrasse, is the sumptuous **Schlosskirche**; it's generally kept locked but a notice will tell you where to get the key.

The most imposing part of the Schloss' gardens is now unfortunately cut off by an arterial road to the south, though at least it does leave a peaceful corner at the edge of town. Here is the graceful **Einsiedelner Kapelle**, a miniaturised version of the great Swiss church of the same name. Türkenlouis' widow, Margravine Augusta Sibylla, went on pilgrimage there to pray for her son Ludwig Georg, who, at the age of six, was still unable to speak; needless to say, her faith worked the trick. Later, the **Pagodenburg** was made as a play-house for the prince and his brother. This was modelled on its counterpart in Nymphenburg on the outskirts of Munich; like the chapel, it was built by the new court architect, Johann Michael Ludwig Rohrer, who, along with the Margravine herself, originally came from Bohemia. Behind is the Jugendstil **Wasserturm**, now a café.

Rastatt's town centre was planned in conjunction with the Schloss but only finished in the mid-eighteenth century. Centrepiece is the elliptical Marktplatz, with several fountains, the **Rathaus** and the **Stadtkirche St Alexander**, the last-named already showing Neoclassical influence. Between here and the Schloss are a number of handsome courtiers' houses. One of these, Herrenstr. 11, houses the **Heimat Museum** (Wed, Fri & Sun 10am–noon & 3–5pm; free), which traces the history of the town and includes displays of medieval art and souvenirs of Türkenlouis.

Schloss Favorite

South of Rastatt, on the way to Baden-Baden, is **Schloss Favorite** (guided tours mid-March–Sept 9–11am & 2–5pm; Oct–mid-Nov 9–11am & 2–4pm; DM3), the summer residence of Augusta Sibylla in her years as regent. Here, J.M.L. Rohrer attempted to create the smaller-scale opulence characteristic of the Central European courts which the Margravine preferred to the French-inspired grandeur favoured by her husband.

The interiors are often riotously ornate, notably the *Spiegelkabinett* with its 330 mirrors, and the *Florentiner Zimmer*, lavishly adorned with coloured marbles, stucco, rare woods and semi-precious stones.

Practicalities

Rastatt's **Bahnhof** is at the eastern end of town; here the scenic *Murgtalbahn* from Freudenstadt connects with the express line down the Rhine. Cheapest **hotel**, at DM30 per head, is *Nagel*, Schloss Str. 15 (☎07222/35262). As can be seen from the smoking chimneys, Rastatt is a **beer** town in the middle of a wine region. The *Braustübl* of *Hofbräu Hatz* is on Poststrasse; the food here is also reasonably priced. Products of the rival *Franz* brewery can be sampled at *Gaststätte Türkenlouis* on Bahnhofstrasse.

Karlsruhe

KARLSRUHE is the baby of German cities. It didn't exist at all until 1715, when **Carl Wilhelm**, Margrave of Baden-Durlach, began the construction of a retreat at the edge of the Hardter Wald. There he could escape from a wife who bored him, in order to pursue his cultural interests – and to enjoy the company of several mistresses. The planned town which subsequently grew up around the palace was given an appropriate appellation – "Carl's Rest". Initially modest in size, its growth was stimulated by its establishment as the capital of the re-united state of Baden in 1771 and by the subsequent elevation of its rulers to the title of Grand Dukes under Napoleon's reorganisation of the European political map. Karlsruhe flourished throughout the nineteenth century, enjoying what was, by German standards, a remarkably liberal atmosphere and becoming a major centre for both science and art. In 1945, however, it finally lost its status as a regional capital; Baden was divided between the American and French occupation zones, and Stuttgart made the obvious choice as seat of government for the embryonic province of Baden-Württemberg. As if by way of compensation, Karlsruhe was nominated as the home of the two highest courts of the Federal Republic, a role which has saved it from sinking to the status of a provincial backwater.

As a standard large industrial city, Karlsruhe is by no means the central target of anyone's travels, but it nonetheless has much to offer – to discerning eggheads at least. The city's own propaganda baldly proclaims that it occupies fifth place in the hierarchy of the country's cultural centres, carefully omitting to say which four surpass it. Whether or not this self-estimation is accurate, the **museums** (which are among the oldest public collections in Germany) are undeniably top class, sufficient reason in themselves to justify a visit.

THE FAN TOWN

Looking at a map or an aerial photograph, Karlsruhe appears as an extraordinarily handsome city, thanks to its superbly rhythmical fan-shaped plan. As in an earlier purpose-built princely town, Mannheim, the hub of the system is the Schloss, here placed in isolation to the extreme north. Again this building is U-shaped, but thereafter the geometric patterns become far more imaginative and complex. The Schloss gardens are circular, with the outer half left in a natural state, while the inner is closed by a crescent of regular buildings; this forms a triangle with the Schloss which takes up exactly a quarter of the grounds. From here radiate nine dead straight avenues (representing each of the Muses); the central axis, Karl-Friedrich-Strasse, runs in a vertical line from the palace's central pavilion, while the two end ones shoot outwards at angles of 45° from the wings, with the others placed at regular intervals in between.

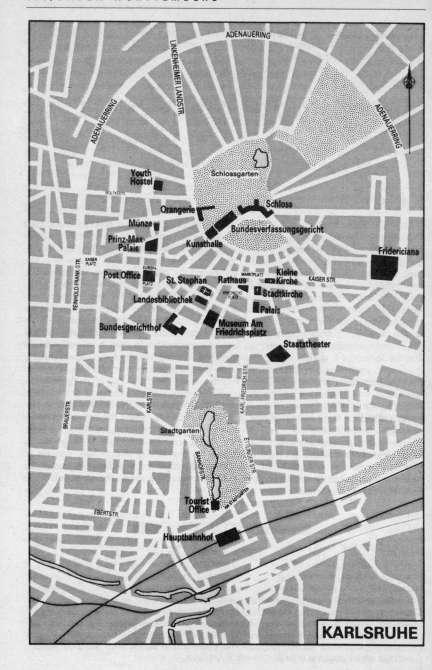

KARLSRUHE

The Schloss and Schlosspark

Although the oldest surviving building, the **Schloss** is actually the second on the site, built in the French-influenced Baroque style of the 1750s. Sadly, it was completely gutted in the last war; the interior has now been modernised to house the **Landesmuseum** (Tues, Wed & Fri–Sun 10am–5.30pm, Thurs 10am–9pm; free). To the left of the entrance is the **archaeology** section. Highlights are a relief of two horsemen from Nineveh; a Sicilian statuette of the goddess *Nike*; and a carving of a gift bringer from Xerxes' palace in Persepolis. Further on are some impressive pieces of Roman sculpture, notably; *Hanging Marsyas* from a villa near Rome; *Mithras Killing the Bull*, which came from near Heidelberg; and a relief of two underwater gods from a settlement not far from Karlsruhe. Many of the museum's finest pieces are in the Renaissance gallery upstairs, including four stunningly bold stained glass windows designed by **Baldung** for the Carthusian monastery in Freiburg and a polychrome limewood *Madonna and Child* by **Riemenschneider**. At the far end of this wing is the **Turkish booty** (*Türkenbeute*), captured by the Margrave Ludwig of Baden-Baden in his seventeenth-century campaigns against the Turks. Unique in Western Europe, this includes embroidery, illuminated books, cutlery, jewellery, leather, woodwork, saddles and weapons of all types. The museum's dazzling Art Nouveau collection is also particularly worth seeing.

In a building immediately to the left of the Schloss is housed the **Bundesverfassungsgericht** (Federal Constitutional Court), the highest judicial authority in the country. This is, in theory, an essential bulwark against the rise of any would-be Hitler, whose accession to power was greatly facilitated by the excessively liberal constitution of the Weimar Republic, which gave full rights to groups pledged to its destruction. The German "Basic Law" has been made much tougher; all political parties must now pledge themselves to the democratic process, or else be outlawed by this court.

The Kunsthalle

At Hans-Thoma-Str. 2, the left side of the circular road round the Schlosspark, is the **Kunsthalle** (Tues–Fri 10am–5pm, Sat & Sun 10am–6pm; free), housed in the mid-nineteenth century Academy of Art.

Early German painting

The magnificent collection of old masters on the first floor is reached via a monumental staircase adorned with a huge fresco by **Moritz von Schwind**, *The Consecration of Freiburg Münster*. Focal point of the gallery is one of the world's greatest pictures, *The Crucifixion* by **Grünewald**. The last and most powerful of his four surviving versions of this scene, it conveys an almost unbearable feeling of tragic intensity. One of the most baffling aspects of Grünewald's art is its inconsistency, and *The Fall of Jesus*, which came from the same altarpiece, has far less emotional impact. Two small monochrome pictures, *St Elizabeth* and *St Lucy*, give a good idea of his early style.

A tiny *Christ with Symbols of the Passion* is a recently discovered **Dürer**; near it hangs a painted version of his famous woodcut *Knight, Death and the Devil* by his pupil **Hans Hoffmann**. Other German paintings to look out for are **Burgkmair**'s *Portrait of Sebastian Brant* (the satirist), **Cranach**'s *Frederick the Wise Adoring the Virgin and Child*, and several works by **Baldung**, among which is *Margrave Christoph I of Baden in Adoration*; Moritz von Schwind included a cameo of the artist painting this work in the stairway fresco. Among the gallery's rarities is *The Raising of Lazarus* by **Wendel Dietterlin**, author of a book of fantastical Mannerist engravings which was immensely influential with late sixteenth-century architects and decorators.

Flemish, Dutch and French painting

The representation of Flemish, Dutch and French painting is equally good. *St Jerome in the Desert* by **Patinir** is one of the few paintings definitely from the hand of this elusive Antwerp master of landscapes with fantastic rock formations. There are also important examples by three other rare painters – **Lucas van Leyden**'s *St Andrew*, **Wtewael**'s *Chicken Inspection*, and **Sweerts**' *Roman Wrestling Match*. **Rembrandt** is represented by a middle-period oval *Self-Portrait*, while there are several examples of **Rubens**. One of **Claude**'s largest canvases, *Adoration of the Golden Calf*, is the star of the seventeenth-century French section, which also includes a diptych of *The Annunciation*, the only known painting by the great Mannerist engraver **Jacques Bellange**, and canvases by Poussin, Le Brun, and the Le Nain brothers. From the following century are four still lifes by **Chardin**.

Nineteenth-century German painting

A notable array of nineteenth-century German painting is dominated by the work of **Hans Thoma**, who served as director of this gallery for twenty years. He was accomplished at both landscape and portraiture but had an unfortunate tendency to drift into sentimentality. **Menzel** and **Feuerbach** are represented by important works, but the gem of this section is **Friedrich**'s *Rocky Reef by a Beach* which, in spite of its tiny size, exudes a truly monumental sense of grandeur.

The Orangerie

The **Orangerie** (same times; free) next door houses paintings by many of the established names of twentieth-century European art, along with a cross-section of nineteenth-century French schools, ranging from Delacroix and Courbet to the Impressionists and their followers. There's a good representation of the *Blaue Reiter* group, notably a couple of fine animal paintings by **Marc**. Another Expressionist masterpiece is **Kokoschka**'s *View of Mont Blanc from Chamonix*, while **Beckmann**'s *Transport of the Sphynxes* is an allegorical canvas alluding to France's liberation from Nazism.

The city centre

At ground level, the streets of the fan-shaped plan are rather less impressive, due largely to the fact that most of the original buildings have been supplanted by undistinguished successors, something for which war damage is partly, but by no means entirely, responsible. Nonetheless, some outstanding architecture survives – including some of the finest **Neoclassical buildings** in Germany. Few buildings from the same generation as the Schloss remain; an exception is the sole place of worship the town then possessed, the **Kleine Kirche** on the main horizontal street, Kaiserstrasse.

Neoclassical Karlsruhe

The next phase of the building of Karlsruhe only occurred with Baden's promotion to an independent Grand Duchy. During the following twenty-five years, a remarkable local architect, **Friedrich Weinbrenner**, completely transformed the city into a worthy capital. As a young man, he had travelled to Rome; having assimilated the style of the ancient world, he employed its grand style in the creation of the great public buildings required by a modern city. Between the Schloss and the start of the central axis, he laid out the rectangular Marktplatz, at the far end of which is an austere red sandstone **Pyramid** containing the grave of Carl Wilhelm. The western side of the square is dominated by the long pink range of the **Rathaus**. Opposite, the Corinthian facade of the **Stadtkirche** looks like an updated version of a Roman temple. Its present interior is modern and functional, the dignified galleried original having been a casualty of wartime bombs. Periodically it's open for exhibitions; otherwise the key is available on weekday mornings at the church offices at Erbprinzenstr. 5.

Immediately south is another square, Rondellplatz, this time circular in shape. It contains the **Palais** (now a bank), whose forms are almost identical to those of the Stadtkirche. In the centre of the square rises an **Obelisk** in honour of the Grand Duke Carl, celebrating his granting of a constitution to the citizens of Baden. West along Erbprinzstrasse is the **Museum am Friedrichsplatz** (Tues 10am–8pm, Wed–Sat 10am–4pm, Sun 10am–5pm; free), the original late Neoclassical home of the Grand Ducal collections. It's now entirely given over to natural history, mostly stuffed animals, but has a good prehistoric section, which includes the only complete skeleton of a hipparion (a forerunner of the horse) yet discovered. Alongside is the **Landesbibliothek** (Mon–Fri 9.30am–6pm, Sat 9.30am–12.30pm; free), which displays its treasures – including many wonderful medieval illuminated manuscripts – in a series of temporary exhibitions.

Further evidence of the enlightened, tolerant nature of the young state of Baden is provided by the Catholic church of **St Stephan** directly opposite. This was built by Weinbrenner, himself a Protestant, at the same time as he was working on the Stadtkirche for members of his own faith. Just as the Rathaus forms a pair with the Stadtkirche, so does St Stephan, but in a wholly different way – the main body of the church is circular while the portico is Doric, the whole being a conscious reinterpretation of the great Pantheon in Rome. Down Ritterstrasse is a heavy late nineteenth-century palace formerly used by the heir to the Grand Duchy; it now houses the second most important law court in Germany, the **Bundesgerichthof** (Federal Supreme Court). This is where the most important postwar criminal trials have been held, including those of several of the Baader-Meinhof gang.

Karlsruhe's third Federal institution is the **Münze** (Mint) on Stephanienstrasse just to the west of the Kunsthalle. Weinbrenner's last building, this is still serving its original purpose, albeit on a much larger scale. Just down Karlstrasse is the **Prinz-Max-Palais** (Tues–Sun 10am–1pm & 2–6pm, also Wed 7–9pm; free), a stolid Wilhelmine mansion now named after one of its former owners, who served a heady five-week stint in the autumn of 1918 as last Chancellor of the Second Reich. In that time, he democratised the constitution, dismissed the military dictator Erich Ludendorff, began peace negotiations, and announced the abdication of the Kaiser before the latter had consented; whereupon he himself resigned and vanished from the national stage. The top floor of the building now contains the local history museum, with maps and prints, plus a model of how the city looked in 1834, when it was at its most splendid. Also exhibited is the *Draisienne*, first exhibited in Paris in 1818 by the Karlsruhe inventor **Karl von Drais**: decide for yourself whether or not it deserves its disputed title as the world's first bicycle.

The **University**, the *Fridericiana*, is located at the far end of Kaiserstrasse. Founded in 1825, this has been a specialist technical institution from the outset. Among its most famous professors were Heinrich Hertz, the pioneer researcher in the field of electromagnetic waves, and Fritz Haber, whose synthesis of ammonia from nitrogen and hydrogen provided the solution which enabled the world demand for chemical fertilizers to be met.

Durlach

DURLACH, 5km east of the city centre, can be reached by train, or by tram #1 or #2. It was the original residence of the local Margraves, and is hence described as the "mother town" of Karlsruhe, of which it's now officially a part, though it retains its own quiet atmosphere. The **Karlsburg** was destroyed in the War of the Palatinate Succession but was rebuilt in the eighteenth century. Part of it now houses the museum of the Pfinz district (Sat 2–5pm, Sun 10am–noon & 2–5pm; free), with displays on local history and on German communities in Slovakia. At the far end of town is the **Turmberg**, which can be ascended by a rack railway. The summit commands great views over the surrounding countryside, and there are a couple of good **restaurants**, *Burghof* and *Schützenhaus*. In Durlach itself is a good old world inn, *Alte Schmiede* on Ochsentorstrasse, which serves a range of salads and specialises in a delicious ten-year-old plum brandy.

Arrival and practicalities

Karlsruhe's **Hauptbahnhof** is situated well to the south of the city centre. Directly facing the entrance is the **tourist office** (Mon–Fri 8am–7pm, Sat 8am–1pm; ☎0721/35530). Ask here if you're interested in a **Rhine cruise**; there's a varied choice of routes from Easter to November, departing from the port at the western extremity of the city. The 24-hour ticket on the **public transport** system is a bargain at DM6. To reach the centre, you can either go from the eastwards-pointing stop with tram #3 or #6 (the latter is circuitous) to Marktplatz, or from the westward-pointing stop with tram #3 or #4 to Europaplatz. **Mitfahrzentrale**'s office is at Rankestr. 14 (☎0721/33666).

Accommodation

The **youth hostel** has a good location just five minutes' walk from the Schloss at Moltkestr. 2b (☎0721/28248). Centrally-sited **hotels** are plentiful, but cater overwhelmingly for the business market. Expect to pay at least DM40–45 per head; rooms at this price are available at *Pension am Zoo*, Ettlingerstr. 33 (☎0721/33678), *Pension Central*, Sophienstr. 6 (☎0721/27324), and *Kolpinghaus*, Karlstr. 115 (☎0721/31434). You can stay for much less in the outlying villages; there's a **campsite** in Durlach by the River Pfinz (☎0721/44060).

Eating, drinking and nightlife

For a university city, Karlsruhe is surprisingly quiet come the evening; only a few scattered pockets seem to spring to life. Some animated student **bars** can, however, be found in and around Ludwigsplatz; *Das Krokodil* and *Café Salmen* both offer raucous music, while the latter serves a good selection of salads. In contrast, *Goldenes Kreuz*, just round the corner on Karlstrasse is a late eighteenth-century beer hall serving excellent food; it's also the flagship of the local *Hoepfner* brewery. Nearby on Erbprinzenstrasse is a small vegetarian restaurant, *Sonne*. The trendiest **cafés**, patronised by artists and art students, are *Rix* on Waldstrasse and *Stephanie*, further north on the street of the same name. Others can be found on Akadamiestrasse, where there are also several pizzerias and an adventurous Arab snack bar, *Arafat Imbiss*. Round the corner in Kaiserpassage is *Restaurant Afrika*, featuring African food, often to the accompaniment of traditional music; there's also a rock pub, *Mad House*. Again this area also offers the alternative of a traditional tavern-restaurant, *Moninger*, named after Karlsruhe's largest brewery, which is particularly renowned for its dark Alt beer.

The main **theatre** is the *Staatstheater* on Baumiesterstrasse, which presents opera, operetta, musicals, ballet and concerts in its main auditorium, plays in the smaller hall. Other venues for drama include *Kammertheater*, Karl-Friedrich-Str. 24 and *Die Insel*, Wilhelmstr. 14, while *Marotte*, Kaiserallee 11, has puppet shows. Other concerts are held at the *Stadthalle* on Festplatz, while **live jazz** is performed at *Jubez*, Am Kronenplatz.

NORTHERN BADEN-WÜRTTEMBERG

The northern part of Baden-Württemberg consists of various territories which were only incorpor~~:~~ into the Grand Duchy of Baden and the Kingdom of Württemberg as a result of the Napole~~..~~ic redistribution of the map of Europe, and whose very different history and geography mean that they're best considered separately.

The fertile **Kraichgau** region, between the Rhine and the Neckar north of Karlsruhe, was particularly associated with the Prince-bishops of Speyer, who established their resplendent new palatial headquarters at **Bruchsal** in the eighteenth century. Further north is the heart of the **Palatinate** (*Pfalz* or *Kurpfalz*), which was ruled by the Count Palatine of the Rhineland, the most senior official in the Holy Roman Empire and one of the seven Electors. The name of the old state lives on in the Land of Rhineland-Palatinate, but its original boundaries were very different. For five hundred years its capital was **Heidelberg** – now the best-loved of all German cities, and a place which definitely warrants several days' stay. The planned town of **Mannheim** was built as the new Palatine capital in the early eighteenth century, with **Schwetzingen** – whose fantastical gardens are unlike any other – used by the court in the summer months. Down the Neckar from Heidelberg is **Bad Wimpfen**, for centuries a Free Imperial City, and one which defies classification; Napoleon give it to Hessen, to which it has never properly belonged.

Like Swabia, **Franconia** (*Franken*) was one of the five great provinces of medieval Germany. Under Napoleon, nearly all of this was incorporated into Bavaria, but the northwestern part – consisting of the **Hohenlohe** plain and part of the **Tauber valley** – was split off and used to beef up both Baden and Württemberg. This includes a section of the famous **Romantic Road**, which mostly lies in Bavaria.

Bruchsal

It was the first time I had seen such architecture. The whole of next day I loitered about the building; hesitating half-way up shallow staircases balustraded by magnificent branching designs of wrought metal; wandering through double doors that led from state room to state room; and gazing with untutored and marvelling eyes down perspectives crossed by the diminishing slants of winter sunbeams.

Patrick Leigh Fermor, *A Time of Gifts*

On his walk to Constantinople, Patrick Leigh Fermor struck it lucky at **BRUCHSAL**, staying as guest of the burgomaster in the resplendent Baroque **Schloss**. His description reflects the fact that this is no ordinary palace; indeed, it's a complete courtly town, comprising over fifty different buildings, which stands as an oasis in the midst of the ugly modern community which now surrounds it.

The Schloss

Construction of the **Schloss** began in 1720 by order of the newly enthroned Prince-bishop of Speyer, Cardinal Hugo Damian von Schönborn, who had fallen out with the local burghers and so decided to move his seat across the Rhine to what was then no more than a hamlet in the heart of the Kraichgau region. A member of a dynasty which specialised in collecting bishoprics (six others were then in family hands), the Cardinal was keen not to be outdone by his brother in Würzburg, who had also put the erection of a magnificent new residence for himself at the top of his list of priorities. Several talented architects were recruited to carry out the work, and the great **Bathasar Neumann** was occasionally seconded from his employment at Würzburg to supply the bravura touches needed to lift the project into the artistic first division.

The Schloss complex, whose cheerful yellow, red and white buildings have been restored to pristine condition following devastation in an air raid at the end of the war, stands on Schönbornstrasse, which leads north to Heidelberg. Along the eastern side of the street are a series of offices, with the Chancellery centre-stage; an army of lackeys lived in the large edifice to the south. At the northern end of the street is the **Damianstor**, while a smaller triumphal arch gives access to the main courtyard. To the left is the **Hofkirche**, whose haughty onion-domed belfry towers over all the other buildings; the interior has unfortunately been modernised. On the opposite side is the **Kammerflügel** where prestigious international **concerts** are often held.

The interior

However, the great reception rooms are all in the central **Corps de Logis** (Tues–Sun 9am–1pm & 2–6pm; DM2). Facing you on entry is Neumann's ingenious monumental **staircase**. This is very different from its Würzburg counterpart, being based on a great central cylinder. The lower section is laid out as a dark grotto, covered with antique-style frescos; you then ascend via walls richly covered with stucco to the airily bright oval landing. Here a brilliant *trompe l'oeil* fresco – an integral part of the overall design – apparently reaches the height of the dome, extending a perspective into the open heavens. Painted by **Januarius Zick**, the most accomplished German decorative artist of the day, it eulogises the history of the Speyer diocese. Neumann and Zick also collaborated on the two rooms off the staircase. The *Fürstensaal* is devoted to the supposedly wise government of the Prince-bishops, while the *Marmorsaal*, which glitters with gold-leaf and coloured marbles, pays tribute to the everlasting nature of the bishopric of Speyer by presenting it in the guise of Mount Olympus.

The Museum Mechanischer Musikinstrumente

It's definitely worth paying the extra money to visit the **Museum Mechanischer Musikinstrumente** (guided tours at 10am, 11am, noon, 2pm, 3pm, 4pm & 5pm; DM5 including Schloss admission) which has recently been installed in some of the vacant rooms. Short demonstrations are given on a cross-section of the 200-odd exhibits, which were regarded as scientific miracles in their own time. Earliest of these are the musical clocks which were much in favour in eighteenth-century courts such as Bruchsal itself, and for which even the greatest composers were forced to prostitute their talents – Haydn wrote a delightful set of miniatures, while Mozart created several profound masterpieces, which have to be played on a full-sized organ for maximum effect. From the turn of the present century are examples of the piano-roll system pioneered by the German *Firma Welte*, which enables the accurate play-back of performances by famous pianists. This technique was later ambitiously adapted for the organ, and there's a marvellous instrument here which was formerly used to entertain guests in the *Hotel Excelsior* in Berlin.

The rest of the town

Other than the Schloss, Bruchsal has very little to offer, the modern centre of town an illustration of how far standards in planning have slipped in recent years. However, it's worth crossing it (via Kaiserstrasse, then uphill over the stream) to see the oldest quarter, dominated by the twin onion towers of **St Peter**, burial church of the Prince-bishops. Designed by Neumann during one of his sorties to the town, its domed interior features elaborate altars and stuccowork.

Practicalities

Bruchsal's **Bahnhof** is a junction on the railway lines linking Stuttgart, Karlsruhe and Heidelberg. To reach the Schloss from there, turn left and continue straight on; you'll reach the gardens within a few minutes. Alternatively, turn right on arriving at Kaiserstrasse; this soon brings you to the end of Schönbornstrasse. A **campsite** and *Naturfreundehaus* are at Karlsruher Str. 215 (☎07251/15106) to the south of the centre. Cheapest **hotel** is *Graf Kuno*, Württemberger Str. 97 (☎07251/2013), charging from DM30 for singles, DM54 doubles. For a meal or a drink, try *Zum Bären*, within the Schloss complex; it serves the best food in town and has a beer garden. The **tourist office** (Mon–Wed & Fri 8am–noon & 2–4pm, Thurs 8am–noon & 2–5pm; ☎07251/79301) is in a modern shopping centre called *Bürgerzentrum*.

Schwetzingen

There's nothing quite like the gardens of **SCHWETZINGEN**. This town, which lies on the railway between Karlsruhe and Mannheim, some 12km west of Heidelberg, was of very minor significance until the 1740s. There isn't even anything remarkable about the **Schloss**, a rather cut-price palace designed by the Heidelberg architect Johann Adam Breunig, whose coat of pinkish-orange paint is a rather desperate attempt to make it appear more striking than it is; it's the gardens which get all the praise and all the visitors.

ELECTOR CARL THEODOR (1724-99)

Schwetzingen's stunning transformation from its long history of mediocrity was due to the Elector Carl Theodor, who inherited the Palatinate from his childless uncle and later became a somewhat reluctant Elector of Bavaria as well, when another branch of the Wittelsbachs died out. As if by compensation, Carl Theodor started several aristocratic lines, ennobling such of his many mistresses as were not high-born; even today, there's a standing joke in the region that his bastard descendants can immediately be identified through having his distinctive nose. His chief political goal was to prevent the excessive dominance of Germany by either Prussia or Austria; to this end, he attempted to do a deal with the Habsburgs to swap Bavaria for Belgium, which would have left him in charge of a sizeable and coherent Rhenish state. This made him a thorn in the flesh of the ever-ambitious Frederick the Great, who derided him as "a lucky dog", commenting bitterly that "without drawing his sword even once that lazy fellow has gained more territory than I have been able to do in three wars, one of which lasted seven years". If Carl Theodor's achievements in this field were ultimately in vain (the Palatinate was carved up just two years after his death), his track record as a patron of the arts has proved far more enduring. The most important decision he took was to make Schwetzingen his summer residence and to embellish it with the pleasure park he craved yet was unable to have in his fortified seat at Mannheim.

The Schlossgarten

The **Schlossgarten** (daily during official summertime 8am–8pm, rest of year 9am–5/6pm; DM2.50) is a supreme triumph of the art of landscaping and of the Rococo style, representing a highly original escape into a world of pure fantasy. It took some thirty years to lay out the gardens and adorn them with a series of whimsical buildings. These aimed at capturing the atmosphere of various far-off civilisations; this fascination with the exotic marks out Schwetzingen as one of the precursors of the budding

Romantic movement. Best time to see the gardens is late spring – the lilac, ivy and chestnut trees are a riot of colour in May, while the linden trees are at their most fragrant during June. High summer can be uncomfortably crowded; off-season, you might have the park to yourself, but, in addition to the absence of bloom, the pavilions are then kept locked.

The Schlosstheater

The **Schlosstheater** (guided tours in summer at times listed on noticeboard; DM2) was added to the main building by **Nicolas de Pigage**, an ingenious architect from Lorraine who arrived in Schwetzingen in 1750 and spent much of the next three decades constructing its garden buildings. In an individual confection, mixing Rococo with Neoclassicism, Pigage built a triple-tiered auditorium in the shape of a lyre, facing a deep stage harbouring complicated machinery underneath. It was originally intended for the performance of French comedies, and Voltaire, a personal friend of the Elector, was a regular visitor. With its grand dimensions, long vistas, straight avenues and symmetrical layout, the French-style **formal garden** is very much a product of the Age of Reason. It's richly endowed with fountains (which play daily in summer), mock-antique urns and a host of statues, some of which are masterpieces.

Just west of here is the **Tempel Apollos**, which served as an open-air auditorium. A sunken garden with sphinxes leads to an artificial mound crowned by a temple in the style of Classical Rome housing a statue of the god. This is the first in a row of buildings by Pigage; alongside is one of his finest works, the **Badhaus** (daily in summer 10am–12.30pm & 1–6pm). Its nine rooms are adorned with rosewood panellings, sculptures, landscape paintings, and Chinese tapestries and silks. The marble bath repeats the elliptical shape of the central drawing room; its water pipes are artistically decorated, and the chamber itself adorned with mirrors and jewels. Next to the Badhaus is an arbour with a fountain of water-spouting birds; it's nicknamed "The End of the World" because of the *trompe l'oeil* perspective, which terminates in a painted diorama. Crossing the moat and continuing northwards, you come to the **Tempel der Botanik**, supposedly representing the trunk of an oak tree, and the **Römische Wasserweg**, a spectacular fake of a fort and aqueduct, deliberately built as an ivy-covered ruin to enhance its illusory effect. Beyond here are the outer reaches of the park, laid out in the contrastingly untamed style of an English garden. By following the path traversing this section, you can return to the main part of the park via the humpbacked **Chinesische Brücke**.

The Tempel Merkurs

Pigage's remaining buildings are at the opposite end of the park. The **Tempel Merkurs** is reached via either of the paths along the side of the artificial lake. Originally, this monument was intended to be redolent of ancient Egypt, but ended up as a pastiche of the clifftop ruin of a European Romanesque castle, anachronistically adorned with scenes of the life of Mercury. From here, there's a spectacular vista over a pond to the pink cupola and minarets of the **Moschee** or Mosque (daily in summer 10am–12.30pm & 1–6pm), the most original structure in the gardens and the last to be built. It's a unique translation of Oriental forms into the language of eighteenth-century European architecture; down the years, Islamic visitors have continually been impressed by it, and the building has even been used for worship. Returning in the direction of the circular section of the garden, you come to the sixteen-columned **Tempel Minervas**, which goes back to the favourite source of inspiration, Classical Rome. The goddess of wisdom is seated inside; she also appears in a frieze above the entrance, poring over a plan of the gardens of Schwetzingen, to which she gives her seal of approval.

Practicalities

The **tourist office** (Mon–Fri 9am–noon & 2–5pm, Sat 9–11am; ☎06202/4933) is on Schlossplatz, in one of the few imposing buildings in the town itself, the eighteenth-century **Palais Hirsch**. This is also where you can book for performances in the Schlosstheater. The **Bahnhof** is five minutes' walk from here down Carl-Theodor-Strasse. **Buses** to and from Heidelberg stop on Schlossplatz; services run every half-hour for most of the day. Although there's no particular reason for staying in Schwetzingen, it makes a good alternative base if Heidelberg is booked solid; **rooms** at around DM30 per head are available at *Stadtschänke*, Carl-Theodor-Str. 31 (☎06202/25614), *Silberner Anker*, Herzogstr. 31 (☎06202/15961), and *Rheintal*, Marktplatz 30 (☎06202/15730), while *Mainzer Rad*, Marktplatz 4 (☎06202/4524) charges DM35.

Asparagus has been cultivated in Schwetzingen for more than three centuries; in season (April–June) it can be sampled in any of the town's restaurants, several of which are grouped close to the Schloss. Each April and May, the Schlosstheater is the setting for an international **music festival**, often focusing on the works of Gluck. Another festival in September is devoted solely to Mozart; there are also regular musical and theatrical performances of all kinds throughout the year.

Mannheim

MANNHEIM was formerly considered one of the most beautiful cities in Germany. Writing in 1826, William Hazlitt called it "a splendid town, both from its admirable buildings and the glossy neatness of the houses. They are too fine to live in, and seem only made to be looked at." A mere stripling among German cities, it was founded in 1606 as a fortress at the strategically important intersection of the Rivers Rhine and Neckar. Its meteoric rise to prominence came with the return of the Counts Palatine to Catholicism; unable to establish a satisfactory relationship with the burghers of Heidelberg, Carl Philipp decided in 1720 to make Mannheim the main seat of his court. A daringly original **planned town** (see below) was laid out, which served as capital of the Palatinate for the next 57 years, becoming one of Europe's most celebrated centres of the performing arts. The nineteenth century saw heavy industrialisation, centred on the harbour trade and shipbuilding, though its most prestigious feature was the auto-mobile factory established by Carl Benz, who demonstrated his first vehicle here in 1886. Alas, the continued prominence of industry, coupled with heavy damage in the last war means that the city's overall appearance is no longer pleasing. However, the highly esteemed **grid-plan** still survives.

THE CHESSBOARD TOWN

The construction of Mannheim was based on a chessboard layout on the strip of land between the two great rivers. A simple system for naming and numbering the streets was adopted, which was later used in a modified form throughout North America. The city is divided into 144 squares, each bearing a letter followed by a number. Streets to the west of the central axis are designated A to K, moving northwards; proceeding in the same direction, those to the east are L to U. The street number indicates proximity to the axis, so that D7, for example, is to the far west, whereas R7 is at the extreme east. Obviously, each house then bears a second number, which indicates its position on the square. At first the system can be confusing, particularly when you arrive at the Hauptbahnhof, which is at the extreme southwest corner of the grid, at a point where the blocks are of widely varying sizes. However, once you get the hang of it, there's really no other European city which it's so simple to find your way around.

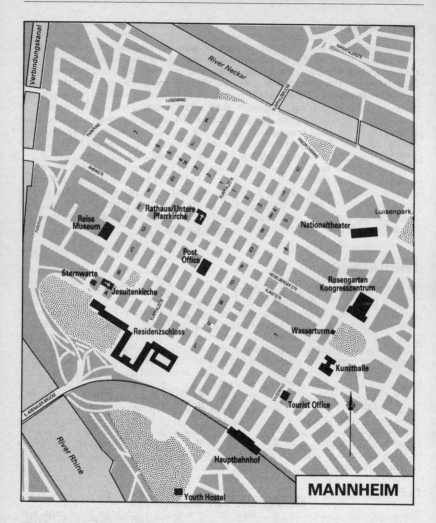

The streets of the grid

The pivot of the planned town is the horseshoe-shaped **Residenzschloss**, the most massive Baroque palace ever built in Germany. Soon after its completion, it became an expensive white elephant – the court transferred to Munich when Carl Theodor inherited the Bavarian Electorate. The dignified exterior is heavily indebted to Palladianism; the interior was far more sumptuous, including rich stuccowork and ceiling frescos by the Asam brothers. These were obliterated by wartime bombs; afterwards, the building was put to functional use to house the University, with only the outside restored in full.

However, as a real labour of love, the **chapel** (daily 9am–5pm) at the end of the western wing, plus the main **reception rooms** (guided tours April–Oct Tues–Sun 10am–noon & 3–5pm, Nov–March same times Sat & Sun only; DM1.50) were re-created from old photographs. The success of this project is highly debatable, but at least the *Rittersaal*, reached via a monumental staircase, provides an effective **concert hall**, which is particularly appropriate as the Mannheim court's greatest achievements were in the field of music. Its orchestra, which pioneered the mellow tones of the clarinet, was regarded in the eighteenth century as the best in the world, while the symphony was developed here into the chief form of instrumental music.

The Jesuitenkirche

On A5, just to the west of the Residenzschloss, is the **Jesuitenkirche**, deliberately constructed as the largest church in town to symbolise the Palatinate court's return to Catholicism; the grandiose facade and the central dome are the most striking features. Immediately to its rear is the **Sternwarte**, an observatory tower now used by artists.

The Zeughaus

Just to the north on C5 is the **Zeughaus**, erected in the penultimate year of Mannheim's period as Palatine capital. It now houses the **Reiss-Museum** (Tues & Thurs–Sun 10am–1pm & 2–5pm, Wed 10am–1pm & 2–8pm; free), with collections of Dutch and Flemish cabinet pictures, of decorative arts and of local history – look out for the old maps and prints which give an idea of the original dignified appearance of the grid-plan streets, something hardly even hinted at today. On the square directly in front of the Zeughaus is a brand new building specially designed to house the most important section of the museum, the archaeology department. This originated as the Elector's private cabinet of antiquities, and ranges from the Stone Age to the early medieval period. Also in the new museum are ethnological displays from Africa, the Islamic countries, India, China and Japan.

Around the Marktplatz

The **Marktplatz**, which occupies the square G1, is the scene of markets on Tuesday, Thursday and Saturday mornings; an enticingly varied picnic can be assembled at a bargain price by shopping here. In the centre rises a large monument presented by Carl Theodor; originally representing the Four Elements, it was re-worked into an allegorical composition in praise of Mannheim by the son of the original sculptor. On the south side of the square is a curious Siamese-twin of a building, erected just before Mannheim became the seat of the court. Sharing a central tower, the eastern part serves as the **Rathaus**, while the western is the **Untere Pfarrkirche**; their physical union is supposed to symbolise the concord between Justice and Piety, between secular and sacred authority.

Outside the grid

The other main square, the Jugendstil **Friedrichsplatz**, is due east from here, just outside the central grid. It was laid out around the **Wasserturm**, which is some fifteen years older, and is the main example of a style which left a considerable mark all over the city. Another fine Jugendstil building is the **Kunsthalle** (Tues, Wed & Fri–Sun 10am–5pm, Thurs 10am–8pm; free) on Moltkestrasse, the next street to the south. This contains one of the best collections of nineteenth- and twentieth-century painting and sculpture in Germany, and is now the city's most obvious single draw. Highlight of the collection is one of the great masterpieces of Impressionism, **Manet**'s *Execution of Emperor Maximilian of Mexico*, the largest and most complete of the four versions he painted of this subject. Other notable works in the same room are **Cézanne**'s *Pipe Smoker*, and still lifes by Renoir and van Gogh. The German section was brutally pruned in the Nazi purges against "degenerate art", but there's a room devoted to Romanticism, including several important examples of **Feuerbach**. *Portrait of the*

Writer Max Herrmann-Neisse is one of **George Grosz**'s best canvases, while there's an outstanding array of modern German sculpture, with **Barlach** and **Lehmbruck** strongly represented, along with a host of avant-garde works. Major temporary exhibitions are frequently held in the gallery.

On the banks of the River Neckar

At the northernmost end of the grid-plan the central axis road continues over the Neckar by the Kurpfälzbrücke. Moored close to the bridge is the 1920s passenger steamer *Mainz*, which now houses a **navigation museum** (Tues–Sat 10am–1pm & 2–5pm, Sun 10am–5pm; free). Nearby is the departure point for **harbour cruises** (June–Aug Mon & Thurs 10am & 2.30pm; duration two hours; DM9). Eastwards along the river is the city's playground, the **Luisenpark** (May–Aug 9am–9pm; rest of year 9am–dusk; DM3). This boasts various flower gardens, hothouses, an aquarium, a menagerie of farmyard animals and water fowl, an open-air stadium for concerts, a gondola course and a watersports centre. There's also the **Fernsehturm** (11am–dusk; DM3) offering the best overall view of the city. Just south of the park on Wilhelm-Varnholt-Platz is the **Planetarium** (showings Tues–Sun 3pm, also Mon & Fri 8pm, Sat & Sun 5pm & 7pm; DM6).

Practicalities and nightlife

The **tourist office** (Mon–Fri 8.30am–6pm, Sat 8.30am–noon; ☎0621/101011) is at Kaiserring 10. For DM1 you can pick up their monthly programme of events, *Mannheimer Veraltungsprogramm*, which includes limited listings for Heidelberg. **Mitfahrzentrale** have an office at N4, 19 (☎0621/21846).

Accommodation

The **youth hostel** is at Rheinpromenade 21 (☎0621/822718); take the underground passageway at the back entrance of the Hauptbahnhof, then turn left; it's only a few minutes' walk away. This convenient location makes it a good base for touring the surrounding area. **Camping** is possible (April–Sept only) on the banks of either of the city's two great rivers. The larger and cheaper site is at NEUOSTHEIM (☎0621/416840) on the Neckar to the east; the other is to the south on Strandbad in NECKARAU (☎0621/ 856240); in spite of its name, it's located on a bend of the Rhine. **Hotels** are overwhelmingly geared to the expense account market, but two well situated exceptions are *Arabella* at M2, 12 (☎0621/23050), with singles at DM30, doubles DM50; and *Rosenstock* at N3, 5 (☎0621/27343), whose singles cost DM35, doubles DM60. Otherwise, there's a clutch of places on Tattersallstrasse just to the north of the Hauptbahnhof; cheapest is *Goldene Gans* (☎0621/105277), with singles at DM40, doubles from DM65.

Nightlife

Mannheim has a vibrant **theatre** tradition; the *Nationaltheater* on Goetheplatz is the successor to the now-destroyed building near the Schloss which was associated with Schiller's youthful *Sturm und Drang* phase. Performances of plays, opera, ballet and musicals are presented, along with special shows for kids. Other venues are *Klapsmühl' am Rathaus* at D6, 3 for cabaret and pantomime, and *Puppenspiele*, Collinistr. 26 for puppets, while **concerts** are held at *Kongresszentrum Rosengarten* on Friedrichsplatz.

Eating and drinkimg

Among a wide choice of places to **eat** and **drink**, *Elsässer* at N7, 8 serves some of the best food in town, while the brewery-owned *Andechst* at N2, 10 has a particularly lively atmosphere. The beer hall of Mannheim's main brewery, *Eichbaum*, is just north of the Neckar at Käfertalerstr. 168; its Weizen beers are renowned. Two vegetarian restaurants are *Heller's* at N7, 13 and *Redlich* at H1, 16, while a good Italian is *Augusta*, Augustaanlage 40. Among many fine cafés is *Herrdegen*, in an eighteenth-century mansion at N2, 8. Look out for the local speciality, *Mannemer Dreck* (Mannheim Mud), invented last century at a time when there was an over-reaction by the police to dogs fouling the pavement; a humorous baker retaliated by making a chocolate teabread in a similar shape, and the recipe has remained popular ever since.

Heidelberg

When the Romantic movement discovered **HEIDELBERG** in the late eighteenth century, the city was very much a fallen star. Capital of the Palatinate for five hundred years, it had never fully recovered from two sackings at the hands of French troops in the previous century; its rulers had abandoned their magnificent, crumbling Schloss in favour of the creature comforts of their new palace in Mannheim. Yet this wistful feeling of decay only enhanced the charms of the city, majestically set on both banks of the swift-flowing River Neckar between two ranges of wooded hills – a real-life fulfilment of the ideal German landscape, and a site known to be one of the earliest inhabited places in the world. Add to all this the fact that the city was home to the oldest university on German soil (which was the custodian of rich and bizarre traditions), and there was an intoxicatingly heady brew which not only stirred the Romantic imagination, but has seduced generations of travellers ever since, to an extent no other German city comes close to matching. To many of the rushed Grand Tour of Europe coach parties of today, Heidelberg *is* Germany, the only place in the country they see – or, perhaps, want to see.

For English-speaking visitors, the distinguished roll-call of predecessors gives Heidelberg special claims on the attention. Earliest of these was the Scots-born princess, **Elizabeth Stuart**, daughter of the first monarch of the United Kingdom, James VI and I. She arrived in 1613 as the seventeen-year-old bride of the Elector Palatine and presided over a spectacular court life for five years, before leaving for Prague and her ill-fated spell as the "Winter Queen". Heidelberg's greatest painter is also Britain's greatest; **J.M.W. Turner** first came to the city in 1836, and, in a series of oils and watercolours, captured its changing moods and magical plays of light in his own inimitable way. Among Americans, **Mark Twain** deserves pride of place; he began the hilarious travels round Europe recounted in *A Tramp Abroad* in Heidelberg in 1878, and his descriptions of the city have never been surpassed. By this time, Heidelberg was already a popular sojourn for Americans visiting Europe, though the numbers were a trickle in comparison with the situation today. After World War II (in which, significantly, the city was spared from aerial bombardment), Heidelberg was chosen as the headquarters of the US Army in Europe. Nowadays some 20,000 American nationals (about one in seven of the total population) live there, mostly in Patrick Henry Village, a purpose-built community to the south.

The telephone code for Heidelberg is ☎06221

Practicalities

Heidelberg is best avoided in high summer; the students, who make such an essential contribution to the life of the city, clear out then and are replaced by hordes of tourists. Surprisingly, it's possible to cover all the essential sights fairly quickly, but you should certainly plan on staying for several days at least, in order to soak up the city's atmosphere. Be warned that first impressions of Heidelberg are likely to make you wonder what all the fuss is about; the **Hauptbahnhof** and inter-city **bus terminus** are situated in an anonymous quarter some 1.5km west of the centre, with a dreary avenue, Kurfürsten-Anlage, leading towards town. The rather harrassed **tourist office** is on the square outside (Mon–Thurs & Sat 9am–7pm, Fri 9am–9pm, Sun 10am–6pm in summer, 10am–3pm in winter; ☎21341/27735).

Accommodation

In the high season, it's worth paying the DM2 fee the tourist office charges for finding a room; although there are **hotels** dotted all over the city, these are often booked solid. If you want to look yourself, glance at the chart outside which tells you where vacancies exist. A couple of budget options, charging upwards of DM20 for a bed in a small dorm, are *Krokodil*, Kleinschmidstr. 12 (☎24059), a short walk away in the direction of the city centre, and *Jeske*, in the heart of the city at Mittelbadgasse 2 (☎23733); the former also has singles from DM50, doubles from DM85. The few other conveniently sited hotels with reasonable rates are *Zum Weinberg*, Heliggeiststr. 1 (☎21792), with singles DM35, doubles DM55; *Brandstätter*, Friedrich-Ebert-Anlage 60 (☎23944), doubles (only) at DM70; and *Elite*, Bunsenstr. 15 (☎25734), singles from DM45, doubles from DM70. All the other cheaper options are well out, and may offer no advantages over commuting from another town. Otherwise, ask in the second-hand clothes shop *Flic-Flac* at Unterestr. 12, where young travellers are helped to find rooms in private houses.

The **youth hostel** is near the Zoo on the north bank of the Neckar, about 4km from the centre at Tiergartenstr. 5 (☎412066); take bus #11. It's large, fairly luxurious and very liberal – not only is there a late curfew, but there's also a bar in the basement. If it's full, as is often the case, there's another hostel in Dilsberg, 15km down the Neckar (see below); the hostel in Mannheim is also close enough to make commuting cost-effective. Both **campsites** are east of the city by the river – *Heide* (☎06223/2111) is between ZIEGELHAUSEN and KLEINGEMÜND; *Neckertal* (☎802506) is in SCHLIERBACH.

Public transport

A 36-hour ticket on the **public transport** network makes a good investment; it costs DM6 for journeys within the city boundaries, DM10 for the full circuit. The Altstadt is mostly pedestrianised; tram #1 takes you from the Hauptbahnhof to Bismarckplatz, at

---

HEIDELBERG VIEWPOINTS

It's the long-range views which have made Heidelberg so famous, and the city is a ready-made subject for picture-postcard **photography**; with its hilly setting, there are plenty of angles to choose from. If you take the trouble to go to the same vantage point at different times of day, you'll see the reason for Heidelberg's hold on painters: the red sandstone buildings change their hue with the movement of the sun, and the shafts of light make magical effects as they illuminate and cast into shadow different parts of the scene. "One thinks Heidelberg by day the last possibility of the beautiful," wrote Mark Twain, "but when he sees Heidelberg by night, a fallen Milky Way... he requires time to consider upon the verdict."

The best-known view is from the northern quays of the Neckar, where you get a full-frontal panorama of the Altstadt nestling snugly below the Schloss, itself sharply etched against the background of the wooded Königstuhl. The spectacle from street level is surpassed by climbing up the slopes of the Heiligenberg via the celebrated **Philosophenweg** ("Philosopher's Walk"), so-called because of the stimulus it offered to the meditation of Heidelberg thinkers. As an alternative, start from the town centre, and follow Neue Schloss Strasse and Molkenkurweg to the *Molkenkur* hotel, whose terrace gives a very different perspective. Further up, the Königstuhl is crowned by the **Fernsehturm** (Television Tower; March–Oct daily 10am–5pm; DM2), commanding a sweeping panorama over the Neckar valley and Odenwald.

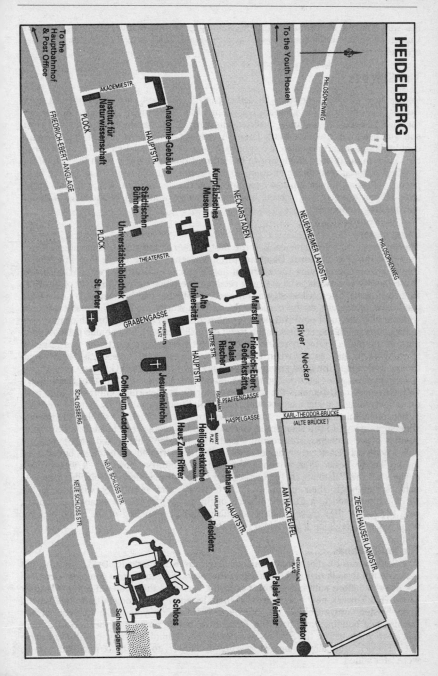

HEIDELBERG

To the
Hauptbahnhof
& Post Office

To the Youth Hostel

PHILOSOPHENWEG

PHILOSOPHENWEG

AKADEMIESTR.

PLÖCK

FRIEDRICH-EBERT-ANLAGE

Institut für
Naturwissenschaft

HAUPTSTR.

Anatomie-Gebäude

Kurpfälzisches
Museum

NECKARSTADEN

NEUENHEIMER LANDSTR.

River Neckar

Städtische
Bühnen

PLÖCK

Universitätsbibliothek

THEATERSTR.

Alte
Universität

Marstall

Palais
Rischer

Friedrich-Ebert-
Gedenkstätte

St. Peter

GRABENGASSE

UNIVERSITÄTS
PLATZ

UNTERE STR.

HAUPTSTR.

PFAFFENGASSE

FISCHMARKT

KARL-THEODOR-BRÜCKE
(ALTE BRÜCKE)

Jesuitenkirche

HASPELGASSE

Collegium Academicum

Haus Zum Ritter

Heiliggeistkirche

MARKT
PLATZ

KORNMARKT

Rathaus

HAUPTSTR.

AM HACKTEUFEL

ZIEGELHÄUSER LANDSTR.

SCHLOSSBERG

NEUE SCHLOSS STR.

NEUE SCHLOSS STR.

Residenz

KARLSPLATZ

NECKARMÜNZ
PLATZ

Palais Weimar

Karlstor

Schloss

Schlossgarten

the western end of the long, straight Hauptstrasse. Alternatively, bus #11 goes to Universitätsplatz on the southern side of the old city, bus #34 to Kornmarkt at the eastern end.

The Schloss

Centrepiece of all the views of Heidelberg is the **Schloss**, one of the world's great castles . . . "with empty window arches, ivy-moulded battlements, mouldering towers – the Lear of inanimate nature – deserted, discrowned, beaten by the storms, but royal still, and beautiful," to quote Mark Twain. A series of disparate yet consistently magnificent buildings of various dates, it somehow hasn't been diminished by its ruined condition; if anything, it has actually grown in stature. Enough remains (with the help of the plentiful pictorial records which exist) to give a clear idea of what it looked like in its prime, yet a new dimension has been added by the destruction, which reveals otherwise hidden architectural secrets and magnifies its umbilical relationship with the surrounding landscape.

Some history

The Schloss originally dates back to the first quarter of the thirteenth century. It was then that the title of **Count Palatine**, the most senior office under the Holy Roman Emperor and one carrying the status of an Elector, was bestowed on a Wittelsbach, Duke Ludwig of Bavaria, whose family retained the office right to the end of the Holy Roman Empire. The earliest significant portions of what can be seen today date from the following century, as the castle evolved into a sturdy medieval fortress capable of withstanding the most powerful siege weapons of the day. In the sixteenth century, the inner courtyard of the Schloss began to be embellished with sumptuous palatial buildings, as its role as a princely residence became of increasing importance; this gathered momentum in mid-century when the Electors converted to Protestantism and began the construction of the most splendid **Renaissance buildings** in Germany.

Lutheranism was later jettisoned in favour of Calvinism, and the **Heidelberg Catechism** of 1562 remains the basic creed for many Reformed churches. This took on an increasingly militant aspect when Elizabeth Stuart's youthful husband, **Friedrich V**, became nominal leader of the Calvinist League, which aimed to establish the irreversible supremacy of Protestantism in Germany and to topple the Habsburgs from their position of pre-eminence in the country's affairs. Friedrich's ham-fisted attempt was not only a personal disaster (he was defeated, exiled and stripped of his titles), but also led to the Thirty Years' War, which devastated the country. However, it was French designs on the Palatinate in 1689 which led to the destruction of Heidelberg and its Schloss; although their claim on the territory was eventually withdrawn, the Electorship passed to a Catholic branch of the family. Unable to establish a rapport with the locals, they moved their seat; the planned re-building of the Schloss never occurred, and Heidelberg was left to vegetate.

The fortifications

The Schloss can be reached by funicular from the Kornmarkt for DM3.50 return, but it's more fun to walk up via the Burgweg; that way, you can make a complete circuit of the exterior before entering. At the northwest corner is the sixteenth-century **Dicker Turm** (Fat Tower), now a semicircular shell, its outer wall, along with its top, having been blasted away. Behind the northern fortifications you get a glimpse of the Renaissance buildings and pass the **Zeughaus**, before coming to the **Redoute**, built just a few years before the Schloss was destroyed. Behind it stands the **Glockenturm** (Bell Tower), originally a single-storey defence tower, to which six residential levels were later added.

Continuing along the eastern side, you see the protruding **Apothekerturm**, an old defensive tower which was later converted into the Apothecary plus residential quarters. Between it and the Glockenturm is a superb oriel window, part of a now-vanished banqueting hall. At the southeastern corner is the most romantic of the ruins, the **Pulver Turm** (Powder Tower), now generally know as the **Gesprengter Turm** (Blown-up Tower). Originally a gunpowder store, it was destroyed by miners who tunnelled underneath and blew it up from the centre. This left a clean break in the now-overgrown masonry; the collapsed section still lies intact in the moat, leaving a clear view into the chambers of the interior, with their once-elegant central column supports.

From here, it's best to proceed to the western side of the Schloss, an artificial plateau formerly used as a gun battery but converted by Friedrich V into a pleasure garden. At its entrance is the graceful Roman-inspired **Elizabethpforte**, a gateway said to have been erected in a single night in 1615 as a surprise for the princess; the sober **Englischer Bau** adjoining the Dicker Turm was also built in her honour. At the western end of the garden is the semicircular **Rondell**, commanding a view over the rooftops of the city.

The Schlosshof

The **Schlosshof** (free access at all times; guided tours of interiors daily April–Oct 9am–5pm; Nov–March 9am–4pm; check on noticeboard for times of departures in English; DM4) is reached by a series of sixteenth-century defensive structures – the Brückenhaus, the bridge itself and the severe **Thorturm** (Gate Tower), the only part of the Schloss not blown up. Immediately to the left of the entrance is the Gothic **Ruprechtsbau**, where you can see two restored chambers, one with an elaborate chimneypiece. After the ruined library comes the **Frauenzimmerbau**, where the women of the court resided; its colossal ground-floor hall has been restored as a venue for concerts. Looking anti-clockwise from the entrance gate, you first of all see the Gothic **Brunnenhaus** (Well-House), a loggia with a graceful star vault. Its marble columns were brought here from Charlemagne's palace, and had previously adorned a Roman building. This is followed by a series of functional buildings – the **Kaserne** (Barracks) and the **Oekonomiebau**, which housed offices and workshops; part of it has been converted to the *Weinstube Schloss Heidelberg*, one of the best restaurants in town, and one surprisingly reasonable in price.

What really catches your eye in the courtyard, however, is the group of Renaissance palaces on the north and east sides. Next to the Oekonomiebau is the mid-sixteenth-century **Ottheinrichsbau**, now just a shell but preserving its vigorous horizontal facade. The magnificent sculptural decoration has successive tiers of allegorial figures representing Strength, the Christian Virtues and the Planetary Deities. In the basement is the **Deutsches Apothekenmuseum** (April–Oct daily 10am–5pm, Nov–March Sat & Sun only 11am–5pm; DM2), an offbeat but worthwhile collection. Among the displays are several complete Baroque and Rococo workshops, an early seventeenth-century travelling pharmacy and a Herbarium. You can also descend to the bowels of the Apothekenturm, which has been rigged out with a furnace and distilling apparatus in an attempt to re-create its old appearance.

The triple loggia of the earlier **Saalbau** forms a link to the celebrated late sixteenth-century **Friedrichsbau**. With its strong vertical emphasis, this is a perfect counterbalance to the Ottheinrichsbau. It's a swaggering Mannerist composition handled with superb aplomb by the Alsatian architect Johannes Schoch; he paid respect to the past by using the three great orders of Classical antiquity, yet also anticipated the Baroque in the intersecting pillars, with their dependency on the effects of light and shade. A series of bucolic, larger-than-life statues is a pantheon of the House of Wittelsbach, beginning with Charlemagne (the alleged founder of the dynasty) and continuing right up to the ruling Elector. Those now on view are copies, but the originals can be seen inside, along with a number of restored rooms which have been decked out in period style. On the ground floor is the intact **Schlosskapelle**, which, in total contrast to the facade, harks back to the Gothic period; not surprisingly, in view of the photo opportunities outside, it's now a popular venue for weddings.

The **Fassbau** (daily April–Oct 9am–7pm, Nov–March 9am–6pm; DM1, but included in price of guided tours) is reached down a passageway in front of the Schlosshof. It contains the celebrated **Grosses Fass** (Great Vat), said to be the largest wine barrel in the world with a capacity of over 50,000 gallons; this is crowned with a platform which did service as a dance floor. Made in the late eighteenth century, the vat is the third in a spectacular line; though a folly and long out of service, it's reputed to have been filled on at least one occasion, when there was a particularly good grape harvest in the Palatinate (whose Elector was entitled to claim a tithe). Facing the entrance, as a ploy to elicit a gasp from visitors when they turn the corner and see the real thing, is the so-called **Kleines Fass** (Little Vat), itself of ample proportions.

The Altstadt

The Altstadt, the historic centre of Heidelberg, is a largely pedestrianised area between the Schloss and the Neckar, bisected by an unusually long main street, Haupstrasse. In comparison with the Schloss, its monuments can seem prosaic: although the old layout of the medieval city survives, the French devastation means that nearly all the buildings are eighteenth-century or later, and are excessively sober in style. To many people, these are familiar from the Hollywood version of *The Student Prince* by the Hungarian-American composer Sigmund Romberg.

Marktplatz and the eastern quarters

The finest surviving buildings in the Altstadt are grouped on Marktplatz. In the middle is the Gothic red sandstone **Heiliggeistkirche**, founded just after the University at the end of the fourteenth century; its lofty tower, capped by a Baroque dome, is one of the city's most prominent landmarks. Note the tiny shopping booths between its buttresses, a feature ever since the church was built – this was a common practice in medieval times but has been frowned upon for so long that examples are now rare. Inside, it's light, airy and uncluttered, but was not always so, as the church was built to house the mausoleum of the Palatinate Electors. Only one tomb now remains – that of Ruprecht III, who became King of Germany in 1400, and his wife, Elizabeth von Hohenzollern. Furthermore, the triforium gallery once housed one of the great libraries of the world, the *Bibliotheca Palatina*; this was confiscated by Field Marshal Johann Tilly as war booty and presented to the Pope. Some items were returned last century, but the finest books remain in the Vatican.

Facing the church is the only mansion to survive the seventeenth-century devastation of the town, the **Haus zum Ritter**, so-called from the statue of Saint George dressed as a knight which crowns the pediment. Built for a Huguenot refugee cloth merchant, it was clearly modelled on the Ottheinrichsbau in the Schloss to which, with its extravagant decoration of caryatids, scrollwork and fancy gables, it stands as a worthy competitor. Now an expensive hotel and restaurant, it completely outclasses its Baroque neighbours, among which is the **Rathaus** on the eastern side of the square.

Plenty more Baroque mansions can be found dotted all over the Altstadt; most notable is the **Residenz** of the Grand Dukes of Baden on Karlsplatz, which now houses the German Academy of Sciences and Letters. Further east, at Hauptstr. 235, is the **Palais Weimar**, now containing the **Volkerkünde Museum** (Tues–Sat 3–5pm, Sun noon–1pm; DM1), which has good African collections. At the end of the street is the Neoclassical **Karlstor**, a triumphal arch in honour of the Elector Carl Theodor, designed by his court architect, Nicolas de Pigage. However, the most important structure this great artistic patron gave to his ancestors' capital is the **Alte Brücke** downstream. Dating from the 1780s, it's at least the fifth on this site; in the last war, it suffered the inevitable fate of being blown up but has been painstakingly rebuilt. Particularly eyecatching is its fairy-tale monumental gateway, which is typical of the sort of building the Elector favoured: the twin towers and portcullis are reminiscent of medieval fortifications, but the ornamental bell-shaped roofs betray a lack of any defensive purpose.

Between here and Marktplatz are several narrow little alleys. At no. 18 in one of these, Pfaffengasse, is the **Friedrich-Ebert-Gedenkstätte** (Tues, Wed & Fri–Sun 10am–6pm, Thurs 10am–8pm; free). It was the childhood home of Friedrich Ebert, the journeyman saddler who, in the traumatic period following defeat in World War I, simultaneously became the first Social Democrat to come to power in Germany and the country's first freely elected leader. This was to be one romantic Heidelberg story without a happy ending; Ebert was unequal to the superhuman task of curbing the reactionary vested interests which held a stranglehold over German society at the time, and a scurrilous hate campaign mounted by the press hounded him to an early grave.

The University quarter

Much of the western half of the Altstadt is occupied by buildings of the **University**, officially known as the *Ruperto-Carola*, in honour of its two founders. It was established in 1386 by the Elector Ruprecht I; this makes it the oldest in what is now Germany.

One side of Universitätsplatz, the Altstadt's second main square, is occupied by the **Alte Universität;** like so many of the city's buildings, it dates back to the first quarter of the eighteenth century, and was designed by the local architect Johann Adam Breunig. To its rear on Augustinergasse is the most celebrated University building, the former **Studentenkarzer** (Student Prison; Mon–Sat 9am–5pm; DM1), which is now a protected monument (see overleaf). Between 1712 and 1914, it was used to detain students (a sizeable proportion, by all accounts) who had been convicted of an offence. Every available square centimetre of the walls of the otherwise spartan cells is covered with graffiti, with a black silhouette self-portrait of the prisoner the most popular motif.

The rest of the Universitätsplatz, in the centre of which is the **Löwenbrunnen** (Lion Fountain), is occupied by the Neue Universität. This was erected in 1931, thanks to American munificence; Henry Ford was a prominent contributor. With the postwar boom in higher education, it has proved to be hopelessly small, and a new campus has had to be laid out along the Neckar northwest of town. The **Universitätsbibliothek** (Mon–Fri 8.30am–10pm, Sat 9am–5pm; free) is down Grabengasse to the south of the square, with the entrance for temporary exhibitions round the corner on Plöck. These vary widely in appeal, but in summer there's generally a display centred on some of the treasures of the collection. Particularly outstanding is the fourteenth-century *Codex Manesse*; apart from containing 137 beautiful miniatures, it ranks as the most important collection of Middle High German poetry. Across the road from the library is the Gothic university church of **St Peter**, while diagonally opposite is the Baroque **Collegium Academicum**, originally a seminary, now a student residence.

The **Jesuitenkirche**, tucked away just to the east of Universitätsplatz on Schulgasse, is in the sombre, classically-inspired style favoured by this evangelising order, who came here with the intention of re-capturing Heidelberg for Catholicism, a mission which doesn't seem to have been particularly successful. Housed in its gallery and the adjoining monastery is a rather moderate **Museum für Sakralkunst** (May–Oct Tues–Sat 10am–5pm, Sun 12.15–5pm, Nov–Apr Sat 1–5pm & Sun 12.15–5pm only; DM2.50).

Following Plöck in a westerly direction, you come to the former **Institut für Naturwissenchaften** at the junction with Akadamiestrasse. Heidelberg's most famous scientist, **Robert Wilhelm Bunsen**, was based there for four decades. His name is

HEIDELBERG UNIVERSITY

Initially, Heidelberg University's fortunes were closely tied to that of the Palatinate Electors; it became a great centre of humanism and the Reformation, but fell into decline in the eighteenth century, to be revived in 1803 by Grand Duke Karl Friedrich as the first state university of Baden. One of its most lasting achievements came soon after: while still a student, **Clemens Bretano** and his brother-in-law **Achim von Arnim** put together the collection of folk poetry known as *Des Knaben Wunderhorn* ("The Boy's Magic Horn") in the years 1805-8. This was to be a key influence on the future evolution of Romanticism, directly inspiring the researches of the Brothers Grimm, whose prose folk-tales (being more amenable to translation) have gained a far wider international fame. However, the work of Armin and Brentano has been spread by the composer Gustav Mahler, who gave the verses idiomatic tunes and cloaked them in succulent orchestral colours, with several finding their way into his symphonies.

In spite of the vicissitudes of German history in the last two centuries, Heidelberg has managed to preserve its academic reputation: it's one of the few universitites largely exempted in criticism of the modern German higher educational system, which is generally seen as something of a failure. Heidelberg is particularly renowned in the natural sciences, where it has nurtured a stream of Nobel Prize winners; it was also here, under **Max Weber**, that sociology was developed as an academic discipline.

Of the many **traditions** associated with the University, the oddest was the fact that, until the present century, its students were not subject to civil jurisdiction. When a crime or breach of the peace was committed, the offender had to be dealt with by the university authorities. Moreover, when found guilty, the student did not need to serve his punishment immediately; he could do so at his leisure. Nor was there any stigma attached to imprisonment – indeed, it was seen as an essential component of the university experience. Nobody knows how this system came into being, but it presumably dates back to the times when most alumni were aristocratic and subject to the mores of *noblesse oblige*.

A second Heidelberg tradition – this time one which spread throughout Germany – was the **Mensur**, or fencing match. Students were divided into confraternities (*Verbindungen*) according to the region of their birth; the members wore a distinguishing cap and were forbidden from socialising with those belonging to other groups. At least three (in practice, far more) duels were held on two days of every week. Each bout lasted for fifteen minutes, excluding stoppages, unless it became dangerous to proceed; if the outcome was inconclusive, it had to be re-staged at a later date. The combatants wore goggles and every vital organ was padded, so that the risk of death was minimal. They were placed at arm's length from each other and fought by moving their wrists alone; to flinch or to step back were the ultimate disgraces. Wounds were frequent, particularly on the top of the head and left cheek; these were treated immediately by a surgeon or medical student. What was really bizarre was that the wounds became highly prized badges of courage; for optimum prestige, salt was rubbed into them, leaving scars which would remain for life. Foreign commentators have continuously poured scorn on this tradition – Patrick Leigh Fermor described it as "duelling which wasn't duelling at all, of course, but tribal sacrification. Those dashing scars were school ties that could never be taken off . . ." Mark Twain characteristically pilloried it for a different reason, pointing out its inferiority to the French concept of a duel, which was supposedly to the death but in reality led to no one being hurt at all. The anachronistic ideal of chivalry that is the *Mensur* precariously staggers on, however, among right-wing toffs, while its effects can still be seen on elderly professorial brows. Rapiers are now the only swords used, with the aim of making high cuts.

Another tradition associated with the fencing corps was the **Kneipe**, a stag party where competition was confined within the group. The idea was to down as many mugs of beer as possible in a given space of time; the winner became the *Bierkönig*. As the rules were concerned solely with emptying the contents of the glass down the throat, and not about retaining the alcohol in the system, those who didn't mind the discomfort of consistently spewing up were able to accomplish prodigious totals of close to one hundred pints in an evening. Several **taverns** which were the scene of these bouts still exist (see p.309).

familiar to school pupils all over the world for popularising that staple gadget of the laboratory, the "Bunsen burner"; he was also the first to separate the colours of the spectrum. Facing you on Hauptstrasse at the end of Akadamiestrasse is the nineteenth-century **Anatomie-Gebäude**, occupying the site of a Dominican monastery which had been hastily converted a few decades before, with its church used for dissections and its sacristy as a morgue.

The Kurpfälzisches Museum

Housed in the **Palais Morass** at Hauptstr. 97, an early eighteenth-century mansion built for a law professor, is the **Kurpfälzisches Museum** (Tues, Wed & Fri–Sun 10am–5pm, Thurs 10am–9pm; DM1). It's best kept until the end of your stay, as it provides an effective summing-up of what you have seen. The archaeology section includes a cast of the jawbone of *Homo heidelbergiensis* (the original is owned by the University); this is estimated to come from the inter-glacial period 500,000 years ago, making it one of the oldest human bones ever discovered. On the first floor is a room devoted to the history of the Palatinate. The intact Schloss can be seen in a large documentary picture from the early seventeenth century; it also turns up in the background of Jan Brueghel's exquisite *Allegory of Summer*. There are sensitive portraits of Elizabeth Stuart and her family by both the Honthorst brothers, dating from her exile in Holland when she was extolled as "The Queen of Hearts" by a whole generation of gallants. From here, you pass through a suite of period rooms before seeing the museum's prize possession, the limewood *Altar of the Twelve Apostles* by **Tilman Riemenschneider**. For centuries masked under a thick coat of polychrome, it was only recognised as the work of the master about a generation ago; it has since been returned to its original unpainted state, revealing a wonderful sense of characterisation and pathos in each of the figures.

Eating, drinking and entertainments

Hauptstrasse and the adjacent side streets are jammed with places of entertainment to suit all tastes; there's no better place for a pub crawl in all of Germany. The much-trumpeted **student taverns** are a must; they're perfectly genuine and are still patronised by the leftovers of the old fraternities, even if parties of tourists now make up the bulk of the clientele, particularly in summer. They're sights in themselves, with their faded photos and daguerrotypes, their trophies, swords, pads, helmets and miscellaneous paraphernalia. However, they're only one facet of Heidelberg's rich culinary and nightlife tradition. The city is also the heart of an important **wine** area; best selection of local vintages is available in *Brunn*, a shop at Bergheimerstr. 35; their own sparkling vintage is called *Perkeo-Sekt*, in honour of one of Heidelberg's great characters, the dwarf who was custodian of the predecessor to the Grosses Fass.

Historic student taverns

Hirschgasse, Hirschgasse 3. On the northern bank of the Neckar, with a hall still used for duelling; the restaurant is nowadays much more expensive and upmarket than the others.

Roter Ochsen, Hauptstr. 217. One of the two most famous of the taverns, its U-shaped interior has been patronised by the confraternities since it was built at the beginning of the eighteenth century. Reasonably-priced food, but open evenings only.

Schnizelbank, Bauamtsgasse 7. The only one of these taverns where the emphasis is on wine rather than beer.

Schnookeloch, Haspelgasse 8. Oldest of the group, founded only a couple of decades after the University; its beer garden offers the chance of a welcome respite from the crowds.

Zum Sepp'l, Haupstr. 213. Along with *Roter Ochsen*, the pub every tourist wants to visit; having been used by the student corps continuously since 1634, it has the longest uninterrupted tradition. More commodious than any of the others, and with the cheapest food.

Other restaurants

Abel's, Haupstr. 133. Relaxed wine bar-cum-restaurant where you can sit outside.

Denner, Bergheimer Str. 8. Restaurant specialising in fish dishes.

Güldenes Schaf, Hauptstr. 115. Features an extensive menu of game dishes.

Kowa, Kurfürsten-Anlage 9. Vegetarian restaurant, open Mon–Fri lunchtimes only.

Kurpfälzisches Museum, Hauptstr. 97. Wine bar in the museum courtyard which also serves excellent food.

Perkeo, Haupstr. 75. A real old-fashioned restaurant, one of the best in town, whose decor has hardly changed in a hundred years.

Schlossquell-Brästübl, Bergheimer Str. 91. The beer hall and restaurant of the main local brewery, whose products are made from spring water and have a soft, delicate flavour.

Vetters Alt-Heidelberger Brauhaus, Steingasse 9. *Hausbrauerei* which makes Pils, Weizen and an extremely powerful Bock; also goes good-value meals.

Wilhelmsplatz, Kaiserstr. 30. Well off the beaten tourist trap, and a good place to meet locals; serves large, cheap meals.

Zieglerbräu, Bergheimer Str. 1b. Excellent traditional *Gaststätte*, featuring very reasonably priced game dishes.

Cafés and bars

Biermuseum, Haupstr. 143. The largest selection of beers in Heidelberg, with 101 varieties to choose from, ten of them on draught.

Café Journal, Haupstr. 162. Best of the bistro-type cafés which are all the rage among present-day Heidelberg students. Has a wide selection of newspapers, and makes a good choice for breakfast.

Café Knösel, Haspelgasse 20. Heidelberg's oldest and most elegant café; speciality is the *Heidelberger Studentenkuss*, a dark chocolate filled with praline and nougat. Also does full meals.

Café Schaftheutele, Hauptstr. 94. Another old world café, with its own garden and celebrated for its marzipan fancies.

Café 7, Marktplatz and Haupstr. 75. Both branches serve the best ice-creams in Heidelberg.

Hard Rock Café, Hauptstr. 142 Very American in feel, this has huge pop video screens, and serves delicious baguettes.

Higher Taste, Kornmarkt 9. Small café serving Indian vegetarian food.

Palmbräuhaus Hauptstr. 18. A modern re-creation of palm court days, complete with resident pianist.

Trinidad, Friedrich-Ebert-Anlage 62. The place to come for exotic cocktails.

Discos and live music pubs

Cave 54, Krämergasse 2. Normally a nostalgic-style disco, except on Tuesdays, when live jazz is featured.

Doctor Flotte, Hauptstr. 130. Raucous bar playing both rock and jazz.

Fischerstübchen, Obere Neckarstr. 2. The favourite disco of the local students.

Regenbogen, Fahrtgasse 18. Women-only disco.

Whisky à Go Go, Oberbadgasse 10. Gay men's disco.

Ziegler, Bergheimer Str. 18. Varied late-nite spot, featuring a varied programme of jazz and rock concerts, cabaret and theatre.

Zigarillo, Bergheimer Str. 147. Crowded disco housed in an old factory.

Classical music and theatre

Classical music concerts are held in the modern *Kongresshaus Stadthalle* overlooking the Neckar. The *Heidelberger Kammerorchester* is a Mozartean-sized orchestra of good standing, even if their programmes tend to be conservative. At the main **theatre**, the *Städtischen Bühnen* on Theaterstrasse (☎58279/20519), there's a varied mixture of plays, opera, operetta, and performances by an experimental *corps de ballet*. Straight drama is also offered at the tiny *Zimmertheater*, Hauptstr. 118, and the *Landfriedhaus*,

Bergheimerstr. 147. Productions for **kids** are performed at the *Heidelberger Kinder und Jugendtheater*, Zwingerstr. 3–5.

Festivals

Heidelberg's most spectacular **festivals** are those using the Schloss as a backdrop. On the first Saturdays of June and September, and the second in July, there are firework displays and historical pageants; these attract horrendously large crowds, but are highly enjoyable all the same. From late July until the end of August, there are open-air concerts and opera performances (inevitably, *The Student Prince* is included) in the Schlosshof at 8pm on most evenings (☎58976 for tickets and information); in bad weather, they're transferred indoors. Throughout the year, various **fairs** are held on Karlsplatz – *Heidelberger Frühling* (early June); *Weindorf* (mid-Sept); *Heidelberger Herbst* (late Sept). The climax of **Carnival** (variable Feb/March) is the Rose Monday parade; there's another procession through the streets on the third Sunday before Easter.

Listings

Bike hire is available at the Hauptbahnhof.

Bookshops Try around Sofienstrasse and Universitätsplatz.

Car breakdown (☎19211) for 24-hour service.

Car hire *Avis*, Karlsruher Str. 43 (☎22215); *Hertz*, Kurfürsten-Anlage 1 (☎23434); *InterRent*, Bergheimer Str. 159 (☎20845).

Cultural institute *Amerika Haus*, Sofienstr. 12 (☎24771).

Gardens *Botanical Gardens*, Im Neuenheimer Feld (Mon–Thurs & Sun 9am–noon & 1–4pm). *Zoo*, Tiergartenstrasse (April–Oct daily 9am–7pm, Nov–March daily 9am–5pm; DM7, kids DM3).

Kids *Märchenparadies* on top of the Königstuhl (mid-March–mid-Oct daily 10am–6pm; DM3, kids DM2) is an adventure playground featuring fairy-tale characters and a miniature railway.

Markets Wed and Sat on Markplatz, Tues and Fri on Friedrich-Ebert-Platz.

Mitfahrzentrale Kurfürsten-Anlage 57 (☎24646).

Neckar cruises leave from the quay beside the Stadthalle mid-May to mid-Sept, run by *Rhein-Neckar-Fahrgastschiffahrt* (☎20181) and *Personenschiffahrt Hornung* (☎480064). A 45-minute local sail costs DM5; the round trip to Neckarsteinach, DM15.

Post office Main branch with Poste Restante is beside Hauptbahnhof; others are on Universitätsplatz and Sofienstrasse.

Shopping Untere Strasse is the trendiest street, featuring some amazing second-hand clothes shops, with quality ballgowns and hats available at knock-down prices. Apart from *Flic-Flac*, mentioned above, look out for *Py*, with an eye-swimming array of sunglasses from the Fifties.

Sports The main swimming pool is beside the Zoo. Tennis has recently become a Heidelberg mania, as the two German superstars, Boris Becker and Steffi Graf, both come from villages just outside the city. The German Grand Prix motor racing takes place at nearby HOCKENHEIM each July.

Travel agencies *American Express*, Friedrich-Ebert-Anlage 16 (☎29001); *HS Reisebüro*, Bismarckplatz (☎27151) does student deals.

What's on The tourist office publishes a weekly *Heidelberg diese Woche*, priced DM0.50.

The route of the Neckar castles

The route along the Neckar from Heidelberg to Bad Wimpfen, 70km southeast, passes through the craggy woodland of central Germany's most extensive forest, the Odenwald. All of this is designated as a national park, the Baden-Württemberg section being known as the **Naturpark Neckartal-Odenwald**. A series of bleak castles on the heights above the river serve as a reminder of a feudal past, as well as a rich source of **legends**. Though this countryside is best seen from a boat, the train makes a good alternative as it keeps close to the river most of the way.

Dilsberg

The quaint old village of **DILSBERG**, now incorporated into NECKARGEMÜND, is just 15km from Heidelberg, to which it's connected by regular buses. It's surrounded by walls, in one of whose towers is a **youth hostel** (☎06223/2133), which makes a possible commuting base. Dilsberg had a reputation for being able to withstand the most determined of besiegers (even managing to hold out against the much-feared Johann Tilly in the Thirty Years' War); tradition has it that this was thanks to a secret subterranean passage under the Neckar which led to a well-stocked storeroom.

The ruined **Burg** (daily 9am–noon & 1–6pm; DM1) is associated with the legend of a practical joke which ended tragically. A young knight, betrothed to the niece of the lord of the castle, was utterly convinced that whoever slept in the "haunted chamber" would not wake up for fifty years. His mischievous friends gave him a sleeping draught and put him to bed in a disused room hanging with cobwebs; they then dressed up as old folk, in order to fool him when he awoke shortly after. Having had their fun, they pulled off their disguises and subjected the shell-shocked youth to ridicule for his naivety – but his mind had already snapped and he was to spend the remaining years of his life in harmless insanity, comforted only by the girl who reminded him so much of what he believed to be his long-dead love.

Zwingenberg

A stretch of the northern bank which follows, including HIRSCHHORN, falls within Hessen; EBERBACH, 23km from Dilsberg, marks the point where the Neckar deviates sharply from its hitherto northerly course, turning westwards towards the Rhine. **ZWINGENBERG**, a further 10km south, has the **Burg** (guided tours May–Sept Tues, Fri & Sun 2–4.30pm, DM3) of the current holder of the now-meaningless title of Margrave of Baden. It occupies a picturesque setting above the village and is impressively complete, with a thirteenth-century keep surrounded by a fifteenth-century defensive wall, along with various embellishments from later periods. Below is the **Wolfsschlucht** (Wolf's Glen), scene of the most famous Neckar legend. Here the devil, disguised as Samiel, a wild huntsman, lured his victims by offering them seven of his magic bullets, which inevitably hit their target. The first six would do what the victims wanted; Samiel killed them with the seventh. Carl Maria von Weber, who visited the glen in 1810, made it the central scene of his opera *Der Freischütz* (the first full-blooded piece of Romanticism in musical history) a decade later.

Neckarzimmern

The region's characteristic sandstone gives way further south to a section of limestone cliffs. **NECKARZIMMERN**, 20km from Zwingenberg, has the oldest of the Neckar castles, **Burg Hornberg** (April–Oct daily 9am–5pm; DM2), home for 45 years of the great sixteenth-century robber baron, Götz von Berlichingen, whose armour is on display. Every so often, he would imperiously descend from his seat to confiscate the cargo of passing ships, distributing the profits to the poor; in his memoirs, he thanked God for delivering particularly rich pickings at the times of greatest need. An earlier story associated with this castle is reminiscent of the Rhenish Lorelei legend – it tells of how the heiress fell in love with a poor Crusader, but was forbidden to marry him and escaped to live in a nearby cave, singing an anguished ballad written by her lover which the locals mistook for the cries of an evil spectre. Ill-luck befell anyone who heard the voice, but all the locals were too cowardly to try to kill the spirit. When the Crusader returned from the Holy Land, he resolved to undertake the task, recognising his own composition only after he had fired the fatal shot.

Gundelsheim and Burg Guttenberg

Just south of Neckarzimmern, the Odenwald gives way to a gentle landscape of vineyards and market gardens. The small medieval town of **GUNDELSHEIM**, 5km on and 15km before Bad Wimpfen, is set in the shadow of **Schloss Horneck**, Baroque successor to a fortress of the Teutonic Knights. The Bahnhof here is the nearest to the most interesting castle of the region, **Burg Guttenberg** (March–Nov daily 9am–6pm; DM6); to reach it, you have to cross the bridge to the other side of the river. This building, with a tall, narrow keep and an impressive curtain wall, dates back to the Staufian epoch, but has been much altered inside. Among its many curiosities are the wooden library, and a herbarium in which the plants are stored in a series of trick compartments.

However, the castle's main claim to fame is for having Europe's largest collection of **birds of prey** – over a hundred in all. Each day at 11am and 3pm, there's an exhilarating demonstration of several of these birds in free flight. Yet all this is not just for show – there has been a highly successful programme for breeding endangered species, and an average of fifty birds per year are released back into the wild. There's also a good restaurant, set on a terrace commanding an extensive view over the valley.

Bad Wimpfen

The prefix "Bad", used by hundreds of German towns as a free advert for the presence of spa facilities, immediately conjures up the image of geriatrics and hypochondriacs pottering around the manicured lawns of soulless, white-walled sanitoria, with only the chirping of birds to disturb the deathly hush. **BAD WIMPFEN** has a spa quarter at its northern extremity which conforms to this stereotype, but is otherwise so totally different it seems strange the authorities want to use such a misleading designation. It certainly shouldn't be needed to draw visitors, as this pocket-sized town with a population of just a few thousand, built high above a bend in the Neckar marginally beyond the point where the Jagst flows in from the east, is a real visual treat, preserving a wonderful array of monuments as testament to its richly varied history. The site has been inhabited since prehistoric times; Romans, Frankish kings and the Bishops of Worms were later rulers, prior to its choice, from around 1200, as a favourite **residence of the Staufian emperors**. Some 150 years later Wimpfen was made a Free Imperial City, an independence it retained, courtesy of the lucrative salt trade, until the advent of Napoleon.

A century ago, Mark Twain found Wimpfen "very picturesque and tumble-down, and dirty and interesting". Only the first and last of these adjectives still hold good, an extensive programme of restoration and scrubbing-up since having turned the town into a very desirable place to live. What's immediately impressive is the **skyline**, one of the most dramatic in Germany: it's best seen from the right bank of the Neckar, where the imperious towers give it the appearance of a miniature medieval Manhattan. This is particularly stunning when illuminated by night, giving you the sensation of being whisked back centuries in time. The very different vistas from the western approach roads are almost equally photogenic.

Wimpfen am Berg

On leaving the **Bahnhof**, turn right and you're immediately on Hauptstrasse, the central street of the upper town, known as *Wimpfen am Berg*. About halfway up is the **Schwibbogen Tor**, which formerly gave access to the **Kaiserpfalz** (Imperial Palace). What isn't immediately obvious is that the medieval town grew up within the area formerly occupied by the court buildings, which were already in ruins. It's even more surprising that substantial portions of the palace remain to this day, ranking among the most important of the relatively few surviving examples of Romanesque civil architecture in Europe. The austere riverside wall, which had the advantage of a formidable natural barrier behind, survives largely intact. At its southern end, it's guarded by the **Nürnberger Türmchen** and the **Roter Turm**, a gaunt box-like structure which was the last line of defence. From here, there's a fine view over the town and valley.

Further along is the **Kaiserkapelle** (April–Oct daily 10am–noon & 2–4.30pm; DM1), now containing a small museum of religious art. The gallery was reserved for the emperor who could, if necessary, make a quick getaway through a passageway to the haven of the Roter Turm. Adjoining the chapel is the sole surviving part of the **Palast** itself – a weather-worn but still elegant row of arcades, each of whose paired columns is carved in a different manner.

The Steinhaus and the Blauer Turm

Also from the Staufian epoch is the large **Steinhaus** (Stone House), which stands out among the later predominantly half-timbered buildings. Originally the home of the castle commandant, it was modernised in the sixteenth century by the addition of Gothic gables. It's currently fitted out as the local **museum** (April–Oct Tues–Sun 10am–noon & 2–4pm; DM2), with exhibits from all periods of the town's history. Diagonally opposite is the symbol of Wimpfen and the most potent reminder of its days of power and glory, the **Blauer Turm** (Blue Tower; April–Oct Tues–Sun 9am–noon & 1.30–5pm; DM2). Named after the tints of the limestone used in its construction, this watchtower was all but destroyed in a fire in 1848 and was only recently made fully secure. At noon on Sundays from April to September, the resounding strains of a trumpeter playing chorales from the top can be heard throughout the streets.

Around the Stadtkirche

The twin towers of the **Stadtkirche** are the last main features of the Romanesque part of Wimpfen's skyline; the rest of the building is a late Gothic hall church. Behind can be seen an emotional *Crucifixion*, similar to the one its sculptor, Hans Backoffen, made for his own tomb in Mainz. Close by is the **Wormser Hof**, part of which is also Staufian; it was the residence of the administrator in the service of the Bishop of Worms, with a barn to store the tithe of agricultural produce he collected. Nowadays, it's home to the 250 historic dolls of the **Puppenmuseum** (Wed, Sat & Sun 2–5pm; DM1).

It's worth sauntering round all the streets of the old town, which curve and plunge their way past half-timbered houses, Baroque mansions and quiet squares with Renaissance fountains. Among the many surprising vistas, that from the **Adlerbrunnen** (Eagle Fountain) at the junction of Hauptstrasse and Salzgasse is particularly fine. The best-preserved street is **Klostergasse**, several of whose buildings have exterior galleries which formerly served as bath houses. Down Bollwerkgasse is the artillery bastion, built in the sixteenth century to designs by Dürer, no less. Restoration work is being carried out on the monumental half-timbered fifteenth-century **Spital** on Hauptstrasse, in order that it can become a museum in due course.

Wimpfen in Tal

The lower town, known as *Wimpfen in Tal*, can be reached in ten minutes by foot from the Bahnhof by following the main road to the left. It's built round the great **Ritterstift St Peter** (Mon–Sat 10am–noon & 3–5pm, Sun 10.30am–noon & 3.30–5pm) which, after a break of five centuries, was re-populated in 1947 by Benedictine monks who had fled from Silesia. Come here during their services, which use the Gregorian chant, and Wimpfen's illusion of transporting you back in time will be complete.

The fortress-like facade of the **church**, with a huge porch and a pair of octagonal towers, dates from the tenth century; the rest of the building is a masterly French-inspired Gothic design. This is generally attributed to the near-legendary mason **Erwin von Steinbach** who built part of Strasbourg Cathedral; in Germany he's been regarded as a real celebrity among the largely obscure architects of the Middle Ages ever since Goethe penned a flowery prose-poem in his honour. Superb original sculptures can be seen on the south doorway and inside the chancel; the latter group includes the then-recently-deceased Saint Francis of Assisi. Access to the **cloister**, which has sections in each of the three phases of the Gothic style, is only allowed to groups who have booked in advance, but you can tag along with one of these (which are frequent during the summer) if you ask at the shop.

Festivals and practicalities

Wimpfen in Tal is the scene of one of Germany's oldest **popular festivals**: it's claimed the week-long *Talmarkt* in honour of Saints Peter and Paul (29 June–5 July) has been celebrated every year since 965. Nowadays, the end is marked by a spectacular fireworks display. Two more fairs dating back to the Middle Ages are held in the centre of *Wimpfen am Berg* – the *Hafenmarkt* for handicrafts at the end of August, and the *Weihnachtsmarkt* in December, which is a cut above the imitative versions found in practically every German town. *Fasching* also has a long tradition here; highlights are the Sunday parade and the evening celebrations on Ash Wednesday.

Accommodation

Provided you're not looking for a swinging nightlife, Bad Wimpfen makes a good place to stay, particularly as accommodation is inexpensive, with over twenty private houses – which are scattered all over town – offering **rooms** at DM25 per head or less; otherwise, the cheapest hotel is *Neckarblick*, Erich-Sailer-Str. 48 (☎07063/7002), with singles from DM32, doubles from DM54. The **youth hostel**, run by a very hospitable family, has an unbeatable location at Burgviertel 21–23 (☎07063/7069) – it's in an old half-timbered house built against the ramparts beside the ruins of the Palast.

Eating, drinking and cruises

There's a clutch of **restaurants** serving hearty *bürgelich* cuisine all down Hauptstrasse; *Klosterkeller* is the best and most expensive, whereas *Traube* at the end of the street is particularly good value. Alternatively, try *Kräuterweible* on Marktrain, well thought of by the locals for its chicken dishes. The **tourist office** (Mon–Fri 9am–noon & 2–4pm, also Sat & Sun April–Sept 10am–noon & 2–4pm; ☎07063/53151) is in the Rathaus on Marktplatz, facing the Stadtkirche. Ask here about **Neckar cruises**, which run both upstream and down throughout the summer months, departing from the jetty beside the Neckarbrücke.

The Hohenlohe

The **Hohenlohe** is the name given to the plain between the Tauber Valley and the Swabian Forest. It's a quiet rural area, with rich farming country interspersed with the inevitable stretches of woodland and cut by two contrasting rivers – the fast-flowing Jagst and the placid Kocher – which follow a remarkably parallel course. There's a stong feudal tradition here, which to some extent lingers on – the area is about as far removed from the thrusting, competitive nature of modern German society as it's possible to be.

Unlike the Prussian *Junkers*, the **House of Hohenlohe** were enlightened, paternalistic landlords, and it seems poetic justice that they've managed to hold on to their possessions while their counterparts found themselves dispossessed after World War II: there are still a dozen historic castles in the family's possession. The area is almost entirely free of tourist hordes and is ideal for quiet exploration: however, it's probably better visited on day trips from a base in Schwäbisch Hall or the Neckar or Tauber Valleys, as there's nothing much to do come the evening. Hostels and campsites are practically non-existent, though there are plenty of **hotel rooms** available in the DM30–40 range. It's really better to have your own car or bike; communications by public transport are generally much better east–west (as the railway lines follow the rivers) than north–south.

Öhringen

ÖHRINGEN, which lies midway along the scenic railway line between Heilbronn and Schwäbisch Hall, was the seat of one of the Hohenlohe scions. The **Schloss**, facing the Marktplatz, is a horseshoe-shaped construction straddling the late Renaissance and Baroque periods, and is now used as offices. It's rather eclipsed by the **Stiftskirche** opposite, the fifteenth-century rebuild of a collegiate church founded in 1037 at the request of Countess Adelheid, mother of the first Salian emperor, Conrad II; her sarcophagus can be seen in the crypt. Far more grandiose are the Renaissance funerary monuments in the chancel, which constitute the necropolis of the local princes. Look out in particular for the *Tomb of Philipp von Hohenlohe and Maria von Oranien* (daughter of William the Silent) adorned with reliefs illustrating episodes from the Netherlands' War of Independence against Spain. Also of note are the late Gothic carved retable of *Madonna and Child with Saints* at the high altar, and the elaborate keystones of the vaults which have portraits and coats of arms of aristocratic families.

East of Marktplatz

Half-timbered houses abound throughout the town centre. In contrast, the *Karlsvorstadt*, to the east of Marktplatz down Poststrasse, is a piece of eighteenth-century town planning, separated from the old quarter by a Neoclassical gateway. On this street is the **Weygang Museum** (Tues–Sun 10am–noon & 2–4pm; DM1), which concentrates on objects made of pewter. Another collection of specialist appeal is the **Motor-Museum** on Stettiner Strasse (April–Oct daily 1–5pm, Nov–March Mon–Fri only 1–5pm; DM3), with classic sports and touring cars, and over fifty historic motorbikes.

Neuenstein

NEUENSTEIN, just 4km east of Öhringen and the next stop on the train, was the headquarters of a different branch of the Hohenlohe family, who built the area's most magnificent **Schloss** (guided tours mid-March–mid-Nov 9am–noon & 1.30–6pm; DM5). Part of the original moated castle can still be seen in the keep and ring walls. However, when this came into the possession of the family in the sixteenth century, it was transformed into one of the most spectacular Renaissance palaces in Germany, a building fully worthy of comparison with the châteaux of the Loire.

To see its resplendent exterior, bristling with elaborate scrollwork gables, to best effect, you have to walk along the main road leading westwards out of town; the vista from the square facing the entrance is considerably less impressive. Actually, this oversized Schloss was seen as a white elephant before the end of the seventeenth century when the line of Hohenlohe-Neuenstein died out; the prince who inherited it converted it into an orphanage, old peoples' home and workhouse, functions it served for nearly 200 years. Inside are several large halls, notably the *Kaisersaal* with its weapons and hunting trophies; there are also rooms furnished in various period styles, and collections of sacred art, furniture and *objets d'art*. However, by far the most arresting room is the late Gothic **kitchen**, one of the best-preserved in existence; the corner set aside for the slaughtering of game is guaranteed to turn the stomach of any vegetarian.

Jagsthausen

Some 20km due north of Öhringen is **JAGSTHAUSEN**, which lies on a different railway line from Heilbronn. Its heavily restored medieval **Burg**, now mostly converted into a hotel, is celebrated as the birthplace of Germany's answer to Robin Hood, **Götz von Berlichingen** (1480–1562), a more recent and more historically substantiated figure than his English counterpart. A man who used the most unscrupulous of methods to achieve his lofty ideals of helping the poor and persecuted, part of Götz's aura derived from the fact that he was apparently impervious to physical pain. While storming the Burg in Landshut at the age of 23, his right hand was torn off, but he was so engrossed in the struggle that he failed to notice. He had a replacement made out of iron which he claimed was just as effective as its predecessor, and it lasted him for the rest of his life. Goethe used the folk-hero's *Memoirs* as the basis for his first important work, a typical if disorganised product of the *Sturm und Drang* movement. This play is invariably featured among the open-air drama performances held annually between June and August (☎07943/2295 for more information). Götz's famous iron hand is the star exhibit of a small **museum** (mid-Mar–Oct 9am–noon & 1–6pm; DM1).

Schöntal

SCHÖNTAL, 6km up the River Jagst, is built within the precincts of a former Cistercian **Kloster** (guided tours April–Oct daily at 11am, 3pm & 4.30pm; DM2). This was founded in the twelfth century, but the present complex largely dates from a Baroque rebuilding programme by Leonhard Dientzenhofer. The church has a particularly handsome facade, its twin towers crowned by bulbous domes. Inside are four outstanding alabaster altarpieces, which are among the finest German sculptures of the seventeenth century. The cloister contains the tomb of Götz von Berlichingen, complete with a carving of his emblem of the iron hand. Also included on the tour are the *Ordensaal*, which is covered with paintings showing the 300 religious and military orders which then existed, and the monumental staircase of the *Neue Abtei*, cleverly fitted into the smallest possible space.

The Tauber valley

At the extreme northeastern corner of Baden-Württemberg, the gentle **River Tauber** cuts through a lush, verdant landscape of undulating hills, often dotted with vineyards, which stands in sharp contrast to the rugged contours of the neighbouring Swabian Jura. It manages to preserve an agreeable atmosphere of rustic peace and quiet, at least outside those towns which are staging posts on the famous tourist route known as the **Romantic Road** (see box on p.166), which closely follows the entire length of the Tauber valley, with the exception of its northernmost stretch.

Wertheim

Situated at the point where the Tauber joins the westward-flowing Main, **WERTHEIM** is the most northerly town in Baden-Württemberg. It's nicknamed "Little Heidelberg", and with some justification, as there are clear similarities between the two – the setting between the riverside and wooded slopes, the prevalence of superb and varied panoramic viewpoints, the twisting alleyways, the ruined castle looming high above. The original town was situated on the northern bank of the Main for fear of flooding, but it moved in the twelfth century when the local counts, realising the strategic importance of the spit of land between the two rivers, used it as the basis for building up a territory between the two ecclesiastical principalities of Mainz and Würzburg. A precarious independence was maintained down the centuries from the prying hands of the bishops, whose unwelcome advances were a major factor in Wertheim becoming one of the earliest bastions of Protestantism.

The town centre

The town is an ideal place in which to wander simply at leisure. On the right bank of the Tauber, the quays are lined with old fishermen's houses; on the **Kittstein Tor** there's a scale recording the water-mark of each flood since 1595. Further up towards the Main is the **Spitzer Turm** (Pointed Tower), the original corner point of the fortifications erected around 1200. The streets immediately behind housed a large Jewish population right up until the days of the Third Reich. At the heart of Wertheim is the **Marktplatz**, lined with half-timbered houses and scene of colourful markets on Wednesdays and Saturdays. Behind is the **Kilianskapelle**, an unusual fifteenth-century double chapel; the lower storey served as an ossuary. Opposite is an earlier Gothic building, the **Stiftskirche**, in whose choir are a series of ornate Renaissance tombs, the pantheon of the House of Wertheim.

A short walk down Mühlenstrasse is a half-timbered house containing the **Glas-Museum** (April–Oct Tues–Sun 10am–noon & 2–4pm; DM1), a surprisingly comprehensive collection. Across the street is the **Historisches Museum** (April–Dec Mon–Fri 10am–noon & 2–4pm, Sat & Sun 2–4pm; free), with wide-ranging displays of Franconian sacred art, traditional costumes, ceramics and local history. There are also a number of paintings of Wertheim by Otto Modersohn, the leading light of the artistic community at Worpswede (see *Chapter Six*); these date from holiday visits in the 1920s, long after the death of his estranged wife, the more talented Paula Modersohn-Becker. The building housing the museum is a Baroque palace built to replace the **Schloss**, a casualty of the Thirty Years' War. From the twelfth-century fortress, the tall watchtower and part of the walls survive; later additions include the twin-towered barbican and the residential quarters. In spite of its condition, it's well worth climbing up for the outstanding view over the two rivers, with the vast stretch of the Odenwald to the west and the wooded Spessart hills to the north.

Bronnbach

BRONNBACH, 7km upsteam and officially now part of Wertheim, is built round its **Kloster** (guided tours, lasting 45 minutes, Easter–Oct daily 9.30am–noon & 2–5pm; DM3), a daughter foundation of Maulbronn. The bulk of the architecture is in the severe Transitional style favoured by the Cistercians, with just a nod towards the Gothic in the church but rather more awareness of the new style in the later cloisters and chapter house. Whereas Maulbronn became Protestant at the Reformation, Bronnbach remained Catholic. This accounts for significant differences in their present appearances: in the early eighteenth century, the passion for Baroque led to a desire to transform the face of the old monastery. The church was adorned with a cluster of ornate altarpieces; these are fine works in themselves but mar the architectural purity. A more successful addition was the *Josephsaal*, a sumptuous refectory used during the summer.

Practicalities

Wertheim's **Bahnhof** is on the left bank of the Tauber, only a few minutes' walk from the centre. There's a **youth hostel** in the hills at Alte Stiege 16 (☎09342/6451), and also a **campsite** (☎09342/5719). Cheapest **hotel** in Wertheim itself is *Hofgarten*, Untere Heeg 1 (☎09342/6426), charging upwards of DM30 per person. Lower rates are available in outlying villages; the **tourist office** (Mon–Fri 9am–12.30pm & 2–5pm, Sat 9am–noon; ☎09342/1066) will find a room free of charge. Best **restaurant** for traditional food is *Bach'sche Brauerei* on Marktplatz; or try *Zepfhahn* on Mammelgasse.

Tauberbischofsheim

At **TAUBERBISCHOFSHEIM**, a further 16km up the river, is the point where the **Romantic Road** begins its short Baden-Württemberg stretch. This picturesque little wine town, a mixture of half-timbered and sandstone buildings, claims tor itself the title of world capital of **fencing**. At the 1976 Olympic Games, the team that was trained here scooped a bucketful of medals, six of them gold – then did even better at the next Olympiad.

The town's other claim to fame is as the home of the first **convent** in the country. This was founded in 730 by the Devon-born Benedictine monk Saint Boniface, known as the "Apostle of the Germans"; the town's name (which means "Bishop's Home on the Tauber") derives from the fact that he became Archbishop of Mainz. Subsequently, the convent became known as **St Lioba** after its first abbess, who was related to Boniface. The name lives on in the restrained Baroque church of a now-suppressed Franciscan successor to the original convent in the middle of town.

A short walk down Klostergasse is a series of sixteenth-century almshouses, while the central **Marktplatz** is lined with a varied group of buildings, including the restored pharmacy and the early seventeenth-century post office. However, the dominant monument in Tauberbischofheim is the **Schloss**, with its stern cylindrical watchtower, at the southern end of town. Construction was begun in the thirteenth century by the Archbishops of Mainz, soon after they had gained full control over the town. The interior, which includes a couple of Gothic halls, now houses the **Heimat Museum** (Easter–Oct Tues–Sat 2.30–4.30pm, Sun 10am–noon & 2.30–4.30pm; DM1). This features prehistoric finds from the area, colourful costumes, and furniture from Renaissance to Biedermeier.

Practicalities

The **youth hostel** is on a hill to the northwest commanding a fine view over the town, at Schirrmannweg 2 (☎09341/3152); follow Wellenbergstrasse to the left of the Bahnhof's exit. **Pensions** charging DM30 or less per head are *Weisses Ross*, Hauptstr. 13 (☎09341/2338), and *Café Stein*, Hauptstr. 67 (☎09341/3204). *Badischer Hof*, Hauptstr. 70 (☎09341/2385), which is slightly more expensive, boasts an excellent **restaurant**; other good places to eat are *Lamm*, also on Hauptstrasse, *Paradies* on Waldtorstrasse and *Pilsstube Ritter* on Bahnhofstrasse, while *Schlosscafé*, again on Hauptstrasse, is the best choice for coffee and cake. The **tourist office** is in the Rathaus on Marktplatz (Mon–Fri 9am–12.30pm & 2–5pm; ☎09341/80313).

Bad Mergentheim

BAD MERGENTHEIM, the next stop on the Romantic Road some 20km from Tauberbischofsheim, is one of the most celebrated spas in the country. Judging from the evidence of excavations, which have led to the uncovering of a Celtic well, the presence of hot salt springs at this point was known to Bronze Age tribes. However, they lay forgotten for over two millennia, until their rediscovery in 1826 by a shepherd who noticed his flock crowding round a trickle of water close to the north bank of the Tauber. Three years later, the first hotel opened and the town has never looked back. The timing of the finding of the springs was fortuitous, as seventeen years before Mergentheim had lost the prestigious role it had held since 1525 – as seat of the **Order of Teutonic Knights** (see below). Apart from Marburg, it's the only place still on German soil offering reminders of the Order which so often played a crucial role in the history of the nation. Even if you normally find spas a turn-off, it's worth coming to see the old part of town, on which the Knights left a characteristic stamp. This is sharply differentiated from the cure facilities, and situated on the opposite side of the river.

THE TEUTONIC KNIGHTS

Originally founded as a hospitaller community in Palestine in 1190, the **Order of Teutonic Knights** (*Deutschritterordern*) quickly took on a religious and military character. It increasingly turned its attention towards the Christianisation of Eastern Europe and to leading the drive to push Germany's frontiers eastwards, taking full advantage of an offer by the Kingdom of Poland to rid it of the threat posed by the heathen Prussians, Jacwingians and Lithuanians. By the early fourteenth century the Knights had exterminated the first two tribes, appropriating the Prussians' name and controlling a powerful Baltic state from the fortress-headquarters at Marienburg (now Malbork; see our guide to *Poland*). They repopulated the territories with German peasants, and grew rich from the profitable grain trade. Prosperity bred complacency, and successive defeats by the now-landlocked Poles, who had formed a new alliance with the Lithuanians, meant that the Knights had to cede half their lands and re-establish themselves at Königsberg in East Prussia. In 1525, the Grand Master Albrecht von Hohenzollern converted to Protestantism and transformed the territory into a secular duchy, initially under Polish control.

Those of the Order still loyal to Catholicism moved their base to Mergentheim, where they had owned land since the thirteenth century. Although it was in irreversible decline and never again a military force, the Order remained a prestigious body and its Grand Master belonged to the highest rank of the German nobility. Mergentheim remained the Knights' base until they were disbanded by order of Napoleon in 1809; however, the Order was re-constituted in Vienna 25 years later, where it remains active as a charitable body.

Around town

The Knights established themselves in the former Hohenlohe castle, which was expanded and rebuilt to form the **Deutschordensschloss**, which in turn was partly replaced in the early eighteenth century. This gargantuan complex of buildings takes up the whole of the eastern part of town; most of it is now used as offices, while the **Schlosspark** beyond, laid out in the English style, forms a south-bank counterpart to the *Kurpark*. In accordance with the tenets of the order, the architecture is severely ascetic, with only the occasional touch of frivolity, as in the bright orange **Torbau** which forms the main entrance. At the corner of the main courtyard is the handsome Rococo **Schlosskirche**, in part the work of the two greatest German architects of the day – Balthasar Neumann designed the twin towers, and François Cuvilliés provided plans for the white stuccoed interior, whose vault is covered by a huge fresco glorifying the Holy Cross.

Opposite the facade of the church is the main range of the Schloss, approached by two Renaissance **staircases**: the northern one has an ingenious corkscrew shape, while its more conventional counterpart leads to the **museum** (March–Oct Tues–Fri 2.30–5.30pm, Sat & Sun 10am–noon & 2.30–5.30pm; Nov–Feb Sat & Sun only; DM3). Apart from the Neoclassical *Kapitelsaal*, the rooms are surprisingly unostentatious and are used for displays on the history of the Order, including valuable treasury items and portraits of all the Mergentheim Grand Masters.

The spacious central Markt is divided in two by the step-gabled sixteenth-century **Rathaus**; the arms of the Grand Master who built it are borne by the hero Roland in the fountain in front. A colourful array of houses of various dates erected by vassals of the Order lines the rest of the square. Tombs of some of the most illustrious of the Knights are found in both the **Marienkirche** just off the southern side of the Markt, and the **Stadtkirche**, down an alley at the opposite end; the latter church, oddly enough, was originally founded by another Order of Crusaders, that of St John of Jerusalem. Beside it stands the **Spital**, whose chapel is adorned with Gothic frescos. On Burgstrasse is the **Automobil-Museum** (Tues–Sun 10am–6pm; DM3), a large collection of vintage cars, ranging from Bugatti to Rolls-Royce, and motorbikes.

Now officially part of Bad Mergentheim, the village of **STUPPACH**, 5km south, possesses one of the supreme masterpieces of German Renaissance painting, **Grünewald**'s *St. Mary of the Snows*, in its otherwise unremarkable Pfarrkirche (daily April–Oct 8.30am–5.30pm, Nov–March 8.30am–noon & 1.30–5pm; DM1). This is part of a triptych, one wing of which also survives and can be seen in Freiburg.

Practicalities

Bad Mergentheim's **Bahnhof** is conveniently situated between the medieval and spa parts of the town, on the same side of the Tauber as the former. One of the Neoclassical pavilions on the north side of the Markt contains the **tourist office** (Mon–Fri 9am–noon & 2.30–5pm, Sat 9am–noon; ☎07931/57135). There's a **youth hostel** at Erlenbachtalstr. 44 (☎07931/6373) in the outlying village of IGERSHEIM (which has its own Bahnhof) to the northeast. The **campsite** is 2km south of town at Willinger Tal (☎07931/2177). Cheapest **pensions** are *Haus Ursula*, Lorenz-Fries-Str. 3 (☎07931/3309), with singles from DM19, doubles from DM33, and the more central *Helen*, Mühlwehrstr. 31 (☎07931/8378), charging upwards of DM30 per head. *Zum Wilden Mann*, Reichengasse 6 (☎07931/7638), where prices start at DM28 per person, has what's arguably the town's best **restaurant**. The main **festival** is the *Stadtfest* in June.

Weikersheim

WEIKERSHEIM, 11km due west of Bad Mergentheim, is the ancestral seat of the **House of Hohenlohe**, which first came to local prominence in the twelfth century and whose various branches ruled for centuries over various tiny tracts of territory between the Free Imperial Cities of Schwäbisch Hall, Heilbronn and Rothenburg ob der Tauber.

The town centre

In the planned central **Marktplatz**, laid out at the beginning of the eighteenth century, is the **Tauberländer Dorfmuseum** (April–mid-Nov Tues–Sun 10am–noon & 2–5pm; DM1.50), which contains folklore displays on rural life throughout Franconia. The square itself was designed as a processional way linking the Stadtkirche, which contains the Hohenlohe pantheon, to their **Schloss** (guided tours daily April–Oct 8.30am–6pm, Nov–March 10am–noon & 2–4pm; DM3). A particular touch of swagger was provided by the arcaded buildings immediately fronting the main entrance, shaped like embracing arms in the manner of the colonnades before St Peter's in Rome. In 1586, when Count Ludwig II re-established Weikersheim as the family's main residence, he decided to replace the old moated castle with a magnificent new Renaissance palace. The Dutch architect Georg Robin chose a daringly original ground-plan based on an equilateral triangle. Only one wing of this, characterised by six magnificent scrollwork gables, was built, as the Hohenlohes turned their money and attention to supporting the Protestant cause in the Thirty Years' War. In the early eighteenth century the complex was completed in the Baroque style, though still retaining some parts of the medieval fortress.

Unquestionably the highlight of the reception rooms is the **Rittersaal**, the most sumptuous banqueting hall ever built in Germany, whose decorations are a hymn of praise to the dynasty and its preoccupations. The huge coffered ceiling is painted with depictions of the glories of the hunt, the entrance doorway is carved with a scene of a battle against the Turks, and the colossal chimneypiece is adorned with a complicated allegory which illustrates the family motto, "God gives Luck". Flanking the fireplace are the reclining stucco figures of Count Ludwig and his wife, sister of William the Silent, above which are their respective family trees. Even more eye-catching are the life-sized stuccos of deer parading along the main walls, joined by an elephant, a beast the craftsmen had clearly never seen.

The **gardens**, which are contemporary with the later parts of the Schloss, are exceptionally well-preserved. They're bounded by chestnut trees and are arranged symmetrically, with formal clipped hedges offset by the blazing colour of the flower arrangements. On the terrace immediately behind the palace is a series of sixteen caricature statues of members of the court, the only surviving set of the many inspired by the engravings of the Lorraine artist Jacques Callot. In the central pond is a representation of *Hercules Fighting the Hydra*: like many other petty German princes, the Hohenlohes fondly saw analogies between themselves and the great hero. Further evidence of their megalomania comes with the **Orangerie** at the end of the garden, which provides a theatrical backdrop to the Tauber Valley beyond. Among the figures represented are what they imagined to be their spiritual ancestors – the emperors of Ancient Assyria, Persia, Greece and Rome, no less.

Practicalities

You can indulge in a spot of **wine-tasting** of the local vintages at the *Gutskellerei* (Mon–Fri 8am–5pm, Sat 9am–5pm, Sun 11am–5pm), just beside the entrance to the Schloss. In the Marktplatz is the **tourist office** (Mon–Fri 9am–noon & 2.30–5.30pm, also Sat 2–4pm in summer; ☎07934/7272). Much the cheapest **hotel** is *Krone*, Hauptstr. 14 (☎07934/8314); alternatively, there's a very superior **youth hostel** on the banks of the Tauber at Im Heiligen Wöhr (☎07934/7025). If you're following the Romantic Road by public transport, note that Weikersheim is the last town until Nördlingen on a passenger rail line: for the next stretch you're dependent on the local buses, or the daily *Europabus*.

Creglingen

CREGLINGEN, 13km upstream from Weikersheim, is an old world village with half-timbered houses, some of which are built directly over the former ramparts. Its renown, however, is entirely based on the isolated **Herrgottskirche** (April–Oct daily 8am–6pm, Nov–March Tues–Sun 10am–noon & 1–4pm; DM1.50), a Gothic pilgrimage chapel founded in the fourteenth century after a ploughman had dug up a miraculous holy wafer in a nearby field. If you're travelling by *Europabus*, a stop is made here; otherwise the quickest and most pleasant way to come from Creglingen is via the path running alongside the brook named after the church.

The Herrgottskirche is architecturally unremarkable but houses the magnificent limewood *Altar of the Assumption*, carved by **Tilman Riemenschneider** in about 1510. Set in a filigree shrine specially constructed in order to catch the day's changing light effects, the main scene ranks as the artist's masterpiece. The four reliefs of the life of the Virgin are of markedly lower quality and are presumably not the work of the master, who employed as many as twenty assistants in order to fulfil the flood of commissions which came his way. However, Riemenschneider certainly made the exquisite predella scenes of *Epiphany* and *Christ Among the Doctors*; the calm, pensive central figure in the group of scholars is almost certainly a self-portrait. A couple of decades after the retable was made, the chapel was given over to the Lutherans; its extraordinary state of preservation is due to the fact that, as the main scene was anathema to Protestant doctrine, it was closed off – not to be re-opened until well into the nineteenth century.

Practicalities

The countryside around Creglingen is described, without a trace of irony, as **Herrgottsländle** (The Lord God's Little Land), as much through local belief that it resembles the Garden of Eden as from the name of the church. In the streams and lakes are good **angling** possibilities, with abundant supplies of trout, eel, perch, pike and carp. Beside the Münstersee some 3km away is a campsite (☎07933/321), while there's a youth hostel on a hillside at the eastern end of Creglingen itself at Erdbacherstr. 30 (☎07933/336). Otherwise, there are several pensions in town, where you should be able to find a room for DM30 or less; among these is *Krone*, Hauptstr. 12 (☎07933/558), which has a superb and inexpensive restaurant. There are also a number of farmhouses offering bargain deals; for more information about these, contact the tourist office in the Rathaus (Mon–Fri 9am–5pm; ☎07933/70111). After Creglingen, the Romantic Road crosses into Bavaria, the next stops being Detwang and Rothenburg ob der Tauber (see *Chapter One*).

travel details

Trains

From Stuttgart to Freiburg (1 an hour; 2hr 45min); Karlsruhe (2; 1hr 10min); Ludwigsburg (frequent; 10min); Marbach (2; 25min); Esslingen (2; 10min); Tübingen (2; 1hr); Rottweil (1; 1hr 30min); Donaueschingen (1; 2hr); Konstanz (1; 2hr 40min); Ulm (3; 1hr); Schwäbisch Gmünd (2; 40min); Schwäbisch Hall (1; 1hr); Heilbronn (1; 45min); Heidelberg (1; 1hr 10min); Frankfurt (10 daily; 2hr 5min); Cologne (1; 3hr 45min); Hamburg (8 daily; 6hr 45min); Hannover (9 daily; 5hr 30min); Mainz (1; 1hr 30min); Mannheim (1; 1hr 30min); Ulm (1; 55min).

From Karlsruhe to Baden-Baden (3 an hour; 20min); Freiburg (2; 1hr); Freudenstadt (1; 2hr); Schwetzingen (2; 40min); Mannheim (frequent; 30min).

From Ulm to Blaubeuren (1 an hour; 10min); Heidelberg (1; 2hr 15min); Mannheim (1; 2hr 25min); Mainz (1; 3hr 5min).

From Heidelberg to Bruchsal (2; 20min); Bad Wimpfen (1; 50min); Cologne (1; 2hr 25min); Mannheim (1;10min); Mainz (1; 1hr 5min); Bonn (1; 2hr 2min).

CHAPTER THREE

HESSEN

Occupying the geographical centre of Germany and manifesting elements of both north and south German culture, **Hessen** claims to be the very heart of the nation. Although one of the parts of the country least visited by foreigners, it's also, paradoxically, one which has created preconceived images of Germany more than any other. This is because of the world-wide familiarity of the folktales collected by the most famous Hessians, the **Brothers Grimm**, which are set in the darkly forested highlands, feudal castles and half-timbered towns so characteristic of the province.

Modern Hessen was flung together by the Americans as an administrative unit after World War II. It represents an approximate revival of a territory founded in the thirteenth century and which reached the height of its power and influence during the Reformation. Its ruler, Landgrave Philipp the Magnanimous, was the undisputed champion of **political Protestantism**, and it was mainly because of his dogged determination, in the face of many reverses, that centralised Imperial power and the threat of a wholesale return to Catholicism were crushed forever. On his death in 1567, however, Hessen was divided into four separate states. Within a short period, they had crystallised into two – Hessen-Kassel and Hessen-Darmstadt – and these formed the main basis of the region's division until modern times, though there were many other later fragmentations. The division proved to be particularly destructive during the Thirty Years' War, in which much of Hessen was devastated.

During the eighteenth century the region's main export was mercenary soldiers, and a large pressganged contingent helped Britain to lose the American War of Independence. The nineteenth century was a period of more conventional commercial activity, with the arrival of the industrial revolution and the founding of big concerns like Opel (originally a sewing machine factory) along the banks of the River Main. It was also a period of political wheeling and dealing as the local princes attempted to play Prussia and Austria off against each other. Hessen-Kassel, hitherto regarded as the senior province, backed the wrong side and was absorbed by the expanding Kingdom of Prussia in 1866. The wilier rulers of Hessen-Darmstadt were able to remain as independent Grand Dukes, and in this capacity joined the Second Reich five years later.

Today Hessen is one of the most prosperous of the German Länder, focused on the American-style dynamism of **Frankfurt**. Although traditional heavy industry still exists around the confluence of the Rhine and the Main, it's the serious money generated by banking and modern communications-related industries in Frankfurt which provides the region's real economic base. The two former capitals, **Kassel** and **Darmstadt**, are likewise industrial. Both suffered heavily in the war, though both are worth visiting for the sake of their many reminders of past periods of artistic patronage. Otherwise, apart from occasional light industrial pockets, most of Hessen's inhabitants live from farming (which is mostly still small-scale) or tourism. By far the most beautiful city is modest-sized **Marburg**, Hessen's first capital and home to one of Germany's most prestigious universities; in conjunction with the other towns of the **Lahn** valley, it's a great place to spend a few days. The same can be said of the Baroque city of **Fulda**, still a major episcopal centre, which offers easy access to the **Vogelsberg** and **Rhön** hills. Hessen's other main hot spot is the **Rheingau**, the scenic but touristy stretch of the Rhine, west of the Land capital **Wiesbaden**, a money-oriented playground and gambling centre.

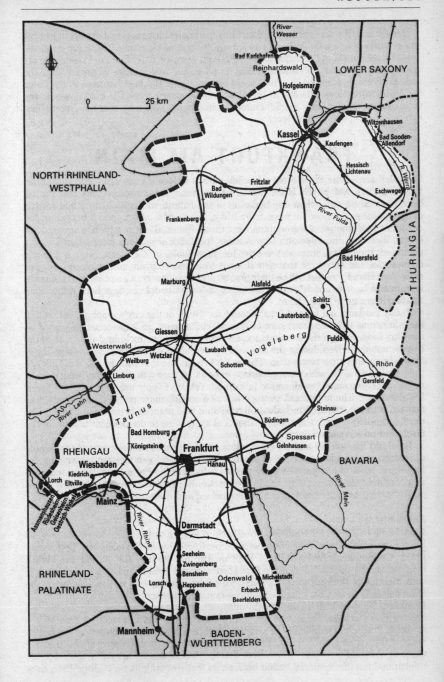

Hessen is easily accessible: Frankfurt has the busiest international airport in Europe and is easily reached by **rail** and **road** from the rest of Germany. There are good rail links between most of the major towns, although remoter areas like the Vogelsberg are best explored by car. **Accommodation** in all of the major cities is pricier than the national average, whereas the rural areas offer some of the best bargains in the country. **Politically**, Hessen is one of the most volatile states: the CDU hold power at the moment, but the left-wing is traditionally strong, and it was here that the Greens first entered government at Land level.

FRANKFURT AM MAIN

Straddled across the River Main a few kilometres before it converges with the Rhine, **FRANKFURT AM MAIN** is the capital city Germany has never actually had, having been cheated on more than one occasion of the role to which its history and central geographical position would seem to entitle it. Yet that hasn't stopped it becoming the economic powerhouse of the country, a cut-throat financial centre which is home to 388 banks, including the all-mighty *Bundesbank* itself. It's a modern international city, a communications and transport centre for the whole of Germany, with a frenetic commercial and social life that sets it apart from its relatively sleepy hinterland. For many travellers Frankfurt will be their first taste of the country; it's a place with a surprising amount to offer and it's worth spending at least a couple of days here rather than treating it as a mere transit point.

Today banking and related jobs account for much of the city's employment, and at times it seems to be one vast hive of commercial activity, an impression enhanced by the ultra-modern high-rise architecture. Over half of the city, including almost all of the centre, was destroyed during the war and the re-builders decided to follow a policy of innovation rather than restoration. The result is a skyline that smacks more of Chicago than the Federal Republic – appropriate enough in a city that has the reputation of being one of the most Americanised in Europe. Yet this is only one of Frankfurt's faces. It's also a surprisingly civilised metropolis which spends more per year on the arts than any other city in Europe, and whose inhabitants like nothing better than to spend an evening knocking back a few jugs of the local apple wine in the open-air taverns of the **Sachsenhausen** suburb.

Frankfurt has an energetic nightlife and is a thriving recreational centre for the whole of Hessen, with a good selection of theatres and galleries, and an even better range of museums, mostly concentrated along the south bank of the River Main. It comes across as a confident and tolerant city, and in the **Bockenheim** district there's a healthy "alternative" scene, not self-consciously institutionalised in the way that Berlin's has become.

Some history

Frankfurt's **commercial tradition** goes back to Roman times, when its importance as a river crossing point and junction between north and south Germany was first recognised. Charlemagne had a fortress built on the old Roman site during the eighth century, and by the twelfth century Frankfurt was well established as a trading centre, with merchants flocking to the Römerberg to sell their goods in the shadow of the royal palace built by Charlemagne's successors. This market evolved gradually into the Frankfurt fair which flourishes to this day, albeit in new premises just outside the centre. The stock exchange was opened in 1585 and it was in Frankfurt that Meyer Amschel Rothschild founded both a banking house and a financial dynasty at the beginning of the nineteenth century. Frankfurt was also the main centre of the postwar German economic recovery. It was here that the Americans set in motion the currency reform that put the shattered nation back on its feet – overnight, on 20 June 1948, they introduced DM10.7 billion worth of new currency, printed in the USA and delivered to Frankfurt under armed guard, to replace the vastly inflated *Reichsmark*.

The city's **political role** has been similarly prominent, albeit with more variable results: its failure to establish itself as the nation's capital symbolises the tragedy of German history, in which authoritarianism has so often triumphed. In 1356, Frankfurt gained permanent status as the place where the Electors met to choose the Holy Roman Emperor, and in 1562 consolidated its position by supplanting Aachen as the scene of the imperial coronations. It was one of only four of the hundreds of erstwhile city-states allowed to retain its independence after the Napoleonic wars. As such, it was chosen as the seat of the National Assembly and seemed set to provide neutral leadership to the fragmented German nation, arbitrating between the competing imperial powers of Prussia and Austria. Hopes for a united Germany run by liberal-minded politicians in Frankfurt reached a head during the revolutions of 1848-9, but were quickly dashed. The city was seized by Prussia in 1866 and has never been so much as a regional capital since then. After World War II, it seemed to be the natural choice as capital of the truncated West German state, but lost out on the casting vote of Chancellor Adenauer, who had campaigned in favour of Bonn, the city nearest his own home, in alliance with Berliners who feared – correctly, as it turned out – that, in the event of a long-term division of the country, Frankfurt would be strong enough to thwart Berlin's chances of ever regaining the status of capital.

> The telephone code for Frankfurt is ☎069.

Arriving and finding somewhere to stay

Frankfurt **airport** is one of the world's busiest (and best), and is a major point of entry into Germany from abroad (**information** Arrival Hall B, Level 1; Mon–Fri 8am–4.30pm; ☎693153). There are regular **rail** departures from the airport **Bahnhof** which will enable you to reach most of Western Germany's cities fairly easily. Trains leave the airport approximately once every ten minutes for the **Hauptbahnhof** (journey time 11min) from where there are even more comprehensive services throughout Germany and beyond. The airport is also linked to the Hauptbahnhof by two S-Bahn lines, run by the city transport company (*FVV*), which is also responsible for bus, tram and U-Bahn services. There's a flat rate of DM2 for all journeys (which includes any transfers) and you buy tickets from the blue machines for trams, S- and U-Bahns or from the driver for buses. From the Hauptbahnhof you can walk to the town centre in about fifteen minutes or take tram #11, which goes right through the heart of the old city centre.

Frankfurt has two main **tourist offices**. There's one in the Hauptbahnhof, opposite track 23 (Nov–March Mon–Sat 8am–9pm, Sun 9.30am–8pm; April–Oct Mon–Sat 8am–10pm, Sun 9.30am–8pm; ☎2128849), where they'll be able to give you general information about Frankfurt, book hotel rooms and organise guided tours. There's also an office for general information at Römerberg 27 (Mon–Fri 9am–7pm, Sat & Sun 9.30am–6 pm; ☎212 38708)).

Accommodation

Accommodation is predictably pricey, thanks to the expense-account businesspeople who come here for the various *Messe* or trade fairs. It can also be quite difficult to find, and it's best to try and sort it out in advance – especially if you're arriving when one of the major fairs is on, such as the Book Fair, usually at the end of September/beginning of October. If you're planning on staying for a while, contact one of the **Mitwohnzentralen**, at Klingerstr. 9 (☎284340) or Wiesenstr. 32b (☎462030), who will

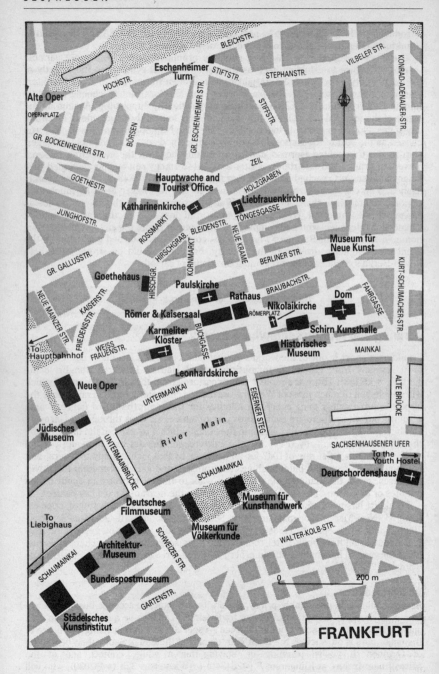

FRANKFURT

arrange the let of an apartment. For shorter stays, the best budget bet is the **youth hostel** at Deutschherrnufer 12 (☎619058) in Sachsenhausen, reached by bus #46 from the Hauptbahnhof. There are also two **campsites** – at Niederräder Ufer 20 (☎673846) to the west of Sachsenhausen (take tram #15) and at An der Sandelmühle (☎570332) in the northern suburb of Heddernheim (take U-Bahn #1, #2 or #3).

As for cheap **hotels** and **pensions**, there isn't much in the city centre under DM50. If you don't mind the sleazy environs, most of the few reasonably priced hotels seem to cluster around the Hauptbahnhof, close to the Kaiserstrasse red light district. These include *Lohmann*, Stuttgarter Str. 31 (☎232534), with singles DM36, doubles DM64; *Brukner*, Stuttgarter Str. 9 (☎253545), with singles DM49, doubles DM82; *Goldener Stern*, Karlsruher Str. 8 (☎233309), with singles from DM39, doubles from DM56; *Ilona*, Mainzer Landstr. 123 (☎236204), with singles from DM42 and doubles from DM68; *Glockshuber*, Mainzer Landstr. 120 (☎742628), with singles from DM55 and doubles from DM95; and *Life*, Weserstr. 12 (☎231014), with singles from DM40, doubles from DM65. Further out, but still within walking distance of the Hauptbahnhof, is *Atlas*, Zimmerweg 1 (☎723946), which has singles from DM48 and doubles from DM68; while *Backer*, Mendelssohnstr. 92 (☎747992),with singles from DM40 and doubles from DM60, has perhaps the most enticing location of the budget options, being close to the University.

The city

Most of central Frankfurt can be covered on foot; almost all the main sights lie within the bounds of the old city walls, which have been turned into a stretch of narrow parkland describing an approximate semicircle around the city centre. From here it's an easy matter to cross the Main into Sachsenhausen, where most of the museums are conveniently located along the southern river bank. Other suburbs are best reached by means of the efficient public transport network.

The Altstadt

Until it was devastated in two massive air raids in 1944, Frankfurt had the largest and most complete Altstadt in Germany. After the war, the most important monuments were carefully restored; other parts were hastily rebuilt in a modern manner. Even so, large gap sites remained until the 1970s, when, after much heated debate, they were filled with a mixture of pastiche medieval buildings and prestigious ultra-modern public commissions. The result is inevitably a compromise – though a satisfactory enough solution under the circumstances.

The Römerberg

As good a point as any to begin your explorations is the **Römerberg**, the historical and, roughly speaking, geographical centre of the city. Charlemagne built his fort on this low hill, on the site of earlier Roman and Alemannic settlements, to protect the ford which gave Frankfurt its name – *Frankonovurd* (Ford of the Franks). Throughout the Middle Ages the Römerberg was Frankfurt's focal point, serving as market place, fairground, venue for every imaginable kind of *Volksfest* and, less frequently, for the celebrations associated with an Imperial coronation. At the start of this century the Römerberg was still the heart of the city, an essentially medieval quarter ringed by half-timbered houses built by the rich merchants and bankers who had made Frankfurt one of Germany's richest centres – its "secret capital", according to Goethe.

At the western end of the Römerberg is the **Römer** building itself, which formerly served as the Rathaus. Its distinctive Gothic facade, with its triple-stepped gables, was more or less all that remained after the war, but the building has been restored with consummate skill. Its two upper storeys house the **Kaisersaal** (Mon–Sat 9am–5pm, Sun 10am–4pm; DM1), the former imperial coronation hall, which contains 52 rather effete-looking nineteenth-century portraits of the German emperors. The building fronts the Römerplatz, the market square, which has the Mannerist **Gerechtigkeitsbrunnen** (Justice Fountain) in the middle. Facing the Römer, a row of seven half-timbered houses was built in the late 1970s using original plans and traditional construction methods. The attention to detail is incredible, but somehow the end effect is slightly jarring and the buildings seem like film-set backdrops.

On the southern side of Römerplatz stands the former court chapel, the **Nikolaikirche**, the only one of seven Protestant churches in central Frankfurt to survive the war. The interior is refreshingly restrained, a real refuge from the noise and rampant commercialism of the rest of the square. Though the church was given a Gothic facelift in the fifteenth century, the lines of the original Romanesque structure are visible on the inside where only the chancel underwent alteration. Opposite is the **Steinerne Haus**, a postwar reconstruction of one of the few stone-built houses of the Frankfurt Altstadt; it now houses a commercial art gallery (Tues 11am–6pm, Wed 11am–8pm, Thurs–Sat 11am–6pm; DM4).

Off the northern side of Römerplatz is the Neoclassical **Paulskirche** (daily 11am–3pm), built in the late eighteenth century as a Lutheran preaching hall. However, it was soon taken over for secular purposes, and it was here that the ill-fated German National Assembly met during the revolutionary upheavals of 1848–49. The church still functions as a meeting hall and looks totally unecclesiastical inside. On the northern wall there's a monument to the victims of the Nazis.

Around the Römerberg

East of Römerplatz is the most controversial of the inner city developments. At its core is an ambitious building called the **Kultur-Schirn**, a general purpose cultural centre consisting of a glass tunnel for exhibitions (which regularly attracts prestigious shows) and a rotunda with more display space and a café. The locals call the place the "Federal Bowling Alley", or, in their more fanciful moments "Murder at the Cathedral", due to its proximity to the Dom. Whether you like it or not will probably depend on how you feel about Post-Modernism, but in many ways it represents a brave attempt to recreate a sense of the Römerberg as the centre of Frankfurt. Running roughly parallel with it, and bounded to the south by Saalgasse, is a row of gabled townhouses which, though essentially modern in design and construction, echo the medieval past of the Römerberg.

Beyond is the **Historische Garten**, where the foundations of some of the Roman, Carolingian and medieval buildings which previously occupied the site have been laid bare to form a little park. Just to the north, in Domstrasse, looms the newly-completed **Museum für Moderne Kunst** (Tues & Thurs–Sun 10am–5pm, Wed 10am–8pm; free), looking like a high-tech slice of cake. This has attracted a fair amount of criticism on the grounds that the collection is as yet unworthy of its setting, though it does include examples of such famous postwar artists as Beuys, Warhol and Lichtenstein.

The Dom

The most significant building in the Altstadt is the red sandstone church of **St Bartholomäus**, popularly if inaccurately referred to as the **Dom**, a courtesy title granted it by virtue of the fact that, being the venue for the election and coronation of the Holy Roman Emperors, it was far more important than most cathedrals. In essence, it's a Gothic hall church built in the thirteenth and fourteenth centuries. The two **portals** – and particularly that on the south side, which retains most of its original sculptures – are the finest features from this period; a curiosity is that the building is almost as broad as it is long. However, the outstanding feature of the Dom is its 95-metre **tower** (April–Oct 9am–12.30pm & 2.30pm–6pm; DM1), added in the early fifteenth century by the brilliantly idiosyncratic municipal architect **Madern Gerthener**, whose quirky genius left a profound mark on the city. The pinnacled summit is one of the most original creations of German Gothic and is a clear attempt to re-think earlier spires, such as those of Freiburg's Münster, in a more modern idiom. Before the construcion of the modern skyscrapers, the tower was the tallest structure in the city, and even today, strict planning rules are enforced to preserve its dominance over the Altstadt, of which there's a superb **view** from the top.

The treasures of the spacious, light-filled interior include a monumental *Crucifixion* group on the west wall by the Mainz sculptor Hans Backoffen; the poignant fifteenth-century *Maria-Schlaf-Altar* in the north transept chapel; the nearby tomb of the royal pretender Günther von Schwarzburg, rival of Emperor Charles IV; and an intricately carved set of mid-fourteenth-century choir stalls. To the right of the choir is the relatively simple and unadorned **Wahlkapelle**, where the seven Electors used to make their final choice as to who would become emperor. The Dom's bells, the second largest of any church in Germany, have been tuned in with all the others in the city, and four times a year they all unite to form a deafening carillon. Housed in the cloister is the **Dommuseum** (Tues–Fri 10am–5pm, Sat & Sun 11am–5pm; DM2), which contains treasury items, historic ecclesiastical garments and an old altarpiece.

Along the River Main

Opposite the southern side of the Dom is the fourteenth-century **Leinwandhaus**, formerly a cloth hall. It now contains three galleries, including the city's photographic gallery (Tues, Thurs & Fri 11am–6pm, Wed 11am–8pm, Sat & Sun 11am–5pm; DM4). From here, it's just a few paces to the banks of the Main. Walking westwards, you come to the **Saalhof**, an amalgamation of architecturally diverse Imperial buildings now housing the **Historisches Museum** (Tues & Thurs–Sat 10am–5pm, Wed 10am–8pm; free except for special exhibitions). Its twelfth-century chapel is all that remains of the old palace complex, which grew up around the Römerberg in the Middle Ages. The museum contains an extensive local history collection, highpoints of which are replicas of the crown jewels of the Holy Roman Empire (the originals are in Vienna) and a facsimile of the Golden Bull of 1356 which ratified Frankfurt's status as venue for imperial coronations. There's a model of the city as it looked in 1912, and an eye-opening section on the devastation caused by the bombing. The **Rententurm**, which dates from 1456 and forms part of the building, is one of the few surviving towers from the old city defences.

A short distance to the west is the **Leonhardskirche**, originally a pilgrimage station on the well-trodden route to Santiago de Compostela in northern Spain. Surviving from this Romanesque church are the octagonal east towers and two beautiful portals, but the latter are now indoors as a Gothic aisle was subsequently built over them. At the end of this is the *Salvatorchörlein*, a chapel whose amazing pendant vault was considered *the* great sight of Frankfurt in the early days of tourism. The replacement chancel, built by Madern Gerthener, preserves most of its luminous stained glass windows; to the side is a magnificent gilded altar from Antwerp with skilfully carved scenes from the life of Christ.

A little further along Untermainkai is the **Karmelitenkloster**, a late Gothic building most famous for Jerg Ratgeb's colossal fresco cycle in its cloisters, depicting scenes from the life of Jesus. Painted between 1514 and 1523, it was badly damaged in the war, but recent work has restored its exquisite colouring and vividness. The southern part of the building now houses the **Museum für Vor- und Frühgeschichte** (same times as Historisches Museum; free), a collection devoted to early and prehistory and to the archaeological work carried out in Frankfurt. Further west, at Untermainkai 14–15, is the **Jüdisches Museum** (same times; free), which recounts the history of Frankfurt's once powerful and wealthy Jewish population.

The northern Altstadt

A few minutes' walk north of the Karmelitenkloster, at Grosser Hirschgraben 23, is the **Goethehaus und Goethe-Museum** (April–Sept Mon–Sat 9am–6pm, Sun 10am–1pm; Oct–Mar Mon–Sat 9am–4pm, Sun 10am–1pm; DM3), the interior of which has been immaculately restored after being completely burned out during the war. This is where Goethe was born and raised, and not surprisingly it's become a popular tourist spot: to Germans, Goethe represents the pinnacle of their distinguished literary tradition, and he's accorded the same sort of reverence that's bestowed on Shakespeare in English-speaking countries. (See also Weimar, *Chapter Eleven*.) The house has been made to look as much as possible like it did when Goethe lived here, and there are a few original objects which somehow survived the war, while the well-stocked library has some autographed examples of his writings.

The **Katharinenkirche**, a little further along on Kleiner Hirschgraben, is where Goethe was baptised and confirmed. Opposite is the **Hauptwache**, an eighteenth-century Baroque building which used to be Frankfurt's biggest (and aesthetically most pleasing) police station. These days it's a pricey city-centre café, while the station of the same name is a junction on nearly all of Frankfurt's S- and U-Bahn lines.

Nearby on the Liebfrauenberg is the **Liebfrauenkirche**, a fifteenth-century church now belonging to a Capuchin monastery, whose monks are well known for their work with the local down and outs. Look inside for the unusual Baroque altar, a huge alabaster and gilt affair which sits well in the dusky pink sandstone interior. Even finer is the original south doorway, now only visible from the inside; its gorgeous and still brightly coloured tympanum of *The Adoration of the Magi* is a masterpiece of the "Soft Style", and is thought to be the work of Madern Gerthener. In the **Markthalle** just behind the church you can buy Turkish produce and stock up on the best fresh fruit and veg in town. To the north is **Zeil**, one of Germany's most expensive and exclusive shopping streets, though the area around Konstablerwache has become notorious for its drugs pedlars: one downside of Frankfurt's prosperity is that it has become the undisputed drugs capital of Germany.

A little to the northwest of the Hauptwache is the **Börse**, Frankfurt's stock exchange. It's open to the public on weekdays from 11.30am to 1.30pm if you fancy a first-hand glimpse of where Frankfurt's conspicuous money comes from. Appropriately enough two of the most expensive shopping streets in the city are just around the corner. **Goethestrasse** is Frankfurt's Bond Street, all expensive jewellers and designer clothes shops, while **Grosse Bockenheimer Strasse**, known to the natives as *Fressgasse* (Guzzle Lane) is home to upmarket delicatessens and smarter restaurants. Look out for *Stefan Weiss*, a butcher's shop that's sometimes described as a "meat boutique", owing to its immaculate interior and high prices.

Both of these streets lead into Opernplatz, home of the grandiose Neoclassical **Alte Oper**, built in 1880 in imitation of, and as a rival to, the opera houses of Paris and Dresden. The present structure is the result of years of work to restore the damage of 1945 – the vestibule and first-floor café, all fake marble and colonnades, recapture something of the late nineteenth-century ambience. With its excellent acoustics, the Alte Oper is often used as a congress hall as well as playing host to classical musicians and the likes of Barbra Streisand and Liza Minelli. Oddly enough you won't see much opera here, apart from the occasional production which doesn't need elaborate staging.

The fringes of the Altstadt

For one of the best **views** of Frankfurt old and new, it's worth taking a walk through the **Taunusanlage** and the **Gallusanlage**, two narrow stretches of parkland running into each other that begin south of Opernplatz and curve round to the Main, following the line of the old city wall. With the Alte Oper to the north, the Hauptbahnhof to the west, the Römerberg to the southeast and all around you the ultra-modern high-rise office buildings which give the city its distinctive skyline, it's a great place to capture a view of the city. But – and it's a big but – this area is the favourite hangout of the city's junkies, who can be seen in their dozens injecting themselves with drugs. All this is something not for the squeamish, and it's best to steer clear of the area by night.

A much more pleasant stroll from Opernplatz is in the opposite direction, through, the **Bockenheimer Anlage** and past a small lake to the **Nebbienische Gartenhäuschen**, a playful little villa built in 1810 by a local publisher to mark his third marriage. At the end of the Bockenheimer Anlage rises the **Eschenheimer Turm**, the highest defensive tower in Germany. There were once 42 towers ringing the city and this is the most imposing of the survivors; its fantastical shape, peppered with oriels and turrets and looking like it was designed in the Hollywood dream factory, marks it out as the handiwork of the ever resourceful Madern Gerthener. Look out for the nine holes in the shape of a figure 9 on the weather vane which, according to legend, were shot into it by a local poacher.

Nearby in Stephanstrasse is the **Petersfriedhof** which for years was Frankfurt's most fashionable cemetery; in the adjacent school courtyard is the grave of Goethe's mother, "Frau Aja". About ten minutes' walk to the south, just off Fahrgasse, is a surviving stretch of the **Staufenmauer**, the twelfth-century city wall which was the grand daddy of all Frankfurt's subsequent defences. Just beyond here, a left turn into Berliner Strasse will lead you to Battonstrasse and the **Jüdischer Friedhof**, which was in use from 1462 to 1828 and contains the Rothschild family vault.

Sachsenhausen

If you want to escape from the centre of Frankfurt, or have a laid-back evening out, then head for **Sachsenhausen** on the south bank of the Main. Although it has been part of Frankfurt since 1318, this city-within-a-city retains a distinctive atmosphere. It's best known as the "apple wine quarter", in honour of its most famous product, which is served in practically every bar in the area, and it's here that you'll find Frankfurt's most civilised nightlife. In **Schweizer Strasse** there's every imaginable kind of speciality shop, while in the old *Schlachthaus* (slaughterhouse) on Deutschherrnufer (opposite the Flösserbrücke) there's a *Flohmarkt* (flea market) every Saturday morning, which claims to be the largest in Europe.

The heart of the quarter

The best way to approach Sachsenhausen is over the **Eiserner Steg**, an iron footbridge which runs from just outside the Historisches Museum. Lazy alternatives, which cross via the Alte Brücke further to the east, are bus #46 from the Hauptbahnhof or, if you're feeling in the mood for a bit of tourist tack, the *Ebbelwei-Express*, an old-time tram with on-board apple wine and pretzels (Sat & Sun afternoon; DM3 inclusive). However you decide to get there, you'll be doing a lot of walking when you arrive as most of Sachsenhausen is pedestrianised.

Just over the Alte Brücke is the **Deutschordenshaus**, a triple-winged eighteenth-century building formerly belonging to the Teutonic Knights, whose Baroque facade cunningly hides a Gothic church. Overlooking the river just a couple of minutes' walk away is the **Kuhhirtenturm** (Cowherds Tower): built in 1490 as part of the Sachsenhausen fortifications, it looks like an elongated fortified barn. Most people go to Sachsenhausen to eat, drink and be merry in the restaurants and bars of **Alt Sachsenhausen**, the network of streets around Affentorplatz to the south. The main attractions are the apple wine houses – recognised by the pine wreath or *Fichtekränzi* hanging outside – where drinkers sit at long wooden benches in an atmosphere that makes it easy to get into conversation. (See *Eating and drinking* below.)

At the southernmost end of the quarter looms the 120-metre **Henninger Turm** (Tues–Sat 11am–11pm, Sun 11am–6pm; DM3.50) of the eponymous Frankfurt brewery. The entrance fee includes access to a museum (open until 7pm) illustrating the history of beer in the city from the Middle Ages to the present day, and to the observation platform, which commands a fine view over Frankfurt. There are also a couple of top-notch restaurants, which are pricey, though not unreasonably so.

Along Museumsufer

Between the Eiserner Steg and the Friedensbrücke to the west is Schaumainkai, popularly known as the **Museumsufer**, as the best museums in Frankfurt, seven in all, are straddled along its bank. First up, at no. 15, is the **Museum für Kunsthandwerk** (Tues & Thurs–Sun 10am–5pm, Wed 10am–8pm; free), which has one of the largest and best collections of applied art in the world. It's housed in a discreetly innovative building designed by the American architect Richard Meier; all sloping ramps in place of stairs and glassless internal windows framing *objets d'art*. The museum is divided into four sections: European, featuring a unique collection of furniture models, glassware and ceramics; Islamic, with some fine carpets; Far Eastern, with lots of jade and lacquerwork plus a liberal sprinkling of porcelain and sculptures; and finally a section devoted to books and writing. In a nineteenth-century villa at no. 29, the **Museum für Völkerkunde** (same times; free) is a small ethnographical museum with an extensive collection of masks and totems from all over the world.

The **Deutsches Filmmuseum** (same times; free) at no. 41 is Germany's biggest and best on the subject, featuring a huge collection detailing the development of films and the film industry. A distinctly "hands-on" approach encourages visitors to get to grips with the various film-related items on display, which range from early bioscopes to modern movie cameras. On a larger scale, there's a reconstruction of the *Grand Café* in Paris where the Lumière brothers showed the first ever public film, and of a Frankfurt cinema from 1912. There's also a good collection of film posters and a very extensive section on film music. Not surprisingly the museum has its own cinema (entry DM6) and there's a good little café in the basement.

A passage leads from the Filmmuseum café to the **Deutsches Architekturmuseum** (same times; free) at no. 43, installed in a self-consciously avant-garde conversion of a nineteenth-century villa. The highpoint of the interior, which has been gutted and restyled in dazzling white, is the "house within a house", which dominates the museum like an oversized doll's house. Somehow it doesn't quite work, and despite a glass roof and clever use of lighting, the building has a very claustrophobic feel which detracts from the actual exhibits themselves, the bulk of which are architectural drawings and models.

More conventional in layout is the **Bundespostmuseum** (same times; free) at no. 53, a big collection of anything remotely connected with postal matters. Conceivably it might be of interest to a philatelist: there are lots of postage stamps, postmen's uniforms, post coaches, post boxes, models of post trains and the like. The museum is also big on telephones, as Frankfurt calls itself the birthplace of the telephone, irrespective of the claims of Alexander Graham Bell.

The Städelsches Kunstinstitut

Very much the star of the Museumsufer, the **Städelsches Kunstinstitut** or **Städel** (same times as the other museums; DM6) at no. 63 ranks as one of the most comprehensive art galleries in Europe. Unlike the galleries of Munich and Berlin, it is not rooted in a royal collection – it was founded in the early nineteenth century by a local banker as an art college, with an assembly of old masters from which students could learn.

MEDIEVAL GERMAN PAINTING

Chronologically, the layout begins on the top floor. Highlights of the **German section** include a naïve but surpassingly beautiful *Garden of Paradise* by an unknown Middle Rhenish master of the early fifteenth century, *The Resurrection* by **Master of the Housebook**, *Job on his Dungheap* by **Dürer**, and two grisailles from a lost altarpiece by **Grünewald**. **Holbein the Elder's** large *Passion Altar*, painted for the city's Dominican monastery, is one of his finest works, with no quarter given in the representation of gruesome detail. **Cranach's** *The Holy Kinship*, which incorporates portraits of some of the leading personalities of the day, is another major altarpiece from the eve of the Reformation. The idiosyncratic art of **Baldung** is represented by a *Baptism of Christ* triptych and *Two Weather Witches*, while in **Altdorfer's** opulent *Adoration of the Magi* the artist typically indulges his love of rich and elaborate detail. The outstanding *Portrait of Simon George of Cornwall* by **Holbein the Younger** is particularly intriguing for the fact that the subject was clean-shaven when the sittings began; the artist had to carry out a skilful modification in order to show the beard his patron subsequently grew.

NETHERLANDISH AND EARLY ITALIAN WORKS

One of the main strengths of the gallery is its wealth of paintings from the early **Netherlandish School**, dominated by the gem of the whole collection, **van Eyck's** *Lucca Madonna*, which shows his legendary precision at its finest. The first great painter of the School, now generally identified as **Robert Campin** but labelled here as the Master of Flémalle, is represented by several works, while his pupil **Roger van der Weyden** features with a magnificent *Virgin and Child with SS Peter, John the Baptist, Cosmas and Damian*. Also in the room are superbly observed male portraits by Memling and Massys, and one of **Bosch's** earliest known works, *Christ Presented to the People*; though restrained by his standards, it already shows his penchant for caricature and facial distortions. The Madonna and Child, a frequent subject in the Netherlandish section, also dominates the **Italian**, where the outstanding treatment is the ethereal image by **Fra Angelico**. Versions by Verrocchio, Moretto da Brescia, Perugino, Bellini, Cima and Carpaccio make fascinating comparisons. Other highlights here are an *Annunciation* by **Carlo Crivelli**, *St Mark* by **Mantegna**, *Portrait of Simonetta Vespucci* by **Botticelli**, and **Pontormo's** *Lady with Lap-Dog*.

SEVENTEENTH-CENTURY PAINTING

Pride of place among **seventeenth-century** paintings goes to Frankfurt's own **Adam Elsheimer**. The largest work ever painted by this master of the small-scale is the *Altarpiece of the Cross*, the seven panels of which have been patiently accumulated over the years. Also here are *The Great Flood* – a miracle of compression – and *The Dream of Joseph*. Poussin, Claude and Rubens, all admirers of Elsheimer, are on display in the next section, which also includes the most purely Baroque work in **Rembrandt's** entire output, the violent *Blinding of Samson* – a striking contrast with the quiet dignity of his very early *David Playing the Harp before Saul*. There's a gloriously luminous **Vermeer**, *The Geographer*, and examples of most of the lesser artists of seventeenth-century Holland. Representation of the eighteenth century is sparser, but there are two scenes from a *Horrors of War* series by **Goya**, and examples of Tiepolo, Canaletto and Chardin. A recent acquisition is a newly discovered **Watteau**, the marvellously frothy *Isle of Cythera*.

EIGHTEENTH- & NINETEENTH-CENTURY PAINTING

Paintings from the **late eighteenth century onwards** occupy the first floor. Of the big French names, **Courbet** (a *View of Frankfurt*), **Degas**, and **Monet** are the ones to look out for. However, German artists predominate. *Goethe in the Roman Campagna* by

Johann Heinrich Tischbein is the most celebrated of the many Romantic portrayals of the writer. The Nazarene Brotherhood figures strongly, notably with a huge detached fresco of *The Introduction of the Arts into Germany*, painted by **Philip Veit**, once director of the Städel. If this isn't to your taste, you might prefer the realism of **Wilhelm Leibl**, whose *Unlikely Couple* is an update of a favourite Renaissance theme – mercenary love.

TWENTIETH-CENTURY WORK

Until the days of the Third Reich, the Städel had perhaps the finest array of modern painting in Germany. However, over 500 paintings were removed in the measures against "degenerate art", and the collection has never recovered, although it now has the benefit of being able to display loans from local industrialists and financial institutions. German highlights include **Beckmann**'s *The Synagogue* (bought by public appeal as an atonement for past sins), **Dix**'s unflattering *The Artist's Family*, **Ernst**'s spooky *Nature in Morning Light* and **Kirchner**'s *Nude Wearing a Hat*; the most notable foreign paintings are **Matisse**'s *Still Life* and **Picasso**'s *Portrait of Fernance Olivier*.

The Liebighaus

Last but by no means least of the museums is the **Liebighaus** (same times; free) at no. 71: the villa which houses it can easily be identified by the bits and pieces of statuary on display in the garden, including *Ariadne on the Panther* by Johann Heinrich Dannecker. The collection is a step-by-step guide to the history of sculpture, and as such is the most important in the country, though only sections of it have been open in recent years due to a long-term restoration project which, by the time you read this, should be complete. Sumerian, Egyptian, Greek, Roman and Coptic examples give a comprehensive overview of the Classical world. German works predictably predominate in the later periods; look out in particular for the late fifteenth- and early sixteenth-century golden period, featuring important carvings by Nicolaus Gerhaert, Hans Multscher and Tilman Riemenschneider.

Westend and Bockenheim

Frankfurt's financial district, the **Westend**, developed as home to the commercial class during the nineteenth century. Until the Nazis came to power many of the wealthier members of Frankfurt's Jewish community (the second largest in Germany) lived here – for example, huge swathes of land between Bockenheimer Landstrasse and Reuterweg were owned by the Rothschild family until the city bought them out in 1938, for a "bargain" price. In the 1960s the property speculators moved in, forcing ordinary people out of their homes so the old buildings could be converted into offices or the sites used for skyscrapers. Scant attention was paid to planning laws as the developers fell over themselves to grab every available inch of land, and from 1970 onwards there was a rash of house occupations and squattings in protest. Fierce clashes with the police ensued, but caused only temporary delays to the process of redevelopment.

Ugliest building in the area is undoubtedly the **Hochhaus am Park** in Fürstenberger Strasse, a totally incoherent structure designed by a succession of architects. The most impressive of the high-rises is the sleek **Deutsche Bank**, a little to the west of the Alte Oper, which dominates the Frankfurt skyline; the bank has an art collection which can be viewed by prior arrangement (☎7150) or, should you so desire, you can just have a look round the foyer and watch the money-makers going purposefully about their business in the shadow of a cascading fountain. At **Siesmayerstrasse 6** you can take a look at a piece of very recent history; this elegant upper-middle-class villa (now fallen on very hard times) was the last squatted house in the Westend to succumb.

Westend has its own stretch of greenery too. In the north-west of the area is the **Grüneburgpark**, a nineteenth-century English-style park which these days is popular with joggers and weekend footballers. On the northeastern edge is the Botanischer Garten, a good place to go for a walk as it has a sort of cultivated wildness to it. It incorporates the manicured **Palmengarten** (daily 9am–4/5/6pm; DM5), which is planted with tropical and sub-tropical trees, plants and flowers.

Bockenheim

Bockenheimer Landstrasse, once Frankfurt's millionaires' row, will take you from Westend to **Bockenheim**, a predominantly working-class district which since the 1960s has been turned into the centre of Frankfurt's alternative scene by a big influx of bohos and students. The area also has a large *Gastarbeiter* population and is best thought of as a Frankfurt version of Berlin's Kreuzberg with the difference that the various groups who have made it their home are not as factionalised and stand-offish as in that city. Leipziger Strasse is the main shopping drag (on U-Bahn line #6) and there are a lot of good bars and restaurants around – the Italian ones are best from a culinary viewpoint but the Greek places are usually best value for money.

The University complex is at the southeastern edge of Bockenheim, which partly accounts for its popularity with students. In the vicinity is the **Senckenbergmuseum**, Senckenberganlage 25 (Mon–Fri 9am–5pm, Wed 9am–8pm, Sat & Sun 9am–6pm; DM3), a massive natural history museum. Even if you're not normally attracted by this subject, it's well worth coming to see the remarkable palaeontology collection, dominated by an awe-inspiring array of dinosaur skeletons.

Höchst

Nowadays a western suburb of Frankfurt, **HÖCHST**, which can be reached by S-Bahn line #1 or #2 from the Hauptbahnhof or Hauptwache, is an ancient town in its own right, as well as being the home of the famous Hoechst chemical company. Although very much in the shadow of the chemical works, the small Altstadt rewards a quick look round. The **Balongaropalast** at Balongarostr. 109 is a slightly over-the-top Baroque townhouse, in whose gardens open-air theatre performances are occasionally held. A little further down the same street, in the **Dalberghaus** (no. 186), Höchst porcelain is once again being manufactured – replica eighteenth-century shepherdess figurines and the like are for sale at unhealthy prices. On Schlossplatz to the south there's a run-of-the-mill Renaissance **Schloss** and the old **Zollturm** (Customs Tower). The latter houses the local museum (daily 10am–4pm; free), which, having been sponsored by Hoechst, tends to dwell on the history of that company. East of here is the Carolingian **Justiniankirche** (Mon–Wed noon–2pm, Thurs–Sun 3–5pm), by far the oldest church in the Frankfurt conurbation.

Bus #54 from the Altstadt takes you down Höchster Farben Strasse and to your left you'll see the huge chemical complex stretching out down to the Main. The cathedral-like administrative offices of the factory were designed by the Jugendstil architect Peter Behrens and must be among the most aesthetically balanced factory buildings anywhere. The bus then goes on to Zeilsheim, which in the immediate postwar years was *the* black market centre of Germany and where, around **Coburger Strasse**, you can still see the little cottages of the **Arbeiter Kolonie Zeilsheim**, a turn-of-the-century model housing development for Hoechst workers.

Eating, drinking and nightlife

Not surprisingly, given its status as one of Germany's main urban centres, Frankfurt has a wealth of gastronomic possibilities catering for even the most esoteric tastes. Whether it's vegan breakfast, Japanese afternoon tea or a gourmet Italian dinner you're

---

APPLE WINE

There's a theory that Europe has a cider belt separating the areas producing wine and beer, and that Frankfurt is the hub of this. This seems tenuous at best, as the apple wine tradition here is historically a relatively recent one, having started in 1750. Made by the same process used in the production of ordinary wine, apple wine is bought in blue-grey stone jugs called *Bembel* and drunk from a *Schobbeglas*. There are four types: *Süsser*, sweet and fresh from the presses in autumn, and relatively weak; *Rauscher*, which will blow your head off if you don't treat it with respect; *Heller*, which is clear and smooth; and the hazy and golden *Alte*. Those in the know order *Handkäs mit Musik* (cheese served with onions and vinaigrette) or *Rippchen mit Kraut* (smoked pork chop with *Sauerkraut*) as a culinary accompaniment to their *Ebbelwei*.

---

after, you'll be able to find it somewhere. As for drink, the city is situated close to several famous wine-producing regions, and is itself an important beer centre: *Binding* is the largest brewery in the country, while *Henninger* is one of the biggest exporters; both produce a wide range of products, though no specifically local style. However, the city's favourite beverage is apple wine (*Apfelwein*; variously known as *Ebbelwei* or *Ebbelwoi* in the local dialect), a cider variant best sampled in the specialist taverns in Sachsenhausen.

Apple wine taverns

Sachsenhausen

Aprikösie, Neuer Wall 3. Old-fashioned, with a secluded courtyard. Closed at weekends.

Buchscheer, Schwarzsteinkautweg 17/Gablonzerstr. 12 (tram #14 or bus #35 from the city centre, or tram #17 from the centre of Sachsenhausen). Set amidst the rose gardens on the southeastern edge of Sachsenhausen and very popular with walkers. Good home cooking and home-produced apple wine.

Eichkatzerl, Dreieichstr. 29. A traditional Sachsenhausen apple wine tavern with a very popular restaurant. Closed Wed and first Thurs of every month.

Gerbemühle, Deutschherrnufer 105. On the banks of the Main, complete with large garden.

Germania, Textorstr. 16. Best of the many traditional taverns on the street.

Klaane Sachsehäuser, Neuer Wall 11. A family place favoured by native Sachsenhauseners.

Nagur, Schweizer Str. A little upmarket but worth dropping in on.

Wagner, Schweizer Str. 71 One of the best of the taverns, with a lively clientele ranging from young to middle-aged. Frequently packed out.

Zu den Drei Stuebern, Dreieichstr. 28/Klappergasse. Mainly patronised by locals; has a small bar-room and pleasant terrace at the rear. Closed Sat.

Zum gemalten Haus, Schweizer Str. 67. A bit on the olde worlde side with its oil-painted facade and stained glass windows, yet quite lively, with long rows of tables outside.

Zum grauen Bock, Rittergasse 30. There tend to be a lot of tourists at this one but it does stay open until 1am.

Elsewhere in the city

Momberger, Alt-Heddernheim 13 (U-bahn lines #1, 2 and 3 to Weisser Stein). Very traditional and full of locals rather than tourists, due to its being out on the northern edge of the city. The apple wine comes straight from wooden vats on the premises and the food is cheap.

Scherer, Lindenau 9 (U-bahn lines #1, 2 and 3 to Weisser Stein). A cosy place in the suburb of Eschersheim; serves ordinary wine too.

Zur Eulenburg, Eulengasse 46 (U-bahn line #4 to Seckbacher Landstrasse). Staid middle-aged clientele, but the food and *Ebbelwei* are as good as any.

Cafés and café-bars

The centre

Altes Café, Kaiserstr. 5. Traditional café with fine cakes and high prices.

Bar Central, Elefantengasse 11. A long-established pillar of the Frankfurt *Szene*. Happy hour from 8pm to 9pm, and good music at all times.

Buchcafé, Kleine Bockenheimer Str. 14. A bookshop which doubles as a café; excellent place to peruse books or read the assorted city papers and magazines.

Café Gegenwart, Bergerstr. 6. Spacious and very trendy hangout whose walls are a forum for avant-garde art. Does good value bistro-type meals.

Café Schwille, Grosse Bockenheimer Str. 50. This traditional *Kaffee und Kuchen* spot is also the place for an early breakfast (it opens at 7am). Good in the summer as there's a terrace. Also branches at Rossmarkt, and next door to the Katharinenkirche.

Eckstein, An der Stadtmauer 7. Arty meeting point with obligatory exhibitions on the walls and occasional live music in the basement.

Rotlint-Café, Rotlintstr. 60. Recommended for breakfasts, this one is just outside the city centre (tram #12 from Grosse Friedbergerstrasse) and is popular with a youngish alternative crowd. Open until 1am.

Bockenheim and Westend

Café au Lait, Am Weingarten 12. Among Bockenheim's trendiest meeting places; also has a great selection of breakfast possibilities.

Café Laumer, Bockenheimer Landstr. 67. One of Frankfurt's oldest cafés, halfway up the Westend's main thoroughfare, now enjoying a new lease of life with a young arty clientele.

Orfeo, Hamburger Allee 45. Favoured by media/creative types. Superb breakfasts and main courses from about DM11.

Stattcafé, Grempstr. 21. Another place which does good breakfast. The emphasis is on healthy eating in an informal atmosphere – popular with the Bockenheim arty crowd. A real focal point, with work from Frankfurt artists on the walls.

Sachsenhausen

Café Bar, Schweizer Str. 14. Despite an unimaginative name, this is the trendiest café in Sachsenhausen, all black (it's also known as the *Schwarzes Café*) and mirrored decor with a posey clientele.

Café Will, Schweizer Str. 59. A very traditional café, much favoured by elderly gents in grey suits, but they do excellent breakfasts as well as a fine array of cakes and ice creams.

Das Lesecafé, Diesterwegstr. 7. Popular with would-be intellectuals, the gimmick here is that you read as you eat and drink. You can select a book from the neighbouring bookshop – or just admire the art on the walls.

Bars

The centre

Club Voltaire, Hochstr. 5. Good food at good prices (you can eat well for DM12), and an eclectic clientele: political activists, artists, musicians, Greens, gays – you'll find them all here in one of Frankfurt's best-established meeting places.

Die Wanne, Opernplatz 12. In the shadow of the Alter Oper, with good food and wine.

Dominicus, Brückhofstr. 1. A vaulted cellar establishment with live music at weekends, whose good wines and free *Schmalzbrot* (black bread) draw a young crowd.

Dünker, Bergerstr. 265 (U-Bahn line #4 to Bornheim Mitte). Originally a sampling house selling wine by the crate, you can now drink in the unpretentious cellar. Closes at 9pm.

Haus Wertheym, Fahrtor 1. A medieval inn on the Römerberg with *Bockbier*, traditional food and a friendly atmosphere. Closed Tues.

Medius-Keller, Neue Mainzer Str. 24. This cosy and usually candle-lit establishment is one of the best wine cellars in Frankfurt – an ideal place for a rendezvous.

Nostradamus, Heiligkreuzgasse 16–18. An atmospheric bar with occasional folk music and Guinness on tap.

Vinum, Kleine Hochstr. 9. Newly opened (though the owner is a member of one of Frankfurt's most venerable wine-merchant families), this is proving to be one of the city's most popular wine bars.

Zwölf Apostel, Rosenbergerstr. 1. Frankfurt's first *Hausbrauerei*, serving organically brewed Pils.

Sachsenhausen

Balalaika, Dreikönigstr. 30. Popular with Brits and Americans – but don't let that put you off. Features live music with a Slavic flavour.

Der alte Hut, Deutschherrnufer 28. Flea market decor and river views make this a popular place to sink a few drinks. 8pm–1am.

Down by the Riverside, Mainkai 7. English-style pub whose soul music attracts hordes of black American GIs.

Sachs, Darmstädter Landstr. 119. A huge old brewery cellar which has been tarted up and now attracts phenomenal numbers of people. Not bad for all that.

Bockenheim and Westend

Bockenheimer Weinkontor, Schloss Str. 92. Popular wine bar, particularly favoured by the singles crowd.

Fidelio, Bockenheimer Landstr. 1. A favourite Westend watering-hole for media and advertising types, with a wine bar atmosphere. Normally open until 1am.

Restaurants

The centre

Alte Kanzlei, Neidenau 50. Alsace specialities – which means things like dandelion salad from DM28. Closed Sat.

Aubergine, Alte Gasse 14. Good food, good service, reasonable prices (by central Frankfurt standards) – lunch DM20, four courses DM45. Open until 11pm.

Avocado–Le Bistro, Hochstr. 27. Fine bistro fare starting at around DM20, complemented by a carefully selected wine list.

Bombay Place, Taunusstr. 17. A tandoori and chicken joint near the Hauptbahnhof.

Buffalo, Alte Rothofstr. 10. City-centre steakhouse, much favoured by GIs and their families. Also does good enchiladas and tacos.

Byblos, Vilbeler Str. 32. A bit over the top – good Lebanese food, plenty of arak and the added attraction of belly dancing from 10.30pm on Fridays.

Casa del Pittore, Zeisselstr. 20). An expensive city-centre Italian, but their fish is excellent.

Da Salvatore, Schöne Aussicht 16. Pizzeria with good views over the Main.

Die Leiter, Kaiserhofstr. 11 (just off Grosse Bockenheimer Strasse). Classy yet not too expensive with pavement tables in the summer. DM15–25.

Eden, Rahmhofstr. 4 . Real heavy-duty vegetarian place patronised by true adherents. Open until 8.30pm but closed Sun.

El Pacifico, Boulterrasse, Sandweg 79 (U-Bahn line #4 to Merianplatz). It's worth going out of the way for the enchiladas and tacos, which even attract jaded Americans.

Estragon, Jahnstr. 49. It's tarragon with everything in this reasonably priced restaurant, which attracts a lot of office workers and fills up quickly.

Gaylord, Elbestr. 24. Excellent Indian food, friendly and helpful staff.

Green Hill, Gutzkowstr. 43. Not particularly cheap but quite tasty vegetarian. Try their tofu stroganoff. Open until 11pm most nights but closed Mon.

Grüner Bambus, Ostendstr. 61. Highly recommended Vietnamese restaurant.

Juchheim's, Am Salzhaus 1. An authentic Japanese teahouse and restaurant. The teahouse is open until 6.30pm and the restaurant until 10.30pm. Closed Sun.

La Galleria, Theaterplatz 2. Widely regarded as the best Italian restaurant in Frankfurt, with first class cuisine at first class prices.

L'Emir, Baseler Platz 2. Great Lebanese place, with a huge selection of appetisers. Occasional belly dancing shows at weekends.

Mikuni, Fahrgasse 93. A Japanese restaurant which makes few concessions to the west.

Nibelungenschänke, Niblungenallee 55 (U-bahn line #55 to Niblungenallee). Typical Greek food at reasonable prices. The clientele is young and the place is usually open until 1am.

Palace Restaurant, Moselstr. 23. Chinese place open till 4am, with great duck dishes from DM22.

Panda, Düsseldorfer Str. 10. The cheapest good Chinese restaurant in the Hauptbahnhof area.

Sawadi, Friedberger Str. 34. Probably the best Thai place in Frankfurt; very popular, so you're not encouraged to linger.

Scarlet Pimpernel, Krögerstr. 7. Good Polish restaurant open Sat and Sun only 8pm–1am.

Tamnak, Berliner Str. 64. Lots of bamboo decor and fine Thai food.

Tse-Yang, Kaiserstr. 67. Pricey but very good Chinese in the middle of the red light district. The Peking duck is especially recommended.

Westend

Bistro Rosa, Grünerberg Weg 25. The walls hung with pictures of pigs lend an element of kitsch, but the food is excellent.

Da Lucio e Mario, Feuerbachstr. 23. Well-established Italian restaurant.

Erno's Bistro, Liebingstr. 15. Westend French with an Alsace accent and business clientele; three course meals for DM40. Open until 10pm; closed at weekends.

Golfo di Napoli, Leipziger Str. 16. Pricey Italian, popular with the Westend yuppies, but the food and atmosphere are good.

Isoletta, Feldbergerstr. 23. One of the more affordable Italian restaurants, popular with the nearby ad agency types during the day.

Knoblauch, Staufenstr. 39/Liebingstr. Friendly, intimate little place where everything comes liberally laced with garlic. DM15–25.

Natur-Gourmet, Eppsteinerstr. 54. Inexpensive vegetarian place mainly patronised by people working locally. Open until 6.30pm.

Rosa, Grüneburgweg 25. Good food for Westend types not so keen on conspicuous consumption. Closed weekends.

Bockenheim

Ban Thai, Leipziger Str. 26. Reasonably priced and very hot Thai dishes.

Gargantua, Friesengasse 3. One of Bockenheim's best, with a three-course meal for DM38. If that's too meagre you could always go for the seven-course one at DM98. Open until 9.30pm; closed Mon and first Sun of the month.

Pizzeria da Chino, Adalbertstr. 29. Decently priced pizzeria. Nothing fancy, but a good place to fill up.

Rapunzel, Schloss Str. 92. German cuisine prepared to a high standard and served in soothing surroundings. Main courses from around DM30.

Union International Club, Am Leonhardsbrunn 12/Ditmarstr. This place is so upmarket that it doesn't even have a sign on its wrought iron gates to say it's a restaurant. You get a couple of courses for about DM35.

Sachsenhausen

Alt Prag, Klappergasse 14. Czech speciality place with *Budweiser* (the original) on tap.

Nachteule, Schifferstr. 3. Open until 4am, this is a late-night institution in Frankfurt, attracting a wide-ranging clientele and serving very healthy portions.

St Hubertus, Gartenstr. 175. A game and wildfowl speciality place with a garden; you should be able to come away with change from DM25.

Wolkenbruch, Textorstr. 26. No-smoking vegetarian serving everything from tofu burgers to wholemeal pizzas. From DM9.

Nightlife

Not surprisingly Frankfurt's nightlife is pretty eclectic, though in this money city quite a lot of what's going on is out of the reach of most pockets. The following is a selective run down of the more affordable venues. Worth knowing about is Kleine Bockenheimer Strasse, aka *Jazzgasse* (Jazz Alley), the centre of Frankfurt's lively jazz scene. Many leading German jazzers cut their musical teeth playing in the bars around here and there's usually live music going on most nights.

Live music venues

Batschkapp, Maibachstr. 24. Open most days of the week 9pm–1am with live music or fairly up to the minute DJ dance sounds.

Brotfabrik, Bachmannstr. 2-4. One of the most innovative venues in the city, featuring live and disco music from all over the world, with salsa particularly featured; entrance fees range from DM5 to DM15. Also has a café and a Spanish restaurant.

Irish Pub, Kleine Rittergasse 11. Every big German city has its Irish pub; Frankfurt's is very popular, with good Irish music. Open until 1am.

Jazz Keller, Kleine Bockenheimer Str. 18a. This atmospheric cellar is Frankfurt's premier jazz venue. Open 9pm–3am. Closed Mon.

Music-Hall, Voltastr. 74. Big venue northwest of the Hauptbahnhof, with regular live music and discos. Open until 3am; also does food.

Schlachthof, Deutschherrnufer 36. Rough and ready rock and jazz joint, housed in Sachsenhausen's old slaughterhouse.

Sinnkasten, Brönnerstr. 5. This place has everything – pool room, cabaret stage, disco and, most importantly, a concert hall where they put on everything from jazz to avant-garde and indie stuff. Open 9pm–2am. Entry DM7.

Discos

Frankfurt's disco scene is heavily dance music-oriented, with most venues serving up house/techno beats for predominantly young crowds. Places tend to stay open until 4am during the week and 5am or 6am at weekends. Entry starts at about DM10.

Central Park, Holzgraben 9. A rock disco, drawing in old hippies and provincial teenagers. Anachronistic, but it makes a change from the norm.

Cooky's, Am Salzhaus 4. Frankfurt's best known and most popular disco. Dance music and chart stuff draws in a youthful crowd. On Mondays there are usually live bands.

Dorian Gray, Airport C, level 0. Oddly located at airport, one of the largest discos in Germany, and not always so easy to get into. Entry DM10; open until 6am. Closed Mon and Tues.

Funkadelic, Brönnerstr. 11. Mainly hard-core dance music which attracts a lot of black GIs.

Omen, Junghofstr. 14. More heavy duty dance music, dished up by the leading lights of the local DJ scene.

Gay Frankfurt

Blue Moon, Eckenheimer Landstrasse. Women's place, full of intense political lesbians.

Keller, Bleigstrasse. Extremely chic with a slightly intimidating atmosphere. Men only.

Madame, Alle Heiligen Strasse. Also for women; a little more laid-back.

Schweig, Schäfergasse. Relaxed and unpretentious – a good way into the Frankfurt gay scene.

Culture

Frankfurt has a predictably lively performing arts scene, centred on the aforementioned *Alte Oper* on Opernplatz (☎13400) and the *Städtische Bühnen* on Theaterplatz (☎256 2335). The latter has one auditorium for **opera** (its productions, with a strong bias in favour of twentieth-century music, are regarded as the most innovative in Germany) and two for **drama**. The company also owns the *Bockenheimer Depot*, housed in the old tramway depot at Bockenheimer Warte (☎2123 7432). Venues of special note include the flourishing *English Theater*, Kaiserstr. 52 (☎2423 1620), which performs **English language** plays in the original, and *Gallus-Theater*, Krifteler Str. 55 (☎738 0037), which has a fair claim to be regarded as the main contribution the *Gastarbeiter* have made to the national culture. *Theater am Turm*, Eschersheimer Landstr. 2 (☎154 51100) is a trendy *Szene* place, while *Tigerpalast*, Heiligkreuzgasse 16–20 (☎20770) performs old-fashioned cabaret. **Satirical cabaret** can be seen at *Die Schmiere*, Im Karmeliterkloster (☎281066), *Die Maininger*, Neue Rothofstr. (☎280227), and *Künstlerhaus Mousonturm*, Waldschmidtstr. 4 (☎4058 9520). Among the city's **orchestras**, pride of place goes to the *Radio-Sinfonie-Orchester-Frankfurt*, which is of international class. Large-scale concerts tend to be held in the *Alte Oper*, or in the *Jahrhunderthalle* on Pfaffenweise (☎360 1240) in Höchst.

Listings

Airlines *Air Canada*, Friedensstr. 11 (☎250131); *Air New Zealand*, Rathenauplatz la. (☎291897); *British Airways*, Rossmarkt 23 (☎290371); *Lufthansa*, Am Hauptbahnhof 2 (☎25700); *Qantas*, Bethmannstr. 56 (☎230041); *TWA*, Hamburger Allee 2-10 (☎770601).

Bike hire from *Per Pedale*, Falkstr. 28, Bockenheim (☎707 2363).

Book Fair Held annually in September/October at the *Messe* in the centre, this is the largest bookfair in the world. On the last day you can often pick up great bargains from the English and American stalls.

Bookshop *British Bookshop*, Börsenstr. 17 (☎281492).

Car hire *Mini Rent*, Eckenheimer Landstr. 91 (☎596 2038); all the big companies have offices at the airport.

Consulates *British*, Bockenheimer Landstr. 42 (☎170 0020); *American*, Siesmayerstr. 21 (☎753040); *Australian*, Gutleutstr. 85 (☎273 9090).

Cultural institute *Amerika-Haus*, Staufenstr. 1 (☎722794).

Duty chemist ☎11500.

Duty doctor ☎7950 2200.

Festivals Main folklore events are the *Waldchestag* at Whit weekend and the *Mainfest* in early August.

Mitfahrzentralen Gutleutstr. 125 (☎2305113); Baseler Str. 7 (☎236444).

Post offices The main post office with Poste Restante is at Zeil 110 and there's one open round the clock in the Hauptbahnhof.

What's on The best magazine is *AZ-Frankfurter Stadt Illustrierte*, which costs DM3.50 from newsagents. The tourist office publishes *Frankfurter Woche*, which theoretically costs DM2 but is usually available without payment. Comprehensive theatre and cinema listings can be found in the free *Strandgut*.

Women's Frankfurt Consult the bi-monthly *Frankfurter Frauenblatt* for information. There's a women's centre at Hamburger Allee 45 (☎7074157), a women's *Mitfahrzentrale* at Konrad-Brosswitz-Str. 11 in Bockenheim (☎771777), and a women's bookshop at Kiesstr. 27.

Around Frankfurt

Frankfurt is an excellent centre for day trips: among the cities on its S-Bahn circuit are Darmstadt, Wiesbaden and the Rhineland-Palatinate state capital of Mainz. The section below describes some smaller places which make more manageable targets for quick escapes from the metropolis.

Bad Homburg vor der Höhe

BAD HOMBURG, a spa town at the foot of the Taunus mountains, can be reached by S-Bahn #5. It's more notable for its somnolent atmosphere than for its monuments, but the **Kurpark** is a good place for a stroll. From the entrance walk down the Brunnenallee to the fake Roman temple which houses the **Elizabeth-Brunnen**, the most famous of the eleven springs. The main bath house is the **Kaiser-Wilhelm-Bad** – for DM20 you can wallow in the mineral baths for two and a half hours and see if it deserves its reputation as a pick-up joint. There's also a **Spielbank** (casino) which the locals claim as the inspiration for its counterpart in Monte Carlo*.

For nearly two hundred years, the town was the capital of the tiny state of Hessen-Homburg which was ruled from the **Schloss** (Tues–Sun 10am–4pm; DM2); this was taken over by the Prussian kings as a summer residence after they annexed the principality in 1866. The Schloss is a fairly typical seventeenth-century palace with only the 55-metre high **Weisse Turm** as a reminder of its original defensive purpose. It was built by Friedrich II, Prince of Homburg, who was the model for Kleist's hero in the eponymous play; his wooden leg, displayed inside, is known as the "Silver Leg" because of its silver joints. There's also a portrait **bust** of Friedrich here, sculpted by the Baroque master sculptor-architect, Andreas Schlüter.

From Bad Homburg it's worth taking a trip to **Saalburg**, a reconstructed Roman fort about 7km northeast of the town (daily 8am–5pm; DM3) – it gives a good impression of how a fortified Roman frontier post must have looked.

Practicalities

The **tourist office** is in the *Kurhaus*, Louisenstr. 58 (Mon–Fri 8.30–6pm, Sat 9am–1pm; ☎06172/12130). Bad Homburg has plenty of hotels, though they tend to be on the pricey side: an exception is *Johannisberg*, Thomasstr. 5 (☎06172/21315), which has singles for DM33, doubles DM60. There's also a **youth hostel**, across from the eastern entrance to the Schlosspark at Meiereiberg 1 (☎06172/23950). The one antidote to the town's penchant for quiet is *Gambrinus*, a "**music pub**" in the Fürstenbahnhof, which features a disco or a live performance every evening.

The High Taunus

The thickly wooded slopes of the **High Taunus** (*Hochtaunus*) are atmospheric and invigorating rather than breathtaking, and the most attractive part can be explored in a day, when travelling betwen Frankfurt and Wiesbaden. The highest peak, the **Grosser Feldberg** (880m), is the tallest mountain in any of the Rhineland schist massifs; from the tower at the summit there's a marvellous panorama. In the nearby village of OBERREIFENBERG there's a **youth hostel** at Limesstr. 14 (☎06082/2440).

Königstein In Taunus

The area's main town is **KÖNIGSTEIN IN TAUNUS**, which can be reached by bus or mainline train from Frankfurt or Wiesbaden. It boasts a moderately exciting ruined **Burg** (daily March 9.30am–4pm; April–Sept 9am–7pm; Oct–Feb 9.30am–3pm; DM2), from whose crumbling keep you can just about see Frankfurt. If you want to spend a little longer in the area there are a few **hotels** and **pensions**, one of the cheapest of which is *Zur schönen Aussicht*, Schneidhainer Str. 30 (☎06174/21525).

---

*The reason for this is that, when gambling was outlawed throughout Germany in 1872, François Blanc, founder of the Bad Homburg casino, left for the Riviera and succeeded in turning it into the new gambling centre of Europe.

Gelnhausen

Some 40km east of Frankfurt, on the main rail line to Fulda, is **GELNHAUSEN**, a small town perched on the slopes of the Kinzig valley and at the fringe of the Spessart an upland forest region which sprawls south into Bavaria. Gelnhausen likes to call itself *Barbarossa-Stadt*, a reference to its foundation by Emperor Frederick Barbarossa in the twelfth century, though it's equally proud of being the birthplace of the seventeenth-century writer Johann Jacob Christoffel von Grimmelshausen, whose semi-autobiographical *Simplicissimus* is the first great German novel – and one of the great tragi-comedies of world literature.

Parts of the defensive walls remain, and you can visit the ruins of Barbarossa's palace, the **Kaiserpfalz** (daily 10am–1pm & 2pm–5pm; DM1), which stand on an island in the middle of the River Kinzig. The other big attraction is the **Marienkirche**, set at the highest point of town, overlooking the Marktplatz. Although built in various stages, it's a magnificent building which graphically illustrates the transition from Romanesque to Gothic. Particularly notable are the strongly contrasted towers, which form an irresistibly photogenic ensemble, and the elaborately decorated chancel. The **tourist office** is at Am Obermarkt (☎06051/820054 or 82000). There's a **youth hostel** at Schützengraben 5 (☎06051/44240) and the cheapest **hotel** is the *Scheim von Bergen*, Obermarkt 22 (☎06051/2755), with rooms from around DM30 per person.

Büdingen

About 10km to the north of Gelnhausen is **BÜDINGEN**, a feudal township which likewise dates back to the time of the Hohenstaufen emperors. Nowadays, it's a health resort but is chiefly worth visiting for its abundant medieval survivals. The **Stadtmauer**, still completely intact, is pierced with decorated Gothic gateways. There's also a still-inhabited **Schloss** (guided tours March–Oct Tues–Sun at 2pm, 3pm & 4pm; DM3). This is in two parts, with a Gothic *Vorburg* protecting the main *Kernburg*, a truly remarkable structure which comes close to being round in shape, but in reality is an irregular polygonal with thirteen sides. It was continuously rebuilt down the ages, so the component parts run the full gamut of architectural styles from the twelfth to seventeenth centuries. The late Gothic **Schlosskapelle**, with its elaborate network vaulting, is particularly outstanding.

SOUTHERN HESSEN

The southern part of Hessen offers a wide variety of scenery, ranging from the wooded heights of the **Odenwald** at the extreme tip of the province to the famous vine-growing areas on the east bank of the Rhine. There are only two cities in this area: the staid spa of **Wiesbaden** and the former ducal residence of **Darmstadt**, which is a place with more than a few surprises in store.

Darmstadt

A cursory inspection of **DARMSTADT** is unlikely to leave you with much of an impression. The only way it differs from any other prosperous German city rebuilt after the war – with featureless modern facades interspersed with the odd incongruous prewar structure – is in the survival of the planned Neoclassical layout, with broad streets and spacious squares. Don't be discouraged, though – Darmstadt has a rich cultural heritage, traces of which have survived both the bombs and the planners.

During the second half of the eighteenth century the *Darmstädter Kreis* (Darmstadt Circle) flourished under the protection of Landgravine Karoline, numbering among its members Goethe, Martin Wieland and Johann Herder. The playwright Georg Büchner spent much of his short life in Darmstadt and wrote his great drama *Danton's Death* here in 1834, while under police observation for suspected revolutionary activities. It was at the turn of the present century, however, that the arts flourished most freely in Darmstadt: Grand Duke Ernst Ludwig (a grandson of Queen Victoria) supported the first and finest flowering of **Jugendstil**, the German form of Art Nouveau. The surviving monuments of this period are the most lasting and visible symbol of the city's support for artistic innovation.

Arrival and practicalities

If you arrive at the **Hauptbahnhof**, which is about 1km west of the city centre, you'll immediately get your first taste of the local Jugendstil heritage as the station was a key part of the style's second phase in the second decade of the century. In a pavilion immediately outside is one of the **tourist offices** (Mon–Fri 8.30am–6pm, Sat 8.30am–noon; ☎06151/132783), but the main branch is in the Neues Rathaus, Luisenplatz 5 (Mon–Fri 9am–6pm, Sat 9am–5pm; ☎06151/132780). **Hotels** are expensive, with nothing below DM40. The cheapest central possibilities are *Zentral-Hotel*, Schuchardstr. 6 (☎06151/26411), and *Pension Wetzstein*, Landwehrstr. 8 (☎06151/20443), both with singles from DM45 and doubles from DM70. In the northern suburb of Ahrheiligen *Pension am Elsee*, Raiffeisenstr. 3 (☎06151/372613), has singles for DM40, doubles DM65. There's a **youth hostel** at Landgraf-Georg-Str. 119 (☎06151/45293), right beside the open-air swimming pool at the Grosser Woog lake and also handily placed for visiting the Jugendstil buildings on Mathildenhöhe. **Mitfahrzentrale**'s office is at Rheinstr. 47 (☎06151/33696).

The city

Between 1567 and 1918, the city was capital of the state of Hessen-Darmstadt, which was promoted to a Grand Duchy, with control over a large chunk of the Rhineland, during the Napoleonic period. The subsequent flurry of building activity to create a worthy capital meant that Darmstadt had its fair share of grand streets and squares, but most were destroyed on the night of 11 September 1944 when it was hit by 300,000 incendiary bombs and 700 high explosive bombs. (A fictionalised account of this raid, told from the point of view of both sides, can be found in Len Deighton's *Bomber*.) The resulting fire-storm, deliberately created following the tried and tested Hamburg pattern, killed 12,000 people. Darmstadt made a remarkably quick recovery, particularly in the cultural arena, but most of its historic quarter was gone forever.

The centre

At the centre of modern Darmstadt sprawls **Luisenplatz**, a windswept shopping plaza criss-crossed by tram and bus lines and notable only for the **Ludwigsäule**, a memorial to Grand Duke Ludwig I. From here, Rheinstrasse leads east to Ernst-Ludwig-Platz, on which stands the **Weisse Turm**, a fifteenth-century defensive tower which was later restyled in fashionable Baroque. Beyond is the spacious triangular Marktplatz, on whose southern side stands the gabled Renaissance **Rathaus**. Round the corner is the **Stadtkirche**: repeated extensions of the fourteenth-century core have created a rather staid but unobjectionable exterior; inside, the only point of note is the immense sixteenth-century alabaster memorial to Landgrave Georg I and his wife, which the immodest nobleman commissioned to replace the church's original altar.

On the north side of Marktplatz is the **Schloss**, an extensive but unexceptional complex which developed gradually over seven hundred years. Reduced to a shell in

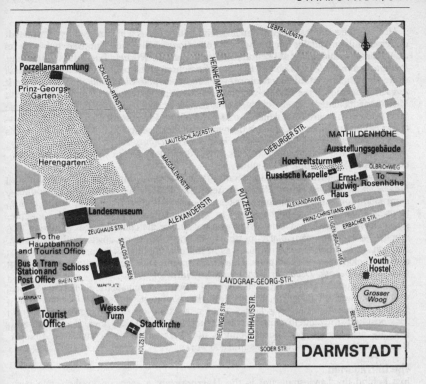

the 1944 bombing raid, it has been diligently restored. The Baroque *Neuschloss* houses a library and the town archive, while the predominantly Renaissance *Altschloss* is home to a technical university and the **Schlossmuseum** (Mon–Thurs 10am–1pm & 2pm–5pm, Sat & Sun 10am–1pm; DM2.50). Basically this is another example of the dreaded German *Heimatmuseum*, but it's redeemed by **Hans Holbein the Younger**'s *Madonna of Jacob Meyer*, painted in 1526, one of the supreme masterpieces of Renaissance painting. It's particularly intriguing in being the last Catholic altarpiece by any of the great German masters of the period, all of whom (including Holbein himself) became Protestant. The picture shows the former Burgomaster of Basel, accompanied by his living and deceased wives, asking the Virgin to intercede on behalf of his sickly baby son, whose features – bizarrely – duplicate those of the Christ child.

The Landesmuseum

Slightly to the north of the Schloss is the **Landesmuseum** (Tues–Sun 10am–5pm, Wed also 7–9pm; free), one of the best general museums in the country. On the ground floor there are examples of decorative art from the Middle Ages, Renaissance and Baroque, including a *Crucifixion* group by **Riemenschneider** and a glittering array of medieval **stained glass**, the most notable being a cycle from the Ritterstiftskirche in Bad Wimpfen. The first floor is devoted to **natural history**: a redundant open-cast shale pit near Darmstadt has proved fruitful ground for excavations, and remains of prehistoric crocodiles, fish and horses recently dug up there are now on view.

However, the Landesmuseum's main claim to fame is as a picture gallery. A wing of the ground floor contains one of the best collections of German Primitives, going back as far as the mid-thirteenth-century altar-table from Worms. **Lochner**'s gorgeous *Presentation in the Temple* shows the Cologne School at its mid-fifteenth-century peak, while the **Master of St Bartholomew**'s *Madonna and Child with SS Adrian and Augustine* belongs to the final flowering of this movement a couple of generations later. Mid-Rhenish painters closely followed Cologne's lead, and one of the finest products of this region is the work from which the **Master of the Darmstadt Passion** derives his name. Several pictures by **Cranach** dominate the Renaissance section, including one of his greatest canvases, *Cardinal Albrecht von Brandenburg as St Jerome*, an allegory which shows the Reformation period's most conciliatory senior Catholic in the traditional pose of Saint Jerome in his study.

Among the old masters on the second floor, the most important is the enigmatic *Magpie on the Gallows*, one of **Pieter Bruegel the Elder**'s last works. The evil-looking contraption for public executions strikes a menacingly discordant note in the sunny landscape, which forms the backdrop to a peasant dance. Presumably, the magpie symbolises the gossip and thus serves as a warning of the consequences of talking too much – something particularly pertinent in the Spanish-occupied Netherlands of Bruegel's day, when the Inquisition was in full cry. Highlights from the seventeenth century include pieces by Rubens, Domenichino and Domenico Feti, and a touching *Lamentation over the Dead Christ* by **Louis Le Nain**.

A number of canvases by the Swiss **Arnold Böcklin** dominate the Romantic section, which also includes *Iphigenia*, one of **Feuerbach**'s finest works. The German avant-garde gets precedence in the galleries of the new extension, though many of the country's best-known twentieth-century artists, such as Corinth, Kirchner, Beckmann and Dix, are also represented. Focal point is the *Werkstatt* of the iconoclastic **Joseph Beuys**, of whom the museum has some 300 works.

The Herrngarten

Just behind the Landesmuseum is the **Herrngarten**, a spacious English-style park which contains the tomb of Landgravine Karoline and a Jugendstil monument to Goethe. At the northeastern end is the **Prinz-Georg-Garten**, a formal Rococo garden. Its pavilion, the Prinz-Georg-Palais, houses the **Porzellansammlung** (Mon–Thurs 10am–1pm & 2–5pm, Sat & Sun 10am–1pm; DM2.50), an extensive porcelain museum. On the ground floor there are examples from the local Kelsterbach factory; a whole room is devoted to the products of the Imperial Russian porcelain factory, and there are also some huge Chinese and Japanese porcelain vases. On the second floor there's a big collection of intricate German pieces and an English room which, in addition to a few Davenport and Wedgwood pieces, inexplicably features a couple of horrendous Silver Jubilee and Royal Wedding souvenirs.

The Mathildenhöhe

The **Mathildenhöhe**, a unique artists' colony on the eastern edge of the city centre, is a living monument to Jugendstil, and if you only have time to see one thing in Darmstadt it should be this. It's only a fifteen-minute walk along Erich-Ollenhauer-Promenade from just behind the Schloss. Alternatively, take tram #4 from Luisenplatz; get off at Grosser Woog, and from there head up Eugen-Bracht-Weg to Europa Platz.

At the centre of the Mathildenhöhe stands a building which fits in well with the Jugendstil buildings but didn't originally have anything to do with the colony itself – the **Russische Kapelle**, a heavily ornamented Russian Orthodox chapel crowned by two gilded domes built in 1898 at the behest of the last Czar of Russia, Nicholas II, who often spent the summer in Darmstadt with his Hessen-born wife. Serbian Orthodox services are regularly held here for Darmstadt's Balkan community.

Work on the Mathildenhöhe colony began in 1901 with the construction of the **Ernst-Ludwig-Haus** (Tues-Sun 10am–6pm; DM4), designed by the Viennese architect Joseph Maria Olbrich for the *Dokument Deutscher Kunst 1901*, an exhibition whose aim was to encapsulate all aspects of the Jugendstil movement. Approached via a broad flight of steps, the building has something of the mausoleum about it, with its imposing portal flanked by monumental figures of Adam and Eve carved by Ludwig Habig. A Jugendstil museum has recently been extablished inside, showing choice products made by the colony – ranging from stained glass windows to jewellery, silverware and porcelain.

To complement the Ernst-Ludwig-Haus, Olbrich built seven houses as artists' residences immediately below on Alexandraweg and Mathildenhöhweg, also in 1901. Four survive in reasonably authentic shape: the others were hit by bombs and have been replaced or inaccurately restored. They vary in style from the slightly subverted villa look of the **Olbrich-Haus** to the angular southern European appearance of the **Kleine Glückert-Haus**, and all have unique and intricate design features which differentiate them from each other. The ethos of the original project is best preserved in the **Grosse Glückert-Haus**, a building in which every internal and external detail has been invested with verve and style. This is the only house in which you're allowed to venture indoors; you can try ringing at the gate, but it's advisable to ask the tourist office to arrange a visit for you. Next door to it is the **Behrens-Haus**, designed by the Hamburg architect Peter Behrens, also in 1901. Its brick-framed white facade and red-tiled roof inject an element of Hanseatic sobreity into the colony, in deliberate contrast with Olbrich's more playful Mediterranean efforts. Only the door, decorated with swirling bronze appliqué work and flanked by rippling turquoise columns, has much in common with the neighbouring houses.

In 1908 work on the huge and gleaming **Austellungsgebäude** (Exhibition Hall) at the top of the Mathildenhöhe was completed. It's still in use, and the first-floor café is equipped with Jugendstil furnishings. Look out for the Olbrich-designed mosaic in the roof of the pavilion halfway up the entrance steps. Next to the Austellungsgebäude rises the **Hochzeitsturm** (Wedding Tower), a 48-metre-high brick tower with a distinctive roof which, when seen head-on, looks like a hand facing palm outwards. It was presented to Grand Duke Ernst Ludwig and his bride by the city three years after their 1905 wedding and has become so popular that it's now Darmstadt's official emblem. A lift takes visitors to the top (Tuesday–Sunday 10am–6pm, DM1.50).

Rosenhöhe

Because most of the Mathildenhöhe buildings are now used by various design institutes and cultural organisations, Darmstadt's practising artists have moved to the nearby **Rosenhöhe** area. This is reached in about ten minutes from the Olbrich-Haus by following Alexandraweg, turning right into Fiedlerweg, left into Seitersweg and then crossing the railway bridge. During the late 1960s a new artists' colony was established here in the **Rosenhöhe Park**, whose original purpose was to provide a last resting place for members of the ruling family of Hessen-Darmstadt. At the entrance to the park is the **Löwentor**, a gate comprising six Jugendstil lions (brought here from the Platonenhain Park on the Mathildenhöhe) standing on top of decorative brick pillars. Nearby is the **Ostbahnhof**, built in the style of a Russian country station at the request of Czar Nicholas II.

Other attractions

Darmstadt's most curious museum is the **Wella Museum**, at Berliner Allee 65, near the Hauptbahnhof. Founded by the Wella hair-care product company, the museum contains 2500 objects crammed into one claustrophobic room, covering every conceivable aspect of hair and beauty care from ancient times to the present. A gruesome selection of surgical instruments is a reminder of the days when barbers doubled as surgeons, and there are some bizarre pictures woven in human hair by nineteenth-century apprentice hairdressers. Visits are by appointment only – ring ☎06151/342459 and ask for Frau Schwab, who provides a guided tour in English.

In the suburb of Kranichstein is the **Jagdschloss** (Tues–Sun 10am–noon & 2–4pm; DM2.50), the Renaissance summer palace and hunting lodge of the Landgraves and Grand Dukes of Hessen-Darmstadt. Inside is a museum devoted to their hunting exploits, featuring paintings of hunting scenes, guns and trophies. To get there take bus #H from the town centre.

Eating, drinking and nightlife

Darmstadt's **nightlife** is somewhat fragmented. There is, however, a good cluster of **bars** and cheap **restaurants** just west of the Herrngarten, while most of the *Apfelwein* places are to the east of the same park. The latter area is where many of Darmstadt's students live, and it makes a good starting point for a pub crawl.

Restaurants

Alt-Hamburg, Landgraf-Georg-Str. 17. Speciality fish and seafood restaurant.

Burg Frankenstein, Mühltal. Way out on top of a 370m hill in the southern suburb of Eberstadt, but the reasonably priced food is among the best in Darmstadt, and the views alone make the trip worthwhile.

Las Palmas, Pallaswiesenstrasse. Good, cheap Spanish restaurant which also serves up German food.

Localen, Dieburger Str. 50. Specialises in cheap but mouth-watering Italian pizzas.

Weinmichels Weinstube, Schleiermacherstr. 10–12. Classiest and best of the city's wine-restaurants.

Zum Goldenen Anker, Landgraf-Georg-Str. 25. Traditional brewery-owned *Gaststätte* serving wholesome meals at bargain prices.

Bars and café-bars

Kronenbräugarten, corner of Dieburgerstrasse and Spessart Ring. Beer garden worth checking out if the weather is good.

Kulturcafé, Hermannstr. 7. Has vegetarian food and occasional theatre or live music.

Oktave, corner of Landwehrstrasse and Viktoriastrasse. Upmarket jazz bar.

Petri, Anheiligerstr. 50. Favourite haunt of hip youngsters.

Rem, Beckerstr. 22. Best place in town for exotic cocktails.

Studentenkeller, Im Schlosshof. Enduringly popular student meeting place, situated in the Schloss courtyard.

Sumpf, Kasinostr. 105. Studenty pub which does fairly cheap snacks.

Worschtküsch, Erbacher Str. 5-7. Excellent jazz bar and bistro housed in a converted butcher's shop near the Mathildenhöhe – it advertises itself as "a pub without standards".

Live music , theatre and festivals

Hottest **nightspot** in town is *Abfahrt*, on Heidelberger Landstrasse in the suburb of Eberstadt, which can be reached by tram #7 or #8 from Luisenplatz. Bands come from all over Germany to play here, and the disco has the best music in town. *Goldene Krone*, Schustergasse 18, has constantly changing acts ranging from cabaret to various kinds of music, while *Forty-Six*, Alsfelder Str. 45, is a late-nite disco, staying open till 3am. The main venue for **drama** and formal **concerts** is the *Staatstheater* on Georg-Buchner-Platz. Local **festivals** include the *Frühlingfest* in March or April, the *Heinerfest* on the first weekend of July and the *Herbstfest* in late September.

The Odenwald

The **Odenwald** is a large upland forest area – which is designated as the *Naturpark Bergstrasse-Odenwald* – occupying almost all of the southernmost part of Hessen and stretching into both Bavaria and Baden-Württemberg. On its westernmost fringe is the misleadingly named **Bergstrasse** (Mountain Road): nowadays it's a tourist route running from Darmstadt to Heidelberg, but to the Romans – who called it the *Strata Montana* – it was a major military road. During the Middle Ages it developed as a trading route, and numerous castles sprang up along it to protect the merchants from outlaws lurking in the marshland around the Rhine. These days the area is known primarily for the fact that spring starts here earlier than anywhere else in Germany, and the best time to visit is in late March or early April, when the fruit trees that line it all suddenly come into bloom. Further east, the hilly countryside of the heart of the Odenwald is punctuated by postcard-pretty half-timbered towns where traditional craft industries continue to flourish.

Along the Bergstrasse

If you take bus #5504 south out of Darmstadt you'll hit a string of small towns which seem to merge into one another. First up is **SEEHEIM**, an innocuous little place with a redbrick, beamed **Rathaus**. Nearby are a couple of castles: **Schloss Alsbach**, at the end of a long winding road, is little more than a circular pile of stones, while the nineteenth-century **Schloss Heiligenberg** is very much intact – it's owned by the Battenberg family, whose English cousins changed their name to Mountbatten. The first place of any real consequence on the Bergstrasse is **ZWINGENBERG**, a romantic little half-timbered town which would make a good overnight stop. The unusual thirteenth-century **Bergkirche** towers over the Marktplatz, set on top of a huge retaining wall. There's a **youth hostel** at Auf dem Berg 41 (☎06251/75938), and rooms at *Gasthof zur Traube*, Heidelberger Str. 23, cost around DM30 per person.

Next stop is **BENSHEIM**, a biggish town with a typically half-timbered centre incorporating all the usual features. It now engulfs the village of **AUERBACH** to the east, whose **Schloss** (Tues–Sun 10am–5pm or dusk) commands a great view out across to the Rhine. Just to the south lies the **Fürstenlager Park**, which is planted with exotic trees and dotted with whimsical eighteenth-century garden pavilions. Although there aren't really any cheap **hotels** in Bensheim, there are a couple of places in Auerbach where you should get a room for around DM30: *Gasthof Auerbacher Haus*, Darmstädter Str. 170 (☎06251/75689), and *Pension Waldschlöschen*, Burgstr. 36 (☎06251/71324).

Just to the southwest of Bensheim is **LORSCH**, which is notable mainly for the **Lorscher Halle**, the gatehouse to what was once one of the most powerful monasteries in Germany. Amazingly, it dates back to 774, and is the best-preserved building to have survived from this period of Carolingian architecture; its patterned stonework, arranged like a mosaic, is of outstanding quality.

HEPPENHEIM, next down the line, is the scene of the big local *Weinfest* on the last weekend in June and the first weekend of July. It has a few quaint half-timbered streets but the overall effect of the town centre is spoiled by an ugly department store. There is, however, a **youth hostel** in the grounds of the ruined **Schloss Starkenburg** (☎06252/77323), a couple of kilometres to the northeast of the town.

The heart of the forest

The central part of the Odenwald is serviced by a branch railway from Darmstadt, on which trains run nearly every hour. It's an easy target for day trips, though the provision of abundant cheap accommodation makes it a good place to spend a restful few days.

Michelstadt

The market town of **MICHELSTADT**, which celebrated its 1250th birthday in 1991, is the undoubted star of the Odenwald. The late fifteenth-century **Rathaus**, which dominates the central Marktplatz, features on every tourist brochure to the region; with its characteristic half-timbering and slightly spooky corner oriels crowned with sharply pointed spires, it perfectly encapsulates the Romantic image of medieval Germany. Just to the west is the **Kellerei**, a courtyard formed by the half-timbered store buildings of the former castle; it now houses the folklore collections of the **Odenwaldmuseum** (Easter–Oct Tues–Sun 10am–noon & 2–5pm; DM2).

At the northern end of town, about 1km from the centre, is the **Einhardsbasilika** (mid-March to Oct Tues–Sun 10–11.30am & 1–5.30pm; DM1), a church dating back to 827, the year of its foundation by the local grandee Einhard, courtier to Charlemagne, and author of a fascinating biography of the emperor. Just to the east is **Schloss Fürstenau**, a moated thirteenth-century castle formerly belonging to the Archbishop-Electors of Mainz; it's privately owned, but you're allowed to go into the courtyard and stroll in the extensive park.

Michelstadt's **tourist office** is at Marktplatz 1 (☎06061/74146). Here you can pick up a list of the twenty or so private houses with **rooms** to let from as little as DM16. Alternatively, there are plenty of **hotels** in the centre, often with excellent restaurants attached: an example is *Ratsschänke*, Neutorstr. 2 (☎06061/652), which charges from DM31 per person. There's also a **campsite** (May–Sept only) at Am Waldstadion (☎06061/3256). The town hosts a number of **festivals**, the most important being the ten-day *Bienenmarkt* at Whit.

Erbach and Beerfelden

Adjoining Michelstadt to the south is **ERBACH**. The town is completely dominated by its huge Baroque **Schloss** (March–Oct 8.30am–noon & 1.30–3pm; DM5), which incorporates part of its medieval predecessor and contains a more interesting than average local museum. Since the eighteenth century, Erbach has been the main German centre for ivory carving, an art celebrated in the **Deutsche Elfenbeinmuseum** (daily 10.30am–noon & 2.30–4.30pm; DM4) at Otto-Glenz-Str. 1. There's the usual provision of private rooms, plus a **youth hostel** at Eulbacherstr. 33 (☎06062/3515), while the **campsite**, *Camping Safari* (☎06062/3159) is in the suburb of Bullau to the southeast.

About 10km further south is **BEERFELDEN**, the centre of which was rebuilt along Neoclassical lines in 1810. Look out for the **Mumlingquelle**, where natural spring water is pumped into a huge trough from twelve outlets, and the **Galgen**, one of West Germany's last surviving gallows and in use until 1806. The **tourist office** is at Metzkeil 1 (☎06068/2071) and there are **camping** facilities at *Fischhäuselquelle*, (☎06068/20710). A reasonable local **hotel** is *Odenwald*, Kräberger Weg 19 (☎06068/3784).

Wiesbaden

Strolling around the centre of **WIESBADEN** it's not difficult to imagine how the city must have looked during its glory days as a nineteenth-century *Kurstadt*, when the aristocracy of Europe flocked here to take the waters at the numerous thermal spas and to gamble away their fortunes in the famous casino. Today the city trades on its past reputation, conjuring up the atmosphere of a bygone era to attract visitors. The Russian nobles who were once the main patrons have been replaced by wealthy Arabs and tanned, *nouveau riche* Germans. It's worth stopping off in Wiesbaden for a few hours just to get a taste of the atmosphere, but the chances are it won't be long before the conspicuous wealth and overt snobbery of the place start to get to you.

The city centre

At the heart of Wiesbaden is the **Kurhaus**; completed in 1906 in a Neoclassical style which would have been fashionable a hundred years previously, it's the bland symbol of a city where appearances are everything. The over-the-top decor of the halls has been the backdrop to many a glittering provincial night out, and the building also houses the **Spielbank** (casino), which has become a handy source of extra revenue for the city. This was opened in 1949, but gambling first started in earnest in 1771 and Wiesbaden's original casino was the inspiration for "Roulettenburg", in Dostoyevsky's novel *The Gambler*. Gambling, however, was suspended between 1872 and 1949 as a result of a ban imposed by Kaiser Wilhelm I after his son, Crown Prince Friedrich III, had formed an "unsuitable" attachment to a woman gambler. On one side of the Kurhaus is the **Staatstheater**, another example of late Neoclassical decadence, while on the other is the **Kurpark**, an English-style park complete with weeping willows, giant chess set and duck ponds. From here you can walk up into the wooded slopes of the Taunus, which rise to the north of the city.

The rest of the city centre, though pleasant enough to look at, doesn't really have much to offer. **Wilhelmstrasse**, the main shopping street, which runs past the Kurhaus into Friedrich-Ebert-Strasse, is full of expensive antique shops and glitzy designer stores. On Schlossplatz stands the **Stadtschloss**, built in the 1840s for the Dukes of Nassau who in the previous century had established Wiesbaden as their main seat. Nowadays, it's the Hessen state parliament: although Wiesbaden had had no connection with Hessen until the Prussians formed the province of Hessen-Nassau in 1867 from various recently annexed territories, the city was chosen as the state capital when the old province was revived in 1946. This decision was largely determined by the fact that its ambience made it far more appealing to politicians and administrators than the obvious choice of Frankfurt, or the rival historical capitals of Darmstadt and Kassel. Facing the Stadtschloss is the seventeeth-century **Altes Rathaus**, the oldest bulding in the city, albeit none too inspiring for all that. In front of it, on Marktplatz, where markets are held on Wednesdays and Saturdays, there's a small fountain topped by a playful looking lion, one of the symbols of the city. Halfway up Mauergasse there's a second-hand shop called *Dagi's Flohmarkt* which has a fine selection of bric-a-brac and old clothes.

You can sample the famous waters at the **Kochbrunnen**, just off Taunusstrasse a few minutes walk from the Kurhaus; despite the much vaunted healing properties you are advised to restrict your intake to one litre per day. The Neoclassical colonnades surrounding the fountains which dispense the water now house a café and crêperie, which slightly undermine the elegant atmosphere. That's really about it for the city centre, apart from the **Städtisches Museum** on Friedrich-Ebert-Strasse (Thurs–Mon 10am–4pm, Tues 10am–9pm; free); it possesses a few paintings by the Russian artist Alexei Jawlensky, a member of the Expressionist *Blaue Reiter* group, but is otherwise a fairly pedestrian collection.

If you have time, you might care to sample the delights of the **thermal baths**. The most atmospheric (and expensive) is the *Kaiser Friedrich Bad*, Langgasse 38-40 (bus #1 or #8), which features a pseudo-Roman pool; the modern *Thermalbad Wiesbaden*, Leibnizstr. 7 (bus #18), is cheaper but has more of a public-baths feel.

The outskirts

On the northern edge of Wiesbaden looms the **Neroberg**, a 245-metre Taunus foothill with an open-air swimming pool and good views of the city. To get there take bus #1 to Nerotal and from there ascend by the water-powered funicular railway. On the summit stands the **Russische Kapelle**, also known as the *Griechische Kapelle*, a nineteenth-century Russian-style chapel instantly recognisable by its five gilded cupolas; it was built as a mausoleum for the Russian-born Princess Elisabeth of Nassau, who died in childbirth at the age of 19.

It's also worth taking a trip south to **Schloss Biebrich**, set on the Rhine in the suburb of the same name (take bus #3, #4, #13, #A3 or #A13 from the town centre). This eighteenth-century Baroque palace, the original Wiesbaden home of the Dukes of Nassau, has a restrained elegance which puts the showy centre of Wiesbaden to shame. Though the building itself is only open to the public for the occasional concert, you can stroll in the fine park. It's also the first embarkation point after Mainz for **cruises** down the Rhine; for more details on these, see *Chapter Four*.

Practicalities and entertainments

Wiesbaden's **Hauptbahnhof** is about 15 minutes' walk south of the city centre, which can be reached by bus #1 or #8. One of the **tourist offices** is in the Hauptbahnhof (daily 8am–9pm; ☎0611/172 9781); the other is at Rheinstr. 15 (☎0611/172 9780). **Hotels** under DM40 are few and far between: you'll have more chance of finding something reasonable in Mainz, an option well worth considering in light of the fact that the two cities share an integrated public transport network on which 24-hour tickets cost just DM5. The cheapest hotels in Wiesbaden itself are *Haus Klemm*, Matthias-Claudius-Str. 25 (☎0611/304313), with singles DM35, doubles DM50, and *Ring*, Bleichstr. 29 (☎0611/400177), which has a few basic singles at DM38, and more luxurious doubles at DM80. Other possibilities exist in the suburbs; in Biebrich try *Schützenhof*, Am Schlosspark 45 (☎0611/66920), which has singles from DM30 and doubles from DM53, or *Beyer*, Mainstr. 25a (☎0611/65866), whose rates begin at DM37 per person. The **youth hostel** is at Blücherstr. 66 (☎0611/48657), best reached by bus #14 from the Hauptbahnhof.

Eating and **drinking** in Wiesbaden can be an expensive affair too. There are plenty of upmarket restaurants and bars, but the best value for money and atmosphere is at *Domizil*, Moritzstr. 52, a reasonably priced "alternative" bar which also serves cheap meals. There's also a good takeaway pizza place in Hermannstrasse, just one door away from the corner of Bismarckring, while *Café Klatsch*, Mariabrunnestr. 9 is the top choice for breakfast. Behind Wiesbaden's glitzy scene, there are quite a few good pubs: *Bebop*, Saalgasse 11, sometimes features blues and jazz, while *Kartoffel*, Nerostr. 33, is a student favourite, as is *Wirtshaus*, Nerostr. 24, which is still patronised by leftovers of the sixties generation. Regular **live music** venues include *Sherry and Port*, Adolfsallee 11, which plays jazz, and *Tanzpalast Park* on Wilhelmstrasse, which doubles as a very exclusive **disco**.

The Rheingau

The Hessen side of the Rhine, running from Wiesbaden to the border with Rhineland-Palatinate at Lorchhausen, is known as the **Rheingau**. Sheltered from the elements by the gentle slopes of the Taunus, the region has developed into one of Germany's foremost wine producing districts, and its vineyards, ruined castles and drowsy little villages make it a favourite destination for coach parties and package tourists. You can cover it fairly well by train from Wiesbaden, but to visit the out-of-the-way corners you really need a car. Road B42, running from Wiesbaden to the Rhineland-Palatinate border and taking in all the little wine villages, has been designated the *Rheingauer-Riesling-Route*, a special interest stretch for wine fans, enabling them to stop off and do a spot of tasting and buying. There's also a walking route, the *Rheingauer-Riesling-Pfad* which runs through the lower slopes of the **Rheingau-Gebirge** – the part of the Taunus which rises from the banks of the Rhine.

Eltville, Kiedrich and around

First stop out of Wiesbaden is **ELTVILLE**, a town famous for its sparkling wines (it's on the main Frankfurt to Cologne railway line and there are plenty of buses in all directions). This is where Thomas Mann's urbane conman Felix Krull spent his youth, but apart from his fictional presence, the town's only cultural highlights are a lot of cute half-timbered houses and a very fresh looking fifteenth-century fresco of *The Last Judgment* in the late Gothic **Pfarrkirche**. The **tourist office** is at Schmittstr. 4 (Mon–Fri 8am–5pm; ☎06123/6891). One of the cheapest **hotels** is *Zur Post*, Rheingauer Str. 46 (☎06123/2231), with rooms from about DM30 per night.

Kiedrich

From Eltville you can take a bus up to **KIEDRICH**, an improbably medieval looking little place dominated by the ruins of **Burg Scharfenstein**. The main tourist attraction is the fifteenth-century church of **St Valentinus** (April–Oct Tues–Sun 2.30–4.30pm), which was once a pilgrimage destination for epilepsy sufferers. Inside, look out for the oldest (1500) working organ in Germany, the *Kiedricher Madonna* (1330) and the intricately carved pews with their vine motifs.

A few kilometres west of Kiedrich, set on the wooded slopes of the Rheingau-Gebirge, is **Kloster Eberbach** (April–Sept 10am–6pm; Oct–March 10am–4pm; DM1.50), founded in 1135 by the Cistercian order, and one of the best-preserved medieval monasteries in Germany. A couple of tombs in one of the fourteenth-century chapels are the only features to detract from the church's austerely grandiose architecture. Behind the church are the leafy cloisters and a ruined well-chapel, surrounded by the former living quarters of the monks. The dormitory, an immense vaulted affair built in the 1240s, is one of the most impressive early Gothic rooms in Europe, and like the church is almost devoid of decoration. In the refectory the huge wine presses once used by the monks are on display; wine production continued after the dissolution of the monastery in 1803, and some of the monastery buildings are now used to press, ferment and store the produce of the "Eberbacher Steinberg", the former monastic vineyard. There are yearly wine auctions and some of the vintages are reckoned to be world class.

Hattenheim, Oestrich and Geisenheim

The road back down to the bank of the Rhine brings you to **HATTENHEIM**, a conventional little Rhine village where there are **camping** facilities at *Zur Brückenschänke*; make enquiries at Hauptstr. 4 (☎06723/2827). From here head west past **Schloss Reinhardshausen**, a castle of sorts turned *Weingut* (wine tavern), to **OESTRICH**, where there's a seventeenth-century wooden river-crane once used to load wine barrels onto ships for transport down the Rhine and beyond. *Gasthaus Schwan*, built in 1628, is an atmospheric little watering-hole, and *Pension Schäferhof*, at Waldstr. 10 (☎06723/1234), is the most reasonable local hotel, with rooms from around DM25 per night. A couple of kilometres down the road is **WINKEL**, which officially belongs to Oestrich. Here you can visit the **Brentanohaus**, which belonged to the step-brother of the Romantic writer Clemens Brentano; Clemens himself spent his summers here, often entertaining the likes of Goethe and other prominent literary figures. Also of note is the **Graues Haus**, the oldest habitable stone house in Germany.

Geisenheim

The main point of interest at the nearby half-timbered village of **GEISENHEIM** is the sixteenth-century **Schloss Schönborn**, where Johann Philipp von Schönborn, Elector and Archbishop of Mainz, negotiated the provisional agreement of the Peace of Westphalia which ended the disastrous Thirty Years' War. Up in the Taunus, a few kilometres outside Geisenheim, there are a couple of castles. The eighteenth-century **Schloss Johannisberg** was restyled along fashionable Neoclassical lines between 1826 and 1833 by the Metternich family, who are still in possession; there's an impressive panoramic view of the region from its southern terrace. **Schloss Vollrads**, with its moated fourteenth-century tower, is one of the best preserved castles in the Rheingau. There are **camping** facilities at Geisenheim (call ☎06722/8515 for details).

Rüdesheim

RÜDESHEIM claims the dubious distinction of being the most visited town in the region, attracting over three million sightseers a year. It's a favourite stopping-off point for coach parties and Rhine cruisers as it conforms pretty well to the general conception of what a typical Rhine town should look like – all crooked narrow streets, half-timbered houses and souvenir shops, sloping down gently from the wooded hills and terraced vineyards above. The big local attraction is the **Drosselgasse**, a street comprised entirely of pubs, and generally full of tourists being ripped off. The twelfth-century **Brömserburg**, a squat and angular fortress, is worth visiting for the **Rheingau-und Weinmuseum** (May–Nov Tues–Sun 9am–noon & 2–6pm; DM3); it contains 21 old presses and a vast collection of wine vessels, including some fine examples of vases that were used to store and transport wine from Roman times through to the Middle Ages. Rüdesheim also has a few reminders of an era when this stretch of the Rhine was a turbulent and contested area, in the shape of a twelfth-century defensive tower called the **Boosenburg** and the circular late Gothic **Adlerturm**. Also of interest are two medieval nobles' houses: the **Brömserhof**, which has a half-timbered tower with the added attraction of a large collection of mechanical musical instruments, and the **Klunkardshof**, which has a particularly well-preserved half-timbered facade.

A reminder of a later phase in the development of Germany is the **Niederwalddenkmal**, a bombastic remnant of the Imperial German Reich. This immense monument 225 metres above the town can be reached either by foot or by chairlift (DM5 single, DM7 return) over the vineyards which swarm up the slopes behind Rüdesheim. The monument itself was built to mark the unification of Germany in 1871 and features a huge allegorical statue of *Germania*, symbol of the emergent and ultimately doomed empire. Nearby are the undeniably romantic ruins of the thirteenth-century **Burg Ehrenfels**, a one-time toll castle, which, in conjunction with the Mäuseturm, a tower built on a mid-river island, was used by the Archbishops of Mainz to control Rhine river traffic.

Practicalities

Rüdesheim's **tourist office** (Mon–Fri 8.30am–12.30pm & 2–6pm, Sat & Sun 2–6pm) is at Rheinstr. 5. The local **youth hostel** is set amidst the vines, a long walk from the town, at Am Kreuzberg (☎06722 2711). There are plenty of **hotels** but they tend to be expensive and most will be booked up during the summer. A couple of cheap possibilities are *Gasthof Winzerschänke*, Marktstr. 27 (☎06722/2733), and *Pension Bach*, Langstr. 13 (☎06722/2512), both from around DM30. On the whole you're probably better off sticking to the smaller places round about as they'll be cheaper and likely to have vacancies. There are two **campsites** in Rüdesheim: *Campingplatz am Rhein* (☎06722/2528 or 2582) and *Landgut Ebental* (☎06722/2518) near Niederwald. At the beginning of July there's a firework display and in mid-August Rüdesheim has its *Weinfest* – during the latter it seems like all of those three million visitors have hit town at once.

Assmannshausen, Presberg and Lorch

Just out of Rüdesheim the Rhine suddenly bends through ninety degrees to flow more or less south–north, and there follows a treacherous stretch of river called the **Binger Loch**, where most of the barges which ply the Rhine normally take a pilot on board to negotiate the channel through the rapids and reefs. The first town you'll come to is **ASSMANNSHAUSEN**, a smaller and less touristy version of Rüdesheim. In the terraced vineyards round about some of Germany's best red wines are produced. For cheap accommodation head to the *Pension Milberg*, Am Rathaus 2 (☎06722/2945), with rooms from around DM30. From Assmannshausen you can ride a chairlift up to **Schloss Niederwald**, an eighteenth-century hunting lodge turned hotel, from where there are good views of the Rhine and its sloping banks.

Presberg and Lorch

While you're in the area you might also care to visit AULSHAUSEN, a secluded little resort village lying in a sheltered side valley, or **PRESBERG**, a few kilometres into the Rheingau-Gebirge – famous for its clean air and as a base for exploring the **Naturpark Rhein-Taunus**, a national park established to protect the area's natural assets from over-exploitation.

The final stretch of the *Rheingauer-Riesling-Route* will take you through to **LORCH**. Facing the Rhine is the **Hilchenhaus**, a sixteenth-century Renaissance mansion featuring a distinctive stepped gable and some ornate carvings. In the Gothic **Martinskirche** there's an ornately carved altar to Saint Martin with painted panels, and late thirteenth-century choir stalls decorated with fantastic animals. Look out for **Burg Nollig**, a fourteenth-century fortified dwelling tower which stands at the point where the River Wisper flows into the Rhine. Cheapest local **hotel** is *Gasthof Henninger Eck*, Rheinstr. 50 (☎06726/692). **Camping** facilities are at *Suleika* (☎06726/9464) and the **youth hostel** is at Schwalbacher Str. 54 (☎ 06726/307).

NORTHERN HESSEN

Northern Hessen is, relatively speaking, off the beaten track. To the west there's the valley of the Lahn, a Rhine tributary, while the east of the province is characterised by forested highland countryside. By far the biggest city is **Kassel,** whose centre is one of the dullest in Germany but is very much worth visiting on account of its art treasures. Far more congenial is **Fulda**, which has preserved its Baroque character intact. The gem of the area, however, is the old university town of **Marburg**, one of the most beautiful places of its size anywhere in Europe.

The Lahn valley

The **River Lahn** forms a natural boundary dividing the upland forest areas of the Taunus and the Westerwald. Most of it lies within Hessen, but a small downstream stretch, shortly before it flows into the Rhine just south of Koblenz, is in Rhineland-Palatinate. A series of historic towns, each conveniently separated by intervals of approximately 20km, punctuate the Hessen section; exploration is made easy by the road and railway which closely follow the river for all but its uppermost stretch.

Limburg

LIMBURG, which lies close to the Land border some 50km north of Wiesbaden, is chiefly famous for a particularly pungent type of cheese. The town is dominated, in every sense, by its unusual **Dom**, which lies on a rocky spur above the river. Despite looking like some sacred counterpart to the fantasy castles erected all over Germany in the Romantic period, it's actually a perfectly genuine medieval church from the first half of the thirteenth century. It illustrates the long-standing national preference for aggressive picturesqueness in architecture at its most outrageous – something to which the orange and white colour scheme contributes as much as the exotic roofline with its beckoning array of towers and spires. In essence, the Dom belongs to the last phase of the Romanesque style. Despite the use of much of the vocabulary of Gothic architecture – which had already been established in France for a century, but which was only beginning to make its mark in Germany – it seems that the builders were unaware of the structural advantages of such features as the pointed arch and the rib vault. Instead, they used them for their novelty value – and for the extra scope they gave for creating extravagant surface effects.

The Burg

Next to the Dom is the **Burg**, a fortification complex dating back to the ninth century, when the local counts chose this spot as the site for a defensive castle. In Domstrasse, within the compound of the Burg, is the **Diözesanmuseum** (mid-March–mid-Nov Tues-Sat 10am–1pm & 2–5pm, Sun 11am–5pm; DM2). The main attractions are the *Dernbacher Beweinung*, a fifteenth-century sculpture depicting the Lamentation of Christ, and the treasury items, notably the *Limburger Staurothek*, a tenth-century Byzantine reliquary in the form of a cross, which was brought back from the Crusades by a local knight. Below the Dom and Burg is the **Altstadt**, the substantially intact medieval centre, which features some predictably fine and venerable half-timbered houses. There's a big cluster around Fischmarkt, including the **Historisches Rathaus**, an extremely well preserved fourteenth-century Gothic building complete with great hall.

Practicalities

Limburg's **Bahnhof** is just south of the Altstadt. The **tourist office** (April–Oct Mon–Fri 8am–12.30pm & 2–6pm, Sat 10am–noon; Nov–March Mon–Thurs 8am–12.30pm & 2–5pm, Fri 8am–12.30pm; ☎06431/203222) is at Hospitalstr. 2. There's a **youth hostel** at the extreme southern edge of town at Auf dem Guckucksberg (☎06431/41493), and a **campsite** (☎06431/22610) at the northern end, on the opposite side of the Lahn. Cheapest **hotels**, all charging around DM35 per person, are *Gasthof Schwedenhof*, Offheimer Weg 11 (☎06431/6848), *Weisses Ross*, Westerwaldstr. 2 (☎06431/8776), and *Zur Reichspost*, Frankfurter Str. 8 (☎06431/6404).

Weilburg

What **WEILBURG** lacks in size, it makes up for in visual appeal. Standing on a peninsula enclosed by the Lahn, its compact centre is grouped around the elegant sixteenth-century **Schloss** (guided tours March–Oct 10am–noon & 1–4pm; Nov–Feb 10am–noon & 1–3pm; DM2), with its warm facade of orange stucco. Once the residence of the Counts of Nassau, the Schloss is a sprawling affair, almost a little town in itself. Major additions were made in the early eighteenth century, when stables were added to the northern part of the building and the **Schlossgarten** was constructed in a series of terraces leading down to the Lahn. The Baroque **Schlosskirche** is one of the most outstanding Protestant churches in Hessen; its elaborate pillared altar, decorated with cherubs and sun-bursts, has an almost Rococo feel to it. Just in front of it, on the **Marktplatz**, is the heavily ornamented Neptunbrunnen. Also worth a look are the five-arched **Steinerne Brücke**, which spans the Lahn just north of the Schloss, and the **Schiffstunnel**, built in the nineteenth century to save ships having to sail right round the peninsula.

Practicalities

The **tourist office** is at Mauerstr. 8 (☎06471/31424). There's a **youth hostel** 2km outside town at Am Steinbühl (☎06471/7116), while the cheapest local **hotel** is *Pension Felsenkeller*, Ahäuser Weg 4 (☎06471/30489), whose rooms start at DM25. Other similarly priced possibilities exist in some of the villages around Weilburg – the tourist office will tell you what's on offer.

Wetzlar

WETZLAR holds an honoured place in the annals of German literature. Between 1693 and 1803 the town was the seat of the *Reichskammergericht*, the highest civil court of the Holy Roman Empire. While working there as a legal clerk, **Goethe** fell in love with Lotte Buff, the fiancée of a close friend. His response to this awkward situation was to run away from it. However, when another friend there, Karl Wilhelm Jerusalem, committed suicide over an unrequited love affair, he was inspired to fuse the two episodes by writing an epistolary novella, *The Sorrows of Young Werther*. It was an immediate sensation; before his twenty-fifth birthday, Goethe had become the most celebrated literary figure in Europe, inspiring a Romantic reaction against the Age of Reason and creating a continent-wide phenomenon of young men wearing blue coats and yellow breeches, suffering from melancholy and contemplating suicide.

The Altstadt

These days Wetzlar is a light industrial town, but the narrow streets of the **Altstadt**, with their half-timbered, grey-roofed houses (many of them only restored to their original state during the last few years), bear witness to a more prestigious past. The Altstadt is centred on three squares – the **Schillermarkt**, the **Eisenmarkt** and the **Kornmarkt** – and crowned by the thirteenth-century **Dom**. Begun in 1235 around the nucleus of an earlier Romanesque church (whose north tower still stands), the Dom evolved over the next century and a half into a strange hybrid of Romanesque and Gothic. In 1370 work was suddenly halted, leaving the west side of the building incomplete. The south tower, the only Gothic part to be finished, was later surmounted with a belfry and turret.

The Hof des Deutschen Ritterordens

The other main attraction in Wetzlar is the **Lottehaus** (Tues–Sat 10am–1pm & 2–5pm, Sun 10am–1pm; free), the house where Lotte Buff lived with her parents, which stands in the **Hof des Deutschen Ritterordens** (Court of the Teutonic Knights). A must for Goethe aficionados, it has been turned into a small museum containing furniture, pictures and books – lots of first editions and translations of *Werther*, not surprisingly. Also in the courtyard is the **Städtische Museum** (same times; free), which details Wetzlar's history as a Free Imperial City from 1180 to 1830, and the development of its iron and optical industries. It was here that Oskar Barnack pioneered today's standard 35mm camera, and the town is home to Leitz, the leading manufacturer in the field.

Practicalities

Wetzlar's **Bahnhof** is about 1km north of the Altstadt and on the opposite side of the Lahn. The **tourist office** is at Domplatz 8 (Mon–Fri 8am–noon & 2–4.30pm, Sat 9.30–

11.30am; ☎06441/405338). There's a **youth hostel** in a lovely secluded setting southeast of the Altstadt at Richard-Schirmann-Str. 3 (☎06441/71068), while there are two **campsites** within easy reach of the town. The first of these, *Niedergirmes*, is north of the Bahnhof (☎06441/34103), the other is at *Dutenhofener See* (☎0641/21245), about halfway to Giessen, near the Bahnhof Wetzlar-Ost. Cheapish **hotels**, each charging around DM30 per person, are *Gasthaus Bill*, Gabelsbergstr. 30 (☎06441/31617), *Mayerle*, Kirchstr. 1 (☎06441 32197), and *Süss*, Neustädter Platz 1 (☎06441/45441). For some of the best **food** and **drink** in town, head north of the Altstadt to the *Wetzlarer Braustube*, Garbenheimer Str. 20, the *Gaststätte* of the local brewery.

Giessen

Before the war **GIESSEN** was as famous for its half-timbered houses as it was for its University, founded in the early seventeenth century and traditionally strong in the sciences. Unfortunately, it was severely battered by bombs and the centre nowadays is a typically bland example of postwar reconstruction. Giessen has also suffered the misfortune of being selected by the US army as a garrison town and supply centre.

The town centre

One of the few timber-framed buildings to have survived, the fourteenth-century **Burgmannenhaus** (Tues–Sun 10am–4pm; free) on Georg-Schlosser-Strasse, has been restored to house the local museum. There are also a few attractions around Brandplatz: the **Neues Schloss** is a late Gothic half-timbered palace and next door to it is the **Zeughaus**, a Renaissance arsenal which now contains part of the University. Nearby is the fourteenth-century **Altes Schloss** (Tues–Sun 10am–4pm; free), now home to a small art collection. Behind it is the **Botanischer Garten**; first created for scientific purposes in the seventeenth century, it's the town's most attractive feature. Otherwise, there's only the **Liebig-Museum** (Tues–Sun 10am–4pm; free) at Liebigstr. 12, which is devoted to the life and work of the nineteenth-century scientist Justus von Liebig, whose teaching laboratory here introduced a systematic approach to the study of chemistry, attracting students from all over Europe. Liebig was eventually lured away to Munich, where he was granted dispensation from the demands of the teaching which had made him famous in order that he could pursue research and writing. Nonetheless, his contribution to Giessen's reputation was such that the University is now named after him.

The Schiffenbergkloster

Just to the southeast of town is the **Schiffenbergkloster**, a ruined monastery in whose walled gardens students conduct "secret" fencing matches at the crack of dawn on Sunday. Concerts are held here on Saturday evenings and Sunday afternoons. You can walk from the centre or take bus #6 from Berliner Platz (departures normally every half-hour, but watch out on Sunday as there are only a couple of buses back in the course of the afternoon).

Practicalities

Giessen's **Bahnhof** is just a short walk southwest of the town centre, while the **tourist office** is at Berliner Platz 2 (Mon–Fri 9am–noon & 2–6pm, Sat 9am–noon; ☎0641/3062489) The **youth hostel** is at the western side of town at Richard-Schirmann-Weg 53 (☎0641 65879); take bus #4 or #7. Cheapest local **hotel** is the *Frankfurter Hof*, Frankfurter Str. 205-207 (☎0641/22782), where rooms cost upwards of DM25. If you happen to find yourself in Giessen at night, head for Ludwigstrasse, which is known as *Kneipenstrasse* by the locals because it's full of pubs. Also worth checking out for occasional live music is the *Eulenspiegel* in Seltersweg.

Marburg

The cradle of Hessen and its original capital, **MARBURG** clusters up the slopes of the Lahn valley some 30km upstream from Giessen in a maze of narrow streets and medieval buildings. There are distinctive lower and upper towns, dominated respectively by two of Germany's greatest buildings, the Elisabethkirche and the Schloss. However, the whole ensemble is in many ways the most remarkable feature, as Marburg has been touched by war less than almost any other city in the country. At the time of the Reformation, **Landgrave Philipp the Magnanimous** abolished the cult of his ancestor, **Saint Elisabeth**, which had hitherto been responsible for the town's status as one of the major pilgrimage centres of Northern Europe. In 1527 he established the University, the first in the world to be subject to the new Protestant faith, and academic affairs have dominated local affairs ever since. Nowadays, nearly a quarter of the population is in some way associated with the University, and the presence of 15,000 students gives it a relaxed and lively atmosphere. Marburg has good rail and road links with Frankfurt, Kassel and Koblenz, and is one place in Hessen worth going far out of your way to visit.

The lower town

Although much of it is now taken up with functional modern buildings of the University, the kernel of the lower town (or *Unterstadt*) survives from the thirteenth century. It was then the property of the **Order of Teutonic Knights** (see Bad Mergentheim, *Chapter Two*), who were at the height of their preoccupation with Germany's eastward expansion and the conversion of the eastern Baltic lands to Christianity by whatever methods were deemed necessary – even genocide. Given their bellicosity, it's all the more ironic that they showed such dedication to Saint Elisabeth (see below), whose life could hardly have presented a greater contrast.

SAINT ELISABETH (1207–31)

A daughter of the King of Hungary, Elisabeth was born in Pressburg (now Bratislava, the capital of Slovakia). While still a child, she was betrothed to Ludwig IV, Landgrave of Thuringia which in those days incorporated most of present-day Hessen. She was married in 1221 and went to live in courtly splendour in the Wartburg above Eisenach. However, she showed no taste for high living, and devoted much of her time to the poor and sick. Despite this being deemed unbecoming behaviour for a princess, legends quickly circulated of the divine powers she possessed to extricate herself from various scrapes: as, for example, the occasion when the loaves she was carrying to feed the hungry turned into a posy of roses when she encountered her husband, or when she was provided with a new cloak by an angel to save her from the disgrace of arriving improperly attired at a banquet after she had discarded her robes to clothe a beggar she had met on the way.

Elisabeth was widowed at the age of twenty when Ludwig died of the plague while on his way to fight the Sixth Crusade. She left Eisenach for Marburg, where she donned the grey habit of a Franciscan nun and devoted herself entirely to the hospital she founded there. So aesthetically strict was her lifestyle that she died of exhaustion four years later. At the behest of her brother-in-law Conrad, co-regent of Thuringia and later Grand Master of the Teutonic Knights, it took only a further four years for her to be canonised. She has ranked among the most popular saints ever since, her life proving a fertile source of inspiration for artists.

The Elisabethkirche

No sooner had Elisabeth gained papal recognition as a saint in 1235, than the Teutonic Knights began the construction of the **Elisabethkirche** (April–Oct Mon–Sat 9am–6pm, Sun 12.30–6pm; Nov–March Mon–Sat 10am–4pm, Sun 12.30–4pm; DM2) on the site of her hospice, encasing her tomb in the process. The first purely Gothic building on German soil, it's also one of the most original and most beautiful. There are no rich figure portals and no elaborate pinnacles and flying buttresses so characteristic of France; instead such favourite national devices as the hall church format (which necessitated heavy wall buttresses), and the trefoil or "clover leaf" plan for the east end were adapted to the new style of architecture for the first time. The twin **towers**, with their relentless upward movement and tall pointed steeples, are also very Germanic and noticeably different from their more varied and elaborate French counterparts.

Inside, the church is like a museum of German religious art, full of statues and frescos, mainly celebrating Elisabeth's piety. Curiously enough, her cult underwent a major revival just before the Reformation, and five magnificent winged **altars** were created by the local master carver Ludwig Juppe and the painter Johann von der Leyten. On the right as you enter is one of these, the *Elisabeth-Altar*, which vividly relates the saint's life. In an alcove to the other side is the tomb of **Paul von Hindenburg**, the *Reichspresident* who appointed Hitler Chancellor in 1933. His body was brought to this decidedly unsuitable location after the war by the Americans; occasionally demonstrations are held outside the church to protest at the unholy pilgrims who have made the tomb a place of neo-Nazi pilgrimage. At the opposite end of this aisle is a curvaceous **statue of Elisabeth** dating from about 1470; it was probably commissioned by her aristocratic descendants, hence the way it depicts her in a pose she herself would have despised – as a richly robed, crowned princess clutching a model of her church.

Just around the corner is the *Elisabeth-Chor*, as the northern part of the clover leaf plan is known. Its centrepiece is the towering **mausoleum** containing her coffin in its original location. Look out for the reliefs on the pedestal, which show her being mourned by beggars and cripples instead of the kings and bishops who normally occupied such a position. Among the **altars**, pride of place goes to that dedicated to the Virgin, in which Juppe skilfully incorporated a much-venerated older sculpture of *The Pietà* into the predella. A number of **murals** illustrating the saint's life, long covered up and only rediscovered this century, can also be seen.

The former sacristy on the northern side of the choir now contains the church's most spectacular treasure, the resplendent mid-thirteenth-century **golden shrine** which contained the relics of Elisabeth until Philipp the Magnanimous had them reinterred. Elisabeth's life is illustrated once more on the reliefs on the lid.

Finally, the *Landgrafen-Chor*, the southern arm of the trefoil plan, serves as the **pantheon** of the rulers of Hessen. The first tomb in the eastern row is to Elisabeth's brother-in-law Conrad, while the fourth, artistically the finest of the group, commemorates Heinrich I, the first Landgrave of Hessen. Also worthy of special note is the only alabaster intruder among the stone tombs, that to Philipp the Magnanimous' father Wilhelm II, who is gruesomely depicted as a decaying corpse.

The rest of the quarter

Grouped around the Elisabethkirche are several other buildings formerly belonging to the Teutonic Knights. Forming a sort of close around the church's east end are the thirteenth-century **Brüderhaus** and **Herrenhaus**, the fifteenth-century **Deutsch-Orden-Haus** and the sixteenth-century **Kornspeicher**. All are now used by the University: the Kornspeicher, formerly a corn store and bakehouse, now houses the **Mineralogisches Museum** (Tues 10am–1pm & 3-6pm, Thurs & Fri 10am–1pm, Sat & Sun 11am–3pm; free), which is more interesting than it sounds, with a glittering array of precious stones.

Up a little hill to the west of the Elisabethkirche is the **Michaelskapelle**, a funerary chapel for the Knights and pilgrims to the shrine. Saint Elisabeth herself was buried in its peaceful little cemetery once the ban on her cult had been imposed.

Following Deutschhausstrasse southeastwards, then turning right into Biegenstrasse, at no. 11 you'll find the **Universitätsmuseum für bildende Kunst** (10am–1pm & 3–5pm, closed Tues; free), which has a Lucas Cranach the Elder portrait of Luther, a Klee, a Kandinsky and a Picasso, and works by German artists, notably the local painter Karl Bantzer. The main part of the campus is in the vicinity, straddling both sides of the Lahn. Cross over to the *Mensa* building and you'll be rewarded with a fine view of the city.

The upper town

Other than its one supreme monument, the most remarkable feature of the upper town (*Oberstadt*) is its atmospheric appearance, with plunging steets, steep stairways, narrow alleys, secluded corners and surprising vistas. The easiest way up is by continuing along the banks of the Lahn from the *Mensa* and crossing over the bridge. However, an equally enticing, if much steeper, approach is to follow the **Steinweg**, an old stepped street hemmed in by half-timbered buildings, from the Elisabethkirche.

Marktplatz and around

Heart of the Altstadt is the **Marktplatz**, with its St-Georg-Brunnen and an appealing line-up of golden half-timbered houses. During term-time the square is the focal point of Marburg's nightlife, but out of term it's very peaceful, except for the twice-weekly markets. Here you might see older women in the traditional costumes still sometimes worn in the area, a hangover from the days when Protestant and Catholic had to be able to tell each other apart – the Protestants wore black, dark brown, blue or green, while the Catholics wore bright colours with plaited hair. The **Rathaus** is a sixteenth-century Gothic building with a gabled Renaissance staircase tower featuring another statue of Elisabeth by Ludwig Juppe, holding the arms of the Landgraves of Hessen. The heraldic symbol is supposed to be a lion, but the sculptor mischievously made it look like a monkey.

In the old schoolhouse just off the Markt is the **Emil-von-Behring-Austellung** (Mon–Fri 8am–4pm; free), a permanent exhibition about the life of the immunology pioneer who was awarded the first ever Nobel Prize for Medicine in 1901 for his work in finding vaccines for diptheria and tetanus. He's one of Marburg's most celebrated professors: other famous names who have held chairs at the University are Denis Papin, the Huguenot refugee who invented the steam engine; Robert Bunsen, populariser of the "Bunsen burner"; Ferdinand Braun, who developed Marconi's invention of the wireless and shared the Nobel Prize with him; and Friedrich Carl von Savigny, father of the modern German legal system. The last of these taught the University's most famous alumni, the Brothers Grimm.

South of Marktplatz

South of the Markt is the **Kiliankirche**, Marburg's oldest church, but one which has been secularised since the sixteenth century. It later served as a school. In the Nazi period it was appropriated for use as the local SS headquarters, and was also the final place to which Marburg's Jews were taken before deportation. Nowadays, it again serves a worthy purpose as the head office of the German Green Cross. Further south is the **Alte Universität**, which took over a Gothic Dominican monastery, of which only the church (9am–6pm, closed Wed) now remains. The rest of the complex was rebuilt in a grandiose neo-Romanesque style, with the centrepiece being the **Aula** (Mon–Fri 11am–1pm & 4–5pm; DM0.30), a ceremonial hall (now used only for occasional public events or the inauguration of a new professor) adorned with frescos depicting the history of the city .

The Marienkirche and the Kanzlei

Nicolaistrasse leads west from Marktplatz to the thirteenth-century **Marienkirche**, from whose terrace there's a good view out over Marburg and the Lahn. Just past here is a stairway called the Ludwig-Bickell-Treppe which provide the shortest route up to the top of the town. Alternatively, you can ascend the slower way to the northeast via the Renaissance **Kanzlei**, which now houses another University collection, the **Religionskundliche Sammlung** (Mon, Wed & Fri 10am–1pm; free), with notable material on the Reformation and Marburg's part in it.

The Schloss

Towering above Marburg at a height of 102m above the Lahn is the **Schloss** (Tues–Sun 10am–1pm & 2–5/6pm; free). There was a castle on this site as far back as the twelfth century, but the present structure was begun by order of Sophie of Brabant to serve as the seat of the Landgraves of the new state of Hessen. Marburg lost its status as capital to Kassel at the beginning of the fourteenth century, but before then a substantial portion of the present Schloss had been built. This included the south wing, at the end of which is the **Schlosskapelle**. Inside, the lurid rose-coloured interior is quite striking; some original murals and part of the mosaic pavement also survive.

From the same period is the **Saalbau** on the northern side. This is notable for illustrating that this Schloss was primarily a residential palace, as opposed to the then standard fortified castle. Although the magnificent great hall, the largest structure of its kind in Germany, is known as the *Rittersaal*, it actually had no military function, instead being a venue for feasts and receptions. The most famous of these was the **Marburg Colloquy** of 1529, where Philipp the Magnanimous failed to unite Protestantism.

The hall's two spectacular Renaissance inlaid wood doorways are among the many additions and embellishments made to the Schloss during the fifteenth and sixteenth centuries, when Marburg periodically regained its position as capital of all or part of Hessen. At the eastern side of the complex, the **Wilhelmsbau**, linked to the main courtyard by a covered bridge, was the last significant part to be built. It now contains the miscellaneous archaeology, applied art and local history displays of the **Museum für Kulturgeschichte** (Tues–Sun 10am–1pm & 2–5pm; free). From the terrace outside there's a wonderful aerial view over the Elisabethkirche and the lower town.

Practicalities

Marburg's **Hauptbahnhof** is on the right bank of the Lahn at the northern end of town, just five minutes' walk from the Elisabethkirche. Immediately outside, at Neue Kasseler Str. 1, is the **tourist office** (Mon–Fri 8am–12.30pm & 2–5pm; April–Sept also Sat 9.30am–noon; ☎06421/201262 or 201249). It has a free room-finding service, which is particularly handy in that there's a surprising dearth of **hotels** with a convenient location. Cheapest, at DM30 per person, is *Reher*, Alte Kasseler Str. 66 (☎06421/65624), which lies further north of and to the rear of the Hauptbahnhof. In the town centre, try *Einsle*, Frankfurter Str. 2a (☎06421/23410), which charges DM40 per person, or *Haus Müller*, Deutschhausstr. 29 (☎06421/65659), which has singles from DM45 and doubles from DM85. The pretty half-timbered *Sonne*, Markt 14 (☎06421/26036), has a few simple singles for DM45, but most of its rooms, including all the doubles, are more luxurious and accordingly priced. There's a larger range of options in the suburbs; in Einhausen, for instance, *Gasthof Barth*, Einhäuser Str. 13 (☎06420/7440), has singles from DM32 and doubles from DM60. The **youth hostel** is at Jahnstr. 1 (☎06421/23461), a little to the southeast of the Altstadt; the **campsite** (☎06421/21331) is a bit further down the river.

Drinking and eating

There's no shortage of places for drinking and eating in this student-dominated town. Among their favourite **pubs** are *Hinkelstein*, Markt 18, a cellar tavern with occasional live music, and *Quodlibet*, Gutenbergstr. 35, which attracts billiards freaks. Others are along the half-timbered buildings on Hirschberg, the street leading off from the Markt, and on Untergasse. Trendy **café-bars** are *Café Velo* on Augustinergasse and *Café Barfuss* on Langgasse, which has an excellent selection of tacos and pasta. However, the coolest street creds hang out at *Roter Stern*, housed in a bookshop at Am Grün 28, which is especially well known for its superb Nicaraguan coffee. Two good **pizzerias** are *Sardegna*, just off Rudolphsplatz, which uses a wood oven, and the nearby *Rustikale*, which also does a good Italian-style breakfast. Near the *Mensa Parkplatz*, just off Kurt-Schumacher-Strasse on the eastern side of the Lahn, is a recommended **vegetarian** place, *Kalimera*. Best traditional German **restaurant** is the aforementioned *Sonne*; alternatively, try the *Stadthalle*, Biegenstr. 15.

Marburg's main **festival** is the bucolic *Marktfrüschoppen* on the first Sunday in July; the *Elisabethmarkt* in mid-October is another notable event. To find out **what's on**, consult the free bi-weekly *Marburger Magazin Express*; it's always worth checking up on **events** held on the Schlosspark's open-air stage. **Boats** can be hired from *Bootsverleih*, Auf dem Wehr (☎06421/26864). There's a **women's centre** at Renthof 18 (☎06421/63570).

The Vogelsberg

The **Vogelsberg** is a quiet region of gently rolling hills, forests and small villages which has long been known to the weekend trippers of Hessen but remains relatively undiscovered by outsiders. A massive extinct volcano about 50km in diameter, the Vogelsberg rises to a maximum altitude of 774m at the **Taufstein** – not a dramatic landscape, but a good place for a bit of rustic recuperation. There are regular bus connections between the small towns and villages, and plenty of youth hostels, campsites and other cheap accommodation.

The High Vogelsberg

At the heart of the range is the area known as the **High Vogelsberg** (*Hoher Vogelsberg*), which has been designated a *Naturpark*. Approaching from Giessen the first town you come to is the small health resort of **LAUBACH**, some 30km to the east. The **Schloss**, which preserves its medieval core amid many subsequent additions and alterations, is still owned by the local counts and normally closed to the public. The only exceptions are the limited opportunities to view the **library** (May–Oct Thurs at 5.30pm) – one of the most valuable private collections in Europe. Otherwise, there's nothing outstanding to see, but the town's relaxed atmosphere makes it a pleasant place to while away the time at a café – try *Göbel* in Friedrichstrasse or *Venezia* in Wildemanngasse. There's a **youth hostel** at Am Ramsberg (☎06405/1376).

Schotten

SCHOTTEN, some 10km east, lies in the middle of the High Vogelsberg. It's a quiet little town, notwithstanding the fact that its *Schottenring* is the oldest motor racing track in Germany. The Gothic **Liebfrauenkirche** is unexpectedly grand for such a rural community; it boasts a delicately carved entrance portal of the Adoration of the Magi and a magnificent late fourteenth-century painted altar depicting both the Passion and the Life of the Virgin. Schotten makes the obvious starting point for exploring the Taufstein's wooded slopes or the nearby **Nidda-Stausee**, a watersports and angling centre with **camping** facilities.There's a **youth hostel** at Lindenweg 17 (☎06044/ 2354), while the cheapest **hotel** is *Adler*, Vogelsbergstr. 160 (☎06044/2437), which has rooms from around DM28 per person.

Alsfeld

The 30km route from Schotten to **ALSFELD** takes you through the core of the *Naturpark*, along a stretch of the German Holiday Road *(Deutsche Ferienstrasse)*, and under the shadow of the Taufstein. Alsfeld itself, which can also be reached by the railway linking Giessen and Fulda, is conventionally attractive and very sleepy – even the punks are well behaved. Its buildings conform to the half-timbered blueprint characteristic of the area, and many of them are so old that they seem ready to pitch forward into the cobbled streets. The town's slightly sinister sixteenth-century **Rathaus**, one of the finest in the country, stands on the minute **Marktplatz**, focal point of Alsfeld's historic quarter. Also here is the Renaissance **Hochzeitshaus**, a rare stone building, originally built for the celebration of weddings and festivals. At Hersfelder Strasse 10–12 are two of the oldest half-timbered houses in Germany. Apart from these, the only other really notable building is the thirteenth-century **Walpurgiskirche**, a grey, geometrical church built onto the remains of an earlier structure. At Rittergasse 3–5 two gaudy Baroque buildings have been combined to house the **Regionalmuseum** (Mon–Fri 9am–12.30pm & 2–4pm, Sat & Sun 10am–4pm) and local **tourist office** (☎06631/18224).

The cheapest **hotel** is *Zur alten Schmiede*, Untergasse 12 (☎06631/2465). For good **food**, and the closest you're likely to get to a lively atmosphere in Alsfeld, make for *Bistro Swing*, which is up a small alley just before the *China Restaurant* on the right-hand side of Obergasse. Alsfeld's only passable café is *Venezia* at Obergasse 23.

The Eastern Vogelsberg

LAUTERBACH, 12km southeast of Alsfeld by road or rail, is another half-timbered town given variety by a couple of notable Rococo buildings. Of these, the **Stadtkirche** was finished off with a Neoclassical tower, while **Schloss Hohhaus** (Tues–Fri 10am–noon & 2-4pm, Sat 10am–noon, Sun 2–4pm; DM1) has rich stucco interiors which now house the local history museum. There's a **youth hostel** in the woods to the east of town at Schlitzer Str. 50 (☎06641/2181). A couple of notable local **festivals** are the *Prämienmarkt*, held in the week of Corpus Christi (variable date in May/June), and the *Gildefest*, which takes place on the first weekend of September every second year.

Schlitz
SCHLITZ, 10km to the northeast, is a little-known, extremely well-preserved medieval town which would be bombarded with day-trippers were it in a more favourable geographical position. Some idea of the strength of the town's defences can be seen from the fact that its **Stadtmauer** is pierced by just two gateways, yet is further protected by no fewer than four castles of varying dates. The keep of the oldest of these, the **Hinterburg** (Easter–Oct 9am–noon & 2–6pm; DM2), can be ascended for a fine panorama over the region. Of the others, the **Vorderburg** occupies the highest part of town, the **Schachtenburg** is half-timbered, while the **Ottoburg** was only added in the seventeenth century and now serves as the **youth hostel** (☎06642/400). Within the walls is a fine array of half-timbered houses, while outside stands the Baroque **Hallenburg**, the palatial residence of the local counts.

Fulda

Lying in a narrow valley between the Vogelsberg and the Rhön, **FULDA** was best known throughout the Cold War period as being at the weak point in NATO's front line (the so-called "Fulda Gap") through which the massed tanks of the Warsaw Pact were supposedly most likely to pour into the heart of Western Europe. With that dubious threat now gone, the city can concentrate once more on its role as a major episcopal centre, the venue for the annual meetings of both the Catholic Bishops' Conference and the German Protestant Convention. Church affairs, indeed, have dominated Fulda's history. Its roots go back to the eighth century when a small town grew up around the abbey founded by Saint Boniface, a monk sent from England to convert the Germans. After his martyrdom in 754 Fulda became a pilgrimage site, and over the years its abbey grew into one of the most important monasteries in Germany. It was here that a couple of monks transcribed the *Lay of Hildebrand*, one of the first recorded pieces of German literature. For centuries, the abbots doubled as secular princes; on their promotion to the rank of bishops they transformed their seat into a Baroque vision of golden turrets and crosses. After the Napoleonic secularisation, Fulda suffered the fate of being annexed by one state after another every few years, before finally being incorporated into Hessen.

The Dom and Around

Fulda's imposing **Dom**, on the western edge of the town centre, is a classic early Baroque structure, free of the excesses of later Bavarian Baroque, but with an attention to detail and complexity of design which gives it a different feel from most German churches. The glory of the spacious and stuccoed interior is the high altar, depicting the Assumption of the Madonna in full-blown gilded splendour and flanked by six marble columns. Behind here is a small and more austere chapel where the monks used to assemble for prayer. Saint Boniface's tomb is in the slightly oppressive crypt beneath the high altar – it's incorporated into a sepulchral black marble altar with carved reliefs depicting the saint's martyrdom and his resurrection on Judgment Day. The **Dommuseum** (April–Oct Mon–Fri 10am–5.30pm, Sat 10am–2pm, Sun 12.30–5.30pm; Nov, Dec, Feb & March Mon–Fri 10am–12.30 & 1.30–4.30pm, Sat 10am–2pm, Sun 12.30–4pm; DM3.50), reached via the crypt, contains Boniface's relics, which include his sword, his head and the book with which he vainly tried to fend off his murderers.

The Michaelskirche

Next door to the Dom is the **Michaelskirche**, built in the shape of a Greek cross as a copy of the Church of the Holy Sepulchre in Jerusalem. It's the only building to have survived the wholesale conversion of Fulda to the Baroque. In comparison to the mighty Dom it's quite inconspicuous, but in some ways is more impressive than its larger rival, incorporating as it does the rotunda of an earlier church; although this has been much altered, two of its eight columns date back to 822. Inside, look out for the fourteenth-century **stone tablet** in the Baroque chapel built on to the northern transept: it illustrates the Passion in an unusual graphic code for the benefit of the illiterate of the time, with symbolic images such as lips to signify Judas' kiss.

The Stadtschloss

Across from the Dom is the former episcopal palace, the cream-coloured **Stadtschloss** (Mon–Thurs, Sat & Sun 10am–12.30pm & 2.30–5pm, Fri 2.30–5pm; DM3). Again the work of Johann Dientzenhofer, it's a huge building with several wings which has housed the municipal offices ever since it was acquired by the city last century.

Highlight of the state rooms is the *Daalbergsaal*, which is painted with a quirky representation of the Four Seasons, with winter in the guise of a harlequin. It's also worth taking a stroll in the **Schlossgarten**, a geometrical ornamental park which leads to the **Orangerie**, the best-looking of Fulda's secular Baroque buildings. Inside, look out for the *Sauerkrautbild*, a ceiling painting showing Greek deities eating sausages. The **Flora-Vase** in front of the Orangerie, named after the floral goddess whose statue crowns it, is a masterpiece of the art of garden sculpture.

Elsewhere in the centre

As for the rest of Fulda town centre, the **Hauptwache**, across the road from the Schloss on Bonifatiusplatz, is a Baroque police station clearly modelled on its Frankfurt counterpart. From here Friedrichstrasse takes you to the **Stadtpfarrkirche**, which pretty much conforms to Fulda house style, and the **Altes Rathaus**, which breaks the mould by having a non-conformist half-timbered facade (a reconstruction of the sixteenth-century original). Just to the south is the Jesuit Alte Stadtschule, now housing the **Vonderau-Museum** (Tues–Sun 10am-6pm; DM3), a collection covering history, archaeology, anthropology, and the fine and applied arts. Directly opposite is the **Alte Universität**, now serving a more humble role as a school. Finally, on Heinrichstrasse at the western end of the town centre, the **Landesbibliothek** (Mon–Fri 10am–noon & 2–4pm; free), has a permanent exhibition featuring a Gutenberg Bible, various illuminated manuscripts and some unusual medieval satirical drawings.

Outside the centre

On St-Laurentius-Strasse, on the western side of the River Fulda (bus #9 from the Hauptbahnhof), is the **Deutsches Feuerwehrmuseum** (Tues, Wed & Fri–Sun 10am-5pm, Thurs 2–9pm; DM3), a collection of fire-fighting appliances and equipment from the eighteenth century to the present. Also on this bank is the **Andreaskirche**, one of four monasteries grouped around Fulda in the shape of a cross. It's worth a visit for the more or less intact eleventh-century frescos in its crypt. In the southern suburb of Johannisberg is the **Denkmalpflege Fortbildungszentrum** (☎0661/45081), one of the world's leading study centres for the restoration and maintenance of historic monuments. If you call and make an appointment they'll be happy to show you around.

More enticing than any of these is the **Petersberg**, a 400-metre-high hill about 4km to the east, which commands wonderful views of Fulda itself and across to the Vogelsberg and Rhön. The hill is crowned by the **Peterskirche**, the finest of the monasteries grouped round the town. Its crypt, with its precious ninth-century frescos, survives from the first building on the spot; the main church was rebuilt in the fifteenth century but has superb Romanesque reliefs on its triumphal arch.

Further delights await at the **Schloss Fasanerie** (guided tours April–Oct Tues–Sun 10am–noon & 1–4pm; DM3), about 6km southwest of Fulda, which is reckoned to be the finest Baroque palace in Hessen. Built at enormous expense in the eighteenth century, the place offers a fascinating glimpse into the capricious changes of taste of the German aristocracy: when it came into the possession of the Electors of Hessen-Kassel, many of the rooms were refurbished to suit their penchant for the Neoclassical style. If you tire of the opulence and the ranks of Fulda porcelain, have a break in the elegant surroundings of the *Schlosscafé*, or take a walk through the magnificent park.

Practicalities

Fulda's **Hauptbahnhof** is at the eastern end of the town centre. The **tourist office** is at Schloss Str. 1 (Mon–Fri 8.30am–noon & 2–4.30pm, Sat 9.30am–noon; ☎0661/102345). There's a **youth hostel** at the southwestern edge of town at Neuenberger Str.

107 (☎0661/73389); the easiest way there is by bus #12 to Stadion. Fulda isn't too bad as far as reasonable **hotels** go. One of the most centrally located is the *Gasthof Grüne Au*, Abtstor 35 (☎0661/74283), in the shadow of the Dom, whose rates begin at DM30 per person. Another fairly central possibility, with similar prices, is the *Pension Hodes*, Peterstor 14 (☎0661/72862). A little out of the centre is the *Gasthof Zum Nussknacker*, Dr-Weinzierl-Str. 2 (☎0661/35937), with singles from DM38 and doubles from DM71.

Eating and drinking

As for **eating** and **drinking**, upwardly mobile types gravitate towards the *Dachsbau Bistro*, Pfandhausstr. 7–9, where food and drink are good but a little on the pricey side. Fulda's "alternative" scene is centred on *Kreuzsaal*, Schlitzer Str. 81, and *Krokodil*, Karlgasse 31; the latter is a fairly upmarket café-bar which stays open until 1am. *Löhertor*, Gerberstr. 9, has just about everything including a disco upstairs and occasional film shows. *Zur Windmühle*, Karlstr. 17, is a traditional pub while *Schoppen-Keller*, Paulustor 6, is a *Weinkeller* with a very mixed clientele and relaxed atmosphere.

The Rhön and Spessart

East of Fulda stretches the **Rhön**, a volcanic region a little more wild and threatening than the Vogelsberg. These hills have become a big hang-gliding centre and there are some good walking and cycling routes. The Rhön is split between Hessen, Bavaria and Thuringia, but Hessen has the **Wasserkuppe**, which at 950m is the highest peak in the range. For exploring the Rhön the best base is **GERSFELD**. It's a small tourist-oriented town with a Baroque **Pfarrkirche** whose altar, pulpit and organ are piled on top of one another to great dramatic effect. There's also a **Schloss**, likewise Baroque, which contains a museum displaying some fragile-looking examples of Fulda porcelain work. The **tourist office** is in the *Kurverwaltung*, Brückenstr. 1 (☎06654/7077), the **youth hostel** at Jahnstr. 6 (☎06654/340), and there's no shortage of reasonable **hotels**. Lowest rates are at *Weinig*, Am Kreuzgarten 4 (☎06654/557), and *Goldener Stern*, Rommserstr. 8 (☎06654/267).

Further west lies the Hessen section of the **Spessart**, Germany's largest continuous upland forest area. The most enticing destination, easily reached by bus or train, is **STEINAU**, a typical little half-timbered town in whose **Hanauisches Amtshaus** the Brothers Grimm spent part of their youth. There's a memorial to them in the town's **Schloss** (Tues–Sun 10am–noon & 1–5pm; DM2), as well as a puppet theatre which performs their stories.

The Fulda-Werra basin

The River Weser, the backdrop to so many of Germany's most famous legends, is formed from the union of two separate rivers, the **Fulda** and the **Werra**, whose basins form much of the most easterly part of Hessen. If travelling between Fulda and Kassel, it's well worth making a detour into this countryside, which for long suffered because of its proximity to the impenetrable East German border, and which remains for the most part little visited by tourists.

Bad Hersfeld

One town which avoided any feelings of Cold War blight is **BAD HERSFELD**, situated some 30km downstream from Fulda and easily reached by train. Its response to the situation was to inaugurate in 1951 an annual **drama festival**, which has become one of the leading permanent fixtures in the German cultural calendar. Lasting from mid-June to mid-August, it takes in both classical drama (this is Germany's most celebrated Shakespeare stage) and modern works (material as diverse as Brecht and *Kiss Me Kate*). The plays are performed against the stirring backdrop of the **Stiftsruine**, the remains of an eleventh-century basilica (the largest Romanesque church in the country), which was destroyed by French soldiers in the eighteenth century. This is much the finest building in town; otherwise, there's the familiar spectacle of a half-timbered **Altstadt** with a Renaissance **Rathaus**.

Practicalities

If you intend visiting for the drama festival, try to sort out tickets and accommodation by the preceding February through the **tourist office** at Am Markt 1 (☎06621/201274). There's also another big annual event, the *St-Lullus-Fest* in mid-October, which claims to the longest established **popular festival** in the country. Bad Hersfeld's **youth hostel** is towards the northern fringes of town at Wehnebergstr. 29 (☎06621/2403), while local **hotels** charging DM30 or less include *Gasthof Jäger*, Homberger Str. 93 (☎06621/3810), and *Gasthof Café Eichhof*, Brelauerstr. 12 (☎06621/2682).

The Werra valley

From Bad Hersfeld you can travel by train via the major railway junction of BEBRA to **ESCHWEGE**, the main town of the Werra valley region, some 60km northeast. The *Johannisfest*, celebrating mid-summer, is a big local **festival**. At other times, the main attractions are a half-timbered **Marktplatz**, a Renaissance **Schloss**, and two Gothic churches – one for the Altstadt and another for the Neustadt. The **tourist office** is at Hospitalplatz 16 (☎05651/304210), and there's a **youth hostel** at Fritz-Neuenroth-Weg 1 (☎05651/60099). In the town centre cheap hotels are in short supply – check with the tourist office for details.

Following the snaking path of the Werra downstream by either road or rail, you come after 10km to **BAD SOODEN-ALLENDORF**, a double town cut in two by the river. Bad Sooden is a salt-spring *Kurort*, while Allendorf is chiefly notable for its half-timbered houses; it formerly suffered the misfortune of being hemmed in on three sides by the East German border. Affordable **hotels** are plentiful: try *Gasthof zum Stern*, Kirchstr. 71 (☎05652/2252), or *Haus Erika*, Am Haintor 22 (☎05652/2278). The **tourist office** in the *Kurverwaltung*, on Landgraf-Philipp-Platz, will be able to give you details of other possibilities.

A further 12km downstream is **WITZENHAUSEN**, the so-called "Cherry Town". The cherry orchards contain some 200,000 trees and crowd right up into the old-fashioned town itself; the place gets particularly busy during the springtime *Kesperkirmes* (Cherry Fair), when the "Cherry Princess" is crowned. The **tourist office** is at Am Markt 1 (☎05542/2506); the cheapest local **hotels**, charging DM30 or less, are *Dovidat*, Burgstr. 20 (☎05542/2506), and *Hotze*, Kasseler Str. 29 (☎05542/3214). There's also a **campsite**, *Werratal* (☎05542/1465).

The Kaufung Forest

Between the valleys of the Fulda and Werra is the sleepy **Kaufung Forest**, now designated as the *Naturpark Meissner-Kaufunger Wald*, which is as yet barely discovered by tourists. The railway line from Eschwege to Kassel takes you through the heart of this landscape, enabling you to stop off at either of the main towns. **HESSISCH-LICHTENAU**, which preserves part of its medieval fortifications and a richly decorated Renaissance Rathaus, is the obvious base for the many walking routes on the **Hoher Meissner** (754m), the highest peak in northern Hessen. **Hotels** at around DM30 per person include *Zur Lichten Aue*, Desselerstr. 6 (☎05602/2087), and *Ratskeller*, Landgrafenstr. 17 (☎05602/2772); other possibilities exist in some of the surrounding villages – check with the local **tourist office** at Landgrafenstr. 52 (☎05602/2061).

About 15km away by rail – and a similar distance from Kassel – is the overgrown village of **KAUFUNGEN** (if travelling by train, get out in Ober-Kaufungen). It stands round a sizeable **Klosterkirche**, which once belonged to a Benedictine convent founded in 1017 by Saint Kunigunde, wife of Emperor Henry II. If you're looking for somewhere to stay in this area, you could do worse than to head for **NIESTE**, a slate-roofed little village just a few kilometres to the north of Kaufungen. The most reasonable **hotels**, charging around DM25 per person, are *Gasthof zum Adler*, Witzenhäuser Str. 24 (☎05605/2642), and *Gasthof zum Niestetal*, Kaufunger Str. 9 (☎05605/2490).

Kassel

Although nowadays chiefly famous for the *documenta*, the huge modern art exhibition held there once every five years, **KASSEL** is basically an industrial city. Its big armaments industry ensured four-fifths destruction of its centre during the war, and consequently most of the buildings there are functional products of the 1950s; as the publicity brochures are only too keen to remind you, Kassel was the first place in Germany to feature the now obligatory pedestrian zone. Yet, despite the unenticing appearance of most of the centre, the city scores in being one of the greenest in Germany. It also preserves plenty of reminders of its period of glory, which began in the late seventeenth century with the arrival of Huguenots expelled from France, continued throughout the following century with the acquisition of all the trappings of a capital city, and culminated in the years 1806–1813, when it was the royal seat of the Kingdom of Westphalia.

Getting around and finding somewhere to stay

Kassel has two main train stations: the **Hauptbahnhof**, at the northern edge of the city centre, is a dead end and is increasingly being overshadowed, especially on express services, by **Bahnhof Wilhelmshöhe**, which is about 1km east of the eponymous park. The main **tourist office** (Mon–Fri 9am–6pm, Sat 9am–1pm; ☎0561/13443) is now in the latter station. They charge a DM3 fee for finding a room, which is well worth paying, given the shortage of cheap **hotels**. Lowest rates in the centre are at *Hamburger Hof*, Werner-Hilpert-Str. 18 (☎0561/16002), near the Hauptbahnhof, which has singles from DM35 and doubles from DM65; similar prices are charged at *Autoreisehotel*, Mombachstr. 19 (☎0561/895947), further north (take tram #1 or #5 from Königsplatz). On the eastern edge of Kassel, the small *Gasthaus Bürgerhof*, Umbachsweg 53 (☎0561/ 522615), charges from DM30 per person, while *Gasthaus zum Sportplatz*, Lilienstr. 108 (☎0561/59060), has singles from DM40 and doubles from DM70; to reach them, take bus #17 from Königsplatz. In Wilhelmshöhe, *Palmenbad*, Kurhausstr. 27 (☎0561/32691), has rooms from DM34 (though most are far more expensive), while *Neue Holland*, not far from the Herkules at Hüttenbergstr. 6 (☎0561/ 33229), has singles at DM40, doubles DM72. There's a **youth hostel**, about fifteen minutes' walk west of the Hauptbahnhof at Schenkendorfstr. 18 (☎0561/776455), and **camping** facilities at Giesenallee 7 (☎0561/22433), on the banks of the Fulda just south of Karlsaue. Given the spread-out nature of the city, it's worth investing in the DM6 **public transport** ticket, which covers any 24-hr period, or the entire weekend.

Wilhelmshöhe

It was Landgrave Carl, the same ruler who invited the Huguenots to settle in Kassel, who began the laying-out of the **Wilhelmshöhe**, a huge upland forest park which is the largest urban example of its kind in Europe. Situated at the western edge of the city, and reached by tram #1 or #4, it remains its most enduring permanent attraction. Although originally intended as a formal garden in the Italian Baroque manner, it was modified by Carl's successors in line with the eighteenth-century preference for the English approach to landscaping, with a predominantly "natural" appearance mingled with an assortment of hidden follies.

The Schloss and the Gemäldegalerie

Curiously enough, the gargantuan **Schloss Wilhelmshöhe** was something of an after-thought, only begun in the 1780s. One of the finest Neoclassical buildings in Germany, it was designed and partly built by Simon-Louis du Ry, the last and most distinguished of a dynasty of local architects of Huguenot extraction. Its *Weissensteinflügel* is now designated the **Schlossmuseum** (guided tours March–Oct Tues–Sun 10am–4pm; Nov–Feb Tues–Sun 10am–3pm; DM2), a fairly predictable collection of opulent furni-ture, glassware, porcelain and other *objets d'art*, many from the time when Napoleon's brother Jérôme held court here as King of the puppet state of Westphalia.

THE GEMÄLDEGALERIE

Far more enthralling is the **Staatliche Kunstsammlung Kassel** (Tues-Sun 10am–5pm; free), which occupies the central block. Its ground floor is given over to Greek and Roman art – look out for the *Kassel Apollo*, a Roman copy of an archetypal Classical Greek bronze. Upstairs is the **Gemäldegalerie** (Picture Gallery), a treasury of old masters which originated in the collection of Landgrave Carl's successor Wilhelm VIII, whose spell as Governor of Breda and Maastricht fuelled a passion for the painting of the Dutch Golden Age. He accumulated what remains one of the world's finest collections of this period, supplemented by seventeenth-century European paintings.

Until recently, the gallery boasted of owning seventeen canvases by **Rembrandt**, but in the light of current research six of these have been demoted to the status of works by followers. Among the undisputed pieces, though, there are still some supreme masterpieces, most notably the profoundly touching *Jacob Blessing his Grandchildren*. This rarely depicted subject shows the patriarch choosing to bless Joseph's second son Ephraim first, on the grounds he was destined for greater things – namely, to be the ancestor of the Gentiles. Rembrandt accordingly showed Ephraim as a fair-haired Aryan-type, in contrast to the dark features of the first-born, Manasseh. From roughly the same period comes one of his greatest portraits, *Nicolaes Bruyning*, vividly conveying the sitter's animated personality. Two paintings from a decade earlier are unique in Rembrandt's oeuvre. *Winter Landscape* is his only nature study executed in bright colours, while the intimate *Holy Family with the Curtain* presents the scene in the manner of a tiny theatre set. *Profile of Saskia* is a demonstration of the young artist's virtuosity, with his first wife, gorgeously decked out in velvet and jewellery, depicted as an icon of idealised womanhood. Hals' *Man in a Slouched Hat* is a late work, clearly showing the influence of Rembrandt married to his own talent for carica-ture, which can be seen more plainly in the earlier *Merry Toper*. Other pieces from seventeenth-century Holland on show include paintings by Terbrugghen and Jan Steen, and more than twenty works by **Philips Wouwerman**.

In spite of Landgrave Wilhelm's strict Calvinism, which drew him to the Dutch School above all others, he assembled a magnificent group of Flemish paintings of the

3ame period. There are some choice canvases by **Rubens**, notably *The Crowning of the Hero*, *The Madonna as a Refuge for Sinners*, the highly unflattering *Nicolas de Respaigne as a Pilgrim to Jerusalem*, and a beautiful nocturnal *Flight into Egypt*. **Van Dyck** is represented by portraits drawn from all phases of his career, while the examples of **Jordaens** show his taste for the exotic on a large scale.

The seventeenth-century Dutch and Flemish collection takes up most of the first and second floors, but the end cabinets are devoted to small-scale fifteenth- and sixteenth-century paintings, mostly from Germany. **Cranach**'s early *Resurrection Triptych* is one of a number of highlights, others being **Dürer**'s *Elsbeth Tucher* (familiar from its appearance on the DM20 note), **Baldung**'s *Hercules and Antaeus*, and an impassioned *Crucifixion*, set in a Danube landscape, by **Altdorfer**. On the top floor a group of Italian Renaissance pictures is dominated by a magnificent full-length *Portrait of a Nobleman* by **Titian**. However, once again it was the seventeenth-century masters who most appealed to the Hessian taste, and there are some spectacular examples of Italian Baroque, finest of which is **Preti**'s *Feast of Herod*. From Spain come outstanding pieces by **Murillo** and **Ribera**, while **Poussin**'s *Cupid's Victory over Pan* represents French art of this same period. **Schönfeld**'s *The Great Flood* is one of the finest of all seventeenth-century German paintings, while there are a couple of examples of the brilliant but short-lived **Johann Liss**: the enigmatic *Scene with Soldiers and Courtesans* and the effervescent *Game of Morra*, a work anticipatory of the Rococo style of a century later.

The rest of the park

Immediately to the north of the Schloss is the **Ballhaus**, a neat little Neoclassical building which King Jérôme, Napoleon's brother, had built as a theatre in 1808. It was turned into a ballroom twenty years later and has the same role (intermittently) today; exhibitions are also sometimes held. Not far away is the **Gewächshaus**, a glass hothouse dating back to 1822.

The **Bergpark**, the original Baroque ornamental garden, features a 250-metre-long, 885-tiered cascade. It's overlooked by the famous **Herkules** (mid-March–mid-Nov Tues–Sun 9am-5pm; DM2), which might look like an eighteenth-century Michelin Man, but which commands a sweeping panoramic view, as well as being a source of great pride to the burghers of Kassel, who have made it the symbol of their town. The statue lounges on top of a bizarre pyramidal structure, which is in turn set into a purely decorative castle called the **Oktogon**. At 2.30pm on Wednesdays, Sundays and holidays in summer, the floodgates at the foot of Herkules are opened and water pours down the cascade and over a series of obstacles to the fountain in front of the Schloss.

Finally, at the park's eastern entrance, at Wilhelmshöher Allee 361, the **Kurhessen-Therme** (Mon, Tues, Thurs & Sun 9am–11pm, Wed, Fri & Sat 9am–midnight; DM14 for 90min or DM36 for the day) is an ultra-modern, open-plan spa complex complete with indoor and outdoor thermal pools, saunas, jacuzzis, cinema and restaurant.

The city centre

In the centre of Kassel, the few remaining historic monuments are rather marooned among the postwar buildings, but there are several museums well worth taking the trouble to see if you're in town. Starting from the west, the **Landesmuseum** (Tues–Sun 10am–5pm; free) on Brüder-Grimm-Platz contains displays of pre- and early history in Hessen, plus the applied arts section of the Staatliche Kunstsammlung. There's also a substantial astrophysics section, including a 1560 observatory and various clocks and astronomical instruments made by Tycho Brahe. Sharing the building is the **Deutsches Tapetenmuseum** (German Wallpaper Museum; same times; free) which is apparently the only one in the world devoted to this subject. Actually, it's far

THE BROTHERS GRIMM

One of the great inseparable partnerships, **Jacob Grimm** (1785–1863) and **Wilhelm Grimm** (1786–1859) were of an impeccable Hessian background. Born in Hanau, they were brought up in Steinau and educated in Marburg, before moving to Kassel, where they spent the longest part of their careers, working principally as court librarians. It was at Kassel that they put together the collection of tales, which they first published in 1812 under the title *Kinder- und Hausmärchen*. This was primarily a work of scholarship; the stories were all of folk origin and were taken straight down from oral sources. The book went through many editions, culminating in the definitive version of 1857, which contained two hundred tales. In the process, the desire of Jacob (the more gifted scholar of the two) to preserve the original unadorned version of the stories underwent increasing modification at the hands of Wilhelm, who had superior literary talents and favoured a certain amount of stylisation and embroidering of the folk idiom.

The collection made the brothers celebrities, and such characters as Cinderella, Rumpelstiltskin, Hansel and Gretel, Snow White and Little Red Riding Hood became familiar to children all over the world. Yet this popular success did not interfere with their dedication to serious scholarship, particularly in their later years as professors at Göttingen (where they were expelled for their liberal views) and Berlin. In 1854, they began to compile the *Deutsche Wörterbuch* – the German equivalent of the Oxford English Dictionary – a task taken up by several subsequent generations of scholars and only finally completed in 1961.

better than it sounds, adopting a generous interpretation of the word to cover all kinds of hangings, with exhibits from all eras and continents.

Only a couple of minutes' walk to the southeast, the **Neue Galerie** (same times; free) at Schöne Aussicht 1 takes up the history of art where the Schloss Wilhelmshöhe collection leaves off. The emphasis is on local artists, notably work produced at Willingshausen–Schwalm, Germany's oldest artists' colony.

Examples from most major European artistic movements are also featured, with a few works by the omnipresent Joseph Beuys. Next door, in Schloss Bellevue, the **Brüder-Grimm-Museum** (Tues–Fri 10am–1pm & 2pm–5pm, Sat & Sun 10am–1pm; free), at Schöne Aussicht 2, tells all about the famous fairy-tale tellers and philologists (see box above); the highlight is their own annotated manuscript version of the *Fairy Tales* – a must if you have any interest in their work.

Museum Fredericianum and the *documenta*

Proceeding along Frankfurter Strasse, you come to the vast open space of Friedrichsplatz, on which stands the oldest purpose-built museum building in Europe, the **Museum Fredericianum**, built by Simon-Louis du Ry before he began work on Schloss Wilhelmshöhe. Nowadays, it's used for temporary exhibitions, and is also the headquarters of the *documenta*, a retrospective of twentieth-century art inaugurated in 1955 which has become a multi-media event embracing everything from painting to video art. In effect, the whole city has become its venue, and many of the spectacular sculptures you see dotted throughout Kassel are leftovers from documenta events of previous years.

The *documenta 8* of 1987 featured the diverse talents of Joseph Beuys, Rainer Werner Fassbinder, Yoko Ono and hundreds of others in one of the most significant avant-garde art events in the world. Beuys was responsible for some of the *documenta*'s zanier moments – one of his schemes entailed planting 7000 oak trees throughout the city, each one marked by a small basalt stone. The *documenta 9* will be held from 13 June to 20 September 1992, after which there won't be another until 1997.

Across from the museum, at Steinweg 2, is the **Ottoneum**, constructed in the first decade of the seventeenth century as the first permanent theatre in Germany. Today it is home to the **Naturkundemuseum** (Tues–Fri 10am–4.30pm, Sat & Sun 10am–1pm, free), itself one of the oldest natural history collections in Europe. If you follow Oberste Gasse or Mittelgasse north from here, you come to the **Martinskirche**. Like all the churches in the city centre, this was devastated during the war, and it has been rebuilt in a compromise style which makes no attempt to restore it to its original form. However, it's worth a quick visit to take a look at the huge Renaissance memorial to Landgrave Philipp the Magnanimous, patron of Luther and founder of Marburg University.

The southeastern edge of the city centre, by the banks of the River Fulda, is taken up by another large Baroque park, the **Karlsaue**. In it stands the **Orangerie**, a long, orange-coloured Baroque palace, which, at the time of writing, was being fitted out as a science museum. Alongside is the **Marmorbad**, an ornate bathing hall adorned with mythological statues and reliefs. Further south is the **Blumeninsel Siebenbergen** (daily April–Oct 10am-7pm; DM1), an island strewn with flowers, trees, and exotic plants and shrubs.

Food, drink and practicalities

The best **bars** and **cafés** in Kassel seem to be in the area around Goethestrasse, a student district on the western edge of the city centre, where a few Jugendstil houses break up the general architectural monotony. *Wirtschaft* on the corner of Goethestrasse and Querallee is a recommended bar, while *Café Berger* opposite is a good *Kaffee und Kuchen* place. *Vis-a-Vis* on the corner of Goethestrasse and Lassallestrasse is an alternative-type café-bar, and at *Werkstatt*, a small café-bar on the corner of Friedrich-Ebert-Strasse and Diakonissenstrasse, there are occasional avant-gardish art exhibitions.

Kassel isn't particularly renowned for its **restaurants**, but the inevitable *Ratskeller*, Obere Königsstr. 8, is a reliable choice, while *Weinhaus Boos*, midway between Bahnhof Wilhelmshöhe and the city centre at Wilhelmshöher Allee 97, has a high reputation for both wine and food.

There are several worthwhile **festivals** in addition to the *documenta*. The *Zissel* in early August is a folklore event centred on the River Fulda, with processions, jousting and live music. On the first Saturday of September, the *Lichtfest* sees Wilhelmshöhe lit by a fireworks display and thousands of torchlights, with a large fair held earlier in the day. The beginning of November marks the *Kasseler Musiktage*, one of Europe's oldest festivals of classical music. Most of the **concerts**, then as throughout the year, are held in the *Stadthalle*, Friedrich-Ebert-Str. 152; the other big cultural venue, for **opera** and **drama**, is the *Staatstheater* on Steinweg.

River cruises are run by two different companies, which have quayside offices either side of the Fuldabrücke: *Personnenschiffahrt Rehbein* (☎0561/18505 or 407710) and *Personnenschiffahrt Söllner* (☎0561/774670). There are several competing **Mitfahrzentralen**, including *Mitfahrladen*, Frankfurter Str. 285 (☎0561/42085), *Mitfahrzentrale des Westens*, Friedrich-Ebert-Str. 107 (☎0561/773305 or 774797), and *Sun Drive*, Frankfurter Str. 197 (☎0561/24031).

Around Kassel

Kassel's position as a transport hub makes it a good base for excursions into the nearby countryside. Besides the destinations listed below, the places in the Fulda-Werra basin are all possible targets for day trips.

Schloss Wilhelmsthal

Just 10km from Kassel, close to the village of CALDEN, is **Schloss Wilhelmsthal** (March–Oct Tues–Sun 10am–5pm, Nov–Feb Tues–Sun 10am–4pm; DM2), the summer residence of the Landgraves, and later of King Jérôme. It was designed by François Cuvilliés, the great Rococo architect of Munich, and modelled closely on his earlier Amalienburg. However, he was not involved in the actual building, which was entrusted to Simon-Louis du Ry, whose first major commission it was, and who added the two side pavilions to the original plan.

The most notable feature of the sumptuously decorated interior is the *Schönheitsgalerie*, a gallery of court beauties painted by Johann Heinrich Tischbein the Elder, the Kassel-based member of the painting dynasty. There's also a fine English-style park, replete with fountains, which could provide an hour's pleasant wandering.

Bad Karlshafen

BAD KARLSHAFEN, which can be reached by frequent buses from Kassel, is a Baroque town straddling the River Weser at the very northern tip of Hessen. Now a *Kurort* and a popular tourist destination, it was founded in 1699 by Landgrave Carl, who planned to build a canal from here to Kassel which would enable Hessian merchant ships to avoid the customs toll imposed at nearby Hann. Münden, which, inconveniently for him, belonged to the neighbouring state of Hannover. Although his grandiose scheme never came to fruition, the town retains a unique ambience which it owes in part to the role originally intended for it – the harbour basin, surrounded by delicately coloured gabled Baroque houses, is particularly atmospheric. Carl encouraged many of the Huguenot refugees to come and run the new harbour town, and Paul du Ry, grandfather of Simon-Louis, was responsible for drawing up the original plans. The role of the Huguenots in the development of the town is recorded in the **Hugenotten-Museum** (Tues–Sat 2–6pm, Sun 11am–1pm & 2–6pm; DM1), Hafenplatz 9a.

The **tourist office** is in the *Kurverwaltung* at Hafenplatz 8 (☎05672/1022) and there's a **youth hostel** at Winnefelderstr. 7 (☎05672/3380). There are plenty of cheap **hotels**, charging DM30 per person or less, the best bets being *Freise*, Mündener Str. 46 (☎05672/2551), and *Haus Weserblick*, Unter den Eichen 4 (☎05672/890). Others in and around the centre aren't difficult to find.

Fritzlar

Some 30km southwest of Kassel, and best reached by train, lies **FRITZLAR**, one of Hessen's finest small towns. As you walk from the Bahnhof towards the centre, you come to the banks of the gently flowing River Eder, from where there's a great view of the skyline in all its medieval aspect, the half-timbered houses nestling behind a largely intact **Stadtmauer** pierced by fourteen towers. The **Dom** occupies the site of a tree sacred to pagan tribes, which was felled by Saint Boniface during a missionary visit to the area in 724. From the eleventh-century successor to the church he founded, there remain the three spacious crypts, one of which contains the shrine of Saint Wigbert, Fritzlar's first abbot.

Most of the remainder of the Dom dates from the thirteenth and fourteenth centuries, and is a mixture of Romanesque and Gothic. The **Schatzkammer** (Mon–Sat 10am–noon & 2–4/5pm) in the cloisters contains valuable treasury items, notably the jewelled cross which belonged to Emperor Heinrich III. North of the Dom is the cobblestoned **Marktplatz**, lined with tall gabled buildings and with a statue of Roland as centrepiece. The **tourist office** (Mon–Thurs 10am–1pm & 2–4.30pm, Fri 10–11.30am) is housed in the Rathaus.

travel details

Trains

From Frankfurt to Wiesbaden (2 an hour; 30min); Darmstadt (3 an hour; 15min); Kassel (2 an hour; 2hr); Marburg (2 an hour; 1hr); Fulda (2 an hour; 1hr); Bremen (1; 4hr 20min); Cologne (1; 2hr 20min); Koblenz (1; 1hr 40min); Trier (1; 2hr 45min); Hannover (1; 3hr 15min); Giessen (1; 40min).

From Wiesbaden to Rudesheim (1 an hour; 35min).

From Kassel to Marburg (1 an hour; 1hr); Fulda (1; 40min); Freiburg (1; 1hr 35min).

CHAPTER FOUR

RHINELAND-PALATINATE AND SAARLAND

O f all the German Länder, the **Rhineland-Palatinate** (*Rheinland-Pfalz*) is the one most overlaid by legend. The **River Rhine** is seen here at its majestic best, and there's hardly a town, castle or rock along this stretch which hasn't made a distinctive contribution to its mythology. According to this myth, this is the land of the national epic, the *Nibelungenlied*, an extraordinary tale of heroism, chicanery, dynastic rivalry, vengeance and obsession, which bites deep into the German soul. It's also the land of the deceptively alluring Lorelei, of the robber barons who presided over tiny fiefs from lofty fortresses, and of the merchant traders who used the natural advantages of the river to bring the country to the forefront of European prosperity.

Nowadays, the Rhine's once treacherous waters have been tamed, enabling pleasure cruisers to run its length, past a wonderful landscape of rocks, vines, white-painted towns and ruined castles. Everything conforms perfectly to the image of Germany promoted by the tourist office; visitors swarm in, and people living on the trade do very nicely. Although the Rhine gorge is the bit most people want to write home about, the rest of the Land does rather well in the picture-postcard stakes too. The **Mosel valley**, running all the way from France to its confluence with the Rhine at **Koblenz**, scores highly for scenic beauty and has the advantage that it's not quite as over-subscribed and spoilt. Further north, the valley of the **River Ahr**, which flows into the Rhine near **Remagen** (of *The Bridge at . . .* fame), manages to rival both of the larger rivers in terms of good looks and touristic allure. Only in the **Hunsrück** and the **Eifel**, the Rhineland-Palatinate's "mountain" ranges, do the otherwise ever-present vines give way to bare heathland and forest, creating landscapes that are at times almost desolate.

Industry exists only in isolated pockets, and **Mainz**, the state's capital and chief city, only just ranks among the forty largest in Germany. Its monuments, though, together with those of the two other Imperial cathedral cities of **Worms** (the font of Germany's once-rich Jewish culture) and **Speyer**, do their bit for the historic side of things, the wealth of their architectural heritage equalling the natural beauty of the surrounding countryside. However, the number one city from the point of view of sights is **Trier**, which preserves the finest buildings of Classical antiquity this side of the Alps.

Trier's Roman survivals are a potent reminder of the area's illustrious **history**. The Rhine itself marked the effective limit of Roman power, and from that period onward the settlements along its western bank dominated national development. Throughout the duration of the Holy Roman Empire, the importance of this area within Germany can be gauged by the fact that two of the seven Electors were the Archbishops of Mainz and Trier, while another was the *Pfalzgraf*, or Count Palatine of the Rhine. (The last-named actually lived in what is now Baden-Württemberg, but his territories have provided the present-day Land with its name.) Like the Romans, the French have often regarded the Rhine as the natural limit of their power, and their designs on the region – ranging from the destructive War of the Palatinate Succession launched in 1689, via

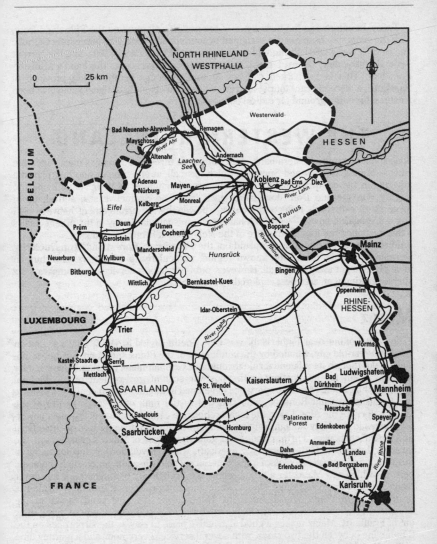

the Napoleonic grand design, to the ham-fisted attempts to foster an independent state there after World War I – have had a profound impact on European history.

As far as **getting around** is concerned, it's one part of Germany where having your own transport is a definite benefit. Otherwise, buses tend to have the edge over trains for seeing the best of the scenery. Despite their associations with over-organised tour groups, the pleasure steamers which glide down the great rivers throughout the summer are certainly worth sampling. **Accommodation**, whether in hotels, youth hostels or campsites, is plentiful, but is best reserved in advance during the high season in the most popular areas.

Today, in contrast to the turbulence of the past, it's all quiet on the Rhineland front, with the economic base heavily sustained by tourism and wine. Predominantly Catholic and rural, it was a CDU stronghold until the shock SPD victory in 1991, and the current Federal Chancellor, **Helmut Kohl**, first came to prominence as the Land's Minister-President. This is in marked contrast to the miniature neighbouring province of **Saarland**, a place of scant tourist interest, whose heavily industrialised valley has been a natural breeding ground for radical political leaders.

THE WESTERN RHINELAND

Spaced out along the western bank of the Rhine are three of Germany's most venerable cities – **Mainz, Worms** and **Speyer** – which have all, at one time or another, played a key role in the country's history, the most potent reminder of their status being the mighty Romanesque Dom dominating each city. The distinctive size and shape of these three cathedrals reflects the curious power-sharing arrangement between civil and ecclesiastical power – with each having an unusually large say in the other's affairs – that sustained the fragile structure of the Holy Roman Empire for so long.

Further west lie the wooded uplands of the **Palatinate Forest** and **Hunsrück**. By German standards, it's a little known region, particularly to foreigners, and thus an ideal place to get away from it all. However, public transport services are comparatively sparse, making it an area best explored by car or bike.

Mainz

"The capital of our dear Fatherland" was how Goethe styled **MAINZ**. That's a position this 2000-year-old city, situated by the confluence of the Rhine and Main, has never officially held, though its influential role throughout German history certainly gave it a far stronger claim for nomination as the postwar seat of government of the Federal Republic than Bonn. Mainz's importance developed in the mid-eighth century, thanks to the Englishman Saint Boniface, who raised it to the rank of the main centre of the Church north of the Alps. Later, the local archbishop came to be one of the most powerful princes in the Holy Roman Empire, holding Electoral status and having the official title of Archchancellor. Further kudos was gained courtesy of Mainz's greatest son, the inventor **Johannes Gutenberg** (see overleaf), whose revolutionary developments in the art of printing made a colossal impact on European civilisation. Since the Napoleonic period – which saw Mainz for a time become the French city of *Mayence* – it has never managed to recover its former status, while its strategic location inevitably made it a prime target of World War II bombers. Nonetheless, it's now Land capital of the Rhineland-Palatinate and is an agreeable mixture of old and new. If you're flying in or out of Frankfurt, Mainz makes a good alternative place to stay as the airport lies on the S-Bahn line between the two cities, with several services every hour and a journey time of less than thirty minutes.

> The telephone code for Mainz is ☎06131

The Dom

Rearing high above all the other buildings in the centre of Mainz are the six towers of the massive red sandstone **Dom** (or **Kaiserdom**), which still ranks as one of the most important Roman Catholic cathedrals in the country. A few years ago it celebrated its

1000th anniversary, even though little remains from this epoch other than the ground-plan, some of the lower masonry and the bronze doors by the normal north entrance; most of what can be seen today is twelfth-century Romanesque.

One of the Dom's most singular features – which is a deliberate ploy to emphasise its mass – is that it's completely surrounded by buildings, stuck right up against its walls. The present picturesque group of houses dates from the eighteenth century, but the **St-Gothard-Kapelle**, two storeys high and of a contrasting grey stone, is from the first half of the twelfth century. Once the archbishops' own chapel, it's now the area set aside for private prayer and is entered from the north transept. The Dom's status as an Imperial cathedral, with a special area required for the Emperor as well as the clergy, can be noticed at once in the **choirs** at both ends of the building, each flanked by one large and two small towers. What's perhaps less immediately obvious, but a further emphasis of its historical importance, is that it follows the precedent of St Peter's in Rome in being orientated from east to west, the reverse of normal.

Inside the Dom

The solemn and spacious **interior** for the most part preserves its architectural purity. Above the nave's arcades is a cycle of murals of the life of Christ. Painted in the gentle Nazarene style – which aimed at recapturing the freshness and faith of medieval paint-

ing – they're a far more successful adornment than most such well-meaning nineteenth-century attempts at "improving" old churches. However, the interior is remarkable above all for serving as a very superior cemetery for the archbishops. These men were no shrinking violets, commissioning grandiose monuments to themselves which adorn the piers of the nave, forming an unrivalled panorama of sculpture from the thirteenth to nineteenth century. Not only is this a must for necrophiles; many of the **tombs** are artistically first-rate.

Among the finest is the poignant late fifteenth-century *Monument to Adalbert von Sachsen*, third from the end on the north side; its youthful subject died before his consecration and is thus not shown in ecclesiastical robes. The same sculptor made the touching *Holy Sepulchre* in the Magnuskapelle. From early the following century are the most grandiose of all the tombs, carved by a local man, **Hans Backoffen**, one of the outstanding crop of German sculptors who bridged the late Gothic and early Renaissance. His masterpiece is the *Monument to Uriel von Gemmingen*, on the last but one pillar of the north side of the nave; two others by him are directly opposite.

The Diözesan Museum

The **Diözesan Museum** (Mon–Wed & Fri 9am–noon & 2–5pm, Thurs & Sat 9am–noon; free), laid out in rooms opening off the cloisters, houses the best sculptures of all. These are fragments from the demolished rood screen, created around 1240 by the anonymous mason – one of the supreme artistic geniuses of the Middle Ages – known as the **Master of Naumburg** from his later work in the eastern German cathedral of that name. In his carvings here, such as the scenes of the Elect and the Damned, and above all in the *Head with Bandeau*, note his beautiful sense of modelling, and the uncanny realism and characterisation which are far in advance of any other sculpture of the time.

Around the city centre

The spacious **Markt** is the scene of markets on Tuesday, Friday and Saturday mornings. Here also is the riotously colourful **Marktbrunnen**, the finest of Mainz's many fountains, a joyful Renaissance concoction adorned with putti and topped by a statue of the Virgin and Child.

Dominating the adjoining Liebfrauenplatz is the resplendent pink Renaissance facade of the **Haus zum Romischen Kaiser**, which houses the offices of the **Gutenberg Museum** (Tues–Sat 10am–6pm, Sun 10am–1pm; free); the actual displays are in a modern extension behind. It's a fitting tribute to a great inventor, making amends for the abysmal treatment he received at the hands of the authorities of his own day.

JOHANNES GUTENBERG (c.1400–68)

An illegitimate son of a canon of Mainz, Gutenberg dreamed of being able to reproduce manuscripts to the same standard of beauty and quality as that achieved by copyists, but without the painstaking physical labour that was involved. Although it's a myth that he invented printing as such – the Chinese had been able to do it for centuries – it was only through his pioneering development of moveable type that the mass-scale production of books became possible. His inventions were of tremendous significance, and were to survive without appreciable technological advancement right up to the present century. However, they led to Gutenberg's personal ruin – his short-sighted creditors, interested only in making a quick profit, wrested his inventions from him by means of a lawsuit. Totally destitute, he thereafter had to rely on charitable handouts to continue his researches.

Until 1978, Mainz had only the second volume of Gutenberg's most famous work, the **42-line Bible**. Made in the 1450s, it's a gravely beautiful production employing magisterial Gothic lettering. The city then managed to repatriate from America the last of the 40-odd surviving complete versions still in private hands, and this has pride of place in the strong room on the second floor. The basement contains a mock-up of Gutenberg's workshop and printing machines of later dates.

Despite war damage, the centre of Mainz, especially around the Dom, contains many fine old streets and squares lined with examples of vernacular building ranging from half-timbered Gothic to Rococo. North of the Dom, the magnificent **Knebelscher Hof** is reminiscent of the Weser Renaissance style of northern Germany, while Kirschgarten and Augustinerstrasse to the south are particularly well preserved. Just off the end of the latter is the sumptuous church of **St Ignaz**, marking the transition from Rococo to Neoclassicism. Outside, a monumental *Crucifixion* group by Hans Backoffen stands over the sculptor's own tomb, which is even more imposing than those he had made for the archbishops. This marks the end of the historic quarter – beyond is a particularly sleazy red light district, the largest vice centre in the Frankfurt conurbation.

Across Schöfferstrasse from the Dom is Gutenbergplatz, with the municipal theatre and a statue to the inventor by the Danish Neoclassical sculptor, Bertel Thorwaldsen; further down the street is the whitewashed Renaissance frontage of the **Domus Universitatis**. Continuing down Ludwigstrasse, you shortly come to Schillerplatz and Schillerstrasse, which are lined with impressive Renaissance and Baroque palaces, now used as offices. Here too you'll find the elaborate modern **Fastnachtsbrunnen**, honouring the annual Carnival festivities, whose celebration here ranks for spectacle second only to Cologne's.

Up the hill by Gaustrasse is the fourteenth-century Gothic church of **St Stephan** (daily 10am–noon & 2–5pm). Although a pleasant enough building with a pretty cloister, it's now chiefly remarkable for possessing what must rank as the most impressive of all the many postwar embellishments found in German churches. In 1976, the parish priest persuaded **Marc Chagall**, the great Russian Jewish artist long resident in France, to make a series of stained glass windows. The theme chosen was reconciliation, symbolising that between France and Germany, Christian and Jew. There are nine windows in all, luminously brilliant in their colouring and quite astonishingly vibrant for an artist in his nineties; they were finished in November 1984, just a few months before Chagall's death.

Along the Rhine

Most of Mainz's remaining monuments of interest are situated in close proximity to the Rhine. The quayside is dominated by the stark black and white lines of the 1970s **Rathaus**, designed by Arne Jacobsen and another impressive modern addition to the city's heritage. Across the road is the so-called **Eiserne Turm** (Iron Tower), once part of the medieval fortifications, now a commercial art gallery; the other surviving city gate, the **Holzturm** (Wooden Tower), is south down Rheinstrasse. Continuing northwards up the same street, you come to the Baroque **Zeughaus** and **Deutschhaus**; behind is the gabled Renaissance facade of the old arsenal, the **Sautanz**. Near here, a copy of the **Jupitersäule** – whose original is in the Landesmuseum (see below) – has been set up.

Further on is the **Schloss**, the enormous former palace of the Archbishop-Electors, a superbly swaggering late Renaissance building with a Baroque extension. The once-famous interiors were completely destroyed in the war; in their place is the **Römisch-Germanisches Museum** (Tues–Sun 10am–6pm; free), a rather confusing collection in which copies of famous antiquities mingle with original pieces.

Far more worthwhile is the **Landesmuseum** (Tues–Sun 10am–5pm; free), occupying the old Imperial stables directly down Grosse Bleiche. The outstanding **archaeol-**

ogy department includes a hall full of Roman sculptural remains, dominated by the original Jupitersäule, the most important Roman triumphal column in Germany. Also here
are fragments from demolished medieval buildings, especially the fourteenth-century
Kaufhaus, one of only two German secular facades of the era to have survived. The
most important paintings are at the very end of the ground-floor gallery. They include a
series of nine canvases of the *Life of the Virgin* from the studio of the mysterious, highly
original fifteenth-century Middle Rhenish draughtsman known as **Master of the
Housebook**; the two Nativity scenes are by the Master himself. Also of note are copies
of Dürer's celebrated *Adam* and *Eve* by his pupil **Baldung**, *St Jerome* by **Cranach**, and
an altar wing by the **Master of St Bartholomew**, whose companion is in London's
National Gallery. Upstairs are seventeenth-century Dutch cabinet pictures, and a
modern section whose main pull, an array of colourful drawings by Chagall, is unfortunately only occasionally on view. There's also a glittering collection of Jugendstil glass.

Eating and drinking

Mainz is unashamedly a wine rather than a beer city, boasting more vineyards within
its boundaries than any other German city. If you fancy a wine crawl, you don't need to
stray far from the vicinity of the Dom: there's an abundance of traditional Weinstuben,
most of them serving meals, on Liebfrauenplatz, Grebenstrasse, Augustinerstrasse,
Kartäuserstrasse and Jakobsbergstrasse.

Alt-Deutsche-Weinstube, Liebfrauenplatz 7. The oldest Weinstube in Mainz, popular with locals of
varying ages. Serves cheap daily dishes, but open evenings only.

Brauhaus zur Sonne, Stadthausstrasse. A traditional beer hall, something of a rarity in this wine-
wedded city.

Café Korfmann, Am Markt 11-13. Elegant café in a decorative Rococo mansion; also a good choice
for breakfast or lunch.

Calvados, Steingasse. Recommendable crêperie serving both sweet and savoury varieties.

Doctor Flotte, Kirschgarten 1. Exotic cocktails are the speciality, though hot and cold meals are
also available.

Haus des deutschen Weines, Gutenbergplatz 3. High quality if pricey restaurant, serving a huge
range of wines from all over Germany.

Kartäuser Hof, Kartäuserstr. 14. Mainz's oldest inn, dating back to the twelfth century, serving
German and international dishes.

Klosterschänke, Kartäuserstr. 3. Housed in a former brewery, so it's appropriate that it has the best
beer garden in the city.

Löschs Weinstube, Jakobsbergstr. 9. Tiny Weinstube offering bargain menus, open evenings only.

Weinhaus Schreiner, Rheinstr. 38. Best of the Weinstuben for top-notch food at reasonable prices.

Zum Salvator, Grosse Langgasse 4. Excellent brewery-owned restaurant.

Practicalities and entertainments

The **Hauptbahnhof** is situated northwest of the city centre. A short way down
Bahnhofstrasse is the **tourist office** (Mon–Fri 9am–6pm, Sat 9am–1pm; ☎233741).
Many of the least expensive **hotels** are close by, though they hardly charge bargain
basement rates. At Bahnhofstr. 15 is *Pfeil-Continental* (☎232179) with singles at DM48,
doubles DM90, while *Terminus*, Alicestr 4 (☎229 8760), has singles at DM45, doubles
DM70. Cheaper and with a better location very near the Dom are *Stadt Coblenz*, at
Rheinstr. 49 (☎227602), and *Zum Schildknecht*, at Heliggrabgasse 6 (☎225755); expect
to pay around DM40 for a single, DM76 a double. For markedly lower prices, you'll have
to stay some distance out. The suburb of GONSENHEIM (reached by trams #10 and
#11, buses #22 and #23) is the likeliest, with two hotels in the range of DM30 for a single,
DM50 for a double – *Roseneck*, at An der Bruchspitze 3 (☎680368), and *Zarewitsch*, at

Kurt-Schumacher-Str. 20 (☎42404). Alternatively, there's the **youth hostel** (☎85332), situated in the wooded heights of Am Fort Weisenau; catch bus #1 or #22. Mainz's **campsite**, *Camping Maaraue* (☎06134/4383), is a short ride to the Brückenkopf-Kastel stop on bus #13 from the Hauptbahnhof.

By far the hottest **nightspot** at the time of writing is *Terminus* on Rheinallee, a sparsely decorated former warehouse which attracts punters from miles around. Main **theatre** venue is the *Stadttheater* on Gutenbergplatz; "alternative" fare is offered at the *Forum Theater Unterhaus* on Münsterstrasse. On the **classical music** front, it's worth looking out for concerts by the *Mainzer Kammerorchester*, who are especially renowned for their performances of Mozart.

Other than Carnival (here known as *Fastnacht* and using a far more intelligible dialect than in Cologne), the principal **popular festivals** are: the *Johannisnacht* in mid-June, which includes fishermen's jousts and firework displays; the *Weinmarkt* jamboree on the last weekend in August and the first in September; and the *Nikolausfest* on the first Saturday in December, featuring a procession of children.

The stretch of the Rhine between Mainz and Koblenz is touristically the most popular. **Steamers** depart from in front of the Rathaus (March–Oct only); also here are the *K-D Linie* offices (☎24511). **Mitfahrzentrale** is at Bonifatiusplatz 6 (☎612828).

Rhine-Hessen

The hinterland of Mainz is an area called **Rhine-Hessen** (*Rhein-Hessen*), chiefly famous as a major wine producing area. Look out for the *Trullos*, small conical white shelters for vineyard workers in among the vines. These are of a type only normally found in Apulia in Italy, and are said to have been built by Italian immigrants 150 years ago.

By far the most attractive town is **OPPENHEIM** which is full of half-timbered houses set in narrow little streets. Most vaunted local feature is the **Katharinenkirche**, one of the most significant Gothic churches between here and Strasbourg. Inside, look out for the *Oppenheimer Rose*, a fourteenth-century stained glass window. The other local church is the **Bartholomäuskirche**, which, despite a dubious-looking exterior, has a spacious Gothic interior and a truly bizarre altar. The only other attraction worth mentioning is the **Deutsches Weinbaumuseum**, Wormser Str. 49 (Tues–Sun 1–5pm; DM1), which has a wide range of exhibits related to vine growing and wine production.

Worms

Here is one of the most memorable places in the West, here was the holy temple of the Romans, the royal fortress of the Niebelung, the palace of Charlemagne, the court of the Prince-bishop of Worms.

Inscription on the Dom in Worms.

A rich web of fact and myth has been spun around **WORMS**, which lies on the left bank of the Rhine some 40km south of Mainz. Originally settled by Celtic tribes and then by the Romans, the city became the heart of the short-lived fifth-century Burgundian kingdom described in the *Nibelungenlied* (see overleaf). It was a favoured royal seat of various subsequent royal dynasties, the scene of the weddings of both Charlemagne and Frederick Barbarossa and of the Concordat of 1122 which settled the power struggle between the papacy and the empire. In the Middle Ages Worms achieved great prosperity and was for a while a venue for sittings of the Imperial Parliament or **Diet**, most famously that of 1521 at which Luther was declared an outlaw. Unfortunately, much of its magnificence was destroyed in successive wars against the French, but several outstanding monuments remain in the midst of the functional modern city centre which has grown up since World War II. As Worms was formerly nicknamed "Little

---

THE NIBELUNGENLIED – GERMANY'S NATIONAL EPIC

Written at the end of the twelfth century, the *Nibelungenlied* describes the fall and virtual genocide of the Burgundian nation at the hands of King Etzel (Attila) the Hun. This was the culmination of the long vengeance planned by Etzel's wife, the Burgundian princess Kriemhild, in retribution for the murder of her first husband Siegfried, the famed dragon-slayer. The saga is actually a brilliant fusion, with a great deal of imaginative embroidering, of two quite separate episodes in Worms' colourful early history. The Burgundians, originally allies of the declining Roman Empire, settled in Worms in 413, but were driven out by Attila in 436 shortly after they had established their independence from Rome. At the turn of the seventh century, Worms was the residence of the Visigoth princess Brunichildis (the inspiration for Kriemhild's rival Brunnhild), one of two sisters who married kings of different parts of the Merovingian Empire; a subsequent quarrel led to a fratricidal war which claimed the lives of all four leading participants.

Jerusalem", being home to a large and influential **Jewish community**, it's appropriate that it preserves the most important reminders to be found in Germany of this once-rich heritage. These vividly bring to life the reality of the Holocaust and the destruction it caused in human and cultural terms.

The Dom

Foremost among the survivors of Worms' bygone days of glory are the seven city centre churches, not one of them built later than 1744. Best of the bunch is the **Dom** (or **Kaiserdom**), a huge twelfth-century building which dominates the skyline even from a distance. From outside, it's highly distinctive in appearance, with its two domed choirs and four corner towers; it also displays great unity, with only a few Gothic additions having been made to the original late Romanesque structure.

The **east choir**, the first part to be built, was the prototype for what was to become a distinctive trick of the local school of architecture – although the exterior walls are straight, they are rounded inside. Peering out from the arcades are statues of lions devouring their prey, their terrifying looks apparently intended to frighten off the devil; look out also for the enigmatic figure of a workman (thought to be a self-portrait of the architect) with a monkey on his shoulder. Even more decorative is the **west choir**, the culmination of the building programme half a century later; with its rose windows, zigzag arcades and rich mouldings it ranks among the most imposing examples of all Romanesque architecture.

On the north side of the nave is the **Kaiserportal**, according to the *Nibelungenlied* the site where Kriemhild and her sister-in-law Brunnhild had words with each other about just who had the right to enter the building first; this petty quarrel led to the murder of Siegfried and the eventual collapse of the Burgundian nation. These days, however, it's the richly decorated Gothic **Südportal** – a veritable Bible in stone – which is the main entrance. Most unusually, the sculptures from its Romanesque predecessor weren't wasted, being placed on the wall immediately indoors.

As you enter the Dom, the sight of Balthasar Neumann's huge Baroque **high altar** provokes a gasp. It's a real Technicolor extravaganza in gilded wood and marble, featuring awe-inspired statues of Saints Peter and Paul with two angels pointing at the Madonna and Child, who seem to be coming straight towards you. There's an austere stained glass window backdrop which, in its simplicity, offsets the altar effectively. Otherwise the Dom is relatively spartan, no more so than in the dark and eerie **crypt**, the last resting place of five generations of the Salian dynasty, whose eight plain sarcophagi sit in oppressive silence. In the south transept a **model** showing the centre of Worms before its destruction by the French is worth a look.

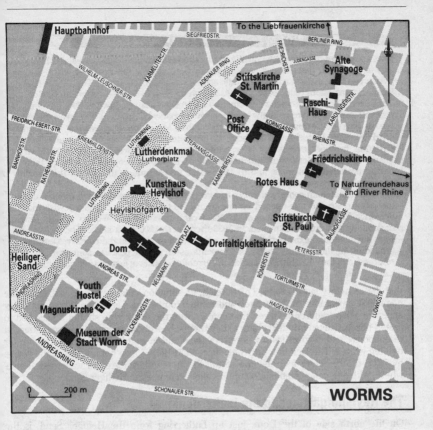

WORMS

South of the Dom

From the Dom, Dechaneigasse leads south to the **Magnuskirche**, the first church in this part of Germany to go over to Protestantism. It dates back to Carolingian times but has been extended and altered so much you could be forgiven for not realising it. Across the square stands the former **Andreasstift**, now housing the **Museum der Stadt Worms** (Tues–Sun 10am–noon & 2–5pm). The Romanesque church forms an appropriate setting for a collection of medieval sacred art; the monastic buildings contain Roman and Frankish antiquities plus the Lutherzimmer, which details the events of the 1521 Diet and includes some of Luther's original writings. Just behind the Andreasstift is a surviving section of the **Stadtmauer**, with the still-intact **Andreastor**.

The Jewish cemetery

A modern ring road parallels the course of the wall. At its extreme southwest corner is the **Heiliger Sand**, the oldest Jewish cemetery in Europe and the most poignant reminder, in its leafy tranquillity, of the influential Jewish community of Worms (see below). The **tombstones**, which have many beautiful inscriptions and carvings, date back as far as 1076. For reasons which have never been explained, they do not have the customary orientation to Jerusalem, the sole exception being that of the martyr Rabbi Meir von Rothenburg at the lowest point of the grounds. Although it's nothing less than a miracle

WORMS AS "LITTLE JERUSALEM"

Jews are known to have settled in Worms by the year 1000, and quickly established what was to be one of their largest settlements in Germany for the next 940 years. A synagogue was built in 1034 and a Talmudic school was also established. The latter's leading luminary was Rabbi Salomo ben Isaak, known as **Raschi**, whose commentaries on the Torah and Talmud are works still cited by Hebrew scholars today. In 1096, the community suffered the first of its many mishaps when fanatical Crusaders destroyed the entire Jewish quarter. Germany's most respected rabbi, **Meir von Rothenburg**, was imprisoned by King Rudolf von Habsburg in order to stifle the zeal for re-settlement in Palestine; he died seven years later, without regaining his freedom. During the Great Plague of 1390 the Jews were attacked by their fellow townspeople who accused them of having poisoned local wells; and in 1615 social unrest among the rest of the populace once again meant persecution.

By the nineteenth century, matters had greatly improved. The ghetto to which the Jews had been restricted was opened up and from 1849 to 1852 Worms had a Jewish mayor, Friedrich Eberstadt. It wasn't until the Nazis came to power that Worms' ancient Jewish community was finally destroyed. In 1933 there were 1100 Jews in the city; by 1945 the Jews had ceased to exist here – all were either dead or had fled the country. Despite the rebuilding of the leading Jewish monuments as an act of postwar contrition, nobody returned, and the city's Jewish population currently consists of just two newcomers.

that the cemetery survived the Third Reich, its situation outside the old walls, and the neglected appearance of the twisted and sunken tombstones, are not as sinister as they appear. Jewish tradition believed that contact with the dead, who should be allowed to rest in peace, caused impurity; hence they themselves chose to locate their cemetery at the opposite end of town from where they lived and to eschew the Gentile fashion for tending graves. The lack of tombstones later than 1940 is also not a result of the Nazis: by 1911, the cemetery had become so full that a new burial ground was created elsewhere, with only long-established families allowed to use the Heiliger Sand.

The Heylshofgarten and the Lutherdenkmal

On the north side of the Dom, just up Lutherring from the Heiliger Sand, is the **Heylshofgarten**, occupying the site of the now-vanished Imperial palace. In April 1521 this was the scene of the *Lutherreichstag*, a convocation of the Imperial Diet hastily set up by the newly-elected Emperor Charles V in response to an anti-reformist bull from the Vatican. At the hearing, Luther refused to renounce his views; he was forced to go into exile and the Reformation was set in motion. Within the park is the **Kunsthaus Heylshof** (May–Sept Tues–Sun 10am–noon & 2–5pm; Oct–April Tues–Sat 2–4pm, Sun 10am–noon & 2–4pm; DM2), a foundation established by the leading family in nineteenth-century Worms' return to prosperity as a leather metropolis. Their exquisite collection of fine and applied arts includes a colourful array of medieval stained glass; a tender *Madonna and Child* by Rubens, along with several modellos by the same artist; a large number of seventeenth-century Dutch cabinet pictures; and a statue of *Adam* by the sixteenth-century Worms sculptor Conrad Meit, one of the few German artists to adopt the full-blooded Italian Renaissance style.

The Lutherdenkmal

Across the Lutherring directly opposite is the **Lutherdenkmal**, a nineteenth-century monument which is the largest ever erected in honour of the Reformation. The memorial, a group of no-nonsense bronze figures with Luther at the centre, shows the great man making his terse declaration before the Diet: "Here I stand. I cannot do otherwise. God help me. Amen." Flanking him are Elector Frederick the Wise of Saxony and

Landgrave Philipp of Hessen, the two powerful princes whose support made the Reformation a practical reality; behind stand the two great scholars, Johannes Reuchlin and Philipp Melanchton. The remaining male figures are the main precursors of Protestantism – Petrus Waldus, John Wycliffe, Jan Hus and Girolamo Savonarola; the seated women represent the first German cities to adopt the new faith.

The eastern quarters

On the other side of the Dom on Neumarkt is the **Adlerapotheke**, a Baroque town house and chemist's shop which is one of the few surviving examples of the Baroque architecture which mushroomed in Worms following its destruction in the Wars of the Palatinate Succession. Also from this period is the nearby **Dreifaltigkeitskirche**, but, although it preserves its handsome frontage, the interior was modernised following a burn-out in World War II. Following Kammerer Strasse northwards, you come to the Romanesque **Stiftskirche St Martin**, whose whitewashed walls and angular tower give it a decidedly singular appearance. Saint Martin was supposedly once imprisoned in a dungeon underneath this church.

The Old Jewish Quarter

Just east of here, centred on Judengasse, is the old Jewish quarter. The **Alte Synagoge** (daily 10am–noon & 2–4/5; free) was reduced to ruins on *Kristallnacht* and further damaged by World War II bombing, but was rebuilt using the old stones and re-dedicated in 1961; it's occasionally used for worship, mostly by the American army's Jewish personnel. The main part of the synagogue, in a late Romanesque style, was built in 1174–5, probably by the same masons as were then working on the Dom, and was for the use of men only. An extension for the use of women, featuring the new pointed arch, was added in 1212, at right-angles to the existing structure. Adjoining the synagogue is the Talmudic teaching room known as the **Raschi-Kapelle**, while in the precincts is the underground **Tauchbad** or ritual bath house (both same times; free). In the **Raschi-Haus**, a former school, meeting-house and dance hall, is the **Judaica Museum** (Tues–Sun 10am–noon & 2–5pm; DM1), with an extensive collection detailing the history of the Jews of Worms.

South to the Stiftskirche St Paul

Further along Judengasse is another well-preserved section of the city wall, with the **Raschiturm** and the **Friesenspitze**. South of here, Karolingerstrasse leads to the junction of Rheinstrasse and Römerstrasse, on which is the dignified Lutheran Baroque **Friedrichskirche**. Beside it stands the **Rotes Haus**, the only surviving Renaissance town house in Worms; when you see its pink curlicued gables you might suspect that the destruction of the others was no accident. A couple of minutes' walk southwest brings you to the **Stiftskirche St Paul**, a rough sandstone Romanesque church. Although the present nave was rebuilt in the Baroque era, the building as a whole, and in particular the chancel and triple-towered westwork, is self evidently a miniaturised version of the Dom. Other surviving parts of the city walls, including the **Burgerturm**, the **Torturm** and **Lutherpförtchen**, are located just to the east.

Outside the centre

Because the centre lies about a kilometre inland, visitors to Worms often fail to realise that the city is actually on the banks of the Rhine. It's well worth walking along Rheinstrasse to the **Torturm**, a massive gateway which straddles the **Nibelungenbrücke** over the river. This historicist extravaganza was built as recently as 1900, but it's effective enough in its purpose: coming into town by the B46 road gives the impression of entering some mysterious medieval world. Below the gateway is the bronze **Hagenstandbild**, which illustrates the scene from the *Nibelungenlied* when the villainous Hagen hurls into the Rhine the cursed treasure of the Nibelungen just after he has murdered Siegfried.

Which just leaves the Gothic **Liebfrauenkirche** in the northern suburbs of the city, set in the **vineyards** which produce *Liebfraumilch*, a bottle of which is invariably left on the table at the end of all bad parties. The German version of this wine isn't anything like the sickly syrup that finds its way on to British supermarket shelves. On the contrary, it's a quality product which has to pass through a control centre: *Blue Nun* and *Madonna* are the best-known labels. The church itself is of cathedral-like dimensions; with its multi-coloured stonework and fantastical towers, the exterior shows the German penchant for the picturesque in architecture at its most extreme, though the delicate tympanum and clean lines of the interior add a welcome note of restraint.

Practicalities

Worms' **Hauptbahnhof** is northwest of the old city; follow Wilhelm-Laueuscher-Strasse straight ahead and you arrive in a few minutes at the Lutherdenkmal. The **tourist office** is at Neumarkt 14 (Mon–Fri 9am–noon & 2–5pm; April–Oct also Sat 9am–noon; ☎06241/25045). There's a **youth hostel** handily located between the Dom and the Andreasstift at Dechaneigasse 1 (☎06241/25780) and also a *Naturfreundehaus* just to the east of the old city wall at Flosshafenstr. 7 (☎06241/23660). **Camping** facilities are on the eastern bank of the Rhine near the Nibelungenbrücke (☎06241/24355).

There are a fair number of reasonably-priced city centre **hotels**, but beware that these tend to be oversubscribed. Directly across from the Hauptbahnhof at Siegfriedstr. 29 (☎06241/6284) is *City*, which charges upwards of DM35 per person. Similar prices are on offer at *Nordend*, at no. 2 on the same street (☎06241/45840); this is a branch of the larger and slightly cheaper hotel of the same name just to the north at Mainzer Str. 90 (☎06241/43057). Close to the Dom are *Weinhaus Weis*, Färbergasse 19 (☎06241/23500), and *Lortze-Eck*, Schlossergasse 10 (☎06241 24561), whose rates both begin at DM30. More likely to have space than any of these is *Wormser Eck*, well to the south of the centre at Klosterstr. 80 (☎06241/6671).

Eating and drinking

Among recommendable places to **eat** and **drink**, *Rheinischer Hof* on the banks of the Rhine below the Torturm, stands out for its setting and food, whether *Kaffee und Kuchen* or a full sit-down meal. Nearby at Rheinstr. 54 is *Fischereck*, which does reasonably-priced fish and chicken dishes. For a cheapish Italian, try *Etna*, Am Ziegelofen 14; for a high-class version of the same there's *Tivoli*, Adenauer-Ring 4. There are also several lively hangouts on Judengasse, such as the trendy *Café Jux* and the bars *Kutscherschänke* and *Schwarzer Bär*. The city gets busy at the end of August and the beginning of September for the *Backfischfest*, a wine **festival** where fried fish is the culinary speciality.

Ludwigshafen

South of Worms is **LUDWIGSHAFEN**, home town of Federal Chancellor Helmut Kohl. It's a sprawling industrial mass, dominated by the BASF chemical works, and forms a virtual continuation of the ex-capital of the Palatinate, Mannheim (see *Chapter Two*), which lies directly across the Rhine. If you happen to find yourself here, your initial impulse will be to get out of town fast, a reaction you'd do well to heed. Ludwigshafen's only real positive point is the **Wilhelm-Hack-Museum** (Tues & Thurs–Sun 9.30am–5pm, Wed 9.30am–9pm; free), a large art museum at Berliner Str. 23 which has a collection of mainly modern art, including works by Kandinsky, Mondrian and Malevich.

Speyer

SPEYER, the final member of the triumvirate of Imperial cathedral cities, is some 50km up the Rhine from Worms. Lying on a minor branch railway line, it's slightly tricky to reach by public transport: coming from Worms, you usually have to change to a DB bus at Ludwigshafen; there's also a service from Heidelberg via Schwetzingen, though this takes about two hours to cover the 21km. Nonetheless, it's well worth making the effort, as Speyer, which in 1990 celebrated the 2000th anniversary of its foundation as a Roman infantry camp, was one of the few Rhenish towns to come through World War II unscathed. Even though its role was once much grander, it stands today as an archetypal episcopal and market town, lively enough never to seem staid, yet not to the extent of spoiling its atmosphere of restrained dignity.

The Dom

Speyer rocketed to a prominent position in the second quarter of the eleventh century, when the Salian dynasty of emperors chose it, alongside Goslar, as their favourite seat. They ordered the construction of a huge new **Dom** (or **Kaiserdom**) as their burial place. This regal building, in the purest Romanesque style, has dominated Speyer ever since; indeed, when it was finished, it was the largest church in the West. At the turn of the twelfth century it was partially rebuilt, notably with the erection of a new stone vault which was far higher than any ever previously attempted. The **towers** were also added, as were the **dwarf galleries** round the exterior which were to become such an essential feature of Rhineland churches. It's easy enough to distinguish the two building phases, as the smooth ashlar of the embellishments contrasts with the rough-hewn stonework of the original. The Dom was badly damaged by French troops in 1689, when Speyer was almost entirely destroyed; half the nave was left in ruins, but it was later brilliantly restored. Only the **westwork**, a romanticised nineteenth-century replacement for the one destroyed by the French, is a let-down, having taken its inspiration from the decorative late Romanesque style of Worms rather than the austere purity which is the hallmark of the rest of the building.

The interior

The interior has been all but stripped of furnishings, in order to focus attention on its awesome, mathematically calculated proportions. Its great glory is the **crypt**: although the earliest part to be built, it remains the largest in Germany, and is justifiably claimed as the most beautiful in the world. With its alternately coloured sandstone pillars and slabbed marble floor, it has an almost Middle Eastern quality. It's divided into three connected spaces and contains the coffins of four emperors and four kings, among them Rudolf von Habsburg (the first of the dynasty to become German king), who is depicted in a magnificently carved sepulchral slab displayed on the west wall of the burial vault.

The Domgarten

Last century, an English-style park, the **Domgarten**, was laid out around the Dom, meaning that there's an uninterrupted view of the great building from all sides. Particularly fetching is that from the **Heidentürmchen** (Heathens' Tower) to the east, one of the rare surviving sections of the medieval city wall; this formerly overlooked the Rhine, but the river has since been diverted to the east. Occupying the centre of the former cloisters on the south side is the sixteenth-century shrine of *Christ on the Mount of Olives*; however, the sculptures are pastiches of the originals, the sole survivors of which are kept under the northwest tower.

Around the Dom

As has been the case for centuries, Speyer's streets fan out from the Dom. Diagonally across Domplatz, housed in a triple-towered mock palace from the early years of this century, is the **Historisches Museum der Pfalz** (daily 10am–5pm; DM2). It includes objects found in the Dom's imperial graves, but the most celebrated exhibit is the Bronze Age *Golden Hat of Schifferstadt*, found in a nearby town. The same building also houses the **Weinmuseum**, featuring every conceivable wine-related object and what is claimed to be the oldest bottle of wine in the world, dating from 300AD. Unfortunately, all the objects described here are packed away and unlikely to be on view again until 1993, leaving only the section on the history of the city to see in the meantime.

Across Grosse Pfaffengasse, on the northern side of the museum, lies the enclosed heart of the former Jewish quarter, which can be entered from Judengasse. The east wall of the **Synagoge** still stands, but the main surviving monument is the **Judenbad** (*Mikwe* in Hebrew; April–Oct daily 10am–noon & 2–5pm; DM1), a twelfth-century ritual bath-house for women. Seemingly built by the same masons who had recently completed the Dom, it's the oldest and best-preserved example in Germany and a poignant reminder of a vanished culture.

On the northern side of the Dom, are the fourteenth-century **Sonnenbrücke**, Speyer's only remaining old bridge, and the **Wirtshcaft zum Halbmond**, a seventeenth-century half-timbered inn with a strange polygonal oriel window. On the other side of Hasenpfulstrasse is the **Kloster St Magdalena**, a Carmelite convent whose church has a tastefully understated Baroque interior. The Jewish-born philosopher Edith Stein, whom the Nazis gassed at Auschwitz, was a nun here from 1923 to 1931.

The rest of the city

Following Grosse Himmelsgasse from the Dom brings you to the **Dreifaltigkeitskirche**, a Protestant example of the many Baroque buildings built in Speyer after the devastation of 1689. Its interior is fairly extravagant but not without subtlety: the most impressive features are the two-storey wooden gallery with its painted side panels and the fanciful painting on the wooden vaulting which adds to the extrovert character of the church. Alongside the Dreifaltigkeitskirche are the **Retscherhof**, the ruined palace of a noble family, and the **Läutturm**, a tall late Gothic tower. Further west, along Korngasse, is **St Ludwig**, the church of a thirteenth-century Dominican monastery. It contains the only surviving medieval altar front in the Palatinate and the winged late Gothic *Bossweiler Altar*.

Speyer's main street, **Maximilianstrasse**, forms a dead straight processional way right across the heart of the city to the Dom, widening towards the end to form a spacious square. Among the colourful Baroque and Rococo buildings which line it are the **Rathaus** (whose interior can usually be visited during normal working hours) and the **Alte Münze**, the former mint. Closing off the western end of the street is the **Altpörtel** (April–Oct Mon–Fri 10am–noon & 2–4pm, Sat & Sun 10am–5pm; DM1), a craggy thirteenth-century gateway which is the only other surviving part of the city walls. A graceful arcaded gallery was built on top in the early sixteenth century, while the steep hip roof which finishes it off was added a couple of hundred years later. From the top, there's a wonderful view over Speyer and the Palatinate.

Down Gilgenstrasse and across Bartholomäus-Weltz-Platz is the **Gedächtniskirche der Reformation** (or **Retscherkirche**), a heavy neo-Gothic church built at the turn of the century in honour of the 1529 Diet of Speyer, at which supporters of Luther made their formal protest against the Edict of Worms, thus gaining the name "Protestants" for the first time. A large statue of the reformer dominates the porch; the interior blazes with a complete set of stained glass windows. A few minutes' walk east at Allerheiligenstr. 9 is the **Feuerbachhaus** (Mon–Fri 4–6pm, Sun 11am–1pm; donation expected), the birthplace of the Romantic painter Anselm Feuerbach, who is chiefly remembered for his sweeping Italianate canvases of mythological scenes. The house is now a wine bar, but upstairs is an exhibition of his paintings and drawings.

Practicalities

Speyer's **Hauptbahnhof** and **bus station** are about 10 minutes' walk northwest of the centre, but most buses continue down Bahnhofstrasse to drop you opposite the Altpörtel. The **tourist office** is at Maximilianstr. 11 (Mon–Fri 9am–5pm, Sat 10am–noon; ☎06232/14395). **Hotels** with a convenient location include *Zum Deutschen Kaiser*, Allerheiligenstr. 37 (☎06232/75630), with singles DM35, doubles DM55; *Zur Grünen Au*, Grüner Winkel 28 (☎06232/72196), with singles from DM40, doubles from DM60); and *Weisses Tor*, Herdstr. 21a (☎06232/71510), which charges DM40 per person. The **youth hostel** is at Leinpfad (☎06232/75380), on the banks of the Rhine a little south of the centre.

Few small German cities offer such a bewildering variety of places to **eat** and **drink**. Top choices for a full sit-down meal are the atmospheric old cellar-restaurant, *Wirtschaft Zum Alten Engel*, just west of the Altpörtel at Mühlturmstr. 27; the nearby *Pfalzgraf*, Gilgenstr. 26b; and the somewhat more expensive rotisserie, *Weisses Ross*, Johannesstr. 2. *Domhof-Brauerei*, Grosse Himmelgasse 6, is a *Hausbrauerei* serving local speciality dishes, while *Zur Alten Münze*, Korngasse 1a, is the top wine bar. For *Kaffee und Kuchen*, try *Café Schumacher*, Wormser Str. 23 or *Altpörtel-Café* in the shadow of the gateway. Speyer claims to have invented the *Bretzel*, the crispy salted bread which is such a German favourite; it gives its name to the main local **festival**, the *Bretzelfest* on the second weekend of July.

The German Wine Road

The **German Wine Road** (*Deutsche Weinstrasse*), Germany's oldest designated tourist route, runs south for 80km from BOCKENHEIM, a small town 14km west of Worms, to SCHWEIGEN–RECHTENBACH on the French border. In this area there are about 23,000 hectares of vineyards and in some places the climate becomes almost sub-tropical, enabling farmers to grow lemons, figs and tobacco as well as vines. As with most German tourist routes, it's meant for cars (look out for the bunch of grapes sign-posts), though with a little planning you can follow it by train and bus. All the towns mentioned in this section have a plentiful supply of reasonably-priced accommodation in pensions.

The first main stop is **BAD DÜRKHEIM**, which is a little too touristy but which is worth visiting on the second and third Sundays in September when it hosts the **Wurstmarkt** (Sausage Fair), a gargantuan wine festival said to be the largest in the world. An appropriately sized cask is brought out, though it's used to contain not the wine but the people drinking it – up to 450 at a time. There's a **campsite** at *Azur-Knaus*, Am Badesee (☎06322/61356), and a small **youth hostel** at Schillerstr. 151 (☎06322/63151).

Some 15km south at the foot of the Haardt hills (a branch of the Vosges) is the half-timbered town of **NEUSTADT**. At the end of the sixteenth century, the Count Palatine Casimir established a Calvinist university here as a competitor to its Lutheran counter-part in Heidelberg; the original building, the **Casimirianum**, can be seen on Ludwigstrasse. On the central Markt is the handsome Gothic **Liebfrauenkirche**, containing tombs of the Counts Palatine. Neustadt has now swallowed up the village of

HAMBACH just to the south, whose neo-Gothic **Schloss** sprang to fame in 1832 when a group of students, protesting against Germany's continued political fragmentation, raised the black, red and gold tricolour for the first time. There's a **youth hostel** here at Hans-Geiger-Str. 27 (☎06321/2289).

From Hambach buses run to the **Kalmit** (673m) about 4km east, which commands incredible views across the plain as far as Speyer. From here head for **ST MARTIN**, a small village with narrow streets and vine-covered restaurants which makes a good place to break your journey. It's dominated by the ruined **Kropsburg**, a thirteenth-century fortress which suffered the usual fate at the hands of the French in the seventeenth century, but which preserves much of the outer wall plus part of the tower.

A couple of kilometres to the south is **EDENKOBEN**. Signs direct you to **Schloss Villa Ludwigshöhe** (April–Sept 9am–1pm & 2–6pm; Oct–March 9am–1pm & 2–5pm; DM2), a nineteenth-century castle built for King Ludwig I of Bavaria, with some good wall and ceiling frescos. These days it houses a small museum, devoted mainly to the work of the German Impressionist painter Max Slevogt. Nearby is **RHODT**, a typical small wine town full of half-timbered *Winzerhäuser* (winehouses); look out for the arches of vines which grow on frames across some of the streets.

The last main stop is **BAD BERGZABERN**, reached by bus by a detour from the Weinstrasse via LANDAU. It was formerly the seat of the Dukes of Zweibrücken, though their Schloss – Renaissance with Baroque additions – is completely overshadowed by their smaller residence, the **Gasthaus zum Engel**, unquestionably one of the finest Renaissance buildings in the Palatinate. The village has a **youth hostel** at Altenbergweg (☎06343/8383).

The Palatinate Forest

Stretching north from the French border as far as the large industrial town of KAISERSLAUTERN, and bounded to the east by the Weinstrasse and to the west by the border with Saarland, the **Palatinate Forest** (*Pfälzer Wald*) is one of the most compelling and unspoiled parts of the province. A sparsely populated, heavily wooded stretch of countryside, it's dotted with castles and half-forgotten villages, and most of it is designated a *Naturpark*. It's popular with walkers and climbers; if you're in more of a hurry, the best way to get around is by car as local bus services are a little sparse.

Annweiler and around

From Landau it's a twenty-minute train journey to **ANNWEILER** from where there are regular bus services to **Burg Trifels** (April–Sept Wed–Sun 9am–1pm & 2–6pm, Oct, Nov & Jan–March 9am–1pm & 2–6pm; DM2). Imperiously set on a jagged crag, this is a rebuild of a typical Hohenstaufen palace. To get there you have to walk up a steep hill, but it's well worth the trek. The Schloss is one of the most venerable in Germany, dating back to the eleventh century, and was supposedly one of Frederick Barbarossa's favourite haunts. In 1193 Richard the Lionheart was imprisoned here and only released on payment of an enormous ransom. It subsequently served as an Imperial treasury and then gradually fell into ruin after its abandonment in 1635; the rebuild (which is surprisingly effective) was carried out between 1938 and 1966. The chapel houses copies of the Imperial crown jewels, while from the **Kapellenturm** there's a tremendous panoramic view of the surrounding area, including the ruins of **Burg Anebos** and **Burg Scharfenberg** to the south. In Annweiler itself are a **youth hostel** at Turnerweg 60 (☎06346/8438) and several cheap **pensions**, including *Radke*, Am Flotz 17 (☎06346/2114), which has singles from DM22 and doubles from DM40, and *Haus Schönblick*, Zum Hönigsack 30 (☎06346/7001), with singles from DM20 and doubles from DM38.

Erlenbach

From Annweiler carry on to **ERLENBACH**, where the main attraction is **Schloss Berwartstein** (March–Nov Mon–Sat 9am–6pm, Sun 1–5pm, Dec–Feb Sun only 1–5pm; DM3.50), a castle with a chequered past. It started life in 1152 when Frederick Barbarossa gave it to the Bishop of Speyer. By 1314 it had become a hideout for local bandits, who caused so much trouble in the area that the authorities had the Schloss destroyed. It was then rebuilt, only to be burned down in 1591. At the end of the nineteenth century it was again reconstructed; looking like an archetypal fairy-tale castle, it now houses a restaurant. You can still see some of the old rooms which were carved out of the rock on which the castle was built. Just to the north of Erlenbach is the ruined **Burg Drachenfels**, which suffered a similar fate to Schloss Berwartstein, but escaped the ignominy of being turned into a restaurant. It too has rooms hewn out of the rock and similarly constructed stone staircases.

Dahn

Nearby FISCHBACH is notable only for the huge US military facility housed there; it's one of the largest nerve gas centres in Europe, a fact which the locals are understandably none too happy about. Unless you're a spy, avoid Fischbach and head instead for **DAHN** (reached by bus #6840 from Erlenbach), where untold delights await. Above the town are the ruins of three castles within one outer wall, set on top of a long, rocky ridge. The biggest and best preserved is **Altdahn**, which features watch-posts, rooms cut out of the rock face, and some semi-intact towers. Only a few rock chambers and the remains of the walls are left of **Grafendahn**, and practically nothing is left of **Tanstein** apart from a few broken stones. Just outside town are the **Braut und Brautigam** (Bride and Groom), two immensely tall pillars of limestone, one slightly higher than the other. Dahn has a **youth hostel** at Am Wachtfelsen 1 (☎06391/1769), while there are **camping** facilities at Im Büttelwoog (☎06391/5622). Cheapest **pensions** are *Frohnbühl*, Erfweiler Str. 13a (☎06391/1535), from DM18, and *Haus Burgenland*, Am Griesböhl 13 (☎06391/5641), which charges DM22 per person.

The Hunsrück

The **Hunsrück**, which rises up between the Rivers Mosel and Nahe, is one of the three huge volcanic schist massifs (the others are the Eifel and the Vosges) to the west of the Rhine. It's not too well served by the rail network and the bus services are meagre in some places – once again this is a region best explored by car. Most of the Hunsrück is forested and dotted with small villages, with the occasional incongruous small industrial town rearing up out of the woods. In the past it was a big source of precious stones and metals, and even today quarrying and related industries are still important to the economic life of the area.

Idar-Oberstein

IDAR-OBERSTEIN, in the Nahe valley on the southern edge of the range, should definitely be on your itinerary. (It has good rail links with BINGEN and the Saarland towns.) Formerly a mining centre for precious stones and minerals, Idar-Oberstein has remained, even with the exhaustion of the old lodes, a centre for stone-cutting and polishing, and for the manufacture of jewellery. In reality, it's two towns joined together: Oberstein, crammed into the steeply wooded Nahe valley, is the historic part, while Idar, sprawling northwards up the narrow Idarbach valley, is more commercial in character.

From Oberstein's Marktplatz, 214 steps lead up to the late fifteenth-century **Felsenkirche** (1 April–15 Oct 9am–6pm; DM2) set into the rocky northern face of the

Nahe valley. Inside, look out for the graphic five-panelled altar painting, dating from 1410, of scenes from the life of Christ, and for the fine stained glass windows, some of which are as old as the church itself. Above the Felsenkirche are the **Schloss** ruins, the jagged remains of two medieval fortresses, from where there's a good view of Oberstein and the Nahe valley.

On Marktplatz itself is the **Heimatmuseum** (daily 9am–5.30pm; DM3), which details the development of the local precious stone and jewellery industry. It shows how stones were once cut and polished using *Schleifmühlen*, huge sandstone wheels powered by the waters of the River Nahe. Look out too for the translucent flakes of *Landschaftsachat*, fragments of agate on which patterns seem to take the form of ghostly landscapes.

In Idar an ugly 22-storey office block in Schleiferplatz houses the **Diamant-und-Edelsteinbörse**, Europe's only diamond and precious stone exchange. On the first floor of the same building is the **Deutsches Edelsteinmuseum** (May–Sept 9am–6pm, Oct–April 9am–5pm; DM5), which is full of precious stones with "before and after" examples of the stone-cutters' art. On the outskirts of Idar in Tifensteinerstrasse is the **Weiherschleife** (Mon–Fri 10am–noon & 2–5pm, Sun & holidays 10am–noon), the last surving water-powered jewel-cutting shop – there used to be over a hundred in the area. Here craftsmen still finish stones in the traditional way, lying on wooden beams and pressing the stones against sandstone grinding wheels.

A little to the west of Idar itself, reached by bus #6435, is the **Edelsteinminen Steinkaulenberg** (15 March–15 Nov daily 9am–5pm; DM3.50), Europe's only precious stone mine. Not for the claustrophobic, this is a huge network of underground tunnels and chambers which have been mined since Roman times and are still a source for the agates you'll see in all the ritzy jewellery shops in town. Between FISCHBACH and BERSCHWEILER (reached by bus #6455), there's the **Kupferbergwerk**, a similar type of complex, but this time a copper mine. Waxwork figures are used to show how copper ore was mined in days gone by (guided tours daily 1 March–15 Nov 10am–6pm, rest of year Sat, Sun & holidays 10am–noon & 1–3pm; DM3.50).

Practicalities

The **tourist office** is at Bahnhofstr. 13 (☎06781/27025) in Oberstein. There's a **youth hostel** at Alte Treibe 23 (☎06781/24366) and quite a few reasonable **hotels** and **pensions** in Oberstein. *Zur Beisszange*, Hauptstr. 584 (☎06781/22041), has singles from DM30 and doubles from DM52, *Pension Schlie*, Amtsstr. 2 (☎06781/25526), charges upwards of DM25 per person, while *Trarbach*, Wüstlautenbachstr. 11 (☎06781/25677), has singles from DM22 and doubles from DM40. There are **camping** facilities in the suburb of TIEFENSTEIN (☎06781/35551; take bus #6443, #6445 or #6446). At the end of June the *Spiessbratenfest* takes place, with pork and steak cooked over an open fire, garnished according to a recipe brought back from South America by German agate miners during the last century.

THE MOSEL VALLEY

The **River Mosel** (better known in English under its French name, *Moselle*), rises in the foothills of the Vosges in France. In its German stretch, it flows between the Eifel and Hunsrück massifs, entering the Rhine at Koblenz. Abroad, it's best known as a **wine-producing** area, and vineyards crowd the south-facing slopes, with more rugged terrain elsewhere. The lethal combination of wine and scenery, plus castles and history, attracts a lot of visitors – making it the kind of place that most Germans under the age of thirty wouldn't be seen dead in. That said, there's a great deal to recommend it – though not in high season, when hordes of tourists turn the most popular destinations – such as **Cochem** – into real hell-holes.

There are still a few corners which have managed to fend off coach trip attacks and retain some of the atmosphere which so impressed the **Romans**, on the edge of whose world the Mosel valley was. They've left their mark all along the valley, particularly in Trier, which has some of the best preserved remains of Classical antiquity in Northern Europe. You'll be able to cover the ground described here in a rushed four to five days; reckon on at least twice as long to see it in detail.

Trier

"Trier existed 1300 years before Rome!" exclaims the inscription on one of the city's historic buildings. In fact, this is a piece of hyperbole: although **TRIER** is the oldest city in Germany, it was actually founded by the Romans themselves. Once the capital of the Western Empire, Trier was also an important early centre of Christianity. This helped give it political clout throughout the Middle Ages and beyond, its archbishop ranking as one of the seven Electors.

Nowadays, Trier has the less exalted role of regional centre for the upper Mosel valley, its relaxed air a world away from the status it formerly held. Despite a turbulent history, an amazing amount of the city's past has been preserved: it presents a veritable encyclopaedia of European architectural styles, with pride of place going to the most impressive group of **Roman monuments** north of the Alps. These alone would be enough to put Trier in the rank of "must-see" German cities, and it's one of the few places in the Rhineland-Palatinate deserving an unqualified recommendation.

> The telephone code for Trier is ☎0651

Arrival and practicalities

The **Hauptbahnhof** is northeast of the centre, and it's about ten minutes' walk along Theodor-Heuss-Allee to the main entry of the old city. Here, at An der Porta Nigra, you'll find the **tourist office** (May–Aug Mon–Sat 9am–6.45pm, Sun 9am–3.30pm; Sept–Oct Mon–Sat 9am–6pm; Nov–April Mon–Fri 9am–5pm, Sat 9am–1pm; ☎48071). For news of **events**, pick up their monthly news sheet, *Der fröhlicher Steuermann*.

The official **youth hostel** is on the banks of the Mosel at Maarstr. 156 (☎29292). Additional possibilities for dormitory accommodation are the *Kolpinghaus Jugendhotel*, just off the Hauptmarkt at Dietrichstr. 42 (☎75131), and the ship *URANUS* (☎35730), which is moored in the Mosel between April and October. There are **campsites** on the western bank of the Mosel at Luxembourger Str. 81 (☎86921) and in the grounds of the Schloss in the suburb of MONAISE (☎86210) on the same side of the river. Additional facilities can be found in the nearby town of KONZ (easily reached by train) at *Saarmündung* (☎06501/3477), situated at the confluence of the Saar and Mosel.

If you want to stay in a **hotel**, the cheapest central option is to go for a cell-like but perfectly adequate room costing DM29 in the *Warsberger Hof*, part of the aforementioned *Kolpinghaus* complex. Other places with a convenient location are *Zur Glocke*, Glockenstr. 12 (☎73109), which charges upwards of DM30 per person, and *Grund*, Paulinstr. 7 (☎25939), with singles DM38, doubles DM70. *Saarbrücker Hof*, Saarstr. 46 (☎57161), at DM30 per person, is south of the old city, but still handy enough for the main sights. Otherwise, the best deals are far out on the other side of the Mosel: try *Haus Magda*, Biewer Str. 205 (☎66372) or *Kappes*, Biewer Str. 209 (☎61001), both charging around DM25 per person.

Augusta Treverorum was founded, probably in 16 BC, as a crossing point on the junction between the imperial frontier along the Rhine and the Gallic-Belgic provinces. Its name, later shortened to *Treveris* (and the French form *Trèves*, which until recently was also the normal English designation), signifies that it lay in the territory of the conquered Treveri tribe. The new settlement quickly developed into a major city, and remained so until it was sacked around 275 AD by the Alemannians. However, it was rebuilt shortly afterwards under **Emperor Diocletian**, who made it into one of his four capitals, the head-quarters of the Western Empire, which stretched from Britain to Spain. Trier's prestige reached its height under **Emperor Constantine**, who lived there from 306 to 316: the time when he adopted Christianity as the official religion, with Trier as the premier bishopric north of the Alps. The city then had 80,000 inhabitants – almost as many as it has today – and was adorned with spectacular new buildings. Decline began with the establishment of Constantinople as the overall Imperial capital, though emperors continued to reside in Trier until 400, when the administration of the Western Empire was moved to Arles. Only its position as a major ecclesiastical centre saved it from falling into irreversible decline and political impotence.

The city

Despite being relatively small in modern terms, some of Trier's sights are fairly far out, and two days are the minimum amount of time required to see everything, though there's a handy concentration in the centre if you've only a day to spare.

The Porta Nigra and the Simeonstift

The **Porta Nigra** (Black Gate) retains its historic function as the main entry point to the old city. By far the most imposing Roman building in Northern Europe, it's also the biggest and best preserved city gate of the Classical period anywhere in the world. Its exact age is uncertain: it's often said to date back to the second century, but seems more likely to have been one of the embellishments ordered by Constantine. The massive sandstone blocks are held together by iron rods set in lead, and it has been weathered black by the passage of time (hence the name, bestowed in medieval times). Towering above the surrounding streets and buildings, it's an awesome symbol of Roman architectural skill and military might. Would-be attackers were trapped between inner and outer gates, enabling defenders to pour boiling oil and moulten lead down from above; the gateway served its purpose well and was never breached.

The Porta Nigra owes its survival to the fact that, during the eleventh century, Saint Simeon, a Greek hermit who was a friend of the powerful Archbishop Poppo, chose the gloomy ground floor of the east tower as a refuge from the world. After his death in 1035 the Porta Nigra was transformed into a **church** in his honour. Various further additions were made, but in 1803 Napoleon ordered their removal, so that only the twelfth-century Romanesque choir and some slightly frivolous Rococo carvings remain from the post-Roman period.

Opening times for the Porta Nigra and the rest of Trier's Roman monuments, other than the Konstantinbasilika, are as follows: April–Sept daily 9am–6pm; Oct daily 9am–1pm & 2–5pm; Nov & Jan–March Tues–Sun 9am–1pm & 2–5pm, Dec Tues–Sun 10am–4pm Porta Nigra and Kaiserthermen only. The Barbarathermen are closed Mon throughout the year. Entry to individual sites is DM2, DM1 students and pensioners, or you can save by buying a ticket valid for all of them for DM6, DM3 students and pensioners.

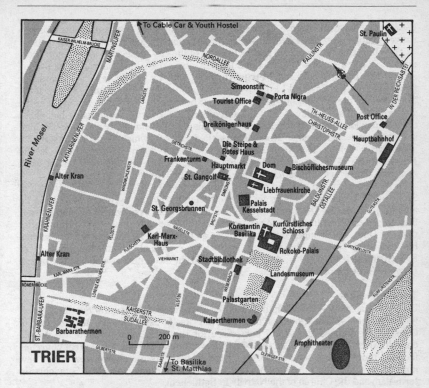

TRIER

Adjoining on the western side is the **Simeonstift**, the collegiate foundation attached to the church. Its cloister, the *Brunnenhof*, is the oldest in Germany, and unusual in that the main walk is on the upper floor, which is supported by the massive arcades below. Today the ground floor houses a restaurant (see below), with the **Städtisches Museum** (Tues–Fri 9am–5pm, Sat & Sun 10am–1pm; DM2) above. This version of the inescapable *Heimatmuseum* is vastly better than usual, thanks to an anarchic layout and some outstanding off the wall exhibits, notably the original sculptures of some of the prominent structures on the Hauptmarkt: the Marktkreuz, the Steipe and the Petrusbrunnen. Also here is a good ancient history section, with Egyptian grave masks and paintings, hundreds of Roman terracotta lamps, a lot of Graeco-Roman statuary and an important collection of Coptic textiles.

Simeonstrasse and the Hauptmarkt

From here, Simeonstrasse runs down to the Hauptmarkt, roughly following the route of an old Roman street. Today it's a busy shopping area, but can boast several medieval monuments. The most notable is the **Dreikönigenhaus** (House of the Magi), white-washed but with garishly painted highlighting, which dates from the first half of the thirteenth century. An early Gothic dwelling tower of the kind found in Regensburg, this was a secure home in uncertain times for a rich merchant family. Then, the ground floor would not have opened on to the street at all: the original front door can be seen at first-floor level, high above the street. It was reached by a wooden staircase which could easily be dismantled in times of trouble, or by a ladder which could be pulled up from the street. Also worth a peep is the huge arcaded Gothic wine warehouse underneath the *Karstadt* department store. These days it houses the store's restaurant, the unimaginatively-named *Historicher Keller*, which isn't particularly worth recommending in itself.

The **Hauptmarkt** remains a real focal point of the city, especially in summer: there are always a few stalls selling fruit and flowers, and Trier's kids and punks like to loll around the brightly coloured **Petrusbrunnen**, with its ornate replica Renaissance figures of the Four Cardinal Virtues. Alongside, atop a slender column, is a copy of the **Marktkreuz**, the original of which was placed here in the mid-tenth century. On the western side of the square is the late Gothic **Steipe**, the former banqueting hall of the town councillors, nowadays appropriately housing a café and pricey *Ratskeller*. Behind it is the stately Renaissance **Rotes Haus** (Red House), which bears the inscription about Trier being older than Rome. A few paces down Dietrichstrasse is the **Frankenturm**, a Romanesque tower-house whose austere, unadorned stonework contrasts sharply with the tarted-up appearance of the Dreikönigenhaus.

At the southern end of Hauptmarkt a Baroque portal leads to the Gothic church of **St Gangolf**, which was built in the fifteenth century by the burghers of Trier in an attempt to outdo the Dom and wind up the archbishops, from whose temporal power they hoped to break free. The tower, added in 1507, actually made the church higher than the Dom, which angered the archbishop so much that he had one of the towers of his cathedral specially heightened to restore episcopal superiority. From here Fleischstrasse leads southwest to the Kornmarkt, in the centre of which is the ornate Baroque **Georgenbrunnen**.

The Domfreihof

Up Sternstrasse from the Hauptmarkt is the **Domfreihof** (Cathedral quarter), which has a history as illustrious as that of Trier itself. Saint Helena, the mother of Constantine, donated the site of her palace for the creation of an immense double church, which was consecrated in 326 AD. It was one of the quartet of great churches founded more or less simultaneously by the emperor as the showpieces of the new imperial religion, the others being Old St Peter's in Rome, the Holy Sepulchre in Jerusalem and the Church of the Nativity in Bethlehem.

Some of its masonry survives in the present quadruple-towered **Dom**, which was started in 1030, though not finished until a couple of centuries later. However, the most tangible reminders of the original church are two granite pillars: one, the *Domstein*, can be seen in front of the southern portal, the other in the courtyard between the Dom and the Liebfrauenkirche. Save for the extension made to the southern tower to make it higher than St Gangolf, the Dom's austerely impressive facade has changed little since the eleventh century.

Inside, there's an incredible sense of space, much enhanced by the ribbed vaulting of the ceiling; the relative plainness of the architecture is enlivened by many devotional and decorative features which have been added down the ages. The delicate Romanesque tympanum in the south aisle is the finest of these, but the most eye-catching items, such as the pulpit and the densely peopled *All Saints' Altar* on the third pillar on the south side of the nave, were carved by **Hans Ruprecht Hoffmann**, an inventive local sculptor who was also responsible for the Petrusbrunnen on Hauptmarkt. The Dom's most important relic is the *Seamless Robe*, supposedly the garment worn by Christ when he was crucified: only rarely displayed for veneration, it's kept in the raised **Heiltumskammer** at the east end, whose over-the-top Baroque decoration adds a rare jarring note. Also upstairs is the **Schatzkammer** (Mon–Sat 10am–noon & 2–4pm, Sun 2–4pm; DM1). This has examples of local goldsmiths' work, notably a bizarre tenth-century portable altar to hold a relic of the foot of St Andrew.

From the airy **cloisters** you get a wonderful view of the ensemble of the Dom and the adjoining **Liebfrauenkirche** next door. The latter occupies the site of the southern section of Constantine's great double church, and thus continues the original idea of there being two separate places of worship in the complex. Begun in 1235, it was only the second church to be built in Germany in the Gothic style, of which it's a wonderfully pure example. The ground-plan is highly original, taking the form of a rotunda with a cross superimposed on it; the vault is supported by twelve pillars representing each of the Apostles. Now darkened by the insertion of modern stained glass windows, the interior contains the Baroque marble tomb of the warlike Archbishop Karl von Metternich. The facade, bristling with statuary, provides about as dramatic a contrast with the neighbouring Dom as it would be possible to devise, although most of the sculptures have had to be replaced by copies.

Facing the north side of the Dom on Windstrasse is the **Bischöfliches Museum** (Mon–Sat 9am–1pm & 2–5pm, Sun 1–5pm; DM1); although inserted into the framework of an older building, this utilises ultra-modern display techniques to superb effect. The most important exhibit is the quite stunningly fresh-looking fourth-century **fresco cycle** from the ceiling of the palace which preceded the Dom. Also of special note is the ninth-century fresco from the vanished Carolingian church of St Maximin, although it has worn its years less successfully. Upstairs is an important collection of **sculptures**, including most of the original statues from the facade of the Liebfrauenkirche, fragments of the Dom's rood screen and the refined *Monument to Archbishop Jakob von Sierck* by Nicolaus Gerhaert von Leyden.

The Konstantinbasilika and around

From the Liebfrauenkirche, Liebfrauenstrasse leads past the ritzy Baroque Palais Kesselstadt to the **Konstantinbasilika** (or **Aula Palatina**; April–Oct daily 9am–1pm & 2–6pm; Nov–March Tues–Sun 11am–noon & 3–4pm; free) on Konstantinplatz. This huge brick structure, once Constantine's throne hall, dates back to 310AD, and is the most impressive of Trier's Roman remains after the Porta Nigra. Its dimensions are awe-inspiring: although 30m high and 75m long, it's completely self-supporting, something which would be difficult enough to achieve even with the benefits of modern technology. Although now comparatively spartan, in Roman times it was richly decorated in accordance with its role (albeit short-lived) as seat of the Roman Empire. Having served successively as royal fortress and archbishop's residence, it was saved from dereliction by order of King Friedrich Wilhelm IV of Prussia in order to serve as the church of the local Protestant community, a role it still has today. At 3pm on most days in summer, there are guided visits to the catacombs below.

Next door is the seventeeth-century **Kurfürstliches Schloss**, once the residence of the Archbishop-Electors but now, more mundanely, a local government office. It's rather overshadowed by its extension, the **Rococo-Palais der Kurfürsten**, which was built in 1756 for an archbishop who felt that the old Schloss wasn't good enough for him. By 1794 Rococo was out and the last Elector moved to a more fashionable Neoclassical residence in Koblenz. Although it took some knocks over the next two hundred years, particularly in World War II, the facade survives and now sits in shockingly pink glory overlooking the **Palastgarten**, which is populated by Rococo statues.

At the southern end of the garden is the **Landesmuseum** (Mon 10am–4pm, Tues–Fri 9.30am–4pm, Sat 9.30am–1pm, Sun 9am–1pm; free), which houses a fantastic collection of Roman relics – one of the best outside Italy – which vividly bring to life all this civilisation's sophistication and complexity. Prize exhibit, kept in the entrance hall, is the *Neumagener Weinschiff*, a stone sculpture found at Neumagen-Dhron in the Mosel valley, showing a wine ship complete with crew. The following rooms have outstanding mosaics, while in the main central hall are many elaborately carved monuments. The *Igeler Säule*, the magnificent 23-metres-high column in the courtyard, however, is only a copy: the original can be seen in the centre of the village of IGEL, 8km down the Mosel.

As a supplement to the Landesmuseum, visit the **Schatzkammer der Stadtbibliothek** (Easter–Oct Mon–Fri 1–5pm, Sat 10am–1pm; Nov–Easter Wed 1–

5pm only; DM2), a couple of minutes' walk to the west at Weberbach 25. Displayed here are two of the world's most beautiful books: the ninth-century *Ada Evangelistary* with an antique cameo of Constantine on the cover, and the tenth-century *Codex Egberti*, partly illuminated in Trier by the Master of the Registrum Gregorii, the first German artist by whom a body of work can be identified.

The Kaiserthermen and the Amphitheater

Behind the Landesmuseum are the **Kaiserthermen**, the Imperial baths built in the reign of Constantine. Although they haven't survived intact, the scale of what was once one of the largest bathing complexes in the Roman world is still apparent. Today only the ruined *Caldarium* (hot bath), with its distinctive strips of brick among the stone-work, is visible above ground. The extensive underground heating system has also survived, and you can walk among the service channels and passages. By the Middle Ages local lords had turned the baths into a castle, which was incorporated into the **Stadtmauer**, surviving sections of which can still be seen nearby. By last century the ruins were gradually disappearing under a pile of rubble, and it was only the efforts of twentieth-century archaeologists that saved them.

From the Kaiserthermen the route to the **Amphitheater** is well signposted. It was built into the slopes of the Petrisberg above the city in around 100AD and is the oldest of the surviving Roman buildings in Trier. The structure has been exposed in most of its original glory, and you can still sense the grandeur of the original, which had a seating capacity of 20,000. It's still possible to see some of the arched cages where the animals were kept and take a look under the arena itself, which is partly supported by timber blocks and has an elaborate – and still functioning – drainage system cut into its base.

The southwestern quarters

An earlier set of Roman baths, the **Barbarathermen**, lie at the opposite end of Südallee from the Kaiserthermen. Built in the second century, they look more as Roman ruins should – piles of rock, vaguely defined foundations and ruined walls. Only the subterranean sections retain their original shape, a seemingly endless maze of passages, channels and chambers. Just to the north, off Lorenz-Kellner-Strasse, is the ugliest building in Trier, the only too visible **Flakturm**, built by the Nazis as a conscious modern update of the city's medieval tower houses. Further east is **Viehmarkt**, a popular student rendezvous point. During digging work to build an underground car park, the remains of another set of Roman baths were found; after much uncertainty, it looks as though a full excavation will be allowed to go ahead.

Just to the west in Brückenstrasse, where at no. 10 you'll find the **Karl-Marx-Haus** (April–Oct Mon 1–6pm, Tues–Sun 10am–6pm; Nov–March Mon 3–6pm, Tues–Sun 10am–1pm & 3–6pm; DM2). In this archetypally bourgeois Baroque mansion the famous revolutionary theoretician and economist (see opposite) was born in 1883 to well to do parents of Jewish extraction: his father was a respected lawyer who had converted to Protestantism, his mother a Dutchwoman who never mastered the German language. Unfortunately the displays here neglect the human angle, concentrating instead on detailed expositions of Marx's political theory. The museum is run by the SPD – something of an irony, as Marx did his best to scupper the party in its early days.

The **Römerbrücke** over the Mosel is the last of the city's Roman remains. In spite of its name, only the basalt supporting pillars are actually Roman, and for the most part it now looks like any other regulation issue bridge, with cars and lorries constantly pounding over it. A little way downstream are the **Kranen**, two old customs cranes which date from the days when the Mosel was the main route for incoming and outgoing goods. The first you come to dates from 1774 and was directly modelled on the

KARL MARX (1818–83)

The revolutions in Eastern Europe in 1989 and the collapse of central government in the Soviet Union in 1991 have dealt a crushing blow to the reputation of Karl Marx, a man who had been elevated to the status of a god throughout the Communist world. Yet, in his own lifetime, there were few hints of the heights to which he would posthumously rise. His career as a campaigning journalist in the Rhenish province of Prussia ended with his expulsion after the revolutionary failure of 1849; thereafter he lived in London and Paris, his subsequent writing activity – notably the vast tract *Das Kapital* – dependent on the charity of his well-heeled co-author Friedrich Engels.

Despite the fact that he rarely attended political meetings, disliked public speaking, was intellectually arrogant, and usually expressed himself in prose of mind-numbing turgidity and verbosity, Marx held what Engels described as a "peculiar influence" on working-class and socialist movements – though at the time he was regarded as only one revolutionary prophet among many. His deification only came as a result of Lenin's adaptation of his theories before and after the Bolshevik Revolution of 1917, though there was a double irony here: not only had Marx predicted that the revolution would first occur in the industrialised West, he himself had what almost amounted to a racial prejudice against Russians, most manifest in his bitter struggles in the International against Mikhail Bakunin. Yet for seven decades attempts were made in Russia and its satellites to engineer Marx's prophecies of the classless society; it was only when these supposedly revolutionary regimes were themselves overthrown by popular revolutions that his powers as a seer finally became discredited.

other, which was built in 1413. Old winding gear is still visible in both and locals claim that they're still in working order.

Outside the centre

The hills around Trier provide many marvellous panoramic views of the city and the Mosel valley. Easiest of access is the **Weiss Haus**, which can be reached by **cable car** (Mon–Fri 9am–6pm, Sat & Sun 9am–7pm; DM4 single, DM5 return), leaving from Zurlaubener Ufer, north of the Kranen.

Two contrasting churches are also very much worth the short detours necessary. On the southern edge of town, about fifteen minutes' walk down Saarstrasse from Südallee, is the **Basilika St Matthias**. In 1127 Crusaders brought back from the Holy Land relics of Saint Matthias (the apostle who replaced Judas Iscariot); this huge church was then built on the site of an existing one to provide sufficient space for the pilgrims who came here to venerate the only one of Jesus' followers to be buried north of the Alps. The whitewashed facade is startling, the original Romanesque modified by the addition of Baroque and Neoclassical features to create a truly sumptuous fricassee; most of the rest of the building is little changed, save for the addition of opulent late Gothic star vaulting. The tomb of Saint Matthias is found at the intersection of the nave and transept; those of the first two bishops of Trier, Saints Eucharius and Valerius, to whom the previous church was dedicated, are in a Roman sarcophagus in the crypt.

At the other end of town is **St Paulin**, designed by Balthasar Neumann in 1757. From the outside it looks quite restrained, sober even, but the interior is an all-singing, all-dancing Rococo extravaganza of colour and light. The eye is assaulted by the complex ceiling frescos and the ornate pillars, dripping with cherubs and scroll work, creating an other-world effect, particularly if you catch it when the sun's rays flood the building thorugh the tall narrow windows. It's all just as Neumann intended: his idea was that entering a church should be like entering heaven. Look out for the carvings on the high altar and the choir stalls by Jacob Tiez, which are some of the best examples of Rococo decoration in the Rhineland-Palatinate.

Eating and drinking

As far as **food and drink** are concerned, Trier has something to suit every taste and pocket. Alongside several high class traditional restaurants are plenty of bars where you can get good and inexpensive food, thanks to the presence of a large and hungry student population; there are also numerous opportunites for wine tasting, if you want to sample the full range of the superb local vintages.

Restaurants

Blesiusgarten, Olewiger Str. 135. Eighteenth-century cellar in the wine-producing district of Olewig, offering a predominantly French menu.

Brunnenhof, Im Simeonstift. Prone to be mobbed by tourists, but the food is of high quality, with the bonus of being able to sit outside in the historic cloister in fine weather.

Da Paolo, corner of Neu Strasse and Pfützenstrasse. Reasonably-priced trattoria.

Hong-Kong-Haus, Georg-Schmitt-Platz. Recommendable Chinese restaurant.

Lenz Weinstuben, Viehmarkt 4. Classy wine bar serving French and regional dishes.

Löwenbrauerei, Bergstr. 46. Behind the Amphitheater, with a shady beer garden and serving homely German food.

Palais Kesselstadt, Liebfrauenstr. 10. Trier's most famous and upmarket restaurant, housed in a magnificent Baroque palace, and with a huge choice of local wines as accompaniment to your meal.

Pfeffermühle, Zurlaubener Ufer 76. Another celebrated, very intimate restaurant, serving French *haute cuisine*. Reservations usually necessary (☎26133).

Weisshaus, Bonner Str. 30. By the cable car terminus and with a wonderful view of Trier, though the food alone is worth the journey.

Zum Christoffel, Simeonstr. 1. Reasonably-priced hotel restaurant specialising in game and lamb dishes.

Zum Domstein, Hauptmarkt 5. Trier's most innovative restaurant, with an adventurous vegetarian menu in addition to the standard *Gutbürgerliche Küche*, while Roman-style dishes are served in the cellar. Bargain menus at lunchtime.

Bars

Asterix, Karl-Marx-Str. 11. Big, relaxed student bar serving an eclectic range of mountainous piles of cheap grub.

Bagatelle, Zurlaubener Ufer. Best of the cluster of riverside pubs near the youth hostel.

Blaues Blut, Pferdermarkt. Bar where the "punk's not dead" crew congregate.

Fetzenreich, Sichelstrasse. The cheapest beer in town – and mainly frequented by students of English and French, so a good place for striking up a conversation.

In Flagrante, Viehmarkt 13. One of the most popular student haunts.

Mephisto, Am Irminen Freihof. Pub serving good value food, which comes complete with a huge beer garden which gets mobbed out in summer.

Rizz, Dietrichstr. 3. The favourite watering-hole of successful local yuppies.

Rubycon, Roonstr. 1. Trier's *Rock und Blues Kneipe* – and fine if you like that sort of thing.

WINE TASTING

The *Weininformationen Mosel-Saar-Ruwer*, Konstantinplatz 11 (daily 11am–5pm) is the most convenient place for a spot of wine tasting: you can sample six different vintages for DM6. However, it's more fun to head out to **Olewig** (east of the Amphitheatre, and reached by bus #6), where eight different cellars (daily 10am–6pm except in early autumn & Christmas) are open for a week at a time on a rotational basis; you can sample four wines for DM4, or eight for DM7. To find out which one is open during your stay, check first with the tourist office, who also have information about the many wine-related events held throughout the year.

Sutträng, Judengasse. Best of the traditional pubs.
Zapotex, Pferdemarkt. Hangout of the local fashion victims.

Listings

Bike hire is available at the Hauptbahnhof, the youth hostel and the *Kolpinghaus*.
Festivals Main events are Carnival (variable date in February/March), the *Altstadtsfest* on the second weekend in June, plus various *Weinfeste* throughout the summer.
Mitfahrzentrale Karl-Marx-Str. 15 (☎44322).
Mosel cruises From Zurlaubener Ufer in both directions (see also box below).
Poste Restante right beside the Hauptbahnhof on Bahnhofsplatz.
Women's centre Saarstr. 38 (☎40119).

The Lower Saar Valley

The **Lower Saar Valley**, the area before the river flows into the Mosel just west of Trier, is part of Rhineland-Palatinate rather than Saarland, and contains a few places well worth the short detour or day excursion.

Saarburg

SAARBURG has that slightly Gallic atmosphere which sets the area between the French border and the Rhine apart from the rest of the country. For many years it was the ball in a long running game of catch between France and Germany in which the result, more often than not, was the torching of the town by French soldiers. Parts of the old fortifications are still intact and there's a ruined **Schloss** with a tall and solid-looking tower looking out over the Saar valley. In the Altstadt the **Leukbach**, a tiny tributary of the Saar, drops twenty metres in a series of cascades between old houses with sickly pink and green facades, and the vines used to make *Saarburger Rausch* wine. One local curiosity is the **Glockengiesserei**, a foundry where bells are cast using methods which have hardly changed over the centuries. It can be visited by arrangement – check with the **tourist office** at Graf-Siegfried-Str. 32 (Mon–Fri 9am–5pm, Sat 10am–5pm; ☎06581/81215) for details. **Cruises** along the Saar and to Luxembourg are run by *Saar Personenschiffahrt*, Laurentiusberg 5 (☎06581/5605).

Saarburg has a **youth hostel** at Bottelter Str. 8 (☎06581/2555), along with **camping** facilities on a hill just to south of town at the *AEGON Ferienpark* (☎06581/2037). A host of pensions average around DM30 single, DM55 double, for example *Haus Saargau*, Saargaussstr. 18a (☎06581/3569), and *Haus Brizin,* Kruterberg 14 (☎06581/2133).

Serrig and Kastel-Staadt

To the south, reached by a regular train service, the village of **SERRIG** is famous for its *méthode champenoise* sparkling wines and for the remains of a Roman temple and settlement. There are more extensive Roman remains in the nearby village of **KASTEL-STAADT**, including parts of a road, the foundations of houses, and fragments of a fortress with water and sewage pipes still intact. High above the village are the **Klause**, hermits' cells set into the rocks that tower over the Saar valley. Next to them is the **Grabkapelle** (Tues–Sun 9am–1pm & 2–6pm; DM1), a funerary chapel designed by Karl Friedrich Schinkel in 1838 to house the remains of King John the Blind of Bohemia, who died in battle during the fourteenth century. The remains of the Luxembourg-born king, which had been shipped from pillar to post over the previous four hundred years, were kept here until after the last war when, bizarrely, they were sent to back to Luxembourg as war reparations.

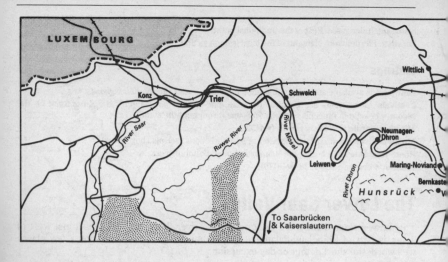

The Mosel Wine Road

From Trier you can follow the **Mosel Wine Road** (*Mosel Weinstrasse*) by bus or car to where the Mosel flows into the Rhine at Koblenz. You can also do the stretch by rail as there are plenty of trains throughout the day – both express services, which run directly from Trier to Koblenz in about ninety minutes, and slower local services, which stop off at many of the small towns. The river meanders through innumerable wine villages and towns in a series of tortuous curves, the slopes of its valley lined with vineyards. If possible do this trip by road, since the railway leaves the valley for substantial stretches and crosses relatively nondescript countryside. However, if you follow the

---

BOAT TRIPS ALONG THE MOSEL

Between May and early October, you can travel the length of the River Mosel from Trier to Koblenz, or just make short local trips; the German Rail Pass allows you to travel on the *K-D Linie* steamers without charge. The same company runs luxury cruises allowing you to see the best of both the Mosel and the Rhine: a three-day trip from Frankfurt to Trier or a two-day one from Trier to Cologne both cost upwards of DM400, meals included.

FERRY COMPANIES AND ROUTES

K-D Linie Rheinwerft, Koblenz (☎0261/31030).	Koblenz–Cochem.
Collée–Hölzenbein Rheinzollstr. 4, Koblenz (☎0261/37744).	Koblenz–Cochem.
Gebruder Kolb Briedern (☎02673/1515); offices in Cochem (☎02671/7387) and Trier (☎0651/263170).	Cochem–Trier.
Hans Michelis Goldbachstr. 52, Bernkastel-Kues (☎06531/8222)	Bernkastel-Kues–Traben-Trarbach.
Gerhard Voss Goethestr. 15, Bernkastel-Kues (☎06531/6316).	Bernkastel-Kues–Leiwen.

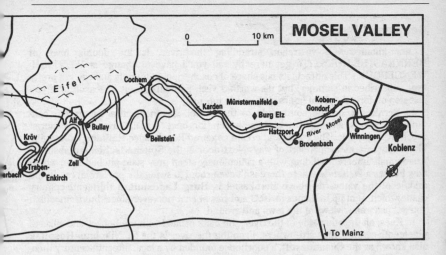

B53 as it criss-crosses the Mosel you won't miss any of the splendid scenery which lines the route. An agreeable alternative is to travel by **boat** – see opposite for details.

Neumagen-Dhron and around

Bus #6246 will take you from Trier to SCHWEICH and from here you can take bus #6230 as far as BULLAY. **NEUMAGEN-DHRON**, the first town you'll hit en route, is best known for its Roman remains and for being the oldest wine-producing town in Germany. These days it's a largish place with a lot of modern buildings, but during the fourth century Neumagen-Dhron was the summer residence of the Emperor Constantine and you can still see the remains of his castle, which originally covered the size of a football pitch. Fronting the **Peterskapelle** is a replica of the *Neumagener Weinschiff*, the original of which is now in the Trier Landesmuseum. The **Heimatmuseum**, Römerstr. 137 (16 April–31 Oct 10am–noon & 2.30–5pm, 1 Nov–15 April 2.30–5pm; DM1) is marginally more interesting than average, with finds from Constantine's castle and local wine-related exhibits, including a huge wooden press.

Also in the museum building is the **tourist office** (☎06507/2001) and through them you may be able to rent private rooms. There are **camping** facilities at Römerstr. 100 (☎06507/3212) and at *Zum alten Leienhaus* (☎06507/3212). For reasonable **accommodation** try *Schander*, Römerstr. 52 (☎06507/5322), or *Pension Krebs,* Römerstr. 65 (☎06507/5377), both upwards of DM20 per person.

Beyond PIESPORT the scenery becomes much more enthralling and there's a succession of tiny wine-producing villages on each side of the river. On the southern bank you'll pass through half-timbered WINTRICH, backed by steep cliffs, and FILZEN with its Franciscan monastery. It's worth taking a little diversion off the beaten track to **VELDENZ**, where a twelfth-century ruined Schloss towers over a village that was once centre of a medieval dukedom. In the village an uninspiring modern church has been tagged onto a thirteenth-century bell tower, with slightly bizarre results. There's a *Weinfest* here on the last Sunday in July. Also meriting a detour is the little town of **MARING-NOVIAND**, in the Eifel foothills on the north side of the river. Just outside town is the **Klosterhofgut Siebenborn**, featuring a dank, vaulted wine cellar and Roman foundations. The local *Weinfest* is celebrated in the streets with much gusto over the fourth weekend in June.

Bernkastel-Kues

A few kilometres downstream, straddling the river, is the double town of **BERNKASTEL-KUES**. (To get here by rail you'll have to change at WITTLICH-WENGEROHR.) This attracts its fair share of coach-tripping tourists and can get pretty over subscribed in summer, but it's worth a visit, particularly out of season or if you just stop off for a couple of hours in the early morning.

In Bernkastel, on the south side of the Mosel, the main attraction is the half-timbered, gently sloping **Marktplatz**, which for once actually lives up to tourist brochure hyperbole. The coffee and cream coloured Renaissance **Rathaus** looks suitably stately in a municipal sort of way. Next door is the **Spitzhäuschen**, an absurdly narrow half-timbered building with a ridiculously steep grey slate pitched roof, which now houses a *Weinstube* where there isn't even room to swing the proverbial cat. In the middle of the vineyards above Bernkastel is **Burg Landshut**, a thirteenth-century castle which went up in flames in 1693 and has been a ruin ever since, but from which you get panoramic views of the town and around.

In Kues, on the other side of the river, the bank is lined with the houses and villas of nineteenth-century vineyard owners. Fronting the river is the **St Nikolaus-Hospital**, also known as the **Cusanusstift**, a poorhouse founded by a local fifteenth-century theologian, Nicolaus Cusanus. These days the Gothic riverside buildings are home to 33 destitute old men – a symbolic figure representing each year of Christ's life. In its heavily ornate **Kapelle** there's a vivid mid-fifteenth century *Crucifixion* triptych by the Cologne narrative painter known as the Master of the Life of the Virgin.

Practicalities

The **tourist office** is at Am Gestade 5 (☎06531/4023) and there's a **youth hostel** at Jugendherbergstr. 1 (☎06531/2395). Bernkastel-Kues has dozens of **hotels** but can get full up because of the volume of summer traffic. Best budget possibilities are: in Kues *Pension Mertz*, Rausstr. 19 (☎06531/6394), from DM25 per person; in Bernkastel *Pension Esslinger*, Kirchhof 8 (☎06531/6617), which charges DM22 per person. Local **camping** facilities are at Am Hafen 2 (☎06531/8200).

For reasonable **food** try *Huwer*, Römerstr. 35, where you'll be able to get a simple, cheap and appetising meal. Not surprisingly, there are dozens of cafés and restaurants in Bernkastel-Kues and the general rule is that the ones in the quieter streets are less likely to be full of tourists being ripped off. During the first weekend in September the biggest *Weinfest* on the Mosel takes place here, when consumption of gallons of the most famous local vintage, *Bernkasteler Doctor*, brings plenty of life to the streets.

Kröv and Traben-Trarbach

From Bernkastel-Kues the Mosel snakes round to **KRÖV**. Here there's a vineyard called *Nacktarsch* – literally "Naked Arse" – which, according to local dialect experts, is a corruption of "nectar". Other things worth knowing about are the standard array of half-timbered houses, including the mid-seventeenth-century **Dreigiebelhaus** (Three Gable House), and the *Weinfest* which takes place in the first weekend in October.

Round one more bend in the river is another double town, **TRABEN-TRARBACH**. In days of old Traben (on the northern bank) was a prime strategic site, which didn't go down too well with the locals, who soon tired of seeing their town destroyed every time one of the two fortresses above the town was besieged. Sighs of relief went up all round when **Schloss Grevenburg**, now reduced to a couple of walls, was blown up in 1697 in accordance with the terms of a recently signed peace treaty. In 1734 **Mont Royal**, built just 44 years previously by Louis XIV, suffered similar treatment, leaving the citizens free to get on with more peaceful pursuits like building half-timbered houses.

Most of these are actually in Trarbach on the opposite bank, where they rub shoulders with more substantial upper-middle-class villas from the nineteenth century. Also on the Trarbach side of the connecting bridge is the **Brückentor**, a hideous monumental gateway designed by the Jugendstil architect Bruno Möhring on what must have been an off-day. Möhring created several other buildings in town in the same style, but only a few are worth seeking out: these include the **Haus Huesgen**, Am Bahnhof 20, and the **Haus Breucker**, An der Mosel 7, both on the river bank in Traben.

Practicalities

The **tourist office** is at Bahnstr. 22 in Traben; pick up their useful map of walks in the surrounding hills. There's a **youth hostel** at Am Letzten Hirtenpfad (☎06541/9278), about 15 minutes' walk from the Bahnhof on the same side of the river. Also in Traben are **camping** facilities at Rissbacher Str. 165 (☎06541/6352), while there's another site 2km down the road at Wedenhofstr. 25 (☎06541/9174 or 1033) in WOLF. On Wildbadstrasse, the road wending upwards from Trabach to KAUTENBACH, are three **hotels** charging around DM25 per person: *Haus Jutta* at no. 227 (☎06541/9544), *Pension Bartz* at no. 161 (☎06541/2349) and *Pension Härdter* at no. 194 (☎06541/6404). In the town itself, best bet is *Gasthof Germania*, Kirchstr. 101 (☎06541/9398), which has similar rates. One recommended local *Weinstube* is *Moselschlösschen* at Neue Rathausstr. 12–16 in Traben. Traben-Trarbach's *Weinfest* is held during the last weekend in July; there's another on the last Sunday in June in Wolf.

From Enkirch to Cochem

Following the southern bank of the Mosel eastwards from Traben-Trarbach will bring you to the village of **ENKIRCH**. This was founded by the Romans, but there's nothing exceptional to see, apart possibly from the sixteenth-century **Drehkäfig**, a cell which was originally built to house young men who had been leading local girls astray. The *Weinfest* here is on the first Sunday in August and there are plenty of places where you can sample the product. Further north, on the opposite bank, is **ALF**. From here it's an easy ascent to the ruins of **Burg Arras**, a tenth-century castle with a semi-renovated tower reached by rickety wooden stairs. There's a fine panoramic view from its restaurant. Local **camping** facilities are in BULLAY at Moselufer 1 (☎06542/22921) and just outside the half-timbered village of EDIGER-ELLER (☎02675/701) further north.

BEILSTEIN is a relatively undiscovered and sleepy little place crowded into a tributary valley on the south bank of the Mosel, with plenty of reasonable **accommodation**. Try *Burg*, Moselstr. 2 (☎02673/1424), from DM18 per person, or *Gute Quelle*, Marktplatz 34 (☎02673/1437), from DM28 per person. The best local **food** and **drink** can be had at the musty old cellar of *Weingut Joachim Lipmann* on Marktplatz, which is open on Monday when most of the competition tends to close. As far as actual sights go, there's only **Burg Beilstein**, a romantic ruin built between the thirteenth and fifteenth centuries and owned by the Metternich family until shortly before its destruction in 1689.

Cochem

Next town of any size is **COCHEM**, on the northern bank of the river, a place which has sold its soul to tourism and should be avoided like the plague in summer. The main attraction is the **Burg** (15 March–31 Oct 9am–5pm; DM3.50), one of the Rhineland-Palatinate's more famous replica castles. If it weren't a complete fake (the eleventh- to fourteenth-century original went up in smoke in 1689, assisted by enthusiastic French soldiers), the Burg, which dominates the town with its cluster of towers and implacable walls, would be quite impressive, but somehow the knowledge that it's only an *ersatz* castle makes it look a bit ridiculous. Inside, the Burg has been decorated in mock medieval style, though there are some fine pieces of Renaissance furniture.

As for the rest of Cochem, it's an averagely uninspiring town, the majority of whose inhabitants seem to live from either the hotel trade or by selling beer *Steins* and funny hats to the coach trippers. There's a regulation issue half-timbered **Marktplatz** with a sober Baroque **Rathaus**. Behind stands the **Martinskirche**, with a tower that looks like a Rococo soldier's helmet. It's a postwar rebuild of an original which dated back to the ninth century. Parts of the old city wall are also still intact, including three chunky city gates. From one of them, **Enderttor**, you can take a chairlift ride (daily 9am–6pm; DM5.50) to the top of the **Pinnerkreuz** hill, from where there's the best view of the town and its environs. Don't be fooled by local urgings to go and see the **Brauseley**, billed as the Mosel's answer to the Lorelei – it's utterly hopeless.

Cochem's **tourist office** is on Endertplatz (☎02671/3971). There's a **youth hostel** at Klottener Str. 9 (☎02671/8633) on the south side of the Mosel. The town has four **campsites**, the most accessible of which are *Schausten*, Endertstr. 124 (☎02671/7528), and *Behrens*, south of the river on Stadionstrasse (☎02671/7762). Most of the numerous **hotels** are pricey and full throughout the season. If you're stuck, try *Haus Karina*, Zehnthausstr. 48 (☎02671/3482), which has singles from DM23 and doubles from DM38, or the *Zur Weinhexe*, Hafenstr. 1 (☎02671/8482), with singles from DM30, doubles from DM50.

Karden, Burg Eltz and around

From Cochem it's another 11km to **KARDEN**, which preserves houses dating back as far as the twelfth century. The **Stiftskirche St Kastor** was under construction for over three hundred years, marking the full transition from Romanesque to Gothic. Although small, its simple white lines make it one of the most visually appealing churches of the Mosel. Inside, there's a fine early seventeenth-century side altar of *The Martyrdom of St Stephen*, and a slightly faded wall painting of Christ which looks startlingly modern. Built into the cliffs behind the town on the south bank of the Mosel are two castles: the restored twelfth-century **Wildburg**, and **Burg Treis**, an eleventh-century ruin.

Beyond Karden the Mosel valley starts to lose its specialness, but you might care to stop briefly in the riverside town of **HATZENPORT**, which is clustered around a pair of Romanesque stone churches and the old restored **Fährturm** (Ferry Tower). In **BRODENBACH** on the far shore there's a **youth hostel** at Moorkamp 7 (☎02605/3389) and a **campsite** at Rhein-Mosel-Str. 63 (☎02605/1437).

Burg Eltz

In any event, make sure you don't miss **Burg Eltz** (1 April–1 Nov 9am–5.30pm; DM6.50), one of only two intact medieval castles in the Rhineland-Palatinate (the other is the Marksburg – see p.416). To get there, catch bus #6039 from Hatzenport to MÜNSTERMAIFELD, from where you can take another bus to Burg Eltz. This castle really is something else: it seems to rise vertically straight out of the woods of the Elzbach valley and bristles with conical towers. It goes back at least as far as the twelfth century, developing over the next four hundred years as a defensive home for the various branches of the Eltz family, who managed to live there peacably for a couple of hundred years until a run-in with Balduin, the Elector of Trier. This resulted in a two-year siege, during which **Burg Trutzeltz** was built by Balduin directly in front in order to lob rocks at the castle. After Burg Eltz fell the Eltz family were allowed to remain in possession as vassals of Balduin and peace returned. Most of what you see today was built during the fifteenth century: inside the walls are a number of residential towers crammed together round an inner courtyard, which escaped destruction by the French in 1689 only because a member of the Eltz family happened to be an officer in the French army.

The **interior** of the castle, which you can only see by guided tour, is more or less as it was during medieval times, complete with original furnishings, wall hangings and paintings. Particular impressive is the *Rübenach Untersaal*, with sixteenth-century Flemish tapestries of unlikely-looking exotic animals and plants, and a number of panel paintings, including Cranach's *Madonna with Grapes*. The **Schatzkammer** (DM2.50 supplement) is full of silver- and gold-ware, glass, porcelain, weapons and armour, including a suit of armour which belonged to Emperor Maximilian I.

Be warned that Burg Eltz is snarled up with tourists in summer; make sure you arrive early, or visit it out of season. Best bring your own picnic – the snack bar is tacky and overpriced.

Kobern-Gondorf and Winningen

KOBERN-GONDORF is a double town trailing out along the Mosel bank 10km east of Hatzenport. The most unusual local attraction is the **Goloring**, a prehistoric circular tomb complex dating from 1200–600 BC. In Kirchstrasse (in Kobern) you can see the **Abteihof**, the oldest half-timbered house in the Rhineland-Palatinate: built in 1321, it looks in suspiciously good shape for its age. Also worth visiting is the castle complex. The **Niederburg** is an extensive pile of crumbling masonry with a more or less intact tower, while the **Oberburg** has the almost perfectly symmetrical Romanesque **Matthiaskapelle**, which once housed the remains of the Apostle Matthias (later transferred to the Matthiaskirche in Trier). In Gondorf there's also an **Oberburg**, but it's been cut in half by the road and railway, which hasn't done a lot for it aesthetically.

The **tourist office** is on the Marktplatz (☎02607/1055). Cheapest **hotels** are *Gasthof Zur Fähre*, Marktplatz 12 (☎02607/571), and *Schwab*, Marktstr. 30 (☎02607/238), both charging around DM30 per person. For **eating** and **drinking**, try *Weingut Thomas Höreth* (☎02607/647), housed in an old mill, complete with wine museum. To get there, take the road up to the Matthiaskapelle, then turn down the road opposite the cemetery. Kobern-Gondorf is big on *Weinfeste*; there's one in late June and early July, another during the second weekend in September and a third in the second weekend in October.

Weinfeste also figure in **WINNINGEN**, the last town of any interest before Koblenz, a half-timbered place which holds the oldest wine festival in Germany at the end of August and beginning of September. At this time, wine flows from the town fountain instead of water. A grisly attraction here is the **Hexenhugel**, (Witches' Hill) a popular picnic spot where, during the Thirty Years' War, twenty-one women were burned alive as witches. Just outside the town is the huge bridge which carries the E31 European highway over the Mosel valley; fortunately, it hasn't destroyed the local atmosphere.

THE RHINE GORGE

Beyond Mainz, the **Rhine** bends westwards and continues its hitherto stately but unspectacular journey. Suddenly, there's a dramatic change – the river widens and swings back to a northerly course, threatening the low banks on either side, while long wooded islands block the view ahead.

This marks the entry to the spectacular **gorge**, which, though it's only a small part of the river's total length of 1320km, *is* the Rhine in popular imagination. The combination of the treacherous waters, whirlpools and rocky banks lining the sharp twists of the river pose a severe test of navigational skill. Nowadays, this has been considerably eased by the digging of channels to control the movement of the river, but it has inevitably thrown up legends of shipwrecks, sirens and mermaids. The lure of the castles of the medieval robber barons, the raw elemental beauty of the landscape itself and the

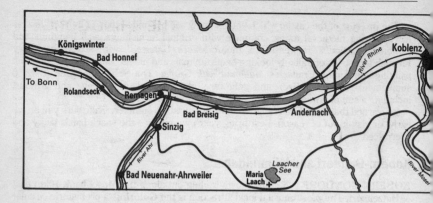

famous wines made from the vines which somehow cling to the lower slopes make for one of Europe's major tourist magnets. Yet the pleasure steamers are still greatly outnumbered by the long, narrow commercial barges, a reminder of the crucial role the river has played in the German economy down the centuries.

The Rhine from Bingen to Koblenz

The first stretch of the gorge, up to the confluence with the Mosel, is undoubtedly the finest, lined with cute half-timbered towns and an extensive range of castles in various states of repair. In high season, this means a flood of organised tour parties. If you must do this part of the Rhine in summer then try and avoid spending the night in the area as **accommodation** under DM30 tends to be heavily booked up, often well in advance. Bearing in mind that the true identity of the region has been sacrificed to hard sell, you could do worse than take the **train** through this stretch and admire the best feature – the scenery – in comfort, but it's undeniably more fun to go by **boat**.

Spring and autumn are undoubtedly the best times to visit the area, and you could easily spend several days meandering around. Rail and road links lie on either side of the river and, although there are no bridges between Bingen and Koblenz, fairly frequent ferry links for passengers should enable you to hop from one side of the river to the other without too much difficulty.

Bingen, Bacharach, Kaub and Oberwesel

Poor relation of Rüdesheim on the other side of the Rhine, **BINGEN** doesn't really have much going for it, other than as the starting-point of the great gorge. Look out, however, for the **Mäuseturm**, a former customs tower on an island in the Rhine in which, according to grisly legend, Archbishop Hatto of Mainz was devoured alive by mice after having burned all the local beggars alive during a famine. Also worth a look is **Burg Klopp**, a former castle of the Electors of Mainz, which towers over the town, commanding a great view out over the Rhine to the Taunus. Even this is not what it seems: the original fortress was destroyed in 1689 and the ruins were blown up in 1711, so that what you see today is a nineteenth-century replica. Housed within its tower is the local **Heimatmuseum** (Tues–Sun 9am–noon & 2–5pm; DM2), whose prize exhibit is a brutal-looking set of Roman doctor's instruments.

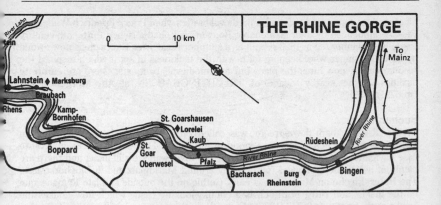

The **tourist office** is at Rheinkai 1 (☎06721/14269). There's a **youth hostel** at Herter Str. 51 (☎06721/32163), in the suburb of BINGERBRÜCK – a place most famous for its railway yards. Bingen itself isn't bad for cheap **hotels**, which could be good news if you want to spend the night in the area but can't really afford the tourist-inflated prices in Rüdesheim. *Krone*, Rheinkai 19–20 (☎06721/17016), has singles at DM30, doubles at DM50, while *Gasthof Frambach*, Gerbhausstr. 25 (☎06721/14986), has doubles (only) at DM56. There are **camping** facilities (☎06721/17160) near the Hindenburgbrücke in the suburb of KEMPTEN.

The fun starts a few kilometres north of Bingen at **Burg Rheinstein** (9am–5/7pm according to season; DM3.50) which, you might think, looks like part of a Victorian Gothic railway bridge. You wouldn't be far wrong – in fact Burg Rheinstein inspired the

---

BOAT TRIPS ALONG THE RHINE

The imperious white vessels of the **K-D Linie** (Rheinwerft, Koblenz; ☎0261/31030; see also listings in Mainz, Bonn and Cologne) have several sailings each way in several directions during the June to September high season; the services thereafter progressively run down, and stop altogether at the end of October, to resume in a skeleton format at Easter or the beginning of April, whichever is the earlier. Published prices verge on the extortionate (Bingen to Koblenz costs DM49), though in practice day returns are generally available for less than this. However, both the German Rail Pass and Eurail (though not InterRail) passes are valid.

In addition, a number of smaller companies offer sailings along shorter stretches:

FERRY COMPANIES AND ROUTES

Bingen-Rüdesheimer Fähr- und Schiffahrtgesellschaft Rheinkai 10, Bingen (☎06721/14140).   Bingen–St. Goar

Hebel Linie Rheinallee 35, Boppard (☎06742/2420).   Boppard–Koblenz–Kobern-Gondorf.

Josef Hewel Bayerhofgasse 11, Boppard (☎06742/2223).   Boppard–Braubach.

Collée-Hölzenbein Rheinzollstr. 4, Koblenz (☎0261/37744).   Koblenz–Bingen.

Merkelbach Emster Str. 57, Koblenz (☎0261/76810).   Koblenz–Braubach.

nineteenth-century trend for replica medieval castles when Prince Friedrich Wilhelm of Prussia, influenced by then fashionable Romanticism, had a ruined thirteenth-century castle he had inherited in 1823 rebuilt as a summer residence. The castle is now owned by an opera singer who, keeping faith with the tackiness of spirit which inspired the reconstruction, now hires the place out for "medieval" banquets. There are **camping** facilities in the nearby village of TRECHTINGHAUSEN at Am Morgenbach 1 (☎06721/6133).

Bacharach

BACHARACH, 10km downstream, was called *Baccaracum* by the Romans after an altar stone to Bacchus which once stood in the Rhine. This was blown up in 1850 to ease navigation of the river, but parts of the old town wall are still intact and there are plenty of half-timbered houses, particularly around Marktplatz and in Blücherstrasse. The **Peterskirche** on Marktplatz is early Gothic on the outside and late Romanesque on the inside, and **Burg Stahleck** is a chunky-looking castle which now houses the local **youth hostel** (☎06743/1266). From the overgrown and half-timbered Posthof square there's a good view of the **Wernerkapelle**, the red sandstone frame of a never-completed Gothic chapel.

The **tourist office** is at Oberstr. 1 (☎06743/1297). A wide choice of hotels can be found on Blücherstrasse, Langerstrasse and Oberstrasse. The local **campsite** is at Strandbadweg (☎06743/1752).

Kaub

From **KAUB**, a few kilometres north on the opposite bank of the Rhine, you get a great view of the **Pfalz** (April–Oct daily, 9am–noon & 1.30–5.15pm; DM1.50 plus DM1.80 for the boat trip), a white walled toll fortress standing on a mid-river island which has become a famous Rhineland symbol. The five-cornered central tower was built in 1327 and the many-turreted outer wall added later. This stronghold enabled the lords of **Burg Gutenfels** above Kaub to extract a toll from passing ships until well into the nineteenth century. Burg Gutenfels as you see it today is a late nineteenth-century rebuild of the thirteenth-century original, in which Gustavus Adolphus lived during the Thirty Years' War.

It was at Kaub that Field Marshal Blücher, the Prussian general who saved the day with his late arrival at the battle of Waterloo, crossed the Rhine during an earlier campaign against Napoleon. He's commemorated in the **Blüchermuseum**, Metzgergasse 6 (Tues–Sun April–Oct 10am–noon & 2–4pm, Nov–March 10am–noon; DM1), which is in the building he used as his headquarters. The rooms are done out in grand Empire style and are full of military bits and pieces from the the Napoleonic Wars and old Prussia. There are **camping** facilities at *Am Elsleinband* on Blücherstrasse (☎06774/560).

Oberwesel

OBERWESEL, back on the left bank just to the north, is overlooked by the huge **Schönburg** castle, now a ruin but, as you'll realise when you walk around its battlements, still impressive. In town, the Gothic **Liebfrauenkirche** is known to the locals as "the red church", after the huge red sandstone blocks used to build it. In the airy interior, look out for the *Niklausaltar*, on which the saint is shown helping three knights who have been sentenced to death for crimes they didn't commit, saving three sisters who have been forced into prostitution by their father, and protecting passengers on board a ship. The town also possesses the best set of fortifications on the Rhine, with eighteen defensive towers still surviving. **Camping** facilities (☎06744/245) are just off the B9 road to the north of town.

The Lorelei, St Goarshausen and St Goar

Next stop is **ST GOARSHAUSEN**, which trails along the eastern bank of the Rhine for a couple of kilometres. On the way you'll pass the **Lorelei**, the famous outcrop of rock where, according to legend, a blonde woman used to sit combing her hair while she lured passing sailors to watery graves with her eerily compelling song. There's a naff statue at the water edge to commemorate the legend. The rock itself has been over-hyped – it's impressive but not staggeringly so. However, there are outstanding views from the top (you can reach it via St Goarshausen itself on bus #6147 or by following the signs marked *Loreley Felsen* if you're travelling under your own steam). Apart from a viewing platform, the summit has a **campsite** (☎06771/7519). Also up here is the *Loreley Freilichtbühne*, an open-air stage that is frequently used for rock concerts.

Above St Goarshausen itself is **Burg Katz** (Cat Castle), the partially reconstructed fourteenth-century fortress of the Counts of Katzenelnbogen, which can be visited by prior arrangement with the **tourist office** at Bahnhofstr. 8 (☎06771/427). Burg Katz was built to rival another castle a few kilometres downstream, which belonged to the Archbishops of Trier and earned the inevitable nickname **Burg Maus** (Mouse Castle) because of its relative puniness. Today Burg Maus is an eagle and falcon station, giving daily displays of bird flight at 11am, 2.30pm and 4.30pm. The *Weinwoche* is during the second and third weeks in September, and there are other *Weinfeste* at the end of September and during the third weekend in October.

St Goar

A ferry will take you back across to the west bank of the Rhine and the town of **ST GOAR**, which is slightly prettier and more touristy than its counterpart. Looming above town is one of the best Rhine castles, the enormous **Burg Rheinfels** (daily April–Sept 9am–6pm, Oct 9am–5pm; DM3) which, until the French blew it up in 1797, was one of the most powerful fortresses on the Rhine. It was founded in 1245 by Count Dieter von Katzenelnbogen, who wanted to look after his Rhine toll-collecting racket, and just ten years later withstood a 9000-man siege by soldiers of the Alliance of Rhenish Towns. During the sixteenth and seventeenth centuries the Landgraves of Hessen extended what was already a formidable castle into an enormous fortification complex which was to prove virtually impregnable: it was the only Rhineland castle that the French were unable to take during the War of the Palatinate Succession. In 1796 the castle surrendered to the troops of Napoleon without a shot being fired, and over the next three years the French did their best to demolish it. Today, the medieval outline can still be seen and you can walk through the underground passages of the later battlements. Models in the **Heimatmuseum** (April–Sept 9.30am–noon & 1–5pm; admission included in Burg entrance fee), which is housed in a rebuilt section, show how the place looked before it was destroyed.

In town the main monument is the **Stiftskirche** on Oberstrasse (predominantly Gothic with a dash of Romanesque) which has some well-restored fifteenth-century murals. The **tourist office** is at Heerstr. 120 (Mon–Fri 8am–12.30pm & 2–5pm; ☎06741/383). There's a **youth hostel** at Bismarckweg 17 (☎06741/388), just outside the town centre, while **camping** facilities are at *Friedenau*, Gründelbachstr. 103 (☎06741/368), and *Loreleyblick*, An der Loreley 29–39 (☎06741/324), neither of which are too far out of town. As with most of the Rhine towns, it's probably better to avoid staying here in high season but there are a few reasonable **hotel** possibilities: *Rhein-Hotel*, Heerstr. 71 (☎06741/485), has singles from DM30 and doubles from DM50 as does *Jost*, Gründelbachtal (☎06741/314). Rooms are also available in private houses – the tourist office has a complete list.

Boppard

At **BOPPARD** the Rhine gorge starts to level out and the valley landscape becomes a gentler one of rounded, vine-covered slopes. The town has its own share of attractions, foremost of which is the **Severuskirche** on Marktplatz, yet another Romanesque-Gothic church, this time of cathedral-like dimensions. A twin-towered structure, brightly painted in white and orange, it was built during the twelfth century to house the remains of St Severus, which had been brought here from Trier. Look out for the ceiling paintings, some of which date back to the thirteenth century, depicting *The Martyrdom of the Theban Legion* and *The Last Judgment*, and for the Gothic stained glass windows, which look almost Chagallesque.

The squat Gothic **Karmelitenkirche**, near the Rhine quay, has a couple of seventeenth-century altars and various tombs of local bigwigs. At the east entrance is a recess which houses the fourteenth-century *Traubenmadonna*. Traditionally, local vine growers place the first ripe bunch of grapes of the year by the statue and leave it there until it withers away.

At the end of Kirchgasse, which is just off Oberstrasse (Boppard's main street), are the remains of the Roman **Stadtmauer**, which has weathered the years remarkably well. Also here are a couple of watchtowers, the only two survivors of the 28 which the Romans built during the fourth century to fend off the locals. At the end of Bingergasse are the remains of more recent fortifications. The **Binger Tor** was built during the Middle Ages and has survived more or less intact, bar the odd bit of crumbling here and there. Between Burgplatz and Rheinallee is the **Alte Burg**, a castle and residence built by the Archbishops of Trier to consolidate their grip in the area. The central keep, with its apertures for the pouring of boiling oil, molten lead and the like, was built around 1327, while the more civilised-looking wings were added during the seventeenth century. These days the building houses Boppard's **Heimatmuseum** (April–Oct Tues–Fri 10am–noon & 2–4pm, Sat 10am–noon, Sun 2–4pm; DM2). Part of this is devoted to the furniture of Michael Thonet, a son of Boppard, who, during the early nineteenth century perfected the technique of laminating wood and earned himself a fortune in the process. At the northern end of town, a chairlift ascends to the **belvedere** known as *Vierseenblick*, which commands a magnificent panorama over the Rhine's most spectacular bend.

Boppard's **tourist office** is at Karmeliterstr. 2 (Mon–Fri 8am–12.30pm & 1.30pm–5pm, Sat 9.30am–noon; ☎06742/10319). There are **camping** facilities at *Sonneck*, just north of town on the B9 right next to the Rhine (☎06742/2121 or 3225). Cheapest central **hotels** are *Sonnenhof*, Kirchgasse 8 (☎06742/3223), and *Weinhaus Patt*, Steinstr. 30 (☎06742/2366) both from DM28 per person.

From Boppard to Koblenz

From Boppard a ferry runs across the Rhine to **KAMP-BORNHOFEN**, above which are two castles known as the **Feindlichen Brüder** (The Rival Brothers). **Burg Liebenstein** is the better preserved of the two, with its Gothic living tower and a keep set on top of a huge rock. The battlements seem to be partly directed at **Burg Sterrenberg**, which is set slightly lower on the other side of a small river valley. Both castles have small restaurants and you could spend a pleasant couple of hours exploring the pair.

About 10km north of Kamp-Bornhofen is **BRAUBACH**. Set in the hills about 25 minutes' walk above the town is the **Marksburg** (guided tours every hour 15 March–15 Nov daily 9.30am–5pm, 16 Nov–14 Mar daily 11am–4pm; DM4), the only medieval castle on this stretch of the Rhine to escape destruction by the French. The fact that this one is an original (showing a few signs of wear and tear) makes it a lot more impressive than the reconstructions you'll already have seen. Most of the building, including the turreted sandstone keep, was built between the twelfth and fourteenth centuries with a few additional defensive features added in the seventeenth century. Inside there's a big collection of weapons from the Middle Ages, including some extremely unpleasant instruments of torture. There are also displays about knightly life in the Middle Ages which throw a bit of light on the absurd way in which the Rhine valley was ruled during medieval times – dozens of counts, often little more than glorified robbers, extracting tolls from Rhine traffic and lording it over their own little fiefs from their castle strongholds. The Marksburg also has the only preserved medieval botanic garden in Germany, and in the souvenir shop they're very proud of the fact that this is the only castle in Europe where you can buy authenticated medieval documents.

Next stop is **LAHNSTEIN**, where the River Lahn runs into the Rhine. Apart from the restored **Burg Lahneck** (Easter–Oct 10am–5.30pm; DM3) above the town there's not much to see here. Lahnstein does, however, have a couple of **campsites**: *Rhein-Lahn-Eck*, Sandstr. 8 (☎02621/50916 or 8390), and *Burg Lahneck* (☎02621/2765 or 2789), in the grounds of the castle. It's also not a bad place to look for a **hotel** room: among several possibilities is *Rheinischer Hof*, Hochstr. 47 (☎02621/2598), at about DM30 per person.

From Lahnstein you can take the ferry (passengers only; if you're driving you'll have to go via the KOBLENZ road bridge) to **RHENS**, above which stands the momentous-sounding but rather pathetic-looking **Königsstuhl** (Seat of Kings). Resembling the base of some unfinished monument, this stone platform is where the German Electors met from 1273 to 1400 to choose their king. In fact, like so many of the Rhine's "medieval" monuments, it's a bit of a cheat. Although the original was put up around 1376, most of what can be seen today dates from as recently as 1842, a witness to the nineteenth century mania for resurrecting Germany's medieval past. Rhens itself is a half-timbered kind of place with substantially intact medieval fortifications and a rather too pristine Rathaus.

Just to the north, practically in Koblenz itself, is **Schloss Stolzenfels** (April–Sept Tues–Sun 9am–1pm & 2–6pm, Oct–March 10am–1pm & 2–5pm; DM3), a Karl Friedrich Schinkel neo-Gothic version of a thirteenth-century Burg which had gone up in smoke in 1688. The interior is a bit over the top, filled to saturation point with suits of armour and medieval weaponry. The most taste-affronting part is probably the *Rittersaal*, though the king's apartments come a close second.

A detour up the Lahn

From Lahstein, it's well worth making a detour up the Lahn, a beautiful valley which provides a welcome escape from the tourist claustrophobia of the Rhine. Most of the river lies in Hessen, though the downstream stretch is in Rhineland-Palatinate.

The first town you come to is **BAD EMS**, a fashionable, elegant and very expensive spa, which still preserves much of the ambience that drew figures like King Wilhelm I of Prussia to take the waters. It has gained an honoured place in German history for this very reason, as it was while resting here in July 1870 that Wilhelm inadvertently sparked off the events which led to the achievement of the long-awaited goal of national unity just six months later. Earlier in the month, his kinsman Leopold von Hohenzollern-Sigmaringen had been proposed for the vacant throne of Spain, but had withdrawn on 12 July under heavy pressure from France. Not content with this, Emperor Louis Napoleon sent his ambassador to Ems the next day to obtain a promise from Wilhelm that no member of the Hohenzollern family would ever again lay claim to Spain. The king refused, and informed Chancellor Bismarck of the outcome of the meeting by telegram. Ever the master tactician, Bismarck saw here an opportunity to have a final showdown with the French which would unite the southern German states with the Prussian-dominated North German Confederation, He published a doctored version of the letter the next day, making it appear that the Prussian king had been slighted. In umbrage, the French declared war five days later, with disastrous consequences for them: within six months they had been routed – and Wilhelm was proclaimed Kaiser of the Second German Reich.

Just up the river is NASSAU, cradle of the famous dynasty of Oranien-Nassau (see Siegen, *Chapter Five*). In spite of its historical associations, there's little of interest left to see today. You're better pressing on to **DIEZ**, seat of one of the family offshoots. The town clusters at the foot of their highly distinctive medieval **Schloss**, an immensely tall building which looks more like a vast tower house. Nowadays, it has been refurbished as the local **youth hostel** (☎06432/2481). Also in Diez is the elegantly Baroque **Schloss Oranienstein** (guided tours daily 9.30–11.30am & 2–4pm; DM2), the family home in more peaceful later years, decked out with lots of seventeenth- and eighteenth-century paintings and furniture. From here, it's only a few kilometres to the Hessen frontier and the episcopal city of Limburg (see *Chapter Three*).

Koblenz

KOBLENZ is always either thronged or deserted, according to the season. Its favourable geographical location at the confluence of the Rhine and Mosel first recommended it to the Romans, who established a settlement here in 14 AD. Nearby, the Lahn flows in from the east, which means that the town lies close to the four distinct scenic regions separated by these rivers – the Eifel, Hunsrück, Westerwald and Taunus – and thus makes an ideal touring base. The town itself polarises opinion – some enjoy its relaxed, rather faded charm; others find it smug and boring. Its connection with tourism actually has deep roots, as it was in Koblenz in 1823 that **Karl Baedeker** began publishing his famous series of guidebooks which aimed at saving travellers from having to depend on unreliable and extortionate local tour guides for information. Old editions of these (the one on *The Rhineland* itself is a good example) are still worth seeking out: their sententious prose evokes a vanished epoch, and their pull-out maps are wonderful to handle.

Around town

The place to begin is the **Deutsches Eck**, where the Mosel flows into the Rhine. In 1897, a colossal equestrian monument in the heroic taste of the time was erected here to Kaiser Wilhelm I. It was destroyed in the last war, but the base, itself a pompous structure with over a hundred steps, was rebuilt and piously dedicated to the unification of Germany. Demolition would have been kinder, as it adds nothing to the view.

Close by is the finest building in the city, the Romanesque collegiate foundation of **St Kastor**, largely twelfth century, whose imposing facade has twin towers with characteristic "bishop's mitre" roofs. A long-term project to restore the interior has left it looking wonderfully fresh. See the elaborate **keystones** of the Gothic vault, especially the one showing the Madonna and Child in a boat. There's a good view of the church from the floral garden of the adjacent **Deutschherrenhaus**.

The Rhine bank is today largely given over to tourist facilities; the curious old **crane**, now converted into a pricey restaurant, is the only thing to catch the eye. Only a few monuments of medieval Koblenz's centre, which bordered on the Mosel, remain; they're rather over-restored in the romantic image of old Germany, with the exterior walls painted in bright colours, but are undeniably picturesque. You come first of all to the **Deutscher Kaiser**, a sixteenth-century tower house which also is now a restaurant. Further on is the Florinsmarkt, with the Romanesque-Gothic **St Florin**, now a

Protestant parish church, the **Schöffenhaus**, a pretty little orange building with corner turrets, and the **Altes Kaufhaus**. This last building now houses the **Mittelrhein Museum** (Tues–Sat 10am–1pm & 2–5.30pm, Sun 10am–1pm; DM1.50), a fairly miscellaneous collection of paintings, sculptures and antiquities. The ground floor has a few German Primitives, including an *Adoration of the Magi* by the Augsburg painter **Jörg Breu** which unashamedly plagiarises a portrait by his fellow-citizen, Holbein the Elder, for the figure of one of the kings. Upstairs are many works by one of Germany's most accomplished Rococo painters, **Januarius Zick**, who eventually settled in Koblenz.

Further along the Mosel bank is the **Alte Burg**, altered to a Renaissance palace and now housing the municipal library, but originally constructed to defend the fourteenth-century **Balduinbrücke**. Turning away from the river, you come to **Münzplatz**, which still preserves the mint master's house. Also in the square is the mansion birthplace of the wily Habsburg statesman **Clemens von Metternich**, high priest of the theory (which was to dominate nineteenth-century politics) that the key to a peaceful Europe lay in maintaining a balance of power among the main states. His peak of influence came during his dominant hosting role at the Congress of Vienna in 1815, which laid down the structure of post-Napoleonic Europe; ironically, his native town was given to Prussia – arch-rival of his adopted Austria – as a result.

Down the pedestrian precinct at the intersection of Löhrstrasse and Markstrasse there's a fine grouping of four houses, each with ornamental oriel windows. Left from here is another large square, Plan, lined with large eighteenth-century buildings. Behind are the exotic Baroque onion-shaped spires of the **Liebfrauenkirche**, a handsome if diffuse church with a galleried Romanesque nave and a Gothic chancel. Just beyond is the **Rathaus**, incongruously housed in a cavernous former Jesuit college.

In the late eighteenth century, Koblenz was expanded to the south in the form of a planned Neoclassical town. The Archbishop-Electors of Trier moved their court here, centred on the huge **Schloss**; three years after its completion, the Elector fled in the wake of Napoleon's advance, never to return. The buildings were gutted during the last war and now serve as offices. A more lasting memento of the period is the stately **theatre** fronted by an obelisk on Deinhardplatz. Its programmes of plays, opera and other events put those of many larger cities to shame.

Ehrenbreitstein

Across the Rhine lies **EHRENBREITSTEIN**, with the original **Residenz** of the Electors, designed by Balthasar Neumann. Looming high above is the vast **Festung** – one of the largest fortresses in the world – with an impressive set of defences which the Prussians painstakingly and quite needlessly rebuilt over a ten year period after Koblenz passed into their hands. It now contains the youth hostel and the **Landesmuseum** (mid-March–Oct daily 9am–5pm; DM1). Even if you don't want to stay here, it's well worth the climb for the sake of the memorable panoramas of the city and its two great rivers. Access is possible (but expensive) by chairlift in season; otherwise, follow the main road along the shore of the Rhine until you come to a path which snakes upwards.

Practicalities

The **Hauptbahnhof** and **bus station** are side by side, to the south west of the historical part of the city. Immediately opposite is the main **tourist office** (May–Oct Mon–Fri 8.30am–6pm, Sat 9am–2am: additional hours in the summer, shorter hours in winter; ☎0261/31304). There's also a branch on the Rhine front at Konrad-Adenauer-Ufer (June–Sept Tues–Sat 11.45am–6.15pm, Sun 11.30am–6.30pm; ☎0261/129 2207). Pick up the large city plan, which has exhaustive listings of hotels, restaurants, pubs, discos and leisure activities on the back.

Accommodation

The previously mentioned **youth hostel** (☎0261/73737) – buses #7, #8, #9 or #10 go closest – must rate as one of the best in Germany; not only is the view superb, but it has recently been given a thorough modernisation too. Usually empty in winter, it's regularly full in summer. The **campsite** is at Lützel, directly opposite Deutsches Eck (April to mid-Oct; ☎0261/802489). A ferry crosses the Mosel here in summer, while another somewhat further south crosses the Rhine. **Hotel rooms** are very reasonable: you can find them at around DM30 for a single, DM55 for a double. In the centre, the best bargains are *Christ*, Schützenstr. 32 (☎0261/37702), and *Weinand*, Weissernonnengasse 4-6 (☎0261/32492). There are also a number in Ehrenbreitstein – *Mäckler*, Helffensteinstr. 63 (☎0261/73725), and *Zur Kaul*, at no. 64 in the same street (☎0261/75256), are the cheapest at DM25 per person. Some of the remoter suburbs, such as Arenberg in the woods, or the Mosel villages of GÜLS and LAY, have the cheapest rooms of all.

There's a **Mitfahrzentrale** office at Rheinstr. 34 (☎0261/18505). The two main **festivals** are Carnival and *Der Rhein in Flammen*; the latter takes place on the second Saturday in August, and features fireworks and bonfires.

Food and drink

For both **eating** and **drinking**, it's well-nigh impossible to escape the tourist syndrome. For sampling the local *Riesling* and *Müller-Thurgau* **wines**, the *Weindorf* near the Rheinbrücke (closed all November) is the best-known centre, grouping four taverns in the form of a village square. It was set up for the 1925 German Wine Exhibition and has been preserved ever since; its function as an attraction for visitors is a bit too obvious. Surprisingly, Koblenz is also a major **beer** centre: the large *Königsbacher* brewery not only makes an excellent bitter tasting Pils, but also has a subsidiary named *Richmodis* in Cologne, enabling it to produce its own very fruity *Kölsch*. There are plenty of bars and restaurants (including many international varieties) in the streets of the old town; those out of the centre, such as in Ehrenbreitstein, have a more genuine local flavour. Numerous **discos** and **nightclubs** are on offer too, though this is hardly the place in which to look for anything very original.

The Rhine from Andernach to Bonn

Soon after leaving Koblenz, the Rhine gorge opens out, cutting between the ranges of the Eifel and Westerwald. If this stretch doesn't quite match the grandeur of the immediately preceding section, it's impressive nonetheless and well worth following by either boat or train. With exceptions, it's also less touristed, and hence **accommodation** prices are less of a rip-off.

Andernach

ANDERNACH, which lies 16km down the Rhine from Koblenz, can trace its history back further than almost any other German town. It celebrated its two thousandth anniversary in 1988, commemorating the foundation of a Roman base for the campaigns against the tribes on the eastern side of the Rhine. Subsequently Andernach became a Franconian royal seat, before passing to the control of the Archbishop-Electors of Cologne, serving as the southern border of their territory until the Napoleonic invasion. Nowadays, it's an odd hybrid, having a fair amount of industry, yet taking advantage of its situation and monuments to double as a holiday resort.

If you're travelling along the Rhine by boat, it's definitely worth alighting for a couple of hours in order to walk round the thirteenth-century **fortifications**, which were laid out on the Roman foundations. The walls survive largely intact, making a solid back for many later buildings, including a well-concealed row of houses. Extra defence on the southern stretch was provided by the **Burg**, the most important town castle in the Rhineland. Blown up by French troops in 1688, a fair amount has nevertheless survived, notably the later embellishments such as the **Pulverturm** and residential palace wing.

Round to the north, overlooking the river, is the **Rheintor**, whose inner gate has weather-worn statues illustrating the best-known local legend, that of the *Andernacher Bäckerjungen* (baker boys of Andernach), who saved the town from occupation by letting loose their bees on the invading army. The most picturesque feature of Andernach's fortifications, however, is the fifteenth-century **Runder Turm** overlooking the Rhine on the northern side of town, whose octagonal upper storeys give it an exotic, oddly Moorish air. Thankfully, the French siege guns failed to penetrate its thick walls, but the enormous dent they made can still be seen clearly. Continuing down the river bank, you shortly come to a remarkable sixteenth-century **crane** whose original wooden mechanism remained in service into the present century and is still in full working order.

Just to the west of the Runder Turm, the tall twin facade towers of the **Pfarrkirche Maria Himmelfahrt** rise majestically above the rest of the skyline. For the most part, it's an archetypal late Romanesque basilica with a pronounced Rhenish accent, though the northeastern belfry, whose rough masonry stands in stark contrast to the supersmooth stonework of the rest of the building, is in fact a survivor of the previous church on the site.

Andernach's main axis, Hochstrasse, runs from here to the Burg; about halfway down is the **Altes Rathaus**, occupying the site of the former ghetto. A *Mikwe* (Jewish bath) was recently discovered underneath the session room; to see it, ask for the key at the **tourist office** (Mon–Fri 8am–12.30pm & 1.30–5pm, Sat 9am–noon; ☎0263/406224) on the adjacent Läufstrasse. Directly opposite is the Gothic **Christuskirche**, a former Minorite monastery with a curiously lopsided interior. A little further down the street is the **Haus von der Leyen**, a Renaissance patrician mansion that now houses the local **museum** (Tues–Fri 10am–noon & 2–5pm, Sat & Sun 2–4pm; DM2). Lack of space means that only a small collection of antiquities is permanently on display, but the changing exhibitions (prominently featured on posters outside) are often surprisingly good.

Practicalities

Andernach hosts a number of **festivals**, including a medieval fair in the Burg (mid-July); *Die Tausende Lichten* (The Thousand Lights), featuring fireworks and illuminations (first weekend in September); and, of course, Carnival. In summer, the town is a popular overnight stop with tour coach operators; hence there are plenty of **hotels**, but these are often fully booked and anyway charge independent travellers inflated prices. There's a clutch of cheaper options along Konrad-Adenauer-Allee overlooking the Rhine, and on Mauerstrasse directly behind; the going rate is upwards of DM35 per person. You should be able to stay for a bit less at *Hubertus*, Im Boden 13 (☎0263/45769), or in the few **private houses** (the tourist office has a list; single rooms are pretty well non-existent). Beware of *Zum Stadtwappen* on Kirchstrasse; it's one of the cheapest options according to official listings, but the proprietress uses any old dodge – from charging for breakfast twice to levying a supplement for proximity to a toilet – to bump up the bill. Most of what passes for **nightlife** goes on in Hochstrasse and the streets leading from it down to the Rhine. **Buses** leave from Am Stadtgraben, the western range of the old wall. The **Bahnhof** is on Kurfürstendamm; to reach the centre, walk straight ahead, then turn right under the railway bridge.

Beyond Andernach

Immediately beyond BROHL, the train's second stop after Andernach, stands **Burg Rheineck**. This fortress, which was rebuilt in the nineteenth century, is no longer open to the public, but if you follow the path to the right, you come to a belvedere commanding an impressive panorama. A further 3km on is **BAD BREISIG**, a popular spa and holiday resort, which makes the cheapest base for exploring this area; rooms can be found for as little as DM20 in private guest houses scattered all over the town, and there's also a **campsite** (☎02633/95645).

From Bad Breisig, the railway leaves the banks of the river for a spell, continuing to **SINZIG**, 6km away, which lies near the end of the valley of the Ahr. There's just one monument of note: the church of **St Peter**, one of the smallest but most original of the Romanesque basilicas of the Rhineland. Even more than usual, the impression is of a dream-like fantasy, an effect accentuated by the white and yellow paint covering the exterior walls. The lofty galleried interior, which uses differently coloured stones for contrast, creates an impression of space out of all proportion to its modest length. On the south side of the chancel is a chapel adorned with noble though fragmentary frescos which are contemporary with the building, while the high altar has a brightly coloured late fifteenth-century *Passion Retable* from Cologne.

Remagen

Back on the Rhine, 4km north, is **REMAGEN**, a town famous for a **bridge** which – apart from its support towers – no longer exists. The towers on the Remagen side have been converted into the **Friedensmuseum** (March–Nov daily 10am–5pm; DM2), which chronicles the story of the bridge by means of old photographs.

In the centre of town, the dominant building is the curious church of **SS Peter und Paul**. At the turn of the century, it was decided that the original Romanesque-Gothic church was no longer sufficiently big for the town's expanding population; accordingly, a new church, imitating the style of the old but on a much larger scale, was tacked at right angles directly on to it. More directly appealing is the enigmatic **Pfarrhoftor**, a double gateway forming the entrance to the parish close. It's covered with carvings made by a Romanesque sculptor of limited technique but fertile imagination.

High above Remagen stands the mid-nineteenth-century **Apollinariskirche**, goal of a popular ten-day pilgrimage at the end of July. The church was built in tandem with the completion of the Dom in Cologne, and is a miniature version of it. Inside, the walls are covered with frescos of the lives of Christ, the Virgin and Saint Apollinaris. According to the old *Baedeker Guides*, in its time this church was representative of the very best

---

THE BRIDGE AT REMAGEN

Remagen's bridge was built during World War I to aid the movement of troops and supplies to the Western Front. On 7 March 1945, an advance regiment of the US Armoured Division reached this point, to find that the bridge – unlike all the others along the Rhine, Germany's most crucial natural defensive barrier – was still intact. The token Nazi force who had been left to guard it was quickly routed, enabling the Americans to establish a base on the opposite bank. Eisenhower declared the bridge to be "worth its weight in gold", while Hitler ordered the execution of four officers for their carelessness in failing to blow the bridge up. In retrospect, the importance of the Remagen episode seems exaggerated, as crossings were made by the Allies further up the Rhine the following week. Moreover, the bridge itself collapsed ten days later due to overloading, killing 28 American soldiers. However, it was symbolically a telling blow and has remained a popular subject for books, the best of which is Ken Hechler's *The Bridge at Remagen*.

modern art and architecture. Though such a view was subsequently sneered at by more "enlightened" opinion, the building can by now be enjoyed for what it is – a true period-piece.

With its central location, Remagen is undoubtedly the best base for this part of the Rhine, and there's a **campsite** (☎02642/22222) right beside the river. The hotels beside the Bahnhof are geared to coach parties and are anyway best avoided as thundering goods trains pass through all night. Far better to go for a room in a **private house** – *Borsch-Genn*, Walburgstr. 23 (☎02642/23109), has singles at DM25, doubles at DM48, and also offers competitive full- or half-board rates, while *Fleschhut*, Birresdorfer Str. 26 (☎02642/22559), has two doubles at DM50 or less.

Rolandseck

ROLANDSECK, a further 6km north, has now been absorbed by Remagen. The railway station building is now designated the **Künstlerbahnhof** (daily 10am–5pm; DM2.50), housing a notable collection of works by Hans Arp, along with changing exhibitions of contemporary art. More sculptures by Arp and by Henry Moore can be seen for free on the lawn outside.

One of the most famous Rhine legends is closely associated with the vicinity of Rolandseck. In the middle of the Rhine, just beyond the village, is the island of **Nonnenwerth**, occupied by a former convent. On hearing news of the death of Roland (Charlemagne's nephew) in an ambush in northern Spain, his betrothed is alleged to have come here, taking her final vows the moment before the hero, miraculously recovered from his wounds – which had killed him off in all alternative sagas – arrived to claim her. Stricken by grief, he built the **Rolandsbogen** fortress on the hill above in order to catch occasional glimpses of her. Whatever the veracity of the story, it's well worth climbing up to the ruin, which commands one of the most extensive views of this part of the Rhine, with Bonn and the Siebengebirge (see Chapter Five, *North Rhineland-Westphalia*) immediately to the north.

THE EIFEL

Strictly speaking the mountains of the **Eifel** range – which are divided between the Rhineland-Palatinate and North Rhineland-Westphalia – are little more than big hills. On the whole, they aren't desperately exciting, which probably accounts for the lack of mass tourism. However, in the part of the Eifel which lies in the Rhineland-Palatinate you'll find a gentle landscape of wooded hills and bare heathland, dotted with volcanic lakes and intersected by quiet, unspoiled valleys. The area is used to visitors, but most of them are Germans who spend their summer vacations abroad and come here for a second break in late spring or early autumn. This means that it's a good place to escape the crowds, particularly if you're otherwise concentrating on a nearby tourist area, such as the Rhine or Mosel.

The only part of the region which has completely succumbed to tourism is the **Ahr valley** in the northeast where truly spectacular scenery brings hundreds of thousands of visitors during a season that lasts from May until late October. North of Trier, in the **Bitburg-Prüm** region, is where you'll find the region at its most unspoilt. The area known as the **Vulkaneifel,** where glassy circular lakes in the craters of extinct volcanoes and massive pillars of volcanic rock compete for attention, has some of the most unusual and spectacular scenery, with the added attractions of well-developed holiday and water sport activities. Best looking town outside the Ahr valley is **Mayen** with its restored medieval centre and spectacular castles. Otherwise much of the Eifel has a slightly sleepy air, its life revolving round the seasonal influxes of visitors and people coming to the various spa towns or *Luftkurorte*.

The Ahr Valley

The valley of the River Ahr rates as one of the most scenic corners of western Germany. The landscape and most of the towns in this valley, which cuts down through from the **Hohe Eifel** to join the Rhine just outside Remagen, are so postcard-pretty that at times you'll find yourself in a real Brothers Grimm landscape of ruined castles, forests and vineyards. No effort has been spared when it comes to providing for mass tourism, and this is where the problems start. From May through to October all those idyllic little towns and villages are filled to overflowing with day-tripping German families, hikers, wine fans and British coach parties, and the only people who really benefit are the owners of tacky souvenir shops and the hotel keepers who rack up their prices and rake the money in.

The best thing to do is to visit the area out of season when you can absorb the atmosphere of the place without the crowds. There really is a lot to take in: the country-side is magnificent once you hit the upper reaches of the valley (particularly around **Altenahr**), and many of the towns and villages look like they've hardly changed in centuries. The area is best explored by taking the train up from Remagen; at first the valley seems flat and nondescript but gradually vineyards start to crowd up to the railway track and the sides of the valley become steeper.

Bad Neuenahr-Ahrweiler

First stop is **BAD NEUENAHR-AHRWEILER**, which threads its way along the Ahr for a few kilometres just before the valley becomes narrower and the spectacular stuff begins. It's really two towns which have grown into each other: Bad Neuenahr is fairly modern and commercially oriented while Ahrweiler is so impossibly old-fashioned that it looks like a film set.

Ahrweiler

From **AHRWEILER's Bahnhof** it's only a few minutes' walk to the centre of town. One of the two **tourist offices** is at Wilhelmstr. 24 (Mon–Fri 8.30am–5.30pm, Sat 9am–noon; ☎02641/5051). The walled kernel of the town dates back to the Middle Ages and seems wildly archaic with its narrow streets and half-timbered buildings. This impression is enhanced as you pass through the **Niedertor**, one of the four medieval city gates. Niederhutstrasse is the town centre's main commercial street with plenty of tacky souvenir shops, along with delicatessens and wine merchants. There are also a few good, albeit slightly pricey, cafés and *Weinstuben*. *Café Sonntag* at no. 69 is fine in a touristy kind of way and *Zum Winzer Michel* at no. 65 is a good place to sample some of the red wines produced in the vineyards you'll have seen as you approached the town. Niederhutstrasse runs into the broad Marktplatz, where you'll find another recommendable restaurant, *Alte Post*, along with another branch of the tourist office.

On the northern side of the square is the thirteenth-century **Pfarrkirche St Laurentius**. Inside are fourteenth- and fifteenth-century frescos and modern stained glass windows, some of which have an almost Expressionist feel to them. At the other end of Marktplatz is the **Weisser Turm**, a defensive tower originally built around 1110 and given a few Baroque embellishments during the seventeenth century. This now houses the **Ahrgau Museum** (April–Oct Fri 10am–noon & 2pm–5pm, Sun 10.30am–noon; DM1) which has a mainly uninspired collection of bits and pieces relating to the Ahrtal area with an emphasis on local wine-production methods through the centuries.

The town centre is ringed by the **Stadtmauer**, built between the thirteenth and fifteenth centuries and still more or less intact despite numerous attempts to breach it during the Thirty Years' War. It's straddled by four towers, of which the largest is the southern **Ahrtor**, overlooking the river Ahr. From here you get a good view across to the **Ursulinenkloster Kalvarienberg**, which sits on the edge of town surrounded by vineyards. This imposing building, resembling a French château, now houses a convent and girls' school.

There are plenty of **hotels**, although the budget end of the market is less well-catered for and obviously in summer it's advisable to check on room availability in advance. *Zur Erholung*, Schützenstr. 74 (☎02641 34936), has a single at DM25, doubles from DM44; *Ippendorf*, Wolfgasse 7 (☎02641/34941), has singles from DM26, doubles from DM48, while *Zur Linde*, Waldporzheimer Str. 69 (☎02641/34319), and *Kronen*, Alveradisstr. 17 (☎02641/34202), respectively charge from DM30 and DM32 per person. The **youth hostel** is on St-Pius-Strasse (☎02641/34924), about 20 minues' walk from the Bahnhof along a well-signposted route; the **campsite** is at Kalvarienbergstr. 1 (☎02641/36250), on the way out to the Ursulinenkloster.

Bad Neuenahr

Though less attractive than its sister town, **BAD NEUENAHR** has a couple of things worth seeing: the **Willibrorduskirche** on Schweizerstrasse, with its Romanesque west tower and the usual melange of architectural details, and the **Beethovenhaus** on Beethovenstrasse, a Baroque townhouse where the composer used to spend his holidays. Beethoven probably came to the town in order to benefit from its thermal springs and the healing properties of the locally bottled mineral water.

Today Bad Neuenahr is still a well-known *Kurort* and spa. The riverside **Kurgarten** (daily 7am–9.30pm; DM2.50) and the classically elegant **Thermal Badehaus** are survivors from an era when wealthy families from all over Europe came here to enjoy the waters and hothouse social life. Another big attraction is the **Spielbank** in Casinostrasse, the largest casino in Germany. The roulette wheels start rolling daily at 2pm and for DM5 admission you can gamble away your life's savings or, if you're more cautiously inclined, just watch the action. The **tourist office** is at Hauptstr. 60 (☎02641/2278), next door to the Bahnhof. Among the huge range of hotels on offer, try *Haus am Lennépark*, Unterstr. 11 (☎02641/24031), with singles from DM28, doubles DM54, or *Zum Ännchen*, Hauptstr. 47 (☎02641/21890), with singles DM32, doubles DM60.

The Upper Ahrtal and the Rotweinwanderweg

Heading west by rail out of Bad Neuenahr-Ahrweiler you pass through a string of little wine-producing villages. The railway runs roughly parallel to the most interesting and scenic stretch of the **Rotweinwanderweg**, a walking route (look out for the distinctive red bunch of grapes signs) which starts at BAD BODENDORF and covers the 35km to ALTENAHR. The Ahr valley is at its most beautiful after Bad Neuenahr-Ahrweiler, where the valley narrows and its steep sides are terraced with vines in an effort to cultivate every available centimetre.

First stop after Bad Neuenahr–Ahrweiler is **WALPORZHEIM**, which is actually an administrative part of the larger town. The local wine speciality is a late-Burgundy type which you can sample in the *Probierkeller* of the *Winzerverein Walporzheim*, Walporzheimerstr. 173 (☎02641/34763), which is the second oldest wine co-op in Germany. Also worth checking out is *Brogsitter's Sanct Peter*, Walporzheimerstr. 134 (☎02641/389911), a wine restaurant belonging to the famous *Weingut St Peter*, a vineyard which was founded in 1246. During the second weekend in August the annual *Weinfest* takes place and the streets run with red wine.

Next along the line are the little wine villages of **DERNAU** and **RECH**. Dernau's *Hotel-Gasthaus Poppelreuther*, Friedenstr. 4, has one single from DM25 and doubles from DM52. Rech also has a good selection of pensions and it's worth bearing these villages in mind if you're in the area in high season when the hotels in the larger towns tend to fill up quickly.

MAYSCHOSS, a couple of kilometres up the line nestles in the Ahr valley and consequently attracts a lot of coach parties. Although the town boasts 500 hotel beds, few of them come cheap; best bets are *Gasthaus Fuhrmann*, Dorfstr. 45 (☎02643/ 7028), which has rooms from DM30 per person, and *Bacchus Keller*, Ahrrotweinstr. 20, whose rates begin at DM33 per person. The main non-wine-related local attractions are the ruined **Saffenburg**, which overlooks the village, and the black marble tomb in the **Pfarrkirche** containing the remains of Katherina Von der Mark-Schleiden, a serving girl turned countess who once ruled the area from the castle.

Altenahr

The next stop is **ALTENAHR**, a town which can only be described as picturesque and whose population seems to increase tenfold in the summer. It's horrendously clogged up then, but if you go off-season you could easily spend a few days here using the town as a base to explore the surrounding area. The landscape is magnificent – the valley is so narrow at this point it almost becomes a gorge and the town is situated on a tortuous bend in the river. If you follow the river eastwards out of town precipitous rock faces soar from the northern bank, and on the southern side steep forested slopes lead up to the craggy peaks of the **Voreifel**. By night, the whole place has an unearthly atmosphere.

Altenahr's **tourist office** is housed in the Bahnhof building (Mon–Fri 10am–noon & 3–5pm, Sat 10am–noon; ☎02643/8848). There are plenty of suspiciously pristine half-timbered facades – and also plenty of souvenir shops and hotels. The best way to appreciate Altenahr's undeniable charms is to trek up to **Burg Are** from whose ruined heights you get a tremendous view of the surrounding area. Burg Are itself was built around 1100 and the ruins have a romantic feel to them – you could easily imagine them as the venue for an illicit lovers' rendezvous in days gone by. Like most castles in this part of Germany it was destroyed by the French in 1690 after a nine-month siege, leaving only ruined walls. The whole town was once fortified but only a few remnants of the former wall and towers remain. There's also a Romanesque **Pfarrkirche** which, despite a few Gothic additions, retains very clear and simple lines.

In addition to the *Rotweinwanderweg*, there are fifteen signposted local **walking routes**. A number of paths lead up from the Bahnhof into the hills and to the nearby village of ALTENBURG. Look out for the **Teufelsloch**, a famous local landmark and viewpoint, where the elements have eroded a giant hole into the rock. From up here you gain a good view of the **Langfigtal** natural park and of the **Breite Ley**, a sheer volcanic rock formation which rises from the Ahr valley just outside town. Another possibility is to take the chairlift which runs from the bottom of Seilbahnstrasse to the 330-metre-high **Ditschardhöhe**, with a café and good views.

The local **youth hostel** (☎02643/1880) is about thirty minutes' walk out of town down the unlit Langfigtal. **Camping** facilities are available just outside town near Altenburg (☎02643/8503). Biggest cluster of **hotels** is on Brückenstrasse, but you'd be well advised to shop around, using the tourist office's list. **Pensions**, for example *Maria Schäfer* at Rossberg 93, can cost as little as DM20 per person.

From Altenahr you can make a five-minute train journey to **KREUZBERG**, where the railway line ends; if you want to go any further, you're reliant on the buses. The **Burg** is an eighteenth-century reconstruction of an earlier one which was destroyed by the French. Near the Bahnhof is another **campsite** (☎02643/8581).

Adenau and The High Eifel

There are regular services (approximately one bus an hour) from Altenahr to **ADENAU** and the thirty-minute journey takes you through the upper reaches of the Ahr valley, via a succession of tiny villages, deep into the **High Eifel** (*Hohe Eifel*). Adenau is a pretty little tourist town straggling along the river valley, notable mainly for the fifteenth- and sixteenth-century half-timbered houses which surround its **Marktplatz**. These are actually the genuine article, as the occasional sagging roof or slightly buckled facade shows, but they have been prettified for the tourists and now house the usual range of cafés, bars and shops. There's also a venerable church here that dates from the eleventh century, but which was altered in the thirteenth century.

The **tourist office** is at Marktplatz 8 (☎02691/2016). Reasonable local **hotels** include *Gästehaus Kupper*, Hauptstr. 15 (☎02691/2156), which costs DM30 per person, and *Poststübchen*, Hauptstr. 22 (☎02691/2589), from DM25 per person.

Nürburg and the Nürburgring

From Adenau, regular buses run to the **Nürburg**, a ruined castle which stands on one of the highest peaks in the Eifel range (678m). The Nürburg was originally the site of a Roman fortress but the ruins you see today are the remains of a twelfth-century fortress destroyed by French soldiers after a long siege in 1690. A few pensions and hotels lie in the eponymous nearby village, of which one of the cheapest is *Pension Hans Loosen*, Burgstr. 28 (☎02691/7418), offering singles from DM28, doubles from DM50.

Easily reached from the village itself is the famous **Nürburgring** race track which, depending on your sensibilities, could well be worth a visit. No longer used for Formula One grand prix racing because of the dangerous track (it was here that Niki Lauda had his near-fatal crash in 1976), it's still used for minor motor races. The main entrance to the ring is just outside Nürburg itself and the track, built between 1925 and 1927, is a 28km long figure-of-eight which winds its way through the forested High Eifel. If you're travelling by car you can take a spin round the track yourself (DM15 for the whole run, DM12 for the 24km northern section or DM6 for a 4.5km short run). For DM75 a professional racing driver will chauffeur you round either of the tracks (☎02691/302154 Mon–Fri for more information about this; ☎02691/302156 or 302158 for news of events).

If you're in the area you might also want to take a look in the **Rennsportmuseum** (daily 10am–6pm; DM8.50). This houses an extensive collection of thoroughbred cars and bikes of the kind that have raced on the Nürburgring for the last sixty years or so.

Mayen and around

The first thing you should know about **MAYEN**, some 30km from Andernach on the main east–west Eifel railway line, is that it was almost completely flattened by the RAF on 2 January 1945 to prevent the Germans from using it as a staging post for troops during the Ardennes offensive. This will save you from disappointment when you find out that all its quaint and charming buildings date from the last forty years or so. The rebuilding programme has been carried out with a great deal of sensitivity and, apart from an ugly department store on the Marktplatz, no great architectural errors seem to have been made.

If you arrive by rail it's a five-minute bus ride from the **Westbahnhof** to the town centre. The bus will drop you off at the **Brückentor**, which, along with the **Obertor** on Boemundring at the other side of town, is all that remains of the once 1600-metre-long city wall. Walking up Marktstrasse towards the Marktplatz you pass the **Pfarrkirche St Clemens**, whose distinctive twisted steeple was caused by poor construction techniques and the influence of the weather. On Marktplatz itself is the Baroque **Altes Rathaus** – the only town centre building to survive the war just about intact – which houses the **tourist office** (daily 8am–12.30pm & 1.30–5.30pm; ☎02651/88260).

From the other end of the square the thirteenth-century **Genoveveburg** glowers over the town. Nowadays it houses the **Eifeler Landschaftsmuseum** (Feb 16–Nov 30 Mon–Sat 9am–noon & 2–5pm, Sun & holidays 10am–1pm; DM2), where a range of Eifel-related exhibits takes you from the Stone Age to modern times. Look out for the before-and-after pictures showing the war damage inflicted on the town. About two-thirds of the **Herz-Jesu-Kirche**, which you can see from the battlements of the Genoveveburg, was destroyed: photographs inside record the destruction and reconstruction.

Close to Mayen is **Schloss Bürresheim** (April–Sept 9am–1pm & 2–6pm, Oct, Nov & Jan–March 9am–1pm & 2–5pm; closed the first working day of every month; DM2), which is the epitome of the German fairy-tale castle. It rises out of the wooded valley of the River Nette and is only about five minutes out of town by bus (leaving from the stop between Im Möhren and Wittbende on the Habsburgring). Begun as a fortress in 1220, it was turned into a residential castle during the sixteenth century, a change clearly reflected in its appearance, the grim stone walls of the original fortress being topped by more fanciful Renaissance turrets.

Best **hotel** bet is *Keupen*, Marktplatz 21–23 (☎02651/73077), which charges upwards of DM27. The **youth hostel** is some way out of the town centre on Knüppchen (☎02651/2355); to get there walk down Göbelstrasse from Marktplatz, turn left on to Stehbachstrasse and then make an immediate right into Im Möhren and follow the road right up the steep hill. As far as **nightlife** goes, Mayen is a dead loss; the only place with any action is *Rote Rooster*, Töpferstr. 3, which attracts a vaguely "alternative" crowd.

Monreal

A few kilometres down the line from Mayen, **MONREAL** is an attractive place, but one that should be given a wide berth during holiday periods. Off-season, its streets of half-timbered houses look like they belong on a biscuit tin lid. Look out for the **Johannisbrücke** which spans the River Elz (a stream really). It's also worth taking time to explore the **Philippsburg** and **Löwenburg**, the two ruined castles which tower over the village. A number of *Wanderwege* start in Monreal; information about these can be obtained from Mayen tourist office.

Maria Laach

By far the most outstanding historical monument in the Eifel is the Benedictine monastery of **Maria Laach**, which lies in an isolated setting of forests, meadows and fields roughly 15km north of Mayen. Its name is derived from the adjacent **Laacher See**, which was formed by a volcanic cave-in, and which still has a raw primeval feel to it. Bus #6032 links Maria Laach with the nearest railway station (NIEDERMENDIG) and with Mayen, while bus #6031 runs there from Andernach.

The **church** is a visual stunner, ranking as the most beautiful of all the great Romanesque buildings of the Rhineland. Its sense of unity is all the more remarkable in that, although begun at the end of the eleventh century, it was not finished until well into the thirteenth century. One of its most distinctive features is its stonework – for the most part it's constructed from the local yellow-brown tufa, but dark basalt was used for architectural highlighting. Each end of the church is girded with an arrangement of three towers, presenting as varied and striking a silhouette as the Middle Ages ever produced.

Even more remarkable is the last part to be built, the **Paradise**, a courtyard placed in front of the building, enclosing the western choir. Apparently intended as a symbol of the innocence of the Garden of Eden, it's unique in Christian architecture, being suggestive of Islamic places of worship, an impression strengthened by the addition of the burbling Lions' Fountain in the middle. The capitals, showing a fabulous bestiary, were carved with a gossamer delicacy by a mason dubbed the Samson Master, who is also known to have worked at Andernach and Bonn.

After all this, the pure Romanesque sobriety of the interior comes as a surprise. However, the early Gothic **baldachin** at the high altar is again reminiscent of the art of Islam and is quite unlike any other such object in Europe. There's also a fine polychrome **tomb** of the founder, Count Palatine Heinrich II, shown in an idealised youthful reclining pose, clutching a model of the church. To see the **crypt**, the earliest part of the building, you have to join one of the regular guided tours (donation expected) conducted by the monks. Their services employ the Gregorian chant; vespers, at 5.30pm, finishes in good time to catch the last bus out. You can **eat** in style at the monastery's own hotel (☎02652/5840), or more simply in the cafeteria alongside. A campsite (☎02636/2485) can be found on the shore of the Laacher See.

The Vulkaneifel

The **Vulkaneifel** (Volcanic Eifel), in the very heart of the massif, was the scene of explosive volcanic activity until about 10,000 years ago, which has done a lot to shape the physical and economic landscape of the region. Both the distinctive circular **crater lakes** (*Maare*) which dot the area so handily for windsurfers and water-skiers, and the natural springs that draw thousands of *Kurort* visitors and keep local mineral water bottlers in business owe their existence to these geologically recent upheavals.

Daun

DAUN, right in the centre of the Vulkaneifel, can be reached from Mayen by bus or train. In the surrounding locality, the post-volcanic crater lakes have been turned into restrained resorts with facilities for sailing, angling and water sports. Daun itself makes a convenient base for exploring the area, with its full complement of cheap hotels. In the centre of town, *Manderscheid*, Wirichstr. 23 (☎06592/2210), has rooms from DM25 per person. Similar rates are available at *Zu den Maaren*, Maarstr. 6 (☎06592/2230), and *Zum Post*, Muhlenweg 7 (☎06592/2151), in GEMÜNDEN, near the town's cluster of crater lakes.

The three lakes **Gemündener Maar**, **Weinfelder Maar** (or **Totenmaar**) and **Schalkenmehrener Maar** are all easily reached from Daun town centre either on foot or by bus. Weinfelder is easily the most compelling. Of the three lakes it's the only one where boating and fishing are forbidden and it has a melancholy, almost threatening atmosphere, enhanced by the forlorn chapel on its bank and the still, dark surface of the water. A little further afield near GILLENFELD is the **Pulvermaar**, the largest of the lakes, which has **camping** facilities on its bank (☎06573/523 or 311).

Going back to Celtic times, Daun's old town centre sits on top of a chunk of volcanic rock – its name means "fortified heights". Though it looks impressive as you approach, closer up it turns out to be a slightly bland market town and *Kurort*. The **tourist office** is in the *Kurzentrum*, Leopold Str. 14 (Mon–Fri 8.30am–6pm, Sat 10am–noon; ☎06592/71477), but the town doesn't really have any sights to speak of. The only substantial surviving part of the old castle, the *Höhenburg*, has been turned into a hotel and apart from that the only place worth a passing look is the Pfarrkirche, just off Wirichstrasse, which dates back to the tenth century.

Ulmen and Kelberg

ULMEN, on the edge of the **Ulmener Maar**, 10km east of Daun, can be reached by bus or train. It merits a call for its ruined castle and lakeside atmosphere, although the planners have thoughtlessly cut the town in two with a motorway. **KELBERG**, a tiny *Luftkurort* surrounded by rolling woodland, also rates a visit, but is a bit more difficult to get to, with only a couple of buses per day from Daun. The Romanesque-Gothic **Pfarrkirche** is pretty enough, if over-proud of its fifteenth-century wooden *Crucifix*.

Gerolstein

West of Daun, at the junction of the railway line from Andernach with that between Trier and Cologne, is **GEROLSTEIN**. Again, its main assets are natural ones: a couple of Dolomite rock pillars which tower over the town in a most spectacular way, harbouring the remains of a 300 million year old coral reef. In the north side of the one called **Munterley** is the **Buchenloch**, a cave which was once home to a band of Neanderthals.

Otherwise, Gerolstein hasn't got much going for it. The Roman **Villa Sarabodis** is interesting enough, but there's not much left. For a bit of light relief you can always visit the factory that produces *Gerolsteiner Sprudel*, one of Germany's favourite mineral waters. For details and opening times, check with the **tourist office** in the Rathaus (Mon–Thurs 7.45am–12.30pm & 1.30–5pm, Fri 7.45am–12.30pm & 1.30–4pm; ☎06591/ 1382).

Manderscheid

From Daun there are fairly frequent buses through the deep wooded valley of the River Lieser, then up the alternating wood- and heathland of the Vulkaneifel to **MANDERSCHEID**. It's yet another touristy little *Kurort*, clinging tightly to the banks of the river. Above the eastern bank of the Lieser are two castles: the **Oberburg** and the **Unterburg**. Together they once formed part of an extensive fortification system which, in the fifteenth century, was thought to be impregnable. It wasn't. Both castles were sacked during the Thirty Years' War and later the troops of Louis XIV finished the job. Fortunately the city authorities have done pretty good restoration work on both buildings.

It's also worth taking a trip to the **Meerfeldermaar** about 5km west of Manderscheid, and to the **Hinkelmaar** on top of the **Moosenberg** just southwest of the town. The Hinkelmaar, although relatively small, looks much more like a former volcano crater than some of the other *Maare*, and at one point you can see where lava once broke through its sides in a sixty-metre-wide stream.

Another attraction in the Manderscheid area is the **Abtei Himmerod**, an eighteenth-century monastery with an impressively austere Baroque church attached. This was once one of the most important religious houses in the Eifel and was favoured by monastically inclined sons of the local nobility until the French dissolved it in 1802 and sold the buildings. It's been well restored, but bear in mind that the place is a day-trippers' destination in the summer.

Manderscheid's **tourist office** is in the *Kurverwaltung* building (Mon–Fri 8am–12.30pm & 2–5pm, May–Oct Sat 10am–noon; ☎06572/2377). The town's **youth hostel** is at Mosenbergerstr. 17 (☎06572/557). Best **hotel** bets are *Kupferpfanne*, Wittlicher Str. 25 (☎06572/4936), from DM25 per person, and *Haus Elisabeth*, Am Hohlen Weg 14 (☎06572/4402) from DM21.

Wittlich

Buses run from Manderscheid south to **WITTLICH**, a conventionally attractive town situated at the point where the Eifel starts to level out and the Mosel valley proper begins. In summer, the town's bars and cafés spill out on to the streets, creating an atmosphere that makes you forget that you're in Northern Europe. Wittlich's special climate enhances the illusion: it's so mild here that the usual vineyards keep company with a tobacco plantation.

The town's **tourist office** is in the southeastern corner of the Baroque Altes Rathaus on Burgstrasse (Mon–Fri 9am–noon & 1–6pm, Sat 10am–noon & 2–5pm; ☎06571/ 4086). The rest of the building is home to the **Städtische Gallerie** which puts on regular exhibitions. In the immediate vicinity, around **Marktplatz**, there are some Baroque houses which do a lot to help create the town centre's unselfconsciously historic feel. Nearby is the **Markuskirche**, an early Baroque church which would be unexceptional were it not for its impressively tall, steep-roofed bell tower. There's also a significant local Roman left-over in the shape of the **Römervilla**, just off Schloss Strasse on the way out of town.

The vibrant local street life gets excessive during the third weekend in August when the **Saubrennerkirmes** is celebrated. This fair is marked by the usual drinking and eating extravaganza, plus the roasting of over a hundred pigs in the market place. This is to mark the grudge held against all pigs by the people of Wittlich ever since it was captured after a long siege – thanks to a pig who ate the turnip being used to hold the town gate shut.

Centrally located hotels include *Schneck*, Trierer Str. 52 (☎06571 5692), with singles from DM27, and *Wittlicher Hof*, Trierer Str. 29 (☎06571/772), from DM35. The town is full of cafés and bars and most of the centrally located ones aren't bad; *Journal*, Neustr. 8, is the trendiest hangout.

Bitburg-Prüm

North of Trier is the administrative region of **Bitburg-Prüm** which has a few relatively undiscovered corners, though it's become a major centre for winter sports enthisiasts.

Bitburg

BITBURG itself is a bit of a dump. Apart from the famous **Bitburger Brauerei** at Romerstrasse 3 (Mon–Thurs 9.30am–1.30pm), which supplies beer to the whole Eifel and beyond, and the **Bierbrunnen**, a copper fountain in the town centre which dispenses beer on festival days, there's not really much to see or do. The town achieved notoriety in 1985, when **President Reagan** laid a wreath at the town's war cemetery, the burial place of 49 SS officers. Coming immediately after his visit to Belsen concentration camp, this insensitive gesture deeply offended Germany's Jewish community. Should you need to stay on, the **tourist office**, Bedastr. 11 (☎06561/8934), will supply further information on the town and its accommodation facilities.

Kyllburg

It's probably best to by-pass Bitburg altogether and head straight for **KYLLBURG**, about 11km to the north by road or rail and easily reached from Trier. This is a *Kurort*, the sort of place that could be the setting for a Thomas Mann novella with its lazy ambience, turn of the century hotels and sun terraces for convalescents. It makes a good base for exploring the surrounding area which, although unexceptional, is tranquil in a low-key way. Main sights are the **Stiftskirche**, with an intact sixteenth-century stained glass window, and the thirteenth-century defensive tower, which has a good vertigo inducing view of the surrounding area (pick up the key from the market garden next door).

The **tourist office** is in the *Kurverwaltung*, Hochstr. 19 (daily 8am–6pm; ☎06563/ 2007). **Camping** facilities are available just outside town at Karl-Kaufmann-Weg 1 (☎06563/2570). The most central **hotel** is *Zur Post*, Bahnhofstr. 30 (☎06563/2216), with singles from DM31, doubles DM52.

It's an easy walk of about 1km from Kyllburg to **Malberg**, a sixteenth-century castle which towers above the attached village in true fairy-tale fashion. A little to the east of Kyllburg is SEINSFELD, with a moated medieval castle. Halfway to Bitburg, just outside the village of NATTENHEIM, is **Villa Otrang** (April–Sept Tues–Sun 9am–1pm & 2–6pm; Oct–Nov & Jan–March Tues–Sun 9am–1pm & 2–5pm; DM2), the best-preserved Roman monument in the area. You get a good impression of the original layout and there are some vivid animal mosaics.

Prüm

From Kyllburg head for **PRÜM** by one of the three direct buses per day, or take the train to Gerolstein and then a bus from there. This is a soporific little ex-market town (the Marktplatz is now a car park) and winter sports centre. The **tourist office** is on Hahnplatz (☎06551/505) directly opposite the main tourist attraction, the Baroque-fronted **Salvatorbasilica**, which was designed by Seitz and Neumann, the team responsible for the St Paulin in Trier. Inside are the obligatory holy relic (a fragment of Christ's sandal) and tomb of local royal personage (Lothar I, grandson of Charlemagne).

In winter Prüm becomes a weekend skiers' mecca with a couple of good runs at the **Wolfschlucht** (just outside town) and on the **Schwarzer Mann**, the highest Eifel ridge, which is in a part of the range known as the **Schnee-Eifel** (or **Schneifel**), about 14km north-west of Prüm. For skiing information, contact Prüm tourist office. Prüm has plenty of central **hotels**, such as *Zum Goldenen Stern* on Hahnplatz (☎06551/3075), which charges from DM30 per person. There's a **youth hostel** (☎06551/2500) on the edge of town, at the top of an agonisingly steep hill.

Neuerberg

For a real taste of the region's raw beauty head for **NEUERBERG** (four buses a day from Prüm), a picturesque little village in the remote Enztal, whose partially ruined castle houses a privately owned **youth hostel**. *Gasthof Balmes*, Kirchgasse 1 (☎06564/2314), is one of the cheaper **hotels**. There are **camping** facilities at Pestalozzistr. 7 (☎06564/2071), while the **tourist office** is at Herrenstr. 2 (☎06564/2017).

THE SAARLAND

The **Saarland**, taking its name from the River Saar which cuts through its length, is the poorest of the western German Länder, traditionally a big coal-mining area which is now suffering from a bad case of post-industrial malaise. It's always been a bit of a political football; much of it belonged to France up until 1815, and a couple of times this century they've tried to get their hands on it again. After World War I the Saarland passed into League of Nations control, which effectively meant that the French took over, with the right to exploit local mines in compensation for damage done to their own mining industry during the war. In the January 1935 plebiscite 90 per cent of Saarlanders voted for union with Nazi Germany. After World War II the Saar once again found itself in limbo, nominally autonomous but with the French government, which was pushing for economic union, calling the shots. In November 1952 the population voted against reunion with Germany, but by January 1957 the increasing prosperity of the Federal Republic had convinced the Saarlanders that their future lay there, and they thus rejoined the fold – much to the chagrin of the French government.

Most Germans see the Saarland only from the vantage point of one of the various motorways that criss-cross it; if you're driving through, it has to be said there aren't really any compelling reasons for getting out of your car. It's unlikely to be a place you'd want to go out of your way to visit, but if you happen to be in the area then there are one or two marginally interesting places and, away from the heavily industrialised areas, the gently rolling wooded landscape is relatively inoffensive. The French have left a small linguistic legacy in the shape of the greeting *Salü* which replaces the normal *Guten Tag* here. Of late there's also been a marked French influence on local **cuisine**, traditionally always a poor man's fare, based on a thousand and one potato variations like *Hooriche* (raw potato rissoles).

Politically, the Saarland has left a mark out of all proportion to its size. Erich Honecker, the veteran GDR dictator toppled in the 1989 revolution, was born in the Saarland town of Neunkirchen, where his sister – untempted by the regime he was so prominent in moulding – is still a Communist Party activist. Furthermore, the Land's current Minister-President, Oskar Lafontaine*, is seen as the main future hope of the SPD, if the party is to recover from its long period in the doldrums at Federal level.

Saarbrücken

The relative poverty of the Saarland is nowhere more apparent than in the capital **SAARBRÜCKEN**, which, despite the efforts of both the German and French governments over the years, is a shabby industrial town. It's the kind of place that lists among its attractions the *Bergwerksdirektion* (Mining Administration Office), and apart from a few central historic buildings is almost unrelievedly modern.

Around town

The town (whose name means "Saar bridges") has a vague harbour feel. What sights there are lie south of the river. There's a nondescript Schloss – which has seen better days – on the square of the same name, with a fifteenth-century **Schlosskirche** containing tombs of the Princes of Nassau-Saarbrücken. (Some of these are replicas – the originals were destroyed in the war.) About the most interesting feature of the Schloss is its park, and that suffers from its view over the autobahn.

The Schloss was designed during the eighteenth century by Friedrich Joachim Stengel, Saarbrücken's municipal architect, who also built the **Altes Rathaus** opposite. Today this houses the **Abenteuer Museum** (Tues & Wed 9am–1pm, Thurs & Fri 3–7pm, Sat 10am–2pm; DM2) which is devoted in roughly equal parts to the lives and cultures of "primitive" peoples and to the ego of its founder Heinz Rox-Schulz who has spent most of his life travelling to far-flung corners of the world collecting and filming. Bizarre items from the collection include a 2000-year-old Peruvian mummy and some shrunken heads.

From Schlossplatz head down Schlossstrasse and turn right into Eisenbahnstrasse. On the right you'll see the plain white mid-eighteenth-century **Friedenskirche** (Peace Church), which has a startlingly austere interior, with just a single crucifix as decoration. Opposite in Ludwigsplatz is the Baroque **Ludwigskirche**, designed by Stengel and generally reckoned to be the best church in the Saarland despite the fact that it was burned down in 1944 and has been extensively restored. It's an odd building, quite low and severe, with a strangely truncated octagonal tower. The interior, including the imposing pulpit, is painted in brilliant white. At no. 15 on the square is the **Museum für Vor- und Frühgeschichte** (Tues–Sat 9am–4pm, Sun 10am–5pm; free), an extensive but dull archaeology collection.

---

*Having narrowly survived an assassination attempt, Lafontaine gave a lacklustre performance as Chancellor-candidate in 1990. Facing a hopeless battle against Helmut Kohl, who had turned the dream of German unification into reality, he tried to play the petty bourgeois card of niggling about the cost of the exercise, prompting the charge that he was wholly unequal to the historical challenge facing the nation.

The **Deutschherrenkapelle** in Moltkestrasse to the west of the city centre is Saarbrücken's oldest building, dating back to the thirteenth century, although you wouldn't know it at first glance, because it has been frequently and radically altered over the centuries. At the eastern end of town, on St Arnualer Markt, is the **Stiftskirche St Arnual**, a solid early Gothic affair, topped by a Baroque tower. Inside are a few tombs of members of the Nassau-Saarbrücken family: the most spectacular are those of Count Johann III and Elizabeth von Lotharingen.

Crossing the **Alte Brücke** brings you to the north bank of the Saar. On the right is the **Staatstheater**, an angular, monumental building, nowadays used for musicals and drama, which is a good example of the kind of architectural thinking that went on in the Third Reich. Head up Saarstrasse to St Johanner Markt, an old town square with some elegant eighteenth-century houses and a Baroque fountain, all designed by Stengel. Nearby is the **Basilika St Johann**, a standard eighteenth-century Baroque church also designed by Stengel and financed by Louis XV of France.

St Johanner Markt and Bahnhofstrasse to the northwest are supposedly where it's at in Saarbrücken – there are a few expensive shops, cafés and restaurants and a general sense that what money there is in the city tends to find its way here. In the **Altstadtgalerie** at St Johanner Markt 24 (Tues–Sun 11am–7pm; free) you'll find mainly eighteenth-century arts and crafts, while the **Moderne Gallerie und Alte Sammlung** (Tues–Sun 10am–6pm; DM2) at Bismarckstr. 11–15 has a passable collection of nineteenth- and twentieth-century art. It includes works by Raoul Dufy, Pissarro, Monet and Franz Marc; on the first floor is a Rodin sculpture, *Despair*.

Practicalities and information

Saarbrücken's **tourist office** is in the *Info-Pavilion*, Trierer Strasse 2 (Mon–Fri 7.30am–8pm, Sat 7.30am–4pm; ☎0681/309 8222). There's a **youth hostel** at Meerwiesertalweg 31 (☎0681/33040), on the northeastern edge of town (bus #15, #16 or #4 from Bahnhofstrasse), and a *Naturfreundehaus* at Piesporter Weg (☎0681/74617). The cheapest central **hotels** are *St Johanner Hof*, Mainzer Str. 3 (☎0681/34902), which has singles from DM30 and doubles from DM60, and *Schlosskrug*, Schnollerstr. 14 (☎0681/35448), from DM35. The local **camping** facilities are at Am Spicherer Berg (☎0681/51780), a few kilometres south of Saarbrücken on the Franco-German border. For non-EC citizens, who may require visas to visit France, the **French consulate** is at Johannisstr. 2 (☎0681/30626). **Mitfahrzentrale** have an office at Rosenstr. 31 (☎0681/67981).

Saarbrücken is a student town and you do get the feeling that there's something going on here, thanks in part to a strong arty contingent who are always trying to get various projects off the ground. A good way too find out **what's on** is to buy the *Stadtzeitung* (DM3), the bi-monthly local listings magazine. There's also a monthly information sheet called *Salü Saarbrücken*, which often has useful tips, available from the tourist office. One unusual event is the *Perspectives du Théâtre* **festival** of young French theatre, held here every May, which usually throws up a few avant-garde offerings. Also worth knowing about is the *Max Ophüls-Preis* film festival held every January. Saarbrücken's **women's centre** is at Türkenstr. 15 (Mon–Fri 8am–6pm, Sun 2–6pm).

Eating and drinking

Venues for **eating** and **drinking** are several. The place to see and be seen in Saarbrücken is *Brasserie Fröschengasse* in Fröschengasse. For cheap Greek food, there's *Paros Gourmet* on Fass Strasse near the St Johanner Markt; for reasonably priced local fare, try *Bastei*, Saaruferstr. 16, on the south bank of the Saar, while *Naturkost*, at the junction of Wilhelm-Heinrich-Strasse and Franz-Josef-Röder-Strasse, is the best bet for health food.

Worth mentioning is the *Kultur Café*, which forms part of the Stadtgalerie just off the St Johanner Markt. Here, as well as being able to sit outside, you can also have art with your coffee as exhibitions are held on the second floor. The centre of the local **gay** scene (men and women) is *Big Ben* in Försterstrasse which is open most evenings. For **live jazz**, go to *Jazzkeller Giesskanne*, Am Steg 3.

Elsewhere in Saarland

The Saarland has a diverse range of attractions, prominent among which are several important fortifications, a couple of Roman sites and a surprising amount of fine scenery, particularly along the banks of the Saar; the towns, such as Saarlouis and Mettlach, are also far more pleasing than the capital itself.

Homburg and around

At the eastern end of the Land, and easily reached by train from Saarbrücken, is **HOMBURG**. There's nothing much of interest in the town itself, but about ten minutes south by rail, just outside the village of SCHWARZENACKER, is the **Römisches Freilichtmuseum Schwarzenacker** (April–Nov Tues–Sun 9am–noon & 2–5pm; Dec–March Wed 9.30am–4.30pm, Sat & Sun noon–4.30pm; DM3), a big open-air museum on the site of an old Roman settlement which has been partly excavated and reconstructed. Also in the vicinity of Homburg are the **Schlossberghöhlen** (guided tours May–Sept Mon–Fri at 4.30pm, Sat 2–6pm, Sun 10am–noon & 2–6pm, Oct–April Sat 3–6pm, Sun 11am–noon & 2–6pm), a series of sandstone caves on twelve levels, covering 5km altogether. They were hollowed out over six centuries and at one time the sand from them was one of the area's main exports. During the seventeenth and eighteenth centuries, the caves were occupied by the French, who turned them into a frontier fortress, while in the last war they served as a massive communal air-raid shelter for the people of Homburg. Nearby there's a ruined **Schloss** set in gloomy wooded grounds.

Homburg **tourist office** is in the Rathaus, Am Forum (☎06841/2066) and there's a **youth hostel** at Sickingstr. 12 (☎06841/3679). The cheapest **hotels** are *Fasanerie Ursula Kiefer*, Kaiserslauterer Str. 21 (☎06841/65848), and *Haus Bergfrieden*, Steinbergstr. 16 (☎06841/244; in EINÖD), both of which have singles from DM30 and doubles from DM50.

About 15km by rail from Homburg (change at Neunkirchen) is **ST WENDEL**, a pleasant little market town whose main attraction is the Gothic **St Wendelinuskirche**, with three towers and richly decorated interior. En route, you might want to break the journey at **OTTWEILER** which has a well-preserved medieval Altstadt. In the village of **OTZENHAUSEN**, just outside Nonnweiler, about 27km north of St Wendel (train to Turkismühl and then take bus #6430 to Nonnweiler), are the remains of a Celtic **Ringwall** or fortified hillside settlement.

Saarlouis

Travelling west out of Saarbrücken you come to **SAARLOUIS**, a biggish town, originally built as a frontier fortress in 1680 by Louis XIV's architect, Sébastian Vauban. The town passed into Prussian hands in 1814 and although its fortress role was abandoned in 1889 much of the old Prussian fortification network, the **Kasematten**, is still intact – the buildings now house shops and bars rather than soldiers and cannons. Saarlouis has long since spilled out of its old confines but the centre still retains a regularity that could only be the product of the military mind, and the town's main square, the **Grosser Markt**, is actually the former parade ground. Appropriately enough, the town's most famous son was a soldier – Marshal Ney, Napoleon's favourite general.

Mettlach and around

Heading north by road or rail will bring you to **METTLACH**, one of Saarland's prettier towns. The Baroque **Abtei**, an eighteenth-century rebuild of a much older structure, really stands out – but unfortunately it can't be visited as it's used as offices and a private museum by a ceramics firm. The more valuable treasures, including a triptych reliquary, can be seen in the **Pfarrkirche St Liutwin**. In the woods of the nearby park, whose entrance is marked by a neat Neoclassical fountain designed by Karl Friedrich Schinkel, is the octagonal **Alter Turm**, a tenth-century Romanesque mausoleum. A couple of reasonable **hotels** in Mettlach are *Haus Becker*, at the corner of Steinbach and Saarschleife (☎06864/289), singles DM35, doubles DM64, and *Kuhn*, Freiherr-vom-Stein-Str. 14 (☎06864/583), from DM25 per person.

Take bus #6300 from Mettlach to the village of ORSHCOLZ, from where you can walk to **Cloef**, a viewpoint overlooking the Saar *Schleife*, a colossal loop in the river which has created a narrow wooded peninsula. There's a **youth hostel** in the village of DREISBACH (☎06868/270; bus #6300 from Mettlach). The same bus goes to **NENNIG**, in the Mosel valley very close to the Luxembourg border, where there's an old **Schloss** and, more significantly, the remains of the **Römischer Mosaikfussboden** (Tues–Sun April–Sept 8.30–11.30am & 1–5.30pm, Oct & Nov, Jan–March 9–11.30am & 1–4pm; DM1). Along with the huge villa to which it belonged, this Roman floor mosaic was unearthed by a farmer in 1852 on the south-eastern edge of the village. The mosaic originally formed part of the villa entrance hall and includes vivid and detailed depictions of gladiatorial combat. There are **camping** facilities at Sinzer Strasse 1 (☎06866/322) in Nennig itself.

travel details

Trains

From Mainz to Koblenz (frequent; 50min); Worms (2 an hour; 40min); Cologne (1; 2hr 30min); Bonn (1; 1hr 15min); Koblenz (1; 50min); Frankfurt (8 daily; 2hr 30min); Karlsruhe (1; 1hr 5min); Idar Oberrstein (1; 1hr 10min); Saarbrücken (8 daily; 2hr 5min).

From Koblenz to Trier (1 an hour; 90min); Cologne (30min; 1hr 50min); Andernach (30min; 15min); Boppard (1; 15min); Bingen (1; 1hr 10min); Rüdesheim (1; 1hr); Saarburg (8 daily; 1hr 40min); Saarbrücken (8 daily; 2hr 25min).

From Saarbrücken to Mainz (1 an hour; 2hr 30min); Koblenz (1; 2hr 30min); Cologne (5 daily; 3hr 30min); Trier (5 daily; 1hr 5min).

CHAPTER FIVE

NORTH RHINELAND-WESTPHALIA

North Rhineland-Westphalia (*Nordrhein-Westfalen*) is only the fourth largest of the Länder in terms of area, but has, with 17 million inhabitants, by far the largest population. As its double-barrelled name suggests, it's historically two distinct provinces, North Rhineland having belonged to the Franks, while Westphalia marked the beginning of Saxon territory. With the industrialisation process in the nineteenth century, any lingering distinction between the two became hopelessly blurred with the mushroom growth of a vast built-up area around the mineral-rich valley of the River Ruhr. This formed a clearly recognisable unit, yet was divided almost exactly in half by the traditional boundaries. After World War II, it was decided to preserve the economic integrity of the *Ruhrgebiet*, as the area came to be known, by uniting the two provinces. In any event, both had lost a great deal of their former distinguishing characteristics by internal migration, a factor subsequently compounded by high immigration from abroad.

Of the thirty-eight German cities registering a population of over 200,000, ten are in the North Rhineland and a further six in Westphalia. Many begin just as another ends, and the Ruhrgebiet is joined to a string of other cities stretching right to the southern border with Rhineland-Palatinate, making up the most densely populated area in Europe. In this conurbation, **Cologne** is by far the most outstanding city, managing to preserve much of the atmosphere and splendours of its long centuries as a free state, at times the most powerful in Germany. The Land's other city of top-class historical interest is **Aachen**, the original capital of the Holy Roman Empire. Next in line comes **Münster**, which would presumably be capital of Westphalia, if such a division still existed. As it is, the Land government meets in self-consciously cosmopolitan **Düsseldorf**, which inspires admiration and revulsion in roughly equal measure. At the southern end of the Land is **Bonn**, capital of the West German state for its 40-year existence, and still (for the time being) the national seat of government; though never suited for the role it was so casually given in 1949, it's a place all too easily maligned.

In spite of the stranglehold heavy industry has traditionally held over North Rhineland-Westphalia, much of the landscape is rural, with agriculture and forestry making key contributions to the economy. The **Eifel** in the Rhineland, and the **Sauerland**, **Siegerland** and **Teutoburg Forest** in Westphalia all offer varied scenery, and are popular holiday spots with the Germans themselves, being such obvious antidotes to urban life. In these areas are some wonderful small towns – **Monschau**, **Bad Münstereifel**, **Soest** and **Lemgo** – which can stand comparison with any in Germany. Their counterparts along the Rhine have been scarred by war, but **Brühl** and **Xanten** are still particularly worth visiting.

Sobriety is the keynote of the province's architecture; new styles were slow to develop, and there was far less of a readiness to replace buildings simply because they were old-fashioned than was the case further south. This means that there's a legacy of

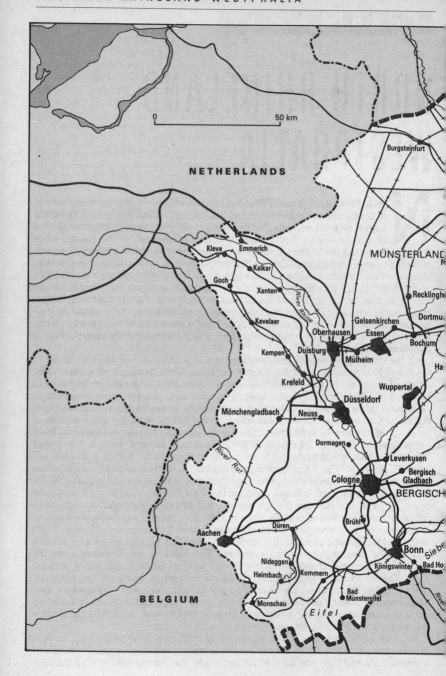

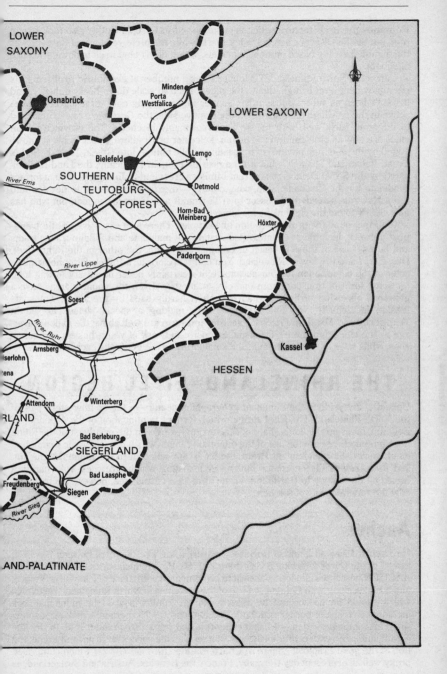

Romanesque architecture which is unsurpassed in Europe. Gothic also took strong root, but the Renaissance barely made a mark, while the preferred form of Baroque was the dignified variety based on Roman models, which didn't lend itself to flowery Rococo offshoots.

Currently, North Rhineland-Westphalia faces a number of **economic problems**. Its unemployment level is high, due to the recent need to scale down heavy industry, and it hasn't been as successful as other Länder in developing and attracting companies active in the new high-tech fields. On the positive side, the *Gastarbeiter* have managed to integrate fairly well, with racism kept reasonably in check. The province's main cities are now as multicultural as London, Leicester or Bradford, a fact tacitly acknowledged by the common practice of translating public notices into Greek, Turkish, Serbo-Croat, Italian and Spanish – but not English or French. Politically, the Land is dominated by the Social Democrats; current Minister-President is **Johannes Rau**, a former candidate for the Chancellorship, who, contrary to expectation, failed to develop into the party's much-needed successor to Willi Brandt and Helmut Schmidt, but who has now clearly found the right niche for himself.

Getting around the province couldn't be simpler. There's an extensive **public transport** network, including two integrated systems of main-line and S-Bahn trains, trams and buses – one of these is based in Cologne and Bonn, the other in the Ruhrgebiet, Düsseldorf and the Lower Rhineland. You can therefore turn the claustrophobic character of the conurbation to your advantage: it's certainly never necessary to wait long for some form of transport from one city to another. Even the country areas have a generous allocation of buses, which are often hardly used by the locals. Transport **freaks**, incidentally, will find oddities worth making a special detour to see in **Wuppertal** and **Minden**. Prices for **accommodation** are well above the national average in the cities, but there's the usual extensive network of youth hostels and campsites, while rates in the countryside and smaller towns are generally excellent value.

THE RHINELAND–EIFEL REGION

Upland countryside is the dominant geographical feature of the southwestern part of the North Rhineland. The **Eifel range**, which forms a continuation of the Ardennes in Belgium, takes up the lion's share of this territory, while on the east bank of the Rhine the **Siebengebirge** are the last of the mountain ranges which give the river so much of its characteristic grandeur. At **Bonn**, the landscape adjacent to the Rhine flattens out, and there begins the enormous built-up conurbation which stretches, with hardly a break, all the way up to Dortmund. Prime attraction of this area, however, is undoubtedly the venerable city of **Aachen**.

Aachen

"In Aachen I saw all kinds of priceless treasures, the like of which no man has seen rarer," wrote Dürer following a visit there in 1560. His enthusiasm can still be echoed; **AACHEN** possesses fabulous riches fit to be compared with those of Istanbul or Venice, and it ranks, along with Cologne, as one of the two cities in North Rhineland-Westphalia which should on no account be missed. Now a frontier post – the municipal area includes stretches of border with both Belgium and the Netherlands, making it something of a smugglers' den – it has metamorphosed from a far grander role. In the late eighth and early ninth centuries the city was seen as the successor to ancient Rome, the hub of the great Frankish empire of **Charlemagne** (*Karl der Grosse*) which comprised pretty well all of present-day Germany, France, the Benelux, Austria and Switzerland, as

The telephone code for Aachen is ☎0241.

well as much of Italy and part of northern Spain. In 794, after 26 years of almost constant campaigning, Charlemagne established Aachen as the main seat of his court. The choice was made partly for strategic reasons, but also because of the presence of hot springs, over which the Romans had first built thermal baths. Exercising in these waters was one of the Emperor's favourite pastimes, and his contemporaries rated him a swimmer without peer. The spa has continually given the city prestige and visitors, but its political power was short-lived, lasting only a generation after Charlemagne's death.

Arriving and practicalities

Aachen's **Hauptbahnhof** is just south of the city centre. One of the **tourist offices** is immediately opposite, at Bahnhofplatz 4 (Mon–Fri 9am–6.30pm, Sat 9am–1pm; ☎180 2965), though the main branch occupies the *Atrium Elisenbrunnen* on Friedrich Wilhelm-Platz (same times; ☎180 2960). **Camping** is possible just to the northeast of

the centre at Pass Str. 85 (☎155495). The **youth hostel** is much further away, situated on a little hill in a suburban park to the southwest, at Maria-Theresia Allee 260 (☎71101; bus #2 direction Preuswald from the Elisenbrunnen, alight at Brüsseler Ring or Ronheide). Two of the cheaper **hotels** are near the Hauptbahnhof: *Karls*, Leydelstr. 10 (☎35449), charges around DM40 for a single, DM65 a double, while *Hesse*, Friedlandstr. 20 (☎34047), has singles at DM37, doubles DM65. Other budget possibilities tend to be far out – *Göbel*, Trierer Str. 546 (☎523244), charges from DM30 single, DM52 double; *Hansa Haus*, Von-Coels-Str. 42 (☎551380), has singles at DM33, doubles DM58; while *Neuenhof*, Vaalser Str. 387 (☎74518), costs from DM39 for a single, DM75 a double. **Mitfahrzentrale** have an office at Roermonder Str. 4 (☎155087).

The city centre

Modern Aachen's historical centre – the interesting bit – is reached from the Hauptbahnhof in about ten minutes by following Bahnhofstrasse and then turning left into Theaterstrasse. It's small and compact, and can comfortably be seen in a day, though you'll need longer to take in more than a few of the city's varied and excellent museums. Badly damaged in the last war, Aachen was also devastated by a terrible fire in 1656. This accounts for the unusually large number of Baroque buildings by north German standards; their restrained, classically-derived style is a world away from the wild fantasies which were then all the rage in Bavaria.

The Dom

Thankfully, although hardly anything remains from Charlemagne's time, Aachen retains its crowning jewel in the former **Pfalzkapelle** (Palace chapel). Now forming the heart and soul of the present-day **Dom**, its presence is enshrined in the French name for the city, *Aix-la-Chapelle*. A ninth-century monk-chronicler, Notker the Stammerer, relates how skilled workmen were brought from many lands in order that this edifice should surpass any previously erected, and concluded that it was "built by human hands, yet with the inspiration of God". Charlemagne's courtier Einhard, who must have watched the building's construction, attributed its splendour to the Emperor's religious devotion, and fills in details of the decoration – "gold and silver, with lamps, and with lattices and doors of solid bronze". He also explained that marble columns were brought from as far as Ravenna, on whose basilica of San Vitale the chapel was largely modelled; indeed, the Pope's authorisation letter to Charlemagne for the removal of marbles and mosaics from the palace there still exists.

THE BUILDING

Even after such descriptions, you can't help being overwhelmed by the Dom's extraordinary symmetry, height and grandeur. Designed by **Odo von Metz**, it's an eight-sided dome, surrounded by a sixteen-sided ambulatory, above which is a two-tiered gallery with eight arcades of columns; the number eight is significant, representing perfection and harmony. The circumference of the octagon is 144 Carolingian feet – the cardinal number of the heavenly Jerusalem – and that of the outer polygon exactly twice that: an impeccable concord and order which are intended to symbolise Heaven. As a result of the cult of Charlemagne (he was canonised by an anti-pope in 1165), and the possession of the so-called Great Aachen Relics (allegedly the swaddling clothes and loin cloth of Christ, the gown of the Virgin and the garb of Saint John the Baptist), pilgrims poured into the city in such numbers that the building needed to be expanded. An airily high and narrow **Gothic chancel** was therefore added, again modelled on a great building from elsewhere in Europe, the Sainte-Chapelle in Paris. Its original stained glass has been lost, but the modern replacements at least give the right effect. Also from this period is a series of two-storey chapels encircling the octagon. The one specially endowed for the use of Hungarian pilgrims was later replaced by a Italianate Baroque design, as successive epochs continued to leave their mark on the Dom; another important addition was the west tower, which was under construction for several centuries.

THE FURNISHINGS

Some of the original furnishings survive: in the vestibule alone you can see the bronze doors with lions' heads mentioned by Einhard, along with a pine-cone which seems to have been a water-spout, and an antique she-wolf. These are rather overshadowed by the embellishments crafted from the costliest of materials with which Charlemagne's successors enhanced the Dom, making it positively drip with treasure. Adorning the main altar is the **Pala d'Oro**, an early eleventh-century altar front with ten embossed scenes of the Passion. Behind, and of similar date, is the **ambo**, a pulpit like no other, fashioned from gold-plated copper adorned with precious stones, reliefs of the Evangelists and ancient Egyptian ivories of profane subjects. Suspended from the dome by means of a mighty iron chain is the enormous twelfth-century **chandelier** given by Frederick Barbarossa. Regrettably, its weight quickly caused the mosaics to crack; those to be seen today are a nineteenth-century attempt at recreating the effect of the originals. The gilded **shrine of Charlemagne** has recently returned to its position at the end of the chancel, following a decade of restoration. Finished in 1215, having been fifty years in the making, it contains the remains of the saint, who is depicted on the front. It also serves as a glorification of the Holy Roman Empire he founded, with portraits of his successors along the sides, instead of the normal biblical personages. The status accorded Charlemagne is further emphasised by the early fifteenth-century statue of him on the pier behind, the only outsider in a cycle of the Virgin and Apostles.

In the gallery is the **imperial throne**, a marble chair with a wooden seat approached by six steps, in the manner of that in Solomon's temple; from here the emperor had a grandstand view of all that was happening below. Although popularly believed to have belonged to Charlemagne, it now seems certain that it's at least a century later in date, perhaps made for the coronation of Otto I, which initiated the tradition of emperors being crowned at Aachen, a practice which lasted until the sixteenth century. In order to see the throne (with an added bonus of a different perspective on the Dom and its furnishings) you've no choice but to join a **guided tour**. These cost DM2 and leave from the **Schatzkammer**, which has its own entrance on Klostergasse; there are at least a couple a day, rising to hourly departures at the height of the season.

The Schatzkammer

The Schatzkammer (Tues–Sat 10am–5pm, Sun 10.30am–5pm, Mon 10am–2pm; in summer, stays open until 8pm on Thurs, 6pm on weekdays other than Mon; DM3) is as much an essential sight as the Dom. Quite simply, it's the richest treasury in Northern Europe, a dazzling feast for the eyes and an unashamed glorification of the wealth and power of the Church Triumphant. For maximum security, the most valuable pieces are kept in the basement. Prominent among them is the greatest of all processional crucifixes, the late tenth-century **Lothair cross**, studded with jewels and bearing an antique cameo of the Emperor Augustus; the Crucifixion is modestly engraved on the reverse. From the beginning of the following century come a **holy water vessel**, carved from an elephant's tusk, and a **golden book cover** with an ivory of the Madonna and Child, which was made as an accessory to the Pala d'Oro in the decoration of the altar. A damaged **ivory diptych** is the only item from the time of Charlemagne, while the large **Roman sarcophagus** carved with a scene of the rape of Proserpine served as the emperor's improbable coffin for 400 years. Finally, there's the thirteenth-century **shrine of the Virgin**, made to house the Great Aachen Relics, but not started until the companion piece dedicated to Charlemagne had at last been completed – another revealing illustration of how important his cult had become.

On the ground floor, pride of place belongs to the **base plates** of the great chandelier, delicately engraved with angels and scenes from the life of Christ. Among many superb **reliquaries**, note the idealised portrait head of Charlemagne. Gifts from such devotees as Margaret of York and Louis of Hungary (who also endowed the chapel for his country's pilgrims) show the international extent of the Aachen cult. The astonishing vibrancy of the local goldsmith tradition down the centuries is proved by the sixteenth-century work of **Hans von Reutlingen**, which stands comparison with any of the older masterpieces.

The Rathaus

Charlemagne's palace once extended across the Katsch Hof, now lined with ugly modern buildings, to the site of the present **Rathaus**. Fronting the Markt, which boasts the finest of the medieval houses left in the city, its facade is lined with the figures of fifty Holy Roman Emperors – 31 of them crowned in Aachen. Above the entrance, Charlemagne shares a niche with Christ and Pope Leo III, who conducted his coronation ceremony in Rome on Christmas Day 800. Built in the fourteenth century on the palace foundations, and incorporating two of its **towers**, the Rathaus is a mix of attempts to restore its original Gothic form with the inevitable Baroque changes of later years. The best bit of the interior (Mon–Fri 8am–1pm & 2–5pm, Sat & Sun 10am–1pm & 2–5pm, but liable to closure at any time for civic receptions; DM1) is the much-restored **Kaisersaal**. Here the Charlemagne Prize is awarded annually to the citizen who is deemed to have made the largest contribution to European unity, an ideal the city sees as having begun during its own imperial days. Five large frescos by the Düsseldorf artist Alfred Rethel give a Romantic portrayal of scenes from Charlemagne's life, but your attention is more likely to be drawn by the crown jewels, dazzlingly displayed at one end. These are only reproductions, however; the originals have been kept in Vienna since the early nineteenth century, when they were commandeered by the Habsburgs (who had been hereditary holders of the title of Holy Roman Emperor for centuries) for their new role as Emperors of Austria. There's also a bronze statue of Charlemagne which was formerly part of the fountain in the Markt; it was replaced in 1969 after constant maltreatment.

The rest of the centre

Southeast of the Markt is another square, the Hühner Markt, where livestock was formerly sold. Here stands the **Couven-Museum** (Tues–Fri 10am–5pm, Sat 10am–1pm, Sun 10am–5pm; DM2), an elegant merchant-class home which has been named after a father and son team of architects who designed many of the city's Baroque buildings. It has been fitted out with mid-eighteenth- to mid-nineteenth-century furnishings gathered from houses of the Aachen-Liège region, giving an idea of the stylish if frivolous priorities of the local bourgeoisie. Look out for the complete apothecary, a lavishly decorated first-floor living room with carved chimneypiece, and the huge Advent crib in the attic.

In a house on Pontstrasse, which leads north of the Markt, **Paul Julius von Reuter** established his famous news agency (still a watchword in the world of the media), using carrier pigeons to cirulate the reports. To commemorate this, the **Internationales Zeitungsmuseum** (Tues–Fri 9.30am–1pm & 2.30–5pm, Sat 9.30am–1pm; free), with a collection of some 120,000 newspapers, has been established at no. 13 in the same street. An exhibition room has been set up to show by means of original editions how the press (German and English language examples dominate) reacted to great stories, from the 1848 revolutions via the two world wars to contemporary conflicts. The obituaries of major figures prove that posterity's verdict is often very different from the instant response, while some curiosities are offered for light relief. If you're seriously interested, you can apply to see particular issues. At the end of Pontstrasse – which functions as the hub of the student nightlife scene – is the **Ponttor**, an awesome early fourteenth-century gateway which was formerly the strongest part of the city's fortification system. Of the ten other gates, the only survivior is the **Maschiertor** just to the west of the Hauptbahnhof.

Before the construction of modern facilities, the hub of Aachen's spa life was the **Altes Kurhaus**, an ornate late eighteenth-century building by the younger Couven, situated east of the Markt at Komphausbadstr. 19. At the time of writing, it was due to provide a temporary home for the **Suermondt-Ludwig-Museum** (Tues–Sat 10am–5pm, Sun 10am–1pm; DM2), pending the refurbishment of its normal premises at Wilhelmstr. 18. The museum has an excellent collection of northern European medieval sculpture, with an extensive array of Pietàs, Madonnas and Passions; these are almost exclusively anonymous and predominantly folksy in style, though some, such as the large Lower Rhenish *St Peter Altar*, achieve a rather more developed artistic sense. Also of special note are the Baroque fancies of **Dietrich von Rath**, the city's last important goldsmith, and the sculptures and stained glass by **Ewald Mataré**, an Aachen artist best known for his role in creating new works for German cathedrals and churches in the period of their restoration following war damage. There are also a number of old masters, including notable works by Joos van Cleve, Cranach, Rubens, Ribera and Zurbarán.

Finally, it would be a pity to leave Aachen without following Charlemagne's example and taking a **swim** in the warm waters. Conveniently located in the old city is the *Römerbad* at Buchkremerstr. 1 (Mon–Fri 7am–7pm, Sat 7am–2pm, Sun 7am–1pm). The temperature of these baths is kept at a constant 32°C and there's no doubt that they're wonderfully refreshing.

The suburbs

One of Aachen's two spa quarters is centred on **Monheimsallee** to the northeast of the Altstadt. At no. 52, there's another thermal bathing hall, the *Kurbad Quellenhof* (same times as the Römerbad), while the *Kurgarten* is the well-tended park you'd expect. However, Monheimsallee is best known for its **casino** (3pm–2am, Fri & Sat until 3am; minimum stake is DM5 at the cheapest roulette table), housed in a Neoclassical building with a glitteringly modernised interior. Note that the management want only the better class of visitor, with full evening dress being the normal attire. If you strike it lucky at the tables, the restaurant provides a tempting outlet for your winnings; it's one of the very best in Germany, glorying in two Michelin rosettes.

Just south of the quarter, housed in a former factory building at Jülicher Strasse 97–109, is the brand new **Ludwig Forum für Internationales Kunst** (Tues, Wed & Fri–Sun 11am–7pm, Thurs 11am–10pm; DM4). This is one of Germany's most vibrant centres for contemporary visual arts, and enables more of the city's superb modern collection to be shown than was possible in its former home in the Altes Kurhaus. What's on display at any one time is obviously a lottery, but all the big names of American painting and sculpture are well represented. Soviet and Eastern European art is another strength – the star piece is **Dimitri Shilinsky's** *Adam and Eve*, depicting the artist and his wife. Also worth seeking out is a papier-mâché by a contemporary German sculptor, **Thomas Lanigan-Schmidt**, *A Rite of Passage – the Leprechaun*, which apparently took eleven years to make.

About fifteen minutes' walk east of the Hauptbahnhof, at Bismarckstr. 68, is a moated medieval castle, **Burg Frankenberg** (Tues–Fri 10am–5pm, Sat & Sun 10am–1pm; DM2). The interior has been restored to house the local history museum; though mainly of parochial appeal, this has interesting models which attempt to recreate the likely original form of Charlemagne's palace. Ceramic products from Aachen are displayed in the tower. On the opposite side of the railway tracks is the suburb of **Burtscheid**, the second spa quarter, which has a distinctive skyline, thanks to a handsome pair of churches built on its heights by the elder Couven. Again, it features thermal bathing facilities and sedate areas of parkland.

Eating, drinking and nightlife

Many of the best places to eat and drink are found in and around the Markt, while the most animated district is the student quarter, centred on Pontstrasse.

Restaurants

Degraa, Fischmarkt 6. *Gaststätte* of the only local brewery, which produces both light and dark beers.

Domkeller, Hof 1. A genuine local, in spite of its location right by the Dom; always full, though it expands to the terrace outside in high summer.

Goldener Schwan, Markt 37. Occupying a fine old house; particularly good at lunchtimes, when special menus are on offer.

Postwagen, Krämerstr. 2. Unquestionably Aachen's most famous pub-restaurant and a sight in itself, both for its cheerful Baroque exterior tacked on to the Rathaus and the cramped and irregular rooms within.

Zum goldenen Einhorn, Markt 33. Has an enormous menu with Italian and Greek cuisine as well as German, the speciality being thin fillets of veal with an enormous choice of sauces.

Zum Schiffgen, Hühner Markt 23. An ideal place for a sedate meal.

Bars and cafés

Be-Bop, Südstr. 54. Enduringly popular café-bar, especially in the evenings.

Hauptquartier, Promenadenstr. 46. The city's most eccentric bar, a living testimony to the enduring popularity in Germany of all things punk.

Leo van den Daele, Büchel 18. Aachen's classiest café, and the best place to sample *Printen*, a spiced gingerbread which is the city's main claim to a culinary peculiarity.

Meisenfrei, Krakaustr. 38. Has a bewildering choice of games to help while away the time.

Molkerei, Pontstr. 141. Bright and cheerful during the day, but lacks atmosphere in the evening.

Salsa, corner of Südstrasse and Beethovenstrasse. Friendly, relaxed haunt of the in-crowd.

Tangente, Pontstr. 141. Sharing a terrace with *Molkerei*, this is an elegant daytime café which transforms itself into a jumping, youthful watering-hole at night.

Tomate, Markt 45. Features regular jazz sessions.

Discos

Club Voltaire, Friedrichstr. 9. The only all-night joint worth mentioning; has a tiny dance floor, with music kept at conversation level.

Make-up, Hirschgraben 31. Haunt of hard rock diehards.

Metropol, Blondelstr. 9. Aachen's top disco, with a bizarre range of music: funk on top of heavy metal via Europop to the jazz and soul played at the café next to the dance floor. Situated on the eastern side of town, and best visited after midnight when the schoolkids have cleared off.

Rotation, Pontstr. 135. Very popular but rather poky disco in the student quarter.

Culture and festivals

The *Eurogress* centre next to the casino is where both rock and classical **concerts** are held. More highbrow culture is available at the *Stadttheater* on Theaterplatz just across from the Elisenbrunnen; either **drama** or **opera** is performed most evenings and standards are good – Herbert von Karajan first made his name as musical director here. *Grenzlandtheater* on Friedrich-Wilhelm-Platz offers modern fare, albeit with an emphasis on established playwrights. The main local **festival** is the *Karlsfest* in honour of Charlemagne at the end of January, while Carnival is celebrated here with typical Rhenish enthusiasm.

The Northern Eifel

The German section of the **Eifel** massif is divided by the Land boundary between North Rhineland-Westphalia and Rhineland-Palatinate; the former's share consists mainly of the **Hohes Venn**, an extensive plateau of impervious rocks which stretches into Belgium. Variation in the scenery is provided by the River Rur, which cuts a deep, winding valley, and by the vegetation of gorse, broom and cotton grass. The area is poor in natural resources: no cities have ever developed, and the nineteenth century saw mass emigration, much of it to the United States. Nowadays, the principal industry is the provision of **activity holidays** – skiing in winter, hiking, angling and sailing in summer – punctuated by dead periods between the seasons.

Monschau

The Northern Eifel's other main draw is a series of well preserved small towns, at least two of which rank among the finest in Germany. One of these is **MONSCHAU**, some 30km south of Aachen. It's only accessible by bus, with slow but fairly frequent services; most of the Eifel railways have closed because of the high cost of maintenance and low usage levels. The town's main attraction is its dramatic setting deep in the Rur valley, with ruined fortresses – the **Burg** and the **Haller** (both with unrestricted access) – crowning two of the hills above. These offer some of the many superb **views** to be had in the area; others can be enjoyed from a belvedere just off the main road to Aachen, or from the commanding heights of the continuation of this road in the direction of Nideggen. The Burg, much the larger of the ruins, is the building from which Monschau developed. Its keep and gateway are Romanesque originals; the ring wall and parapets date from a strengthening of the defences in the fourteenth century, while the large *Eselsturm* (Asses' Tower) is from a couple of hundred years later, as is the central *Palast* which has been restored to serve as a **youth hostel** (☎02472/2314).

The lower part of Monschau is an almost completely preserved townscape, dominated by the magnificent **multi-storey mansions** lining the Rur, whose slate roofs are sometimes pierced by two tiers of dormer windows. Though half-timbering is used extensively, these houses aren't as old as they might appear – they date from Monschau's main period of prosperity, centred on cloth production, which followed the Thirty Years' War. The most ornate of all, the **Rotes Haus** (Red House), adds a rare splash of colour to the town, which is otherwise so monochromatic that it seems to grow organically out of the landscape. Built by a merchant in the 1750s, it's now a **museum** (guided tours Good Friday–mid-Nov Tues–Sun at 10am, 11am, 2pm, 3pm & 4pm; DM3); it features a Rococo staircase with an elaborate iron railing, and is fully furnished in the same style. The nearby **Troistorff Haus** on Laufenstrasse, which is now used as municipal offices, is smaller, but has a fancier exterior and another fine stairway.

Practicalities

The **tourist office** (April–Oct Mon–Fri 9am–6pm, Sat 9am–12.30pm, Nov–April Mon–Thurs 9am–noon & 1.30–5pm, Fri 9am–12.45pm; ☎02472/3300) is at Stadtstrasse 1 beside the main bridge. For DM2 you can book here to visit the **Senfmühle**, where mustard is still made using last century's equipment. The town has another historic workshop in the **Glashütte** (glassworks) at Burgau 14 (March–Oct Mon–Fri 10am–5.30pm, Sat & Sun 10am–6pm; DM2.50). There are **campsites** at Perlenau (☎02472/636) and at Grünentalstr. 36 in the adjoining village of IMGENBROICH (☎02472/3931), while a second and more luxurious hostel is at Hargardgasse 5 in HARGARD (☎02472/2180), some 3km away. **Private houses** with rooms to let, generally at around DM40 a double, can be found on Kirchstrasse, Laufenstrasse and Oberer Mühlenberg. **Hotels** charging DM30 per person or less include *Alt Montjoie*, Stadtstr. 18 (☎02472/3289); *Burgau*, St-Vither-Str. 16 (☎02472/2120 or 2284); *Burghotel*, Laufenstr. 1 (☎02472/2332); and *Haus Flora*, Laufenstr. 134 (☎02472/2289). The **cafés** and **restaurants** which crowd the town centre are mostly of a high standard. Try the products of the local *Felsenkeller* brewery; its speciality is *Monschauer Zwickelbier*, a dark, cloudy, bottom-fermented beer supposedly rich in vitamin B.

The Lake District

The area east of Monschau is known as the **Sieben Seen** (Seven Lakes), all of which are artificial. As an alternative to reaching them by bus, there's the *Rurtalbahn*, a painfully slow but enormously scenic railway which closely follows the course of the Rur. This begins at **DÜREN**, an industrial town midway between Aachen and Cologne; now totally modern, its main claim to fame is that it was where Holbein executed his ill-fated portrait of Anne of Cleves (see p.496). The other terminus is **HEIMBACH**, on the eastern bank of the **Rursee Schwammenauel**, the largest reservoir in west Germany, which attracts loads of tourists in summer with its possibilities for angling, water sports and cruising. Heimbach is a spa town and in some ways resembles Monschau, its ruined Burg towering over streets of half-timbered dwellings; but in fact it's far less genuine – most of the houses are modern. If you want to stay, there are several **campsites** and plenty of cheap **rooms** to let, but there's no hostel.

NIDEGGEN, some 11km north, is much more imposing, perched like an eyrie high above the valley. The **Burg**, residence of the Dukes of Jülich, dates partly from the twelfth century, but was transformed into a palace in the Renaissance period; it survives as a ruin, and there's free access to the courtyard and tower, which commands an extensive view. Other sections have been drastically restored to house the local **museum** (Tues–Sun 10am–5pm; DM2). Within the precincts is the **Pfarrkirche**, a pure example of Romanesque architecture, adorned with frescos of the same period. A large section of the town **walls** has been preserved, including two fortified gateways; there are also a number of characteristic half-timbered houses. The **youth hostel** is at Rather Str. 27 (☎02427/226), while **rooms** at DM30 or less per person are available in numerous hotels and private houses. There's a **campsite** in BRÜCK (☎02427/508), 2km below Nideggen, on the banks of the Rur near the Bahnhof.

Bad Münstereifel

BAD MÜNSTEREIFEL is easiest reached from Bonn, lying at the dead end of a branch rail line. For all its concealed position, deep in the valley of the River Erft, it's a place of considerable character, rivalling Monschau in quality; though not so homogeneous, nor so picturesquely sited, its monuments are more enjoyable. Prominent among these is the thirteenth- to fourteenth-century **Stadtmauer**, which survives intact. Straight ahead from the Bahnhof is the formidable northern gate, the **Werther Tor**; the corresponding position to the south is guarded by the **Orchheimer Tor**. To the east and west, the fortifications rise high into the hills, giving extra protection to the town huddled along the banks of the river. On the eastern side are the **Burg** (the only ruined feature) and the **Johannistor**; the western front now forms the boundary of the *Kurgarten* with its spa facilities, and is defended on its southern corner by the **Heisterbacher Tor**. You can walk freely along this stretch of rampart, which offers wonderful views over the town and the surrounding foothills of the **Ahrgebirge** range (see *Chapter Four*). For a wholly different perspective, it's worth following the footpath round the walls.

Münstereifel ("minster in the Eifel") derives its name from the fact that the town developed from a Benedictine monastery; this was founded in 830 and quickly became a popular place of pilgrimage through possession of the relics of the Roman martyrs Chrysanthus and Daria. The present **Stiftskirche** (named after the saints, whose graves are in the crypt) is a magnificently severe twelfth-century Romanesque church, which dominates the skyline of the lower town. Across the Kirchplatz is the striking red facade of the **Rathaus**, a masterpiece of Gothic civil architecture which began life in the mid-fourteenth century as a guild house. On Langenhecke to the rear of the church is the **Heimat Museum** (April–Oct Tues–Sun 9am–noon, also Wed 2–4pm; Nov–March Sat 10am–noon, Sun 10am–noon & 2–4pm only; DM1). The building itself, once the home of a lay-brother of the monastery, is more interesting than the local history displays inside – contemporary with the church, it's possibly the oldest intact house in Germany.

As well as these public buildings, Münstereifel offers one of the most satisfying townscapes in the region, enhanced by its rustic setting on the banks of the River Erft, which is never more than a stream; almost every street within the walls is worth exploring. Look out for the half-timbered mid-seventeenth-century **Haus Windeck** on Orchheimerstrasse, the first floor of which is now a café. Also of interest is the seventeenth century **Jesuitenkirche** facing the Markt, built in an anachronistic Gothic style.

Practicalities

The **tourist office** is at Langenhecke 2 (Mon–Fri 9am–5pm, Sat 10am–noon & 2–4pm, Sun 10.30am–12.30pm; ☎02253/505182). Private houses with **rooms** to let at around DM20 per person can be found all over town, just look out for the *Zimmer frei* signs. The **youth hostel** is high in the hills about 2km east of town at Herbergsweg 1–5 (☎02253/7438) just before the village of RODERT, while the **campsite** is to the south on the banks of the Erft (☎02253/8282). There are plenty of reasonably priced places to **eat** and **drink**, particularly along the main Wertherstrasse. Watch out for lunchtime set menus, which are often tremendous bargains; this is particularly true of the *Burggaststätten* in the castle ruins, which specialises in *vom heissen Stein* dishes.

The surrounding countryside is good for **hiking**; get a free tourist board brochure which outlines the best routes. The most popular excursion is to the world's largest **radio-telescope** situated just outside the hamlet of EFFELSBERG, 8km southeast. Visitors are admitted only in groups, but individuals can join these; as limits are placed on the numbers allowed on each guided tour, it's best to phone ahead (☎02257/30117; Tues–Fri 10am, 11am, 2pm, 3pm & 4pm, Sat 9am, 10am, 11am & noon; DM2).

Bonn

The name of **BONN** is indissolubly associated with the West German state, having served as its capital from the time the country was set up in 1949 until the unification of 1990, when Berlin was restored to its former role. Although still the seat of government, it will lose that honour before the decade is out, and, in a colossal blow to the supreme self-confidence it has acquired, it's in grave danger of slipping back to its prewar obscurity. In some ways this is no more than it deserves, as it was the most unlikely and unloved of European capitals: just "A Small Town in Germany" according to the title of John le Carré's spy thriller, or "The Federal Village" in the condescending eyes of the inhabitants of grander German cities. Yet, for the time being at least, it remains worth a visit of a day or two if taken on its own merits as an historic town given an extra dimension as a result of being in the political spotlight.

> The telephone code for Bonn is ☎0228

The town centre

Prior to its elevation to the role of capital, Bonn was chiefly famous as the birthplace of **Ludwig van Beethoven**. The house where he was born at Bonngasse 20 is one of the few old buildings in the centre to have escaped wartime devastation. It contains an unfussy and intelligently presented **museum** (April–Oct Mon–Sat 9am–1pm & 3–6pm, Sun 9am–1pm, Nov–March Mon–Sat 9.30am–1pm & 3–5pm, Sun 9.30am–1pm; DM2) dedicated to the great composer. Beethoven served his musical apprenticeship at the Electoral court of his home town, though he left it for good at the age of 22. Bonn has zealously built up the best collection of memorabilia of its favourite son. There's a bunch of uncomfortable portraits of the tormented genius (who was a reluctant sitter), along with manuscripts and correspondence. The three instruments with which he was associated as a professional performer are represented in the form of the console of the organ (now destroyed) on which he played as a youth, his last piano, and his viola. Most poignant of all are the ear-trumpets which a friend made specially in order to combat his advancing deafness.

Around the Markt

At the end of Bonngasse is the **Markt**, with a pink Rococo **Rathaus**, one of two large squares in the midst of the pedestrian shopping precinct. The other square is dominated by the huge Romanesque **Münster** whose central octagonal tower with its soaring spire is the city's most prominent landmark.

The Landesmuseum and the Schloss

The pick of Bonn's somewhat provincial museums, the **Landesmuseum** is behind the Hauptbahnhof at Colmantstr. 14–16 (Tues, Thurs & Fri 9am–5pm, Wed 9am–8pm, Sat & Sun 11am–5pm; DM3). Star piece is the **skull of Neanderthal Man**, found in a valley near Düsseldorf (see p.487), and calculated to be some 60,000 years old. Among a generally mediocre collection of paintings on the first floor, look out for five panels by the painter known as the **Master of the St Ursula Legend** after the dispersed series from which these came. There's also a rare work by **Elsheimer**, *Three Marys at the Sepulchre*.

Bonn's other dominant building is the Baroque **Schloss**, an enormously long construction which was formerly the seat of the Archbishop-Electors of Cologne and is

LUDWIG VAN BEETHOVEN (1770-1827)

No composer has ever made a greater impact on the history of music than **Ludwig van Beethoven**. The successor to the Viennese classical tradition of Haydn and Mozart, he developed the three great forms of the period – the symphony, the string quartet and the piano sonata – to their ultimate limits. His work reflects his libertarian concerns, and shows for the first time the ability of music to convey a humanitarian message without the aid of text, thus setting the scene for the Romantic composers of the next hundred years. From 1800, Beethoven had problems with his hearing, an affliction which was partly responsible for the transformations he wrought in orchestral sound; the menacing power of some of his symphonies was so different from anything previously composed that many contemporaries were – literally – physically scared of them. By the time he finished his *Ninth Symphony*, in which instrumental and choral music were woven into one for the very first time, he had become completely deaf, yet he continued to compose, notably three valedictory string quartets of awesome emotional intensity.

now used by the University. To the south, the Schloss is bounded by the open spaces of the Hofgarten, at whose far end is the **Akademisches Kunstmuseum** (Mon–Wed, Fri & Sun 10am–1pm, Thurs 10am–1pm & 4–6pm; DM1) housed in a Neoclassical pavilion designed by Schinkel. This has an eerie collection of casts of famous antique sculptures, originally made for the benefit of art students.

Poppelsdorf and the southwest

Also branching out from the Schloss is the kilometre-long avenue of chestnut trees which leads to **POPPELSDORF**, where the Frenchman **Robert de Cotte**, who had undertaken modifications to the Schloss, was commissioned to build a second Electoral palace. He responded with an ingenious *trompe l'oeil* design, concealing the circular courtyard within a rectangular ground plan. Again, the palace is now occupied by University departments, the grounds serving as the **Botanical Gardens** (summer Mon–Fri 9am–7pm, Sun 9am–1pm, winter Mon–Fri 9am–4.30pm). For a sociological as well as architectural stroll, wander in the streets immediately to the east, such as Schloss Strasse, Kurfürstenstrasse, Argelanderstrasse and Bismarckstrasse: these represent a remarkably complete picture of turn-of-the-century town planning for the better-off sections of the middle-class.

To the other side of Poppelsdorf's Schloss at Sebastianstr. 182 is the **Robert-Schumann-Haus** (Mon & Fri 10am–noon & 4–7pm, Wed & Thurs 10am–noon & 3–6pm, Sun 10am–1pm; free) containing a collection of memorabilia of the Romantic composer. In spite of a blissfully happy marriage to the pianist Clara Wieck, which inspired so many of his yearning, passionate song settings and so much of his virtuoso piano music, Schumann had a history of psychological instability, culminating in a complete mental breakdown and attempted suicide when he threw himself into the Rhine. At his own request, he spent the last two years of his life confined to the sanatorium adjoining the house.

Continuing south from Poppelsdorf, a road leads uphill to the isolated pilgrimage church of **Kreuzberg**. The original seventeenth-century chapel was given the full Rococo treatment a hundred years later, including the addition of the Holy Steps behind the altar, an imitation in the lavishly ornate style of Balthasar Neumann of those now in Rome on which Christ allegedly ascended to receive Pilate's judgment. Beyond here, the city fans out into a number of old villages, often separated by open countryside. Among them is **VENUSBERG**, which has a game reserve with wild boar and both red and fallow deer.

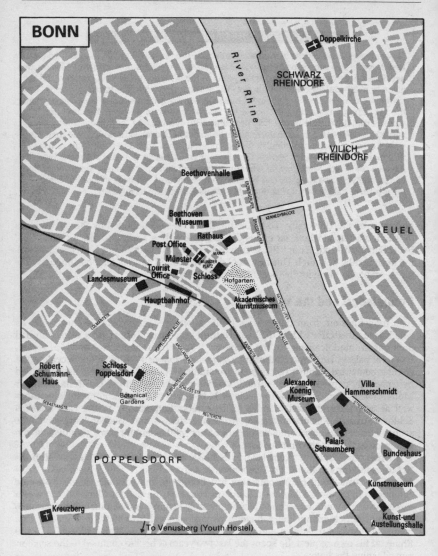

The Government Quarter

Bonn's government quarter can be reached either by following Reuterstrasse from Poppelsdorf, or by taking Adenauerallee from the Hofgarten: the distance is about the same. Saddled with its "temporary status", it was not custom built, but utilised a series of existing structures. Ironically enough, work had just started on new buildings when the sudden fall of Communism in East Germany in 1989 shook the city out of its complacent assumption that it was going to be a long-term capital.

THE STRUGGLE TO BECOME CAPITAL

When Germany was finally unified through Prussian military might in 1871, **Berlin** became the first official and undisputed capital the country had ever had. The partition of Berlin after World War II meant that the city could no longer fulfil its role, though the eastern sector became the official capital of the GDR. Meanwhile **Bonn** – hitherto a provincial university town – was chosen as capital of the West German state. In a sense, this was a deliberately crass choice in line with the "provisional" nature of the new country (see "History" in *Contexts*). Konrad Adenauer, the first Chancellor, lived nearby and championed its cause as a matter of personal convenience, forming an unholy alliance with West Berlin representatives, who were desperate to thwart the claims of **Frankfurt** (the only other city considered for the role), astutely realising that the latter might be powerful enough to deny Berlin's re-instatement as capital.

For all the swiftness of the unification process when it finally happened, four decades of national partition had made the name of Bonn virtually synonymous with that of the new, responsible face of Germany. Thus, although Berlin was confirmed as capital in 1990, Bonn fought to remain the seat of government. The campaign was vitriolic: the Bonn lobby contrasted its proven record at the heart of a prosperous, democratic and peace-loving country with Berlin's tainted history as the successive headquarters of a militaristic absolute monarchy, then Nazi and Communist totalitarian dictatorships; the huge costs of making the move were also cited, as was the fact that, now that the Eastern Territories were accepted as lost forever, Berlin's geographical position was no longer sufficiently central. In retaliation, Berlin's supporters rubbished Bonn as a backwater inappropriately sited for the great challenge of rebuilding the shattered economy and society of eastern Germany. Chancellor Helmut Kohl, like Adenauer a native of the Rhineland, surprisingly endorsed Berlin, which in June 1991 won a narrow majority in the deciding parliamentary vote.

Both the **Villa Hammerschmidt** and the **Palais Schaumburg** are pompous Empire buildings from the last century, once private dwellings of the mega-rich but now the official residences of the Federal President and Chancellor respectively. You aren't allowed near them, never mind inside. Further south, the **Parliament buildings** are in the Bauhaus style of the 1930s; this time admission is possible, but only for groups by written appointment, though you can try joining a party who have booked to be shown around the Bundesrat (Upper House) – more trouble than it's worth, unless you're passionately keen on German politics. Indeed, the whole quarter offers even less than you'd expect, and the best reason for coming is the wonderful **view** over the Rhine and the Siebengebirge on the opposite bank.

In the summer of 1992 a new **museum** opens on Friedrich-Ebert-Allee, containing the collection that has previously been held in the town's Kunstmuseum: this includes a good selection of Expressionist paintings and drawings, many by the brilliant **August Macke** who spent part of his brief life in the city.

Bad Godesberg

When Bonn was officially expanded in 1969, it gobbled up a string of small villages, giving it a foothold on the eastern bank of the Rhine for the first time. It also annexed the old spa town of **BAD GODESBERG** (reached by U-Bahn #16 or main-line train) to the south, stretching its boundaries to the Land border. Bad Godesberg's character had already made it a favoured location for many of the diplomatic missions, who found its grandiose Empire-style villas just the sort of headquarters they were looking for. The town is also a famed conference centre, and has hosted at least two fateful events – the series of meetings between Chamberlain and Hitler in 1938 which paved the way for the Munich Agreement in which "peace in our time" was bought at Czechoslovakia's expense; and the 1959 conference of the Social Democrats, when the party, bidding to end a period of three decades in opposition, disavowed its earlier connections with Marxism, class warfare and anti-clericalism, and became part of the postwar consensus rooted in acceptance of the idea of a "social market economy".

Rearing high over the town is the **Godesburg**, the most northerly of the great series of castles crowning promontories above the Rhine, built in the thirteenth and fourteenth centuries by the Archbishops of Cologne and blown up in 1583. Today it's mostly a hotel: the cylindrical **keep** is still intact and can be ascended (April–Sept Tues–Sun 10am–6pm; DM0.30) for a panoramic **view**, including a distant glimpse of Cologne and the Siebengebirge. Views, indeed, are Bad Godesberg's major attraction; you'll find plenty more if you saunter down the *Rheinufer*, the promenade along the river bank. Otherwise, there are two spa parks in the town centre, separated by fashionable buildings, prominent among which is the late eighteenth-century **Redoute**, formerly the ballroom of the Electors, now a renowned restaurant.

Schwarzrheindorf

The only one of Bonn's outer villages worth making a special detour to see is **SCHWARZRHEINDORF**, on the right bank of the Rhine to the extreme north, reached by bus #540 or #550. It boasts a relatively little-known but outstanding monument in the form of the **Doppelkirche**, a former manorial church (Mon–Fri 9am–6.30pm in summer, 9am–5pm in winter; Sat & Sun 9am–5pm). Built in the mid-twelfth century, this offers an intriguing insight into the social and religious preoccupations of the medieval world. The exterior cleverly disguises the fact that it encases two separate chapels, the upper reserved for the lord, the lower for the use of the labourers. Apart from its architectural idiosyncracies, the church has rare Romanesque **fresco** cycles. Turning on the light by the door reveals *The Vision of Ezekiel*, *The Transfiguration* and *The Crucifixion*, while upstairs the great visions of *The Apocalypse* were painted for their lordships' contemplation. The upper chapel is only accessible on Saturdays and on Sunday afternoons, but its frescos can always be seen through an aperture. A short walk to the east is another old township, **VILICH**, with an abbey church and a rebuilt moated Schloss.

Practicalities and nightlife

The **Hauptbahnhof** lies plumb in the middle of the city, the central pedestrian area opening out immediately before it. To the right is the **bus station**, whose local services, along with the trams (which become the U-Bahn in the city centre), form part of a system integrated with that of Cologne. As the attractions are well spaced out, it's better to buy tickets in blocks of four, or a 24-hour pass which costs DM7 for Bonn alone. There's also a three-day pass available, at DM13 for Bonn only, DM21 for the whole circuit. Also shared with Cologne is the **airport** (☎02203/402222 or 402256 for flight information), which can be reached by means of a half-hourly bus service. The **tourist office** (April–Oct Mon–Sat 8am–9pm, Sun & holidays 9.30am–12.30pm; Nov–March Mon–Sat 8am–7pm; ☎773466) is at Münsterstr. 20 at the entrance to the shopping area. Pick up the handy *Bonn from A to Z*, which has a good map and listings in English.

Accommodation

There's a choice of two **youth hostels**. Much the larger is in Venusberg, at Haager Weg 42 (☎281200); bus #520, #521 or #528. The alternative – one of the most luxurious in Germany – is at Horionstr. 60 in Bad Godesberg (☎317516); bus #515, leaving from the tram terminus beside the spa town's own Bahnhof, passes right in front. **Camping** is possible all year round at Im Frankenkeller 49 (☎344949) in MEHLEM on the banks of the Rhine south of Bad Godesberg. Best bargains among the more central **hotels** are *Virneburg*, Sandkaule 3a (☎636366), with singles from DM35, doubles from DM65, and *Bergmann*, Kasernenstr. 13 (☎633891), with singles at DM40, doubles DM70. Bad Godesberg has a whole clutch of places at similar or lower rates; cheapest are *Wessel*, Bonner Str. 22 (☎351230); *Zum Stern*, Drachenburg 68 (☎348631); and *Gästehaus Scholz*, Annettenstr. 16 (☎379363).

Nightlife

Bonn's **nightlife** is largely dependent on the University; out of term and at weekends the centre is little better than a ghost town come the evening. In the Altstadt, the best traditional restaurants are *Em Höttche*, Markt 4 and *Im Bären*, Acherstr. 1. Three of the trendiest hangouts are situated together at the junction of Bornheimerstrasse and Berliner Platz – *Bla Bla*, the garishly decorated meeting-place of punk diehards; the less outlandish *Namenlos*; and the disco *Novum*. *Jazz Galerie*, Oxfordstr. 24, features live sessions most evenings, while the brasserie *Köller*, Heerstr. 1, has a yuppyish appeal. To the west, *Aktuell*, Gerhard-von-Are-Str. 4, is a particular haunt of journalists. More youthful pubs are *Zebulon*, Stockenstr. 19, patronised mainly by arts students, *Headline* on Sterntorbrücke, and *Mondrian* on Kasernenstrasse, which is particularly trendy and has the advantage of drinks being cheaper than usual. It's also worth traipsing south to Königstrasse, where you'll find the candlelit *Kerze*, bristling with alcoves and partitions; it's patronised by a mixed age range and serves excellent, if pricey, Italian dishes. *Südstadt-Kneipe* on the same street offers a selection of reasonably priced cocktails and food to a background of good music.

To find out what's on in the fields of **theatre**, **concerts** and **exhibitions**, consult the fortnightly *Kulturkalender* produced by the tourist office; a broader perspective is taken by the monthly *De Schnüss*, available from newsagents. The Bonn highbrow cultural scene is good but by no means outstanding: top international musicians sometimes appear at the *Beethovenhalle* at Fritz-Schroeder-Ufer, while the *Opernhaus* (which also hosts ballet) is at Am Boeslagerhof. Among the theatres are *Europatheater* at Mauspfad and *Kabarett* at Gaurheindorfer Str. 23. The main alternative cultural centre is *Brotfabrik* at Kreuzstrasse in the right-bank suburb of BEUEL; it features exhibitions, cinema, readings and feminist events. *Pantheon* at Am Bundeskanzlerplatz in the government quarter is on the same lines, and also holds a disco at weekends, while *Biskuit-Halle* on Wesselwerke is the main venue for visiting live bands.

Listings

Bookshops There's a wide selection in and around Am Hof (behind the Schloss).

Embassies *British* at Friedrich-Ebert-Allee 51 (☎234061); *Irish* at Godesberger Allee 119, Bad Godesberg (☎376937); *American* at Deichmanns Aue 29, Bad Godesberg (☎3391); *Canadian* at Friedrich-Wilhelm-Str. 18 (☎231061); *Australian* at Godesberger Allee 107, Bad Godesberg (☎81030); *New Zealand* at Bonn-Center (☎214021).

Festivals Every three years (1992, 1995) there's an international Beethoven festival in September. The main folklore event is the *Pützchensmarkt*, a colourful fair held annually on the first weekend of the same month in Beuel.

Markets Daily on the Markt; every third Saturday of the month, there's a flea market on Rheinaue.

Mitfahrzentrale Herwarthstr. 11a (☎693081).

Poste Restante Münsterplatz 17.

Rhine cruises These depart from Brassentufer just south of Kennedybrücke: *K-D Linie* (☎632134), *Bonner Personnenschiffahrt* (☎636542).

The Siebengebirge

The **Siebengebirge** (Seven Mountains), on the eastern bank of the Rhine just before the **Land** boundary with Rhineland-Palatinate, rank as one of the river's most suggestively grand stretches, steeped in the lore of legend and literature. According to one story, the mountains were created by seven giants clearing the dirt from their shovels; in size-wise contrast, they're often regarded as the site of the most famous of the Grimms' fairy tales, *Snow White and the Seven Dwarfs*.

Despite the name, there are about thirty summits in this extinct volcanic range, which stretches for about 15km north to south and 5km east to west. From Bonn, six of the main peaks can be seen; the number seven, with its traditional mystical significance, applies only to those visible from a point further north. Of the group, **Drachenfels** (321m), **Wolkenburg** (325m) and **Lohrberg** (435m) are all of a mineral called trachyte; **Petersberg** (331m), **Nonnenstromberg** (336m) and **Grosser Ölberg** (461m) are of basalt, a later formation; while **Löwenburg** (455m) is of dolerite. For centuries, stone from these mountains was quarried to construct the great buildings of the Rhineland, notably the Dom in Cologne; this activity was brought to an end in 1889, when the whole area was designated as the first national park in Germany. In accordance with the country's taste in such matters, the Siebengebirge are covered with thick woods, which means that views are very restricted most of the time, though all the more spectacular when you do reach a belvedere. This wasn't always so; old prints show the upper parts of the peaks free of trees, and generally crowned with a fortress.

The resorts

"One day suffices to explore the most interesting points in this district, unless the visit be for geological purposes," intoned last century's Baedeker Guide. This particular piece of advice still holds good, and the Siebengebirge make an easy outing from Bonn, to which they're connected by U-Bahn #64 and #66. Alternatively, you could base yourself at either **KÖNIGSWINTER** or **BAD HONNEF-RHÖNDORF**. These two holiday resorts have avoided the fate of Bad Godesberg on the opposite bank of being swallowed up by the city. Königswinter is about the nearest Germany comes to a Bournemouth or a Scarborough in its relaxed, rather dated air, awash with amusement arcades and Tin Pan Alley dance halls. As befits a spa, Bad Honnef is more upmarket, preserving its *Kurhaus* in a fine park. It was the chosen residence of **Konrad Adenauer**, first Chancellor of the Federal Republic, whose home at no. 8c in the street named after him is now a memorial **museum** (Tues–Sun 10am–4.30pm; free).

Practicalities

Hotel rooms in both towns are plentiful and, being geared to vacationing families, are generally good value; they're certainly worth considering as an alternative to paying Bonn's inflated prices. In Königswinter, Hauptstrasse and Grabenstrasse have the main concentration of cheap places; those on Rheinallee are a good notch higher in class. Bad Honnef has a **youth hostel** at Selhofer Str. 106 (☎02224/71300) at the very southern end of town, and a couple of **campsites**. The cheapest hotel is *Zur Dorfshänke* on Aegidiusplatz (☎02224/8889), with singles at DM28, doubles at DM48. It's worth trying to time your visit to coincide with one of the numerous **festivals**, the most spectacular of which is *Der Rhein in Flammen*, a display of fireworks and illuminations held on the first Saturday in May; a week later, the cutting of the first crop of asparagus is celebrated. Bad Honnef's *Weinfest* is held on the first weekend in September; exactly a month later comes Königswinter's *Winzerfest*.

KONRAD ADENAUER (1876-1967)

A local government stalwart of the Catholic Centre Party during the Weimar Republic, **Konrad Adenauer** seemed to be merely a stop-gap leader when he finally entered the national stage at the age of 73. In the event, his impeccable record as an anti-Nazi (he had been deposed as mayor of Cologne) and his moderate right-wing politics happened to be exactly in tune with the country's mood in the postwar period, and he remained in power for fourteen years, only retiring when his coalition partners made this a condition of their continued support. Adenauer's high reputation rests on his twin achievements of the "Economic Miracle" and the international rehabilitation of Germany, though there's little doubt that his inflexible attitude towards the Russians was a contributory factor in cementing the division of the nation into two hostile states.

The mountains

Although the lowest of the mountains, **Drachenfels**, situated immediately behind Königswinter, is by far the most interesting; unfortunately, it's heavily touristed and even more heavily exploited. Don't be tempted by the rack railway, built in 1883 using a system pioneered in Switzerland; it may be an ingenious piece of engineering, but the fare is a rip-off, the more so as the footpath is paved and makes for a steep but easy ascent. Beware also of the many cafés lining this path; some charge fair prices, others emphatically don't, so check carefully before ordering. About a third of the way up is the **dragon's cave**, traditionally supposed to be the home of the fearsome monster slain by the hero **Siegfried**; by immediately immersing himself in its warm blood he gained a horny skin which would have rendered him invincible had a falling leaf not left a spot as vulnerable as Achilles' heel. From this legend comes the name of the wine, *Drachenblut* (dragon's blood), made from the grapes cultivated on these slopes. the most northerly vineyard in western Germany. Best pass by the cave, featuring a kitsch presentation of live reptiles and a model of the dragon, for which a stinging DM4 entrance fee is asked. Your money is better spent on **Schloss Drachenburg** (guided tours Tues–Sun 10am– 6pm; DM2), which may not be too wonderful aesthetically speaking, but is a good example of the nineteenth-century German love of macabre Gothic fantasy. From the terrace there's a really spectacular **view**, which more than makes up for the ghastly tribulations en route. There's an even wider panorama from what's left of the Romanesque **Burg**, a ruin since the Thirty Years' War, at the summit of the mountain. Apart from being able to trace the Rhine's path both upstream and down, you can see over the Eifel to the west, and get a different perspective on the Siebengebirge to the familiar one from across the river; on an even half-decent day, the spires of Cologne can also be distinguished.

Gimmicks are thankfully wholly absent in the rest of the mountains in the range, and a series of well-marked hiking trails enables you to choose your own route round. **Petersberg** is probably the best known; its summit is occupied by a grandiose luxury hotel often used for state visits; it was Chamberlain's base for his ill-fated talks with Hitler in Bad Godesberg. **Löwenburg** is allegedly haunted by a wild huntsman, doomed to an eternal chase as punishment for his cruelty when alive. **Grosser Ölberg** is the most enticing after Drachenfels, commanding the next best views. Although furthest from the Rhine of all the peaks, it has the advantage of being the highest, and of including panoramas over the Taunus to the east.

Kloster Heisterbach

From here, it's only a short descent to the area's sole great monument, the ruins of the early thirteenth-century Cistercian **Kloster Heisterbach**, built, like so many of this order's foundations, in the Transitional style between Romanesque and Gothic. One of the first priors, Caesarius, was a chronicler of legends, which he collected in the *Dialogus Miraculorum*. The most famous of these – which was retold by Henry Longfellow and must have inspired Washington Irving's *Rip van Winkle* – concerns a monk who, while out for his daily walk, was meditating disbelievingly on the text of Psalm 90, "a thousand years in thy sight are but as yesterday"; on returning for vespers, he found that a whole century had elapsed since his departure. Heisterbach was pulled down at the beginning of the nineteenth century following the Napoleonic suppression, but the apse and its ambulatory were spared when the explosives failed to ignite. This tiny fragment had an impact on the Romantic imagination out of all proportion to its size; depictions of lonely, overgrown and crumbling abbeys set in wooded valleys, often illuminated by moonlight, became one of the favourite subjects of the movement's painters. Nowadays, the eighteenth-century monastic buildings are occupied by a convent of Augustinian nuns, who have built a modern church. They also run a café-restaurant, specialising in a huge choice of irresistible home-made gateaux.

Brühl

Midway between Bonn and Cologne, set inland from the Rhine, lies **BRÜHL**, a town which developed from a castle founded by the Archbishop-Electors in the thirteenth century. The eighteenth-century successor to this is the most sumptuous palace in the Rhineland, seemingly a little piece of Bavaria wafted mysteriously northwards. It makes the town one of the most interesting in the province, but isn't the reason two million people swarm here each summer, nor why **kids** are likely to rate Brühl the highlight of a holiday in Germany.

Phantasialand

The main draw nowadays is **Phantasialand** (April–Oct daily 9am–6pm; adults DM22, kids DM20), the first amusement park in Europe to rival Disneyland and a clear example of how strong the transatlantic influence has become in Germany. It's laid out on the site of an open-cast mine, at the extreme southern end of town, and can be reached by regular **bus** services from Brühl's Bahnhof. Provided you find the place palatable (not everybody does), and are prepared to enter into the spirit of fun and silliness, there are enough attractions to last a full day. These range from re-creations of prewar Berlin, a Wild West town and China of a thousand years ago, through rides on a Viking ship, an overhead monorail, a 1.3km waterfall and the world's largest roller-coaster. Be warned that even the park's owners admit that there are an uncomfortably large number of visitors on Sundays and throughout July and August.

The town centre: Schloss Augustusburg

In its own day Brühl's heart and soul, the **Schloss Augustusburg** (guided tours lasting 1 hr, Feb–Nov Tues–Sun 9am–noon & 1.30–4pm; DM1.50) must have seemed as much of an extravaganza as Phantasialand does now. Such is its splendour that it's *the* favourite venue for state visits and the Federal President's official binges; unfortunately, this means it's liable to unexpected periods of closure for up to three weeks at a time. It's very much a personal creation of the eighteenth-century Archbishop-Elector **Clemens August**, a member of the Bavarian Wittelsbach dynasty. From an early age, he had been earmarked for an ecclesiastical career in order to advance the family's power base. In this, he was brilliantly successful, though he showed no piety whatsoever, living a life of unashamedly pampered luxury and gaining a reputation as a womaniser – he was summoned to Rome by the Pope to explain the presence of two particularly beautiful singers at his court, and his death came after he had danced the night away rather too energetically. He favoured Brühl as the seat of his court because of its ideal situation for his favourite hobby, falconry, and was determined to rebuild the medieval moated Schloss which had been destroyed by French troops in 1689.

Initially the design was in dignified Baroque: building was later entrusted to **François Cuvilliés**, who eliminated all features reminiscent of a fortress and transformed the complex into a pleasure palace facing a formal French-style garden. As the final *pièce de resistance*, the greatest architect of the day, **Balthasar Neumann**, was recruited to draw up plans for the ceremonial **staircase** – an eye-grabbing fricassee of marble and stucco, crowned by a fresco glorifying the Virtues. The decorative scheme of this and the following Hall of Guards and Music Room, which are almost equally sumptuous, is a complicated series of allegories in honour of the Wittelsbach dynasty.

Adjoining the west front of the Schloss is the **Orangerie**; now housing a café and an exhibition room, it forms a processional way to **St Maria zu den Engeln**. Built as a Franciscan monastery in the simplest form of Gothic, the church's interior was greatly pepped up for its new function as court chapel by the insertion of a lavish **high altar** – taking up the entire chancel – designed by Neumann.

The Max Ernst museum

Max Ernst, the Dadaist and Surrealist painter, was born in Brühl, a fact commemorated by a small **museum** (Mon–Thurs 10am–noon & 2–4pm, Fri 10am–noon; free) housed in his birthplace, a villa facing the northern wing of the Schloss. It has a few early oil paintings, but the bulk of the material is graphic work, displayed in a changing series of exhibitions.

Practicalities

Within the former monastic buildings of St Maria zu den Engeln are the Rathaus and **tourist office** (Mon–Wed 8am–noon & 2–4pm, Thurs 8am–noon & 2–6pm, Fri 8am–noon; ☎02232/79345). They keep a list of **rooms** to let, costing from DM25 to DM30 per person. Most centrally placed is *Harth*, Wallstr. 103 (☎02232/47227); if you prefer a location near Phantasialand, try *Maeder*, Akazienweg 14 (☎02232 32314), or *Schmidt*, Akazienweg 19 (☎02232/32295). Alternatively, two **hotels**, both close to the Schloss, charge between DM30 and DM40: *Clemens-August-Stube*, Römerstr. 86 (☎02232/22041), and *Brühler Hof*, Uhlstr. 30 (☎02232/42711). Brühl's prices are generally so much lower than those in both Cologne and Bonn that it's worth considering as an alternative base – both cities can be reached quickly either by tram (from the town centre) or train (from the opposite side of the Schloss). **Concerts** by top international musicians in the Schloss *Galerie* are the main cultural attraction, while October sees a **festival** of international puppet theatre. There are two **beers** to try – Brühl is sufficiently close enough to Cologne to be allowed to brew its own *Kölsch* (see p.471), named *Giesler*, while the local Pils is predictably named *Clemens August*.

COLOGNE (KÖLN)

Although now in the political shadow of the neighbouring upstarts of Bonn and Düsseldorf, **COLOGNE** stands as a colossus in the vast urban sprawl of the Rhine-Ruhr conurbation, being unquestionably one of the great German cities, and currently the fourth largest with a population of just under one million. The huge Gothic **Dom** is the country's most visited monument, while its assemblage of Roman remains and medieval buildings is unsurpassed and the museums bettered only by those in Berlin, Dresden and Munich. The annual **Carnival** festival in the early spring is one of Europe's major popular celebrations. The city also ranks high as a **beer** centre: there are 24 breweries (more than in any other city in the world), all producing the distinctive *Kölsch*.

Originally founded in 33 BC, Cologne quickly gained importance. It was the birthplace of Julia Agrippa, wife of the Emperor Claudius who in 50 AD raised it to the status of a colony (hence its name) with full rights as a Roman city. Subsequent development owed much to ecclesiastical affairs – a bishopric was founded in the fourth century and Saints Severin, Gereon and Ursula were all martyred in the city; churches were soon dedicated to each and built over their graves. The cult of Saint Ursula was especially popular, being associated with the alleged death of her 11,000 virgin companions (though the true figure was probably a more realistic eleven). In the twelfth century, Cologne forcibly acquired the relics of the Three Magi from Milan, thus increasing its standing as one of the greatest centres of pilgrimage in northern Europe.·

Medieval Cologne, a city of 150 churches, became enormously prosperous because of its strategic situation on the Rhine at the intersection of trade routes. The largest city in Germany, it was one of the great European centres of learning and boasted a distinctive school of painters. Decline inevitably set in, but something of a comeback was made in the eighteenth century with a recipe imported from Italy which involved distilling flower blossoms in almost pure alcohol. Although originally meant as an aphrodisiac, this was to achieve world-wide fame as a toilet water under the euphemism by which customers ordered it – water from Cologne, *eau de Cologne*.

The modern city has reclaimed its old role as a major trade and business centre, and has also become Germany's radio and television metropolis. As a welcome contrast to the class-consciousness and frantic status-seeking of its neighbours, it has an openness about it similar to that of the city states of Hamburg and Bremen. To this is added a general atmosphere of fun and irreverence more characteristic of the Mediterranean than Germany.

The telephone code for Cologne is ☎0221.

Arrival and practicalities

The **Hauptbahnhof** is right in the centre of the city, immediately below the Dom. Moving on is never a problem as some 1000 trains per day stop there. The **bus station** is directly behind, with international services on the lower tier. For the **airport** (☎402222/402256 for flight information) take bus #170; there are departures approximately every 20 minutes, with a journey time of less than half an hour.

The **tourist office** is at Unter Fettenhennen 19, directly in front of the Dom (May–Oct Mon–Sat 8am–10.30pm, Sun & holidays 9am–10.30pm, Nov–April Mon–Sat 8am–9pm, Sun & holidays 9.30am–7pm; ☎221 3345). Apart from the usual maps, there's an excellent array of free leaflets and brochures on every aspect of the city. For a **hotel room**, best advice is to stump up the DM2 they charge to find you a place. Accommodation is plentiful, but it's scattered all over the city and is mainly geared to the expense account brigade attending the numerous trade fairs. This does mean, however, that some of the better hotels offer cut-price rates at slack times; an example is *Gülich*, Ursulaplatz 13–19 (☎120015), which halves its prices. If you prefer to look yourself, the following are centrally placed and charge in the region of DM35–45 for a single, DM65–75 for a double: *Stapelhäuschen*, Fischmarkt 1–3 (☎212193); *Im Kupferkessel*, Probsteigasse 6 (☎135338); *Schmidt*, Elisenstr. 16 (☎211706); *Einig*, Johanisstr. 71 (☎122128); and *Henn*, Norbertstr. 6 (☎134445). Whole streets of medium-price hotels can be found immediately at the back entrance of the Hauptbahnhof. You can obviously pay less if you're prepared to stay further out.

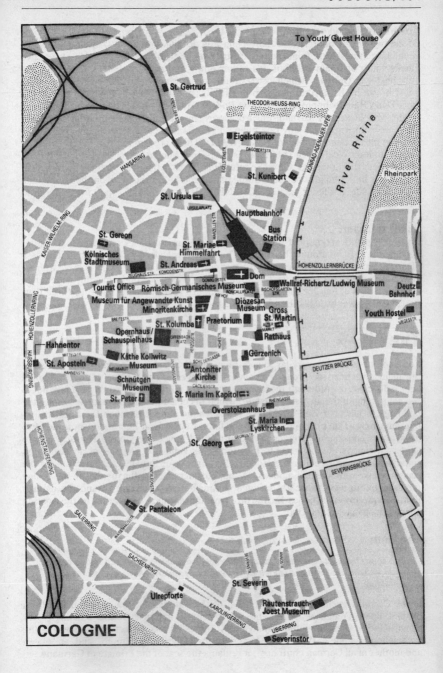

To Youth Guest House

THEODOR-HEUSS-RING

River Rhine

Rheinpark

St. Gertrud

Eigelsteintor

St. Kunibert

St. Ursula

Hauptbahnhof

Bus Station

St. Gereon

Kölnisches Stadtmuseum

St. Mariae Himmelfahrt

St. Andreas

HOHENZOLLERNBRÜCKE

Dom

Tourist Office

Römisch-Germanisches Museum

Wallraf-Richartz/Ludwig Museum

Deutz Bahnhof

Museum für Angewandte Kunst

Minoritenkirche

Diözesan Museum

Youth Hostel

Gross St. Martin

St. Kolumba

Praetorium

Opernhaus/Schauspielhaus

Rathaus

Hahnentor

Gürzenich

St. Aposteln

Käthe Kollwitz Museum

Antoniter Kirche

Schnütgen Museum

St. Peter

St. Maria Im Kapitol

Overstolzenhaus

St. Maria In Lyskirchen

St. Georg

DEUTZER BRÜCKE

St. Pantaleon

SEVERINSBRÜCKE

St. Severin

Ulrepforte

Rautenstrauch-Joest Museum

Severinstor

COLOGNE

Youth hostels and camping

Of the two **youth hostels**, the more central is at Siegesstr. 5a in DEUTZ (☎814711), about 15 minutes' walk from the city centre over the Hohenzollernbrücke, or just two blocks south of Deutz Bahnhof. It's rather dingy and claustrophobic, though it's the only hostel in Germany which takes credit cards. Much more enticing is the youth guest house in the northern suburb of RIEHL (☎767081; take U-Bahn #5, #16 or #18 from Dom/Hauptbahnhof, and alight at Boltensternstrasse): this has modern spacious rooms with lockers, a bar and, unsurprisingly, much higher prices. As far as **campsites** are concerned, the only one open all year is located at Peter-Baum-Weg in the extreme northeastern suburb of DÜNNWALD. There are two more in POLL (south of Deutz); that on Weidenweg (☎831966) is open from May to September and is intended for families; the other, on Alfred-Schutte-Allee (☎832337) is for schoolchildren, and only opens in the holiday periods. Immediately south, but this time on the right bank, is the final site at Uferstr. 53a in RODENKIRCHEN (☎392421), open from March to October.

Public transport

Cologne's **public transport** network uses a mixture of buses and trams; the latter become the U-Bahn around the centre. The system is shared with Bonn, and it's possible to take a stopping tram between the two cities – useful if you intend to leave from or arrive at somewhere which isn't central. Ticket prices are high, making it better to invest in strips of four, or those valid for 24 hours (DM7 Cologne only), or three days (DM13 Cologne only, DM21 the whole circuit).

The city

You don't need to walk very far to see the main attractions of Cologne – the Dom and the main museums are grouped conveniently together, with some of the traditional beer halls close by. Although most visitors venture no further, it would be a pity not to see something of the medieval Altstadt, which occupied an enormous area; among the buildings to have survived are twelve Romanesque churches, much the finest collection anywhere. Don't expect to get more than a superficial impression in under two days, and a considerably longer period is needed to see everything. The best way to start your tour is to cross over to the right-bank suburb of Deutz – or at least to go some distance across either the Hohenzollernbrücke or the Deutzer Brücke – for the classic **view**, with the tall houses of the burghers lining the banks of the Rhine (crossed by no less than eight bridges within the city boundaries), and the chunky Romanesque tower of Gross St Martin providing an ideal counterfoil to the soaring openwork steeples of the Dom.

The Dom

> "... it was the most beautiful of all the churches I have ever seen, or can imagine. If one could imagine the spirit of devotion embodied in any material form, it would be in such a building."

Lewis Carroll's gushing tribute is typical of the extravagant praise which has been heaped upon Cologne's **Dom**. One of the most massive Gothic buildings ever constructed, it dominates the city in every sense, its size reflecting its power – the archbishop was one of the seven Electors of the Holy Roman Empire, and, as "queen and mother of all German churches", it remains the seat of the Primate of Germany.

Some history

The history of the present building is an odd one, for, although the foundation stone was laid in 1248, it was only finally completed in 1880; most of what can be seen today was put up in two concentrated periods of activity separated by five centuries, yet in an almost identical architectural style. Impetus for the creation of a new cathedral came with the arrival of the alleged relics of the Magi and the subsequent increase in pilgrims. A spectacular **shrine** was commissioned to house the relics, begun in 1181 by **Nicholas of Verdun**, the greatest goldsmith of the day, and finished in 1220 by local craftsmen. What was now needed was a fitting palace to house this memorial to the kings, whose relics were deemed important for symbolical reasons – they were the first earthly monarchs to be acknowledged by the King of Heaven, therefore whoever guarded them must hold a special place in the kingdom of Christ on earth. It was decided to adopt the ethereal new Gothic style of architecture for the cathedral, rather than the late Romanesque style still in vogue in the Rhineland, but to surpass earlier French models in size and splendour.

The exterior

The chancel, designed by **Master Gerhard**, was completed in 1322, but thereafter the sheer ambitiousness of the plans began to take its toll. In 1560, the project was abandoned, with only the south tower and the lower parts of the nave and facade having been built. That might have been the end of the story, had it not been for the impact of the Romantic movement in the early nineteenth century, which led to a campaign for the completion of the cathedral, boosted by the discovery of two pieces of parchment which showed the medieval builders' designs for the facade. From 1842, in a remarkable act of homage from one age to another, the work was carried out in a style that would have been completely familiar to the original masons.

Today, pollution has made it hard to distinguish the two sections, and the facade, of which you get a great uninterrupted view from the square in front, has an overwhelming, crushing power. Originally, the **spires** were, at 157 metres, the tallest structures in the world, but they were soon dwarfed by the Eiffel Tower and are no longer even the highest in Cologne. All the same, you need a fair bit of energy to climb up the south tower to the base of the steeple for a fine **panorama** over the city and the Rhine (daily 9am–4/5/6pm according to season; DM2).

The interior

Enter by the west door and your eye is immediately drawn down the great length of the building to the **high altar** with the shrine to the Magi, which illustrates the history of the world as described in the Bible, with Epiphany given due prominence. It's one of three artistic masterpieces to be found here; the others are in the chapels at the entrance to the ambulatory. On the north side is the ninth-century **Gero crucifix**, the most important monumental sculpture of its period. The corresponding chapel to the south has the greatest achievement of the fifteenth-century Cologne school of painters, the *Adoration of the Magi* triptych by **Stefan Lochner**. His refined, idealised and other worldly style finds a perfect outlet in this truly gorgeous scene; the wings feature two of the Cologne martyrs, Saints Ursula and Gereon, with their companions. Look out also for an elaborate sixteenth-century carved retable from Antwerp in the south transept, a colossal wooden *St Christopher* nearby, and (at the intersection of the north transept and the nave aisle) the fourteenth-century *Clares altar*. The whole **chancel** is outstanding, preserving an unparalleled set of furnishings contemporary with the architecture – choir stalls; painted wooden panels; vibrant statues of Christ, the Virgin and the Apostles; and a delicate altar front. To penetrate beyond the barrier for a marginally better view of these, you have to take one of the free **guided tours**

(German only) which leave from below the organ in the north transept. Times of departures on any given day are prominently displayed on various boards – normally they're at 10am, 11am, 2pm and 3pm except Sunday mornings.

Stained glass windows are an essential component of a Gothic cathedral, and Cologne has a marvellously varied assemblage. The oldest, dating from 1260, is in the axis chapel of the ambulatory and is a "Bible" window, pairing New Testament scenes with a parallel from the Old Testament; another is two chapels to the south. In a wholly different, far more monumental style is the late Gothic glass on the north side of the nave, designed by some of the leading local painters. These in turn contrast well with the brilliantly coloured nineteenth-century Bavarian windows opposite, a gift from King Ludwig I towards the Dom's completion.

The Schatzkammer and Diözesanmuseum

The **Schatzkammer** (Mon–Sat 9am–4/5pm, Sun 1–4/5pm; DM2) has a few lovely Ottonian manuscripts, but is far less interesting than the **Diözesanmuseum** just outside in Roncalliplatz (Mon–Wed, Fri & Sat 10am–5pm, Sun 10am–1pm; DM1). A beautiful **Lochner**, *Madonna of the Violets*, forms the centrepiece; in a glass case, and easily missed, is his little *Nativity*. Also displayed here are most of the sculptures which adorned the portal of the south tower, the only one dating from the medieval building period. Carved in the workshop of **Michael Parler**, a member of the famous dynasty of masons (see Schwäbisch Gmünd, *Chapter Two*), they've been replaced in situ by faithful copies. Other highlights include an eleventh-century crucifix which bizarrely uses an antique lapis lazuli of a woman as the head; the *St Severin medallion* with a portrait of the saint; and two priceless textiles – a sixth-century Syrian silk illustrating a hunt, discovered in the shrine of Saint Kunibert, and a Byzantine cloth embroidered with lions.

Museums around the Dom

Cologne's two most important museums are housed in ultra-modern buildings right beside the Dom; neither should be missed. Unless you have a student card (which allows half-price admission), it makes sense to invest in the DM6 Museums Pass, which allows continued entry to these and to all the other municipal collections on any three days (not necessarily consecutive) in a week.

Wallraf-Richartz/Ludwig Museum

Bischofsgartenstr. 1. Tues–Thurs 10am–8pm, Fri–Sun 10am–6pm; DM3.

This houses the city's collection of paintings. On the first floor is the Wallraf-Richartz Museum of old masters, centred on the unique holdings of the fifteenth-century **Cologne school** (see "Painting and Graphics" in *Contexts*). Look out for the backdrop depictions of the medieval city, often featuring the unfinished Dom. **Stefan Lochner** is the most admired artist of the school, and his *Last Judgment* is a major work, enormously inventive in its detail, gentle and fantastic in its view; *Madonna in a Rose Garden* and the portable triptych *Madonna in a Walled Garden* show his treatment of what must have been far more congenial subjects. From the preceding generation, the **Master of St Veronica** is the most accomplished painter, with two contrasting versions of the *Crucifixion*, one as delicately refined as an illuminated manuscript, the other with monumental figures. The best vignettes of Cologne are by the **Master of the Glorification of the Virgin**, but the gems of the whole display are the two large triptychs made for the Carthusians by the **Master of St Bartholomew**, who represented the final flowering of the school at the beginning of the sixteenth century. His figures are executed as if in imitation of sculpture and have a haunting, mystical quality.

Displayed alongside the Cologne masters are other German paintings, including a small **Dürer** *Fifer and Drummer* and several typical examples of **Cranach**. There are also a number of Flemish and Italian Primitives, among which a *Madonna and Child* by **Simone Martini** stands out. Grouped around the staircase are the largest works, including two canvases by **Rubens**, *Juno and Argus* and *Stigmatisation of St Francis*. The latter was painted for the Capuchins of Cologne and is now hung back to back with *St Francis in the Porzincula Chapel* by **Murillo**, offering a fascinating comparison of treatment by two of the great masters of the Counter-Reformation.

The corridor and galleries beyond have a rich representation of seventeenth-century Dutch artists, including what is probably the very last of **Rembrandt**'s great series of self-portraits, in which he depicted himself in the guise of a laughing philosopher (or perhaps the satirical painter Zeuxis) from ancient Greece. There's a comprehensive array of French painting from the seventeenth century to Impressionism, while the nineteenth-century German school is dominated by a large collection of the local artist **Wilhelm Leibl**, leader of the Realist movement.

THE LUDWIG MUSEUM

The Ludwig Museum of twentieth-century art occupies the remainder of the galleries, including all of the second floor. It's a shock to go up from the fifteenth-century altarpieces and be confronted by Brillo boxes, Pepsi Cola and Campbell's Tomato Juice, the favourite subjects of **Andy Warhol**, which are the centrepiece of a notable display of Pop Art which also includes examples of Tom Wesselmann and Roy Lichtenstein. **Claes Oldenburg** is represented by *The Street*, which occupies a whole room. Many other eye-catching pieces of sculpture, including the uncanny fibre-glass creations of the Realists and **Ed Kienholz**'s *Portable War Memorial* (a devastating satire on his country's cultural values) are housed in the basement.

Among German works, there's a fine batch by **Kirchner**, notably a group portrait of *Die Brücke*; around it hang examples of these very painters. **Max Ernst** provided a similar memento of the Surrealists, including co-opted dead members, Raphael and Dostoyevsky. By the same artist is an iconoclastic ringing of the changes on the theme of the *Madonna and Child*; the furious mother administers a sound thrashing on the infant's buttocks while Ernst and friends look on. **Beckmann**, **Nolde** and **Kokoschka** are all strongly represented; look out for the latter's *View of Cologne*. There are three superb portraits by **Dix**, including one of himself, and a number of sculptures in various media by **Barlach**. Two rooms are devoted to **Picasso**, who is represented by sculptures and ceramics as well as paintings from most phases of his career. In contrast, there's only a single spectacular **Dalí**, *Perpignan Station*, the elaborate symbolism of which is explained in a descriptive label. Beside it hangs one of the most famous Surrealist canvases, *Presence of Mind* by **Magritte**. An impressive array of Russian paintings includes a large **Chagall**, *Moses Destroying the Tablets of the Law* .

The third museum in the premises, the **Agfa-Foto-Historama**, shows old photographic equipment and a changing selection of prints from the vast holdings of the famous company, whose headquarters are in nearby Leverkusen.

Römisch-Germanisches Museum

Roncalliplatz 4. Tues & Fri–Sun 10am–5pm, Wed & Thurs 10am–8pm; DM3.

This important archaeological museum is specially constructed around the star exhibit, the **Dionysos Mosaic**, excavated here in 1941. The finest work of its kind in Northern Europe, it adorned the dining room of a patrician villa of about 200 AD, and is made from over a million pieces of limestone, ceramics and glass, covering an area of some seventy square metres. Its astonishing state of preservation is due to the protective covering it received from the burnt-out remains of the building falling on it when sacked by a Germanic tribe in the fourth century.

The other main item is the **tomb of Poblicius**, a veteran who had served in the 5th legion. Dating from about 40 AD, this is an even more recent discovery. It stands about 15 metres high and has been re-erected beside the mosaic, although considerably more restoration has been necessary. If you're broke, you don't need to pay to see these two objects – there's a good view to be had by peering in from the square.

Otherwise, the museum is arranged thematically. The collection of **glass** is reckoned to be unsurpassed anywhere in the world; it includes a tiny idealised portrait of Augustus Caesar made in 27 BC. From the second century, the Cologne workshops developed their own distinctive forms, with coloured serpentine threads used for decorative effects. This style culminated around 330 AD in the *diatreta* glass, decorated with a delicate network design. Perhaps of more general appeal is the dazzling array of **jewellery** on the first floor, most of which was found in Frankish graves.

The Altstadt and the Romanesque churches

The vast area that was medieval Cologne suffered grievous damage in the last war. Much of what you now see is modern, due to the need to rebuild the city as quickly as possible to return it to economic viability. Where there wasn't a pressing need for buildings to be reconstructed, as in the case of the churches, time was allowed in order to undertake faithful restoration projects, and these are still going on. What has been achieved is undoubtedly impressive – to realise this you only need to look at the photographs displayed in each church showing its state at the end of the war – although there's no denying that much has been irretrievably lost and that the city has been altered for the worse.

With that proviso, there's a lot to enjoy, and the twelve **Romanesque churches**, which range in date from the tenth to the thirteenth century, form one of the most coherent groups in a single architectural style to be found in any European city. Each has interesting features, but if you blanch at the prospect of seeing them all, the extraordinary **St Gereon** is the one that shouldn't be missed for its architecture, while **St Maria im Kapitol** has the finest furnishings, and **Gross St Martin** and **SS Aposteln** have justifiably famous exteriors. Where there are standard times for visiting the churches, these are listed in brackets; beyond these hours the vestibule may still be kept open, allowing at least a restricted view inside. To avoid cultural indigestion, it's obviously best to spread your exploration of the Altstadt over two or three days.

The east

For nearly 600 years the tower of **Gross St Martin,** surrounded by four turrets, was the dominant feature of the Cologne skyline, not being usurped by the Dom's spires until last century. The rest of the church seems rather truncated for such a splendid adornment, although the interior (daily 10am–6pm) has been returned to its simple original form. Such old houses as remain are in the streets nearby; seen at close quarters, it's rather obvious that many are recent reproductions.

A short distance beyond is the Alter Markt, one of three large squares in the heart of the city. From here, you can see the irregular octagonal tower of the **Rathaus**, a building which is a real jumble of styles, yet with marvellous features. Its core is fourteenth-century Gothic; the following century the tower was added in a more flamboyant idiom, while in the 1570s a graceful loggia, a rare example of Renaissance architecture in the Rhineland, was provided as a frontispiece. To see the historic parts of the interior – the *Hansa Saal* from the first building period and the tower rooms with doorways of inlaid woods – you have to take an hour-long guided tour (Mon, Wed & Fri at 3pm; free). Although it's in German only, you can pick up an explanatory leaflet in English.

Just in front of the entrance to the Rathaus is an unprepossessing door which leads down into the **Mikwe**, a Jewish ritual bath house dating from about 1160, the only remnant of the ghetto which was razed soon after the expulsion order of 1424. It's officially open on Sundays 11am–1pm, but from Monday to Friday you can ask for the key during office hours at the porter's desk in the Rathaus. More subterranean sights can be seen just a short distance away in the form of the foundations of the **Praetorium**, the Roman governor's palace and the **Roman sewer**, a surprisingly elegant vaulted passageway some 100 metres long. The entrance to both of these is at Kleine Budengasse (Tues–Sun 10am–5pm; DM2, but included on the Museums Pass).

Proceeding southwards, you pass the burnt-out **Alt St Alban**, left as a war memorial; the **Gürzenich**, best known as the home of the Carnival balls; and the tower which is all that survives of **Klein St Martin**. Behind is **St Maria im Kapitol**, not seen to advantage from outside as it was built in a severe convent style and is now hemmed in by modern houses, but with a majestic interior (daily 10am–6pm) complete with a full circuit for processions around the aisles. Look out for the **wooden doors**, contemporary with the architecture and among the most precious works of their kind, depicting Christ's Nativity, Teachings and Passion in a restrained, loving way.

Continuing in a southerly direction, go down Rheingasse to see **Overstolzenhaus**, the finest mansion in the city, a step-gabled patrician home contemporary with the later Romanesque churches. A short walk from here is the sailors' church of **St Maria in Lyskirchen** (daily 10am–12.30pm & 3–5pm); their *Schöne Madonna* of about 1420 is one of several fine works of art. The vaults are covered with thirteenth-century frescos of scenes from the Old and New Testaments and lives of saints; they're seen to best effect if you climb the stairs to the gallery. From here, head up Grosse Witschgasse and Georgstrasse to **St Georg** (daily 8am–6pm), an eleventh-century pillared basilica which resembles early Christian churches. The westwork, added the following century, looks squat and stumpy from without, but is impressively spacious when you're inside.

The south

It's then a walk of some fifteen minutes due south to the **St Severin** quarter. The church itself (daily 7.30am–noon & 3–6.45pm) is mainly of interest to archaeology buffs, on account of the **Roman-Frankish graveyard** which has been found directly underneath; it can be visited on guided tours (Mon & Fri 4.30pm; free). Just beyond the church is the Severinstor, part of the medieval fortifications which were largely demolished last century when the Ring was built. A short walk to the east, at Ubierring 45, is the **Rautenstrauch-Joest Museum** (Tues–Sun 10am–5pm, 1st Wed in month 10am–8pm; DM2). This large ethnological museum's particular strengths are Indo-China and Pre-Columbian America; West Africa, the Pacific and Indonesia are also well represented. There are often special exhibitions; when these occur, the Museums Pass isn't valid for even the permanent displays.

Following the ring road in a northwesterly direction, you pass the **Ulrepforte**, another turreted gateway. Further along, turn right at Waisenhausgasse and you arrive at **St Pantaleon** (daily 9am–5pm), the oldest surviving church in the city, dating from the end of the tenth century. It's chiefly notable for its massive westwork with vestibule; this was messed about in the Baroque period, before being returned to its original shape in a pioneering archaeological reconstruction last century. Inside, there's an airy Flamboyant Gothic rood screen, crowned by a seventeenth-century organ in a Rococo case.

The west

North up Poststrasse and Peterstrasse is **St Peter**, a Gothic church with gleaming stained glass windows. The magnificent *Crucifixion of St Peter*, painted by **Rubens** for the high altar, is now displayed in a chapel by the entrance. Next door is **St Cäcilien**, a Romanesque convent church which now houses the **Schnütgen Museum** (Tues–Sun

10am–5pm, 1st Wed in month 10am–8pm; DM2), a collection of religious art (except paintings) of the Rhineland. The setting greatly enhances the objects, and it's an ideal place to while away an hour or so. Major pieces of Romanesque sculpture include: the church's own tympanum, carved in a heavily antique style; the wooden *Crucifix* from St Georg; and the mysterious *Siegburg Madonna*. From the Gothic period the museum's most important possessions are the original carvings from the Dom's altar front and a polychrome console bust of a woman.

Across the road and down Antongasse is the tiny Gothic **Antoniterkirche**, now a Protestant parish church, best known for housing one of the most famous of twentieth-century sculptures, **Barlach**'s *Memorial Angel*. This is a cast made from the plaster of the original, which was created for the 700th anniversary of the Dom in Güstrow but destroyed in the perverse Nazi measures against "degenerate art". Around the church is the main shopping centre; the streets follow the same plan as their Roman predecessors, but almost all the buildings are modern. Up Herzogstrasse are the ruins of the Gothic **St Kolumba**, which wasn't restored after the war; instead Gottfried Böhm inserted a minute chapel within the shell in 1950.

Further down the same street is another Gothic church, the severe **Minoritenkirche**. It contains the tomb of John Duns Scotus, the Scots-born theologian who was the leading intellectual in early fourteenth-century Cologne. Ironically, he's the origin of the word "dunce": his defences of traditional religious orthodoxies so enraged his radical fellow-countrymen at the time of the Reformation that they used his name as a personification of stupidity. Alongside the church is the **Museum für angewandte Kunst** (Tues 10am–8pm, Wed–Sun 10am–5pm; DM3), a comprehensive array of applied art from the Middle Ages to the present day. The Jugendstil section is particularly impressive, though the incongruous highlight of the museum is an exquisite little panel of *The Nativity* by **Memling**. A short distance west of the Antoniterkirche lies Neumarkt. Housed in a bank at no. 18 is the **Käthe-Kollwitz-Museum** (Mon–Wed 9am–4.30pm, Thurs 9am–6.30pm, Fri 9am–3.30pm; free). It has a large display of graphics and a few sculptures by Käthe Kollwitz, one of the leading female artists of this century. Her preference for black-and-white media helps give her work an enormous pathos, evident in her variation on the *Mother and Child* theme, and her denunciations of the follies and sufferings of war.

The far end of Neumarkt is dominated by the superb early thirteenth-century apse of **SS Apostein** (Holy Apostles – an unusual dedication outside the Orthodox world). This is an archetypal Rhenish basilica with all the characteristic features – clover-leaf chancel with dwarf-gallery, central octagon with turrets and, above all, the great western tower with its "bishop's mitre" roof. Despite its apparently homogeneous design, building actually began in the eleventh century; the interior (10am–1pm & 2–6pm, closed Tues) is surprisingly plain. Nearby is another of the city gates, the **Hahnentor**, which resembles a castle's barbican.

The north

Due north of SS Aposteln is **St Gereon**, most idiosyncratic of the twelve Romanesque churches and a truly great building. Its kernel was an oval-shaped fourth-century chapel; in the eleventh and twelfth centuries a crypt, chancel and twin towers were added. Then, in the early thirteenth century, the Roman masonry was harnessed to form the basis of a magnificent four-storey decagon with ribbed dome vault, a work which has no parallel in European architecture. At this time, the adjoining baptistery was also built and adorned with frescos. Make sure you come here when the whole of the church is open (daily 10am–noon & 3–5pm) to see the decagon's interior, which seems more graceful and less massive than from outside; the modern stained glass is a controversial addition. The crypt preserves its original mosaic floor.

From here, you can return towards the Dom, passing a fragment of Roman wall and the Zeughaus, which houses the **Kölnisches Stadtmuseum** (Tues, Wed & Fri–Sun 10am–5pm, Thurs 10am–8pm; DM2), which focuses on the history of local trade and industry, along with sections on Carnival and eau de Cologne. Some good models show the city's building development. A little further east, **St Andreas** has the **Maccabeus shrine**, a piece of early sixteenth-century craftsmanship, doubtless inspired by the Dom's shrine to the Magi. Another casket contains the relics of Saint Albertus Magnus, the thirteenth-century scholar who was the star teacher at Cologne's renowned Dominican College; his pupils there included Saint Thomas Aquinas, later to develop into the greatest philosopher of his time and arguably of the entire medieval period. A short way along Marzellenstrasse is the pink exterior of **St Mariae Himmelfahrt**, a seventeenth-century Jesuit foundation and Cologne's only Baroque building of note. Its galleried interior is lavishly decorated – unusual for the Rhineland, where Bavarian excesses never caught on.

A bit further down the same street, turn left into Ursulaplatz, where **St Ursula** (daily 9.30am–noon & 1–4.30pm), with its prominent sturdy tower, still retains some Romanesque features, along with Gothic and Baroque accretions. Unless you're squeamish, try to get hold of the sacristan, who will show you the **Goldene Kammer**, an ornate Baroque chamber gruesomely lined with reliquaries. He can be elusive, but should be available at the fixed times (Mon & Thurs 11am–noon, Wed & Fri 3–4pm, Sat 4–5pm). From here, the **Eigelsteintor**, another impressive survival of the medieval fortifications, is reached via the street of the same name. Dagobertstrasse then leads east to **St Kunibert**, the final fling of the Romanesque in the early thirteenth century, completed just as work began on the Dom. It's also the last church to be restored following war damage, with the nave and massive westwork having only recently been joined up. Inside (daily 7am–noon & 3–6pm), note the stained glass windows in the apse, which are contemporary with the architecture. On the piers of the transept are the two dramatic polychrome figures of an *Annunciation* group, an important piece of Gothic carving by **Conrad Kuyn**, master mason at the Dom in the early fifteenth century.

Outside the centre

If you want to stray beyond the confines of the Altstadt, Cologne's suburbs offer a wide choice of **parks** and some of the most exciting **modern architecture** in Germany.

Some modern architecture

In every way, the dominant building outside the centre is the **Fernsehturm** (Telecommunications tower; daily 9am–11pm; DM4, including ascent by lift to the viewing platform), in the Stadtgarden west of the Ring. Completed in 1980, at 243 metres it's considerably higher than the Dom, and in spite of the pricey admission it's definitely worth going up for the breathtaking views over the city and the Rhine. Very close by, within the Stadtgarden, is **Neu St Alban**, one of several highly praised modern churches in Cologne, with a mystical quality reminiscent of early Christian churches. Also near the Ring, but to the north, is **St Gertrud** on Krefelder Strasse, with an amazing tapering tower. It's the work of **Gottfried Böhm**, whose father **Dominikus** was a pioneer of radical church design in the inter-war period. An example of the latter's 1930s Expressionism is **St Engelbert**, a centrally planned building of eight identical concrete shells, located very near the youth guest house on Riehler Gürtel. His **St Maria Königin** in the southern suburb of MARIENBURG, is one of the most accomplished of a new generation of churches built to serve the needs of the residential quarters then being built.

Green Cologne

Although there are few areas of green in the city centre, about a quarter of Cologne is given over to open spaces. Most popular is the **Rheinpark** in Deutz on the right bank of the Rhine, a legacy of large garden shows, with the *Tanzbrunnen*, round which showbiz concerts are held in summer. It's linked by cable car (April–Oct Sat–Thurs 10am–7pm; DM4) over the Rhine to the **Botanical Gardens** (daily 8am–dusk), near the **Zoo** and **Aquarium** (daily 8.30am–6pm in summer, 9am–5pm in winter; DM6). Other parks are in the far suburbs. To the south are the recreational *Volksgarten* and a forestry reserve at **RODENKIRCHEN** (daily 9am–4/6/8pm according to season) with trees, plants and shrubs from around the world. The right bank has nature reserves at **DÜNNWALD**, **BRÜCK** and **PORZ**, the last featuring birds of prey (daily April–Sept 9am–7pm, Oct–March 9am–5pm).

The western suburbs

From the Hahnentor, Aachner Strasse runs in a dead straight line westwards to the outer suburbs. Just beyond the Ring, a short walk down Universitätstrasse brings you to the **Museum für ostasiatische Kunst** (Tues–Sun 10am–5pm, 1st Fri in month 10am–8pm; DM2). Devoted to the arts of China, Japan and Korea, this is yet another of Cologne's collections which has been given specially designed modern premises, appropriately enough by a Japanese architect and with a traditional Japanese garden.

Further along Aachner Strasse, in the suburb of WEIDEN, is the city's final important Roman munument, the **Grabkammer** (Tues–Thurs 10am–1pm, Fri 10am–5pm, Sat & Sun 1–5pm; DM2), a second-century burial chamber. It contains marble busts of a couple and a young woman which are contemporary with the building, and a sarcophagus from the following century with carvings of the seasons.

Drinking and eating

Cologne crams over 3000 **pubs, bars and cafés** into a relatively small area. Most *Eckkneipen* or "corner pub" are of a uniform drabness and are generally worth avoiding: much more promising are the *Brauhäuser*, brewery-owned **beer halls** which largely date from the turn of the century, though claiming a much longer pedigree. Whilst smaller than their Munich counterparts, they have similarly cavernous interiors with sparse decor. They're staffed by horribly matey *Köbes*, who all year round keep up the the Carnival tradition of making insulting and corny jokes. Inevitably, these pubs are often overrun with visiting businessmen and Dom-gawping tourists, but they're definitely worth sampling as they offer some of the cheapest **eating** possibilities in the city, specialising in the local cuisine. Don't be misled by the dialect, however – *Halve Hahn* is not the half chicken you'd expect but a rye roll with cheese, while *Kölsche Kaviar* is less of a bargain than it appears when you realise it's a black pudding, again with rye bread.

The Brauhäuser – and other eating possibilities

Three of the *Brauhäuser* are very close to the Dom; consequently they're the most prone to be packed with visitors. *Alt Köln* at Trankgasse 7–9 has a quite different interior to the others, a picturesque folly with wooden alcoves and galleries representing a romantic recreation of a series of old German taverns. *Früh am Dom*, Am Hof 12–14, and *Brauhaus Sion* round the corner at Unter Taschenmacher 5 are archetypal. For a less touristy atmosphere and arguably better food, you'd be better trying those a bit further away – the two called *Päffgen*, at Heumarkt 62 and Friesenstr. 64; *Haus Töller* at Weyerstr. 96; and *Zur Malzmühle* at Heumarkt 6.

KÖLSCH

Kölsch beer is as much a piece of the local life of Cologne as the Dom or Carnival, and may only be produced in the breweries located in and around the city. It's clear, light, highly fermented and aromatically bitter, with a strong accentuation of hops. Invariably, it's served with a substantial head in a tall, thin glass (*Stange*) which holds only a fifth of a litre. This gives it a rather effete image among macho beer drinkers from elsewhere in Germany who tend to revile it, in contrast to the religious reverence it's accorded in Cologne. The denigratory view seems rather jaundiced, and there's no doubt that the modest capacity of the glasses ensures that the beer is always fresh.

If you've a really serious interest in the city's liquid culture, head out southwards to the *Küppers Kölsch Brauhaus* beyond the Südstadt at Altenburgerstr. 157, where a **museum** has been set up, including the re-creation of an old brewery (guided tours Saturday only, leaving every hour 11am–3pm; ignore the sign outside and the tourist office leaflets which say it's open until 4pm). Afterwards you can have a drink in the beer garden or in the tavern reconstructed to resemble those in the city centre.

Ethnic restaurants

Most of Cologne's **ethnic restaurants** are either expensive or mediocre, but the following are exceptions: *Tchang*, Grosse Sandkaul 19 (Chinese); *Maharani*, Hohenzollernring 53 (Indian); *Bali*, Brüsseler Platz 2 (Indonesian); *Yakitori*, Friesenplatz 7 (Japanese); and *Café-Especial*, Deutz-Neuhöffer Str. 32 (Mexican).

Nightspots: bars and venues

There are four distinct quarters of Cologne with a recommendable concentration of nightspots. The most obvious is the area around Gross St Martin in the **Altstadt**; this tends to catch visiting tourists and businessmen, but the best places do manage to create their own distinctive atmosphere. Down the road from the University (in the southwestern part of the city), the **Quartier Lateng** is more like the real thing as far as mingling with locals is concerned, even if it has lost its trendy edge. The **Südstadt**, or St Severin quarter, now has the most stylish bars and cafés, and the biggest crowds. For once, it pays to follow them – it's their sheer exuberance that make the place. The more relaxed **Belgisches Viertel** (the streets around the Ring, just to the west of the centre) is nowhere near as packed or self-consciously trendy. Currently dominated by arty types, it's also a centre of the **gay scene**, has the most original **discos** and could yet become the in place. Here's a selection of the best establishments listed by street within each quarter. Also included are some recommendations for **breakfast**, often available until the afternoon, although on Sundays it's a popular finish for late-night revellers.

Altstadt

Alter Wartesaal, Am Hauptbahnhof. A die-hard of the disco scene which has lost some of its freshness; music a mixture of Europop and Gothic.

Biermuseum, Buttermarkt 39. A favourite haunt with tourists and correspondingly pricey; there are eighteen sorts of beer on tap.

Kännchen, Am Bollwerck 13. Tiny traditional pub.

Kauri, Auf dem Rothenberg 11. Conveniently sited disco with good selection of funk and blues; free entry but drinks extortionate.

Künsterklause Timp, Heumarkt 73. Mainly noted for a fairly tacky transvestite cabaret, but is very lively and packed out on Saturday nights; can be stroppy about letting women in.

Papa Joe's Em Streckstrumpf, Buttermarkt 37. A cosier, smaller, equally good version of *Klimperkasten*; invariably standing room only, with music beginning at 8.30pm and special Sunday sessions at 11am.

Papa Joe's Klimperkasten, Alter Markt 50. The deservedly popular place to go for traditional live jazz which is belted out to an appreciative audience from 8pm onwards. Very expensive drinks but young clientele at weekends; more businessmen at other times.

The Corkanian, Altermarkt. Large Irish pub serving Guinness and Kilkenny often featuring live Irish music. Packed out, especially at weekends.

Quartier Lateng

Café Central, Jülicher Str. 1. Stylish café which is one of the best places for breakfast; good selection of newspapers.

Café Orlando, Engelbertstr. 9. Quiet café just off Zülpicherstrasse, offers breakfast and health food; 1950s decor with old juke box.

Filmdose, Zülpicher Str. 39. One of the most original fun pubs in Cologne when busy (at weekends); otherwise a bit depressing. It has a tiny stage for cabaret and also shows films in English.

Gilberts Pinte, Englebertstr. 1. Notorious student dive, home to a thousand *Stammtische*, but with plenty of atmosphere.

Juke Box, Luxemburger Str. 83. Best place to come to hear local live bands; free entrance, but jammed solid at weekends.

Luxor, Luxemburger Str. 40. Disco with a healthy mixture of black dance music and chart stuff; also a popular live venue. Free entry after 11pm.

Palä, Palanterstr. 12a. Backstreet café with a wide selection of ice-creams and breakfasts.

Peppermint Lounge, Hochenstauffenring 23. One of the most popular late-nighters, springing into action around midnight; also good for a late breakfast.

Vanille, Zülpicher Str. 25. Lovely café with kitsch decor; good for food (especially breakfast) and cocktails; keeps a selection of newspapers and has occasional disco evenings.

Weinhaus Kyffhäuser Keller, Kyffhäuser Str. 47. As recommendable a place as any in Cologne for a glass of wine, with over forty varieties to choose from.

Südstadt

Bi Pis Bistro, Rolandstr. 61. In the unlikely setting of the Boy Scout offices; older, left-wing clientele and regular poetry readings.

Chlodwig-Eck, Annostr. 1. On a backstreet off the Ring; very in.

Climax, Ubierring 18. A place to spot the in-crowd; very dark with ear-splitting music.

Lichtblick, Kurfürstenstr. 8. Easy-going café away from the crowds; good breakfasts.

Linus New Pub, Ubierring 22. In the forefront of the Südstadt scene with good music under subdued lights; beware of being short-changed on beer measures.

Opera, Altenburgerstr. 1. Huge, overlit barn of a place with very young punters queuing to get in at the weekends; good music and plenty of atmosphere.

Schröders, Altenburgerstr. 11. Very chic; rather like a French brasserie with bright lights and mirrors.

Spielplatz, Ubierring 58. More in the style of a beer hall, with a lot more character than some of its newer counterparts.

Belgisches Viertel

Alcazar, Bismarckstr. 39a, Snug and candlelit, with tasty if overpriced menu; somewhat older clientele.

Broadway Café, Ehrenstr. 11. At the entrance to the Broadway cinema; good breakfast from late morning onwards.

Café Limelight, Bismarckstr. 44. Small and cosy artists' pub, totally unpretentious, yet with poetry readings, plays, cabaret and live music.

E.W.G., Aachener Str. 59. Chaotic pub packed out with students.

Hammersteins, Antwerpener Str. 34. The place to meet Cologne's yuppies; best known for excellent but exorbitant restaurant.

Neuschwanstein Diskothek, Mittelstr. 12. At time of writing the best disco in Cologne, with an excellent mix of music.

Schulz, Bismarckstr. 17. Right at the heart of the gay scene; very reasonably priced bar and café.

Stadtgarten, Venloer Str. 40. Home of the *Kölner Jazzhaus Initiative*, so most of the jazz is modern and experimental; there's also a good restaurant.

Wunderbar, Venloer Strasse. Thurs–Sun 4.30am–9am. Last stop on an your all-night pub crawl; it's rumoured that you're thrown out if you fall asleep.

Zorba the Buddha, Brüsseler Str. 54. Spacious café-restaurant with good quality vegetarian food; breakfast served 10am–3.30pm.

Zorba the Buddha, Hohenzollernring 40. Disco with good selection of mainstream music. Dance floor sometimes clears at midnight so that the Bhagwan owners, decked from head to toe in red, can let rip with percussion instruments.

Zorba the Buddha die Kleine, Brabanter Str. 15. Smaller and quieter than the above, with older customers.

Nighlife: culture

For listings of what's currently playing in the fields of music, theatre and films, consult the billboards (which are found all over the city); the posters are changed weekly for the cinemas, every ten days for other entertainments.

Classical music

Classical music performed to the highest international standards can be heard at the brand new *Philharmonie* (☎240 2100) in the same building as the Wallraf-Richartz/ Ludwig Museum on Bischofsgartenstrasse. There are two local symphony orchestras – the *Gürzenich* and *Westdeutsche Rundfunk*, the latter being attached to the national radio, whose headquarters are in Cologne. The radio studios were one of the pioneer centres of electronic music, being particularly associated with the work of Karlheinz Stockhausen (probably the world's most controversial living composer), who is still a Cologne resident. As a contrast, look out for performances by *Musica Antiqua Köln*, Germany's leading specialist ensemble for Baroque music played on period instruments. The *Opernhaus* at Offenbachplatz (☎212581) is currently directed by the American James Conlon. This square's name, incidentally, commemorates the fact that Jacques Offenbach, who conquered Paris with his frothy operettas, and who wrote the ultimate can-can, was a native of Cologne. There are any number of free concerts in the churches; these are all listed in a monthly programme which you can usually pick up in any of the churches themselves. Performances are of a good amateur standard at least, and often considerably more than that. One regular series, featuring a seasonally appropriate Bach cantata, takes place at the Antoniterkirche on the first Sunday evening of each month. Check at the *Musikhochschule* (near St Kunibert) for more free recitals, sometimes by top professionals. Large-scale **pop concerts** and other spectaculars which attract large audiences tend to be held at the *Sporthalle* in Deutz. Best places to hear **jazz** are the *Stadtgarten* and the two pubs called *Papa Joe's* (see above).

Theatre and cinema

The leading **theatre** is the *Schauspielhaus* on Offenbachplatz (☎212651); *Schlosserei* is part of the same complex, but with a more experimental programme. Alternatively, there are *Kammerspiele*, Ubierring 45 (☎212651), and the tiny *Theatre der Keller*, Kleingedankstrasse (☎318059), both of which offer classical and contemporary works. For mime and cabaret, try *Atelier Theatre*, Roonstr. 78 (☎561591). Productions suitable for **kids** are at *Comedia Colonia*, Löwengasse 7–9 (☎247670), and *Kleine Komödie*, Turiner Str. 3 (☎122552), while *Kefka* on Albertusstrasse (☎2401688) is Europe's only theatre devoted solely to pantomime. *Puppenspiele*, Eisenmarkt 2–4 (☎212095), has celebrated marionettes, but be warned that the unintelligible Kölsch dialect is used.

The most ambitious **cinema** programmes are those of *Die Cinemathek* (☎21136), which is actually part of the Museum Ludwig.

Carnival – the facts

While there's no doubt that Cologne is worth visiting at any season, by far the best time to come is during **Carnival**. It's celebrated here with a verve normally associated with Mediterranean countries, and is a useful corrective to the common misapprehension that the Germans are an excessively serious and respectful people. For the *drei tollen Tage* ("three crazy days"– Thursday, Sunday and Monday of Carnival week), life in the city comes to a complete stop and everyone, from punks to grannies, dons make-up and costume, taking to the streets as clown, fool, harlequin or historical personality.

History and customs

The present highly organised festival (here always known as *Karneval*, as opposed to *Fasching* in Southern Germany) dates back to 1823, but its true origins are lost in the mists of time. In part it derives from a pagan exorcism of evil spirits in the transition from one season to another, and in part from a Christian tradition of periods of fasting, which were invariably preceded by counterbalancing periods of merriment. This latter factor governs the timetable of the festival, which has moveable dates; the climax occurs in the week preceding Ash Wednesday, immediately before the stringencies of Lent. However, the Carnival season actually begins as early as "the 11th of the 11th", ie 11 November, a date which was seen as having a foolish significance. From then on, Cologne holds both costume balls and *Sitzungen* (sessions); at the latter, speeches are made in rhyming couplets in the local *Kölsch* dialect (incomprehensible to outsiders, but fairly close to Dutch).

The Carnival

The real business begins with **Weiberfastnacht** on the Thursday prior to the seventh Sunday before Easter. A ceremony in the Alter Markt, starting at 10am, leads to the official inauguration of the festival with the handing over of the keys of the city by the Mayor at 11.11am precisely to *Prinz Claus III*, who assumes command for the "three crazy days". Whereas in other cities he's aided by a Princess, in Cologne he has two companions, the peasant *Bauer Knut* and the virgin *Jungfrau Karla* who is played by a man and is emphatically not his betrothed. The fun can then begin in earnest; in repentance for the chauvinism of earlier centuries, this particular day is now given over to the supremacy of women, who are allowed to take the liberties of their choice. At 3pm there's the first of the great **processions**, beginning at Severinstor, based on the **legend of Jan and Griet**. The former was Jan von Werth, a seventeenth-century cavalry officer who saved the city from ruin in the Thirty Years' War. Griet was the Cologne girl who had spurned him, prompting him to assume a military career; they were not to meet again until she, as an ageing spinster, saw him enter the city as a general at the head of his troops. In the evening, the great series of **costume balls** begins, the most prestigious being those in the Gürzenich. However, there are plenty of spontaneous bouts of singing, dancing and boisterous conviviality in the streets and taverns as an authentic alternative.

For the next two days, the city returns to relative normality during daylight hours, although fancy dress is still much in evidence, and on the Saturday morning there's the **Funkenbiwack**, featuring the *Rote und Blaue Funken* (Red and Blue "Sparks"), men

---

---

dressed up in eighteenth-century military outfits; they disobey every order – a symbol of Cologne's long tradition of anti-militarism. The celebrations come to a climax with the two big costumed processions with floats; on Sunday the **Schull- un Veedleszög**, largely featuring children, forms a prelude to the more spectacular **Rosenmontagzug** (Rose Monday Parade). The latter is unquestionably the highlight of the celebrations, a riot of colour featuring over 7000 people, half of them musicians, and 300 horses; and costing some DM1 million to mount. This is only partly due to the costumes; a dominant feature is the fact that 40 tons of sweets, 100,000 chocolates, 100,000 packets of popcorn and innumerable bunches of flowers and containers of eau de Cologne are hurled into the crowd. The first part of the procession is a pageant on the history of the city; then comes the satirical section in which local, national and international politicians appear in effigy; finally there's the gala in honour of the Cologne Carnival, with the spectacular retinues of the peasant, the virgin and the Prince bringing up the rear. It's all done with a proper sense of Germanic thoroughness, taking no less than four hours to pass by. After this, the festival runs down; there are numerous smaller parades in the suburbs on Shrove Tuesday, while the restaurants offer special fish menus on Ash Wednesday.

Carnival practicalities

Although the city gets jam-packed with visitors during Carnival time, many are day-trippers and there's no problem finding **accommodation**, but bear in mind that both youth hostels are likely to be full at the weekend. A greater difficulty comes in deciding where **to stand** during the processions; if you want the backdrop of the Dom, make sure you come several hours before they start (12.30pm on Sunday, noon on Monday) and choose a position on the elevated terrace. Alternatively, go somewhere towards the beginning or end of the route (the tourist office provides free maps), where the crowds are thinner. You could consider hiring one of the grandstand **seats**, positioned all along the course of the route; these are expensive for the Rose Monday Parade, but definitely good value at DM5 on the Sunday. Remember to keep well wrapped up; even when the weather is sunny, it's likely to be cold. Don't expect to do anything else during the "three crazy days"; all the museums and most of the shops are closed, and even the Dom's doors are firmly locked except for the occasional service. Above all, join in the fun; it isn't essential to get dressed up (though it helps), and don't hesitate to follow the crowds, usually congregated round a big drum – it's the impromptu events as much as the set pieces which make this such a great festival. Note that there's a special deal allowing unlimited travel on the public transport network between Weiberfastnacht and Shrove Tuesday. For advance **tickets**, write to *Festkomitee des Kölner Karnevals*, Antwerpener Str. 55. **Dates** of forthcoming Rose Mondays are as follows: 22 Feb 1993; 14 Feb 1994; 27 Feb 1995; and 19 Feb 1996.

Listings

Airlines *British Airways*, Marzellenstr. 1 (☎135081); *Lufthansa*, Bechergasse 2–8 (☎8264).

Bookshops The streets circling Neumarkt have a dense concentration of bookshops; try also around the Dom, on Komodienstrasse or the area around the University. Specially recommended is *Büchermarkt*, Ehrenstr. 4, which stocks a huge range of cut-price titles on the arts, including many in English.

Car hire *Avis*, Clemensstr. 29 (☎234333); *Hertz*, Bismarckstr. 19–21 (☎515084); *InterRent*, Christophstr. 2 (☎132071); *Europa Service*, Am Malzbüchel 1–3 (☎219797); *Condor*, Wilhelm-Mauser-Str. 53 (☎581055); also a number of offices at the airport.

Car repair *Colonia*, Matthias-Brüggen-Str. (☎591009) and *Mauritius Garage*, Mauritiuswall 11–13 (☎219608) both offer 24-hour service. Petrol is available round the clock from *BV Aral*, Augustinerplatz (☎210363).

Cultural institutes *British Council* at Hahnenstr. 6 (☎236677); *Amerikahaus* at Apostelnkloster 13–15 (☎209010 or 241367).

Duty chemist (☎11500).

Duty doctor (☎720772).

Eau de Cologne (*Kölnerwasser*) The most popular souvenir of a visit to the city, this can be bought in innumerable stores. About twenty companies make the product; *Farina*, founded in 1709 and still in business today, is one of the original manufacturers; *Mülhens* is another firm with a long pedigree.

Exhibitions International-class displays are often held at the *Joseph Haubrich Kunsthalle*, Joseph-Haubrich-Hof 1 (☎2212335).

Festivals Everything else inevitably stands in the shade of Carnival (see previous page). However, the Corpus Christi celebrations (variable date in May or June) are also impressive, featuring a barge procession along the Rhine.

Markets The large squares in the Altstadt provide a fitting setting for frequent markets; there's a weekly one all day Friday in Alter Markt, and a *flea market* in the same location every third Saturday. Special occasions are: – the *flower market* in Alter Markt on weekends in late April and early May; the *junk market* in Neumarkt in mid-May and again in mid-September; the *Weinwoche* (actually nearer a fortnight) in Neumarkt in late May/early June; and the *Weihnachtsmarkt* in both locations throughout Advent.

Mitfahrzentrale Saarstr. 22 (☎233464); there's a women-only branch (along with a feminist bookshop) at Moltkestr. 66 (☎523152).

Post office The main office with Poste Restante is on An den Dominikanern, and has a 24-hour service, except for parcels, which must be sent from the depot on Marzellenstrasse. A branch in the Hauptbahnhof is open daily 7am–10pm.

Rhine cruises *K-D Linie* at Frankenwerft 15 (☎2088318); *Rein-Mosel* at Konrad-Adenauer-Ufer (☎121600); *Colonia* at Lintgasse 18–20 (☎211325).

Sports The main outdoor ground is at Aachener Strasse in the western suburb of MÜNGERSDORF; *FC Köln*, one of Germany's most successful football teams, plays here, and there's an international athletics meeting in August or early September. An ice rink and swimming stadium are at Lentstr. 30 in Riehl, and a huge *Sporthalle* for indoor events is at Mülheimer Strasse in Deutz.

Travel agencies Many are to be be found in the vicinity of the Dom, including *Thomas Cook* at Domkloster 2 (☎202080).

What's on The tourist office publishes a comprehensive monthly programme, detailing important forthcoming events, *Köln-Monatsvorschau*, priced DM1.50. Best listings mags are *Stadt Revue* and *Kölner Illustrierte*, available from newsagents at DM5 each.

THE LOWER RHINELAND

The **Lower Rhineland** (*Niederrhein*) is the name given to the predominantly flat area north of Cologne; the great river thereafter offers no more dramatic scenery. Industrialisation, though significant, is held in check most of the way up to **Düsseldorf**.

Immediately beyond, however, begins the most developed industrial region in the world, consisting of the Ruhrgebiet (whose westernmost cities, such as Duisburg and Essen, overlap with this area) and the corresponding towns across the river, such as **Krefeld** and **Mönchengladbach**. After this, there's a dramatic change to a countryslde very close in spirit to nearby Holland. There are no more cities, but a number of small historic towns, notably **Xanten** and **Kalkar**.

Zons and Knechtsteden

The curious village of **ZONS**, sometimes designated *Feste Zons* in honour of its original function as a fortified customs post on the Rhine, lies 25km downstream from Cologne. It's now part of the municipality of DORMAGEN, an industrial town of no interest in itself, and is some 3km east of the latter's Bahnhof, to which it's connected by regular bus services.

In 1372 the Archbishop of Cologne, Friedrich von Saarwerden, decided to levy taxes on the profitable shipping route through his domain, and began the building of a walled town on the site of his predecessors' long-destroyed castle. For all Zons' history of bad luck – it's repeatedly been ravaged by fires and floods down the centuries – the original **fortifications** remain largely intact. They rank as one of the most important surviving examples of a medieval defensive system in Germany, though it now requires a bit of imagination to visualise their original setting, as silting means they're now some way back from the Rhine.

Zons is the sort of place you'd expect to be overrun by sightseeing coaches, but, on weekdays at least, it's remarkably quiet. The best views are obtained by walking around the outside of the circuit. Beginning at the bus stop, turn right and you shortly come to the **Mühlenturm**, the upper section of which was converted into a windmill early in its history. From here, you continue along the south side of the town, which has a double wall, the outer having been added for protection against flooding. At the corner are the ruins of **Schloss Friedestrom**, including the gateway, the chunky keep, and a courtyard which forms a fitting setting for open-air theatre and pageants (every Sunday afternoon mid-June to mid-Sept; also other random days). The eastern wall has two cylindrical defensive towers, along with an octagonal watchtower; at its far corner is the **Rheinturm**, the medieval entrance to the town and the place where customs dues were collected. Three watching posts pierce the northern wall, which terminates in the battlemented **Krötschenturm**. In the town centre there's one more tower, the round **Juddeturm**, which served as both prison and look-out. Around the Rheinturm are the few old houses which have survived the natural disasters; everything else is Baroque or later. The handsome **Herrenhaus** contains the local museum (Tues–Fri 2–7pm, Sat & Sun 10am–12.30pm & 2–6pm; free) which mounts temporary exhibitions alongside its own collection of Jugendstil art.

Practicalities

Zons' **tourist office** (Mon–Fri 8.30am–noon, also Tues 2.15–4.15pm, Thurs 2.15–5.15pm; ☎02106/3772) is housed in the modern building behind the Juddeturm. Much the best **restaurant** in town is *Altes Zollhaus* on Rheinstrasse by the Rheinturm; unfortunately it's also the most expensive. Plenty of cheaper alternatives can be found down Schloss Strasse; some of these have **rooms** to rent, but the prices asked tend to be well over the odds. Otherwise, there are two **campsites** at STÜRZELBERG 1km to the north – *Strandterrasse* (☎02106/71717) and *Pitt-Jupp* (☎02106/42210). Throughout the summer, regular daily **boat trips** (☎02106/42149 or 42349) run to Benrath; there are very occasional sailings to Cologne.

Kloster Knechtsteden
Also within the municipality of Dormagen is the Romanesque **Kloster Knechtsteden**, built in the austere style favoured by its Premonstratensian founders, but enlivened by a central octagon flanked by twin towers. It stands in an isolated setting 3km west of the Bahnhof, reachable by a frequent bus service. As in the great imperial cathedrals, there's a choir at both ends of the building; the eastern one is a late Gothic replacement, while that to the west is adorned with mid-twelfth century **frescos** showing *Christ as Pantocrator*, surrounded by angels and the Evangelical symbols, with portraits of the Apostles below. If you fancy a quiet night away from the cities, the *Klosterhof* (☎02106/80745) just outside the monastery gate has singles at DM40, doubles at DM75, along with a bar-restaurant.

The Bergisches Land

The green countryside on the right bank of the Rhine east and north of Cologne is known as the **Bergisches Land**; it was formerly the Duchy of Berg, whose capital was Düsseldorf. In the nineteenth century this pastoral landscape (much of which is now designated a *Naturpark*) became punctuated by a series of bleak manufacturing towns, which were responsible for putting Germany at the forefront of industrial development.

Prominent among these towns is **LEVERKUSEN**, a northern continuation of Cologne, which is virtually a fiefdom of one of the country's largest companies, the Bayer chemical conglomerate. Here aspirin was invented in 1899, and polyurethane products first introduced to the world in 1937. In the past decade it has swallowed up the town's other famous company, the Agfa photographic plant. Adjoining Leverkusen to the east is **BERGISCH GLADBACH**, best known for its paper products.

Altenberg

Set in isolation in a wooded valley of the River Dhün just a few kilometres north of Bergisch Gladbach is **ALTENBERG**, with the area's only outstanding monument, the so-called **Bergischer Dom**. In spite of this name, it's not a cathedral but a monastery built by the Cistercians, whose rule prescribed secluded settings of this kind. In 1133 the Count of Berg moved his seat and donated his ancestral home, set on the hill above, to this reforming order of monks, who used the stones to construct their first church. What makes the present building, begun in 1255, particularly interesting is that it's contemporary with, and of similar stature to, the Dom in Cologne, only this time it was completed in just over a hundred years. In accordance with the austere Cistercian tradition there's no tower and little in the way of decoration. Nevertheless, it's still enormously photogenic, seeming to blend effortlessly into the landscape; the best view is from the hill to the east, where you see the choir with its corona of chapels (the earliest and finest feature) to best advantage.

Few buildings so perfectly encompass the basic tenets of the Gothic style: there are no grand gestures; everything is spacious, bright and harmonious, a visible manifestation of the order's quest for spiritual tranquillity. The chancel has wonderful original silvery-grey **stained glass** windows which have geometric motifs only. This same type of glass, but with floral shapes, fills the big lights of the north transept, beaming down on the tombs of the Counts (later Dukes) of Berg. Relaxation of the normal Cistercian rejection of representational subjects is confined to the giant facade window, the largest in Germany: it depicts *The Heavenly Jerusalem* in predominantly golden tones, a particularly memorable sight when illuminated by the setting sun.

Getting there

Buses run regularly between Altenberg and Bergisch Gladbach, or the monastery can be reached in an hour from the centre of Cologne, if you strike lucky with connections: take U-Bahn #5 to the terminus at HOHENHAUS, from where there are up to a dozen buses per day. If you want to sample some of the atmosphere of rural peace, make sure you come on a weekday. On Sundays, Altenberg acts as a magnet for urban dwellers seeking their weekly retreat; a curiosity is that both Catholic and Protestant services are held. This was a condition laid down last century by the Prussian King Friedrich Wilhelm IV when he arranged for the church's repair and return to worship, after a period of disuse and decay following the Napoleonic suppression. Ask at *Küchenhof* (one of three bar-restaurants currently occupying the outbuildings) for the key to the early thirteenth-century **Markuskapelle**, the oldest surviving part of the complex.

Wuppertal

WUPPERTAL stands at the northernmost end of the Bergisches Land group of industrial towns, and some 30km east of Düsseldorf. The overriding justification for a detour is to see its public transportation system – little recommendation, you would think, but the **Schwebebahn** (hanging railway), a monorail suspension system without wheels, is genuinely unique. What even the local tourist office admits would otherwise be just another dull industrial town is given a freakish character – sonic as well as visual – by this creaking railway, suspended on high by a steel structure supported by 472 triangular girders, and hailed by Jean Cocteau as the "flying angel". Wuppertal didn't exist as such when the line was built between 1898 and 1900 to link the various towns strung along the valley of the River Wupper – BARMEN and ELBERFELD being the largest. These communities united in 1929, yet still preserve distinct identities; Wuppertal hasn't evolved a recognisable city centre.

The brainchild of **Carl Eugen Langen**, who failed to interest Berlin and Munich in his idea, the *Schwebebahn* runs directly above the river between fifteen of its nineteen stations. It then passes over the main thoroughfares of SONNBORN and OBERWINKEL to the west, leaving them permanently dank. The sleek orange and blue cars are fourth generation; at weekends in summer, one of the original models is run. This is the only gimmick associated with a genuine local facility which is both fast (it's immune from delays) and efficient (services run every few minutes). Above all, it has proved the safest public transport system ever devised, never having seen a serious accident. Travel along the whole route for a complete picture of the town, and look out for the *Werther Brücke* station, which preserves its original Jugendstil decoration.

Around town

Almost incidental to the delights of the *Schwebebahn*, Wuppertal has a decent collection of nineteenth- and twentieth-century art in the **Von der Heydt Museum** at Turmhof 8 (Tues 10am–9pm, Wed–Sun 10am–5pm; DM1), not far from Elberfeld Bahnhof. Highlights include a study for **Manet**'s masterpiece, *Déjeuner sur l'Herbe*, and works by Delacroix, Daumier, van Gogh and Seurat; there's also a good display on a local man, **Hans von Marées**, who is now rated one of last century's most important German artists. Nearby, on Poststrasse, is the **Uhrenmuseum** (Mon–Fri 10am–noon & 4–6pm, Sat 10am–1pm; DM3), a collection of over a thousand clocks.

Of more marginal interest is the **Museum für Frühindustrialisierung** (Museum of Early Industry; Tues–Sun 10am–1pm & 3–5pm; free) at Engelsstrasse in Barmen. In front stands the **Engels Haus** (same times; free), an elegant late eighteenth-century building which belonged to a family of textile entrepreneurs. It now serves as a memorial to their celebrated black sheep **Friedrich Engels**, who was born nearby. As a young man, he was sent to England to work at the sister factory of *Ermen & Engels* in Manchester; there he became fascinated by the plight of the urban proletariat, and on his return to Barmen in 1845 wrote his celebrated *The Condition of the Working Class in England*. Soon afterwards, he began collaborating with Karl Marx, returning to work as a capitalist in Manchester in order to provide funds for their joint revolutionary writings. Though very much the junior partner in these, Engels always had a large input on matters concerning nationalities, diplomacy, the military and business practices – even in the books such as *Das Kapital* in which Marx appears as sole author.

Barmen really seems to relish its reputation as an anti-establishment town, as it was also the scene of the 1934 Synod of the "Confessing Church", Protestant opponents of Hitler. At this meeting, the church declared its independence from state control, proclaiming itself the only true heir of the Lutheran tradition, in contrast to the bogus Reich Church most clergymen had been forced into joining. Their guiding force, **Pastor Martin Niemöller**, was later incarcerated in a concentration camp, but gained a reputation outside Germany as one of the most effective anti-Nazis, and survived to become a leading pacifist and international churchman after the war.

Practicalities

Wuppertal's **tourist office** (Mon–Fri 9am–5.30pm, Sat 9am–12.30pm; ☎0202/563 2270) is just across from Elberfeld Bahnhof, beside the bus terminus. The *Schauspielhaus* on nearby Bundeallee presents plays and operas, but is best known for Pina Bausch's *Tanztheater,* by some way Germany's leading **modern dance** company. Her erotic, expressionistic programmes make free use of techniques drawn from mime and the circus. If you want to spend the night in town, the **youth hostel** is at Obere Lichtenplatzer Str. 70 (☎0202/552372), a few minutes' walk to the south of Barmen's Bahnhof; hotels are plentiful but tend to be on the expensive side. Reasonably priced places to **eat** and **drink**, on the other hand, can be found all over the city, especially in the large pedestrian precinct in the centre of Elberfeld; try the local *Wicküler* beer. There's a **Mitfahrzentrale** office at Luisenstr. 46 (☎0202/450316).

Düsseldorf

DÜSSELDORF is Germany's richest city, and in many ways the paragon of the postwar face of the Federal Republic – orderly, prosperous and self-confident. Few places can have a name so inappropriate to their present status: the "village on the Düssel" is now a thriving Land capital of 600,000 inhabitants on both banks of the Rhine, crossed here by no less than six bridges. Since the war, it has developed a cosmopolitan and strangely un-European character, consciously modelling itself on the thrusting "get up and go" American approach to life, and acting as the main foreign outpost of Japanese commerce's quest for world market supremacy.

Never as industrialised as its neighbours in the Ruhr, Düsseldorf has concentrated on its role as the region's financial and administrative centre, and from this it derives its prosperity, in accordance with the inevitable pattern of the money manipulators creaming off an outsized share of the profits. Alongside one of the country's largest stock exchanges are the headquarters and offices of innumerable multinational giants. At least two of these, the **Thyssen-Haus** in the heart of the city and the **Mannesmann-Haus** on the banks of the Rhine, are dominant landmarks in the way that towers of churches and town halls were in medieval cityscapes – an analogy both significant and disturbing.

The telephone code for Düsseldorf is ☎0211.

The extent to which you'll like or loathe Düsseldorf depends very much on your reaction to the way it has sold its soul to the corporate dream. If luxury shops are your scene, there are none more stylish between Paris and Berlin. The city likes to think of itself as Germany's leading fashion centre, with sartorial elegance and other ostentatious displays of wealth serving as indicators of individual standing in its fiercely competitive high society. Even for a short visit, it's an expensive option, but there's no doubt that the **nightlife**, at least, is one of the most varied and enjoyable in the country.

Arrival and practicalities

The **Hauptbahnhof** is situated in the southeast part of the city centre; from here, the shopping streets begin to fan out. S-Bahn trains leave at twenty minute intervals for the **airport** to the north (☎421223 for flight information). Note that, unlike neighbouring cities, most of Düsseldorf's attractions are within walking distance of each other, so the DM8.50 24-hour ticket on the public transport network is really only of use if you specifically want to see the outlying suburbs. The **tourist office** (Mon–Fri 8am–6pm, Sat 9am–1pm; ☎350505) is on Konrad-Adenauer-Platz, directly facing the Hauptbahnhof; it has free maps and monthly programmes of events.

To book a **hotel room**, head for the separate booth within the station (Mon–Sat 8am–10pm, Sun 4–10pm). Best check here for any good deals on offer, as accommodation is overwhelmingly geared to the business traveller, and prices are far above the

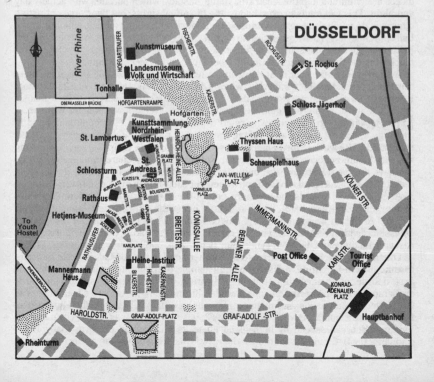

national norm, even in the suburbs. Those in the vicinity of the Hauptbahnhof are as cheap as any, especially *Manhattan*, Graf-Adolph-Str. 39 (☎370244), which has some singles at DM40 and doubles from DM70, and *CVJM*, Graf-Adolf-Str.102 (☎360764), where singles cost DM46, doubles DM82. More realistically, expect to have to pay over DM50 per person to stay in a hotel. Faced with such prices, it's worth remembering that the **youth hostel**, at Düsseldorfer Str. 1 in OBERKASSEL (☎574041) has single rooms at DM28 as well as the normal dormitory facilities. From the station, take bus #835 or walk down Graf-Adolf-Strasse and continue in a straight line, crossing the Rheinkniebrücke; it's the first building on the other side. Alternatively, there are two **campsites** (April–Sept only): *Oberlörick* (☎591401), also on the left bank of the Rhine, is reached by U-Bahn #76, #705 or #717 to Belsenplatz, then bus #828; for *Unterbacher See* (☎899 2038), out at the eastern extremity of the city, take bus #781.

The city centre

The **Altstadt**, close to the Rhine, reflects the meaning of Düsseldorf's name in its modest proportions. Never one of Germany's great cities from an architectural point of view, it's chiefly renowned today for its remarkable range of places of entertainment. Immediately to the east is a planned **green belt**, created by French landscape gardeners in the eighteenth and nineteenth centuries when Düsseldorf was a seat of the Electors Palatinate, who succeeded the defunct line of the Dukes of Berg, the city's founders.

The Altstadt

Over 200 restaurants, beer halls, wine cellars, bistros, snack bars, jazz centres and discos are crammed into the small area of the Altstadt, which pulsates with activity day and night. This fact tends to overshadow the historical sights, but two very contrasting churches do catch the eye. **St Lambertus**, a fourteenth-century brick building in the hall church style, is easily recognisable because of its tall twisted spire, now ousted from its former physical and spiritual dominance over the city by the huge corporate tower blocks. Inside, there's a graceful Gothic tabernacle, and a fifteenth-century *Pietà*.

A short walk to the east is **St Andreas**, a Jesuit foundation of 1629 which is one of the chief reminders of the period when Düsseldorf was the seat of the Electors Palatinate: its galleried interior, ornately decorated with stucco, served as their mausoleum. The most famous and genuinely popular of the Electors was Johann Wilhelm II, better known as **Jan Wellem**, who ruled from 1679 to 1716. He's commemorated in the huge open area named after him in the heart of the city, and by a masterly equestrian statue (the work of his Italian court sculptor Gabriel de Grupello), erected during his own lifetime outside the Renaissance **Rathaus**. In the square immediately to the north is the **Schlossturm**, the only remnant of the old fortifications; it has been restored to house a small **navigation museum** (Tues–Sun 10am–5pm; DM2).

At Schulstr. 4, towards the southern end of the Altstadt, is the **Hetjens-Museum** (Tues–Sun 10am–5pm; DM3), which boasts of being the only one in Germany entirely devoted to the art of ceramics. It's a tidy collection, albeit one mainly for aficionados. Düsseldorf's favourite son, the poet **Heinrich Heine** (see box), is commemorated by a research institute and museum (Tues–Sun 10am–5pm; DM2) nearby at Bilkerstr. 14.

Overlooking the Rhine at the extreme southern end of the Altstadt is Peter Behrens' **Mannesmann-Gebaude**, a distinguished example of corporate architecture from the first decade of this century, but now dwarfed by the **Mannesmann-Haus**, the skyscraper which pioneered the postwar identification of Düsseldorf's appearance with the power of multinational companies. Nonetheless, the radio tower, the **Rheinturm**, built just to the south between 1979 and 1982, has now taken over as the city's highest building. You can ascend by high-speed lift to its observation platform (daily 10am–midnight; DM4), though it's doubtful if the view is inspiring enough to justify the price.

HEINRICH HEINE (1797-1856)

One of Germany's most celebrated and intriguing men of letters, Heine modified the traditional Romantic themes of his day by using a biting sense of irony. The recurring image of the *Doppelgänger* in his work reflects his lifelong feeling of isolation – as a poet in a family of merchants, a Jew and Protestant convert among Catholics, a Francophile who eventually settled in Paris yet remained German at heart, and as a revolutionary familiar with Marxism who kept faith with the bourgeois liberal tradition. His early *Buch der Lieder* provided the dying Schubert with the texts for his last songs, and was to be a similar source of inspiration for subsequent composers, notably Schumann, Brahms and Wolf. Later, his *Reisebilder*, combining factual descriptions, poems and political comment, initiated a new and much-imitated form of travel writing.

The museum quarter

Housed in an ultra-modern gallery in Grabbeplatz just north of St Andreas is the **Kunstsammlung Nordrhein–Westfalen** (Tues–Sun 10am–6pm; DM5). The genesis of this collection was a remarkable act of postwar contrition by the authorities. **Paul Klee**, the abstract painter, was a professor at the Düsseldorf Academy from 1930 until dismissed in the Nazi purges of 1933. In atonement for this, around ninety of his works were purchased from a private American source in 1960; shortly afterwards, a rapid acquisitions policy, of twentieth-century art only, was adopted. The Klee collection remains the obvious draw, although only about two-thirds of the works are on show at any one time. Even if you aren't attracted to this painter, there are many other highlights, such as one of **Picasso**'s most famous representational works, *Two Sitting Women*; **Léger**'s large *Adam and Eve*; **Kirchner**'s *Negro Dance*; **Modigliani**'s *Diego Rivera*; and self-portraits by **Kokoschka** and **Chagall**. Already the collection resembles a who's who of modern art, and it continues to grow.

The **Kunstmuseum** (Tues–Sun 10am–5pm; DM5), directly north of the Altstadt at Ehrenhof 5, has extensive displays on three floors. This could very nearly have been one of Europe's finest art galleries, as the Electors owned a marvellous array of paintings which followed the court to Munich in 1806 and soon formed one of the bases of the Alte Pinakothek. A great **Rubens** masterpiece, an altarpiece of *The Assumption*, never made the journey because of its size; it now puts almost all the other old masters on the first floor completely in the shade. Among the few paintings not wholly outclassed are *Venus and Adonis* by the same painter; a *St Jerome* attributed to **Ribera**, and *St Francis in Meditation* by **Zurbarán**. Also on this floor is a series of powerful lithographs by **Otto Pankok** called *The Passion*, though in fact Christ's whole life is depicted. Their gloomy, highly-charged emotionalism, with hateful mobs and angst-ridden victims, directly reflects the contemporary horrors of the Holocaust. Upstairs, there's a modern section which complements that in the Kunstsammlung, along with an extensive show of the nineteenth-century historical painters of the **Düsseldorf Academy**. Now long out of fashion, they suffer from failing to find a sense of inspiration to match their undoubted technical skill. More pleasing is the sparkling **glass** section on the ground floor, dominated by Art Nouveau and Art Deco pieces from Germany, France and America.

Directly in front of the Kunstmuseum is the **Landesmuseum Volk und Wirtschaft** (Land Museum of People and Industry; Mon, Tues, Thurs & Fri 9am–5pm, Wed 9am–8pm, Sun 10am–6pm; DM1), displaying economic and social facts about the world by means of charts and graphs. Primarily an educational institution, its presentation is sound but dry. The final specialist museum of note is the spanking new **Löbbecke Museum und Aquazoo** (daily 10am–6pm; DM6) at Kaiserwerther Str. 380, north of the city centre; take U-Bahn #78 or #79. Combining an aquarium with serious scientific displays, it's an ideal outing if you have kids.

The green belt

As the culmination of the transformation of Düsseldorf by the Electors Palatinate into a city of parks, ponds and canals, the main thoroughfare, the **Königsallee**, was laid out at the beginning of the nineteenth century. It's one of Germany's most famous streets and is chic rather than beautiful; down one side are banks and offices, with expensive stores, representing all the trendiest names in international designer-made goods, lining the other. People shop here with an incredibly self-conscious air; in antithesis to the intended effect, the prevailing hallmark is one of vulgarity, and it's appropriate that the architectural setting is so mediocre. Only the late Jugendstil **Kaufhaus** has any merits as a building, though it has suffered from an interior modernisation. Diagonally opposite its rear entrance is **Wilhelm-Marx-Haus**, the earliest visible expression of Düsseldorf's infatuation with the New World, hailed as the first skyscraper in Germany when it was erected in the 1920s.

The largest of the parks is the **Hofgarten**, shaped like a great stiletto-heeled shoe, and now incongruously cut in several places by busy streets. Towering over it is the **Thyssen-Haus**, by far the most arresting of the corporate structures which so altered the city skyline in the 1950s, offering a fascinating play of light on its three huge silvery-green slabs. Beside it, the daring white curves of the **Schauspielhaus**, built in 1970, provide an effective counterpoint, as well as a reminder that, in this city, the public structures stand very much in the shadow of big business.

At the far end of the Hofgarten is **Schloss Jägerhof**, a Baroque palace which sustained severe damage in the last war. Its interior decorations have been refitted as the **Goethe Museum** (Tues-Fri & Sun 10am–5pm, Sat 1–5pm; DM3) reckoned to be the best collection of memorabilia of the great poet and playwright after those in Frankfurt and Weimar. Unless you're an avid fan, the contents will seem fairly mundane, though it's worth glancing over the section on works of art inspired by his most celebrated drama, *Faust*. Just to the north of the Schloss is the city's finest modern church, **St Rochus**. Outside, it resembles a giant beehive; the interior is deliberately dark, in an attempt to recreate the old mysteries of religion.

Eating and drinking

Walking through the Altstadt – "the longest bar in Europe" according to the tourist office – is an enjoyable activity in itself, especially on summer days when it's even more crowded than usual and virtually every pub and restaurant offers the opportunity for imbibing *al fresco*. **Eating** is one of the few things it's possible to do cheaply in Düsseldorf, thanks to the various ethnic communities. Cuisines on offer include Italian, Balkan, Spanish, Argentinian, various forms of Oriental, and fish specialities. By far the most popular **drink** is the distinctive local **Alt** beer, dark in colour and tending towards sweetness in some varieties, caused by the higher quantity of malt used than in lagers.

The heart of the Altstadt

This area is given over almost entirely to diverse places for eating and drinking, and is, unsurprisingly, by far the most touristed.

Aldo-Snack, corner of Kurzestrasse and Mertensgasse. Pick of the ubiquitous pizzerias, scoring over its rivals by providing oils and spices for you to add yourself.

Csicos, Andreasstr. 9. Highly-rated but pricey Hungarian restaurant.

Hühner-Max, Mertensgasse 10. Has the air of a transport café but serves tasty German dishes (main courses only) at very low prices.

Im Goldenen Kessel, Bolkerstr. 44. Flagship of the *Schumacher* brewery, renowned for its food.

Irish Pub, Hunsrückenstr. 13. Surprisingly genuine reminder of Hibernia, owned and staffed by expatriates; Alt here takes second place to *Guinness*.

Marktwirtschaft, Marktplatz. An excellent place to spend a quiet evening among the well-heeled youth of Düsseldorf.

Tante Anna, Andreasstr. 2. Historic restaurant-cum-wine bar with 150 vintages to choose from.

Weisser Bar, Bolkerstr. 33. Popular pub patronised by a curious mixture of young Düsseldorfers and young tourists, and staffed by relics of the '68 generation.

Zum Schlüssel, Bolkerstr. 45. *Hausbrauerei* which has spawned the much larger *Gatzweilers* brewery; products from both are available in the cavernous and well-patronised interior.

The northern Altstadt

You only need to move a few streets further north to escape from the tourists into an area preferred by locals.

Im Füchschen, Ratingerstr. 28. *Hausbrauerei* producing a relatively bitter Alt; also serves filling and reasonably priced meals

Im Goldenen Ring, Burgplatz 21. Traditional tavern serving excellent food.

Ratinger Hof, Ratingerstr. 10. Germany's first and most notorious punk bar; although the premises look ready to collapse, its reputation lives on, as it blasts out ear-splitting music and continues to be patronised by diehards of the cult

Schlossturm, Mühlenstr. 2. Particularly enjoyable on fine days, offering a sheltered view over the Rhine from the cobbled square outside.

Zum goldenen Einhorn, Ratingerstr. 18. An enduringly popular spot with the youth of the city, especially in summer when it opens its leafy little beer garden.

The southern Altstadt

This quarter is even more off the beaten tourist track and correspondingly laid-back. It's the best area if you're looking for live jazz.

Dr Jazz, Rheinstrasse. Jazz hangout, with different bands each evening.

Front Page, Mannesmann-Ufer 9. Cosy piano bar.

Miles Smiles, Akademiestr. 6. Jazz bar which also offers decently priced snacks and cocktails.

Zum Schiffchen, Hafenstr. 5. Traditional beer hall serving excellent food.

Zum Uerige, Bergerstr. 1. A real drinking man's pub, this is perhaps the most famous *Hausbrauerei* in all of Germany, producing the ultimate in Alt beer. As a bonus, it has its own sausage kitchen, though this is in the only food served.

Outside the Altstadt

To escape tourists altogether, you have to look a bit further afield. The first two bars listed here are tucked away in the shopping area between the Altstadt and the Hauptbahnhof; the others are on the left bank of the Rhine.

Café Bernstein, Oststr. 158. Stylish place for a nightcap, largely patronised by a distinctive Düsseldorf group – monied student couples.

Ferdinand Schumacher, Oststr. 123. *Hausbrauerei* which is the parent of the aforementioned *Im goldenen Kessel*.

Nachtcafé, Collenbachstrasse. One of the few places in Düsseldorf open all night.

Sassafras, Düsseldorfer Str. 90. Café-bar with a youthful and unpretentious clientele.

ZAKK (*Zentrum fur Alternative Kunst und Kultur*), Fichtenstr. 40. As its name suggests, a bar with a difference, drawing visitors from neighbouring cities to its exhibitions, video showings and other arty events.

Discos

Atmosphere, Am Hauptbahnhof. Open Saturdays only, it's a safe bet, if rather conservative in terms of both clientele and music.

Big Apple, Kurzestrasse. Specialises in golden oldies.

Relax, Jahnstrasse. Popular with gay men, although less so on Saturday nights when about a quarter of the punters are women.

DÜSSELDORF'S FESTIVALS

It's worth trying to time your visit to coincide with one of Düsseldorf's three main **popular festivals**. The **Carnival** celebrations (seven weeks before Easter) are ranked third in Germany, although those in nearby Cologne are the best of all. The celebrations are supposed to signify the end of winter; its beginning is heralded by **St Martin's Eve** on 10 November, marked by an enormous procession of lantern-bearing children. In late July, the **Grosse Schützenfest** (riflemen's meeting) is a *kermis* along the banks of the Rhine lasting for eight days. Simultaneously, there's a huge funfair (claimed to be the largest of its type in the world) offering gut-churning rides on the Ferris Wheel, the Big Dipper and other machines. The most celebrated local tradition is **cartwheeling** by local lads in the streets of the Altstadt. This is in honour of an urchin who saved the day when a wheel became loose on the popular Elector Palatinate Jan Wellem's wedding coach, but the reason it survives is the less romantic one of extorting money from tourists. In spite of serving as an unofficial symbol of the city, you're unlikely to see any demonstrations out of season.

Soul Centre, Bolkerstrasse. Of the two dozen discos in the Altstadt, one of only a couple deviating from playing standard modern fare.

Tor 3, Ronsdorfer Str. 143. South of the centre in the district of BILK, this huge barn of a place is the city's leading disco. It has few concessions to comfort, but its customers are young, friendly and out to enjoy themselves with a vengeance.

Music and theatre

Pop concerts and large-scale spectaculars are staged at the *Philipshalle*, Siegburger Str. 15 (☎899 7744) in the southern district of OVERBILK. There's also a strong local tradition in **classical music**. Both *Deutsche Oper am Rhein*, Heinrich-Heine-Allee 16a (☎370981), and the *Düsseldorfer Symphoniker* enjoy good provincial standing, even if present standards are short of the heydays last century when both Mendelssohn and Schumann did stints in charge of the city's musical affairs. The normal venue for concerts is the *Tonhalle*, Hofgartenufer (☎899 6123).

Choice in **theatre** is wide, with drama offered at the *Schauspielhaus*, Gustav-Grundgens-Platz 1 (☎363011), *Kammerspiele*, Jahnstr. 3 (☎378353), and *Theater an der Luegallee*, Luegallee 4 (☎572222). Cabaret and satire feature at the bizarrely spelt *Kom (m)ödchen* on Hunstückenstrasse. (☎325428), with comedy programmes at *Komödie*, Steinstr. 23 (☎325151). For **kids**, there are the *Puppentheater*, Heimholtzstr. 48 (☎371368), and the *Marionettentheater*, Bilkerstr. 7 (☎328432). Offbeat fare is presented by two youth companies based in a wing of Wilhelm-Marx-Haus at Kasernenstr. 6 – *Junges Theater in der Altstadt* (☎327210/37) and *Junge Aktionsbühne* (☎899 5465). Also in these premises is *Filminstitut Black Box*, most adventurous of the city's many **cinemas**.

Listings

Airlines *British Airways*, Berliner Allee 26 (☎80021); *Aer Lingus*, Berliner Allee 47 (☎80231); *Air Canada*, Königsallee 30 (☎80451); *TWA*, Berliner Allee 22 (☎84814/5).

Consulates *British*, Georg-Glock-Str. 14 (☎434281); *American*, Cecilienstr. 5 (☎490081); *Canadian*, Immermannstr. 3 (☎353471).

Mitfahrzentrale Kölner Str. 212 (☎774011).

Poste Restante Immermannstr. 1.

Women's bookshop Becherstr. 2.

Women's centre Kölner Str. 216 (☎782479).

Düsseldorf's environs

It's easy enough to escape the cosmopolitan atmosphere of central Düsseldorf, and a few tranquil spots within and just outside the boundaries of the city make for good day trips.

Benrath

Top of the list is **BENRATH** to the south, best reached by S-Bahn. The **Schloss** and its park were commissioned by the Elector Carl Theodor in the mid-eighteenth century; the unusual harmony of the whole complex is due to the fact that the architect, the French-born **Nicholas de Pigage**, was also a landscape gardener. The central building, in a style hovering between Rococo and Neoclassical, represents a very clever piece of *trompe l'oeil* construction – for all its seemingly small size, it contains eighty rooms. Guided tours (Tues–Sun 10am–4pm, leaving at half-hourly intervals; DM2), take in the sumptuous reception and garden rooms on the ground floor, as well as some of the private apartments upstairs. Afterwards, you can stroll in the formal gardens and see the surviving block of the old palace.

Neanderthal

One of the slowest trains in western Germany wends its way up the River Düssel to METTMANN, stopping at **NEANDERTHAL** en route. This valley is named after the seventeenth-century Protestant poet **Joachim Neander**, who liked to meditate there. Though he only lived to the age of thirty, he became rector of the Latin School in Düsseldorf and wrote a number of hymns which have crossed the barriers of language and denomination, most notably *Lobet den Herren* ("Praise to the Lord, the Almighty, the King of Creation"). During his lifetime, the valley was a rugged canyon, not easily accessible; subsequently, the landscape was changed completely by limestone mining, and it was this that led to a sensational discovery which made Neanderthal famous. In 1856, workers dug up bones from the bottom of a cave; these were later identified as belonging to an earlier form of mankind than *homo sapiens*, one still bearing a slight facial resemblance to the ape. The term **Neanderthal Man** has since been used to describe the tribes of humans who were wiped out by the last Ice Age. A small **museum** (Tues–Sun 10am–5pm; DM1) explains the living conditions of these hunting peoples; there are also a few prehistoric bones (though the original discovery is now in Bonn – see p.450), and hypothetical reconstructions of what the race looked like, including a model of Neanderthal Man wearing the clothes of 1980s city gent. The valley has a game reserve, including animals such as bison which haven't evolved much since prehistoric times, but the landscape around is now irretrievably ruined, and the Düssel – little more than a ditch in the city – is still nothing grander than a stream here.

Neuss

On the west bank of the Rhine, Düsseldorf's suburbs merge imperceptibly into **NEUSS**, officially a separate large industrial town with extensive dockyards; it's best reached by train, as the fare is the same as for the trams. From the **Hauptbahnhof**, turn left and then left again into Krefelder Strasse, the start of the central shopping axis, which subsequently changes its name to Büchel, then Oberstrasse. About halfway down is the Markt, where you'll find the town's sole outstanding monument, the **Münster** or **St Quirinus**. It represents the apotheosis of the Rhineland Romanesque style, built in the early thirteenth century at a time when Gothic was established elsewhere. There's all the exuberance characteristic of the end of an era – blind arcades are employed in playful patterns, and the clover-leaf shape favoured by Rhenish architects is used in the design of the windows as well as in the plan of the chancel. The dome provides a touch of almost Oriental exoticism; together with its four turrets and the facade's belfry, it makes a memorable silhouette.

In complete contrast is the early twentieth-century **Dreikönigenkirche** to the south of the town centre. Following war damage, it was embellished with a wacky hanging vault by the father and son team of Dominikus and Gottfried Böhm. The church also has a complete set of stained glass windows by the Dutch artist **Johan Thorn-Prikker**, one of the Jugendstil community based in Hagen; those in the chancel and transept are figurative and glow like jewels; the later geometric ones in the nave show his move to an abstract style. Neuss' only other building worth catching is the **Obertor** (part of the thirteenth-century fortifications), situated at the far end of the main shopping street. Along with a modern extension, it now houses the **Clemens-Sels-Museum** (Tues–Sun 10am–5pm; DM2), an average local collection with some surprises, such as paintings by the Pre-Raphaelites and French Symbolists.

Hotels in Neuss are a fallback if Düsseldorf seems too expensive, though none is an outstanding bargain. There's also a **youth hostel**, close to the Rhine at Macherscheider Str. 113 (☎02101/39273) in the suburb of UEDESHEIM. For a cheap and filling lunch, try the seventeenth-century tavern *Em Schwatte Päd*, at the point where Büchel changes to Krefelder Strasse; on the same street nearer the Hauptbahnhof is a good brewery pub-restaurant, *Im Kessel*.

Mönchengladbach

MÖNCHENGLADBACH, 30km west of Düsseldorf, is, like Bonn, an average-sized provincial town which has been catapulted to prominence since World War II. The new role for this old textile and machine manufacturing community is the rather less enviable one of serving as NATO's operations base for Northern and Central Europe, and as the headquarters of the British Army on the Rhine. A purpose-built suburb has been created at **RHEINDAHLEN** to the west of the centre; it's a real Little Britain, and a guaranteed antidote to any pangs of homesickness. Not only does English reign supreme as the language; everything, bar the local buses and the use of the Deutschmark as currency, breathes the British way of life, as the colony does its utmost to forget that it's living on German soil. There are cricket and rugby pitches, halls for Scout and Brownie packs, Anglican and Presbyterian churches; the main thoroughfare is styled *Queens Avenue*, while the side streets tend to commemorate trees rather than deceased political leaders. The troops will remain in Germany until what's left of the Soviet Union withdraws all its forces from the former GDR.

The town centre

Though not the most obvious destination unless you're visiting a friend or relative, Mönchengladbach does have some notable attractions, including the most audacious publicly owned art gallery in Germany, the **Museum Abteiberg** (Tues–Sun 10am–6pm; DM3), an ultra-modern building right in the heart of the old part of the town, which is reached in about fifteen minutes from the Hauptbahnhof by turning left on exit and going straight up Hindenburgstrasse, the main shopping street. Inaugurated in 1982, it was intended from its conception a decade earlier to be a major piece of modern architecture. The twin aims were to make it a distinctive yet harmonious feature of the cityscape, and an integral part of the modern art collection displayed within. An architect who is also an artist, the Viennese **Hans Hollein**, was chosen to see the project through, and the acquisitions policy has eschewed nearly all the century's best-known artists, and supported the avant-garde in a big way. **Joseph**

Beuys, who first sprang to fame following an exhibition in Mönchengladbach, is copiously represented; other artists include Lucio Fontana, Cy Twombly, Richard Sella, Sigmar Polke and Arman Fernandez. If you're keen on the iconoclastic and experimental nature of modern art, this museum warrants a special trip; but if you've even a suspicion of allergy, best keep well away.

Directly behind is the **Münster**, successor to the tenth-century Benedictine abbey from which the town derives its name (*Mönchen*=monks). The present building was erected throughout the thirteenth century, straddling the late Romanesque and early Gothic periods and culminates in the chancel by **Master Gerhard**, who was also master mason at the Dom in Cologne. Its central "Bible" window, pairing fourteen New Testament scenes with episodes from the Old Testament which were believed to anticipate them, is the only surviving piece of original glass. Notwithstanding the fact that three of the bottom panes have had to be replaced, it ranks as one of the loveliest in Germany. The **Schatzkammer** (Tues–Sat 2–6pm, Sun noon–6pm; DM2) displays the church's treasures, the most valuable of which is a twelfth-century portable altar from Cologne. You may have to ask to see the crypt and the sacristy: the former, unusually large for its time, is the oldest part of the church. The sacristy is a handsome Gothic room with delicately carved capitals and an amazingly well-preserved stone pavement.

Nightlife and practicalities

Mönchengladbach has quite a swinging **nightlife**, much of it self-evidently geared to its foreign residents. On the Alter Markt itself is *Nostalgia-Pub Cannape*, while some of the bars round the corner on Aachener Strasse have live jazz. However, most of the action, in the evenings at least, takes place on the steeply plunging Waldhausener Strasse, which is almost entirely given over to an enormous choice of ethnic restaurants, steak houses, snack bars, taverns, cafés, ice-cream parlours and discos, ranging from *Soul Centre* to those playing the latest heavy metal. *Dicker Turm* has snug little bars on three floors of a rebuilt tower which was once part of the fortifications. The favourite **beer** is the dark **Alt**, particularly that made by *Hannen*, who have a large brewery here.

Unfortunately, the central **hotels** are mostly on the pricey side, but try *Steffens*, Waldhausener Str. 160 (☎02161/32386), which costs DM30 per person. If it's full, you'll probably have to pay a lot more, or else stay far out. *Faassen*, Vorster Str. 233 (☎02161/559182), and *Kasteel*, Vorster Str. 529 (☎02161/559694), in the suburb of HARDT (bus #13 or #23), both charge around DM30 to DM35 per person and have restaurants, the latter's being particularly good. Also in Hardt, but a further 1km south in the woods, is the **youth hostel** at Gritzkesweg 125 (☎02161/559512); continuing in a straight line from here, you come before long to the Rheindahlen garrison, so its location is less isolated than it might appear. Full lists of other accommodation possibilities are available from the **tourist office** at Bismarckstr. 23–27, between the Hauptbahnhof and Alter Markt (Mon–Fri 9am–6pm, Sat 9am–1pm; ☎02161/22001), which also publishes a free monthly programme of events.

Borussia Mönchengladbach gave the city an additional claim to fame in the 1970s when, most improbably, it supplanted Bayern Munich as Germany's leading **football** club for several seasons; the cognoscenti rated the tussle with Liverpool in the European Cup final of 1977 one of the matches of the decade. They've now gone off the boil, but if you want to see them in action their ground is at *Bökelberg,* north of the centre. Surprisingly, the favourite spectator sport is not soccer but horse-drawn wagon racing, a modern version of the Roman chariots, held at the *Trabrennbahn* stadium. The list of **festivals** is headed by Carnival, which is unusual in featuring its main parade on Shrove Tuesday, meaning you can move on to it after the main celebrations have finished elsewhere.

Krefeld

KREFELD, some 20km northeast of Mönchengladbach, has long been a by word in the world of fashion, thanks to its standing as Germany's leading textile town. Although the industry originally developed by Huguenot refugees was centred on linen, and rayon is now the basis of much of the output, Krefeld is renowned above all for its luxury silk and velvet products, forming the principal European rival to the great French centre, Lyon. The town is also a Rhine port, thanks to the absorption of adjacent **UERDINGEN**, now overrun by the belching chimneys of the giant Bayer chemical works. As at upstream Leverkusen, this company's dominance even extends to owning the eponymous local football team.

Around town

In the centre of Krefeld proper, a shopping area of startling anonymity, is the **Kaiser-Wilhelm-Museum** (Tues–Fri 10am–5pm, Sat & Sun 11am–5pm; DM2) on Karlsplatz. Its ponderous architecture from the last years of the nineteenth century stands in sharp contrast to the modern art which occupies the lion's share of the space within. **Joseph Beuys** and **Yves Klein** are both extensively featured, and there are examples of all the main Pop artists in a strong American representation. Graphic work takes up a large part of the display, and includes **Matisse**'s *Jazz*, a luxuriantly coloured set of twenty stencilled cut-outs, and **Miró**'s *Makemono*, a folding lithograph on silk, which has equally brilliant kaleidoscopic effects. There's a good **Monet**, *Sunset over Westminster*, sculptures by Rodin, Barlach and Lehmbruck, and a display of Jugendstil glass, ceramics and metalwork. More surprisingly, there's a decent representation of the Italian Renaissance, including some good sculptures.

Open for temporary exhibitions only, when the same times are in force, are **Haus Lange** and **Haus Esters** at 91–97 Wilhelmshofallee, northeast of the centre and reached by bus #91 or #97. Built between 1928 and 1930 by **Mies van der Rohe** – now firmly enshrined as the patron saint of property developers – they're among the earliest examples of the International Modern movement in architecture.

Practicalities

All of Krefeld's sights can be covered in a day, so there's no particular reason to stay overnight, the more so as there's no hostel or indeed much in the way of cheap **accommodation**, the many hotels in the centre all being geared to the business set. Check with the **tourist office** on Theaterplatz (Mon–Fri 8am–6.30pm, Sat 8am–1pm; ☎02151/29290) for any good deals; from the **Hauptbahnhof** go straight ahead along Ostwall. There are innumerable places to **eat** and **drink** in the main streets; *Et Bröckske* on Marktstrasse is a pub renowned for good food at reasonable prices. **Mitfahrzentrale** have an office at Rheinstr. 95 (☎02151/802081).

Linn

It would be idle to pretend that Krefeld is anything other than a typical industrial conglomeration, but its fine museums provide justification for a visit. The main concentration of these is in the suburb of **LINN**, reached from the centre by tram #44, or from any other town by S-Bahn. Formerly a separate community, it manages to preserve something of its old character, above all in the streets round Andreasmarkt, where a new home has been built for the long-established **Deutsches Textilmuseum** (April–Oct Tues–Sun 10am–6pm, Nov–March Tues–Sun 10am–1pm & 2–5pm; DM3; same price and times apply to everything else in Linn). With some 20,000 items this is appropriately the leading collection in the country, with works from all countries and periods. For conservation reasons, these can only be displayed in rotation in the form of small temporary exhibitions. You can see any other object by application; if you've a serious interest in the subject, best write ahead. At the end of the square is the entrance to **Burg Linn**, a moated castle founded in the twelfth century but remodelled in the fifteenth century. Left in ruins in 1702, it has been partly restored and furnished in period style. The **Butterturm**, formerly the prison, can be climbed for an extensive view. In front of the moat is the **Jagdschloss**, once part of the outer bailey but revamped in the 1730s as a hunting lodge, once it had been decided that the main castle was redundant. Its rooms have been fitted out with original objects from the homes of leading local families of the eighteenth and nineteenth centuries, while there's a display of mechanical musical instruments on the ground floor (demonstrated mornings only). Finally, a modern building houses the **Niederrheinisches Museum**, which has important archaeology collections. Particularly outstanding are those excavated in nearby Gellep, whose sandy soil ensured a remarkable state of preservation – most spectacular are the contents of an intact sixth-century Frankish prince's grave.

Kempen, Kevelaer and Goch

Beyond Krefeld and the adjoining manufacturing town of MOERS immediately to the north, the Lower Rhineland loses its urban nature and increasingly resembles the neighbouring Netherlands in character. This is true not only of the flat landscape and predominantly brick architecture, but also of the local dialect, which is the original Low German from which the Dutch language is derived.

Kempen

KEMPEN, a railway junction just 10km northwest of Krefeld, is the presumed birthplace of one of the best-selling writers of all time – not that **Thomas à Kempis** ever enjoyed fame or fortune during his life, or would have wanted to. A modest, retiring man, he spent seventy of his ninety years in the same Dutch Augustinian monastery, where he wrote *The Imitation of Christ*, a book whose influence on the Christian world is surpassed only by the Bible itself. There's none of the deep intellectualisation common in theological tracts, nor the ecstatic mysticism which limits the appeal of so many religious writings. Instead, the author deliberately addressed the common reader, using simple yet poetic prose to stress the importance of a spiritual and aesthetic lifestyle. An exhibition on Thomas à Kempis – including an example of the first Latin edition of his masterpiece, published in 1487, sixteen years after his death – is the centrepiece of the **Museum für Niederrheinische Sakaral Kunst** (Museum of Sacred Art; Tues, Wed & Fri–Sun 11am–5pm, Thurs 11am–7pm; DM2) which occupies the old Franciscan Paterskirche and its monastic buildings in the town centre.

Neary is the **Propsteikirche**, a bulky fourteenth-century Gothic church with a striking pink Romanesque tower. It's richly adorned with works of art collected during the town's heyday in the fifteenth and early sixteenth centuries: the three large altarpieces came from Antwerp while the superb tabernacle and Renaissance organ were made in Cologne. The streets of Kempen only just scrape the description of photogenic; there remain a number of old houses, parts of the fortifications, and the medieval Burg, which was completely rebuilt last century in the Romantic manner. If you want to stay, the cheapest **hotel** in town is *Haus Becker*, Thomasstr. 9 (☎02152/519269), with singles at DM35, doubles DM60.

Kevelaer

KEVELAER, some 30km north on the main railway line to KLEVE, is Germany's premier **place of pilgrimage**, drawing some 500,000 believers each year in a "season" lasting from May to October. Just before Christmas 1641, a local pedlar, Hendrick Busman, heard voices charging him to build a chapel on the site. Shortly after, his wife had a vision of the chapel containing the image of *The Blessed Virgin of Luxembourg* which she had seen carried by two soldiers; this picture had been attributed with healing properties during a plague in Luxembourg. Within six months, Busman had built a simple shrine with his own hands, in which the miraculous icon was placed; the cult quickly grew, and three years later the far more substantial **Kerzenkapelle** (Chapel of the Candles) was built in an archaic Gothic style to house the pilgrims. A decade later, Busman's construction was replaced by the elaborate hexagonal **Gnadenkapelle** (Chapel of the Favours), in which the image was displayed facing the square outside. The fame of the pilgrimage spread so much in the nineteenth century (largely due to a hoax by Heinrich Heine, a Jew and Protestant convert) that a vast neo-Gothic **Basilica** had to be built to accommodate the crowds who flocked from all over the country.

No doubt it's a reflection of the Germanic nature that Kevelaer lacks the sheer, unadulterated bad taste that's the hallmark of other leading Marian shrines in Europe, such as Lourdes, Fátima and Knock. Unlike them, it can't really be recommended as worth seeing for shock value, which means you're unlikely to want to stay for long – unless you're keen on waiting for a miracle. Apart from the pilgrimage churches already mentioned, the only other attraction is the **Niederrheinisches Museum für Volkskunde** (daily 10am–5pm, Nov–April closed Mon; DM2). There's a **youth hostel** at Schravelen 50 (☎02832/8267); **hotels** are scattered all over town and, being geared to the pilgrim market, seldom ask for more than DM30 per person.

Goch

A further 10km north lies **GOCH**, ominously described in Patrick Leigh Fermor's *A Time of Gifts*; the town was his introduction not only to Germany, but also to the newly-established Third Reich. His descriptions of an outfitter's shop, a tavern and an SA parade vividly convey the Nazi regime's obsessiveness, regimentation and, above all, double-think – he found it impossible to square the delightful renditions of the folk songs commandeered for Party use with the thuggery and philistinism practised by those who sang them.

Only the **Steintor** survives of the 28 towers and gates which once defended Goch; it houses the local **museum** (Tues–Sun 10am–noon & 3–5pm; DM1), which features archaeological finds and sacred art. Round the corner on Steinstrasse is the resplendent brick facade of one of the finest patrician mansions in the Lower Rhineland, the sixteenth-century **Fünfgiebelhaus** (House of the Five Gables), now the Rathaus. From the square beyond, you can see the tower of the only other interesting monument in town, **St Maria Magdalena**, a large Gothic church, also of brick, which is closely related to those in nearby Kalkar and Kleve; when locked, ask for the key at the parish offices in front of the facade. If you want to spend the night, the most convenient **hotel** is *Gocher Hof* on Bahnhofsplatz (☎02823/1460), which charges DM30 a head.

Xanten

XANTEN, set just back from the Rhine some 45km north of Krefeld, is one of the oldest settlements in Germany. In about 100 AD *Colonia Ulpia Traiana* was founded as a residential town (the only one in the Rhineland other than Cologne) in succession to the nearby garrison of Vetera, centre of operations for the campaign to subdue the eastern Germanic tribes. It in turn was abandoned with the collapse of the empire, and followed by a new community built immediately to the south around the graves of Christians martyred in 363 during the last wave of purges. The graves were popularly but implausibly believed to contain Saint Victor and members of the Thebian Legion; the name given to the town is a contraction of the Latin *Ad Sanctos Martyres* (To the Holy Martyrs). Writing at the end of the twelfth century, the anonymous poet of *The Nibelungenlied*, describing semi-mythical events centuries earlier, characterises Xanten as "great", "splendid" and "far-famed", the birthplace and court of the invincible hero Siegfried, Lord of the Netherlands, Norway and the mysterious Nibelungland, home of the fantastic gold treasure of the Rhine which was to form the basis of the very different version of the legend unfolded in Wagner's epic *Ring* cycle 700 years later.

The town

Xanten is something of a Peter Pan, its current population of 16,000 little more than the probable size of the Roman town. It kept its medieval aspect until the last war, when it was badly bombed. Modern Xanten has successfully risen from the debris to appear once more as one of Germany's neatest country towns (the recipient of several prestigious conservation prizes), if one which is sometimes rather too crammed with daytrippers from the industrial hotbed to the south for its own good.

The centre
The town's **fortifications** survive in part, still defining the town's perimeter on the north and east sides. They're pierced by several towers, many of which have been converted into luxury flats, including the grandest of the group, the **Klever Tor**, whose double gateway formed the northwest entrance to the town. Just up Nordwall, the next tower underwent a more radical conversion in the eighteenth century, being re-shaped to form a windmill. Immediately facing it is Brückstrasse, best preserved of the old streets.

Between here and the Markt, the **Dom** lies cocooned in its own close or "Immunity", so named from its status as a haven from external laws and taxes. An atmosphere of otherworldly peace still reigns in this confined space – but only at certain times of the day, as it now doubles as a school playground. From afar, the massive facade dominates the town; it was the only part of the Romanesque cathedral spared when a sober Gothic replacement was put up in the late thirteenth century. Subsequent builders tampered with it right up until 1525, by which time the towers had been considerably heightened. If you go around to the rear, you'll see a polychrome fifteenth-century statue to the Dom's patron saint, Saint Victor; whether one of the ancient tombs discovered in the crypt excavations earlier this century is really his burial place is a matter resolved more by faith than cold logic. The five-aisled **interior** (10am–noon & 2–5/6pm) gives a rare opportunity of sampling the genuine, cluttered feel of a medieval cathedral, thanks to the extraordinary range of objects it has preserved – expressive pier statues of saints, a rood screen, choir stalls, a hanging *Double Madonna*, stained glass windows and a crowd of altars. Particularly notable are the four carved and painted late Gothic winged retables in the aisles, one from Antwerp and three from nearby Kalkar; finest is that on the south side, with scenes from the life of the Virgin springing from a superb *Tree of Jesse* by Henrik Douverman. The same sculptor made the reliquary busts for the high altar, which also incorporates the twelfth-century shrine of Saint Victor.

In the southwest corner of the close is the **Regionalmuseum** (Tues, Thurs & Fri 10am–5pm, Wed 10am–8pm, Sat & Sun 11am–6pm; DM3), which serves as something of a repository for the Dom, with the treasury kept in the basement, and works of art no longer required for display on the ground floor. It also has extensive archaeology and local history collections, but be warned that these are presented in an extremely didactic fashion, and that the most important finds from local excavations are housed in its parent museum in Bonn. From here you can pass out into the **Markt**, something of a hotchpotch of styles, with houses ranging from Gothic to Rococo. At the far end, turn left down Karthaus, named after the former Charterhouse whose Baroque facade is the dominant feature of the street.

The Archäologischer Park

From here, continue along Rheinstrasse; across the main road is the site of Colonia Ulpia Traiana, now the **Archäologischer Park** (daily 9am–6pm; DM3). This was the only Roman town in Northern Europe which was never built upon; that it subsequently disappeared is due to the fact that its stones were ideal building materials for later constructions, including the Dom. In the 1970s a proposal was made to develop the area into a recreation zone, but in return for sparing the site the authorities insisted that the excavations be given populist appeal. Thus, instead of merely uncovering ground plans, full-blooded conjectural reproductions of the main buildings of the town were attempted. The result is controversial to say the least, and purists will be horrified by the Disneyland touches. However, if you normally find archaeological sites hamstrung by scholarly timidity, this will come as a revelation, giving a graphic picture of the true size and scale of a Roman town. Eventually, the aim is to go as far as recreating the original riverside setting, which has now completely disappeared; at the moment, the **walls** with their massive fortifications, notably the **Harbour Gate** at the very far end of the park, form the most impressive feature. Just inside the main entrance, an **inn** has been reconstructed; here the presentation goes outrageously over the top with toga-clad waiters serving the sort of meals it's alleged the Romans would have eaten. The **amphitheatre**, which is partly original, now serves as a successful venue for open-air theatrical performances; the **temple**, on the other hand, has been rebuilt only as a ruin.

Practicalities

From the **Bahnhof**, the centre is only a few minutes' walk via either Hagenbuschstrasse or Bahnhofstrasse. Services on the line northwards to Kleve are often replaced by buses, which leave from the forecourt. The **tourist office** (mid-March–mid-Oct Mon–Fri 10am–5pm, Sat & Sun 10am–4pm; rest of year daily 11.30am–4pm; ☎02801/37238) is located in the Rathaus at the corner of the Markt and Karthaus. Helpfully displayed in their window is a list of more than a score of private houses with **rooms** to let; these are the cheapest option, as there's no hostel. Nearly all cost around DM25 per person; you can choose a central location, or there are many in a more rural setting which are still within walking distance. The least expensive hotel is *Galerie an de Marspoort*, Marsstr. 78 (☎02801/1057), with singles from DM40, doubles from DM60. There are plenty of places to eat and drink in the centre, though Xanten doesn't score highly for either gastronomy or nightlife. To the east of town, towards the Rhine, are peaceful **nature trails** in protected countryside, while to the north is the **Xantener Nordsee**, a watersports centre, with a range of boats for hire (summer only).

Kalkar (Calcar)

Quiet, somnolent **KALKAR** was built on a sandbank completely surrounded by an arm of the Rhine, but heavy silting has meant that it's now well inland. It lies on the least busy of the three railway lines linking the Ruhrgebiet with Holland, midway between Xanten and Kleve; thanks to possessing one of Germany's most remarkable churches, it rivals the former as the most interesting of the Lower Rhenish towns.

The town

The central **Markt** square lost much of its character to wartime bombs, but some old houses have been restored to provide fitting company for the **Rathaus**, a brick building with a prominent octagonal turret. Behind, a step-gabled merchant's residence, connected by a modern extension to the oldest house in the town, contains the **Stadtmuseum** (Tues–Sun 10am–1pm & 2–5pm; DM1). This has an excellent collection of manuscripts and charters, along with the work of painters, most notably the Expressionist **Heinrich Nauen**, who lived in the town. Off the opposite end of the Markt is the well-restored facade of the **Beginenhof**.

None of this prepares you for the splendours of **St Nicolai**, built to the side of the Markt at the same time as the Rathaus. From the outside, it looks quite ordinary – a plain fifteenth-century brick building, enlivened only by its tall tower. The gleaming white interior (April–Oct Mon–Fri 10am–noon & 2–6pm, Sat 10am–noon & 2–5pm, Sun 2–5pm, Nov–March daily 2–5pm; DM1) is another matter altogether, bristling with such an astonishing array of **works of art** that it's now designated a "church-museum". It seems odd that what has never been more than a parish church in a town which has never been very large could have garnered such riches, but medieval Kalkar became wealthy through a cloth industry that used locally produced wool. The rich burghers showed their appreciation for this natural bounty by funding a school of woodcarving which flourished continuously for about a century from 1450, producing one great altarpiece after another, whose purpose was to illustrate the lives of Christ and the saints for the enlightenment of a largely illiterate congregation. Fifteen large retables and numerous other statues and paintings originally embellished the church; some were sold last century, but all the important pieces remain in situ.

It's worth taking time to examine the myriad details to be found in the big showpieces; all display an amazing level of technical virtuosity. **Henrik Douverman**, who made the *Altar of the Seven Sorrows of the Virgin* in the south apse, the *Double Madonna Candelabrum* in the middle of the nave and the superbly expressive *St Mary Magdalene* in the north aisle, has long been recognised as a highly individual artist, one who proved the continuing vitality of late Gothic forms well into the sixteenth century. However, many of his little-known predecessors, who were forced to submerge their artistic personalities in co-operative ventures, showed equal skill, nowhere more than in the crowded main *Passion Altar*, begun by the founder of the school, **Master Arnt**, and continued by **Ludwig Jupan**; these carvers were also responsible respectively for the *St George Altar* and the *Altar to the Virgin* fronting the entrance to the chancel. Painted panels were added to many of the retables to fill out the story; particularly fine are the colourful scenes on the *Passion Altar* by **Jan Joest**; the setting of *The Raising of Lazarus* is, incidentally, Kalkar's Markt.

Practicalities

From the **Bahnhof**, St Nicolai's tower is clearly visible and is only a few minutes' walk away, but you're more likely to arrive by one of the far more extensive **bus** services, which conveniently stop in the Markt. The **tourist office** (Mon–Fri 9am–noon & 2–5pm; ☎02824/13138) is hidden away down Grabenstrasse at the back of the Rathaus; they have a list of the few private houses with **rooms** to let. There's an unofficial **youth hostel** in a quaint windmill setting just past the museum down Hanselaer Strasse, but it's only randomly open. Otherwise, there are two **hotels** on the Markt – *Seydlitz* (☎02824/2411) is perfectly adequate at DM30 per person; *Markt-Klause* (☎02824/2252), in a historic building, has singles at DM40, doubles from DM70. The latter also has the second best restaurant in town, with eminently reasonable prices; it's only surpassed by the much more expensive *Ratskeller* directly opposite. Just north of Kalkar is the

Wisseler See, a natural lake which is a watersports centre; it also has a **campsite** (☎02824/6613).

Kleve (Cleves) and Emmerich

KLEVE was obliterated during the war, its status as a frontier town making it a prime target for aerial bombardment. All that remains of the old city are the main public buildings, now heavily restored and, it could be argued, stripped of their soul in the process.

The town

Unusually for the area, Kleve is built on hills, dominated by a cliff (which gives the town its name) crowned by the **Schwanenburg** (Swan Castle), which is closely associated with the legend of Lohengrin, Knight of the Holy Grail. It was the seat of the once-powerful local dukes, whose dynastic aspirations reached a climax in 1539 with the marriage of Anne of Cleves to king Henry VIII of England – only to end in humiliation the following year (see below). The present castle dates from the fifteenth century, but has had so many subsequent alterations it's difficult to categorise its style. Nowadays, it serves as law courts and local government offices, but you can ascend the **tower** (April–Sept daily 11am–5pm, Nov–March Sat & Sun only same times; DM2) for extensive views.

Immediately opposite, the former stables house the town library, while behind is **St Mariae Himmelfahrt**, a large brick church similar to Kalkar's St Nicolai. In terms of artistic treasures, however, it's very much a poor relation, though its **high altar** was made by the star member of the neighbouring town's school of woodcarving, Henrik Douverman. There's also a special burial chapel for the dukes, housing some fine tombs with recumbent figures. Little else remains of the old city, which has been transformed into a bland modern shopping centre.

West of the centre, and reached via the street named after it, is the **Tiergarten**, a terraced garden, laid out in 1656 in the Italian style. The garden features a rotunda, an amphitheatre, a canal and, as the centrepiece, a statue of Pallas Athenae. This is a copy, the original having been moved for preservation reasons to the municipal museum, **Haus Koekkoek** on Kavarinerstrasse in the town centre (Tues–Sun 10am–1pm & 2–5pm; free). Also on show in the museum is a Book of Hours made in the workshop of the **Master of the Hours of Catherine of Cleves**, one of the most important illuminators of the late Middle Ages; the wonderful manuscript after which he's named became part of the transatlantic drain of works of art, and is now in the Pierpoint Morgan Library in New York. The town's other great artist was **Joos van Cleve**, who settled in Antwerp, developing a style heavily indebted to the Italian Renaissance, but modified by a Northern European brittleness. A *Male Portrait* by him has recently been placed on loan here by the Federal government in order that his work may once more be seen in the place of his birth.

THE "FLANDERS MARE"

In 1539, the English king, **Henry VIII**, was on the lookout for a new queen following the death of his third wife, Jane Seymour. He sent his painter, Hans Holbein the Younger, round a number of courts to make likenesses of prospective brides, one of whom was Anne, daughter of the Duke of Cleves. It seems the artist – normally anything but a flatterer – was placed in an impossible position by having to execute the portrait quickly, and to the approval of his hosts. Henry was sufficiently pleased with the result (which can be seen in the Louvre in Paris) to contract a marriage, but disliked the "Flanders mare" from the moment he set eyes on her, and sent her back home in ignominy six months later; the unfortunate Holbein was dismissed from royal service for his part in the debacle.

Practicalities

Kleve's **tourist office** (Mon–Fri 9am–5pm; ☎02821/84254) is in the Rathaus further down Kavarinerstrasse. The **youth hostel** makes an inexpensive base for touring the Lower Rhineland, and is the only one, apart from Kevelaer, in the area. It's a fair way out, at the top of a hill at St. Annaberg 2 (☎02821/23671); take bus #57. Most convenient of the cheaper **hotels** is *Burg*, Hafenstr. 32 (☎02821/12188), where you'll pay around DM40 per person; the nearest **campsite** is at Wisseler See to the south (see p.496).

Emmerich

Whereas the towns on the left bank of the lower stretch of the Rhine are set back from the river, those on the opposite side tend to be commercial ports. **EMMERICH** is the most interesting of these; it's just 9km from Kleve, to which it's linked by the longest **suspension bridge** in Germany, an effortless structure spanning some 1300 metres. The town was very badly damaged in the war, but the restoration has been highly successful; the centre once again has a spick and span appearance, its confident brick buildings making it seem even more Dutch than the other Lower Rhenish towns. Two hundred thousand vessels use the port annually; the importance of river trade to local life is celebrated in the **Rheinmuseum** at Martinikirchgang just off the main square (Mon–Wed 10am–noon & 2–4pm, Thurs 2–6pm, Fri & Sun 10am–noon; free); the **tourist office** (same times; ☎02828/2470) is also here. Cheapest hotel in Emmerich itself is *Zur Grenze*, s'Heerenberger Str. 298 (☎02828/2367), at DM38 per person; there are several similarly priced alternatives in the suburb of ELTEN.

Towards the river, the former monastery of **St Martini** looks at first sight to be one of the Gothic brick hall churches so typical of the region. In fact, it's a real oddity: two quite distinct and fragmentary buildings, the newer section erected at right angles to the remains of its Romanesque predecessor, whose architecturally pure crypt survives intact. Housed in a strong room is the **Schatzkammer**, a treasury fully worthy of a great cathedral (no set opening times; if closed, ask at the priest's house behind the church; DM1). The most valuable item is the *Ark of St Willibrord*, an elaborately embossed eleventh-century chest-reliquary remodelled four centuries later, and there are many other wonderful pieces. Look out for the imaginative carvings adorning the fifteenth-century stalls in the church itself – especially the depiction of two dogs fighting over a bone.

THE RUHRGEBIET

The **Ruhrgebiet** is the most heavily industrialised region in Europe, a continuously-built-up area stretching unbroken for some 65km east to west, and up to 30km north to south, in the middle of which is the traditional boundary between the Northern Rhineland and Westphalia. It takes its name from the River Ruhr, which flows right through the region to its confluence with the Rhine, and owes its extraordinary development to fabulously rich mineral deposits, often located close to the surface. The constituent towns, most of which were little more than villages until last century, do their best to preserve some kind of identity, but, apart from the fact that it's hard to determine where one ends and the other begins, they're mostly very similar in feel. Though certain cities are associated with a particular product or service (**Essen** and **Mülheim** with steel, **Gelsenkirchen** with coal, **Duisburg** with its docks, **Dortmund** with beer, **Bochum** with cars), each has a broad economic mix with heavy industry providing the lead.

The region is generally been glossed over in other English-language guidebooks and, on the face of things, it might seem you'd have to be out of your mind to want to come here. Yet – once allowances are made for their less salubrious aspects – Dortmund and Essen, at least, can be enjoyed just like any other historic city. There's also no doubt that although recent years have brought many problems to the Ruhrgebiet, caused by the worldwide need to scale down old industries, they've led to a vast improvement in the region's physical appearance. Only a fraction of the mines and factories which formerly blotted the landscape now survive; the redundant plants have been removed, often to be replaced by parkland. Moreover, the prosperity brought by industry has funded a **vibrant cultural scene** – Bochum is one of Germany's leading centres for theatre, while there are highly diverse art museums in many of the cities.

The Ruhrgebiet has played a crucial role in modern German (and hence world) history. Industrialisation came for the most part after the area had fallen under the control of Prussia, the great predatory power of the nineteenth century. It followed hard on the heels of the British lead, but avoided many of the pioneering country's mistakes. Weapons manufactured in the Ruhr helped win the battles which led to German unification; they also featured strongly in the arms race which led to World War I. Most ominously of all, it's doubtful if Hitler would ever have gained a truly national foothold, let alone come to power, had he not received the financial backing of many of the area's captains of industry.

Duisburg

With **DUISBURG**, separated from Düsseldorf by just a few kilometres of open county-side, the Ruhrgebiet begins with a vengeance. Until the early nineteenth century, this small walled town of about 5000 inhabitants had changed little since the great geographer Gerhard Mercator worked there in the sixteenth century. The Industrial Revolution saw it expand out of all recognition with the production of coal, iron and steel; above all, it developed as a harbour for cargo, thanks to its key location at the point where the Ruhr enters the Rhine. It still ranks as the world's largest inland port, although recent years have seen a movement towards a post-industrial economy, with the closure of all but one of the seven pits, and steel production highly modernised. The city centre has been tidied up and largely given over to pedestrians, a green belt has been created, and the population has decreased by about 70,000 to its present level of 540,000 as people have been able to afford more congenial accommodation outside the conurbation. Alas, it's a case of too little too late; in spite of glossy brochures presenting the city in the most favourable light, there's no escaping that it has extraordinarily little in the way of general attractions. Medieval Duisburg has almost completely disappeared: the **Salvatorkirche**, a rather ordinary large Gothic church where Mercator is buried, is virtually the only reminder of time past. It's not a city you're likely to want to stay in for long, and the only reason for coming at all is if any of its sights (which boil down to the river port and the museums) is in your field of interest.

The harbour

One of the oddball attractions of Duisburg is to take a **harbour cruise**; these run from April to October, last a couple of hours and cost DM10. Be warned that the views are a world away from the legendary landscapes further up the Rhine: coal tips, scrap heaps, gaunt warehouses and belching chimneys straight out of a Lowry painting are the order of the day. The two main departure points are the Schwanentor near the

Salvatorkirche in the city centre (3pm daily, with an additional cruise at 10am on Sundays), and the Schifferbörse in the heart of the docklands at RUHRORT (2pm daily, also 11am on Sundays). Each has an extra departure at 5pm and 4pm respectively on Sundays between May and August, and on weekdays during the schools' summer vacation. Bookings can be made at the offices on Mülheimer Str. 72–74 (☎0203/3950). As a supplement, visit the **Museum der Deutschen Binnenschiffahrt** (Museum of German Inland Navigation) housed in the former Rathaus in Ruhrort (Tues & Fri–Sun 10am–5pm, Wed & Thurs 10am–4pm; DM1) for its large collection of ship models and a medieval dug-out canoe.

The centre

The other museums are in Immanuel-Kant-Park in the city centre. Modern art freaks should overlook Duisburg's shortcomings in order to visit the **Wilhelm-Lehmbruck-Museum** (Tues 11am–8pm, Wed–Sun 11am–5pm; DM3), Germany's premier collection of twentieth-century sculpture. Its centrepiece is the legacy of the sculptor **Lehmbruck** himself, born to a Duisburg mining family, who committed suicide in 1919 at the age of 38. There are many examples here of his classically beautiful portrait busts, but it's his more ambitious compositions of elongated, writhing figures, such as *The Fallen One* (*Der Gestürzte*), *Mother and Child*, *Kneeling Woman* (*Kniende*) and *The Brooder* (*Sinnende*) which make a more lasting impression. There's also work by the most prestigious international sculptors of the century – Rodin, Barlach, Giacometti, Henry Moore, Archipenko, Marini, Lipchitz, Arp and Naum Gabo. An attractive feature is the way artists chiefly famous as painters are represented by their much rarer sculptures – the Fauvist **Derain** abandons his usual bright palette in *The Twin*; the Surrealists **Dalí** and **Magritte** provide two of the most memorable pieces in *Head of Dante* and *L'Avenir des Statues*; while their colleague **Max Ernst**'s *Un Ami Empressé* and *Objet Mobile* are shown alongside two of his canvases. In the entrance hall are the most spectacular exhibits, **Joseph Beuys**' *End of the Twentieth Century* and **Duane Hanson**'s *Vietnam War Piece*, a devastating attack on the folly of the conflict, with a horrifyingly real depiction of five American soldiers dead and dying in the mud. The gallery above has a light-hearted recent acquisition in *Das Märchenrelief* by **Jean Tinguely**, which needs to be set in motion for full effect; ask an attendant.

The modestly sized **Niederrheinisches Museum** (Tues & Thurs–Sat 10am–5pm, Wed 10am–4pm, Sun 11am–5pm; DM2) is for the most part of average interest only, with the usual archaeology and local history exhibits, including a series of models on how the city has developed. These are completely outclassed by the (German only) display on the work of **Gerhard Mercator**, born in Flanders of German stock, who settled in Duisburg in 1552 and remained there until his death 42 years later. His most enduring legacy is the Mercator projection, still in use in a modified form today in both sea and air transport; this enabled maps to be drawn accurately on a flat surface and meant sailors could steer a course by plotting straight lines, instead of continually resorting to the compass. The most eye-catching items here are the terrestrial globe of 1541 and its celestial counterpart of ten years later, works of art as much as science whose beauty can be attributed to Mercator's early training in Antwerp as an engraver.

Practicalities

The **Hauptbahnhof** is at the eastern end of the city centre, reached from Immanuel-Kant-Park by Friedrich-Wilhelm-Strasse. Turning right from here is the beginning of Königstrasse, where you'll find the **tourist office** (Mon–Fri 8.30am–6pm, Sat 8.30am–12.30pm; ☎0203/283 2025); pick up the free monthly programme of events *Heute in Duisburg*. The city presents high-class performances at the *Theater der Stadt* (opera

---

MÜLHEIM AND THE THYSSEN DYNASTY

Adjoining Duisburg to the east is **Mülheim**, where the River Ruhr is crossed by seven bridges. Mülheim's growth was tied so closely to the spectacular success of the steel mills founded by **August Thyssen** (1842–1926) that it became a virtual family fiefdom. Thyssen's eldest son Fritz was the first prominent industrialist to see Hitler as the man the upper classes were looking for – someone who would stamp out democracy and trade unionism at home, and restore military glory abroad. He helped fund the Nazi Party from 1925 and was later instrumental in persuading other magnates to follow his example, although he was later to repent of his actions. His brother Heinrich, on the other hand, left Germany at an early age in favour of a succession of other European countries. He became well-known as an art collector, establishing what will probably be the last ever private collection of old masters to rival those of the world's great museums. This was broken up after his death, but was reassembled and expanded by his son, who put the paintings on public display at his Swiss mansion in Lugano. A few years ago, German bids to provide a new home for the gallery (accompanied by special pleading on the grounds that the paintings had been acquired as a result of wealth created in the country) were rejected in favour of an offer from the Spanish government.

---

and drama) and the *Mercatorhalle* (concerts of all kinds), both of which are just round the corner. This part of the city is also the best place to look for other entertainments – *Kino Hollywood* at Königstr. 63–65 is rather trendy, and there are plenty of places to **eat** and **drink**. The obvious beer to sample is the locally produced *König* Pils, made in the largest brewery in Germany still in private hands. Should you wish to stay, the **youth hostel**, Kalkweg 148 (☎0203/724164), is in the suburb of Wedau, near the main recreation parks; take bus #934, #936 or #944. **Hotel rooms** in the centre tend to be expensive; check with the tourist office for any good deals, or be prepared to stay far out.

Essen

ESSEN is the largest city of the Ruhrgebiet, and the fifth in Germany, a sprawling conglomeration of some 700,000 people. For centuries it was a small town under the control of its convent's abbesses, but it sprang to prominence as the steel metropolis in the industrialisation process last century, being effectively run by the most powerful of all Germany's commercial dynasties, the **Krupp** family, whose real-life story of wealth, influence and intrigue makes the fictional heroes of American soap operas seem puny in comparison. Essen is proud of its heritage, boasting northern Europe's oldest parish church, largest synagogue and tallest town hall; indeed, the city's publicity manages to make it sound a very enticing destination. While that's a somewhat exaggerated claim, Essen does nevertheless have a handful of worthwhile attractions – it's one Ruhr city which definitely merits a day or more of anybody's time.

The city centre

The centre of Essen consists largely of an enormous shopping precinct. At the northern end are two dominant features of which the tourist office is wildly proud, though in truth neither is an asset: the domed **Alte Synagoge** is a horrendously ugly monstrosity from the early years of this century, remarkable mainly for having outlasted the Third Reich; it now houses a documentary centre on the suffering of the Jews under the Nazis (Tues–Sun 10am–6pm; free). The other building, the **Rathaus**, a 1970s skyscraper, doesn't rate as one of the gems of modern architecture either.

In this setting, the **Münster** (or **Dom**) seems rather incongruous. A ninth century foundation, it functioned as a collegiate church for aristocratic women until the Reformation; since 1958, it has been the cathedral of a new diocese centred on the Ruhr. The west end is an eccentric tripartite eleventh-century structure apparently modelled on the Dom at Aachen; the rest of what must have been a magnificent building was destroyed by fire and replaced by an unexceptional Gothic hall church. A stupendous collection of **treasures** by Ottonian craftsmen nonetheless makes the Münster a place of outstanding interest. Most prominent of these is the **Golden Madonna** of 965, the first known work of its kind. Housed in its own locked chapel beside the entrance to the crypt, it's highly venerated – at least as many people come to see it for devotional as for aesthetic reasons. The simplicity of form (in contrast to material) makes for a highly charged emotional impact similar to that found in the art of primitive tribes.

Also in the church is a large seven-branched candelabrum from about 1000, but the other star pieces are all in the **Schatzkammer**, housed in rooms off the south transept (Tues–Sun 10am–4pm; DM1), which should on no account be missed. Here are four dazzling **processional crosses** of the tenth and eleventh centuries; gospel book cover with scenes carved in ivory; the crown of Otto III; and many other priceless items. Joined to the front of the Münster by means of an atrium is the **Johanniskirche**, a miniature Gothic baptismal church containing a double-sided altarpiece by Barthel Bruyn; whether you see the Christmas or Easter scenes depends on the time of year. Between the Münster and the Hauptbahnhof, in a multi-storey building on Rathenaustrasse, is the **Deutsches-Plakat-Museum**, the largest collection of posters in the country (Tues–Sun noon–8pm; DM2).

South of the centre

The main museum complex, however, is located well to the south of the city centre at Goethestr. 41; to reach it, take Kruppstrasse westwards at the back of the Hauptbahnhof, turn left at Bismarckplatz into Bismarckstrasse and continue straight ahead. Here are two separate collections – the **Ruhrland Museum** and the **Folkwang Museum** (Tues–Sun 10am–6pm; combined ticket DM3). The former has the usual local displays, with geology on the ground floor, customs, folklore and industries upstairs. Far more enticing is the Folkwang Museum, one of Germany's top galleries of nineteenth- and twentieth-century art. Two rooms are devoted to the French Impressionists and their followers, including versions of **Monet**'s favourite subjects, *Rouen Cathedral* and *Water Lilies*; an outstanding **Manet** *Fauré as Hamlet*; and four good examples each of **Gauguin** and **van Gogh**. In the German section, two works by **Friedrich** stand out among the Romantics, while there are examples of all the main figures of the present century, with **Nolde**, **Rohlfs** and **Kirchner** being particularly well represented; Kirchner's *Three Women in the Street* ranks as one of the key paintings in the development of the Expressionist movement.

The southern part of Essen has a surprising green belt. This begins with the **Gruga Park** (April–Sept 8am–midnight, Oct–March 9am–dusk; DM3), which incorporates the Botanical Gardens and large recreation areas. Beyond are extensive forests on both sides of the **Baldeneysee**, a long, narrow reservoir formed out of the River Ruhr. It's a popular leisure centre in summer, with watersports and walking trails. In this area are the grounds of the **Villa Hügel**, built for the **Krupp** family between 1868 and 1872, and serving as their home until 1945. You have to buy a ticket at the entrance to the park, just behind the S-Bahn station; it covers admission to both houses (Tues–Sun 10am–6pm; DM1.50). This idyllic setting gives little clue to the significance of the family, who personify many of the tragedies of modern German history, their genius for both engineering and organisation being channelled into the most destructive of ends.

THE KRUPP DYNASTY

Alfred Krupp (1812–87) brought the dynasty to national prominence 250 years after his ancestors had established themselves as Essen's foremost family. He was in some respects a model employer, pioneering sick pay, free medical treatment, pensions and retirement homes for his workers. On the other hand, he also had a paranoid obsession for inventing ever more deadly weapons; he has appropriately been dubbed "the father of modern warfare" and his field guns were largely responsible for Prussia's victory over France in 1871 which sealed the unity of Germany. His son Fritz gave a hard business edge to this policy, developing an unrelenting cycle of inventing new offensive weapons, followed by defences against them, only to make these superfluous by the creation of even more powerful means of attack. These were sold to all and sundry in the arms race which reached its inevitable conclusion in World War I, and ensured international honours and fabulous riches for the family to offset the disappointment of German defeat. The next head of the clan, Gustav Krupp von Bohlen, provided Hitler with essential funding; he and his son Alfried were also enthusiastic participators in the Holocaust, making extensive use of concentration camp labour in producing new weapons for the Nazi onslaught on world civilisation. Both were sentenced as war criminals at Nürnberg, but the Americans later took pity, and Alfried once more assumed command of an organisation which continued to grow spectacularly, with his own personal fortune estimated at one thousand million dollars. Eventually he stretched his interests too far; the family lost control of their empire in 1967, but their name lives on in the corporation which succeeded it.

The smaller of the houses has a technicolor PR-type presentation of the achievements of the corporation; upstairs, the family history of the Krupps is described, with the darker episodes carefully glossed over. In the large house, to which it's linked by a pavilion, you can wander at leisure around some of the forbidding, high-ceilinged, wood-panelled rooms, hung with tapestries and portraits of the leading lights of the day, including the Kaisers, who were close friends. Every so often (generally June–Oct in even-numbered years) there's a blockbuster international **loan exhibition** on a major artistic theme.

Practicalities

Essen's **Hauptbahnhof** is situated bang in the city centre, only a couple of blocks south of the Münster. The **tourist office** (Mon–Fri 9am–8pm, Sat 10am–8pm, Sun 10am–noon; ☎0201/235427) is also within the station, but it's easy to miss, being at the extreme southwest side – ie in the opposite direction to the city centre.

Accommodation

Availability of **hotel rooms** tends to depend on whether or not there's a trade fair on: Essen's prices are a bit lower than in many of the nearby large cities. In the centre, *Lindenhof* at Logenstr. 18 (☎0201/233031) has the best location amongst the cheaper places; singles are DM45, doubles DM80. A little further out are: *Hermannseck* at Eltingstr. 30 (☎0201/314937) at DM30 per person; and *Nordstern* at Stoppenberger Str. 30 (☎0201/31721) with singles at DM38, doubles DM72. The **youth hostel** (☎0201/491163) is in Werden, a long way from the centre, but in a delightful location in the woods; this suburb is worth seeing anyway, with a twelfth century Romanesque basilica church, the Abteikirche St Liudger. To reach it, take the road passing uphill directly in front of the abbey, and carry straight on; it lies well above the houses. Also in Werden, but on the opposite side of the river near the S-Bahn station, is one of the three **campsites** (☎0201/492978). The others aren't far away, being situated side by side on the south shore of the Baldeneysee in FISCHLAKEN. Most of the city's **restaurants** seem to have their eyes on the business market. However, *Kleiner Adler* at the corner of Akazienallee and Schwarze Meer, between the Munster and the Hauptbahnhof, offers hearty helpings of traditional cuisine at very reasonable prices, as well as a separate menu of game dishes – more expensive but superb. To mix with a younger clientele, try the cosy and crowded *Franziskus Keller* at I. Weber-Str. 6 just beyond the market square; it has cheap daily specials.

Nightlife and transport

Listings of events, cinema, theatre, exhibitions and all kinds of music are found in *Live Essen*, available from newsagents, or you can sometimes pick up a free copy at venues. **Pop concerts**, musicals and other large-scale shows are held at the *Grugahalle*, at the northern end of the eponymous park. **Classical music** is performed in both the *Villa Hügel* and the *Saalbau*, south of the Hauptbahnhof down Huyssenallee; the *Opernhaus* behind hosts opera, theatre and dance. Alternative dramatic programmes are presented at *Studio Theater am Rathaus*. Essen's **public transport** system is comprehensive, embracing buses, trams (some of which become the U-Bahn for part of their route) and the S-Bahn. Given the size of the place, a 24-hour ticket can be a good investment as it doesn't take many journeys to cover the DM8.50 price. Buying tickets in batches of four is also worthwhile if you're planning on spending more than a day in the city. **Mitfahrzentrale** is at Heinickestr. 33 (☎221031).

Bochum

BOCHUM lies right at the heart of the Ruhrgebiet, sandwiched between the two giants of Essen and Dortmund; it marks the transition to the part of the area which is traditionally Westphalian. Appropriately enough it's the place to come to learn about the achievements of Germany industry, boasting as it does two of the best specialist technical museums in the country; if these don't appeal, to be honest there's little else to justify a visit here, other than the remarkably vibrant **theatres**, which manage an improbable rivalry to the likes of Berlin and Munich. A pleasant if anonymous shopping area forms the centre, devoid of any sense of history bar the rather ghostly reminder provided by the **Propsteikirche**, a Gothic hall church now standing forlornly in its own grounds. Even more than usual, Bochum seems a loose federation of disparate built-up areas, the green spaces between them (often the sites of abandoned mines) all the more necessary for the locals because of the complete lack of access to open countryside. In spite of the traditions in heavy industry, the leading employer is now the car plant of Opel, General Motors' European subsidiary.

Around town

Arriving at the **Hauptbahnhof**, the **tourist office** (Mon–Fri 8.30am–6pm, Sat 8.30am–noon; ☎0234/13031) is found in the front part of the building. The centre is straight ahead from here: turn right and follow the inner ring road all the way to the **Deutsches Bergbaumuseum** (German Mining Museum; Tues–Fri 8.30am–5.30pm, Sat & Sun 9am–1pm; DM5): you can't miss it, as its sixty-metre high winding tower is a dominant feature of the skyline. Established in 1930, this legitimately claims to be the most important collection of its kind in the world, and is both exhaustive and inventive in scope. Budget at least two hours for a visit, as the ticket includes a 45-minute conducted tour (German only, hourly departures) around the demonstration pit in the bowels of the earth immediately below. Less frequently, there are opportunities to ascend the tower.

Bochum's other main attraction is the **Eisenbahn Museum** (Railway Museum; Wed & Fri 10am–5pm, Sun 10am–1pm; DM4), run by the national preservation society. Take the S-Bahn to Dalhausen, and turn left at the exit; it's then about 1.5km ahead. Some of the trains are in open yards, but most are grouped in two sheds. The first contains the locomotives themselves, with some real beauties, especially the oldest item, an imperious black and red monster from the 1920s. In the second hall are the passenger carriages, the comforts of the first class contrasting strongly with the hard benches in the third. Also here is an example of Deutsche Bundesbahn's most singular contribution to transport history, the *Schiene-Strasse-Bus*, a bizarre hybrid which looks like a coach but is also equipped with wheels for travelling along rails; it was widely used in forest areas until the late 1960s.

The **Museum Bochum** (Tues–Fri noon–8pm, Sat & Sun 10am–6pm; free) is just round the corner from the Bergbaumuseum on Kortumstrasse; the displays here, mounted in a series of changing exhibitions, are devoted to post-1945 art only. There's a branch at **Wasserburg Kemnade**, a moated castle at the southeastern extremity of the city (Tues 9am–3pm, Wed–Fri 1–7pm, Sat & Sun 11am–6pm; free). Although heavily restored, a couple of ornate chimneypieces remain, and a large collection of historical musical instruments has been installed, including such rarities as a pedal piano and a gusli. Adjacent is a **farmhouse museum** (same times, but May–Oct only).

Between here and the centre are the eye-catching futuristic buildings of the **Ruhr-Universität**, the main institution for technical education in the region, and a good place to meet people, although weekends are best avoided as the campus tends to be deserted. Specific reasons for coming include the **Botanical Gardens** on the southern side (daily April–Sept 9am–6pm, Oct–March 9am–4pm), and the **Universitäts-museum** (housed under the library; Tues–Fri noon–3pm, Sat & Sun 10am–6pm; free) with a collection of antiques, notably glass and sculptures, and some modern art.

Practicalities and entertainments

There are abundant places to **eat** and **drink** in the city centre. Two local beers to try are *Vest* and *Fiege*; the *Stammhaus* of the latter brewery is at Bongardstr. 23, and is equally renowned for its food. Somewhat cheaper, but just as good, is the *Bochumer Brauhaus* on Rathausplatz. If you're out at the Eisenbahn Museum, *Central Hof* is one of several places around Dalhausen Bahnhof offering inexpensive, homely cooking. Bochum has no youth hostel, but those in Essen and Hagen are both within easy commuting range. The nearest **campsite** is by the banks of the Ruhr in the adjacent town of HATTINGEN. Cheapest **hotels** with a central location are *Wiesmann*, Castroper Str. 191 (☎0234/591065), and *Sandkühler*, Flurstr. 1 (☎0234/581588), both DM30 per person. The **Mitfahrzentrale** office is at Ferdinandstr. 20 (☎0234/37794).

For listings of **events**, pick up the tourist office's free monthly *Wann, Wo, Was*. Bochum has a high reputation for **theatre**; the repertory company based at the *Schauspielhaus* on Königsallee ranks as one of the top four in the country. Puppet shows and concerts by the *Bochumer Symphoniker*, a body of good provincial standing, also feature at this venue. The *Ruhrlandhalle* on Stadionring hosts large-scale spectaculars; next to it, the *Starlighthalle* was completed in 1988 specifically to cater for a run of Andrew Lloyd Webber's *Starlight Express*, a venture marking Bochum's bid for national leadership in West End-type productions – rather a neglected area in Germany since the war. For **live jazz**, the place to go is *Bahnhof Langendreer*, at the extreme east end of town; this also hosts a festival each March.

Dortmund

The name of **DORTMUND** immediately brings **beer** to mind – it was first granted
brewing rights in 1293, and even jealous rivals are forced to admit it's the national
drink's number one city. Six top breweries are based here – *Kronen, Union, Ritter,
Thier, Stifts* and *Actien (DAB)*. Their chimneys form a distinctive feature of the skyline;
those of *Union* are right in the centre and about the first landmark you see on arrival at
the **Hauptbahnhof**. In all, six million hectolitres are produced annually, a total
surpassed in world terms only by Milwaukee. Much of it is for export, which has led to
the word being used to categorise certain types of beer. The Hauptbahnhof and the
pedestrian streets around it, incidentally, should be **avoided after dark** as they're the
forum for some pretty heavy drug dealing types.

Alone among Ruhr cities, Dortmund, now with a population of over 600,000, was
important in the Middle Ages when it was an active member of the Hanseatic League;
this helps give it a rounded and distinctive character which all its neighbours somehow
lack. Provided you're prepared to overlook the obvious limitations of a place where
wartime bombs wreaked horrendous damage and where heavy industry is still prominent, it's a surprisingly interesting and enjoyable city in which to spend a day or two.

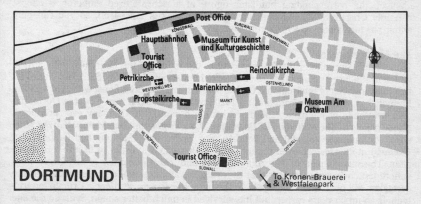

The city centre churches

The inner ring road, whose sections all bear the suffix "wall", follows the line of the
vanished thirteenth-century fortifications and thus defines the perimeter of the medieval city. Only a fraction of this area was left standing after the war, and not a single
secular building from the Hansa days remains. The four civic churches, however,
survived the onslaught in a battered condition, and a painstaking restoration
programme which lasted into the 1980s has returned them to their former state.
Although they're now marooned in a modern shopping centre, the layout of the old
streets and squares has been followed, thus minimising the visual loss. None of the
churches is architecturally outstanding, but their assemblage of Gothic art treasures
justifies a visit to the city – if the beer isn't a sufficient draw.

The Petrikirche and Propsteikirche

Directly facing the Hauptbahnhof is the **Petrikirche** (Wed 3–6pm, Fri 9am–2pm, irreg-
ularly open on other weekday afternoons), boasting a colossal **Antwerp altar** from
around 1520, which opens out to show expressively carved scenes of the Passion and

Legend of the Cross, featuring no fewer than 633 separate figures. These can be seen between autumn and Whit; during the summer they're hidden behind the more modest painted section narrating the earlier part of Christ's life. A short walk down the central axis of Westenhellweg is the **Propsteikirche**, the one church retained by the Catholics when Dortmund embraced the Reformation. On the high altar is a colourful and crowded triptych from about 1490 by the Westphalian painter **Derick Baegert**, aided by his son **Jan**. Straddling the scenes of *The Holy Kinship*, *The Crucifixion* and *The Adoration of the Magi* is a view of a medieval town proudly girt with numerous towers and spires – the earliest known depiction of Dortmund, and a poignant memorial to its long-lost splendours.

The Reinoldikirche

Continuing across Hansastrasse, Ostenhellweg leads to a large square overshadowed by the **Reinoldikirche**, named after the city's patron saint who was stoned to death in Cologne, whereupon his coffin is supposed to have rolled all the way to Dortmund under its own steam – perhaps just as well for the preservation of his memory, given that Cologne was already well endowed with holy martyrs. He's depicted as a young knight in a superb fourteenth-century wooden statue guarding the entrance to the chancel; the corresponding but later figure of a richly attired emperor is almost certainly Charlemagne. Unfortunately the choir area is fenced off, so you can only admire its furnishings at a respectful distance.

The Marienkirche

Immediately opposite is the **Marienkirche**, the oldest of the churches, with a nave which is still largely Romanesque (Tues–Fri 10am–noon & 2–4pm, Sat 10am–1pm). Its two masterpieces of International Gothic painting are the city's finest works of art. The high altar triptych dates from around 1420 and is by **Conrad von Soest**, a Dortmund citizen in spite of his name, and as endearing a painter as Germany ever produced. These panels of *The Nativity*, *The Dormition of the Virgin* and *The Adoration of the Magi* show the uniquely graceful and delicate "Soft Style" (see "Painting and Graphics" in *Contexts*) at its greatest, even though all were truncated in order to fit into a Baroque altar. The inner wings of *The Annunciation* and *The Coronation of the Virgin* have suffered such heavy paint loss that they're generally kept under cover, although the caretaker will open them if you ask. In the nave, the *Berswordt Altar*, a Crucifixion triptych, is about 25 years earlier, but has survived in much better shape. See also the late Gothic stalls – their irreverent carvings include, appropriately enough, a man downing a mug of beer.

The museums

The **Museum für Kunst und Kulturgeschichte** (Museum of Art and Cultural History; Tues–Sun 10am–6pm; free), very near the Hauptbahnhof at the beginning of Hansastrasse, occupies a rather wonderful Art Deco building of the 1920s which was formerly a savings bank. Its highlight is a series of reassembled **interiors** – an eighteenth-century Westphalian pharmacy, the *Fliesensaal* (tiled room) with hunting scenes in Delft tiles, and a panelled music room from a bourgeois residence in Bremen. Among the notable paintings is a stunning, sombre **Friedrich**, *Night on the Sea*, along with a couple of smaller works. In the basement the archaeology display is dominated by the *Dortmunder Goldschatz*, a hoard of fourth- and fifth-century gold coins found locally.

On the inner ring road is the **Museum am Ostwall** (same times; free), devoted to the municipal collection of modern art, with changing exhibitions on the ground floor. Upstairs is a comprehensive display of Expressionism, dominated by what's arguably

August Macke's masterpiece, *Grosser Zoologischer Garten*, which experiments with the new Cubist forms in an anachronistic triptych format. Most eye-catching of the experimental sculptures is **Wolf Vostell**'s *Thermo-Elektronischer Kaugummi* of 1970. Occupying a whole gallery, this has 13,000 forks and spoons grouped behind two barbed wire fences, and – believe it or not – features 5000 pieces of chewing gum. From here, continue along Ostwall and turn left into Märkischestrasse; you eventually come to the *Kronen Brauerei*. In 1982, Dortmund's long felt need for a **brewery museum** was at last satisfied by a display set up in the premises here (same hours as the other museums; free).

The Westfalenpark

A little further south the city's large green belt begins; it would be attractive were it not marred by the uncomfortable proximity of some of the most satanic-looking mills still in operation. You have to pay to enter the **Westfalenpark**; buy the DM3 ticket which includes admission to the **Fernsehturm** (Television tower) at the entrance gate, as it costs more if you decide you'd like to go up later on. It's 212 metres high, an older and simpler structure than those in Cologne and Düsseldorf. There's a high-speed lift which whisks you up to the platform with its extensive and starkly contrasting panorama over the industries of the Ruhr and the rolling landscape of its playground, the Sauerland. Also within the park is the **Deutsches Rosarium**, featuring thousands of roses from all over the world.

Drinking, eating and nightlife

Inevitably, the **beer halls** must head the list of entertainments, and the city centre is ideal for a pub crawl; there's no need to move very far to sample the products of all the different breweries. The **Markt** is the obvious place to begin; here *Krone* claim to have had an uninterrupted presence since 1430, an even longer pedigree than the Hofbräuhaus in Munich. It's therefore disappointing that what's there today has a modern interior with plastic decor and elaborate swinging chairs, whose main line of business is an expensive rôtisserie (which admittedly has a high reputation). Next door, *Wenker's*, named after the most eccentric of Dortmund brewers, is much more animated, being a great favourite with the youth of the city. The drink to order is *Utrüb*, a blonde ale top-fermented with plenty of yeast sediment left in. Two watering-holes in a more traditional vein on the same square are *Kiepenkerl*, which serves *Union*, and *Zum Alten Markt*, whose allegiance is to *Thier*, and which also has reasonably priced food cooked in the old Westphalian style. Another *Thier* pub, *Gänse Markt*, is just round in the corner beside the Marienkirche in what was once the goose market. Facing the Reinoldikirche, *Zum Ritter (Restaurant Marché)* is a good value self-service restaurant, using fresh market ingredients, extremely popular at lunchtimes.

The **Ostwall** has another concentration of places to eat and drink, beginning with *Café Knüppel* at the corner with Ostenhellweg, a genteel salon in which to take coffee and cake. In contrast, some noisy beer halls and discos are directly opposite, while a *Victorian Pub* features among the more staid ale houses down the road. Further west along the ring, you come to Hoherwall, with *Hövels Hausbrauerei* offering a beer garden and some of the best food in town. Hansastrasse also has promising possibilities, notably *Schwarzer Rabe*, arguably Dortmund's top restaurant.

For the most decadent nightspot, you have to head to the old village of **SYBURG**, now the most southerly suburb. On the heights between a ruined Romanesque Burg and its restored parish church stands the vast modern palace of glass that is the **casino** (slot machines open from 1pm, the real stuff from 3pm). During gaming hours regular bus services run from the Hauptbahnhofs of both Dortmund (#444) and Hagen (#544).

Even if you don't want to play, it's a good place to do a spot of people-watching, particularly at weekends. It's possible to wander around the building without hassle. If you're a gambler, entry to the slot machines is DM1; formal registration is necessary for the tables, where minimum stakes are DM2 at roulette, DM10 for black jack, and DM40 for baccarat.

To find out about **events**, consult either *Blick in die Stadt* or *Dortmunder Bakanntmachungen*; both cost a nominal amount from newsagents. **Theatres** include the *Schauspielhaus* and its *Studio* on Hiltropwall, and the *Theatre am Ostwall*, while the *Opernhaus* is on Hansastrasse. There are plenty of **cinemas** in the centre, again on Hansastrasse and the parallel Brückstrasse. The huge *Westfalenhalle* southwest of the centre is used for **sports** and other blockbuster shows such as **jazz** and **pop concerts**.

Practicalities

In front of the Stadtgarten at Südwall 6 is the main **tourist office** (Mon–Wed 8am–4pm, Thurs 8am–6pm, Fri 8am–noon; ☎0231/542 25666). More convenient, but with fewer leaflets, is the branch opposite the Hauptbahnhof (Mon–Fri 9am–6pm, Sat 9am–1pm; ☎0231/542 22174). There's a **campsite** at Syburger-Dorfstr. 69 (☎0231/774374), not far from the casino. The youth hostel closed a few years ago, but those in Hagen and Cappenberger See are near enough to make commuting cost effective. For **hotel rooms**, most of the better bargains are in outlying suburbs; exceptions are *Carlton*, Lütge Brückstr. 5–7 (☎0231/528030/9), DM40 per person; *Sport-Hotel*, Mallinckrodtstr. 212–4 (☎0231/821047/8), and *Atlanta,* Ostenhellweg 51, (☎0231/579518/9), both upwards of DM39 per person. The **Mitfahrzentrale** office is at Grünestr. 3 (☎0231/822067).

Hagen

Like nearby Wuppertal, **HAGEN** would be a characterless large town were it not for an imaginative and rather brilliant act of initiative around the turn of the present century. **Karl Ernst Osthaus**, a local industrialist and patron of the arts, was instrumental in persuading a group of talented international designers in the Art Nouveau style to come to Hagen. Prominent among them were the architects Peter Behrens of Hamburg, Henry van de Velde from Belgium and Mathiew Lauweriks from Holland, along with another Dutchman, the decorator Johan Thorn-Prikker. The artists' colony thus founded was a fitting successor to the one in Darmstadt, Germany's other main centre of what was always called Jugendstil, to which Behrens had also belonged. Nor were other styles shunned; the Expressionist painter Christian Rohlfs was summoned and stayed until he died in 1938, seventeen years after Osthaus' own premature death put an end to his ambitious plans for a complete garden city.

The Jugendstil buildings

Your first glimpse of this legacy comes at the **Hauptbahnhof**; illuminating the exit is a large stained glass window by Thorn-Prikker, an allegory entitled *The Obeisance of the Crafts before the Artist*. From the square in front, turn right and then follow Elberfelder Strasse straight ahead, eventually taking any of the small side streets into the parallel Hochstrasse, where you'll find the **Karl-Ernst-Osthaus-Museum** (Tues, Wed, Fri & Sat 11am–6pm, Thurs 11am–10pm, Sun 11am–4pm; free). The exterior is in the stolid end-of-century Wilhelmine style, but the interior, created a few years later by van de Velde, has all the sense of fantasy and romance characteristic of the best Art Nouveau. Originally this contained Osthaus' private art collection, the Folkwang Museum, which was hung in an unconventional thematic manner. After his death, it was sold en bloc by his heirs to the city of Essen, where it can still be seen. Since the acquisition of the building by the Hagen authorities in 1945, belated attempts have been made to re-create the original effect by acquiring works in line with Osthaus' tastes. There's a good representation of Expressionism and other twentieth-century German art, with several examples of **Rohlfs**, whose studio was housed here, along with works by **Macke** (*Women in Front of a Hat Shop*), **Dix** (the erotic *Artist and Muse*), **Kokoschka** (*The Actor Sommarunga*), Kirchner, Nolde, Beckmann and Schmidt-Rottluff.

To the east of the centre, reached by bus #502, is the projected garden suburb of **Hohenhagen**, of which only an incomplete crescent known as **Stirnband** was built. The nearer side of this consists of a row of houses by Lauweriks, homogeneous in style but each given its own identity. Still in private ownership, they are undoubtedly the ulti-mate in des. res. within the Ruhrgebiet. Fronting the other entrance to the crescent is **Haus Cuno** by Behrens, now an academy of music; on weekdays it's worth sticking your head round the door to see the impressive stairwell. The rest of this street really forms a processional way to the vast **Hohenhof**, designed as Osthaus' own residence by van de Velde. This is one of the great achievements of the Art Nouveau movement, a dream home if ever there was one, and a building which seems to change dramati-cally from every angle of vision. Now owned by the city, it's a cultural centre, but the interior is generally only accessible on Saturdays between 2pm and 6pm. Try to come then to see the intricacies of its decorations, which include furniture designed by its architect, stained glass windows by Thorn-Prikker and a huge canvas, *The Elect*, by the Swiss **Ferdinand Hodler**.

The outskirts

Hagen's only other attraction is the **Freilichtmuseum** (April–Oct Tues–Sun 9am–6pm; DM3) south of the city in SELBECKE; take bus #507. Laid out in the valley of the Mäckingerbach, this marks the point where the industrial Ruhrgebiet gives way to the rural Sauerland. There are some 65 traditional buildings, but it differs from other museums of the same type in that the emphasis is technical, rather than social or archi-tectural. Horny-handed old sons of toil demonstrate all kinds of historical equipment, ranging from machinery for producing iron and steel, through printing and papermak-ing, spinning, weaving and dyeing, to baking and mustard production; it's possible to buy many of the products made here. There's also a windmill near the entrance; as it's some distance from the other buildings, check first for the times when it's going to be put into action. Just to walk round the site takes quite a while, and you need to budget at least three hours for a visit – longer if you want to see all the crafts demonstrated.

Practicalities

The **tourist office** (Mon–Fri 9am–6pm, Sat 9am–1pm; ☎02331/13573) occupies a pavil-ion in Mittelstrasse, the continuation of Elberfelder Strasse. Most of the nightlife gets going in the streets around here, and **concerts** are held at the *Stadthalle* on Wasserloses Tal. For **live jazz**, go to *Tuba Keller* on Hohenzollernstrasse; the pub above has a beer garden, while that behind, *Loüster*, swarms with young locals and is the best choice if you want an animated atmosphere with blaring rock. Traditional beer halls serving hearty food are *Andreas am Museum* (named after Hagen's own beer) on Hochstrasse, *Alt Nürnberg* on Elbersufer, and *Stadtschänke* on Friedrich-Ebert-Platz.

The **youth hostel** is at Eppenhauser Str. 65a (☎02331/50254; bus #502 or #503), just a few minutes' from Stirnband. Although there's no **campsite** in the city boundaries, that at Syburg (see above) is only a few kilometres away, reached by bus #544. **Hotel rooms** are cheaper than in most other Ruhr cities; in the centre, *Gasthof Bürgerkrug*,

Werdestr. 2–4 (☎02331/26779), has singles from DM25, doubles at DM50; *Haus Teimann*, Eppenhauser Str. 195 (☎02331/53504), charges from DM28 per person; while *Danne*, Hochstr. 76–78 (☎02331/32626), and *Targan*, Hugo-Preuss-Str. 5 (☎02331/16863), both cost around DM34 for a single, DM60 for a double. Given the fact that the places you'll want to see are so far apart, a day ticket on the **public transport** system, costing DM8.50, is worth considering; it allows you to go as far afield as Syburg. There's a **Mitfahrzentrale** office at Södingstr. 3 (☎02331/337555).

Recklinghausen

The northern part of the Ruhrgebiet, before the vast built-up area gives way to the open spaces of Münsterland, is known as the district of **RECKLINGHAUSEN**, after its principal town; the other main communities – none of them with much to offer – are MARL, CASTROP-RAUXEL and HALTERN. Recklinghausen itself, though small-scale compared to the cities to the south, does its best to appear distinctive. Originally founded as a royal seat by Charlemagne, it was a Hanseatic city in the Middle Ages, dominated by blacksmiths and cloth merchants. There's nothing major in the way of surviving monuments, but you still get something of the feel of the old town amidst all the usual later accretions – certainly, there's more of a sense of continuous history here than is to be found anywhere else in the Ruhr. Streets in the centre still follow the old twisting and turning pattern and there are a number of half-timbered houses, some fragments of the city wall, and, as centrepiece, the **Petruskirche**, predominantly Gothic, but incorporating parts of its Romanesque predecessor as well as sundry modifications by subsequent builders. From the Baroque period, the **Engelsburg** on Augustinessenstrasse is a handsome mansion built round a courtyard; it's now the best hotel in town. Round the corner on Geiststrasse is the **Gastkirche**, formerly an almshouse chapel, containing several striking altarpieces.

Recklinghausen's pride and joy, however, is its **Ikonmuseum** (Tues–Fri 10am–6pm, Sat & Sun 11am–5pm; DM2.50) at Am Kirchplatz beside the Petruskirche. This isn't just another example of the seemingly inexhaustible German capacity for creating museums on the most abstruse of subjects – it really is the finest collection of this simple yet haunting and powerful art form outside the Orthodox world. The star piece is the huge late sixteenth-century Russian *Calendar Icon of the Year*, a tour de force illustrating the main stories of the Bible, as well as portraying hundreds of saints, arranged according to their feast day. From the following century comes *The Credo*, executed using techniques reminiscent of Western manuscript illuminators, and a masterly *Enthroned Christ*, a signed work by the Cretan **Elias Moskos**. The earliest works, from the fifteenth-century Moscow and Novgorod schools, have perhaps the most overtly emotional appeal; among the finest are the symbolic *Christ the Unsleeping Eye* and *St Nicholas with Scenes from his Life*. In addition to over 400 icons displayed by subject, there are extensive collections on the decorative arts of the Orthodox and Coptic churches.

Festivals and practicalities

Cultural life in Recklinghausen centres on the *Ruhrfestspiele*, a **festival** of concerts, plays, exhibitions and discussions held annually in May and June. Run in conjunction with the national Federation of Trade Unions, it's an indication of how events regarded as highbrow in other countries appeal to all sectors of German society. The *Festspielhaus*, in the Stadtgarten to the west of the city centre, was opened in 1965 as the specially designed home for the festival. For the rest of the year, the normal **concert** hall is the *Saalbau* on Dorstener Strasse, while the main venue for **drama** is *Theater im Depot* on Castroper Strasse.

Recklinghausen has no **tourist office** as such, but you can pick up maps and leaflets at the Rathaus during working hours; the museums also keep a stock. The cheapest **hotels**, charging around DM30 per person, are *Haus Korte*, Castroper Str. 365 (☎02361/43201), and *Kolpinghaus*, Herzogswall 38 (☎02361/22640). Nearest **campsites** are at HALTERN to the north – *Dülmener See*, (☎02594/2125), *Hoher Niemen* (☎02364/2511) and *Seegesellschaft Haltern* (☎02364/3360); the first two are open all year, the last April to September only. For an animated **pub**, try *Boente* on Augustinessenstrasse, where you can sample the products of the local *Kornbrennerei* brewery in a large beer garden.

WESTPHALIA

Westphalia (*Westfalen*) is named after one of the three main Saxon tribes; by the early Middle Ages, the term came to be used for all of Saxony west of the River Weser. Despite this long tradition as a definable part of Germany, it's never really been governed as a unit, and the boundaries have often been changed dramatically – the short-lived Kingdom of Westphalia, established by Napoleon for his brother Jérôme, consisted mostly of Hessen, while the present political division of the country has seen parts of the historic province transferred to Lower Saxony. Apart from the cities in the Ruhrgebiet which are traditionally Westphalian (Dortmund, Recklinghausen, Gelsenkirchen, Hagen and Bochum), there are three distinct constituent parts – the fertile **Münsterland** plain to the north; the predominantly rural **Sauerland** and **Siegerland** to the south; and the depression to the east bounded by the vast stretch of the **Teutoburg Forest**. The last-named now incorporates what was formerly one of the smallest states of the German Reich, the **Principality of Lippe**. Of the cities, the two largest, **Bielefeld** and **Münster**, could hardly be more different: the former is predominantly industrial whereas the latter is the epitome of middle-class prosperity. **Paderborn**, like Münster, is an important episcopal centre. However, many of the most memorable towns in the area – **Soest**, **Lemgo** and **Höxter** – are modest in size.

According to its tourist board, Westphalia is associated with "the solid and substantial things in life". In architecture, the characteristic features are moated castles, lofty hall churches and half-timbered farm buildings. Gastronomically, it's famous for hams, spit roasts, beer, schnapps and, above all, rye bread. Westphalia is an archetypal German province and a favourite holiday destination with the Germans themselves. In spite of a fair number of Britons visiting friends and family in the military bases, there's no more than a trickle of tourists from abroad – a definite plus from the viewpoint of authenticity.

Münster

Northern Westphalia is dominated by the province's former capital, **MÜNSTER**, one of the most varied and enticing of the cities spread across the flat German plain. It has an unusually rich architectural heritage, including examples of all the main styles from Romanesque to Baroque. Industry has been confined to the peripheries, and the chic shops crowding the centre are an unabashed celebration of the affluent consumerism enjoyed by a population which is overwhelmingly middle-class. The University is the third largest in Germany; one consequence of this is that the city has come firmly under the rule of the bicycle. However, the dominant influence on Münster has been the Church, its very name – the equivalent of the English word "minster" – deriving from the evangelising monastery of **Saint Liudger** who was consecrated bishop in 805 as part of Charlemagne's policy of converting the Saxon tribes to Christianity. Apart from the years 1534–5 when it was taken over by the fanatical Anabaptist sect, it has remained intensely loyal to Roman Catholicism, even during the Third Reich, when the

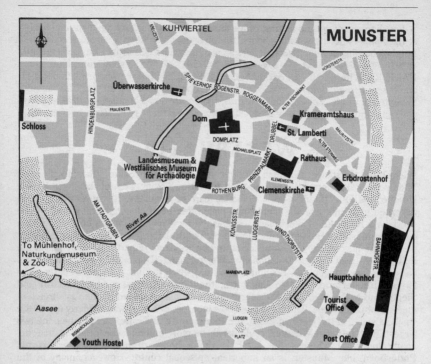

city's bishop, **Clemens August von Galen**, was one of the regime's most courageous and persistent opponents. In 1936, he organised a popular revolt which succeeded in overturning an edict to remove crucifixes from school buildings – an apparently trivial incident, but one of the few occasions the Nazis gave in to domestic opponents. This defiance counted for nothing with the Allied bombing missions, which administered particularly brutal treatment on Münster, but the city recovered well, adopting a much praised rebuilding programme.

Arrival and practicalities

The **Hauptbahnhof** is directly to the east of the city centre, which is reached by heading straight down Windthorststrasse. **Bus services** both within the city and to other places in the province leave from the string of stops on both sides of Bahnhofstrasse. Directly opposite is the main **tourist office** (Mon–Fri 9am–8pm, Sat 9am–1pm, 1st Sat in month 9am–6pm, Sun 10.30am–12.30pm; ☎0251/510180); there's also a branch within the Rathaus (Mon–Fri 9am–5pm, Sat 9am–4pm, Sun 10am–1pm; ☎0251/492 2745). The **youth hostel** is at Bismarck Allee 31 (☎0251/43765) in a good location by the right bank of the Aasee; bus #13 goes closest. **Camping** is possible from mid-March to mid-October at Dorbaumstr. 35 (☎0251/329312) in the northeastern suburb of HANDORF. **Hotel rooms** emphatically don't come cheap. Most convenient among the better buys is *Zum Schwan*, Schillerstr. 27 (☎0251/661166), facing the back of the station, at DM47 for a single, DM85 for a double; the pub downstairs offers *vom heissen Stein* dishes at a very reasonable cost. Centrally sited alternatives are *Zur Krone*, Hammerstr. 67 (☎0251/73868), at DM40 per person, and *Odysseus*, Engelstr. 60 (☎532775), singles DM35, doubles DM60; unless you're prepared to pay a bit more, you'll have to stay far out. At the extreme southwest of the city proper are *Lohmann*, Mecklenbeckerstr. 345 (☎0251/71525), with singles at DM35, doubles DM65, and *Haselmann*, Flasskamp 41 (☎0251/717055), at DM40 upwards. There's also a concentration of hotels in the outlying town of HILTRUP directly to the south, which are generally cheaper than in the city. **Mitfahrzentrale** is at Papenburger Str. 6 (☎0251/661006).

The Prinzipalmarkt

Münster's population is swollen by the British and American soldiers whose bases ring the suburbs. They may be unpopular with the locals, but their justification for being there – the maintenance of the peace and balance of power in Europe – happens to be the historical role of which Münster is most proud. In the centre of the main street, the **Prinzipalmarkt**, stands the magnificent Gothic **Rathaus**, scene of the signing in 1648 of the **Peace of Westphalia**, which brought to an end the multitude of religious, constitutional and dynastic conflicts known as the Thirty Years' War. For the previous five years, the Catholic parties had been in congress at Münster; the highly complex negotiations which took place represent the beginnings of modern diplomacy as still practised. In honour of the treaty, the room where it was signed was renamed the **Friedensaal** (Peace Hall); it's filled with exquisite carving and is the one part of the Rathaus generally open to the public (Mon–Fri 9am–5pm, Sat 9am–4pm, Sun & holidays 10am–1pm; DM1.50).

Next door, the **Stadtweinhaus**, a Renaissance building with an abutting Italianate portico, has also been returned to its former splendour. The rest of what must once have been one of the most handsome main thoroughfares in Europe is rather more of a compromise; alongside faithfully rebuilt houses are some which are mere approximations, while others are deliberately modern reinterpretations using the old motifs.

At the end of Prinzipalmarkt is **St Lamberti**, a good example of the spacious hall church style characteristic of Westphalia. Its elegant openwork spire, one of the chief landmarks of the city, reflects the nineteenth-century German obsession with embellishing Gothic buildings. High up on the older part of the tower hang three wrought-iron cages; in them were displayed the bodies of the Anabaptist leader **Jan van Leyden** and his two principal lieutenants, following the crushing of their "Reich" (which, like Hitler, they believed would endure for a millennium) by the Prince-bishop's army. Apart from insisting on adult baptism, this sect believed in the common ownership of property and in heeding the biblical injunction to be fruitful and multiply – the leader himself took no less than sixteen wives. The iconoclastic tendencies of the Anabaptists led them to destroy the beautiful sculptural decoration which was a key feature of the city's medieval churches; one of the rare examples left in situ is the elaborate *Tree of Jesse* over St Lamberti's south doorway. Facing the church's apse on Alter Steinweg is the **Krameramtshaus**, a late sixteenth-century building in the Dutch style it's the oldest guild hall to have survived; nowadays it serves as the main public library.

Domplatz

The vast **Domplatz**, on which markets are held on Wednesdays and Saturdays, is reached in just a few strides from Prinzipalmarkt down either Domgasse or Michaelisplatz. Almost any point on the square offers a superb view of the huge thirteenth-century **Dom**, built in less than forty years in a style bridging the transition from Romanesque to Gothic. The only entrance is via the porch (or "Paradise"), which is adorned on the inside with statues of Christ and the Apostles which date from the very beginning of the building period; the pier figure of Saint Paul, the Dom's patron, is from 300 years later, the first of several subsequent additions to make up a full programme worthy of a Gate of Heaven, to which such doorways aspired.

The Dom's **interior** is highly unusual, the nave having just two bays of massive span. It's jam-packed with sculptural memorials and other works of art. What really catches your eye is the **astronomical clock**, made in the 1530s, in the southern arm of the ambulatory. Based on the most precise mathematical calculations available at the time, it shows the orbit of the planets and the movement of the fixed stars, as well as fulfilling the normal function of charting the course of the sun and the moon; the lowest section is a calendar. The leading Münster painter of the day, **Ludger tom Ring the Elder**, decorated the clock with the Evangelical symbols, delicate scenes of the Labours of the Months and a gallery of entranced spectators. If you brave the crowds at noon, you can hear the carillon and see the emergence of the Magi to pay tribute to the infant Christ.

At the far end of the cloisters the **Domkammer** (Tues–Sat 10am–noon & 2–6pm, Sun 2–6pm; DM1) houses the treasury. Pride of place goes to the eleventh-century gold reliquary of St Paul, studded with jewels a couple of hundred years later; other outstanding pieces are the thirteenth-century processional cross and fourteen bust-reliquaries of the prophets.

Museums on Domplatz

The Domplatz, which also contains several Baroque mansions, serves as the city's museum centre. The **Landesmuseum** (Tues–Sun 10am–6pm; free) houses works of art of mostly Westphalian origin, but is of far more than parochial significance. On the ground floor is a really outstanding collection of **medieval sculpture**, including the original statues from the Überwasserkirche (see below). From the Dom is the massive group of *Christ's Entry into Jerusalem*, which adorned the upper part of the facade destroyed in the war. The latter is the work of **Heinrich Brabender**, a long-forgotten name who now appears as one of the most individual of the remarkable group of late Gothic German sculptors. Also by him is a series of Passion scenes made for the Domplatz; despite their weary appearance – the Anabaptists smashed them only a few years after they were made – the wonderful dignity and characterisation of the figures can still be appreciated. Also on display are examples of the quite different art of his son **Johann Brabender**, who was fully Renaissance in style and happiest on a small-scale, as in sensitive and delicate works such as *Calvary* from the Dom's rood screen and *Adam and Eve* from the Paradise. A dimmed room is devoted to **stained glass**, which can be examined in far more favourable conditions than in a church.

Upstairs, the history of Westphalian painting is traced, beginning with the "Soft Style" of **Conrad von Soest** and the **Master of Warendorf** in the early fifteenth century. From the next generation is **Johann Koerbecke**, whose masterpiece, the *Marienfeld Altar*, contains background depictions of Münster. The Renaissance section is dominated by the diverse interests of the **tom Ring** family; apart from the portraits for which they are best known, there are religious works by Hermann and pioneering still lifes by Ludger the Younger. On the second floor are two rooms of Expressionist paintings, with a good cross-section of the work of **Macke**. The **Westfälisches Museum für Archäologie** (same times; free) in the interconnected building is chiefly of documentary interest; there's a notable lack of objects likely to give much pleasure.

The rest of the city

A short distance to the west of the Dom stands the **Liebfrauenkirche**, usually known as the **Überwasserkirche** (Church by the Water) since it stands beside the Aa, Münster's tiny river. Like St Lamberti, it's a fourteenth-century hall church, with a floridly decorated tower. Its superb sculptures proved particularly repugnant to the Anabaptists, who smashed and buried them; some 350 years later, they were dramatically rediscovered but were considered too fragile to return to their original location. From here, Frauenstrasse leads to Schlossplatz with the resplendent eighteenth-century **Schloss** of the Prince-bishops, its two side wings reaching out like embracing arms. The front facing the **Botanical Gardens** (daily 7.30am–5pm) is quite different, but the interior was completely destroyed in the war, and has been modernised for use by the University. Its architect, **Johann Conrad Schlaun**, was almost single-handedly responsible for making Münster the capital of north German Baroque, which was far more restrained than its southern counterpart. A couple of other buildings by him can be seen at the opposite end of the city centre; they can be reached from the Rathaus by following Klemensstrasse. The **Erbdrostenhof**, a nobleman's mansion, again shows his talent for the grand manner; it has survived in better shape than the Schloss and is currently being restored to house a museum.

Southwest from the centre

Heading southwest from the centre, the sausage-shaped **Aasee**, some 6km in circumference, is the most popular recreation area in the city, particularly at the weekend when the yachts and motorboats of prosperous locals crowd the water. At the lower end of the left bank is the **Mühlenhof**; though small, it's one of Germany's longest-established open-air museums (mid-March–Nov daily 9am–5pm, rest of year Mon–Sat 1.30–4.30pm, Sun 11am–4.30pm; DM3; take bus #14). On a fine day, it's worth a plod round the twenty or so agricultural buildings from the province which have been re-erected here, the centrepieces being a trestle windmill of 1748 and an early seventeenth-century millhouse, fitted out with authentic furnishings.

Eating, drinking and nightlife

Not the least of Münster's attractions is the wonderful choice of **bars**, **cafés** and **restaurants**. The most obvious place to begin is around the Prinzipalmarkt, but an equally notable nightlife area is the **Kuhviertel** just beyond the Überwasserkirche; this is usually described as the Latin quarter, but students no longer predominate. Look out for the amazing range of **beers** – Pils, Alt, Weizen, Malz and *Spezial* – made by *Pinkus Müller*, although small, and the only one left in Münster, it's among the most highly-regarded of all German breweries. Alt, whether from Pinkus or imported from that other snobbish city, Düsseldorf, is Münster's most popular drink; it's generally mixed with syrup (*mit Schuss*) or with a punch of fresh raspberries and peaches (*Altbierbowle*).

Prinzipalmarkt and around

Altes Brauhaus Kiepenkerl, Spiekerhof 45. Named after the statue of the pedlar outside, this has a ground floor beer hall and elegant upstairs café.

Café Kleimann, Prinzipalmarkt 48. Occupying one of the finest of the old guild houses, it makes a cheaper alternative to *Otto Schucan* for *Kaffee und Kuchen*.

Otto Schucan, Prinzipalmarkt. This pricey café serves delicious coffee and has an irresistible display of cakes; it attracts a varied clientele – students, businessmen and elderly women.

Palmen Café, Aegidiimarkt 1. Best selection of teas in town.

Stuhlmacher, Prinzipalmarkt 6. The city's most celebrated pub, it has a wide selection of beers, and is ideal for a spot of people-watching, particularly in the early evening. Its restaurant is expensive, however, and you can eat better elsewhere.

Kuhviertel

Cavete, Kreuzstr 38. Youthful watering-hole with loud music and a selection of inexpensive pastas and puddings.

Das Blaue Haus, Kreuzstr. 16. A direct competitor of *Cavete* in every respect.

Fischbrathalle, Schlaunstr. 8. Long-established fish restaurant; remember that it closes around teatime.

Pinkus Müller, Kreuzstr. 6-10. The brewery's restaurant is decked out in traditional style; it fills up heavily from mid-evening – notably with members of the American community. Not the cheapest, but the best place in town for a traditional Westphalian meal.

Pinkus Müller Biergalerie, Kreuzstr. 4. Main drinking-den of the local brewery.

Elsewhere in the city

Altes Gasthaus Leve, Alter Steinweg 37. Gastronomically, the pick of the old-fashioned beer halls clustered along this street.

Cadaqués', Ludgeristr. 62. The bistro cooking here is best sampled in the freshly cooked lunchtime specials – but to be avoided if you're in a hurry.

Der Bunte Vogel, Alter Steinweg 41. Another beer hall, though a bit trendier than usual .

Gambrinus, Königsstr. 34 . Lively pub which does good value schnitzels cooked in a score of different ways.

Hardies, Mauritzstr. 30. One of the main student pubs, with a large but not exclusively gay clientele.

Kruse Baimken, Am Staatgraben 52 (by the north bank of the Aasee). *The* place to come on a fine evening, when you may find close on a thousand people, including many of the beautiful set, relaxing in its beer garden.

Scala, Hörsterstr. 51. Student café, which forms, with the adjacent Italian *Bier-Café Roma* and *Pasadena Piano Bar*, what the army call the "Bermuda Triangle".

Treibhaus, Steinfurter Str. 66. Less self-conscious alternative to *Kruse Baimken* further to the north; also does low priced meals.

Discos

Byblos, Hörsterstrasse. Part of the "Bermuda Triangle" area, and featuring an American night on Saturdays.

Club Leo, Roggenmarkt. In the basement of a clothes shop, patronised chiefly by punters in their early 20s.

Der Elephant, Roggenmarkt. Down an arcade, this caters mainly for older swingers. ·

Festivals and culture

The main **popular festival**, known as *Send*, is a fair held for five days at a stretch three times annually (March, June and October) in the Hindenburgplatz in front of the Schloss. Carnival is also celebrated, if not with the same gusto as in the Rhineland, while the *Lambertusfest*, beginning on 17 September, is a festival for children. Surprisingly, Münster isn't especially renowned for its highbrow culture, although there's a modern *Stadttheater* at Neubrückenstrasse, while the *Halle Münsterland* on Albertsloher Weg to the south of the centre hosts large-scale events.

Münsterland

Münsterland is the name given to the large tract of Westphalia stretching from the Rhine to the Teutoburg Forest, bounded by the Netherlands and Lower Saxony to the north, and by the Ruhrgebiet to the south. Its rich soils are agriculturally highly productive, and it remains predominantly rural, with no large towns other than the capital. Being almost unrelievedly flat, it's emphatically not a province you visit for scenery, but it boasts over fifty **historic castles** (known as *Wasserburgen* – see overleaf*)*, quite the densest concentration to be found in Germany, and the nearest the country comes to rivalling the French Loire châteaux.

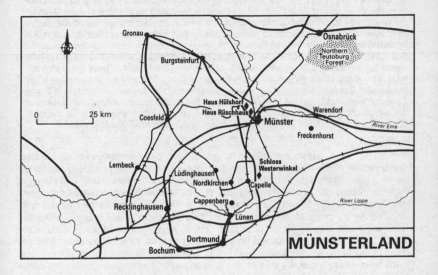

Visiting the Wasserburgen

The local tourist offices are keen to promote the Wasserburgen, whose virtues they flaunt by means of irresistible photographic posters. However, there are pitfalls which you should be aware of, as it's easy to end up frustrated and disappointed. Firstly, the vast majority of the castles remain private dwellings, generally still in the hands of old aristocratic families who are alive, well, and managing very nicely without the need of extra cash from prying outsiders. Few show much enthusiasm for the tourist board's initiatives; many castles can be seen from the outside only, and in some cases even that is kept out of bounds by the erection of large hedges and impenetrable gates. Secondly, the alluring posters are nearly all aerial views, and for good reason – from above the castles invariably look far more arresting than they do from the ground, where it's never possible to see the complete layout of the complex, and where your own photos often have to be made from very narrow angles. Thirdly, the interiors of those castles which are open for visits never measure up to the exteriors, where the umbilical relationship of the water to the buildings plays such an essential role.

Offputting as all this sounds, it should be stressed that the best of the castles, which are described below, are very much worth visiting and offer the easiest access. It definitely pays to be well organised; that way you can hope to see several in a day, as it's unlikely you'll need more than a couple of hours at any single one. Although there's a comprehensive local bus service, the timetabling isn't ideal for castle-crawling. If you haven't a car, consider **hiring a bike**, available almost everywhere and at competitive

---

THE WASSERBURGEN

The *Wasserburgen* are so named because their most characteristic feature is a surrounding tract of water. This form was developed in the sixteenth century by local landlords for strongholds to protect their fiefdoms, and was necessitated by the lack of natural strategic points which more undulating countryside would provide; it superseded the earlier technique of building on artificial mounds, which had been rendered highly vulnerable by advances in gunpowder and firearms. A couple of centuries later, in more peaceful times, Baroque country houses were built in this countryside, some of them as replacements for their redundant predecessors, others completely new. These generally still included a moat, although now for aesthetic reasons only. **Voltaire** set the opening of his great satire *Candide* in one of these estates, lampooning the degenerate lifestyle of Baron Thunder-ten-tronckh and his 25-stone wife, and the intellectually bankrupt philosophy of the complacent tutor Dr Pangloss who convinced everyone they were living "in the most beautiful and delightful of all possible mansions, in this best of all possible worlds".

---

prices. The most convenient place to go is the *Gepäckabfertigung* at Münster Hauptbahnhof, which charges DM10 per day; this is halved if you're initially taking the bike on a train. Many other stations in the province offer the same deal, and plenty of private firms have daily rates of DM8 or less. A full list is published in the tourist office's *Gastgeberverzeichnis – Münsterland* brochure, a handy companion for touring the province. If you've a serious interest in the castles, this lists them all and tells you when and where you must write or phone in advance for an appointment. Münster itself is the obvious base to choose; you should be able to find a **room** for no more than DM35 per person in any of the smaller towns, but they're uniformly dull places come the evening. **Youth hostels** are unusually thin on the ground, and, like the more numerous campsites, are not in the best locations.

Around Münster

You don't need to venture far out of Münster for your first taste of these châteaux, as **Haus Rüschhaus** (guided tours every half-hour April–mid-Dec Tues–Sun 10am–12.30pm & 2.30–5pm; DM3) stands just beyond the end of the built-up area, and can be reached by bus #5. The present building was designed and built from 1745 to 1748 by **Johann Conrad Schlaun** as a summer house for himself. It's quite an eccentric little construction, mostly homely in feel, but with touches of Baroque swagger, as in the sloping roofline and the sweeping facade which in fact fronts a fully practical barn, integrated into the house as was the norm in traditional local farmsteads. The *Italian Room*, named after the capriccio scenes on the hand-made wallpaper from Paris, provides the only decorative note in the house. Originally Schlaun's bedroom, it was transformed to its present state by later owners, the family of Germany's leading nineteenth-century authoress, **Annette von Droste-Hülshoff**, who lived here for 20 years from 1826, during which time she produced much of her finest work. Best known for her charming poetic vignettes of nature, she spent the first three decades of her life in the original seat of her aristocratic family, **Haus Hülshoff** (March–Oct daily 9.30am–6pm; DM2 for park, DM2 for house). Bus #563/4 goes there from Münster, or you can walk from Rüschhaus in about half an hour by continuing straight ahead and turning left down the footpath just past the highway junction; don't follow the road, which adds a considerable distance to the journey. This castle is a classic example of the Renaissance *Wasserburg* design, the outer barrier (*Vorburg*) being a severe, low-lying building with square corner towers, the inner building (*Hauptburg*) an airy L-shaped dwelling in the Dutch style, to which a neo-Gothic chapel was added last century. There's also an attractive park, recently re-created after old designs. Whether it's worth the extra to see inside the *Hauptburg* is debatable; you're only allowed to visit a suite of six rooms, authentically furnished in the early nineteenth-century style familiar to the poetess.

Burgsteinfurt

The most varied castle in Münsterland is found in the town of **BURGSTEINFURT**, some 35km northwest of Münster, on the main railway line to GRONAU. It's still the home of the Dukes of Bentheim, who introduced the Calvinist faith to northern Germany; although the present incumbent is more generous with access than most private owners in the area, the organisation of visits has been left in the hands of a particularly feckless **tourist office** based at the former Rathaus. This bunch don't seem at all interested in individual visitors, and your best bet is to latch on to one of the many tour groups who are escorted round in the summer months. Obviously, it's sensible to phone ahead (☎02551/1231) to find out when these are, but be warned that the staff are uncooperative and that, without an appointment, all you can see is part of the exterior. That said, it's a fascinating building, with all manner of fragments from diverse periods surviving in a ramshackle way, the courtyard alone serving as an encyclopaedia of European architectural history. From the twelfth century comes a Romanesque double chapel, the lower of which remains in its simple original state, while the upper has been adapted according to Protestant tenets. On the left-hand side, a Renaissance wing was built, centred on a superb two-storey oriel window. To the south is the **Bagno**, a spacious public park laid out in the English manner, which offers good distant views of the castle.

Lembeck

LEMBECK, about 50km southwest of Burgsteinfurt, can be reached by train from there or Münster via COESFELD. The castle, set back from the village, is also still in private hands, but the fact that part of it is now a hotel means that access is easier than normal (guided tours daily mid-March to mid-Nov every hour 9am–5pm; DM3). In spite of the impressive severity of the exterior, conforming to the old *Wasserburg* design, it seems to be the first in the province to have been built more for pleasure than defence, a fact suggested by the exuberant helmets on the towers and by the very obvious vulnerability of the rear, connected by a small causeway to the gardens. Just to the east of Lembeck is the **Naturpark Hohe Mark**, a protected area of gently sloping forests, a veritable oasis in the midst of so much flatness.

Lüdinghausen

There's a choice of bus or train from Münster to **LÜDINGHAUSEN**, 30km south; the buses are better, as the railway route is circuitous and the Bahnhof a long way out. The moated castle named after the town itself has been too messed about down the years to be of much interest, but **Burg Vischering** at the northern boundary is the archetypal *Wasserburg*, as well as the only one wholly given over to tourism, being designated the **Münsterland Museum** (March–Oct Tues–Sun 8.30am–12.30pm & 2–5.30pm, Nov–Feb Tues–Sun 10am–12.30pm & 2–3.30pm; DM2). Its *Hauptburg*, horseshoe in shape, with a singular octagonal tower in the centre of the courtyard, was beautified around 1620 by the addition of the *Erker*, the abutting Renaissance section with an elegant oriel window. Directly facing this are the spreading branches of a trumpet tree, the most remarkable of several rare species planted in the grounds. As usual, the interiors are plain by comparison, but the *Rittersaal* with wooden beamed ceiling has been restored to good effect. There's an exhibition on life in the medieval castles of the region; other folklore displays, this time on the farms and the towns, are to be found in the *Vorburg*.

Nordkirchen

If you've only a day to spare on the castles, the best way to spend it is by combining a visit to Lüdinghausen and **NORDKIRCHEN**, 8km southeast. This redbrick giant is by far the largest and most spectacular of the group, a manifestation of the fantastic wealth of the **Plettenberg** dynasty of Prince-bishops who decided to replace their old fortress with a palace in the French manner. Every tourist brochure refers to it as the "Westphalian Versailles", a nickname it has had since its conception in 1703, when it referred to the older and much smaller palace at Versailles, on which Nordkirchen was directly modelled. Now, the comparison actually smacks of false modesty, as it's aesthetically far superior to the Sun King's overblown, megalomaniacal monstrosity.

The complex is on one island only (instead of the two normally required for a *Wasserburg*), and exhibits all the sense of order characteristic of the Age of Reason. It's almost completely symmetrical and is specially designed to produce a spectacular main vista, an effect achieved by breaking up the main block into sections and preceding them with long, narrow pavilions. Behind, there's a formal garden with Baroque sculptures. Nowadays, Nordkirchen belongs to the Land government, which has adapted it as a college for financial studies; consequently there's free access at all times, and what you can see from outside definitely justifies a visit. Official opportunities for viewing the **interior** aren't generous (guided tours Sat & Sun 2–5pm, usually on the hour; DM2). However, there are many private visits on weekdays throughout the summer, to which you're allowed to tag on; consult the list posted in the porter's office or, better still, phone ahead (☎02596/1001). The rooms are less grandiose than you might imagine from outside, but have the full pomp of the Baroque in their rich stucco-work, ceiling paintings, wood panelling and plentiful furnishings.

There are no buses out of Nordkirchen on Sundays, and only one on Saturday afternoons (to Lüdinghausen), which entails taking the 2pm tour. The nearest station, on a line with a very restricted weekend service, is at CAPPEL, 5km east. If you travel this way, you can also visit **Schloss Westerwinkel** (April–Oct Tues–Fri 2–5pm, Sat & Sun 2–6pm; DM3), situated a further 2km east. Although only a few years older than Lembeck, it's still Renaissance and strongly fortified, with a *Hauptburg* built on a square ground-plan; the interiors, however, reflect the tastes of the nineteenth-century owners.

Cappenberg

CAPPENBERG, 12km south of Nordkirchen, stands just outside the industrial town of LÜNEN, which marks the beginning of the Ruhrgebiet. There's been a **Schloss** here since the ninth century; the present building is Baroque, and for many years it was home to the art treasures of Dortmund. With the creation of a new museum in the city, it has been freed to host temporary exhibitions of various kinds (Tues–Sun 10am–5pm; free). Far more significant is the **Stiftskirche** directly in front, founded by the brothers **Gottfried** and **Otto von Cappenberg** in atonement for the part they had played in helping Lothair of Saxony sack the city of Münster in 1121, destroying most of the Dom in the process. Their confessor, Norbert von Xanten, suggested that a fit form of repentance would be the establishment of a German headquarters for the Premonstratensian order he had recently founded in France. The plain architecture favoured by these monks, Romanesque with later Gothic additions, gives no hint of the riches within, which include two of the supreme masterpieces of German medieval art. Displayed in a safe in the south transept is the stunning **head-reliquary of Frederick Barbarossa**, the oldest surviving portrait of a German emperor made from life. Actually intended to contain a relic of Saint John the Evangelist, it's probably the work of an Aachen goldsmith of about 1160. In the choir is the early fourteenth-century **founders' memorial**, depicting them as rather jolly youths with virtually identical features clasping a model of the church. At around the same time, a tomb was made for the now-canonised Gottfried; it's kept in the south transept. Other important works of art are the polychrome Romanesque triumphal cross and the elaborately carved Gothic stalls (each of the misericords is worth looking at). Below the castle complex is a private-owned **Wildpark** offering various nature trails. A further 2km on, actually within Lünen, is the artificial boating lake named **Cappenberger See**; there's a **youth hostel** (☎02306/53546) at Richard-Schirrmann-Weg on its northern shore.

Freckenhorst and Warendorf

FRECKENHORST, 25km east of Münster, also has an important Romanesque **Stiftskirche**. This time it's the architecture which is most striking, even if it's ruggedly impressive rather than beautiful. The massive solemn facade is particularly memorable, with two cylindrical corner towers huddling up against the great belfry. At the east end, a pair of square towers form a perfect counterpoint. In the crypt is the thirteenth-century **tomb of Geva**, a memorial to the woman who founded the original convent in the ninth century. The most important work of art is the **baptismal font**; the upper register is adorned with masterly carvings of scenes from the life of Christ, with fantastic animals below. On the walls around are paintings from a dismembered "Soft Style" retable of about 1430 by the **Master of Warendorf**.

Others from the same series can be seen in the Landesmuseum in Münster, but the central panel, a colourful *Calvary* surrounded by four other Passion scenes, remains in its original location, **St Laurentius** in **WARENDORF**, 3km north. This is a typical Westphalian hall church, which also has some fine sculptures, notably the three figures from the portal who have been moved just inside for protection, and the group of *St Peter, St Paul and a Canon* at the far end of the north aisle. The adjacent Markt is lined with old buildings, including the **Rathaus**, whose upper floors are open as a museum (Tues–Fri 3–5pm, Sat 10.30am–12.30pm, Sun 10.30am–12.30pm & 3–5pm; free).

Soest

About thirty minutes from Dortmund by train, **SOEST** was a city of similar importance at the time of the Hanseatic League. Nowadays it's a whole world away in spirit, never having expanded much beyond its walls, which survive minus their battlements, and it preserves a medieval air and layout. It ranks as one of Germany's most delightful towns, yet could so easily have been incorporated into the Ruhr conurbation. This proximity to the industrial heartland led to Soest being heavily bombed during the war, but restoration has been so deft that the scars have healed completely and there's scarcely a street within the fortifications which doesn't live up to the tourist board image of Romantic Germany. All the main buildings were constructed from a local sandstone whose deep lime greens bestow a distinctive character on the town and are well offset against the many red-roofed and whitewashed half-timbered houses. The play of light on these surfaces produces such magical effects it's little wonder that Soest has nurtured more than its fair share of German artists.

The town

Both the **Hauptbahnhof** and the **bus station** are located just outside the northern stretch of the city walls. Turn left from either along Bahnhofstrasse and then right into Wiesenstrasse; the twin spires of the Gothic **Wiesenkirche** (Our Lady of the Meadows) are straight ahead (summer 10am–12.30pm & 2.30–6pm ; winter 10am–noon & 2–4pm). This is a key building in German architectural history, when the favoured but problematic hall church design finally acquired an elegance to match any other style of building. Although only a parish church, it's a cathedral in miniature, with an interior nothing short of stupendous. Slender unadorned piers thrust effortlessly up to the lofty vault, and the walls seem to be made of nothing but dazzlingly brilliant stained glass. These were inserted over a period ranging from just after the church's construction in the fourteenth century to the early sixteenth century, when money ran out before the south side could be glazed. The masterpiece of this assemblage, placed over the north portal, is from the final period, showing *The Last Supper* with a Westphalian menu of beer, ham and rye bread. As a bonus, the church houses a richly varied collection of works of art, including three large triptychs.

The Hohnekirche

On higher ground to the rear stands the **Hohnekirche** (Our Lady on the Hill; summer 9.30am–noon & 1–5pm; winter 1–4pm only). The same Protestant congregation owns both this and the Wiesenkirche, taking refuge in the cosier surroundings of this squat, box-like structure for the winter months. It's a Romanesque attempt of about a century earlier at creating a hall church; the rather plain result was, however, greatly enlivened by a sumptuous fresco decoration, much of which has survived. Also here are a couple of fine works of art in the *Passion Altar* by the late fifteenth-century Westphalian painter known as the Master of Liesborn, and the remarkable *Scheibenkreuz*, a four-metre high triumphal cross from about 1200, adorned with delicate reliefs of the life of Christ.

The centre

The centre is soon reached from here by returning to Wiesenstrasse, continuing via an old water mill up Am Seel, where you'll find the **tourist office** (Mon and Wed–Fri 8.30am–12.30pm & 2.30–4.30pm, Tues 8.30am–12.30pm & 2.30–5.30pm, Sat 9.30am–noon; ☎02921/103323). Dominating the skyline here is the noble tower of St **Patrokli**, generally (if inaccurately) referred to as the **Dom**. This forms part of a resplendent Romanesque westwork, which is so grandiose a frontage that the rest of the building comes as an anticlimax, for all that it's a spacious and homogeneous construction. The upper gallery houses the **Dommuseum** (Sat 10.30am–12.30pm & 2–4pm, Sun 11.30am–12.30pm & 2–4pm; DM1.50), with the church treasure and some lovely stained glass, including precious twelfth-century examples.

Only a few yards in front stands the **Petrikirche** (Mon–Fri 9.30am–12.30pm & 2.30–6.30pm, Sat 10am–2pm), towering over the square of the same name which also contains the **Rathaus**, the only significant Baroque addition to the city. Again with a westwork as its most notable feature, the Petrikirche is Romanesque with the addition of a Gothic chancel. On the third piers of the nave are two *Crucifixion* frescos attributed to **Conrad von Soest**, a major figure of the fifteenth century, and one of the few early German masters known by name. An important painting definitely by this artist, *St Nicholas Enthroned with SS Catherine, Barbara and the two Johns*, occupies the altar of the tiny Romanesque **Nicolaikapelle**, situated behind the east end of St Patrokli. In spite of an unprepossessing exterior, the inside of the chapel is a real gem, another variation on the hall church theme, with rounded column shafts dividing the space into two equal aisles. It's generally locked (officially open 11am–noon on Tues, Wed, Fri & Sun, but hours not always adhered to); if so, ask for the key at the **Wilhelm-Morgner-Haus**, the local cultural centre based in a modern building directly in front (Mon–Sat 10am–noon & 3–5pm, Sun 10.30am–12.30pm; free). This is named after Soest's own Expressionist painter, whose short career overlapped with the presence in the city of two of the movement's leading lights, Christian Rohlfs and Emil Nolde. A number of Morgner's canvases can be seen on the first floor, revealing a versatile talent which was to end at the age of 26 on a Flanders battlefield.

The rest of town

From here, follow Ulricher Strasse southwards, turning left into Burghofstrasse. You shortly come to a complex of buildings, including a rare Romanesque house and the **Burghof**, a sixteenth-century mansion now housing the local history museum (Tues–Sat 10am–noon & 3–5pm, Sun 11am–1pm; DM1). The main feature is the *Festsaal* on the ground floor, whose walls are covered with white stuccowork; the Biblical subjects are original, the battle scenes and emperors skilful modern pastiches. Another small museum is housed in the **Osthofentor** (April–Sept Tues–Fri 2–4pm, Sat 11am–1pm, Sun 11am–1pm & 3–5pm; Oct–March Wed 2–4pm, Sun 11am–1pm; DM1), a stately Renaissance gateway which once formed the northeast entrance to the town, and a rare surviving adornment of the walls. The display here is mostly concerned with medieval warfare; what looks like a spectacular modern sculpture in the attic turns out to be a fancy arrangement of 25,000 crossbow bolts.

Practicalities

Although Soest has been spared the ruthless commercial exploitation of so many picturesque old German towns, it's not immune from tourism, particularly at the weekends, when day-trippers from the Ruhr stream in. One consequence of this is that there's a bewildering choice of **restaurants** – over a hundred in all, few of them especially cheap. For budget eating, the pizzerias offer good value; you'll find a couple on Brüderstrasse not far from the Hauptbahnhof. At the opposite end of the scale, *Pilgrim Haus* on Jacobistrasse is Westphalia's oldest inn, with an uninterrupted tradition from the early fourteenth century; though expensive, the food could hardly be bettered. Otherwise, many old-world **cafés** provide a relaxed atmosphere for coffee and cake; a good choice would be *Sauerland* on Filzenstrasse, which has been run by the same family for two centuries. However, the food you should on no account miss is Soest's own contribution to culinary history, the famed **pumpernickel**, a strongly-flavoured black rye bread popular throughout Germany at breakfast time. It's made by leavening the dough for 24 hours, then baking it for as long again, until the sugars in the rye turn dark. For the genuine article, go to *Wilhelm Haverland*; their factory on the Markt has been in operation since 1799, and you can choose from several different recipes in their side-street shop behind. There's no local beer, but you can't go wrong with the wide range of Dortmund and Sauerland brews on offer in the taverns. Soest's main **festival** is a colourful market held on All Saints' Day (1 Nov).

Accommodation

The **youth hostel**, Kaiser-Friedrich-Platz 2 (☎02921/16283), is just outside the southern section of the city wall. There's no **campsite**, but those around Möhnesee (see p.527) are just a few kilometres away and connected by regular bus services. **Hotel rooms** are almost invariably reasonable in price. Lowest rates are at *Lindenhof*, Niederbergheimer Str. 74 (☎02921/73551), southeast of the old city, from DM27, and *Zum Schwarzen Raben*, just south of the Dom at Ulricher Str. 15 (☎02921/16309), at DM28 per person.

The Sauerland

The **Sauerland** forms an extensive part of eastern Westphalia, stretching from the edge of the Ruhrgebiet across to the border with Lower Saxony. Literally translated, the name means "Bitter Land", though it's unclear whether this comes from the fierce Saxon tribes who once inhabited the region and put up a doughty resistance to Charlemagne, or from the poor soils and hostile, rugged terrain; there's also the possibility that the name is a simple corruption of "South Land". It's rural, upland country,

THE DAMBUSTERS

The importance of the Ruhr dams to the economy of the Third Reich was highlighted by the famous **"Dambusters"** episode of World War II (told in Paul Brickhill's book and in the popular film which, however, wasn't shot on location). At the time, these massive concrete structures would hardly have been grazed by existing explosives. In order to penetrate them, the inventor Barnes Wallis developed enormous ten ton bombs which skipped across the water surface like a pebble, sinking behind the defensive nets and lodging themselves against the weakest point of the dams' walls. These "bouncing bombs" were dropped with devastating effect by the Lancasters of 617 Squadron, commanded by Wing Commander Guy Gibson, on 17 May 1943. Such havoc was caused by the ensuing flooding, which destroyed 123 factories, 25 bridges and 3000 hectares of arable land, that it was estimated to have taken the equivalent of several months' work by 100,000 men to repair the damage – a telling blow to the whole Nazi war effort and a major propaganda coup. This, at any rate, is how the evidence has traditionally been presented: latest research suggests that the claims were exaggerated, and that the Möhne dam, far from being wrecked, was eventually repaired. Fifty-six members of 617 Squadron were killed in the raid– "If only I'd known," Barnes Wallis said when he discovered the RAF losses, "I'd never have started this."

supposedly containing a thousand mountains; nowadays it serves as an obvious holiday and recreation area for the teeming millions who live in the nearby cities of the Rhine-Ruhr conurbation. The Sauerland's attractions are quintessentially German – above all, it's good **hiking** country, with nearly 12,000km of marked footpaths, and four national parks fall wholly or largely within its boundaries. Dotted with rivers and artificial lakes, it's also one of the country's main centres for **angling** and more strenuous **activity holidays**, such as surfing, rowing, canoeing, sailing and hang-gliding, while riding in covered wagons Wild-West style has also been made into a regional speciality. Much of the Sauerland is of a surprisingly Alpine character for a place so far north, and **winter sports** help to keep its tourist trade going all year round.

On the surface, the Sauerland is the mirror opposite of the Ruhrgebiet. However, though there are no major cities, there are many medium-sized industrial towns. **Beer** is a leading product – the soft local spring water is a crucial ingredient; as a result, many aficionados rate Sauerland brews superior even to those of nearby Dortmund. *Warsteiner*, dubbed "the queen of beers" for its delicate taste, is currently being heavily promoted abroad; *Veltins* is popular throughout Germany, while *Iserlohner* and *Hirsch* are also very fine. Sauerland water, moreover, plays a key role in the economy of the Ruhrgebiet, and the great **dams** of the region are key features of the German inland waterway system.

Some practicalities

The Germans have kept the Sauerland largely to themselves, and it's fairly easy to see why. Such towns as exist are by no means outstanding, and they're all short on major sights. The scenery may be consistently impressive, but it lacks the legendary associations of the Rhine, the grandeur of the Bavarian Alps or the distinctiveness of the Black Forest. Nonetheless, the area makes a good choice if you want to escape the obvious destinations for a while. It's also easy on the budget, as you don't need to look far for cheap **accommodation** – campsites and youth hostels are peppered all over the district, while private houses with rooms to let at around DM20 are legion; there are also many farmhouses offering inclusive deals at bargain rates. If you're attracted to the region, get hold of the free annual tourist board publication *Gastgeberverzeichnis – Sauerland* which has exhaustive listings on all forms of lodgings, plus full details of sports and activities.

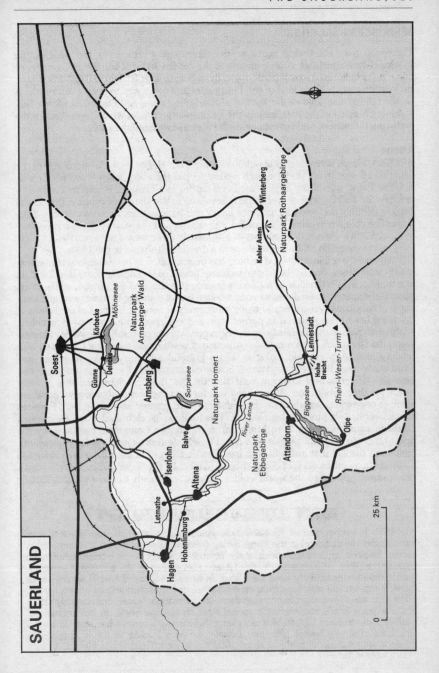

Märkisches Sauerland

There are four constituent parts to the Sauerland. Furthest to the west is the **Märkisches Sauerland**, corresponding to the old Duchy of Mark. This is sometimes taken to include Hagen itself; more logically, it begins with HOHENLIMBURG, where the continuously built-up land of the Ruhrgebiet first gives way to open countryside. A scenic railway line follows the course of the River Lenne and continues all the way south to Siegen. On the east bank is the Lennegebirge range, which forms part of the **Naturpark Homert**; to the west begins the **Naturpark Ebbegebirge**.

Altena

ALTENA, which is reached in about 30 minutes from Hagen, is the obvious star of the Sauerland towns, thanks to its superb setting deep in the valley, high above which is its massive **Burg**, one of the largest medieval castles in Germany. Begun in the twelfth century, the buildings were erected at intervals up to the sixteenth century; the central keep is strongly protected by an outer bailey and no less than three consecutive gateways. The complex inevitably crumbled with disuse, and there were plans last century to rebuild it in a phoney Romantic style. Fortunately these were f never carried out, and the present condition of the castle is due to a drastic restoration in the 1900s.

Schirrmann's original hostel (see box) has been ossified as one of several **museums** in the castle (Tues–Sun 9.30am–5pm; inclusive ticket DM3). The day room is in the style of a traditional Westphalian farmstead; adjoining it is the area for groups, while downstairs is the spartan main dorm, its solid wooden bunks standing in triple tiers, and looking as if they could yet withstand many more years of service. Several of the rooms in the Burg have been restored in period style and equipped with impressive furniture. Highlights include the *Stadthalle* by the entrance, with its carved Renaissance chimneypiece; the Great Hall, with a notable collection of pewter; and the chapel, adorned with retables from Antwerp and Cologne, and a graceful fifteenth-century *Madonna and Child* made from Bamberg sandstone. Scattered throughout the rooms are important examples of **arms and armour**, reflecting the fact that the Sauerland was a major centre for their production. Altena itself was for long the world's leading wire-making town; so prestigious was this that the craftsmen were granted exemption from Prussian military service – a rare privilege indeed. This tradition is celebrated in the **Deutsches Drahtmuseum** (German Wire Museum) in the former Commander's House by the ticket office; to be frank neither this nor the **Schmiedemuseum** (Smithy Museum), honouring the fact that iron smelting has been carried out in the Altena area since the ninth century, offers very exciting subject matter. In the outer bailey there's what's rather cheatingly called the world's oldest functioning **youth hostel** (☎02352/23522);

THE BIRTH OF YOUTH HOSTELLING

In 1909, a teacher named **Richard Schirrmann** established the world's first ever permanent **youth hostel** in the Burg, having previously operated from a schoolroom in town. Inspired by the simple idea of the need to provide low-cost accommodation for young travellers, Schirrmann's choice of Altena is explained by the fact that the countryside around is particularly good for hiking. In time, hundreds of hostels sprang up all over Germany, and have long been an established and important feature of national life. The idea was slow in catching on elsewhere (an international federation was only set up twenty years later), but eventually spread right around the world, to the gratitude of millions of travellers, not all of them young. Schirrmann's reward has been to have a plethora of streets named after him (usually the ones leading to the local hostel) – indeed, he's commemorated just as prolifically in western Germany as Marx and Lenin once were in the GDR.

its location makes it the most attractive place to stay in town, but there are only forty beds and it's regularly full. Another, much larger hostel is at Linscheider Bach 2 (☎02352/22815) at the extreme northern end of town, but note that there's no campsite and hotels are, by regional standards, relatively expensive.

Iserlohn

ISERLOHN, the Sauerland's largest town, can be reached circuitously from Altena by either bus or train, but it's more fun to take the direct 9km path over the hills. Still a centre of the iron industry, Iserlohn has a couple of moderately interesting churches, both with carved altars – Gothic **St Marien**, dominating the town from its hill, and the Romanesque **Bauernkirche**. Beside the latter is the **Heimat Museum** (Tues, Wed & Fri–Sun 10am–5pm, Thur 10am–7pm; DM1), housed in a ritzy Baroque mansion. The main attraction, however, is the **Dechenhöhle** in the outlying village of LETHMATHE, arguably the most outstanding of several **stalactite caves** in the Sauerland (daily guided tours lasting 45 minutes, April–Oct 9am–5pm, Nov–March 10am–4pm; DM4). Discovered last century when the railway line was being constructed, the geological formations are reckoned to be anything from 300 to 350 million years old. Inevitably, the chambers have been given nicknames according to the shapes they supposedly resemble; particularly impressive are the *Palm Tree Grotto*, with its single, tapering stem, and the *Kronleuchter*, so called for looking like an abstract version of the famous Romanesque crown-shaped chandeliers in Aachen, Hildesheim and Comburg.

Nordsauerland

Soest is sometimes counted as part of the **Nordsauerland**, an area centred on a 10km-long artificial lake, the **Möhnesee**. The northern bank has been developed as a holiday resort area for angling and watersports, and there are **campsites** all along this shore. **Cruises** depart from GÜNNE, DELECKE and KÖRBECKE from April to October. Between these first two villages is the famous **dam** which, though not the largest, was the prime target of the "Dambusters", due to its proximity to the industrial centres. Controlling the flow of the River Heve into the River Ruhr, it's 650 metres long and 40 metres high; when it was breached, 134 million tons of water gushed out into the countryside. Now long repaired, it's one of four footbridges interspersed at fairly regular intervals allowing you to cross over to the opposite bank of the lake. This has been left in its natural state, and a southerly arm, the **Hevesee**, is a protected area for birdlife. The **youth hostel** (☎02924/305) lies directly across from Körbecke. Immediately beyond is the beginning of the **Arnsberg Forest**, an upland *Naturpark* of beech, birch and larch, which stretches for some 30km east to west, and up to 15km north to south.

Hochsauerland

The **Hochsauerland** is much the largest of the four districts, beginning immediately beyond the Arnsberg Forest and continuing east to the boundary with Lower Saxony and south to the Siegerland. ARNSBERG itself is traditionally considered the "capital" of the Sauerland, and is the administrative centre for the whole region. It's built on a spur of land on a bend of the River Ruhr, rising neatly upwards in tiers. To the north are the ruins of the **Schlossberg**, scene of a two-day festival in late May or early June. The southern part of the old town is dominated by the **Propsteikirche**, a Gothic church with rich Baroque furnishings, beside which stands the ornate **Hirschberger Tor**, a rare example of north German Rococo. Numerous half-timbered houses line the streets of the town, while the **Sauerland Museum** (Tues–Sat 9.30am–5pm, Sun 9.30am–1pm; free) occupies the Renaissance **Landberger Hof**. There's a **youth hostel** at Rumbecker Höhe 1 (☎02931/10627) on the east side of town, by the Arnsberg Forest.

The **Sorpesee**, another artificial lake, lies 10km to the south. Again, it's a centre for angling and watersports; cruises run from May to September, departing from LANGSCHEID on the northern shore. There are a string of **campsites** and a **youth hostel** (☎02935/1776) on the western bank, which is actually very close to Balve in Märkisches Sauerland. To the east and south of here is the bulk of the aforementioned **Naturpark Homert**; apart from its numerous trails, it's a good area for birdwatching, with some 450 resident species.

Further south is the **Naturpark Rothaargebirge** (Red-Haired Mountains), a range covered with conifers and deciduous woods, which separates the Sauerland from the Siegerland to the south. It's best known as winter sports country; the main resort, **WINTERBERG**, can be reached by train from Arnsberg via a branch line from BESTWIG. As well as the *pistes*, Winterberg has an indoor skating rink, and bobsleigh and toboggan runs, while international dog-sleigh races are held each January. The town stands at the foot of the **Kahler Asten**, which at 841 metres is the highest peak in the Sauerland; it's covered with snow for about a third of the year, and the average winter temperature is freezing point. You can ascend to a belvedere for a huge, if not particularly inspiring, panorama of the district. There's a **youth hostel** not far from the mountain in ASTENBERG (☎02981/2289); Winterberg itself has an abundant choice of **rooms** in private houses at only marginally higher rates.

Südsauerland

The heart of the **Südsauerland** is the largest of the reservoirs, the appropriately named **Biggesee**, which lies below the Ebbegebirge range. A branch of the main Hagen–Siegen railway runs from FINNETROP down the western bank of the lake. **ATTENDORN**, on the northern shore, is an old Hanseatic town. Its fourteenth-century **Rathaus**, apart from being the only secular structure of its period in the entire region, is a striking building, with elaborate gables on both its short ends, and an open lower storey which was intended to serve as a market hall. The upstairs rooms now house the **Heimatmuseum** (Tues–Fri 9am–1pm & 3–5pm, Sat 9am–1pm, Sun 11am–1pm; DM1), which contains a notable collection of pewter figures. **St Johannes** is a four-teenth-century Gothic hall church incorporating the tower of its Romanesque predecessor. It's nicknamed the "cathedral of the Sauerland" due to its pre-eminence among the region's churches. Just to the north of town is the **Attahöhle** (daily April–Oct 9am–5pm, Nov–March 10am–4pm; DM4), a particularly impressive stalactite cave. To the east is **Burg Schnellenberg**, the largest of the few surviving hilltop castles in Westphalia. Part of it has been rebuilt as a luxury hotel, but a section has been preserved as a **museum** with a collection of weapons (April–Oct Tues–Sun 10am–5pm; DM1).

There are two **campsites** just outside town, and there's a **youth hostel** at Heldener Str. 5 (☎02722/2455). **Festivals** include the best Carnival celebrations in the Sauerland, and various parades during Holy Week, while the first Saturday in August sees *Der Biggesee in Flammen* (The Biggesee in Flames), with fireworks and illuminations. **Cruises** are run on the lake between Easter and mid-October from both Attendorn and **OLPE**, the highly developed watersports resort on the southern bank. There are three **campsites** in the latter's surrounding area, plus a **youth hostel** in nearby STADE (☎02761/6775).

LENNESTADT, on the main Hagen–Siegen line almost due east of Attendorn, lies at the junction of the *Naturparks* Homert, Ebbegebirge and Rothaargebirge. South of the town, a minor road leads shortly to the **Hohe Bracht**, at 584 metres the finest vantage-point in the Südsauerland, commanding a sweeping view from its belvedere tower over the three ranges as far as Kahler Asten. An alternative for a broadly similar panoramic view is the **Rhein-Weser-Turm**, some 12km southeast of Lennestadt.

Siegen and the Siegerland

The Rothaargebirge range provides a horizontal dividing line separating the Sauerland from the **Siegerland** to the south. This region is a somewhat bizarre mixture of a heavily industrialised valley (in many respects similar to South Wales) and a holiday resort area which, even more than the Sauerland, the Germans have reserved for themselves. It's a land of hills and mountains, cut right across the middle by the River Sieg which flows due westwards, entering the Rhine just north of Bonn.

Siegen

SIEGEN is the capital of this district and the only place within a radius of about 100km which can properly be called a city. Iron and steel production were the reasons for its development last century; relative isolation meant that its growth was checked, and even now its population is barely over 100,000. One of Siegen's main assets is its setting, rising from the banks of the river high into the hills above; this has recently been enhanced by the construction of a spectacular **viaduct** (the biggest in the country) which carries the A45 autobahn – linking the Ruhrgebiet with Hessen – 104m above the Sieg.

THE HOUSE OF NASSAU-SIEGEN

Before industrialisation, Siegen was chiefly associated with the fortunes of the **House of Nassau-Siegen**, a line founded in the late thirteenth century by the local count, Otto I. In 1530, the name was changed to **Oranien-Nassau**, following intermarriage with an aristocratic family from Orange in Provence. Subsequently, this dynasty had a profound impact on the course of Northern European history, thanks to the acquisition of land in the Low Countries. **William the Silent** (1533–84), who was born in nearby Dillenberg, was the creator of the modern Dutch state, driving out the occupying Spanish forces and establishing a new Protestant and mercantile power. Later luminaries included Johann Moritz, the seventeenth-century governor of Brazil and another William (1650–1702), who became King of Great Britain and was to play such a prominent part in Irish history that he continues to inflame folk memories to this day.

Siegen's castles – and their history

A curiosity of Siegen is that it has two castles originally belonging to the Nassau-Siegen/Oranien-Nassau family, one at the top of the town, the other a few hundred metres below. This is due to the fact that the line split in 1623 over continued support for the Reformation; thereafter, the Catholic branch lived in the **Oberes Schloss**. The original fortified Burg has been much modified down the centuries and isn't particularly picturesque, but its ramparts command the best views over the town, while the gardens, in honour of the Dutch connection, are planted with 60,000 tulips. Part of the building has been adapted to house the **Siegerland Museum** (Tues–Sun 10am–12.30pm & 2–5pm; DM3). This contains varied collections, including a realistic model of a mine 14 metres under the courtyard. There's also a display of memorabilia on the **Busch** brothers, a remarkable twentieth-century Siegen family whose anti-Nazism gave further impetus to their international careers. Adolf and Hermann founded the Busch Quartet with two friends; their 78rpm recordings, particularly of Beethoven, have never been surpassed in terms of interpretation, and many can still be bought in modern remasterings. They also blazed a pioneering trail by championing the playing of Baroque music by authentic-sized chamber groups, instead of in the souped-up arrangements which had been the norm for the previous century. Fritz Busch was a

IR PETER PAUL RUBENS (1577-1640)

Sir Peter Paul Rubens' father Jan, a Calvinist sympathiser, was forced to flee his native Antwerp, settling in Cologne, where he entered the service of Princess Anna of Saxony, second wife of William the Silent. Eventually he graduated from being her adviser and diplomatic agent to sharing her bed when her husband was at war. An untimely pregnancy led to his unmasking; lucky to escape with his life, he was banished to Siegen, where the great painter was born in 1577. A year later, the family was allowed to return to Cologne; after Jan Rubens' death, they went back to Antwerp. Not only was the young artist quickly reconciled with Roman Catholicism, he was later one of the most ardent propagandists of the Counter-Reformation; he further went against his father in becoming a faithful diplomatic servant of the Spanish imperial power. A man who was almost indecently successful (he ran the equivalent of a picture factory, which churned out canvases by the hundred, all bearing the master's characteristic stamp even when he had contributed little to their actual execution), Rubens was an incorrigible social climber, a grovelling toady to all political and spiritual authority. This stance is clearly seen in his paintings, as is his chauvinistic attitude to women, whom he eyed lustfully as fodder for his insatiable sexual appetite. Yet it's a measure of his greatness as an artist that these offputting opinions don't seem to matter – his works can be enjoyed for their phenomenal technical skill, carefully planned design, glorious colours and unabashed *joie de vivre*.

leading conductor who was prominent in the establishment of opera at Glyndebourne, which has become a key feature of the summer season for London high society, while Willi was one of Germany's best actors.

However, the museum's main draw is its display on the art of **Peter Paul Rubens** (see above) who, by a sheer fluke, can be counted a native of Siegen, though he was in no sense a German. His qualities are all present in a late masterpiece here: somewhat pompously named *The Victorious Hero Seizes the Opportunity for Peace*, it's an allegory featuring Perseus with the head of Medusa, Minerva, Abundance, Opportunity and Time. From a decade earlier, *Roman Charity* illustrates the legend of Cimon, who was saved from starving to death in prison by being breast-fed by his daughter Pero. There's also a haughty *Self-Portrait* from about the same time, and five more original works.

The **Unteres Schloss**, the seat of the Protestant line, originally occupied an abandoned Franciscan monastery. This was destroyed by fire in 1695 and replaced by the present extensive Baroque complex. It's now largely occupied by offices, but the royal crypt has survived. Between the two castles is the Markt, with the eighteenth-century Rathaus and the **Nikolaikirche**, one of the most distinctive of the extravagant series of late Romanesque churches founded in the Rhineland and around. The kernel of the building is a thirteenth-century galleried hexagon – the only example of this design in Northern Europe. Two centuries later, the handsome red and white tower was added, forming a highly successful complement. Inside is a baptismal plate made in Peru, a legacy of the time when the Oranien-Nassau family, who used the Nikolaikirche as their court chapel, were playing an important role in the colonisation of South America. Lower down the hill is the **Martinikirche**, the unremarkable late Gothic successor to one of the most important Ottonian churches in Germany, from which the mosaic pavement has been preserved.

Practicalities

The **tourist office** (Mon–Fri 9am–1pm & 2–6pm, Sat 9am–noon; ☎0271/593517) is located immediately in front of the **Hauptbahnhof**. To reach the Altstadt from here, walk right through the pedestrian precinct and turn left uphill at the end.

Mitfahrzentrale have an office at Freudenberger Str. 15 (☎0271/54083). There's a **youth hostel** at Am Alten Friedhof 1 (☎0271/52215) within the grounds of the Upper Schloss. Cheapest **hotel**, charging DM25 per person, is *Schäfer*, Rosterstr. 111 (☎0271/334222), while DM28 is the going rate at the following: *Gasthof Rörig*, Eintrachtstr. 9 (☎0271/332484); *Gasthof Meier*, St-Johann-Str. 3 (☎0271/332609); and *Laterne*, Löhrstr. 37 (☎0271/57034). The last named, occupying one of the few surviving half-timbered houses in Siegen, has one of the best **restaurants** in town; there are several rather more inexpensive places to eat and drink on the same street, which dips downwards from the Markt. Local **beers** have the advantage of using the clear, pure mountain water of the Siegerland; *Krombacher* is well known throughout Germany, whereas consumption of *Irle*, which is no less fine, is confined mainly to this district. In the lower part of town, on Koblenzerstrasse, is the *Siegerlanderhalle*, the venue for **concerts** of all kinds.

The Siegerland

FREUDENBERG, 11km northwest of Siegen, to which it's linked by regular bus services, is an archetypal picture-postcard town which seems to feature on just about every German calendar. In 1540 the town, then less than a century old, was destroyed by fire; the streets built thereafter as replacements have survived almost intact – row upon row of black and white half-timbered houses, whose steeply pitched slate roofs bear witness to the harshness of the winter climate. It's a popular recreation resort all year round, and there are plenty of pensions where it's possible to stay for as little as DM20 per person – try along Oranienstrasse, the most impressive street of all.

There's also a string of holiday centres on the slow but striking railway line skirting the Rothaargebirge, linking Siegen with **FRANKENBERG** in Hessen. Snow can fall early in the winter – often before it arrives in the Alps – whereupon the towns are besieged by skiing parties. **BAD BERLEBURG** is the best-known resort, its spa facilities giving it a balancing pull in summer; it also has one of the few large-scale historical monuments in the region in its Baroque **Schloss** (guided tours daily at 10.30am & 2.30pm; DM2.50). Closer to Siegen are HILCHENBACH and ERNDTEBRÜCK; from the latter a different railway line leads to **BAD LAASPHE**, another spa with half-timbered buildings reminiscent of Freudenberg. All resorts have good hiking possibilities, while accommodation is both plentiful and cheap.

Paderborn

The cathedral and market city of **PADERBORN** lies some 55km northeast of Soest, just before the North German plain gives way to the Teutoburg Forest. It's a characterful place with a variety of archaeological and artistic attractions to add to the geological curiosity from which it derives its name, meaning "source of the Pader". This, the country's shortest river at a mere four kilometres in length, rises in a park in the heart of the city. It's formed by the surfacing of more than 200 warm springs, which pour out over 5000 litres of water per second. These originate as subterranean streams in the **Eggegebirge** range to the east; they're suddenly forced out into the open at this point by the abrupt change in topography from the plateau to a lowland whose soil contains an impermeable layer of marl. Although the visual impact is less startling than might be supposed, the park is an idyllic spot and makes the obvious place to begin your tour, offering as it does the best view of the city's two main churches – the twin-towered former **Abdinghof** monastery in the foreground, with the massive single steeple of the **Dom** rearing up behind.

CHARLEMAGNE IN PADERBORN

Paderborn was first brought to prominence in the eighth century by that great lover of hot springs, **Charlemagne**. He established a royal seat, which became a base both for his first parliaments and for his campaigns against the Saxons. In 799, Pope Leo III, having narrowly escaped an assassination attempt, visited the emperor here; the alliance subsequently forged led to the foundation of the Holy Roman Empire and Charlemagne's coronation in Rome the following year. This was to prove an event of major significance in European history, giving the papacy a new, less overtly political role, and defining the basic power structure for German internal affairs which was to last for the next millennium.

The city

During postwar rebuilding of the city, the foundations of the **Carolingian Kaiserpfalz**, the site of these momentous meetings, were discovered just to the north of the Dom; they had been hidden from view since a fire destroyed the building in the year 1000. Soon it became the most exciting archaeological site in the country, and was excavated in the 1960s, revealing the ground plan of a sizeable complex which included a King's Hall, a church, a monastery and courtyards. Also unearthed was an open-air throne, now under cover beneath the Dom's north portal; you can see it by peering in through the protective glass. To the rear was found the replacement **Ottonian Kaiserpfalz** (Tues–Sun 10am–5pm; DM1), dating from immediately after the 1000 fire and itself desecrated by another fire in 1165. This time the controversial decision was taken to go beyond a routine excavation, and to try and recreate its original form in as scholarly a manner as possible. In 1976 the palace made its belated reappearance, its pristine stonework making an odd contrast with the venerable status of the design. It now houses the regional archaeology museum, but interest centres on the structure itself, as no original palaces from this epoch survive. You pass through a subsidiary building to the vestibule; to the right is the two-storey Ikenbergkapelle, while to the left is the Great Hall, which takes up the lion's share of the complex. Standing on its own near the entrance is the only authentic remnant of the palaces, the tiny **Bartholomäuskapelle**. Surviving documents relate that it was built in 1017 by Greek workmen, although it is more likely that these visitors were Byzantine masons from Italy. As the very first hall church erected in Germany, it can claim to be the initiator of what was to become the pre-eminent national architectural form. Despite a glum exterior, it's very dapper inside, a classically inspired design of three aisles of rounded pillars crowned with flowery Corinthian capitals.

The Dom

In preparation for Pope Leo's visit, Charlemagne ordered the construction of a no-expense-spared church which was almost immediately raised to the status of a cathedral; ever since, the city's history has been dominated by its ecclesiastical role. The present **Dom** is a cavernous and somewhat monotonous thirteenth-century Gothic hall church whose tower, slit by innumerable little windows, is a remnant of its Romanesque predecessor. It's entered by the southern porch (or "Paradise") whose portal is adorned with French-style figures. More refined carvings from a now vanished doorway can be seen on either side of the transept window; look out for the cartoon-like fables – a boar blowing a horn, a hare playing the fiddle, a crane removing a bone from a wolf's throat, and a fox dressed as a scholar to receive his diploma. Inside, the Dom resembles a museum of seventeenth-century heroic sculpture to the glory of the Prince-bishops, much of it by one of Germany's few Mannerists, **Heinrich Gröninger**. His masterpiece, almost facing you on entry, is the grandiose *Monument to Dietrich* *von Fürstenberg*, complete with depictions of the buildings this bishop commissioned to transform the face of the city. The Dom's most enduring attraction returns to the animal theme and comes in the form of a puzzle, which you should try to work out in advance. Follow the signs marked *Hasenfenster* into the cloister garden; the tracery of one of the windows is the emblem of Paderborn, and a mason's trick which was celebrated in its day. This shows three hares running around in a circle, but although each clearly has two ears of his own, it has only been necessary to carve one per creature.

The Markt

The south side of the Dom faces the open space of the vast Markt, lined with tall Baroque houses and the Romanesque **Gaukirche**. In this setting, the lead-plated glass palace which houses a couple of shops, a café and the **Diözesanmuseum** (Tues–Sun 10am–5pm; DM1) creates a strident impact, the more so as it masks some of the wonderful views of the Dom. This brash modernist intrusion into the old city clearly had its supporters, as its architect was Gottfried Böhm, who immediately afterwards was asked to rebuild the Ottonian Kaiserpfalz. The interior, rising abruptly in tiers, is a cleverly thought out design to provide a majestic setting for the museum. In the basement, the **Schatzkammer's** most valuable pieces are two inlaid reliquary cabinets, made for the Dom and the Abinghof in about 1100, and the Baroque shrine of Paderborn's patron, Saint Liborius. The Dom's old bells are invitingly displayed with hammers, allowing you to indulge in a bit of instant campanology. Most of the collection exhibited upstairs is junk, but pride of place at the summit is rightly given to the *Imad Madonna*, a hierarchic mid-eleventh-century wooden statue named after its bishop donor.

The rest of the city

The remaining sights can be covered by means of a short circular walk. Following Schildern at the southwest corner of the Markt, you come to the city's most handsome building, the **Rathaus**, bedecked with arcades, gables and oriel windows, and fronted by a zappy facade. Erected in the early seventeenth century in the Weser Renaissance style, it was modelled on the patrician **Heisingsches Haus** just down the street. The top storey contains a small natural history museum (Tues–Sun 10am–6pm; free), focusing principally on the region's ornithology. Up the hill from here is the **Jesuitenkolleg** from the end of the same century, whose church, like the one in Cologne, has a vast galleried interior with anachronistic Gothic pointed arches.

Further along Kamp is the sober **Dalheimer Hof** by the Westphalian Baroque architect, Johann Conrad Schlaun. Going back downhill along Kesselerstrasse, you see the Romanesque **Busdorfkirche**, whose main joy is its tiny cloister. A couple of minutes' walk down Heierstrasse, then left into Thisaut, is the oldest remaining half-timbered house, **Adam-und-Eva-Haus**, now the local museum (Tues–Sun 10am–6pm; free). The most eye-catching exhibits are a couple of exquisite drawings of the city by Schlaun, and a display of engravings by **Heinrich Aldegraver**, a native of Paderborn who was one of Dürer's most faithful followers. From here, the Dom is back in view and only a few minutes' walk away.

Practicalities

The **Hauptbahnhof** is southwest of the centre; turn right at the exit and keep going straight. En route to the Markt you'll pass the **tourist office** on Marienplatz (Mon–Fri 9am–6pm, Sat 9am–1pm; ☎05251/26461). For once, the **youth hostel** is conveniently sited just a few minutes' walk from the main attractions at Meinwerkstr. 16 (☎05251/22055), the continuation of Heierstrasse. Most **hotel rooms** are reasonably priced; among the cheapest are *Hubertushof*, Hubertusweg 51 (☎05251/4463), and *Bürgerkrug*, Detmolder Str. 394 (☎05251/4254), both upwards of DM27 per person. The two **camp-**

sites are both in the northern outreaches of the city – *Am Waldsee* at Husarenstr. 130 (☎05251/7372) and *Stauterrassen* at Auf der Thune 14 (☎05251/4504). The tourist office publishes a free monthly programme of **events**, *Paderborn von Tag zu Tag*. Pubs offering **live music** are *Tuba*, Kasseler Str. 26, *Das Treibhaus*, Detmolder Str. 21, and *Kukoz*, Tegelweg 3–5. Concerts, musicals, dance, opera and jazz make up the varied fare at the ultra-modern *PaderHalle* on Maspernplatz. Pick of the **cinemas** is *Studio*, Westernstr. 34, which frequently features films in English. The main **popular festivals** occur in July, including a *Schützenfest* on the second weekend. There's also a beer week in October. Best place **to eat** is the *Ratskeller* in the Rathaus.

Bielefeld

BIELEFELD, some 35km north of Paderborn, clusters around the narrow middle strip of the Teutoburg Forest. It's strongly reminiscent of the cities of the Ruhrgebiet in history, feel and appearance, and is the overwhelmingly dominant economic centre of eastern Westphalia. Founded in the thirteenth century by the Counts of Ravensberg, the town gained prosperity in the late Middle Ages through the linen trade. The nineteenth century saw a mushroom growth, due to the increased importance of this traditional industry, plus various new engineering products associated with it. Development was facilitated by the fact that nearby Minden, with a far more favourable geographical location, was emasculated by its role as a garrison town.

The city

The **Hauptbahnhof** is to the north of the city centre; directly opposite is the **tourist office** (Mon–Fri 9am–6pm, Sat 9am–1pm; ☎0521/178844). From here, continue straight ahead down Bahnhofstrasse to Jahnplatz; this takes you on to the ring road, which encloses the modestly-sized Altstadt. Continuing down Niederwall, you come to the **Rathaus**, an ugly imitative monstrosity from the beginning of this century which contains another tourist office (same times Mon–Fri only; ☎0521/178899); next door, and built simultaneously, is the luxuriant Jugendstil **Stadttheater**, the city's main venue for opera and drama.

At the end of this road, Spiegelstrasse leads up towards the **Sparrenburg**, built between 1240 and 1250 as the seat of the Counts of Ravensberg. It's on the edge of the Teutoburg Forest, which runs right through the modern built-up area. Heavily restored, the castle has the twin attractions of a round tower which can be ascended for a panoramic view, and some 300 metres of underground passageways and dungeons (March–Nov Tues–Sun 9am–1pm & 2–6pm; combined ticket DM2). In the courtyard is a statue to Margrave Friedrich Wilhelm of Brandenburg, the man who established Bielefeld's prosperity by introducing the *Leinenlegge*, a quality control for linen.

Below the Sparrenburg to the north is the so-called "new town", grouped around the **Neustädter Marienkirche**, a handsome Gothic church built in the late thirteenth and early fourteenth centuries, and now standing, much in the manner of an English cathedral, in splendid isolation on a green. Its tall twin towers are crowned by unusually long and sharply pointed lead steeples; they look so venerable it's hard to believe they were devastated in an air-raid and had to be rebuilt almost from scratch.

The church, which contains outstanding **works of art**, is unfortunately kept locked; ring at the door of the halls directly in front for the caretaker. On the high altar is a masterpiece by the same Westphalian "Soft Style" artist who painted the *Berswordt Altar* in Dortmund. It shows the *Madonna and Child with Saints*, surrounded by a dozen small panels, mostly of scenes from Christ's life; the wings were cut up and sold last century, and are now in museums all over the world. A major but nameless fourteenth-century sculptor (whose works can also be seen in Cappenberg and Marburg) carved the frieze of apostles above the altar, which belonged to the former rood screen. He also created the magnificent *tomb of Otto III von Ravensberg and Hedwig von Lippe*, featuring a touching yet unsentimental portrayal of their previously deceased son. The other elaborate Ravensberg family monument is clearly modelled on this tomb, even though it was made over a century later.

On nearby Artur-Ladebeck-Strasse is the smooth red sandstone pile of the **Kunsthalle** (Tues, Wed, Fri & Sun 11am–6pm, Thurs 11am–9pm, Sat 10am–6pm; DM2.50, Fri free). The building itself, erected in the 1960s, was intended to be a signifi-cant addition to the city's heritage; it was designed by **Philip Johnson**, Mies van der Rohe's principal American follower, who was himself one of the leading lights in propa-gating the International Style in architecture. This implantation of an overtly New World building has been greeted with a fair amount of critical derision, but the authori-ties are convinced of the long-term wisdom of their choice. The collections, worth seeing if you're in town but not special enough to justify a detour, are typical of current German taste. Most of the Expressionists are represented, with good examples of Beckmann, Kirchner, Nolde and Macke; there are sculptures by Rodin, Barlach, Archipenko, Lipchitz, Caro and Moore (some inside, others in the garden), and several rooms of European and American abstract painting.

What remains of the Altstadt is just a short walk from the Kunsthalle – turn right into Obernstrasse at the end of Artur-Ladebeck-Strasse. The Markt is lined by the patri-cian houses originally built by the most prosperous linen merchants. Oldest is the late Gothic **Crüwell House** of 1530; the others are in the cheerful Weser Renaissance style of the following century. Round the corner on Postgang is the Gothic **Altstädter Nicolaikirche**, which contains a spectacular sixteenth-century altar from Antwerp, featuring some 250 figures in the carved depictions of the Passion. Behind the church is the *Leineweber* (linen weaver) statue; he is depicted with the traditional characteris-tics of a long pipe and walking stick.

Festivals and practicalities

If Bielefeld is rather thin on historic monuments, its numerous **popular festivals** provide a counterbalance. Best of these is the *Leineweber Markt* on the last weekend in May, which includes street theatre, jazz and rock concerts, as well as folklore displays. Open-air music of all kinds is played throughout the city during the summer, while every third Saturday from May to October sees a flea market; the location varies, but the Markt itself is regularly the venue. In mid-July, the *Sparrenburgfest* in the castle features tournaments and a medieval fair, while there's a week-long *Weinfest* in mid-September.

For a full list of the month's **events**, pick up the tourist office's free programme. Apart from the Stadttheater already mentioned, drama is also performed at the *Theater am Alten Markt*, while there's a *Puppenspiele* (puppet theatre) at Ravensberger Str. 12. Concerts are given at *Oetkerhalle* on Stapenhorststrasse. Bielefeld's most original venue, however, is the **Alten Ravensberger Spinnerei**, east of Jahnplatz on Heeper Strasse, a grandiose nineteenth-century linen mill, well worth seeing in its own right as a rare survivor of the sort of factory which once dotted large German industrial towns. Lovingly restored, it's now a cultural centre, featuring exhibitions, film shows and musi-cal recitals.

The **youth hostel**, Oetzer Weg 25 (☎0521/22227), is 4km south of the centre in an isolated location within the Teutoburg Forest; take tram #2 to its terminus, then bus #121, but note that the latter stops running soon after the evening rush hour. There are two **campsites**, both on the edge of the forest, at Vogelweide 9 (☎0521/450336) and Beckendorfstrasse (☎0521/3335). Centrally located **hotels** are almost entirely geared to business visitors; cheapest is *Hunning*, Kreuzstr. 9 (☎0521/62293), at DM40 per person. The tourist office can supply lists of alternatives in the suburbs (there's a whole clutch in BRACKWEDE to the south), but you'd be better off looking for a room in a more congenial small town nearby, such as Lemgo or Detmold. One of the city's best **restaurants** is *Sparrenburg* within the castle; another good choice is *Im Bültmannshof*, Kurt-Schumacher-Str. 17a. The **Mitfahrzentrale** office is at Helmholtzstr. 26 (☎0521/68978).

Minden

Minden is a mighty fortress,
A strong weapon and protection.
With Prussian fortresses, however, I'd
Prefer to have no connection.

So scoffed the libertarian Heinrich Heine, savagely parodying Luther's great Reformation hymn *Ein' feste Burg ist unser Gott.* MINDEN's strategic importance, at an easily fordable point of the River Weser, has meant that military affairs have dominated its history: the old ramparts were converted into a full blown fortress by the Swedes during the Thirty Years' War; it was the scene of a decisive battle in 1759 in which the British and Prussians defeated the French; and, during the Napoleonic Wars, it was equipped with the very latest defensive systems as a leading Prussian frontier town, a role it retained until this became superfluous with the unification of Germany in 1871. The city kept its historic appearance until the last war, when its strategic importance inevitably led to severe aerial bombardment.

The Wasserstrassenkreuz

Minden's role as a fortress meant it could not expand and industrialise, but its favourable geographical position led to its development as the hub of the German inland water transport system, and it's from this function that its main present-day attraction derives. In the northern part of the city, you'll find the **Wasserstrassenkreuz** (Waterway Junction) which is unique in Europe. Most eye-catching feature is the surrealistic **Kanalbrücke** (Canal Bridge), a 375-metre long aquatic flyover built between 1911 and 1914; it allows the *Mittellandkanal* – which stretches right across North Germany, linking the Rhine with the Elbe – to pass directly over the Weser. The heart of the system is the fortress-like **Schachtschleuse** (Great Lock) which shifts 12,000 cubic metres of water while transferring ships from canal to river or vice versa in just seven minutes. Alongside is the exhibition hall (Mon–Sat 9am–5pm, Sun 9am–6pm; DM1.50) which explains the layout and working of the *Wasserstrassenkreuz* by means of models and diagrams. A series of paths enable you to explore the area on foot, but it's far more fun to take a **cruise**. Run by the *Mindener Fahrgastschiffahrt* (☎0571/41046; Wed, Thurs, Fri 3pm, May–Sept Sun & holidays 10.15am, duration 90min; DM8), these leave from the jetty immediately opposite the Great Lock. Check locally for shorter trips; it's also possible to combine a trip round Minden's waterways with a cruise down the Weser – see Hameln, *Chapter Six.*

The city centre

The **Hauptbahnhof** is on the right side of the river; its situation, a good twenty minutes' walk from town, is explained by the fact that it was built as part of the Prussian fortifications. Along with the three small forts grouped in a semicircle around it, it's one of the few survivors of that period, as the citizens had no more love for their citadel than did Heine, and dismantled it as soon as it was declared redundant.

The Altstadt is dominated by the **Dom**, whose massive westwork, with two subsidiary towers stuck like glue to the main belfry, is in the severest form of Romanesque. The main body of the building, however, is a hall church, erected in the late thirteenth century in a pure early Gothic style; this has a light and airy feel, thanks to the huge windows decorated with highly elaborate tracery. On the south transept wall is a frieze of Apostles, the remnant of a former Romanesque rood screen; from the same period is the bronze *Minden Crucifix*, the Dom's most important work of art. However, the one currently displayed here is a copy; the original is in the **Domschatz** in the *Haus am Dom* opposite (Tues, Thurs, Sat & Sun 10am–noon; Wed & Fri 3–5pm; free).

Just beyond lies the Markt, whose north side is taken up by the **Rathaus**. Its lower storey, featuring an arcaded passageway, is contemporary with the Dom; the upper part is late Renaissance. Continuing up the steps from here takes you to the best preserved part of the Altstadt, centred on Martinikirchhof. On this square are two survivors of the Prussian garrison buildings, the **Körnermagazin**, where weapons were stored, and the **Martinihaus**, which served as the bakery. Also here is the **Schwedenschänke**, used by the Swedish troops as their refectory during the Thirty Years' War. **St Martini** itself is the pick of Minden's gaunt and blackened parish churches, with a dignified interior housing notable furnishings – late Gothic stalls, Renaissance pulpit and wrought-iron font – and a magnificent organ, partly dating back to the sixteenth century.

Just off the square on Brüderstrasse is the **Alte Münze**, formerly the house of the master of the mint; today, less suitably, it's a Greek restaurant. A rare example of Romanesque civil architecture, it owes its survival to the fact that it was subsequently embellished according to the tastes of the time (with a stepped gable in the Gothic period, and an oriel window in the Renaissance). Mansions in the characteristic Weser Renaissance style are dotted all over the quarter – the finest are on Bäckerstrasse, Am Scharn, and Papenmarkt. The densest concentration, however, is on Ritterstrasse, where five houses have been adapted to contain the **Minden Museum** (Tues, Wed & Fri 10am–1pm & 2.30–5pm, Thurs 10am–1pm & 2.30–6pm, Sat 2.30–5pm, Sun 11am–6pm; free). Displayed in two courtyards are fragments of sculptural decoration from buildings such as these; see in particular a wonderful *Story of Samson*. Upstairs, along with the usual folklore displays, there's a room devoted to the **Battle of Minden**. A turning point in the Seven Years' War, its outcome was to a large extent decided by a successful assault by the British infantry on the French cavalry, the first time such a rash reversal of roles had been attempted – even if it only happened through a misunderstanding of orders.

Practicalities

The **tourist office** is at Grosser Domhof 3 (Mon–Wed & Fri 8am–1pm & 2–5pm, Thurs 8am–1pm & 2–6pm, Sat 9am–1pm; ☎0571/89385). Among the best places to **eat** and **drink** are *Domschänke* on Kleiner Domhof, and *Laterne* on Hahlerstrasse. Look out also for *Zum Fischbäcker* on Obermarktstrasse, which fries fish in a manner worthy of Yorkshire and offers bargain lunchtime menus. If you want to spend the night in town, *Marienhöhe*, Marienglacis 45 (☎0571/22854), is much the cheapest **hotel** in the centre at DM30 per person. Other options tend to be far out – an example is *Grashoff*, Bremer Str. 83 (☎0571/41834), charging DM26 for singles, DM48 for doubles; it's in the suburb of TODTENHAUSEN, site of the Battle of Minden.

Around Minden

There's a much wider choice of accommodation possibilities in **PORTA WESTFALICA**, a scattered holiday resort and spa 8km upstream, just one stop away on the train. Across the river from the Bahnhof is the **campsite** (☎0571/72743; April–Oct only). The **youth hostel** is at Kirchsiek 30 (☎0571/70250); turn right on leaving the Bahnhof, then first left, and continue straight ahead. There are also numerous **rooms** on offer in private houses for DM25; a full list is available from the *Haus des Gastes* in the *Kurpark*. Porta Westfalica lies between the two ranges of the **Wiehengebirge** to the west and the **Wesergebirge** to the east. The former is crowned by the stolidly grandiose **Monument to Kaiser Wilhelm I**, whose view is rivalled by the **Portakanzel** directly opposite. Higher up on the right-bank side, you get the best view of all from the **Fernhsehturm** (Television tower) on the Jakobsberg. Plenty of marked **nature trails** pass through both ranges.

The countryside to the **north and west of Minden**, on the other hand, is flat and ideal cycling country (bike hire available at the city's Hauptbahnhof). It's peppered with **windmills** – 37 historic examples survive. Get hold of the glossy tourist board brochure *Die Westfälische Mühlenstrasse* (English insert available), and the separate leaflet detailing when the mills are operating – this is done in rotation on weekend afternoons from April to October. Various **farms** in the area offer lodging from as little as DM20, or DM30 full board.

Lemgo

LEMGO, 12km north of Detmold and 25km east of Bielefeld, would be a strong contender in any competition to find the prettiest town in northern Germany. It scores heavily on two points – it's never been bombed, nor has it suffered from mass tourism. Many of the buildings from its sixteenth-century Hanseatic heyday survive, and are now immaculately cared for, with the merchant class which built them from the profits of foreign trade now replaced by a mixture of retailers, wealthy commuters (over half the population works elsewhere) and public bodies. With its surprising vistas and architectural groupings, and the myriad delicate details on the buildings, it's as if the town had been specially made for the benefit of photography.

Around town

The **Bahnhof**, on a small branch line from Bielefeld, is just to the south of the historic kernel of the city; most **buses** leave from the bays in front, but not the services to and from Detmold, which stop a couple of minutes' walk to the right along Paulinenstrasse. At the end of this road, turn right into Breitestrasse and you're immediately in one of Lemgo's finest thoroughfares, soon arriving at the spectacular **Hexenbürgermeisterhaus** (Witches' Burgomaster House) on the left hand side. The facade, with its elegantly tapering gables, its *Fall of Man* over the doorway and its two quite different oriel windows (something of a Lemgo speciality) adorned with the Seven Cardinal Virtues, ranks as one of the supreme masterpieces of the joyous Weser Renaissance style. It was built in 1571, three years after the completion of the rest of the house, by a local man, **Hermann Wulf**, who was an uncommonly fine architect to judge from this and his other buildings in the town, but whose provinciality has denied him lasting fame. Originally commissioned by a merchant family, the house's present curious name derives from an occupant in a later, more mordant period, the notorious **Hermann Cothmann**. He was burgomaster of Lemgo at the height of the hysterical campaign against supposed witches between 1666 and 1681, apparently sentencing some ninety women to death.

Inside, an above average **Heimatmuseum** (Tues–Fri & Sun 10am–12.30pm & 1.30–5pm, Sat 10am–1pm; DM1.50) appropriately includes a room devoted to gruesome instruments of torture, from the inquisition stool with its seat of protruding nails, through thumb and leg screws, to less brutal items such as the barrel which formed a moveable version of the stocks. However ridiculous these now seem, it's worth reflecting just how much suffering they caused, and in an age still basking in the glow of the Renaissance. On a happier note, there are rooms furnished in period style, and an exhibition on a considerably more enlightened Lemgo citizen of the same period, **Engelbert Kämpfer**. A pioneering traveller in Russia, Persia, Java and Japan, Kämpfer had deluxe accounts of his journeys printed and published in his native town, which was then a leading centre of book production.

Just off Breitestrasse down Stiftstrasse is the **Marienkirche**, the Gothic hall church of a convent which was suppressed when Lemgo went over to the Reformation. It has one of the richest musical traditions in Germany, so any concert will be worth hearing – there's a small international festival in the first week of June. The choir is celebrated, the **swallow's nest organ** even more so. Built between 1587 and 1613, initially by a Dutchman, and then by two brothers from Hamburg, it's rated amongst the sweetest-sounding instruments in Europe. If you aren't lucky enough to hear it, the woodwork is still an artistic treasure in its own right, although sadly stripped of its original bright polychromy. Also from the Renaissance is the **font**, the work of a local sculptor, **Georg Crossmann**, with unashamedly sensual figures of the Four Christian Virtues. Behind it are statues of the nobleman Otto Zur Lippe and his wife, masterpieces of late fourteenth-century funerary art.

Beyond the end of Breitestrasse, past the so-called Squires' Houses, you reach the **Wippermannsches Haus**, the only one of the great merchant buildings in the extravagant late Gothic style, which must have been due to the archaic tastes of its owner, as it's a few years younger than the Hexenbürgermeisterhaus. Nowadays it houses the **tourist office** (Mon–Fri 9am–5.30pm, Sat 9am–noon; ☎05261/213347); pick up their brochure in English which has a map and good photographs. It's then just a few paces to the **Markt**, one of Germany's finest squares, lined with a wealth of superb structures from the fourteenth century onwards. The **Rathaus** complex on the east side represents the changing building fashions in its photogenic jumble of arcades, pinnacles and gables. Its northern corner, the old **apothecary**, is still used as a chemist's shop, and has a magnificent oriel window. The gossamer carvings, again the work of Crossmann, include a frieze of ten famous scientists with their engraved words of wisdom, while the columns of the upper windows show the Five Senses.

The south side of the square is fronted by the early seventeenth-century **Ballhaus**; beside it is the sixteenth-century **Zeughaus**, whose rear wall is painted in psychedelic zigzags. You won't find photographs of the west side of the Markt in tourist brochures, and for good reason – the effect of its stately Renaissance edifices was long spoiled by two unworthy later buildings. In the 1970s, it was decided to pull the latter down and replace them with structures in a style that was modernist, yet imbued with motifs from Lemgo's past. The result won a prestigious architectural prize, though something less stridently self-confident might have fitted in better. There can be no complaints, however, about the northern frontage of the square, which also forms part of Lemgo's central axis, Mittelstrasse. Appropriately, this is the street most evocative of the Hansa; half-timbering was used extensively, and some of the mansions have nicknames deriving from their decoration, such as *House of the Planets* and *Sundial House*. The buildings on the right also have handsome backs, forming part of the close of the Gothic **Nicolaikirche**, whose twin towers were later varied by the addition of contrasting lead spires. Its interior, a characteristic hall design, has an assortment of works of art in all manner of different styles, including another font by Crossmann.

To see a house like no other in Lemgo (or anywhere else), continue to the end of Mittelstrasse, then straight ahead down Bismarckstrasse to Hamelner Strasse, where you'll find the **Junkerhaus** (Tues–Fri & Sun 10am–5pm, Sat 10am–1pm; DM1.50). It's the obsessive single-handed creation of a totally eccentric local architect, painter and sculptor, **Karl Junker**, who was determined to bequeath his own vision of a dream house as a modern counterpart to the sixteenth-century mansions he knew so well. From the outside, it looks like the witch's cottage from *Hansel and Gretel*, while the interior is spookier than anything Hammer House of Horror ever produced. The omnipresent sinuous and virtuoso monochrome woodcarvings are the stuff of nightmarish fantasies, produced by a man who was a Surrealist before such a movement existed. Returning down Hamelner Strasse, go sharp left into Pagenhelle before the start of Bismarckstrasse; shortly you come to **Schloss Brake** (Tues–Sun 9am–6pm; DM4), a moated Renaissance castle of the Counts of Lippe.

Practicalities

From here, the **campsite** (April–Nov only; ☎05261/14858 &12206) can be reached by following the path of the river back towards the town. There's no hostel; the tourist office has a list of **rooms** in private houses from about DM20 per person, although these are all situated in the outskirts. The cheapest **hotels** with a central location are *Bahnhofswaage*, Am Bahnhof (☎05261/3525), at DM35 per person; *Zum Landsknecht*, Herforder Str. 177 (☎05261/68264), at DM30 per person, whose restaurant does French-style cuisine; and *Hansa-Hotel*, Breitestr. 14 (☎05261/4889), which charges upwards of DM30 per person. **Cafés** and **restaurants**, including all the usual ethnic varieties, abound throughout the town centre.

Detmold and the Southern Teutoburg Forest

DETMOLD, capital of the former Lippe Principality, makes the obvious base for seeing the varied attractions of the southern part of the **Teutoburg Forest** (*Teutoburger Wald*). If you're understandably baffled by the competing claims of Germany's innumerable forests, most of which seem to offer much the same as any other, then this is truly one with a difference, adding extra natural, historical and artistic delights to the usual fare of wooded trails, for which there's such a national penchant.

Detmold

An old jingle, quoted ad infinitum in tourist brochures and on billboards all over town, describes Detmold as *eine wunderschöne Stadt*. That ranks as something of an exaggeration, but it's an agreeable place nonetheless, with a far more laid-back approach to life than is usual in Germany. Arriving at either the **Bahnhof**, on the line between Bielefeld and the important junction of Altenbeken, or the **bus station** alongside, turn left along Bahnhofstrasse, then right into Paulinenstrasse; the largely pedestrianised historic area lies a short walk down to the left. Langestrasse and the streets around, such as Bruchstrasse, Schülerstrasse, Krummestrasse and Exterstrasse, are lined with large half-timbered **old houses**, many now containing the most obvious places to **eat** and **drink**, interspersed with self-confident stone buildings of the Wilhelmine epoch. However, easily the most attractive street is the venerable and smaller-scale Adolfstrasse, running parallel to and east of Langestrasse.

North of the Markt is a green area centred on the **Residenzschloss** (guided tours daily April–Oct every half-hour 9.30am–noon & 2–5pm, Nov–March at 10am, 11am, 2pm & 3pm; DM4), which is surrounded by water on three sides. The keep of the medieval fortress was incorporated into the present Renaissance structure, which was progressively shorn of its defensive features down the years. It remains in the possession of the descendants of the Counts (later Princes) of Lippe who built it; unfortunately, their attitude to visitors is extremely high-handed – you're shunted around as quickly as possible and treated in a condescending way by the lackeys. The interior is not what you'd expect from outside; its rooms were transformed in the eighteenth and nineteenth centuries according to the tastes of the time, but their most valuable adornment is a superb set of seventeenth-century Brussels tapestries of *The Life of Alexander the Great*, woven from cartoons made by the great French designer Charles Le Brun.

From here, the **Landesmuseum** (Tues–Fri 9am–12.30pm & 2–5.30pm, Sat 9am–12.30pm, Sun 10am–5.30pm; DM2) is reached down Ameide, to the rear of the Schloss. It's housed in two buildings, with natural history in one, archaeology, local history and folklore in the other. The second building has a number of reconstituted period rooms, and comprehensive displays on the history of fashion and on local agriculture, incorporating a rebuilt tithe-barn and granary.

This makes a good prelude to the spectacular **Freilichtmuseum** (April–Oct Tues–Sun 9am–6pm; DM3), the most important open-air museum in Germany, which is being laid out at the southern side of the town; to reach it, go in a straight line down the Allee, the continuation of Langestrasse. When complete (which will not be for several years) it will comprise 168 redundant original buildings from rural Westphalia; currently over ninety are in place. These are grouped together according to region, thus giving a clear picture of the different construction styles. As a centrepiece, there will be three complete simulated villages, although only that from the Paderborn area exists as yet; other parts of the province are represented by a more modest selection, generally constructed round a large manor house. Apart from farmsteads and workshops of diverse kinds, you can see watermills and windmills, humble privys, wayside chapels and a complete school. The whole way of life associated with these buildings is preserved as well – thus the traditional crafts of weaving, spinning, pottery, milling and forging are demonstrated, farmyard animals are reared, and the gardens are planted to give a practical yield of vegetables. Several hours are needed to do justice to the museum; reasonably priced lunches are available at the eighteenth-century inn *Zum Wilden Mann* on the main street of the Paderborn village, less substantial fare at *Tiergartenkrug* near the Tecklenburg and Minden group of houses.

Practicalities

The **tourist office** (Mon–Thurs 9am–noon & 1–5pm, Fri 9am–5pm, Sat 9am–noon; ☎05231/767328) is located in the Rathaus just off the Markt on Langestrasse. They have full lists of the extensive choice of **private rooms** available all over the surrounding area, which cost from as little as DM15. Most of these are only practical if you've got your own transport; the solitary one in Detmold itself is *Pillath* at Nachtigallenweg 21 (☎05231/25709) which is still a good bargain at DM25 per person. The cheapest **hotels** are *Hermann*, Woldemarstr. 17 (☎05231/22527), at DM30 for a single, DM56 a double, and *Meier*, Bahnhofstr. 9a (☎05231/33007/23026), at DM30 per person. There's a **youth hostel** at Schirrmannstr. 49 (☎05231/24739) right on the edge of town; from Paulinenstrasse, turn right into Freilingrathstrasse, then left into Brahmsstrasse, and follow its continuation, Schützenberg, to the end.

Around Detmold

Four of the **Teutoburg Forest**'s top sights are within 10km of Detmold; at a push, it's possible to see all in a day, following a southerly route. Unless you've got your own transport, however, a fair amount of walking is necessary.

The Hermannsdenkmal

Firstly, there's what can be regarded as Germany's equivalent of the Statue of Liberty, the **Hermannsdenkmal** (daily April–Oct 9am–6.30pm, Nov–March 9am–4.30pm; DM1), situated on the **Grotenburg** to the southwest of the town; two buses go out

---

ARMINIUS – THE FIRST GERMAN HERO

Having served for three years in the Imperial army, **Arminius**, a warrior prince of the Cherusci tribe, originally allies of the Romans, became wise to the fact that, by stealthy means, the Germanic peoples were in danger of being subjugated in the same way as the Gauls. In 9 AD he inflicted a crushing defeat on the Roman army in the Teutoburg Forest, using techniques akin to modern guerilla warfare. He then tried to forge an alliance with the southern Germanic tribes, which might have spelt real disaster for the Empire, but was frustrated by their quisling leadership. Nevertheless, two more Roman campaigns to subdue Germania were repelled, leading them to abandon the attempt. The hero was murdered by his own in-laws in 21 AD and was forgotten for centuries, only to be rediscovered and eulogised by the Romantic movement, who saw him not only as a great liberator, but also (rather fancifully) as the first man with the vision of a united Germany, which was at long last to be achieved.

---

daily, or it can be reached on foot by gently ascending paths from the suburb of HIDDESEN. The monument commemorates **Arminius** (or "Hermann", see above) and is as near as possible to the scene of his greatest victory. The completion of the project was entirely due to the single-minded dedication of the architect-sculptor **Ernst von Bandel**, who worked at it on and off from 1838 to 1875, according to the availability of funds. Resting on a colonnaded base, the monument is crowned with an idealised vision in copper of the hero brandishing his sword on high; the total height to the tip of the sword is 53 metres, and the figure weighs a little matter of 76,865kg. From the platform there's a superb **view** over the whole range of the Teutoburg Forest.

The Vogelpark and Adlerwarte

Following Denkmalstrasse you descend in less than 2km to the first of two ornithological treats, the **Vogelpark** (Bird Park; variable date in March/April–Oct 9am–6pm daily; DM4) with over 2000 varieties from all over the world, from miniature hens hardly bigger than insects to the large South American nandu. Particularly impressive is the collection of parrots and cockatoos, showing off a kaleidoscopic range of colours, and sufficiently domesticated to be left uncaged.

From here, you can follow the footpath to the right and continue in a straight line to the **Adlerwarte** (Eagle Watch; daily 8.30am–6pm, or until dusk in winter; DM3) in BERLEBECK. This eyrie, commanding a fine panorama over the forest, serves as a breeding station and clinic for birds of prey, with around ninety of these magnificent creatures kept here permanently. Displayed on chains or in cages are all kinds of eagles – imperial, golden, prairie, sea, bald, martial, and the enormous and rare harpy – as well as falcons, hawks, kites, buzzards, vultures, condors, griffons and various breeds of owls. The site was specially chosen because of its suitability for **free flight**, and the demonstrations of this (April–Oct 11am & 3pm, Nov–March 11am & 2.30pm) are a memorable experience on no account to be missed. There are three directions the bird can choose to ascend; it then glides out of sight for a while before returning to make a flawless swoop on the bait in the hand of the falconer, whose every movement it can follow from as far as 2km away.

The Externsteine

The **Externsteine**, a further 3km south just before the town of HORN-BAD MEINBERG, is a jagged clump of sandstone rocks set by an artificial lake, a striking contrast to the wooded landscape to be found all around. It's one of Germany's most evocative sites, with origins lost in the twilight world. The pregnant sense of mystery is increased by the enigmatic mixture of natural and man-made features, whose precise meaning and significance has teased and baffled generations of scholars.

Adorning the bulky rock at the far right is a magnificent large **twelfth-century relief** of *The Descent from the Cross*, which was carved on the spot, making it quite unlike any other known sculpture of the period. Although Romanesque in style, it's imbued with the hierarchical Byzantine spirit, one of the few German works of art, illuminated manuscripts apart, so influenced. Some limbs have been lost, but its state of preservation is otherwise remarkable. Directly below is a worn carving, probably representing Adam and Eve entwined around the serpent. To the side is a series of caves, now closed off; one of these bears an inscription saying it was consecrated as a chapel in 1115. There's also a stairway leading up to a viewing platform at the top. The next rock, fronted by an open-air pulpit, retains its natural peak, below which is a roofless chapel with a circular window exactly aligned to catch the sunrise on the summer solstice. It's too upright to accommodate a staircase, but you can ascend from the top of the stumpy rock to the left by means of a little bridge bent like a bow; from the ground it looks precarious, but it is totally secure. The fourth rock, bearing a plaque depicting the coat of arms of the Counts of Lippe, is again crowned with apparent danger, in this case a large stone which seems ready to fall down, but which is actually fastened with iron hooks, following the repeated failure of attempts to dislodge it.

Many pundits are convinced that the Externsteine served as a centre of pagan worship; others maintain that the site's religious origins go back no further than the twelfth century, and that it's a re-creation of the Holy Places of Jerusalem, inspired by Crusaders' tales. Part of the charm of the place is that firm evidence for such theories remains tantalisingly elusive. What's known for sure is that it was an anchorite hermitage throughout medieval times, and that it then passed to the local counts, serving successively as a fortress, a pleasure palace and a prison, undergoing many alterations in the process, before being restored to its present form – assumed to be the original – early last century.

Höxter

HÖXTER, about 45km southeast of Detmold, is the easternmost town in Westphalia. Lower Saxony is soon entered if you follow the course of the River Weser, whether downstream to Hameln or upstream to Hann. Münden, two places which are far closer to it in feel than anywhere in its own province.

Abtei Corvey

The main claim on your attention is the once powerful **Abtei Corvey**, just over 1km from the town centre, and reached by either following the river eastwards, or going in a straight line down Corbiestrasse. A ninth-century Carolingian foundation, it was a famous centre of scholarship, its greatest legacy being *The History of the Saxons*, written around 975 by the monk-chronicler **Widukind**. He gave the newly conquered barbarian race an appropriately grand origin in veterans of Alexander the Great's army, and vividly related their story right up to his own day. The **Abteikirche** (daily 9.30am–1pm & 2–6pm; DM0.70) actually retains the great westwork of the original building, one of the few pieces of architecture of this period to have survived anywhere in Europe. The towers and the gallery between them are twelfth-century modifications, but inside you can see the solemn entrance hall with the *Kaisersaal* above, surviving much as the early emperors would have known them, except that the organ now blocks the view downstairs. In any case, the church they looked down on was so badly ravaged in the Thirty Years' War that it had to be replaced by a completely new building, which dates from 1667–71. Although normally described as Baroque, the architecture is Gothic in every respect, for all that this style was by then a total anachronism. In contrast, the complete set of painted wood furnishings are so much of their own day, with no later intrusions in evidence, that it's easy to feel transported three centuries back in time.

To the side of the church is the extensive complex of monastic buildings, built a generation later in the plain Baroque favoured in Northern Germany. After the Napoleonic secularisation it became a ducal **Schloss** and is now a museum (April–Sept daily 9am–6pm; DM3). Temporary exhibitions are featured, and there are displays on folklore and local history, but you're likely to derive most pleasure simply from being allowed to roam loose through umpteen rooms. On the upper floor, the *Festsaal* forms an elegant setting for classical concerts by star international artists in May and June; in the adjacent rooms are displayed some of the 80,000 volumes from the abbey's famous library. From 1860 until his death fourteen years later, the poet **Heinrich August Hoffmann von Fallersleben** (see box) served as their custodian, and there's an exhibition on his work. The *Schloss Restaurant* offers some of the best food in town, and is reasonably priced, provided you stick to the set menus.

DEUTSCHLAND ÜBER ALLES

Hoffmann von Fallersleben is best known for what soon became the national anthem of a united Germany, *Das Lied der Deutschen*, as set to the finest piece of music ever used for such purposes, Haydn's stately and spacious *Emperor's Hymn*. Its opening line *Deutschland, Deutschland über alles* became notorious under the Nazis, who were unaware that the melody was based on a Croatian folk song, and was thus part of the hated and "inferior" Slav culture. In reality, there's nothing sinister about the words, which are liberal in sentiment; what might seem to be an assertion of national superiority is actually a clarion call to abandon the petty feuding of the old states in favour of German unity. The third stanza was retained by the West German state as its national anthem, and recently there were moves to reinstate the first verse to celebrate unification of the country. Alas, the frontiers delineated – "from the Maas to the Memel" – are very out of date: the latter is now in Lithuania.

The town centre

The centre of Höxter itself is dominated by the twin towers of the red sandstone **Kilianikirche**, a Romanesque building clearly modelled on Corvey; inside is a Renaissance pulpit adorned with fine alabaster reliefs. Otherwise, the town is notable for the prevalence of **half-timbered houses**, which include the mid-sixteenth-century **Küsterhaus** facing the church, in which the **tourist office** (Mon–Fri 8am–1pm, 2–5.30pm, Sat 9am–noon; ☎05271/63244) is now situated. Beyond is the **Rathaus**, a late Renaissance structure from the following century, adorned with octagonal turret and oriel. It's rivalled in splendour by the earlier **Dechanei** (Deanery), an asymmetrical double house reached down Marktstrasse. Although it's the busiest street, Westerbachstrasse is astonishingly well preserved, offering a complete panorama of half-timbering down the centuries, from late Gothic (eg no. 43, *Haus Ohrmann*) to Neoclassical (eg no. 40). There's little doubt that the Renaissance buildings steal the show, particularly *Tilly Haus* (no. 33–37), *Corveyer Hof* (no. 29) and *Altes Brauhaus* (no. 28). The last named remains Höxter's most famous **beer hall**, specialising in *vom heissen Stein* dishes. Other old-world pubs include *Adam-und-Eva-Haus* on Stummrigenstrasse, originally a Renaissance mansion, and *Strullenkrug* on Hennekenstrasse. The latter building is early nineteenth-century, but the site, with the largest beer garden in town, has a much longer tradition. Facing it is Rodiewerkstrasse, with another varied collection of old houses of various dates.

Practicalities

The **Bahnhof** is surnamed Rathaus with good reason; it's just a stone's throw from the centre, right beside the River Weser. Services on this branch line are slow; a pleasant alternative (May–early Oct only) is to travel to Hameln or Hann. Münden by **boat**; there's a departure point near the Bahnhof and another at Corvey. The **campsite** (☎05271/2589) has a good location on the right bank of the Weser opposite the town. Alternatively, there's a **youth hostel** at An der Wilhelmshöhe 59 (☎05271/2233): from the far end of Westerbachstrasse, cross over to Gartenstrasse; after a couple of minutes' walk, turn left and follow the road to the end. **Hotel rooms** are all reasonably priced; even the aforementioned *Corveyer Hof* (☎05271/2272), the classiest option, need cost no more than DM36 per person. *Braunschweiger Hof*, Corbiestr. 5 (☎05271/2236), *Zum Landsknecht*, Stummrigestr. 17 (☎05271/2477), and *Zum Weserstrand*, Stummrigestr. 38 (☎05271/2477), all charge around DM28 per person. A room in a private house may cost as little as DM16; the tourist office has a complete list. The main **festival**, as in many other towns in the area, is the *Schützenfest* in early July.

travel details

Trains

From Cologne to Aachen (3 an hour; 45min); Bonn (4; 20min); Düsseldorf (frequent; 25min); Siegen (1; 1hr 35min); Wuppertal (1; 30min); Hagen (2; 50min); Dortmund (frequent; 1hr 10min); Essen (frequent; 50min); Münster (frequent; 1hr 45min); Soest (4 daily; 2hr 20min); Bielefeld (2; 1hr 30min); Hannover (frequent; 2hr 50min).

From Düsseldorf to Mönchengladbach (frequent; 30min); Wuppertal (2; 40min); Duisburg (frequent; 15min); Kleve (1; 1hr 25min); Dortmund (frequent; 1hr); Essen (frequent; 30min); Münster (frequent; 1hr 30min); Soest (4 daily; 1hr 20min).

From Kleve to Xanten (1 an hour; 40min); Kalkar (1; 10min).

From Dortmund to Essen (frequent; 25min); Bochum (frequent; 10min); Hagen (2; 30min); Münster (2; 30min); Aachen (8 daily; 1hr 50min); Bielefeld (2; 40min); Minden (10 daily; 1hr 15min); Hannover (1; 2hr).

From Bielefeld to Lemgo (1 an hour; 1hr); Detmold (1; 1hr 15min); Hannover (frequent; 1hr 30min).

From Münster to Düsseldorf (2 an hour; 1hr 20min), Hagen (1; 1hr 5min); Wuppertal (1; 1hr 25min); Essen (frequent; 55min); Osnabrück (frequent; 25min); Bochum (frequent; 45min); Bremen (frequent; 1hr 15min).

CHAPTER SIX

BREMEN AND LOWER SAXONY

he Land of **Lower Saxony** (*Niedersachsen*) only came into being in 1946, courtesy of the British military authorities. In forging this new province, the former **Kingdom of Hannover** – which had shared its ruler with Britain between 1714 and 1837, but which had later been subsumed into Prussia – was used as a basis. To it were added the two separate ex-duchies of **Braunschweig** and **Oldenburg**, plus the minute but hitherto seemingly indestructible **Principality of Schaumburg-Lippe**.

In spite of this diverse patchwork, and some anomalies (**East Friesland** is very much an area apart, while **Osnabrück** properly belongs in Westphalia), the Land actually has strong historical antecedents. It forms the approximate area inhabited by the Saxon tribes, other than the Westphalians, at the time of the Roman Empire and the succeeding Dark Ages. Thus it more accurately bears the name "Saxony" than the two new eastern Länder which together were so designated from the Middle Ages right up to the post-World War II settlement. In accordance with the general north-south divide, the Reformation took strong root in most of Lower Saxony. **Politically**, however, it's very finely balanced, and is something of a national barometer, with the SPD narrowly having ousted the CDU from power in 1990.

Geographically, Lower Saxony is highly diverse. It contains much of Germany's sparse provision of **coastline** and **islands**, behind which stretches a flat landscape, often below sea-level. Further south is the monotonous stretch of the North German Plain, but this gives way to the **Lüneburg Heath** to the east, and to highland countryside further south, in the shape of the hilly region around the **River Weser** and the gentle wooded slopes of the **Harz** mountains.

That Lower Saxony is not particularly well-known to English-speaking visitors is in some ways surprising. Apart from the Hanoverian connection, there are long-standing trading and dynastic bonds with Britain, while the island of **Helgoland** was actually once part of the United Kingdom. Furthermore, one of literature's great comic characters, Baron Münchhausen of **Bodenwerder**, was originally introduced to the world through a book written in English. Other semi-historical figures from Lower Saxony are if anything even more familiar, especially the rat-catching Pied Piper and the jester Till Eulenspiegel. The province is also one of two associated with another famous (and very German) legend – the witches' sabbath of *Walpurgisnacht*.

Lower Saxony is the second most extensive Land after Bavaria, but has a very low population density. None of its cities is as big as the old Hanseatic port of **Bremen**, an enclave within the province, but a Land in its own right, in continuation of its age-long tradition as a free state. Otherwise, there are just two cities with a population of over 200,000. Much the larger of these is the state capital, **Hannover**, which only really came to prominence in the seventeenth century, and which is to be visited more for its museums and magnificent gardens than for its monuments. **Braunschweig** is altogether more venerable, and still preserves considerable reminders of its halcyon period at the end of the twelfth century.

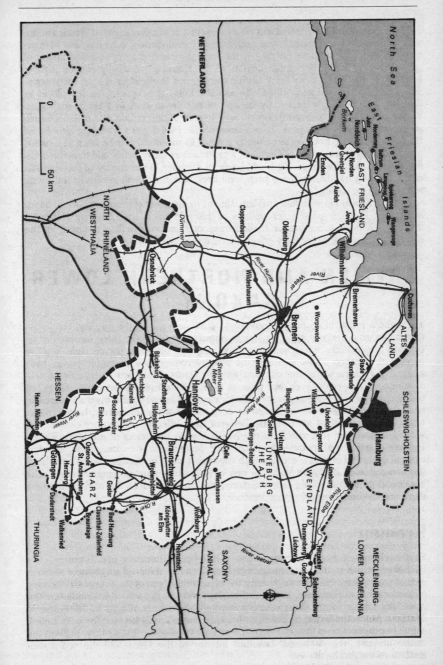

The province's smaller towns and cities present a fascinating contrast. **Hildesheim**, with its grandiloquent Romanesque architecture (revolutionary in its day, and of enormous influence throughout Europe) is the most outstanding from an artistic point of view. Nowhere is the mercantile heyday of the Hansa more vividly evoked than in **Lüneburg**, with its masterly brick Gothic showpieces. **Wolfenbüttel** is an early example of a planned town, and, with **Celle** and **Bückeburg**, is among the few places in Germany to be strongly marked by Italian-inspired Renaissance and Mannerist styles. Very different is the exuberantly ornate architecture of the archaic Weser Renaissance style, which reached its peak in and around the Pied Piper's stamping ground of **Hameln**. A mining town quite unlike any other in the world can be seen at **Goslar**, while **Göttingen** boasts one of Germany's most famous universities, and thus the liveliest nightlife in the province. **Einbeck**, home of *Bockbier*, is a reminder of the strength of the brewing tradition in these parts, and beer aficionados will generally find themselves spoilt for choice.

Getting around is seldom a problem, thanks to the usual efficient network of buses and trains. The only possible exceptions to this rule are in the Lüneburg Heath (in much of which there's a ban on fuelled transport) and in travelling to and from the islands off the coast, where ferry prices are relatively expensive.

BREMEN AND NORTHERN LOWER SAXONY

Throughout much of its past **Bremen** was governed not by the nobility, but by its merchants, as a free city state – a sharp contrast to most of the three hundred or so German principalities, some quite tiny, that were run by feudal barons right into the nineteenth century. Those centuries of self-government and economic power have marked the character of the city and its inhabitants. There's a certain air of self-assuredness, superiority even, and pride in their political independence that marks out the Bremen people – a hangover that's inextricably linked to the town's **Hanseatic** past. Bremen still governs itself (and its deep-water harbour at **Bremerhaven**, 60km north), as the **smallest state in the Federal Republic**. It's the country's oldest and second largest port too, safe from the North Sea on the banks of the River Weser. Imports of exotic commodities from far-flung destinations – cotton, coffee, tobacco, tropical fruits and cereals – coupled with the export trade in wool and wood have been the foundation of Bremen's status as one of Germany's most prosperous cities. The hinterland is entirely within Lower Saxony, and the city makes the obvious base for exploring the northern part of this province.

Bremen

Of the cluster of North German cities – Hamburg, Hannover and Bremen – it's **BREMEN** which is the most manageable. Though a city, it has an atmosphere reminiscent of an English country town, lacking the commercial buzz of Hamburg, and the ugly redevelopment of Hannover. In one or two days you can get a good impression of the place: the former fortifications where a windmill still stands, almost in the centre of town; the **Schnoorviertel**, crammed with former fisher-family houses; the bold, mural-painted backs of houses near the river; the elegant villas of the last century. Right in the centre of town, the darkened, beautiful interior of the **Dom** and the sumptuous **Rathaus** shouldn't be missed.

Some history

It was in the eighth century that the Holy Roman Emperor Charlemagne dispatched the Anglo-Saxon Willehad to the Weser to convert the Saxons there to Christianity; seven years later a bishop of Bremen was appointed, and in 789 the first church was built where the Dom stands today. A further two hundred years on, the city was granted free market rights, giving independent merchants the same **trading rights** as those working on behalf of the crown, a vital step for Bremen's economic expansion. The city was an important centre for the church in the eleventh century, and over the centuries saw considerable conflict between civic and ecclesiastical interests. In 1358 Bremen joined the Hanseatic League and, having survived a virtual cessation of trade during the Thirty Years' War, was granted free city status in 1646.

This was renewed in 1949 when Bremen, together with Bremerhaven, was declared a *Land* of the Federal Republic of Germany. Since then, it's had a reputation for being the most politically radical part of the country, with the SPD having held power without a break. One of their most significant acts was the establishment of a university, which has set up an alternative, multi-disciplinary curriculum in opposition to the normal conservative, highly specialised bent of the country's higher educational system. In 1979, Bremen was the scene of the key breakthrough by the Green Party – for the first time, they achieved a large enough share of the vote to enter a regional parliament, and successfully used this as a springboard towards becoming a major force in national politics.

> The telephone code for Bremen is ☎0421.

Practicalities

The **Hauptbahnhof** is just to the north of the city centre; immediately outside stands the **tourist office** (Mon–Thurs 8am–8pm, Fri 8am–10pm, Sat 8am–6pm, Sun 9.30am–3.30pm; ☎30800), best source of information for what's on in town, and with a room booking service. There's a second, smaller office at Hilmanplatz 6 (☎8000). Pivotal **tramline** is the #5, which starts from the airport, heads close to the Rathaus and Hauptbahnhof, and runs northwards parallel to the Bürgerpark. The *Bremen Kärtchen*, a **24-hour go-anywhere ticket** is available for DM6; this and other tickets may be bought at the booth outside the Hauptbahnhof. Bremen is flat and therefore ideal for exploring by **bike**, which you can hire right outside the Hauptbahnhof, on the left-hand-side of the square as you come out. *Fahrrad Station* (Mon–Sat 9am–1.15pm & 3–5.30pm; ☎302114) DM10.50 per day; between DM30 and DM50 deposit on each bike.

Accommodation

Bremen's **youth hostel** is very well located in the western part of the old town at Kalkstr. 6 (☎171369), and there's a good central **campsite**, *Internationale Campingplatz Freie Hansestadt Bremen*, Am Stadtwaldsee 1 (☎212002), on the north side of the Bürgerpark close to the university; buses #28 to Stadtwaldsee or #23 to the university go in the right direction. Another budget option is the *Seemannsheim* at Jippen 1 (☎18361); though sailors are given priority, there's seldom any problem getting a room; women are accommodated in more salubrious and slightly more expensive quarters than men. The densest and most convenient cluster of **hotels** in the centre of town is near the Hauptbahnhof; not suprisingly these are expensive, with prices ranging from DM50 upwards per person. Less costly but still fairly close to the centre is *Heinisch*, Wachmannstr. 26 (☎342925; on #5 tramline, or ten minutes' walk

BREMEN

from the Hauptbahnhof), singles from DM48, doubles from DM80. Just east of the Ostertor are: *Weidmann*, Am Schwarzen Meer 35 (☎494055), singles from DM40, doubles DM80; and *Kosch*, Celler Str. 4 (☎447101), singles from DM40, doubles DM70. Also worth trying is the *Weltevreden*, Am Dobben 62 (☎78015), singles from DM50, doubles from DM90. The location of this hotel is very convenient, since it's about half-way between the city centre and the Ostertorviertel, heart of Bremen's nightlife. Across the Weser, but not too remote, is *Haus Hohenlohe*, Buntentorsteinweg 86/88 (☎558027), with singles from DM45, doubles DM70.

The Altstadt

Although more than half a million people live here, Bremen doesn't give the impression of being a large city – partly because the main area of historical interest is the **Altstadt**, on the Weser's northeast bank. The former fortification that surrounded it, the **Wall**, is now an area of green park, with a zigzagging moat forming a curve around the perimeter of the old city. To the north, the **Ostertorviertel** (known as *das Viertel* – "the Quarter") was the first part of the city to be built outside those city walls, and is today the liveliest part of town, the area to head for at night. North of the Hauptbahnhof, the **Burgerpark** and **Schwachhausen** areas are worthy of a stroll for their many streets of villas, each discreetly advertising Bremen's turn-of-the-century wealth. The Burgerpark is twice the size of London's Hyde Park, and apart from being beautiful in itself, contains old wartime bunkers too sturdy to be blown up, which have been decorated by local artists and now sport political murals.

From the Hauptbahnhof, getting to the old town is a simple matter of walking straight ahead and crossing the bridge over the Wall into the pedestrian zone. A life-size bronze of pigs, a swineherd and his dog marks the beginning of the Sögesrasse (Sow Street), along which swine used to be driven to the market. This is Bremen's main shopping street, and, as a standard Euro-shopping precinct, it's not particularly inspiring. The single place worth stopping off for is Bremen's bastion of *Kaffee und Kuchen*, the *Café Knigge*, up on the right-hand side. Left at the top is the **Liebfrauenkirche**, a lovely hall church with contrasting Romanesque and Gothic towers that's swathed by the flower market, with a number of booths around its walls – the flashy built-in sausage stand is the most incongruous.

Around the Rathaus

The **Marktplatz** ahead is relatively small and is dominated by the **Rathaus**, whose highly ornate **facade** – rich in mouldings, life-size figures and bas-reliefs, and with the undersides of its large rounded arches set with enormous "jewels" – is in Weser Renaissance style. It was added to the original Gothic structure between 1609 and 1612, two hundred years after the latter was first built. One of the most splendid of north Germany's buildings, it fortunately survived World War II unscathed. You can only visit the interior as part of a guided tour (Mon–Fri at 10am, 11am & noon; Sat–Sun 11am & noon; 30mins, free), and it's worth it to see the extremes of Bremen's civic pride: rooms awash with gilded wallpaper and busy, ornate carving. Downstairs the **Ratskeller** is as usual pricey, but wine buffs can buy a glass or two from the cellar's collection of 600 vintages, some stored in the eighteenth-century barrels which double as partitions.

On the left as you face the Rathaus is a ten-metre-high stone **statue of Roland**, nephew of Charlemagne, who brandishes the sword of justice and carries a shield bearing the inscription (in the *Plattdeutsch* dialect): "Freedom do I give you openly". Erected by the burghers in 1404 as a symbol of Bremen's independence from its archbishop, he's the city's traditional protector; as long as Roland stands, they say, Bremen will remain free. Roland's pointy kneecaps were used as a medieval measurement-check by local housewives: the distance between the two is the exact length of one *Elle*, by which cloth was sold. In 1989 he was de-Nazified, when a lead casket containing Nazi documents, a Hitler-era time-capsule placed there in 1938, was removed. Poor Roland now spends his time staring at the much-disputed modern facade of the **Haus der Bürgerschaft** (Parliament Building), one of the ugliest edifices ever to disgrace a German town centre.

A happier postwar addition to the square is the bronze group of the **Bremen Town Band** by the local sculptor, Gerhard Marcks. Rising like a pyramid, it shows a cock standing on a cat standing on a dog standing on a donkey, and is an illustration of an old folk tale retold by the **Brothers Grimm**. In fact, this is the town band that never was: en route to the city, the animals arranged themselves in the way depicted and started to make music. In so doing, they frightened a group of robbers away from their hideout and took over the comfortable house for themselves, remaining there ever after.

The Dom

On a small rise beyond the Rathaus stands the twin-towered **Dom**, formerly the seat of one of medieval Germany's five archbishops, but now a Protestant church. Any youngish men you see sweeping the steps are doing it because they have reached their thirtieth birthday without finding themselves a wife – this is the traditional penance (or, perhaps, a way of advertising their availability). The dom itself has been restored recently, its brooding interior beautiful in architectural styles ranging from eleventh-century Romanesque to late Gothic. There are crypts at both ends of the building (one for the use of the emperor, the other for the archbishop), though that to the west had to be truncated when the huge twin-towered facade was erected in the thirteenth century. Just above the entrance is the early sixteenth-century **organ gallery**, adorned with statues, including Charlemagne and Willehad, by the Münster sculptor Heinrich Brabender. In the eastern crypt are more works of art, notably an eleventh-century *Enthroned Christ* and a magnificent thirteenth-century bronze **font**. Off the south-east corner is the **Bleikeller** (Mon–Fri 10am–5pm; Sat 10am–noon; Sun 2–5pm; DM2), where lead for the roofing was stored; it was opened up a while ago, and some bodies, perfectly preserved due to the lack of air, were discovered. Unusually, it's open to visitors, the "mummies" providing a popular – if macabre – attraction.

Elsewhere on Marktplatz

Surviving buildings from Bremen's Hanseatic heyday are rare, but include the restored patrician houses lining much of the rest of the Marktplatz, and the **Schütting**, the ritzy, sixteenth-century Flemish-inspired mansion with contrasting gables, which was where the guild of merchants convened. Round the corner on Langenstrasse is the equally imposing, step-gabled **Stadtwaage**, the municipal office for weights and measures.

Off the south side of Marktplatz is a strange street which seems to combine elements of Gothic, Art Nouveau and fantasy: the **Böttcherstrasse** or Coopers' Street. Once a humble alleyway in which barrel-makers lived and worked, it was transformed in the 1920s by the Bremen magnate **Ludwig Roselius**, who made much of his fortune from *Kaffee Hag*, the first-ever decaffeinated coffee. He commissioned local avant-garde artists (notably Bernhard Hoetger, whose characteristic plump figures are reminiscent of Chinese laughing Buddhas) to effect the change. In among the bronze reliefs, the arches and turrets are a number of craftspeoples' workshops and booths, and a musical clock depicting the history of transatlantic crossings. During the Nazi era, the whole street was to be demolished because it was considered corrupt art. But the charismatic Roselius persuaded the authorities to let it stand as a warning example, so to speak, of all that was considered bad in the arts.

The only old house in Böttcherstrasse is no. 6, a fourteenth-century step-gabled building with a sixteenth-century facade, that's now known as the **Roselius Haus**. Roselius bought the property at the turn of the century, and converted it into a **museum** (Mon–Thurs 10am–4pm, Sat & Sun 11am–4 pm; DM2.50). Though it gives an interesting opportunity to see the interior of a Hanseatic merchant's house, its collection of medieval art and furniture is not especially well displayed; the best works are paintings by Cranach the Elder and the Younger and an alabaster statue of *Saint Barbara* by Riemenschneider. Adjoining is the **Paula-Becker-Modersohn-Haus** (Mon, Tues & Thurs 10am–4pm, Wed 11am–4pm), which contains a number of paintings by that artist, who lived and worked in the nearby village of Worpswede.

The Schnoorviertel

Tucked away between the Dom and the river is a small, extraordinarily well-preserved area of medieval fisherfolks' houses known as the **Schnoorviertel**. Dating from the fifteenth century, this is Bremen's oldest surviving quarter: it's worth a wander through the small streets, far too narrow for modern traffic to pass, to see the variety of buildings and to get a feeling for the city's past. Predictably, in being preserved the area has been prettified and now houses pricey specialist shops selling antiques, crafts and toys. Thankfully, it still manages to be a residential area too, avoiding a gentrification that would have left it soulless.

The Kunsthalle

Just east of the Schnoorviertel at Am Wall 207 is the **Kunsthalle** (Tues 10am–9pm, Wed–Sun 10am–5pm; DM6), one of the oldest municipal art galleries in Germany. The ground floor is mostly given over to changing displays of modern art, but also contains a Jugendstil room containing valuable collections of graphic art. Sadly, most of the outstanding group of watercolours by **Dürer** were destroyed in the war, but a small panel of *St Onofrio* by this artist can be seen in the first room upstairs, along with **Altdorfer**'s earliest surviving work, *The Nativity*, and several examples of **Cranach**. The adjacent galleries contain Dutch and Flemish paintings: *Noli Me Tangere* is a successful co-operative composition between **Rubens** (who painted the figures) and **Jan Brueghel** (who did everything else); there's also the striking full-length *Portrait of Duke Wolfgang Wilhelm of Pfalz-Neuburg* by **van Dyck**, and a *Portrait of a Man* attributed to **Rembrandt**. In the small cabinet rooms to the side are works by earlier European masters, notably Italians, of which the most important are *Madonna and Child* by **Masolino** (one of very few works by this artist to have left Italy) and *A Doctor* by **Moroni**.

However, the gallery's main draw is its superb array of nineteenth-century and early twentieth-century painting. Among the French School, there are five canvases by **Delacroix**, including *King Rodrigo*. A room is devoted to the Nabis: the most impressive works here are *Homage to Cézanne* by **Maurice Denis** and **Vuillard**'s designs for the decoration of the former Champs Elysées Theatre. Other highlights are an important early **Monet**, *Camille*, and **Manet**'s *Portrait of the Poet Zacharie Astruc*. Pick of the German works are **Beckmann**'s *Apache Dance* and *Self-Portrait with Saxophone*, **Kirchner**'s *Street Scene by Night,* and a comprehensive representation of the Worpswede colony, with some forty examples of **Paula Becker-Modersohn** on view around the landing.

Three more museums

Next door to the Kunsthalle is the **Gerhard-Marcks-Haus** (Tues–Sun 10am–6pm; DM2) which contains sculptures, drawings and watercolours by the artist. Apart from the monument to the Bremen Town Band, Marcks is best known for the bronze doors and other works of art he made for a number of German cathedrals and churches to replace those lost in the war. Another collection of specialised appeal is the **Übersee-museum** (Tues–Sun 10am–6pm; DM2), right beside the Hauptbahnhof, which has a large range of ethnological exhibits drawn from all over the Third World.

Of more general interest is the **Bremen Landesmuseum** (Tues–Sun 10am–6pm; DM2), unfortunately rather a long way from the centre of town at Schwachhauser-Heerstr. 240. Laid out in an imaginative and informative manner, this traces the history of Bremen and its port, and has a collection of decorative arts. Among the most important exhibits are the original statues of Charlemagne and the seven Electors from the Rathaus facade. If you're out this way, it's well worth continuing to the nearby **Botanical Gardens** which, in season, are ablaze with some 800 different species of rhododendrons and azaleas.

Eating, Drinking and Entertainment

Eating

Given the number of good **café-bars** in Bremen, it's difficult to single out individual choices. One or two **restaurants**, however, do stand out.

Alte Gilde, Ansgaritorstr. 24. In the vaulted cellar of a seventeenth-century house, this is a reliable all-round recommendation for full meals, whether fish or otherwise.

Bistro Brasil, Ostertorsteinweg 83 in the Ostertorviertel. Has a tropical, all-night atmosphere.

Café Am Wall, Am Wall 164. Has a lively atmosphere and vegetarian food

Café Caruso, Friesenstr. 6–7 is another good choice, with a decent range of food and a friendly atmosphere.

Deutches Haus, Am Markt 1. Top-notch fish specialities served in a grand patrician house.

Flett, Böttcherstr. 3. In one of the fantasy houses in Bremen's most famous street (stained glass windows and oriental carpets feature among the decor), this is another leading choice for fresh seafood dishes.

Friesenhof, Hinter dem Schüting 12. Excellent brewery-owned *Gaststätte*.

Restaurant Souterrain, Sielwall 50. Good, basic pizza place .

Vivaldi Café, Schwachauser-Heerstr. 4 (in Schwachhausen). Highly popular, with a range that often includes vegetarian dishes.

Sowieso Bistro, Schwachhauser-Heerstr. 281. Both this, and the *Cartoon Café* nearby, are relaxed and handy for light meals.

Drinking

Bremen is one of Germany's most famous **beer cities**; the brewers' guild, founded in 1489, is the oldest in the country. It's the home of the internationally famous *Beck's*, one of the most heavily exported brews in the country, though it's a comparative newcomer, having existed for just over a century. *St Pauli Girl* is another brand well-known abroad, but the products of *Haake-Beck* are the ones to go for in the city itself. They make both a filtered and an unfiltered Pils (the latter known as *Kräusen*), as well as the refreshing *Bremer Weisse*, which is usually sweetened with fruit syrup. Best choice of beers is at *Kleiner Ratskeller* on Hinter dem Schütting. The *Ratskeller* itself (see p.551), according to an old statute, can serve only **wine** – but offers an astonishing choice of over 600 wines, one of the largest collections in Germany.

The best place to head for **bars and nightlife** is the Ostertorviertel, in particular along the Ostertorsteinweg, and in the short yard called *Auf den Häfen*, near the junction of Humboldtstr. and Am Dobben; which is similar in atmosphere to London's Camden Lock, except much smaller and without the water. Bars, restaurants and studios squeeze next to each other, and on summer evenings, people sit outside long into the night. Two popular *Kneipen* in the quarter are *Brommy*, Hemelinger Str. 7, and *Gerken*, Feldstr. 77. Another good place, with a beer garden attached, is the *Leierkasten*, Pagentorner Heimweg, between Staderstrasse and Friedrich-Karl-Strrasse. For Sunday morning jazz (traditional), head for the *Waldbühne* in the Bürgerpark. Best reached by bicycle, this small stage and beer garden is not far from where the railway crosses the road Am Stadtwald.

Late night bars to check are: *Airport*, Am Dobben 70; *Bierakademie*, Herdentorsteinweg 4`(open 24hrs); and *Café Noir*, Herdentorsteinweg 2; (open 24hrs). The last two are right by the station, so expect a very mixed crowd.

Music and theatre

Excellent concerts of **classical music**, mainly of chamber music and appearances by international guest orchestras, are arranged by the *Philharmonische Gesellschaft*. Tickets (between DM15–30) from *Praeger and Meier*, Böttcherstr. 7 (☎325173), are usually in short supply, but it's worth a try, especially as a limited number are available at half-price for students. The *Jazz Club Bremen* in the Tivoli building by the Hauptbahnhof has live concerts, mainly of traditional styles, on Fridays and Saturdays. Main **theatres** are *Theater am Goetheplatz* (☎365 3333), which hosts major dance performances, operas and musicals, and *Concordia* (☎365 3333), Schwachhauser-Heerstr. 17, which specialises in modern and experimental works. The *Bremen Shakespeare Company* at the *Theater am Leibnizplatz* (☎500333), is the only company in Germany to have seven of Shakespeare's play in rep at any one time.

Info

Best source of nightlife info is the tourist office, which has pamphlets listing events, and is the city's main ticket-booking agency. The monthly **listings magazines** *Bremer Blatt* and *Kursbuch* and the fortnightly *Prinz* are each around DM3, but a free magazine *Lokal Spezial* can be picked up in restaurants/cafés – useful for addresses rather than actual events. German-speakers staying longer might be interested in *Bremen bei Nacht* (DM5).

Listings

Bike hire At the station, Bahnhofplatz Ostseite (☎302114), Mon & Wed 9am–1.30pm & 3–6pm plus May–Sept Sun 9am–1.30pm & 3–6pm.

Books *The Cosy Bookshop*, Dobbenweg 10, (☎703709); Mon–Fri 3.30–6pm; Sat 10am–1pm; closed during school holidays. Second-hand English books for around DM5; swaps possible.

Car rental *Inter-Rent* (☎170941)

Festivals Leading folklore events are the *Eiswette* on 6 Jan (Epiphany), and the *Freimarkt*, which begins with a procession in mid-Oct, and continues for a fortnight.

Gay line (☎704170).

Harbour cruises Departures March–Oct from *Martini–Anleger* (☎321229), through the pedestrian tunnel at the end of Böttcherstrasse. Tours last 75min and cost from DM10.

Mitfahrzentralen *Bremer Mitfahrzentrale* (in the Ostertorviertel), Humboldstr. 6 (☎72011). *Mitfahrladen und Reiseladen*, Weberstr. 44 (☎72022/72167). For women, the *Mitfahrzentrale für Frauen* is run from the women's bookshop at Friesenstr. 12 (Fesenfeld; ☎74033).

Poste Restante At junction of An der Weide and Löningstrasse, beside the Hauptbahnhof.

Sports *SV Werder Bremen* have been one of the most successful football teams in the country in recent seasons. They play at the *Weserstadion* in Osterdeich, on tram lines #2, #3, & #10; ☎498106 for fixtures and details. Indoor sporting events are held in the *Stadthalle*, just behind the Hauptbahnhof.

Taxis (☎14141).

Womens' centre (☎349573).

Bremerhaven

BREMERHAVEN is the Federal Republic's busiest fishing port, founded in 1827 as Bremen's deep-water harbour. Unless you're a naval buff, it has nothing that can't be seen better, and more conveniently, elsewhere.

Pride of the town is the **Deutsches Schiffahrtsmuseum** (National Museum of Navigation) in Von-Ronzelen-Strasse (Tues–Sun 10am–6pm; DM4). This traces the history of German sailing from prehistoric times to the present; star exhibit is a fourteenth-century Hanseatic log which was dredged up from the port of Bremen. Outside in the harbour, several historic vessels are moored, including *Seute Deern*, the last German wooden sailing ship, and the Arctic explorer *Grönland*. There's also a wartime U-boat, the *Wilhelm Bauer*, the only one of its kind still in existence.

The only conceivable alternative attraction if you're waiting for a boat is the **Museum für kunst des 20 Jahrhunderts** at Karlsburg 4 (Tues–Sat 3–6pm, Sun 11am–1pm). Otherwise it's a short hop by train to Bremen or Hannover, or by boat to Helgoland (day return DM55, standard return DM68; trip takes 3hrs). If you do need to stay, the **tourist office** (☎0471/42095) at von-Ronzelen-Strasse 2, can advise on rooms.

Around Bremen

If you're staying in Bremen and want a trip out, the most obvious places to head for are the coast and area around **Stade**, and the former artists' colony of **Worpswede**. **Verden** is a worthwhile stop-off if you're heading towards Hannover or the Lüneburg Heath.

Verden

Between Bremen and Hannover – or Bremen and the Lüneburger Heide – the small city of **VERDEN** on the River Aller is at first sight not particularly interesting. But hidden away at the end of a tedious shopping centre is North Germany's oldest brick-built church, and a Dom that dates back to the twelfth century.

The Dom

However you approach it, the **Dom** is very impressive indeed. The interior has a feeling of great space; it was one of the first full-scale churches in Germany to be built in the hall style, with nave, aisles and choir all the same height. Its lightness is increased by the apparent slenderness of the columns, your eye drawn up their vertical mouldings. Just outside and opposite the Dom is a rather good café, *Das Andere Café*. The **Johanniskirche** on Ritterstrasse, built during the twelfth century and gothicised in the fifteenth century isn't as impressive, but has a homely feel and a few medieval frescos.

Verden has always been an equestrian centre, with major horse auctions taking place here three times a year (around 19 April, 13 July & 18 October). Horsey types from all over the country are drawn to the **Deutsches Pferdemuseum** here (Andreasstr. 7; Tues–Sun 9am–4pm) – a rather serious institution with a huge collection of equine artefacts, and a valuable library in the Hippological Institute.

Practicalities

The **tourist office**, Ostertorstr. 7a (☎04231/12317), straight ahead and right from the Hauptbahnhof, sells cycle touring maps (DM7 each) of places within easy reach on a few days' tour. One tour leads to the **Vogelpark Walsrode** (daily mid-March–Oct 9am–7pm; DM10), a large park around 30km south-east of the town, where about 5000 indigenous and exotic birds are on view in large birdhouses. Here the countryside begins to take on the characteristics of the Lüneburger Heath.

Verden is very small, and nowhere is more than ten minutes' walk from the Bahnhof. There are plenty of **places to stay**: a modern youth hostel is at Saumurplatz (☎04231/61163), and at the inexpensive end of hotels is *Der Oelkenhof*, Im Dicken Ort 17 (☎04231/62963).

Worpswede

About 25km outside Bremen in the **Teufelsmoor** (the forbiddingly-named "Devil's peat bog") is the intriguing village of **WORPSWEDE**. Back in the 1880s this was a simple farming village, where the inhabitants scraped together a living. The artists Fritz Mackensen and Otto Modersohn came here then, and over the next ten or so years Worpswede developed into an artists' colony, a movement run on roughly similar lines to the Pre-Raphaelites. The famous poet Rainer Maria Rilke was closely associated with them, as was his wife, Clara Westhoff.

It was **Paula Becker**, who subsequently married Modersohn, who became the most significant of the set – her powerful, depressing pictures depicting the grim realities of peasant life, poverty and death stand out from the pretty, though comparatively facile, impressionistic scenes of the others. The exhibition hall in the centre of town that sometimes shows her work was built in 1927 in a flamboyant style, reminiscent almost of a Thai temple.

Practicalities

If you make a trip to Worpswede you're not limited to the exhibitions by the original artists – many craftspeople are based here and have studios, and although the town is quiet it has various restaurants and cafés – and a **youth hostel** (☎04792/1360). You can reach Worpswede by bus #140 from Bremen Hauptbahnhof; a **light railway** runs from BREMERVÖRDE, and it's possible to come from Bremen by (infrequent) **boat** in summer. Ask at the tourist office in Bremen for exact times of both services.

The Altes Land

The blunt stump of land between the Elbe and the Weser is not easy to explore without your own transport – it's gentle countryside, though, scattered with interesting villages whose charm partly lies in being off the beaten track.

The area closest to Hamburg, the so-called **Altes Land**, sees most visitors. Traditionally the Altes Land is Hamburg's garden – fruit and vegetables are the main crops of a sheltered cultivated area that's picturesque and pleasant to meander through by bike or car on a sunny day, with plenty of places to stop off for a hearty German lunch. Such a trip is easily combined with a visit to the small town of **BUXTEHUDE**, though the town itself is of slender interest, with but a few restored houses from its Hanseatic past.

Stade

About 26km north and west of Buxtehude, the little port of **STADE** used to be in Swedish hands back in the seventeenth century, and the **museum** (Tues–Sun 10am–5pm) in the *Schwedenspeicher* (Swedish Warehouse) in the harbour records that history. Every summer the Swedish connection is celebrated in the town with the Schwedenwoche (Swedish week), normally held in the second week of June. One or two surprisingly grand house facades indicate that Stade was once relatively affluent – as it is today, thanks to industry on its outskirts. There's a strange atmosphere to the town, though; the old harbour (the **Westwasser**) and houses there that form the heart of the town were under threat of demolition back in the 1960s, and, following a successful protest that stopped the area being turned into a car park, a lot of renovation was carried out. The job was done so well, so thoroughly, that Stade now has an odd, artificial, almost toytown feel to it. The large **Cosmaekirche**, topped by an onion-shaped spire, dates from the thirteenth century and may be open for a look inside. Also by the old harbour is the **Goebenhaus** (birthplace of Prussian Field Marshal von Goeben) which has a reasonably priced café with home-made snacks and cakes.

WESTERN LOWER SAXONY

This area takes in points west of Bremen, as far as the border with the Netherlands – much of it is agricultural land, and the main area of interest is **East Friesia** (*Ostfriesland*). Over the centuries the Friesians have resolutely avoided complete absorption by their German neighbours, retaining their own language and cultural identity. They inhabit a low-lying, fertile province that was prey to constant inundation by the sea; it was a miserable sort of existence, as **Pliny** observed around 50AD:

> *Here a wretched race is found, inhabiting either the more elevated spots or artificial mounds where they pitch their cabins. When the waves cover the surrounding area they are like so many mariners on board a ship, and when again the tide recedes their condition is that of so many ship-wrecked men.*

Not surprisingly, the Friesians got pretty fed up with this sort of life and as soon as the technology arrived began to build the dykes that have culminated in the sea-barrier that extends right round the coast from **Emden** to **Wilhelmshaven**.

East Friesia may have poor weather and interminably flat countryside, but it has spawned an ingenious tourist sub-culture taking advantage of the "bracing maritime climate . . . that regenerates the blood and nerves" while "a walk along the foreshore will provide natural inhalation treatment", as the local tourist brochure puts it. If you want more, you can pay for the privilege of being submerged in genuine North Sea mud in a number of large health spas, or join organised walks across the mudflats (the *Watt*) that encircle the coast – something you certainly shouldn't attempt on your own.

There are less esoteric alternatives: several **towns**, such as **Norden**, merit a visit; great stretches of land are designated **nature reserves** and there are two long-distance **footpaths** connecting Emden with Wilhelmshaven. The first follows the Ems-Jade canal, the second the coastline taking the name of Klaus Störtebeker, a fifteenth-century Friesian pirate and Robin Hood-type character whose name is much lauded locally. If you're coming from Osnabrück, you can get further info from *Wiehengebirgsversand d.v.*, Bierstrasse 25, 4500 Osnabrück.

The **East Friesian islands**, with their long sandy beaches, lie just off the coast and are immensely popular holiday resorts. Each island has a full range of tourist facilities and trains connect the ferries to most major German cities. With the possible exceptions of **Norderney** and **Juist**, this popularity has more to do with the country's truncated coastline than any special charm.

Oldenburg, on the eastern edge of Western Lower Saxony, has eighteenth-century buildings worth seeing in passing, while to the south the main town is the old episcopal centre of **Osnabrück**, a major railway junction.

Most inland **travel** can be done by bus, though it's worth noting that services can be sparse on Sundays; **ferry** details are listed in the text, though services can be erratic, dependent on time of the year and north sea tides.

Emden

EMDEN is West Germany's fourth largest seaport and the principal town of East Friesia, with a population of some 50,000. A trading centre from the time of Charlemagne, Emden was becalmed when the river Ems changed its course during the seventeenth century, and only revived some 300 years later with the digging of the Dortmund-Ems canal and the building of a new harbour. Heavily bombed in World War II, there's precious little left of the old town; what remains marks Emden as a pleasant but unremarkable place, important chiefly because of its Volkswagen plant. The **Bahnhof** and **bus station** are five minutes from the centre – turn right after the water tower down Ringstrasse and first left – where you can find the **tourist office** (Mon–Fri 9am–1pm & 3–5.30pm, Sat 10am–1pm; ☎04921/20094) moored in an old light-ship. They will help with **accommodation**, or you can try the cheapest place in the centre of town: *Pension Ewald*, Neutorsgang 7, charging DM30 per person. The **youth hostel** is at An der Kesselschleuse 5 (☎04921/23797) on the eastern outskirts and the **campsite** *Knock* is 8km west along the coast road.

The centre

The centre of Emden has one or two minor attractions. There are the remains of the medieval church of Cosmas and Damian; a rather incongruous Renaissance gate stuck by the water-side and a **Museum für Moderne Kunst** on Hinter dem Rahmen 13 (Tues 10am–8pm, Wed–Fri 10am–5pm, Sat & Sun 11am–5pm) that concentrates on Expressionism. The **Ostfriesisches Landesmuseum** (Mon–Fri 10am–1pm & 3–5pm, Sat & Sun 11am–1pm; closed Mon Oct–April), right in the middle of town in the former Rathaus, has a selection of local items and one of the largest collections of **armour** in Europe. Finally, the tourist office will provide details of **boat trips** around the waterways that once protected Emden – a pleasant way to spend an afternoon.

Greetsiel

The strip of agricultural land to the west of Emden, known as the **Krummhörn**, was reclaimed from the sea between the Wars; at its northern tip is the picturesque fishing village of **GREETSIEL**. All roads lead to Rome, and all tourist coaches in Ostfriesland probably lead to Greetsiel, a shrimp-fishing village since the fourteenth century, with cobbled streets, hump-backed bridges, windmills and teashops, but – in season – definitely not for those with a low coach-party tolerance. There's plenty of accommodation for visitors, mainly in bed and breakfast arrangements, and the **tourist office** at Sielstr. 17 (☎04926/1331) can arrange places to stay, though it gets difficult if you leave it too late in the day. The **youth hostel** is at Kleinbahnstr. 15 (☎04926/550) with **camping** fairly close by at Loquard (☎04927/595). Don't miss *Is Teetied* opposite the church in Greetsiel, an East Friesian style olde tea shoppe with many good things to eat. Friesians may account for only two per cent of the population, but they drink twenty-five percent of the nation's tea; they like it strong, poured over special giant sugar crystals (*klöntjes*) and topped up with cream. **Buses** connect Greetsiel with Norden and Emden, though Sunday services are poor.

Just down the road, FREEPSUM is Germany's lowest point, 2.3m below sea-level. From nearby **DIEKSKIEL** you can go out on the Watt with a *Wattführer*, an experienced guide who will lead you through the treacherous mud-flats; emphatically not something you should try on your own.

Borkum

The island of **Borkum** is the largest and most westerly of the East Friesian islands. A popular holiday spot, it has all the facilities of a resort including a casino, an indoor swimming-pool with sea-water and artificial waves, a marina and long sandy beaches. **Ferries** for Borkum leave from the harbour (*Aussenhafen*) just south of Emden four times daily in summer, twice daily in winter (journey takes 2hr 30min; return ticket DM44, DM22 for a return day trip). There are onward connections from the ferry terminal to Emden and other major German cities. Despite the calm effected by a ban on cars during the tourist season, frankly, Borkum has nothing special to offer and does not warrant the long and expensive trip – other islands are more appealing and more easily reached. However it's possible to reach Holland from Borkum on a ferry sailing to the Dutch island of Eemshaven: tickets cost DM35 (DM20 for a day trip). For further details call ☎04921/890722, and see our guide to *Holland, Belgium and Luxembourg*.

Aurich, Norden and Norddeich

AURICH is the administrative centre of East Friesia, and an easy bus ride from Emden. Once the seat of the province's nobility, the town is quite grand, in spite of its small size, with a large, pink Schloss and some impressive Baroque buildings to its credit. The old part of town is still surrounded on two sides by a **moat**, and in the town centre is the enormous **Marktplatz**, created in the early sixteenth century by Count Edzard. You have to go the **Historisches Museum** at Burgstr. 25 (Tues–Sat 10am–noon & 3–5pm, Sun 3–5pm) to see a reconstruction of the houses that used to edge the square. Their graceful lines are marred these days by several incongruous postwar additions, notably the grey lump of the savings bank that still makes local hackles rise. Close to the museum are some of the town's best **Renaissance facades**; the **Lambertikirche**, with the solid, square tower typical of this region (though in this case topped by a spire) has an altar carved in Antwerp around 1500.

It's easy to walk across town, and although the **youth hostel** (Am Ellernfeld, ☎04941/2827), for example, is on virtually the other side of town from the Bahnhof, it's still no more than twenty minutes away on foot. In yet another corner is the **Pferdemarkt**, the original site of Aurich's market from the thirteenth century until the creation of the new square but now a car park and the main place for **bus** arrivals and departures. The **tourist office** (☎04941/4464) is here, too, and has accommodation lists. Along the Oldersumer Strasse is an **old windmill**, the Stiftsmühle, built in 1858 and now open to visitors (May–Sept Tues–Sat 10am–noon & 2–5pm, Sun 2–5pm).

About 5km west of Aurich, in the peat-bog (*Moor* in German) of the Südbrookmerland, is the **Moormuseum Moordorf**, (Victoburer Moor 7a, Südbrookmerland-Moordorf; May–Oct Tues–Sun 10am–5.30pm; DM2), dedicated to 200 years of history of the **Moordorf colony**. The museum records the tough life in the colony, whose inhabitants depended on peat fires for heating and cooking. The museum is housed in an old cottage and other small buildings; peat-digging and traditional crafts are often demonstrated.

Norden

At the centre of **NORDEN** stands the medieval **Ludgerikirche**, built between the thirteenth century and fifteenth century. Its **organ**, made in the 1680s and housed in an elaborate Baroque case, is one of the most beguiling instruments in the world, ranking as the masterpiece of northern Germany's greatest exponent of the craft, Arp Schnitger. The tall, narrow building near the church is its freestanding belltower. Together they dominate the huge **Marktplatz**, half of which is grassed over and dominated by shady, mature trees, forming an odd, or at least unfamiliar, picture in this part of the world. Along the paved part of the market place are two Renaissance houses, and several other facades of similar age. Up the Osterstrasse is perhaps the best of the town's Renaissance buildings, a late sixteenth-century **burgher's house**, which today contains an excellent and reasonably priced Italian restaurant, *Vesuvio*. Also near the church are the **Heimatmuseum** (Wed & Fri 3–5pm, Sat 10am–noon) and the **tourist office** (June–Aug Mon–Fri 8am–5pm, Sat 10am–5pm; Sept–May Mon–Fri 8am–2.30pm; ☎04931/17202), which can help with accommodation.

Perhaps because of the large square, perhaps because it has escaped the standard German pedestrian zone, Norden has an individual, if a little sleepy, atmosphere. It's a far more pleasant place to be based than its seaside neighbour Norddeich, especially if you stay at the *Hotel zur Post*, a sort of alternative hotel rescued from a dilapidated state by the two women who now run it. The downstairs adjoining **café-bar** appears to be the centre of Norden life (and is next to the post office on the market place).

Norddeich

Ten minutes by bus from the Marktplatz is **NORDDEICH**. **Ferries** run from here to the islands of Juist and Norderney, and the train, timed to coincide with the boats, goes right up to the jetty (**Norddeich-Mole**). If you are going to Baltrum, a bus meets appropriate trains to take passengers to the ferry at Nessmersiel. Alternatively, you could stop off in Norddeich itself, though it's an ugly rambling town with precious little to recommend it. Almost every house takes **bed and breakfast** visitors – just look out for "*Zimmer frei*" signs. The **youth hostel**, at Strandstr. 1 (☎04931/8064) is signposted, and has camping facilities. From Norddeich-Mole there are trains to a range of German cities, and even direct services to Amsterdam and Copenhagen.

The Islands: Juist and Norderney

Depending on the tides, between one and three ferries leave Norddeich Mole for the island of **Juist** every day; the trip takes eighty minutes and costs DM22 for a day return, DM36 for a period return. One of the most attractive and popular of the East Friesian islands, Juist is a narrow strip of land 17km long and a few hundred yards wide. A sandy, dune-fringed beach extends the entire length of its northern shore and even on hot summer days privacy is not hard to find. The only **settlement** is halfway along the island near the ferry terminal. It's a rather drab suburban affair, but at least it's not dominated by high-rise hotels and, best of all, there are no cars. Criss-crossed by foot and cycle paths, Juist has the full range of tourist facilities with dozens of bars and restaurants, a large covered swimming-pool and a nature reserve (the "Bill").

Juist practicalities

Accommodation can be a little tricky in summer, but the **tourist office** (Friesenstr. 18, April–Sept Mon–Sat 8am–noon & 3–5.30pm; Oct–March Mon–Sat 8am–noon; ☎04935/809222) in the Rathaus is more than willing to help. Reckon on about DM30 per person. The **youth hostel** (March–Oct only) at Loogster Pad 20 (☎04935/1094) has 400 beds and family rooms. **Camping** is not permitted anywhere on the island. The following *Ruhezeiten* (literally "periods of quiet", for which read "You shall not enjoy yourselves, you shall not party, you will obey orders") must be observed: summer daily 1–4pm & 9pm–8am, winter 10pm–7am.

Juist's main **post office** is at Friesenstr. 12. A useful **travel agent** for details of sailings to local islands and the mainland is the *Reisebüro Kiesendahl*, Strandstr. 2 (☎04935/1096). For a tour of the celebrated Juist **mud-flats** and the protected wildlife areas, contact Wattführer Heino Behring on ☎04935/1443.

Norderney

The most popular and distinctive of the East Friesian islands, **Norderney** is also the most accessible. Depending on the season, **ferries** make the fifty-minute journey from Norddeich Mole to Norderney between nine and thirteen times a day; a period return costs DM19. **NORDERNEY** town is at the western end of the island, a short bus ride or a fifteen-minute walk from the ferry terminal. The **tourist office** (May–Sept Mon–Fri 8am–12.30pm & 2–6pm, Sat 10am–12.30pm & 2–4pm; ☎04932/502), just off the main square at Bülow Allee 5, will arrange **accommodation** – though things get tight in high season. There are two **youth hostels** (open March–Oct), one at Südstr. 1 (☎04932/2451; members only; bus from ferry or 35min walk down Zum Fahranleger to Deichstrasse then on to Südstrasse), the other way to the east of the town and not on any bus route, at Am Dünensender 3 (☎04932/2574) with attached **camping** facilities. Both hostels fill quickly in season. There are two further **campsites**, one of them on the eastern edge of town, and the other several kilometres further on.

Slightly self-conscious, Norderney is the oldest spa on the German North Sea coast and was once a favourite royal holiday residence. The **central square** with its manicured gardens, elegant cafés and Neoclassical buildings has retained a certain nineteenth-century grace, though most of the town is a dull mixture of modern architectures. Its only surprise is a huge pyramid of stones piled up in the middle of an ordinary suburban side street. Crass in the extreme, this is in fact a **monument to Kaiser Wilhelm** and his efforts to unify Germany; sixty-one stones marked with their state of origin.

Norderney tries hard to cater for all tastes. In summer the bars are packed with serious drinkers, middle-aged couples tuck into apple strudels and gamblers fill the casino with no time to eat or drink. Meanwhile, earnest joggers trot round the myriad footpaths, families sunbathe on the long sandy beach, pensioners take the cures and cyclists tour the nature reserve. If that's not enough, there are innumerable gourmet restaurants, a couple of small museums and the first-ever covered swimming-pool to have seawater and artificial waves. For an account of the very different lifestyle of the islanders in the first half of last century, read the second part of Heinrich Heine's *Reisebilder*. Norderney also inspired *The North Sea*, a cycle of poems by the same author.

More Islands: Baltrum, Langeoog, Spiekeroog, Wangerooge

With none of the polished sophistication of their westerly neighbours, these four islands have four things in common: sandy beaches to the north and mud-flats to the south; drab modern settlements with a suburban air; nature reserves; and **bus/ferry** connections from Norden's Bahnhof.

Baltrum

Baltrum is the smallest and least remarkable with three coaches from Norden Bahnhof to the ferry point at NESSMERSIEL per day. Buses arrive in time for each of the three ferry departures, though you can expect crossings to be delayed in rough weather.The **tourist office** (☎04939/8048) in the Rathaus has full details of ferry time-tables and supplies an **accommodation** list: there's a **campsite** on the edge of the nature reserve and a quiet atmosphere not found at the busier resorts, partly a result of cars being banned on the island.

Langeoog

Buses also leave Norden Bahnhof for **BENSERSIEL**, the ferry port for **Langeoog**, between three and five times daily – though in this case the bus is not synchronised with the ferry. The ferry costs DM23 return, takes fifty minutes and connects with the island's toytown railway to the main settlement. The best place to stay must be the **youth hostel** (April–Sept) some 3km to the east, pleasantly sited behind the Melkhörn sand dunes – ring ahead in high season (☎04972/276). Otherwise, check the **notice-board** outside the Rathaus for daily vacancies in local rooms. The village is particularly dull and Langeoog's only claim to fame is its enormous colony of seabirds found in the **nature reserve** at the east end of the island.

Spiekeroog

The same bus from Norden continues along the coast to **NEUHARLINGERSIEL** for **Spiekeroog** – two to four ferries per day, fifty minutes. Attractions here include an island railway and a seventeenth-century church.There's also a **youth hostel** (15 March–30 Oct; ☎04976/329; phone booking before arrival preferred). The tourist office at Nooderpad 25 (☎04976/170) supplies information on rooms, and tells you how to get to the **Inselkirche** (Island Church), the oldest (1696) church on the East Friesian Islands. It contains wreckage from one of the ships of the Spanish Armada, wrecked off the coast nearby in 1558.

Wangerooge

The bus continues to **HARLESIEL** for **Wangerooge**. **Ferries** make the seventy-minute trip two or three times daily in summer and once in winter; return tickets cost DM41. The **tourist office** (April–Sept Mon–Sat 9am–noon & 3–4.30pm, Oct–March 9am–noon; ☎04469/890) will help with **accommodation** – reckon on about DM35 per person – and there's also a **campsite** (☎04469/307). The main settlement is in the middle of the island, connected by rail to the ferry terminal; a branch-line goes to the western tip where you can find the **youth hostel** (open May–Sept; ☎04469/439).

Founded in 1804, the old resort was swept away by high tides some fifty years later and precious little has survived from its Victorian past. One of the more attractive islands, Wangerooge has all the usual tourist facilities, a small museum in the old lighthouse, and several **bird sanctuaries**.

Along the coast

Other villages along the coast vary in character – the fishing villages with their old-fashioned boats, such as DORNUMERSIEL and the inland harbour of CAROLINENSIEL – are inevitably more picturesque than the newly built resorts like BENSERSIEL. The **bus services** to all these places are fairly good, but tend to dovetail with island ferry sailing times, so it's best to pick up a local bus timetable. Carolinensiel has a **Sielhafenmuseum**, devoted to boat-building, fishing, dyke-building and other activities on the Lower Saxon North Sea coast. It's in an old corn warehouse, right on the harbourside (mid-June to mid-Oct). More or less opposite is a rather imposing hotel with strange staff, but there's a **youth hostel** at Herbergsmense 13 (☎04464/252).

Jever

Strictly speaking, **JEVER** is not part of East Friesia but belongs to its rival Friesia, or the Jeverland. The town's heroine is Fräulein Maria, an energetic and gifted sixteenth-century countess who gave Jever city rights, had the fortifications built, founded a school and commissioned several works of art. Later, through marriage and conquest, Jever came under Russian, Dutch and French rule. The rather magnificent pink **Schloss**, begun in the fifteenth century and subsequently extended, is now a very good **museum** (March–Dec Tues–Sat 10am–1pm & 3–5pm, Sun 11am–1pm & 3–5pm). Look out, if you go, for the carved oak ceiling of the audience room, which Fraülein Maria had made by the Antwerp artist Cornelis Floris. Otherwise, exhibitions of crafts and reconstructed rooms are the museum's main features. It might be possible to go up the tower for a **view** of the town and across the castle gardens, planted with some beautiful trees.

The centre

On the way through narrow streets towards the centre of the old town and the church, you pass the sixteenth-century **Rathaus**. The **Stadtkirche** has been burned down and rebuilt at least nine times in its 900-year history. It last had a fire in 1959, when over half of the church was completely destroyed and replaced, for better or worse, with a contemporary design. The enormous monument by Floris that Fraülein Maria had erected for her father somehow survived, and can be seen in the remains of the Baroque church, now integrated into the new building. A work of architecture as much as sculpture, it's particularly remarkable for the extraordinary mixture of materials used – wood, marble, sandstone and clay. From May to September there are weekday tours of the **Jever brewery**; turn up by 10.30am at the brewery in Elizabethufer 17. The Pils is celebrated as the most bitter-tasting beer made anywhere in Germany, and is a popular drink among northern Germans.

Jever's **tourist office** is in the Johannis-Ahlers-Haus on the Altermarkt (Mon–Fri 9am–5pm, Sat 9am–1pm; ☎04461/71010). It offers the usual accommodation facilities and the usual array of glossy leaflets on the town.

Halfway between Jever and Wilhelmshaven is the village of SILLENSTEDE, and if you have your own transport you might want to stop off to look at the **Floriankirche**, a twelfth-century Romanesque church made of granite blocks – its organ is renowned, too, and there are concerts here on Saturday evenings.

Wilhelmshaven

As German unification gathered momentum, Wilhelm I of Prussia coveted British naval supremacy and decided to build a westward naval base and dockyard on the North Sea coast. This purpose-built military town was to be the epitome of efficiency with an integrated rail, canal and dock system. The result was **WILHELMSHAVEN**, founded in 1853 and a key determinant in German naval planning by the end of the century. Heavily bombed in World War II, the centre was rebuilt as an ugly, concrete shopping centre and there are few reminders of Wilhelmshaven's imperial past. The dockyards are still the main employers, but the naval base is no longer of any great strategic significance and the town has a rather desolate, insular atmosphere.

The town has a number of curiosities within easy walking distance – the high Victorian elegance of the houses on Kielerstrasse, south of Peterstrasse; the old harbour; the naval base; and the Kaiser Wilhelm bridge with its symmetrical Prussian sentry-boxes. The nearest **"beach"** is at Südstrand, though it's really a mole with a few inches of sand. Finally, Wilhelmshaven has a flourishing punk scene, attracting surprisingly good British bands.

Practicalities – and onward travel

The **Hauptbahnhof** and adjoining **bus station** are in the middle of town, ten minutes from the **tourist office** (Mon–Fri 9am–6pm, Sat 9am–1pm; ☎04421/25281)) at Börsenstr. 55b – turn left out of the station, immediately left up Virchowstrasse and then take the third left. They will phone round for **accommodation** and provide town maps. Alternatively, you can try the convenient *Hotel Flacke* at Virchowstr. 30 (DM35 per person), or the **youth hostel** at Freiligrathstr. 131 (☎04421/60048), a couple of kilometres north of the city centre; the nearest **campsite** is about 4km further on by the sea. In emergencies there's a large, wooded park at the far end of Virchowstrasse where you could try to bed down – though this is illegal.

Most tourists bypass Wilhelmshaven. Holiday-makers heading for the islands of Langeoog, Spiekeroog and Wangerooge go through the railway junction of SANDE a few miles to the west, whilst those travelling to HELGOLAND go straight through the town to the ferry terminal. There are **railway** connections from Wilhelmshaven to a wide range of German cities via Sande and **bus** services to the surrounding small towns. Services are, once again, poor on Sundays.

Helgoland

Ferries leave Wilhelmshaven once a day between April and September for the three-hour trip to **Helgoland** (or Heligoland). A single fare costs DM52. Alternative sailings depart from BREMERHAVEN, NORDDEICH/NORDERNEY (once weekly) and CUXHAVEN. The red limestone island of Helgoland stands on its own seventy kilometres from the mouth of the Elbe, and was once an important naval base and coaling station. Occupied by the British, it only came into German hands in 1890, when it was swapped for Zanzibar. Bombarded during World War II, the inhabitants were forcibly evacuated in 1947, and the remaining fortifications blown up. For five years it served as a bombing target for the RAF, until finally returned to Germany in 1952. Reconstruction began immediately and Helgoland has become a popular holiday resort with all the usual facilities – and duty-free status. The craggy cliffs are dramatic, but frankly Helgoland is not special enough to warrant the time and expense of getting there – other more accessible islands are just as enjoyable. If you do make it here the **tourist office** (☎04725/80862) will help with **accommodation** – ring ahead in high season – and there's a **youth hostel** (☎04725/341) open from April to October.

Oldenburg

South of Wilhelmshaven, **OLDENBURG** is a pleasant enough place to change trains, but unlikely to qualify as a major stopping-off point otherwise. A former ducal residence town, it's now mostly modernised and criss-crossed with large shopping streets, busy with people on shopping trips from the surrounding countryside. As the town has a student population, there's plenty going on in the evenings. Oldenburg keeps busy with various festivals throughout the year, the **Kramermarkt** in October being the annual high point.

The centre

Arriving by train it's soon obvious that Oldenburg is not expecting visitors – no signposts to the town centre, no hint of where you might spend the night or find a map of the town. Turning immediately right out of the station, along the Mosle Strasse, leads to the northernmost part of the moated Altstadt. Alternatively, heading straight out of the station takes you to the end of the harbour, a busy inland port linked to the North Sea and, by canal, to the Netherlands. You can then turn right and follow the old moat to the left, crossing it at some point into the southern part of the Altstadt, thereby avoiding the shoppers and arriving in the area of Schlossplatz, Markt and Berg Strasse, the "cultural" end of town.

Tourist information (☎0441/15744) is at Lange Str. 3 in the **Lappan**, the fifteenth-century tower of the medieval Heiligen-Geist-Hospital.

In the Schlossplatz, the seventeenth- and eighteenth-century **Schloss** houses the **Landesmuseum für Kunst und Kulturgeschichte** (Tues–Fri 9am–5pm Sat & Sun 9am–1pm; free) whose lure is a large collection of paintings, interiors and ceramics – and, most celebrated of all, the **Tischbein room**. The name of Tischbein is often associated with that of Goethe, who was apparently inspired by the painter's idyllic scenes. Duke Peter Friedrich Ludwig of Oldenburg was a patron of Tischbein, hence the large collection here. Modern art is housed in the **Augusteum** (same times; free), a separate building on the corner of Elisabeth Strasse and the Damm.

Up in the market place is the thirteenth-century **Lambertikirche**, whose Gothic exterior has been built round and over, and is today scarcely visible. The interior was completely reworked, under Peter Friedrich Ludwig's orders, in the 1790s into a classical round shape based on the Pantheon in Rome. It's rather like a Wedgewood vase turned inside out – quite astonishing.

The area around Berg Strasse is good to look at; Berg Strasse itself has a few crafts shops, and runs down to the Theaterwall. The present **Staatstheater** was built at the end of the last century and was extensively renovated in 1974 as a venue for concerts, ballet and opera performances, as well as drama. To the south of the old town is the **Schlossgarten**, which used to be the source of vegetables, eggs and milk for consumption in the Schloss. It was subsequently laid out as an English-style garden, and is a good place to relax and picnic.

Practical details

The **youth hostel** is at Alexander Str. 65 (☎0441/87135), north of the Pferdemarkt, and summer **camping** facilities exist by the Flötenteich lake, up in the northeast part of town, by bus from the town centre to Nadorst.

The least expensive **hotels** are quite a way out of town, with the exception of *Mandel* (doubles from DM75) at 91er Str. 2 whose proximity to the railway may lead to sleepless nights, and *Sprenz* (doubles from DM80) at Heiligengeist Str. 15, which is by the Pferdemarkt. Two private addresses offer bed and breakfast: *Frau Bundkiel*, Friedrich-Rüder-Str. 30 (☎0441/12340), about ten minutes' walk south of the Schloss, and east of the Schlossgarten; or *Frau Kretz*, Cäcilien Str. 2 (☎0441/77520): cross the moat by the theatre – Roon Strasse – and turn right. Both of these cost DM25. Other than this, the tourist office has the usual reservation service.

For **eating**, the café in the Schlossplatz has salad-style dishes, and Lange Strasse and Achtern Strasse have a good selection of places: try *Campino* at Achtern Str. 57 for pizza, sandwiches and salads; *Laterne*, at Heiligengeist Str. 19; *Le Journal*, Wallstr. 13, and *Kartoffelkiste* at Artillerie Weg 56. For **drinking**, head for the Kurwick Strasse; there's also *Ulenspegel* (open late) at Burg Str. 12 and *Hannenfass*, Baumgarten Str. 3, whose speciality is Altbier, and which features music on Wednesdays. At the same address is *Sunup's* (a disco-café-bar), or there's *Bebob*, hard by the station.

Best way to get around town is on foot, but you can **hire bikes** at *Fahrrad Bonke* in the Haupt Strasse, or *Die Speiche* in Donnerschweer Strasse. The tourist office sells a cycle map, and the cycle paths are extensive and good. Lastly, the **Mitfahrzentrale** is at Nadorster Str. 38 (☎0441/885656).

Around Oldenburg

A relaxed 20km bike ride, or a twenty-minute train trip east leads to **HUDE**, where remains of a natty thirteenth-century Cistercian **kloster** stand by a water mill. There's a **youth hostel** at Linteler Str. 3 (☎04408/414).

From Hude, you could then cycle, stopping at the thatched village of DÖTLINGEN (there's also a direct bus that takes just over an hour from Oldenburg) to **WILDESHAUSEN**. The small settlements dotted around here make up a so-called "square mile of prehistory" consisting of bronze-age graves (at PESTRUP), burial chamber and stones at KLEINKNETEN and more stones at RECKUM. The **Alexanderkirche**, Wildeshausen's medieval church, has thirteenth- and fifteenth-century frescos, and the town hall is Gothic, too. The **youth hostel** is at Am Filleberg 9 (☎04431/2223).

CLOPPENBURG, some 15km west, is worth making for, to see the **Freilichtmuseum** (March–Oct Mon–Sat 8am–6pm; Sun 9am–6pm, Nov–Feb Mon–Sat 9am–5pm, Sun 10am–5pm; DM3.50). This has a collection of about 100 historic rural buildings from all over Lower Saxony re-erected on one site, with craftspeople demonstrating old techniques. A little further south, you might want to stop off to see the **Schloss Dinklage**, which still has its moat

Osnabrück

OSNABRÜCK stands somewhat apart from the rest of Lower Saxony, at its extreme western end. Geographically and historically, it really belongs to Westphalia, and it has many parallels with Münster, which is just 55km to the south. Each city is now home to a large British army base, and has a sizeable student population. Both owe their foundation to Charlemagne; in the Middle Ages, both were ruled by a prince-bishop, and were important trading centres. Subsequently, they shared the hosting of the long negotiations – regarded as the birth of modern diplomatic practices – which led to the signing of the **Peace of Westphalia** in 1648, bringing the Thirty Years' War to an end. One curious agreement resulting from these talks was that Osnabrück was to be ruled in future by a Catholic and a Protestant bishop in turn. The Welf family provided the latter incumbent; the ambitious Duke Ernst August of Hannover was one holder of the see, and his son, the future King George I of Britain, was born in the city. When the bishopric was secularised under Napoleon, the Hanoverians annexed its territories. After World War II, Osnabrück therefore joined the rest of Hannover in the new province of Lower Saxony, though the fact that the city's publicity is handled by the Westphalian tourist office is an indication of where loyalties lie.

As a railway junction on major north–south and east–west lines (a legacy of the old trading routes), Osnabrück is very easily accessible. Much of the city is modern: heavy damage was caused by bombing in the last war, and restoration has been less successful than in Münster. Some highly characterful streets and squares do remain, but it's a pity that more thought wasn't given to the planning of the bland shopping areas with which they're now intermingled.

The Dom

The **Dom** has a spacious setting in the middle of its own square in the heart of the city. If, as is often claimed, cathedrals should represent the character of the city around them, Osnabrück's readily fits the bill. Built in fits and starts between the twelfth and sixteenth centuries, it's something of a curate's egg. The facade **towers** are a fascinatingly unlikely combination – the late Gothic one on the southern side is almost twice the width of its Romanesque neighbour – but they are outclassed by the dignified octagon (the oldest part of the present building) over the transept crossing.

The interior

Inside, the Dom presents a pleasingly sober, predominantly Gothic appearance. Among a number of notable **works of art**, the early thirteenth-century bronze font and the exactly contemporary polychrome wood *Triumphal Cross* are outstanding. The latter's name is something of a misnomer, as Christ is here depicted as a pathetic, suffering, all-too-human figure. In the south transept is a monument to a provost, which was made by the north German Baroque architect, J.C. Schlaun. Wonderful gilded wrought-iron gates guard the entrance to the ambulatory, at the end of which is the *Margarethenaltar*, a limewood retable by the sculptor who also carved the *Madonna of the Rosary* in the north transept. The identity of this emotional artist, who was still working in the late Gothic style well into the sixteenth century, remains elusive: he's known simply as the **Master of Osnabrück**.

The Diözesanmuseum

Further works by this carver can be seen in the **Diözesanmuseum** (Tues–Fri 10am–1pm & 3–5pm, Sat & Sun 10am–1pm; DM1.50), housed in rooms above the cloister. The most eye-catching item here, however, is the gilded *Kapitelkreuz*, made in the early eleventh century and studded with two pontifical rings, a couple of Roman cameos and a variety of coloured gems. The early seventeenth-century confessional, from a nearby convent, was made in the wake of the Tridentine reforms and is the earliest example in northern Europe of what was to become a very familiar structure. Other highlights are a tenth-century ivory comb, silverware and the figures from the demolished rood screen.

The Markt

Just beyond the Dom is the other main square, the triangular-shaped **Markt**. Its colourful step-gabled mansions are modelled on the merchant houses of the Hanseatic ports, while in the centre there's a fountain which gushes with beer whenever there's a festival on. On the northern side of the square is the Gothic **Marienkirche**, which takes the hall church design to its logical conclusion by omitting the transept. Inside are a fourteenth-century *Triumphal Cross*, a sixteenth-century *Passion Altar* from Antwerp and numerous tombs – including that of Justus Möser, whose researches into Westphalian folklore in the eighteenth century were to serve as a trail-blazer for the Romantic movement.

Closing the end of the Markt is the early sixteenth-century **Rathaus**, from whose steps the Peace of Westphalia was proclaimed; the present stairway dates from the nineteenth century, as do the large statues of German Emperors, among which Kaiser Wilhelm I is lined up alongside his medieval predecessors. During normal working hours, you can go inside to see the wood-panelled *Friedensaal* and its generally glum portraits of the representatives of Sweden and the Protestant German principalities, who deliberated here while their Catholic counterparts met in Münster. Ask at the porter's desk to see the **Schatzkammer**, which contains valuable documents and treasury items. Star piece is the magnificent fourteenth-century *Kaiserpokal*, a goblet adorned with coloured glass and figurines. Also notable is the late sixteenth-century *Schützenkette*, a trophy awarded to the winner of the annual marksmen's festival.

The rest of the city

Facing the rear of the Rathaus on Bierstrasse is the pretty half-timbered frontage of Osnabrück's most famous inn, *Walhalla*. It features extensively in Erich Maria Remarque's *The Black Obelisk*, a novel describing the traumatic hyper-inflation of 1923. Neither this nor any of his subsequent books ever matched the spectacular success of his first novel, *All Quiet on the Western Front*, which was the one German book to match the eloquence of the British literature of World War I. Most of Osnabrück's surviving **old houses** are nearby – on Marienstrasse, Hegerstrasse, Grosser Gildewartare, Krahnstrasse and Bierstrasse itself. The first three form a yuppified pedestrian precinct, where antique shops and bistros vie with each other for prominence. At the end of Bierstrasse is the former **Dominikanerkirche**, now a cultural centre which often features exhibitions of contemporary art. It also contains a weather-worn late Gothic statue of Charlemagne, the only survivor of the original cycle from the Rathaus facade. Beyond here, several fragments of the city wall can be seen round the ring road, including the Neoclassical **Heger Tor**, celebrating the victory at Waterloo.

Diagonally opposite is the **Museum für Kulturgeschichte** (Tues–Fri 9am–5pm, Sat 10am–1pm, Sun 10am–5pm; DM1.50). On the ground floor, the local history collections are of interest for such fragments as the original medieval sculptures from the *Brautportal* of the Marienkirche. Upstairs there's a large collection of works by the local Jewish artist **Felix Nussbaum**, a member of the *Neue Sachlichkeit* art movement, which rejected Expressionism in favour of a starkly realistic form of representation. He died in Auschwitz, aged 40, in 1944.

Continuing southwards along Heger-Tor-Wall, you soon see on the left the tall tower of the **Katharinenkirche**, a church broader than it is long. In the big square behind is Osnabrück's most original building, the **Leidenhof**. The sixteenth-century merchant owners converted their original fourteenth-century stone house into a miniature palace by the addition of a staircase tower and a new wing, whose facade resembles a gigantic cardboard cut-out. What really catches the attention, however, are the zigzags painted on the two Renaissance additions, making them look strangely modernistic.

South of here, Neuer Graben and Neumarkt mark the boundaries of the Altstadt, though the Neustadt beyond (which had its own set of fortifications) was founded as early as the beginning of the eleventh century. Across from the Leidenhof is the yellow **Schloss** of the prince-bishops, built in an Italianate Baroque style. The interior has been modernised to house part of the new University. Down Johannisstrasse is the twin-towered **Johanniskirche**, another thirteenth-century Gothic hall church, whose chancel contains a fine fifteenth-century cycle of sandstone figures of the Apostles.

Practicalities

Osnabrück's **Hauptbahnhof** is ten minutes' walk southeast of the city centre, which is reached by following Möserstrasse straight ahead, then crossing the River Hase. The **tourist office** (Mon–Fri 8.30am–6pm, Sat 8.30am–1pm; ☎0541/323 2202) is at no. 22 on the Markt. There's a brand new **youth hostel** to the south of town at Iburger Str. 183a (☎0541/54284); take bus #23 or #25 from Neumarkt, and alight at Kinderhospital. In addition, there are two **campsites** in the environs – *Niedersachsenhof* (☎0541/77226) and *Attersee* (☎0541/124147). Cheapest centrally-placed **hotels** are *Vennemann*, Johannisstr. 144 (☎0541/572589), which charges DM27 per person; *Jägerheim*, Johannistorwall 19c (☎0541/21635), whose rates begin at DM30; and *Nord-Hotel*, Hansastr. 31 (☎0541/64133), which starts at DM32. Plenty more with similar rates can be found a bit further out. The **Mitfahrzentrale** office is at Martinstr. 9 (☎0541/42947).

Many of the best places to **eat** and **drink** (there's a fine *Osnabrücker Pils*) are in the old streets to the rear of the Rathaus. A couple of more traditional places, each offering Westphalian cuisine at reasonable prices, are *Der Landgraf* on Domhof and *Dom-Restaurant* on Kleine Domfreiheit. The *Lagerhalle* on Rolandsmauer is the most popular **nightspot** in town, featuring live rock, jazz and folk music, along with regular disco evenings. Main **theatre** venue is the Jugendstil *Städtische Bühnen* opposite the Dom, while the modern *Stadthalle* on Schlosswall is used for **concerts**.

EASTERN LOWER SAXONY

In the east of Lower Saxony, the landscape transforms itself from coastal plain to the rolling **Lüneburg Heath** (*Lüneburger Heide*), which contains the constrasting towns of **Lüneburg** and **Celle**, as well as several nature reserves. This extends eastwards to an area known as the **Wendland** that juts into the former GDR, and south towards the state capital of **Hannover** and the province's second city, **Braunschweig**. Continuing in a southerly direction, you soon come to more elevated land: **Hildesheim** stands in the foothills leading to the Harz, while there are fine rolling landscapes around **Hameln** in the valley of the River Weser further west.

Lüneburg

Of all the many medieval trading cities built by the Germans on and near the Baltic coast between Hamburg and Riga, only **LÜNEBURG** has survived virtually unscathed. It was all but ignored by the World War II bombing missions which destroyed so much of northern Germany, having by then declined into economic insignificance. Yet in the Middle Ages the city was immensely wealthy, profiting from the fact that it was (literally) built on **salt** – then a rare and essential commodity, almost worth its weight in gold. At its peak, the Lüneburg saltworks had 2000 employees (which probably made it the largest commercial enterprise in Europe); the city's magnificent brick buildings were funded from exports of the salt to Scandinavia, Burgundy, Poland and Russia, and the other trading links which ensued. Gabled facades, from Gothic to Baroque, still line the streets of the centre. Many have a pronounced tilt, as a result of subsidence caused by disused mines: the salt deposits haven't been worked since 1980, leaving the saline springs of the spa quarter as the only active reminder of a tradition dating back to the tenth century. However, Lüneburg is far from being the museum-piece it might appear. Its population almost doubled in 1945 as a result of an influx of refugees from the confiscated Eastern Territories, and it has again become a lively regional centre.

The Markt

The **Markt** is the focus of the town's commercial life, particularly on Tuesdays, Wednesdays and Saturdays, when markets are held. In the middle of the square is a sixteenth-century bronze **fountain** with a statuette of the moon goddess Luna, after whom Lüneburg (which means "fortress of Luna") is somewhat improbably named. On the square's north side is a fine Renaissance mansion, in which the poet Heinrich Heine spent part of his boyhood, and the Baroque **Schloss**, now the seat of the regional court of justice. The latter was always something of a white elephant: though Lüneburg was nominally capital of one of the Welf family's duchies, its merchants wielded such power from the fourteenth century onwards that they forced their aristocratic rulers to make Celle their main base, while Lüneburg functioned in practice as a city-state, even if never officially recognised as such.

The Rathaus

A clear indication of where the true balance of power lay can be seen by comparing the Schloss with the far more grandiose **Rathaus** (guided tours Tues–Fri at 10am, 11am, noon, 2pm & 3pm, Sat & Sun at 10am, 11am, 2pm & 3pm; DM5), which occupies the west side of the Markt. Its Baroque facade is a mere frontispiece to the largest and most impressive medieval town hall in Germany. The *Grosse Ratssaal*, the old council chamber, is the most famous part. Originally from the fourteenth century, it was embellished a hundred years later with richly traceried windows bearing stained glass portraits of nine great heroes. Another century later, it received its impressive wall and ceiling decoration, which included a scene of *The Last Judgment* in honour of its new function as the court of justice. Other highlights include the tiny *Körkammer* where the burgomasters (four of whom are depicted in the windows) were elected, and the *Fürstensaal*, the former dance hall, with its charming fifteenth-century candelabra made from stags' antlers, and seventeenth-century portraits of the local dukes. However, the finest room of all is the *Grosse Ratsstube*, which ranks as one of Germany's most important Renaissance interiors thanks to the pyrotechnic woodwork – benches, panelling and, most notably, the doorways – carved by Albert von Soest. At the end of the tour, you're allowed to linger over the municipal silverware, by far the finest collection in Germany. Unfortunately, what you see here are only replicas: the originals are now in the Kunstgewerbemuseum in Berlin.

Am Sande and around

Lüneburg's largest square is the elongated **Am Sande**, whose name reflects the fact that it was laid out on a sandy marsh. It lies almost due south of the Markt, and is reached along the partly pedestrianised Bäckerstrasse. On the way, take a peek inside the late sixteenth-century **Rathsapotheke**, whose orderly interior forms a perfect complement to the elaborate gable and portal outside. Am Sande itself has the most impressive group of burghers' mansions in town, illustrating the seemingly inexhaustible variations the local builders worked on the theme of the brick gable. Particularly impressive is the **Schwarzes Haus** (Black House) on the west side of the square, so called from the colour of its glazed brickwork. Formerly an inn and brewery, it's now the seat of the local chamber of commerce.

St Johannis

The opposite end of Am Sande is closed off by the impressively large brick church of **St Johannis**. This was begun in the thirteenth century, but the tall tower (which leans a couple of metres out of true), was only erected in the early fifteenth century. The **organ** is celebrated – the case and some of the pipework are early eighteenth-century, but it incorporates much of its mid-sixteenth-century predecessor, one of the oldest instruments in the country. It can be heard briefly each Friday at 5.30pm; from mid-June to late October, longer recitals are given on Thursdays at 8pm. Almost equally precious is the **high altar**, a co-operative work by several fifteenth-century artists from Hamburg and Lübeck. Its reverse side, illustrating the lives of SS John the Baptist, Cecilia, George and Ursula, was painted by Hinrik Funhof with a delicacy worthy of comparison with the great Flemish masters of the period. Two more notable retables are housed in the chapels to either side; look out also for the *Madonna and Child* candelabrum in the north aisle, which has a marked similarity to those in the Rathaus.

Some museums

From the rear of St Johannis, follow the River Ilmenau south for a couple of minutes, and cross over by Wandrahmstrasse, on which stand an old mill and the **Museum für das Fürstentum Lüneburg** (Tues–Fri 10am–4pm, Sat & Sun 11am-5pm; DM2). This features a good collection of medieval artefacts, including the tomb of a local duke, along with the predictable folklore and local history displays. The most intriguing exhibit is a copy of the once-famous thirteenth-century map of the world from the nearby convent of Ebstorf, the original of which was destroyed in a bomb raid on Hannover.

Just off the eastern end of Am Sande, at Heiligengeiststr. 39, the **Kronen-Brauerei-Museum** (daily 10am–noon & 3–5pm; free) has been set up in the former premises of the only brewery left out of the eighty the town once had. A free English leaflet guides you round the four floors of equipment, enabling you to see every stage of the traditional beer-making process. You can end your tour in suitable style by enjoying the products of the modern brewery – the smooth *Lüneburger Pils* or the very dry *Moravia Pils* – in the historic beer hall, complete with garden, which is right next door.

At no. 10 on Ritterstrasse, the next street to the south, is the **Ostpreussisches Landesmuseum** (Tues–Sun 10am–5pm; DM2), which owes its existence to Lüneburg's large influx of refugees, many of whom came from the Baltic state of East Prussia, which in pre-war years was the most far-flung part of Germany. In 1945, it was divided horizontally along the middle, with the southerly half allocated to Poland (to whom the whole territory had once belonged), while the remainder, including the capital city of Königsberg (which was renamed Kaliningrad), was made a province of Russia.* The museum illustrates East Prussian history from the German viewpoint, in the process showing why bitterness at the Russian annexation remains so acute: natives of Königsberg include such stalwart Germans as the philosopher Immanuel Kant (who is said to have left the city only once in his life, and then only very briefly), the Romantic writer E.T.A. Hoffmann, and the artists Lovis Corinth and Käthe Köllwitz.

The western quarters

At the edge of the Altstadt, several minutes' walk west of the Ostpreussisches Landesmuseum, is the site of the old saltworks. The surviving installations have been turned into the **Deutsches Salzmuseum** (Mon–Fri 10am-6pm, Sat & Sun 10am–5pm; DM3), which tells you everything you are every likely to want to know about the extraction, history, geology and economics of salt. In addition, you get to see the city's sole surviving salt-pan, which is put into production each day in summer at 3pm. Continuing southwards, you come to the **Kurzentrum**, a modern spa complex set in an extensive park, which seems strangely at odds with the rest of the city. Thermal and mud baths, saunas and a solarium are all on offer daily at very reasonable rates, should you wish for a break from cultural indigestion.

In the opposite direction from the Salzmuseum is another brick Gothic hall church, **St Michael**; it stands on J.S.-Bach-Platz, which is so named because the great composer was a pupil at the school established in the monastic buildings after secularisation. The church itself was once celebrated for its *Goldene Tafel* (Golden Table) treasures, but what is left of these can be seen in the Kestner Museum and Landesgalerie in Hannover; nowadays the building is chiefly remarkable for the tottering appearance it presents as a result of its insecure foundations. From here, you can ascend **Kalkberg**, the low-lying hill to the west; the Welf fortress which once stood here has completely disappeared, but in compensation there's a fine long-range view over Lüneburg and its surroundings. The best route back to the Markt is via Auf dem Meere, a street lined with old craftsmen's houses.

---

*The break-up of the Soviet Union has left the future of the Russian part of East Prussia, now a stranded enclave between Poland and Lithuania, as a little-known yet potentially explosive political issue. Germany would undoubtedly be prepared to pay handsomely to get it back, yet the memories this would rekindle make it a prospect no other country is likely to welcome.

The Wasserviertel and Kloster Lüne

Following Bardowicker Strasse north from the Markt, you come to the fifteenth-century parish church of **St Nicolai**, where the sailors and artisans used to worship. Its tower, a neo-Gothic replacement of the original, can often be ascended in summer (though hours are irregular) for a view over the city, and in particular of the old port or **Wasserviertel** which lies just to the east. Walking there along Lüner Strasse, you pass one of the city's oldest houses, formerly the town house of Kloster Lüne. With its peaceful riverside setting, trees, bridges, mills and other imperious buildings, it's the most evocative spot in town, creating a picture about as far removed from a modern-day harbour as it is possible to imagine. Formerly a herring warehouse, the **Altes Kaufhaus** had to be rebuilt after a fire in 1959, but still has its cheery Baroque facade. Opposite is the **Alte Krane** (old crane), which received its present form in the 1790s, though it dates back at least as far as the fourteenth century.

Kloster Lüne itself (guided tours 1 April–15 Oct Mon–Sat 9–11.30am & 2.30–5.30pm, Sun 11.30am–12.30pm & 2–5pm; DM4) lies 2km northeast of the Wasserviertel. The present complex dates largely from the late fourteenth and early fifteenth centuries, though the half-timbered outbuildings were added later. It became a Protestant convent at the Reformation, but has served as a plush retirement home since the early eighteenth century. Best time to visit is in the last week of August – the only time the valuable **collection of embroideries** is displayed.

Practicalities

Lüneburg's **Hauptbahnhof** has two terminals facing each other across Bahnhofsplatz. The quickest way to reach the centre is to go north along Lüner Weg, then turn left into Lünertor Strasse; this brings you to the Wasserviertel. Alternatively, turn right at the southern end of Bahnhofsplatz into Altenbrückertor Strasse, which takes you straight to Am Sande. Under the Rathaus' front arches is the municipal **tourist office** (May–Sept Mon–Fri 9am–1pm & 2–6pm, Sat & Sun 9am–1pm; Oct–April Mon–Fri 9am–1pm & 2–6pm, Sat 9am–12.30pm; ☎04131/309593). A regional office for the Lüneburg Heath, whose *Gastgeberverzeichnis* brochure has exhaustive accommodation listings, is at Am Sande 5 (☎04131/42006). If you want to **hire a bike** to explore the area, go to *Laden 25*, Am Werder 25.

Accommodation

Of the centrally sited **hotels**, the best bet is probably *Scheffler*, in an old half-timbered house just off the Markt at Bardowicker Str. 7 (☎04131/31841); it charges DM43 per person and has an excellent restaurant. Other possibilities include *Stadt Hamburg*, Am Sande 25 (☎04131/44438), whose rates are in the range DM30–45, and *Lübecker Hof*, Lünertorstr. 12 (☎04131/51420), whose range is DM33–52. In addition, there's a **youth hostel** at Saltauer Str. 133 (☎04131/41864) well to the south of town, best reached by bus #1. The **campsite** (☎04131/791500) is by the banks of the River Ilmenau even further south; catch a bus towards DEUTSHEVERN.

Food, drink and festivals

Among places to **eat** and **drink**, the top choices are the inevitable *Ratskeller* in the Rathaus and the aformentioned *Kronen-Brauhaus*, Heiligengeiststr. 39. Best place for breakfast is *Campus-Café*, Am Sande 3, which also does full meals. For a relaxed *al fresco* summer atmosphere, when tables are put out on the street, try the bars along Stintmarkt, on the western side of the Wasserviertel. Main **festivals** are the *Schützenfest* in mid-July and the *Stadtfest* in late August.

The Lüneburg Heath and the Wendland

Part wooded, but mainly uncultivated open heathland, the **Lüneburg Heath** (*Lüneburger Heide*) is grazed by large flocks of *Heidschnucken*, goaty-sheep descended from the Corsican *mouflon*. It's the grazing by these large, long-haired and curly-horned creatures that maintains the heath by keeping down the seedlings. In late August the heather erupts in deep purple swathes, adding a mass of colour to the heath's otherwise subtle palette. Picturesque villages, with timber-and-brick houses and churches, are also dotted around, forming an idyllic backdrop for festivals, the annual coronation of the queen of the heath, and shepherds who still wear their traditional green outfits. The only blots on the pastoral horizon are the large British troop **exercise areas and gunning ranges**, a legacy of the fact that it was here, on 4 May 1945, that Field Marshal Montgomery received the unconditional German surrender.

The Naturschutzpark Lüneburger Heide

One of the British bases is unfortunately right on the edge of the **Naturschutzpark Lüneburger Heide**, a 200 square kilometre nature reserve in the northwest of the region, where the heathland and villages are least changed. Motor traffic is forbidden in much of this park, but there are networks of footpaths and cycle paths (hiring a bike is usually easy in most towns) and it's lovely cycling country; horse-riding is another possibility. Bees buzz over the heather, and the local honey is renowned – as are the potatoes, oddly enough. Places to stay (mostly at low rates) abound, so you can probably rely on finding accommodation as you go; most towns have a tourist office.

Public transport in and to the area is fiddly: by train, you would have to go from Lüneburg south to the industrial town of UELZEN, then west to SOLTAU, from where buses and occasional historic diesel trains run to the park. A far easier approach is to take the direct bus from Lüneburg to **UNDELOH**, an attractive village in the heart of the park which boasts a half-timbered church going back to the twelfth century. There's a youth hostel here at Heimbucher Str. 2 (☎04189/279), plus some two dozen hotels and pensions. From Undeloh, you can walk 4km south to ultra-quaint **WILSEDE**, along a road banned to wheeled traffic. An old farmhouse, *Dat Ole Huss*, has been opened as a museum illustrating the ways of the past. You can also climb up northern Germany's highest hill, the Wilseder Berg, for all-round views of the heath. Because of their abundant accommodation, two other possible bases for exploring the area are the health resorts of **EGESTORF**, which lies just outside the western fringe of the park, and **BISPINGEN** , which is beyond the southern boundary. The latter is a particularly pretty village with a fourteenth-century church; it also has a youth hostel, at Töpinger Str. 42 (☎05194/2375).

The southern heath

Down towards Celle, there's another protected area of landscape, the **Naturpark Südheide**. This has far more trees than its counterpart to the northwest, even including an extensive area of natural woodland, the Unterlüss Forest, which is crossed by marked hiking trails. The main base for this area is the recuperative health resort of **MÜDEN**, which has a youth hostel at Wiesenweg 32 (☎05053/225), and plenty of cheap pensions.

On the main road between Soltau and Celle, 16km southwest of Müden, is **BERGEN**. At Am Friedenplatz 7 in the town itself is a small **Freilichtmuseum** (Mon–Thurs 9.30am–noon & 3–5pm, Fri 9.30am–noon; DM2), which brings together a number of old farm buildings from throughout the region. Some 6km south, and reach-

BERGEN-BELSEN CONCENTRATION CAMP

Some 50,000 people died in **Bergen-Belsen**, many as a result of starvation and disease, or by the personal whim of the infamous camp commandant, Josef Kramer, the "Beast of Belsen". When the camp was liberated some 13,000 unburied bodies were found lying in heaps; many of the 30,000 survivors were on the point of death. The film made of the camp's liberation still appalls: a number of Germans, who were forced to watch it and realise the atrocities that had been carried out in their name, subsequently committed suicide. In Britain the film was shown in every cinema in the country, revealing the horror of the "Final Solution" to the public for the first time.

Reaching the camp from Celle is difficult: buses run from Monday to Friday at 11.55am, 1.40pm & 3.45pm; the journey takes an hour and the last return bus leaves at 4.05pm. By car, the camp is 22km northwest of Celle on the B3; turn left when you reach Bergen. It's also reachable by turning off the main E4 route between Hannover and Hamburg at the Soltau-Sud junction.

able by Celle-bound buses, is the infamous **Konzentratsionslager Bergen-Belsen** (see above), well-known from the diaries of the young Dutch Jewess, Anne Frank. Nowadays it's a monument run by the state office for political education. The buildings were destroyed at the end of the war by the British, for fear of a typhus outbreak, but the mass graves remain, and a visit to the site of such horror is deeply disturbing. Just down the road is a British army base, and the sound of their heavy guns going off makes events of 45 years ago seem eerily close.

The Wendland

The easternmost part of Lower Saxony is known as **Wendland** after a Slavic tribe called the Wends, whose mark can be seen in the large number of villages with decidedly un-Germanic names. The old border with the GDR was mostly defined by the **River Elbe**, but then cut right back in, leaving a V-shaped wedge jutting into what is now Saxony-Anhalt. For obvious reasons, it's one of the least visited parts of Germany, content to remain as a tranquil backwater, but it has important natural attractions: a large part of the area is designated as the *Naturpark Elbufer-Drawehn*.

The Elbufer

If you're got your own transport, the easiest approach from Lüneburg is to travel 25km east to the little riverside town of **BLECKEDE**, and follow the Elbe upstream; bikes have the advantage over cars, as cycle tracks closely follow the river, which is here barely touched by tourism. There's also a railway into the region, though this doesn't reach the Elbe until **HITZACKER**, a lovely little town built on an island where the River Jeetzel joins the Elbe. At Wolfsslucht 2 (☎05862/244) you'll find the area's youth hostel; in addition, there are plenty of reasonably-priced pensions. The train terminates a few kilometres away at the slightly larger town of **DANNENBERG**, which has a twelfth-century tower and streets of half-timbered houses; here you'll find the regional campsite (☎05861/4183).

Further upstream is **GORLEBEN**, which was often in the national headlines. Back in the 1970s the government decreed the salt-mines here to be a suitable storage place for nuclear waste. There was massive public resistance, not only for ecological and safety reasons, but because of the provocative location by the border. An "independent" state – *Freies Wendland* – was even established as part of the protest, and the alternative/green influence still has a high profile. The final port of call is tiny **SCHNACKENBURG**, the former West Germany's easternmost community; it qualifies officially as a town because it used to be a toll point for Elbe shipping.

The "round villages"

The other main area of interest in the Wendland is centred on the town of LÜCHOW, which lies 15km south of Dannenburg. Around here, the Wends left their mark on the landscape in the form of distinctive round villages called *Rundlingdörfer*. Basically, a cluster of about ten thatched, timbered houses are arranged close together in a circular pattern, all facing inwards so the village could be better defended. The *Rundlingsdörfer* are tucked away in the trees, off the main roads – look out for signposts indicating a "Rundlingsdorf". Most of them are still lived in, but the inhabitants are used to being peered at by visitors. Some offer **pension accommodation** – in GÖTTIEN for instance (near KÜSTEN, just west of Lüchow) you can stay at *Der Eichenhof* (☎05841/3156).

Celle

Somewhere between Lüneburg and **CELLE** (pronounced "Tseller") is an invisible line – as you go south you leave behind the magnificent brickwork of the Hanseatic towns and flat land, and enter the domain of timber-framed buildings so characteristic of central Germany. Thus while Lüneburg and Celle are the northern and southern hubs of the Lüneburg Heath, these two old and beautiful towns seem to have come from different worlds. Which in fact they did, for while Lüneburg resembles the Baltic merchant cities it had such close contact with, the ducal town of Celle was centred much more on palace and military life. Celle's abundance of sixteenth- to eighteenth-century timbered buildings has been impressively preserved, and whole streets are intact.

The Schloss

The **Schloss** (guided tours daily at 9am, 10am, 11am, noon, 2pm, 3pm & 4pm; DM1) dominates the town, and the main streets run towards it with a gesture of subservience. Originally built in the late thirteenth century, it became the main residence of the Dukes of Braunschweig-Lüneburg in 1371, when the independently-minded burghers of Lüneburg flexed their collective muscle and chucked out their feudal overlords. In 1530, the building was completely rebuilt in the Renaissance style; the present white-washed exterior, with its idiosyncratic corner towers, decorative gable and lofty, confined courtyard, dates almost entirely from this period.

Sole survivor of the medieval castle, and highlight of the tour, is the **Schlosskapelle**, which was cleverly incorporated into the southeastern tower facing the town, its pointed Gothic windows being the only giveaway as to its presence there. Its architectural simplicity was obscured in the second half of the sixteenth century by an integrated programme of Mannerist decoration that's still stunningly fresh and vibrant. The cycle of 76 paintings, commissioned from the Antwerp artist **Marten de Vos** (once an assistant to Tintoretto in Venice), forms a complete illustrated Bible, in accordance with the new Protestant doctrines. The two galleries are adorned with portrait sculptures of Old and New Testament figures, and wacky pendants of varying shapes and sizes hang from the vault. Both the pulpit, with reliefs of the Passion, and the organ, resplendent with painted shutters, are intrinsic parts of the scheme, and are beautiful works of art in their own right.

Early in the eighteenth century the Duchy of Lüneburg was reunited with Hannover (which had split off the previous century) when Sophie Dorothea, daughter of the last Duke of Lüneburg, married the future George I of Britain. Thereafter, Celle was no more than the second-string German residence of the Hanoverian dynasty, and a place where those who had fallen from grace could readily be dumped. In the 1770s the

Schloss became home for a few years to an exiled queen, Caroline Mathilde of Denmark, who was banished following an indiscretion with a courtier. Her **suite of rooms** can be visited independently (Mon–Sat 10am–4.30pm, Sun 10.30am–12.30pm; DM1).

An especially pleasant way to sneak a look inside other parts of the Schloss is to go to a performance at its **theatre** – dating back to 1674, it's the oldest one in Germany to have a resident company. Concerts and plays are performed throughout the year, except during July and August. Tickets and information are available (mornings only) from the box office at Schlossplatz 13. Unfortunately, the powers-that-be don't allow you near the handsome Baroque auditorium unless you're attending a performance.

The Altstadt

Celle's other outstanding feature is its sheer quantity of original **half-timbered buildings** – 480 in all. The town is trying to resolve the problem of how to protect them, while keeping the centre alive at the same time. Unless businesses are given the chance to modernise property, the council believes, an alternative commercial centre will soon be set up in a different part of town, and the Altstadt will become a museum-piece. A careful check is supposedly made on modifications that are carried out, but it's still jarring when you see a beautiful seventeenth-century building fitted with a chain-store's shop front, or a concrete structure faced with mock timber (as with the *C&A* building).

Around the Stadtkirche

All this notwithstanding, every street in the Altstadt is a visual treat, and well worth including in a gentle stroll. The place to begin is Stechbahn (formerly a yard used for tournaments) which runs from the centre of Schlossplatz; here you see a Renaissance house with oriels and the early sixteenth-century court pharmacy, the **Löwenapothek**. Opposite the latter is the **Stadtkirche**, whose tower (Tues–Sat 3–6pm; DM0.50) commands the best view of the town – a trumpeter plays a chorale from here at 6.30am & 6.30pm every day. The church itself, originally Gothic, has a Baroque interior and serves as the pantheon of the local dukes. Behind is the **Rathaus**, whose fourteenth-century *Ratskeller* is the oldest pub in northern Germany. Most of the building, however, is in the carefree Weser Renaissance style, and is distinguished by two beautifully contrasted oriel windows: one at street level, the other an extension of a gable.

Celle's old houses

The most outstanding half-timbered house in Celle is the **Hoppener Haus** at the corner of Rundestrasse and Poststrasse. Built for a courtier in 1532, it's richly carved with allegorical figures, monsters, scrollwork and scenes of rural life. In front stands a lion fountain, known as the *Piepenposten*. The oldest dated house, at Am Heiligen Kreu 26, states that it was built in 1526, though Neue Str. 32 (originally fifteenth-century but with a Renaissance oriel) has the best claim to be regarded as the most venerable house in town. Look out for the corner of Nordwall and Bergstrasse, where someone built their home on top of a piece of the original city wall. Among later Baroque stone buildings is the **Stechinellihaus** on Grosser Plan, named after an influential Italian architect and courtier who lived in a house on this site.

The **Bomann-Museum** (Mon–Sat 10am–5pm, Sun 10am–1pm; DM1), in a grandiose Jugendstil building at the corner of Schlossplatz and Stechbahn, is above average for a local collection. Its displays on regional trades, history and folklore feature several reconstructed farmhouses and (in the courtyard) a half-timbered house fully furnished in the Biedermeier style.

The rest of the town

Just outside the eastern edge of the Altstadt is the old ghetto, though the colourful Baroque half-timbered houses themselves hardly offer any clue as to the area's former status. Within one of these houses, Im Kreise 24, is the **Synagoge** (Mon–Fri 3–5pm). Its decoration was destroyed on *Kristallnacht*, but, most unusually, it wasn't burned down. After the war it was well restored, and it stands today as one of the very few historic Jewish temples left in Germany.

Not far from here, bounding the southern side of the Altstadt, is the **Französischer Garten** (French Garden), which was laid out in the seventeenth century and later adapted in the informal English manner. Within the park is the **Bieneninstitut** (Mon–Fri 9am–noon & 2–4pm; free), the main bee-keeping station in Lower Saxony. Beyond is the **Ludwigskirche**, the only Neoclassical church in northern Germany designed by the great Berlin architect Karl Friedrich Schinkel. Its exterior is marred by the later addition of a pair of towers, but the interior is a gem – a miniature, updated version of the columned basilicas of the Romans.

West of the Schloss, on the road between the town and the Hauptbahnhof, are more half-timbered houses, plus a number of Baroque palaces in the French style. The most impressive of these, complete with gate-house, courtyard and a handsome facade bearing the ducal coat of arms, is the **Justizvollzugsanstalt**. This, strange to say, served as the local prison and workhouse.

South of here, reached down Breite Strasse, is the **Niedersächsische Landgestüt** (Lower Saxon Stud Farm), which was founded by King George II in 1735. It can be visited outside the season, when the 250 or so stallions are put out to stud (mid-July to mid-Feb Mon–Fri 8.30–11.30am & 3–4.30pm; free), but the best time to come is during the big autumn **festival**, the highlight of Celle's social calendar. Held on the last Sunday in September and the first in October (or, on occasions, the last two in September), plus the Wednesday preceding these, each programme lasts for three hours, and features a parade of the stallions, as well as a quadrille performed by coaches and ten.

Practicalities

The **tourist office** (mid-May–mid-Oct Mon–Fri 8am–6pm, Sat 9am–1pm & 2–5pm, Sun 10am–noon; rest of year Mon–Fri 8am–5pm, Sat 10am–noon; ☎05141/1212) on Schlossplatz will find a **room** for you free of charge. Hotels within the Altstadt are uniformly expensive, and you'll have to stay some way outside to save money. Cheapest option, at DM30 per person, is *Gudehus*, Celler Str. 11 (☎05141/51528). Rates beginning at DM40 are available at *Schnarr*, Fuhrberger Landstr. 17 (☎05141/41355), *Am Landgestüt*, Landgestütstr. 1 (☎05141/217219), and *Blühende Schiffahrt*, Fritzenwiese 39 (☎05141/22761). Alternatively, there's a **youth hostel** at Weghausstr. 2 (☎05141/53208); turn left on leaving the Hauptbahnhof and continue straight ahead for about 2km, or take bus #3 to Dorfstrasse. The **campsite** is at *Silbersee* (☎05141 31223) in VORWERK, a suburb at the northern end of town.

Eating and drinking

Among places to **eat** and **drink**, pride of place goes to the *Ratskeller*. It's on the expensive side, but worth it in view of the superb food and historical setting. Almost as good are *Union* on Thaerplatz and *Schwarzwaldstube* on Bergstrasse. After a long gap, the town is once more a centre of **beer** production. You can sample *Celler Urtrüb* and the powerful *Cellenser Bock* at the brewery's own *Gaststätte Urtrüb-Klause* at Nordwall 56. For a beer garden atmosphere, there's *Bier-Akademie* on Am Weissen Wall; for a wine bar, try *Utspann* on Im Kreise.

Wienhausen

WIENHAUSEN, a village of half-timbered houses 10km southeast of Celle, to which it's connected by regular buses, clusters around a remarkable **Kloster** (guided tours April–Sept Mon–Sat at 10am, 11am, 2pm, 3pm, 4pm & 5pm, Sun at 11.30am, 1pm, 2pm, 3pm, 4pm & 5pm; Oct same times except Mon–Sat at 4pm & 5pm; DM5). Founded in 1231 by Agnes von Meissen, daughter-in-law of Henry the Lion, the convent became Protestant at the Reformation, and is still in use today. The superb brick buildings are something of an anomaly this far south. Their severity stands in contrast to the brightness of the nuns' chancel, the walls of which are covered with a well-preserved cycle of fourteenth-century frescos illustrating the life of Christ and the legend of the Holy Cross, along with secular subjects. In the centre of the choir is a wooden *Holy Sepulchre*, complete with a figure of the dead Christ, which dates from the late thirteenth century.

The Kloster's most valuable treasures are its **tapestries**. Woven by the nuns in the fourteenth and fifteenth centuries, they rank among the greatest ever made. Unfortunately, they're only put on display for eleven days around Whitsun each year; check with the tourist office in Celle for the exact dates.

Hannover (Hanover)

At first, for some reason or other, Hanover strikes you as an uninteresting town, but it grows upon you. It is in reality two towns: a place of broad, modern, handsome streets and tasteful gardens, side by side with a sixteenth-century town, where old timbered houses overhang the narrow lanes; where through low arches one catches glimpses of cobbled courtyards, once often thronged, no doubt, with troops of horse, or blocked with lumbering coach and six, waiting its rich merchant owner and his fat placid frau . . .

Jerome K. Jerome, *Three Men on the Bummel.*

Though written at the turn of the century, this description of **HANNOVER** is still apposite. Initial impressions of this city are unlikely to be very promising, and despite having had the benefit of a long special relationship with Britain (see overleaf) and having played an important part in European cultural history to boot, it hasn't generally been given a good press in guidebooks. Hannover was something of a late developer, only coming to the fore in the second half of the seventeenth century, and much of its best architecture belongs to the nineteenth and early twentieth centuries. Another oddity is the fact that Hannover's showpiece is not a great cathedral (it's never had one), palace or town hall, but a **series of gardens**. However, these are no ordinary gardens – they're among the most impressive in Europe, preserving their spectacular original Baroque features almost intact. Add this to a number of first-class **museums** and a vibrant cultural scene, and there's plenty in Hannover to keep you occupied for a couple of days.

> The telephone code for Hannover is ☎0511.

Arriving and practicalities

The **Hauptbahnhof** is right in the centre of town; to the rear is the **bus station** for long distance routes. On Ernst-August-Platz, the square facing the Hauptbahnhof, is the **tourist office** (Mon–Thurs 8.30am–6pm, Fri 8.30am–7.30pm, Sat 8.30am–3pm; ☎168 3903). Among the brochures you can pick up is *The Red Thread*, a horribly chatty but very useful free booklet guiding visitors round the main sights via a painted red line which runs along the pavements, across roads and down subways.

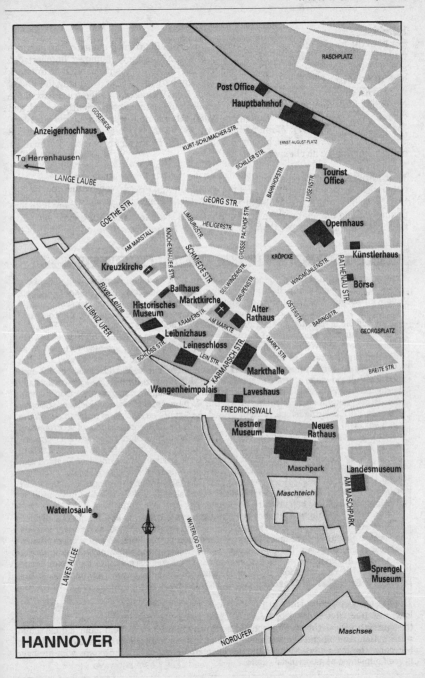

RASCHPLATZ

Post Office
Hauptbahnhof

Anzeigerhochhaus

GOSERIEDE

KURT-SCHUMACHER-STR.

ERNST-AUGUST-PLATZ

SCHILLER STR.

To Herrenhausen

LANGE LAUBE

Tourist
Office

BAHNHOFSTR.

LUISENSTR.

GEORG STR.

Opernhaus

GOETHE STR.

LIMBURGSTR.

HEILIGERSTR.

GROSSE PACKHOF STR.

AM MARSTALL

KNOCHENHAUER STR.

SCHMIEDE STR.

KRÖPCKE

Künstlerhaus

Kreuzkirche

WINDMÜHLENSTR.

RATHENAU STR.

Börse

SELWINDERSTR.

GRUPENSTR.

OSTERSTR.

BARINGSTR.

Ballhaus

Bibel Leine

Marktkirche

Historisches
Museum

Alter
Rathaus

GEORGSPLATZ

LEIBNIZ UFER

KRAMERSTR.

AM MARKTE

Leibnizhaus

MARKT STR.

Leineschloss

BREITE STR.

SCHLOSS STR.

LEIN STR.

KARMARSCH STR.

Markthalle

Wangenheimpalais

Laveshaus

FRIEDRICHSWALL

Kestner
Museum

Neues
Rathaus

Maschpark

Landesmuseum

AM MASCHPARK

Maschteich

Waterlosäule

LAVES ALLEE

WATERLOO STR.

Sprengel
Museum

NORDUFER

Maschsee

HANNOVER

Hotels

For DM5 the tourist office will book you a **hotel**. As a flourishing centre of the lucrative trade fair industry (the April *Messe* is the largest in Europe), Hannover hoteliers can afford to charge fancy prices. Provided there isn't a fair on, it's probably best to check with the tourist office first to see if there are any bargains going. Normally the lowest rates, with singles DM40, doubles DM70, are at *Haus Tanneneck*, to the southeast of the city centre at Brehmstr. 80 (☎818650). The following are more conveniently located, and charge from DM45–50 for singles to DM80–90 for doubles: *Hospiz am Bahnhof*, Joachimstr. 2 (☎324297); *Flora*, Heinrichstr. 36 (☎342334); *Reverey*, Aegidiendamm 8 (☎883711); and *Gildehof*, Joachimstr. 6 (☎15742). There are plenty of more distant alternatives, but they're no cheaper.

Youth hostels and campsites

Otherwise, there's a **youth hostel** at Ferdinand-Wilhelm-Fricke-Weg 1 (☎322941); take U-Bahn #3 or #7 (direction Mühlenberg), and alight at Fischerhof, from where it's a five-minute walk to the left over the bridge. Alongside is a **campsite**. More expensive than these, but still a bit cheaper than any hotel, is the *Naturfreundehaus* on the edge of the

---

HANOVERIAN HISTORY . . . AND THE BRITISH CONNECTION

In the seventeenth century, the territories of the Welf House of Braunschweig-Lüneberg were split up, and a new duchy, clumsily named Braunschweig-Calenberg-Göttingen, came into being. This was commonly known as **Hannover**, after the old Hanseatic market and brewing town which was its principal city. A new summer residence for the court was slowly laid out at the village of Höringehusen, a few kilometres from Hannover's Altstadt.

Ernst August, who acceded to the duchy in 1679, was a man of high ambition. He charged Gottfried Wilhelm Leibnitz, the great philosopher and scientist who served as librarian and historian to the Welfs for forty years, with the task of proving that the House was descended from the Italian Este family. The successful conclusion of this entitled the duke to claim a new Electorate in the Holy Roman Empire, which was formally bestowed in 1692. Even more significant was Ernst August's marriage to **Sophie von der Pfalz**, daughter of Elizabeth Stuart, the "Winter Queen" (see Heidelberg, *Chapter Two*). In 1701, the English parliament passed the Act of Settlement, in order to cut off the Catholic "Old Pretender" and his heirs and ensure the continuation of a Protestant monarchy. Sophie was named as next in line to the throne after Princess (later Queen) Anne. In the event, Sophie died just before Anne in 1714, and her son **Georg Ludwig** became King George I of the United Kingdom, the parliamentary union of England and Scotland having been concluded seven years previously. As well as a monarch, Britain gained one of the greatest composers of all time: anticipating the accession, the court director of music, **Georg Friedrich Händel**, was already well established in London by the time his employer had taken up residence.

Until 1837, Britain and Hannover shared the same ruler. At first, monarchs divided their residency between the territories (George I understandably so, as he never learned to speak English), but gradually they neglected their original seat. When William IV died without issue, however, the union came to an end. The exclusion of women from the succession in Hannover meant that another Ernst August ascended to its throne (since 1814 it had been a kingdom in its own right) whereas his niece Victoria became the British Queen. This led to another bright period in Hannover's history, during which the city was transformed in Neoclassical style by the court architect, **Georg Ludwig Friedrich Laves**. In the event, it turned out to be a false dawn. During the Seven Weeks' War of 1866, the blind King Georg V opted to back neither Prussia nor Austria; the rampaging Prussian victors responded by driving him into exile and annexing his kingdom. Hannover thereafter remained part of Prussia until 1946, when the old duchy became the main component of the newly created Land of Lower Saxony, with the city itself reinstated as a provincial capital.

wooded Eilnriede park at Hermann-Bahlsen-Allee 8 (☎691493); take U-Bahn #3 (direction Lahe) or #7 (direction Fasanenkrug) to Spannhagenstrasse. Another establishment belonging to the same association is at Am Fahrhortsfelde 50 (☎580537) in the distant suburb of Miesburg: take bus #3 to Lahe, then continue with bus #31 to Waldfriedhof or #32 to Meyers Garten.

Getting around

There are only two fares on the entire **public transport** network; it's well worth buying tickets in strips of six for DM10, or investing in a DM6 24-hour pass. Some trams stop on Ernst-August-Platz, while others go underground to form the U-Bahn in the city centre, with stops at the Hauptbahnhof and Kröpcke.

The city centre

Hannover has had to reconstruct itself after being almost totally demolished by World War II bombing. The northern part of the city centre is a vast shopping area of mostly pedestrianised streets and arcades. Further south is the modest-sized Altstadt, beyond which is the inner ring road, on and around which are the best museums and an attractive green belt.

The northern city centre

The view on arrival at the Hauptbahnhof isn't exactly prepossessing, with a bland pedestrian precinct stretching ahead. Underneath runs the **Passarelle**; mostly under cover, but with sections in the open-air, it's meant to be a sort of subterranean bazaar-cum-piazza. While the prime sites at the flashy end are occupied by expensive shops, towards the station it predictably becomes seedier; many shop sites are empty, and walking through at night is a little disconcerting.

Standing at Hannover's most popular rendezvous, the *Café Kröpcke*, the most imposing building in view is the **Opernhaus**, a proud Neoclassical design which is arguably the finest of the city's Laves-designed showpieces. Nearby are other self-confident public buildings from later in the century, close in style to British architecture of the time. On Sophienstrasse, the yellow and red brick **Künstlerhaus**, originally a museum, is now a lively arts centre, while the neo-Renaissance **Ständehaus**, built as a guild hall, now houses the state treasury department. The **Börse** on Rathenaustrasse actually imitates the Tudor style – proof that British influence continued long after the end of the monarchical link.

If you're keen on modern architecture, make a detour along Georgstrasse to Goseriede to see the **Anzeigerhochhaus**. This newspaper office, made of brick-clad reinforced concrete and topped with a green copper dome, is an example of the 1920s Expressionism of Fritz Höger. Even if it's hardly the skyscraper it purports to be, and is less dramatic than the same architect's Chilehaus in Hamburg, it's nonetheless an arresting, balanced, and well thought-out design. The dome now houses the city's most adventurous cinema.

The Altstadt

A few minutes' walk south of the Anzeigerhochhaus are a few streets of rebuilt **half-timbered houses**. These convey something of the impression of the medieval town, which had already been much altered before the devastation of the last war; its form is easier to imagine if you've seen nearby Celle, which is preserved almost intact. The first major building in their midst is the fourteenth-century **Kreuzkirche**, which has a peaceful, close-like setting. At the high altar is a *Passion Triptych* by Cranach. One of the chapels is used by the local Serbian community, and is decorated with icons – a stark contrast with the Protestant sobriety of the rest of the church.

On Pfersdestrasse to the south is the **Beginenturm**, the last surviving remnant of the city walls. It has been incorporated in the fabric of the modern building housing the **Historisches Museum** (10am–8pm, Wed–Fri 10am–4pm, Sat & Sun 10am–6pm; free), one of Germany's most imaginative local history museums. On the ground floor to the left are the four **state coaches** of the House of Hannover. These are still family property – even the gold carriage, adorned with Rococo paintings and carvings, which was made in London in 1783 and used for state openings of the Westminster Parliament. Upstairs, there's a telling contrast to these limousines in the form of the *Hanomag*, a tiny two-seater convertible developed in 1928, which was a sort of trial run for the *Volkswagen* as a family car. A series of pictures, town plans and models illustrates the changing face of Hannover, while several reconstructed interiors from farmhouses in the province give an insight into rural life.

Just across the road is the **Ballhof**, a seventeenth-century half-timbered sports hall which is now the main repertory theatre. On nearby Holzmarkt (not its original location) the **Leibnitzhaus** has been re-erected following its total destruction in the War. This magnificent Renaissance mansion was the home of **Gottfried Wilhelm Leibnitz**. A historian by profession, Leibnitz was active in a vast range of intellectual fields: he developed Pascal's calculating machine, arrived independently at the theory of differential calculus at the same time as Newton, charted the origins and migrations of mankind, and made enormous contributions to the disciplines of jurisprudence, philosophy, theology, geology and linguistics.

The Altstadt's dominant building is the fourteenth-century **Marktkirche**, one of the most southerly of the series of brick hall churches characteristic of the Baltic lands. Its bulky tower, terminating in a spire of unusual design, has long been the emblem of the city. Originally, it was meant to be much higher, but an old chronicle reports that it was finished off quickly because "the masons had become tired and sick in the purse". The unadorned interior walls are now closer to how the building originally looked than has been the case for some 300 years. There's a noble carved *Passion Retable*, made around 1500, at the high altar; miraculously, the fourteenth- and fifteenth-century stained glass in the east windows has survived, and has recently been cleaned and restored. Across the square is the high-gabled fifteenth-century **Altes Rathaus**, whose elaborate brickwork is enlivened with colourful glazed tiles.

Friedrichswall and around

The line of the former city wall is now occupied by the inner ring road, forever seething with traffic. On Friederikenplatz stands the **Leineschloss**, which is now the Land parliament. Its dignified porticos, modelled on the temples of ancient Greece, were added by Laves, who carried out a thorough transformation of the original structure. Immediately to the east, two more buildings by him – the **Wangenheim-Palais** and the **Laveshaus** – stand side-by-side; the latter was his own home. Down Lavesallee is yet another of his works, the **Waterloosäule**, a triumphal column commemorating the part played by the Hanoverian troops in the final defeat of Napoleon. It was mainly thanks to them that Wellington's central line held long enough for Blücher's Prussian forces to reach Waterloo and turn the tide in favour of the beleaguered British.

Opposite the Laveshaus is the **Kestner Museum** (Tues, Thurs and Fri 10am–4pm, Wed 10am–8pm, Sat & Sun 10am–6pm; free). This compact decorative arts museum is named after its founder August Kestner, a Hanoverian diplomat in Rome; he was the son of Charlotte Buff, Goethe's first love and a central character in his novella *The Sufferings of Young Werther*. On the first floor, the medieval collection features treasures and textiles from Lower Saxon convents; outstanding are surviving items from the *Goldene Tafel* of St Michael in Lüneburg, and the magnificent gilded bronze head-reliquary of an unknown saint, made around 1200 for Stift Fischbeck. The remaining galleries have an eclectic array of exhibits, ranging from Renaissance bronzes through eighteenth-century porcelain to a luxuriant selection of Art Nouveau *objets d'art* from America as well as Europe. Upstairs are examples of the ancient Greek, Etruscan, Roman and Cypriot civilisations, along with a more comprehensive Egyptian collection.

Next door is the **Neues Rathaus**, a gargantuan early twentieth-century Art Deco cum-neo-Gothic fantasy, which is held into its marshy foundations by over 6000 piles of beechwood. It's definitely worth a peek inside; there are occasional guided tours but no one seems to mind if you just wander round, up and down the spiral staircases. Between April and October (9.30am–noon and 2–5pm; DM2) you can ascend to the dome for what are the best **views** of the city. However, the main attraction is the lift which takes you up – it follows an inclined path and is apparently one of only two in Europe like this. Look out for the models of Hannover at various stages of its history; the one of the bombed wartime city is a shocking record of the damage it suffered.

Directly behind the Neues Rathaus is the **Maschpark**, with a small artificial lake. Farther on is a much larger man-made lake, the **Maschsee**, which serves as the locals' main playground. You can saunter down its tree-lined promenades, take a cruise on a pleasure steamer, or else hire a rowing boat or canoe.

The Landesmuseum

The **Landesmuseum** (Tues, Wed & Fri–Sun 10am–5pm, Thurs 10am–7pm; free) occupies stolid-looking premises facing the east side of the Maschpark. Its main draw is the Landesgalerie on the second floor, wihich has an excellent collection of paintings from the Middle Ages to the early twentieth century. On the left are two rooms of Primitives, of which the most notable is a *Passion Altar* by the first German artist known by name, **Master Bertram**. Most of the other works are by his anonymous Saxon contemporaries; particularly striking are *Two Scenes from the Life of St Paul* by a Hildesheim artist dubbed **Master of the Lambertikirche**, and the retables from which the **Master of the Golden Table** and the **Master of the Barfüsser Altar** get their names. In the following rooms, the star painting is an exquisite *Portrait of Philipp Melanchton* by **Hans Holbein the Younger**, displayed alongside its lid, which is one of the few surviving examples of Holbein's skill as a decorative artist. Hanging beside it is a lurid *Luther on his Deathbed* by **Cranach**, and a small *Christ Carrying the Cross* attributed to **Dürer**. A decent display of Italian Renaissance work includes pictures by Botticelli, Raphael, Pontormo and Bronzino.

The large *Bacchus and Venus* by the Antwerp Mannerist **Bartholomeus Spranger** is an allegory illustrating an old proverb: "Wine and women bring two sorrows to life". It's one of the most imposing paintings created in the erotic style cultivated at the turn of the seventeenth century at the court of the Emperor Rudolf II in Prague – and in the tiny neighbouring principality of Schaumburg-Lippe. As a total contrast, the peaceful classical world is evoked in **Poussin**'s *Inspiration of Anacreon* and **Claude**'s *River Landscape with Goatherd*. Pick of the seventeenth-century Flemish paintings are **Rubens**' *Madonna and Child*, **van Dyck**'s *A Gentleman of Santander, the Governor of Antwerp*, and *Men Bathing by Moonlight* by **Michael Sweerts**; the last, characteristically for this artist, is a highly original subject, with wonderful luminous effects. There's a good cross-section of the Dutch school, including one of **Rembrandt**'s rare excursions into nature painting, *Landscape with the Baptism of the Eunuch*, another masterly exposition of contrasts of light and shade. Also of special note is *A Woman in Profile* by his most talented pupil, the short-lived **Carel Fabritius**.

A comprehensive array of the varied styles practised in nineteenth-century Germany includes a set of four small canvases illustrating *The Times of Day* by **Friedrich**; **Leibl**'s haunting *Peasant Girl*; several humorous paintings by Spitzweg; and numerous examples of the Impressionists Liebermann, Corinth and Slevogt. A specially dimmed room shows the giant cartoons made by the members of the **Nazarene Brotherhood** for the decoration of the Casa Bartholdy in Rome.

On the first floor of the museum, the **archaeology** department has as its showpiece the bodies of prehistoric men preserved naturally in the peat bogs of Lower Saxony. The varied contents of several excavated graves are another highlight, along with an array of Bronze Age jewellery. On the same floor is a **natural history** section with a wide variety of stuffed animals and a full-scale reconstruction of a dinosaur, while downstairs there's an **aquarium** with live fish from all round the world.

The Sprengel Museum

Further down the road, on Kurt-Schwitters-Platz, is the **Sprengel Museum** (Tues 10am–10pm, Wed–Sun 10am–6pm; DM2). Named after the chocolate magnate Bernhard Sprengel, whose gift of his private collection formed the basis of the museum, this ranks as one of the most exciting places in Germany in which to see modern art. An unusually high proportion of the display space is given over to changing exhibitions of photography, graphics, and various experimental art forms, but there's also a first-rate permanent display of twentieth-century painting and sculpture.

Centrepiece of the museum is a huge range of the work of one of this century's most controversial and influential artists, Hannover's own **Kurt Schwitters**. His pleasing early landscapes and still lifes come as a surprise if you're only familiar with the famous Dadaist collages, which, in an attempt to create art out of non-art, tack all kinds of junk on to the canvas. The artist coined the term *Merz* to describe these, and set himself the target of creating a *Merzbau*, a work of art which would fill a house. Both completed versions of this were destroyed in the Nazi measures against "degenerate art", but an accurate reconstruction can be seen here.

Other highlights of the museum include a cross-section of **Picasso**'s work; complete rooms devoted to **Klee** and **Arp**; sculptures by Barlach and Henri Laurens; an updated *Prodigal Son* by **Beckmann**, along with self-portraits painted forty years apart; Surrealist paintings by Magritte, Tanguy and Ernst; and a huge range of Expressionists, with Munch, Nolde, Kirchner and Kokoschka all well represented.

Herrenhausen

The royal gardens of **Herrenhausen** (as Höringehusen came to be known) can be reached from the centre by U-Bahn #1 or #2. However, it's advisable to walk either there or back, as the route goes through two of the four gardens which make up the set; before venturing out, make sure you pick up the free tourist office leaflet which has an excellent plan of the complex.

The Welfengarten and the Georgengarten

Proceeding north from town along Nienburger Strasse, the least remarkable of the gardens – the **Welfengarten** – lies to the right, dominated by the huge neo-Gothic pile of the **Welfenpalais**, now occupied by the University. To the left, the dead straight avenue of lime trees named Herrenhäuser Allee cuts through the **Georgengarten**. This is a *jardin anglais* of the type beloved by the Romantics, featuring trees arranged in an apparently natural setting, and an artificial lake, crossed by two graceful little bridges designed by Laves.

Also within this park is the Neoclassical **Georgenpalais**, home of the **Wilhelm-Busch-Museum** (Tues–Sun 10am–5pm, closes at 4pm Nov–Feb; DM2). Local people flock to the temporary exhibitions on the ground floor, which centre on the work of an artist who has made a significant contribution to satirical expression – Daumier, Doré and Cruickshank have all been featured in recent years, as well as contemporary cartoonists. Upstairs, there's a permanent display on **Wilhelm Busch**, who lived and worked in Hannover last century. He was a capable painter of landscapes and genre scenes, but gained worldwide popularity through his illustrated books, notably *Max* *and Moritz*. In these, he invented what has become a stock vocabulary for strip-cartoonists, using patterns of oscillation to express movement, and conventional signs to depict each emotion.

The Grosser Garten

The Georgengarten was created as a foil to the magnificence of the formal **Grosser Garten** (daily 8am–8pm in summer; 8am–4.30pm in winter; free), which is justifiably the city's pride and joy. It's best to time your visit to coincide with the playing of the **fountains** (May–Sept Mon–Fri 11am–noon & 3–4pm, Sat & Sun 10am–noon & 3–5pm) or when the **illuminations** are switched on (May–Sept Wed, Fri & Sat at dusk). Credit for the splendour of the layout goes to the Electress Sophie, who called them "my life", and her gardener, the Frenchman Martin Charbonnier, who completely transformed the initially modest garden into a spectacular showpiece which drew on elements of the French, Italian and Dutch traditions. Sadly the original palace was totally destroyed by Allied bombing in the war, but the **Galerie**, a festive hall adorned with frothy frescos of Virgil's *Aeneid*, and the **Orangerie** have survived.

Just inside the entrance gate is one of the most striking features, the **Gartentheater**. Temporary structures for music and drama were commonplace within royal gardens, but this one was permanent, featuring an auditorium in the form of an amphitheatre. The hornbeam hedges cleverly doubled as scenery and changing rooms, while a series of gilded statues on pedestals served as stage props. Plays by Molière and Racine, and music by Handel formed the staple repertoire of this theatre in its early days, and are still performed during the summer season. Immediately to the east is the **Grande Parterre**, whose eight sections are planted with geometric arrangements of flowers and shrubs. In front stands the Italianate **Grosse Kaskade**, belonging to the original garden, plus a sundial and grotto, while the maze is at the far end.

Behind the Grande Parterre is a modern embellishment: eight small plots have been laid out to illustrate different styles of landscape-gardening down the centuries. Particularly notable is the **Renaissancegarten**, which reproduces a section of the now-vanished *Hortus Palatinus* in Heidelberg. West of here is the secluded **Boskettgärten**, used by courtiers for intrigues and romantic encounters. The rear section of the Grosser Garten consists of a series of radiating avenues bounded by hedges and trees, each ending at a fountain. As a centrepiece, there's the **Grosse Fontäne**, which spurts Europe's highest jet of water, at 82 metres.

The Berggarten and the Fürstenhaus

Across Herrenhäuser Strasse to the north of the Grosser Garten is the **Berggarten**, set up to tend rare and exotic plants. Its collection of orchids was considered the finest in Europe, and many are still cultivated in its hothouses. Behind these are a rock garden, a pergola garden and an iris garden; the last-named is in full bloom in April and May. Even more glorious is the central "Paradise" of rhododendrons. At the far end of the Berggarten is the **Mausoleum** of the House of Hannover, a late work by Laves in the sternest Neoclassical manner. A graphic illustration of how the architect's style had developed is provided by the domed **Bibliothekspavilion** at the entrance, which he designed thirty years earlier in a carefree idiom still showing echoes of the Baroque.

Some compensation for the loss of the palace is provided by a number of courtly buildings to be found to the west along Herrenhäuser Strasse. The so-called **Fürstenhaus** (daily April–Sept 10am–6pm; Oct–March 10am–5pm; DM3.50) has been adapted as a sort of museum of the House of Hannover; whether it's worth paying the steep entrance fee depends on what value you place on royal mementoes. There's one striking room entirely covered by a panorama of a hunt, and some fine portraits, including likenesses of King George III and Queen Sophie Charlotte as seen by both Thomas Gainsborough and Johann Zoffany.

Eating, drinking and nightlife

As you'd expect in such a cosmopolitan city, there's a huge choice of places to eat and drink, with the Altstadt and the streets around being the liveliest area come the evening. Hannover's **beer** tradition continues unabated: *Lindener Gilde*, the best-known local brewery, has operated uninterruptedly since 1546, its main product being *Broyhan-Alt*, which is named after the sixteenth-century Hannover man who allegedly invented export beer. The Pils of the rival *Herrenhausen* brewery is also worth seeking out.

Altdeutsche Bierstube, Lärchenstr. 4. Hannover's best traditional *Gaststätte*, situated northeast of the Hauptbahnhof.

Brauhaus Ernst August, Schmiedestr. 13. New *Hausbrauerei* occupying the site of the original *Broyhan* brewery. Already one of the most popular spots in town, it serves reasonably priced meals and an excellent unfiltered Pils.

Hannen-Fass, corner of Knochenhauerstrasse and Schuhstrasse. Hugely popular student bar which offers mountainous piles of cheap pub grub.

Hoa Binh, An der Strangriede. Vietnamese restaurant in the University quarter, with a good line in vegetarian dishes.

Klatschmohn, Lange Laube 20. Speciality vegetarian restaurant.

Kröpcke, Kröpcke. This famous café is a real Hannover institution – as well as one of its main landmarks.

Leine-Domizil, Karmarschstr. 50. Café-bar which makes a good choice for breakfast or a snack; has live music most evenings.

Mandarin-Pavillion, Marktstr. 45. One of the best Chinese restaurants in Germany; has bargain menus at lunchtimes.

Markthalle, Karmarschstrasse. The best place to come for a daytime snack or a quick lunch: German, Italian, Spanish and Turkish stallholders sell terrific examples of their cooking, as well as provisions to take away.

Mövenpick, Georgstr. 35. Self-service restaurant in the shopping arcade behind the tourist office: has a huge selection of mouth-watering dishes, both hot and cold.

Seerestaurant Panorama, Arthur-Menge-Ufer 3. Housed in the decadent surroundings of the casino, this classy restaurant with lakeside views of the Maschsee is more affordable than you might expect.

Weinloch, Burgstr. 33. Liveliest of the several good pubs to be found in this street in the heart of the Altstadt.

Nightlife

Recommendable **discos** are *Osho* on Raschplatz, *Cheers* on Andreasstrasse and *Check In* on Goethestrasse, while the main venue for **pop concerts** is the *Pavilion* on Raschplatz. Many of the best **classical music** performances are to be heard in the Protestant churches; these are listed in a bi-monthly leaflet. The *Knabenchor Hannover* is currently at least as good as its famous Viennese counterpart; in spite of the name it generally performs with adult male voices as well as boys. Concerts by the *Staatsorchester* alternate with operas at the *Opernhaus*. The best place for **theatre** is the *Ballhof*, other venues include *Theater am Aegi* on Aegidientorplatz and *Landesbühne* on Bultstrasse. More experimental dramatic fare is offered at the *Künstlerhaus*, which also rivals the *Anzeigerhochhaus* for the best **cinema** programmes in town.

Listings

Cultural institute *Amerika Haus*, Prinzenstr. 9 (☎327284).

Exhibitions In addition to the venues listed in the text, worthwhile shows are held at *Forum des Landesmuseums*, Am Markt 8; *Kestner-Gesellschaft*, Warmbüchenstr. 16; *Kubus*, Theodor-Lessing-Platz 2.

Festivals Hannover's *Schützenfest* (marksmen's festival) for ten days in late June/early July is the most spectacular of the many held in northern Germany. It features processions with floats, fireworks, and a considerable intake of alcohol, notably the *Lüttje-Lage*, in which you drink simultaneously from two glasses – one containing beer, the other schnapps – placed one inside the other.

Markets As well as the general markets on and around Am Markt, there's a flea market each Saturday morning on Hohen Ufer.

Mitfahrzentrale Weisse-Kreuz-Str. 18 (☎312021).

Poste Restante Beside the Hauptbahnhof on Ernst-August-Platz.

Sports There's a huge *Sportpark* with indoor and outdoor stadiums and swimming pool on the west bank of the Maschsee.

Schaumburg

The tiny principality of **Schaumburg-Lippe** (formerly Holstein-Schaumburg) was one of the great survivors of imperial Germany. By skilful diplomacy it managed to avoid being swallowed up by unwelcome suitors, and kept its place on the map until 1946, when it became a part of Lower Saxony; now stripped of the latter half of its double-barrelled name, it holds the status of a *Landkreis* (district) within the province. Both of the towns which have served as its capital lie on the main rail line between Hannover and Osnabrück. They're chiefly notable for having the finest Mannerist art and architecture on German soil, created by some of the same artists who worked at the famously degenerate court of Emperor Rudolf II in Prague.

Stadthagen

Situated some 45km west of Hannover, **STADTHAGEN** was the original capital of Schaumburg-Lippe, a role it regained after World War II. As an administrative centre as well as a market town, it's the more animated of the two towns, though it has less in the way of sights. The handsome Renaissance **Schloss** at the southern end of the town centre is now used as offices and can thus only be seen from outside. Focal point of the town is now the inevitable **Marktplatz**, which offers a palatial Renaissance Rathaus clearly modelled on the Schloss, several grandiose half-timbered burghers' houses and a deliberately over-the-top Rococo mansion.

Set in a close just off the square is **St Martini**, a rather gaunt Gothic hall church. This possesses an intricate fifteenth-century high altar and a Renaissance pulpit, but would be considered unremarkable were it not for the extraordinary seven-sided **Mausoleum** built onto the east end in the 1620s, in celebration of the promotion of the rulers of Schaumburg-Lippe from the rank of counts to princes of the Holy Roman Empire. The Dutchman **Adrian de Vries**, the most accomplished and least controversial of the imperial court artists of Prague, was commissioned to provide the sumptuous marble and bronze decorations. He responded with his masterpiece, the **Monument to Prince Ernst**, which occupies centre-stage. This features a superbly vivacious scene of the Risen Christ surrounded by angels, lions and sleeping guards, as well as the family coats of arms and a medallion portrait of the prince.

Practicalities

Stadthagen's **Bahnhof** is at the northern end of town, a twenty-minute walk from the centre. The **tourist office** (☎05721/7820) is just off Marktplatz at Rathauspassage 1. Cheapest **hotels** are *Gasthaus Bruns*, Niedernwöhrener Str. 1 (☎05721/75001), at DM27 per person, and *Zur Amtspforte*, Obernstr. 31 (☎05721/75746), whose rates begin at DM32. There are plenty of places to **eat** and **drink** on and around Marktplatz: try the historic *Herrenhäuser*.

Bückeburg

At the turn of the seventeenth century, the capital of Schaumburg-Lippe was moved 18km west to **BÜCKEBURG**, then a mere hamlet. This remains the seat of the former ruling family, who, like so many German aristocrats, are left with plenty of wealth and possessions as compensation for their loss of political power; their continued presence here means that Bückeburg still preserves much of the atmsophere of its former role as a princely capital. Worth bearing in mind is that all the town's sights can be visited on Mondays – one of very few places in the country where this is so.

The Schloss

The **Schloss** stands in its own very extensive grounds at the edge of the town centre. On the bridge over the moat, look out for the two superb bronzes of *Venus and Adonis* and *The Rape of Prosperine*, both the work of Adrian de Vries. From here, you can cross over into the courtyard. The wing facing you was rebuilt after a fire in the eighteenth century – walk round to the right to catch a glimpse of the resplendent Renaissance sections of the exterior, which were added to the original fourteenth-century tower-house in the mid-sixteenth century. Continuing onwards, you come to the sombre neo-Romanesque **Mausoleum** (April–Oct daily 9am–noon & 1–6pm; DM2) whose dome has what's apparently the largest mosaic in Germany.

Good-value **guided tours** (daily 9am–noon & 1–6pm; DM6) of the Schloss itself take in the photogenic inner courtyard and the most imposing apartments. These are eclectic, to say the least, passing in quick succession from a grandiose Wilhelmine banqueting chamber with a huge Venetian-style fresco, through an intimate Rococo smoking room, to a Renaissance hall hung with superb Brussels tapestries. The **Schlosskapelle** is a real eye-grabber: originally Gothic, it was adapted in the Mannerist period for Protestant worship. As if to give the lie to the belief that the new faith was inimical to worldly beauty, it was decorated in the most extravagant manner possible: every inch of the walls is covered with frescos, and there's a complete set of gilded and carved furnishings. In the same period, the even more sumptuous **Goldener Saal** was built as a secular counterpart. Its doorway, rising to the full height of the room, is flanked by huge statues of Mars and Flora, with Mercury floating above in the company of cherubs and goddesses. Luxuriant pine-cones hang from the coffered and painted ceiling.

The town

The brothers Hans and Ebbert Wulf of Hildesheim, who had carried out the decoration of the Schlosskapelle and Goldener Saal, were afterwards commissioned to build Bückeburg's other focal building, the **Stadtkirche**, which lies at the top of the main Lange Strasse. This competes with Wolfenbüttel for the title of first full-scale Protestant church ever to be built. It's much the more unified building of the two, and is a real masterpiece of design, notwithstanding the Latin inscription running across the facade which declares that it is: "An Example of Piety, not of Architecture". Apart from its facade the exterior is a glum affair, but the **interior** (May–Sept Mon–Fri 10.30am–noon; Oct–April Wed 2–4pm only) is stunning. Massive Corinthian pillars shoot right up to the vault, and your eye is drawn to the gleaming gold case of the massive organ at the far end, at which Johann Christoph Friedrich Bach, son of J.S., presided for 45 years. In adapting the old hall church formula to the Protestant emphasis on preaching, brightly painted galleries were added all round, and the **pulpit** placed in the centre; the latter is one of the most beautiful in the country, its base lined with gold-plated reliefs of the life of Christ. The fiery figures of Moses and Saint Paul keep the preacher company during his sermon, whereas the cherubs on the sounding-board serve as an antidote to any overly serious discourse. Even more impressive is Adrian de Vries' **font**, where the Holy Ghost, hooked up by wires, hovers above the Baptism of Christ.

Housed in a half-timbered house with a jarring modern extension on Sablé Platz, the pedestrian area between Lange Strasse and Bahnhof Strasse, is the **Hubschraubermuseum** (Helicopter Museum; daily 9am–5pm; DM4), apparently the only one of its kind in the world. A reminder of the proximity of the German and British military bases, it incorporates an educational display on vertical flight technique, and is well labelled in English. Following a section on the history of man's attempts to fly, there are dozens of original machines, representing all the famous names in helicopter design.

Practicalities

Bückeburg's **Bahnhof** lies at the northern end of town; it's a straight ten-minute walk down Bahnhofstrasse to the Schloss. The **tourist office** (Mon–Fri 8am–12.30pm & 2–5pm, Sat 9–11am; ☎05722/20624) is at Lange Str. 45. Best **restaurant** in town is the *Ratskeller* in the Rathaus directly opposite the Schloss gates. There are several cheaper alternatives on Lange Strasse, among them the **hotels** *Berliner Hof* at no. 31 (☎05722/3324) and *Brauhaus*, on the corner with Braustrasse (☎05722/4634), which each have rooms at around DM35 per person. Nearest **youth hostel** is at Porta Westfalica (see *Chapter Five*), two stops away on the train; there are **campsites** there and at Doktorsee (☎05751/2611) near RINTELN, some 10km south of Bückeburg.

Hameln (Hamelin)

"A pleasanter spot you never spied" was how Robert Browning characterised the venerable town of **HAMELN**, situated on the River Weser 45km southwest of Hannover. His verse rendition of the **legend of the Pied Piper** has made the place one of the best-known towns in Germany as far as English-speaking people are concerned – and earned him the eternal gratitude of the local tourist board.

THE PIED PIPER LEGEND

There are various versions of the Pied Piper legend, which was first chronicled in 1384, the exact centenary of when the event allegedly took place. A mysterious stranger dressed in a multicoloured coat appeared in Hameln and offered to rid the town of its plague of rats and mice. Upon promise of payment, he played on his pipe and lured the vermin to the Weser, where they all drowned. The ungrateful burghers reneged on the reward and sent the rat-catcher packing. He returned one Sunday morning when the adults were at church, dressed in a weird yellow and red huntsman's costume. This time it was the town's 130 children who answered the magnetic strains of his pipe, and they followed the stranger out of town and out of sight, apparently disappearing into a cavern, never to be seen again. The only children who were saved were a cripple and a deaf-mute.

Many **interpretations**, none of them conclusive, have been placed on this story. It may symbolise the plague epidemics that were a fact of life in medieval Europe – the term "children" of a town was often used in old chronicles as a synonym for "citizens". Alternatively, it's possible the piper was actually a land agent charged with finding settlers – the Count of Schaumburg had a plantation in Moravia, while there are communities in Transylvania which claim descent from the children of Hameln. Another plausible theory is that the events were linked to the disastrous Children's Crusade of 1212, when youngsters from all over Europe joined in an attempt to conquer the Holy Land from the Infidel by peace – something their seniors had failed to do by force. One of the two main leaders was a boy from Cologne called Nicolas, and it's quite likely that there were recruits to the cause from Hameln.

Inevitably, the Pied Piper legend – perhaps the most endurably fascinating of Germany's rich store of folk-tales – always looms large, which makes Hameln an ideal outing if you have kids. However, there are more serious attractions as well: along with nearby Lemgo (see *Chapter Five*), it's the best place to see the distinctive **Weser Renaissance** style, a form of civil architecture which typically features large projecting bay windows, richly decorated gables ornamented with pyramids and scrollwork, ornamental fillets with coats of arms and inscriptions, and lavish grotesque carvings, many of which are appropriately dubbed *Neidköpfe* – envious "neighbours' heads". During the 1960s a comprehensive restoration programme was started, which has left Hameln looking in immaculate shape.

Osterstrasse and the Markt

For centuries Hameln was no more than a small milling and market town, which lay within a heavily fortified circular town wall. In the wake of the Thirty Years' War, its potential for growth was stunted by the strengthening of its defences by the Hanoverians, to the extent that it acquired the nickname of "the Gibraltar of the North". Napoleon ordered the demolition of the fortress in order that the town could expand. The only surviving sections of the fortress are two isolated medieval towers at the north end of town (the **Pulverturm** and the **Haspelmathsturm**) and the **Garnisonkirche**, a church built in the Lutheran Baroque style for the use of the Hanoverian troops, but now deconsecrated and used as a savings bank. It guards the entrance to **Osterstrasse**, the town's central axis – and one of Germany's finest streets.

Facing the Garnisonkirche on the left is the **Rattenfängerhaus** (Rat-catcher's House). Built for a local councillor at the beginning of the seventeenth century, its name is due solely to an inscription on the side wall documenting the legend. Its facade is one of the most original in Hameln, the delicacy of its ornamental details (which include plenty of jealous neighbours) standing in deliberate contrast to the massiveness of the overall design. The interior is only marginally less impressive; it now houses what's probably the best **restaurant** in town. Though not cheap, it's excellent value, and there's a wide selection of ice-cream-based dishes if you don't want to splash out on a full meal.

Further up the street to the right is the **Leisthaus**, built about fifteen years earlier for a merchant by the local mason Cord Tönnies. The statue of Lucretia in a niche above the oriel window offers a profane contrast to the figures of the Seven Christian Virtues on the frieze below, a juxtaposition of sacred and secular that is typical of the German Renaissance. In this case inspiration was obviously provided by the carvings on the timber supports of the sixteenth-century **Stiftsherrnhaus** next door, which feature the planetary deities along with the Apostles and other Biblical personages; its ground floor is now one of the best of the many fine **cafés** found along the street.

The rest of the Stiftsherrnhaus, along with all of the Leisthaus, is given over to the **Museum Hameln** (Tues–Fri 10am–4.30pm, Sat & Sun 10am–12.30pm; May–Sept stays open until 4.30pm on Sun; DM1). Among the collection of religious art on the first floor, the most striking items are a set of statues of the Apostles which formerly stood on the rood screen of the Münster, and the *Siebenlingsstein*. The latter commemorates another Hameln legend, that of the birth of septuplets to a local family in 1600; though the parents and elder siblings are shown praying at the foot of a crucifix, there was again no happy ending, as all the babies died soon afterwards. Elsewhere, you can see a number of period interiors, documentation on the history of the town and, of course, a display on the Pied Piper story.

At the end of Osterstrasse is the huge **Hochzeithaus** (Wedding House), a festival hall erected in the early seventeenth century, whose main features are its high end gables and elaborate dormer windows, under each of which there is a doorway, which formerly led into a shop. On the side facing the Markt, a **carillon** has been installed. At 1.05pm, 3.35pm & 5.35pm each day, its figures enact the Piper's two visits to Hameln. Opposite is the **Dempterhaus**, built a few years earlier for the burgomaster after whom it's named. The **Marktkirche** rather detracts from the scene; it was Hameln's only major loss to wartime air raids, and has been poorly rebuilt with smooth stones which clash with the remains of the original masonry.

The rest of the town

Among many fine buildings on Bäckerstrasse, which begins off the left-hand side of the Markt, two stand out. The Gothic **Löwenapotheke**, still in use as a chemist's shop, illustrates that the Weser Renaissance style sprang from quite plain origins – the basic form is similar, but there's almost no decoration, apart from the hexagonal star on the gable, which was intended to ward off evil spirits. Further along is the **Rattenkrug**, which was built by Cord Tönnies a couple of decades before the broadly similar Leisthaus. Originally the home of a burgomaster, it has long served as an inn.

Halfway down Wendenstrasse, a fine narrow street opposite the Löwenapotheke, is the **Lückingsche Haus**, whose profuse carvings mark it out as the best example of the revival of half-timbering which occurred in the mid-seventeenth century. Also worth seeing is Alte Marktstrasse, which joins Bäckerstrasse by the Rattenkrug. Its most notable building is **Kurie Jerusalem**, a large half-timbered store from about 1500 which was long derelict, but has been magnificently restored as a play-centre (where kids can be left if you want to go sightseeing without them in tow). Further down is the **Redenhof**, the only remaining nobleman's mansion in Hameln. Dating from the mid-sixteenth century, it's surprisingly plain in comparison with the contemporary houses of the prosperous burgher families. Old buildings of more conventional design can be found on Hummerstrasse and Neue Marktstrasse.

At the end of Bäckerstrasse, overlooking the Weser, is the **Münster**, successor to a Benedictine monastery founded around 800. It's something of a mix of styles – the eleventh-century crypt and the squat octagonal lantern tower survive from a Romanesque basilica which was converted into a Gothic hall church from the thirteenth century onwards, the austere belfry only being added some 200 years later. Inside, the raised chancel is the most striking feature.

Practicalities

Hameln's **Bahnhof** is situated well to the east of the centre, which is reached via Bahnhofstrasse and Deisterstrasse. The municipal **tourist office** (May–Sept Mon–Fri 9am–1pm & 2–6pm, Sat 9.30am–12.30pm & 3–5pm, Sun 9.30am–12.30pm; Oct–April Mon–Fri 9am–1pm & 2–5pm; ☎05151/202517) is situated in the Bürgergarten just before the entrance to the old part of town. They keep plenty of brochures in English, but the most useful is an index-folder in German with all sorts of helpful tips, even including the best times of day for photographing the main buildings. A branch is opened in the Hochzeithaus in the summer months, while there's a separate office for the whole Middle Weser region at Inselstr. 3 (☎05151/26832).

Accommodation and other details

During the tourist season, it's a good idea to spend the night in Hameln; that way you can see the town before or after the day-trippers have come and gone. The **youth hostel** is well placed about five minutes' walk north of the old town at Fischbecker Str. 33 (☎05151/3425), at the point where the Hamel (no more than a stream) flows into the Weser. On the latter's western bank is the **campsite** (☎05151/61157), which is open all year round. There are surprisingly few **hotels**, and they're not particularly cheap; lowest rates, at around DM40 per head, are at *Kretschmer*, Süntelstr. 35 (☎05151/24271), *City*, Neue Markstr. 9 (☎05151/7261), and *Altstadtwiege*, Neue Marktstr. 10 (☎05151/27854). However, there are about a dozen **private houses**, some in the heart of the old town, with rooms to let at around DM25 per person; the tourist office has a full list. Many of the best places to **eat** and **drink** occupy historic buildings mentioned in the text. Another good choice is *Pfannenkuchen* on Hummenstrasse, which offers a huge choice of delicious pancakes, while there's a top-class Chinese restaurant, *Peking*, at 164er Ring 5.

The Pied Piper legend is enacted in a **historical costume play** held in the town centre at noon every Sunday from mid-May to mid-September; performances last thirty minutes and are free. **Cruises** on the Weser (bear in mind that strong currents mean the upstream journeys are painfully slow) are run by *Weisse Flotte* and *Oberweser Dampfschiffahrt*, with departures from the jetty by the Münster. Each Thursday in summer, the former company runs a special service to Hannover via the *Wasserstrassenkreuz* in Minden (see *Chapter Five*).

The Weser Country around Hameln

As a supplement to a visit to Hameln, it's well worth taking in some of the nearby sights. Two destinations in particular stand out; both are easy to reach, and needn't take up too much time.

Fischbeck

Situated 8km north of Hameln and connected by regular bus services (passenger trains no longer stop there), **FISCHBECK** is dominated by its **Stift**. This women's collegiate church was founded in 955, and has preserved an unbroken tradition ever since, thanks to having turned Protestant in the mid-sixteenth century. Today, five elderly canonesses keep up its charitable work, only taking their vows once they have retired from a professional career. One of their tasks is to show visitors round the complex; admission is by **guided tour** only (Easter–mid-Oct Tues & Fri 9am–11am & 2–4pm, Wed, Thurs, Sat & Sun 2–4pm; DM4). It's best to phone ahead first (☎05152/8603), or check at Hameln's tourist office, to ensure admission; ask for a tour in English – one of the guides is a fluent speaker.

The present church was built in the twelfth and early thirteenth centuries as a columned basilica in the manner of the churches of the early Christians, but was ravaged by fire soon after it was built. A drastic restoration at the turn of the century removed most of the Baroque accretions, but some additions remain – such as the wooden balconies from where the canonesses, in true aristocratic manner, observe the services. Architecturally the finest part of the Stift is the **crypt**, whose capitals are all carved in a different manner. The **cloister** is a Gothic structure, with the houses of the canonesses on its upper storey.

Fischbeck has several outstanding **works of art**, but there's only a copy of the most famous, a gilded head-reliquary of a saint; the original is now in the Kestner Museum in Hannover. Earlier this century, the long-lost polychrome wood *Statue of the Foundress Helmburg* was discovered and placed in the chancel. Made around 1300, it's an imaginary, idealised portrait, showing her as a young woman, instead of the elderly widow she was when she founded the Stift, a story illustrated in a late sixteenth-century tapestry in the south transept. On a wooden beam high above the end of the nave is a thirteenth-century *Triumphal Cross*, while beside the pulpit there's an extraordinary wooden *Seated Man of Sorrows* – carved around 1500, it radiates an enormous sense of pathos. According to legend, it was made for the Stift by an itinerant craftsman in gratitude for having been cured there of the plague.

Bodenwerder

BODENWERDER, 25km downstream from Hameln, is a good choice of destination if you want to take a short cruise on the Weser. Its name is synonymous with **Baron Münchhausen**, the King of Liars, who is one of Germany's most famous literary characters. He's been rather a forgotten figure elsewhere – even after Terry Gilliam's no-expenses-spared cinematic version of the Baron's tall tales. Münchhausen's mansion, now the Rathaus, contains a small **museum** (April–Oct daily 10am–noon & 2–5pm; DM1) in his honour. Outside is a fountain illustrating one of his most famous exploits (which consistently defeats the film-makers) – stopping to water his prize Lithuanian horse, he found that the liquid was pouring out of its body, the rear end having been shot off in battle. (Needless to say, the two parts of the steed were later successfully reunited.) On the first Sunday of each month between May and September, some of Münchhausen's exploits are re-enacted.

If you want to stay in Bodenwerder, there's a **youth hostel** in the hills to the east of town on Richard-Schirrmann-Weg (☎05533/2685) and a **campsite** at Schünemann (☎05533/4938), along with an abundant range of **pensions** and **private rooms**.

BARON MÜNCHHAUSEN

The real-life **Karl Friedrich Hieronymous von Münchhausen** was an eighteenth-century soldier of fortune who fought for the Russians against the Turks, before retiring to his ancestral seat, where he regaled credulous listeners with monstrously boastful tales of his adventures. One of his audience was **Rudolph Erich Raspe**, himself a real rogue, who embroidered the stories further and published them under the Baron's name in Britain. For all his failings, Raspe was highly talented – he had been a protegé of Leibnitz in his native Hannover – and the book is stylishly written, perfectly capturing the understated manner of a boring old raconteur launching every few minutes into yet another totally implausible anecdote. The Baron's numerous adventures included stranger travels than even Gulliver's – he made two trips to the moon (one of them unintentional), a journey all the way through the earth's crust, and a voyage through a sea of milk to an island of cheese. In less far-flung parts, he shot a stag with a full-sized cherry tree between its antlers (thus obtaining haunch and sauce at the same time), served as a human cannonball in the war against the Turks, and single-handedly saved Gibraltar from falling into Spanish hands by tossing the enemy's 300 pieces of artillery into the sea. While his exploits have been made famous by Terry Gilliam's 1988 movie, *The Adventures of Baron Münchhausen*, look out for the Goebbels-financed film of the same name – an incredibly futuristic wartime fantasy.

Hildesheim

HILDESHEIM, which lies 30km southeast of Hannover, stands unrivalled as Lower Saxony's premier city of art. Some of the finest buildings in all of Germany are to be found there, and its importance to European culture can hardly be exaggerated. During the eleventh-century Ottonian period, the **Romanesque style** – emerging hesitantly elsewhere – achieved a state of perfection here, not only in architecture, but in sculpture and painting as well. Five hundred years later, the city was adorned with a multitude of **half-timbered buildings** whose sheer artistry far surpasses those of any other German city.

Because of this legacy, old guides used to consider Hildesheim as one of the "must" cities of Germany. Looking at more modern books, the usual impression given is of a place of moderate interest only. Needless to say, the reason for this slump in reputation was war damage. Hildesheim was bombed just a month before the German surrender

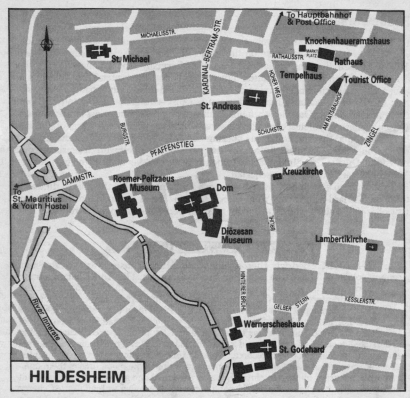

HILDESHEIM

in 1945, and the consequent fire, fuelled by the wooden buildings, caused damage which even some exemplary restoration cannot disguise, and left the surviving monuments marooned among typically bland, functional modern developments. However, the 1980s saw Hildesheim make an astonishing comeback. Fortified by commercial prosperity, the city council made the bold decision to recreate what had hitherto been regarded as irretrievably lost. They were given a fillip by UNESCO's decision to list the two main churches, both of which had been shattered in the war, among the monuments of the world which must be protected at all costs.

Marktplatz

In 1983 work began on resurrecting the picturesque jumble of buildings around the central **Marktplatz**, which has now re-emerged, following its almost complete destruction in the war, as Germany's most imposing market square. Only two of the buildings are original: the early Gothic **Rathaus** at the eastern end, which was only partially destroyed and hurriedly rebuilt, and the fifteenth-century **Tempelhaus** at the southeast corner, which somehow remained intact while all its neighbours collapsed. The most likely explanation for the latter's puzzling name and distinctive shape is that it was inspired by a Crusader's description of buildings he had seen in the Holy Land. Some softening of the rather spare, flat textures occurred with the addition of a late sixteenth-century oriel window bearing carvings of the Prodigal Son. Nowadays, the building houses a bookshop and the offices of the *Hildesheimer Allgemeine Zeitung*, the longest continually running daily newspaper in Germany. The Renaissance **Wedekindhaus** next door, the Baroque **Lüntzelhaus** and the part-Gothic, part-Baroque **Rolandstift** (formerly a home for poor girls), were restored by the local savings bank to serve as its headquarters. Directly opposite, Trusthouse Forte have rebuilt the mid-seventeenth-century inn known as the **Stadtschänke**, along with the aptly named **Rokokohaus** and the early sixteenth-century **Wollenwebergildehaus** (Wool Weavers' Guild House) to serve as their second hotel in Germany. The council themselves paid for a copy of the Renaissance **Marktbrunnen**, which is topped by a figure of a knight and has the municipal arms depicted on the basin.

As the culmination of the restoration project, the small **Bäckeramtshaus** (Bakers' Guildhall) of 1800 and the colossal early sixteenth-century **Knochenhaueramtshaus** (Butchers' Guildhall) on the west side of the square were re-created from scratch. The latter had earned for itself the title of "the most beautiful half-timbered house in the world", a title few would dispute on seeing its highly distinctive architecture and seemingly inexhaustible range of carvings on Christian, pagan and humorous subjects. Part of it now houses a restaurant (see below); the upper storeys contain the local history displays of the **Stadtgeschichtliches Museum** (Tues & Thurs–Sun 10am–6pm, Wed 10am–9pm; DM3).

St Michael

Hildesheim's supreme building, the mould-breaking church of **St Michael**, is about ten minutes' walk west of the Marktplatz, reached via Michaelisstrasse. Perched on a little hill and girded with six towers, it's not too fanciful to see it as a depiction of the heavenly Jerusalem. Originally a Benedictine monastery, St Michael's was very much a personal creation of **Bishop Bernward**, who ruled the see of Hildesheim between 993 and 1022. Confidant of Emperor Otto II and tutor to Otto III, Bernward was a well-travelled and erudite man who is known to have taken a direct part in the art and architecture he fostered in Hildesheim.

The nave

The nave forms the centrepiece of St Michael's meticulously thought out design. An important innovation was the move away from the columned basilica of the Romans to a new system, subsequently known as the **Lower Saxon style**, whereby each bay is demarcated by a hefty square pillar, between which are placed two columns. These are topped by another new device, the cubiform capital, from which spring the arches, coloured in alternate white and red to impart a sense of rhythmic movement. The height of the roof is exactly twice the length of each bay of the nave, a marriage of art and mathematics which is the key to the serenity of the church. Shortly after Bernward was canonised in 1192, substantial embellishments were made in order to make it a worthy resting-place for his relics. Seven elaborately carved capitals were made for the nave, and in the west transept a **choir screen** was erected; only part of this remains, yet its stucco carvings rank among the masterpieces of German sculpture.

The ceiling

An even more spectacular addition was the **ceiling**, which is one of only two Romanesque painted wooden ceilings to have survived. Fortunately, it had been removed for safety during World War II, and its fresh state of preservation is remarkable – three-quarters of its 1300 separate oak panels are original. Executed in the style of contemporary illuminated manuscripts, its programme is based on the imagery of the tree, a decision prompted by the fact that the church's most sacred relic was a piece of the Holy Cross. In the first main scene, Adam and Eve are shown beside the

Tree of Knowledge. Next comes the sleeping Jesse, from whose loins springs the rod which passes through descendants such as David and Solomon before arriving at the Virgin Mary and Christ himself.

The crypt

Saint Bernward's body is interred in a stone sarcophagus in the ground-level **crypt** at the western end of the building; this necessitated a rebuilding to accommodate a raised chancel, which impaired the previously perfect architectural unity of the church. The Catholics were allowed to retain the crypt when St Michael became Protestant at the Reformation; it's only open for mass, but you can peek in by opening the door to the left of the choir screen. Another later addition was the Gothic **cloister** to the north of the church, of which only one wing survives.

The Dom

As a building, the **Dom**, which is set in its own close and reached via Burgstrasse, is a poor relation of St Michael's, but its hauntingly romantic cloister and superb art treasures convinced the UNESCO inspectors that it was an equally important piece of cultural heritage. The exterior is largely a fake, with prominent Gothic side chapels and a Romanesque facade and towers that are a modern guess at how the building might have looked before it was completely transformed in the Baroque epoch. Inside, the architecture has been restored to its original eleventh-century layout, a close adaptation of the forms pioneered at the great monastery fifty years before.

The interior

One of Saint Bernward's particular enthusiasms was the art of bronze-casting, and he established a foundry which was to flourish for centuries. Its first major product was a pair of **processional doors**, originally made for St Michael's, but moved a few years later to the Dom's main entrance, where they were installed on the inside. They tell the story of Adam and Eve on the left-hand side, and of Christ on the right, each episode unfolding with a lively attention to anecdotal details. Soon afterwards, the craftsmen made the **triumphal column**, now in the southern transept. Rather more obviously inspired by Roman victory monuments, this illustrates the lives of Jesus and Saint John the Baptist in a manner akin to strip cartoons. Around 1065, the huge **wheel-shaped chandelier** was suspended from the vault of the nave. Mantled with alternate towers and gateways, it's yet another representation of the heavenly Jerusalem and was to serve as the prototype for the even more ornate candelabra in Aachen and Gross Comburg. In the baptismal chapel is the **font**, made in 1225, it rests on personifications of the four sacred rivers, while the basin and lid illustrate various Biblical stories, mostly with a watery theme.

The cloisters

The **cloister** (April–Oct Mon–Sat 9.30am–5pm, Sun noon–5pm; DM0.50) most unusually is built onto the transepts, forming a protective shield round the apse, on which grows the **thousand-year-old rosebush**, to which the legend of Hildesheim's foundation is inextricably tied. In 815, Ludwig the Pious, a son of Charlemagne, hung the royal chapel's relics of the Virgin on the tree while he was out hunting near *Hildwins Heim* (the home of a farmer named Hildwin). When he tried to remove them, they would not budge; taking this to be divine instruction, he decided to endow the mother church of a new diocese on the very spot. Whether this is really the original bush is disputed, but it's certainly many centuries old, and does seem to lead a charmed life – it burst into flower not long after the air-raid which had flattened most of the Dom itself, and has blossomed every year since. In the centre of the cloister garden is the **St-Annen-Kapelle**, a beautiful fourteenth-century miniaturisation of a Gothic cathedral, with an arresting set of gargoyles spouting from its walls. The sumptuous Renaissance **rood screen**, which fenced off the Dom's chancel until 1945, can be seen in the Antoniuskapelle off the cloister's southern walk.

The Diözesanmuseum

Hildesheim's **Diözesanmuseum** (Tues & Thur–Sat 10am–5pm, Wed 10am–7pm, Sun noon–5pm; DM4) contains the second richest ecclesiastical treasury in Germany. Among the highlights are several works dating from the time of Saint Bernward – the *Golden Madonna* (actually wooden but covered with gold-leaf), a pair of candlesticks, and two crucifixes named after the bishop himself. Equally imposing are various twelfth-century pieces – the *Cross of Henry the Lion*, three shield-shaped crucifixes and a set of enamel plates. The eagle-lectern was made around the same time as the font, while the *Chalice of St Bernward*, though it has no real connection with the bishop, is an outstanding piece of goldsmith's work from around 1400.

The Roemer-Pelizaeus Museum and Andreasplatz

Adjoining the north side of the Dom's close is the old Franciscan monastery, which now contains the **Roemer-Pelizaeus Museum** (Tues–Sun 10am–4.30pm; DM3). Refreshingly different from the standard provincial museum, this hosts an international **loan exhibition** on a major archaeological topic each year, when the opening times are extended. What's on display is subject to change, but you're sure to be able to see part of the collection of **Egyptian antiquities**, which is one of the best in Europe and in itself enough to justify a visit to Hildesheim. The most famous exhibit is the white limestone funerary monument of Hem-iuni from 2530 BC. Other outstanding sculptures include statuettes of Amenophis III and Teje (parents of Akhenaton), a statue of the fearsome half-man, half-jackal Anubis (the god of death) and the reliefs from the tomb of Seschem-nefer IV. The museum's other main strengths include a comprehensive collection of Chinese porcelain and a varied array of exhibits from the Peru of the Incas.

Proceeding eastwards along Pfaffenstieg and Schuhstrasse, you see the tall tower of **St Andreas** on the left. Within its exhilaratingly lofty Gothic interior, Luther's friend Johannes Bugenhagen converted the city to the Reformation. The church itself actually gained from the air-raids – it was rebuilt according to the ambitious schemes of the original masons, which had never previously been fully put into effect. On the other hand, this hardly makes up for the almost complete loss of the square round the church, formerly regarded as a worthy rival to Marktplatz.

The southern Altstadt

The southern part of Hildesheim was largely spared from war damage, and presents several streets of half-timbered houses as a reminder of what the whole of the old city once looked like. At the top end of Brühl, the nearest of these streets to the centre, the one surviving secular building from the time of Saint Bernward can be seen. Originally a fortified reception hall-cum-law court, it was converted into a collegiate foundation known as the **Kreuzkirche** in the late eleventh century, and now forms part of the otherwise Baroque parish church of the same name, making a truly odd combination. To the west of the southern section of Brühl runs the parallel Hinterer Brühl, an almost completely preserved old street. Look out for the early seventeenth-century **Wernesches-Haus**, with its allegorical depictions of the Virtues and Vices, and representations of historical personalities.

St Godehard

At the end of the street is **St Godehard**, a former Benedictine monastery church built in the mid-twelfth century to commemorate the recent canonisation of the man who had succeeded Saint Bernward as Bishop of Hildesheim. Unusually well preserved, it boasts a pair of round towers on its facade, with a larger version of these over the transept. There's a delicate stucco relief over the north doorway showing Christ between Saint Godehard (holding a model of the church) and Saint Epiphanus. The interior proves the durability of the style pioneered at St Michael's, the only advance being the rich carvings on the capitals. Star piece of the church's rich treasury is a magnificent early twelfth-century psalter illuminated at the sister English monastery of St Albans; it's periodically kept here, but is sometimes shown at the Diözesanmuseum.

Along Gelber Stern

East of St Godehard is another fine old street, Gelber Stern, among whose buildings is the mid-sixteenth-century **Haus des Waffenschieds**, the guild house of the armourers, decorated with carvings of the tools of the trade. At the end of the road is Lappenberg, which runs perpendicular to the south; it has a complete row of craftsmen's homes. Nearby stands the **Kehrwiederturm**, the only surviving example of the gates which once surrounded the inner city. To the east is Kesslerstrasse, arguably the most imposing of the old streets, lined with impressive Renaissance and Baroque mansions. The largest and finest of these is the **Dompropstei** (Deanery) at no. 57, set in its own spacious yard. Just north of here is the **Lambertikirche**, which contains a lovely early fifteenth-century "Soft Style" retable painted by an unknown local master.

The suburbs

Another well preserved old quarter is the **Moritzberg**, on a hill to the west of the city centre, and reached along Dammstrasse, Bergsteinweg and Bergstrasse. It's grouped round yet another Romanesque church, **St Mauritius**. Although dating from the second half of the eleventh century, this favoured the traditional format of a columned basilica, which is still evident despite the fact that the interior is now cloaked with Baroque decoration. The crypt and cloister, however, have been preserved in their original state. Unfortunately, there isn't much of a view from these heights; for that you have to go to the **Galgenberg**, at the opposite end of the city.

Eating and drinking

Other than around Marktplatz, there's no obvious concentration of good places to eat and drink in Hildesheim, but there are plenty of enticing possibilities dotted around the city.

Bürgermeisterkapelle, Osterstr. 60. Excellent hotel restaurant.

Die Insel, Dammstr. 30. The best café in town, with scrumptious home-made cakes; also does full meals.

Hildesheimer Brauhaus, Speicherstr. 9. *Hausbrauerei* serving its own organically brewed Pils; also often features live music, for which there's a DM3 entry fee.

Hive's Fass, Andreas-Passage. Very popular bistro, with adjoining beer garden.

Knochenhaueramtshaus, Markt 7. Snacks can be had on the ground floor, full meals on the mezzanine, while the basement is a *Bierkeller*, open evenings only.

Krehla, Moritzstr. 9. Up on the Moritzberg; serves light meals, but is best-known for the seven kinds of home-made fruit wines.

Kupferschmiede, Am Steinberg 6. In a secluded forest setting 5km south of town, this is one of the most famous restaurants in northern Germany, offering both *nouvelle cuisine* and hearty Germany fare. One for a splurge, although the set menus are far from extortionate; reservations recommended (☎05121/262351).

Ratskeller, Markt 1. Far less expensive than its counterparts in most other cities (there are cheap daily specials at lunchtimes) – yet it can rival any of them in quality.

Schlegels Weinstube, Am Steine 4–6. Cosy, highly atmospheric little wine bar-restaurant in a half-timbered sixteenth-century building directly opposite the Roemer-Pelizaeus Museum. Open weekday evenings only.

Schwejk, Osterstr. 16. Bohemian-style cooking and Czech beers are featured here; best at lunchtimes, when there are bargain menus.

Practicalities

The **Hauptbahnhof** is at the northern end of the city; best way to reach the centre is to follow Bernwardstrasse, then Almstrasse, but be warned that these characterless shopping precincts make rather an inauspicious introduction. Tucked away behind the Marktplatz on Am Ratsbauhof is the **tourist office** (Mon–Fri 9am–6pm, Sat 9am–1pm; ☎05121/15995). To find out more about the city and its wealth of monuments, invest DM1 in the *Hildesheimer Rosenroute*, a detailed guide along the tourist trail traced on the streets by a trail of white roses. **Mitfahrzentrale** have an office at Annenstr. 15 (☎05121/39051).

Accommodation

Cheapest **hotel** with a decent location is *Kurth*, Küsthardtstr. 4 (☎05121/32817), at DM30 per person. *Zum Klee*, Renatastr. 4 (☎05121/83685), charges from DM39, *Gasthaus Ostertor*, Ostertor 4 (☎05121/35291), from DM40, while rates at *Weisser Schwan*, Schuhstr. 29 (☎05121/12053/4), and *Am Hagentor*, Kardinal-Bertram-Str. 15 (☎05121/35566), start at DM45. The nearest **campsite** is way to the east of town at DERNEBURG (☎05062/565). Unfortunately, the **youth hostel** isn't much more convenient; it occupies a rustic location high in the wooded hills above Moritzberg at Schirrmannweg 4 (☎05121/42717), and is a good hour's walk from the centre. No bus goes anywhere near, though #1 and #4 will take you part of the way.

Nightlife and festivals

Jazz fans should head for Hildesheim at Whit weekend, when the *Jazz-Time* festival presents the whole gamut of styles, both in formal concerts and impromptu open-air events. All kinds of **music** are featured along with **drama** in the varied programmes of the *Stadttheater* on Theaterstrasse; there are also regular recitals and concerts in the Protestant churches. Main **popular festivals** are the *Frühlingsfest* for nine days in March, the *Weinfest* for a week in mid-May, and the ubiquitous *Schützenfest* in mid-June.

Braunschweig (Brunswick)

Today **BRAUNSCHWEIG** is the epicentre of the most heavily industrialised part of Lower Saxony, but it preserves plenty of reminders of the far grander role it once played. During the twelfth century it was the chosen residence of **Henry the Lion** (*Heinrich der Löwe*), one of the most powerful princes in Europe, who commissioned innumerable monuments and works of art to grace his capital. Over the next few centuries the city became increasingly important as a commercial centre; its trade connections stretched into Russia, Scandinavia, Flanders and England, and the consequent wealth was put to use creating buildings worthy of the city's power and status. In the mid-eighteenth century Braunschweig had yet another brilliant period. The first technical university in the world, the *Collegium Carolinum*, was established there in 1745. When the local dukes took up residence again the following decade, having been absent for over 300 years, their superb art treasures were put on public display and the city became a flourishing cultural centre.

Arriving at the **Hauptbahnhof**, you may well wonder where the magnificence has gone – don't worry, the station is some distance to the southeast of the centre. It's quite a walk, so best take tram #1 or #5 to the "island" which forms the historic heart of the city. This is still completely surrounded by water – a man-made system based on the two arms of the River Oker – and contains several distinct medieval districts, which were formerly governed separately. Each of these quarters was centred on a market square and usually had its own parish church. Severe bomb damage in the last war means that the old buildings are now interspersed with plenty of ugly modern shops and offices, but it's still possible to visualise the medieval layout.

Burgplatz

To look at the city in chronological order, the **Burgplatz** in the middle of the "island" is the place to start. It's full of memories of Henry the Lion (see below), who was at the peak of his power at the time the square was laid out. In 1166, he commissioned the **Burglöwe** (Lion Monument) to form its centrepiece. Perched high on a pedestal, this bronze statue, which was originally gilded, was the first freestanding sculptural monument to be made since the days of the Romans. Even though it has been replaced twice, the lion still stands as a potent reminder of the long centuries of power enjoyed by the Welfs.

HENRY THE LION

Henry the Lion (1129/30–95) was born into the greatest of all dynastic feuds of the Middle Ages – that between his own family, the **Welfs**, and the **Hohenstaufens**, who then held a stranglehold on the office of Holy Roman Emperor. His father, Henry the Proud, had been a major loser in this conflict, having been divested of his titles of Duke of Saxony and Bavaria. By allying himself with his cousin, Emperor Frederick Barbarossa, "The Lion" quickly regained both duchies, and seemingly brought the feud to an end. His early career brought one success after another: he founded both the city of Munich and the port of Lübeck, and began the process of creating a powerful Baltic state. However, he became too powerful for his own good, posing a threat to the feudal structure of the Holy Roman Empire. He fell out with Frederick over the price of his continued support of imperial policy in Italy and the Holy Land – his demand that the Free Imperial City of Goslar and its lucrative silver mines be made over to him was clearly excessive – and consequently was stripped of his titles and confined to his ancestral lands of Braunschweig-Lüneburg. The Welfs' feuding with the Hohenstaufens thereafter continued to bedevil medieval Germany – and dominated politics in Italy, where, under the names of the Guelphs and the Ghibellines, their followers championed the cause of papal and imperial power respectively. Nonetheless, the Welfs retained control over at least part of their heartland right up to the present century.

The Dom

Seven years later the **Dom** (daily 10am–1pm & 3–5pm) was begun, and was substantially complete before the end of the century. Its craggy, fortress-like external appearance (which seems to be another symbol of the power of the Welfs) is the prototype of a distinctive Braunschweig style, which was followed in all the other medieval churches of the city. Another feature copied throughout the city was the later insertion of a Gothic bell-gable between the two towers, which further increases the sense of the facade's massiveness.

The interior is far lighter in feel. This is partly due to the well-preserved Romanesque **frescos**, dating from around 1220, which were hidden behind plaster for

BRAUNSCHWEIG

centuries. The portraits of saints in the nave, executed with the finesse of manuscript miniatures, are particularly fine. An even more crucial addition was the opening out of the north side of the Dom in the mid-fifteenth century by masons who seem to have been familiar with English Tudor architecture; the two new aisles are separated by a row of writhing **columns** which twist in alternate directions. On the end wall is the sole survivor of the previous cathedral which stood on this site, a Byzantine-inspired wooden *Crucifixion* signed by a certain Master Imerward. At the entrance to the choir a seven-branched **candelabrum**, donated by the founder, springs from a base of four crouching lions. In front is the limestone **tomb** of Henry the Lion and his second wife Matilda, daughter of Henry II of England. The beautifully carved reclining figures, made a good generation after their deaths, impart a sense of peaceful repose which is in contrast to the turbulence of their lives. Memorials to other members of the Welf dynasty are housed in the crypt.

The rest of the square

Facing the Dom is Henry's castle, **Burg Dankwarderode** (Tues–Sun 10am–5pm; free). Named in honour of the semi-mythical ninth-century founder of the city, it was constructed at the same time as the Dom. Its unusually complete appearance is mainly due to a nineteenth-century restoration, which follows the original form far more faithfully than most projects inspired by the Romantic reverence for the Middle Ages. Appropriately, it now houses a museum of medieval art and artefacts, of which the star attraction is the original of the Burglöwe. Other highlights include an eighth- or ninth-century walrus-tooth casket, the eleventh-century arm-reliquary of Saint Blasius (patron of the Dom), and the cloak of Otto IV, son of Henry the Lion – and the only Welf to become Holy Roman Emperor.

The Burgplatz used to be a courtyard in its truest sense – the houses that used to stand around its edge belonged to the courtiers. Two half-timbered sixteenth-century successors to these survive – the **Guildehaus** and the **Minsterialhof**, the latter now the seat of the local chamber of commerce. The Neoclassical mansion in the opposite corner of the square was originally a publishing house, but now accommadates the **Landesmuseum** (Tues, Wed & Fri-Sun 10am–5pm, Thurs 10am-8pm; free). This contains local history displays on the Braunschweig region; in the entrance hall is the second version of the Burglöwe.

Altstadtmarkt

The other significant cluster of Braunschweig's past is found in and around the **Altstadtmarkt** to the west. A corner of this is taken up by the former **Rathaus**, which ranks as one of the most beautiful and original secular buildings in Germany. Consisting of two wings arranged in an L-shape, its present form dates back to the early fifteenth century, when the open upper arcades, with their flowing tracery and statues of the Welfs, were added. The graceful lead **Marienbrunnen** in the middle of the square was made around the same time; it's topped by a shrine-like structure with the Virgin and Child and the four Evangelists.

Opposite stands the **Gewandhaus** (Drapers' Hall), its grandeur reflecting the importance of the medieval tailors. The facade is a Dutch-influenced Renaissance composition of extraordinary elaborateness, whose gable, shaped like an equilateral triangle, is crowned by a figure of Justice. Alongside is the half-timbered seventeenth-century **Zollhaus**, once used by customs officials and the military. Also on the square is the Baroque **Stechinellihaus**, designed by the Italian court architect after whom it's named, who was also responsible for many buildings in Celle.

St Martini (Tues–Fri 10.30am–12.30pm, Sat 9am–noon), originally a twelfth-century basilica, stands at the far end of Altstadtmarkt. The finest and earliest of Braunschweig's parish churches, it follows the usual pattern of being modelled on the Dom, but altered inside to form a spacious hall. It also gained some fine sculptures in the fourteenth century, notably the group of the Wise and Foolish Virgins on the north doorway. Another addition is the Gothic chapel dedicated to Saint Anne, housing a Renaissance pulpit that shows Saint Martin dividing his coat in order to clothe a beggar.

The other historic quarters

North of Burgplatz, reached via Casparistrasse or Bohlweg, is the old district of Hagen, centred on Hagenmarkt. Its fountain bears a nineteenth-century statue of Henry the Lion carrying a model of the church of **St Katharinen**, which he also founded. Closely modelled on the Dom, St Katharinen's interior was later transformed into a spacious Gothic hall church. The same is true of **St Andreas** further to the west, which was the parish of the Neustadt district. Across from this church is the **Liberei**, a fifteenth-century library building which is the only example of Gothic brick architecture in the city. Further west is yet another similar-looking parish church, **St Petri**. Nearby, on Bäckerklimt, is the bronze **Eulenspiegelbrunnen**, commemorating the legendary jester Till Eulenspiegel (see opposite). The owls and monkeys on the fountain represent the shapes into which he would work dough as an apprentice in a nearby bakery. The shop itself was bombed in 1944, but similar breads remain a local speciality to this day.

Raised above the old city on a slight hillock at its southern edge is the former Benedictine monastery of **St Aegidien**, the only church in Braunschweig built in a pure Gothic style. Its handsome pulpit retains the original late Gothic reliefs by Hans Witten, a sculptor who was the equal of the more famous Riemenschneider and Stoss, but whose reputation suffers from the fact that most of his work is in remote Saxon

> ### TILL EUELENSPIEGEL
>
> One of Germany's most famous semi-historical characters, Till Eulenspiegel (the name means "Owl Mirror") was born of peasant stock in the village of Kneitlingen near Braunschweig around 1300. Disrespectful of all forms of authority and realising the inherent foolishness of the human condition, he lived by his native wit, consistently putting points over on pompous aristocrats, merchants, churchmen and scholars with his practical jokes and punning sense of humour. Anecdotes about him were popular all over medieval Europe, and were first published in book form in the early sixteenth century. His name has since been enshrined in the German word for tomfoolery (*Eulenspiegelei*) and the French name for a rogue or scoundrel (*espiègle*). He has also inspired two major works of art – a brilliant orchestral showpiece by Richard Strauss and an epic poem by a winner of the Nobel Prize for Literature, Gerhart Hauptmann.

towns. The monastic buildings now house the **Jüdisches Museum** (Tues–Sun 10am–5pm; free), which vividly illustrates German Jewish culture down the centuries. There's even a full scale reconstruction, complete with all the original fittings, of a Baroque synagogue dismantled earlier this century.

Braunschweig's other significant district is the Altewiek a few blocks further north. This is now usually known as the Magniviertel after the church of **St Magni** which forms its core. The few half-timbered streets in the city which completely escaped destruction in the air-raids are found around here; the semicircular group immediately behind the church, and the blind alley called Herrendorftwerte, just to the east, are particularly evocative.

The Herzog-Anton-Ulrich-Museum

North of the Magniviertel, on Museumstrasse, is the **Herzog-Anton-Ulrich-Museum** (Tues & Thurs–Sun 10am–5pm, Wed 10am–8pm; free). Of outstanding quality for a regional museum, it's particularly intriguing in that it reflects the personal artistic tastes of the duke after whom it's named, who was responsible for building it up some 300 years ago. The collection was opened to the public in 1754, thus making it the first museum in Germany.

Dutch and Flemish painting

In the first floor picture gallery, pride of place goes to the Dutch school, and in particular to one of **Rembrandt**'s most psychologically acute works, *A Family Group*. It was painted at the very end of his life, and shows his style at its most advanced and daring, with its loose brushwork supplemented by extensive use of the palette knife, its heavy chiaroscuro effects, and the informal arrangement of its subjects. Rembrandt's very personal vision of Biblical stories is represented here by a tender nocturne of *The Risen Christ Appearing to Mary Magdalene*. The dramatic *Landscape with Thunderstorm*, bathed in warm golden hues, shows yet another side of his diverse genius.

Vermeer's *Girl with the Wineglass* displays a level of technical virtuosity fully equal to, but very different from, Rembrandt's. Probably executed with the help of a *camera obscura*, it captures the three-dimensional space of the interior to uncanny effect. Two other highlights of the Dutch collection include a subtly delicate late fifteenth-century portable altar known as the *Braunschweig Diptych*; and a sharply observed *Self-Portrait* by the country's leading sixteenth-century artist, **Lucas van Leyden**. Most of the specialist painters of the seventeenth century are represented; *The Marriage of Tobias and Sara* by **Jan Steen** and three landscapes by **Jacob van Ruisdael** are particularly notable. Among Flemish works of the same period are several pieces by **Rubens**, a fine **van Dyck** and a fetching **Teniers**, *The Alchemist's Workshop*.

German painting

The most important German work in the gallery is *Portrait of Cyriacus Kale* by **Holbein the Younger**; it was painted in London, where the Braunschweig-born sitter worked at the Hansa trading headquarters, as the inscription states. A strong representation of **Cranach** includes a lively workshop cycle of *The Labours of Hercules*, and a *Hercules and Omphale*. The latter is by Cranach's hand alone, as is the *Portrait of Albrecht von Brandenburg-Ansbach*, which depicts the cross-eyed Hohenzollern who had been Grand Master of the Teutonic Knights. By the time this picture was painted, Albrecht had converted to Protestantism, secularised his Order's holdings and become Duke of Prussia – events which were crucial in his family's ultimately successful drive to win leadership of the German nation. A delicate *Morning Landscape* by the short-lived **Elsheimer** rounds off this section.

The rest of the museum

Duke Anton Ulrich's taste in Italian painting seems to have been confined to the sixteenth-century Venetians and the bombastic artists of the Baroque. The most fascinating work is what's labelled as a *Self-Portrait* by the mysterious father-figure of Venice's Renaissance, **Giorgione**. One of the few surviving paintings widely accepted as genuine, it's probably a cut-down version of a *David with the Head of Goliath*. Important examples of the later Venetian Renaissance include works by Veronese, Tintoretto and Palma il Vecchio.

In the **decorative arts** section on the top floor Italy features rather more extensively, with a notable array of bronzes and porcelain, plus a valuable onyx vase from Mantua. Other particular strengths are Chinese lacquerwork, Limoges enamels, and jewellery, ceramics and furniture from all over Europe.

Practical details

Braunschweig has two **tourist offices**: one is just outside the front door of the Hauptbahnhof (Mon–Fri 8am–6pm, Sat 9am–noon; ☎0531/79237); the other is housed in a pavilion on Bohlweg (Mon–Fri 8.30am–6pm, Sat 9am–noon; ☎0531/46419). The **youth hostel** is at Salzdalumer Str. 170 (☎0531/62268) to the south of the city, reached by bus #11 or #19 to Krankenhaus. It has a few single rooms, which are well worth considering, given the shortage of cheap **hotels**. In the centre, the only two budget options are *Gästehaus Kohlmarkt*, Kohlmarkt 2 (☎0531/41766), with singles from DM43, doubles from DM76; and the YMCA-run and rather institutional *Am Wollmarkt*, Wollmarkt 9-12 (☎0531/46139), with singles DM45, doubles DM87. Further out, the best bets are *Heyer*, Hannoversche Str. 1 (☎0531/54041), whose rates begin at DM28, and *Jägerhof*, Volkmarsweg 16 (☎0531/36657), with singles from DM33, doubles from DM65. If you're staying far out, note that there's a 24-hour **public transport** ticket for DM5. **Mitfahrzentrale** have an office at Bohlweg 42–43 (☎0531/14041).

Eating

The best **restaurants** in town are the pricey *Haus zur Hanse*, Güldenstr. 7, which features French-style cooking, and the more reasonable and archetypally German *Gewandhauskeller* in the aforementioned Gewandhaus. A common accompaniment to local dishes is a dark sauce known as *Mumme*, which derived from a famous malt **beer** which was extensively exported to England until the eighteenth century. Nowadays, the products of the city's main breweries, *Wolters* and *Feldschlösschen*, are relatively conventional, though there's also a *Hausbrauerei*, Schadt's, at Höhe 28. **Vegetarians** are well catered for by the *Vegetarisches Restaurant*, Stephanstr. 1, and by the *Kartoffelhaus* on Burgplatz which, as its name implies, specialises in potato-based dishes.

Nightlife

Braunschweig has a strong **theatre** tradition; in the now demolished building on Hagenmarkt the first part of Goethe's *Faust* received its premiere in 1829. The building was replaced a few decades later by the *Staatstheater* on Am Theater (between Museumpark and Theaterpark), which remains the leading venue for highbrow performances. Shows with an alternative slant are presented at *FreiBiZe* in the Bürgerpark. This community centre occupies the old waterworks, which are themselves of note as an early example of industrial architecture. **Concerts** of all kinds are held at the modern *Stadthalle* on Leonhardplatz, not far from the Hauptbahnhof. There's a **festival** of modern chamber music each November, while the main annual folklore event is a medieval market held in Burgplatz in late May or early June.

East of Braunschweig

East of Braunschweig, on each of the two main rail routes into the former GDR, are a couple of very contrasting diversions, both well worth a short stopover.

Königslutter Am Elm

KÖNIGSLUTTER AM ELM lies some 20km away in the shadow of the beech forest of Elm. The one monument worth seeing here is the former **Abtei**, set at the opposite end of town from the Bahnhof. Founded by Emperor Lothar III in 1135, its earliest and finest parts were built by Romanesque masons from Lombardy. The small scale and infinitely varied sculpture is an outstanding illustration of the thoughts and obsessions of the medieval mind. It can be seen on the exterior of the apse, adorned with grotesque human masks, imaginary beasts and hunting scenes, and on the north doorway, whose twisted columns are guarded by menacing lions. It's also present in the north walk of the cloister, each of whose columns is of a different shape and design from any other. The interior of the church is covered with frescos – an overenthusiastic nineteenth-century attempt, admittedly using some rather ghostly traces as a starting-point, to recreate the original appearance.

THE PEOPLE'S CAR

The impetus behind the setting-up of the **Volkswagen** company (which was initially state-owned) came directly from Hitler, who wanted a small, reliable car that anyone could afford to buy and run. It was Ferdinand Porsche – a name indelibly associated with vehicles aimed at the very opposite end of the market – who in 1936 provided the design for the distinctive little machine whose hallmarks were its sloping bonnet and its starting crank, and which popularly came to be known as the *Beetle*. Two years later, the factory was built; it was destroyed during the war, whereupon the story might well have ended.

In the event, Volkswagen became a fairy-tale postwar success, and one of the linchpins of West Germany's "economic miracle". The Beetle's cheapness and durability made it a huge export hit, and up to 20 million models were produced in a year. In 1961, 1.5 million small shareholders were given the chance to share in the profits when the government sold off its majority holding. However, the company ran into serious difficulties in the 1970s: no attempt had been made at diversification, and sales of the Beetle plummeted as increased general affluence led to a demand for more luxurious cars. To halt the decline, the drastic decision was taken to scrap the old faithful altogether (though it's still made under licence in Mexico), and to develop a new range of models, based on the more upmarket but still modest *Golf*. It was also decided to make extensive use of robots in the construction process. Finally, the CDU government, normally far less infatuated with privatisation programmes than its Conservative counterpart in Britain, disposed of all its remaining shares in 1988. These measures have by and large been successful, even if the Midas-touch formula of the past is now accepted as having been lost for ever.

Wolfsburg

WOLFSBURG, 30km further north, is an archetypal company town. As late as the 1930s, it was a hamlet of 150 souls, clustered round a part-Gothic, part-Renaissance moated Schloss. Nowadays 130,000 people live there, almost exactly half of them employees of the giant *Volkswagenwerk* (see previous page). **Guided tours** of the factory are offered every weekday afternoon, generally at 1.30pm: turn up at 12.30pm at Wachla 17, or phone ahead first (☎04921/886 2390). Other than this, the town boasts significant examples of modern architecture which have, inevitably, attracted widely diverging opinions from the critics. The most important are the **Kulturzentrum** in the heart of town and the **Heilig-Geist-Kirche** 1km south – both by the internationally acclaimed Finnish architect Alvar Aalto – and the **Stadttheater**, a late work by one of Germany's leading twentieth-century designers, Hans Scharoun.

Wolfenbüttel

Reached in just a few minutes from Braunschweig via what was, when it opened in 1838, the first state-owned railway line in Germany, **WOLFENBÜTTEL** is a place which deserves to be far better known. One of the Welf duchies had its seat there from 1432 to 1754, and even today it preserves much of the layout and atmosphere of a ducal *Residenzstadt*. Indeed, it offers the most evocative example of the petty courts which once dotted the politically fragmented map of the Holy Roman Empire. When the local dukes moved back to Braunschweig, Wolfenbüttel seems to have fallen into a deep slumber; it came through World War II unscathed, and no fewer than 600 historic half-timbered houses survive, as well as plenty of large public buildings. It's also the earliest example in Germany of a **planned town** – in fact, it evolved from several consecutive plans, all of whose outlines are still visible. This subsequently became a favourite idea with German princes – Freudenstadt, Mannheim, Ludwigsburg and Karlsruhe were all built in this way – but none is anywhere near as intact as Wolfenbüttel.

Schlossplatz

From the Bahnhof, cross over the River Oker, then turn left along Schuwall, coming to the spacious **Schlossplatz**, whose eastern side is lined with the plain timber-framed buildings characteristic of the town.

The Schloss

Directly opposite is the huge, dazzlingly white **Schloss**. Apart from the moat and some re-used masonry, nothing remains of the medieval moated fortress, whose present form is a conflation of Renaissance and Baroque rebuilding. The most distinguished feature is the Renaissance **tower**, whose unusual design includes a gabled clock-face on each side; it was built in the early seventeenth century by **Paul Francke**, who was responsible for many of the buildings in the first phases of the planning of Wolfenbüttel. This apart, the exterior of the Schloss dates from a century later and was designed by the highly inventive **Hermann Korb**.

The upper arcades of the Palladian-style inner **courtyard** were originally open, following normal Italian practice; however, they were filled in soon after, when the incompatibility of open arcades and northern weather became apparent. Round the back of the Schloss, a troupe of English actors under Thomas Sackville established themselves as the first permanent theatre company in Germany in 1590. This ushered in a golden era for the performing arts in Wolfenbüttel, but the opera house built there the following century has unfortunately not survived. The surprisingly modest **state apartments** (Tues, Thurs & Sun 10am–1pm, Wed 3–5pm, Fri & Sat 10am–1pm & 3–6pm; free) are worth a quick look to get an impression of how the dukes lived.

The Zeughaus

On the north side of Schlossplatz is the **Zeughaus**, again by Francke. Its cheerful crimson exterior, decorated with richly carved gables, hardly suggests its original function as an arsenal, whose cavernous lower storey once housed the biggest and most powerful cannons in Germany. Immediately behind is the grandest of Wolfenbüttel's half-timbered buildings, a huge mid-seventeenth-century storehouse.

The Herzog-August-Bibliothek

Nowadays, the Zeughaus hosts temporary exhibitions from the pride of the town, the **Herzog-August-Bibliothek** (daily 10am–5pm; combined ticket DM5), whose headquarters are in the nineteenth-century pseudo-*palazzo* diagonally opposite. The Dukes of Braunschweig-Wolfenbüttel were true bibliophiles; by the mid-seventeenth century the scholarly August the Younger had built up the largest library in Europe, consisting of 130,000 volumes, all catalogued by himself. When the philospoher Leibnitz served as custodian of the Welf family collections, he collaborated with Hermann Korb in designing a magnificent wooden rotunda to house the books, but this was demolished last century when larger premises became necessary. Several rooms of the main library have been laid out as a museum, with changing selections from its holdings of rare books, as well as other specialities such as Renaissance maps and globes and twentieth-century artists' sketchbooks. A strongroom holds a display on the library's greatest treasure, the **Gospel book of Henry the Lion** (see below), but unfortunately the initial intention to put on public display the original manuscript itself has not been honoured.

THE WORLD'S MOST EXPENSIVE BOOK

Arguably the most sumptuous manuscript produced in the Romanesque period, Henry the Lion's Evangelistary or **Gospel book** was commissioned around 1180 for use in the Dom in Braunschweig. Among its 24 beautifully coloured full-page miniatures is a scene showing Christ crowning Henry and his English wife Matilda; the saints in paradise include Thomas à Becket, recently murdered as a result of a misunderstood remark made by his friend Henry II, Matilda's father. Last century, the Welf family reacquired this heirloom, but sold it after the last war to a secretive private collector. In 1983, it was auctioned by Sotheby's in London; desperate to gain this key piece of their heritage, the Land government of Lower Saxony headed a consortium which splashed out £10 million, setting a world record price for a work of art. It remains the most expensive book in the world.

The Lessinghaus

The **Lessinghaus** (same times and tickets) in front of the Bibliothek was the official residence of the librarian. A triple-winged summer house, it was finished just three years before the dukes decided to abandon Wolfenbüttel as a residence. Its present name comes from the second famous holder of the librarian's post, the hugely influential playwright **Gotthold Ephraim Lessing**, who spent the last eleven years of his life there; a collection of memorabilia pays tribute to him. The main work from his Wolfenbüttel years is *Nathan the Wise*, a piece particularly interesting in the light of subsequent German history – its wholly admirable hero is a Jew.

Alte Heinrichstadt

East of Schlossplatz is the original late sixteenth-century planned town, the **Alte Heinrichstadt**. One of its focal points is the **Stadtmarkt**, a square lined with half-timbered buildings, in the centre of which is a bronze statue of Duke August the Younger, depicted leading his horse rather than riding it.

Off the north side of the square, on the street named after it, is the **Kanzlei** (Chancellery). Though somewhat messed about, it's notable as being the only surviving building by the Dutchman Hans Vredeman de Vries, the leading architectural theoretician of the Northern European Renaissance. The Kanzlei now houses the mildly interesting **Archäologisches Museum** (Tues–Sat 10am–5pm, Sun 10–1pm; free) of the Braunschweig region. Almost all the other streets around here are worth walking along; look out for **Klein-Venedig** (Little Venice), so named because it fronts a canal.

The Hauptkirche

As a climax to the Alte Heinrichstadt, the **Hauptkirche** was begun in 1608 by Paul Francke; after two decades of restoration, it's now looking in pristine shape. Notwithstanding the dedication to *Beatae Mariae Virginis*, it was not only Lutheran from the outset, but was the first parish church to be built specifically for the Protestant faith (although Bückeburg's Stadtkirche, started three years later, was actually finished first). It's an extraordinary confection, mixing late Gothic, Renaissance and Mannerism, while the main portal – designed like a triumphal arch with statues of two of the dukes ensconced between Moses and Aaron below, and Christ at the summit – has all the swagger of the emergent Baroque style. On the long sides of the building are a series of profusely decorated gables, while on the facade and in the vestibule are hundreds of delicately carved reliefs of animals and demons.

The church's light and spacious **interior** (Tues–Fri 10am–1pm & 3–6pm, Sat 10am–1pm & 2–4pm) doubles as the ducal pantheon. In accordance with Protestant needs, the nave takes up the lion's share of the space, the short chancel being reserved for the administration of the two central sacraments – baptism and the Eucharist. Regular recitals are held on the early Baroque organ, first presided over by the composer **Michael Praetorius**, who is buried below. He's best known for his beguiling arrangements of over 300 foot-tapping dance melodies, collectively known as *Terpsichore*; many of these have again become familiar, having served as television signature tunes to period plays.

Other quarters

East of the Hauptkirche is the **Neue Heinrichstadt**, centred on the Holzmarkt; for the most part, its buildings faithfully follow the style of the earlier part of town. In the early eighteenth century, Hermann Korb finished off the square in an ingenious fashion by inserting the oval **Trinitiaskirche** between the two redundant gateways at the far end, transforming the latter into a pair of towers for the church in the process.

Further east, across the Oker, a huge new town of manufacturing workshops called the **Juliusstadt** was once planned. However, it never got beyond a couple of streets. Instead, the far more modest craftsmen's suburb of **Auguststadt** was laid out at the opposite end of Wolfenbüttel, to the west of the Schloss. Its houses are remarkably similar to those in the "better" part of town, and the half-timbered **Johanniskirche**, set beside its detached belfry in a shady green, brings a touch of rusticity to the quarter.

Practicalities

Wolfenbüttel's **tourist office**, which publishes a useful free English-language walking tour of the town, is down an alley off the south side of Stadtmarkt (Mon, Tues & Thurs 8am–12.30pm & 2–4pm, Wed 8am–12.30pm, Fri 8am–12.30pm & 2–6pm; ☎05331/

27593). There used to be a youth hostel in a wing of the Schloss, but this has closed and may not re-open, leaving the **campsite** by the open-air swimming-pool on Langestrasse as the only real budget option. **Hotels** are all on the expensive side, but try *Kersten*, Rosenmüllerstr. 8 (☎05331/86487), or *Waldhaus*, Adersheimerstr. 75 (☎05331/43265), both at around DM40 per person. Places to **eat** and **drink** include *Alt-Wolfenbüttel*, an old inn on Kramerbuden, just off the Stadtmarkt, and *Karlsberg* on the site of the old bastion overlooking Lange Strasse at the eastern end of town.

SOUTHERN LOWER SAXONY

South of Wolfenbüttel, Lower Saxony's landscape soon makes a significant change to the gentle wooded slopes of the **Harz** mountain range. This was long a famous mining area, thanks to rich deposits of gold, silver and other less precious minerals, but these have, in the present century, become exhausted. At the edge of the mountains, the old imperial city of **Goslar** is the area's main draw, a place as evocative of medieval Germany as any you'll find. Nothing else within the Lower Saxon section of the Harz is of comparable quality, but just beyond the range are a number of impressive old half-timbered towns, such as **Einbeck**, the home of *Bockbier*, **Duderstadt** and **Hann. Münden**. As a complete contrast to these, there's the university city of **Göttingen**, which isn't particularly notable for its monuments but boasts the most exciting atmosphere of any town between Hannover and Frankfurt.

Goslar

The stereotype of a mining town immediately conjures up images of rows of grim iden-tikit terraced houses paying obeisance to the gargantuan, satanic-looking machinery in whose shadow they lie. **GOSLAR**, which stands in a superb location at the northern edge of the Harz, could not be more different. Admittedly, the mining here was always of a very superior nature – silver was discovered in the nearby 600-metre-high **Rammelsberg** in the tenth century, and the town immediately prospered, soon becoming the "treasure chest of the Holy Roman Empire", and a favourite royal seat. As a Free Imperial City in the later Middle Ages, Goslar, though never very large, ranked as one of the most prosperous communities in Europe, with lead and zinc now added to the list of ready-to-hand mineral deposits. Despite two fires sweeping through the streets in 1800, much survives as a reminder of this heady epoch. The presence of a POW hospital during World War II spared it from Allied bombing, ensuring that the entire town now enjoys the status of a protected monument. With just cause too, as Goslar claims to have more **old houses** (over 1500, with 168 pre-1550) than any other town in Germany.

Arrival and practicalities

Goslar's **Bahnhof** and **bus station** are at the northern edge of the Altstadt, just across from the Neuwerkkirche. It's only about ten minutes' walk to Marktplatz, where you'll find the municipal **tourist office** at no. 7 (May–Oct Mon–Fri 9am–6pm, Sat 9am–2pm; Nov–April Mon–Fri 9am–1pm & 2–5pm, Sat 9am–2pm; ☎05321/2846). A separate regional office for the entire Harz region is at Marktstr. 45 (☎05321/20031).

Accommodation

At either office you can pick up a comprehensive list of **hotels**, **pensions** and **private rooms**. If travelling in a group and intending to stay for at least three days, the best deal is to rent a holiday home; most atmospheric are the luxury appartments in the *Burg*

Zwinger, Thomasstr. 2 (☎05321/41088 or 85135), which can work out at as little as DM20 per person per day. Should you prefer the convenience of a hotel, the early eighteenth-century *Zur Börse*, Bergstr. 53 (☎05321/22775 or 22220), is one of the prettiest; singles cost from DM45, doubles DM75. Among the pensions, *Gästehaus Möller*, a few minutes' walk west of the Bahnhof at Schieferweg 6 (☎05321/23098), charges from DM30 per person; this price includes as good a breakfast as you'll find in Germany. Also recommended is *Gästehaus Noack*, in a tranquil location south of the Altstadt at Rosenberg 26 (☎05321/22585); here singles begin at DM26, doubles at DM51. The **youth hostel**, Rammelsbergerstr. 25 (☎05321/22240), is at the foot of the mine, not too far from the centre, but a long trek from the Bahnhof. Nearest **camping** is the well equipped *Sennhütte*, Clausthalerstr. 28 (☎05321/22498 or 22502), in the Gose valley, several kilometres along the B241 in the direction of Clausthal-Zellerfeld.

Marktplatz

Although it hosts an attractive market with fish and pastry specialities on Tuesdays and Fridays, Goslar's **Marktplatz** is best seen empty to fully appreciate the gorgeous visual variety of its buildings, ranging from creamy-textured walls, via pretty half-timbering to sober red and grey slate. The rather comical-looking gold-plated **Reichsadler** (Imperial Eagle) sits perched on top of the fountain in the middle of the square. Sculpted in Romanesque style in the early thirteenth century, this is now the third copy, but, remaining completely faithful to the original, it still looks more like a cock uncertainly poised for take-off than a fearless bird of prey.

The Glockenspiel

At 9am, noon, 3pm & 6pm, the modern **Glockenspiel** – rather appropriately housed on top of the municipal treasurer's building – explains how Goslar rose to be the richest town in Europe during the late Middle Ages. First to appear are a knight and his horse; the latter, according to legend, pawed the ground of the Rammelsberg, and uncovered silver traces. When the boom began, the emperors moved in, and Otto I is presented here with a lump of silver by the knight. The remaining groups show miners hacking their way from the Middle Ages through to the nineteenth century, finishing with their present-day counterparts proudly displaying their state-of-the-art equipment. Rather a sad twist, then, that due to depletion of the various ores, Europe's oldest mine – with nearly 3000 employees – closed down for good in 1988.

The Rathaus

Across the square is the **Rathaus** (guided tours daily June–Sept 9am–5pm; Oct–May 10am–4pm; DM2), whose *Huldigungssaal* (Hall of Homage) ranks as one of the best preserved secular interiors of the Middle Ages. The name is rather misleading, as homage was actually paid in the great hall where the admission desk is now situated. Its superb gold-starred, marine-blue panelled ceiling dates from the original construction of the building in the latter half of the fifteenth century; the chandeliers, carved from antlers and carrying figures of the emperors, were transported from the Dom a few decades later. The *Huldigungssaal* itself was the assembly hall of the city council from 1500 onwards and later used for the town's archives. Its richly decorated panels, painted by an unknown artist over 400 years ago, show scenes from the life of Christ and portraits of various citizens of Goslar. Several valuable relics are hidden in altar niches and closets behind the panelling. Among them are a precious gold and silver tankard from the fifteenth century, elaborately embellished with mining and hunting scenes, and the *Goslarer Evangeliar*, a thirteenth-century manuscript with exquisite Byzantine-inspired Romanesque miniature paintings; sadly only a facsimile of the latter is now displayed. The original *Reichsadler* is also on view.

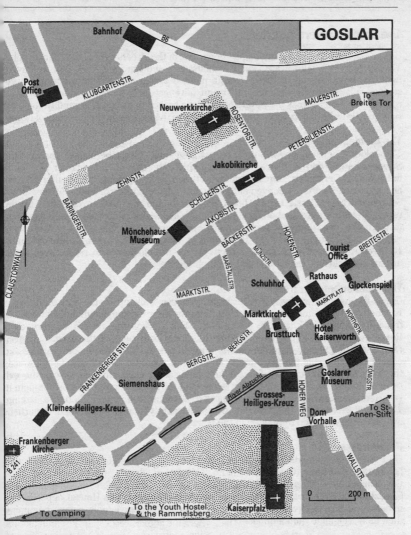

GOSLAR

Bahnhof
B6
Post Office
KLUBGARTENSTR.
Neuwerkkirche
ROSENTORSTR.
MAUERSTR.
To Breites Tor
PETERSILIENSTR.
Jakobikirche
ZEHNSTR.
SCHILDERSTR.
BÄRINGERSTR.
JAKOBISTR.
Mönchehaus Museum
BÄCKERSTR.
Tourist Office
BREITESTR.
CLAUSTORWALL
MARSTALLSTR.
MÜNSTR.
HOKENSTR.
Schuhhof
Rathaus
Glockenspiel
MARKTSTR.
MARKTPLATZ
Marktkirche
WÖRTHSTR.
Brusttuch
Hotel Kaiserworth
FRANKENBERGER STR.
BERGSTR.
BERGSTR.
Siemenshaus
Goslarer Museum
KÖNIGSTR.
River Abzucht
Grosses-Heiliges-Kreuz
HOHER WEG
To St-Annen-Stift
Kleines-Heiliges-Kreuz
Dom Vorhalle
Frankenberger Kirche
B 241
WALLSTR.
0   200 m
To Camping
To the Youth Hostel & the Rammelsberg
Kaiserpfalz

Around the Rathaus

Opposite is the **Hotel Kaiserworth**, previously the guild house of tailors and cloth-makers. Here Baroque and Gothic tumble down on top of Renaissance arches, while the frontage bears eight statues of German emperors, with a naked man excreting a gold coin thrown in for good measure. Just behind the Rathaus is the **Marktkirche**, dedicated to the Roman martyrs Saints Cosmas and Damian, patrons of the medical profession. The architecture, a mix of Romanesque and Gothic, with twin towers and rough-hewn masonry, is typical of Goslar. Inside, look out for the bronze baptismal font, created by a local artist, Magnus Karsten, in 1573: just about every major Biblical event is represented on it in magnificent detail.

The southwestern quarters

Goslar's **half-timbered** beauty begins in earnest in the streets behind the Marktkirche. The styles to look out for are Gothic, Renaissance and Baroque, many homes having two and sometimes all of these: Gothic pointed arches are transformed into three-stepped inlays, usually dull red, gold and olive green in colour; sombrely brilliant rosettes cartwheel across the rafters of the Renaissance houses, while gaudily coloured Baroque devils lie like flattened gargoyles bereft of their power in their prisons of beam.

The Siemenshaus

The oldest houses lie in the Bergstrasse and Schreiberstrasse areas; the **Siemenshaus** (Mon–Fri 9am–noon; free), which was built by a forefather of what is today one of Germany's largest suppliers of medical equipment, electrical appliances and armaments parts, is conveniently situated on the corner of both. Further down Schreiberstrasse, classic Gothic brick houses abound, the style exemplified by the early sixteenth century embodied at no. 10, with its lavishly decorated chimney passing through the two single-roomed storeys. From here, turn left into Frankenberger Strasse and continue down to Frankenberg Plan, on which stands the **Kleines-Heiliges-Kreuz**, set in spacious gardens where the old folk who retire there – and dozens of chickens – can amble about at their leisure.

The Frankenberger Kirche

Going through the archway to the right, you can walk up to the **Frankenberger Kirche**, once the church favoured by miners for their weddings, which is situated in tranquil solitude on the little hill above. Built during the twelfth century as a Romanesque basilica, the later Gothic additions form part of the town's western ramparts. The gigantic Baroque carved wooden passion altar verges on pastiche and could easily dominate the place until you begin to take in a few other details: towards the back of the church, two fierce lions stand facing each other to absorb the evil believed to have come from the west; some faint thirteenth-century frescos compete in vain for attention against an over-charged Baroque pulpit, and there's a strange *Triumphal Cross*, with a deathly-white Christ macabrely topped with a wig of the artist's own hair, a device used frequently in the Harz area.

Peterstrasse

On Peterstrasse immediately to the east are some of the most intriguing of the town's houses: the **Kuhhaus** (Cow House) at no. 27 is named after its previous function, while the **Kürbishaus** (Pumpkin House) at no. 23 is named after its shape. In the **Klauskapelle** to the right and the **Schmiedhaus** (Blacksmith's House) opposite, the miners would respectively pray and collect their sharpened tools before beginning their daily trek up to the Rammelsberg.

The Kaiserpfalz

Dominating a spacious park at the southern end of the Altstadt is the **Kaiserpfalz** (Imperial Palace; daily May–Sept 9.30am–5pm; March, April & Oct 10am–4pm; Nov–Feb 10am–3pm; DM2.50). By far the largest and most important Romanesque royal palace to have survived anywhere in Europe, its exterior is still a potent symbol of the power and wealth enjoyed by Germany's medieval rulers. Built at the beginning of the eleventh century to be home to a succession of greedy emperors enticed by the riches hidden in the Rammelsberg behind it, the Kaiserpfalz continued to flourish for nearly 300 years, hosting important Imperial Diets and benefiting from Goslar's proximity to the crossroads of the two major trade routes of the Middle Ages – from Flanders to

Magdeburg, and from Lübeck to Venice. A fire which gutted the palace in 1289 and a decline of interest around the same time by the emperors kept the building in a state of disrepair over the next few centuries, humbling it even to the point where it was used as a barn and stables during the seventeenth century. Kaiser Wilhelm I came to the rescue in 1868, paying for it to be reconstructed to its former state.

The Reichsaal and the Ulrichskapelle

By present-day standards, the building seems over-restored. This is particularly true of the interior, where the vast **Reichsaal**, whose enormous arched window openings must have given birth to many a draughty Diet during the palace's heyday, was covered, floor to ceiling, with Romantic paintings. Various emperors are depicted being valiant (in battle), pious (distributing riches to the poor), conquering the earth and being blessed by heaven. The hall is most of what remains of the Kaiserpfalz, with the early twelfth-century **Ulrichskapelle** on its southern side. This chapel, the most authentic part of the complex, is an ingenious piece of design: the ground-plan is a Greek cross, but the upper storeys are shaped as a Byzantine-style octagon. In the centre stands the tomb of Emperor Heinrich III, though it contains only his heart: the rest of his body lies in Speyer.

Behind the palace (where, if you face it directly, the irregular shaped stones to the left are the only ones remaining of the originals), the *Goslar Warrior* by Henry Moore lies reclining with his shield on his toe; this is a legacy of the first of the annual prizes awarded by the city to a famous modern artist. Beyond it a pretty semi-walled rose garden, dotted about with firs and shady spreading trees, leads down to a small bridge, the Abzucht stream, and a stone-walled tower. Formerly used to defend the town from invaders, it can now be lived in only by those families with the money and inclination to defend it from the attacks of time.

Hoher Weg

On the opposite side of the Kaiserpfalz, facing the Hoher Weg, the enormous car park stretching below you was once the site of the eleventh-century **Dom**, pulled down in 1822 due to lack of funds for restoration. Only the **Vorhalle** (daily June–Sept Mon–Sat 10am–1pm & 2.30–5pm, Sun 10am–1pm; Oct–May 11.30am–2.30; DM0.60; enquire at the Kaiserpfalz reception if closed) with its facade of stucco statues survived. Inside is the original part bronze **imperial throne**; it was used symbolically at the opening assembly of the Second Reich in Berlin in 1871. Other relics from the church are housed in the Goslarer Museum (see below). The Dom's stones are now embedded in any number of houses, having been sold at the time of demolition to townsfolk who subsequently built their homes with them.

Directly in front of the Dom, Hoher Weg leads down to the **Grosses-Heiliges-Kreuz** at no. 7, one of the oldest hospices in Germany. Built in 1254, it's currently undergoing badly needed repair; in the meantime, a tasteful but uninspired ceramics and trinkets shop downstairs and a rather good photo-montage of the town upstairs provide a pleasant enough diversion. If you have a penchant for rare and beautiful dolls, the **Museum für Musikinstrumente mit Puppenmuseum** (March–Oct daily 10am–6pm; Nov–Feb Mon–Fri 10am–6pm, Sat 10am–2pm; DM2) a little further down the road might briefly quench your thirst.

Goslar's most famous house, the sixteenth-century **Brusttuch**, lies at the bottom of Hoher Weg, almost opposite the Marktkirche. It's an outstanding example of the "Wild Man" style, whose theme of "natural" unbridled sexuality was a great favourite with German Renaissance artists and craftsmen. The beams of the top storey are crammed with satirical carvings of figures from medieval life, folklore, religion and mythology: mischievous cherubs firing arrows at angels, dignified ladies perched on top of goats, and a carelessly suggestive dairymaid churning the butter and squeezing her buttocks at the same time. Facing it across Marktstrasse is the **Bäckergildehaus** (Bakers' Guild House), a far more sober, yet equally imposing example of half-timbering.

The northern quarters

Immediately north of the Marktkirche is the **Schuhhof**, the site of the former shoemakers' guildhall and market. Fires over the centuries have ravaged one part of the square, but the surviving side has three and four storey half-timbered houses from the seventeenth century. Münzstrasse on its western side contains more architectural beauties, including a seventeenth-century coaching inn, the **Weisser Schwan** at no. 11, where a tin figure museum (daily 10am–5pm, Thurs until 9pm; DM2.50) depicts the history of Goslar à la Lilliput.

The Mönchehaus Museum

At the end of the street, turn into Jakobistrasse, where, at no.15, a Renaissance craftsman's house has been the subject of one of the most polished and professional pieces of restoration in Goslar. The **Mönchehaus Museum** (Tues–Sat 10am–1pm & 3–5pm, Sun 10am–1pm; DM2.50) lies just beyond, at the corner with Mönchestrasse. A black and white half-timbered sixteenth-century building, it's the curious home to Goslar's permanent modern art exhibition, featuring works by recipients of the city's annual prize. The contrast works amazingly well indoors, with de Koonings, Tinguelys and Vasarelys hanging amidst the oak beams; the effectiveness of the huge metal sculptures parked in the garden is more debatable, but it's good to see something in Goslar with an experimental touch.

Two churches

On the square at the eastern end of Jakobistrasse is the Catholic parish church, the **Jakobikirche**. Only the west wing remains from the original Romanesque structure, which was rebuilt in Gothic style. Inside, there's a moving *Pietà* by the great but elusive early sixteenth-century sculptor, Hans Witten. North along Rosentorstrasse, the **Neuwerkkirche** (Mon–Thurs & Sat 9.30–11.30am & 2.30–4.30pm, Sat 9.30am–11.30am) stands in a peaceful garden. Built as a Cistercian convent during the late twelfth and early thirteenth centuries, the church's main exterior features are its two polygonal towers and the delicate late Romanesque carvings on the apse. Inside, there are works of art dating back to the period of construction, notably the choir screen and some rather clumsily retouched frescos. The curious stone **handles** high up on the pillars of the nave are unique in the history of architecture and have a didactic purpose: those on the south have grotesque carvings and represent the temptations of the devil; the wreaths on the north symbolise the eternity for which the soul should strive.

The Abzucht and the Stadtbefestigung

From Marktplatz, go south along Worthstrasse, where a fairly successful attempt at an artists' quarter has been constructed along and around the banks of the **Abzucht**, the tiny stream that passes through the southern part of Goslar. On the corner of Abzuchtstrasse and Königstrasse is the **Goslarer Museum** (May–Sept Mon–Sat 10am–5pm, Sun 10am–4pm; Oct daily 10am–4pm; Nov–April Mon–Sat 10am–4pm, Sun 10am–1pm; DM2.50). This contains the usual local history displays, including a section on mining in the Rammelsberg. However, the collection is taken out of the ordinary by some superb treasures from the Dom, including a couple of stained glass windows and the exotic *Krodoaltar* – which looks more as if it were fashioned deep in the heart of Africa than in eleventh-century Europe.

The Abzucht bubbles along the cobbles to occasionally bump into one of the handful of rickety water mills still remaining of an original twenty-five; follow the red stones in the middle of the pathways to find the sites of the former mills, now replaced by houses. Look out for the **St-Annen-Stift** (daily 9am–noon & 3–6pm; knock at the door for entrance); dating from 1488, this hospice is the oldest half-timbered building in Goslar. Inside, you can view the chapel with its medieval woodwork and seventeenth-century wall paintings.

From here, it's a short walk down St Annenhöhe to see the best-preserved parts of the **Stadtbefestigung** (city ramparts). It takes about two hours to walk the complete circuit, which is interspersed with many stretches of greenery. If pressed for time, go down zingerwall to see the **Zwinger** (daily 9am–5pm; DM2), an ivy-covered, thick-walled tower once used by the town's artillery. It commands a fine view over Goslar and the Harz; there's also a display of medieval weapons and a restaurant. The most imposing part of the town's fortifications is the bulky ensemble of the **Breites Tor** at the northeasternmost corner, the sight of which alone must have been enough to scare off any would-be invaders.

The Rammelsberg

Of the various walks in the vicinity of Goslar, the most interesting is the geological trail round the **Rammelsberg** (the tourist office publish a leaflet). A more pressing reason for visiting the mountain which provided the city with its wealth is that a **Bergbaumuseum** (guided tours daily 9.30am–6pm; DM6; take bus #C from the centre) has been set up in double-quick time in the famous mine. The visit begins in the hall-like changing-room, now used as an exhibition explaining the historical background; here you don a miner's overalls and helmet before descending into the bowels of the earth. As yet, only a small section is open; be warned that you'll need an exceptional command of German to understand the guide's highly technical explanations.

Eating and drinking

Goslar's food and drink scene seems primarily geared to the fact that many of the town's visitors are taking a relaxing holiday – hence the presence of so many cafés. However, if you're prepared to look around, you'll find establishments to suit every taste and pocket.

Barock-Café Anders, Hoher Weg 4. Best place in town for *Kaffee und Kuchen*; walk straight to the back of the café to sit outside, where there's a leafy vista of the Harz.

Brauhaus Goslar, Marstallstr. 1. This new *Hausbrauerei*, serving an excellent unfiltered Pils, has revived Goslar's medieval brewing tradition after a long gap. It's one of several bars grouped round a courtyard which have collectively become the liveliest spot in town.

Christall, Bäckerstr. 106. The long menu here features plenty of inventive vegetarian dishes.

Historisches Café, Markt 4. Another good choice for those with a sweet tooth, particularly when the weather is good and you can sit outside on the square.

Kaiserwerth, Markt 3. Top-class hotel restaurant; on the expensive side, though not unreasonably so.

Kontrast, Worthstr. 10. One part of this specialises in health food stuff; the somewhat more pricey bistro next door serves crêpes and light French dishes.

Pupasch, Schilderstr. 4. Characterful old pub in a half-timbered building across from the Jakobikirche.

Weisser Schwan, Münzstr. 11. Part of this famous old inn is given over to a Balkan grill-house that's a cut above the German norm.

Worthmühle, Worthstr. 8. Does excellent hot provincial cooking at very low prices.

Zebra, Bäckerstr. 18. Cheap and cheerful new wave hang-out.

The Harz mountains

Nowhere, other than in Berlin itself, was the reality of the postwar division of Germany more evident than in the **Harz** mountains, the first barrier encountered by the icy winds which sweep across the North German Plain. A popular holiday destination since the idea of a vacation away from home took off in the course of the nineteenth century, the Harz were divided right through the middle by the notorious barbed-wire frontier. Most roads came to a dead end, and adjacent villages were completely cut off from each other, often to the ruination of local economies. A fascinating contrast was presented by the two sides, which for once was not (the frontier apart) entirely to the east's disadvantage. For one thing, many of the towns on the Lower Saxon side were converted into modern resorts which are characterless in comparison with their eastern counterparts. For another, the mountain steam railways which are still such an attraction in the former GDR were closed down here and replaced by buses: the only trains left are those running along the northern and western fringes of the range. Despite the many changes which have occurred since the re-unification, the differences between the two sides of the Harz remain a vivid illustration of the effects of four decades of national division.

The range has a climate which is euphemistically described as "bracing". Although this means that there's lots of rain and fog, with heavy snowfall in winter, it doesn't deter hordes of mainly elderly holidaymakers who have earned the region the derisive sobriquet *Rentnergebirge* (pensioners' mountains). Perhaps they're drawn by the relatively gentle slopes of the mountains ("the skiing here is for babies," according to another insult) which make the Harz ideal for healthy but undemanding **walking** holidays.

Clausthal-Zellerfeld

The most direct route into the Harz from Goslar will take you to **CLAUSTHAL-ZELLERFELD**, some 20km to the southwest. If you're driving, it's best to take time to admire the scenery: the direct B241 road winds and climbs its way through dense forest flanked by a number of small, hidden lakes. Buses tend to follow a more circuitous route via HAHNENKLEE, a big winter sports resort built round a Scandinavian-style stave church from the first decade of the present century.

Two old towns merged into one, Clausthal-Zellerfeld is a characterful place where half-timbered houses are interspersed with those faced with coloured slate. It was the main mining centre of the Upper Harz, but the last pit shut down in 1931. The tradition is exhaustively documented in the excellent **Oberharzer Bergwerksmuseum** (daily 9am–5pm; DM4.50) at Bornhardtstr. 16 in Zellerfeld, the northern part of the double town. Included in the entrance fee is a tour through the life-sized model of a pit which has been erected in the garden; make sure you ask for the English-speaking guide, as the language used is very technical. You can wander at your leisure round the other mining buildings, which have been moved here from their original locations. Star piece is the *Pferdegaipel*, a shaft which was worked by horses: it's the only one of its kind in Germany.

Clausthal clusters around the **Marktkirche**, the largest wooden church in Central Europe. Built in the first half of the seventeenth century, its main body is of fir, while the tower is made of oak. Inside are notable furnishings, of which many, including the double gallery, the retable and pulpit, are also fashioned from wood. Across the street is the **Technische Universität**, Germany's most unlikely university, which grew out of the mining academy established here in the eighteenth century. Its **Mineraliensammlung** (Mon 2–5pm, Tues–Fri 9am–noon; free) is reckoned to be one of the largest and best collections of minerals in the world.

racticalities

he **tourist office** is in the old railway station building in the gulley between the towns
: Bahnhofstr. 5a (Mon–Fri 9am–noon & 2–5pm, Sat 9am–noon; ☎05323/7024). Should
ɔu wish to linger they'll organise accommodation and, in winter, ski and sledge hire.
here are over a score of **private houses** with rooms to let, usually at no more than
M20 per person; there are also plenty of **hotels** charging around DM30, a couple of
xamples being *Zur Börse*, Schulstr. 47 (☎05323/2121) in Clausthal and *Gästehaus
reisinger*, Marktstr. 27(☎05323/81423) in Zellerfeld. The **youth hostel** is at the
xtreme eastern end of Clausthal at Altenauer Str. 55 (☎05323/2293). One of the **camp-
ites** is south of here at Lange Brüche 4 (☎05323/1300); another is at the northwestern
inge of Zellerfeld at Spiegeltaler Str. 31 (☎05323/81712). For **eating**, a good choice is
ie *Gaststätte* of the Bergwerksmuseum, which features game specialities; in Clausthal,
y *Goldene Krone*, Kronenplatz 3. Top choice for **drinking** is *Anno Tobak*, a student
vourite at the top end of Osteroder Strasse, diagonally opposite the Marktkirche.

Along the former border

he old border between East and West Germany may have lost its barbed wire, but it
etains its inherent fascination, particularly while vestiges of the former division
ɪrvive. One of these is the disrupted transport network: the plush spa of **BAD
IARZBURG** is a dead end for the railway lines from both Goslar (which is only ten
ıinutes' away) and Braunschweig. If you want to continue eastwards to Wernigerode,
ɔu have to change to a bus, as the GDR authorities chopped off the old line just before
ie border. Still, this is at least a major improvement on the situation up to 1989, when
•ng circuitous journeys were necessary to cover distances of only a few kilometres.

orfhaus

he 15km hiking trail from Bad Harzburg to the crossroads hamlet of **TORFHAUS**
sed to be one of the most prized Cold War thrills, passing as it did right alongside the
·on Curtain. Even now, it has an eerie fascination, at least as long as the ghostly watch-
•wers, which may or may not be preserved for posterity, remain as a blight on the land-
:ape. Torfhaus, which can also be reached by bus, offers the best views of the
elebrated **Brocken** (see *Chapter Ten*), rendezvous of the witches on *Walpurgisnacht*
30 April), a festival celebrated in all the towns in the Harz. The path from here was re-
pened soon after the Berlin Wall came down, and makes an enticing alternative to the
asier approach from Schierke. If you want to do some serious hiking in the area,
'orfhaus' **youth hostel** (☎05320/242) makes an obvious base. A further 5km south,
ıere's another crossroads at the **Oder-Teich**, an artificial lake made in the eighteenth
entury. Here you can take a swim, or buy locally produced honey from one of the stalls.

Sraunlage

RAUNLAGE, which lies 8km south of the Oder-Teich, is a resort which was deliber-
tely built up as a showpiece of capitalist values – with dozens of souvenir shops and
:cores of pseudo-Alpine hotels and pensions – right on the Communist doorstep. If
ɔu're in the area, the town would probably make a good place for an overnight stop
ecause, if nothing else, it's not lacking in facilities. It's a *Kurort* and popular destination
ot only with the OAP crowd but also with young families who come here for the skiing.
'here are five pistes on the **Wurmberg** (965m), which were made tantalisingly visible
ɔ the unfortunates over the border. You can ride a cable car to the top (from where
ıere's a grandstand view over the region) and back for DM10. A full list of accommoda-
on possibilities is available from the **tourist office** in the *Kurverwaltung*, Elbingeröder
tr. 17 (☎05520/1054). The **youth hostel** is at Von-Langen-Str. 63 (☎05520/2238).

The western fringe

WALKENRIED, at the extreme southwestern corner of the Harz, used to be anothe dead end, but was forunate enough to have its rail link to Nordhausen in Thuringia restored even before German re-unification was formally achieved. This little healthy resort, arguably the most attractive on the western side of the Harz, has one of the area's few notable historic monuments – a Cistercian **Kloster** which was once among the most powerful in Germany. Built in the early thirteenth century in the Transitional style favoured by this order, the church is very ruinous, though impressive fragments of the facade and one of the transepts remain to give an idea of its former grandeur **Guided tours** (Easter–Sept Mon–Sat 10am–noon & 2–5pm, Sun noon–5pm; rest o year Sat & Sun only at 2pm & 3pm; DM3) are run round the monastic buildings, which have recently been restored to their original form. Highlights are the graceful north walk of the cloister, idiosyncratically divided into two aisles, and the former chapte house, now fitted out as the Protestant parish church. The village is chock-a-block with pensions and private houses with **rooms** to let; a full list is available from the *Kurverwaltung*, Steinweg 4 (☎05525/357). There's also a **campsite** (☎05525/778) a the eastern fringe.

Herzberg

About 20km northwest via the railway skirting the Harz is **HERZBERG**, one of the few places in the Harz not wholly given over to tourism – a fact reflected in the higher than normal accommodation prices. Overlooking the town is the **Welfenschloss** (April–Sept Tues–Fri 10am–12.30pm & 1–5pm, Sat & Sun 10am–12.30pm & 1–6pm; Oct–March Tues–Fri 11am–12.30pm & 1–4pm, Sat & Sun 11am–12.30pm & 1-5pm; DM2), a half-timbered seventeenth-century castle built in the "Wild Man" style seen in Goslar inside is one of the tin figure museums so beloved of the Germans. A biggish lake in the town centre helps give the place a distinctive atmosphere.

St Andreasberg

Herzberg lies in the lower reaches of one of the Harz's main beauty spots, the thickly wooded **Sieber valley**. It's best explored on foot, but an attractive alternative is to take a bus up to **ST ANDREASBERG**, the highest town in the Harz: the road at times runs parallel to the valley and at times features spectacular corkscrew bends. At the foot of the town's steep hill is its main attraction, the old silver-mine known as **Bergwerkmuseum Grube Samson** (guided tours daily at 11am & 2pm; DM2.50).

Osterode

The railway junction of **OSTERODE**, 10km northwest of Herzberg, was the home town of the great sculptor Tilman Riemenschneider. It boasts a pretty centre of half timbered houses along with a few grander municipal buildings, of which the most visible is the Baroque **Kornhaus**: built by the Hanoverian kings as a precautionary measure against famine crippling the local mining industry, it could hold 2000 tons of grain – hence its palatial dimensions. Look out also for the shark's rib above the entrance to the **Rathaus** which is supposed to ensure protection against flooding. The *Ratskeller* underneath is the town's best **restaurant**, and is particularly recommendable at lunch time, when bargain menus are on offer. For a full accommodation list, contact the **tourist office,** which is housed in the elegant Villa Schachtrupp in a park just west of the town centre at Dörgestr. 40 (☎05522/6855). In addition to a plentiful supply of pensions and private rooms, there's a **youth hostel** towards the eastern edge of town at Scherenberger Str. 34 (☎05522/5595). Further along the road, in the shadow of the Söse-Stausee, a reservoir ringed by wooded hills, is the **campsite** (☎05522/3319).

Einbeck

EINBECK, which lies just to the west of the Harz, is something of a mecca for **beer** lovers, being the original home and the most authentic producer of Germany's most famous strong brew, *Bockbier*. The town is almost equally well-known for its half-timbered houses, characteristically painted in yellow, red, green and black – around 120 survive from the sixteenth century alone.

BOCKBIER

In the Middle Ages Einbeck boasted no fewer than 700 breweries – virtually all of which were tiny part-time operations run within the household. Many of the houses where beer was brewed can still be identified: two clues to look for are double doorways (one of which was used for rolling the barrels through), and dense groupings of dormer-like ventilation openings in the attic, where the raw ingredients were stored. Made from wheat and fermented from the top, what became known as *Einpöckisches Bier* was a strong brew designed for export, with fermentation taking place in the course of the journey to the customer. Its most famous historical appearance came at the Diet of Worms in 1521 when Luther used it to fortify himself during his heroic stand against the full might of the Empire and the papacy. In time, the drink became known as *Bockbier* (after a corruption of the town's name); it was introduced into the Hofbräuhaus in Munich, and has long been as popular in Bavaria as in Lower Saxony. Two crucial differences between the modern and old version are that it's now made from barley, and fermented from the bottom. Nowadays, the *Einbecker-Brauerei* is the only brewery left in the home town of this headily potent beer. It produces both light (*Hell*) and dark (*Dunkel*) varieties, as well as the special brown *Maibock*, available only in springtime. All of these have a smooth, dry, and highly satisfying flavour. Curiously enough, locals tend to prefer its other, more conventional products: a *Brauherren-Pils*, and a *Spezial*.

The Marktplatz

The hub of life in Einbeck is the **Marktplatz**, which is surrounded by well-kept and obviously genuine sixteenth-century houses. Look out for the **Brodhaus** and the **Ratsapotheke**, which stand next door to each other like two superannuated old men opposite the **Ratswaage** (Weigh House) and the vaguely sinister-looking **Rathaus**. The Rathaus could well have served as a model for the witch's house in the Hansel and Gretel story, thanks to three low conical spires which sprout out of the stairwell and the two sharply contrasted oriel windows. Dominating the square from its central position is the **Marktkirche**, a box-like Gothic hall church with a striking red sandstone Baroque facade.

Elsewhere in town

Immediately to the west lies **Tidexerstrasse**, the most impressive street in town, with a gloriously picturesque ensemble of half-timbered houses. However, the finest house of all is no. 13 in **Marktstrasse**, whose whole facade is covered with intricate allegorical carvings, drawing on Christian and Classical themes. Many of the figures are remarkably expressive and you get the impression that the artist used local characters as models. Another handsome street, Steinweg, leads north to another red sandstone Gothic church, the **Stiftskirche St Alexandri** (Mon–Fri 10am–noon). Its set of choir stalls, bearing the date of 1288, is the oldest in Germany, though the main treasure is a magnificent Romanesque chandelier. The only interesting museum is the **Fahrradmuseum**, Papenstr. 1–3 (Tues 3–5pm, Wed 10am–noon, Thurs 4–6pm, Fri & Sat 10am–noon,; free), a collection of bikes which has everything from the wooden wheeled boneshakers of 1817 to the very latest racers. It's also worth taking a walk round the surviving sections of the **Stadtmauer**; much of the fortification network is intact and you can stroll along the massive earthworks which were constructed to increase the protection afforded by the wall itself.

Practicalities

Einbeck's **Bahnhof** is 4km from the centre in the castle-crowned village of SALZDERHELDEN. **Buses** have replaced the former branch railway into the town, but beware that these do not necessarily connect with the arrival and departure of trains. The **tourist office** is in the Rathaus (April–Sept Mon–Fri 9am–1pm & 2.30–6pm, Sat 10am–noon; Oct–March Mon–Thurs 9am–1pm & 2.30–5pm, Fri 9am–1pm; ☎05561/316121). There's a small **youth hostel** at Tiedexer Tor 3 (☎05561/2155). Of the **hotels** with a central location, the most reasonably priced are *Gästehaus Herkur*, Bismarckstr. 4 (☎05561/2300), which starts at DM25 per person, and *Stadt Hannover*, Möncheplatz 10 (☎05561/5496), which charges upwards of DM30 per person. For a bit more luxury, try *Gilde-Hof*, Marktplatz 3 (☎05561/2160); rooms cost from DM40, while the *Gaststätte* is one of the best restaurants in town and a good place to sample the local beers.

Göttingen

GÖTTINGEN is positively metropolitan in contrast to the surrounding area. It owes its exciting, buzzing atmosphere to its large student population (30,000 out of a total populace of 130,000), who have made sure that the nightlife here almost has a big-city feel to it. In fact, a lot of students come to Göttingen after studying in Berlin, and they seem to have brought some of the latter's pace with them. Students here flirted briefly with the spirit of '68 but today they're more interested in patronising the town's *Musikkneipen* and jazz clubs by night while studying for well-paid, secure careers during the day. Things quieten down a little outside term time – but there's usually something going on.

The Markt and around

The central Markt is dominated by the **Altes Rathaus**, a massive sandstone structure which has an almost Venetian feel to it, quite at odds with the half-timbered buildings nearby. Most of what you can see today dates back to the fourteenth and fifteenth centuries, when Göttingen was at the height of its commercial prosperity, but it was never completely finished, as resources had to be diverted to constructing the municipal fortifications. The only way of seeing much of the building is by taking a **guided tour** (Wed & Sat at 3pm). At other times, you'll have to be content with looking at the medieval-looking frescos and coats of arms painted on the inner walls; these turn out to be little over 100 years old, having been commissioned by the authorities during the restoration of the building during the 1880s. When the weather is good the *Rathskeller* takes over part of the Markt and you can have a drink or a meal while looking at the **Gänseliesel**, "the most kissed girl in the world", a bronze statue of a goose-girl erected at the beginning of the century, to whom, according to tradition, the students must give a few smackers when they pass their finals.

Behind the Altes Rathaus is the **Johanniskirche** (May–Oct daily 10.30–11.30am), a twin-towered fourteenth-century Gothic church which has a certain decrepit elegance even though its impact is diminished by the shops that crowd in around it. Theological students are allowed free accommodation in one of the **towers**, but they have to

GÖTTINGEN'S ACADEMIC TRADITION

Göttingen was a decayed market town when King George II of the United Kingdom, in his capacity as Elector of Hannover, founded the **University** in 1737. A free-thinking, liberal atmosphere was immediately promoted, in sharp contrast to the authoritarian traditions of the country's other seats of learning; this enabled Göttingen to establish a high reputation very quickly, which it has maintained ever since. In its early days, it was particularly associated with poets, such as the group known as the *Göttinger Hain-Bund*, early Romantics who wrote on folklore, nature and homely themes, and **Gottfried August Bürger**, holder of the chair of Aesthetics, whose ballads (especially *Leonore*, with its vivid image of Death), were enormously influential. The University's literary reputation continued in the nineteenth century with the appointment of the **Brothers Grimm** to professorships – while there Jacob wrote an exhaustive study, *Teutonic Mythology*, , which was to inspire similar studies of national folklore all over Europe. Unfortunately, this tradition, along with Göttingen's liberal standing, was severely tarnished by the dismissal of the brothers and five colleagues in 1837 for failing to kow tow to the reactionary new constitution introduced into the Kingdom of Hannover.

Mathematics and science have, if anything, been even stronger academic specialities in Göttingen. In the eighteenth century, the leading figure was **Georg Christoph Lichtenberg**, who invented the prototype of the Xerox copying machine and the hot-air balloon. He was also a dedicated Anglophile and a brilliant satirical writer; his *Book of Aphorisms* is a storehouse of worldly wisdom, whose clarity and precision puts all subsequent German philosophy to shame. Throughout the first half of the last century, **Carl-Friedrich Gauss** (the face on the new DM10 note) dominated the University's intellectual life. His name is given to a unit of the field of magnetic intensity, and, in partnership with Wilhelm Weber, he invented the electromagnetic telegraph. In the next generation, the chemist **Friedrich Wöhler**, best known for his pioneering work with aluminium, preserved the university's position at the forefront of world science. The present century has seen a string of Nobel Prizes awarded to Göttingen professors. Since World War II, the town has been the headquarters of the fifty separate high-powered scientific research units of the **Max-Planck-Institut**, named in honour of the discoverer of quantum theory, who passed his last years here.

endure the sound of the bells from the other tower and miserable living conditions (no running water or WC), as well as granting admission on Saturdays between 2pm & 4pm to anyone wanting to climb up for a view of the town. Behind the church is the medieval **Johannesviertel**, more or less a slum district until the 1970s, when the city finally got round to tarting it up. At the point where Johanniskirchhof runs into Paulinerstrasse is the former **Paulinerkirche**, originally built by Dominican monks in 1331, which in 1529 was the scene of the first Lutheran church service in Göttingen. Used as the provisional home of the University when it first opened, the building now houses part of its library.

The rest of the town

Following the pedestrianised main street, Weender Strasse, north from the Markt, brings you to the Jakobikirche (May–Oct daily 11am–1pm), another Gothic church, dominated this time by a single tower which was designed by a member or associate of the famous Parler dynasty of masons. From Judenstrasse at the back of the church, turn right into Ritterplan, where the only aristocratic mansion left in the town has been refurbished to house the **Städtisches Museum** (Tues–Fri 10am—5pm, Sat & Sun 10am–1pm; free). As you'd expect, this has a Göttingen bias, with a big collection of religious art and plenty of examples of locally produced glass and porcelain.

The University is spread out all over the town, though its most imposing buildings are found in the eastern part of the Altstadt, and around its green belt. Finest of all is the Neoclassical **Aula** on Wilhelmsplatz, a couple of blocks south of the Städtisches Museum and a similar distance east of the Markt; this graduation hall was built to celebrate the centenary of the University's foundation. Many of the departments have their own museum; unfortunately, these tend to be open only one day a week, or by appointment. One definitely worth trying to catch is the **Völkerkundliche Sammlung**, Theaterplatz 15 (Sun 10am–1pm; free), which includes part of the collection assembled by Captain Cook in the South Seas and a bizarre array of 400 fertility symbols and mother-god effigies.

Anybody who knows anything about German history won't be able to resist the **Bismarckhäuschen** (Tues 10am–1pm, Thurs & Sat 3-5pm; DM1), a small tower on the southern edge of the town centre which forms part of the old city wall. In 1833 this was home to the seventeen-year-old Otto von Bismarck, then a student in the city. The man who later became the "Iron Chancellor" and who finally realised, by a mixture of brute force and astute politicking, the long-established ideal of a united Germany, was forced to live here, having been banned from the city centre for drunkenness and "misbehaviour of various kinds".

Going north along Angerstrasse, you come to the **Marienkirche**, which stands on what used to be the boundary between the Altstadt and the so-called Neustadt, built as a rival town outside the original city walls by a local nobleman in an attempt to challenge the increasingly powerful burghers. The citizens' response to this threat was an astute one. They waited until the nobleman went bankrupt and then bought the Neustadt from him, incorporating it into Göttingen itself. The Marienkirche looks quite unecclesiastical, which probably has something to do with the fact that its bell tower used to be one of the gateways to the Neustadt; indeed, the street still passes through an archway cut in it.

Eating and drinking

Above all, Göttingen is a city where you can enjoy yourself. There are dozens of cafés, bars and restaurants which, thanks to the heavy student presence, tend to be high on atmosphere and low in cost.

Blue Note, Wilhelmplatz 3. Slightly upmarket jazz/blues bar which seems to be favoured by medical and law students drawn by its snob appeal.

Can Can, Kornmarkt 9. A chrome decor basement café, which, thanks to its cheap baguettes and live music in an animated atmosphere, is highly popular with undergraduates.

Havana Moon, Rote Str. 18. Very trendy Texan-style bar.

Junkerschänke, Barfüsserstr. 5. Göttingen's best restaurant, housed in a beautiful fifteenth-century half-timbered building; rather pricey, but worth it.

Naturell, Lange-Geismar-Str. 40. Inventive vegetarian and wholefood restaurant (Mon–Fri 11am–7pm, Sat 11am–2.30pm).

Nörgelbuff, Groner Str. 23. Favourite haunt of the more bohemian members of the student community; features occasional live music and theatre.

Taormina, Groner-Tor-Str. 28. Recommended pizzeria which stays open until 1.30am.

Zum Altdeutschen, Prinzenstr. 16. Göttingen's most famous student pub, even if these days its clientele seems to be dominated by tourists.

Zum Schwarzen Bären, Kurzestr. 12. Romantic *Gaststätte* dating back to the sixteenth century, complete with stained glass windows and cosy little alcoves; the food is first class and fairly reasonable in price.

Zum Szültenbürger, Prinzenstr. 7. Another celebrated student tavern, with basic dishes such as *Schmalzbrot* as an alternative to full meals.

Practicalities

Göttingen's **Hauptbahnhof** lies just to the west of the centre, which is reached by going straight ahead via the underpass, then along Goetheallee. The main **tourist office** (April–Oct Mon–Fri 9am–6pm, Sat & Sun 9am–4pm; Nov–March Mon–Fri 9am–1pm & 2–6pm, Sat 9am–1pm; ☎0551/54000) is on the first floor of the Altes Rathaus. Most of Göttingen's centrally-sited **hotels** are on the pricey side. The cheapest with a decent location are: *Zur Rose*, Kurze Geismarstr. 37 (☎0551/57050), with singles from DM36 and doubles from DM65; *Stadt Hannover*, Goetheallee 21 (☎0551/45957), which charges from DM43 per person; and *Pension am Theater*, Planckstr. 12 (☎0551/59362), whose rates begin at DM40. To the north of the centre, handily placed for the University, are *Zum Schwan*, Weender Landstr. 23 (☎0551/44863), with singles from DM39, doubles from DM59 and *Berliner Hof*, Weender Landstr. 43 (☎0551/31340), with singles from DM38, doubles from DM70. The **youth hostel** is 3km east of the centre at Habichtsweg 2 (☎0551/57622); take bus #18. **Mitfahrzentrale's** office is at Obere-Masch-Str. 18 (☎0551/44004).

The main **cultural** venues are the *Deutsches Theater* and the *Stadthalle*, which face each other across Theaterplatz, and the more experimental *Junges Theater* on Hospitalstrasse. Each June, Göttingen celebrates the music of Handel in the *Händelfest*, one of Europe's best and most adventurous celebrations of the work of a single composer; many long-forgotten masterpieces have successfully been dusted down here and brought back into the repertoire.

Duderstadt

DUDERSTADT lies just over 30km east of Göttingen in the upper part of the **Eichsfeld** region, a remote land which time forgot and whose inhabitants were, according to popular prejudice, a little slow on the uptake because of centuries of in-breeding. Most of this area became part of the GDR; in thanks for being spared this fate, Duderstadt styled itself the centre of *Die Goldene Mark* (The Golden Borderland). As a result of the success of Willi Brandt's *Ostpolitik*, the town was chosen as one of the places where the hitherto impenetrable border could be crossed; the communication links set up then have proved to be a great boon since unification.

Around town

For much of its history, Duderstadt was an enclave belonging to the Archbishop-Electors of Mainz, and it therefore likes to claim that it's the northernmost part of south Germany. The **half-timbered houses** (some 500 in all) have a unique subtlety which somehow stands out from that of all the other towns in the area. Typically, they're brightly coloured and decorated with carvings (including many impressive figures) and inscriptions, messages from the past which still have an uncanny vitality. The best examples are in **Hinterstrasse**, where there's a rich mix of architectural styles reflecting phases in the town's history of partial destruction followed by intense reconstruction.

Duderstadt's central axis, Markstrasse, widens to form a square at each end. Untermarkt to the west is dominated by the Protestant parish church of **St Servatius**, which was given a Jugendstil look inside after being burned out in 1915. On Obermarkt, its Catholic counterpart, **St Cyriakus**, is a handsome Gothic hall church with impressive Baroque furnishings inside, notably the tall candelabra with figures of angels, which are often carried on religious processions. Between the two churches is the **Rathaus** (April–Oct Mon–Fri 8.30am–1pm & 2–5pm, Sat & Sun 9.30am–12.30pm & 2.30–4.30pm; Nov–March same times Mon–Fri only; DM2), whose thirteenth-century kernel can be appreciated from inside, though the exterior has been masked behind such superb embellishments as the late Gothic turrets and half-timbering, and the elaborate Renaissance balcony and stairwell. Outside the Rathaus stands the **Mariensäule**, a sandstone statue of the Virgin Mary set on top of a tall pillar whose base is flanked by palm trees, creating an incongruously Mediterranean atmosphere.

The other main sight is the **Westertorturm**, the original northwestern gateway to the town. Its high, narrow roof has, over the years, gradually turned on its own axis and taken on a characteristic spiral appearance. This makes the best point to begin a walk round the surviving parts of the fortifications, from where there are many surprising views of the town.

Practicalities

Duderstadt is not on a railway line, but there are frequent **bus** connections with Göttingen; those run by DB leave from the station below the Westertorturm, but others depart from Untermarkt. The **tourist office** is in the Rathaus (times as above; ☎05527/841200); this is the best place to ask about **private rooms**, which average around DM20 per person. **Hotels**, and in particular cheap ones, are in rather short supply; *Schutzenhaus*, August-Werner-Allee 28 (☎05527/5506), has a few rooms beginning at DM25 per person; otherwise expect to pay around DM40 at *Alte Post*, Jüdenstr. 20 (☎05527/8967), or *Deutsches Haus*, Hinterstr. 29 (☎05527/4052); the latter also has one of the best **restaurants** in town. Alternatively, there's a **youth hostel** at Schutzenring 6 (☎05527/3833). **Camping** facilities are available at *Campingplatz Forsthaus Nesselröder Warten* (☎05508/364) in NESSELRÖDE, which lies on the Duderstadt–Göttingen road. Main local **festival** is the inevitable *Schützenfest* on the second weekend in July.

Hann. Münden

Playing the time-honoured game of listing the Seven Wonders of the World, the great German traveller-scholar Alexander von Humboldt – who had seen a fair bit of the globe for himself – listed **HANN. MÜNDEN** as ranking among the seven most beautifully sited towns. Even if this judgment seems tinged by excessive patriotism, there can be no doubt about the charm of the setting, below thickly wooded hills at the point where the **River Weser** is formed by the merging of the **Fulda** and **Werra**. The town's rather odd name, by the way, is the official contraction of "Hannoversch Münden", the name it bore when it was part of the Kingdom of Hannover; the locals have no truck with the abbreviation "Münden" which sometimes appears on maps.

Around town

Hann. Münden has even more **half-timbered houses** than Duderstadt – over 700 in all. Separated by some six centuries of history, they completely dominate the face of the town, and their main attraction lies in the effect of the overall ensemble – individually, they're less impressive than their counterparts elsewhere. Look out, however, for no. 34 on the main street, Lange Strasse. This was the home of the town's most celebrated citizen, **Johann Andreas Eisenbart**, an eighteenth-century doctor whose controversial medical techniques enabled him to gain a reputation as a miracle-worker. A commemorative statue of him stands outside, while his life is the subject of an open-air costume play held each Sunday between mid-May and the end of August.

Curiously enough, Hann. Münden's few set pieces are all of a more solid stone construction. The most impressive of these is the **Rathaus**. This dates back in part to the fourteenth century, but the side facing the Markt was rebuilt at the turn of the seventeenth century in the cheerful Weser Renaissance style by Georg Crossmann, the creator of many similar buildings in Lemgo. The facade is masterly, with the ornate gables, resplendent doorway and the obligatory two-storey oriel window all competing for pre-eminence. Across Kirchplatz is **St Blasius**, an unusual-looking Gothic hall church with a hexagonal tower and a very steeply pitched roof of red slate. The only other major monument is the **Welfenschloss** (May–Oct Tues–Fri 10am–noon & 2.30–5pm, Sat 10am–noon & 2.30-4pm, Sun 10am–12.30pm; DM1), an L-shaped Renaissance palace overlooking the Werra; the name is a reminder that one branch or other of the Welf family ruled the town for most of its history. It now houses the standard local history displays, but also boasts fresco cycles dating from soon after the time of the building's construction, among the few in Germany from this period.

Behind the Schloss is the **Werrabrücke**, a bridge which dates back at least as far as the fourteenth century. From here, you can cross over not only to the far side, but also to **Doktorwerder**, an island with a sculpture garden. Of the other islands around the confluence, the largest is **Unterer Tanzwerder**, which is likewise a popular recreation area. Here also are the landing stage for cruise boats, a swing bridge over the Fulda, and the **Weserstein**, a stone marking the birth of the great river at the point where, according to the rather trite inscription, "the Fulda and Werra kiss".

To appreciate the beauty of Hann. Münden's setting, and the harmonious layout of the town with its sea of red roofs, you really need to see it from above. One possibility is to go up the **Rotunde** (mid-May to mid-Sept daily 10.30am–12.30pm & 3–5pm; DM1), one of several towers remaining from the disembodied medieval fortification system. For a really magnificent bird's-eye view, cross the Fulda by the Pionierbrücke, and climb up to the old tower known as the **Tillyschanze** (May–Oct daily 10am–dusk; DM1).

Practicalities

Hann. Münden lies on the express railway line between Göttingen and Kassel, 35km from the former, 23km from the latter; the **Bahnhof** is ten minutes' walk east of the town centre. The **tourist office** is in the Rathaus (May–Sept Mon–Fri 8.30am–5pm, Sat 8.30am–12.30pm; Oct–April Mon–Thurs 8.30am–12.30pm & 1–4pm, Fri 8.30am–12.30pm; ☎05541/75313); after closing time, an information point is kept open daily until 8pm or 9pm according to season. In addition to an abundant supply of **private rooms**, there are a couple of cheapish **hotels**: *Gasthaus Zur Hafenbahn*, Blume 54 (☎05541/4094), which starts at DM23 per person, and *Gasthaus Im Anker*, Bremer Schlagd 18 (☎05541/4923), whose prices begin at DM25. The **youth hostel** is way to the north of town at Prof-Oelkers-Str. 10 (☎05541/8853), while the **campsite** has a handier location on an island in the River Fulda named Oberer Tanzwerder (☎05541/122257). Best place to **eat** is the *Ratskeller* in the Rathaus, which offers French-style cuisine as well as the usual solid German fare. In summer, several daily **river cruises**, leave from Unterer Tanzwerder; these go downstream to Höxter and Hameln, or upstream to Kassel.

---

travel details

Trains

From Bremen to Bremerhaven (1 an hour; 50min); Oldenburg (2; 35min); Wilhelmshaven (2; 1hr 40min); Emden (1; 2hr); Norddeich (1; 2hr 50min); Osnabrück (1; 2hr); Hannover (2; 1hr).

From Hannover to Einbeck (1; 1hr); Hildesheim (3; 25min); Göttingen (3; 1hr); Braunschweig (2; 50min), Celle (3; 25min); Lüneburg (2; 1hr 20min), Wolfenbüttel (2; 1hr 10min); Hann. Münden (1; 2hr); Hameln (1; 50min); Goslar (1;1hr 20min).

Ferries

From Emden to Borkum (summer 4 daily, winter 2; 2hr 30min).

From Norddeich Mole to Juist (1–3; 1hr 20min), Norderney (9–13; 50min).

From Bensersiel to Langeoog (3–5; 50min).

From Neuharlingersiel to Spiekeroog (2–4; 50min).

From Harle to Wangerooge (summer 2–3 daily, winter 1; 1hr 10min).

From Wilhelmshaven to Helgoland (summer 1 only; 3hr).

CHAPTER SEVEN

HAMBURG AND SCHLESWIG-HOLSTEIN

Jutting up between the North and Baltic Seas, and stretching as far as the Danish border, **Schleswig-Holstein** is the most northerly of Germany's Länder. One of the Federal Republic's few coastal regions, it's not surprising that maritime influences have defined the Land: in the Dark Ages the town of **Schleswig** thrived as a Viking trading centre and that era is now recorded in an excellent museum. During the medieval period the port of **Lübeck** was one of the main pivots of the Hanseatic League, and today it's the region's most impressive town, the architectural heritage of its former mercantile glory revealed in the houses of patrician families, the warehouses in which their goods were stored, and the churches they built with the wealth they accrued. **Flensburg** has similar trading connections, and shows the influence of Danish occupation – throughout its history, control of Schleswig-Holstein has shifted back and forth between Germany and Denmark.

Inland Schleswig-Holstein is a mix of dyke-protected marsh, peat-bog and rich alluvial farmland. No mountains or fairy-tale castles here, nor jovial thigh-slapping dances: northernmost Germany contrasts starkly with the south, and a Bavarian would feel less at home than someone from England. Areas like **Angeln** in the northeast are dotted with half-timbered houses and ancient villages, and though there's little else in the way of specific "sights", and public transport is at best erratic, it's an area easily explored by bike.

Both the coastal region east of Angeln and the western North Friesian coast have miles of sandy beaches and a surprising amount of sunshine (indeed, the island of Sylt has the highest amount of sunshine anywhere in Germany). The **North Friesian Islands**, scattered along the west coast, are also popular in summer for sun and sand; venture here in winter and you'll be rewarded with bracing sea air and what the brochures kindly term "health-promoting walks": however unlike their sisters, the East Friesian Islands, they are not promoted as organised health resorts – which, on the whole, is to your advantage. The **coastal towns** are more than just a springboard for the islands: **Niebüll** has two surprisingly fine collections of art, and **Husum** has charm tempered by its working fishing harbour.

Hamburg, a Land in its own right, exists like an island in the south of the state, a city infamous for the prostitution and sleaze of the Reeperbahn. That's about as much as most people care to know about the place, but Hamburg has plenty to offer: not least a sparkling nightlife and a city centre that's made up of enjoyably contrasting and easily explorable neighbourhoods.

It's possible to travel directly to Hamburg **by ferry** from Hull or Harwich, the latter also having ferry connections to Esjberg in Denmark. Arriving at one port and leaving from the other, ten days to a fortnight would allow you to travel through Schleswig-Holstein, taking in the best of each coast and the major towns. For more details on ferries, see *Basics*.

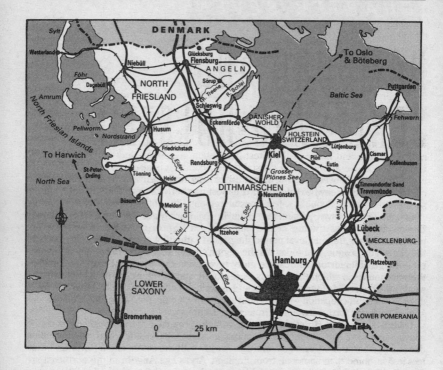

Hamburg, like the other city-state of Bremen, is a sure-fire **SPD stronghold**. Current Minister-President of Schleswig-Holstein is **Björn Engholm**, who in 1991 was elected national chairman of the SPD; it's quite likely that he will be the party's Chancellor-candidate against Kohl at the next general election. He came to power in 1988, bringing to an end four decades of CDU rule in the province. The previous election in 1987 had been racked by scandal when the then Minister-President, Uwe Bartschel, was accused of phone-tapping, smears and other dirty tricks: though he denied this, his subsequent suicide seemed to affirm his culpability. Although the CDU were able to continue in power, they were dependent on the single Danish-speaking deputy guaranteed to the ethnic minority under the state constitution – hence the need for the election a year later.

HAMBURG

The River Elbe marks the southern border of Schleswig-Holstein, and 90km inland stands the port of **HAMBURG**. Exhilaratingly different from any other German city, Hamburg has always been a city state, free to trade as it pleased, unencumbered by dukes and princes. Even now it officially bears the title of *Freie und Hansestadt:* "Free and Hanseatic City".

During World War II Hamburg was massively bombed by the Allies. As the first city that bombers flying from England would pass over on the North Sea route into central Germany, Hamburg was often attacked. But on July 28, 1943 it became the first Reich city to suffer a **firestorm**, when the combination of high explosives and incendiary bombs turned eight square miles of the city centre into one huge conflagration, with winds the speed of hurricanes uprooting trees and sucking people into the inferno. On that night, over 42,000 civilians were killed – more than the total of British dead during the entire Blitz.

Hamburg's wealth enabled it to recover quickly in the postwar years, and though today its reputation is tainted by tales of the red-light area, that's only a small part of what the city is about. It's a stylish media centre, a huge modern seaport, a scene of radical protest, and home of the latest generation of a long-standing merchant class. Unless you arrive at one of the coastal ports, Hamburg is also where you're likely to begin your travels around Schleswig-Holstein: allow two or three days to explore the centre and suburbs, and as many nights as your pocket (and constitution) will stand to soak up its nightlife.

In spite of the vast proportions of the city's outline, only one third is actually built up. The rest is either parks, lakes or tree-lined canals. To cycle around, you'd never believe you were in one of Germany's major industrial cities, the largest after Berlin: not only because of the open spaces and water everywhere, but also because of the abundant greenery. Municipal policy dictates that two thousand new trees have to be planted each year, and the result is a very pleasing effect, with almost every road lined with trees, keeping the city green and the air cleaner.

The telephone code for Hamburg is ☎040.

Orientation and practicalities

Central Hamburg is neatly recognisable on any map, as it's bordered by large roads which trace the original city's fortifications. It has a semicircular shape, with its base facing the River Elbe and Hamburg's massive **port**, while the rest of the city fans out around the centre's rounded contours. Bulging out to the northeast is the city's glamorous **Alster lake**, lined by some of the poshest quarters in town. To the west of the centre, lie the quarters of **St Pauli** and **Altona**, and just north of these the **University quarter**, which together form the heartland of Hamburg's best nightlife. Finally, there are some famous **suburbs** worth visiying, chiefly Blankenese, Övelgönne and Neuengamme.

Arriving and getting around

Ferries from Harwich (20hrs 30min) and Hull (24hrs) arrive at the **St Pauli Landungsbrücken**, which has a U-Bahn station attached, and is very close to the centre of town. There's a **tourist information** kiosk (daily 9am–4pm; ☎300 51200) between bridges 4 and 5.

Arriving at the **airport**, you'll find easy access into the city, either by taking the bus which connects with the Hauptbahnhof every twenty minutes, or by taking the slightly cheaper option of a municipal bus to Ohlsdorf, and then either a U- or S-Bahn to your required destination. There's a **tourist information** booth at the airport in terminal 3 (daily 8am–11pm; ☎300 51240). If you want to book a hotel room immediately, you can

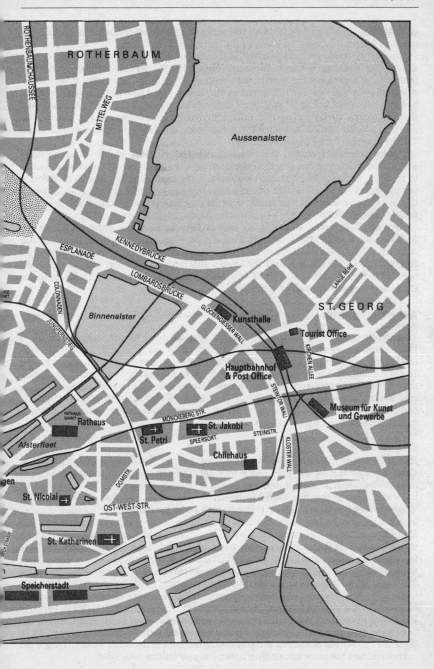

go to terminal 2, where there's a free-phone service for all hotels listed on the information board there. Naturally they will be the more expensive hotels.

Arriving by **train**, you find yourself at the **Hauptbahnhof**, close to the city centre, and within walking distance of some cheap hotels, if not the youth hostels. Immediately opposite is the **tourist information** office (daily 7am–11pm; ☎300 51230), which offers a wide variety of brochures and maps, some free, and also makes hotel bookings on your behalf. If you need more extensive advice and information, and shorter queues, then head for the main office in the *Bieberhaus* on Hachmannplatz, right next to the station to your left, as you come out facing Kirchenallee (Mon–Fri 7.30am–6pm, Sat 8am–3pm; ☎300 51244).

Public transport around the city is quick and efficient by the U- and S-Bahn system, for which you can buy tickets either from the machines in the entrance halls, or from the staffed public transport windows in the same vicinity. Your best option, if you plan to travel around a lot in one day, is to buy a day pass for around DM6.20, which is also valid on the buses. The family ticket is excellent value, costing a little less than double the single pass.

Best of all, however, would be to **rent a bicycle** from the tourist office in the *Bieberhaus* (available May 1–Sept 30; Mon–Fri 8am–6pm; Sat 9am–3pm; DM10 per day or DM20 for the weekend). They're good quality bikes, and considering Hamburg's long distances and predominantly flat terrain, this mode of transport gives the quickest opening to the city, for very little effort – much less tiring than hours of walking to see sites which are scattered all over the city.

Accommodation

In spite of a good variety of types of accommodation, it can be surprisingly difficult to find somewhere easily affordable if you don't want to use the youth hostels. It's true that there are plenty of cheapish hotels in the St Georg quarter, next to the Hauptbahnhof, but the unsuspecting will as likely as not end up in a brothel: it's impossible to tell them apart from "normal" hotels. For budget accommodation, best bet is to ring the city's *Mitwohnzentralen* before you arrive. These offer an excellent service, being agencies that provide rooms in shared flats, and furnished or unfurnished apartments, both for short-term and long-term stays.

Youth hostels

Hamburg has two **youth hostels**. Ignore any listings which name others, such as *Commodore* or *Mui* for example, since they only cater to organised groups and do not offer rooms to independent travellers.

First choice of the two available would be the large *Auf dem Sintfang*, Alfred-Wegener-Weg 5 (☎313488), S- or U-Bahn stop Landungsbrücken. The location is excellent, not just for the city's attractions, but also because it's perched on a steep incline above the port, with panoramic maritime views. Accommodation is in dormitories with up to eight beds in them, and prices are DM18.40 per night for junior members, DM20.40 for seniors, breakfast and sheets included. The place is rather basic, with no extra facilities other than the day rooms; there's also a 1am curfew, and the staff wake you up at 7.30am, to be out by 9am. But it's cheap, and serves warm meals for around DM5.50.

Slightly more expensive (DM21 juniors, DM25 seniors, sheets and breakfast included), is the *Jugendgästehaus Horner Rennbahn*, Rennbahnstr. 100 (☎651 1671), S-Bahn stop Horner Rennbahn. It's out in the eastern suburb of Horn, right next to the horserace track in a very light and airy modern building that's peaceful enough when there isn't a race on. Standards are slightly higher than in the other hostel, though the curfew remains the same and getting up time is only half an hour later.

Mitwohnzentralen

Hamburg has three **Mitwohnzentralen**, all providing the same service for similar fees: rooms will usually be around DM25 per night; flat prices vary according to area and size, though the fee is normally worked out on the basis of one month's rent.

Die Mitwohnzentrale, Lobuschstr. 22 (☎391373), U-Bahn stop Altona.

Mitwohnzentrale Rutschbahn, Rutschbahn 3 (weekdays 4–7.30pm; Sat 11.30am–2pm; ☎418018), U-bahn stop Hoheluft.

Mitwohnzentrale Hamburg, Haubachstr. 8 (☎389 5118; weekdays 9am–1pm and 2–6.30pm), U-Bahn stop Altona.

Camping

All of Hamburg's five **campsites** are located on the northwest edge of Greater Hamburg, best reached by car. However, the first listed site is relatively close to S-Bahn stop Schnelsen, the next three are near Eidelstedt station, and the last quite close to Stellingen station.

Campingplatz Schnelsen-Nord, Wunderbrunnen 2 (☎559 4225).

Campingplatz Anders, Kieler Str. 650 (☎570 4498).

Campingplatz Buchholz, Kieler Str. 374 (☎540 4532).

Campingplatz Ramcke, Kieler Str. 620 (☎570 5121).

City Camping Park, Kronsaalsweg 86/Kieler Str. (☎540 4994).

Hotels

Although the St Georg quarter is slightly sleazy in parts, especially along Steindamm, there are areas which are quiet and residential within easy walking distance of the centre. Prices listed below are all the lowest on offer in the various hotels.

Annenhof, Lange Reihe 23 (☎243426). A friendly, small place run by a husband and wife team; singles start at DM38, doubles at DM64.

Esplanade, Colonnaden 45 (☎342961). In the more salubrious shopping area, west of the Binnenalster lake; singles DM60, doubles DM80.

Royal, Holzdamm 51 (☎243753). Simple and old-fashioned; singles DM50, doubles DM80.

Sarah Petersen, Lange Reihe 50 (☎249826). Singles around DM45, doubles DM60.

Steen's Hotel, Holzdamm 43 (☎244642). Charmingly located in a quiet, pretty corner of St Georg; singles DM80, doubles DM90.

Wedina, Gurlittstr. 23 (☎243011). Rather stuffy but well-located on the southeastern edge of the Aussenalster, within easy walking distance of the Hauptbahnhof; singles DM60, doubles DM90.

Fanning out from the city centre, but still in convenient proximity, are three hotels worth trying in the university quarter: *Adria*, Johnsallee 63 (☎442959), singles DM50, doubles DM70; *Fink*, Rothenbaumchaussee 71–73 (☎440571), singles DM38, doubles DM80; and *Grindel*, Grindelallee 32 (☎451281), singles DM45, doubles DM70.

The city centre

Most of the centre of **Hamburg** was consumed in a great fire in 1842: the flames ran out of control for several days, which is why you don't find many buildings dating from before that period. Add to that the British "Operation Gomorrah" in 1943, when half of the city was destroyed by bombs, and it's a wonder there's anything over fifty years old left to see at all. As it is, there are a great many nineteenth- and early twentieth-century buildings remaining, tucked in between prize-winning modern developments, and hidden within this central mêlée, you'll also find the sole surviving seventeenth-century houses of the city.

The Altstadt east of Alsterfleet

The centre arches in a great semi-circle over the baseline of the Ost-West Strasse, about 2km long. This semi-circle can then loosely be divided by the slanting Alsterfleet canal, which separates the original Altstadt quarter from the later-grown Neustadt, the other side of the water. Most maps no longer record this difference, since nowadays they have melted into one. But the division is still useful for the visitor new to the city.

The oldest part of Hamburg is around the ruined tower of **St Nikolai**, formerly one of Germany's finest neo-Gothic churches, designed by Sir George Gilbert Scott, only to be flattened by his countrymen about a hundred years later. Today its blackened stump stands as an anti-war memorial. Close by is the **Trostbrücke**, which connected the old city with the Neustadt, the "new" quarters west of the Alsterfleet canal, which developed in the early Middle Ages. The two statues on the bridge are of Saint Ansgar, Hamburg's first archbishop, and Count Adolf III, founder of the new quarters, and more importantly for the city's future development, instrumental in the signing of the imperial decree which gave Hamburg the right to tax-free import of goods and transport of passengers from the sea to its port, 90km inland along the River Elbe. Thus the city's future as one of Europe's largest and most important commercial ports was sealed as early as the twelfth century. Today the bridge appears somewhat incongruous, surrounded as it is by modern office blocks. On the other hand, its unexpected appearance, picturesquely reflected in the Nikolaifleet canal below, is all the more pleasant a surprise.

Follow the canal south, perhaps crossing the busy Ost-West Strasse at Holzbrücke and you find the remaining eighteenth-century merchant homes, with their grand facades facing the street and the red-brick, gabled backs facing the canal, where goods were directly hoiked into the merchant's attic store rooms. The most famous examples are the row of houses along the **Deichstrasse**, which also happens to be where the Great Fire broke out. The best place to see the crooked backs of the houses is from the Hohe Brücke. For views of similar architecture, head back up **Cremon**, or **Riemerstwiete**, two streets further east.

Continuing east, you come to **St Katharinen**, which is less interesting for its reconstituted architecture than for the continuous exhibition which it runs. If your German is up to it, the *Multivision Hamburg* (Mon–Sat hourly 11am–5pm, except 1pm, Sun, noon–4pm except 1pm; DM5) is an accessible introduction to the city's history and development, with many famous names and events portrayed with a vivid slide show, and suitably dramatic music. Even if you don't speak German, the pictorial nature of this show makes it an interesting moving picture gallery.

The Chilehaus

Heading northeast along the Dovenfleet, with the waterfront warehouses on your right, you soon reach the U-Bahn station Messberg, and directly opposite, the remarkable **Chilehaus**. Built with the traditional red bricks of north German architecture, this unconventional house was created in the early 1920s and remains one of the most original works of the period. It was designed by the Expressionist architect Fritz Höger, whose idea it was to mirror Hamburg's ocean-going ships in this large office block. As you wander around it – ideally from the other side of the road for best views – you begin to recognise the contours of a great ship, the staggered balconies high above recalling the various decks and the sharp corner of its eastern extremity cleverly representing a ship's bow. If the name seems incongruous, that's because it has nothing to do with the building, but recalls the country in which the architect originally made his fortune.

St Jakobi and St Petri

Across the Burchardsplatz and up the Mohlenhofstrasse, you come to another of central Hamburg's five church towers, which traditionally characterise its skyline. This is **St Jakobi**, which frankly doesn't make a memorable impression, but which does contain the precious treasure of Arp Schnitger's seventeenth-century **organ**, considered a masterpiece of its time and still in frequent use; (it's currently being restored, and is due for completion in 1993). Unfortunately, postwar rebuilding did not attempt to recreate the original, so that the interior is in drab 1950s style, with only the outside recalling the building's former glory. The same can be said for all of the city's churches, with the glorious exception of St Michaelis, described on p.636.

Directly behind St Jakobi lies the **Mönckebergstrasse**, which is the main artery of the city's commercial shopping, with one high-street name following another, the occasional *McDonalds* or *Burgerking* eagerly lapping up tired shoppers and tourists alike. Follow this street west, and you're heading to the hub of the city centre, which clusters around the grandiose Rathaus. On the way you pass **St Petri**, originally the oldest of the city's churches, believed to have its origin in an eleventh-century chapel. Destroyed in the Great Fire and then again in 1943, it nevertheless retains much of its nineteenth-century neo-Gothic architecture, and most famously, boasts Hamburg's oldest piece of craftwork: the fourteenth-century bronze **door-knocker** on the central western portal.

Around the Rathaus

A stone's throw away from here, the **Rathaus** sits heavily in all the boastful splendour of the German neo-Renaissance. Built to display the superior quality of Hamburg's civil parliament, there is something faintly self-conscious about the building's style. Perhaps they were trying a little too hard to create the proper symbolism when both the city's patron saints and maritime images were lined alongside each other around its rooftop rim. City guides will tell you the building has more rooms than Buckingham Palace: what they don't mention is that they're much smaller. Nevertheless, when the city's parliament isn't in session, guided tours around its stately rooms offer an instructive view of Hamburg's uniquely glamorous municipal headquarters. (Tours in English Mon–Thurs every 30min 10.15am–3.15pm, Fri–Sun hourly 10.15am–1.15pm.)

In front of the Rathaus, the **Rathausmarkt** is usually teeming with tourists and shoppers alike, sampling whatever goodies the variety of stalls happen to be offering that month, while the elegant **Alsterarkaden** provide for leisurely strolls past expensive shops, leading out onto the **Binnenalster**, which is the petite forerunner of the larger **Aussenalster** lake, beyond the city centre. The arcades were built to echo those on Venice's Piazza San Marco, though it's pretty evident that a few arcades don't make up a Venetian square. If you're interested in seeing Germany's first **stock-market**, and Hamburg's financial heart, then head along the arcades away from the lakes, and you'll soon find yourself round the back of the Rathaus on the Adolphsplatz. Founded in 1558, the stock-market reflected the fact that Hamburg's cosmoplitan world of trade and commerce was bilingual, in those days commonly using both German and Dutch. The present building is a restored version of the Neoclassical one built in the mid-nineteenth century, and extended in the early part of this century. Guided tours take place Mon–Fri at 11.15am.

The Neustadt west of Alsterfleet

Turning away from the Rathaus and towards the Binnenalster, you cross the Reesendammbrücke, which has been there in some form or other since the thirteenth century. The present model was built in the 1840s, but in the early Middle Ages this was the site of a corn-mill, which dammed the Alster river's water to turn its wheel. From then onwards, there's always been a small lake here – the larger one beyond created a few hundred years later – and Hamburg's high society, then as now, delighted in promenading around its edges. The finest and most expensive promenade is traditionally the **Jungfernstieg**, named after the young women who used to twirl their brollies here. Head north, along the Neuer Jungfernstieg, and you'll find the splendid houses of the city's bankers and businesses, as well as Hamburg's best address: the **Hotel Vierjahreszeiten**. It boasts that it's the second best hotel in the world after one in Malaysia, and even if that no longer holds true, you can be sure that prices are way beyond your pocket . . .

If you're tempted by any of the **boat trips** (between April and October) offered along the Jungfernstieg, the best is undoubtedly the *Kanal-Fahrt* (daily at 9.45am, 12.15pm, 2.45pm, & 5.15pm; 2hrs; DM17, DM8.50 kids). This tour will take you round both the Alster lakes, and also along the River Alster itself, passing many of the city's finest villas and sailing clubs, and presenting a view of Hamburg otherwise impossible to see.

The Hanseviertel

The streets spreading out behind the Jungfernstieg, towards the Gänsemarkt and down Neuer Wall, Bleichen and ABC-Str., are collectively known as the **Hanseviertel**. This is an area of shops and offices, and the city's flashest shopping arcades. Their scale is not as gigantic as the London equivalents springing up around Docklands, but they are much ritzier. Unsurprisingly, traditionally elitist cultural events take place nearby, in the **Staatsoper** on the Dammtorstrasse.

Heading southwest from the Hanseviertel you enter a more residential area the other side of Kaiser-Wilhelm-Strasse. Streets worth strolling along are Breiter Gang or Wexstrasse, where you'll not only find attractive houses, but also the odd bar or restaurant you might fancy. **Grossneumarkt**, in particular, is a favourite haunt for inner city eating and drinking. Not far from here, the **Peterstrasse** presents one of Hamburg's most beautiful streetscapes, being a small stretch of completely restored eighteenth-century townhouses, built in traditional red-brick style, with gabled tops tapering towards the sky. Walking along this street gives you an idea of what most of the city must once have looked like. If you're interested in musical heritage, you could visit the **Brahms Gedenkstätte** at Peterstr. 39, (Tues–Fri noon–1pm, Thurs 4–6pm), which holds some documentation of the life and work of the composer, who was born in Hamburg and spent many unsuccessful years here.

St Michaelis

Just around the corner, you'll find Hamburg's city symbol and finest church: **St Michaelis**. Seated on a small hill, its copper-plated tower is visible from most parts of the city. Happily, this is the one church that has not only been rebuilt on the outside, but also on the inside, so that present-day visitors can still marvel at its superb northern Baroque elegance. Inside, you find the typically Lutheran design, which directs the congregation's eyes not to the altar, but to the pulpit. There are no fewer than three organs regularly used for services, the smallest and most recent (1960s) tucked into the wall, to the left of the altar. The best bird's eye view of the city is from the church tower **look-out platform**, at 82metres (May–Oct daily 9am–5.30pm; Nov–Apr Thurs–Tues, 10am–4pm, Sun 11.30am–4pm; DM2, lift DM3).

The Krameramtswohnungen

A rather touristy but nevertheless worthwhile visit is to the **Krameramtswohnungen** (Krayenkamp 10, Tues–Sun, 10am–5pm), round the corner from St Michaelis. This tiny backyard of seventeenth-century housing is the last remaining in the city. It was built as retirement homes for the widows of shopkeepers, who were forbidden to carry on their husband's trade after his death and were housed here by the guild. They were still in use until the early 1960s, but now all but one of them has been turned into a trinket shop or art gallery. For DM1.50, you can squeeze inside the single house remaining in its original form and see just how small people were only a few hundred years ago.

The Port: from Fischmarkt to Speicherstadt

Hamburg's **port**, founded in the late twelfth century, was the making of the city. Without it, Hamburg would never have become one of Europe's four major ports, and the world's largest depot for oriental carpets, as well as Germany's leading market for coffee, tea and spices from all over the world. Ever since Emperor Frederick Barbarossa granted free trade and a customs exemption for all goods brought in by ship in 1189, wealth and municipal status have been assured. These days, of course, the port's significance is tempered by the worldwide recession in ocean-going trade, as well as the decline in related industries such as ship-building. The authorities have tried to make their wharfs competitive by cutting labour and mechanising the handling of containerised cargo: even supertankers can be in and out within less than twenty-four hours, whereas manual unloading used to take at least a week.

The human cost of these measures has been great, and unemployment is higher here (and in the north generally) than in most other parts of the country. But the work-force has a history of powerful organisation, and there were systemised strikes as early as the 1840s. In the 1880s came the longest strike the city has seen, when 18,000 harbour workers went out for ten weeks, in protest against the massive re-housing that was necessitated by the demolition of their homes to make way for the *Speicherstadt* (see below), the port's tax-free warehouses. In the turmoil immediately following the First World War, there was more action: a sailor's revolt in November 1918, two days after the one in Kiel. In 1923 came the **Hamburg uprising**, with fighting on the streets at the height of the postwar crisis of inflation and hunger. These days, however, political action and violence has moved away from the port and into the city. The focus of attention is still on the waterfront though, since it is the embattled Hafenstrasse that is at the heart of present-day conflict with the authorities (see below).

The Fischmarkt and Hafenstrasse

The best time and place to begin an exploration of the length of Hamburg's harbour is to go to the **Fischmarkt**, not far from St Pauli Landungsbrücken, early on a Sunday morning. Between 5am and 10am (7–10am in winter), the former fishmarket hall and a large part of the waterfront around it are given over to a weekly circus of shopping and selling, where you can buy anything from fish to live ducks, potted palms, clothes or tacky trinkets. The bars and *Imbiss* stands in the vicinity open for the occasion, filled with shoppers and late-night survivors alike, all tucking in to the sounds of early morning jazz and stall-holders bellowing out their wares. If you can make it, it's a spectacle worth seeing, though be prepared for the push and shove of hordes of other people. By 10am, the market is supposed to end, in accordance with an old law that was to ensure trade didn't compete with Sunday church services. In fact, it lingers on for a good hour more, but many of the most colourful traders have sold out by then, no longer performing their crowd-drawing sales pitches.

The short stretch of waterfront road that connects the Fischmarkt with the Landungsbrücken is the infamous **Hafenstrasse**. With its occupied houses, you won't have failed to notice it: the walls are covered with slogans and occasionally creative murals, many of the windows are smashed from past raids, and, depending on the state of seige, doors are barricaded and look-outs peer from top floor windows. The houses stand on prime land, and have been the battleground between developers and squatters for some years now. For the moment, things are quiet and tourists come to take pictures and gaze on the motley crew of inhabitants, something of an exotic attraction. But serious violence flares up at regular intervals, and in 1990, the city's authorities braced themselves for a final, semi-successful armed onslaught. If you want to find out more, you could venture into the collective kitchen, known as the *Volksküche*, or the intermittent cafés run in some of the houses.

Around the Landungsbrücken

Back down by the **Landungsbrücken**, you pass the many bridges leading to the floating pontoon lined with expensive *Imbiss* stands and restaurants, as well as the many boats offering **harbour tours** (*Hafenrundfahrten*) for about DM12. Make sure you go on one of the small ferries and not the large double-decker, since only the small ones take in the canals of the **Speicherstadt** as well as the port itself. If you want to see the hulls of mighty container ships close up, then this is the tour for you. **Tours in English** go from Brücke 1 between March and November, daily at 11.15am, DM14, DM7 kids. For **alternative tours** highlighting environmental problems, phone ☎241031.

If you prefer to explore a late nineteenth-century three-master, then the distinctive green-hulled **Rickmer Rickmers** (daily 10am–6pm DM2.50) is moored opposite the S-Bahn station. Built in 1896, this ocean-going barque had a history of international sailing before it was impounded by the British in 1916. They used it as part of their maritime war effort, and once World War I was over, gave it to the Portuguese. Eventually, some Hamburg businessmen found the boat mouldering away off the coast of Portugal; they brought it back in 1987, restored it to its original beauty, and now it's regarded as one of the city's most important treasures. There's also a gourmet restaurant on board, but its prices are steep.

A brisk fifteen minutes' walk further along the waterfront will take you to the separate world of the nineteenth-century **Speicherstadt**. The world's largest self-contained warehouse complex, it was built between 1885 and 1910 in the beautiful red-brick style of local architecture. Strolling along its canals and cobblestone streets, you're transported into another time and world, when ships still used to unload goods by the bundle and box. Sacks of coffee can be seen piled high, thousands of oriental carpets lie rolled up, scents of teas and spices waft out of open doors, and bulky men can be seen heaving goods by the traditional hooks used a hundred years ago. All the buildings are under protection, so there are no lifts or other machinery to assist present-day workers. Goods can be stored here over many years tax-free, until the merchant thinks he'll get the best price.

The Alster Lakes and River

The Alster lakes, in the heart of Hamburg, make up the main recreational area of the city. Whether with ice-skating in winter or sailing and boating in summer, the large **Aussenalster** is always a busy place, while the smaller **Binnenalster** is frequented mainly by commercial boats and pedestrians promenading around its salubrious edges. Together, the two lakes encompass an area of about three square kilometres that no fewer than nine thousand boats are licenced to use. Not surprisingly, there are times during the height of the summer season when the tourist boats can hardly squeeze through. The shoreline around both lakes is open to the public, and the footpaths along it are pleasantly incorporated into park landscapes which offer plenty of scope for picnics and sunbathing.

To walk around the lakes would take about three hours, and take you past many of the city's finest villas, clubs and consulates, especially along the **western shore**, where the rich have traditionally built their lakeside homes. The areas known as **Rotherbaum** and **Harvestehude** are two of the most exclusive residential parts of Hamburg, and if you enjoy nineteenth-century and Jugendstil architecture, it's worth exploring some of the streets around here: especially those branching off from the Klosterstern, such as Harvestehuder Weg and side streets. Around Pöseldorfer Weg and Milchstrasse, parallel with Harvestehuder Weg, is an area known locally as **Pöseldorf**, though no map marks it out as such. This has become a particularly trendy and upmarket spot, where media types hang out in expensive cafés and pose in the similarly pricey restaurants. The **eastern shore** presents an equally well-heeled facade, but look beyond it and you soon find yourself in the sleazy streets of St Georg. Only further to the northeast does the surrounding area become respectably residential, gradually meeting up with the exclusive villas spilling over from Harvestehude.

Along the River Alster

The course of the **River Alster** stretches for a good 50km further, heading first north, through Hamburg's suburbs, and then twisting and turning its way westwards until HENSTEDT. There's a marked footpath (yellow triangles) that follows the course of the river, but the trip to Henstedt is not something you could manage in one day, unless you go by bike and are very energetic. However, for countrified bike excursions, you don't need to go too far out. The 18km stretch from the tip of the Aussenalster to the Wohldorf lock runs through shady park landscapes as well as past river scenes little changed for centuries. There's no need to retrace your route back into the city either, since public transport is available at various points. For example, the U-Bahn stops Ohlsdorf or Klein Borstel are not far from the Fuhlsbüttel lock; six kilometres further on is the Poppenbüttel S-Bahn stop; and not far from the Wohldorf lock is the Ohlsted U-Bahn stop. Maps of the entire route are available from the tourist office, in the brochure entitled *Die Alster*.

St Pauli, Altona and Univiertel

Beginning along the shore of the River Elbe and curving northeast towards the base of the Aussenalster, the three quarters of St Pauli, Altona and Univiertel embrace the western curve of the city centre's traditional edge. St Pauli and Altona are the southern-most part, melting smoothly into each other, while the Univiertel sits compactly north of St Pauli. Collectively, they form the main stomping ground for night-time revellers of all kinds, while cheap day time meals are easy to find in both St Pauli and the Univiertel.

St Pauli

St Pauli, defined by the River Elbe, the Holstenstrasse towards Altona and the railway tracks to the north, is nearest to the city centre, and was originally home to Hamburg's sea-related trades and crafts. The infamous **Reeperbahn**, for example, was where the ropemakers once lived; and the Grosse and Kleine Freiheit (Big Freedom and Little Freedom) are streets so-named not because of the live sex shows you see there today, but because in medieval times, craftsmen were free to practise their trade here. To a large extent, St Pauli is a working-class, residential area to this day, with the sex industry confining itself to the very small area of the Reeperbahn and short streets running off either side, especially those leading towards the port. North of the Reeperbahn, squares such as the **Paulinenplatz**, are a pleasant ramshackle of old housing blocks, their neglected, fly-blown atmosphere mostly unvisited by outsiders.

Lately, St Pauli has been infiltrated by a new set of after-dark revellers, since many bars and clubs have been taken over by avant-garde theatre operators and off-the-wall entrepreneurs. In the middle of the Reeperbahn, for example, you find one of the city's trendiest alternative cabaret and theatre bars, called *Schmidt*. Not far away, at Gerhardstrasse 2, the *La Paloma* bar has been transformed into a smoke-filled art gallery, with the owner's and local artists' works clinging to every space available. A few steps on, notwithstanding its red lighting, the *Mary Lou*, at Hans-Albers-Platz 3, is yet another hang-out for the new set in St Pauli. For detailed listings see p.646–47.

Altona

Heading west, **Altona** follows directly on from St Pauli. Like the former, it has its share of river, partly lined with industrial fish-processing plants, but also with the leafy environs of the **Palmallee** and **Elbchaussee**: grand avenues lined with nineteenth-century villas. Its western border is roughly defined by Fischers Allee, while to the north it spreads almost as far as Frucht-Allee. Although much of Altona is unremarkable for the visitor, being a large residential area. It has an interesting history, originally a Dutch settlement on the edges of German Hamburg, it has always been a haven of free-thinkers and religious tolerance. (Visit the Altonaer Museum, p.644, for extensive displays on the quarter's history). It was a place of racial tolerance too, and as maritime trade brought more and more foreigners to Hamburg, many chose to settle in Altona. A legacy of those times are the many excellent and cheap Portuguese restaurants near the harbour. In this century, Altona became a favoured home for the Turkish, Greek and Arabic "guestworkers" of the city, hence the many kebab shops and fragrant take-away kiosks around Altona Bahnhof, especially along Ottenser Hauptstrasse.

Traditionally, Altona's residents were not much more upmarket than St Pauli's. But the developers have slowly been moving in on the beautiful, but decaying nineteenth-century housing blocks, and certain areas are rapidly becoming rather chic with prices to match. One such street is the **Friedens Allee**, this is still unremarkable at its north-western end but stroll along the short stretch beginning not far from Altona station, and ritzy, neon lit shops cluster among restaurants and bars that exude sophisticated understatement. However, it's not all super-cool around here. The nearby Barnerstrasse is home to one of the city's most favoured and enduring live music venues, the *Fabrik*. Heading over towards the Univiertel, to the northeast, the **Schulterblatt,** near the Sternschanze S-Bahn stop, is home to quite a few popular student *Kneipen*, as well as excellent cheap restaurants. A very different atmosphere prevails around here, not so much trendy as relaxed and unpretentious. The **Schanzenstrasse**, which splits away from Schulterblatt, is also worth checking out, and for all bar and café listings, see p.646–47.

The Univiertel

One S-Bahn stop further, to Schlump, and you're virtually in the **Univiertel**. The streets of most interest are **Grindel Hof Strasse** and **Rentzelstrasse**: this is where you'll find the largest variety of reasonably priced restaurants and café-bars. Also here, is the city's most popular "alternative" cinema: the *Abaton*, which also has a large bar-restaurant upstairs, regularly packed. Stray too far away from these two streets, and you soon find yourself in quiet residential avenues, such as the Rothenbaumchaussee. It's a very small area that holds the stage around here, but for choice and variety, it's the best place to be for uncomplicated eating and drinking, where dress code or image are of little significance.

Suburbs: Övelgönne, Blankenese and Neuengamme

Expeditions to the edge of Hamburg take you to opposite ends of the spectrum: to the west are riverside Övelgönne and Blankenese, with exquisitely restored fishermen's houses, which are now home to the very wealthy; and to the east, Neuengamme, site of one of the concentration camps that operated around the city during World War II, now a sobering museum.

Övelgönne

Heading west along the Elbe, away from the city centre, a road and then a path lead first to **Övelgönne** and then to Blankenese. Both were originally suburbs which housed fishermen and sea captains in beautiful, tiny houses. Today, these areas are among the most popular with the well-heeled, who pay silly prices to squeeze themselves into the "quaint" houses with wide views across the river. The route along the water is very pleasant, with plenty of sandy beaches along the way, and both can easily be visited within the space of a morning's relaxed cycling. Alternatively, catch a boat from St Pauli as far as Övelgonne, using the *HADAG Niederelbedienst* (the Lower Elbe boat service run by *HADAG* shipping), which will take your bicycle for a half-fare; bus #183, from Altona Bahnhof, will also take you to Övelgonne, or the S-Bahn to Blankenese.

A particular attraction of Övelgönne, worth a visit in its own right, is the **Museumshafen**, where around twenty old-time working boats are moored: each one has been lovingly restored, from early twentieth-century fire brigade boats to nineteenth-century wooden fishing trawlers, to double-masted freighters. It's a private museum, run by enthusiasts, who willingly show visitors around if they happen to be there. If nobody is around, you can still stop off at the *Flosscafé* (daily 2–10pm), where a small exhibition describes the ecological problems of the Elbe resulting from industrial pollution. Less earnest and more upmarket is the café *Strandperle* on the beach, which is a favoured summertime hang-out among the "in-crowd". If your purse can stand the strain, there are also some excellent fish restaurants around here.

Blankenese

Blankenese, a twenty-minute cycle ride further along the river, is remarkable chiefly because it is situated on a small yet steep hill, a great rarity in this flat part of Germany. Long gone are the times when it was home to retired fishing folk, who watched the constant flow of ships sailing by. Now, villas squeeze tightly in alongside the older houses, and steep roads and stairway paths wind in among them. It's very picturesque, and down by the beach of beautiful white sand, refined cafés and restaurants cater to your every need. Nearby, there's also a fragrant park of ancient trees, now home to many deer, which you may spot on a stroll around here. The woods conceal many cafés as well, notoriously hard to find – the *Witt Hüs* has music, many sorts of tea and wonderful, wholesome cakes; its address is Elbchaussee 499a, but you'll need to ask directions.

Neuengamme

Neuengamme, the other side of Hamburg, on its eastern edge, is reached via the S-Bahn to Bergedorf, and then buses #227 or #327. The concentration camp **KZ-Gedenkstätte Neuengamme** is open from 10am till 5pm every day but Mondays, and has no entrance fee as it's a political education centre. Nothing remains of the old buildings: it's the exhibition of photos and documents that recreates the horrors of the past, recording the story of resistance and as much opposition as could exist. Hamburg's other concentration camp was at Fuhlsbüttel (now the airport), and some 50,000 people, including over 6000 Hamburg Jews, died in these two camps.

While in Bergedorf, which is otherwise not interesting, you could look at its lovely thirteenth-century **Burg**, close to the S-Bahn. Originally surrounded by a moat, the gabled, red-brick castle was situated on an important medieval trade route, its role primarily tax-collecting rather than noble residence. Inside is a local museum (Tues, Thurs & Sun 10am–5pm), which concentrates on regional folklore and costumes, as well as traditional rural arts and crafts.

Hamburg's museums

Hamburg has some excellent museums, of which the **Kunsthalle** is the most famous. But there are many others, catering to interests as varied as art or postal services, as well as general historical collections. The most important are conveniently located around the edge of the city centre, and entry fees for all are around DM5.

The Kunsthalle

Glockengiesserwall, Tues–Sun 10am–5pm

The collection of paintings and sculpture ranges from medieval to contemporary, and is often augmented by special exhibitions, in which case there's a compulsory supplement to the entrance fee. Upstairs to the right are the earliest works; the layout continues in a broadly chronological manner.

MEDIEVAL GERMAN PAINTING

One room is entirely devoted to three retables by **Master Bertram**: an important figure in German art, he was the country's first painter identifiable by name, and worked for most of his life in Hamburg. His masterpiece is the huge folding altar, mixing paintings and sculpture, which was made for St Petri. The panel showing *The Creation of the Birds and Beasts* is outstanding; the characterisation of each creature grouped round the benevolent Almighty is delightfully fresh, but a prophetic warning note is struck – already the polecat has attacked a sheep. In the next room is part of the dismembered *St Thomas à Becket Altar* by Bertram's successor, **Master Francke**. Painted for the league of merchants who traded with England, it shows a very different style – the figures are more monumental, the structure tauter, the mood more emotional. The most interesting work here from the Renaissance period is **Cranach's** *The Three Electors of Saxony*. This uses the religious format of the triptych, with a continuous landscape backround, in order to show the deceased dukes, Frederick the Wise and John the Fearless, alongside the then ruler, John Frederick the Magnanimous.

FLEMISH PAINTING

The Flemish section begins with a tiny *House Altar* by **Isenbrandt** and the coolly beautiful *Mary Magdalene Playing the Lute* by the mysterious Antwerp painter dubbed **Master of the Female Half-Lengths** because of his preferred way of depicting his subjects. Also on view is a mature religious masterpiece by **van Dyck**, *The Adoration of the Shepherds*. Most of the specialist painters of seventeenth-century Holland are represented, but they're rather overshadowed by two examples of **Rembrandt**. *The Presentation in the Temple* is one of his earliest surviving works: he was only 21 when he painted it, yet there's no sign of immaturity or lack of confidence. From five years later, when Rembrandt was established as a fashionable society portraitist, comes *Maurits Huyghens*.

SEVENTEENTH- AND EIGHTEENTH-CENTURY EUROPEAN PAINTING

Highlights among the display of seventeenth- and eighteenth-century European painting are: **Claude's** *Dido and Aeneas at Carthage*; a pair of **Tiepolos**, *The Agony in the Garden* and *The Crowning with Thorns*; **Canaletto's** *Capriccio with a View of Padua*; **Belloto's** *Ideal View with Palace Steps*; **Goya's** *Don Tomas Perz Estaha*; and *The Creation of Eve* by the eccentric Swiss artist **Heinrich Füssli**, whose sensationalism makes a fascinating contrast with the paintings of Bertram from four hundred years earlier. There is one outstanding sculpture from this period – a bust of a cardinal by **Bernini**.

NINETEENTH- AND TWENTIETH-CENTURY GERMAN ART

The nineteenth-century German section is one of the museum's main strengths. Of a dozen works by **Caspar David Friedrich**, three rank among his most haunting and original creations. *Wanderer above the Mists* shows an isolated figure with his back to the viewer, contemplating an eternity of sky and clouds; overpowering and intimate at the same time, it stresses the awesome, unfathomable power of the natural world. This same theme is present to even greater effect in *Eismeer*; inspired by the voyages of polar exploration, which were then beginning, it depicts a ship half-submerged against a cracked iceberg, and has a menacing aura of timelessness. However, it also has political significance, since the picture symbolises lost hopes after the 1848 Revolution. In contrast, *The First Snow of Winter* imparts a dimension of grandeur to a quite ordinary landscape scene.

Another German artist with a distinctive vision of the world was the short-lived **Philipp Otto Runge**, most of whose best work can be seen here. His most arresting images are portraits of children (usually his own). Chubby-cheeked, over life-size and bursting with energy, they're placed at eye-level to face the viewer head-on. Very different, but equally effective, is the realist approach of **Wilhelm Leibl**, the German equivalent of Courbet. *Three Women at Church*, with its phenomenal detail, super-smooth texture and uncanny evocation of the rapt concentration of the subjects, is rightly considered his masterpiece.

The German impressionists, **Max Liebermann** and **Lovis Corinth** are each allocated a room, close to a choice collection of their French counterparts, including a version of **Manet**'s *Fauré as Hamlet* which is less finished but livelier than the one in Essen. Among the Expressionists, look out for two masterpieces by **Munch**: *Girls at the Seaside* and *Girls on the Bridge*. Pick of the usual range of twentieth-century paintings are **Otto Dix**'s *Der Krieg* triptych, a powerful anti-war statement, and **Paul Klee**'s translucent *Goldfish*, an abstract composition with a rare sense of poetry. The **Kunstverein** next door (Tues–Sun, 10am–6pm) has changing exhibitions of modern and contemporary art.

Museum für Kunst und Gewerbe

Arts and Crafts Museum, Steintorplatz; Tues–Sun 10am–6pm

Just a stone's throw away from the Kunsthalle, on the other side of the Hauptbahnhof, this museum has excellent and well displayed collections of art from ancient Egypt, Greece and Rome, through to this century. In fact, it has a bit of everything, and is the ideal place to dip into a variety of epochs and artistic and craft styles, and find something new you didn't know you liked.

The Art Nouveau/Jugendstil collection is very extensive and undoubtedly one of the most important ones of this style. What makes it particularly memorable is that the museum pieces have been arranged to create entire rooms, so that you get an idea of how things looked in people's homes. Also impressive are the sections dedicated to Chinese and Japanese art: traditional Japanese tea ceremonies are held in an authentic room; advance booking is best for these.

Deichtorhallen

Altlander Strasse; Tues–Sun 11am–6pm

Five minutes' walk south of the Steintorplatz, this museum of modern art is housed in the former fruit and veg market halls. The original wrought-iron and glass structures have been restored only recently, and inside, you'll now find the proudest new addition to Hamburg's art collections. There is no permanent show here, but a challenging programme of travelling exhibitions, both national and international. Always worth a look.

Automuseum

Kurt-Schumacher-Allee 42; daily 10am–5pm

A delightfully nostalgic private museum, where you can see anything from the earliest Rolls Royce, to such beauties as the 1937 *BMW327*. There are plenty of less glamorous, but equally nostalgic sights too, such as postwar *Fiats* and *VWs*. One of the many other highlights of the museum is the collection illustrating the development of bicycles and motorbikes over the course of the century.

Museum für Hamburgische Geschichte

Holstenwall 24; Tues–Sun, 10am–5pm

Situated at the other side of the city centre's semicircle, this museum will tell you everything you could possibly want to know about Hamburg's origins and history, its people and times. There are meticulous recreations of historic quarters in model form, and a large variety of model boats through the ages. An intriguing and unexpected section on the *Reeperbahn* dwells not on the commercial sex which makes it notorious these days, but on its original role as home to the ropemakers who supplied the giant ropes used by the port's ships.

Also part of the museum is the **Historic Emigration Office** (hours as above, but closed 1–2pm Tues–Sat, all day Sun). This section contains the most complete records anywhere in the world of European emigration to the New World. For the period 1850–1914, there are complete records of name, age, sex, occupation and place of origin of each and every passenger. If you want to find your ancestor's records, all you need to know is their name and year of emigration, and the staff will find them for you, for a fee.

Postmuseum

Stephansplatz/Dammtorwall; Tues–Fri 10am–3pm; Thurs until 6pm

A rather eclectic exhibition of the history of post and telephone networks, concentrating on maritime connections of all sorts. Also has stamp collections and old telephones of all shapes and sizes. Added bonus is a look-out platform on the third floor of the building.

Museum für Völkerkunde

Rothenbaumchaussee 64; Tues–Sun, 10am–5pm

Around the Univiertel you'll find four museums dedicated to the sciences. This one is perhaps the most interesting for the general visitor. Here you'll find well-presented displays from Africa and the South Pacific, as well as the Americas and Russia. Given Hamburg's maritime associations with the most far-flung places on earth, the collections are very extensive indeed. What is refreshing is that the museum tries to avoid pandering to voyeuristic attitudes, by not presenting cultures as exotic, but as present-day societies with present-day concerns. The effects of tourism on Pacific cultures is just one display that encourages new attitudes.

Altonaer Museum

Museumstr. 23, Tues–Sun, 10am–6pm

Well into the nineteenth century, until it was smothered by the growth of Hamburg, Altona was a separate Dutch community. The museum shows the Dutch heritage of the region, a facet often unknown to visitors. Not only Hamburg, but the entire region towards the present border is portrayed down the ages, concentrating on the regional trades, such as boat-building, farming, fishing, and all the many different crafts associated with ships and the sea.

Eating and drinking

When it comes to **eating and drinking** in Hamburg, it's always worth making your way out of the city centre. It is true that there are plenty of reasonable restaurants around the Grossneumarkt; but the choice and variety is just so much greater, and the prices lower, if you head to the nearby **Univiertel** or the so-called **Schanzenviertel** around Schulterblatt and Schanzenstrasse. For *Imbiss*-type food, the stalls on the main square in front of the Rathaus offer pricey but delicious snacks; the St Georg area near the Hauptbahnhof is cheaper and downmarket, as is the Reeperbahn in St Pauli. Another place for quick snacks is the pedestrian area outside Altona station.

Restaurants

There are two local specialities to try. *Aalsuppe*, generally made with plums and mixed vegetables as well as eels, is one of the most outstanding soups you'll encounter in Germany. *Labskaus*, a traditional sailor's dish, is more controversial, not to say indigestible; it's a hash which typically contains pickled corned beef, herring, beetroot, mashed potato, onions and gherkins, all topped with a fried egg. Otherwise the endless variety of fish dishes are the most typical meals around here.

Traditional food

Traditional Hamburg restaurants are found throughout the city. From a choice of many, the following are always worth trying for traditional local dishes, as well as standard German fare.

Aalberg, Strandweg 33. In Blankenese, down by the river. This is one of the city's best German/fish places, with carp a speciality. Main dishes are around DM25-50: best left for a splurge.

Alt Hamburger Aalspeicher, Deichstr. 43. The best place to sample *Aalsuppe*; fish dishes range around DM20-30, so not cheap, but always excellent. Try to avoid the place during lunch-hour when hordes of businessmen descend.

But'n Dammdoor, Mittelweg 27. Favoured by a number of prominent Hamburgers, but nevertheless offers great meals between DM10 and DM15.

Fischerhaus, Fischmarkt 14. Offers no-nonsense fish dishes down by the Fischmarkt, not necessarily at cheap prices.

Kanzelmeyer, Englische Planke 8, and **Old Commercial Room**, Englische Planke 10. Classic tourist restaurants in the shadow of St Michaelis, but with very good food.

Other cuisines

At Nali, Rutschbahn 11. Turkish restaurant with a large menu and friendly atmosphere: main dishes around DM15.

Campus Grindelhofstr. One of the best places for cheap sit-down snacks as well as meals.

Curry-Hütte, Grindelhofstr. Basic daytime curries.

Deichgraf, Deichstr. 23. Not exclusively Italian, but very good value with dishes starting at around DM10.

Medded, Bahrenfelder Chaussee 140. Egyptian food that's a bargain at the price. From DM10.

Objektiv Grindelhofstr., corner with Dillstr., Serves luxurious snacks and small dishes for reasonable prices.

Sagres, Vorsetzen 42. One of the many Portuguese eating-houses around the harbour, this is a homely place, popular with Portuguese dock workers – which means giant portions. Try the swordfish with paella.

Taverna Romana, Schulterblatt 53, First-rate Italian restaurant which also serves a few Greek dishes, prices between DM10-30.

The Old Spaghetti House, Gänsemarkt-Passage, on the Poststr. Cheap and cheerful, with pasta dishes around DM13, salads DM10.

Tre Fontane, Mundsburger Damm 45. Cosy and equally well-priced Italian (closed Tues).

Vegetarische Gaststätte, Neuerwall 13. Yummie veggie fodder from DM12 and up. Closes at 7.30pm Mon–Fri, 5pm Sat & Sun.

Bars

Hamburg's favoured **bars** are an ever-changing scene, but the following are the best (at the moment), that make up the heart of the city's nightlife. These days it centres around the St Pauli area and many places don't open before 10pm. Student-favoured bars, which are drinking haunts as well as good for cheap meals, can be found in the Univiertel and the Schanzenviertel. In the former, your best bet is to stroll along Grindelhofstrasse, Rentzelstrasse and Grindelallee, where you're bound to find something to suit your taste and purse.

Abaton, Grindelhofstr. Has an innovative cinema attached, and is a large and noisy place that gets very busy with students at night.

Arcadas, Grindelhofstr. Basically a traditional *Gaststätte* turned over to university types, very popular for lunch.

Café im Buch, Beim Grünen Jäger 21, St Pauli. Mixes excellent food (vegetarian too) with the occasional amateur cabaret.

Dehn's, Ost-West Str. 47. A *Hausbrauerei* that serves its own unfiltered dark malt beer.

Dschungel, Schanzenstr. 28. Strange mixture of ancient punks and neo-hippies, slightly off the beaten track.

Eisenstein, Friedensallee 9, in Altona. Situated in an old factory, bare stone walls and a high ceiling are the setting for people to show just how important they are, or at least how good they are at looking like it. Excellent pizzas.

Erika's Eck, Sternstr. 98. The favoured haunt of late-night drinkers who work in the nearby slaughterhouse. (Open until 3am, when it serves the largest and cheapest breakfast in the city.)

Filmhaus, Friedensallee 7. Popular with creative types and media people. The interior is plain, with simple wooden tables and chairs comfortable enough for a whole night's drinking. The food is good, though the atmosphere gets very smokey.

Frank und Frei, Schanzenstr. 93. A big, slow-paced favourite with students.

Gaststätte Sparr, Hamburger Berg 4. Best visited early on or very late, this is home to the local underground scene, or even just the plain set who wear nothing but black.

Holiday Bar, Hans-Albers-Platz 1. Nothing happens too quickly here, lest anyone should appear too eager.

La Paloma, Gerhardstr. 2. Open 24 hours, is an intimate place mixing art on the walls with heavy drinking.

Luxor, Max-Brauer-Allee 251. Friendly staff attend to serious posers.

Mitternacht, Gerhardstr. 16. This is the one that started the trend into St Pauli in the mid 1980s. These days its popularity is waning, but it's still hanging in there.

Molotow, Spielbudenplatz 5. Post-punk and tough new sounds are the background music in this increasingly popular haunt.

PickenPack, Schulterblatt 3. A good place for an evening's unpretentious drinking, as well as filling meals.

Prinzenbar, Kastanienallee 20. Stuccoed angles and chandeliers are the setting for drinking to good soul sounds, as well as occasional live shows.

Nil, Neuer Pferdemarkt 5, St Pauli. A successful bar-restaurant with a pleasantly mixed crowd.

Souterrain, Papenhuderstr. 26. Popular, even though it is over on the eastern edge of the Aussenalster (nearest U-Bahn stop Mundsburg).

Tempelhof, Hamburger Berg 12. Very popular seedy bar, which retains the swivel-chairs and lowered lights, and still mixes party troopers with red-light customers.

Unit, Talstr. 3–5. Has regular live gigs of all sorts and plenty of good music.

Vienna, Fettstr. 2, tries to create the atmosphere of a bistro-cum-sitting-room.

Zartbitter, Schanzenstr. 2–4. Has seen better times, but still draws the crowds at night.

Café-bars

Most **café-bars** have food as well, most notably excellent breakfasts and snacks (expect to pay around DM8–12). Each reflects the area it's in: you can expect places like Pöseldorf to be pricey and full of yuppies, while the Univiertel and Schanzenviertel are more studenty; and Altona is plain, with mixed crowds.

For traditional *Kaffe und Kuchen*, try *Café Oertel*, Esplanade 29; the *Condi* in the Hotel Vierjahreszeiten on Neuer Jungfernsteg; or the *Alsterpavilion* on the Jungfernstig, which has a rather middle-aged clientele but pleasant views across the Binnenalster.

ALTONA

Café Treibeis, Gaustr. 25 (Werkhof). "Alternative" hang-out, and a good place for weekend breakfasts, which can be had for between DM5 and DM12.

Loretta, Thadenstr. 78. Another breakfast orientated café, with the Sunday buffet offering loads of smoked salmon and other goodies for DM18.

Maybach, Heussweg 66. On the northern edges of the quarter, this has a beer garden too, a rarity in these parts.

CITY CENTRE

Café Schöne Aussichten, Gorch Fock Wall (in the park). An excellent summertime place, with tree-shaded terrace.

Gestern & Heute, Kaiser-Wilhelm-Str. 55. Legendary for the variety of its breakfasts, this place is open around the clock.

Loft, Grosse Bleichen 21 (in the Galleria). Exclusive daytime café for monied people.

ST GEORG

Café Gnosa. Lovely 1930s café with good food. Popular with the gay community.

Café Urlaub, Lange Reihe 63. Breakfast and billiards.

Geel Haus, Koppel 76. One of the better places around here.

Max und Consorten, Spadenteich 7. Situated on a deceptively pretty square, whose trees shade daytime prostitutes.

SCHANZENVIERTEL

Café Stenzel, Schulterblatt 61. Very mixed crowd frequent this pleasantly chaotic place.

Unter den Linden, Julius Str. 16. The place where the art avant-garde meet over their coffee and cakes.

UNIVIERTEL

Café Backwahn, Grindelallee 148. Five different breakfasts from around DM5.

Stradiwadi, Rentzelstr. 17. Relaxed café-theatre, with courtyard terrace round the back.

Nightlife

For the most up-to-date information on where to go, what's on and music venues of all kinds, consult the magazines *Szene Hamburg*, *Prinz* or *Oxmox*.

Discos

Bendula, Stresemannstr. 206. Afro-Caribbean music from 10pm Wed–Sun DM10 at weekends, cheaper in the week.

Gala, Mittelweg 22. Popular with trendy media types and a place to be seen. Tues–Sun 10pm onwards.

Grünspan, Grosse Freiheit 58. Long-established late-closing hard rock disco. Fri 9pm–7am, Sat 9pm–8am.

Kaiserkeller, Grosse Freiheit 36. Part of the *Grosse Freiheit* building, and one of the city's largest discos. DM4 admission includes a drink, open daily 9pm–4am.

Mambo Jambo, Marktstr. 140, Schanzenviertel. The place to go for African music. Tues-Fri 10pm–4am, Sat 10pm–6am.

Top Ten Club, Reeperbahn 136. Holds the distiction of being the city's latest opening disco: 10pm–9am, Fri–Sat 10pm–noon.

Live music venues

Cotton Club, Alter Steinweg. Traditional jazz club.

Dennis Swing Club, Papenhuderstr. 25. Jazz venue, though expect Dixieland rather than modern jazz.

Docks, Spielbudenplatz 19–20. Worth checking, but the acoustics here are dodgy, and it can get very stuffy.

Fabrik, Barnerstr. 36. One of the longest-enduring live music venues in Hamburg, this place is always worth checking out.

Grosse Freiheit, Grosse Freiheit 36. The city's main venue for rock/contemporary live music, with big-name bands mostly playing at weekends. The admission charge depends on who's performing.

Logo, Grindelallee 5. Mainly English and American underground bands.

Markthalle, Klosterwall 9–12. Along with *Fabrik*, venue for better-known European bands.

Werkstatt 3, Nernstweg 32. Located in Altona, this is a centre for alternative projects which often acts as a stage for Third World bands. Friday and Saturday evenings are tropical dance nights.

Classical Music

Hamburg's musical tradition can match that of any city in the world. The present *Staatsoper* at Dammtorstr. 28 (☎351555), not far from the famous but now vanished old building on the Gänsemarkt, once run by Telemann, is one of the top half-dozen **opera** houses in the world: Munich is its only German rival. In recent years, it has benefited from the inspired management of Rolf Liebermann. The **ballet** company attached to the house, run by the American John Niemeier, is also considered to be the best in the country at the moment.

There are three **orchestras** – the *Hamburger Philharmoniker*, the *Hamburger Symphoniker* and the *Nord-Deutscher-Rundfunk* (the house orchestra of the locally-based national radio station); the main concert hall is the *Musikhalle*, Karl-Muck-Platz, ☎346920. The *Monteverdi-Chor*, who excel in music of the Renaissance and Baroque eras, keeps up the city's choral tradition. It's also worth looking out for what's being performed in the churches, especially St Jakobi.

Theatre

The *Deutsches Schauspielhaus* at Kirchenallee 39 (☎248713) is one of the country's leading **theatres**. It's the successor to the *Nationaltheater*, one of whose first employees was the great eighteenth-century playwright and critic Gotthold Ephraim Lessing. Current director is the Englishman Peter Bogdanov.

Among the many venues for drama, some of the most renowned are: *Thaliatheater* at Gerhard-Hauptmann-Platz (☎322666); the *Kammerspiele* at Hartungstr. 9 (☎445620); *Ernst-Deutsch-Theater*, Mundsburger Damm 60 (☎2270/1420); and *Theater im Zimmer* at Alsterchaussee 30 (☎446539). For kids, there's the *Kindertheater* at Richard-Lind-Weg 17b (☎738 3858); or *Puppentheater* at Reinbeker Weg 32 (☎720 3288). Plays in English are performed at the *English Theatre of Hamburg*, Lerchenfeld 14 (☎225543). In contrast, the local *Plattdeutsch* dialect is used at *Ohnsorg Theater* at Grosser Bleichen 23 (☎3508/0321); and at *Hansa Theater*, Steindamm 17 (☎241414), which also presents circus-type shows.

During the **summer open-air theatre festival** (usually in July), make sure you head for performances at the *Kampnagelfabrik* in the park by the Dammtor S-Bahn stop, next to Rothenbaum Chaussee. For the most interesting **cabaret** in the city, head for the *Schmidt*, Spielbudenplatz 24 (☎314804), on the Reeperbahn.

Gay Scene

Not surprisingly, Hamburg has a lively **gay scene**. Other than talking to people in bars and cafés, the best way to find out what's on is to study the city's two gay publications, the magazine *Du und Ich* and the free sheet *Gay Express*, both available in most gay bars. Good starting points for **men** are: the *Café Gnosa* (see Café-bars, above); *Adagio*, Max-Brauer-Allee 14 (closed 2–5pm); *Image*, Poststr. 39; and *Café Spund*, Mohlenhof Str. 3.

For **women**, the best place to find out what's on and where to go around town is probably the *Frauenbuchladen*, Bismarkstr. 98 (☎420 4748), which also runs a café. Other women's cafés, not necessarily exclusively lesbian, are: *Café Meg Donna*, Grindelallee 43; and *Frauenkneipe*, Stresemannstr. 60; and *Frauenkulturcafé*, Peterstr. 36 (Tues–Sun, 4pm–midnight). A **women-only disco** worth checking out is the *Camelot*, Hamburger Berg 12, in St Pauli.

Listings

Airport information (☎508 2557)

American Express Rathaus Markt 5 (☎331141).

Brewery tours The famous *Holstenbrauerei*, Holstenstr. 224, has regular free tours (Mon–Fri except in Aug) round the premises, concluding with a chance to sample the products.

Car rental *Hertz* Kirchenallee 34-36 (☎280 1201); *Topcar*, Gertrudenstr. 3 (☎335998).

British Council Rothenbaumchaussee 34 (☎446057)

Consulates *British* at Harvestehuder Weg 8a (☎446071); *Irish* at Heilwigstr. 33 ☎489250); *American* at Alsterufer 28 (☎411710); *Canadian* at Spitalerstr. 11 (☎330247).

The Dom Not a cathedral but a funfair on the Heiligengeistfeld, close to the St. Pauli U-Bahn station, that is held in spring, summer and autumn sessions.

Emergencies *ADAC* (☎23990); *Doctor* (☎228022); *Dispensing chemist* Ballindamm 39 (☎335333) Mon–Fri 8am–6.30pm, Sat 9am–2pm.

Festivals No means a Hamburg speciality, but the *Übersee Tag* on 7 May celebrates the founding of the port in 1189.

Laundrettes *Wasch Center* chain, all open daily 6am–midnight at: Steilshooperstr. 317; Ohlsdorfer Str. 1-3; Mülenkamp 37; Hammer Landstr. 84; Pagenfelder Platz 5; Eppendorfer Weg 119; and Nobistor 34.

Mitfahrzentrale Högerdamm 26a (☎234123). There's also a women's *Mitfahrzentrale* at Grindelallee 43 (☎450556).

Poste Restante Kirchenallee exit out of Hauptbahnhof.

Sports *Hamburger SV* are one of Germany's best football teams; sailing regattas are frequently held on the Aussenalster; there are various international events, such as a tennis championship in late May, and an equestrian event in early June.

Swimming The beautiful baths at Bismarckbad in Altona are the city's most luxurious, and have women-only days. For outdoor swimming the smaller lakes around Hamburg (such as the Grossensee, Mönchsteich and Bredenbeker Teich) are the best: getting to them is, however, tricky – ask at the tourist office for details.

Views The *Fernsehturm* on Lagerstrasse (daily in summer 9am–11pm, in winter 10am–10pm; DM4 including ascent by lift) is now the highest building in Hamburg; an alternative is the tower of St Michaelis.

Taxis (☎611122).

Travel firm *Studenten-Reisen*, Grindelberg 1 (☎410 1089).

Women's Centre Schmilinskystr. 7 (☎245002).

SCHLESWIG-HOLSTEIN

A land between two seas, **Schleswig-Holstein** is Germany's northernmost province, and almost belongs more naturally to Scandinavia and the lands around the Baltic than to Germany. Chiefly it's an agricultural region, with large areas of forest and moorland: there's practically no heavy industry, and only three major cities. **Kiel**, destroyed in the war and now drably rebuilt, is the capital of the Land; this is where the government sits, and where there's the one university. It's a newcomer though – **Schleswig**, one-time capital of Denmark, and **Lübeck**, once one of Northern Europe's most important merchant centres, have longer pedigrees, and consequently the most historical interest.

Long, dark winters here are cold and depressing. In summer, though, the landscape vibrates with blues and greens, the corn dotted with poppies and cornflowers, the fields burning with the bright yellow of rapeseed. It's beautiful countryside to meander through by any means, most perfectly by cycling: along the coast, frequent local boat services provide enjoyable alternatives.

Schleswig-Holstein has two contrasting coastlines: the flat, battered **North Sea coast**, protected by large dykes, and the gently lapped and undulating **Baltic shore**. The **North Friesian Islands** offer a relaxing, if uneventful, break from the mainland.

The most obvious **route to take**, assuming that you are coming from and returning to Hamburg, is up the North Sea coast and down the Baltic – though with so many ferries heading off to Scandinavia, it's tempting to move on.

BIKE HIRE

It's worth knowing that **bikes** can be hired on a daily basis during summer months for about DM15 per day from the Bahnhofs at Büsum, Flensburg, Meldorf, Niebüll and Schleswig – a great way of seeing the countryside of Schleswig-Holstein.

Lübeck

In medieval times, **LÜBECK** was one of Europe's most important merchant cities and ports, dominating the highly lucrative trading routes along the Baltic. Although long overshadowed by the North Sea harbours of Hamburg and Bremen, which replaced it as international seaports, the city proudly displays the magnificent architectural wealth of its merchant days – Germany's oldest town hall still in use, beautiful merchants' houses, fine Gothic brick-built churches, and quaint old charitable institutions – many of which employ a highly decorative form of brickwork. Indeed, Lübeck's leadership in the artistic sphere was as pronounced as it was in commerce, influencing the appearance of cities along the entire length of the Northern European coast, from Amsterdam to Tallinn. The importance of Lübeck's heritage was given official recognition in 1987 by UNESCO's decision to place its entire Altstadt on the list of the world's most significant monuments – the first place in Northern Europe to be so honoured. This award was not only a tribute to the past, but also to the skill and efficacy of modern German restoration techniques: although the city had been severely bombed in World War II, with a quarter of the centre completely destroyed, such surviving evidence of this is mostly due to its having been left as a deliberate reminder.

In the Cold War years, Lübeck was the only important city to be sited alongside the notorious barbed wire frontier. Paradoxically, this stimulated a revival in its fortunes after a long period of decline: nearly 100,000 refugees came here to settle, not only from the lost Eastern Territories, but also from the GDR itself, before the frontier was finally sealed. Even if its days of glory are no more than a memory, it's still a vibrant city with a wide range of attractions which merits a visit of at least a couple of days.

The telephone code for Lübeck is ☎0451.

Arriving and finding somewhere to stay

The Hauptbahnhof lies just a few minutes' walk west of the Altstadt. Within the station itself is one of the **tourist offices** (Mon–Sat 9am–1pm & 3–7pm; ☎72300); there's another on the Markt (Mon–Fri 9.30am–6pm, Sat & Sun 10am–2pm; ☎122 8106).

Accommodation

Lübeck has hardly any accommodation in private houses. However, the **YMCA** have a hostel, the *Interrail-Point-Sleep-In* , in a renovated historic house in the middle of the Altstadt, at Grosse Petersgrube 11 (☎78982). It costs DM12 per night, DM16.50 including breakfast, and sleeping bags can be hired for DM3. Reception is open 9–11am, 5pm–midnight, and booking, or at least arriving early, is strongly recommended in summer. Failing that, the official **youth hostel** is at Gertruden Kirchhof 4 (☎33433) – go out of the Altstadt through the Burgtor, then bear left for about 200 metres. A

LÜBECK AND THE HANSEATIC LEAGUE

In the eleventh century, a small Wend settlement had been established at the point where the Trave is joined by the Schwartau.. It was destroyed by a rival Slav tribe in 1138, to be replaced five years later by a trading town owing allegiance to the Counts of Holstein. This move was none too popular with **Henry the Lion**, the powerful Duke of Saxony, whose own economic situation was adversely affected by the success of the new Baltic port. After it had burned to the ground in 1157, he forced the count to hand the site over to him, re-establishing it as a city and harbour two years later, and as a bishopric the year after that. He gave it special privileges, whereby the merchants ran the town council independently of ducal control and administered their own system of justice. The so-called **statutes of Lübeck** were later adopted by over a hundred other Baltic towns, and set the trend for medieval German cities being far freer in outlook and atmosphere than the feudalistic principalities. In 1226 Lübeck was officially recognised as a Free Imperial City of the Holy Roman Empire and grew quickly in wealth and trading power; within a century of its birth, it had become the richest city in Germany and the Baltic's premier port .

In 1243, Lübeck formed a trading alliance with Hamburg; this in time, under the name of the **Hanseatic League**, extended to nearly all other ports along the Baltic, as well as to inland cities such as Braunschweig, Lüneburg, Magdeburg and Cologne. A fairly informal grouping, it was initially inspired by the need for mutual protection against pirates, and as an instrument to settle disputes and squabbles among the member towns – matters which Germany's weak central authority was unable to influence. However, in time the Hanseatic League developed into the equivalent of a cartel, excluding non-members from any share in the lucrative Baltic trade and opening a network of trading centres abroad, the most important being in London, Bruges, Bergen and Novgorod. Lübeck was accepted as the leader and spokesman of the League, though it began to lose its supremacy to Danzig in the latter half of the fifteenth century. Throughout the following century, the League itself declined, as valuable herring stocks diminished, as the balance of power in Europe shifted, as the Dutch – with their superior vessels and forward-looking philosophy of free trade – began to bite deeply into the old monopoly, and as trading routes changed due to the discovery of the Americas and new shipping routes to the East. The Thirty Years' War, which drained energy and resources, and left the powerful nation-states of Sweden and the emergent Brandenburg-Prussia in control of much of the Baltic, finally killed it off. Down to just nine members, it met for the last time in Lübeck in 1669. However, Lübeck, along with Hamburg and Bremen, remained a significant port and trading centre. It was only in 1937 that it lost its status as a free city and was incorporated into Schleswig-Holstein.

private hostel option is *Rucksackhotel Backpackers*, just south of the Burgtor at Kanalstr. 70 (☎74807); this charges DM18 for a dorm bed, and also has doubles for DM65, triples for DM85, though all these prices exclude breakfast. Otherwise, the cheapest **hotel**, with singles DM35, doubles from DM60, is *Schönwald*, Chasotstr. 25 (☎64169 or 64162), but it's a long way out, so phone ahead first (English spoken). In the Altstadt itself, the best bargains are *Zur Burgtreppe* at Hinter der Burg 15 (☎73479), whose rates begin at DM40 per person, and *Gästehaus Lentz* (☎71049), which has singles DM35–55, doubles DM50–85; the latter is an annex of the much more expensive *Alter Speicher*, Beckergrube 93 (☎704804). In the vicinity of the Hauptbahnhof, there are a number of reasonably priced possibilities: *Bahnhofshotel*, Am Bahnhof 21 (☎83883), has singles from DM35, doubles from DM65; *Petersen*, Hansestr. 11a (☎84519), has singles from DM45, doubles from DM80; *Marienburg*, Katharinenstr. 41 (☎42512), has singles from DM45, doubles from DM70. The **campsite** is at Steinrader Damm 12 (☎893030) in the suburb of Schönböcken; take bus #7 or #8.

The city

Almost everything worth seeing in Lübeck is in the **Altstadt**, an egg-shaped island still surrounded by the water defences of the Trave and the city moat. Its streets, while not conforming to a pre-arranged plan, are nevertheless arranged very symmetrically, so it's easy to find your way around. For a general view of the magnificent skyline, walk northeast from the Hauptbahnhof to the Marienbrücke: better still, take one of the cruises round the harbour area; details of these are found in the *Listings* section.

The Holstentor, the Petrikirche and around

Entry to Lübeck was once through, but is now along, the side of, the **Holstentor** (Holstein Gate; April–Sept Mon–Sat 10am–5pm; Oct–March 10am–4pm; DM3), whose two sturdy circular towers with turret roofs, joined by a gabled centre section, form the city's emblem and – because of the Holstentor's appearance on the old DM50 note – its most familiar sight. Built in 1477, it leans rather horrifyingly these days, but that shouldn't put you off calling in at its small historical museum, which provides a useful introduction to the city and Hanseatic history. On the waterfront to the right of the Holstentor is a row of lovely old gabled buildings – the **Salzspeicher** (salt ware-houses). They were built in the sixteenth and seventeenth centuries to store precious salt, extracted in Lüneburg and destined for Scandinavia.

Straight ahead over the bridge and up Holstenstrasse, the first church on the right (just down a side street) is the Gothic **Petrikirche**, one of the many buildings to suffer during the massive Allied bombing of 29 March 1942. It no longer functions as a place of worship; instead, the whitewashed, five-aisled interior is put to use for changing exhibitions of contemporary art. A lift goes to the top of the **tower** (April–Oct daily 9am–6pm; DM2), and Lübeck's centre is compact enough for this to be very useful for getting to grips with the layout of the city.

In the shadow of the church, at Kleine Petersgrube 4–5 is the **Museum für Figurentheater** (Tues–Sun 9.30am–6.30pm; DM3), which claims to be the world's larg-est collection of puppet theatre material, with examples from all over Europe, Asia and Africa. Each day the museum is open, special matinees for kids are staged at 3.30pm in the adjoining *Marionettentheater*; performances intended for adults are held on Fridays and Saturdays at 7.30pm. The next street along, **Grosse Petersgrube**, curves and inclines more than is normal is Lübeck, but nevertheless ranks as one of the finest in the city, with a superb array of mansions showing all the different vernacular styles from Gothic to Neoclassical.

The Rathaus

Across Holstenstrasse from the Petrikirche is the Markt, two sides of which are occupied by the imposing **Rathaus**, which illustrates Lübeck's characteristic brickwork – with alternating rows of red unglazed and black glazed bricks – at its most inventive. The north wing, which dates from the mid-thirteenth century, has a high superstructure with spire-topped turrets and two huge holes to lessen wind resistance; its side facing the Markt was further enlivened by the addition of a Renaissance loggia made of very white-coloured stone from the city's old trading partner, the Swedish island of Gotland. At the turn of the fourteenth century, the east wing, with an arcade leading to Breite Strasse behind, was added. Its extension, the *Neue Gemach*, was begun around 1440; it's the finest part of all, providing a highly refined variation on the earlier theme of wind-breaks and corner turrets, with the bonus of coats of arms embedded in the brickwork. On the Breite Strasse side, it was further embellished with an extremely elaborate stone staircase in the Dutch Renaissance style and an oriel window.

Guided tours (Mon–Fri at 11am, noon & 3pm; DM2) go round some of the interi-ors, though it has to be said that these don't quite match what you see from outside. The most notable rooms are the late Baroque *Audienzsaal*, with its allegorical paintings and Renaissance doorway, and the neo-Gothic *Bürgerschaft*. Leaving by the north side, you get a good view of the original thirteenth-century building, and can also see the **Kanzleigebäude**, the chancellery building tacked on in the fifteenth century.

The Marienkirche

Rearing up behind the north wing of the Rathaus is the city's largest and finest church, the **Marienkirche**. It's certain that the two buildings were intended to be seen as a coherent architectural group, as the Marienkirche was where the city's richest citizens worshipped – and they planned from the outset that it should overshadow the bishops' Dom not only by its prominent situation, but in its architectural splendour as well. Built at a leisurely pace between the early thirteenth and mid-fourteenth centuries, it's a tall, soaring building in the French Gothic style – but in brick, rather than stone, which gives it a very different and authentically German appearance. Its twin square **towers** are topped by spires to a height of 185m, while the nave is supported by flying buttresses that rise from the verdigris roofs of the side aisles. In the 1942 bombings the Marienkirche was severely damaged and burnt out – an exhibition inside shows photographs of the devastation and also of the restoration; even more dramatically, the bells in the southern tower chapel have been left smashed on the ground, the way they fell during the bombing. War damage was a mixed blessing: the roof timbers and spires were destroyed, threatening the whole structure; both organs and many other items, including the chancel screen and much other fine woodwork, were lost. On the other hand, original Gothic **wall paintings** which had been covered for centuries were revealed and restored – indeed the entire interior was laid bare for a restoration to its original simplicity.

Today the interior is very light, with a feeling of great loftiness. Detail of the fine ribbing and vaulting is picked out against the pale grey chalk wash in the old terracotta and grey-green colours. All this makes a good backdrop for the church's **art treasures**. The fifteenth-century high altar, in front of which is a pretty fourteenth-century font, is of modest dimensions, but a number of impressive works, dating from the late fifteenth and early sixteenth centuries, can be seen in the ambulatory. These include a life-size carving of Saint John the Evangelist (unfortunately only partly restorable after war damage); a series of powerful Passion reliefs by the Münster sculptor Heinrich Brabender; and a beautiful locally made gilded tabernacle. In the axial chapel is a magnificent carved and painted altar from Antwerp in a gilded wood frame, depicting the life of the Virgin Mary, while in the Alenkapelle, the chapel adjoining the northern transept, is a grave slab of a merchant cast by Lübeck's greatest artist, Bernt Notke. Before leaving, have a look inside the **Briefkapelle** at the southwestern end of the nave, a masterly miniature church which is used by the congregation during the winter.

Mengstrasse and Breite Strasse

On the north side of the Marienkirche is **Mengstrasse**, which is lined with an impressive row of patrician houses. At no. 4 is the Baroque **Buddenbrookhaus**, which was where the famous literary brothers Heinrich and Thomas Mann (see below) grew up. It takes its name from the latter's youthful novel of mercantile life in the city, but unfortunately serves today as a bank rather than the museum it is so cut out to be. Further up the street, nos. 48 and 50 are together designated the **Schabbelhaus**, Lübeck's most famous – and most expensive – restaurant. Crammed full of antiques, it's one of several eateries in the city regarded as sightseeing attractions in their own right.

Another of these is the **Café-Konditorei Niederegger**, facing the Rathaus across Breite Strasse, which is internationally famed for its vast displays of **marzipan**. This is the oddest hangover from the city's trading heyday: the confection was first produced in Lübeck in the Middle Ages from fine almonds imported from Italy. Herr Niederegger perfected the art in 1806, and this mind-boggling variety is the result of the uninterrupted continuation of his business. At the opposite, northern end of Breite Strasse are two impressive Renaissance halls – the **Haus der Kaufmannschaft**, the offices of the local chamber of commerce, and the **Haus der Fischergesellschaft**, the former guild house of the fishermen. The latter is another of the city's best-known restaurants, and is

THE MANN LITERARY DYNASTY

One of the giants of modern European literature, **Thomas Mann** (1875–1955) was equally adept at writing short stories and epic novels. His greatest achievement is *The Magic Mountain*, a blockbuster set in a Swiss sanatorium that symbolically examines the sickened state of early twentieth-century Europe. Another favourite theme, the conflict between the artist and society, is superbly expressed in his most famous story, *Death in Venice*. Although not a political animal, his opposition to Nazism, expressed in the story *Mario and the Magician*, led him to leave Germany voluntarily in 1933. He settled in the USA, where he wrote of Biblical exile in the vast trilogy, *Joseph and his Brothers*. Never really happy in the New World, he returned to Switzerland after the war. His last works include *Doktor Faustus*, which updated the Faust legend to the Nazi period, and one of the German lanaguage's few comic novels, *The Confessions of Felix Krull, Confidence Man*.

Heinrich Mann (1871–1950) was initially preoccupied with similar themes, albeit with the addition of a good deal of erotic fantasy. However, he was given more to social and political comment than his soul-searching younger brother, and many of his novels are clear statements of his socialist views. His most famous work is his devastating attack on reactionary German pedagoguery, *Professor Umraut*, which was filmed as the Marlene Dietrich classic, *The Blue Angel*. Its scope was widened in his best novel, *Man of Straw*, which lays bare the true nature of life under the Second Reich.

Three of Thomas Mann's children became writers, and the short-lived **Klaus Mann** (1906–49) is increasingly regarded as a major literary figure in his own right. He also tackled the Faust theme in *Mephisto*, while his early *The Pious Dance* is a graphic portrayal of the decadent homosexual underworld of Berlin in the days of the Weimar Republic.

decked out inside with all sorts of seagoing paraphernalia; predictably, it's on the programme of every tour group.

Across the street stands the **Jakobikirche**, traditionally the parish church of the seafaring community. In comparison with the Marienkirche, it's modest in scale, the only obvious point of similarity being the Gothic wall paintings on its square pillars. Nonetheless, it's rich in works of art, the finest being the **Brömse Altar** in the chapel to the right of the entrance, which features a carving of *The Crucifixion* by Heinrich Brabender and delicate little Flemish-style paintings. The carved oak **organ lofts** are also impressive; a beautifully worked spiral staircase leads up to the large Baroque organ in the west gallery, though its smaller counterpart in the transept, dating back in part to the fifteenth century, is the more precious instrument of the two.

Grosse Burgstrasse and Königstrasse

Guarding the extreme northern end of the Altstadt, but unlike the Holstentor still on the island itself, is the formidable-looking **Burgtor**, a square tower topped by a bell-shaped roof. The side buildings of the gateway were originally used for stabling the horses of people arriving in the city at this point. Behind it, in black and red Lübeck neo-Gothic style, is the **Versorgungsamt** – a town administration office of the 1890s.

Following Grosse Burgstrasse back towards the city centre, you come to the thirteenth-century **Heiligen-Geist-Hospital** (April–Sept Tues–Sun 10am–5pm; Oct–March Tues–Sun 10am–4pm; free), one of the earliest and best-preserved hospices of the medieval period, whose rhythmic facade is characterised by its gables and tall pepperpot turrets. Inside, the vaulted chapel is richly decorated with frescos, retables and a Gothic rood screen bearing delicate paintings telling the story of Saint Elizabeth. The tiny chambers leading off the main hall were built in the nineteenth century as an improvement on the previous communal space which you can glimpse through the gateway; today the hospice is still used as a home for the elderly.

Königstrasse, the southern continuation of Grosse Burgstrasse, is dominated by stately mansions of the Baroque period and later. The **Gemeinnützige Gesellschaft** at no. 5 was another charitable institution; some of its superbly elegant interiors are now used as a restaurant. Two patrician homes, the **Drägerhaus** at no. 9 and the **Behnhaus** at no. 11, have been combined to form the **Museum für Kunst und Kulturgeschichte** (Museum for Art and Cultural History; April–Sept Tues–Sun 10am–5pm; Oct–March 10am–4pm; DM3, free Sun). It's surprising to see how large these houses are inside, compared with the narrow street frontage; tax was once paid on a building's width rather than than its overall size, which led to houses being built long and narrow. The Drägerhaus has impressive interiors with original nineteenth-century furniture, clocks, porcelain, and other *objets d'art*, plus a room documenting the lives of the Mann brothers. A gallery of nineteenth- and early twentieth-century paintings occupies the Behnhaus. This includes a room devoted to Lübeck's own **Johann Friedrich Overbeck**, founder and guiding light of the influential Nazarene movement (see "Painting & Graphics" in *Contexts*). There's also a lovely *Coastal Landscape by Evening Light* by Friedrich, and fine examples of the Expressionists Kirchner and Munch.

At the corner of the next block is the **Katharinenkirche** (April–Sept Tues–Sun 10am–1pm & 2-5pm; DM3, free Sun), formerly the church of a Franciscan convent – the city's only monastic foundation from the days of the Hansa to have survived intact. In the niches of the facade are nine life-size figures. The first three on the left (*Woman in the Wind, The Beggar* and *The Singer)* are by **Ernst Barlach**: he was commissioned to make the series in the early 1930s, but these were all he had completed by 1932, when his work was banned by the Nazis. The other six were added after the war by **Gerhard Marcks**: you can have a closer look at them in Schloss Gottorf in Schleswig, where another set of terracotta castings from the same moulds is exhibited. In due course, the entire convent will be open as a museum, but in the meantime you can view the inside of the church, whose main peculiarity is its two-storey chancel, the lower of which functioned as a crypt, even though it's at ground level. On the west wall is a large altarpiece of *The Raising of Lazarus* by **Tintoretto**, brought from Venice by a Lübeck merchant. Nearby stands a cast of Bernt Notke's masterpiece, a spectacular group of *St George and the Dragon*, the original of which is in Stockholm.

The eastern quarters

Down Glockengiesser Strasse to the side of the Katharinenkirche, you can step through what appear to be doors in the wall into two of Lübeck's finest courtyards, whose small almshouses were built by seventeenth-century benefactors; these are the exact parallel of their Amsterdam counterparts, and another reminder that two or three centuries ago the ports of the North Sea and Baltic had more in common with one another than with their national hinterlands. The **Füchtings-Hof** at no. 23 was built for the widows of sea captains and merchants; the slightly earlier **Glandorps-Gang** and **Glandorps-Hof** further down at no. 39 were intended for the widows of craftsmen. Another attractive example is the **Haasenhof**, a couple of blocks to the south at Dr-Julius-Leber-Str. 37. At the junction of this street with Königstrasse is the **Löwen-Apotheke**, the oldest remaining house in the city. Two groups of Gothic almshouses can be seen in streets further south – **Von-Höveln-Gang** at Wahmstr. 73–77 and **Dornes-Hof** at Schlumacher Str. 19.

Presiding over the quiet, village-like streets of the southeastern quarter (an area into which few tourists venture) is the handsome single tower of the **Aegidienkirche**, Lübeck's smallest parish church, whose congregation was made up of craftsmen, small-holders and the less affluent merchants. There was a strong musical tradition here, and the early Baroque organ can rival any in Lübeck. What really catches the eye, however, is the richly decorated Renaissance **choir gallery** which shuts off the chancel from the nave. A Protestant variant on the old Catholic idea of the rood screen, its very positioning emphasises the importance of music in Lutheran worship, while its paintings interpret Biblical stories in line with the doctrines of the new faith.

Round the corner, the **St-Annen-Museum** (April–Sept Tues–Sun 10am–5pm; Oct–March Tues–Sun 10am–4pm; DM3, free Sun) is housed in the surviving parts of the late Gothic St-Annen-Kloster, an Augustinian convent which burned down last century. It has a first-rate collection reflecting domestic, civic and religious art and history from the thirteenth to the eighteenth century. The star piece is the magnificent *Passion Triptych* which **Memling** painted for the Dom. There's also a room full of retables commissioned by the various guilds for their chapels; the finest, predictably enough, is that made for the artists' own Guild of Saint Luke, which has attractive paintings illustrating the life of their patron by the leading Lübeck master of the late fifteenth century, **Hermen Rode**. The courtyard, surrounded by very Dutch-looking buildings, is one of the most restful spots in the city; its garden contains many imposing monumental Baroque statues, including the original figures from the Puppenbrücke, the bridge leading from the Hauptbahnhof to the Holstentor.

The Dom and around

At the extreme southern end of the Altstadt is the only surviving reminder of Henry the Lion's city, the huge brick-built **Dom**. It was completed in 1230, with its two 120m towers, as a Romanesque basilica; a couple of decades later, the pure early Gothic porch or "Paradise" was added on the south side to serve as the main entrance. Soon after, work began on replacing the original chancel with a spacious Gothic hall. The whitewashed interior is dominated by an enormous **triumphal cross**, the first important work of **Bernt Notke**, who was a celebrity throughout the Baltic lands in the late fifteenth and early sixteenth centuries. Probably a painter as well as a sculptor, he specialised in the grandiose, making highly original works to adorn churches in Denmark, Sweden and Estonia. This one is a complicated allegory on the salvation offered by the cross, which rests on an elaborate beamed structure bearing superbly expressive figures of saints and angels. Notke was also responsible for the carvings on the **rood screen** behind, to which an astronomical clock was appended in the seventeenth century. Among the Dom's numerous other adornments, look out for the ornate Renaissance pulpit in the main nave, the fifteenth-century *Müllerkrone* candelabrum in the north aisle, the winged retables in the transept, and, in the chancel, the memorials to bishops and noblemen, which range from simple Gothic tombs to commemorative chapels in the swankiest Baroque.

Just north of the Dom is the Renaissance **Zeughaus**, which has recently been restored to house the **Völkerkundemuseum** (Tues–Sun 10am–4pm; DM3, free Sun), whose ethnology displays feature Africa, Asia and the South Seas. Finally, it's worth walking round the back of the Dom, where a pleasant green area has been laid out around the banks of the large pond known as the **Mühlenteich**.

Eating, drinking and entertainment

Lübeck's attractions are far from being only historical: the city is also a renowned gastronomic and musical centre, and there are always plenty of nighttime diversions.

Restaurants

Many of Lübeck's most prestigious restaurants – from the point of view of both food and setting – have been described in the text above. All are pricey, though less expensive menus are often available at lunchtimes. However, the city has plenty of cheaper alternatives, many of them of comparable quality.

Aubergine, Hüxstr. 57. Vegetarian and wholefood café-restaurant.

Brauberger, Alfstr. 36. *Hausbrauerei* serving low-cost meals and its own unfiltered beer

Historischer Weinkeller, Am Koberg. Wine bar-cum-restaurant in the cellars of the Heiligen-Geist-Hospital.

Jever Stuben, An der Obertrave 11. Offers changing daily fish specials, and is particularly good value at lunchtime.

Lübecker Hanse, Kolk 3–7. Housed in a beautiful old building by the Petrikirche, this excellent if pricey restaurant features French cuisine as an alternative to the standard German fare.

Ratskeller, Am Markt. This is the most innovative Ratskeller in Germany: in addition to excellent traditional dishes, they have a long vegetarian menu, and also brew their own naturally fermented beer, *Lübsch-Pils*.

Schmidt's, Dr-Julius-Leber-Str. 60–62. Inexpensive café-restaurant in the heart of the student quarter, with a wide choice of dishes.

Stadtrestaurant, Im Hauptbahnhof. Despite its unpromising-looking setting on the first floor of the Hauptbahnhof, this serves food of a standard rivalling any of the city's most famous restaurants.

Tipasa, Schlumacher Str. 14. A great student favourite, run by Afghanis and featuring a large, everchanging and reasonably priced menu of bistro-type dishes, plus wonderful pizzas and bread made in the roaring wood-fired oven. If you're pressed for time, it has a fast service takeaway next door.

Cafés and bars

Café Amadeus, opposite the Marienkirche. Good for rolls and salads – and for finding out what's on in town.

Café Belmondo, Am Bahnhof. A pleasant café with snacks, and a good place to wait for a train.

Café Nidegger, Breite Str. 89. The celebrated marzipan shop has an elegant backroom café, plus a first-floor dining room; there are various breakfast possibilities from DM6, lunches from DM12.

Charly Rivels Sohn, Glockengiesser Str. 91. Café-bar frequented by Lübeck's artistic set.

Engel, Engelsgrube 59. Music-bar in a street which is one of the liveliest in town come the evening.

Im alten Zolln, Mühlenstr. 93. The most atmopheric of the city's traditional pubs; also does meals.

Discos

There's no cover charge for any of these during the week: expect to pay DM3–5 at weekends, when they can be very full.

Body and Soul. Wahmstr. 28. As the name suggests, concentrates on soul music. Sun–Thurs 8pm–3am, Fri & Sat 8pm–4am.

Das Riverboot, Beim Holstentor In a river boat moored by the Puppenbrücke. Tues–Sun 8pm–2am.

Galaxis, Falkenstr. 45. Housed in a huge converted factory. Wed–Sat 7pm–1am.

Tiffany, Kreuzweg 5. Conveniently close to the Hauptbahnhof, this is for the real night owls. Mon–Thurs 8pm–3am, Fri–Sun 8pm–5am.

Culture

No German city is better known for its **organ recitals** – a tradition dating back to the early seventeenth century, when the Danish composer Diderik Buxtehude became one of the first musicians to achieve fame as a virtuoso solo instrumentalist, drawing huge crowds to his improvisatory recitals at the Marienkirche. The Marienkirche's two modern organs (one of which is the biggest mechanical musical instrument in the world) are used alternately for recitals each Saturday at 6.30pm, while one or other of the Jakobikirche's historic organs is played on Saturdays at 5pm. Other **music** performances can be heard at the *Musikhochschule*, Grosse Petersgrube 17–29. Main **theatre** venue is *Bühnen der Hansestradt Lübeck*, Beckergrube 10–14

Listings

Bike hire Schwartauer Allee 39 (DM5 per day; ☎42660).

Car hire *Autohansa* have an office in the Hauptbahnhof.

Cruises *KuFra Schiffahrtslinien* (☎26561 or 74489) offers cruises round the city and harbour, and to Travemünde, departing from Untertrave. *Lübecker Fahrgastschiff Manfred Quandt* (☎393734 or 73884) features the same destinations, plus the Elbe-Lübeck Canal and the Dassower See in Mecklenburg; all these depart from the Holstentorterrasse, whereas those to the Ratzeburger See leave from Moltebrücke on the other side of the Altstadt. *Personnenschiffahrt Reinhold Maiworm* (☎35455) leaves from the same location for the Ratzeburger See, with the option of continuing on to Ratzeburg itself.

Festivals Main events are: *Markt Anno Dazumal*, an old-time fair held in the Rathausmarkt for 10 days in early May; a two-week *Volksfest* in mid-July; and the *Altstadtfest* on the second weekend in September (odd-numbered years only). The Advent celebrations are a cut above the norm, thanks to the setting of the *Kunsthandwerker-Weihnachtsmarkt* in the Heiligen-Geist-Hospital, and the fairy-land displays of the *Weichnachtsmärchenwald* outside the Marienkirche.

Mitfahrzentrale Fischergrube 45 (☎71074).

Post offices near the Hauptbahnhof (on the left as you come out) and in the Marktplatz by the Rathaus (with Poste Restante).

What's on The tourist office publishes a free monthly brochure, *Lübeck Heute*.

Around Lübeck: Ratzeburg and Travemünde

The main outing south of Lübeck is to **RATZEBURG**, reachable from Lübeck by train or by occasional boat trips in summer – check with the tourist office. Until re-unification, Ratzeburg was only just in the Federal Republic: it sits on an island (joined to the bank by a couple of bridges) in the Ratzeburger See, and part of the east bank formed the border with the erstwhile GDR. Apart from its position, which is both pictu-resque and rather vulnerable looking, Ratzeburg's charms include the twelfth-century **Dom**, a triple-naved basilica founded by Henry the Lion which survived a major fire in the seventeenth century that destroyed virtually the whole of the town.

Its other main sight is the **Ernst-Barlach-Museum** (Tues–Sun 10am–noon & 3–6pm), dedicated to the sculptor who created the figures on the facade of Lübeck's Katharinenkirche. As time goes on, it seems more evident that Barlach, who lived for several years in Ratzeburg before moving to Güstrow, ranks among the most signifi-cant artists of the twentieth century. His bronzes and wood-carvings, using techniques borrowed from the medieval and Renaissance German masters, show a warm human-ity and convey a haunting sense of pathos. Barlach carried his Expressionism into other media – he was a fine graphic artist, and also an accomplished playwright, being particularly concerned with the awesome theme of the cosmic relationship between God and mankind.

Travemünde

Just to the north of Lübeck is **TRAVEMÜNDE**, Lübeck's rather glamorous seaside resort. Go there in winter and you might find the odd playful seal on the fine sandy beach. In summer, though, Travemünde is hardly the place to go to get away from it all. The beach is packed full of busy *Strandkörbe* (hooded basket-seats rented out like deck chairs to keep off the breeze), sailing boats and windsurfers ply the water, and the fashionable **casino** makes fat profits (not least on its terrace, *the* place to sit for cool drinks and ice cream). The town itself is still quite attractive, but it is dominated by the shipping and fishing quays; this is the main port for ferries to and from Scandinavia. From the beach it's odd to watch large ships apparently sailing right onto land, whereas they are actually entering the mouth of the Trave. If you walk northwards up the beach, it eventually peters out and is replaced by cliffs, the Brodtemer Ufer. This is where everybody goes to get a rare view of the Baltic from above sea-level.

The Coast: Travemünde to Kiel

Along the coast north of Travemünde are several resorts – the beaches are good, with fine sand, and camping facilities abound. **TIMMENDORFER STRAND** is fairly elegant, in the style of Travemünde, but others, such as **HAFFKRUG**, are more like fishing villages still. By and large the beaches are narrow, and backed by thick pine forest – especially around **KELLENHUSEN** (just inland from here CISMAR has a thirteenth-century monastery). The railway runs over a bridge to the island of **Fehmarn**, where ferries from PUTTGARDEN go over to Scandinavia. The island would be worth a small trip for its own sake: it has plenty of beaches and camping. West of Fehmarn you are in the Kieler Bucht – Kiel Bay. **LÜTJENBURG** makes a good stopover; it's very small, but is pretty, and you can visit the ancient burial ground (*Hünengrab*) nearby.

Kiel

KIEL had to be almost completely rebuilt following wartime bombing; consequently, there's not much point in looking for charm amongst its sober 1950s three and four-storey blocks. A member of the Hanseatic League from 1284 to 1518, Kiel was always overshadowed by Lübeck in that era. However, once the **Kiel Canal** was opened up in 1895 to provide a shipping link between the Baltic and the North Sea, the town's importance as a strategic naval harbour was confirmed. The canal is now the world's biggest and busiest shipping lane. It was the sailors of Kiel who, late in 1918, mutinied and started a march to Berlin, an intrinsic part of the German revolution. That's more or less forgotten these days, and the face Kiel now presents to the world is of a modern port and university town. Twice host to the Olympic Games watersports (1936 and 1972), it stages a major **annual regatta** (the *Kieler Woche*, last week in June). The town is also known for a nice line in smoked sprats – known as *Kieler Sprotten*.

Virtually all buildings of historical or architectural interest that do remain have been rebuilt following wartime damage – the Gothic and neo-Gothic Nikolaikirche, the Jugendstil Petruskirche and the renowned Jugendstil **Rathaus** with its 67m high tower and tremendous views (guided tours May–Oct 10.30 & 11.30am).

Other than this, you'll have to content yourself with one of several museums: housed in a rare surviving example of a nobleman's timbered town house at Dänische Str. 19 is the **Kieler Stadtmuseum** (Tues–Sun 10am–6pm) of city history. More relevant to Kiel's seagoing connections are the **Kieler Stadt- und Schiffahrtsmuseum** (Nautical Museum; daily 10am–6pm; 15 Oct–15 April Tues–Sun 10am–5pm) in the old fish market hall at Wall 65, and the **Institut für Meereskunde Kiel** (Oceanography Museum; 1 April–30 Sept daily 9am–7pm; 1 Oct–31 March daily 9am–5pm; DM2.20) at Düsternbrooker Weg 20, where there are large **aquaria** and seals. The **Kunsthalle** at Düsternbrooker Weg 1 has a large collection of works from Northern Europe (Thurs–Sat & Tues 10am–6pm, Sun 10am–5pm, Wed 10am–8pm; DM2).

Kiel's most interesting museum is perhaps the **Schleswig-Holstein Freilichtmuseum** (Open-Air Museum; April 1–Nov 15 Tues–Fri 9am–5pm, Sun 10–6pm; also July 1–Sept 1 Mon 9am–5pm; Nov 16–March 31 Sun & hols 10am–6pm in fine weather only; DM5) 6km southwest of town at MOLFSEE. Here thirty or so beautiful old sixteenth- to nineteenth-century farmhouses and barns from around the Land have been reassembled piece by piece in regional groups to give a picture of 500 years of Schleswig-Holstein rural life. A pottery, bakery, four mills, a forge and a dairy are all worked in the old ways by craftspeople, and their produce is on sale. Many of the houses, incidentally, have tiny cabin beds in which whole families used to sleep; in winter they slept sitting up and huddled together against the cold.

Like Flensburg, Kiel is situated on a fjord (though "inlet" is a more realistic term as this is nothing like as dramatic as the Norwegian variety) and has some good nearby **beaches** that can be reached from the city by boat. (Though you might prefer the emptier beaches a little further away unless you're staying in Kiel itself for a long time.) LABOE, HEIKENDORF and MÖLYENORT are the main beach resorts: at Laboe a 75m monument stands in memory of sailors lost in the two world wars, and a 1943 U-boat is open in the summer months as a **museum**.

Practical details

The **bus station** and the **tourist office** (at Auguste-Viktoria-Str. 16; ☎0431/62230) are both opposite the **Hauptbahnhof**. The tourist office can arrange hotel, pension and private bed and breakfast accommodation. **Hotel and pension** prices in Kiel start at around DM85 for a double: remember that during the Kieler Woche rooms will be extremely difficult to come by. The **youth hostel** is at Johannesstr. 1, Kiel 14 (☎0431/735723). There's also **camping** at the *Falkenstein* site: ask at the tourist office.

Being Schleswig-Holstein's only university town, Kiel is fairly lively. The place to go for music and to find out what else is going on is *Die Pumpe* at Hass Str. 22. In the Bergstrasse is a multi-storey **disco**, with different music on each floor and live music at weekends. For **food**, try one of northern Germany's most mouth-watering sandwich bars at Holsteinstr. 92 (Mon–Fri 7am–6.30pm, Sat 7am–2pm).

From Kiel's Bahnhofsbrücke, the landing stage by the station, **harbour trips** run from July to September, and daily trips go up the Kiel Canal in the second half of August.

The Holstein Switzerland

The so-called **Holstein Switzerland** (*Holsteinische Schweiz*), just south-east of Kiel, has nothing resembling the Alps, so presumably gets its name on account of the **lakes**, of which there are about 140 in all. **The Grosser Plöner See** is the biggest of over a dozen major lakes in this area. The main towns are Plön, Eutin and Malente, all of which are designated *Kurorte*, centres for health-orientated holidays, and offering their many visitors all sorts of sports and leisure facilities. Round about, though, are many smaller and quieter places, linked by boat, footpaths and cycle ways; yet again, the bicycle is an ideal way to get about. **PLÖN** is dominated by its grand late Renaissance **Schloss** – it's open to visitors and usually has art exhibitions and classical concerts. Likewise **EUTIN** has a Schloss, and hosts jazz and opera festivals in the summer season. Though **NEUMÜNSTER** is a sizeable place, it's one of Schleswig-Holstein's few industrial towns, and not somewhere to aim for. It does have a "free-range" zoo on its northwest outskirts, where indigenous animals such as wild boar roam freely.

Rendsburg and the Dänischer Wohld

Thirty kilometres inland from Kiel, **RENDSBURG** has a history as a fortified town and trading centre dating back to the eleventh or twelfth century. Its historic buildings are clustered around the **Altstädter Markt**: the sixteenth-century timbered **Rathaus** is interesting because of its archway, beneath which the street runs. It now houses a small **local museum** (Tues–Sun 10am–5pm), supervised by a curious pair of elderly citizens, and the town's **tourist office** (☎04331/21120). The twelfth-century **Christkirche** is close by and has as the centrepiece of its ornate interior a seventeenth-century Baroque altar; its chancel is also seventeenth-century.

However, it's not so much Rendsburg's old buildings that are impressive as much as three feats of transport engineering – the **Kiel Canal**, the tunnel beneath it and the railway bridge above. Bizarrely, one of the best views of Rendsburg is the aerial view from the train. The Lübeck–Flensburg railway line performs some intriguing gymnastics to cope with crossing the Kiel Canal high enough for shipping to pass beneath, yet getting back to ground level for the Rendsburg railway station a few kilometres further on; a large, gently sloping railway loop is the solution. A four-lane tunnel takes traffic beneath the Canal, and **Europe's longest escalator** runs down to the tunnel for pedestrians.

It's fascinating to watch the enormous ships, often from the CIS and Poland, gliding past weirdly out of scale with the landscape. Even before seagoing ships had access to Rendsburg, however, the town was on an important meeting of ways, as the Eider canal passed through here. It joined the Kiel fjord with the Eider river, providing a North Sea-Baltic link, but for small vessels only. It was completed in the late eighteenth century and Rendsburg grew significantly as a result.

Towards the coast from Rendsburg is the **Dänischer Wohld**, the area between Eckernförde and Kiel. The Kiel Canal runs through it, and the train stops at GETTORF, good for exploring the villages nearby. There are cliffs, quite high in places, along the coast, and the villages are not as developed for tourists as in the Kieler Bucht. Try DÄNISCH-NIENHOF (buses from Kiel) for a stop-over.

Schleswig

It's quite astonishing just how different **SCHLESWIG** is from neighbouring Flensburg. An administrative centre, it has a sleepy, civil-servant pace and lacks Flensburg's commercial bustle. Dozing gently at the water's edge on the beautiful Schlei, Schleswig could almost trick you into thinking nothing had ever happened there. It did, though – in the eighth and ninth centuries the **Vikings**, whose trade routes stretched from the Black Sea to Greenland, had their main North European trading centre here, at a settlement called **Haithabu**. Following the demise of the Vikings around 1000, a new town was founded which became the seat of the Dukes of Gottorf and of Schleswig, and was for a time the seat of the government of Denmark.

The Altstadt

What is now Schleswig's **Altstadt** nestles around the twelfth-century Romanesque and Gothic **Dom**, which has an eleventh-century granite basilica as its foundations, and towers from the last century. (There's an excellent pamphlet in English that provides full details on the interior.) What immediately demands your attention is the 12-metre high **Bordesholm Altar** by Hans Brüggemann, one of Europe's most astonishing pieces of wood-carving. Commissioned by the Duke of Gottorf and carved from oak between 1514 and 1521, it shows nearly 400 figures on a background so intricate it resembles filigree, and it's worth taking binoculars to get a closer look. Legend has it that the Duke had the unfortunate artist blinded after completion of the work, so that he would never again create anything so beautiful. The altar originally stood in the church in the village of Bordesholm, close to Kiel; the enormous carving of **St Christopher** by the door is also Brüggemann's work.

Other specific sights in the Altstadt are few: the oddly ecclesiastical **Rathaus** was built as a Franciscan monastery on the site of the eleventh-century royal court; the ground floor is open daily. Down by the waterside a cluster of tiny fifteenth-century houses makes up the **Holm**, an old fishing village: there's another monastery in the Johanniskloster: phone first to arrange a visit, which costs DM1 (☎04621/26263).

Elswhere in town

Schleswig's unmissable target in the west of town is **Schloss Gottorf**, a white castle with three fortress-like wings from the sixteenth century and a later, more graceful château-style wing from the seventeenth century. (April–Oct daily 9am–5pm, though Mon only the Nydamhalle and medieval art sections are open; Nov–March Tues–Sun 9.30am–4pm.) It stands on an island in the Burgsee, a small lake created by damming off part of the Schlei. Today it's home to the **Landesmuseum**, whose collections are divided around the Schloss itself. The **Nydamhalle** is a separate new building to the left of the castle, housing the pre- and early history sections. Its major treasure is a huge **Nydam boat**, an Iron Age oak rowing boat from around 350AD, and there are wo giant oak gods, male and female, from around this period, as well as many other rtefacts. Another, rather grisly display is of the *Moorleichen*, **peat-bog corpses** over wo thousand years old. The skin and hair of the corpses have been preserved by the eat and tanned like leather. Most shocking are the facial expressions, ranging from he beatific look of someone who was presumably dead before burial, to the utter nguish of another, whose fate can only be imagined.

In another building on the other side of the Schloss is the surprisingly good collection f **twentieth-century art**, which includes work by Munch, Kokoschka, Macke, Nolde, Marcks and others. The main museum in the Schloss itself contains art and crafts from he seventeenth century onwards, somewhat tediously displayed but quite a treasure rove if you feel up to it. Try to see the private chapel, the Gothic hall (medieval art) and he painted *Bauernstube*, a room in rustic style.

Haithabu

More ancient history is on hand at the Haithabu site, which has recently been turned nto a fascinating **Viking Museum** (April to end-Oct daily 9am–6pm; Nov–March Tues–Fri 9am–5pm Sat & Sun 10am–6pm; DM3, ticket also valid for Schloss Gottorf).You can get there in summer by boat (a twenty-minute ride) from the Stadthafen, the town quay that's directly south of the Dom, with a ten-minute walk at he other end, or by bus (in the direction of Kiel). The impetus for excavations at Haithabu was the discovery of a Viking longship, whose retrieval took several years. The ship is now displayed, with models showing how it was constructed, along with a multitude of subsequently unearthed artefacts that give some idea of life in a major Viking centre. The settlement was protected by a ten-metre-high semicircular rampart, and the museum buildings that now stand there are constructed, Viking-fashion, like upturned boats.

Practicalities

The **tourist office** at Flensburgerstr. 7 (May–Sept Mon–Fri 9am–6pm, Sat 9am–noon; closed at lunch in winter; ☎04621/87363) has details of private **bed and breakfasts**. Some of these addresses are in the Holm, but are probably snapped up fast. You could try Frau Tesmer, Süderholmer Str. 48 (☎04621/26388), or Frau Stammberger, Am St. Johanniskloster 4 (☎04621/25195). For small **hotels**, try *Zum Stadtfeld*, Stadfeld 2a (☎04621/23947), or the *Wikinger*, Michaelis Str. 54 (☎04621/25514). Both are just north of the old town and cost around DM30 per person. **Camping** in Schleswig is 3km out in the village of Haddeby, near the Viking Museum (☎04621/32450), and there's a **youth hostel** at Spielkoppel 1 (bus #1 or #2 from the station to opposite the theatre, then walk up the steps known as the Lollfusstreppe (☎04621/23893).

Food and drink

For **food**, the Rathausmarkt has places to sit out when it's warm, and there are several good eating places here. The *Senatorkroog* is a bit on the expensive side, but has a good atmosphere and excellent cooking – especially fish. Between the Holm and the Dom, at Fischbrückstrasse, is the *Ringelnatz* café – a little house, each room with its own character, serving good value food, teas, beer and so on.

Transport

Bikes can be hired from the Bahnhof in summer months, or from the Stadthafen. **Boat hire** is also available at the Stadthafen (Plessenstr.1), or from the sailing school, Segelschule Schlei. In summer **boat trips** run up and down the Schlei, but not every day: get the latest timetable from the tourist office. LINDAUNIS is one boat destination, and has a beautiful sixteenth-century thatched house, the **Lindauhof**.

Around Schleswig

From Schleswig you might follow the River Schlei by boat or bus through the countryside to the sea, via LINDAU, LINDAUNIS and ARNIS (claiming to be Germany's smallest town) to KAPPELN. The coast between there and Eckernförde has **swimming beaches**. DAMP 2000 is a modernistic resort built in the early seventies, but the rest is much more natural, until you get to **ECKERNFÖRDE**, which has a *Kurzentrum* (health resort facilities) tacked on to the **Altstadt** and harbour. The old part of town is pretty enough, and the **Nikolaikirche** worth looking into for its carved, dark oak, and beautifully painted choir ceiling and altar. A new **local museum** (Tues–Sun 10am–5pm; irregular hours Oct–March) has just been opened up in the old Rathaus, mainly with collections to demonstrate life earlier this century. One room is a typical *Flüchtlingszimmer* or refugee-room, with a collection of simple belongings and mementos brought on a long trek from the east. It is a reminder that, just after the war, Schleswig-Holstein became the new home of many **refugees** who left behind virtually all their worldly goods and trekked for weeks or months to avoid living in the Soviet sector. **Eating** in Eckernförde seems to centre around the Frau-Clara-Strasse. The **youth hostel**, at the southern end of town (Sehestedter Str. 27; ☎04351/2154), has views over the sea. The **tourist office** has lists of bed and breakfast accommodation, and is situated in the entrance to the sea-water swimming-pool in Preusserstrasse.

Flensburg and Glücksburg

German today, of course, though only a few kilometres from the Danish border, **FLENSBURG** was once Denmark's richest merchant city, with two hundred ships plying the Baltic Sea. With boats coming and going, Denmark so close and the past connection of trade with the West Indies, Flensburg, small as it may be, is not the parochial town its size may suggest. It stands at the head of the gentle Flensburger Fjord, originally just along the waterfront, though later building has crept slowly up the surrounding hillsides. Ten years ago Flensburg was rather shabby, but renovation programmes have rescued many of the **merchants' houses**, yards and **old warehouses**. The only pity is that the town is separated from the water, and effectively cut in half by wide, fast roads which ensure that traffic dominates outside the pedestrian zones.

The town

Most of the interesting buildings are either on the **Holm,** the Grosse Strasse and the Norder Strasse, which together make up a two-kilometre-long **pedestrian zone** running roughly from the Südermarkt (South Market) to the Nordertor (Northern Gate), or between this road and the water. Buses to Flensburg, or into town from the Hauptbahnhof will deliver you at the bus station, from which a footbridge leads over the road and straight towards the Holm. If you plan to see everything in one go, turn left and go down to the Südermarkt with its fourteenth-century **Nikolaikirche** and nearby twelfth-century **Johanniskirche**. If you then head back up the Holm you come to house no. 19/21 on the corner of the Nikolaistrasse, a sixteenth-century merchant's house and courtyard and, a little higher up on the opposite side at no. 10, another impressive facade. At the back of no. 24 is the seven-storey **West Indies Warehouse**, dating from the eighteenth century but extensively restored.

It was the West Indies' sugar trade, combined with Flensburg's pure spring water, that got the Flensburg **rum business** underway – at the last count there were 58 varieties being produced here, and if you are around in the winter, you should try to benefit from them. Apart from the distillery trade, Flensburg's commercial bases have been its port, ship-building, whaling and oyster-fishing. At the Nordermarkt, Neptune's fountain pumps out the famous rum-making **spring water**.

The Marienkirche that also stands here was begun in the thirteenth century, and between it and the square are **covered arcades**, the *Schrangen*, where traders' stalls stood from the sixteenth century. The Kompagnie Strasse goes down to the right, to the Kompagnietor, where a plaque reveals something of the Northern mercantile philosophy that behaving justly will, with the help of God, always bring large profits.

Back on the main street, at Nordertor 6, the helpful **tourist office** is situated in a gabled house (open Mon–Fri 9am–5pm June–Sept; rest of year Mon–Fri 9am–1pm; ☎0461/25901). Further along on the left is a flight of stone steps known as the Marientreppe, and if you can make it up the 150 or so steps there's a good view across the harbour to the other side of town, which was traditionally more for working people than the rich merchants who lived on this side of the water.

The **Schiffahrtsmuseum** (Schiffbrücke 39; Tues–Sat 10am–5pm, Sun 10am–1pm) was opened a couple of years ago in the old customs house, and shows the history of the harbour and its trade, along with fetching model ships made by sailors. On up past the sixteenth-century **Kaufmannshaus** you come to the Nordertor, the so-called "gateway to the North", a step-gabled building put up in 1595. If you still have the energy, there's the **Städtisches Museum** at Lutherplatz 1 (Tues–Sat 10–5pm, Sun 10am–1pm; free) recording town history and everyday life.

Practicalities

Flensburg's **youth hostel** is at Fichte Str. 16 (☎0461/37742) which is quite a way out of town in the suburb of Kielseng, near the stadium, buses from the bus station to Glücksburg will take you there. **Hotels** in town, all with prices around DM30–35 per person, are the *Hotel am Stadtpark*, Nordergraben 70 (parallel with the Holm; ☎0461/24900); *Hotel Zoega*, Norderstrasse 33 (☎0461/23508); and *Flensborg-Hus*, Norderstr. 76. **Camping** is not available; there is, however, a **Mitwohnzentrale** at Jürgensplatz 1 (Mon–Fri 9am–noon & 3–7pm, Sat & Sun 10am–1pm; ☎0461/17961).

Eating and entertainment

The pedestrian zone, especially around the Nordermarkt, has plenty of eating places – *Das Kleine Restaurant* at Grosse Str. 73 has good salads, and there are snacks at the *Eis und Milch Bar* on the corner of Grosse Strasse and Kompagniestrasse.

To find out what's going on, pick up the monthly *Flensburger Programm* from the tourist office, or the alternative magazine called *Hallimasch*. Both will probably mention the *Galerie Musikkneipe* at Holm 66, which has live music – quite well known names – and food. There are also concerts at the *Lagerhaus*, Segelmacher Str. 10; the very fine **café** here seems in danger of closing. *Kunstwerk*, Norderstr. 107–109, is a café-*Kneipe* that does **breakfasts** till well into the afternoon.

Glücksburg

A little further down the Flensburg fjord towards the sea is **GLÜCKSBURG**, a fairly typical therapy town with beaches, forest walks, a first-rate sea-water swimming-pool and a 400-year-old **Schloss** – a little austere, but actually rather impressive, especially when floodlit, because it stands in a lake; you may recognise it from the 10 Pfennig postage stamp. Visiting is by guided tour only (summer 10am–4.30pm, winter 10am–noon & 2–4pm: tours in German, but you might find someone to speak English; closed Jan–Feb). The Schloss has a large collection of tapestries, leather wallcoverings and paintings. **Classical music concerts** are held there during the summer. Finally, tourist information on Glucksburg is available from Sandwigstr. 1 (☎04631/921).

Angeln

The land to the east of the railway line between Flensburg and Schleswig is **Angeln**, home of the Angles who came to Britain in the fifth century. They must have felt at home there: Angeln's slightly hilly landscape, with clusters of woodland and fields divided by hedgerows and pocked with marshes is far more reminiscent of England than of most of Germany. Many of the place names around this area are Danish in origin: names ending *-by* are familiar in English, of course (Grimsby, for example), but in German it's not pronounced *bee* but rather as in de*but*. The larger villages here have some unimpressive modern buildings, but in the smaller hamlets, and along the lanes, you come across plenty of **traditional farmhouses**. Unique to Angeln are the **early churches** built of enormous blocks of granite – the oldest, with a thirteenth-century font, is in **SÖRUP**, roughly 20km south and east of Flensburg. HUSBY, NORDERBRARUP, EGGEBEK, MUNKBRARUP, OEVERSEE and STRUXDORF all have thirteenth-century Romanesque churches too. Many small areas are designated nature reserves, such as the peat-bog of **Satrupholmer Moor**. The **Torsberger Moor** is the site of major archaeological finds of early Germanic settlements, though the best place to find out more and actually see anything of this is in the Schloss Gottorf museum in Schleswig.

Getting around this area is not exactly straightforward: trains will take you from Flensburg to Sörup and on either to Schleswig or via Süderbrarup to Eckernförde. Buses, however, are notoriously rare. The best way to explore the countryside is under your own steam – hire a bike in Flensburg or Schleswig and you can explore the coastline (beaches and campsites all the way along) as well as the villages with their Danish-sounding names. Flensburg tourist office has a cycle map called *Rad und Wanderwege*, indicating touring routes in this area. Most of the roads are pretty quiet, and there are some special routes, such as the old railway line from Tarp to Süderbrarup.

South of the Schlei, thus not really in Angeln, is the **Hüttener Berge nature reserve** (birdlife and wild deer). Again, a bike would be the ideal way to explore here.

North Friesland

North Friesland, East Friesland and Dutch Friesland are all closely linked – culturally and linguistically. They share a history of battling to preserve their precious, flat land and islands from the sea's stormy threats, their trees are bent by the constant on-shore wind, while indoors hot tea and stiff alcohol help the winter pass. With the exception of Sylt, this part of Germany is little visited, and for obvious reasons: towns are few, the landscape bleak and the coastline not a prime choice for summer bathing. But a few days here can be well spent: given time, North Friesland's rugged individuality becomes more and more likeable, and, if you're into getting back to nature, its flora and fauna (birds especially) are hard to beat. The towns of Niebüll and Husum have enough to detain you for a morning at least, Niebüll forming a jumping-off point for Sylt, the largest and best-developed of the North Friesian Islands.

Niebüll

A one-horse town in Schleswig-Holstein's farthest-flung northwest corner isn't top of anyone's list of places to visit, but **NIEBÜLL** has one or two surprises. First, it's from here that the train runs across that thin strip of land to the island of Sylt; secondly, there are two terrific museums each dedicated to artists who fell foul of the Third Reich – Emil Nolde, and less famously, Richard Haizmann.

INTO DENMARK

From both Flensburg and Niebüll it's very easy to get across the border into Denmark. Boats run regularly from Flensburg to SØNDERBURG, and there are regular bus connections. It's definitely worth making a **short trip** by bus from either Flensburg or Niebüll to TØNDER, the **oldest market town** in Denmark, first mentioned in the twelfth century. The semicircular old town has at its heart the lovely **Kristikirk**, with **small gabled houses** round about. Some, such as in the Uldgade, are so tiny you can touch the roof. On the last weekend of August Tønder hosts a large international **jazz and blues festival**, but all through the summer there are music performances in the market place. The extremely helpful **tourist office** (they speak excellent English – proof that you're in Scandinavia) is at Ostergade 2A (☎721220), right in the centre of the old town. For further information and advice, see our guide to *Scandinavia*.

The **Richard-Haizmann-Museum** (April–Oct Tues–Sun 10am–noon & 2–5pm) in the Rathaus is dedicated to the artist's sculpture, pottery and pictures. Haizmann was exiled to Schleswig-Holstein in what was termed "inner emigration" following the banning of his work by the Nazis. Some of it had been displayed in the famous 1930s Berlin exhibition of so-called degenerate art and was subsequently destroyed. Haizmann's work bears the influence of oriental and African art, and is beautifully displayed in a museum created by the curator and the artist's widow, who struggled for many years to open a museum, achieving her ambition only days before her death.

The **Nolde Museum** (March–Oct Tues–Sun 10am–6pm; Nov 10am–5pm; Dec–Feb closed; DM4) stands alone in the countryside at SEEBÜLL (about 5km from Niebüll) in the house and gallery that Nolde built in the 1950s. These were the years when Nolde could be acknowledged again after his work had been condemned by the Nazis. A novel by postwar author Siegfried Lenz, *Die Deutschstunde* (The German Lesson), has as a main character an artist, painting in secret during the war, who was based on Nolde. The museum – marred by its unhelpful staff – can be very full in summer, but if you are there on a quiet day you may have the luxury of enjoying Nolde's vibrant colours on your own. His expressionistic paintings have some themes that are quite brutal and hard to take – the brilliant flower and landscape series are simpler, but powerful, nonetheless. In accordance with Nolde's wishes, the shop sells books and postcards, but no reproductions. A bus runs out to the museum from Niebüll, and the way is clearly signposted if you are travelling by car or bike.

Niebüll itself has little else to see: there's a small **Friesian museum** at Osterweg 76 (open only by arrangement with Frau Scheck: ☎04661/3656) which is laid out to resemble a seventeenth-century farmouse, and a small **natural history museum** open from May to mid-September, at Hauptstr. 108. You can stay at the **youth hostel** at Deezbülldeich (☎04661/8762) or try the *Insel-Pension*, close to the station at Gotteskoogstr. 4 (☎04661/2145).

Husum

HUSUM's small **harbour** is virtually in the middle of town and must have given welcome shelter to generations of fishermen returning from the stormy North Sea. As a town, it's a mixture of small-scale grandeur and workaday simplicity, filled with fishy smells that waft in from the harbour, and with a sufficient scattering of interesting buildings to catch the imagination.

Husum is perhaps best known in association with the name of **Theodor Storm**, a nineteenth-century novelist, poet and civil figure (it was Storm who gave the town its rather unfair title "die graue Stadt am Meer" – the grey town by the sea), who was especially active in Schleswig-Holstein's struggle to remain independent of the expanding Prussian empire. It says much about the town that the three most lauded sights are Theodor Storm's birthplace, his later home (now the Theodor Storm museum), and the Theodor Storm memorial in the Schlosspark – you may even find yourself staying at the Theodor Storm youth hostel.

One of Husum's busiest times of the year for tourism is the spring, when the **Schlosspark** turns into a great sea of mauve crocuses – they were originally planted in the Middle Ages by monks who had a monastery on this site, possibly as a source of saffron. Other visitors pass through Husum on their way to Helgoland (a ferry runs from here) or on trips to the Halligen islands. Especially in winter, Husum, small as it is, provides a welcome change from the blustery bleakness of the Friesian landscape – it's when you think of the isolated houses out on the dyke or on the islands that Husum's importance suddenly becomes clear.

Arrival – and the town centre

Both bus station and Hauptbahnhof are within easy walking distance (up the Herzog-Adolf-Strasse and then left) of the centre of town – the centre being the area south of the castle and north of the harbour, marked by the broad Grosse Strasse which opens out into the **Markt**: both are lined with large houses, mainly eighteenth- and nineteenth-century (though there are one or two beautiful seventeenth-century gabled buildings reminiscent of Lübeck), most of which now have shops on their ground floors. Here too is the step-gabled fourteenth-century **manor house**, supposed to be the oldest building in the town, though its sandstone pillars and doorway were added in the seventeenth and eighteenth centuries. On the north side stands the seventeenth-century **Rathaus**, with the **tourist office** (☎04841/666133) on its ground floor. They have a lot of local information (including a good free English pamphlet, *A Stroll Through the Town*), and provide hotel and pension lists, though not a booking service.

If you turn northwards by the town hall you come into the **Schlossgang** (castle walk), a narrow walkway leading up past small houses, a couple of cafés and craft/giftshops to the **Schloss**. The small house over on the left, the former **gatehouse**, is actually more attractive than the Schloss at a distance – it has retained its ornate Renaissance features, whereas the Schloss itself, built at the same time, underwent extensive modification in the eighteenth century, giving it a **Baroque interior** with fine sandstone and alabaster fireplaces. There's now a **museum** (April–Oct Tue–Sun 10am–noon & 2–5pm) here too, with collections of furniture and everyday objects from North Friesland.

Back past the Grosse Strasse, and a hundred metres or so further south is the **Schiffbrücke**, an inner harbour busy with fishing boats; it's also the place where the ferry takes shelter in winter. One famous catch landed here is *Husumer Krabben* – not crabs, confusingly, but very tasty little brown shrimps. (They are found in abundance on local menus, especially in the form of *Husumer Krabbensuppe*, a soup that often comes topped with whipped cream.) In summer a **shrimp stall** is open on the quayside, selling the freshly boiled catch. The harbour is lined on three sides by eighteenth- and nineteenth-century houses, amongst which the *Hotel zur Grauen Stadt am Meer* stands out. It has a very good restaurant serving **local fish** – rather *bürgerlich*, but better value than the touristy fish restaurant on the corner nearby. Another good place for food and drink near here is the *Café Schöneck* on the corner, with steps leading up to its door. All the rooms inside are crammed with ancient Friesian furniture, and masses of old pictures (which are for sale). It has very good soups, a vast array of warming alcoholic hot drinks, and Danish pastries far above the usual standard to be found south of the Danish border.

Up the small street beside this (the Wasserreihe) on the right is the **Theodor-Storm-Museum** (generally Tues–Sat 10am–4pm; DM1.50), in the house he owned from 1866–1880 when at the height of his career. With many original documents and manuscripts, and as the base of the Theodor Storm society, it is obviously chiefly of interest to Storm fans. However, the house is worth catching as an example of nineteenth-century middle-class lifestyle in this area, as the rooms still have their original furnishings. Storm's wood-panelled study, where he produced about twenty of his novels, has a display of documents, such as correspondence with the Russian novelist Turgenev and other literary figures. The Wasserreihe itself is a narrow and characterful street, with several typical **fishing family houses**.

Another of Husum's museums is the **Ostenfelder Bauernhaus Museum** at Nordhusumer Str. 13 (June–Oct Tue–Sun 10am–noon & 2–5pm), a reconstructed seventeenth-century farmhouse. Also situated here is the **North Friesian Museum** in the Nissenhaus (Herzog-Adolf-Str. 25, April–Oct Mon–Fri 10am–noon & 2–5pm, Sun 10am–5pm; closes at 4pm Nov–March). It was founded in the early 1930s by local-boy-made-good Ludwig Nissen, who made his fortune in the United States, and is especially interesting on the geological background of the area, flood control and town history. It also houses a valuable collection of American paintings, unfortunately hidden away.

Practicalities

Most of the **hotels** start at DM40 per person, and the *Hotel zur Grauen Stadt am Meer*, mentioned above (☎04841/2236) is good if it fits your budget. *Gästehaus Fischer*, Brinkmann Str. 41 (☎04841/2686), is cheaper at DM28. Many private houses offer bed and breakfast at DM15–20 per person – these often fill in summer, so it's best not to turn up late in the day. The **youth hostel** is at Schobüller Str. 34 (☎04841/2714), in the northeast corner of the town. There are two **campsites** near Husum – a bus runs hourly in summer to the one at Dockkoog, right by the beach.

As well as the restaurants already mentioned, there's no lack of traditional **places to eat**. *Dragseth's Gasthof* at Zingel 11 is a sixteenth-century house with a small gallery and tea shop – offering a good selection of food including vegetarian dishes. The *Husumer Speicher* is a converted warehouse at Hafen Str. 17, and this is where live music and entertainment happen in Husum. You'll find a **launderette** at Norderstr. 12 and **bicycle hire** at *Peter Schurr*, Schulstr. 4 (☎04841/4465). **Ferries** to Helgoland and the Halligen islands leave from the Aussenhafen (outer harbour) – along the Hafenstrasse from the Schiffbrücke and beyond. There's a regular bus service from the station to the island of Nordstrand.

The North Friesian Islands

The **North Friesian Islands** lie scattered off the coast, storm-battered for centuries and until recently the home of a small population of fisherpeople and farmers eking out a fragile existence: today tourism is by far the biggest source of income. The land is so flat directly offshore that the sea retreats to reveal large areas of mud-flat – the **Watt*** – which have their own sensitive ecosystem, including masses of birdlife. The main islands are Föhr, Amrum and Sylt, which although little more than a strip of land running north–south, is touristically the most developed and sophisticated. They are all family holiday centres, with holiday homes and riding, tennis and windsurfing facilities. In season, all are likely to be very busy.

---

*It's possible – tides permitting and only under the supervision of an experienced guide – to walk across the Watt from Amrum to Föhr. For more information and details of tours, contact the *Schutzstation Wattenmeer* in Hörnum (Tues–Sun 10am–noon & 3–5pm; ☎04653/1093).

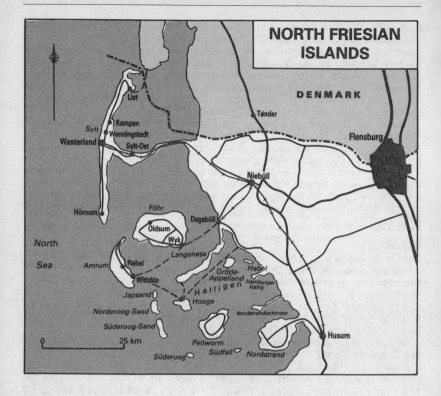

Sylt

Sylt is a different kettle of fish altogether from the other homely islands. It's a favourite among monied Germans, who visit to mix business with pleasure and impress their guests with second homes in the sun. As a result, the island is heavily populated during the major holidays (including Christmas and Easter), and prices for both eating out and accommodation can be high. Such is the demand for **rooms** here that unless you have booked a couple of months in advance – regardless of when you visit – you could be unlucky. To add to complications, there's no central tourist office – each resort on the island has its own agency. However, a last minute (but not cheap) **accommodation booking service** operates on ☎04651/19412.

Westerland

WESTERLAND is Sylt's main town and the hub for bus and train connections. It's considered rather chic and glamorous: a place to dress up for an evening in the **casino** on Andreas-Nilsen-Strasse rather than stomp around in wellington boots. For trad German food try *Alte Friesenstube*, Gaadt 4, housed in one of the oldest buildings on the islandOutside of Westerland the island is quieter (though full of holiday houses). Above all there's plenty of **fine sandy beach** here; the island is shaped rather like a T on its side – Westerland is on the stalk (west side) and the cross-stroke runs north to south for about 40 kilometres in a narrow strip, under a kilometre wide, lined with beaches, dunes and small cliffs (*Rote Kliffen*) which make for a good hiking route.

North of Westerland

North of Westerland is **KAMPEN**, an exclusive enclave of 650 monied inhabitants. Formerly a place of inspiration for such writers as Thomas Mann, Emil Nolde and Karl Zuckmayer, its tiny streets are today packed with antique shops, gourmet restaurants and expensive clothes shops. It's doubtful whether such a large amount of luxury is spread so thick on so small an area anywhere else in Germany.

Between Kampen and List is Sylt's most famous stretch of beach, **Buhne 16**, a haven for naked (but gold-dripping) sun worshippers. After sunset the place to be is *Gogärtchen* on the strip known as "Whiskystrasse".

LIST, with a population of 2000 and a tiny harbour, has Germany's largest expanse of sand dune around it. There's little to do here save sample some fresh fish or catch one of the daily ferries to the port of HAVENBY on the Danish island of RØMØ.

Practicalities

A regular **bus service** runs between Westerland, Kampen and List. Sylt is joined to the mainland at Niebüll by a narrow causeway along which **trains** run – if you want to take a car, it has to be loaded onto the train first. Accommodation is best found through the tourist office in Westerland (☎04682/861). The only **youth hostel** is at Friesenplatz 2 (☎04653/294) in HÖRNUM at the southern tip of the island. **Ferries** to the islands of Amrum and Föhr leave from Hörnum.

Föhr

Föhr is Sylt's nearest neighbour, but quite different in character. Outside of a few bars and cafés nightlife is non-existent, and accommodation is reasonably easy to come by. Ferries from DAGEBÜLL on the mainland arrive at **WYK**, the island's main town. It's a peaceful old place with a thirteenth-century church, a harbour and precious little else. Depending on finances you can either **hire a taxi** for around DM11 and go for a one-hour ride around the island (try the taxi office at Birkenweg 11, or call ☎04681/3705 for more details on this), or **hire a bike** (from one of the numerous shops displaying a *Fahrrad Verleih* sign; around DM15 per week). First place to cycle to should be the village of **NIEBLUM** to the west, an exceptionally quaint and picturesque place of old gabled and thatched cottages along cobbled streets, with an ancient (thirteenth-century) church. Listen to the local dialect: a mixture of Plat-Deutsch, Hoch-Deutsch and Friesian, which is itself a mix of Danish, Dutch and English. There's a **campsite** and a **youth hostel** in Wyk at Fehrstieg 41 (☎04681/2010).

Amrum and Pellworm

Amrum, is a less exciting prospect than the previous islands. Ferries land at the town of WITTDÜN, where, if you're not careful, you'll find yourself stuck since ferries and local buses aren't synchronised. The village has a one-horse feel, though you can hire bikes and there's a tourist office on the edge of the harbour carpark. Walks, beaches, seabirds and sports are the order of the day here, and the bracing breeze becomes quite enjoyable in the end. The **youth hostel** in Wittdün is at Mittelstr. 1 (☎04681/2355). Most visitors book into hotels and bed and breakfasts for a week or more, so it is easiest to ask the tourist office about vacancies in season – they may be hard to come by.

Pellworm

Pellworm, to the southeast of Amrum (ferry from Nordstrand), has thirteenth- and seventeenth-century churches bearing witness to its history, and hardly anything else. Few visitors bother with the island because of its lack of attractions and facilities. The future may be anticipated by Pellworm's huge **solar collector** (it's one of Germany's sunniest places, which bodes well for visitors), generating 280,000 kilowatt hours per year. A small **Watt museum** holds the former local postman's lifetime collection of finds from the Watt. Tourist information (☎04844/544) is right by the harbour.

The Halligen

Smaller, and almost at sea-level, is another, distinct group of undyked islands – the **Halligen**. These last remnants of land are scarcely above sea-level; as you approach them by ship all you see are a few houses apparently sitting on the waves. Once you set foot on dry land you discover that these houses are built on specially constructed hummocks that stay dry when the rest of the land is washed over by winter storms. The land is really good only for grazing sheep, and bed and breakfast is a major source of income for the Hallig inhabitants nowadays. Even more than on the mainland, few young people are interested in staying on to maintain old ways of life, and the Halligen seem set for a slow but sure period of decline.

The islands

The main Halligen are inhabited, but the tiny Hallig Habel is a nature reserve, with just one family present in summer; the even smaller Norderoog is a **bird breeding sanctuary**, and also just has a summertime warden. The main islands, **Nordstrand** and Pellworm (together with Hamburger Hallig and Nordstrandischmoor), used to form a larger island known as **Alt-Nordstrand**, or just Strand, with five quays and some fifty-nine churches and chapels – a major settlement in its time. A tidal wave in 1634 created today's geography. Nordstrand is now connected to the mainland by a narrow causeway, as are Nordstrandischmoor and Hamburger Hallig; the latter has become a virtual peninsula because of silting up on both sides of its link with the mainland.

Hallig Langeness is similarly connected to Hallig Oland, which in turn has a mainland connection, but Föhr, Amrum and Pellworm, plus Hallig Hooge, are reached by peak-season **ferries** running from Dagebüll and Schlüttsiel (run by *WDR* lines) and from Nordstrand (*Kurt Paulsen*). All the tourist offices and some railway stations have leaflets and posters with details of ferries. It doesn't take long to look round a Hallig – so unless you feel like communing with wind and water the few hours between boats may be all the time you want to spend there.

Eiderstedt and Friedrichstadt Halbinsel

Directly north of the Eider estuary is the peninsula (*Halbinsel*) of Eiderstedt. This is where **TÖNNING** and **ST PETER ORDING** are to be found. These are both little harbour towns, not spectacular, but possible bases for exploring the countryside. Tönning, for instance, is right by the Katinger Watt, while St Peter Ording has 12km of beaches, backed by forest and dunes. Both towns have extensive camping facilities.

FRIEDRICHSTADT is certainly worth a look – a small corner of Holland apparently transported to North Friesland. It was built in the 1620s by Dutch settlers with the encouragement of Duke Friedrich III, who rather hoped it would develop into a major commercial town. It didn't, but the town, complete with its canals and bridges, remains a small gem of Dutch Renaissance architecture in an unlikely setting.

Between the Eider and Hamburg

Between the Elbe and the Eider is the area of **Dithmarschen**, with **Heide** at its centre. Coming here from the west, incidentally, you can bypass Hamburg by crossing the Elbe by ferry from Wischhafen (north of Stade) to Glückstadt.

The railway line between Friedrichstadt and Hamburg travels via Heide to **Meldorf**, then Itzehoe, providing a good exploring route. With your own transport it's possible to stop off and explore the area around **Marne** (the Art Nouveau town hall is worth a look if you go) and the "koog" area near the coast – **Friedrichskoog**, for example, is a small, pretty shrimp-fishing town with beaches.

Dithmarschen

The region encircled by the waters of the North Sea, the Eider, the Kiel Canal and the Elbe is **Dithmarschen**. Though Heide is the market town today, nearby Meldorf was originally more important. **Dyking** of Dithmarschen began around the fifth century AD. Maybe the struggle to preserve the land they worked from the ravages of the sea made the Dithmarschen peasants especially defensive of their property – in the thirteenth century they expelled the nobility from Dithmarschen and founded an independent peasants' republic. The nobility never returned, and Dithmarschen gained a reputation for being an individualistic stronghold.

West of Heide is the seaside town of **BÜSUM**, which has good beaches, but is a fairly staid, family resort. Better are the far less busy **beaches** that run north of Büsum as far as the Eider. Boats run daily from Büsum to Helgoland in the summer. This whole coast is dyked and the mouth of the Eider barred against tidal floods (which used to rush 100km inland) by the *Eidersperrwerk*, which has a similar function to the Thames barrier. (You can cross the barrier by road, towards Tönning and St Peter Ording.)

Dithmarschen is covered by a network of some 1500km of signposted **cycle paths**, so you can tour away from the traffic, which is in any case light. **Cycle maps** are available from the tourist offices and bookshops; three maps, DM9.80 each, cover the area.

HEIDE itself is little more than a blip on the horizon, and distinguished only by its vast market square and the ancient stones that mark a burial ground from 2600BC. These stones and the small **museum** at Brahmstr. 8 (prehistory and local history; April–Sept Tues–Fri 9am–noon & 2–5pm, Sun 10am–5pm; Oct–March Tues–Fri 2–5pm, Sun 10am–5pm; free) are close to the unusual water tower. **Hotels** start at around DM35 per person (such as *Hotel zur Markthalle* on the market place), but there are plenty of private bed and breakfast possibilities for about DM15. You can ask at the **tourist office** in the Rathaus (signposted from the market place; ☎0484/699117) for addresses.

MELDORF was once the capital of the Dithmarschen peasants' republic, and was the first town in the area to have a church, in 826. On the site of that church now stands the Johanniskirche – thirteenth-century but modified last century. Finally, at the **Dithmarscher Landesmuseum** in Bütjestr. 4 (March–Oct Tue–Fri 9am–5.30pm, Sat & Sun 11am–4pm; Nov–Feb Sat & Sun only), you can be enthralled by models showing how the dyking and drainage process works.

travel details

Trains

From Hamburg to Lübeck (2 an hour; 40min); Kiel (2; 1hr 30min); Rendsburg (2; 1hr 35min); Schleswig (2; 1hr 50min); Flensburg (2; 2hr 15min); Husum (2; 2hr).

From Kiel to Lübeck (1 an hour; 1hr 25min); Flensburg (1; 1hr 10min); Rendsburg (10 daily; 30min); Schleswig (9 daily; 50min); Husum (9 daily; 1hr 25min).

Ferries

From Nordstrand to Pellworm (winter 3 daily; summer 5 daily; 45–60min).

From Dagebüll to Föhr (winter 7 daily, summer 10 daily; 45min; Amrum (winter 5 daily, summer 8 daily; 2hr).

From Schlüttsiel to Hallig Hooge (1; 1 hr 15min); Hallig Langeness (1; 1hr 15min); Amrum (1; 2hr 15min).

From Hamburg to Harwich (1 every other day; 20hr 30min).

CHAPTER EIGHT

MECKLENBURG-LOWER POMERANIA

Mecklenburg-Lower Pomerania (*Mecklenburg-Vorpommern*) is eastern Germany's maritime province. The tideless Baltic Sea laps at the slim coastline of some 370km, while the rivers Elbe and Oder form natural borders to the west and east; to the south is a spacious lakeland which is the most thinly populated part of Germany. The Land is something of a compromise creation: most of its territory once belonged to the former Grand Duchy of Mecklenburg; the remainder is the German rump (not deemed to be viable as a Land in its own right) of the ancient and much-disputed province of Pomerania, the vast majority of which was ceded to Poland in 1945. Probably because of its diversity, it looks like shaping up to be the most politically unpredictable of all the Länder: although the CDU hold power, even the support of their FDP coalition partners is insufficient to give them an overall parliamentary majority, and the reformed Communists continue to enjoy an unusually high degree of support.

From **Wismar** at the western end of the province, the coastal landscape gradually changes from flat indented shores to the windswept dunes behind **Rostock**, the chief port and largest city. Further east, marking the start of the surviving German part of Pomerania, is **Stralsund**, whose grand Hanseatic buildings look across a narrow channel to **Rügen**, Germany's largest island, characterised by dramatic landscapes as chalky cliffs rise steeply from the sea. Beyond here, the coast curves southeastwards towards the sandy island of **Usedom**, and the Polish border. During the summer the coast is overrun by holiday-makers, but for the rest of the year the region returns to a peaceful emptiness, and a Sunday afternoon atmosphere descends on even the larger towns.

Inland, the great **Mecklenburg Lake Plateau** tilts gently south, with few major towns disturbing the rural landscape until Berlin, about 300km away. This, eastern Germany's granary, is a real backwater and has changed little since debt-enslaved peasants worked the land for their aristocratic masters. The GDR era left a surprisingly small mark around here, mainly manifesting itself in the shape of ugly blocks of flats next to villages. The greatest change is about to come, as western-style tourism discovers the potential of this quietly scenic part of the country. For the moment, however, it's a beautiful land of innumerable lakes and ancient forests almost untouched by human habitation.

The Land capital and former ducal residence of **Schwerin** in the northwest seems disproportionately sophisticated and elegant in such a rustic region; it escaped the ravages of wartime bombs, so its Baroque and Neoclassical architecture is romantically faded but not derelict as in so many other places. Not far southwest lies **Ludwigslust**, which was temporarily the dukes' main seat in the eighteenth century, and is still home to the region's most unspoilt castle. A little further northeast, picturesque **Güstrow** was the ducal summer residence, and makes an ideal base for exploring the lakes. **Neubrandenburg**, 100km east of Schwerin, is on the very edge of the lake district, with a few medieval remnants, but the Baroque townscape of **Neustrelitz,** 30km or so to the south, makes a more attractive destination.

TRAVELLING IN THE FORMER GDR

The places described in this and the following four chapters, with the exception of western Berlin, constituted, until 1990, the Communist-run **German Democratic Republic** (GDR). Although the two German states are now fully united, differences between them are still very marked, and the east is undergoing a process of change which will take until the end of the century at least to complete. Therefore, some information in these chapters is likely to date quickly, and it's important to be aware of the following:

• **Streets** are being renamed, with all Communist references purged. This has already been done in some towns; others are using a mixture of old and new names, while some have yet to take the step. We've used the most up-to-date names in the guide.

• **Telephoning** presents a major headache; not only is the eastern network still separate, it uses a nightmarish system of variable codes for both incoming and outgoing calls. Because of this, it has been impossible to include codes in these chapters; you must always enquire what it is at a post office or exchange from the place where you intend to make the call.

• **Service** was a concept completely foreign to the GDR mentality. Many people have quickly adapted to the new market demands, but expect to have to put up with plenty of surly indifference, even in tourist offices, hotels and restaurants.

• **Hotels** listed here are liable to closure, whether permanent (because no buyer can be found) or temporary (for refurbishment). Equally, many new hotels are likely to be opened, as supply falls well below demand, particularly in the cities. The **youth hostel** situation is similarly fluid; already many have been closed, and may not re-open.

• **Private rooms**, in contrast to western Germany, are now readily available almost everywhere, and are an excellent means of making contact with the locals, who still look on western tourists as having novelty value.

• **Restaurants** are likewise affected by moves towards privitisation. For the most part, the standard of food served is generally well below what you'd expect in western Germany.

• **Public transport** services will probably be sharply curtailed in the next few years. The most drastic effect is likely to be on the railway network, which retains a myriad number of uneconomic branch lines.

• **Roads** are generally in a far poorer state of repair than in western Germany; petrol stations are fewer.

• **Museums and monuments** will often be closed in whole or part, as attempts are made to remedy years of neglect. Expect the opening times and admission prices we've given to be subject to considerable fluctuations. Some castles and palaces are currently the subject of claims by dispossessed former owners; if these are successful, they may be shut to the public in future.

• **Prices** quoted are based on rates in spring 1992, but these may be subject to wild fluctuations, particularly in the case of hotels undergoing refurbishments. In general, though, prices of almost everything are lower than in the west, and are likely to remain so for a few years yet.

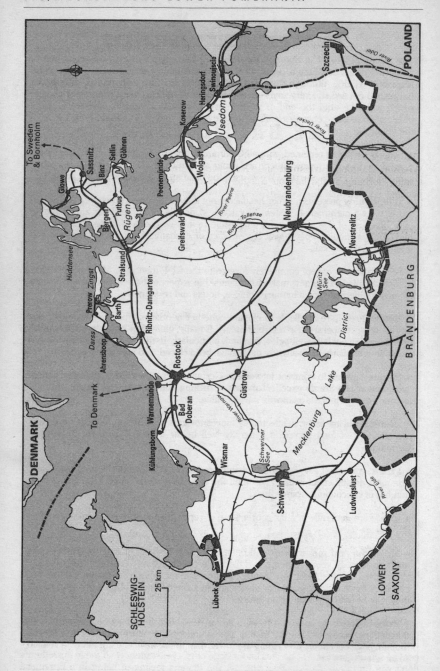

Travel along the coast and inland is fairly easy by train and there are many regional bus routes. In the heavily touristed areas, such as the Baltic coast and the main spots in the lake district, plentiful **accommodation** in private rooms is readily available at reasonable prices. The larger towns also have at least one hotel to their name, and new places are opening up all the time. Camping shouldn't be a problem with a large number of official sites and an ever-increasing number of smaller private ones.

THE BALTIC COAST

The towns of the Baltic coast had their heyday in the Middle Ages. At that time **Wismar, Rostock, Stralsund** and **Greifswald** were important centres of merchant trading, forming a vital link on Northern Europe's east-west shipping routes. They became so rich that they could override traditional domination by the aristocracy, instead joining the **Hanseatic League**, a federation of towns along the entire German coast that represented their economic interests nationally and abroad. But once merchant shipping spread to the Americas and the Far East, the Baltic Sea routes lost their importance and the coastal towns went into decline: the final nail in the coffin was the disastrous Thirty Years' War, which resulted in this entire stretch of coast going to the Swedish Empire. Wismar and Stralsund, in particular, were turned into Swedish garrison towns and exploited for all they were worth, though little evidence of this period remains today.

The medieval townscapes took a battering in 1944, and suffered from lack of attention in the immediate postwar years, when aesthetics took a back seat to rehousing the population in soulless modern estates. However, restoration work is well underway in the historic showpieces: the entire city centre of Stralsund, which has the richest architectural heritage, had already had a preservation order placed on it by a diligent GDR government department. Rostock, home to the former GDR's merchant navy and shipbuilding industry, is the region's gateway to the world, and its port is now open for passenger services as well as freight traffic. It's also one of the oldest university cities in Germany, and cultural life is more vigorous here than anywhere else along the coast, making it the best base for combining urban attractions with beachcombing and day trips inland.

Wismar

History has been a bit mean to **WISMAR** – during the golden age of the Hansa the town was briefly rich and influential, but the general decline of the late Middle Ages was exacerbated by the Swedish occupation of 1648–1803. The Swedes considered it a vital base against the Danes and diverted all the town's resources to turning the place into a massive fortress – but almost as soon as the Wismarines had finished building the fortifications, the Danes moved in and made them dismantle the whole thing brick by brick. Once that was done, the Swedes took over again in 1720, but the town had been leeched to such an extent that it wasn't much use to them anymore. As if to add insult to injury, Wismar was mortgaged to the Duke of Mecklenburg in 1803, and not reclaimed when the lease expired a hundred years later. The town has never really recovered, despite the fact that its beautiful centre draws plenty of weekend trippers from Hamburg and Lübeck.

While the empty feel of a few years ago has already disappeared, with more new cafés and restaurants than anywhere else along the Baltic coast, Wismar remains rather an odd place. All the trappings of a great municipality are there – a massive central square, grand town houses and a large port – yet somehow all these ingredients don't add up to city flair; instead you get the distinct feeling of being in a provincial backwater, though the crumbling medieval and Baroque townscape still has something splendid about it.

The centre

The hundred-square-metre **Marktplatz** is one of the largest in Germany and was the venue for massive jousting sessions in medieval times; now it's the site of a permanent market. Showpiece of the square, though somewhat obscured by all the stalls, is the domed wrought-iron **Wasserkunst**, the pavilion of the former town well, which until 1897 was the only source of drinking water. Nearby is a building known as the **Alter Schwede**. Built in 1380 and Wismar's oldest house, its red-brick pillars are a good example of the coastal Gothic style. In contrast to the gabled south and east sides of the square, the northern end is dominated by the slate-blue of the Neoclassical **Rathaus** – not particularly attractive in itself, but it balances out the proportions well.

Standing forlorn in the middle of the Marienkirchhof, the next square to the west, is the disembodied tower of the **Marienkirche**, the rest of which was destroyed in the war. At the square's southeastern corner is the **Archdiakonat**, a fine example of red and black brickwork from the fifteenth century. Kellerstrasse leads west to the **Fürstenhof**, a striking palace showing Italian Renaissance influence in its two friezes. Beyond is the hefty torso of the **Georgenkirche**, which was blown up by overzealous Communists at the end of the war. It stood as a ruin until the demise of the GDR, whereupon a comprehensive restoration programme started, with the aim of returning it to its original state.

The **Nikolaikirche** at the northern end of the Altstadt was the only one of the three brick Gothic parish churches to remain intact in 1945. As with the Markt, its monumental proportions seem highly exaggerated for this small town: indeed its 37m interior makes it the tallest church in the whole of eastern Germany. On Schweinsbrücke, immediately south of the church, is the **Schabbell-Haus** (Tues–Sun 10am–4.30pm; DM2), a Dutch-style Renaissance mansion built by a local brewer and town councillor. It now contains the obligatory local history museum, which is chiefly notable for the gory collection of medieval torture instruments. Grisliest of the lot are two shrivelled human hands in a wooden bowl, which came from a murder victim and were used to confront the perpetrator in court – an accusing finger from the grave so to speak, successfully used to extract a confession.

Practicalities

Wismar's **Bahnhof** is just outside the northeastern end of the Altstadt; the **bus station** is 300 metres south, at the junction of Bahnhofstrasse and Lübsche Strasse. The **tourist office** (Mon–Fri 10am–5pm; Sat 11am–3pm; ☎2958) is between the Nikolaikirche and the Markt at Bohrstr. 5a; ask here for help in finding accommodation in **private houses**. Otherwise, there are three **hotels**: *Stadt Wismar*, Breite Str. 10 (☎2498); *KG-Hotel*, Am Markt (☎2240); and *Zur Sonne*, Lübsche Str. 51 (☎2104). Nearest **youth hostel** is 8km away in the village of BECKERWITZ (☎362), which can be reached by bus; **campsites** within striking range can be found in TIMMENDORF, ZIEROW, GRAMKOW and BOINSDORF (on the coast), and NEUKLOSTER inland. The best places for **eating** and **drinking** are on and around the Marktplatz. Try the historic *Alter Schwede* at Am Markt 22 or, for fish, the *Gastmahl des Meeres*, Altböterstr. 6. Recommended **cafés** are *Hanseat Café*, Am Marktplatz, and *Café Minks*, Krämerstr. 19.

The nearest stretch of reasonable Baltic **beach** is on the island of **Poel**, about 10km north of town. Its best section is at Schwarzer Busch – but don't expect too much, since it's only a very thin strip of sand that gets very crowded. You can buy ferry tickets from Wismar to Poel from the tourist office; there's also a bus link.

Rostock

Approaching **ROSTOCK** by boat – which is possible after a ferry journey from Wismar, Travemünde or Gedser in Denmark – you'd never guess you were heading for the German Baltic's largest port. Instead, the little fishing village of Warnemünde presents its sandy beach, and tugs are the largest boats around. However, you then swing round to the River Warnow's wide estuary, whose deep-sea port employs over 10,000 people; Rostock itself stands a few kilometres further down, on the southern riverbank. It presents an intriguing architectural mix – medieval and 1950s architecture in the centre, nineteenth-century villas in the suburb of Steintor-Vorstadt, and modern housing estates for the rest.

Practicalities

The main **tourist office** is at Lange Str. 5 (Mon–Fri 8.30am–5pm; ☎22619); there's another in Warnemünde at Am Fährbahnhof (☎52609). Accommodation in **private homes** (around DM15–30 per person) is best found in Warnemünde and the coastal villages between Rostock and Bad Doberan, but the tourist office has some city centre rooms on its books. There's also a *Zimmernachweis* **accommodation agency** at Hermann-Duncker-Platz 3 (☎3800) in front of the Hauptbahnhof.

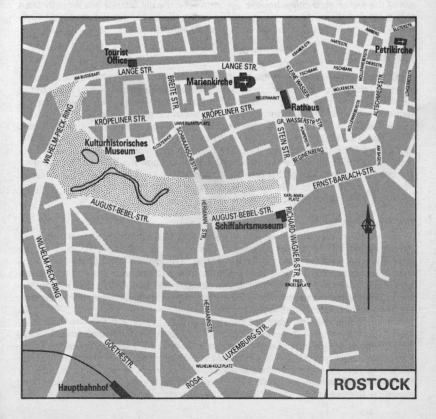

Rostock is the one town in the province where **hotels** are plentiful. Prices are around DM45–100 for singles, DM65–150 for doubles, depending on the facilities. In town, *Warnow*, Hermann-Duncker-Platz 4 (☎37381) is the best choice. There are two places near the Haputbahnhof: *Hotel am Bahnhof*, Gerhart-Hauptmann-Str. 13 (☎36331), and *Nordland*, Steinstr. 7, which takes bookings via the *Hotel am Bahnhof*. In Warnemünde, the most popular hotels are along the beach – the *Strandhotel*, Seestr. 12a (☎5335), and the *Promenadehotel*, Seestr. 5 (☎52782), both in the medium price range. The **youth hostel** (☎5326) is housed in the same old ship as the Schiffbaumuseum (see p.682).

Eating and drinking

The city centre fish **restaurants** like *Ostseegaststätte*, Lange Str. 9, and *Gastmahl des Meeres*, August-Bebel-Str. 111 do some pretty good cheap dishes. Otherwise, the *Zur Kogge* bar/restaurant at Wokrenterstr. 27 is cosy in an obvious, tourist-catering sort of way, and the *Ratsweinkeller* in the Rathaus on Neuer Markt is very popular with the locals. Also worth investigating is *Zum Kugelfisch*, Kröpelinstr. 80, an atmospheric harbour bar. In Warnemünde, try the fish restaurants *Fischerklause*, Am Strom 18, and *Atlantik*, Am Strom 107, or *Teepot*, Am Leuchtturm, which is equally renowned for its food, its startling modern architecture and its seaward views.

Most of the city centre **cafés** are along Kröpelinerstrasse and around the Universitätsplatz, but the best is in the *Alte Münze* round the back of the Marienkirche, one of the few original coffee-houses; unfortunately, the old interior has recently been ripped out, but the cakes are still great. Hip young things hang out at the *Grafik Café*, Schnickmannstr. 7, which also puts on regular art exhibitions.

The Altstadt

A good cross-section of Rostock can be seen if you've opted for the alternative approach by train. Taking tram #11 or #12 from the Hauptbahnhof, situated well to the south of the Altstadt, you pass fading villas on Rosa-Luxemburg-Strasse before entering the medieval sector via the **Steintor**, one of three surviving gates of the old fortifications. **Neuer Markt** is the city's main square, and the fifteenth-century Gothic **Rathaus**, which had a Baroque facade slapped on it in the eighteenth century, stands opposite slim gabled Renaissance houses. The area between here and the Warnow was all but razed by wartime bombs, and almost everything you see now has been built over during the last forty years. **Lange Strasse** was intended to be the showpiece of socialist rebuilding, but its only notable quality is its size: overwide, and lined by large red-brick buildings, it dwarfs the people and cars below.

The Marienkirche

If you're feeling energetic a good way to get an idea of the town's scale is to climb the 200-odd steps up the **tower** (Mon–Fri 10am–noon & 1.30–4.30pm; free) of the **Marienkirche,** just northwest of Neuer Markt. The church itself (Tues–Sat 10am–noon & 3–5pm; Sunday 11.15am–noon) is built in the late Gothic style using the characteristic red bricks of North German architecture. It was intended to rival its counterpart in Lübeck, but the nave collapsed, leaving a rather strangely proportioned interior, with the nave the same length as the transept.

Among the furnishings, look out for the Baroque **organ** and the late thirteenth-century bronze **font**. But the unique feature of this church is the **astronomical clock**, the only one of its kind left in Europe. Originally made in 1472, it's been running continuously since 1643, when it was modernised in accordance with the latest state of scientific knowledge. Its upper clockface is divided into 24 hours, as well as rings showing monthly star signs and the work associated with each one. The lower, older face consists of thirteen concentric circles showing time and planetary movements.

West of Neuer Markt

Kröpeliner Strasse cuts through the pedestrianised heart of the city to the west of Neuer Markt. Look out for the **Spitalpfarrhaus** at no. 82, the finest brick gabled Gothic house remaining in the city; formerly belonging to the medieval hospital, it's now the public library. Beyond lies **Universitätsplatz**, where people loll around the Brunnen der Lebensfreude (Fountain of Happiness), playing music and drinking, surrounded by market stalls and open-air cafés. Around here are the main buildings of the University, founded in 1419 as the first in northern Germany. Although nothing remains from this period – most of the structures are examples of the varied but heavy-handed historicist tastes of last century – there's a fine **Barocksaal** on the east side of the square, which is regularly used as a concert hall. Across from it is the **Blücherdenkmal**, erected in 1819 immediately after the death of the city's most illustrious son, the Prussian Field Marshal Gebhard Leberecht von Blücher. Both the statue and the bas-reliefs were carved by the great Berlin Neoclassical sculptor Johann Gottfried Schadow; the latter depict Blücher's most important victories, among them Waterloo.

Just to the west of Universitätsplatz is the **Kloster Zum Heiligen Kreuz**, a former Cistercian monastery which has been refurbished to house the **Kulturhistorisches Museum** (Tues–Sun 10am–6pm; DM2). Its ground-floor exhibits include eighteenth-century trunks and fourteenth- and fifteenth-century religious artefacts and retables. The rest of the museum has mediocre paintings from the coastal school of painters. On the first floor are works from both before and after World War II from the artists' colony in nearby Ahrenshoop. The second floor covers the late nineteenth- and early twentieth-century period, during which Ahrenshoop was first "discovered".

The southern fortifications

At the end of Kröpeliner Strasse stands the **Kröpeliner Tor**, the most impressive of the city's gateways; its lower part dates back to the late thirteenth century, while the more elegant upper storey was added around 1400. From here, you walk southeast-wards through the landscaped Wallangen, laid out alongside a well preserved segment of the medieval walls. Between here and the previously mentioned Steintor is a rose garden, while immediately to the east of the latter is another surviving section of wall, including the **Kuhtor**, the oldest of the gates.

A couple of minutes' walk south of the Steintor, at August-Bebel-Str. 1, is the **Schiffahrtsmuseum** (9am–5pm, closed Fri; DM2), which is mainly concerned with the region's seafaring history. It contains collections of model boats and sailing craft from the days of the Hanseatic League to the battleships of Kaiser Wilhelm.

East of Neuer Markt

The eastern sector of town is perched on a hill a little apart from the rest. The twisting cobbled streets of this old working-class neighbourhood display the names of many former trades like leather-dyeing, fishing and milking. Less honourable occupations get a look in too – Diebstrasse means "thief street". Very little restoration work has been done, and few visitors find their way here, but despite the neglect, a walk around the run-down streets has its own attractions, and the **Petrikirche** on the Alter Markt is a wonderfully peaceful spot. Its tall spire, by which ships would navigate their way to harbour, was blown off during the war, and now only a stump remains. There's a fine view of the Warnow from the terrace, while the last important part of the fortifications stretch southwards from here almost as far as the Kuhtor.

Warnemünde

WARNEMÜNDE, now Rostock's seaside suburb but still preserving the distinctive feel of a separate town, is best reached by S-Bahn (the Bahnhof, incidentally, is just a stone's throw from the ferry terminal). It has all the charm of a faded photograph: crumbling nineteenth-century holiday villas line the streets, and the fresh greenery of trees contrasts poignantly with the peeling paint. Along Am Strom by the picturesque mini-harbour, small fishermen's houses stand sideways to the sea to avoid biting winds, and along the seafront a boulevard stretches for about a kilometre, with cafés on one side and a white sandy beach on the other. It's not exactly St Tropez – the ugly *Hotel Neptun*, a five-star monstrosity built to obtain hard currency from westerners, disfigures the far end of the seafront – but it's still one of the country's favourite holiday spots. If you'd like to see what the old fishermen's homes looked like inside, there's a doll's house of a **museum** at Theodor-Körner-Str. 31 (Tues–Sun 9am–noon & 2–5pm; DM1).

Between Warnemünde and the centre of Rostock, the **Schiffbaumuseum** (July & Aug Tues–Sun 8.30–6pm; rest of year Tues & Thurs–Sun 8.30am–4.30pm, Wed 10am–4.30pm; DM3) is on an old merchant navy ship, known as the *Friedensschiff*, moored about a kilometre east of S-Bahn stop Lütten-Klein. Walking around the ship's engine room is the best feature unless you're fascinated by the history of shipbuilding and the tools and parts of the trade.

Bad Doberan and around

One excursion from Rostock which should definitely not be missed is to the little town of **BAD DOBERAN**, 17km to the west, which is built round the **Münster** (Tues–Sat 11am–noon; also tours at 9am, 10am, 2pm & 3pm), formerly the church of one of Germany's most powerful Cistercian monasteries. It's arguably the most distinguished of all the brick Gothic buildings in the Baltic lands, even managing to rival the great cathedrals of France in its sweeping elevation and elegance. Although the furnishings are overshadowed by the architecture, the winged fourteenth-century high altar and the tall tabernacle are both impressive adornments.

The **Kamp**, formerly a common, was transformed into an English-style park surrounded by late Baroque and early Neoclassical buildings when Bad Doberan became the summer residence of the Mecklenburg court. Look out also for **Goethestrasse**, a cemetery of eighteenth- and nineteenth-century mansions: their state of disrepair is pitiful, the neglected ones standing out like rotten teeth against the few that have been restored. Among the accommodation possibilities is a **youth hostel** (☎2439) on the Tempelberg at the western edge of town.

Bad Doberan has one other major attraction in the Lilliputian **narrow-gauge steam railway** known as the *Molli*, which runs for 15km from the Hauptbahnhof to the coastal resort of Kühlungsborn. It travels down Goethestrasse before leaving the town behind in a swirl of white smoke and chugging through a forest towards the nearby beaches.

Heiligendamm and Kühlungsborn

The first main stop on the *Molli* is **HEILIGENDAMM**, a grand remnant of Germany's imperial past. Founded in 1793 by Duke Friedrich Franz I, this was the country's first seaside resort, where the rich and aristocratic came to enjoy the newly-fashionable pastime of swimming in the sea. Until recently, the handful of hotels were holiday homes for the GDR's workers, each firm getting its alloted one or two weeks to send its employees here. For the moment, the place stands in sepulchral silence, its beach baskets empty and forlorn – so get there soon. If you want to stay, the **tourist office** is in the Fritz-Reuter-Haus on Professor-Vogel-Strasse.

For a bit more noise and bustle you need to carry on by train to **KÜHLUNGSBORN**, which is one of the Baltic coast's largest holiday resorts. The **tourist office** here is in the *Kurverwaltung* building at Strasse des Friedens 26 and there's a **youth hostel** at Puschkinstr. 4 (☎270).

Fischland, Darss and Zingst

Seen on a map, the peninsula of **Fischland**, **Darss** and **Zingst** looks like a crooked finger hooking itself around the mainland coast midway between Rostock and Stralsund. Bounded to the north by the Baltic and to the south by a series of shallow bays or *Bodden*, this isolated area makes a good destination either as a day trip or overnight stop. Like the whole Baltic coast, the peninsula gets crowded but isn't invaded in summer in the same way that the holiday islands of Rügen and Usedom are – probably because the beaches are less sandy, the scenery a little more rugged and communications sparser.

Fischland

The isthmus of **Fischland** is the most rewarding part of this area. From Rostock travel by rail to RIBNITZ-DARMGARTEN, from where bus #210 covers the whole area.

Wustrow

First stop is **WUSTROW**, a sleepy little settlement overlooking the **Saaler Bodden**. Just past the village entrance it's worth climbing the tower of the **Dorfkirche**, built on the remnants of Slavonic defences, which offers expansive views of the whole island (if the doors are locked the key is available from the parish house in the first street on the right after the church itself). Otherwise simply wander the streets taking in the reed-roofed houses, an architectural characteristic of the area. There's a small **tourist office** opposite the church at Thälmannstr. 3; you'll also find a cheapish café in the same building. A left turn off the main road just beyond the tourist office/café leads into Strandstrasse where there's a signposted *Zimmernachweis* or **accommodation agency** for booking private rooms. From the village's small harbour behind the church a cruise-boat plies the *Bodden* chain .

Ahrenshoop

From Wustrow the windswept cliffs of the **Hohes Ufer** lead to the quiet resort of **AHRENSHOOP** (bus #A210 also runs between the two villages), which developed into an artists' colony at the turn of the century. Eventually artistic overpopulation and the realisation that the area only offered a limited number of themes led to the painters decamping in search of new inspiration, but exhibitions are still held in the *Kunstkaten* and *Bunte Stube* **galleries** on Strandweg (fourth turning on the left from Dorfstrasse, Ahrenshoop's main street, when coming from the south). The local beach, just a hundred metres north of Dorfstrasse, is narrow and a little stony, protected from the Baltic waves by a series of groynes, and remains underpopulated.

The **tourist office** is in the small *Kurverwaltung* building, Kirchnersgang 3 (Mon, Wed, Fri 8am–noon & 1–6pm; Tues & Thur 8am–noon; ☎234). A decent **accommodation** possibility is the friendly *Pension Charlottenhof*, Grenzweg 2/3 (☎302), from DM20 per person. The best place for **eating and drinking** is the *Café Buhne 12*, Grenzweg 12 (first on left after village entrance from south; Fri–Wed 2–11pm), an arty place overlooking the sea at the head of the Hohes Ufer. The food (DM10–25), which includes fish specialities, is excellent. **Bike hire** is available from Reiner Gielow, Dorfstr. 21.

Darss

Darss is a heavily forested area, jutting out into the sea north of Fischland. From Ahrenshoop the main road snakes around the edge of the Darss forest, passing through the traditional fishing villages of BORN and WIECK.

Prerow

About 3km northeast of Wieck is the resort of **PREROW**, an inoffensive little place protected from the Baltic by a line of sand dunes. A couple of big youth-holiday camps here until recently bore the names *Ernst Thälmann* and *Kim Il Sung*, and it's perhaps their presence that gives Prerow a slightly dull, regimented feel. From Wiecker Weg, the main road into town, head down Strandstrasse and Waldstrasse. Prerow doesn't really have a centre, it just straggles along these two streets, and the beach is about 300m north of the latter. From Waldstrasse follow Im Schuning to an inauspicious-looking cluster of cafés and kiosks marking the "entrance" to the beach, where fine sands draw in the crowds.

Other attractions are the **Darss Museum**, Waldstr. 48 (May–Oct daily 9am–5pm; Nov–April Wed & Fri 9am–noon & 1–4pm; DM2), devoted to the history of Darss and the seafaring past of its people, and the eighteenth-century **Seemannskirche,** or "Seamen's Church", on the Zingst road heading west out of town. This simple church has a surprisingly elaborate Baroque altar, and its graveyard is littered with simple monuments that form a sociological history in stone. As with other villages on the peninsula, wandering the side streets can be rewarding with lots of unusual architectural features (colourfully painted doors, carved window frames and ornate weathercocks) adorning the reed-bedecked wooden houses. From Prerow there are number of walking possibilities; a woodland path marked by posts with horizontal red lines leads from Bernsteinerweg (opposite Küsters Allee) on the northwest corner of town through the woods to **Darsser Ort** headland with its isolated lighthouse, while another path traverses the sand dunes west of town in the direction of Zingst.

Prerow's **tourist office** is in the *Kurverwaltung* building at the junction of Strandstrasse and Waldstrasse (Mon–Fri 10am–6pm), and there's an **accommodation agency** at Strandstr. 14. Alternatively try the *Pension Linde*, Waldstr. 33 (☎327), where rooms with a WC and shower are available at DM25 per person. The pension also has a restaurant and bike hire facilities. For **eating and drinking** try the *Dünenhaus* looking out over the beach. **Bike hire** is available at Bebelstr. 37.

Zingst

The village of **ZINGST**, just over 5km east of Prerow, is eminently missable, but its beach, which runs west for 10km, is excellent with fine yellow sand, backed by high dunes. Accommodation possibilities here include a a **youth hostel** at Glebe 14 (☎465). The wooded eastern end of Zingst is a nature conservation area, home to numerous rare plants and birds, and at the end of the road there's a small exhibition house hidden away in the woods behind the car park.

Stralsund

STRALSUND, which marks the point of entry into what has traditionally been regarded as Pomerania, is far more provincial than Rostock. Nonetheless, it's still one of the best places to stay along the whole coast, particularly as it's possible to make day trips to the adjacent holiday island of Rügen (see p.693), now linked by a causeway carrying both road and rail traffic. First impressions of the city don't flatter, as it's ringed by horrid concrete suburbs, but the Altstadt, despite four decades of neglect, is still wonderfully evocative of its Hanseatic past, preserving a wealth of outstanding buildings. Life in Stralsund has always been very closely tied to the fishing trade: the German Baltic's main fishing fleet is based here, and the local shipyard specialises in building fishing trawlers and the enormous fish-processing ships that work the North and South Atlantic.

The Altstadt

Stralsund's Altstadt stands on what is almost an island, with the sea and two natural ponds – the **Frankteich** and the **Knieperteich** – forming a kind of moat; the skyline, framed by the towers of the great brick Gothic churches, is best seen from the southern shore of the willow-lined Frankenteich. From the Hauptbahnhof the Tribseer Damm traverses the isthmus separating the ponds: across the water, the state of dereliction is pretty advanced in many parts, and houses stand abandoned to their crumbling fate. In the places where bombs dropped during World War II left gaping holes, the rubble has just been shoved aside for makeshift car parks or children's playgrounds. However, the preservation order imposed by the GDR state has meant that the decaying Gothic, Baroque and Renaissance buildings are slowly being restored.

The Marienkirche

Beyond Tribseer Damm, Tribseer Strasse leads shortly to Neuer Markt, one of two town squares, where stands the town's largest church, the **Marienkirche**. It's a good idea to begin your tour by ascending its **tower** (Mon–Fri 10am–5pm, Sat 10am–12.30pm & 2.30–5pm, Sun 2.30–5pm; DM1) for an excellent view of the medieval townscape, as well as of Rügen a couple of hundred metres across the water. The church itself is a late fourteenth-century Gothic basilica, but the interior has extensive Baroque alterations and the red brickwork has been painted cream, giving the nave a light and airy atmosphere unusual for this region. The organ was built by the Lübeck master Friedrich Stellwagen in the 1650s, but somehow its slim, high structure, almost reaching the ceiling, has an elegance more reminiscent of Jugendstil than Baroque. An unusual item for the region is the **font**, which, instead of the traditional bronze type, is a marble basin standing on an elevated round pavilion made of wood, giving it the appearance of a fancy garden tea-house.

The central streets

The former **Katharienkloster**, on Mönchstrasse just north of Neuer Markt, houses the renowned **Meeresmuseum** (Museum of the Sea; May–Sept Mon–Thurs 9am–4pm, Fri–Sun 9am–5pm; Nov-April Wed–Sun 10am–5pm; DM3), which covers everything from basic facts about the planet's seas to the history of local fishing across the ages. There are also several aquaria with exotic fish, and a section devoted to the sealife of the Baltic Coast. Usefully (and unusually) there's extensive information in English. The **Kulturhistorisches Museum** in the same building (Tues–Sun 10am–5pm; DM3) contains an important hoard of tenth-century treasure dug up on the island of Hiddensee; a wonderful collection of eighteenth- and nineteenth- century children's toys and doll's houses; and a well-documented section on life in Stralsund since 1945.

On Böttcherstrasse, three blocks to the east, is the **Jacobikirche**, the youngest of the three brick Gothic parish churches. Badly damaged in the war, it still hasn't been fully restored. From here, follow Jacobiturmstrasse north to **Badenstrasse**, Stralsund's finest street, lined with mansions ranging in style from Gothic to Neoclassical.

The Alter Markt and around

Immediately beyond Badenstrasse is the Alter Markt, on whose south side stand the **Nikolaikirche** and the **Rathaus**, which form an integrated architectural pairing of the sacred and secular, thereby copying a formula pioneered in Lübeck, the chief city of the Hanseatic League. The Rathaus – and in particular its mid-fourteenth-century showpiece facade crafted from delicately glazed red bricks – is one of the most original creations of Gothic civil architecture. While it is quintessentially German, the Nikolaikirche's huge flying buttresses and paired towers (one later topped with an incongruous Baroque dome) show definite French influence, albeit given a Baltic accent by the use of bricks. Inside the church are a number of fine works of art, including a tastefully restrained high altar designed by Andreas Schlüter. Other buildings of note on the square are the late Gothic **Wulfamshaus** at no. 5 and the Baroque **Schwedische Kommandatur** at no. 14.

To the north and west, along **Fährstrasse, Schillstrasse** and **Mühlenstrasse**, are many of the best of Stralsund's medieval town-houses. Mühlenstr. 3 is particularly worthwhile, since you can go inside and see the unusual interior of this typical Hanseatic merchant's residence: there are no partitioning walls inside, only three open-plan levels, which were used as combined living and storage quarters. At the southern end of the same street is the **Küter Tor**, one of the two surviving city gates. From here, it's worth following the course of the old fortifications, passing firstly along the shore of the Knieper Teich, then continuing via the **Knieper Tor** to the **Johanniskloster**, a former Franciscan monastery which now houses the city's archives.

Practicalities

The **tourist office** at Alter Markt 15 (Mon 2–5pm, Tues 9am–12.30pm & 2–6pm, Wed & Thurs 9am–12.30pm & 2–5pm, Fri 9am–12.30pm & 2–4pm; May–Oct also Sat 8.30–11am; ☎590) offers the usual private room-finding service, and also sells tickets for the *Weisse Flotte* cruise boats that go to Rügen, Hiddensee and down the coast towards Greifswald. There are three **hotels** to choose from: best located is the *Schweriner Hof*, on the Neuer Markt (☎5281); next choice is the *Baltic*, Frankendamm (☎5381), an old concrete box of an *Interhotel* (both have doubles from DM110); last is *Am Bahnhof*, Tribseer Damm (☎2659), by the Hauptbahnhof with doubles from about DM70. The town **youth hostel** is handily placed at Am Kütertor 1 (☎2160); there's another 6km away in the village of DEVIN (☎2358), reached by bus #3. For information on the local **campsites**, head for the *Campingzentrum Ostsee*, Barther Str. 64b (☎5015).

The *Scheelehaus*, a hospitable little **restaurant** in one of the old town-houses at Fährstr. 23, is the best place in Stralsund for a full meal. Consider, too, the nearby *Ratskeller* in the domed cellar of the Rathaus. The *Schweriner Hof* (see above) is in the same price range, but is best for afternoon coffee and cake, while the *Fischgrill*, Ossenreyerstr. 49 is said to be one of the best fish restaurants on the eastern German Baltic. There are also a number of **bar-discos**, whose single merit is that they exist at all. Choose from the *Störtebekerkeller*, Ossenreyerstr. 49, *Trocadero*, Katharinenberg 13, and the *Tanzcafe Hotel Baltic*, Frankendamm 17.

Greifswald

The Hanseatic city of **GREIFSWALD** was founded by Cistercian monks from the nearby Eldena monastery during the thirteenth century. A university was founded in 1465 and nowadays it's the academic atmosphere that predominates, but the town is known to all too many Germans as the location of one of the ex-GDR's notoriously dangerous Soviet-designed nuclear power stations. There was a near-disaster here in 1976 and further jitters were caused when a fighter plane crashed nearby in 1990. The plant was finally closed down with the demise of the GDR, though the problems of how to dismantle the reactor safely remain.

Around town

Greifswald is a strangely uninspiring place despite the fact that most of its historic centre survived the war and the ravages of GDR town planning. Its appearance should, however, improve dramatically before long, as it's one of five cities in the new Länder which have been earmarked to receive generous restoration funds. Centre of town is the **Markt** (reached from the **Hauptbahnhof** via Bahnhofstrasse and Lange Strasse), a bustling square crammed with stalls selling cut-price tat. Around it are some well restored medieval buildings, most noteworthy of which is the **Rathaus**. Originally built in Gothic style during the fourteenth century, it was given a facelift following an eighteenth-century fire, resulting in an unusual greenish façade more Renaissance in flavour. Directly opposite are a brace of impressive Gothic **gabled houses**, quintessentially north German in appearence.

Following Lange Strasse west from the Markt, turn into Martin-Luther-Strasse where the graceful spire of the **Dom** rises up above the run–down surrounding streets. The brilliant white of the interior is relatively unembellished in true Lutheran style, with only a few modern allegorical frescos and carvings by way of decoration. It's worth climbing the tower (irregular hours; DM2) though you may be dissuaded by the ominous-looking cracks in its structure and the even more off-putting medieval wooden staircase of the final section. Following Domstrasse west from the Dom leads into the **University quarter** – mainly comprising solidly dull nineteenth-century buildings.

On Bruggestrasse, at the eastern end of town, is the thirteenth-century **Marienkirche**, unmissable with its distinctive square tower. This is Greifswald's oldest church and the absence of a choir gives it quite striking internal dimensions. Not far from here is the **Museum der Stadt**, Theodor-Pyl-Str 1-2 (Tues–Sun 10am–6pm; DM1), housed in a former monastery building, and devoted to the history of the town and the University. Highpoint are a number of drawings and paintings by Greifswald's most famous son, the great Romantic artist Caspar David Friedrich.

Practicalities

Greifswald's **tourist office**, at Lange Str. 126 (Mon–Fri 10am–6pm, Sat 9am–noon; ☎3460) can offer the usual private room-booking service – with rates from as little as DM10. At the time of writing there was only one **hotel** in the town centre, the *Boddenhaus*, Karl-Liebknecht-Ring 1 (☎5241), at DM55 per person for standard middle-of-the-range facilities. The **youth hostel**, which is under threat of closure, is at Pestalozzistr. 11/12 (☎3133) south of the town centre; take bus #A from the bus station opposite the Hauptbahnhof. **Eating and drinking** possibilities are still fairly limited. *Zur Hütte*, Am Markt 12, does everything from *Kaffee und Kuchen* to light meals while the *Ratsweinkeller*, Am Markt 1, beneath the Rathaus, is good for something a little more substantial. Those in search of budget-priced student-fodder should head for the *Mensa am Wall*, Schützenstrasse, just west of the Marienkirche.

Wieck and Eldena

A few kilometres east of Greifswald lie two villages heavily promoted as excursion destinations. Bus #H will drop you off on the edge of **WIECK** in the vicinity of the nineteenth-century Dutch-style **wooden drawbridge**, which spans the Ryck and is still in use. Nearby are a couple of *Gaststätten*, the shiny new *Zur Fähre* on the northern bank of the river and the more modest *Zur Brücke* on the south. Wieck itself is a fishing town of the active rather than the tourist variety, as the smell of herring wafting from the harbour testifies. It's worth strolling along **Dorfstrasse** on the far side of the bridge and taking a look at some of the surviving fisher-cottages.

The only point of interest in **ELDENA** is the ruined **Kloster**, located on the Wolgast road, once home to wealthy Cistercian monks who exercised considerable influence over the area. A frequent subject of Caspar David Friedrich's paintings, the monastery dates back to the twelfth century, though little beyond skeletal red-brick walls survives. Originally founded by the Danes, it was later destroyed by Swedish soldiers and much of the masonry carted off as building material. The arched doorways and empty windows of the ruin, backed by tall trees, are undeniably romantic and evocative, and, more prosaically, make a good spot for a picnic.

Wolgast

The relaxed little harbour town of **WOLGAST** lies 24km east of Greifswald on the southern shore of the Peene Strom, the narrow sound separating the German mainland and the holiday island of Usedom. Best viewed as a stopover of a few hours en route to Usedom, Wolgast was for centuries a residence of the Dukes of Pomerania, developing into an important trade centre during the eighteenth and nineteenth centuries. Much of its old fabric survives in the network of narrow streets that slope down to the harbour from the central square, and the town remains important as a harbour with a large working shipyard.

Around town

Wolgast's **Hauptbahnhof** is at the southern edge of town, but it's better to alight at **Wolgast Hafen**, the harbour stop. First thing you'll notice on leaving the station are the huge nineteenth-century half-timbered grain silos on the harbour – the largest on the Baltic coast. To the north of the station is a bridge leading across to the **Schlossinsel**, a small island between the mainland and Usedom, once the site of Wolgast's castle, a structure long since vanished. From here head up Burgstrasse, which runs into Wilhelm Strasse before opening out onto **Rathausplatz**. The pretty little **Rathaus**, with its fluid Baroque facade (it looks almost like an upturned boat) and surrounding nineteenth-century buildings do much to give Wolgast its appeal. A fountain in front of the Rathaus is decorated with scenes depicting the town's history .

Wolgast's main attraction though is the nearby **Petrikirche**, a huge, angular, almost Romanesque-looking structure (it's Gothic in reality), that dominates the town's skyline. It was the court church of the Dukes of Pomerania and is the last resting place of nine of them. The most notable interior decorative feature is the action-packed *Totentanz* (Dance of Death) frieze, depicting death in various guises; from soldier to well-dressed noblewoman. The skeletal figure is shown as ever-present, like a card game kibitzer, and indeed in one scene is even depicted as a card player.

At Rathausplatz 6 is the **Kreismuseum** (Tues–Fri 9am–5pm Sat & Sun 9am–4pm; DM1), a local history museum housed in Wolgast's oldest building, the half-timbered *Kaffeemühle* or "Coffee Grinder" – so called because of its distinctive shape. Much of the museum is devoted to the work of artist Philipp Otto Runge, an important painter of the early Romantic school and contemporary of Caspar David Friedrich. There's also a small display about the development of the V2 at nearby Peenemünde (see p.690), plus changing exhibitions by young local artists.

Practicalities

Wolgast's **tourist office** (Mon–Fri 8am–6pm & Sat 8am–1.30pm; ☎2310) at Lange Str. 1 is fairly well stocked with brochures and can provide the usual private room-booking service. Local **hotels** like the *Park Hotel*, Bahnhofstr. 90c (☎2278), which has the ambience of a secret police barracks, are doing a good job of pricing themselves out of the market. For **eating** and **drinking** the *Ratskeller* in the *Rathaus* is a reliable stand-by. *Vier Jahreszeiten*, August-Dähm-Str. 14, is a big *Gaststätte* that keeps the flag flying for pork and potatoes, while nearby, in a nineteenth-century folly tower, is *Belvedere*, a good Italian (DM10–25). For *Kaffee und Kuchen* head for *Café Biedenweg* on Lange Strasse, which bakes its own tempting varieties.

Usedom

Directly north of Wolgast, **USEDOM** is Germany's second largest island. It has some fine beaches but is very much in the shadow of Rügen as a Baltic holiday destination, lacking the latter's variety of landscape. Fifty kilometres in length and varying in width from less than a kilometre to about 25km, the island has a random shape, like the pattern of spilled water, and is separated from the mainland by the Peene Strom, which, though little more than a narrow channel for most of its length, expands suddenly and takes a big bite out of the southern shore as the **Achter Wasser** bay. At its eastern end Usedom is abruptly cut off by the Polish border, leaving about a fifth of its area, including the port of Świnoujście (formerly German Swinemünde), in Polish hands.

These days Usedom is popular with working-class eastern Germans, though before the war it was the haunt of Europe's rich and its resorts ranked among Germany's most fashionable. Places to head for are **Koserow** which has the finest stretch of beach and **Heringsdorf** which retains some of the ambience that drew the pre-war glitterati. **Bansin** and **Ahlbeck** have some fine Baltic shorefront architecture, but remain steadfastly downmarket, despite the get-rich-quick efforts of various speculators to inject them with new life. At the western end of the island is **Peenemünde**, site of the Nazi rocket research station where Werner von Braun developed the V2 (see below). Only now emerging from decades of semi-isolation, the town has a desolate atmosphere and is the location of a bizarre museum devoted to von Braun's efforts.

As everywhere on the Baltic coast, there's little chance of being able to find a room in July or August without booking in advance. Transport is reasonable, with rail links from Wolgast to Ahlbeck and buses serving the main destinations. Usedom is fairly flat and so well-suited to cycling, although the volume of car traffic in summer is heavy.

Peenemünde and around

Peenemünde can be reached by rail or bus #616 from Wolgast Hafen, though connections are scant. If you're coming by car or bike, cross the Wolgast bridge onto Usedom and turn left off the main road in the direction of TRASSENHEIDE. Just north of here, to the right of the road, is a **monument** to forced labourers from occupied Europe who died building the Peenemünde weapons complex, or who were killed in the August 1943 Allied air-raid. A couple of kilometres down the road is KARLSHAGEN, a slightly drab resort with a reasonable stretch of beach. Just beyond the village is a roadside board with a large map illustrating the layout of *Sperrgebiet Peenemünde* or "Peenemünde Restricted Zone". Until a couple of years ago the derelict buildings nearby were a control point from which unauthorised visitors could be kept out.

From here the road curves gently round, with occasional roadside signs on the edge of the woods warning of unexploded munitions. To the right of the road makeshift concrete barriers and old tank obstacles don't deter people from picking their way through the trees to the Baltic beach, although it's scarcely worth the effort as this stretch is dirty and jellyfish-ridden.

Peenemünde

At the extreme northwestern end of Usedom, hidden in the woods, is the shabby little town of **PEENEMÜNDE**. It's a depressing place whose raison d'être since the 1930s has been the military. They arrived in April 1936 to build the rocket testing centre at which the V2 rocket was subsequently developed, and after the collapse of Nazi Germany the Russians, followed by the GDR's *Nationaler Volksarmee*, took over. The naval and air base at Peenemünde was only closed down in 1990, leaving the place with the devastated air of a steel town after the works have been closed. Until the Wende, Peenemünde and its immediate vicinity were more or less completely out of bounds to

PEENEMÜNDE AND THE V WEAPONS

Peenemünde can thank Werner von Braun's mother for today's melancholy state of affairs. When von Braun was looking for a secluded stretch of Baltic coast on which to build a rocket research station for his Nazi masters, it was she who suggested the little fishing backwater. As soon as the site was approved the locals were kicked out and a vast testing complex erected, complete with airfield, laboratories, launch-pads and housing for an army of scientists, technicians and workers.

Throughout the 1930s a variety of experimental rockets were tested at Peenemünde. The Luftwaffe were busy with their pilotless jet-plane project which became the V1, while von Braun was directing the army's attempt to develop a long-range liquid-fuel rocket to be known as the A4 (subsequently termed the V2 or *Vergeltungswaffe 2* – "Reprisal Weapon 2") The research was dogged by problems, with the airforce and army squabbling endlessly over funding, and though massive resources were channelled into the A4, a successful launch was not achieved unil October 1942.

At the end of the year it was decided to put the rocket into production as soon as possible. On July 7, 1943 Hitler personally made the A4 a priority, a decision reinforced by the RAF's destruction of Hamburg on July 24, an event which demanded massive retaliation of a similar scale on British cities.

Meanwhile the British government, well informed about what was happening on Peenemünde and only too aware of the potentially massive destructive capacity of the A4, were laying plans for an attack on the research complex. On August 17–18, 1943 a small night raid on Berlin drew German fighter cover away from the north coast, allowing 600 RAF heavy bombers to attack Peenemünde.

The raid caused extensive damage to the research station and put the German rocket testing programme out of action until October. Seven hundred and thirty two lives were claimed by the attack, the majority of the dead being forced labourers from the occupied countries, many of whom were killed in the mistaken bombing of their accommodation at nearby Trassenheide. Included in this toll were a number of Luxembourgers who had been supplying the Allies with intelligence reports about German activities. However, the delay to the rocket programme caused by the attack was a great set-back to the Germans. Perhaps the most important result was that the V1 offensive was held up until after D-Day; had the pilotless bomb been unleashed against the invasion fleet as it lay at anchor in Britain's southern ports, the course of events could have been altered radically.

The V1 offensive finally began on June 12, 1944 from sites in northern France. It was to kill 5000 British civilians and cause considerable loss of production and damage to morale, at a time when many Britons thought the war was entering its final phase. The first V2 hit London on September 5, 1944, launched from a site near the Hague, and raids continued until March 1945 (causing a total of 2700 deaths). Cities like Paris, Brussels and Antwerp also suffered heavily from the V weapons.

Work continued at Peenemünde until March 1945 when it was decided to evacuate the site. The Red Army arrived on May 4, 1945 to pick over what was left of the complex. Werner von Braun and his colleagues had already fallen into the hands of the Americans, who soon put them to work on their own missile projects, and later on the NASA space programme – von Braun was chief designer of the Apollo rocket that put man on the moon.

outsiders, and even today much of the environs is still closed off, guarded by a skeleton force of *Bundeswehr* troops. The area's only future can be in tourism, though apart from the remains of the rocket research station there's not much here.

At the end of the main road and well signposted, is the **Informations Zentrum** (Tues–Sun 9am–5pm; DM3, student DM1.50), a museum devoted to Peenemünde's wartime role. Rather disingenuously advertising itself as the *"Wiege der Raumfahrt"* – "Birthplace of Space-Travel", it's undeniably interesting, but the presentation will leave you somewhere between unease and anger. The director is a former GDR airforce major and the emphasis is very much on the technological achievements of von Braun and the way in which the US space programme developed from them. Scant attention is paid to the purpose for which the V weapons were developed, or to the use to which they were finally put.

Near the entrance is an incongruous example of Mecklenburg thatched roofing that seems to have strayed in from another museum, given that adjacent exhibits include a pair of Mig fighters from the ex-GDR airforce. Prominently displayed in this open air-section are a sinister-looking V1 and V2. The backdrop to all this is an immense red-brick power station, built during the thirties for the research complex. Beyond the power station, the erstwhile pride of the GDR navy sits in the Peenemünde harbour, awaiting the breakers in serried rows.

The museum proper is housed in the power station control bunker. Most of the exhibited material is wholly innocuous, devoted to the Birthplace of Space Travel concept – a conceit akin to claiming that the Allied strategic bombing campaign was the prelude to mass-market commercial passenger flight. Amid all this a few models and maps show what the complex looked like before the Allied bombing raid, but there's little attempt to set it in context.

The rest of Peenemünde looks like it hasn't really recovered from the 1943 bombing; a mess of ugly flats overshadowed by the shell of the liquid oxygen plant. All roads lead to barriers with signs warning of *Schusswaffengebrauch* ("weapons in use") with armed guards standing behind them, in scenes reminiscent of the worst days of the old GDR. The bulk of the research complex site, including the various test stands, lies in a military zone still forbidden to the general public.

Zinnowitz and Koserow

Leaving all this and heading east leads you to a string of seaside towns. First up after rejoining the main road is **ZINNOWITZ** (bus #616 and rail from Wolgast and Peenemünde), Usedom's largest resort, with a long promenade lined by grandiose-looking white hotels. Sadly, most of these are big, institutional places only just emerging from forty years as factory and trade union holiday centres, and best avoided. There's a **campsite** just off the main road on the eastern edge of town.

Koserow

A better bet is **KOSEROW** (bus #606 and rail from Zinnowitz and Wolgast), a few kilometres to the east. At first sight this village of modern houses straggling along the road seems to have little to offer. However, beyond the pine-covered slope rising above it is a wonderful stretch of sandy beach backed by low cliffs. If you're contemplating spending any time on Usedom, Koserow makes an excellent base; there's virtually nothing to see here, but the beach (nudist for substantial stretches) has a delightfully secluded feel, and the volume of visitors, though heavy, is not unbearable.

The **tourist office** is at the village entrance on the main road at Hauptstr. 5 (Mon–Fri 9am–noon & 3–8pm, Sat & Sun 9am–noon), and can book **private rooms** starting at about DM10. The only other option is the *Ferienhotel Waldschloss*, Fritz-Behn-Str. 17, which charges from DM26 per person (including breakfast). It's been used as a sanatorium for the last 40 years or so, but renovation is planned, and the building's turrets and gables and leafy location just a couple of hundred metres from the beach compensate for leaky plumbing. A handy **campsite** is at Hauptstr. 15.

For **eating and drinking** try *Kelch's Speisegaststätte*, Karlstr. 9, which does decent fish dishes (open until midnight; DM10–30), in the first street on the right after the tourist office. At the other end of town, at the foot of the 60-metre Streckelberg (Usedom's highest elevation) is *Zum Streckelberg*, good for a post-beach ice-cream or beer and offering edible though uninspired meat-and-potato dishes for DM5–20 (open Wed–Sun only). Hidden in the trees above the western end of the beach is the *Salzhütten*, a small restaurant with outside seating, and more or less on the beach itself are a number of *Imbiss* kiosks and small cafés. Koserow's **bike hire** facilities are at *Fahrrad Ortmann*, Meinholdstr. 34, en route to the Streckelberg.

Bansin, Heringsdorf and Ahlbeck

Fifteen kilometres down the main road from Koserow, the resorts of Bansin, Heringsdorf and Ahlbeck (all served by bus #606 and rail line) merge into one another in rapid succession, though despite the blurring of the boundaries between them, each town retains its separate identity.

Bansin

BANSIN is very much a family holiday destination with an excellent, but inevitably crowded, sandy beach. There's really not much to detain the visitor, though Seestrasse, the town's main drag, running from station to beach, is lined by impressive turn-of-the-century houses in brilliant white with wrought-iron balconies. The street terminates at a small square with a clock which marks the main entrance to the beach.

Should you wish to stay here the **tourist office** (Mon–Fri 9am–noon, 1–6pm, Sat & Sun 9am–noon) for booking private rooms is at Seestr. 64. As in Zinnowitz, most of the local **hotels** haven't recovered from long years serving as workers' holiday homes, though the *Pension Zum Geiseltal*, Bergstr. 26, isn't bad, starting at DM20 per night with breakfast. For **eating and drinking** the *Bauernstube*, Seestr. 42, dishes up stodgy meals, as does the *Gaststätte Schiffbruch* in an upturned boat at the western end of the promenade. The latter offers reasonable fish dishes and free-flowing beer, but avoid the Thursday accordion sessions. If you want to load up on calories the *Eisdiele* at Strandpromenade 22, overlooking the beach near the clock tower, does good ice-cream.

Heringsdorf

Best of the resort triumvirate is **HERINGSDORF**, which retains something of its pre-war atmosphere to complement its near-impeccable looks. Described by Baedeker as "the most fashionable of the Baltic sea-bathing places", Heringsdorf is the oldest resort on Usedom and enjoyed international fame, attracting aristocratic and wealthy holiday-makers from all over Europe, despite its rather unprepossessing name – "Herring-Village" – a leftover from its origins as a small fishing port.

The centre of Heringsdorf is **Platz des Friedens**, reached by following Friedenstrasse from the Bahnhof. The town's architecture is mostly in the familiar Baltic resort style of abundant white facades and attractive balconies, though Platz des Friedens is disfigured by an enormous residential/shopping complex. Fortunately the surrounding buildings are more in keeping with the rest of the town – like the **Kulturhaus**, once a decadent casino, now a worthy theatre and arts centre.

From here the beach and promenade are only a minute or two away. Before the war the Kaiser Wilhelm Pier once stretched out over 500 metres into the Baltic from this point, complete with motorboat moorings and a steamer dock for Rügen-bound boats. It's long since disappeared and these days the beach is tightly packed with *Strandkörbe* or "beach baskets", the engagingly archaic-looking wood-enclosed seats that litter Rügen's beaches. Heading west, the **Strandpromenade**, decked out with well-regimented flower beds, leads past the **Kunstpavilion**, an odd structure looking like a futurist bandstand enclosed by glass, that plays host to temporary art exhibitions.

At the western end of Strandpromenade take a sharp left into Strandstrasse, followed by a right into Maxim-Gorki-Strasse. Here you'll find the **Maxim-Gorki-Gedenkstätte**, Maxim-Gorki-Str. 13, a small museum devoted to Maxim Gorky and the time he spent in Heringsdorf in 1922. It's housed in the former *Pension Irmgard*,

where the author stayed during his sojourn, a period in which he wrote the autobiographical volume *My Universities*. Returning to Platz des Friedens via Badstrasse and
Kulmstrasse offers a chance to appreciate Heringsdorf at its best; quiet leafy streets
straggle up a hill, flanked by small villas with flaking facades set in little gardens.

The **tourist office** is at Dehlbrückstr. 61 (Mon–Fri 9am–1pm & 2–6pm, Sat & Sun
8am–noon), though there will be almost no chance of finding a room in this popular
resort during high season. Most **hotels** fall into the expensive category, though *Stadt
Berlin*, Ernst-Thälmann-Str. 38, near the station offers reasonable rooms at DM30 per
person, as does the slightly run-down *Waldblick*, Kulmstr. 28. For **eating and drinking**
try *Zur Klause*, Strandstr. 6, near the Gorky museum which does a reasonable selection
of inexpensive dishes, or the *Terrassencafé*, Kulmstr. 29, with a good view of the sea.
Bike hire is available from *Uwe Pilgrim*, Brunnenstr. 10, near the petrol station.

Ahlbeck

AHLBECK, has virtually nothing to offer that you won't have encountered already on
Usedom. Admittedly, the town looks good with some ornate villas and grand hotels
and there's a pleasant-enough promenade and sandy beach, but somehow the atmosphere is that of a Baltic Bognor. The town's much promoted **Seebrücke** or pier turns
out to be little more than a glorified pavilion on stilts at the end of the beach. Hopes were
raised when an American businessman bought it in 1990, but so far nothing has come of
plans to turn the shabby restaurant into an establishment worthy of Ahlbeck's past.

Two kilometres east of Ahlbeck is the Polish border. Following the 1945 redrawing
of Europe's boundaries, the eastern tip of Usedom was given to Poland, and the erstwhile German harbour of Swinemünde is now Polish ŚWINOUJSCIE. For non-British
budget travellers (British citizens need a visa to visit Poland, costing £20) it might be
worth investigating accommodation possibilities on the Polish side, where prices (for
everything) are lower than in Germany.

RÜGEN

Rügen is Germany's largest island and has been a favourite summer destination since
bathing first became fashionable during the nineteenth century. Its long, sandy
beaches and airy forests make it an ideal family holiday destination and even in GDR
days Rügen drew over a million visitors a year. Today the area is trying hard to adapt
an overburdened infrastructure to an ever-increasing volume of tourists, as the island
features in western German travel agents' brochures for the first time in years.

Geographical divisions split the island into four distinct areas: **Southeast Rügen**
with the best, and most heavily populated, stretches of beach; **Jasmund** with its
forested national park and chalk cliffs overlooking the Baltic; windswept **Wittow** in the
north; and **West Rügen**, a gentle landscape of farmland and woods.

West Rügen is also home to the island of **Hiddensee**: this isolated strip of land a few
kilometres off-shore has a landscape of surprising contrasts, and an idyllic, car-free
atmosphere that makes it the best destination on Rügen. Also not to be missed are
wind-battered **Kap Arkona** at the northeastern corner of Wittow with its Schinkel-
designed lighthouse and, nearby, the secluded fishing village of **Vitt**. Another important destination is the **Stubbenkammer** cliffs, the most spectacular of Jasmund's
chalk-faces. Of Rügen's towns, the main places to head for are in South Rügen: **Binz**
and **Sellin** are archetypal faded resorts with tree-lined boulevards and grandiose but
crumbling villas, many of which are now in use as hotels, while **Putbus** is, in effect, a
giant Neoclassical folly built during the early 1800s to the greater glory of a local duke.
Island capital **Bergen** is fairly forgettable, as is the port of **Sassnitz** in Jasmund unless
you're en route to Sweden or the Danish island of Bornholm by ferry.

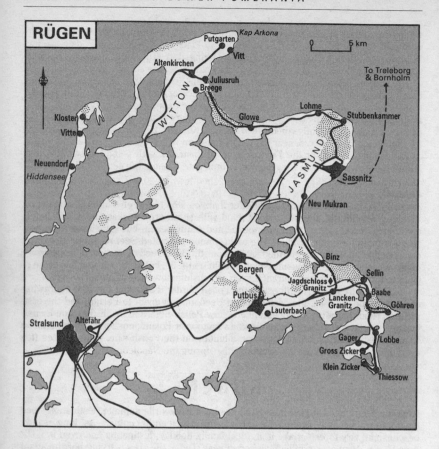

Practicalities

Getting to Rügen poses no problems; bus #A417 runs from Stralsund to Bergen (from where there are train and bus links to the rest of the island) and Sassnitz at 7.45am, 12.55pm and 4.15pm. If the timetable doesn't fit in with your plans, catch bus #1, #2 or #6 from the Bahnhof to Rügendamm and hitch. There are also train services from Stralsund to these towns. For a more atmospheric introduction to the island, take the ferry service from Stralsund to Altefähr on Rügen's southern coast. Island **transport links** are fairly good, with rail services on the eastern half of the island and bus links to more out-of-the-way destinations. Travelling around the island becomes considerably easier if you have your own car; cycling is a possibility but Rügen is hilly, roads are often potholed or surfaced with cobblestones, and local driving habits are erratic (there are no cycle paths to speak of).

The flip-side of Rügen's popularity is that **accommodation is virtually unobtainable** during the months of July and August without advance booking, a fact which makes Rügen a destination best visited off-season. Rügen is particularly atmospheric and empty in winter when the Baltic often freezes over to create an eerie ice-scape. Summers are usually hot, though the west coast of the island is sometimes subjected to battering winds and the whole of Rügen regularly experiences sudden but brief storms.

South Rügen

South Rügen offers a soporifically pleasant landscape of fields and woods, but the main attraction is its kilometres of fine beach. The best stretches start in **Binz** and run northwards, with further strands between the resorts of **Sellin** and **Thiessow**. Generally speaking, these are the places to make for. Island capital **Bergen** has little to offer, though, it's a communications junction most visitors will pass through at least once. **Putbus**, the other main inland town, is worth a brief visit, as is the nearby harbour-village of **Lauterbach**.

Bergen

Rügen's capital **BERGEN** is an undistinguished town of 20,000 and the destination of rail and main road routes from Stralsund. Its possibilities are just about exhausted in the time it takes to have a cup of coffee or a meal while awaiting an onward connection, though the **Marienkirche** on Karl-Marx-Platz in the centre of town (reached from the station via Bahnhofstrasse and Marktstrasse) is worth a quick look. Despite its unremarkable appearance this originally Romanesque building with substantial Gothic additions is the oldest on the island, dating back to the days when its inhabitants were Slavs. Embedded in the church's western wall is a **Slavonic gravestone**, blurrily depicting a bearded man.

Heading northwest from Karl-Marx-Platz along Vieschstrasse, past a memorial to the victims of the Nazis, brings you to Bergen's only other sight, the **Ernst-Moritz-Arndt-Turm** (Mon–Fri 10am–5pm, Sat & Sun 10am–6pm; DM1). This red-brick viewing tower set on top of a pimply hill offers fine views of surrounding tree tops and not much else, while the interior contains a cursory display about Ernst Moritz Arndt, a locally born writer and German patriot active during the Napoleonic Wars.

Practicalities

Bergen's **tourist office** is at Karl-Marx-Platz 12 (Mon–Fri 9am–8pm, Sat 9am–2pm; ☎21129). It might be worth enquiring about private rooms here if you're stuck for **accommodation**, though even Bergen fills up during the summer. For **eating and drinking** try the *Ratskeller* on Marktstrasse next to the post office which serves reliable pork and potato staples, or the *Café Meyer*, Damm-Str. 1, for coffee and cakes.

Putbus

About 8km south of Bergen by rail (or bus #406 from Bergen station) is the sad little town of **PUTBUS**, built as a residence by local aristocrat Prince Wilhelm Malte during the early nineteenth century. Today, despite its undeniably attractive layout and architecture, this *Kurort* town has a sterile, vaguely depressing atmosphere, with only the extensive Schlosspark providing some sort of relief from the prevailing melancholia.

Heart of it all is the **Circus**, a large but shabby roundel, with a plain pillar at its centre commemorating the founding of the town. Around are grand houses with peeling facades, most of which have been converted into apartments and defaced by satellite dishes. Alleestrasse runs west from the Circus past the spick and span whiteness of the Neoclassical **Theater**, Rügen's only theatre. Its flamboyant exterior, bedecked with an exaggerated portico and pseudo-Classical friezes showing poets, lyre-players and assorted muses, belies its present status as a venue for light classical concerts and farces. Next to the theatre is the **Marktplatz**, ringed by stolid nineteenth-century buildings, with a monument at its centre commemorating Prussia's military triumphs over Austria, Denmark and France.

On the other side of Alleestrasse is the **Schlosspark**, bisected from north to south by the chestnut tree-lined Kastanienallee. The Schloss itself was demolished in 1962, just before a visit to the area by Walter Ulbricht, the then GDR leader. Allegedly, the local party bosses hoped to score points with the SED top brass by eradicating this symbol of the feudal past. Fortunately some fine looking ancillary buildings remain and the park is worth wandering through in its own right. The leafy lanes of the park and the banks of the **Schwanenteich**, a small lake with adjacent ruined stables, make for good strolling and there's an attractive Neoclassical church at its western end, adjacent to the small **Tierpark** or zoo. Towards the eastern end of the park (just off Kastanienallee) is the down-at-heel **Orangerie**, once a winter refuge for exotic plants from the park, and now housing exhibition rooms and the tourist office (see below). On the eastern side of Kastanienallee is the **Rosencafé**, a pavilion-like former garden house, now a restaurant.

Practicalities

Putbus' **tourist office** is housed in the Orangerie (July & Aug Mon–Fri 7am–noon & 1–6pm; rest of year Mon & Wed–Fri 7am–noon & 1–4pm, Tues 7am–noon & 1–6pm). The best value-for-money **hotel** is the tiny *Pommernstübchen*, Bahnhofstr. 7 (☎278), at DM25 per person (without breakfast) for a basic room with corridor bathroom. For **eating and drinking** the *Rosencafé* serves edible meals from DM8–15, as does the *Kurhaus* at the western end of Alleestrasse; both have terraces which are good in summer if you've doused yourself with mosquito repellent. Another possibility is the similarly priced *Jägerhütte* just beyond the Tierpark in the Schlosspark where game specialities are on the menu. There's also a small if spartan *Eiscafé* in one of the Orangerie gatehouses. Putbus is a terminus for the *Rasender Roland*, a **narrow gauge steam railway** that runs from here to Binz, Sellin, Baabe and Göhren, the main resorts on Rügen's southeastern coast (see travel details at the end of this chapter). The station is at the end of Bahnhofstrasse, on the eastern edge of town.

Lauterbach

Just south of Putbus is **LAUTERBACH** (trains from Putbus Bahnhof or bus #406 from the Circus), a small fishing and sailing harbour. Lauterbach was chosen as site of Wilhelm Malte's very own purpose-built resort, and his opulent **Badehaus** still stands on the eastern outskirts. A luxurious-looking marble bath-tub stands in front of the entrance to this colonnaded Neoclassical bathhouse, but that's the only reminder of its former function. During GDR days it was holiday home for steel workers from Eisenhüttenstadt, but following the demise of the Worker's and Peasant's State they were booted out in favour of developers who plan to turn the place into a swanky hotel. The large wooded park behind the Badehaus is starting point for a pleasant coastal walking route. For the less energetic Lauterbach also has a decent **restaurant** in the shape of the *Hafenklause*, Am Hafen/Dorfstr. 1, which does reasonably priced fish dishes.

Vilm

Lauterbach is the staring point for boat trips around the island of **Vilm**, which has been closed to the public for the better part of the last fifty years. During GDR days its designation as a nature reserve served mainly to camouflage its role as an exclusive holiday island for the SED hierarchy (revelations in the press about "Erich Honecker's private island" served further to discredit the SED chief after his fall from power). Vilm was briefly opened to the public after the *Wende* but then closed once more, since it was felt that indigenous rare animal and plant species were being harmed by the renewed tourist traffic. Only the scientists of a government-sponsored conservation centre now have free access to the island, a fact which causes resentment among some locals.

Binz and around

Fourteen kilometres east of Putbus by narrow-gauge railway is the town of **BINZ**, an officially designated *Ostseebad,* or "Baltic Resort", that's been in business since the days of the Kaisers and retains much of its nineteenth-century atmosphere. The town's tree-shaded streets are lined by solid mansions with wrought-iron balconies and fancy gablcs – symbols of the self-confident society whose playground it was. These houses were originally built as holiday residences for wealthy families, and most were confiscated by the GDR government for use as workers' rest homes. They are now being sold off for conversion into hotels and apartments, ventures which promise to be lucrative, given the heavy volume of summer visitors.

Binz has two **Bahnhofs** – that for the *Rasender Roland* is southwest of the centre, while the one for the main line to the ports of Neu Mukran and Sassnitz is to the north. From the former, Bahnhofstrasse leads down into **Hauptstrasse**, the town's main shopping street. At the end of Hauptstrasse is Binz's apparently endless sandy **beach**, scattered with *Strandkörbe*. Nearby is the impeccably grand **Kurhaus**, whose terrace looks out over the Baltic. The only jarring note is struck by the spaceage watchtowers used by the lifeguards.

The beach stretches north for about 10km to the cranes of Neu Mukran, while in the opposite direction it curves southeast for a kilometre so before disappearing at the foot of tree-covered cliffs. At the southern end of the beach a sewage-polluted stream flows into the sea and notices warn that it's advisable to avoid swimming for 50m either side of it – you may wish to be even more cautious. Better perhaps to follow the path through the cliff-top woods to the headland viewpoints of **Silvitzer Ort** and **Granitzer Ort**, and enjoy the Baltic at a safe distance.

Practicalities

The **tourist office** (Mon–Fri 9am–noon & 1.30–6pm, Sat 9am–noon) is at Heinrich-Heine-Str. 7, though they haven't really got a great deal to offer. For private rooms head for the *Zimmervermittlung* at Bahnhofstr. 28 (☎2215). Cheapest **hotel** possibility is the *Haus Nymphe*, Wilhelm-Pieck-Str. 28 (☎2570), starting at about DM30 per person, though it's fairly basic. Still at the budget end of things is the *Ostseehotel*, Strandpromenade 38, on the front – slightly shabby but serviceable, charging from DM35 per person. Another resonable option on the front is the *Pension Zur Strandpromenade*, Strandpromenade 46 (☎2742), at DM40 per person, and the friendly *Pension Schwanebeck*, Margaretenstr. 18 (☎/2013), whose rates begin at DM45, and which has a good restaurant. For something a little more classy – and pricey – try the *Strandhotel Rügen*, Strandpromenade 49 (☎2033), with singles DM72, doubles DM119. Binz has the island's only **youth hostel** at Strandpromenade 35 (☎2423), while the **campsite** (☎5141) is just north of town at Prora in the woods between the main road and the beach. **Bike hire** is available at Schmachterseestr. 1 (9–11am), near the town's petrol station.

Eating and drinking won't be a problem here – there are plenty of restaurants and cafés. *Restaurant Vineta*, Hauptstr. 20, does the usual meat-and-potato variations at DM6–20. *Dünenhaus Binz*, Strandpromenade 23, on the front, springs no culinary surprises either but does resonable food at similar prices and has a pleasant terrace. Nearby the *Speiserestaurant Grand*, Strandpromenade 22, does game and fish dishes but works out a touch more expensive. For your *Kaffee und Kuchen* and ice-cream needs try the *Eiskonditorei*, Hauptstr. 29, or the *Café Sahara* on the Strandpromenade where things get a little more lively in the evening with dodgy (usually) live music. Binz has the only real **nightlife** possibilities on Rügen, in the shape of *Im Goldenen Löwe* with a disco until 3am and a *Nachtbar* that stays open until 6am.

Jagdschloss Granitz and Lancken-Granitz

Of possible inland excursions from Binz, the **Jagdschloss Granitz** (daily 9am–5pm; DM2) is another Wilhelm Malte folly, built on top of the 107-metre Tempelberg and reached by taking the narrow-gauge railway to *Haltepunkt Jagdschloss*. Quite why Malte, the founder of gloomy but attractive Putbus, chose to erect this ugly building, which looks like a Gothic water pumping station, is a bit of a mystery. Within, a vertiginous cast-iron staircase leads up the viewing tower to a prospect of Binz and the Jasmunder Bodden freshwater lake to the west, and the island of Vilm. The Jagdschloss also houses a small museum, devoted mainly to portraits of Malte's ancestors.

Older vestiges of the past can be found near the village of **LANCKEN-GRANITZ** (reached by taking the narrow-gauge railway to *Haltepunkt Graftitz* and walking south for about 1km, or by bus #414 direct from Binz). Turn right at the signpost marked *Ziegensteine* at the southwestern edge of the village; after about 1km there's a car park (unsignposted), from where a path leads across the fields to a number of prehistoric grave sites. The first, under a massive oak tree, dates back to 2300 BC and consists of two huge stone slabs laid over uprights to create a grave chamber. Nearby are a couple of similar but less well defined examples, and the surrounding fields and woods hide a number of grave mounds and indeterminate piles of stone.

Sellin and Baabe

About 4km east of Lancken-Granitz is **SELLIN** (narrow-gauge railway connection from *Haltepunkt Graftitz*, or bus #414), another fine example of turn-of-the-century holiday-making grandeur. The main drag here is the magnificent **Wilhelmstrasse** (from the Bahnhof follow Ostbahnstrasse and then turn left into Granitzer Strasse), which slopes up in some style to the top of low cliffs overlooking the beach. The street is lined by wonderful late nineteenth-century edifices, many of which are in use as hotels and pensions. Steps lead down to the beach, which, though littered with *Strandkörbe*, is marginally less crowded than that at Binz.

The **tourist office** is at Wilhelmstr. 40 (Mon–Fri 9am–noon & 1–6pm, Sat 9am–4pm) and there's a **Mitwohnzentrale** at Luftbadstr. 17. **Hotel** possibilities include *Pension Sellin*, on Wilhelmstrasse (☎304), with doubles from DM64. Another good bet is the *Strandhotel*, Wilhelmstr. 24 (☎394), which starts at DM35 per person. Sellin also boasts one of the ex-GDR's premier luxury hotel complexes, the *Cliff Hotel*, Siedlung am Wald (☎80). Here, party bosses enjoyed holidays in style, taking full advantage of their own tennis courts and private beach (served by a lift). Now it's open to anybody who can afford DM90 and upwards per person; there are also eight bars, restaurants and cafés to choose from. Sellin's **eating and drinking** possibilities could otherwise be better, but check out the *Bräustübl Sellin*, Wilhelm-Pieck-Str. 23, which does warm meals, *Kaffee und Kuchen* and ices. Directly above the beach, the *Strandhotel* has a reasonable, if none too fancy, restaurant/café (DM5–15). Another possibility is the *Gaststätte Berliner Hof*, Granitzer Str. 48, open all day for everything from breakfast to evening meals.

Moving down the coast leads to **BAABE**, a purpose-built modern resort that has all but obliterated an original fishing settlement. Though there are few attractions, Baabe itself has an excellent beach. There's also a huge **campsite**(☎293) more or less on the beach at the southern edge of town.

The Mönchgut peninsula

Baabe marks the beginning of the **Mönchgut**, a jagged three-pronged peninsula fanning out to the south. The landscape is one of gentle hills and fields, cut into by a series of sheltered bays on its western side, and sloping down to long beaches in the east. The Mönchgut has a character all of its own, enhanced by the fact that it has its own microclimate with the lowest annual rainfall on the island. The combination of good weather and beaches ensures that it's densely populated in summer, with numerous campsites and holiday complexes to cater for the crowds.

The area has an unusual history. From the thirteenth century onwards the area was owned by the Cistercian monastery of Eldena near Greifswald. They initiated a period of semi-isolation, requiring that the locals should be self-sufficient in everything. Despite this the Mönchgut prospered and evolved its own distinct customs and folk-costumes. The monks disappeared with the coming of the Reformation but the area retained its distinct identity and unusual social developments ensued. Women, for example, enjoyed a degree of equality almost unknown elsewhere in Germany.

Today, getting around the area is no problem, with bus #414 running through the resorts of Göhren and Lobbe, all the way to Thiessow and Klein Zicker at the southern end of the peninsula.

Göhren

GÖHREN is a windswept little resort straddling an exposed headland a few kilometres southeast of Baabe. The **Bahnhof** (southern terminus of the *Rasender Roland*) is more or less on the seafront, and your best bet is to head straight for the beach as the town itself is a little shabby. Just offshore is the **Buskam**, a glacier-deposited rock, once used as an altar by the Slav inhaitants of the island. The name is derived from the old Slavonic "bogis kamien", meaning "God's Stone". It's the biggest of Rügen's many *Findlinge* – rocks left by the passage of Ice-Age glaciers.

In town the only attractions are a couple of museums. From the station head up Strandstrasse and turn into Wilhelm-Pieck-Strasse where you'll find the **Mönchguter Museum** (May–Sept Tues–Sun 9am–5pm; Oct–April Tues–Fri 9am–noon & 1–5pm; DM3), a mildly diverting display of local folk costumes and material about the development of tourism and other indigenous industries like fishing and piloting. A few doors down on the same street is the **Museumshof** (May–Sept Tues–Sun 9am–5pm; Oct–April Tues–Fri 9am–noon & 2–4pm), essentially an old barn crammed with diverse and improbable-looking agricultural implements. There's another museum, the **Rookshus** (May–Sept daily except Tues 9am–5pm; winter closed; DM2), a seventeenth-century fishing cottage, on the road to Lobbe. Just out of town, off the main road in the dunes of the southern beach, is the **Museumsschiff Luise** (opening hours and price as the Rookshus), an old beached freighter, fascinating if you like boats, missable otherwise.

Göhren's **tourist office** is on Schulstrasse (Mon, Wed & Thurs 7am–5pm, Tues 7am–6pm; ☎201). For **accommodation** try *Zum Hövt*, Hövtstr. 8 (☎306), which starts at DM30 per person. The **campsite** (☎222) is hidden away in the woods a stone's throw from the sea, just northeast of the Bahnhof; with a capacity of 4000, it's the largest on the island and can get pretty hellish in high season. **Bike hire** is available at Hövtsr. 10. **Eating and drinking** possibilities include *Kaiser's Hofkneipe*, Waldstr. 11, for meat- and potato-type dishes, *Göhrener Café-Bar/Mönchguter Fischerstübchen*, a combined café/restaurant next to the post office on Wilhelm-Pieck-Strasse whose main line is fish dishes, and *Zur Muschel Bar* on the Strandpromenade, again specialising in fish.

Down the peninsula

South of Göhren, sandy beaches fringed with stones run all the way to the southern end of the peninsula. However, the presence of a massive **campsite** (☎222) just south of LOBBE and innumerable holiday homes, mostly still associated with factories and concerns all over the ex-GDR, means that these are often vastly over-subscribed. One way of escaping the crowds is to take a left turn off the main road about a kilometre south of Lobbe, and make for the tiny, one-street village of **GROSS ZICKER**. A path beyond the car park at the western end of the settlement ends at a stretch of isolated, sandy beach which, though popular, seems empty after the crowds on the eastern beaches. From Gross Zicker there's also access to the 66-metre **Bakenburg**, the Mönchgut's highest point, with correspondingly good views. To the north, in the village of **Gager**, is a **campsite**, just 150 metres from the sea.

Thiessow and around

At the southern end of the Mönchgut is the low-lying village of **THIESSOW**, which lives mainly from fishing, with a little tourism on the side. Local seamen also act as pilots for vessels sailing through the shallows separating Rügen from the mainland. To reach the nearest stretch of beach, cut through the woods just north of the village. A decent **pension** possibility is at Hauptstr. 5 (DM25 per person), and there's a **campsite** just west of the main road on the way into town (☎8226). The *Strandcafé* on the northern beach does decent food and excellent ice-cream, while *Mönchguter Fischerklause*, towards the southern end of the village at Hauptstr. 69, has good fish dishes. Absolute end of the road is the village of **KLEIN ZICKER**, just under 2km west of Thiessow. Crammed into the space at the foot of a hill on an odd blob of land sticking out into the sea, the place is a mecca for watersports enthusiasts, particularly surfers.

Jasmund

Rügen's most striking scenery is to be found in **Jasmund**, an area of undulating woods and fields jutting out into the Baltic on the island's northeastern shore. The celebrated white cliffs of **Stubbenkammer** have become Rügen's unofficial symbol, partly because of the romanticised paintings of Caspar David Friedrich. Running back from the coast is the forested pocket of **Stubnitz**, where easy walking routes criss-cross a woodland landscape more reminiscent of Europe's centre than its northern coast. Jasmund's only major town, **Sassnitz**, is the departure point for ferries to Denmark and Sweden.

Neu Mukran and Sassnitz

About 5km north of Binz, reached by bus #414, are the **Feuersteinfelder** or "flint fields". Here, a largish area just west of the main road is strewn with blue-black flints of various shapes and sizes, thought to have been cast up from the sea by prehistoric storms. Just to the north is one of the ex-GDR's last big prestige projects, the sprawling container port of **NEU MUKRAN**, linked with the Lithuanian port of Klaipeda. Neu Mukran was built in the early 1980s at the instigation of the Soviet Union, which wanted a cargo route from the west that bypassed politically unreliable Polish ports. Now, ironically, much of the cargo consists of withdrawing Soviet soldiers and their equipment.

The larger port of **SASSNITZ**, 5km or so to the north, is fairly forgettable, other than as a transit point. No longer the "prettily situated ... most frequented seaside resort in Rügen", of the pre-war Baedeker, Sassnitz is nowadays a predominantly new and ugly town of 20,000 people who live mainly from the harbour and fish-processing. A few villas remain from the port's turn-of-the-century glory days, but most look to be on the verge of collapse. In 1917 the famous sealed train provided by the imperial German government for Lenin passed through Sassnitz, en route to St Petersburg and the October revolution, and until just after the Wende the **Lenin-Waggon**, a carriage similar to the one used to transport him (the original having long since disappeared), stood in front of Sassnitz station stuffed with Lenin memorabilia. It was a popular sight with western visitors, but less so for the locals who disposed of it as soon as they were able – rumour has it that it's now gathering dust in Dresden. From Sassnitz **harbour** (well signposted near the southern entrance to town) there are regular sailings to the Danish island of Bornholm and the Swedish port of Trelleborg.

Stubbenkammer and around

Unless Scandinavia-bound, your best bet is to leave Sassnitz behind and head for the area's real attractions, the **Stubbenkammer** chalk cliffs of the coast, and the surrounding **Stubnitz** forest, all within the **Nationalpark Jasmund**. There are two ways to do this. The most obvious option is to head direct to Stubbenkammer by road (bus #408 or #419, a pleasant if hilly ride through the woods. The alternative is to follow the coastal path from the northern end of Sassnitz. Mostly it's a cliff-top walk, but occasionally the route dips down into steep-sided stream valleys. The *Gaststätte Waldhalle*, a few kilometres beyond the edge of Sassnitz, is a handy place to interrupt your journey. Adjacent is the **Wissower Klinken**, first of the really large chalk blocks, best appreciated from the cliff-top viewpoint on the **Ernst-Moritz-Arndt-Sicht**, a little way to the north.

Kleine Stubbenkammer and the Königstuhl

The path continues for several kilometres to the **Kleine Stubbenkammer** with the best views of the mighty **Königstuhl**, a vast pinnacle of chalk standing free from the main cliff-face. Königstuhl means "king's seat", and legend has it that in days of yore whoever could climb the seaward side of the 117-metre cliff would become king of Rügen and occupy a stone throne at the top. These days the place swarms with visitors, most of whom choose an easier means of access via the narrow footbridge (DM1) from the car park at the head of the road from Sassnitz. The view from the Königstuhl is, inevitably, splendid though you may have to fight for a space by the rail at the summit. The lines of parked cars along the approach road usually stretch back for several kilometres and the army of day trippers is served by a *Gaststätte*, a couple of *Imbiss* stands and souvenir shops. From the Königstuhl footbridge a precipitous path meanders down to the beach, which stinks and is strewn with rotting seaweed. The last couple of metres are descended by ladder.

The Herthasee

Shortly before the Königstuhl, a track branches off into the forest from the main road. A path leads from this junction to the mysterious **Herthasee**, a dark lily-bedecked pool hidden in the woods, said to have been the bathing place of the Germanic goddess Hertha, who rewarded the efforts of local farmers with rich harvests. According to the tale, after bathing Hertha would drown her mortal servants and their spirits gather on the shore each night. North of the Herthasee is the **Herthaburg**, a small hill with a large stone block nearby, which is thought to have served Rügen's early Slav inhabitants as a sacrificial altar.

Elsewhere on Jasmund

The rest of Jasmund has less to write home about. In the woods at the edge of the hamlet of NIPMEROW (bus #408 from Stubbenkammer), a few kilometres to the east, there's a **campsite** (☎0292/9230), while the otherwise boring village of **LOHME**, a couple of kilometres north, has a short stretch of beach which makes a good place to escape the summer crowds. **Accommodation** in Lohme is limited to a few **private rooms**, and there's no tourist office or *Zimmervermittlung*, so look out for *Zimmer Frei* signs. At the western end of Jasmund is GLOWE, distinguished by the transmitting masts of Radio Rügen, broadcasting mainly for the benefit of ships at sea and monitoring distress frequencies in the Baltic. Glowe is gateway to the **Schaabe**, a sandy isthmus planted with Scotch Pine, separating the Grosser Jasmunder Bodden from the sea. The beaches along the Baltic side are excellent, though the presence of an enormous **campsite** just west of Glowe means that they are rarely empty. This campsite is one of the largest on the island, though at the time of writing it was slated for closure.

Wittow

Wittow is Rügen's northern extremity, wind-battered and sparsely populated, with the headland of **Kap Arkona** and the hidden village of **Vitt** as its main tourist pulls. The area has some decent stretches of beach but these tend to be more exposed and generally less hospitable than those elsewhere on the island. Fish figures highly on local menus and is, generally speaking, well worth sampling.

Breege-Juliusruh and Altenkirchen

Wittow begins at the western end of the Schaabe with the twin village of **BREEGE-JULIUSRUH** (bus #419 from Stubbenkammer and Glowe). Largely given over to holiday camps, the only real reason to stop here is to take advantage of the beaches, a continuation of the Schaabe strands to the south. With your own transport, Breege, overlooking the Breeger Bodden inlet, is just about worth a quick diversion from the main road to look at the thatched *Kapitänshäuser*, eighteenth- and nineteenth-century fisher houses lining the main street, and to stop off for a bite at the *Fischerstube*, a fish speciality place (eels mainly – grilled, jellied and in soup) on the harbour. Should you wish to stop over, the *Gasthof Zum Breeger Bodden*, Dorfstr. 55, has rooms from DM35 per person. Juliusruh has little to offer apart from access to the beach and a ceramics factory producing kitsch objects.

En route from Breege-Juliusruh to Kap Arkona it's worth stopping off briefly in the village of **ALTENKIRCHEN** (bus #419 from Breege-Juliusruh) to take a look at the thirteenth-century **church** that gives the village its name (roughly "Old Church"). It's one of the most venerable on the whole Baltic coast, and richly decorated with thirteenth-century frescos, only uncovered during the late 1960s.

Kap Arkona

At the northern end of Wittow is **Kap Arkona**, whose cliff-top lighthouses and Slavonic fort draw streams of visitors. Make for PUTGARTEN (bus #403 from Altenkirchen), an inoffensive but uninspiring little place from where the Kap Arkona lighthouses are clearly visible.

Just north of the village, parking spaces are provided along the roadside for the carloads of visitors, most of whom dump their vehicles and walk the last 500 metres or so. The **new lighthouse**, dating from the turn of the century and looking very business-like with its orange and black stripes, is the first to assert itself. Moving closer, the **old lighthouse** is more likely to attract your attention. Designed by the ubiquitous Schinkel in 1826 it doesn't really look much like a lighthouse at all, but this three storey red-brick building, with its inset windows and verdigris-dusted dome, does justice to its creator. At the time of writing both lighthouses were out of bounds to the public, with Schinkel's creation shrouded in restorer's scaffolding; by the time you read this it may be accessible.

Nearby is evidence of much earlier human activity in the shape of the **Jaromarsburg**, the grass-covered ramparts of an ancient Slavonic fort, now barely recognisable. West of the lighthouses a path skirts the seaward edge of a forbidden military zone (once part of the GDR frontier "defences" but now in the hands of the *Bundeswehr*) to the **Gellort**, the ex-GDR's northernmost point, hardly an overwhelming sightseeing experience but a bracing enough stroll. If you find yourself feeling hungry, repair to the **seafood kiosk** just below the last leg of the approach road to Kap Arkona where they do excellent herring and fried potatoes with beer, soft drinks or coffee to wash it all down.

Vitt

It might be better, though, to save your appetite for a visit to the village of **VITT**, which has one of the island's best *Gaststätten*. This small fishing port lies hidden in the trees about a kilometre southeast of Putgarten at the end of a rudimentary concrete road. The best approach is to walk from Kap Arkona, although multi-seated horse-drawn carriages run to and from Putgarten charging DM3 return (signs at the beginning of the road from Putgarten forbid cars, but there's a car park near the entrance to the village). Also at the village entrance is a small thatched **chapel** with an octagonal ground-plan (the hand of Schinkel once again). The interior is almost bare with only naive wall-paintings of fishing-village life as decoration. From the chapel a path leads down into a small valley and the village itself, a cluster of improbably well-preserved and unspoiled thatched cottages. Vitt survives almost unchanged since the nineteenth century, seemingly oblivious to the tourists who flock here to wonder at its unique atmosphere, which owes much to the absence of cars, supermarkets and other facets of modern life. Throughout the GDR period it was a much sought-after holiday address, particularly among artists and writers: its popularity is increasing every year, though it hasn't attracted any grandiose development schemes – so far. Vitt's **beach** is stony and not particularly attractive, but it's quiet, the water is fairly clean and there's not a *Strandkörb* in sight.

Practicalities

Vitt's justly famous *Gasthof zum Goldenen Anker* is one of the best **restaurants** around, serving up wonderful fish and seafood dishes (particularly eel). Inside it's intimate and a model of *Gemütlichkeit*, while outside you can sit on benches in good weather. The chances of finding somewhere to **stay** in Vitt are practically nil, at least in summer. There are no pensions or hotels; what few rooms do exist are privately rented, usually to long-standing regular visitors, but should you wish to try your luck head for the small crafts shop run by Käthe Graf at Vitt No. 8, who may just be able to find you accommodation. **Rowing boats** can be hired from the small harbour or you can let a local sea-dog do the work for you in a motorboat.

Hiddensee

Another artist's holiday destination of long standing is the idyllic car-free island of **Hiddensee**, a 16km-long finger of land that stands like a barrage between Rügen and the Baltic. This is, without doubt, Rügen's most worthwhile and appealing corner, and the only real tourist draw in **West Rügen**.

Hiddensee experiences a heavy volume of visitors, but with a little leg-work or pedalling it's not difficult to escape the crowds. Despite its small size, the island has a startling variety of landscapes. The northern **Dornbusch** area is a plug of high ground topped by scrubby fields and sandy woods, while the central part of the island, focussing on the **Dünenheide**, is low-lying heath, giving way to a tapering strip of ever-shifting sand dunes called **Gellen**. Hiddensee has only a few thousand inhabitants, most of whom are concentrated in the villages of **Kloster**, **Vitte** and **Neuendorf**, though the number of inhabitants swells considerably during the summer. Kloster is easily the most appealing of the Hiddensee villages, and the best way to explore the rest of the island is to hire a bike here (DM4–6) and pedal your way around. Though most visitors come to Hiddensee as day trippers, the relatively small number of available beds means that, as elsewhere on Rügen, it's impossible to find somewhere to stay on Hiddensee during July and August.

From the thirteenth century onwards life on Hiddensee was dominated by the Cistercian order of monks, who, while the island's lay inhabitants plundered grounded ships, were not averse to mixing it with mainland fishermen for the prize of exclusive rights to the island's waters. The Reformation ended all that and the island later passed into Swedish hands until Prussia took over in 1815. Not to be left out of the general nineteenth-century tourism boom, Hiddensee used its superior natural charms to lure a better class of visitor, and the island attracted its share of artists and writers.

Getting there

The best approach to Hiddensee is via the small port of **SCHAPRODE** on Rügen's western shore (bus #410 from Bergen). Most vistors pass straight through this little village en route to the jetty for Rügen-bound boats. If you find yourself with time to kill, stick your nose in the late Romanesque **Dorfkirche**, a red-brick thirteenth-century church with a richly decorated pulpit and altarpiece that are strongly reminiscent of south German Baroque.

The first Hiddensee ferry leaves Schaprode at 8am and there are nine further departures until 7pm (journey time 30mins–1hr 15mins; DM8 return, bikes DM1). It's best to head for Kloster – some boats only go as far as Neuendorf or Vitte – though the island is small enough to make walking or cycling from one village to the other a viable option. Last departures from Hiddensee for the mainland are at 5.30pm (check these times though, as they may well change). It's also possible to travel to Hiddensee from the port of WIEK on Wittow (three departures in each direction daily; DM15 return), and from Stralsund on the mainland (15 sailings daily: 9 to KLOSTER via VITTE 1hr 30min, DM20; 6 to Vitte, 45min, DM20).

Kloster

Hiddensee's most popular destination is the little town of **KLOSTER**, straddling the northern end of the island. It's incredibly unspoilt, and is at its best when the daytime crowds have disappeared. There's easy access from the village to the west coast of the island which basically forms an 8km long beach.

From the small harbour where ferries from the mainland dock a lane leads into Kloster. A left turn at the village pond leads along Hauptstrasse, the nearest thing the town has to a main street. To the north of Hauptstrasse is the **Inselkirche** (Island church), in whose graveyard is buried **Gerhart Hauptmann** (1862–1946). Hauptmann, one of the many writers and artists who moved to Rügen in the nineteenth century, belonged to the Naturalist movement of the 1880s, and his dramas focused mainly on the lives and struggles of ordinary people. The realism of his most famous play *Vor Sonnenaufgang* (Before Sunrise), a "social drama" dealing with the human impact of industrialisation, caused a sensation at its première, and though his earlier works remain his most famous, Hauptmann's influence on modern German drama has been extensive. Signposts point the way to the **Gerhart-Hauptmann-Gedenkstätte** (daily 10am–4pm; DM1), the writer's former home, which is also known more picturesquely as *Haus Seedorn*. It's now packed with photos, manuscripts and theatre posters, though some of the rooms have been left as they were when the playwright lived and worked in them.

A little further along Hauptstrasse, just before the beach, is the **Museum der Insel Hiddensee** (daily 10am–3pm; DM1), the island museum, packed with archaeological bits and pieces and ceramics. The **beach**, protected by blocks of rock, can be windswept and wave-battered, but on a good day it's perfect, and if you're willing to walk you can soon leave your fellow visitors behind as the sands stretch south for a good 8km. To the north the beach rounds a headland, continuing for several kilometres at the base of the steepish cliffs of the Dornbusch.

Practicalities

At the time of writing Hiddensee had no **tourist office**, although onc should have opened by the time you read this. The most obvious **accommodation** possibility in Kloster is the *Pension Dornbusch* (☎248) on the harbour. Not far from the Hauptmann museum is *Haus Wieseneck* (☎316) with reasonable rooms at DM30 per person; another alternative is *Haus am Hügel* (☎234). For **eating and drinking**, *Pension Dornbusch* has a reasonable restaurant with views over the harbour, while the nearby *Fischrestaurant Haus Hitthin* is a also a good bet, though a bit more pricey. The *Inselbar* in the *Pension Haus Hiddensee* on Hauptstrasse, is a friendly place with decent food and stays open until midnight. For **bike hire** try *Fahrradverleih Gerhard Wannewitz*, Leuchtturmweg 5, reached by heading straight on at the village pond rather than turning left.

The Dornbusch

A recommended mini-cycle tour takes in the **Dornbusch** area to the north of Kloster. These gentle hills are the most appealing part of the Hiddensee and dominated by a lighthouse that warns ships of the island's presence. Take the road north to the miniscule hamlet of **Grieben**, where the *Gaststätte zum Enddorn* and its large garden entice thirsty cyclists. Those who don't succumb to its temptations will have their resolve tested again a little further along by *Hella's Eiscafé*, an ice-cream place in a thatched cottage. From the "main" road – in reality a crudely concreted track – there are a couple of turnings in the direction of the **lighthouse**, reached after a steep climb, but worth the effort for the excellent views of the island. Adjacent to the lighthouse is a military installation, once part of the GDR's coastal defences – though its purpose was to keep people in rather than out. These days its still in business (though no longer for the purpose of preventing citizens from striking out for Scandinavia on air mattresses) and signs warn of the risk of being shot if you approach, much to the anger of many German visitors.

Skirting the edge of the nearby woods leads to a clearing and the *Gaststätte zum Klausner*, the island's best eating and drinking place. The food is simple but good (and cheap), and best enjoyed at the outside tables during summer. The *Gaststätte* has a few double rooms for DM50, and rents out rustic-looking twin-bedded bungalows at DM10 per person, though these have no showers or toilets – you have to use the ones in the *Gaststätte*. From *zum Klausner* a steepish path leads back down into Kloster, making for wobbly cycle descents into the village.

Vitte and Neuendorf

A kilometre or so south of Kloster is **VITTE**, Hiddensee's biggest settlement and a kind of island capital. Despite this there's not much here, local builders having been less than discriminating in their efforts, though the **Blaue Scheune**, an old fisher-house painted completely blue, is worth a look for occasional art exhibitions. Main **hotel** possibility is the *Ferienhotel Vitte* (☎384). **Bike hire** is available from *Fahrradverleih Ludwig Müller* near the *Kaufhalle* supermarket opposite the harbour.

South of Vitte is the **Dünenheide**, an area of heathland which is at its best in August when the abundant heather blooms purple. A road leads across it via the *Heiderose*, a pleasant *Gaststätte* and good point to take a breather. Looked after by the *Gaststätte* management are a group of holiday bungalows in the woods between the road and the Baltic. Four people can rent one of these bungalows for DM65–75, including breakfast.

Neuendorf

Southernmost of the island's three villages is **NEUENDORF**, a quiet little place which makes a good starting point for wandering the **Gellen**, a sandy spit jutting out south towards the mainland. For crowd-haters, this is the island's most peaceful part. On the western shore, just south of Neuendorf, is a bathing beach, though on the Gellen itself you're restricted to marked paths as the whole area is a nature reserve.

Accommodation is, at the time of writing, pretty much limited to the *Hotel am Meer* (☎201), a GDR-era luxury hotel with a swanky restaurant. An alternative place for drinks and light snacks is the *Strandcafé*. For **bike hire** enquire at the *Freizeitcenter Neuendorf*, Neuendorf No. 20.

THE MECKLENBURG LAKE DISTRICT

The **Mecklenburg Lake District** represents one of Europe's last great unspoiled areas of natural beauty. Here, in a landscape of endless fields dotted by innumerable lakes and criss-crossed by quiet country lanes, life is still dominated by the agricultural calendar rather than the tourist season. The area stretches roughly 100km between the towns of **Schwerin** and **Neubrandenburg** on its west to east axis, and about 80km north to south between **Güstrow** and **Wittstock**. Numerous small lakes dot the landscape between Neubrandenburg and Berlin. In all, there are about 650 lakes in the region, of which the Müritz See and the Schweriner See are the largest. Many of the hitherto undisturbed lakeshores are home to unique wildlife, though these habitats are now being disturbed by the rush to turn the larger lakes into watersports resorts.

Schwerin used to be the capital of the Grand Duchy of Mecklenburg and the town retains some of its old air with its lakeside Schloss and grandiose municipal architecture. Until the early nineteenth century it was the centre of the *Junker* life – the landowning elite of the era dividing their time between here and Berlin while their serfs worked the great landholdings. Not far south, picturesque **Ludwigslust** boasts the finest castle of the region. Another destination is **Güstrow,** former summer residence of the Dukes of Mecklenburg and offering easy access to the Malchiner See. At the eastern end of this region are the towns of **Neubrandenburg** and **Neustrelitz** The former lost most of its original architecture under a hail of bombs, with only the medieval wall and gates surviving, while the latter, despite a well preserved Baroque centre, is struggling to find a way out of the GDR era.

Having your own **transport** makes exploration immeasurably easier, as the public transport network is limited. **Accommodation,** on the other hand, shouldn't be a problem: private rooms are readily available in many of the lakeside villages and most of the larger towns have at least one hotel. **Campers** are well catered for with plenty of established sites and new ones opening all the time.

Schwerin

SCHWERIN, 65km southwest of Rostock, was founded in 1160 by Henry the Lion, and is one of the region's oldest towns, though few reminders of its medieval origins survive. It sits at the centre of ten lakes, largest of which is the 22km long **Schweriner See.** Ferries operate here during summer, or you can hire a boat for more independent exploration. The town owes its pleasant atmosphere partly to the fact that it's surrounded by water and partly to the relative absence of conspicuous decay and postwar GDR architecture. All this is complemented by a number of cultural attractions: three museums, a resident philharmonic orchestra and two respected theatres. Schwerin is worth a day in its own right, and makes an ideal base for discovering the northwest.

The centre of Schwerin divides into three distinct quarters around the **Pfaffenteich,** a kind of glorified village pond. West of the Pfaffenteich, around the Hauptbahnhof, are the straight-laced **town-houses of Paulusstadt,** while to the east is the working-class district of **Schelfstadt.** To the south is the **Markt,** the true nucleus of the town.

Practicalities

Schwerin's **tourist office** at Markt 11 (Mon–Fri 10am–5pm, Sat 10am–1pm; ☎83830), has timetables and ferry tickets, and can also fix you up with private accommodation. There's a clutch of hotels near the station; *Stadt Schwerin,* Grunthalplatz 5 (☎812498), is the best with doubles from DM75, although the similarly priced *Hotel Polonia,* Grunthalplatz 15–17 (☎866 4045), and the *Niederlandischer Hof,* Karl-Marx-Str. 12–13 (☎83721), are both reasonable. Cheaper, but drearier, is the *Bahnhofshotel,* Grunthalplatz 11–12 (☎83778), with doubles from DM50. The nearest **campsites** are in the villages of Rabensteinfeld and Retgendorf, on the southern and northeastern shores of the Schweriner See respectively. There are also some rudimentary sites on the western shore of the lake.

For **eating and drinking** the fish restaurant *Gastmahl des Meeres,* Grosser Moor (near the Markt), is good and economical. Also worth trying are the traditional *Alt Schiveriner Schankstuben,* Schlachtstr. 9, and the *Theatercafé* in Grosser Moor. The local youth head for *Achteck,* Wittenburgerstrasse, which also has occasional discos.

The Markt and around

The Markt is lined by seventeenth- and eighteenth-century buildings, including the **Rathaus** which had a mock-Tudor facade added a couple of hundred years after its construction but is otherwise unremarkable. Also on the square is the town's smallest museum, the **Heimatmuseum** (10am–5pm; DM0.50) with a photographic record of the postwar decades. Just north of the Markt is the **Dom** (Tues–Sat 10am–noon, Sun 2–4pm), offering excellent views from its tower. After taking in the city panorama head south down Puschkinstrasse and Schlossstrasse to the **Alter Garten**, a largish square flanked on one side by a Neoclassical theatre building.

The Staatliche Museum

At the eastern end of the Alter Garten is the **Staatliche Museum Schwerin** (Tues–Sun 10am–5pm; DM2), easily the town's most important museum and renowned for its large collection of seventeenth-century Dutch paintings The works of Adrian van Ostade and Hendrik Avercamp stand out in particular, and one of the most notable works is his *Ice Landscape,* an all-embracing view of seventeenth-century Dutch society as represented by skaters on a frozen lake. Still-life works rate a whole room to themselves, although only the incredibly detailed animal and plant studies of **Otto Marseus van Schrick** are worth a closer look. Other collections include eighteenth-and nineteenth-century landscapes and portraiture from Mecklenburg, porcelain from the Meissen factory, glassware examples and a display of late medieval religious art.

The Schloss

Schwerin's neo-Gothic apparition of a **Schloss** (Tues-Sun 10am–5pm; DM2) stands on a small island in a western inlet of the Schweriner See. Gloriously over the top, it was built to the extravagant taste of one of the Grand Dukes of Mecklenburg during the nineteenth century. The ground-plan is octagonal with each exterior corner punctuated by a fanciful tower, while on the inside there's a strange jumble of things to see ranging from a few restored state rooms to an exhibition of works by local painters. Best of the paintings are **Carl Malchin's** evocative nineteenth-century landscapes and, from this century, **Erich Venzmer's** stark views of sodden Mecklenburg flatlands.

Schelfstadt

East of the Pfaffenteich, the run-down **streets of Schelfstadt** are the most interesting part of town to wander through. At their heart is the **Schelfldirche,** one of the most significant Baroque churches in the entire north of Germany, and looking strangely incongruous in this dilapidated area. Completed in 1713, it has an unusual shape with four wings and a flat roof, quite unlike the Baroque churches of southern Germany.

Ludwigslust

LUDWIGSLUST is a tiny town, 35km south of Schwerin. Major transport routes seem to pass it by, but Ludwigslust is in fact one of the most attractive corners of Mecklenburg. This is due to its role, from 1756 to 1837, as residence of the local dukes, who built a magnificent Schloss and sumptuous park here. Today, admittedly, the place is in a fairly rough state of repair but the Baroque Schloss easily outclasses those of Schwerin and Güstrow. The town itself is predominantly Baroque in style with a nine-teenth-century Neoclassical overlay.

The **Schloss** (guided tours Tues-Sun 11am, lpm, 2pm; DM3), in its Baroque splen-dour, contrasts sharply with the lowly houses of the lumpy streets around. It's a brick structure with sandstone embellishments, but its most notable features are the larger-than-life-statues that run around its roof, looking ready to totter onto the cobbles below. The interior, thanks to long years in service as municipal offices during the GDR era, is a little disappointing, with leaky ceilings, rotten woodwork and chipboard partitions dividing up the entrance hall. At the time of writing only four sparsely furnished rooms were open to the public, but the enthusiasm of the official guide makes up for the paucity of what's on display. Much of the castle's original treasure has disappeared over the years – in one room only the lids of a terrine set remain, the bowls having been allegedly plundered by Red Army cooks in postwar years. Highlight of the tour is the **Goldener Saal,** one of the few rooms that has not been allowed to deteriorate over the last forty years. Glittering with mirrors and gilt, it makes a stunning setting for concerts. Golden vases, cherubs and columns abound – all, however, made from papier-mâché, a result of a cost-cutting exercise by one of the dukes. Outside, the extensive **Schlosspark,** packed with exotic trees and artificial cascades, is an ideal place to stroll away a few hours.

Practicalities

The tiny **tourist office** is at Schlossstr. 6 (Tues–Fri l0am–lpm & 2–6pm; Sat l0am–lpm; ☎2355). The town's three **hotels** tend to be booked up well in advance: *Mecklenburger Hof,* Ernst-Thälmann-Str. 42, and *Parkhotel,* Kanalstr. 19 (☎2815), both have doubles from about DM50; *Stadt Hamburg,* Letzte Str. 46 (☎2506), has doubles from about DM40. A lakeside **campsite** can be found near the village of NEUSTADT-GLEWE, a couple of kilometres northeast of Ludwigslust. Good bets for **eating and drinking** include the *Ratskeller,* Nummerstr. 1, and the *RostockerHof,* Schweriner Str. 39, which do standard German dishes.

Güstrow

GÜSTROW, about 60km northeast of Schwerin, used to be the summer residence of the Dukes of Mecklenburg who built themselves yet another fancy Schloss here. A provincial little place which escaped the attentions of the wartime bombers and thus remains pretty much intact, it first became a popular retreat during the sixteenth century, though it had been flourishing on levies raised from passing merchants for a couple of centuries before that.

Güstrow is certainly worth a day or two, and makes one of the most popular destinations in the region – not least because of the gorgeous countryside to the east and south and easy access to lakes like the Malchiner See and Krakover See. Before the war it was the home and workplace of **Ernst Barlach**, Germany's greatest twentieth-century sculptor. Another artistic claim to fame is the fact that it's the birthplace of **Uwe Johnson**, a GDR author who went into exile in 1959 following conflict with the authorities. His work dealt with the psychological shock of Germany's division and the development of fear and mistrust on opposite sides of the border between the two Germanys – themes that have assumed new relevance of late.

Around town

The predominantly eighteenth- and nineteenth-century houses that make up the town today are in good shape, and many retain original features like brass shop signs or elaborately carved doors. Güstrow appears to be wealthier than many other towns in the region, and this is most evident in the fact that its churches – which during GDR days depended on donations for their upkeep – are in relatively good repair.

In the middle of town on the Markplatz, the **Pfarrkirche** is chiefly interesting for its changing art exhibitions. Hiding away a few streets to the south on Franz-Parr-Platz is the Gothic **Dom**, whose most significant interior features are striking sixteenth-century statues of the apostles in the nave, and a cast of an **Ernst Barlach sculpture,** the *Schwebende* (or "Flying Angel" as it's known in English), commemorating the fallen of World War I. It's a copy of the original work which was melted down by the Nazis who categorised Barlach's work as decadent. Barlach lived in Güstrow in a kind of internal exile until his death in 1938, and his studio is now a museum*. For more information about the town's history head for Güstrow's **Stadtmuseum** (Mon–Fri 9am–noon & 1–5pm; DM2) near the Dom at Franz-Parr-Platz 7.

The **Schloss** on Franz-Parr-Platz (Tues–Sun 9am–noon & 1–5pm; DM3) has had a chequered history. Dating from the sixteenth century, it fell into disrepair a century or so after construction, and was only used again in 1811 when Napoleon's troops set up a field hospital here on their way to Russia The Nazis later used it as a prison, destroying what was left of the original furnishings and decor. The end result is that the castle looks better from the outside than within, though a spacious **museum** inside devoted to German, Italian and Dutch art of the sixteenth century tries to redress the balance.

Practicalities

The **tourist office** is at Markt 23 (Mon–Fri 10am–5pm), but to book **private accommodation** you need to head for Gleviner Str. 33 (Mon–Fri 10am–noon & 1–4pm; ☎61023). The large *Stadt Güstrow*, Markt 2/3 (☎4841), and the *Zentralhotel*, Baustr. 10 (☎63012), both have doubles from around DM50. There's a **youth hostel** at Gustrower Chausee (☎2486), in KRAKOW AM SEE, a lakeside village about 22km south of town; Güstrow's nearest **campsite** is in the village of LOHMEN, about 15km to the south. For **eating and drinking** the *Schlossgaststätte*, Franz-Panr-Platz 1, and the *Ratskeller,* do the usual north German staples, while the *Fischerklause,* Lange Str. 9, is a fish restaurant offering a rest from relentlessly pork-dominated menus. The *Café Borulin*, Markt 2/3, has a dodgy disco by night, if you're in need of a little more excitement.

---

* If you're interested in his work, the **Barlach Atelierhaus** (Tues–Thurs & Sun 9am–noon & 1–5pm; free), Barlach's former lakeside studio, can be reached by taking bus #4 from the Bahnhof. On display are over a hundred of his sculptures and drawings.

Neubrandenburg

At the eastern end of the Mecklenburg lake district is **NEUBRANDENBURG,** interesting chiefly for its medieval fortifications, which are among the most imposing in northern Europe. These largely survived the wartime air-raids that levelled the rest of the town, which was rebuilt in grandiose GDR concrete style during the 1950s and 60s. It's a place to stop in very briefly en route to or from the Baltic coast or the nearby lakes.

Neubrandenburg was founded during the thirteenth century at an important trade route junction, and soon grew rich enough to build extensive fortifications to protect the populace from the robbers and hustlers who lurked in the Mecklenburg woods, preying on travellers and merchants. Today the city walls remain almost completely intact, circling the town centre and broken only by Friedrich-Engels-Strasse, a huge roundabout that whisks through-traffic around Neubrandenburg's heart.

From the Hauptbahnhof Ernst-Thälmann-Strasse leads into the town centre. Near the station itself (turn right into Friedrich-Engels-Strasse) you can see the *Wiekshauser,* half-timbered houses set into the walls. The fortification system has four **gates** in total; the **Neuer Tor**, the **Friedlander Tor**, the **Stargarder Tor** and the **Treptower Tor** – all fine examples of Gothic brickwork. Take them in by walking around the outer edge of the city centre. Within the walls, the twelfth-century **Marienkirche** and the fourteenth-century **Johanniskirche** are the only significant pre-war survivors.

West and south of town are many of the region's lesser-known lakes. The area around the village of **FELDBERG** (which has a youth hostel), 20km to the south is particularly rewarding. Following inauspicious-looking dirt roads into the woods often leads to hidden beauty spots and silent lakes and pools.

Practicalities

The friendly **tourist office** at Ernst-Thälmann-Str. 35 (☎6187) can help with **accommodation**. The only **hotel** is *Vier Tore* on Karl-Marx-Platz (☎5141), with doubles from around DM80 a night. There's a **youth hostel** at Ihlenfeldstr. 73 (☎3761) and another in the village of BURG STARGARD about 10km southeast of town. The nearest **campsite** is at Am Breiten Luzin in FELDBERG (see below). **Eating and drinking** possibilities are rather limited, though the *Weinstuben am Wall,* Ringstr. 4, is reasonable and *Tor Café* in the Friedländer Tor makes a good place to break your circuit of the walls.

Neustrelitz

About 35km south of Neubrandenburg by rail is the odd town of **NEUSTRELITZ**, custom-built capital of the smaller of the two duchies into which Mecklenburg was divided from 1701 until 1934. First impressions are good – streets of Baroque buildings radiate out from a central circus to striking effect and the town slopes down towards the tree-lined shores of the appealing Zierker See. On closer acquaintance, however, Neustrelitz seems to be suffering from extreme post-GDR depression. The locals are distinctly unfriendly and – though this could be a reaction to the presence of large numbers of Red Army soldiers who give the place an occupied feel – the net result is that visitors are left feeling slightly ill at ease.

All of this is a great shame as Neustrelitz is an interesting town dating back to the beginning of the eighteenth century. The town was built to a geometrical street plan around a small hunting lodge transformed into a palace by the Duke of Mecklenburg-Strelitz in 1730. Though it initially benefited from its position on trade routes between the coast and Berlin, Neustrelitz never really rose above sleepy backwater status as the absence of significant post-eighteenth-century development attests.

The town

From the Bahnhof, Strelitzer Strasse leads to the **Marktplaltz**, the town's central focus. Unlike the market-places of other eastern German towns it has yet to be reclaimed by commerce, and for the time being remains dominated by a massive Soviet **war memorial**. As the withdrawal of the ex-Soviet army continues it will only be a matter of time before this relic of their presence is relocated or demolished; take a look while it's still here. Hidden away behind all this is the Baroque **Stadtkirche** which was designed according to plans drawn up by a doctor in the service of one of the Grand Dukes.

From here the town streets radiate out in all directions. Head down Gutenbergstrasse to the **Schlosspark,** a lakeside ornamental garden laid out in the English style by the landscape architect Lenné. The Schloss itself was destroyed in 1945 and though no traces remain, its **Orangerie,** built in 1755 as a winter home for exotic plants, survives. It was transformed into a concert hall by Schinkel during the nineteenth century and the gaudy interior is still more or less intact. Best place to appreciate this is the **restaurant** (see below) where copies of Classical statues and reliefs are backed by vivid orange walls. A stone's throw from the Orangerie is the **Schlosskirche** which, though ostensibly neo-Gothic, has an almost Jungendstil look to it. At the northwestern end of the Schlosspark, just past a small Neoclassical temple, the Zierker See begins. Its shores are great for strolling, and there are a couple of decent *Gaststätten* (see below) and boat hire facilities.

Practicalities

The **tourist office** in the Stadtraat building on the Markt (☎4921) has plenty of **private rooms** on its books, and can also offer information about local lake trips and walking trails. Chances are you won't want to stay overnight, but the town has a few acceptable **hotel** possibilities, including the tolerably seedy *Hotel am Bahnhof*, Strasse des Friedens 1, and the marginally more appealing, family-run *Zur Klause*, Strelitzer Str. 53 (☎2770). Also available are bike hire facilities at Strelitzer Str. 46 – a good way to explore the lakeside paths.

Best place to **eat and drink** is the *Inselgaststätte Helgoland* on an island near the town's pleasantly run-down harbour area (just north of the Schlosspark). The island is linked to the lakeshore by a footbridge and you can watch the sun go down over the Zierker See in a little garden while enjoying a beer and dishes from the eastern German pork-and-potato cookbook (DM5–16). The *Orangerie* restaurant's luridly opulent decor is more interesting than the food (DM8–20). Also worth a visit are the *Restaurant Reuter Stube*, Seestr. 8, and the *Gaststätte Zentrale Pension* on Marktplatz, once home to Engelbert Humperdinck (the late nineteenth-century composer of light opera, not the late 1970s ballad singer of sideburns and flares fame).

travel details

Trains

From Wismar to Rostock (12 daily; 1hr 30min); Schwerin (7 daily; 30min).

From Rostock to Bad Doberan (16 daily; 25min); Berlin (12 daily; 3hr); Güstrow (numerous daily; 40min); Magdeburg (9 daily; 4hr); Neubrandenburg (13 daily; 2 hr 30min); Neustrelitz (13 daily; 2hr);

Sassnitz (15 daily; 1hr); Schwerin (12 daily; 1hr 15min); Stralsund (via Bergen: 15 daily; 1hr 15min); Warnemünde (numerous daily; 25min); Wismar (11 daily; 1hr 45min).

From Stralsund to Berlin (17 daily; 4hr 30min); Neubrandenburg (10 daily; 1hr 50min); Neustrelitz (7 daily; 2hr 20min); Rostock (15 daily; 1hr 20min); Sassnitz (10 daily; 1hr 10min).

From Greifswald to Berlin (13 daily; 2hr 30min); Stralsund (numerous daily; 25min); Wolgast (change at Züssow: 11 daily; 25min).

From Wolgast to Ahlbeck (12 daily; 1hr 30min); Züssow (for Greifswald and Stralsund: 10 daily; 30min).

From Bergen to Lauterbach (via Putbus: 9 daily; 40min); Lietzow (for Binz: 12 daily; 10min); Sassnitz (10 daily; 45min).

From Lietzow to Binz (12 daily; 20min).

From Putbus to Göhren (*Rasender Roland* narrow-gauge line via Binz, Jagdschloss Granitz, Sellin and Baabe: 9 daily; 1hr 10min).

From Sassnitz to Rostock (via Bergen: 2 daily; 3hr 30min); Stralsund (via Bergen: 11 daily; 1hr)

From Schwerin to Berlin (7 daily; 3hr); Bützow (for Güstrow: 12 daily; 1hr); Ludwigslust (hourly;

30 min); Magdeburg (6 daily; 3hr); Rostock (15 daily; 2hr 30min); Wismar (11 daily; 1hr).

From Neubrandenburg to Berlin (10 daily; 2hr 10min); Güstrow (8 daily; 2hr); Neustrelitz (17 daily; 45min); Stralsund (10 daily; 1hr 50min).

From Neustrelitz to Berlin (numerous daily; 1hr 30min); Neubrandenburg (numerous daily; 45 min); Rostock (13 daily; 1hr 40min); Stralsund (10 daily; 2hr 30min).

Ferries

From Warnemünde to Gedser (6 daily; 2hr); Travemünde (daily; 9hr); Wismar (daily; 5hr).

From Stralsund to Kloster (9 daily; 1hr 30min); Vitte (6 daily; 45min).

From Wiek to Hiddensee (3 daily; journey times vary).

CHAPTER NINE

BERLIN AND BRANDENBURG

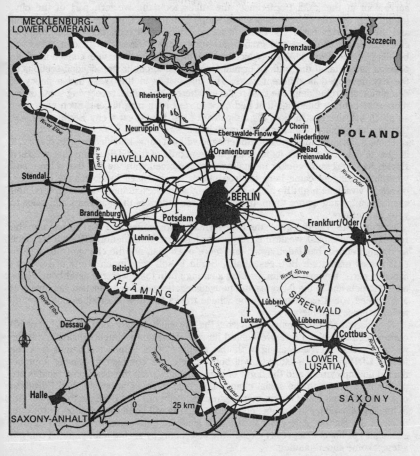

Berlin is like no other city in Germany, or, indeed, the world. For over a century its political climate has either mirrored or determined what has happened in the rest of Europe: heart of the Prussian kingdom, economic and cultural centre of the Weimar Republic, and, in the final days of Nazi

Germany, the headquarters of Hitler's Third Reich, it is a weather vane of European history. After the war, the world's two most powerful military systems stood face to face here, sharing the spoils of a city for years split by that most tangible object of the East–West divide, the Berlin Wall. As the Wall fell in November 1989, Berlin was once again pushed to the forefront of world events. And it's this weight of history, the sense of living in a hothouse where all the dilemmas of contemporary Europe are nurtured, that gives Berlin its excitement and troubling fascination.

It was, of course, **World War II** that defined the shape of today's city. A seventh of all the buildings destroyed in Germany were in Berlin, Allied and Soviet bombing razing 92 percent of all the shops, houses and industry here. At the end of the war, the city was split into French, American, British and Soviet sectors, according to the agreement at the Yalta Conference: the Allies took the western part of the city, traditionally an area of bars, hotels and shops fanning out from the Kurfürstendamm and the Tiergarten park. The Soviet zone contained what remained of the pompous civic buildings, churches and grand museums around Unter den Linden. After the building of **the Wall** in 1961, which sealed the Soviet sector and consolidated its position as capital of the young German Democratic Republic, the divided sections of the city developed in different ways. The authorities in the West had a policy of demolition and rebuilding; the East restored wherever possible, preserving some of the nineteenth-century buildings that had once made Berlin magnificent. Even now, after so much massive destruction, it's indicative of just how great a city Berlin once was that enough remains to fill pages of a guidebook.

Though Berlin is impossible to understand without some knowledge of its history, it is easy to enjoy. For years its isolation in the middle of the GDR meant that **western Berlin** had a pressure-cooker mentality: this, combined with the fact that a large and youthful contingent came here to drop out or involve itself in alternative lifestyles, created a vivacious **nightlife** and a sense of exhausted excitement on the streets. And even if you try and ignore them, the constant reminders of the war years add spice to your wanderings.

Now that the Wall has gone, the two Germanys are unified and the city has won the role of German capital, western Berlin seems less sure of its identity. The border, once so rigidly defined, has faded away, and more often than not the change from west to east passes unnoticed. But, essentially, Berlin is still very much a city of two very separate parts, **eastern Berlin** forming a strange twin to its western neighbour. Here, on the streets and in the factories and housing estates, you'll see constant reminders of a discarded social experiment – one whose traces the new authorities are urgently trying to erase from memory.

The postwar schizophrenia that marred the city will hopefully soon vanish, but **unification** seems destined to leave behind its own damage: the huge subsidies that the western sector received, along with the massive social support schemes that the former GDR granted its citizens, will both be removed completely, causing unprecedented unemployment and the flight of big companies from the city. Some pundits are predicting a return to the social chaos of Weimar days, as an established European order comes to an end. Others, more optimistic, point out that Berlin is the capital city of the largest country in Europe, one whose exports will be of greater total worth than those of the United States. But in the final analysis, no amount of facts and figures, economics or history can really explain the place; only by seeing it for yourself can you attempt some understanding.

If you're spending any time in Berlin, and want to get the full picture on the city and the towns that surround it, our *Berlin* guide is essential reading.

Inevitably, **the pace of change** in Berlin, particularly the eastern part of the city, means that certain sections of this chapter are going to be out of date even as you read them, such is the speed of transformation. It can only be a matter of time, for example, before many eastern streets revert to their pre-1933 names.

One great advantage of unification is that, for the first time since the 1930s, the area **around Berlin** and the newly-designated Land of **Brandenburg** can easily be visited. **Potsdam** and the magnificent palace of Sanssouci is the obvious day trip, and the city of **Brandenburg** itself has its attractions, as does the lake- and forest-strewn countryside. It's important to visit now, since the "lost-in-time" feel of some of the small towns and villages, like **Neuruppin**, will soon be gone for ever.

BERLIN PRACTICALITIES

Because the city is only now recovering from its schizophrenic state, divided between two nations, a few special points need thinking about before making a trip to **BERLIN**, east or west. Obviously, since Germany is now united as one nation, at no point do you need to show passports when travelling into the city – something that still takes getting used to if you knew Berlin in the days of the Wall.

> The telephone code for the area that was formerly West Berlin is ☎030. Plans are afoot to align the erstwhile GDR's antiquated phone system with that of the west, but until then, to call numbers formerly in East Berlin from West Berlin, dial ☎0372; to call numbers in West Berlin from East Berlin dial ☎84930. See also p.677.

Arriving

All scheduled and charter flights arrive at **Tegel airport** (☎410 11), whence frequent #9 buses run directly to the Bahnhof Zoologischer Garten (**Zoo Station**) in the city centre (journey time 35min; DM3). Alternatively, take the #9 bus to Jakob-Kaiser-Platz U-Bahn and transfer to the U-Bahn system (the bus ticket is valid for the U-Bahn journey: see p.721). Taxis cover the distance in half the time and cost DM15–25.

It seems likely that **Schönefeld airport** in the former East Berlin will gradually become the city's second airport: for the moment, though, you'll probably land there if arriving from a central or Eastern European destination. Transit coaches connect the airport to Zoo Station, and to Tegel airport.

You'll also arrive at the Zoo Station if coming by **train**. International **coaches** mostly stop at the central bus station, west of the centre near the Funkturm; regular #94 buses or the U-Bahn from Kaiserdamm station link it to the city centre, a journey of about fifteen minutes.

Accommodation

Since the fall of the Wall, interest in Berlin has dramatically worsened the chance of getting an inexpensive room. It's essential to book at least three months in advance to be guaranteed accommodation, particularly at the budget places on the western side of the city. Remember, too, that the city's hotels fill completely during important trade fairs and festivals, and at Easter and Christmas. The majority of affordable accommodation is in the western section of the city, and it's easiest to look for a room there: if you definitely want to stay in the east, see "Accommodation in Eastern Berlin", on pp.720-1.

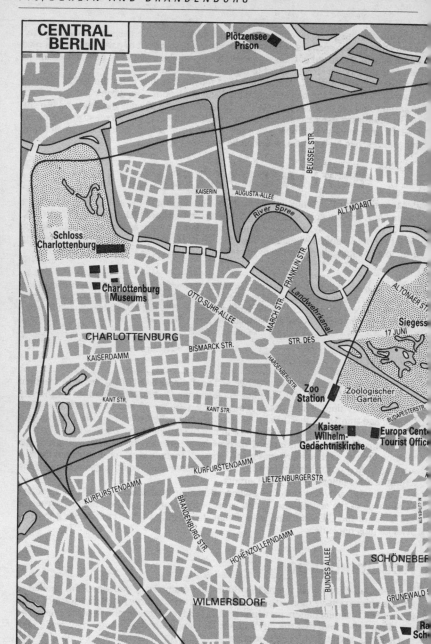

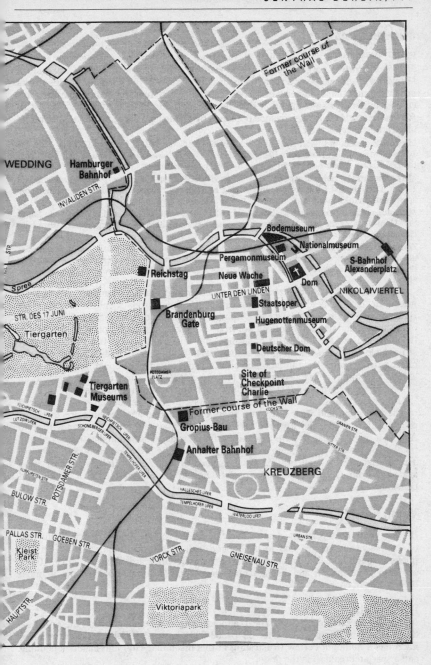

Mitwohnzentralen

Easily the best way of finding a place to stay is by contacting one of the *Mitwohnzentralen* organisations (see *Basics*). The shortest period of time a *Mitwohnzentrale* will book a room for is usually one week. But considering this works out to roughly DM30–45 per person per night, it clearly represents an important cost-cutting option over anything other than the cheapest dormitory hostel beds. Almost all *Mitwohnzentralen* will take advance bookings by phone, and vary only in the number of places they have on their files.

Mitwohnzentrale, 3rd floor, Ku'damm Eck, Kurfürstendamm 227–8, 1/12 (☎88 30 51). Mon–Fri 10am–7pm, Sat & Sun 11am–3pm. Biggest and best of the *Mitwohnzentralen*, and an easy walk from the Zoo Station. Also has rooms for women in women-only apartments.

Mitwohnzentrale, Holsteinischestr. 55, 1/31 (☎861 8222). Mon–Fri 10am–7pm, Sat 10–11am, Sun 1–2pm. Friendly and fairly central, specialising in inner-city rooms. They also have women-only apartments on their lists.

Mitwohnzentrale Kreuzberg, Mehringdamm 72, 1/61 (☎786 6002). Mon–Fri 10am–7pm, Sat & Sun 11am–4pm. As the name suggests, their rooms tend to be in the Kreuzberg/eastern part of the city only, and therefore cheaper.

Zeitraum Mitwohnzentrale, Horstweg 7, 1/19 (☎325 6181). Mon–Fri 9am–1pm & 3–8pm, Sat noon–4pm. Well organised Mitwohnzentrale that specialises in providing inexpensive accommodation for budget travellers. Rooms from DM25 per night, even less if you're a student and book ahead.

Compared to the *Mitwohnzentralen*, most other forms of accommodation seem over-priced or inconvenient. The **tourist office** in the Europa Center, (entrance on Budapester Strasse, 1/30; daily 8am–11pm; ☎ 262 6031; additional office in Zoo Station) offers a hotel and pension **booking service** for DM3, though their options, especially in the high season, are limited to mid-range and upmarket places. However, you may strike lucky and get something for around DM40 single, DM70 double, or be offered a cheap private room. The tourist office also provides an advance booking service: write at least a fortnight before you arrive to *Verkehrsamt Berlin*, Europa Center, 1000 Berlin 30, stating the length of your stay and how much you're prepared to spend.

Otherwise, your chances of finding somewhere directly are good, if you're prepared to phone around and wear out some shoe leather. Summer weekends are the most problematic periods, and if you're arriving on a Friday night any time from June to August it makes sense to have at least the first few days' accommodation booked in a hotel if you haven't been able to reserve a room from the *Mitwohnzentralen* in advance. The tourist office's leaflets *Tips für Jungendliche* and *Berlin Hotelverzeichnis* (also available from German National Tourist Offices) have useful lists of hotels and pensions.

Youth hostels

Berlin's youth hostels are used extensively by school and sporting parties from the rest of Germany, and rooms tend to be booked well in advance: hence it's essential to phone through first. The **Informationszentrum Berlin**, Hardenbergstr. 20 (☎310040; see also "Information and listings magazines" pp.724-5) can book rooms in most hostels free of charge.

IYHF hostels

All require an IYHF card (see *Basics*), although this can be bought from the organisation's offices in Tempelhofer Ufer 32 (☎362 3024; nearest U-Bahn Möckernbrücke). Each has a midnight curfew (frustrating in this insomniac city) and includes bedding and a spartan breakfast in the price.

Jugendgästehaus, Kluckstr. 3, 1/30 (☎261 1097). Bus #29, direction Oranienplatz. Most central of the IYHF hostels, handy for the Tiergarten museums, and very solidly booked. DM20 for those under 25, DM23 otherwise; key deposit DM10. 9am–noon lockout.

Jugendherberge Wannsee, Badweg 1, 1/38 (☎803 2034). S-Bahn #3 to Nikolassee. Very pleasantly located, with plenty of woodland walks on hand near the beaches of the Wannsee lakes but far from the city centre – and with a curfew that renders it useless if you're enjoying the nightlife. DM22 for under 25s, DM25 otherwise; key deposit DM20.

Jugendherberge Ernst Reuter, Hermsdorfer Damm 48–50, 1/28 (☎404 1610). U-Bahn #6 to Tegel, then bus #15 towards Frohnau. So far from town that it's the least popular of the hostels and therefore least likely to fill in summer: worth bearing in mind as an emergency option. Under 25s DM17, otherwise DM20; key deposit DM10.

Other hostels

Bahnhofsmission, Zoo Station, 1/12 (☎313 8088). Church-run mission with limited accommodation for rail travellers (you may need to show your ticket) for one night only. No risk that you'd want to stay for any longer, mind, since the rooms are windowless and dingy and the atmosphere starchily puritan. DM15 per person for a 4-bedded cell with a meagre breakfast; rise and shine by 6am. A desperate option, but worth trying if you're penniless or arrive in town very late.

Jugendgästehaus am Zoo, Hardenbergstr. 9a, 1/12 (☎312 9410). Zoologischer Garten U- and S-Bahn. Excellent location, extremely popular. Singles DM35, doubles DM60, four people in a room DM25. No curfew.

Jugendgästehaus Genthiner Strasse, Genthiner Str. 48, 1/30 (☎261 1481). #29 bus direction Oranienplatz. Located near the grimmer section of the city's canal, but just ten minutes' away from the nightlife of Winterfeldtplatz. Singles DM35, doubles DM66, triples DM90, breakfast included. No curfew; key deposit DM20.

Studentenhotel Berlin, Meiningerstr. 10, 1/62 (☎784 6720). #73 bus to Rathaus Schöneberg, or Eisenacherstrasse U-Bahn. Dormitory accommodation at the relaxed edge of the city's action. Doubles DM30 per person, including breakfast. No curfew; key deposit DM20.

Hotels and pensions

Singles under DM75

Centrum Pension Berlin, Kantstr. 31, 1/12 (☎31 61 53). Great location, two minutes' walk from Savignyplatz and five minutes' bus ride from Zoo Station. Renovated with style, and great value at DM40 single, DM65 double.

Hotel Alpenland, Carmerstr. 8, 1/12 (☎312 9370 or ☎312 4898). Well situated and an excellent choice at this price. Singles DM60–70, doubles DM90–130.

Hotelpension Hansablick, Flotowstr. 6, 1/21 (☎391 7007). A short hop from the Tiergarten, this is one of the few "alternative" hotels in town, being run by a collective. Singles DM75, doubles DM95; up to five people in a room DM40; breakfast included.

Hotelpension Pariser Eck, Pariserstr. 19, 1/15 (☎881 2145 or 883 6335). Adequate lodgings in a pleasant, leafy back street. Ten minutes' walk from the Ku'damm and with some classy cafés nearby. Singles DM50–75, doubles DM70–120; breakfast included.

Hotelpension am Lehninerplatz, Damaschke-str. 4, 1/31 (☎323 4282). Youth hostel-type atmosphere bang in the middle of an area that's lively at night. Dormitory accommodation in a four- or five-bedded room DM25–35 (including breakfast); singles (two rooms only) DM53 or DM63; doubles DM43–48. The single and double rooms don't include breakfast.

Hotelpension Südwest, Yorckstr. 80, 1/61 (☎785 8033). Dreary part of town, but close to Kreuzberg hill and an area that's buzzing at night. Singles DM35, doubles DM60.

Pension Kreuzberg, Grossbeerenstr. 64, 1/61 (☎251 1362). Close to Kreuzberg hill at the smarter end of that neighbourhood. Singles DM40, doubles DM65.

Pension am Savignyplatz, Grolmanstr. 52, 1/12 (☎313 8392). In the midst of Savignyplatz's nightlife; pleasantly seedy. Singles DM37, doubles DM65–75.

Pension am Viktoria-Luise-Platz, Viktoria-Luise-Platz 12a, 1/30 (☎211 4095). A quiet haven in the older part of town, with some interesting bars to explore nearby. Singles DM52, doubles DM74.

DM75 upwards

Unless otherwise stated, the following each include breakfast in the price.

Hotel Artemisia, Brandenburgischestr. 18, 1/15 (☎87 89 05). The first women-only hotel in the city. Dormitory-type accommodation in a three-bedded room DM43, singles DM85–95, doubles DM120–180. Fills up quickly, so it's advisable to book in advance.

Hotel Bogota, Schlüterstr. 45, 1/12 (☎881 5001). Pleasant luxury at sensible prices. Singles DM56–95, doubles DM92–155.

Hotel Charlot, Giesebrechtstr. 17, 1/12 (☎323 4051). Neatly restored, efficiently run hotel near Adenauerplatz. Excellent value for money at DM60–110 single, DM95–155 double.

Hotel Dittberner, Wielandstr. 26, 1/15 (☎881 6485). Old-fashioned finery in comfortable surroundings and at affordable prices. Singles DM90, doubles DM110–150.

Hotel Meineke, Meinekestr. 10, 1/15 (☎882 8111). Typical Berlin hotel with an amiable atmosphere, about a minute's walk from the Ku'damm. Singles DM120–135, doubles DM200.

Hotel Riehmers Hofgarten, Yorckstr. 83, 1/61 (☎78 10 11). Situated in an old Gothic red-brick building in a part of Kreuzberg unscathed by war damage, this is an excellent choice for exploring the less commercial parts of the city. Singles DM150, doubles DM190.

Hotelpension Imperator, Meinekestr. 5, 1/15 (☎881 4181 or 882 5185). Good-value central, intimate hotel, situated on one of the most exclusive yet friendly streets in the city. Singles DM60–85, doubles DM85–120; breakfast not included.

Campsites

None of western Berlin's three **campsites** is close to the centre: however, they're all inexpensive (prices are a uniform DM5 per tent plus DM6 per person per night), well run and, with one exception, open year-round.

Camping Dreilinden, Albrechts Teerofen, 1/39 (☎805 1201). From Oskar-Helene-Heim U-Bahn, take a #18 bus in the direction of Kohlhasenbrück. Open April 1–Sept 30. Two and a half kilometres from the nearest bus stop, this site is inadvisable unless you have transport. Free showers and a small restaurant.

Camping Haselhorst, Pulvermühlenweg, 1/20(☎334 5955). #10 bus in the direction of Haselhorst. The most accessible campsite but the least picturesque. A few minutes' walk from the Havel lakes, and not far from Spandau Citadel. Facilities include a restaurant, bar, showers (DM0.50) and a small shop. Four week maximum stay.

Camping Kladow, Krampnitzer Weg 111–117, 1/22 (☎365 2797). Bus #34 direction Gatow or #35 direction Kladow, then change at Ritterfeld Damm for the #35E. Friendly campsite with the best facilities of all the three sites, including a free crèche, bar, restaurant, shop and showers (DM0.50). Six week maximum stay.

Accommodation in Eastern Berlin

In eastern Berlin the **cheapest accommodation option** is private rooms. These can be arranged via the tourist office, who have large numbers of private householders on their lists. Another source is the **bed and breakfast agency** run by Frau Neugebauer, Wilhelm-Pieck-Str. 206, 1040 (☎2812 5841), who can put you in touch with private householders who rent out rooms from DM25 per person. Alternatively you can cut out the intermediary and go straight to the landlords and ladies with *Herzlich Willkommen – 27,500 Privatquartiere in der DDR* (Mair DM19.50; from any bookshop). Rooms, while nothing fancy, are a bargain compared to even the cheapest hotel.

Accommodation in a private home can be arranged in advance via *Berlin Homestays*, a British company that specialises in finding private rooms in households in eastern Berlin. They offer more than just an accommodation deal, attempting to match visitors up with hosts who share their interests and will be prepared to offer some insight into the city. For details, contact Karen Lawrie, 4 Nuffield Close, Bicester, Oxon, OX6 7TL (☎0869/242011).

Hostels, camping and hotels

A couple of **youth hostels** lie to the east of the city. Closest to town is the **Egon-Schultz-Jugendtourist-Hotel**, Franz-Mett-Str. 7, 1136 (☎512 9127; U-Bahnhof Tierpark), while on the edge of the city is the **Jugendherberge Berlin-Grünau**, Dahmestr 6, 1134 (☎681 4422; reached by taking bus #6 as far as the school).

Of the designated **campsites**, easiest to reach is the *Intercamping* site by the Krossin See, just outside the village of Schmöckwitz on the southeastern outskirts of the city. To reach the site from the centre take the S-Bahn to Grünau and then tram #86 to the end of the line. From here it's a two-kilometre walk if you can't catch one of the occasional buses.

Since 1989 private campsites have mushroomed – often little more than a space in someone's garden. For a complete list of private sites in and around Berlin and in the rest of the ex-GDR get hold of a copy of *DDR Privatplätze für Camping und Wohnmobile* (Alexandra Verlag, DM19.80).

Hotels in the former eastern sector remain prohibitively expensive and, in comparison to the west, thin on the ground. If you want to stay in a hotel, it's probably better to try and find one in the western part of Berlin. The following eastern Berlin hotels represent good value for money at DM50–100 per person per night: *Berliner Hof*, Friedrichstr. 113a, 1040 (☎282 7478), a small, central hotel with corridor bathrooms, breakfast available; *Märkischer Hof*, Linienstr. 133, 1040 (☎282 7155), sixteen rooms, some of which have showers, breakfast available; *Novalis*, Novalisstr. 5, 1040 (☎282 4080), cheapish central possibility with eight rooms, some with showers, breakfast available.

Getting around

Berlin is a large city, and sooner or later you'll need to use its efficient if expensive transport system. The **U-Bahn**, running both under and over ground, covers much of the centre and stretches into the suburbs: trains run from 4am to between midnight and approximately 12.30am, an hour later on Friday and Saturday.

The **S-Bahn** system was severely damaged in World War II, and renovation has only recently begun. These days the service is far less frequent than the U-Bahn system, but better for covering long distances fast – say for heading out to the Wannsee lakes. The city **bus network** covers most of the gaps in the U-Bahn system: **night buses** run at intervals of around twenty minutes, although the routes sometimes differ from daytime ones; the *BVG* (see below) will supply a map.

Eastern Berlin's **tram network** survives from prewar days, though thankfully the rolling stock is a little more modern. Tram termini in the centre of town are at **Am Kupfergraben** near Friedrichstrasse and **Hackescher Markt** near Marx-Engels-Platz. Tickets are available from machines at the termini or from U-Bahn stations.

Tickets

Tickets for the western U- and S-Bahn system and the bus network can be bought from the orange-coloured machines at the entrances to U-Bahn stations. These take all but the smallest coins, give change and have a basic explanation of the ticketing system in English. Though it's tempting to ride without a ticket, be warned that plain-clothes inspectors frequently cruise the lines (particularly, for some reason, at the beginning of the month), meting out on-the-spot fines of DM60 for those without a valid ticket or pass.

Single tickets (*Einzelfahrschein Normaltarif*) common to all the systems cost DM3, irrespective of how far you want to travel; they're valid for two hours, enabling you to

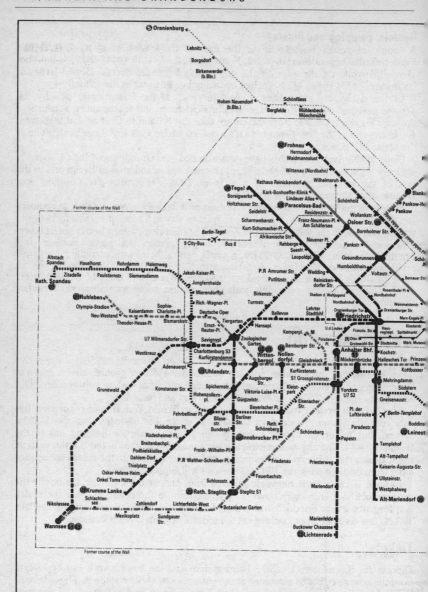

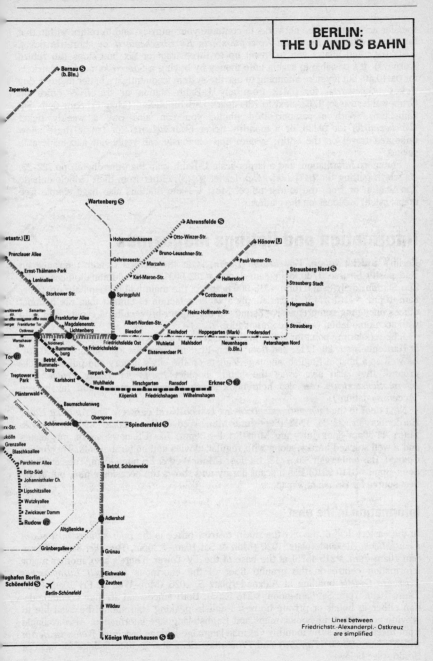

**BERLIN:
THE U AND S BAHN**

Bernau Ⓢ
(b.Bln.)

Zepernick

Wartenberg Ⓢ

etastr.) Ⓤ

Prenzlauer Allee

Ernst-Thälmann-Park

Leninallee

Storkower Str.

archlewski- Samariter-
str   str
berger Frankfurter Tor
Ostkreuz

Warschauer
Str.

Tor Ⓢ

Treptower
Park

Plänterwald

In
rx-Str.

uköln
Grenzallee
Blaschkoallee

Parchimer Allee

Britz-Süd

Johannisthaler Ch.

Lipschitzallee

Wutzkyallee

Zwickauer Damm

Rudow

Flughafen Berlin
Schönefeld Ⓢ ✈

Grünbergallee

Altglienicke

Ahrensfelde Ⓢ

Hohenschönhausen   Otto-Winzer-Str.

Gehrenseestr.   Bruno-Leuschner-Str.
                 Marzahn

Karl-Maron-Str.

Springpfuhl

Frankfurter Allee
Magdalenenstr.
Lichtenberg

Albert-Norden-Str.

Biesdorf   Kaulsdorf
Friedrichsfelde Ost   Wuhletal   Mahlsdorf
Ⓢ Friedrichsfelde   Elsterwerdaer Pl.

Nöldnerpl.
Rummels-
burg

Betrbf.
Rummels-
burg

Karlshorst   Wuhlheide   Hirschgarten   Ransdorf   Erkner Ⓢ ⓔ

Tierpark

Biesdorf-Süd

Köpenick   Friedrichshagen   Wilhelmshagen

Baumschulenweg

Oberspree

Schöneweide Ⓢ Spindlersfeld Ⓢ

Betrbf. Schöneweide

Adlershof

Grünau

Eichwalde

Zeuthen

Berlin-Schönefeld

Wildau

Hönow Ⓤ

Strausberg Nord Ⓢ

Strausberg Stadt

Hegermühle

Strausberg

Paul-Verner-Str.

Hellersdorf

Cottbusser Pl.

Heinz-Hoffmann-Str.

Hoppegarten (Mark)   Fredersdorf

Neuenhagen   Petershagen Nord
(b.Bln.)

Former course of the Wall

Königs Wusterhausen Ⓢ ⓔ

Lines between
Friedrichstr.-Alexanderpl.- Ostkreuz
are simplified

transfer across the three networks to continue your journey, and to return within that time on a different route. An *Einzelfahrschein Kurzstreckentarif*, or short-trip ticket, costs DM2 and allows you to travel up to three train or six bus stops (no return journeys). It's possible to save a little money by buying a *Sammelkarte* of four tickets for DM10.40, but if you're intending to use the system frequently it's better to buy a **day ticket** (*Tageskarte*) for DM12 from any U-Bahn station or the *BVG* office on Grunewaldestrasse, 1/62, next to Kleistpark U-Bahn station (Mon–Fri 8am–6pm, Sat 7am–2pm). With a passport-sized photo, you can also buy a weekly ticket (*Wochenkarte*) for DM28, or a monthly ticket (*Monatskarte*) for DM70: these allow unlimited travel on the entire system and obviously can represent a considerable saving.

For more information, and a larger-scale U-Bahn map than the one on pp.722–23, it's worth getting the *BVG Linienplan* leaflet (DM3), either from their cubicle outside Zoo Station or from the tourist office. Most U-Bahn stations also have simple free maps; ask at the kiosk on the platform.

Information and listings magazines

Berlin's **tourist office**, *Verkehrsamt Berlin*, is in the Europa Center (entrance on Budapester Strasse, 1/30; daily 8am–11pm; ☎262 6031), with additional offices in the Zoo Station (daily 8am–11pm; ☎313 9063) and in the main hall of Tegel airport (daily 8am–10pm; ☎4101 3145). It can supply a wider selection of bumph than the national offices, including comprehensive listings of the higher-brow cultural events, and help with accommodation (see "Accommodation").

A better starting point for gathering more general info is the **Informationszentrum** at Hardenbergstr. 20, 1/12, 2nd floor (Mon–Fri 8am–7pm, Sat 8am–4pm; ☎31 00 40). As well as a host of English-language leaflets on the city's history and political background, they also give away the handy booklet *Berlin for Young People*. The *Informationszentrum* can also help book youth hostel accommodation (again see "Accommodation").

Next door to the *Informationszentrum* are two **cultural centres**. The *Amerika Haus*, Hardenbergstr. 22–24, 1/12 (Sept–June Mon, Wed & Fri 11.30am–5.30pm, Tues & Thurs 11.30am–8pm; July–Aug Mon–Fri 1–5.30pm) has US newspapers, magazines and a well stocked library, along with regular movies and cultural events. The *British Council*, Hardenbergstr. 20, 1/12, 1st floor (Mon, Wed & Fri noon–6pm, Tues & Thurs noon–8pm; ☎3110 9910) has a scant library and shows the occasional film, but is the best source for British newspapers.

Information in the east

In the eastern half of the city the **main tourist office** is the *Informationszentrum am Fernsehturm*, Alexanderplatz, 1026 (Mon & Sat 10am–8.30pm, Tues–Fri 8am–8.30pm, Sun 10am–7pm; ☎215 4575) at the base of the TV Tower. There's also another major information centre on the ground floor of the enormous *Reisewelt Europäisches Reisebüro GMBH* building at Alexanderplatz 5, 1026 (Mon–Wed & Fri 10am–6pm, Thurs 10am–7pm, Sat 9am–noon; ☎215 5255). Both offices can arrange accommodation either in hotels or private homes. English-speaking staff should be available to provide you with guidebooks, maps and English-language information. Also available from these offices is the monthly German-language listings brochure *Wohin in Berlin* which costs DM1.80 (*Tip*, *Zitty* and *Prinz* magazines also include listings for eastern Berlin – see below).

Listings magazines

Berlin has two essential **listings magazines**, which come out on alternate weeks. *Zitty* (DM3.40) is marginally better than *Tip* (DM3.70): both have day-by-day details of gigs, concerts, events, TV and radio, theatre and film, alongside articles on politics, style and the Berlin in-crowd, and useful classified ads. The most recent listings mag is the monthly *Prinz* (DM3). Unable to compete with either *Tip* or *Zitty*, *Prinz* entices readers with titillating covers, and is worth picking up only for its restaurant listings.

The monthly *Berlin Program* (free from the tourist office, otherwise DM2.70) has more condensed listings alongside info on opening times, and national and international train, bus and plane timetables.

The best large-scale **map** of the city (west and east) is the ingeniously-folded *Falk Plan* (DM8.80), which contains an excellent gazetteer and enlarged plans of the city centre. We've only been able to show major streets on our maps: the *Falk Plan* is an essential complement.

WESTERN BERLIN

Until November 1989, the **western areas of Berlin** formed the distinct and artificially created city of West Berlin, a pocket of western capitalism kept alive at great effort and expense by interested parties. Under the four-power agreement, American, British and French troops occupied the city, and the Federal Government in Bonn poured in aid in the form of grants, subsidies and loans. Like the opulent shops that line the Kurfürstendamm, the city was intended as a showcase of western values and wealth in the centre of Soviet-occupied territory. And, sealed off from the GDR, it developed an intensity that gave West Berlin its excitement. Now, though some of the excitement has been replaced by uncertainty over how the former East and West will meld, Berlin is still one of Europe's most atmospheric cities.

No one in their right mind comes here for light-hearted sightseeing: in its western reaches especially, Berlin is a profoundly scarred city, and even in the flashiest sections of the new centre, around the **Memorial Church**, it still seems half-built, the modern buildings somehow making it look less finished and more ugly. Unlike Paris, Amsterdam, or Munich, this isn't a city where you can simply stroll and absorb the atmosphere. You need to plan your trips and target your points of interest, using the city's transport system to cover what can be longish distances. Those points of interest are, almost without exception, sombre: the **Reichstag**, looming symbol of the war years; the remains of the **Wall**, facet of its aftermath; and several **museums** which openly and intelligently try to make sense of twentieth-century German history.

The brighter side is that this isn't the only face of modern western Berlin. By night the city changes, awakening into a **nightlife** that's among the best in Europe – the bars here are by turn raucous, shady, stylish and promiscuous, the discos and clubs blasting their stuff well into the early hours; restaurants are excellent, cheap and of unequalled variety.

Culturally, the city has enjoyed the advantage of massive subsidies from Bonn and a legacy of great art collections. By far the finest of these is in the suburb of **Dahlem**, where a museum complex holds everything from medieval paintings to Polynesian huts. Elsewhere, there's bound to be something to your taste. About a third of western Berlin is either **forest** or **park**, and some of these green stretches are surprisingly beautiful: in the centre, **Schloss Charlottenburg** and its gardens are a great place to loll away a summer afternoon, and, on the city's western outskirts, the **Havel lakes** and the **Grunewald forest** have a lush, relaxed attraction that's the perfect antidote to the city's excesses.

The centre

Wartime damage has left western Berlin with the appearance of a badly patched-up skeleton: beneath the surface the former street plan survives, but in a haphazard fashion and fractured by the erstwhile course of the Wall. The city centre is marked by the **Zoologischer Garten**, or more properly the combined U-Bahn, S-Bahn and train **Zoo Station** adjacent. A stone's throw from here is the centre's single notable landmark, the rotting tusk of the **Kaiser-Wilhelm-Gedächtniskirche** (Kaiser Wilhelm Memorial Church); the **Kurfürstendamm**, an upmarket shopping boulevard, targets in on the church from the west. North and east of the Zoo is the **Tiergarten** park, ending in the east with the old **Reichstag** building and the reopened **Brandenburg Gate**. Near the **Tiergarten Museum district** the former border cuts east to run above **Kreuzberg**, western Berlin's enclave of immigrant workers, "alternative" living, and the most vibrant area at night. **Schöneberg**, a mostly residential area, forms the other point of interest in this part of the centre; to the northwest the museums and gardens around **Schloss Charlottenburg** provide a respite from the modernism of the centre's filing-cabinet office buildings. In between, the city is mostly residential and suburban and, unless you've opted for a pricey hotel, is where you're likely to find **accommodation**.

Zoo Station, the Kurfürstendamm and the Tiergarten

Whether you come by train, coach or bus from Tegel airport, chances are you'll arrive at Bahnhof Zoologischer Garten – **Zoo Station**. Perched high above the street, and with views across to the Zoo, the train station is an exciting place to end a journey, conjuring memories of prewar steam trains under its glassy roof. At street level, though, it's an unkempt and conspicuously lavatorial-smelling place that until recently was run by the East Berlin authorities. By day, but chiefly by night, it's the meeting place for the city's drunks and dope pushers, but has been much cleaned up since a few years back when it was a marketplace for heroin dealing and child prostitution.

The Kurfürstendamm

Step out east from Zoo Station and you're in the centre of the city's maelstrom of bright lights, traffic and high-rise buildings. A short walk south and you're at the eastern end of the **Kurfürstendamm** (known as the **Ku'damm**), a 3.5-kilometre strip of ritzy shops, cinemas, bars and cafés that zeros in on the centre like the spoke of a broken wheel. The great landmark here, the one that's on all the postcards, is the **Kaiser-Wilhelm-Gedächtniskirche**, built at the end of the last century and destroyed by British bombing in November 1943. Left as a reminder, it's a strangely effective memorial, the crumbling tower providing a hint of the old city. Adjacent, a new **chapel** (daily 9am–7.30pm) contains the tender *Stalingrad Madonna*, while the blue glass campanile at the back has gained the local nickname of the "Lipstick" or the "Soul-Silo".

The area around the church acts as a focal point for western Berlin's punks and down-and-outs, who threaten the well-heeled Ku'damm shoppers with demands for cash. It's a menacing, unfriendly spot and **Breitscheidplatz**, the square behind, isn't much better, a dingy concrete slab usually filled with skateboarders and street musicians. This area marks the beginning of Tauentzienstrasse, with the **Europa Center**, a huge shopping centre that contains the *Verkehrsamt* (tourist office), on its northern side and a gimmicky **Multivision** film, slide and model history of the city on the second floor (daily 9am–3pm; DM6). It's worth a climb to the **observation platform** (daily 9am–11pm; DM2), under the rotating Mercedes-Benz symbol, for a preliminary reconnoitre of the centre. Further down Tauentzienstrasse is the *KaDeWe*, an abbreviation of the German for "the Department Store of the West": this it isn't, though it's still an impressive statement of the city's standard of living.

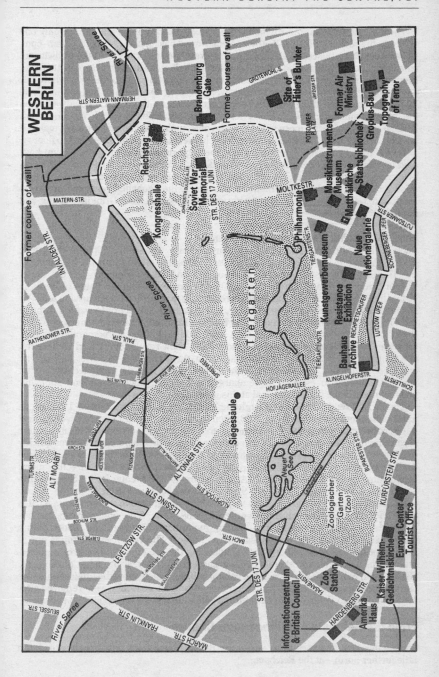

WESTERN BERLIN

Brandenburg Gate

Former course of wall

GROTEWOHL-S.

Site of Hitler's Bunker

EBERT STR.

Former Air Ministry

Gropius-Bau

Topography of Terror

POTSDAMER PLATZ

Reichstag

Soviet War Memorial

MOLTKESTR.

Musikinstrumenten Museum

Staatsbibliothek

Kongresshalle

JOHN FOSTER DULLES ALLEE

STR. DES 17 JUNI

Matthäikirche

HERMANN-MATERN-STR.

River Spree

MATERN-STR.

Philharmonie

TIERGARTENSTR.

PUTSBAMER STR.

Former course of wall

INVALIDENSTR.

River Spree

Kunstgewerbemuseum

Neue Nationalgalerie

SCHÖNEBERGER UFER

RATHENOWER STR.

PAUL STR.

LÜTZOW UFER

Tiergarten

Resistance Exhibition

REICHPIETSCHUFER

CALVIN STR.

LÜNEBURGER STR.

BEVELSWEG

BELLEVUE UFER

SPREEWEG

Bauhaus Archive

TIERGARTENSTR.

SCHILLERSTR.

KLINGELHÖFERSTR.

KIRCH STR.

KÖSTLINER UFER

TILE STR. IMÜLLER STR.

ALTONAER STR.

HOFJÄGERALLEE

Siegessäule

KLOPSTOCK STR.

TÜRM STR.

ALT MOABIT

ESSENER STR.

LESSING STR.

BACH STR.

Neuer See

BURGSTER STR.

KURFÜRSTEN STR.

BOCHUM STR.

Zoologischer Garten (Zoo)

Europa Center Tourist Office

ELBERFER STR.

LEVETZOW STR.

WALDSTR.

MULLINGER STR.

FRANKLIN STR.

MARCH STR.

STR. DES 17 JUNI

BACH STR.

Informationszentrum & British Council

FASANENSTR.

Zoo Station

HARDENBERG STR.

Kaiser Wilhelm-Gedächtniskirche

BEUSSEL STR.

River Spree

Amerika Haus

There's little to do on the Ku'damm other than spend money, and there's only one cultural attraction, the **Käthe-Kollwitz-Museum** at Fasanenstr. 24, 1/15 (11am–6pm; closed Tues; DM6; buses #9, #19 or #29). The drawings and prints of Käthe Kollwitz are among the most moving to be found from the first half of this century. Born in 1867, she lived for almost all her life in Prenzlauer Berg in the eastern part of the city, where her work evolved a radical left-wing perspective. Following the death of her son in World War I, her woodcuts, lithographs and prints became explicitly pacifist, often dwelling on the theme of mother and child. When her grandson was killed in World War II her work became even sadder and more poignant. The museum's collection of her work makes it possible to trace its development, culminating in the tragic sculptures on the top floor.

By the time you reach **Adenauerplatz**, the slick showrooms of the Ku'damm have died out and the bars become affordable: although the clientele tends towards brash kids and sloshed squaddies, it's not a bad starting point for an evening's boozing. Best of all for eating, drinking and nightlife, though, is the squashed rectangle of streets south and west of Zoo Station, focusing on **Savignyplatz** (see "Drinking, eating and nightlife").

The Zoologischer Garten and the Tiergarten

Back in the centre, the **Zoologischer Garten** (daily 9am–sunset, 9pm at the latest; DM7.50, Aquarium DM7, combined ticket DM11, kids half-price) forms the beginning of the **Tiergarten**, a restful expanse of woodland and lakes originally laid out under Elector Friedrich III as a hunting ground and destroyed during the Battle of Berlin in 1945 – though so successful has been its replanting that these days it's hard to tell. The zoo itself is much like any the world over, and expensive too: better to wander through the Tiergarten tracing the course of the **Landwehrkanal**, an inland waterway off the River Spree. Near the Corneliusbrücke a small, odd sculpture commemorates the radical leader **Rosa Luxemburg**. In 1918, along with fellow revolutionary Karl Liebknecht, she declared a new Socialist Republic in Berlin along the lines of Soviet Russia. The pair were kidnapped by members of the First Cavalry Guards: Liebknecht was shot while "attempting to escape", Luxemburg was knocked unconscious and shot, her body dumped in the Landwehrkanal at this point.

The broad avenue that cuts through the Tiergarten is the **Strasse des 17 Juni**, its name commemorating the day in 1953 when workers in the East rose in revolt against the occupying Soviet powers, demanding free elections, the removal of all borders separating the two Germanys, and freedom for political prisoners. Soviet forces quickly mobilised, and between two and four hundred people died; the authorities also ordered the execution of twenty-one East Berliners and eighteen Soviet soldiers – for "moral capitulation to the demonstrators". At the centre of the avenue is the **Siegessäule** (April–Nov Mon 1–6pm, Tues–Sun 9am–6pm; DM1.20; bus #16 or #24), the victory column celebrating Prussia's military victories that was shifted to this spot from what is today's Platz der Republic on Hitler's orders in 1938. Though the boulevard approaches exaggerate its size, it's still an eye-catching monument: 67m high and topped with a gilded winged victory that symbolically faces France. The view from the top is one of Berlin's best – the Brandenburg Gate announcing the grandly restored streets of eastern Berlin, the Reichstag standing like a gnarled protector at the edge of the park. Have a look, too, at the mosaics at the column's base, which show the unification of the German peoples and incidents from the Franco-Prussian War: they were removed after 1945 and taken to Paris, only to be returned when the lust for war spoils had subsided.

From the Reichstag to Checkpoint Charlie

Strasse des 17 Juni comes to an end at the Brandenburg Gate, but it's better to start a little further north – at the Reichstag.

The Reichstag – and the legacy of the Wall

Built in the late nineteenth century to house the German parliament, burned in 1933, and the scene of Hitler's wresting of control of Germany in the same year, the **Reichstag** today seems lost in a sea of irony. Inscribed with the words *Dem Deutschen Volke* (To the German People), the former symbol of national unity for years stood hard by the border that underlined its division; in front, on the broad green square, Turkish workers picnic and Americans play softball. But it's not difficult to imagine the scenes the building has witnessed: in November 1918 the German Republic was declared from a balcony here, while Karl Liebknecht was proclaiming a Socialist Republic in eastern Berlin – and cementing his and Rosa Luxemburg's fate. Nowadays the Reichstag, restored following a wartime gutting, once again houses the united Germany's parliament, and contains the fascinating exhibition *Questions on German History* (Tues–Sun 10am–5pm; free; bus #69 or #83), which chronicles the alliances and divisions, the war and rebuilding that led to Berlin's insular existence. Inevitably the best sections are those on the Third Reich: photos of the 1936 Olympic Games, anti-Jewish propaganda, horrific pictures of the Plötzensee executions, and much documentary evidence of the war years. Most of the commentary is in German, so it's well worth shelling out DM6 for the written English guide or DM2 for an audio tape.

Immediately behind the Reichstag, it's now only just possible to make out the course of the **Berlin Wall**, which for 28 years divided the city; to the left of the entrance, a series of plaques marks the names (where known) of those killed trying to swim to the West across the nearby River Spree. Erected overnight on August 13, 1961, to cordon off the Soviet sector and corral the British, American and French sectors of the city inside the GDR, the Wall underlined the city's schizophrenia and marked its *raison d'être* – the "stabilisation of the impossible". Late in 1989 the East German government, spurred by *glasnost* and confronted by a tense domestic climate, realised it could keep the impossible stable no longer. Travel restrictions for East German citizens were lifted on November 9, 1989 – effectively, the Wall had ceased to matter, and pictures of Berliners East and West hacking away at the detested symbol filled newspapers and TV bulletins around the world. Now the Wall has almost vanished, and the few sections of it that remain are protected from tourist chisels by barbed wire and by its official status as an "historic landmark". It's worth following it south from the Reichstag – and reviewing a little history as you go (see "The Wall – Some History", overleaf).

The Brandenburg Gate

Head south from the Reichstag by the edge of the Tiergarten and you follow the former course of the Wall down to the **Brandenburg Gate** (*Brandenburger Tor*), another of Berlin building dense with meaning and historical associations. Originally built as a city gate-cum-triumphal arch in 1791 and modelled on the Propylaea in Athens, it became, like the Reichstag later, a symbol of German unity, looking out to the Siegessäule and guarding the leafy passage of Unter den Linden, the continuation of what is now Strasse des 17 Juni, in eastern Berlin. In 1806 Napoleon marched under the arch and took home with him the **Quadriga**, the horse-drawn chariot atop the Gate. It was returned a few years later, and the revolutionaries of 1848 and 1918 met under its gilded form; later the Gate was a rallying point for Nazi torch-lit marches. After the building of the Wall placed the Gate in the Eastern sector, nearby observation posts became the place for visiting politicians to secure a handy photo-opportunity – the view was apparently emotive enough to reduce Margaret Thatcher to tears in 1987. With the opening of a border crossing here just before Christmas 1989, the East–West axis of the city was symbolically recreated and the post-Wall mood of eagerness for unification was strengthened. Yet, despite all the recent joy, it's easy enough to see why some, mindful of historical precedent, still view the Gate with a frisson of unease.

Walk through the Gate and you're in what used to be East Germany, with all the attractions of Unter den Linden lying before you (see "Eastern Berlin", pp.746–48), but before continuing, cross to the north side of Strasse des 17 Juni for a look at the **Soviet War Memorial** to the Red Army troops who died in the Battle of Berlin. Built from the marble of Hitler's destroyed Berlin HQ, the Reich's Chancellery, it's flanked by two tanks that were supposedly the first to reach the city.

Around Potsdamer Platz

The stretch of land south of the Brandenburg Gate on the eastern edge of the Tiergarten is seemingly wasteland, with nothing to remind you that this, **Potsdamer Platz**, was once the heart of Berlin and a prewar hub of the city's transport and night-life. The old tramlines can still be seen, running headlong into a near-featureless no-man's-land that's now filled with streams of traffic passing east and west. Nearby, to the north of the Platz, a small hummock of land marks the remains of **Hitler's bunker**, where the Führer spent his last days, issuing meaningless orders as the Battle of Berlin raged above. Here he married Eva Braun and wrote his final testament: he personally was responsible for nothing; he had been betrayed by the German people, who had proved unequal to his leadership and deserved the future he could now envisage ahead of them. On April 30, 1945, he shot himself, his body hurriedly burned by loyal officers. In the wrangles after the war to prove his death, the Soviet Army apparently came up with Hitler's teeth, which they had managed to retrieve from the charred remains and have verified by the Führer's dentist. The latest on this apocryphal tale is that the teeth are now stored away in a museum in eastern Berlin.

Since unification, the question of what to do with the remains of the bunker has reopened. Some say it should be preserved as a museum; others that it would become a shrine for rightist and neo-Nazi groups and should thus be destroyed. In June 1990, during preparations for a performance of "The Wall" by Roger Waters of Pink Floyd, engineers found another bunker further north, filled with weapons and covered with SS murals depicting Nazi might. Whether these too will be destroyed is, as yet, undecided. Plans to redevelop the whole area as an international headquarters for Mercedes-Benz have also been attacked, this time by the Jewish lobby, who reminded town planners that the car firm had been strong financial supporters of the Nazis..

South and east from Potsdamer Platz

Dodging the cars that run down the newly opened Leipziger Strasse and crossing south you come across one of the few remaining stretches of the Wall. Now protected from souvenir hunters, it's illegal to chip a bit off; if you want your own **piece of the Wall**, try one of the street sellers at Checkpoint Charlie, the Reichstag or near the Brandenburg Gate, but be warned that the less scrupulous traders will pass off bits of brick splashed with paint as the true Wall. The real thing is a pale-based aggregate of flint, pebbles and other hard stones.

South and east of Potsdamer Platz, the woodland of the Tiergarten falls away and you enter a semi-desolate area that has never really recovered from 1945 devastation. A magnificently restored exception is the **Martin-Gropius-Bau** at Stresemannstr. 110, 1/61 (Tues–Sun 10am–8pm or later; main collections DM4, though times and prices for temporary exhibitions vary; bus #24 or #29), now the city's main site for large, prestigious exhibitions. Also contained in the building are the main sections of the **Jüdisches Museum** (Tues–Sun 10am–10pm), with a frightening section on the war years, and large collections of German **applied and fine art**. Its small café is a useful stopping-off point and necessary pick-me-up before tackling an adjacent exhibition, **The Topography of Terror** (Tues–Sun 10am–6pm; free). This is housed in a newly built structure a little way from the Gropius-Bau, for nothing is left of the buildings that once stood here. Formerly known as Prinz-Albrecht-Strasse, Niederkirchenstrasse was the

THE WALL – SOME HISTORY

After the war, Berlin was split between its conquerors, as Stalin, Roosevelt and Churchill had agreed at Yalta. Each sector was administered by the relevant country, and was supposed to exist peacefully with its neighbour under a unified city council. But almost from the outset, antagonism between the Soviet and other sectors was high. Only three years after the war ended the Soviet forces closed down the land access corridors to the city from the Federal Republic, in what became known as the **Berlin Blockade**: it was successfully overcome by a massive Western **airlift** of food and supplies that lasted nearly a year. This, followed by the 1953 uprising, large-scale cross-border emigration (between 1949 and 1961, the year the Wall was built, over 3 million East Germans fled to the Federal Republic – almost a fifth of the population) and innumerable "incidents", led to the building of what was known in the GDR as the "anti-Fascist protection wall".

When the four powers were deciding on sectors, one of the parish maps of Greater Berlin of 1920 was used to delineate them: the Wall followed the Soviet sector boundary implacably, cutting through houses, across squares and rivers with its own cool illogicality. One oddity about the Wall was that it was actually built a few metres inside GDR territory; the West Berlin authorities therefore had little control over the **graffiti** that covered it like a static New York subway car. The Wall was an ever-changing mixture of colours and slogans, with the occasional burst of bitterness: *"My friends are dying behind you"*; humour: *"Last one out please turn off the lights"*; *"Why not jump over and join the Party?"*; and stupidity: *"We shoulda nuked 'em in '45"*.

Over the years, at least eighty people were **killed** endeavouring to cross the Wall. Initial escape attempts were straightforward and often successful – hollowing out furniture, ramming checkpoint barriers and simple disguise brought many people over. However, the authorities quickly rose to the challenge, and would-be escapees became more resourceful, digging tunnels, constructing gliders and one-man submarines, building their own hot-air balloons. By the time the Wall came down, every escape method conceivable seemed to have been used – even down to passing through Checkpoint Charlie in the stomach of a pantomime cow – and those who were desperate to get out of the GDR preferred the long wait and complications of applying to leave officially to the risk of being gunned down by a border guard. The guards, known as *Grepos*, were under instructions to shoot anyone attempting to scale the Wall, and to shoot accurately: any guard suspected of deliberately missing was court-martialled, and his family could expect severe harassment from the authorities.

When the end came, it happened so quickly that Berliners East and West seemed not to believe it; but within days of the announcement that citizens of the GDR were free to travel, enterprising characters were hiring out hammers and chisels so that souvenir hunters could take home their own chip of the Wall. Today, especially in the city centre, it's often hard to tell exactly where the Wall ran: odd juxtapositions of dereliction against modernity, or an unexpected swathe of erstwhile "deathstrip" are in many cases all that's left of one of the most hated borders the world ever knew.

base of the Gestapo, the SS and Reich Security offices: in buildings along here Himmler planned the Final Solution, the deportation and genocide of European Jews, and organised the Gestapo, the feared secret police. The exhibition is housed in what were once the cellars of the Gestapo headquarters, where important prisoners were interrogated and tortured. Though the photos here tell their own story, you'll need the English translation (DM2) or the glossy guidebook (DM10) for the main text of the exhibits.

Checkpoint Charlie

The wasteland behind the Gropius-Bau is currently in the initial stages of development into a permanent monument to the victims of the Gestapo, possibly with a study centre and museum. Until this opens there's nothing to detain you, and it's a ten-minute walk (or #29 bus ride) down Wilhelmstrasse and Kochstrasse to **Friedrichstrasse**, once one of the city's great streets, packed with cafés and shops, now a dusty avenue heavily pockmarked by wartime shell damage. **Checkpoint Charlie**, an allied military post and one of Berlin's more celebrated landmarks, stood at Friedrichstrasse's northern end until July 1990, when it was declared redundant and removed, probably to be reassembled in a west German museum. The building lent its name informally to the adjacent GDR border crossing which, with its dramatic "YOU ARE NOW LEAVING THE AMERICAN SECTOR" signs and unsmiling border guards, used to be the archetypal movie-style Iron Curtain crossing.

Tangible evidence of the trauma the Wall caused is still on hand at the **Haus am Checkpoint Charlie** at Friedrichstrasse 44, 1/61 (daily 9am–10pm; DM5; nearest U-Bahn Kochstrasse or bus #29), which tells the history of the Wall in photos of escape tunnels, and with the converted cars and home-made aircraft by which people attempted, succeeded, and sometimes tragically failed to break through the border. Films document the stories of some of the eighty people killed by the East German border guards, and there's a section on human rights behind the Iron Curtain, but it's a scruffy, rather dated collection, and not quite the harrowing experience that some American visitors seem to expect. For more details, pick up a copy of *It Happened at the Wall* or *Berlin – from Frontline Town to the Bridge of Europe*, both on sale here.

Walk a little down Kochstrasse and you'll see a high-rise building marked "**Axel Springer Verlag**". The late Axel Springer, extreme right-wing newspaper and publishing magnate (the newspaper *Bild* was his most notorious creation), deliberately had his offices built here, right next to the border, as an act of provocation towards the GDR authorities.

The Tiergarten Museum Complex

To the west of Potsdamer Platz, the **Tiergarten Complex** (also known as the *Kulturforum*) is a recently-built mixture of museums and cultural forums that could easily fill a day of your time.

The Neue Nationalgalerie

Far and away the finest building here is the **Neue Nationalgalerie**, Potsdamer Str. 50, 1/30 (Tues–Fri 9am–5pm, Sat & Sun 10am–5pm; main collection free; bus #29 or #83), a black-rimmed glass box that seems almost suspended above the ground, its clarity of line and detail having all the intelligent simplicity of the Parthenon. Designed by Mies van der Rohe in 1965, the upper section is used for temporary exhibits, often of contemporary art, while the underground galleries contain paintings from the late eighteenth century onwards. Many, though by no means all, of the works are German, including thoroughly nineteenth-century examples by **Menzel**, **Courbet** and **Feuerbach**. After the bright splodges of **Lovis Corinth** and a clutch of **Monet**s, the galleries move on to the portraits and Berlin cityscapes of **Grosz** and **Dix**. **Kirchner** spent time in Berlin before World War I, and his *Potsdamer Platz* dates from 1914. There's also work by Miró, Karel Appel, Jasper Johns and Francis Bacon: a fine, easily assimilated collection.

The Philharmonie

North of the Nationalgalerie the **Matthäikirche** stands in lonely isolation on a blitzed landscape that now forms a car park for the **Philharmonie**, home of the Berlin Philharmonic and, until he retired and subsequently died in 1989, its renowned conductor Herbert von Karajan. Looking at the gold-clad ugliness of the building, designed in the 1960s by Hans Scharoun, it's easy to see how it got its nickname among Berliners of "Karajani's circus". Should you wish to reserve a ticket, the box office is open

Monday to Friday from 3.30pm to 6pm, Saturday and Sunday 11am to 2pm (☎261 4843): chances of getting a seat for major concerts under the orchestra's new conductor, Claudio Abbado, are slim unless you've booked months in advance, but it's worth trying your luck for other performances under guest conductors.

Two museums and a library

Continuing the musical theme, the **Musikinstrumenten Museum** (Tues–Sat 9am–5pm, Sun 10am–5pm; free) at Tiergartenstr. 1, 1/30, just below the Philharmonie, comes as something of a disappointment. Its collection of (mostly European) keyboards, wind and string instruments from the fifteenth century to the present day is comprehensive and impressively laid out, but it's all strictly look-don't-touch stuff, with guards vigilant for the slightest tinkle. Content yourself with the pre-recorded tapes that give a taste of the weird and wonderful sounds the instruments make.

Much better is the **Kunstgewerbemuseum** (Museum of Applied Arts; Tues–Fri 9am–5pm, Sat & Sun 10am–5pm; free) at Matthäikirchplatz 10, 1/30, an encyclopaedic but seldom dull collection of European arts and crafts. The top floor contains wonderful Renaissance, Baroque and Rococo silver and ceramics, along with Jugendstil and Art Deco objects, particularly furniture. The first floor holds the Middle Ages to Early Renaissance collections, with some sumptuous gold pieces. The highlights, though, are Lüneburg's municipal silver and the treasures of Enger's Stiftskirche, and, in the basement, a small but great assembly of Bauhaus furniture and a display of the evolution of product design.

Lastly, the **Staatsbibliothek** (Mon–Fri 9am–9pm, Sat 9am–5pm; free access), across Potsdamer Strasse from the other buildings, has over three and a half million books, occasional exhibitions, a small concert hall, a cheapish café and a wide selection of British newspapers. The final building to be designed by Hans Scharoun, the *Staabi*'s most recent claim to fame came when it was used as an important backdrop in Wim Wenders' poetic film elegy to the city, *Wings of Desire*.

Kreuzberg

The area directly south and east of the Martin-Gropius-Bau is **Kreuzberg**, famed for its large immigrant community and self-styled "alternative" inhabitants, nightlife and goings on. Effectively there are two Kreuzbergs: the **west**, the area bounded by Friedrichstrasse, Viktoriapark and Südstern, is a richer, fancier, more sedate neighbour to the **east**, which is sometimes referred to as SO 36 after its postal code. East Kreuzberg is western Berlin's "happening" quarter, a mix of punks and old hippies, and the place to hang out and hit the really raucous nightspots, names like *Trash* and *Bronx* giving you an idea of the atmosphere. Though there's precious little in the way of things to see, it is, in many ways, the city's liveliest neighbourhood.

West Kreuzberg

First **the west**. It's only a short walk south, cutting down Stresemannstrasse, from the Gropius-Bau to the remains of the **Anhalter Bahnhof**, a sad reminder of misguided civic action that some would term civic vandalism. The Anhalter Bahnhof was once one of the city's (and Europe's) great rail termini, forming Berlin's gateway to the south. Completed in 1870, it received only mild damage during the war and was left roofless but substantial in 1945. Despite attempts to preserve it as a future museum building, it was blown up in 1952 – essentially because someone had put in a good offer for the bricks. Now only a fragment of the facade stands, giving a hint at past glories. The patch of land that the station once covered is today a park, and though there's nothing to see save the paths of the old rail tracks at the far end, it's an oddly atmospheric spot.

A brisk walk east from here, through streets levelled during wartime bombing, takes you to another Kreuzberg highspot, the **Berlin Museum** at Lindenstr. 14, 1/61 (Tues–Sun 10am–10pm; DM3.50; buses #24, #29 and #41), which attempts to show the history and development of the city through paintings, prints and crafts. The best exhibits are from this century, particularly the collections of wartime posters and kids' toys, and Klaus Richter's portraits of Hitler and Göring. One unmissable attraction is the **Kaiserpanorama**, a large mid-nineteenth-century stereoscope designed to allow several viewers to see its rotating slides simultaneously. Usually it's loaded with pictures of prewar Berlin, giving a vivid portrait of the lost city. Until a permanent site can be found, the museum also holds part of the **Jüdisches Museum**, a small but moving collection of Judaica chronicling the history and tragedy of Berlin's Jewish community: of 60,000 Jews living in the city in 1939, 50,000 died in the concentration camps. The remainder of the collection is in the Martin-Gropius-Bau (see p.730). More whimsically – and the reason most people come here – there's a mock-up of an old Berlin bar, the *Alt-Berliner Weissbierstube* (closes at 4pm at weekends, and is often crowded), which serves a traditional Berlin buffet – distinguished by being very heavy on pork – washed down with pale beer.

An alternative and easier approach to the area is to catch the U-Bahn to Möckernbrücke station on line #1, an enjoyable above-ground ride through old warehouses and towering postwar redevelopment. Walking south from the station, over the Landwehrkanal and turning right along Tempelhofer Ufer, you pass one of the decaying but still ornate **public toilets** erected in the early years of this century: gents can pop in for a Bismarckian moment of relief. A little further on, at Trebbiner Str. 9, 1/61, is the **Museum für Verkehr und Technik** (Museum of Transport and Technology; April–Sept Tues & Wed 9am–6pm, Thurs & Fri 9am–9pm, Sat & Sun 10am–6pm; Oct–March Tues–Fri 9am–6pm; DM3.50, students/children DM1.50; bus #29), one of the city's most entertaining museums and a button-pushers' and kids' delight. The technology section has plenty of experiments, antiquated machinery and computers to play with, alongside some elegant old cars and planes. The transport museum, a collection of ancient steam trains and carriages, is even more impressive, the polished behemoths brought to rest in what was once a workshop of the old Anhalter Bahnhof.

Reaching the **Viktoriapark** (the "Kreuzberg", as it's popularly known) from here means a half-hour's walk, retracing your steps to the U-Bahn and heading south down Grossbeerenstrasse. On the slopes of a hill, the park is one of the city's most likeable, a relaxed ramble of trees and green space with a pretty brook running down the middle, and on summer afternoons there's no better place to stretch out and relax. To one side is the *Golgotha Café* and disco (see "Drinking, eating and nightlife"), packed on summer evenings; on another side is what claims to be Germany's northernmost vineyard; and atop the hill is the **Cross** (though it's more of a Neoclassical spire) from which Kreuzberg gets its name, designed by Schinkel to commemorate the Napoleonic Wars. The view is a good one, too, made all the more pleasant by the wafting aromas from the *Schultheiss* brewery on the southern slopes. The well-restored streets that side the hill, along with Yorckstrasse to the north, have a scattering of cafés, their tone and clientele reflecting the residents of the neighbourhood, who are on the whole slightly older than those of East Kreuzberg. Between Hagelbergerstrasse and Yorckstrasse, **Riehmer's Hofgarten** is an impressive turn-of-the-century bourgeois residential block, though the modern steel and glass Yorck Cinema doesn't fit well in the ensemble.

South and east of the Viktoriapark, the housing fades away to the flatlands containing **Tempelhof Military Airport**. Built by the Nazis, and once Germany's largest airport, it's still possible to see the Nazi eagles that decorate the buildings. Today it's used mainly by the US air force, and it was here that the Allies flew in supplies to beat the Berlin Blockade of 1948–9 – an act that was to strengthen anti-Soviet feeling among West Berliners and increase the popularity of the occupying forces. At the height of the fifteen-month airlift a plane landed every minute, and the **Luftbrückendenkmal**, a memorial at the entrance to the airport symbolising the three air corridors used, commemorates the seventy airmen and eight ground crew who died in crashes while attempting to land. The memorial represents half a bridge: the other half, "joined by air", is in Frankfurt.

East Kreuzberg: SO 36

Despite its reputation as a hotbed of radical protest and alternative lifestyles, (a leftover from the days when West Germany's disaffected youth came to Berlin, since those living in the city were exempt from military service), you don't need any interest in revolution or city machinations to enjoy the eastern part of Kreuzberg. The **nightlife** here is the city's wildest, and it's an enjoyable area to wander through by day, stopping off at one of the innumerable Turkish snack bars for a kebab, breakfasting on a 9am vodka-and-beer special at a café, or just taking in the feel of the place – which is much like an Istanbul market in an Eastern bloc housing development.

Catching U-Bahn line #1 to **Kottbusser Tor** or **Schlesisches Tor** stations is a good introduction to Kreuzberg. The area around Kottbusser Tor is typical: a scruffy, earthy shambles of Turkish street vendors and cafés, the air filled with the aromas of southeast European cooking. Cutting through Dresdener Strasse, past the Babylon cinema (a venue, incidentally, that often shows films in English), takes you to Kreuzberg's main strip, **Oranienstrasse**, which from Moritzplatz east is lined with café-bars, art galleries and clothes shops, and in a way forms an "alternative" Kurfürstendamm. Stop off at any of the bars along here for a taste of what the locals call a *Szene* place – somewhere that's in and happening.

South of Kottbusser Tor U-Bahn, it's a few minutes' walk down Kottbusser Damm to the canal. Turning left here and walking along Paul-Lincke-Ufer in an eastwards direction elicits a peculiar mix of emotions, with the beauty of the natural surroundings long halted by the derelict, deserted factories of eastern Berlin on the other side. The Wall cut through here, and the sense of despondency, of the separation that it brought, is only slowly dissipating.

Around the Schlesisches Tor things are more residential, although for years the nearness of the Wall heightened the tension of the area. The River Spree here was in GDR territory, a strange situation for those residents of West Berlin whose apartments backed directly on to it. At night the areas around both the Schlesisches Tor and the Kottbusser Tor seem a little sharper, darkness giving them an edge of danger and a sense of concealed, forbidden pleasures.

The Landwehrkanal runs south of Oranienstrasse, and below that the broad path of Hasenheide-Gneisenaustrasse marks the transition from east to west Kreuzberg. Around the Südstern (which has a convenient U-Bahn station) is another clutch of café-bars, and Gneisenaustrasse has some good restaurants; but the flavour of east Kreuzberg has gone, and things feel (and are) a lot tamer.

Schöneberg and around

Like Kreuzberg, **Schöneberg** was once a separate suburb, one that was swallowed up by Greater Berlin as the city expanded in the late eighteenth and nineteenth centuries. Blown to pieces during the war, it's now a mostly middle-class residential area, stretching below the Tiergarten and sandwiched between Kreuzberg to the east and Wilmersdorf to the west. Things to see are few, but what is here is both fascinating and moving.

Schöneberg officially begins south of Kurfürstenstrasse, but just north of the Landwehrkanal, on the edge of Tiergarten at Klingelhöferstr. 13–14, is the **Bauhaus Archive** (11am–5pm; closed Tues; DM3.50; bus #29 to Lützowplatz). The Bauhaus school of design, crafts and architecture was founded in 1919 in Weimar by Walter Gropius. It moved to Dessau in 1925 (see p.828) and then to Berlin, to be closed by the Nazis in 1933. The influence of Bauhaus has been tremendous, and you get some idea of this in the small collection here. There's work too by Kandinsky, Moholy-Nagy, Schlemmer and Klee, each of whom worked at the Bauhaus. The building, incidentally, was designed by Gropius himself.

Around Nollendorfplatz

Back in the middle of Potsdamer Strasse, it's a short detour west to **Nollendorfplatz**. which, on its southern side, holds the proto-Deco **Metropol disco** (see "Drinking, eating and nightlife"). Nearby, at Nollendorfstrasse 17, is the building in which **Christopher Isherwood** lived during his years in prewar Berlin, a time that was to be elegantly recounted in perhaps the most famous collection of stories about the city ever written – *Goodbye to Berlin*.

Schöneberg has since been reborn as a fancy, even chic neighbourhood; the would-be Isherwoods of the moment hang out in SO 36, or Prenzlauer Berg in eastern Berlin. At night, this part of Schöneberg, particularly the area around **Winterfeldtplatz**, is a good one for eating and especially drinking: tidily bohemian, less sniffy than Savignyplatz, and much more middle-of-the-road than SO 36. On Wednesday and Saturday mornings the square holds an excellent general **market**.

Rathaus Schöneberg

Schöneberg's most famous attraction actually has the least to see: the **Rathaus Schöneberg** on Martin-Luther-Strasse, the penultimate stop on U-Bahn line #4. Built just before World War I, the Rathaus became the seat of the West Berlin parliament and senate after the last war, and it was outside here in 1963 that **John F. Kennedy** made his celebrated "Ich bin ein Berliner" speech on the Cold War political situation, just a few months after the Cuban missile crisis. What the president didn't realise as he read from his phonetically written text was that he had actually said "I am a small dough-nut", since *Berliner* is the name given in west Germany to those cakes. So popular has this subtext become that the city's souvenir shops sell little plastic doughnuts bearing the historic words. The day after Kennedy was assassinated, the square in front of the Rathaus was given his name – a move apparently instigated by the city's students, among whom the president was highly popular.

If you've time and interest you can climb the Rathaus tower (Sun only 10am–3.30pm) and see the replica **Liberty bell** donated to the city by the US in 1950, though it's more pleasant, and certainly less strenuous, to take a stroll in the small **Volkspark**, a thin ribbon of greenery that runs west from here.

Charlottenburg: the Schloss and museums

The district of **Charlottenburg** stretches north and west of the centre of town, reaching as far as the forests of the Grunewald. To the west it contains a number of things worth seeing (detailed under "West from the centre"), but far and away the most significant target, one that needs a day at least to cover, is the **Schloss Charlottenburg and Museum complex** on Spandauer Damm. The Schloss is open Tuesday to Sunday from 9am to 5pm; tickets, which include entrance to all other Schloss buildings, cost DM7; the buses which run nearest are #54 and #74.

Schloss Charlottenburg and its museums

Schloss Charlottenburg comes as a surprise after the unrelieved modernity of the city streets. Commissioned as a country house by the future Queen Sophie Charlotte in 1695 (she also gave her name to the district), the Schloss was expanded and added to throughout the eighteenth and early nineteenth centuries to provide a summer residence for the Prussian kings, the master builder Karl Friedrich Schinkel providing the final touches. Approaching the sandy elaborateness of the Schloss at the main court-yard, you're confronted with Andreas Schlüter's **statue** of Friedrich Wilhelm, the Great Elector, cast as a single piece in 1700. To see the Schloss's central section, which includes the restored residential quarters, you're obliged to go on the conducted tour that's in German only, which makes it worth buying the detailed (English) guidebook before you start. The tour is a traipse through increasingly sumptuous chambers and bedrooms, filled with gilt and carving. Most eye-catching are the **porcelain room**, packed to the ceiling with china, and the **chapel**, which includes a portrait of Sophie Charlotte as the Virgin ascending to heaven.

It's just as well to remember that much of the Schloss is in fact a fake, a reconstruction of the former buildings following wartime damage. This is most apparent in the **Knobelsdorff Wing**, to the right of the Schloss entrance as you face it; the upper rooms, such as the Rococo "Golden Gallery" are too breathlessly perfect, the result of intensive restoration. Better is the adjacent "White Hall", whose destroyed eighteenth-century ceiling painting has been replaced by a witty contemporary paraphrase. Next door, the "Concert Room" contains a superb collection of works by **Watteau**, including two of his greatest paintings, *The Embarcation for Cythera* and *The Shop Sign*.

Downstairs, the Knobelsdorff Wing currently contains the **Galerie der Romantik** (Tues–Fri 9am–5pm, Sat & Sun 10am–5pm; free), a collection of nineteenth-century paintings from the German Romantic masters, and the Classical and Biedermeier movements that will eventually be transplanted to a planned extension of the Neue Nationalgalerie in the Tiergarten. Most dramatic are the works of **Caspar David Friedrich**, all of which express a powerful elemental and religious approach to landscape, particularly *Morning in the Riesengebirge* and *The Watzmann*.

This room also contains works by **Karl Friedrich Schinkel**, the architect responsible for the war memorial in Kreuzberg and, more notably, the Neoclassical designs of the Altes Museum and many other buildings standing today in eastern Berlin. His paintings are meticulously drawn Gothic fantasies, often with sea settings. *Gothic Church on a Seaside Bluff* is the most moodily dramatic.

The western wing of the Schloss once sided an Orangerie (much depleted after the war) and the **gallery** there now houses major exhibitions. Also in the west wing is the **Museum Vor- und Frühgeschichte** (Museum of Pre- and Early History), an unexciting collection of archaeological finds from the Berlin area.

If this isn't to your taste, there are few better ways to idle away a morning in Berlin than to explore the **Schloss Gardens** (open daily, till 9pm in summer). Laid out in the French style in 1697, the gardens were transformed into an English-style landscaped park in the early nineteenth century; after severe damage in the war, they were mostly restored to their Baroque form. On the western side of the gardens a long, tree-lined avenue leads to the hushed and shadowy **Mausoleum** (April–Oct Tues–Sun 9am–noon & 1–5pm; DM0.50) where Friedrich Wilhelm III is buried alongside his queen Luise, his sarcophagus making him seem a good deal younger than his seventy years. Later burials here include Kaiser Wilhelm I, looking every inch a Prussian king.

Other museums

Though you could spend an idle morning wandering around the Schloss and its gardens, just across the way a group of excellent museums beckons. Best of these is the **Ägyptisches Museum** (Schlossstrasse 70; Mon–Thurs 9am–5pm, Sat & Sun 10am–5pm; free), the result of innumerable German excavations in Egypt from the early part of the century. The museum's pride and joy is the *Bust of Nefertiti* on the first floor, a treasure that has become a symbol for the city as a cultural capital. There's no questioning its beauty – the queen has a perfect bone structure and gracefully sculpted lips – and the history of the piece is equally interesting. Created around 1350 BC, the bust probably never left the studio in Akhetaten in which it was housed, acting as a model for other portraits of the queen (its use as a model explains why the left eye was never drawn in). When the studio was deserted, the bust was left there, to be discovered some 3000 years later in 1912. Elsewhere in the museum, atmospheric lighting focuses attention on the exhibits, which are of a uniformly high standard. Look out for the expressionistic, almost futuristic *Berlin Green Head* of the Ptolemaic period, and the *Kalabsha Monumental Gate*, given to the museum by the Egyptian government in 1973.

Across Schlossstrasse, the **Antikenmuseum** (Tues–Fri 9am–5pm; free) holds Greek and Roman collections, notably the Roman silver treasure found at Hildesheim. Other highlights include a collection of Greek vases that's considered by those in the know to be among the finest in the world. Just south of the Antikenmuseum, the **Bröhan-Museum** (Tues–Sun 10am–6pm; DM3) houses a great collection of Art Deco and Jugendstil ceramics and furniture, laid out in period rooms dedicated to a particular designer and hung with contemporary paintings.

Continuing westwards, Charlottenburg breaks out into open country and forest, with the Olympic stadium and tower the main draws (see below).

West from the centre

While there's more than enough to detain you in western Berlin's centre, the western **suburbs** hold a disparate group of attractions of considerable historical interest; and once you're out of the claustrophobic city, the verdant countryside and lakes come as a surprise, a reminder of Berlin's position in *Mitteleuropa* – and of the fact that one third of the city is greenery and parkland. Thanks to the efficient U- and S-Bahn system it's possible to reach Berlin's western edges in under three-quarters of an hour, making the contrast between inner-city excitement and rural relaxation all the stronger.

Dahlem: The Museum Complex

The suburb of **Dahlem** lies to the southwest of central Berlin in the district of Zehlendorf, a neat village-like enclave that feels a world away from the technoflash city centre. Mostly residential, it's home to the Free University, the better-off bourgeoisie and a group of museums that's the most important on the western side of the city – and among the best in Europe.

Housed in a large new building, the **Dahlem Museum** can be overpowering if you try and do too much too quickly: it's wiser to make a couple of trips here, taking time out to visit the Botanical Gardens nearby (detailed below). If you are pushed for time, the musts are the Picture Gallery and South Seas Ethnographic Collection. To reach the museums, take U-Bahn line #2 to Dahlem-Dorf and follow the signs; the main block is on Arnimallee, and open from Tuesday to Sunday 9am to 5pm. Admission to all the collections is free.

The Picture Gallery

The Gemäldegalerie or **Picture Gallery** is the highlight of the Dahlem Museum. Originally part of the prewar Kaiser-Friedrich Museum, during the war years its paintings were stored throughout the city for safekeeping, with the result that part of the collection is now contained in the Bodes Museum and Nationalgalerie on eastern Berlin's Museum Island. But this doesn't detract from the gallery's scope or quality: arranged in chronological order, it covers the early medieval to late eighteenth-century periods, the section of early **Netherlandish Painting** and later **Dutch and Flemish** works being the most authoritative. Plans are afoot to relocate the Picture Gallery in the *Kulturforum*, the group of museums centred on the Neue Nationalgalerie in the Tiergarten, though whether those parts of the collection currently in the east will be reunited hasn't yet been decided.

NETHERLANDISH PAINTING

The collection of **Netherlandish Painting**, works painted in the Low Countries in the fifteenth to late sixteenth centuries, begins with the artist credited with the creation of European realism, **Jan van Eyck**: his beautifully lit *Madonna in the Church* is crammed with architectural detail, the Virgin lifted in the perspective for gentle emphasis. **Petrus Christus** may have been a pupil of van Eyck, and certainly knew his work, as *The Virgin and Child with St Barbara and a Carthusian Monk* reveals: in the background are tiny Flemish houses and street scenes, the artist carefully locating the event in his native Bruges.

Much of the next room is given over to the work of **Rogier van der Weyden**, which shows the development of the Eyckian technique to a warmer, much more emotional treatment of religious subjects in works like his *Bladelin Altarpiece*. The two other major paintings in this room are both by **Hugo van der Goes**: the *Adoration of the Shepherds* (painted when the artist was in the first throes of madness) and the *Adoration of the Magi* – also known as the *Monforte Altarpiece*. Room 148 moves into the sixteenth century and the works of Jan Gossaert, Quentin Massys and **Pieter Bruegel the Elder**, whose *Netherlandish Proverbs* is an amusing, if hard-to-grasp, illustration of over a hundred sixteenth-century proverbs and maxims.

MEDIEVAL AND RENAISSANCE GERMAN PAINTING

Following the Netherlandish sections are the **German Medieval and Renaissance** rooms, which reveal the contrast between German and Netherlandish treatment of religious subjects: almost always, the German works are darker and more crudely drawn. Crudest of all is the large *Passion Altar* of 1437, made in the workshop of the great Ulm sculptor **Hans Multscher**, an ancient precursor of Expressionist painting. There's an interesting contrast with *Solomon before the Queen of Sheba*, painted in the same year by **Conrad Witz**, who was far more subtle in his aim of developing German painting away from its hitherto idealised forms.

These apart, the best works here are by **Altdorfer**, one of the first fully realised German landscape painters and **Dürer** – a marvellous group of portraits. By **Holbein the Younger** are five superbly observed portraits, most celebrated of which is *The Danzig Merchant Georg Gisze*, featuring a still-life background which is a real tour-de-force of artistic virtuosity. Pick of the many examples of **Cranach** is the tongue-in-cheek *The Fountain of Youth*: here, old women emerge from the miraculous bath as fresh young girls, whereas the men are rejuvenated merely by association.

ITALIAN RENAISSANCE PAINTING

To the right of the rooms containing the German works is the collection of **French and German** painting of the sixteenth, seventeenth and eighteenth centuries. But to continue in chronological order, carry straight on to the **Italian Renaissance** section. This collection is particularly strong on works from the Florentine Renaissance: **Fra Filippo Lippi**'s *The Adoration in the Forest* is rightly one of the most admired of all the paintings of the period. Another much-prized work is the gorgeously colourful *Adoration of the Magi* by the rarely seen **Domenico Veneziano**, which perfectly captures the full regal splendour of the subject. There's work here, too, by Giotto, Correggio, Verrocchio, Masaccio, Mantegna, Raphael and Titian, and, most importantly, by **Botticelli**, whose *Virgin and Child with the Two St Johns*, *Portrait of a Young Woman* and *St Sebastian* are among the highlights of this section of the gallery.

DUTCH AND FLEMISH PAINTING

On the next floor the museum reveals its second strength in the **Dutch and Flemish** collection. This begins with the large portraits of Van Dyck and the fleshy canvases of Rubens, and continues with a fine group of **Dutch interiors**, hung together and inviting comparison. The paintings of **Vermeer** are the most easily identifiable: *Man and Woman Drinking Wine* uses his usual technique of placing furniture obliquely in the centre of the canvas, the scene illuminated by window light.

The subsequent rooms trace the development of Dutch art through the works of Maes, Terborch, Dou, Jan Steen and Frans Hals, and, in perhaps the largest collection of his work in the world, the paintings of **Rembrandt**. Recently, his most famous picture here, *The Man in the Golden Helmet*, was proved to be the work of his studio rather than the artist himself, though this does little to detract from the elegance and power of the portrait.

Continuing through the painting galleries, there's work by Goya, Caravaggio (*Cupid Victorious*, heavy with symbolism and homo-eroticism), Poussin and Claude, and a concluding clutch of Canalettos.

Other collections and sights

The **Sculpture Court** adjoining the Picture Gallery on the upper floor forms a good complement to the paintings: it's chiefly German and most authoritative in its sections detailing the Middle Ages – including work by the masters of the medieval period, Tilman Riemenschneider and Hans Multscher.

The **Ethnographic sections** of the Dahlem Museum are worth a visit in their own right: rich and extensive collections from Asia, and the Pacific and South Sea Islands of Melanesia and Polynesia, imaginatively and strikingly laid out. In particular, look out for the group of sailing boats from the South Sea Islands, dramatically lit and eminently touchable. Other collections within the museum include **Islamic**, **Asian**, **East Asian** and **Indian art** (the largest collection in the country, with an especially good Nepalese section) – dip in according to your tastes.

The Plötzensee Memorial

Berlin sometimes has the feel of a city that has tried, unsuccessfully, to sweep its past under the carpet of the present. When concrete reminders of the Third Reich can be seen, their presence in today's postwar city becomes all the more powerful. Nowhere is this more true than in the buildings where the Nazi powers brought dissidents and political opponents for imprisonment and execution – the **Plötzensee Prison Memorial**.

Plötzensee stands in the northwest of the city, on the border between the boroughs of Charlottenburg and Wedding. To get there, take bus #23 from Tiergarten S-Bahn station to the beginning of Saatwinkler Damm (ask for the "Gedenkstatte Plötzensee" stop) and walk away from the canal along the wall-sided path of Hüttigpfad.

The former prison buildings have now been refurbished as a juvenile detention centre, and the memorial consists of the buildings where the **executions** took place. Over 2500 people were hanged or guillotined here between 1933 and 1945, usually those sentenced in the Supreme Court of Justice in the city. Following the July Bomb Plot, 89 of the 200 people condemned were executed here in the space of a few days: Hitler ordered the hangings to be carried out with piano wire, so that the victims would slowly strangle rather than die from broken necks, and spent his evenings watching movie footage of the executions. Many of those murdered were only vaguely connected to the conspirators; several died simply because they were relatives. Today the execution chamber has been restored to its wartime condition: on occasion, victims were hanged eight at a time, and the hanging beam, complete with hooks, still stands.

Though decked with wreaths and flowers, the atmosphere in the chamber is chilling, and as a further reminder of Nazi atrocities an urn in the courtyard contains soil from each of the concentration camps. The memorial is open from March to September 8am–6pm, October & February 8.30am–5.30pm, November & January 8.30am–4.30pm & December 8.30am–4pm.

Points westward: the Funkturm, Olympic Stadium and beyond

Reaching the **Funkturm**, the skeletal transmission mast that lies to the west of Charlottenburg, is an easy matter of catching U-Bahn line #1 to Kaiserdamm, or bus #66, #92 or #94 from Zoo Station. Since being built in 1928 as a radio and TV transmitter, it has been popular with Berliners for the toe-curling views from its 138-metre-high observation platform (daily 10am–11pm; DM4). With the aluminium-clad monolith of the **International Congress Centre** immediately below, it's possible to look out across deserted, overgrown S-Bahn tracks to the gleaming city in the distance – a sight equally mesmerising at night.

You may have to queue to catch the lift up to the observation platform; much less popular is the **Museum of Radio and Broadcasting** (Tues–Sat 10am–6pm, Sun 10am–4pm; free), housed in a former studio to one side of the tower. Tracing the development of radios, record players and televisions from the beginning of broadcasting in Germany in 1923 until World War II, it's as much a history of design as technology, made all the more entertaining by a scattering of period rooms and a mock-up of the first-ever German radio studio.

To reach the Olympic Stadium from here, catch the #1 U-Bahn three stops westwards to the station of the same name. From there, it's a fifteen-minute signposted walk to the stadium itself.

The Olympic Stadium

Built for the 1936 Olympic Games, the **Olympic Stadium** (8am–sunset; DM2) is one of the few Fascist buildings left intact in the city, and remains very much in use. Whatever your feelings about it, it's still impressive, the huge Neoclassical space a deliberate rejection of the modernist architecture then prevalent elsewhere.

If you cut south and west around the stadium, down the road named after Jesse Owens, and take a right onto Passenheimer Strasse, you reach the **Glockenturm** or bell tower (April–Oct daily 10am–5.30pm; DM2.50). Rebuilt after wartime damage, it's chiefly interesting for the stupendous **view** it gives, not only over the stadium but also

---

THE 1936 OLYMPICS

Hitler used the international attention the **1936 Olympics** attracted to show the "New Order" in Germany in the best possible light. Anti-Semitic propaganda and posters were suppressed in the city, German half-Jewish athletes were allowed to compete, and when the Olympic flame was relayed from Athens, the newsreels and the world saw the road lined with thousands wearing swastikas and waving Nazi flags. To the outside world, it seemed that the new Germany was rich, content and firmly behind the Führer.

Though the Games themselves were stage-managed with considerable brilliance – a fact recorded in Leni Riefenstahl's poetic and frighteningly beautiful film of the events, *Olympia* – not everything went according to official National Socialist doctrine. Black American athletes did supremely well in the games, **Jesse Owens** alone winning four gold medals, disproving the Nazi theory that blacks were "subhuman" and the Aryan race all-powerful. But eventually Germany won the most gold, silver and bronze medals (there's a memorial at the western end of the stadium), and the games were deemed a great success.

north to the natural amphitheatre that forms the **Waldbühne**, an open-air concert site (see "Drinking, eating and nightlife"), and across the beginnings of the Grunewald to the south. Central here is **Teufelsberg** (Devil's Mountain), a massive mound that's topped with a faintly terrifying fairy-tale castle that is a US signals and radar base. The mountain itself is artificial: at the end of the war, the mass of debris that was once Berlin was carted to several sites around the city. Beneath the poplars, maples and ski runs lies the old Berlin, about 25 million cubic metres of it, presumably awaiting the attention of some future archaeologist. In the meantime, it's popular as a place for weekend kite flying, and skiing and tobogganing in winter.

Spandau

Spandau, situated on the confluence of the Spree and Havel rivers, about 10km as the crow flies northwest of the city centre, is Berlin's oldest suburb – it was granted a town charter in 1232, and managed to escape the worst of the wartime bombing, preserving some pretty medieval streets and an ancient moated fort, the Zitadelle. But the word Spandau immediately brings to mind the name of its jail's most famous – indeed in later years only – prisoner, **Rudolf Hess**, Hitler's former deputy who flew to Scotland in 1941 on a bizarre peace mission, and who apparently hanged himself here in 1989.

However, there's little connection between Hess and Spandau itself. The jail, 3km away on Wilhelmstrasse, was demolished to make way for a supermarket for the British armed forces, and the chief reason to come here today is to escape the city centre, wander Spandau's village-like streets, and to visit the explorable, if not totally engrossing, **Zitadelle** at Strasse am Juliusturm, 1/20 (Tues–Fri 9am–5pm, Sat & Sun 10am–5pm; DM1.50), a fort established in the twelfth century to defend the town. The Zitadelle has a small *Heimatmuseum*, a pricey *bürgerlich* restaurant and the **Juliusturm**, from which there's a good view over the ramshackle Zitadelle interior and the surrounding countryside. If nothing else, it's a pleasant spot to picnic away a hot summer's day.

Other than this, **Spandau town**, a ten-minute walk from here, is of minor interest, at its best around its church (where there's a good *Konditorei*), in the playful sculptures of its modern marketplace, and in the recently restored street called **Kolk** (turn right off Am Juliusturm opposite Breite Strasse). Quickest way of getting to Spandau from the city centre is to take U-Bahn line #7 to the Zitadelle station – or to Altstadt Spandau station then doubling back to the Zitadelle. It's also possible to catch **boats** from Spandau to Tegel, Wannsee and elsewhere; see below for details.

Woodlands and lakes: the Grunewald, Havel and Wannsee

Few people associate Berlin with walks through dense woodland or swimming from crowded beaches, though that's just what the **Grunewald** forests and beaches on the **Havel** lakes have to offer. The Grunewald is 32 square kilometres of mixed woodland that lies between the suburbs of Dahlem and Wilmersdorf, and the Havel lakes to the west; it's popular with Berliners for its bracing air and walks. Seventy percent of the Grunewald was cut down in the postwar years for fuel, and subsequent replanting has replaced pine and birch with oak and ash, making it all the more popular.

The Jagdschloss Grunewald

One possible starting point is the **Jagdschloss Grunewald** (April–Sept 10am–6pm; March & Oct 10am–5pm; Nov–Feb 10am–4pm; closed Mon; DM2.50) a royal hunting lodge built in the sixteenth century and enlarged by Friedrichs I and II. Today it's a museum, housing old furniture and Dutch and German painting, including works by

Cranach the Elder and Rubens. To reach the Jagdschloss, take bus #60 from Blissestrasse U-Bahn to the stop at Pücklerstrasse and head west down that street into the forest. Near the Pücklerstrasse stop, incidentally, you'll find the **Brücke Museum** at Bussardsteig 9 (11am–5pm; closed Tues; DM3.50), a collection of works by the group known as *Die Brücke* ("The Bridge") who worked in Dresden and Berlin from 1905 to 1913, and whose work was later banned by the Nazis. The big names are Kirchner, Heckel and Schmidt-Rottluff, who painted Expressionist cityscapes and had considerable influence over later artists.

Strandbad Wannsee and the Pfaueninsel

An alternative approach to the Grunewald, and with the added attraction of beginning at a strip of **beaches**, is to take the #1 or #3 S-Bahn to Nikolasee station from where it's a ten-minute walk or a quick bus ride to **Strandbad Wannsee**, a kilometre-long strip of pale sand that's the largest inland beach in Europe, and one that's packed as soon as the sun comes out. From here it's easy to wander into the forests, or, more adventurously, catch one of several **ferries** that leave a little way from the S-Bahn station (ask there for directions). It's possible to sail to Potsdam, Spandau (DM6), to Kladow, across the lake (your S-Bahn ticket is valid; otherwise DM2.70) or to the **Pfaueninsel** (Peacock Island; daily April & Sept 8am–6pm; May–Aug 8am–8pm; March & Oct 9am–5pm; Nov–Feb 10am–4pm; ferry DM4), whose attractions include a mini-**Schloss**, containing a small **museum** (April–Sept Tues–Sun 10am–5pm; Oct Tues–Sun 10am–4pm). No cars are allowed on the island (nor, incidentally, are dogs, ghetto-blasters or smoking), which has been designated a conservation zone and is home to a flock of peacocks.

EASTERN BERLIN

It's no surprise that, despite the rapid pace of change since reunification, the **eastern part of Berlin** retains a distinct identity. For nearly forty-one years it was the official capital of the German Democratic Republic, one of eastern Europe's staunchest Communist regimes, and twenty-eight of those years were spent in a state of isolation unprecedented in the modern world. Add to this a badly decayed infrastructure, an economy that has been virtually closed down and a population eager, for the most part, to pretend that the last forty years never happened, and the result is a phenomenon that almost defies comprehension. Yet, oddly, in many ways this part of the city *is* Berlin, home of its historic heart, a fact that was easily forgotten after the Berlin Wall went up on August 13, 1961 and East Berlin was reduced to a kind of psychological grey area for westerners.

The division of Berlin into zones of occupation in 1945, although seemingly arbitrary, actually followed local government boundaries, and the Soviet sector, later to become East Berlin, encompassed the city centre *Bezirk* (or district) of Mitte, the political and cultural core of imperial Berlin, and location of the two medieval fishing villages out of which the city originally grew. This carving up of the city left East Berlin home to the lion's share of the city's treasures, including Karl Friedrich Schinkel's Neoclassical architectural legacy, and most of the old museums.

East Berlin developed along very different lines to West Berlin. After the war, as American aid flooded into West Berlin, the East Berliners watched the Russians dismantle and ship east practically everything that was still in working order – even whole factories. Despite this they managed to rebuild their skeletal city with little outside help, preserving much more of its historic identity than did their counterparts in West Berlin.

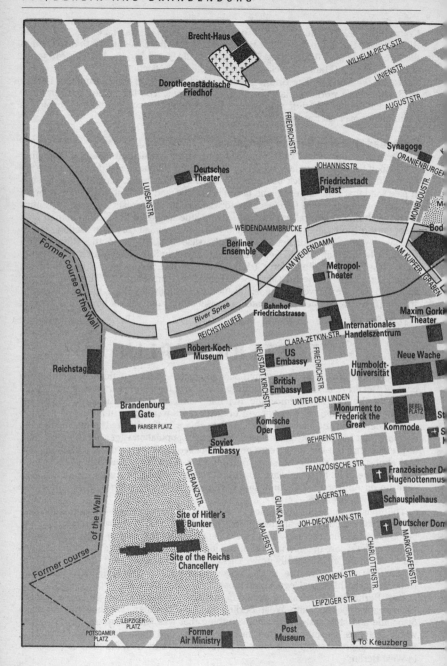

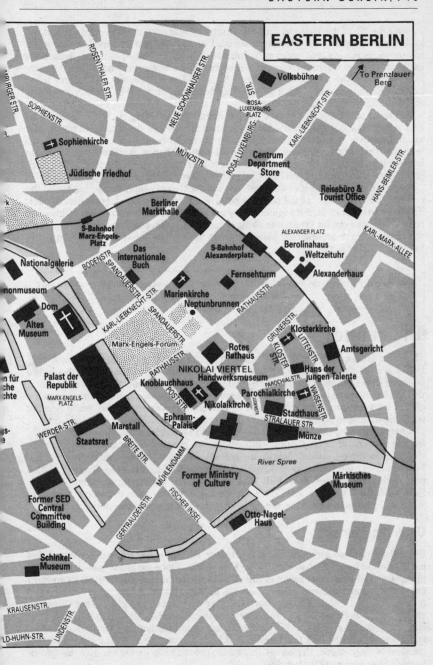

EASTERN BERLIN

To Prenzlauer Berg

Volksbühne

ROSENTHALER STR.

NEUE SCHÖNHAUSER STR.

ROSA-LUXEMBURG-PLATZ

KARL-LIEBKNECHT-STR.

HANS-BEIMLER-STR.

Sophienkirche

SOPHIENSTR.

MÜNZSTR.

ROSA-LUXEMBURG-STR.

Centrum Department Store

Jüdische Friedhof

Reisebüro & Tourist Office

Berliner Markthalle

S-Bahnhof Marx-Engels-Platz

BODENSTR.

SPANDAUERSTR.

Das internationale Buch

S-Bahnhof Alexanderplatz

ALEXANDER PLATZ

Berolinahaus

Weltzeituhr

KARL-MARX-ALLEE

Nationalgalerie

Fernsehturm

Alexanderhaus

RATHAUSSTR.

nonmuseum

KARL-LIEBKNECHT-STR.

SPANDAUERSTR.

Marienkirche

Neptunbrunnen

Dom

GRUNERSTR.

Klosterkirche

Altes Museum

Marx-Engels-Forum

RATHAUSSTR.

LITTENSTR.

KLOSTER STR.

Amtsgericht

n für
che
chte

Palast der Republik

MARX-ENGELS-PLATZ

Rotes Rathaus

NIKOLAI VIERTEL

Handwerksmuseum

PAROCHIALSTR.

Hans der jungen Talente

Knoblauchhaus

POSTSTR.

Parochialkirche

WAISENSTR.

JÜDENSTR.

Nikolaikirche

Stadthaus

se-

WERDER-STR.

Marstall

Ephraim-Palais

STRALAUER STR.

Münze

Staatsrat

BREITE STR.

MÜHLENDAMM

River Spree

Former Ministry of Culture

Märkisches Museum

Former SED Central Committee Building

GERTRAUDENSTR.

FISCHER INSEL

Otto-Nagel-Haus

Schinkel-Museum

KRAUSENSTR.

LINDENSTR.

LD-HUHN-STR.

With the fall of the Wall and unification the city was once again opened up, and the rapid transformation from showpiece socialist capital into part of a modern European metropolis is already well under way. Increasingly, in the unified city, the distinctions between east and west have blurred – it seems only a matter of time before the opinions, based on the 45-year-old divide of the city, that necessarily still inform these pages, will no longer hold true: part of the excitement of being in Berlin, particularly the eastern part, is the speed of change.

But more noticeable on a visit to the city centre is the feeling of change in the air as east and west merge together. Although for many people the future seems at best uncertain, never has debate about what may lie ahead been so open, or so vocal. Go into any bar in the centre and, if you speak a little German, it's likely you'll fall into conversation about the new Germany and its role in the Europe of the 1990s: it's a fascinating time to be here and you may find yourself staying longer than you'd planned.

In purely tourist terms it's important to avoid the trap of simply wandering round the centre of eastern Berlin, as the outlying parts of the city also have a great deal to offer. To gain a true impression it's important to get away from the well-trodden sightseeing routes and head out for Prenzlauer Berg or any another area detailed under "Out from the centre". These are the best places to meet the locals – the only real way to get to know this part of Berlin.

Until the city's telephone network is integrated, the code when phoning the eastern part of Berlin from the west is ☎9.

The centre

The most atmospheric approach to eastern Berlin starts under the city's most celebrated symbol, the **Brandenburg Gate** (see p.729), and leads up the stately boulevard of **Unter den Linden**. A few hundred metres beyond the Brandenburg Gate, the Unter den Linden intersects with **Friedrichstrasse** cutting north–south across this part of the city. A left turn from here leads north to **Bahnhof Friedrichstrasse**, while heading south via what used to be Checkpoint Charlie brings you into Kreuzberg in the west.

Continuing along the Unter den Linden from the Friedrichstrasse intersection leads, by way of some of Berlin's finest eighteenth- and nineteenth-century architecture, to the **Museuminsel**, island home to eastern Berlin's leading museums. At the Museuminsel, the Unter den Linden becomes **Karl-Liebknecht-Strasse**, which passes the **Palast der Republik** (the former GDR parliament building) and the **Fernsehturm** TV tower and leads to **Alexanderplatz**, once the nerve centre of Weimar Berlin, now a concrete and glass wilderness with few redeeming features.

Unter den Linden

From the Brandenburg Gate follow the **Unter den Linden**, a broad boulevard that leads into the heart of what used to be East Berlin. Once the main east–west axis of imperial Berlin and site of many of the city's foreign embassies, until 1989 its western extremity marked the end of the road for East Berliners. A low barrier a hundred metres or so short of the Brandenburg Gate cut it off from Charlottenburger Chaussee (today known as Strasse des 17 Juni), its prewar continuation leading to the city's west end. Since the demise of the Wall, new life has been breathed into Unter den Linden, and it's now crowded with tourists heading both east and west. With the opening of a number of ritzy shops, the street is rapidly re-assuming its prewar role as one of Berlin's most important thoroughfares.

Unter den Linden, meaning "beneath the lime trees", was named after the trees that line the street's central island; the present generation dates from a period of postwar planting. A few hundred metres along is the Friedrichstrasse intersection: before the war this was one of the busiest crossroads in the city, a focal point for cafés and hotels. Like most of the rest of Weimar Berlin it vanished in the debris of the war, and although these days the **Lindencorso**, a restaurant, café and bar complex, attempts to keep the flag flying, the area is a shadow of its former self.

A couple of hundred metres beyond here is an equestrian **monument to Frederick the Great**, the enlightened despot who laid the foundations of Prussian power (see Potsdam p.774). After the war the statue of "Der alte Fritz", as the king was popularly known, was removed from Unter den Linden, and only restored to its city centre site in 1980 after a long exile in Potsdam.

This monument is the vanguard of a whole host of historic buildings, survivors of nineteenth-century Berlin, restored over the last 45 years or so from the postwar rubble. On the left-hand side of the street is the **Humboldt Universität**, a restrained and dignified Neoclassical building from 1748. Alumni of the university include Karl Marx, Friedrich Engels and Karl Liebknecht. The philologists Jacob and Wilhelm Grimm (better known as the Brothers Grimm) and Albert Einstein are some of the better-known former staff members.

Around Bebelplatz

Directly opposite the university is **Bebelplatz**, formerly Opernplatz, the scene on May 11, 1933, of the infamous *Buchverbrennung*, the burning of books that conflicted with Nazi ideology. Thousands of books went up in smoke, including the works of "un-German" authors like Erich Maria Remarque, Thomas Mann, Heinrich Mann and Erich Kästner, along with volumes by countless foreign writers. Perhaps the most fitting comment on this episode was made with accidental foresight by Heinrich Heine during the previous century: "Where they start by burning books, they'll end by burning people."

On the western side of Bebelplatz is the **Alte Bibliothek**, a former royal library known colloquially as the **Kommode** (chest of drawers), thanks to its curved Baroque facade. Lenin spent some time here poring over dusty tomes while waiting for the Russian Revolution, and despite the fact that only the building's facade survived the war, it's been immaculately restored. On the north side of the square, the **Deutsche Staatsoper** by Georg von Knobelsdorff, another flawless eighteenth-century Neoclassical building, was designed as Berlin's first theatre. Like virtually everything else around here it has been totally reconstructed and is now eastern Berlin's leading opera house (see "Drinking, eating and nightlife").

Just behind is another Knobelsdorff creation, the **St Hedwigs-Kathedrale**, which was built for the city's Catholics in 1747 and is still in use. Reduced to a shell on March 2, 1943, the cathedral was not reconstructed until 1963, a restoration that left it with a modernised interior. Next door to the Deutsche Staatsoper is the **Palais Unter den Linden**. Originally built in 1663 and given a Baroque face-lift in 1732, this became a leading venue for modern art exhibitions in 1919. In 1933 the Nazis closed it, declaring hundreds of Expressionist and contemporary works housed in it to be examples of "*entartete Kunst*" or "degenerate art". One wing of the palace now houses the **Operncafé**, formerly one of East Berlin's tackier bar/restaurant/disco complexes but now reborn in grandiose style (see "Drinking , eating and nightlife").

Karl Friedrich Schinkel (1781–1841) was the architect who, more than anyone, gave nineteenth-century Berlin its distinctive stamp, and his **Friedrichwerdersche Kirche**, at Am Werderschen Markt, now houses the **Schinkel-Museum** (Wed–Sun 10am–6pm). Here, a permanent exhibition in the church's upper gallery gives a full rundown of Schinkel's designs, setting his work in the context of the times. Schinkel's most famous surviving creation, the **Neue Wache**, can be found opposite the Deutsche Staatsoper. Resembling a stylised Roman temple, it was built as a sort of Neoclassical police station for the royal watch, and served as a guardhouse until 1918. In 1930 it was converted into a memorial to the military dead of World War I, and in 1957 the GDR government extended this concept to include those killed by the Nazis, dedicating the building as a "Memorial to the Victims of Fascism and Militarism". Inside, a memorial flame flickers over a granite slab covering the remains of an unknown soldier and an unknown resistance fighter. Next door, housed in one of eastern Berlin's finest Baroque buildings, the old Prussian Arsenal or *Zeughaus*, is the **Museum für Deutsche Geschichte**, Unter den Linden 2, 1086 (Mon–Thurs 9am–6pm, Sat & Sun 10am–5pm, but temporarily closed at the time of writing). The highly political and subjective nature of its content was to cause problems after the *Wende* and, despite attempts to redress the balance with a special exhibition about German victims of Stalinist persecution during the period, it was closed down just after reunification to enable a full "reassessment" of the past. In the **Schlüterhof**, the museum's inner courtyard, look out for the 22 contorted faces of dying warriors which adorn the walls, the work of the great Baroque sculptor Andreas Schlüter,

North of Unter den Linden

Heading north at the Unter den Linden/Friedrichstrasse junction takes you along **Friedrichstrasse** itself towards **Bahnhof Friedrichstrasse**, once the biggest border crossing point for East Berlin-bound travellers. Just before the train station, the street passes under the Friedrichstrasse railway bridge, where a plaque on the western side commemorates two young Wehrmacht soldiers executed for "desertion" by the SS during the last hopeless days of the Battle of Berlin; it's one of many reminders of the cataclysm which shaped this city and which has left indelible scars on its fabric.

North of the bridge, on the right, at Friedrichstr. 101 is the **Admiralspalast**, a Jugendstil building and rare prewar survivor. Amid the predominantly concrete architecture of the immediate area its partially gilded facade, divided by fluted columns and inset with bas-reliefs, comes as a real surprise. Originally built as a variety theatre in 1910, it became an important political meeting hall in the immediate postwar years, being one of the few buildings in the area to have survived the bombing.

South of Unter den Linden

South of the Unter den Linden is the grid-like street pattern of Friedrichstadt, one of a number of seventeenth-century city extensions that took Berlin beyond its original walled core. Following Charlottenstrasse south from Unter den Linden leads to the **Platz der Akademie**, an historic cluster of restored buildings that was once considered one of the most beautiful squares in Europe.

The Französischer Dom

On the northern side of Platz der Akademie you'll find the **Französischer Dom**, built as a church for Berlin's influential Huguenot community in the late seventeenth century, and still in use as a place of worship. Today, part of the ground floor houses the **Hugenottenmuseum** (Mon, Wed & Sat 10am–5pm, Thurs 10am–6pm, Sun 11.30am–5pm; DM1.05), detailing the flight of the Huguenots from France after the revocation of the Edict of Nantes and the subsequent settling of 20,000 Huguenots in Berlin. Inside the **tower** (daily 10am–6pm; free) is a smart restaurant, and a balcony running round the outside offers fine views of this part of town and beyond. At the southern end of the square, the **Deutscher Dom** was built around the same time for the city's Lutheran community, and is the stylistic twin of the Französischer Dom. Between the two churches is Schinkel's Neoclassical **Schauspielhaus** with a facade featuring intricate relief work.

Along Leipziger Strasse

From here, Charlottenstrasse continues south to **Leipziger Strasse**, once a main Berlin shopping street linking Alexanderplatz and Potsdamer Platz, and now showing the first signs of impending revival, particularly in the area around the junction with Friedrichstrasse. The only apparent survivor of prewar Leipziger Strasse, the **Spittelkolonadden**, a semicircular colonnade on the right towards its eastern end, turns out to be a copy of part of an eighteenth-century structure that once stood on the opposite side of the street.

At the western end of Leipziger Strasse is Göring's **Air Ministry**, a forbidding structure with a fortress-like air. Göring promised Berliners that not a single bomb would fall on the city during the war; if this were to happen, the Reichsmarshal said, he would change his name to Meyer – a common Jewish surname. Ironically, the Air Ministry was one of the few buildings to emerge more or less unscathed from the bombing and Red Army shelling. After the establishment of the GDR it became the SED regime's *Haus der Ministerien* (House of Ministries), and was venue for a mass demonstration on June 16, 1953 that was to be a prelude for a general but short-lived uprising against the communist government the next day.

Beyond the former Air Ministry, Leipziger Strasse runs into **Potsdamer Platz**, reopened to traffic in the aftermath of November 9, 1989, and the site of what in prewar days was said to be the busiest square in Europe. Now once again traffic streams through, and another once-desolate corner of Berlin has been reborn.

The Museum Island and around

At the eastern end of Unter den Linden the Schinkel-designed **Karl-Liebknecht-Brücke** (formerly the Marx-Engels-Brücke, and before that the Schlossbrücke) spans the Spree. The classical statues which line each side of the bridge represent scenes from ancient Greek mythology, and earned the bridge the popular epithet of *Puppenbrücke* or "Puppet Bridge".

Around the Palast der Republik

The bridge leads onto **Marx-Engels-Platz** (formerly Schlossplatz), former site of the **Berliner Schloss**, the old Imperial Palace, the remains of which were demolished after the war. On November 9, 1918, following the abdication of the Kaiser, Karl Liebknecht proclaimed a Socialist Republic from one of the palace balconies (now preserved in the facade of the Staatsrat building, see below). The Berliner Schloss was badly damaged during the war but probably not more so than a number of other structures which were subsequently rebuilt. However, as a reminder of the still-recent imperial past, the Schloss was an embarrassment to the Communists and they dynamited the ruins in 1950. Much of the space it once occupied eventually ended up as a car park for the **Palast der Republik**, which was built on the southeastern side of Marx-Engels-Platz during the early 1970s to house the *Volkskammer*, the GDR's parliament.

The huge angular building with its bronzed, reflecting windows was completed in less than a thousand days, and was a source of great pride to the Honecker regime. The interior is a masterpiece of tastelessness and the hundreds of lamps hanging from the ceiling of the main foyer explain its nickname, *Erichs Lampenladen* – "Erich's lamp shop". Shortly before reunification an asbestos hazard was discovered in the building, and in October 1990 it was shut down indefinitely. Current speculation in the city suggests that it may well soon suffer the same fate as the Schloss.

On the southern side of Karl-Liebknecht-Platz is the former GDR **Staatsrat**, an early 1960s building enhanced by the inclusion in its facade of the royal palace **balcony** from which Karl Liebknecht proclaimed the German revolution in 1918. Immediately to the east of the Staatsrat is the **Neue Marstall**, an unimaginatively extravagant turn-of-the-century construction, built to house the hundreds of royal coaches and horses used to ferry the royal household around the city. These days the ground floor is in use as an exhibition hall, and it's worth dropping by for displays covering interesting aspects of Berlin history.

Karl-Liebknecht-Platz marks the mid-point of a city-centre island in the Spree, whose northwestern part, extending peninsula-like from the square, is known as the **Museumsinsel (Museum Island)**, location of the best of eastern Berlin's **museums**. Your main problem will be finding enough time to see everything: it almost goes without saying that your best bet is to pick out one collection in particular rather than trying to cram them all into a single day. Note, too, that with the exception of the Pergamonmuseum, all museums are **closed on Mondays**, and you'll frequently find whole sections of collections closed for "technical reasons".

The Pergamonmuseum

The **Pergamonmuseum** (Mon–Thurs, Sat & Sun 9am–6pm, Fri 10am–6pm; DM2.05) is a massive structure, built in the early part of this century to house the treasure trove of the German archaeologists who were busy plundering the ancient world. The museum is divided into four sections, the most important of which, the **Department of Antiquities**, contains the **Pergamon Altar**: a huge structure dedicated to Zeus and Athena, dating from 180 to 160 BC, which was unearthed in Turkey and brought to Berlin in 1903. The **frieze** shows a battle between the gods and giants, and it's a tremendously forceful piece of work, the powerfully depicted figures writhing in a mass of sinew and muscle. The section also contains other pieces of Hellenistic architecture (albeit on a smaller scale), including a **market gate** from the Turkish town of Miletus and various examples of Greek sculpture.

The **Western Asian Section** has items going back four thousand years to Babylonian times, including the enormous **Ishtar Gate**, the **Processional Way** and the facade of the **Throne Room** from Babylon, all of which date from the reign of Nebuchadnezzar II in the sixth century BC. While it's impossible not to be awed by the size and remarkable state of preservation of the deep blue enamelled bricks of the Babylon finds, it's as well to remember that much of what you see is a mock-up, built around the original finds.

The museum's **Islamic Section** contains the facade of a Jordanian **Prince's Palace** at Mshatta from 743 AD, presented to Kaiser Wilhelm II by the Sultan of Turkey, as well as a host of smaller but no less impressive exhibits from Arabia and Persia. Finally, the **East Asian Collection** has a large collection of ceramics, lacquer-work and jade, spanning four thousand years.

The Altes Museum

Directly to the north of Marx-Engels-Platz is the **Altes Museum** (Wed, Thurs, Sat & Sun 9am–6pm, Fri 10am–6pm; free), perhaps Schinkel's most impressive surviving work and now home to a reasonably diverting art collection. The **ground floor** is usually given over to temporary exhibitions, while the **second floor** houses sections devoted to postwar and GDR art; some of the crasser propagandist works have been withdrawn from display. The museum also houses the Kupferstichkabinett (Print Collection), a large collection of engravings and prints containing exquisite drawings by Botticelli, and nineteenth- and twentieth-century German and French graphics and prints; at the time of writing, none of these are on show.

The Neues Museum and Nationalgalerie

Just behind the Altes Museum is the **Neues Museum**, one of eastern Berlin's few remaining war ruins, which is being gradually restored to house the overflow from other museums. Next door, just north of Bodestrasse, is the **Nationalgalerie** (Wed, Thurs, Sat & Sun 9am–6pm, Fri 10am–6pm; DM1), which now contains eastern Berlin's largest art collections. The first-floor **nineteenth-century section** is full of dull portraiture and landscapes, a legacy of the conservatism of Kaiser Wilhelm II, who vetoed a decision by the gallery to buy Impressionist works: apart from a couple of Cézannes it's pretty uninspiring. The **twentieth-century section** is good on the Expressionist and *Neue Sachlichkeit* (New Objectivity) movements, with work by the Dresden and Munich Expressionist collectives *Die Brücke* and *Der Blaue Reiter*, including paintings by Ernst Ludwig Kirchner, Max Pechstein and Karl Schmidt-Rotluff. Also worth seeking out are works by Otto Dix and Emil Nolde, and Ernst Barlach's fluidly expressive sculptures.

The Bodemuseum

At the northeastern tip of the Museumsinsel is the **Bodemuseum** (Wed–Sun 10am–6pm; DM1), housed in an impressive neo-Baroque building. The collection itself is highly traditional and divided into several distinct sections. The **Egyptian Museum/Papyrus Collection** contains art and papyri from 5000 BC to the third century AD. The **Early Christian and Byzantine Section** has an extensive range of objects, mainly religious in nature, from the pre-medieval eastern Mediterranean. Particularly interesting are the sixth-century mosaic from the church of San Michele in Ravenna, the Eastern Orthodox icons and the Coptic art exhibits. In the **Picture Gallery** there's a large collection of German, Italian, Dutch and Flemish paintings – mostly dull but with one or two important old masters. More worthwhile is the **Museum for Ancient and Early History**, which has archaeological material from all over Europe right up to the eleventh and twelfth centuries, including the **Heinrich Schliemann Collection**, which consists of items unearthed by the great German archaeologist on the site of ancient Troy during the nineteenth century. Tragically, the best of the Schliemann Collection was lost during the war, either crushed in the rubble of the supposedly impregnable Tiergarten flak tower, where many of the city's finest treasures had been stored for safekeeping, or spirited off to the Soviet Union as war booty. At the time of writing attempts are being made to establish which pieces were taken east, and to make arrangements for their possible future return. The **Sculpture Gallery** has eighteenth-century pieces with a few notable late Gothic German and early Renaissance Italian examples.

Elsewhere on Museum Island

From the Bodemuseum it's a short walk back to Karl-Liebknecht-Platz. Adjacent to the Altes Museum is the **Dom**, built between 1894 and 1905. With its distinctive dome and towers it was intended to serve the House of Hohenzollern as a family church, and its vault houses ninety sarcophagi containing the remains of various members of the line. The building was badly damaged during the war, but has undergone a long period of reconstruction: although it's not completely open to the public yet, it is possible to step inside and see the interior.

Alexanderplatz and around

Alexanderplatz is the commercial hub of eastern Berlin. If Unter den Linden represents the glories of Berlin past, then Alexanderplatz and the area around it represent the glories of eastern Berlin present, although only time will tell whether the concrete giganticism of the new capital will wear as well as the efforts of Schinkel and his contemporaries. To get to "Alex" from the Palast der Republik, head up the shopping strip of **Karl-Liebknecht-Strasse**, to the right of which lies the **Marx-Engels Forum**, a severely well-ordered park, with a dire bronze representation of the founders of Marxism at its heart.

The Rotes Rathaus and the Marienkirche

Beyond here, across Spandauer Strasse, is a large open space on which stands the **Neptunbrunnen**, a fountain incorporating statues of Neptune and his courtiers. Across Rathausstrasse, to the southeast of the fountain, is the **Rotes Rathaus** (tours Sat 11.15am, 11.30am, noon & 12.30pm from the main entrance), the "Red Town Hall", so called because of its bricks rather than its politics. It's a grandiose, almost Venetian-looking building, which has lost some of its impact now that it's been hemmed in by new buildings. From the Rathaus the pedestrianised Rathausstrasse leads past a series of "luxury" shops, legacy of the old regime's efforts to jazz up the city centre, to Alexanderplatz.

To the north of the Neptunbrunnen is the **Marienkirche**, Berlin's oldest parish church. The nave dates back to about 1270, and the interior is an excellent place to escape the increasingly frenetic street life of the area and listen to a free organ recital (daily 3.30–4pm). Look out, too, for the fifteenth-century *Totentanz*, a 22-metre frieze showing the dance of death, and an immense bronze font.

The Fernsehturm

The Marienkirche, like every other building in the vicinity, is overshadowed by the gigantic **Fernsehturm** or TV tower (May–Sept daily 8am–11pm; Oct–April daily 9am–11pm, second and fourth Tues in month 1–11pm; DM3) that dominates the eastern Berlin skyline like a displaced satellite sitting atop a huge factory chimney. The 365-metre tower was completed in 1969 and does have a couple of positive features: it makes a good orientation point, and there's a tremendous view (40km on a rare clear day, although the summit is often shrouded in cloud) from the observation platform.

Above the observation platform is the *Tele-Café*, whose main attraction is that it turns on its own axis once every hour (you have to buy a DM5 ticket for the privilege of being able to sit here). When the sun shines on the globe of the tower, the reflected light forms a cross visible even in western Berlin, much to the reported chagrin of the old authorities and amusement of Berliners, who call it the "pope's revenge".

Alexanderplatz

Immediately northeast of the Fernsehturm is **S-Bahnhof Alexanderplatz**, a good point from which to catch trains out to the eastern suburbs, and around which myriad *Imbiss* stands and street stalls have sprung up since unification.

Alexanderplatz itself, named after the Russian Czar Alexander I and made famous by Alfred Döblin's novel of life in the Weimar era, *Berlin Alexanderplatz*, is a huge, wind-swept pedestrianised plaza surrounded by high-rises. Alexanderplatz has always figured prominently in the city's history. In 1848 it was barricaded by revolutionaries, and during the revolution of 1918 sailors occupied the Alexanderplatz police headquarters and freed the prisoners. More recently, Alexanderplatz was the focal point of the million-strong city-wide **demonstration** of November 4, 1989, which formed a prelude to the events of November 9. Hundreds of thousands of people crammed into the square to hear opposition leaders speak. Veteran writer Stefan Heym summed up the mood in his speech to the crowd: "Power belongs not to one, not to a few, not to the party and not to the state apparatus. The whole people must have a share."

Dominating Alexanderplatz are the ugly **Hotel Stadt Berlin**, from whose 37th-floor *Panorama-Restaurant* there's an undeniably stupendous view (make a reservation on ☎2190 – it's popular and the food is reasonable), and the huge and even uglier **Reisebüro** building where you'll find a useful tourist information office. In the centre of Alexanderplatz is the sorry-looking **Brunnen der Völkerfreundschaft** (Friendship of the Peoples Fountain), which used to be a hang-out for prostitutes, who promoted friendship between the peoples in their own ways. A more famous monument is the **Weltzeituhr** (World Clock) in front of the Alexanderhaus. Eastern Berlin's most famous rendezvous point, this tells the time in different cities throughout the world, and looks like a product of the same architectural school responsible for the Fernsehturm.

Under the former regime, commercial life on Alexanderplatz centred around the **Centrum** department store, always well-stocked by GDR standards, but now left at a disadvantage by the competition of *KaDeWe*, *Karstadt*, et al. These days things seem to be happening more at street level, with the clusters of stalls selling everything from cheap jeans to *Bockwurst* jostling for space around the edges of the plaza.

The Nikolaiviertel and around

Slightly to the southwest of the Rotes Rathaus lies the **Nikolaiviertel**, a recent development that attempts to recreate the old prewar heart of Berlin on the site of the city's medieval core, which was razed overnight on June 16, 1944. The Nikolaiviertel consists partly of exact replicas of historic Berlin buildings which didn't make it through to the postwar era, such as *Zum Nussbaum* (see "Drinking, eating and nightlife"), a convincing enough recreation of a celebrated sixteenth-century *Gaststätte,* and partly of stylised buildings not based on anything in particular, but with a distinct "old Berlin" feel to them.

At the centre of it all is the Gothic **Nikolaikirche** (Tues–Sun 10am–6pm; DM2.05), a thirteenth-century church, restored to its twin-towered prewar glory. It now houses an exhibition about medieval Berlin. Nearby, at Poststr. 4, is the **Knoblauchhaus**, built in 1759 and now a wine bar.

Nearby on Mühlendamm is the rebuilt Rococo **Ephraim-Palais** (Tues–Fri 9am–5pm, Sat 9am–5pm; DM1), housing a museum that details the growth of Berlin from "Electoral residence to bourgeois great city of the nineteenth century". Nearby at Mühlendamm 5 is the **Handwerksmuseum** (Tues–Sun 10am–5pm), a small but not unentertaining museum about the various trades practised in old Berlin.

Around the centre

The periphery of eastern Berlin's centre is best explored on foot. Its main points of interest lie in the run-down residential crescent running from just north of Bahnhof Friedrichtrasse to Rosa-Luxemburg-Platz, and the most fascinating sections of all are along **Oranienburger Strasse** and nearby **Grosse Hamburger Strasse**, the heart of Berlin's prewar Jewish community.

North from Bahnhof Friedrichstrasse

From the station, Friedrichstrasse itself runs north across the River Spree over the wrought-iron **Weidendammbrücke**. Immediately to the left on Bertolt-Brecht-Platz is the **Berliner Ensemble** theatre (see "Drinking, eating and nightlife"), the official Brecht theatre, although now only the invocation of Brecht's name bears witness to the greatness of the man who was once the main driving force behind modern German drama. After spending much of the Nazi era in American exile, Brecht returned in 1949 with his wife, Helene Weigel, to take over direction of the theatre, marking his return by painting a still-visible red cross through the coat of arms on the royal box.

A little way to the north along Friedrichstrasse is **Oranienburger Tor**. Roughly opposite here is the **Dorotheenstädtische Friedhof**, eastern Berlin's VIP cemetery, which contains the graves of Bertolt Brecht and Helene Weigel, the author Heinrich Mann, John Heartfield (the Dada luminary and interwar photomontage exponent), the philosopher Georg Hegel, whose ideas influenced Marx, and Berlin's great Neoclassical architect Karl Friedrich Schinkel. Just beyond the cemetery is the **Brecht-Haus**, Chausseestr. 125, 1040 (Tues, Wed & Fri 10am–noon, Thurs 10am– noon & 5–7pm, Sat 9.30–11.30am & 12.30–2pm), Brecht's last home and workplace. It now houses a Bertolt Brecht archive and has half-hourly guided tours of the rooms where the playwright worked and lived. Helene Weigel lived here until her death in 1971, and a small collection of artefacts commemorates her life.

Oranienburger Strasse

Altogether more lively is **Oranienburger Strasse**, running southeast from Oranienburger Tor. One of Berlin's seediest red-light districts by night, since the *Wende* Oranienburger Strasse has also become the centre of a thriving alternative culture scene, thanks largely to the *Tacheles e.V*, an art-house collective who have taken over a large abandoned cinema on the southern side of the street just beyond the Oranienburger Tor junction. The exterior is usually festooned with works-in-progress, and the building has become home and workplace to an ever-changing band of international "alternative" artists, kindred spirits and hangers-on. Inside the building, which looks like a bomb site, is a café/bar (see "Drinking, eating and nightlife") and regular gigs and events take place here .

Further down Oranienburger Strasse is the **Neue Synagoge**, which served as Berlin's central synagogue for over sixty years. it was burned on *Kristallnacht*, the night of November 9–10, 1938, when the Nazis launched an all-out assault on Germany's Jewish community.

Wartime bombing caused additional damage to the Oranienburger Strasse synagogue, leaving little more than its shattered facade as a desolate reminder of the savagery of Nazi rule. Here, clearly visible from the street, a plaque entreats passers-by to "Never forget". However, it looks as though the building may yet be reborn: restoration work is in progress and it's planned to turn it into a *Centrum Judaicum*, an institution for the study and preservation of Jewish culture.

The Jewish Cemetery and the Sophienkirche

At the eastern end of Oranienburger Strasse, turn left into Grosse Hamburger Strasse, where on the immediate right you'll see the location of Berlin's oldest **Jewish cemetery**, established in 1672, and the first Jewish old people's home to be founded in the city. The Nazis used the building as a detention centre for Jews from the city, and 55,000 people were held here before being shipped off to the camps. The open space behind is the site of the cemetery itself which was destroyed by the Gestapo in 1943; part of their desecration involved digging a slit trench, which they shored up with gravestones, through the site.

Continuing along the street, past turn-of-the-century neo-Baroque apartment blocks with shrapnel-pitted facades, brings you to the entrance gateway of the **Sophienkirche** on the right-hand side. This church, dating back to 1712, is one of the city's finest Baroque buildings, and the only central Berlin church to survive the war more or less undamaged.

East from the centre: Prenzlauer Berg and Treptow

Away from the centre of eastern Berlin is another city, located in the *Bezirke*, or **districts**, which are each very different in character. Following are accounts of just two districts: for more detailed accounts see *Berlin: The Rough Guide*. The tenements of **Prenzlauer Berg**, a part working-class, part bohemian district that fans out northeast of the city centre, have long been a centre of "alternative" culture and lifestyles. This area is also home to the best cafés, bars and nightlife in the eastern part of the city. With enough time, it's worth heading out to **Treptow** and its massive Soviet war memorial and riverside parks.

Prenzlauer Berg

One eastern *Bezirk* that should on no account be missed is **Prenzlauer Berg**. This run-down working-class district radiates out from the northeastern edge of the city centre in a network of tenement-lined cobbled streets divided by a series of major traffic arteries. Before the *Wende*, Prenzlauer Berg, like Kreuzberg in West Berlin, enjoyed a big influx of "alternative" lifestyle adherents and artists who chose this district to live on the edge of established GDR society – which, given the all-embracing nature of the state, was not as easy as in "alternative" West Berlin. It was no coincidence that during the Honecker years more cars here flew white ribbons from their radio aerials, signalling that the owners had applied to emigrate to the west, than anywhere else in the city. **Squatting** has always played an important role in the life of the area, even under the old regime, and in the face of Berlin's ever-increasing accommodation crisis it will doubtless continue to do so. Since the events of late 1989, large numbers of west Berliners have come here, hoping to recreate the squat-based counter-culture *Szene* that thrived in the west a decade ago. This, coupled with the opening of various new cafés and galleries, has turned Prenzlauer Berg into one of the most exciting parts of the city.

By the turn of the century Prenzlauer Berg had become one of Berlin's most densely populated tenement districts. During the war it was fought over (bullet holes and shrapnel scars on the building facades testify to this) but not flattened, and most of the *Mietskaserne* (tenement blocks) put up in the late nineteenth and early twentieth centuries to house the city's rapidly expanding factory worker population are still standing. Many of the blackened buildings, with their overgrown *Hinterhöfe* (courtyards), look as if they haven't been renovated since the war, and in many cases this is probably so: behind crumbling facades paint peels in gloomy stairwells, and every year a few lives are claimed as overhanging balconies crash onto the streets below. Over the last few years of its existence, the GDR city tourist authorities wised up to the potential appeal of the Prenzlauer Berg, and although they didn't exactly encourage visitors to go into the seedier parts, they started to include the more accessible and presentable streets on the tourist itinerary.

The quickest way to **get to Prenzlauer Berg** is to take the U-Bahn from Alexanderplatz and head for either Dmitroffstrasse or Schönhauser Allee U-Bahn stations. For a more atmospheric approach take tram #46 from Am Kupfergraben, or tram #49 from Hackescher Markt. Either of these will take you through some of eastern Berlin's lesser-known back streets and provide a good impression of the *real* city. They'll also take you past the **Zionskirche**, which was a live music club until neo-Nazi skinheads broke up a gig here in October 1987, in an early manifestation of the revival of the extreme right that spilled out into the open after the *Wende*.

Schönhauser Allee and around

It's a fairly easy walk to Prenzlauer Berg from Rosa-Luxemburg-Platz. The district
starts at the beginning of Schönhauser Allee and if you follow this street for about 600
metres you'll find yourself on **Senefelder Platz**. A stone's throw from here is the
Jüdischer Friedhof, Prenzlauer Berg's Jewish cemetery (Mon–Thurs 8am–4pm;
male visitors are requested to keep their heads covered), just to the right of
Schönhauser Allee. Over 20,000 people are buried here but, thanks to the Nazis, their
last rest is an anonymous one; shortly before the end of the war the gravestones were
smashed into the ground, and now only ivy-covered fragments remain.

Beyond the junction of Schönhauser Alle, Dmitroffstrasse, Kastanienallee and
Eberswalde Strasse, **Schönhauser Allee** assumes its true identity as Prenzlauer
Berg's main drag, an old-fashioned shopping street with, thanks to its cobbled streets
and narrow shop facades, a distinctly prewar feel. This effect is enhanced by the U-
Bahn, which goes overground and becomes an elevated railway shortly before
Dmitroffstrasse station, leaving much of Schönhauser Allee in the shadows.

Schönhauser Allee extends northwards for a couple of kilometres towards Pankow,
lined by shops and street stalls. Just to the southeast of Schönhauser Allee U-Bahn
station, at the intersection of Stargarder Strasse and Greifenhagener Strasse, is the
Gethsemene Kirche, which was an important focal point for reformist activities
during the summer 1989 exodus from the GDR, and during the months leading up to
the *Wende*. Given the peaceful nature of Schönhauser Allee today, it's hard to imagine
that as recently as October 7, 1989 the police were beating non-violent demonstrators
here, during the anti-government street protests that followed the celebrations of the
GDR's fortieth anniversary. Just over a month later, however, the nightmare was over,
and it was in Prenzlauer Berg that ordinary East Germans first experienced the reality
of the passing of the old order when, at 9.15pm on November 9, 1989, a couple walked
through the nearby **Bornholmer Strasse border crossing** into West Berlin, becoming the first East Berliners to take advantage of the opening of the Wall .

These days, however, it's in the maze of run-down streets east of Schönhauser Allee
that Prenzlauer Berg's real attractions lie. Here you'll find some of the best cafés and
bars in the eastern part of Berlin (see "Drinking, eating and nightlife"); the area is best
explored by turning into Sredzkistrasse from Schönhauser Allee.

Kollwitzplatz and Husemannstrasse

A right turn from Sredzkistrasse into Knaackstrasse leads to **Kollwitzplatz**, focal point
for Prenzlauer Berg's main sights, named after the artist **Käthe Kollwitz**, who lived in
nearby Weissenburgerstrasse (now called Kollwitzstrasse) from 1891 to 1943.
Kollwitz's home was destroyed in an air-raid, but today a sculpture entitled *Die Mutter*,
based on one of her drawings, stands in the little park on the square. Her work
embraced political and pacifist themes and can be best appreciated in the Käthe-
Kollwitz-Museum in western Berlin (see p.727)). Lately a number of new bars and
fringe theatres have opened around Kollwitzplatz, and it's become a centre of the local
Szene, one that looks set to turn Kollwitzplatz into the eastern Berlin equivalent of
Winterfeldplatz, or perhaps even Savignyplatz.

Running north from Kollwitzplatz is **Husemannstrasse**, a nineteenth-century tenement street which has been restored to its former glory and turned into a kind of living
museum in a unique and encouraging attempt to preserve the grandeur of old Berlin.
The five-storey blocks with their stately facades and wrought-iron balconies give a good
impression of what the rest of this part of Berlin *could* be like if more resources were
available. For the time being, however, Husemannstrasse is an island in a sea of decay.

The street also has a couple of eastern Berlin's better museums. The **Museum
Berliner Arbeiterleben um 1900** (Museum of Working Class Life in 1900; Tues,
Thurs & Sat 11am–6pm, Wed 10am–8pm), Husemannstr. 12, 1058, housed in a

restored tenement building, concentrates on the living conditions of Berlin's working-class population around the turn of the century, which, you might be tempted to conclude after a stroll through the streets of Prenzlauer Berg, haven't changed much since. A couple of doors down from here is the **Friseurmuseum**, Husemannstr. 8, 1058 (Tues 10am–5pm, Wed 10am–6pm, Mon & Thurs on request), Berlin's eminently interesting hairdressing museum. The proprietor (it's a private museum) is of the same opinion and will give you a guided tour of his domain – which includes exhibits on everything to do with hairdressing from prehistory to the present.

Treptow – the Sowjetisches Ehrenmal

The main reason to come to **Treptow** is to see the huge and sobering **Sowjetisches Ehrenmal**, Berlin's main Soviet war memorial. Standing in the **Treptower Park**, a well-known interwar assembly point for revolutionary workers about to embark on demon-strations, it commemorates the Soviet soldiers killed during the Battle of Berlin in April and May 1945, and is burial place to 5000 of the Soviet Union's estimated 305,000 casual-ties during the Battle for Berlin. To get there, take the S-Bahn to Treptower Park station. From here it's just a few hundred metres to the memorial's arched entrance on the south side of Puschkin Allee. A little way to the south of the entrance is a sculpture of a grieving woman representing the Motherland, to the left of which a broad concourse slopes upwards towards a viewing point flanked by two vast triangles of red granite, fashioned from stone bought from Sweden by the Nazis to furnish Berlin with projected victory monuments. From the viewing point the vista is dominated by a vast symbolic statue, a typically Soviet piece of gigantism fashioned out of marble from Hitler's Chancellery. Over eleven metres high and set on top of a hill, it shows an idealised Russian soldier clutching a saved child and resting his sword on a shattered swastika. Inside the plinth is a memorial crypt with a mosaic in true socialist realism style, show-ing Soviet citizens honouring the dead. In the long sunken park area which leads up to the statue are the mass graves of the Red Army troops, lined by sculpted frescos of styl-ised scenes from the Great Patriotic War.

DRINKING, EATING AND NIGHTLIFE

Nowhere is more than a stone's throw from a **bar** in western Berlin. Just about every street corner has a small *Kneipe*, ranging from lugubrious beer-swilling holes to slick, upscale hang-outs for the city's night people. You'll find that most bars stay open later than elsewhere in Germany: it's quite feasible to drink around the clock here, the result of a law that requires bars to close only for an hour a day for cleaning. In the east, things aren't quite so lively – here the new cafés and bars springing up along Oranienburger Strasse and in Prenzlauer Berg are the places to head for.

The city's compressed, cosmopolitan nature means that the range of **restaurants** in the west is wider than in any other German city: indeed, the national cuisine takes a back seat to Greek, Turkish, Balkan, Indian and Italian food, and plenty of places exist where a meal costs under DM15. Almost all the better bars serve food, too, and this can be a bargain – though beware the most chic places, where that interesting-looking item on the menu turns out to be a plate of asparagus tips for DM25. For cheap, on-your-feet snacks, hit an *Imbiss* kiosk – a few marks for a *Wurst* or burger. Food in the eastern parts of the city tends to compare unfavourably with what's available in the west, with few places offering comparable range, quality or value – a state of affairs that will, hope-fully, slowly change.

Since the time of the Weimar Republic, and even through the lean postwar years, Berlin has had a reputation for having some of the best – and steamiest – **nightlife** in Europe, an image fuelled by the cartoons of George Grosz and films like *Cabaret*. Today, western Berlin is still a city that wakes up when others are going to sleep, with some energetic nightclubs and one of Europe's great orchestras.

Drinking

Though it's fun enough to dive into any bar that takes your fancy, western Berlin has three focal points for drinking, each with enough bars to tackle through the course of an evening, and each with a subtly differing character. Those **around Savignyplatz** are the haunt of the city's conspicuous good-timers; **Kreuzberg** drinkers include political activists, punks and the Turkish community, in a mix that forms this area's appeal. The area **around Nollendorfplatz and Winterfeldtplatz** is the territory of sped-out all-nighters and the pushing-on-forty crew. Elsewhere in **Schöneberg** bars are on the whole more mixed and more relaxed. Unless you're into brawling soldiers or pissed businessmen, avoid the Ku'damm and the rip-off joints around the Europa Center.

In the **eastern part** of the city, don't expect the variety or gloss found in the west. Even more than in the west, bars here tend to be male-only territory: better to head for a café, much more a focal point of life in the east, and places where people come to exchange ideas rather than just drink. Best of all try one of the **newer cafés or bars**, often based around squats or occupied buildings.

Berlin **drink specialities** include *Berliner Weisse*, a watery top-fermented wheat beer that's traditionally pepped up by adding a shot of fruity syrup or *Schuss*. Ask for it *mit grün* and you get a dash of woodruff, creating a greeny brew that tastes like liquid silage; *mit rot* is a raspberry-flavoured kiddy drink that works wonders at breakfast time.

Savignyplatz and around

Dralles, Schlüterstr. 69, 1/12. Notably more expensive than other bars in the area, this is *the* place to see and be seen: the 1950s decor is chic and understated, the clientele aspire likewise. Go beautiful and loaded, or not at all . . .

Rosalinde, Knesebeckstr. 16, 1/12. Upmarket café with an unusual variety of breakfasts: their Fitness Frühstück (muesli, fresh fruit and nuts) does the trick after a rough night out, and there's hot food until 2am.

Schwarzes Café, Kantstr. 148, 1/12. Kantstrasse's best hang-out for the young and chic, with a relaxed atmosphere, good music and food (including breakfast day and night, with a "Black special" of black coffee, a Sobranie Black Russian cigarette and black bread). Although perhaps dating, still a classic Berlin bar (open 24hr, closed Tues 8am–8pm).

Shell, Knesebeckstr. 22, 1/12. The archetypal Berlin posing parlour, the air thick with the sipping of Perrier and the rustle of carefully organised Filofaxes. Slick, starchy and self-consciously superior. Vegetarian food.

Zillemarkt, Bleibtreustr. 48, 1/12. Wonderful if shabby bar that attempts a fin-de-siècle feel. Unpretentious and fun, and a good place to start Savignyplatz explorations – it's by the S-Bahn. Serves breakfast till 6pm.

Zwiebelfisch, Savignyplatz 7, 1/12. Corner bar for would-be arty/intellectual types. Lots of jazz and earnest debate. Good cheap grub.

Kreuzberg

Arcanoa, Zossener Str. 48, 1/61. Drink almost supine in treehut-like contraptions after ordering from a bar that has a stream running through it.

Cazzo, Oranienstr. 187, 1/36. Trendy *Szene*/gay bar, and a good place to sample the austere cosiness of contemporary Kreuzberg.

Homo-Bar (aka *Oranienbar*), Oranienstr. 168, 1/36. Famed Kreuzberg watering-hole, which despite a recent name change is by no means solely a gay bar. The interior is half-plastered (as are most of the clientele), giving it a sort of post-nuclear chic.

Milchbar, Manteuffelstr. 41, 1/36. Typical late-night meeting place of black-clad *Szene* groupies. One of the more "in" spots of Kreuzberg – though it's hard to figure out why.

Wunderbar, Körtestr. 38, 1/61. Large and animated bar with pool room and youthful, varied customers. Essential for the first drink of the evening when arriving at Südstern U-Bahn, just across the street.

Around Nollendorfplatz and Winterfeldtplatz

Bar am Lützowplatz, Lützowplatz 7, 1/30. Distinguished in having the longest bar in the city, this also has Berlin's best selection of whiskies (63) and a superb range of moderately priced cocktails. A dangerously great bar.

Café Einstein, Kurfürstenstr. 58, 1/30. Housed in a seemingly ancient mansion, this is about as close as you'll get to the ambience of the prewar Berlin *Kaffeehaus*, with international newpapers and breakfast served till 2pm. Occasional live music and other activities, plus a good garden. Expensive and a little snooty.

Café M, Goltzstr. 34, 1/30. Though littered with tatty plastic chairs and precious little else, *M* is Berlin's most favoured rendezvous for self-styled creative types and the conventionally unconventional. The cool thing to drink is Flensburger Pils, from the bottle. Usually packed, even for its famous breakfasts.

Slumberland, Goltzstr. 24, 1/30. The gimmicks here are sand on the floor and a tropical theme. Laid-back, likeable, and one of the better bars of this area.

Schöneberg

Estoril, Vorbergstr. 11, 1/62. A favourite Schöneberg bar that serves good tapas with drinks.

Pinguin Club, Wartburgstr. 54, 1/62. Tiny and cheerful bar with 1950–60s America supplying its theme and background music.

Zooloo Club, Hauptstr. 5, 1/62. Compact, little-known bar packed after 11pm with local Schönebergers. Rather wonderful, in a low-key sort of way.

Elsewhere in western Berlin

Blisse 14, Blissestr. 14, 1/31. Café-bar designed especially, but not exclusively, for disabled people. A good meeting place.

Café Adler, Friedrichstr. 206, 1/61. Small café whose popularity came from the fact that it is next to the site of the Checkpoint Charlie border crossing. Serves breakfasts and meals.

Café Hardenberg, Hardenbergstr. 10, 1/12. Large, old-fashioned café with excellent and cheap food that draws in local students. Recommended.

E&M Leydicke, Mansteinstr. 4, 1/30. Claims to be the oldest *Kneipe* in western Berlin and, though some of the decorations look suspiciously recent, it does have the feel of an old-fashioned bar. Geared towards tourists.

Klo, Leibnitzstr. 57. 1/12. This one you'll love or hate. A theme bar based on or around things lavatorial (drinks are served in urine sample bottles). If you share the German fascination for anything related to potties and peeing you'll probably wet yourself laughing; otherwise it's pricey and a bit tacky. Entry DM0.25.

Kumpelnest 3000, Lützowstr. 23, 1/30. Carpeted walls and a mock-Baroque effect attract a rough-and-ready crew of under-30s to this erstwhile brothel. Gets going around 2am. Fine fun, and the best place in the area.

Saftladen 2, Wegenerstr. 1, 1/31. When the booze gets too much for you this could be the place: it specialises in alcohol-free drinks, some of which are quite inventive.

Eastern Berlin

Assel, Oranienburgerstr. 21, 1040. A stylish but unpretentious basement bar/gallery with occasional live music and cheap food at DM4–10. One of the highlights of the area.

Café Arkade, Französische Str. (opposite Am Platz der Akademie), 1080. Major city centre rendezvous for the affluent and arty, and, increasingly, for passing tourists.

Café Papillon, Greifenhagernerstr. 16, 1058. Another eastern Berlin must, with a great atmosphere and a young crowd. There's a garden at the back which is part of a tenement *Hinterhof* (courtyard). Closed Fri.

Café Westphal, Kollwitzstr. 63, 1055. One of the first post-Wall places to open, its original rough and ready feel has given way to a more trendy ambience following a recent refurbishment. Popular with local *Szene*-types, who, thankfully, don't affect the offhand coolness of many of their western counterparts. Excellent breakfasts at weekends from 10am.

Gambrinus, Linienstr. 134, 1040. Very typical and very cheap, this one has succumbed to the craze for pseudo-old Berlin interiors, but remains popular with its working-class clientele.

Inseraten-Café-Bar, Schönhauser Allee 58a, 1058. Decor is late-Honecker Rococo, but otherwise not a bad little café. Also serves as a kind of "Exchange & Mart" – on the bar there's a book containing small ads covering everything from old clothes to lonely hearts.

Kaffeestube, Poststr., 1020. A Nikolaiviertel café which tries to evoke the atmosphere of a prewar coffee house. Open 10am–6pm but closed the first Wednesday of each month.

Metzer Eck, Metzer Str. 33, 1055. Founded in 1913, *Metzer Eck* is popular with the Prenzlauer Berg *Szene* crowd. It's also a favorite with actors, whose photos adorn the walls.

Offenbachstuben, Senefelderstr./Stubbenkammerstr., 1058. Highly recommended for both food and drink, a young, eclectic crowd makes this one of the best places to head for in Prenzlauer Berg. Also popular with the gay crowd. Closed Sun and Mon.

Prenzl-Bohne, Senefelder Str. 27, 1058. An *autonome* café offering spiky post-punk ambience. Hosts occasional exhibitions by local artists and fashion designers. Open Mon & Thurs–Sun 3pm–5am.

Silberstein, Oranienburger Str. 27, 1040. Eastern Berlin's trendiest bar, thanks in part to over-the-top designer furniture fashioned out of tree trunks and Trabant crankshafts by a sculptor from the Tacheles e.V. An arty and fashion-conscious clientele, but fun all the same.

Tante Olga, Linienstr. 71, 1054. An old Berlin pub that's for real. A backstreet spit 'n' sawdust establishment of living room proportions, with just a few sit-down tables and a *Stehtisch*, a circular counter around which you can stand.

Zum Hackpeter, Dmitroffstr./Knaackstr., 1058. An excellent *Kneipe* that remains resolutely true to the spirit of the area, and awaits the discovery that it surely deserves. Bockwurst, etc available for about DM3. Closed Mon and Tues, otherwise open until midnight.

Zum Nussbaum, Propstr./Am Nussbaum, 1020. In the heart of the Nikolaiviertel, overshadowed by the red-brick Nikolaikirche, this is a replica of a prewar pub that was destroyed in an air-raid. The garden in the front is a good place to drink yourself under the table in summer. Food DM6–10.50.

Zur Letzten Instanz, Waisenstr. 14–16, 1020. One of the oldest and best city bars, the kind of place where you end up getting into heated political discussions with complete strangers. Wine upstairs, beer downstairs, and in summer there's a beer garden.

Gay men's bars

The most concentrated area of gay men's bars is between Wittenbergplatz and Nollendorfplatz, south of Kleiststrasse. For more detailed listings, pick up a copy of either Berlin von Hinten *or* Siegessäule, *available from most bars.*

Anderes Ufer, Hauptstr. 157, 1/30. Quiet Schöneberg café-bar favoured by students and alternative types. Women welcomed. Serves breakfasts.

Blue Boy Bar, Eisenacher Str. 3, 1/62. Tiny, convivial and relaxed bar, far less raucous than many that surround it.

Fledermaus, Joachimstaler Str. 14–19, 1/15. Bar and coffee shop popular with tourists as well as locals; one of the city's most relaxing gay bars.

Hafen, Motzstrasse 19, 1/30; adjacent to *Tom's Bar*. Currently *the* cruising bar in the city. Always packed, open till late.

Tom's Bar, Motzstr. 19, 1/30. Dark, sweaty and wicked cruising bar with a large back room.

Zufall, Pfalzburger Str. 10a, 1/15. Mixed gay and lesbian bar: ring the bell to gain admission. Open till late.

Women's cafés and bars
Many of Berlin's women-only bars have a strong lesbian following, though straight women are welcome everywhere.

Begine, Potsdamer Str. 139, 1/30 (women only). Stylishly decorated bar-bistro/gallery with limited choice of inexpensive food.

Die Zwei, corner Martin-Lutherstr. and Motzstr., 1/30. The city's tackiest best, a determinedly (non-exclusive) lesbian bar with music from Marlene via Iron Butterfly to Madonna and a similarly wide range of clientele. Unmissable.

Lipstick, Richard-Wagner-Platz 5, 1/10 (women only Mon, Fri & Sat; open to all on first Fri of month). Lesbian cocktail bar that welcomes straight women; stylish and lively disco. Difficult to find – look out for the white entrance door.

Pour Elle, Kalckreuthstr. 10, 1/30 (closed Mon; women only except Tues). Intimate disco-bar frequented by the straighter sort of (generally older) lesbian. Pricey.

Steps, Grossbeerenstr., 1/61. Basement bar with women-only evenings Tuesday (for motorbikers' meeting) and Friday. Monthly disco.

Eating

You can spend as much or as little as you like on **food** in Berlin; it's one item, at least, that won't break the bank. The following listings detail budget options and sit-down restaurants, and the prices quoted are for main courses, exclusive of starters, drink or tips. All, apart from those listed in the final section, are in western Berlin. Don't forget that many of the **bars** listed above can be excellent (and inexpensive) choices for food, especially breakfast, which may be served till afternoon – or later.

Snacks

Cheapest way of warding off hunger pangs is to use the small **Imbiss** snack stands found on many street corners, where for a few marks you can fill up on *Currywurst* and chips. Many butchers' shops sell meaty snacks at low prices, and around Zoo Station are any number of budget-priced burger bars and pizzerias.

For something a bit more substantial but not that much more expensive, try any one of four sit-down **Imbiss restaurants**, which charge between DM5 and DM12 a meal, or, at lunchtime, either of the city's **mensas**, offically for German students only but usually open to anyone who fits that general description, and always to those with ISIC cards.

Ashoka-Imbiss, Grolmanstr. 51, 1/12 (off Savignyplatz). Daily 11am–midnight. About the best of the lot, dishing up good portions of tremendous-bargain Indian food. Vegetarian options.

Einhorn, Mommsenstr. 2, 1/12 and Wittenbergplatz 5, 1/30. Vegetarian wholefood at its best, in a friendly and relaxed atmosphere – though it's standing only and closes at 6pm daily. DM6–9.

Ernst-Reuter-Platz Mensa, Ernst-Reuter-Platz, 1/12. Mon–Fri 11.15am–2.30pm. Small mensa of the nearby Technical University, with limited choice of meals. Around DM3, *ISIC* required.

Mensa of the Free University, Habelschwerdter Allee, at the junction with Thiel Allee, 1/33 (nearest U-Bahn #2 to Dahlem-Dorf). Mon–Fri noon–2pm. Only worth considering if you're spending the day at the Dahlem museums. Around DM3, *ISIC* advisable.

Nachtigall Imbiss, Ohlauerstr. 10, 1/36. Arab specialities including the delicious *Schaurma kebab* – lamb and hummus in pitta bread. Good salads for vegetarians.

TU Mensa, Hardenbergstr. 34, 1/12. Mon–Fri 11.15am–2.30pm. Meals around DM4, buy your meal ticket before getting your food. Inferior quality to the Free University mensa, but much more central.

Restaurants

German and Austrian

Auerbach, Köpenickerstr. 174, 1/36. German and Swabian cuisine (which includes such pasta-based delights as *Maultaschen* and *Käse Spätzle*) in an elegant, old-fashioned setting. From DM18.

Exil, Paul-Lincke-Ufer 44, 1/36 (☎612 7037). Popular with the Kreuzberg arts crowd for its attractive site next to the canal and its moderate to expensive Viennese food. Something of a bohemian meeting place. Booking advisable.

Florian, Grolmanstr. 52, 1/12. Leading light of the new German cuisine movement in Berlin, this is as much a place to be seen in as to eat. The food, similar to French *nouvelle cuisine*, is light, flavourful – and expensive. DM20 and up.

Tegernseer Tönnchen, Mommsenstr. 34, 1/12. Bavarian cuisine – which means enormous dishes of *Wursts* and *Schnitzels* washed down with pitchers of beer. Given the quantity placed in front of you, excellent value at DM10–17.

French, Italian, Spanish and Greek

Aroma, Hochkirchstr. 8, 1/61 (☎786 2989). Well above average, inexpensive Italian with photo gallery and Italian films on Tuesday evenings. One of the best places to eat in east Schöneberg, it's advisable to book after 8pm. DM8–14.

Chapeau Claque, Pfalzburgerstr. 55, 1/15. Discreet and elegant French restaurant. Upmarket menu with prices to match. DM20 and up.

Cour Carrée, Savignyplatz 5, 1/12. Deservedly popular French restaurant with fin-de-siècle decor and garden seating. DM15–DM25.

Lissos, Pfalzburgerstr. 83, 1/15. One of the first Greek restaurants in Berlin, the original Gastarbeiter diners now having been replaced by hordes of Alternatives and students. DM10-20.

Osteria No.1, Kreuzbergstr. 71, 1/61 (☎786 9162). Classy, inexpensive and therefore highly popular Italian restaurant run by a fun Italian collective. DM10–20; booking advisable.

Egyptian, Indian and Southeast Asian

Der Ägypter, Kantstr. 26, 1/12. Egyptian falafel-type meals. Spicy, filling and an adventurous alternative to the safe bets around Savignyplatz. Good vegetarian selections. DM10–15.

India-Haus, Feurigstr. 38, 1/62. Solid quality Schöneberg Indian, with first-rate veggie options. From DM12, booking advisable.

India-Palace, Leibnizstr. 35, 1/12. Incredible variety and low prices. DM10–14.

Merhaba, Hasenheide 39, 1/61. Highly rated Turkish restaurant that's usually packed with locals. A selection of the starters here can be more interesting than a main course.

Restaurant am Nil, Kaiserdamm 114, 1/19 (near Sophie-Charlotte-Platz). Moderately priced Egyptian, easy-going service. DM10–30.

Tuk-Tuk, Grossgörschenstr. 2, 1/30 (☎781 1588). Amiable Indonesian near Kleistpark U-Bahn. Enquire about the heat of your dish before ordering. Booking advisable. DM10–20.

Mexican and Latin American

Carib, Motzstr. 31, 1/30. Classical Caribbean cuisine, friendly service, lethal rum cocktails. DM10–22.

La Estancia, Bundesallee 45, 1/31. Very good value for money Latin American restaurant, patronised mainly by environmentally and politically conscious Berliners. DM8–15.

Patio, Gorlitzer Str. 32, 1/36. Popular Mexican with all the usual staples. When it's good it's very good, but it has a reputation for erratic standards. DM18.

El Perron, Carmerstr. 13, 1/12. Solid Latin American food, and good fun when patrons leave their tables to tango. DM15–30.

Som Tropical, Kaiser-Friedrich-Str. 40, 1/12. Small South American restaurant with live music at weekends. DM7–20.

Vegetarian and other

Abendmahl, Muskauerstr. 9, 1/36 (☎612 5170). Congenial atmosphere, excellent veggie (but including fish) dishes and reasonable (DM20) prices, make it one of the most enjoyable places to eat in the city.

Jewish Community Centre Restaurant, Fasanenstr. 79, 1/12. Wonderful kosher delights in a good atmosphere.

La Maskera Koburger Str. 5, 1/62 (just south and east of Rathaus Schöneberg). Among the best vegetarian places in town, with an Italian slant adding colour to the food and atmosphere. Wholemeal pizzas and pasta, along with egg and tofu dishes. DM8–20.

Schnecken und Knoblauch, Oranienstr. 47a, 1/61 (☎614 6816). Unusually broad range of meals – Arabic, German, specialist seafood, Italian – in a warm, candle-lit atmosphere. Inexpensive (DM8–20) and excellent; booking advisable.

Thurnägel, Gneisenaustr. 57, 1/61 (☎691 4800). Small, smart, convivial place in west Kreuzberg. DM10–20; booking necessary.

Eating in the East

Restaurants in eastern Berlin can get crowded, and where it's advisable to try and make a reservation beforehand the listing includes the phone number – although given the shambolic state of the eastern phone network it might be better to drop by in person.

The choice of food in most eastern Berlin restaurants is pretty much standard – overdone meats and underdone fish – and, at the moment, a meal out can still be a very drab affair when compared to eating in the west. However, things are improving and there are exceptions – in the places listed below you have a good chance of eating well at a reasonable price.

Ermeler Haus, Am Märkischen Ufer 10, 1020 (☎275 5113/275 5125). Inside this Spree-side building check out the *Raabediele*, an unpretentious basement restaurant where you can get well priced traditional German dishes in slightly folksy surroundings, and where there are usually a few tables free. DM15–25. On the first floor you'll find a pricier and somehow less congenial wine restaurant; DM15–35.

Fioretto, Oberspreestr. 176, 1170 (Köpenick; ☎657 2605). Köpenick's immensely popular Italian joint – one of the best restaurants in the east. Book in advance. DM10–25. Closed Sun and Mon. Open until 2am.

Französischer Hof, Am Platz der Akademie, Wilhelm-Külz-Str./Otto-Nuschke-Str., 1080. The decor is typical of the last days of the GDR – expensive-looking but somehow rather bland. However, you can enjoy a superb view of the Französischer Dom as you dine. The German specialities are better than average and there's a good wine list. DM10–60.

Gerichtslaube, Poststr. 28, 1020. Three possibilities in this reconstruction of Berlin's medieval courthouse; the *Bierschänke* and *Weinschänke* are basically spruced up tourist restaurants with inflated prices. The food in both is all right, although not exactly imaginative; DM 10–20. The *Weinschänke* has an extensive wine list with everything from low-grade Algerian engine oil to vintage French (the latter at a price, of course). Best value for money is the pizzeria above these two which does a passable, if slightly esoteric, interpretation of pizza. DM7.50–15.

Haus Budapest Berlin, Karl-Marx-Allee 91, 1020. In this supposedly Hungarian restaurant most of the dishes are German, but with paprika. It's quite classy in an old-fashioned sort of way and not too pricey. DM8–20.

Neubrandenburger Hof, Wilhelm-Pieck-Str./Borsigstr., 1040. Good food, good value for money and easily reached from the Bahnhof Friedrichstrasse area. One of the few restaurants in central Berlin deserving an unqualified recommendation. Speciality of the house is Mecklenburg cuisine. DM5–20.

Pfeffermühle, Gaudystr. 6, 1058 (Prenzlauer Berg; ☎448 1635). Everything comes heavily sprinkled with pepper here (the name means Pepper Mill). One of the most popular in Prenzlauer Berg, so try and book a table.

Restaurant Moskau, Karl-Marx-Allee 34, 1020 (☎270 0532). Don't be put off by the airport lounge architecture of the building that houses eastern Berlin's best Russian restaurant, as the food, ambience and nimble fingers of the pianist more than make up for it. The Chicken Kiev is excellent.

Restauration 1900, Kollwitzplatz, corner of Husemannstrasse, 1058. One of the few places in the East that can compete with its western counterparts. Imaginative *Neue Deutsche Küche* at affordable prices (DM15–25).

Schwalbenest, Am Marstall (above the *Café Flair*), 1020. Excellent food (particularly the fish) in a congenial atmosphere. DM11–30. Open until midnight.

Music and nightlife

Perhaps inevitably, it's in the western parts of the city that you'll find the most exciting nightlife: venues cover a breadth of tastes, and are rarely expensive. **Clubs and discos** range from slick hang-outs for the trendy to dingy, uninviting punk dives. As ever, it's the tension the city seems to generate that gives the nightlife its colour. In the east there are few bearable discos – the best venues for **alternative nightlife** and **live music** events tend to be the former FDJ (party youth organisation) **clubhouses**.

Berlin's reputation as a leader of the avant-garde is reflected in the number of small, often experimental **theatre groups** working here. The scene is an active one, though bear in mind that many theatre companies take a break in July and August. **Classical music** has long been dominated by the world class Berlin Philharmonic, though other orchestras play in the city, and several museums and historic buildings often host chamber concerts and recitals. Vanishing subsidies have cast a shadow over the theatres, orchestras and opera houses in the east, though it's likely that the big name venues (like the Berliner Ensemble and Deutsches Theater) will weather current storms.

Two of the city's venues are unclassifiable: the *Waldebühne* is a large outdoor amphitheatre on the Hollywood Bowl model, just west of the Olympic Stadium. It presents everything from opera to movies to hard rock – unbeatable in summer. The *Tempodrom*, two tents in the Tiergarten, hosts concerts and circuses in the larger tent, cabaret and more intimate performances in the smaller.

TICKET AGENCIES AND OFFICES

Ticket offices or *Theaterkassen* are usually the easiest way of buying tickets for all major music, theatre and dance events in both western *and* eastern Berlin. They charge a hefty commission (up to 17 percent) on the ticket price.

Europa Center, Tauentzienstr. 9, 1/30 (☎261 7051).

Hertie, Wilmersdorferstr. 118–120, 1/12 (☎312 9502).

KaDeWe, Tauentzienstr. 21, 1/30 (☎24 10 28).

Kant-Kasse, Kantstr. 3–4, 1/12 (☎881 3603).

Discos and clubs

Western Berlin's discos are smaller, cheaper and less exclusive than their counterparts in London or New York – and fewer in number. You don't need much nous to work out that the places along the Ku'damm are tourist rip-offs: the real all-night sweats take place in Kreuzberg and Schöneberg, where glitz is out and post-punk cool in. Don't bother turning up until midnight at the earliest, since few places get going much before then. Admission is often free – when you do pay, it shouldn't be much more than DM10. Like most cities, Berlin's turnover in nightspots is rapid: expect the following listings to have changed at least slightly by the time you arrive.

Abraxas, Kantstr. 134, 1/12 (☎312 9493). Tues–Sun 10pm–5am. Free during the week, DM6 Fri & Sat. Hot and sweaty dance floor, specialising in salsa and Latin American sounds.

Basement, Mehringdamm 107, 1/61 (☎692 5592). Daily 10pm–6pm; free. Competitively trendy atmosphere, occasional performance happenings.

Big Eden, Kurfürstendamm 202, 1/15 (☎882 6120). Sun–Fri 7pm–4am, Sat 7pm–7am. Enormous disco popular with teenagers – check out the dance floor first on the video monitors on the street outside. Admission for women is, rather tackily, free: it's also free for everyone Sun–Thurs, but drinks are expensive. Bit of a tourist trap.

Blue Note, Courbièrestr. 13, 1/30 (☎24 72 48). Tues–Sun 10pm–5am. DM6 entrance on Fri & Sat. Eclectic mix of rock, Latin and (chiefly) jazz sounds. Small dance floor, best after midnight.

Cha-Cha, Nürnberger Str. 50, 1/30 (☎214 2976). Tues–Sun 11pm–6am. Tues, Wed, Thurs & Sun entrance DM5; Fri & Sat DM10. Currently the number one *Szene* spot in the city, ousting even *Dschungel*, next door.

Dschungel, Nürnberger Str. 53, 1/30 (☎246 698). Daily except Tues, 11pm–3am. DM10, free on Mon. The Berlin nightclub scene how you always imagined it. Mixed crowd of nightpeople, all heavily into style, posing and dancing to the excellent music. Not cheap, but essential.

Metropol, Nollendorfplatz 5, 1/30 (☎216 4122). Fri & Sat 10pm–4am; DM10. The city's largest – though rather ordinary – disco, in a marvellous Art Deco building. Occasional live bands.

90° ("Neunzig Grad"), Dennewitzstr. 37, 1/30. Currently chic American-owned club at the far eastern end of Kurfürstenstrasse. Acid House sounds from 10pm. DM10.

Quartier, Potsdamer Str. 96, 1/30 (☎262 9016). Club-cum-arts-centre that has an acid house disco at weekends.

Sox, Oranienstr. 39, 1/36 (☎614 3573). Daily except Tues, 11pm onwards. Small but lively split-level bar/disco in the centre of the Kreuzberg action; music has something for everyone, especially devotees of funk and rap.

Trash, Oranienstr. 40, 1/36. Tues–Sun 11pm onwards. Current home of Berlin youth's weirder elements. Black walls, black clothes and UV lights, hip-hop/new wave sounds.

UFO, Grossgörschenstr., corner of Potsdamer Str., 1/30. Thurs–Sun from 11pm. acid and house music in a venue identifiable by the large silver triangle above the door. DM10.

Live music

The way to find out exactly what's on and where is to look in the listings magazines *Tip*, *Zitty* and *Prinz*, in *Berlin Program*, or on the innumerable fly posters about town.

Major venues

The following are the sort of places you can expect to find international supergroups playing. Book well-in-advance for anything even vaguely popular. Invariably you can't buy tickets from the places themselves but need to go to one of the ticket agencies listed above.

Alte TU-Mensa, Hardenbergstr. 34, 1/12 (☎311 2233). Part of the Technological University.

Deutschlandhalle, Messedamm 26, 1/19 (☎30381). Like the *Eissporthalle* below, part of the Congress Centre west of the city.

Eissporthalle, Jafféstr. 1, 1/19 (☎3038 4387). Another large site. The *Sommergarten im Messegelände* nearby (around the Funkturm) has, as the name suggests, outdoor concerts in summer.

ICC Berlin, Messedamm, 1/19 (☎30381). Vast, soulless hall for trade fairs that often hosts gigs.

Radrennbahn, Rennbahnstr., 1120 (Weissensee). This eastern Berlin cycle-racing track accommodates stadium-sized bands; in the past James Brown, ZZ Top and Genesis have appeared here.

Waldbühne, corner of Glockenturmstr. and Passenheimer Str., 1/19 (☎304 0676). Open-air spot in a natural amphitheatre near the Olympic stadium that features movies, bands, classical concerts and other diverse entertainments. Great fun on summer evenings, but arrive early as it gets crowded.

Werner-Seelenbinder-Halle, Fritz-Reidel-Str., 1055 (Prenzlauer Berg). Venue for bands too big for the clubhouses but not quite in the Radrennbahn league.

Contemporary

Remember that many bars and cafés often have live music: skim through *Zitty*, *Tip* and *Prinz* magazines for up-to-the-minute listings.

Blockshock, Körtestr. 15, Hasenheide 54, 1/61 (☎694 2265). Place for live bands in the heart of the Kreuzberg underground movement, though thanks to action by its complaining neighbours, no longer as lively as it was.

K.O.B., Potsdamer Str. 157, 1/30. A pub in a (now legally) squatted house which on weekdays hosts interesting groups at low prices (DM5). R&B, jazz and psychedelic sounds play here, but the favourites are local anarcho- and fun-punk bands.

The Loft, part of the *Metropol*, Nollendorfplatz 5, 1/30 (☎216 1020). Features a whole range of independent artists, with a view to innovation and introducing new music. Also organises larger concerts in the *Metropol* itself.

Metropol, Nollendorfplatz 5, 1/30 (☎216 4122). Well-known, if not mega, names play frequently in this large dance space.

Quartier, Potsdamer Str. 96, 1/30 (☎262 9016). Reasonably famous bands, theatre and cabaret are on offer at this all-seated venue. Check the listings mags for details of what's on.

Tempodrom, near the *Kongresshalle* on John-Foster-Dulles-Allee, 1/21 (☎394 4045). Two tents, the larger hosting contemporary bands of middling fame.

Clubhouses and venues in the east

Eastern Berlin's former *FDJ* clubs, and local *Kreiskulturhäuser* (arts centres) are, at the moment, probably the most useful places to know about if you're hoping to track down the best that eastern Berlin has to offer in terms of nightlife and live music. The clubhouses also stage frequent **gigs** by local bands and play host to the occasional visiting act from abroad; expect to pay between DM5 and DM10 entrance.

Berliner Prater, Kastanienallee 7–9, 1058 (Prenzlauer Berg; ☎448 5020). One of the biggest and best-known Prenzlauer Berg places, this local arts centre stages middle-of-the-road (but invariably well-attended) events of all kinds. During the summer many of these take place in the large beer garden.

Club Checkpoint Null, Leipziger Str. 55, 1080 (☎208 2995). A multi-media cultural centre staging off-the-wall events – film shows, theatre, gigs – with a cheap bar. An ideal place to find out more about what's going on in this part of the city.

Die Insel, Insel des Jugends, 1193 (Treptow; ☎27255). A reliable venue for thrashy/punky gigs and related events, situated on an island in the Spree in the Treptower Park. There's also a cinema and gallery here.

Haus der jungen Talente, Klosterstr. 68–70, 1020 (☎210 9201). The city centre's premier arts venue, which puts on just about everything: concerts, film shows, theatrical productions, dance, cabaret and exhibitions by young artists. The musical accent is on jazz, though the venue also plays host to occasional all-night acid house parties that attract hundreds of eastern and western ravers. Definitely worth checking out.

JoJo, Wilhelm-Pieck-Str. 216, 1040. Favoured by a young crowd, discos, gigs and arts events of all kinds are the order of the evening here. Jazz and world music feature heavily, but you're equally likely to find punk bands. Open until about 5am at weekends.

Sophienclub, Sophienstr. 6, 1020 (☎282 452). This intimate (read crowded) central club plays host to the best local bands and often puts on discos. Recommended.

Tacheles e.V, Oranienburger Str. 53–56 (☎282 6185). Originally a squat in a derelict cinema, this "art-house" is all things to all people. Offering workspace for artists, rehearsal areas and a hang-out in which a new Berlin *Szene* could be starting to take shape, this place has attracted people from all over Germany, Europe and North America. Frequent gigs, raves and parties occur, and this could be your best route into eastern Berlin's cultural underground and nightlife scene.

Jazz, Folk and Blues

Blues Café, Körnerstr. 11, 1/30 (☎261 3698). Hiding away in a small street off Potsdamer Strasse, this low-profile café is the place to head for if you like your blues pure and original.

Flöz, Nassauische Str. 37, 1/31 (☎861 1000). Basement club that's the meeting point for Berlin's jazz musicians and a testing ground for the city's new bands. Also offers occasional salsa and cabaret. Can be wild.

Go-In, Bleibtreustr. 17, 1/12 (☎881 7218). The place for folk music on an international level, with musicians from the Philippines to the Pyrenees, from India to Scotland.

Quasimodo, Kantstr. 12a, 1/12 (☎312 8086). Berlin's best jazz spot, with daily programmes starting at 10pm. A high quality mix of international stars and up-and-coming names. Small, good atmosphere.

Classical

For years classical music in Berlin meant one man and one orchestra: Herbert von Karajan and the Berlin Philharmonic. Since his death in 1989 the orchestra has retained its popularity under new conductor Claudio Abbado, and tickets for their near-acoustically perfect home, the **Philharmonie**, are extremely difficult to get. Try calling the box office at Kemperplatz, Matthäikirchstr. 1, 1/30 (Mon–Fri 3.30–6pm, Sat & Sun 11am–2pm; ☎261 4883) as far in advance as possible.

Thankfully, the Philharmonic is by no means the only option. The **Berlin Rundfunk-Sinfones-Orchestra** also plays at the Philharmonie, and, as well as opera and ballet, the *Deutsche Oper*, Bismarckstr. 34, 1/12 (☎341 0249), has good classical concerts with tickets selling for as little as DM10 for a seat in the gods. The *Urania*, An der Urania 17, 1/30 (☎24 90 91), has a wide-ranging programme and reasonably priced seats. In the eastern part of town, the **Berlin Sinfonie Orchester**, formerly one of the GDR's most prestigious orchestras, is based in the *Schauspielhaus*, Platz der Academie, 1086 (box offices: large concert hall ☎227 2129; small hall ☎227 2122; ticket returns ☎227 2156; Mon–Fri 2.30–5.30pm). Many smaller orchestras play at sites in and around the city. As ever, see *Zitty* and *Tip* for listings.

Theatre

Sad to say, the mainstream **civic and private theatres** in Berlin are on the whole dull, unadventurous, and expensive – and though it's often possible to cut costs by buying student standby tickets, you'll find little in English save for the work of small, roving theatre groups. However the city is still a major venue for **experimental work**, and if your German is up to it a number of groups are worth the ticket price; check under "Off-Theater" in *Tip* or *Zitty* for up-to-the-minute listings.

Civic and private theatres

Berliner Ensemble, Bertolt-Brecht-Platz 1, 1040 (box office ☎282 3160 or 288 8155: Mon 11am–5pm, Tues–Fri 11am–1.30pm & 2–6pm, Sat 5–6pm). The official Brecht theatre offering a recommended, if slightly lack-lustre, diet of staple Brecht fare like *The Caucasian Chalk Circle*, *Galileo Galilei*, etc. They also dish up Dario Fo, Shakespeare and a droll version of Zuckmayer's *Der Hauptmann von Köpenick*.

Deutsches Theater, Schumannstr. 13a–14, 1040 (box office ☎287 1225 or 287 1226). Eastern Berlin's best theatre until a few years ago, thanks to the inspired direction of Alexander Lang, although the place has never quite got over his departure (he left the GDR before the *Wende*).

Die Distel, Friedrichstr. 101 (in the Admiralspalast), 1080 (☎207 1291) and at Degnerstr. 9 (at the *Venus* cinema in Höhenschönhausen, 1092; ☎376 5179). An heir to Berlin's legendary interwar cabaret tradition, this cabaret ensemble used to put on politically daring shows during the old days, and now addresses the issues raised by life in a united Germany.

Deutsche Oper Berlin, Bismarckstr. 35, 1/10 (☎341 4449). Major mainstream opera and ballet.

Schaubühne am Lehniner Platz, Kurfürstendamm 153, 1/31 (☎89 00 23). State-of-the-art equipped theatre that hosts performances of the classics and some experimental pieces. Its high reputation means that booking ahead is advisable.

Schiller-Theater, Bismarckstr. 110, 1/12 (☎319 5236). The best state-run theatre in western Berlin. Three stages and as experimental as can be. Fabulous building too. Occasional half-price standbys for students with ID.

Theater des Westens, Kantstr. 12, 1/12 (☎312 1022). Musicals and light opera, the occasional Broadway-style show. Beautiful turn-of-the-century building, often sold out.

Experimental and free theatre groups

BELT, Stierstr. 5, 1/41 (offices ☎801 3467). The Berlin English-Language Theatre group. No permanent home but occasionally play in cafés and smaller clubs. Check *Zitty* or *Tip* or phone for further information.

Berlin Play Actors (offices ☎784 7362). Another English-speaking group playing in various places about town. Very high standard of acting.

Freie Volksbühne, Schaperstr. 24, 1/15 (☎881 3742). Not as radical as it once was, but with a reputation for excellent stage designs.

UFA-Fabrik, Viktoriastr. 13, 1/42 (☎752 8085). The most famous, and most efficiently run, cultural factory, with just about every aspect of the performing arts on offer. The UFA-Fabrik acts as an umbrella group for all kinds of performances – theatre, dance, music and film – and it's always worth checking out what's on.

Listings

Airline offices *Air France*, Europa Center, 1/30 (☎26 10 51); *British Airways*, Europa Center, 1/30 (☎69 10 21); *Dan Air*, Tegel Airport, 1/51 (☎4101 2707); *EuroBerlin*, Kantstr. 165, 1/12 (☎884 1920); *Lufthansa*, Kurfürstendamm 220, 1/15 (☎88755); *TWA*, Europa Center, 1/30 (☎262 2003).

Baby sitting services *Babysitter-Service*, Claudiasstr. 6, 1/21 (☎393 5981). *Hernzelmännchen der Freien Universität Berlin*, Unter den Eichen 96, 1/46 (☎831 6071).

Bike hire is available from several shops, though (unlike in cities in what used to be West Germany) not from the railway station. Try *Fahrradbüro Berlin*, Hauptstr. 146, 1/41 (near Kleistpark U-Bahn; ☎784 5562), which charges around DM10 per day, DM50 per week; DM50 deposit and passport needed. In the east bikes can be hired from *Alternative Dieinstleistung*, Prenzlauer Allee 10 (Wed–Sun 10am–8pm). To take your bike on U- or S-Bahn train, you need to buy an additional DM2 ticket.

Bookshops Best selection of Penguins, English paperbacks and books on the city can be found at *Kiepert*, Hardenbergstr. 4–5, 1/12, and the *British Book Shop*, Mauerstr. 83–84, 1080.

Car hire Least expensive firms are *Allround*, Kaiser-Friedrich-Str. 86, 1/10 (☎342 5092); *First & Second Hand Rent*, Lohmeyerstr. 7, 1/10 (☎341 7076); and *Mini-bus Service*, Zietenstr. 1, 1/30 (☎261 1456). International firms have offices at Tegel airport and are listed in the phone book.

Chemists Prescriptions can be filled at any *Apotheke*; outside normal hours a notice on the door of any *Apotheke* indicates the nearest one open. Otherwise try *Europa-Apotheke*, Tauentzienstr. 9, 1/30 (☎261 4142); 9am–6.30pm daily.

Consulates *Britain*, Uhlandstr. 7–8, 1/12 (☎309 5292); *Ireland*, Ernst-Reuter-Platz 10, 1/12 (☎3480 0822); *Canada*, Europa Center 12th floor, 1/30 (☎261 1161); *United States*, Clayallee 170, 1/37 (☎832 4087).

Disabled travel It comes as no surprise to hear that facilities in the western part of the city are better than those in the east. Most of the major western museums have wheelchair access, as do many other public buildings. The full colour U- and S-Bahn map also indicates which stations are accessible by wheelchair.

Emergency doctor (☎310031).

Emergency dentist (☎1141).

Exchange facilities The exchange at the main entrance to the Zoo Station (Mon–Sat 8am–9pm, Sun 10am–6pm) will cash travellers' cheques and give cash advances on major credit cards, though subject to a minimum of DM200.

Laundrettes Dahlmannstr. 17, 1/12 (Mon–Fri 9am–1pm & 3–6pm); Uhlandstr. 53, 1/15 (6.30am–10.30pm); Hauptstr. 151, 1/62 (7.30am–10.30pm). Other addresses are listed under *Wäscherei* in the yellow pages.

Mitfahrzentralen Südstern 14 (☎693 6095); Kurfürstendamm 227 (☎882 7606). *Frauenmitfahrzentrale*, Potsdamer Str. 139 (☎215 3165). Many more listings can be found in *Tip* and *Zitty* magazines.

Postcodes All Berlin addresses are suffixed by a postcode. In our **western Berlin** listings this appears in abbreviated form: eg 1/12 on the end of an address would be written as 1000 BERLIN 12; 1/61 as 1000 BERLIN 61. In **eastern Berlin** the code is listed as a four-digit number: eg 1048 would be written as 1048 BERLIN.

Post office Handiest is at Zoo Station (Mon–Fri 8am–6pm, Sat 8am–noon), with one counter open 24 hours. This is also the place for **Poste Restante** facilities: Postampt Bahnhof Zoo, 1000 Berlin 12.

Taxis congregate outside *KaDeWe*, on Savignyplatz and by the Zoo Station in the west, and in the east at the northern entrance to Friedrichstrasse station, at the *Centrum* department store and entrances to Alexanderplatz S-Bahn station and the *Hotel Stadt Berlin* nearby, and at the *Palasthotel* on the Unter den Linden. To phone for a taxi in western Berlin, call ☎6902 or ☎26 10 26; in eastern Berlin, ☎3644.

Travel agents *ARTU*, Hardenbergstr. 9, 1/12 (☎310 0040) and Nollendorfplatz 7, 1/30 (☎216 3091). Youth and student travel specialists. *Express Travel*, Seeburgerstr. 20, 1/20 (☎331 4034). A British travel agent operating out of Spandau. *SEA Travel*, Gneisenaustr. 53, 1/61 (☎693 7027) offers good deals worldwide.

Women's centre Stresemannstr. 40, 1/61 (☎251 0912). Friendly and well organised help and information centre that offers advice on a wide range of subjects.

BRANDENBURG

Brandenburg is geographically the largest of Germany's five new Länder, though it has a very low population density, largely because it is shorn of Berlin, its epicentre and traditional capital, which is now a Land in its own right. The province was founded as a margraviate or frontier district by **Albert the Bear** (*Albrecht der Bär*) in 1157 from land bequeathed to him by a Pribislav-Henry, a Slav king who had converted to Christianity. Its importance to the predatory German nation's desire for eastward expansion was recognised by its Margrave being designated one of the seven Electors of the Holy Roman Empire. In 1415, this title was bestowed on the **Hohenzollern** family, and from then until 1918 the fortunes of the two became inextricably linked, with Brandenburg being the heartland of the expansionist military state of Brandenburg-Prussia, whose name was shortened to Prussia in 1701.

The Brandenburg landscape consists of undulating farmland and sandy forests which are unexceptional but by no means unattractive: the villages, in particular, with their cobbled streets and brick cottages, reflect a lifestyle seemingly out of the pages of a history book. In lieu of Berlin, the old royal residence of **Potsdam** on its outskirts has taken over as Land capital, and its outstanding group of Baroque palaces is the province's prime draw. West of here lies the long-overshadowed city of **Brandenburg** which, despite the ravages of war and pollution, preserves an important medieval heritage. The only other major towns, **Frankfurt an der Oder** and **Cottbus**, are similarly scarred, though the latter has the good fortune to lie close to the province's one area of outstanding natural beauty, the water-strewn **Spreewald**, which is still inhabited by the Sorbs, Germany's only indigenous Slav minority.

Travel throughout the province is easy, thanks to the continued survival of an extensive public transport network. Most places make easy day trips from Berlin — which is fortunate, as tourist facilities are, as yet, very rudimentary. In the field of **politics**, Brandenburg is the most left-leaning of the new Länder, and the only one where the SPD is currently in power. Minister-President **Manfred Stolpe** played a prominent public role as the Protestant church's senior lay spokesman during GDR days, and has survived many attempts to tar him with the charge of collusion with the Stasi.

Potsdam

"The first fine day should be devoted to Potsdam, without which a complete impression of Berlin can scarcely be obtained," claims the prewar Baedeker, a nod to the fact that **POTSDAM**, although not officially part of Berlin, was the natural completion of the Hohenzollern city, forming a unity with Charlottenburg and the old centre along the Unter den Linden. Despite the fact that it lay just to the southwest of Berlin, until 1990 it was difficult to reach Potsdam: visa regulations made visiting a complicated affair and many people left it off their itineraries. Since the withering away of the border, however, the town has enjoyed an enormous influx of visitors from the west, and you'll almost certainly find that you need two or three days to take everything in.

Some history

Under the Hohenzollerns the small village of Potsdam became a royal residence and garrison town, roles that it enjoyed right up until the abdication of Kaiser Wilhelm II in 1918. World War II left Potsdam badly damaged and 4000 people were killed in the bombing raid of April 14, 1945, which left the town centre in ruins and destroyed many fine Baroque buildings. Immediately after the war, Potsdam was chosen by the victorious Allies as venue for a **conference** where, on August 2, 1945, the division of Germany and Europe was confirmed. Subsequently, under the SED regime, it was decided to demolish the ruins of much of the old town and undertake extensive modern building programmes in pursuit of a "new, socialist Potsdam". These account for the ugly eastern half of the town centre, and although attempts were made to preserve the architectural integrity of the town during the 1980s, the Communists always felt ill at ease with its historical role and imperial associations.

With the opening of the border in 1989, Potsdam's links with the rest of Berlin were once again revived. But reminders of the immediate past remain: the residents of the grim red-brick barracks that ring the town are Soviets, and Red Army men trudge the cobbled streets or cycle along in ungainly fashion as the traffic sweeps past. If the Soviet withdrawal from Berlin continues according to plan they'll be gone by 1994; in the meantime their presence is part of what makes Potsdam unique and far more atmospheric than many more attractively restored towns in the former West Germany.

Practicalities

Visiting Potsdam couldn't be easier. There are excellent transport links from Berlin and the local tourist office can arrange accommodation in either private rooms or hotels – but note that rooms evaporate when the summer crowds descend.

Arrival and information

Coming in by road from western Berlin, bus #6 or #99 from S-Bahnhof Wannsee will deposit you at **Bassinplatz** near the centre of Potsdam. Alternatively, bus #18 runs from S-Bahnhof Wannsee to the Glienicke Bridge, where you can pick up trams #3 and #7 to the **Platz der Einheit**, the former Wilhelmsplatz, Potsdam's central square and traffic hub. Otherwise, a continuation of S-Bahn line #3 from western Berlin will drop you at **S-Bahnhof Potsdam Stadt** from where it's only a few minutes' walk north over the Lange Brücke and along Friedrich-Ebert-Strasse to the Platz der Einheit. A more atmospheric approach is provided by the twice-daily *Weisse Flotte* sailings from Wannsee (see p.743).

Just south of the Platz der Einheit is Potsdam's **tourist information office**, at Friedrich-Ebert-Str. 5 (daily 8am–6pm, Wed closed noon–1pm; ☎21100). It's well equipped with maps and from 1pm onwards books rooms in private accommodation.

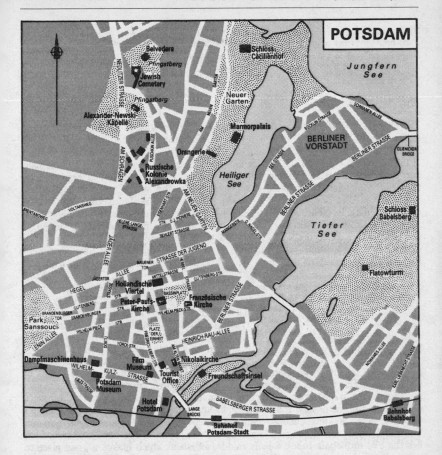

Accommodation

Ideally, you should spend at least a couple of days in Potsdam. If you're on a budget the best bet is to book a **private room** through the tourist office at Friedrich-Ebert-Str. 5 (see above), which will cost about DM35 per person. Potsdam's **youth hostel** is at Eisenhartstr. 5 (☎225125), near the main entrance to the Neuer Garten – again, reservations via the tourist office. There are a number of **hotels**, although, as everywhere in the former GDR, there's no guarantee that the listings given below will still stand by the time you arrive. Potsdam also has a couple of **campsites**. For information, head for the *Zentrale Campingplatzvermittlung*, Am Alten Friedhof (Tues 9am–noon & 2–5.30pm, Thurs 9am–noon & 2–4pm, Fri 9am–noon; ☎22248) where they'll be able to direct you to the nearest available space.

HOTELS

Hotel am Jägertor, Hegelallee 11 (☎21834). The best option in central Potsdam, with singles from DM80, doubles from DM110.

Hotel Babelsberg, Stahndorfer Str. 68 (☎78889). A value-for-money old-fashioned hotel with singles at DM40 and doubles at DM60 (on the Babelsberg side of the Havel).

Hotel Schloss Cecilienhof, Im neuen Garten (☎23141). Housed in a wing of Schloss Cecilienhof, a luxurious but pricey option with singles from DM130 and doubles from DM170.

Jugendtouristenhotel Werder, Strasse am Schwielowsee 110 (☎2850). Cheapest local possibility with singles at DM35 and doubles at DM70. However, it's some way out of Potsdam itself, in the small lakeside town of Werder about 6km to the southeast.

The Altstadt

The **Platz der Einheit** (formerly Wilhelmsplatz) makes a good starting point for any exploration of the town, although only a few non-concrete buildings survive in its immediate vicinity, hinting at a world long since vanished. The fancy-looking building at the southeast corner of the square is a neo-Baroque **post office**, to the immediate north of which stood the Wilhelm III synagogue until it was wrecked on *Kristallnacht*, and later completely demolished – a plaque marks the spot. From the post office, Heinrich-Rau-Allee and **Am Alten Markt** lead to the **Nikolaikirche**. This stately, domed building, its Neoclassical lines at odds with its surroundings, will probably have attracted your attention already if you've come into town from the S-Bahn station. It was originally built according to plans drawn up by Schinkel, and the impact of its exterior is echoed within – the walls are decorated with paintings of New Testament scenes and the effect of the dome is, if anything, more impressive than from the outside.

Diagonally opposite the Nikolaikirche is another survivor, Potsdam's former **Rathaus,** which was built in Palladian style during the mid-eighteenth century. Until 1875 the circular Rathaus tower served as town jail: it lost its town hall function in 1885, and was taken over by a bank, which remained there until the bombs came. Under the old authorities the building became a *Kulturhaus* or arts centre, a role it retains for the time being – inside you'll find a theatre, a couple of galleries and a number of cafés.

Just southwest of the Nikolaikirche is a random collection of concrete blocks, with more than a passing resemblance to a nuclear power station in the early stages of construction. This is Potsdam's controversial **new theatre**, commissioned at immense cost before the *Wende*, with a projected completion date of 1993 to mark the town's millennium: with funds now at a premium, its fate looks uncertain. East of the Platz der Einheit only a few ailing eighteenth-century town houses survive on Heinrich-Rau-Strasse, although this area is the oldest part of Potsdam. East from here lies the **Freundschaft Insel**, a leafy mid-Havel island which makes a good place to take a break from street-pounding, with its ornamental garden, café and boat hire facilities.

West of the Platz der Einheit

Slightly more tangible vestiges of old Potsdam survive in a few of the streets west of the Platz der Einheit. **Yorckstrasse** boasts a number of fine – albeit slightly run-down – **Baroque houses**, as does **Wilhelm-Staab-Strasse**. The **Neuer Markt** quarter just to the south of Yorckstrasse also has a couple of good-looking survivors, including some improbably grand eighteenth-century coaching stables with an entrance in the form of a triumphal arch, which are now home to a haulage firm. At Am Neuen Markt 1 is the **Kabinetthaus**, a small palace which was the birthplace of Friedrich Wilhelm II, the only member of the Hohenzollern family actually born in Potsdam.

The Marstall and around

A little to the northwest across Wilhelm-Külz-Strasse is the former palace **Marstall** or royal stables, the oldest town centre survivor. Originally built as an orangery, it was prettified by Knobelsdorff in the eighteenth century. Today the Marstall houses

Potsdam's **Filmmuseum**, Am Karl-Liebknecht-Forum (Tues–Sun 10am–5pm; DM4; ☎24106), formerly the "Film Museum of the GDR". Drawing on material from the UFA studios in nearby Babelsberg (later DEFA, the GDR state film company – an institution with an uncertain-looking future at the time of writing), the museum presents both a technical and an artistic history of German film from 1895 to 1980, with some particularly fascinating material concerning the genres of the immediate postwar period. There's a vaguely hands-on feel, with a few visitor-operated Bioscopes and numerous screens playing clips. The museum **cinema** is the best in Potsdam, and there's also a good café.

A little to the west of the Marstall, a prefabricated office building occupies the site of the **Garnisonkirche**, the eighteenth-century Baroque garrison church, last resting place of many prominent members of the Hohenzollern family. On March 23, 1933, the Reichstag was re-convened here following the fire and the subsequent elections which had given the Nazis a small majority (see p.948). The building was later wrecked during the bombing, and its burnt-out shell finally demolished in 1968, despite protest from both home and abroad, another victim of the old regime's discomfort with relics of the Prussian and imperial German past.

From here it's worth making a quick detour down **Kiezstrasse**, where a number of eighteenth-century Rococo houses have been beautifully restored, including no. 14 which houses *Der Froschkasten*, one of Potsdam's better bars. The nearby high-rises on the Neustädter Havebucht don't compare very favourably, but do hide in their midst the **Dampfmaschinenhaus**, probably the most imaginative pump-house in Germany. At first sight it looks like a mosque, with a chimney in the shape of a minaret.

The Baroque Quarter

North of the Platz der Einheit, the area bounded by Schopenhauer Strasse, Hegel Alle, Hebbelstrasse and Wilhelm-Pieck-Strasse is Potsdam's **Baroque Quarter**, built between 1732 and 1742 on the orders of Friedrich Wilhelm I. At the southeastern corner of **Bassinplatz** is the **Französische Kirche**, completed according to plans by Knobelsdorff in 1753, in imitation of the Pantheon in Rome, a recurring theme of the period. At its western end, Bassinplatz is graced by the nineteenth-century **Peter-Pauls-Kirche**, with a replica of the campanile of San Zeno Maggiore in Verona.

The ornate Baroque houses, built with slight variations in detail to avoid monotony, lie to the west of here on and around **Brandenburger Strasse**, Potsdam's pedestrianised main shopping street. The whole quarter was intended as a settlement for tradespeople in the then rapidly expanding town. To the north and west of the Baroque Quarter are the most impressive of Potsdam's three surviving town gates – the **Jägertor** or "Hunter's Gate" (at the end of Otto-Nuschke-Strasse), and the **Brandenburger Tor** (at the western end of Brandenburger Strasse), a triumphal arch of 1733 which has a playfulness lacking in its Berlin namesake.

The Holländisches Viertel

Just to the north of Bassinplatz is the **Holländisches Viertel** or "Dutch Quarter", the best-known and most appealing part of Friedrich Wilhelm I's town extension. In the area bounded by Gutenberg Strasse, Strasse der Jugend, Friedrich-Ebert-Strasse and Hebbelstrasse are 134 gabled red-brick houses put up by Dutch builders for the immigrants from Holland who were invited to work in Potsdam by the king. In fact, not that many Dutch took up the invitation, and many of those who did returned home when the promised employment dried up following Friedrich Wilhelm's death, allowing Germans to move into their houses. A disturbingly large number of the houses look derelict, but some excellent restored examples can be found along Mittelstrasse, particularly at the junction with Benkertstrasse.

Park Sanssouci

Park Sanssouci, Frederick the Great's fabled retreat, stretches out for two kilometres west of the town centre, and its gardens and palaces are what draw most visitors to Potsdam. In 1744 Frederick ordered the construction of a residence where he would be able to live "without cares" – "sans souci" in the French spoken in court. The task was entrusted to the architect Georg von Knobelsdorff who had already proved himself on other projects in the town and in Berlin. **Schloss Sanssouci**, on a hill overlooking the town, was completed in the year that work began, while extensive parklands to the west – the **Rehgarten** – were laid out over the following five years. As a finishing touch Frederick ordered the construction of the **Neue Palais** at the western end of the park to mark the end of the Seven Years' War. Over the following hundred and fifty years or so, numerous additions were made, including the **Orangerie** and the laying of Jubiläumstrasse (now known as Maulbeerallee) just south of the Orangerie in 1913. The park is at its best in spring when the trees are in leaf and the flowers in bloom, but these days it's all too often overrun by visitors. To avoid the crowds, visit on a weekday, preferably outside summer, when you'll be better able to appreciate the place.

Schloss Sanssouci

To approach **Schloss Sanssouci** (April–Sept 9am–12.45pm & 1.15–5pm; Feb, March & Oct closes 4pm; Nov–Jan closes 3pm; closed first Mon of month; DM6) as Frederick the Great might have done, make for the eighteenth-century **obelisk** on Schopenhauer Strasse that marks the main entrance to the park. Beyond, Hauptallee runs through the ornate Knobelsdorff-designed **Obelisk-Portal** – two clusters of pillars flanked by the goddesses Flora and Pomona – to the **Grosse Fontäne**, the biggest of the park's many fountains, just to the north. The approach to the Schloss itself leads up through terraced ranks of vines which are among the northernmost in Germany.

Frederick had very definite ideas about what he wanted and worked closely with Knobelsdorff on the design of his palace, which was to be a place where the king, who had no great love for his capital Berlin or his wife Elizabeth Christine, could escape both. It's a surprisingly modest one-storey Baroque affair, looking out over the vine terraces towards the the high-rises of the Neustädter Havelbucht. Frederick loved the Schloss so much that he intended to be buried here and had a tomb excavated for himself in front of the eastern wing, near the graves of his Italian greyhounds, animals whose company he preferred to that of human beings during the last, increasingly eccentric years of his life. When he died, however, his nephew Friedrich Wilhelm II had him interred in the Garnisonkirche in Potsdam itself, next to the father Frederick hated. Towards the end of World War II, the remains of Frederick and his father were exhumed and eventually taken to Schloss Hohenzollern in Swabia for safekeeping from the approaching Soviet army: only in 1991, after unification, were the remains returned and buried in Frederick's preferred site .

Inside, the Schloss is a frenzy of Rococo, spread through the twelve rooms where Frederick lived and entertained his guests – a process which usually entailed quarrelling and arguing with them. The most eye-catching rooms are the opulent **Marmorsaal** (Marble Hall) and the **Konzert Zimmer** (Concert Room), where the flute-playing king had eminent musicians play his own works on concert evenings. Frederick's favourite haunt was his **library** where, surrounded by his two thousand volumes – mainly French translations of the classics and a sprinkling of contemporary French writings – he could oversee the work on his tomb. One of Frederick's most celebrated house guests was **Voltaire** who lived here from 1750 to 1753, acting as a kind of private tutor to the king, finally leaving when he'd had enough of Frederick's bizarre behaviour. In revenge Frederick ordered that Voltaire's former room be decorated with carvings of apes and parrots.

The **west wing** of the Schloss was added in 1840, and its thirteen rooms housed ladies and gentlemen of the court. Nearby on the terrace is a wrought-iron summer house protecting a weatherbeaten copy of a Classical statue, while just to the south an eighteenth-century sculpture of Cleopatra looks over the graves of Frederick's horses.

Around the Schloss

West of Schloss Sanssouci, overlooking the ornamental **Holländischer Garten** or Dutch Garden, is the **Bildergalerie** (Mid-May to mid-Oct 9am–noon & 12.45–5pm; DM4), a restrained Baroque creation that, it's claimed, was the first building in Europe to be erected specifically as a museum. The collection's most famous work is Caravaggio's *Incredulity of St Thomas*; there's also a wonderful *Supper at Emmaus* by his Dutch follower, Terbrugghen. Rubens and van Dyck are both extensively represented; the most important works by the former are *St Jerome in his Study* and *The Four Evangelists*; by the latter are portraits of members of the British court, plus a couple of mythological works, *Rinaldo and Armida* and *Venus in Vulcan's Workshop*.

On the opposite side of the Schloss, from a point near the Cleopatra statue, steps lead down to the **Neue Kammern** (April–Sept 9am–12.45pm & 1–5pm; Feb, March & Oct closes 4pm; Nov–Jan closes 3pm; DM4), the architectural twin of the Bildergalerie, originally used as an orangery and later as a guest house. Frederick was prepared to go to some lengths to achieve the desired carefree rural ambience for Sanssouci and retained an old wooden windmill as an ornament just north of the Neue Kammern. Four years after his death, this was replaced by a rustic-looking stone construction, the **Historische Mühle**, which is being restored for projected reopening in 1993 as a museum of trades and crafts. The **Ruinenberg**, rising to the north of Schloss Sanssouci, looks like a cluster of Classical ruins, but in fact these fragments are artificial, designed to render a little more interesting a reservoir built during the eighteenth century to feed the fountains in the park.

The Orangerie

From the western corner of the Sizilianischer Garten, **Maulbeerallee** (Mulberry Alley), a road open to traffic, cuts through the park to the ascent to the **Orangerie** (mid-May to mid-Oct 9am–noon & 1–5pm, closed every fourth Monday; DM5). This Italianate Renaissance-style structure with its belvedere towers is one of the more visually impressive buildings in the park, and is certainly more outwardly imposing than the Schloss. A series of terraces with curved retaining walls sporting water spouts in the shape of lions' heads lead up to the sandy-coloured building, whose slightly down-at-heel appearance lends it added character.

The western wing of the building is still used for its original purpose, as a refuge for tropical plants in winter, and during the summer it's possible to ascend the western tower, from where there are great views of the Neues Palais and depressing vistas of Potsdam's high-rises to the east. The Orangerie also houses a gallery, the **Raphaelsaal**, with copies of Raphael's most famous masterpieces. Part of the Orangerie is given over to private flats, occupied by members of the park staff – which must be just about the best addresses in Potsdam.

The Belvedere, Drachenhaus and around

From the western wing of the Orangerie, the arrow-straight, lime tree-lined **Krimlindenallee** leads up towards a ruined Rococo **Belvedere**, the last building to be built under Frederick the Great. Now shrouded in scaffolding, it was the only building in the whole park to suffer serious war damage, and restoration work is due to be completed in 1993. A couple of hundred metres short of the Belvedere a path branches off to the left, leading to the **Drachenhaus**, a one-time vintner's house built in the style of a Chinese pagoda for the small vineyard nearby. Today there's a genteel café inside, an ideal point to interrupt your wanderings. Southwest of the Drachenhaus a pathway leads across the park to the **Spielfestung**, the toy fort to end all toy forts, which was built for the sons of Wilhelm II and even armed with miniature Krupp cannons. Returning to the path, follow it to the **Antikentempel**, originally built in 1768 to house part of the art collection of Frederick the Great. This domed rotunda is now the last resting-place of a number of members of the Hohenzollern family, including the Empress Auguste Victoria, and of Hermine, the woman whom Wilhelm II married in exile and who was known as the "last Empress".

The Neues Palais

To the west through the trees rises the **Neues Palais** (April–Sept 9am–12.45pm & 1.15–5pm; Feb, March & Oct closes 4pm; Nov–Jan closes 3pm; closed every 2nd and 4th Mon; DM6), another massive Rococo extravaganza from Frederick the Great's time, built between 1763 and 1769 to reaffirm the might of Prussia and its king after the Seven Years' War. At the centre of the palace is a huge green-weathered dome, topped by a gilded crown. The edges of the roof are lined with statues, which were specially mass-produced by a team of sculptors to adorn Frederick's new creation.

Much of the palace can still be visited, although it's pot-luck as to which rooms you'll get to see on any particular day. The southern wing (which these days houses a small café) contains Frederick's apartments and the theatre where the king enjoyed Italian opera and French plays. A francophile to the point of near mania, Frederick believed that the Germans were philistines incapable of producing great art. The last imperial resident of the Neues Palais was Kaiser Wilhelm II, who packed sixty railway carriages with the contents of the palace when he and his family fled in November 1918, following the revolution and abdication. Across the courtyard behind the Neues Palais are the **Communs**, a couple of pointless Rococo fantasies joined by a curved colonnade. They look grandiose, but their purpose was mundane: they were built for the serving and maintenance staff of the Palais.

The Rehgarten and Charlottenhof

From the Neues Palais, Ökonomieweg leads east through the **Rehgarten** or Deer Garden, former court hunting ground, where you'll find the **Chinesisches Teehaus** (mid-May to mid-Sept 9–11.45am & 12.30–5pm; DM1.50), a kind of Rococo pagoda housing a small museum of Chinese and Meissen porcelain and surrounded by eerily lifelike statues of oriental figures.To the south, a broad expanse of rough parkland, **Charlottenhof**, contains **Schloss Charlottenhof** (mid-May to mid-Oct 9am–12.30pm & 1–5pm; closed every 4th Mon; DM4), a Roman-style building designed by Schinkel and Ludwig Persius for Friedrich IV. Its interior is impressive: the hallway is bathed in blue light filtered through coloured glass decorated with stars, a prelude to the **Kupferstichzimmer**, whose walls are covered in copies of Italian Renaissance paintings. East of here through the woods and across a race-track-shaped clearing called the **Hippodrom** is the **Fasanerie**, another nineteenth-century Italian-style edifice.

The Grüner Gitter and around

At the southwestern corner of Sanssouci is the **Grüner Gitter** or Green Gateway entrance to the grounds, where there's an **information kiosk**. Immediately to the north of this entrance way is the Italianate **Friedenskirche**, designed by Persius for Friedrich Wilhelm IV and completed in 1850. With its 39-metre campanile and lakeside setting it conjures up the southern European atmosphere that Friedrich Wilhelm was striving to create when he ordered the construction of the church using the San Clemente basilica in Rome as a model. Adjoining the church is a domed Hohenzollern mausoleum containing the tombs of Friedrich Wilhelm IV and his wife Elizabeth, and Friedrich III and his wife Victoria.

North of the centre

Heading north from the Nauener Tor along Friedrich-Ebert-Strasse will bring you to some of Potsdam's most fascinating, yet least-known, corners. The beginnings are inauspicious – on the left is a mid-nineteenth-century Italianate villa, once the house of a royal gardener, behind which lie the former district headquarters of the *Stasi*, while the neo-Baroque affair to the north is a turn-of-the-century local government office.

Alexandrowka

However, after about fifteen minutes' walking you'll reach **Alexandrowka**, a settlement of Russian-style wooden houses, built for a group of Russian military musicians who found themselves marooned here after the Napoleonic Wars. Its incongruity makes it one of the most intriguing sights in town, a collection of two-storey dwellings with steeply pitched roofs, laid out in the form of a St Andrew's cross. In 1826, Friedrich Wilhelm III gave the order that houses should be built for these men and their families. Eight houses were built on the arms of the cross, four more at the semicircular linking roads at each end, with an overseer's residence in the middle. The names of the original occupants and subsequent inhabitants (a few of them descendants of the Russians, even today) are carved into the housefronts. Some of the oldest inscriptions are in Cyrillic script. This whole area remains a focus of the Russian presence in Potsdam. The Red Army occupies huge barrack buildings along Voltaireweg and Pappelallee, formerly the property of the *Wehrmacht* and before that the Imperial German Army, while Soviet officers and their families inhabit numerous blocks of flats locally, including ones along Puschkin Allee, just east of the Alexandrowka.

Alexander-Newski-Kapelle

Directly to the north of the settlement is the **Kapelle des heiligen Alexander Newski**, a church built for the Russians in 1829, set on top of the closely wooded Kapellenberg hill. Access is either by scrambling up the hillside, or via a track branching to the right off Nedlitzer Strasse which leads to a rudimentary car park. The chapel is a compact building in pink stucco edged with white, topped by a central onion-domed tower, with smaller domes at each corner. The chapel is usually accessible at weekends, but if there's anyone about during the week it's often possible to take a look round. The interior is festooned with icons, many of them gifts from the Czarina Alexandra, who started life as Princess Charlotte of Prussia. The priest's wife oversees a little stall selling replica icons and holy medals, and often plays Russian Orthodox choir tapes which enhance the already ethereal effect.

The Pfingstberg

Immediately to the north of the Kapellenberg is the wooded **Pfingstberg** hill, another little-known Potsdam curiosity which, like the Russian settlement and the Kapellenberg, is undergoing a process of gradual rediscovery. At the foot of the Pfingstberg is the walled **Jüdischer Friedhof** or Jewish cemetery. Officially, only organised visits are possible (every Sunday at 10am – you can enquire at the tourist information office in town for details), but it's easy enough to gain access to the overgrown graveyard via the numerous gaps in the wall. The cemetery was given by the town to Potsdam's growing Jewish population in 1763 – until then they had to bury their dead in Berlin. As recently as 1933 the Jewish community of Potsdam numbered several hundred, of whom just two returned after the war. The forgotten state of the cemetery stands today as a symbol of their fate: the wall has been patched in haphazard fashion and a few attempts have been made to keep the weeds at bay. It's in urgent need of restoration, for which the authorities have promised to make money available.

From the cemetery the path leads on up the hill to the ruined nineteenth-century **belvedere**, a vast and improbable-looking edifice, built to plans drawn up from Friedrich Wilhelm IV's sketches of the folly-like castles constructed in Italy during the Renaissance. Its walkways and towers give great views of Potsdam itself, and of the landscape north as far as Spandau and Charlottenburg, and west as far as the town of Brandenburg. Unfortunately, it's almost impossible to enjoy them today. Although virtually undamaged by the war, the belvedere was allowed to collapse into ruin by the pre-*Wende* city authorities, because (according to some Potsdamers) it afforded such good views of the border and West Berlin. The small ruin just to the southeast of the belvedere is the **Pomonatempel**, Schinkel's first-ever finished building, constructed in 1800 when he was a nineteen-year-old student of architecture. Originally a neat Neoclassical temple fronted by a four-columned portico, it's now no more than four shattered walls left by time, the weather and vandals.

The Neuer Garten

To the west of the Pfingstberg is the **Neuer Garten**, another large park complex, which includes Schloss Cecilienhof, venue of the Potsdam conference. The main entrance is at the eastern end of Johannes-Dieckmann-Allee, beyond which a road snakes through the park. A couple of hundred metres east of the road, overlooking the Heiliger See, is the **Marmorpalais** or Marble Palace, built for Friedrich Wilhelm II who died a premature death here in 1797, allegedly as a result of his dissolute lifestyle. Until 1990 it was home to the GDR's main military museum: at the moment the building is under restoration, pending reopening with a less martial theme.

Schloss Cecilienhof
Towards the end of the road through the wooded grounds of the Neuer Garten is **Schloss Cecilienhof** (daily 9am–4.15pm; closed every 2nd and 4th Mon; DM3), which looks like a mock-Elizabethan stately mansion transplanted from the Home Counties. Building work on this "English-style" palace, the last to be commissioned by the Hohenzollern family, began in 1913 and was completed in 1917, the war evidently having done nothing to change the architectural style. Cecilienhof would only rate a mention in passing, were it not for the fact that the **Potsdam Conference**, confirming the decisions made about the postwar European order earlier that year at Yalta, was held here from July 17 to August 2, 1945. The conference was as much symbolic as anything else, providing a chance for Truman, Stalin and Churchill (replaced mid-conference by Clement Attlee) to show the world that they had truly won the war by meeting in the heart of the ruined Reich.

Centre of attraction within is the **Konferenzsaal,** or conference chamber, where the Allied delegates worked out the details of the division of Europe and which resembles the assembly hall of a minor public school. Everything has been left pretty much as it was in 1945, with the huge round table specially made in Moscow for the conference still in place, despite the fact that on July 27, 1990, there was an arson attack on the hall. The fire brigade arrived within a few minutes and extinguished the fire, but not before considerable damage had been done. A remarkably quick restoration job has left few traces of what happened. It's still not known who was responsible for the attack, but local *Faschos* – neo-fascists – are thought to be the most likely culprits.

It's also possible to visit the delegates' work-rooms furnished in varying degrees of chintziness. The study of the Soviet delegation is about the most tasteless, but the British room (with a bronze stag at bay in the fireplace and furniture that looks like it was bought as a job lot from a defunct presbytery) comes a close second. Cecilienhof has been used as a hotel since 1960 and there's an expensive restaurant which is also only for the deep of pocket (for information on both see "Practicalities").

On the opposite shore of the Heiliger See to the Neuer Garten is the **Berliner Vorstadt**, formerly an elegant Potsdam suburb, whose crumbling villas were given over to various party and social institutions under the SED regime. Here, too, were numerous Imperial army barracks, housing elite units like the Garde du Corps and Hussars, which are now in Soviet hands. At the end of Berliner Strasse, leading back to Berlin, is the **Glienicke Brücke**, the famous spy-swap bridge which inspired many a cold war film scene. Here in 1962 U-2 pilot Gary Powers was traded for a Soviet agent, while more recently in 1986, Jewish dissident Anatoly Scharansky was freed into the West by the Soviet authorities in an early manifestation of Gorbachev's glasnost. The bridge was reopened to normal traffic at the beginning of 1990, and today there are few reminders of the era when people living in the immediate vicinity needed special permits simply to come and go from their own homes.

Eating, drinking and nightlife

Eating and drinking pose few problems in Potsdam. There's a reasonable array of **restaurants**, and most places are pleasant enough, though few would gain any stars in a gourmet's guide to the Berlin area. In town the major and most convenient concentration of possibilities is along Brandenburger Strasse, although it pays to go a little further afield.

Restaurants

Altes Jagdschloss, Am Jagdschloss Stern. At the eastern end of Babelsberg, housed in a building that seems to have changed little since the eighteenth century. The traditional Brandenburg dishes are reasonable, but it's the atmosphere that makes the place. Expect to pay around DM8–17. Closed Thursday.

Asiatisches Restaurant, Berliner Str. 133 (☎24629). Potsdam's swish Chinese restaurant, run by the former chef of the GDR embassy in Beijing. Closed Sunday.

Badische Weinsuben, Gutenbergstr. 90. A new place offering the cuisine of Baden; a little on the pricey side at DM7–25, but worth it.

Hotel Schloss Cecilienhof in Schloss Cecilienhof (☎22928). The poshest and, not surprisingly, most expensive restaurant in Potsdam. DM45 secures dishes allegedly served up to Churchill, Stalin and Truman during the Potsdam conference, but the high prices do not always guarantee the quality of the food.

Minsk-Nationalitätengaststätte, Max-Plank-Str. 10, am Brauhausberg (☎23490). This ugly-looking modern establishment on the Babelsberg side of the Havel serves surprisingly good pseudo-Byelorussian cuisine. Clear views across to Potsdam are an additional attraction; DM8–20.

Strandterrassen, Kleines Schloss, Park Babelsberg (☎75156). A lakeside place worth investigating. Standard German dishes at DM8–25. Wed–Sun noon–9pm.

Cafés and bars

Café Heider, Friedrich-Ebert-Str. 28–29 (☎22646). A former hang-out of opposition types that retains its old clientele and also boasts the widest selection of cakes in town. Open till 9pm; closed Monday.

Cafe im Filmmuseum, Am Karl-Liebknecht-Forum 1. One of Potsdam's best cafés, and a good place to take a break after visiting the museum.

Drachenhaus, Maulbeerallee (☎21594). A pleasant and genteel little café in the grounds of Schloss Sanssouci itself, housed in a pagoda-style building once used by royal vintners.

Froschkasten, Kiezstr. 4 (☎21315). One of the best and oldest bars in Potsdam, a *Kneipe* that also serves good food. Closed Sunday and Monday.

Milchbar Babette, Brandenburgerstr. 71 (☎21648). Centre of Potsdam's thriving café scene. Open 10am–7pm, until 8pm Sun, Mon & Tues. Also open as a cocktail bar Wed–Sun until 1am.

Die Rebe, Feuerbachstr. 1 (☎24002). A very pleasant wine-*Kneipe* serving food, just southwest of the Brandenburg Gate. It's open until midnight but closed Sunday and Monday.

Nightlife

For **nightlife** the best bets are, as usual, the former *FDJ* clubhouses. Best of these is the *Jugendclubhaus Lindenpark*, Stahndorferstr. 76–78 (☎78990), over in Babelsberg, with regular "alternative" discos and live bands, usually of a thrashy nature. *Fabrik*, Gutenberg Str. 105, is also an alternative venue for gigs and events. The *Haus der Jugend*, Berliner Str. 49, stages promising events. More bizarre are the discos held in the *Haus der Offiziere*, Schopenhauer Strasse/Hegelallee, every Saturday from 7pm: this building is the Soviet officers' clubhouse.

Listings

Bike hire *Fahrradvermietung Golm*, Geiselbergstr. 27. Mon–Fri 3–8pm, Sat & Sun 9am–8pm; closed Tues.

Boat hire on the Freundschaftsinsel, and at Auf dem Kiewitt 21a.

Boat trips *Weisse Flotte*, Lange Brücke, Am Interhotel (☎4241 or 21090). Tickets and information May–Sept daily 8–11am & 11.30am–5.45pm; April–Oct daily 10am–3.30pm. Regular sailings to Wannsee, Caputh, Werder, Ferch and Templin. Single DM6.50, return DM10.

Car hire *Interrent*, Rudolf-Breitscheidstr. 15 (☎75075); *Happy Car*, Böcklinstr. 1 (☎25086).

Post office Main post office: Heinrich-Rau-Allee 16–18 (☎380).

Womens' centre *Frauenzentrum*, Leninallee 189 (☎22383), with café on Friday and Saturday.

Babelsberg

On the eastern bank of the Havel is the town of **BABELSBERG**, now officially part of the Potsdam administrative district. Crossing the Lange Brücke from Potsdam, it's hard not to notice a square tower rising up out of the trees atop the **Brauhausberg** hill on the Babelsberg side. This is the former local SED headquarters or **"Kreml"** (Kremlin), to give it its local nickname. Orginally built as a military college at the turn of the century, it later served as a state archive building – a dark oval patch on the side of the tower marks where the SED symbol used to be.

The Telegrafenburg and the Einsteinturm

Like Potsdam, Babelsberg has a few secrets ripe for rediscovery. Above the Lange Brücke, Albert-Einstein-Strasse leads up onto the **Telegrafenberg**. In the late nineteenth century an astronomical **observatory** was built here, but much more striking is the nearby **Einsteinturm**, a twenty-metre-high observatory tower designed by Erich Mendelsohn in 1920. An unavoidably phallic piece of Expressionist architecture, it looks like an element from a Dalí dreamscape and is the most remarkable modern building in the Potsdam area. Experiments testing the theory of relativity were carried out here in the presence of Einstein, and scientific work continues today with research into the sun's magnetic field. At the moment the building is in a dodgy state, but various initiatives have been started to get together funds for renovation.

On the eastern side of the Telegrafenberg are a couple of musts for cemetery fans: the **Neuer Friedhof**, laid out in 1866 according to plans drawn up by the architect Lenné and, below it on the other side of Heinrich-Mann-Allee, the eighteenth-century **Alte Friedhof** with its Classical mausoleum and overgrown monuments, including one to Eleonore Prochaska who joined the Prussian army in 1813 disguised as a man, successfully fooling her comrades, and later dying in the war against Napoleon.

The DEFA studios and Jagdschloss Stern

Babelsberg's other point of interest may well have closed by the time you read this. From Lutherplatz in the town centre take bus #A, #B or #E along Ernst-Thälmann-

Strasse. North of the road, just before S-Bahnhof Drewitz, are the **DEFA film studios**, a huge complex, originally founded in 1917. As the UFA film studios during the 1920s this was the heart of the German film industry, rivalling Hollywood as a centre of cinematic innovation. Films produced during the heyday of UFA included Robert Wiene's Expressionist masterpiece *Das Cabinet des Dr Caligari* ("The Cabinet of Dr Caligari"), Fritz Lang's *Metropolis* and *Der Blaue Engel* ("The Blue Angel") starring the young Marlene Dietrich. Under the Nazis the anti-Semitic *Jud Süss* was filmed here in 1940, followed a few years later by the special effect-laden colour epic *Münchhausen*. Later, as the DEFA studios, it was the heavily subsidised centre of the GDR film industry, but since the *Wende* its fate hangs in the balance, despite a heavily promoted "Save the Studio" campaign. Guided tours are possible: enquire at *Urania Potsdam*, Brandenburger Strasse 38 (☎395 3078).

Brandenburg

BRANDENBURG, the city from which the province takes its name, lies on the main Berlin–Hannover rail line just over 30km west of Potsdam. For all its illustrious past – it was founded by the Slavs in the sixth century, made the seat of a precarious missionary German bishopric in the tenth century, before becoming the capital of the margraviate established by Albert the Bear in 1157 – its recent history has been a catalogue of misfortunes. These began when the Nazis chose it as the site of a concentration camp; future GDR dictator Erich Honecker served twelve years there, and among those murdered were 10,000 victims of a compulsory euthanasia programme for the mentally handicapped. The Nazis turned Brandenburg's industry – hitherto based on the production of bikes and motor vehicles – over to military purposes, ensuring the city was a prime target of Allied bombers; it was further damaged by the Red Army in 1945, when the defenders mounted a futile last-ditch resistance. After the war, the Communists made it the metropolis for the steel industry their dogma demanded; as a result, the medieval skyline was disfigured by the addition of sixteen smoking chimneys (four of which found their way on to the municipal coat of arms) and drab blocks of flats to accommodate its workers. Many historic buildings were left as ruins, while others rotted under the impact of some of the worst air pollution in Europe.

Yet Brandenburg still has much to offer. It's one of the most beautifully sited cities in Germany, occupying three islands at a point where the broad course of the Havel fashions a wondrous lake-strewn landscape, and its surviving monuments represent North German brick architecture at its most inventive. One of five cities in the former GDR chosen for comprehensive restoration projects, it will hopefully re-emerge before long as the attractive place it once was.

The Neustadt

Arriving at the Hauptbahnhof, Ernst-Thälmann-Strasse brings you to the first of the three island quarters, the **Neustadt** or New Town. It's new only in a relative sense, having been founded as the commercial quarter at the end of the twelfth century, a generation after the previously Slav Altstadt had been re-established as a German town. Despite conspicuous gaps left by the war, its narrow streets retain much of their old feel. The first building in view is the cylindrical **Steintor**, one of four surviving gateways out of the ten the two settlements once possessed between them; in summer, it's open for special exhibitions on the city's history. Following the curvaceous Strasse der Junge Pioniere northeast from here, you come to the **Paulikloster**, a thirteenth-century Dominican monastery left in ruins during World War II.

Right in the middle of the island is the Neustädtischer Markt, now returned to its age-old role as a market square. It's dominated by the **Katharinenkirche**, a Gothic pile from the turn of the fifteenth century. Outside, the walls are crammed with spouting gargoyles and frilly gables tacked on for purely decorative effect, with the varied colouring and positioning of the bricks helping to transform the surface effects yet further. The fantastical but fading interior design tends to overshadow the church's treasures, which include a finely carved fifteenth-century altar and a fourteenth-century stained glass window in the choir which was fortuitously removed from the Paulikloster in 1942.

The Altstadt

Hauptstrasse runs northwestwards over the Havel into the **Altstadt**, which occupies only a small portion of a much larger island. Immediately over the river is the **Johanniskirche**, another brick Gothic church still remaining – for the time being, at least – in the burnt-out state it was left at the end of the war. Further along, at Hauptstr. 96, is the **Freyhaus** (Wed–Fri 9am–5pm, Sat & Sun 10am–5pm; DM1), a Baroque mansion which now houses the district museum. This array of local ephemera is more interesting than you might expect, particularly the displays on the archaeology of the Havelland, the graphic art section, and a fascinating toy collection.

At the end of Hauptstrasse Plauer Strasse leads north to the Altstädtischer Markt, over which looms the fourteenth-century **Altstädtisches Rathaus**, whose facade is topped with an unusual stepped gable. In front of it stands a mighty five-metre-high **statue of Roland**, medieval symbol of Brandenburg's status as a market town. He previously stood guard in front of the Neustädtisches Rathaus opposite the Katharinenkirche, but was brought here after its destruction in World War II.

Continuing northwards, you come to the parish church of the Altstadt, the **Gotthardtkirche**. Its facade is in the austere Romanesque style favoured by the Premonstratensian monks who were its first congregation, but behind it stands a light and airy Gothic hall church erected in the fifteenth century. Inside, look out for the thirteenth-century font and the lovely Burgundian tapestry showing the hunting of the unicorn. On the square facing the church is the **Schulhaus**, a half-timbered former school building from the sixteenth century.

The Dominsel

The **Dominsel**, the smallest of the three islands on which the historic quarters of Brandenburg are built, escaped the worst of the bombing and is by far the most visually pleasing part of town. From the Gotthardtkirche, you have to approach it cicuitously via yet another island, occupied mainly by sports fields, to the north; there's a more direct approach along Mühlendamm from the Neustädtischer Markt. Taking the latter approach, the first monument you come to is the **Petrikapelle**, a thirteenth-century chapel given a spectacular interior transformation three hundred years later, with the addition of the intricate late Gothic vault resting on hexagonal pillars.

The Dom

The **Dom** itself is set in a tranquil close and looks oddly parochial considering the great evangelising role it once played. Begun around 1150 as a Romanesque basilica, it was slowly converted to Gothic in the fourteenth and fifteenth centuries though many parts of the old structure were retained, notably the arcades of the nave. The most atmospheric part of the Dom is the **crypt**, where you can see the poignant original triumphal cross, supplanted *in situ* by a more monumental Gothic group. Even more eye-catching are the **capitals**, whose carvings of fabulous beasts and eerie half human creatures show the vivid flights of imagination of which the medieval mind was capable. A contrastingly sombre note is struck by a series of metal plates, each accompanied by an appropriate biblical quotation, commemorating local clergymen murdered by the Nazis. It's a fitting reminder of the high-profile political role the Dom has played, most recently during the *Wende* of 1989 when the church was regularly filled for recitals given on the magnificent Baroque **organ**, attracting large financial donations for the democratic cause in the process.

In the south transept is a beautifully carved and painted **Bohemian altar** from around 1375, whose radiantly joyous saints mark a refreshing change from the anguished figures normally found in religious art. This was originally the high altar, but it was displaced in favour of a large retable brought here when Kloster Lehnin (see below) was secularised after the Reformation. In front of the latter stands a delicately modelled fourteenth-century **font**, with scenes from the childhood of Christ on its basin, and more fantastic animals on the base. On the north side of the choir, look out for the appropriately named **Bunte Kapelle** (Painted Chapel), another survivor from the Romanesque period.

The **Dommuseum** (guided tours Mon, Tues & Thurs at 10.30am & 2.30pm, Sat at 2.30pm; DM1), entered from the north transept, occupies the conventual buildings of the Premonstratensian collegiate foundation which moved here from the Gotthardtkirche. There's a superb array of medieval textiles, including a *Hungertuch* of 1290, made to cover the altar during Lent. Even finer is the collection of manuscripts, of which the star piece is the **Brandenburg Evangelistary**, a sumptuous late Romanesque gospel book adorned with colourful miniatures. The original is displayed with one page open; a facsimile of the whole book is kept for examination at leisure.

The lakes

Extending northwards for ten kilometre from the Dominsel is the **Beetzsee**, the most accessible of the many lakes that dot the area. Its attractions are low-key, but if you've decided to make your visit to Brandenburg more than just a perfunctory one its birch-lined shores offer good walking possibilities, and the landscape of meadows dotted with pools, tiny forgotten hamlets and crumbling Junker residences is one of scenes from a prewar photograph album. If it's a little more action you're after, there are water-skiing facilities near the village of BRIETZOW.

On the western side of Brandenburg, the Havel flows into a lake, whose various sections are given different names: the isle-strewn southeastern part, for example, is called the **Breitlingsee**, while the western stretch, known as the **Plauensee**, is where the river exits on its 60km journey north to its confluence with the Elbe. On the latter's far shore stands **PLAUE**, a favourite summer destination among Brandenburgers. Entering this small town you pass first through the Kietz, a former fishing settlement of low cottages. Plaue has a small church – originally Romanesque but reworked during the sixteenth century – and a lakeside Schloss with extensive gardens.

Practicalities

Brandenburg's **tourist office** is at Plauer Str. 4 (Mon–Fri 9am–noon & 2–5pm; ☎237743). Here they can arrange **private rooms**; it's also worth asking about the **hotel** situation, which was in a very fluid state at the time of writing. In GDR days, the only option was the *Havel-Tourist*, Katharinenplatz 1 (☎23703), whose rates begin at DM35 for singles, DM60 for doubles. However, there are now a number of cheaper alternatives, such as *Zum Bären*, Steinstr. 60 (☎24179), and *Pension Genorv*, Magdeburger

Str. 12 (☎522493). Other places to stay include the **youth hostel** at Havellerstr. 7 (☎521040) on the Dominsel, and the *Wichernhaus*, a church-run residence at Hauptstr. 66 (☎522287). There are also a number of **campsites** on the lakes around the city; most convenient is *Die Malge* on the Breitlingsee, which also has bungalows for rent. Two more can be found on the nearby islands; yet another, the *Margaretenhof*, is on the peninsula jutting into the Plauensee.

For **eating** and **drinking**, by far the best bet is the excellent *Ratskeller* in the Altstädtisches Rathaus, which is open until midnight seven days a week. The *Stadtcafé*, Hauptstr. 26–28, is a typical example of a GDR attempt at a trendy western-style café, but isn't bad for all that. A local oddity is the *Jugendklubhaus Philipp Müller*, Steinstr. 42, which has a vegetarian and health-food restaurant; there are also discos here several times a week. **Cruises**, run by *Weisse Flotte*, depart from Salzhofufer, on the Altstadt side of the river.

Lehnin

About 20km southeast of Brandenburg, and equally accessible from Potsdam, the time-warped village of **LEHNIN** clusters round its huge **Kloster**, which was founded in 1180 by Cistercian monks on what was then a swampy marsh deep in a forest populated mainly by heathen and hostile Slavs. Despite many vicissitudes, the **church** survives intact and offers a graphic illustration of the way the Romanesque style of the east end, the first part to be built, had given way to Gothic by the time the building was completed in 1260. Although the simple majesty of the elevation is the most impressive feature, there are also a few notable works of art, including a Romanesque triumphal cross and the tomb slab of Margrave Otto IV, son-in-law of Emperor Rudolf von Habsburg, the founder of medieval Europe's most powerful dynasty. The complex of restored monastic buildings has been given a new lease of life in the form of a geriatric home run by Protestant nuns; as the church is often kept locked, you may have to ask at the porter's lodge here for admission.

Oranienburg

About 20km out of Berlin (veering slightly northeast) is **ORANIENBURG**, a drab-looking place of 23,000 inhabitants, home to little more than moribund industry and a nondescript **Schloss**. The one thing that sets Oranienburg apart from dozens of other towns around Berlin is a monument that recalls the grimmest chapter in German history – Sachsenhausen concentration camp.

Sachsenhausen Concentration Camp

The camp, officially known as the **Nationale Mahn- und Gedenkstätte Sachsenhausen** (Tues–Fri 8.30am–4.30pm, Sat & Sun 9am–4.30pm) is in the northern suburb of Sachsenhausen. It's reached from S-Bahnhof Oranienburg by following Strasse des Friedens east, turning left into Strasse der Einheit and then following Strasse der Nationen, which leads to the entrance.

Some history

Opened as a memorial on April 23, 1961 by the GDR government, it's an inevitably sobering place: as the official guidebook puts it, "Every footstep of this earth is soaked with the blood and death-sweat of tens of thousands of martyrs from many different nations". The camp was originally opened in July 1936 (replacing an earlier ad hoc camp housed in a local brewery from 1933 to 1935) as a *Schutzhaftlager* or "Protective Custody Camp", specifically to house opponents of the Nazi regime – mainly communists, socialists and trade unionists. New categories of prisoner were added with every year of National Socialist rule; people convicted of "anti-social" behaviour, homosexuals and finally Jews, of whom 6000 were brought to Sachsenhausen after the brutal *Kristallnacht* attacks of November 9–10, 1938. The war years saw thousands of new internees arrive from the occupied countries and the beginning of organised mass murder, as opposed to the relatively arbitrary killings and executions of the 1930s.

At the end of the war the SS evacuated the camp, moving 33,000 prisoners north towards the Baltic where it was intended to herd them aboard boats which would then be sunk. Known as the *Todesmarsch* (Death March), this pitiless forced march across northern Germany claimed the lives of 6000 prisoners, most of whom died by the roadside (today plaques across the region commemorate them). Fortunately the survivors fell into Allied hands before the SS could put the final stage of their plan into effect. A further 3000 prisoners, most of them only barely alive, were found in the camp hospital when the liberating Soviet army arrived at Sachsenhausen on April 22, 1945.

MVD SPECIAL CAMP No. 7

In August 1945 the MVD, the military branch of the Soviet secret police, reopened Sachsenhausen as "MVD Special Camp No. 7". Originally for war criminals, former Nazis and *Wehrmacht* officers, it gradually filled with people who were simply opponents of the occupying regime including, after 1946, large numbers of Social Democrats who had protested about the forced merger of their party with the Communist party. Among all these prisoners were a few who had previously been interned here by the Nazis. By the time the camp was finally closed on March 10, 1950, about 60,000 prisoners had passed through, of whom some 20,000 died, mainly of hunger and lung diseases. In a recent postscript to this episode, mass graves containing the bodies of Germans executed by the MVD were unearthed in nearby woods in the spring of 1990.

The camp

From the **site entrance** a tree-lined road leads to a **museum** devoted to resistance to the Nazis. Just north of here is **Turm A**, the gatehouse entrance to the camp proper with a stretch of the original electrified camp fence running either side of it.

Beyond Turm A is the **Apellplatz** or parade ground, where the prisoners were gathered for roll call and often kept standing for hours on end or forced to witnesss executions on the camp **gallows**. Behind the gallows, in four semicircular rows were the **barrack blocks**, originally intended to hold 130 prisoners in cramped conditions but each filled by the end of the war with up to 500 men. Only two remain: one now houses the camp **museum**, and the left-hand one is a memorial hall and **cinema** where a film about life in the camp is shown every hour, on the hour. The positions of the other barracks are marked with granite blocks. Beyond them is an open space leading to the stylised camp **memorial**.

Many of the victims commemorated by the memorial died nearby at **Station Z**, where the Germans turned the process of executing Soviet prisoners of war into an almost industrial one, dispatching tens of thousands of men with shots to the back of the neck. At the opposite side of the camp are two surviving barrack blocks used to house **Jewish inmates**, with a special exhibition devoted to their sufferings. Just beyond here are **cells** where prominent prisoners, mainly workers' leaders and patriots from the occupied countries, were held in isolation, usually pending execution. One of the inmates best known to posterity is the anti-Nazi cleric, **Pastor Martin Niemöller**, who was one of the few to survive incarceration here.

Practicalities

There's a **tourist office** of sorts in the *Rat der Stadt*, Strasse des Friedens 92 (☎327/ 5071), while **hotel** possibilities are limited to the expensive *Hotel Melniker Hof*, Strasse des Friedens 48 (☎327/5106), which also has a reasonable **restaurant**. There's also a **youth hostel** at the entrance to the village of Friedrichsthal, just north of Oranienburg.

Neuruppin

Easily enough reached by road or rail from Oranienburg is the lakeside town of **NEURUPPIN**, the birthplace of the writer Theodor Fontane and the architect Karl Friedrich Schinkel. Neuruppin is a predominantly eighteenth-century town of 27,000 inhabitants, whose historic centre is all the more appreciable for being slightly faded. Although renovation will doubtless eventually render the facades spotless and cover the cobblestones, in its present state Neuruppin epitomises the flaking, down-at-heel charm of provincial eastern Germany.

The centre

The town is laid out on a grid-like pattern around three large squares: a result of carefully planned reconstruction following a great fire in 1787. From the **Hauptbahnhof** access to the town is via Bahnhofstrasse, which leads into Schinkelstrasse and ends at the large square of **Kirchplatz** on which sits the **Pfarrkirche St Marien**, a tatty-looking Baroque-influenced church from the early nineteenth century. Karl Friedrich Schinkel's father was superintendent of the Pfarrkirche's predecessor and there's a monument to the more famous son behind the church in the shape of the **Schinkel Denkmal**. Schinkel was born in 1781 and lived in Neuruppin through the time of the great fire and rebuilding, something that may have influenced his later choice of profession. In his adolescence he was sent to school in Berlin, and, having studied architecture, entered the Prussian civil service as a surveyor, later rising to take overall control of the Prussian building office. The mark he left on Berlin is tremendous. He completely transformed the old capital, doing much to give the city its predominantly Neoclassical feel, best exemplified by buildings along and around the Unter den Linden like the Neue Wache and the Altes Museum. Lesser works by the architect crop up all over north Germany, and there seems to be hardly a town in the region untouched by his hand.

Not far from the Schinkel monument is the **Fontanehaus**, the chemist's shop with a stone lion above its doorway at Karl-Marx-Str. 84, which was the birthplace of Neuruppin's other famous son, the author Theodor Fontane – though these days there's little about the building to betray its past.

THEODOR FONTANE 1818-98

Fontane was born in Neuruppin in 1819 to a couple of Huguenot descent. His career as a writer of fiction began relatively late in life. Before publishing his first work he was employed as a pharmaceutical dispenser, later serving as a war correspondent during the Austro-Prussian War of 1866 and the Franco-Prussian War of 1870–71. He wrote a couple of books describing his war experiences and four volumes describing his travels in the Province of Brandenburg, before going on to produce some of the finest novels of late nineteenth-century German literature. His best-known work is *Effi Briest*, published in 1895, the story of an upper-class Prussian woman drawn into an adulterous affair with predictably tragic consequences. Fontane, by his sympathetic portrayal of the protagonists, turns what could easily have become a rather trite reworking of the *Madame Bovary* story into a thinly veiled critique of the inflexible social mores of Prussian society of the time and their devastating effect on the individual.

A few steps along Karl-Marx-Strasse from the Fontanehaus is Neuruppin's Neoclassical **Gymnasium**, the school attended by both Schinkel and Fontane. A similarly grandiose edifice is the **Heimatmuseum** at August-Bebel-Str. 14–15 (the pre-1933 Ludwigstrasse), Neuruppin's town museum (Tues–Fri 8.30am–noon, Sat 8.30am–noon, Sun 10am–noon & 2–4pm). This building was one of the first in Germany to be erected specifically as a museum (the Bildergalerie in Potsdam came first) and contains, naturally enough, extensive material about Neuruppin and its surroundings, as well as sections devoted to Schinkel and Fontane. Just behind the Heimatmuseum is the **Tempelgarten**, a park where Frederick the Great often retreated from his duties as commander of a local army regiment, after being sent here as a young Crown Prince by his father. The park is named after its circular **Neoclassical temple**, the first work of the architect Georg von Knobelsdorff. Towards the southwestern end of Karl-Marx-Strasse is **Ernst-Thälmann-Platz**, a bleak parade ground previously known as Königsplatz, around which large numbers of attractive Baroque buildings survive. At the very end of the street is the **Fontanedenkmal**, a bronze statue of Fontane surveying the main road into town.

A few hundred metres south of Karl-Marx-Strasse is **See Ufer**, a broad lakeside promenade on the shores of the **Ruppiner See**, the lake that threads south of town for about 10km. Overlooking See Ufer, the spire of the thirteenth-century **Klosterkirche** offers clear views of the lake and town – particularly of the medieval buildings in the immediate vicinity that survive from before the great fire, like the **Hospitalkapelle St Lazarus** in Seichenstrasse, a small chapel whose entrance portal has an unusual terracotta relief of Christ tied to a pillar (rather than a cross).

Practicalities

Neuruppin's **tourist office** at Wichmannstr. 5 (☎2613) can arrange accommodation in private rooms and boat trips on the Ruppiner See. The town has a couple of **hotels** but at the time of writing both were temporarily closed; the *Stadt Neuruppin*, Karl-Marx-Str. 90 (☎3030), and the *Märkischer Hof*, Karl-Marx-Str. 50 (☎2801). Both have reasonable restaurants, but if neither is open try *Zum Brauhof* on Karl-Marx-Strasse or the *Café Huth*, Karl-Marx-Str. 85 (closed Mon).

Rheinsberg

About 30km north of Oranienburg is **RHEINSBERG**, at the southern tip of a network of lakes dotted with campsites and watersports facilities. Rheinsberg itself is a pleasant enough eighteenth-century town, mouldering quietly on the shore of the eponymous **Rheinsberger See**. The main sight is Knobelsdorff's lakeside **Schloss** (signposted from the station and located at the point where the town slopes down towards the lake), a three-winged building in smudged white now in use as a sanatorium for diabetics – although there are plans to turn it into a museum. An earlier building on the same site was the residence of Frederick the Great from 1736 until he acceded to the throne in 1740. Frederick spent his time in Rheinsberg (which he was later to claim was the happiest in his life) in the study of science and art.

The lakeside grounds of the Schloss are accessible (daily until 9.30pm) and dotted with odd monuments including, just to the west of the Schloss itself, a red-brick **pyramid** memorial to Frederick the Great's brother Heinrich, who moved into the Schloss after his brother moved out and spent the next sixty years here, enjoying the company of attractive young men and redesigning the gardens. Near the lakeshore is one of his works, a strangely ugly **stone grotto** containing a jumble of urns and statue pediments. The **obelisk** on the opposite shore to the Schloss celebrates the Prussian generals who fell in the Seven Years' War.

Occasionally the concert room of the Schloss is opened up for classical concerts. If you're fortunate enough to be here when one of these is being staged, look out for the allegorical ceiling picture *Der Tag vertreibt die Nacht* (Day Drives Away the Night), showing a barn-owl (representing Friedrich Wilhelm I) being driven away by the advance of Aurora (representing Frederick the Great and/or Heinrich).

Immediately east of the Schloss is the **Platz der Befreiung**, a large square ringed by chestnut trees, where locals and visitors alike sit watching the world go by in summer. Around the square are clustered the town's best eating and drinking possibilities (see below). To many Germans Rheinsberg is best known through the author Kurt Tucholsky (1890–1935) and his book *"Rheinsberg – Bilderbuch für Verliebte"*, the story of a pair of young lovers – Claire and Wölfchen – who visit the town, and an exhibition at Lange Str. 30 (March–Oct Mon–Fri 8am–5pm, Sat 3–6pm) commemorates Tucholsky's life and work. Also worth a quick look is the medieval **Pfarrkirche** with its sixteenth-century interior.

Practicalities

Rheinsberg doesn't have a **tourist office** as such, but information is available from the *Rat der Stadt* building on Lilienthal Str. 2 (☎211). For **eating and drinking**, try one of the collection of places around Platz der Befreiung. Best of the lot is the *Deutsches Haus* on Seestrasse, an excellent (and usually full) restaurant incorporating a *Kaffee und Kuchen* café, but the *Ratskeller* on Platz der Befreiung is also worth investigating. Near the former is the lakeside *Café Seepavillion*, Seestrasse (closed at the weekend). Also worth trying is the *Goldener Anker*, Karl-Marx-Str. 25, a reasonable *Gaststätte* on a street running parallel to the lake just northeast of the Schloss.

As far as **accommodation** goes, the *Hotel am Rheinsberger See*, Zechlinerhütter Landstr. 10 (☎2711), located on the lakeside road running north out of town, might be worth investigating, although it was temporarily closed at the time of writing. There are **campsites** at the Warenthiner Ablage and Prinzenstrand on the southern shore of the lake.

Eberswalde-Finow and around

EBERSWALDE-FINOW is a medium-sized industrial town of minimal interest, situated on a branch of the Oder-Havel canal; only a couple of hotels and a huge Soviet base put it on the map. The only sights worth mentioning are the early Gothic **Pfarrkirche St. Maria Magdalena** and the **Heimatmuseum**, Kirchstr. 8 (Mon–Fri 10am–noon & 2–5pm), a local history museum. There are, however, a few places in the immediate environs of the town that are worth investigating and the *Gasthaus am Walde*, Strasse der Junge Pioniere (☎65218), on the southern road into town, makes a possible accommodation base. A room with a shower and WC will set you back DM50 per person, and there's a restaurant. The management also rents out bikes at DM10 per day. For information about other hotels and private accommodation, enquire at the **tourist office** at Wilhelm-Pieck-Str. 26 (☎23168) in the town centre.

Chorin

Hiding in the woods about 10km northeast of Eberswalde-Finow is the tiny village of **CHORIN**, which is struggling, like so many rural settlements around Berlin, to find its way out of the 1950s. Alight at Bahnhof Kloster Chorin, the first of the two train stations, to see the Cistercian **Kloster**, which, in accordance with the ideals of its founders, is set in a secluded setting outside the village by a small lake, the Amtssee. First established on this site in 1273, it was constructed at a leisurely pace throughout the following two centuries. There's no more picturesque or evocative ruin in all of Germany — partly because it's hardly a ruin at all. Credit for this goes to Schinkel, who last century carried out major structural repairs on the long-abandoned monastery, then in danger of collapse. Both the church and the monastic quarters are substantially intact, though the former now gapingly opens out directly on to the cloister — helping create a much expanded auditorium for the **concerts** which are regularly held throughout the summer months. Architecturally, the finest feature is the highly idio-syncratic **facade**, the last part of the church to be built. A dazzling exercise in patterned brickwork, it contrasts sharply but effectively with the solemn grandeur of the structure behind.

Chorin has a **youth hostel**, set down a track off the main Angermünde road in the woods near the monastery. It's signposted, but again you may have to ask directions. Beds go for about DM12, and you can get breakfast and an evening meal. Best bet for **eating and drinking** is the *Klosterschänke* on the main road at the western edge of the village (closed Tues & Thurs, open until 10pm on Sat & Sun, otherwise 6pm).

Niederfinow and the Schiffshebewerk

Ten kilometres east of Eberswalde at **NIEDERFINOW** is one of the area's more unex-pected sights, the **Schiffshebewerk**, a barge-lift of titanic proportions on the Havel-Oder canal. It can be reached by bus from Niederfinow railway station, although it's a pleasant enough walk of only a couple of kilometres (cross the bridge near the station and head north).

The Schiffshebewerk is used to transport barges from the western upland section of the canal down into the Oder valley and vice versa, replacing an antiquated system of locks. It was opened in 1934, and at the time of its construction was the largest struc-ture of its kind in the world. It subsequently became an important staging post on the canal network linking Germany and Poland, reducing the time taken to lower and raise vessels from several painstaking hours to about fifteen minutes. At first view the lift is quite incredible, like an immense Meccano construction, and as you get closer it becomes even more impressive: an enormous steel trough capable of accommodating a 1000-tonne barge, raised and lowered by an electric-powered system of counter-weights, within a casing of steel girders.

For a closer look at how it works, follow the crowds up the steps on the western side of the road. These will bring you to the upper canal level and a walkway that runs around the outside of the barge-lift. From here you can observe the whole process as barges enter the huge trough and are lowered down into the valley below. Just north of the Schiffshebewerk is one of the original locks, a puny affair in comparison. The struc-ture attracts its fair share of visitors and there's a large car park with souvenir shop and *Imbiss* stands in the shadow of its massive girders. If you want something more substantial to eat or drink, head back towards the station and the *Gaststätte zur Schleuse*, at the junction of Fritz-Böhme-Strasse and August-Kunert-Strasse.

Falkenberg and Bad Freienwalde

From Niederfinow a string of linear settlements straggle southeast towards the Polish border. In the holiday town of **FALKENBERG** a few households let out private rooms. If you don't see any signs, enquire at the *Ausfluglokale Amalienhof* (also known as *Kochis Restaurant*), Thälmannstr. 68, a restaurant and ice-cream parlour.

Just a few kilometres to the east of Falkenberg (and next stop on the Eberswalde–Finow–Frankfurt an der Oder railway line) is **BAD FREIENWALDE**, a spa town on the edge of the Oder marshes, once favoured by the Great Elector. Just before the town proper begins is the **Moor-Badeanstalt**, a spa complex designed by Schinkel and Langhans and still much used by rheumatism sufferers. In the town itself the **Oderland Museum** at Uchtenhagenstr. 2 (Oct–March Tues–Fri 9am–noon & 2–5pm; April–Sept Tues–Fri & Sun 10am–noon & 2–5pm) has the usual local archaeological finds and an interesting section about the reclamation of the Oderbruch.

The wooded margins of the uplands just to the south of town afford great views across the Oder valley towards Poland. On top of the **Apothekenburg** sits a Neoclassical **Schloss** built by Friedrich Wilhelm II in 1797–1798, who was a frequent visitor to the town. After his death the Schloss served as a hunting lodge for many years before being bought in 1909 by Walter Rathenau, the future foreign minister of the Weimar Republic (he was assassinated by Freikorps officers in 1922 for attempting to promote trade links with the Soviet Union). In the Lenné-designed grounds you'll find the *Schlosscafé* which is the best local place to eat and drink. Beyond the Schloss the woods make for good, unstrenuous walking – a popular destination is the **Baasee**, a small lake with a traditional *Gaststätte*. For **accommodation**, try the *Pension Rathbauer*, Goethestr. 13 (☎2067). There's also a **youth hostel** at Hammerthal 3 (☎3875). East of Bad Freienwalde is a series of villages, more forgotten and sunk in the past than any you've yet seen, lost in the huge fields that roll towards the Oder river and the border with Poland.

Frankfurt an der Oder

Eighty kilometres east of Berlin is **FRANKFURT AN DER ODER**, the last stop before Poland. Frankfurt was almost totally destroyed during the war and though the subsequent rebuild was reasonably well thought out there isn't much to hang around for: the town's only real interest is as a stop-off en route to destinations beyond the border. Despite the prevailing architectural modernity Frankfurt is a very old place, dating back to the thirteenth century when German merchants founded a settlement and built a wooden bridge over the Oder. During the medieval period the town developed into an important trade centre, and its yearly fair attracted merchants from all over north Germany and Poland.

Today the **Marktplatz** remains the focal point of the town, flanked by the Gothic **Rathaus** and the shell of the **Marienkirche**, a gloomy reminder of wartime destruction. A few hundred metres east of Marktplatz at Julian-Marchelewski-Str. 17 is the **Kleist-Gedenkstätte** (Mon–Fri 10am–noon & Sat, Sun 10–noon & 2–4pm), a museum devoted to the life and works of the poet and playwright **Heinrich von Kleist** who was born in the town. Not far away is the **Friedensglocke** or peace bell commemorating

---

HEINRICH VON KLEIST (1777–1811)

Born into an old Prussian military family, **Heinrich von Kleist** began his career as a soldier, but resigned his commission and adopted a wandering lifestyle. Depite taking his own life at the age of 34 in a bizarre suicide pact with a woman dying of cancer, he bequeathed an astonishingly varied body of literature, which speaks more forcefully to the modern reader than that of any other great German writer of his time. His plays range from *The Golden Jug*, an hilarious comedy in which a crooked village judge tries a case in which he is the real culprit, via *Penthesilea*, a tragi-comic mythological spoof, to *Prince Friedrich von Homburg*, in which Prussia's Great Elector appears as Justice and Mercy personified. In contrast to the emotional tone of the plays, Kleist's short stories are narrated with detached objectivity. Often set in exotic locations, they characteristically feature dramatic twists of plot, with scenes of lyrical intensity alternating with episodes of savage brutality.

the 1953 ratification of the Oder-Neisse border between Poland and the GDR, though neither the said demarcation nor the country that lies beyond it are particularly popular around these parts. When Polish citizens received the right to visit Germany without visas in the spring of 1991, supporters of the far right in Frankfurt demonstrated and attacked Polish-registered cars. More or less opposite the Friedensglocke on Bachstr. 11 is the Bezirksmuseum Viadrina (Wed–Fri & Sun 10am–5pm; DM1) in a grandiose Prussian *Junker* house.

On the right bank of the Oder is the former German suburb of Damm, now Polish SLUBICE. A footbridge leads across the Oder into Poland, though British subjects need a Polish **visa** to cross the border.

Practicalities

Frankfurt's **tourist office** is at Karl-Marx-Str. 8a (☎325216), and can offer only a few **private rooms** as this is not really a tourist town. The swankiest local **hotel** is the *Stadt Frankfurt*, Karl-Marx-Str. 192 (☎3890)with singles from DM85 and doubles from DM120. A better bet is the *Jugendtourist Hotel* Wilhelm-Pieck-Str. 1 (☎3810) at about DM35 per person. The town also has a **youth hostel** at Platz der Republik (☎381337).

The Spreewald

The **Spreewald**, a unique forest area bisected by the River Spree, 100km southeast of Berlin, should be one of the most interesting excursions from the city, though the sheer volume of visitors tends to give the place the atmosphere of an inland Blackpool. It falls into two parts: the **Unterspreewald** and **Oberspreewald**, north and south of the town of Lübben respectively. Although the Unterspreewald, east of the town of **Schlepzig**, is pleasant enough, the real action is in the Oberspreewald, a 500-square-kilometre area of deciduous woodland. The woods, which are broken up in places by land given over to market gardening, are watered by 300 channels (fed by the River Spree) known as *Fliesse*, and criss-crossed by man-made canals, creating an environment that Theodor Fontane described as "Venice as it might have been 1500 years ago". Most of the local populace are Slavic **Sorbs** (see overleaf) with their own language and traditions, and Sorbish street signs add more than a hint of exotica to an already unusual region. Unfortunately, the Spreewald was discovered a long time ago and tourists flock here in unbelievable numbers during the summer, overrunning the local *Gaststätten* and block-booking seats on the punts that ferry visitors around the area (motorised craft are banned). Nevertheless, the Spreewald remains an eye-opener for the visitor, and most western tourists are surprised to find that, scenically at least, the area actually lives up to tourist-brochure hyperbole. Walking is just as good a way of getting around as taking a punt, but it's essential to get hold of the local *Wanderkarte*, as it's all-too-easy to get lost or disorientated.

Lübben (Lubin)

LÜBBEN (easily reached by rail from Berlin) is the first major town in the Spreewald and from its harbour it's possible to take punt trips into both the Unter- and Oberspreewald. The town has a **Schloss** and a sixteenth-century church, the **Paul-Gerhardt-Kirche** (named after the religious poet buried there), but has the air of never having quite recovered from wartime damage. At the harbour the *Strandcafé*, Heinrich-Heine-Strasse (☎2590), has a small **tourist office** that can fill you in on excursion options. **Accommodation** possibilities in Lübben include the *Spreeblick*, Gübbener Str. 53 (☎3278), and *Am Hain*, Bahnhofstr. 35 (☎3140). The local **youth hostel** is at Zum Wendenfürsten (☎2669).

Lübbenau (Lubnjow)

Perhaps a better starting point for exploring the Oberspreewald is **LÜBBENAU**, a large town of 24,000 inhabitants, a 15km train journey southeast of Lübben. It gets incredibly crowded, though, giving the impression that all of the one million visitors who come here each year are passing through at once. Lübbenau's origins are also Slavonic and it was defended by a wooden wall, later destroyed by the Germans who built a castle here. The original castle was in turn replaced by the over-the-top Neoclassical **Schloss** visible today, which was built just after the Napoleonic Wars by Count zu Lynar, who then exercised feudal control over the town. The Lynar family owned much of the area until 1945, when their castle was turned into a school. In a Baroque building near the Schloss is the **Spreewaldmuseum** (May–Oct Tues–Sun 9am–5pm), which details the history of the town and area.

Punt trips run from the **Hafen der Freundschaft**, Lübbenau's harbour. The harbour here also has an **information office**, mainly dealing with details about boat trips (☎2225). Boatmen catering to the ever-growing number of tourists offer punt trips through the network of canals and channels. It's best to be there as early as possible (around 8–8.30am) as there are bound to be very heavy crowds during the tourist season. The range of trips on offer last anywhere between two and ten hours, depending on how much of the area you want to see. For **eating and drinking**, try the *Zum grünen Strand der Spree*, a reasonable though often packed *Gaststätte* (open until 7pm). A recommended local **pension** is the *Deutsches Haus*, Ehm-Welk-Str. 38–39 (☎2435).

Lehde (Ledy)

One way to escape the crowds is to walk to the nearby village of **LEHDE**, which will take about thirty minutes. Until 1931 the village could only be reached by punt or by crossing the ice of the frozen channels in winter. Lehde's **Freilandsmuseum** is packed with information about the area's history and customs. Farmhouses typical of the region have been brought here from other parts of the Spreewald and light is thrown on local construction techniques: the foundations of these half-timbered houses

---

THE SORBS

A West Slav tribe whose language resembles both Czech and Slovak, **the Sorbs** have lived throughout their history in the province known as **Lusatia** (*Lausitz*), which still maintains a tenuous position on maps of Germany. In the fifteenth century it was divided into Upper Lusatia (*Oberlausitz*) and Lower Lusatia (*Niederlausitz*): the former is now in Saxony (see Bautzen p.927); the latter (of which the Spreewald forms the northern part is in Brandenburg. Although the Germans have been dominant in Lusatia since the tenth century and currently outnumber the Sorbs by more than five to one, as many as a hundred thousand Sorbs still live throughout the region. There were nationalist stirrings in the nineteenth century, leading in 1912 to the formation of the *Domowina* (a word equivalent to the German *Heimat* or "homeland", a cultural and political organisation which is still the main vehicle for Sorbist aspirations.

They were particularly persecuted under the Nazis when Göring proposed expelling them to turn the Spreewald into a gigantic game hunting park stocked with elk and bison. Things improved under the GDR, when the Sorbs were allowed a degree of cultural autonomy, with their language given equal status with German. However, they were mercilessly exploited for tourist purposes: their vivid costumes and popular **festivals** added a much-needed dash of colour to that grey puritan land. The latter include Carnival, horseback Easter processions and, on 30 April, the *Hexenbrennen*, a variant of the Witches' *Walpurgisnacht* found in the Harz.

were built on large stones which in turn rested on timber poles driven deep into the marshy ground. Inside, examples of furniture (look out for the large beds designed to accommodate a whole family) and household objects offer an impression of how the Sorbish populace lived during the last century and displays detail their unique farming methods.

For **eating and drinking** in Lehde, try the *Café Venedig* or the *Zum Frohlichen Hecht* (☎2782) – the latter is also a **pension** although like everywhere around here it gets booked out quickly in summer.

Cottbus (Chośebuz)

At the southern end of the Spreewald stands **COTTBUS**, formerly the capital of one of the three *Bezirke* into which Brandeburg was divided in GDR days. It has a long industrial tradition, the twin pillars of the local economy being the textile industry, established by Dutch settlers in the Middle Ages and later developed by Huguenot refugees, and coalmining, which was the chief cause of the city's rapid growth last century. Because of this pedigree, Cottbus was seen by the Communists as something of a role model for the rest of the country. That's not a view likely to be held by anyone beholding its crumbling old tenements and Stalinist-style blocks of flats today, though a few monuments in the Altstadt and the park-lined banks of the Spree are sufficiently diverting to justify a short visit.

Around town

The Hauptbahnhof is situated well to the southwest of the centre in a particularly unsalubrious neighbourhood, so it's well worth taking tram #1 to Stadtpromenade, then walking east along Marktstrasse. Heart of the town is the **Altmarkt**, which is lined with an impressive series of Baroque mansions, dating from immediately after one of the many disastrous fires which have ravaged the town. Just north of the square is the Gothic **Klosterkirche** (or **Wendische Kirche**), whose tower is, most unusually, placed at the east end. Formerly part of a Franciscan monastery, its alternative name comes from the fact that it has latterly been used for services in Sorb. A later and more visually impressive Gothic church, the **Oberkirche**, stands northeast of the Altmarkt. Its high altar, fashioned in marble, wood, alabaster and sandstone, is a hymn of late Renaissance extravagance, effectively offset by the simplicity of the simple whitewashed architecture.

Between here and the Spree is the **Münzturm**, where the town's first coins were minted. It's one of three towers surviving from the old fortifications: the others are the **Lindenpforte**, through which the path from the Stadtpromenade to the Altstadt leads, and the **Spremberger Turm**, at the far end of Spremberger Strasse, which goes south from the Altmarkt. En route to the latter, you pass close by the **Schlosskirche**, the Baroque church of the Huguenot community. West of here, on Schillerplatz outside the confines of the Altstadt, is the impressively large **Stadttheater**, which claims to be the only authentically Jugendstil theatre in the country.

Practicalities

The **tourist office** is at Altmarkt 29 (Mon–Fri 9am–noon & 2–5pm; ☎24254). As an overnight stop, Cottbus is less enticing than the smaller towns of the Spreewald, particularly as most of the **hotels** are currently able to charge fancy rates. If you want to stay, try *Schwan*, Bahnhofstr. 57 (☎22334), or *Zur Sonne*, Taubenstr. 8 (☎22500), or ask at the tourist office for a private room. There's also a **youth hostel**, occupying an old half-timbered house at Klosterplatz 2 (☎22558). Choice for **eating** and **drinking** is better than you might expect. Try *Zur Postkuche*, Schlossplatz 1, or *Am Stadttor* on Stadtpromenade for a full meal. For *Kaffee und Kuchen*, there's the *Café am Altmarkt*, Altmarkt 10, while *Lipezk* on Stadtpromenade is a Russian-style tea-house, complete with samovar. Underneath the last-named is a disco; other **nightlife** possibilities include the *Jugendclub Töpfertrum* opposite the Klosterkirche, which has folk, jazz and Latin American evenings, and the *Clou Nachtbar*, Oberkirchplatz 10, a bar with a dance floor.

travel details

From Berlin-Hauptbahnhof to Dessau (6 daily; 2hr 15min); Dresden (1; 2hr 30min).

From Berlin-Lichtenberg to Lübbenau (Spreewald; 5 daily; 1hr 10min); Leipzig (10 daily; 2hr 20min); Cottbus (5 daily; 1hr 45min); Lutherstadt Wittenberg (1; 1hr 35min).

From Berlin-Zoologischer Garten to Brandenburg (frequent; 1hr 30min); Potsdam (frequent; 50min); Hamburg (8 daily 3hr 30min); Hannover (12 daily; 4hr 25min); Munich (2 daily; 7hr 20min).

CHAPTER TEN

SAXONY-ANHALT

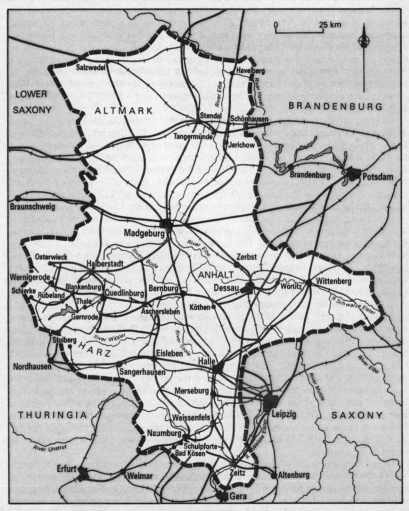

T here was much talk about the re-instatement of the five "historic" Länder when the fall of Communism entailed the creation of eastern states which would slot into Germany's highly successful federal framework. In the case of **Saxony-Anhalt** (*Sachsen-Anhalt*), the description was a complete misnomer, as the province had first come into existence, courtesy of the Soviet military authorities, in 1947. Five years later it was abolished in line with the GDR's policy of concentrating power in the centre, with regional government reduced to small, impotent units. Despite this unsatisfactory pedigree, there was genuine popular demand that this somewhat artificial Land should be revived and it has duly taken its place on the new political map of the country.

The **"Saxony"** in the Land's title is a throwback to the old Prussian province of that name. It came into existence after the 1815 Congress of Vienna, which forced the Kingdom of Saxony to cede about half of its territories as a punishment for having supported Napoleon; these were then united with a number of secularised bishoprics Prussia had acquired after the Thirty Years' War. **Anhalt** was a duchy founded by descendants of Albert the Bear, the first Margrave of Brandenburg. For centuries it was splintered into a number of petty principalities; these finally united in 1863, and the province served as a constituent state of Germany up to the Second World War. However, it was clearly too small to be a viable modern unit – hence the Soviet decision to couple it to a new partner.

Given its diverse make-up, it's hardly surprising that Saxony-Anhalt is the most varied of the new German Länder. The northernmost tract is the **Altmark**, the first piece of Slav territory taken over by the Germans in the great drive to the east they launched in the early medieval period. It's a varied landscape, with stretches of heath and sandy marshes in addition to farmland. The **River Elbe** defines its eastern border; the same river washes the **Börde**, the plain to the south. This has some of Germany's richest and most productive soils, though the otherwise monotonous agricultural countryside is punctuated by **Magdeburg**, one of only two major cities in the Land and its new capital.

Continuing southwards, the **Harz**, Germany's northernmost mountain chain, is approached via gentle foothills. Thickly covered with forests, the Harz proper is by far the best-known part of the Land. The home of the *Walpurgisnacht* legend, it's archetypally German in character, containing some outstanding scenery plus a clutch of well-preserved old towns. Beyond here, eastern Germany's largest area of heavy industry can be found in and around **Halle**, the Land's largest city, and **Dessau**, the historical capital of Anhalt. Further up the valley of the **Saale**, at the southern end of the province, the scenery becomes more rustic, the towns smaller.

Because the early history of the territories which make up Saxony-Anhalt is closely associated with missionary activity towards heathen Slavs, the Land is unusually rich in medieval cathedrals and monasteries. The archbishops' Dom in Magdeburg ranks among the finest in all of Germany, yet its counterparts (all now demoted to parish churches) in **Halberstadt**, **Havelberg**, **Merseburg** and especially **Naumburg** are worthy rivals. For all the impact these had on the history of Germany, their influence pales beside that of **Wittenberg**, the little university town from where Martin Luther launched and directed the Protestant Reformation which changed the whole course of European history. Two other modest-sized places, **Quedlinburg** and **Tangermünde**, had short spells as the capital of Germany; each retains a striking medieval appearance, and respectively has some of the best half-timbered and brick architecure to be found in the country.

Travel throughout the region presents few problems; the transport network itself is one of the main draws of the Harz, which retains the most comprehensive network of **narrow-gauge steam railways** to be found anywhere in Europe. The popularity of this with foreigners in GDR days is one reason the tourist facilities are so much better here than anywhere else in the Land – elsewhere, the provision of private rooms often plugs what would otherwise be a desperate shortage of beds for short-stay visitors. Because of the slight dominance of rural over urban society, the Land is **politically** somewhat to the right, though the CDU failed to gain an outright majority in the 1990 elections.

THE ELBE-HAVEL REGION

The highlights of northern Saxony-Anhalt are thinly spread. In the Börde, **Magdeburg** is the only destination of note; as well as its Dom, it boasts a range of historical and technical monuments, and is one of the best places in which to observe the unfolding of the myriad changes which were set in motion by the *Wende* of 1989. The Altmark's chief town, **Stendal**, has reclaimed its role as a bustling market centre, though its monuments are rather overshadowed by those of nearby **Tangermünde**, which, but for a twist of fate, might have developed into a great metropolis. East of the Altmark, lies a thin strip of land around the confluence of the Elbe and the Havel that was controversially allocated to Saxony-Anhalt rather than Brandenburg; this includes the outstanding yet little-known town of **Havelberg**.

Magdeburg

Thanks to its pivotal position on the key communications network between Berlin and Hannover, **MAGDEBURG** received strong West German backing in its acrimonious tussle with Halle for the status of capital of Saxony-Anhalt just before national unification. This support proved crucial in the city's ultimately successful campaign; had Magdeburg lost out, it would have been one more reverse in what had been a long run of bad luck. Its first calamity came in the Thirty Years' War: during the Catholic siege and occupation of 1631, over two-thirds of the population perished, and the vast majority of the city was burnt to the ground. A spectacular recovery was made after the Peace of Westphalia, but the grandiose Baroque centre which then emerged suffered a similar fate to its medieval predecessor in the Anglo-American air raids of 1945.

Under Communism, Magdeburg had the reputation of being the greyest of grey cities. The surviving historic monuments in the centre – with the partial exception of the imperious Dom, the largest church in eastern Germany – were engulfed in a rash of new buildings in the brutalistic style of architecture favoured by the Stalinist regime; the antiquated infrastructure of heavy industry was retained with no thought for the environment or for the future. While many unsalubrious aspects inevitably remain, the city, buoyed by its new role as a regional capital, has undergone an astonishingly swift transformation, developing a vibrant get-up-and-go atmosphere which is wholly at odds with its recent past.

Arrival and practicalities

The **Hauptbahnhof** is situated just a few minutes' walk west of the city centre. There are also several suburban stations on the small S-Bahn network which can be useful if you're staying far out or intending to visit some of the outlying sights. The **tourist office** (Mon, Tues, Thurs & Fri 9am–6pm, Wed 10am–6pm, Sat 9am–noon; ☎35352) is at Alter Markt 9. Unless you've booked in advance, finding accommodation can be a major headache, particularly during the week, when the influx of business people outstrips the number of available beds. This is despite the opening up of a large number of **private rooms**, costing in the range of DM25–35, which can be booked via the tourist office. Even if there are none vacant when you call, it's worth trying again just before closing time, when those as yet unclaimed (and there generally are a few) are then re-let. Of the **hotels**, which are all centrally sited, the only ones with afford-able rates are *Grüner Baum*, Wilhelm-Pieck-Allee 38–40 (☎32166), at DM34 per person; *Haus des Handwerks*, Gareistr. 10 (☎51422), with singles DM42, doubles DM67; and *Jugendtouristenhotel*, Leiterstr. 10 (☎33881), with singles DM40, doubles DM72. The last

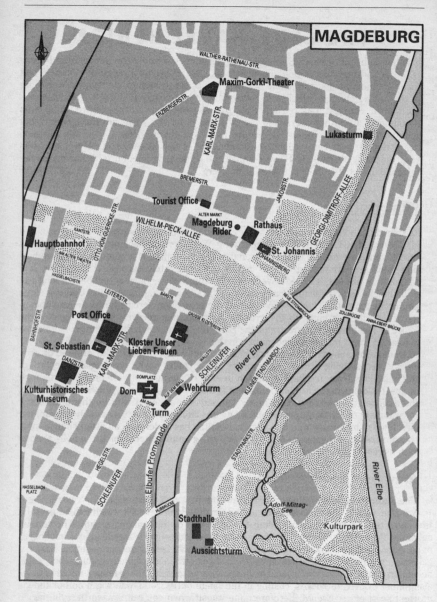

of these doubles as a **youth hostel**: with a IYHA card you get lodging in a triple-bedded room for DM21.50 if you're under 27, DM25.50 if older; whether or not you have to share depends on demand. There's a **campsite** (☎20144) on the banks of the Barleber See at the extreme northern end of the city; take the S-Bahn to the station of the same name.

The Dom

Through all Magdeburg's vicissitudes, the **Dom** (daily 10am–noon & 2–4/5pm) has somehow managed to survive with but little damage to its fabric. The present building is the immediate successor to the monastic foundation which Emperor Otto the Great raised in 962 to the seat of a prince-archbishop charged with the main responsibility for spreading Christianity – and, as a spin-off, Germany's frontiers – deep into Slav territory to the east. Appropriately enough, therefore, it's one of the country's most impressive cathedrals, its lofty Gothic architecture complemented by a truly dazzling array of sculpture. There's also the bonus of a superbly landscaped setting above the Elbe, the only sour note being the insidious blocks of Stalinist-style flats built on one side of the vast Domplatz, which clash horribly with the dignified Baroque palaces opposite, recently refurbished to house the Land parliament and ministries.

The building

Construction of the Dom began in the early thirteenth century with the building of the ambulatory and its chapels in a pure if primitive Gothic style still bearing the marks of the Romanesque sense of mass. Soon after, the masons who had built the Swabian monastery of Maulbronn took over the construction of the main part of the chancel, introducing more refined and progressive architectural forms. They in turn were succeeded by architects who built the transepts and nave in the High Gothic manner of the great French cathedrals, doubling the length of the bays to create an impression of space, and designing large traceried windows which flood the building with light.

With the construction of the northern **porch** (or "Paradise") in the mid-fourteenth century, the body of the Dom was substantially complete. However, work on the facade, whose distinctive **towers**, with their spire-crowned octagonal turrets, are such a feature of the city's skyline, wasn't concluded until 1520. Soon after, the prince-archbishop was ousted in favour of a Protestant bishop, as Magdeburg became one of the stoutest promoters of the Reformation.

The sculptures

Were it a museum of sculpture, the Magdeburg Dom, with its range of masterpieces from Romanesque to modern, would be regarded as the best in Germany. The chapels of the ambulatory, whose capitals are inventively carved with depictions of fabulous beasts, luxuriant foliage and cortorted human heads, contain a number of notable **tombs**. Oldest of these are the bronze monuments to two twelfth-century archbishops. There's also a touching stone memorial to a fourteenth-century successor to these, Otto von Hessen, the great-grandson of Saint Elisabeth, and a highly elaborate Flamboyant Gothic cenotaph belatedly honouring Empress Edith, wife of Otto the Great.

The last-named contrasts with the plain, box-like tomb of the Emperor himself, which sits in solemn grandeur in the middle of the choir. Also surviving from his original cathedral are the beautiful coloured **marble columns** from Ravenna, which were re-used to support the statues of saints placed high up between the piers of the tribune gallery. These figures, together with the unique little scenes in the niches below, belong to the period in the mid-thirteenth century when the Magdeburg workshop, along with its counterparts in Bamberg and Naumburg, was producing some of the greatest sculpture of the Middle Ages. The most arresting figure made here is the **statue of Saint George**, placed on a pedestal on the south side of the choir; although now truncated, the masterly originality of what was probably the first representation of a negro in Western art is still very apparent. Only marginally less fine are the companion figure of Saint Catherine, the Dom's other patron, and the Annunciation group at the chancel entrance. They rather overshadow the fourteenth-century **choir stalls**, whose carvings mix serious and frivolous subjects in equal measure, and the highly decorative fifteenth-century **rood screen**, fine though these are in their own right.

A more substantial production of the earlier Magdeburg sculptors is the **portal** of the Paradise, which features superbly dramatic portrayals of the Wise and Foolish Virgins, and the enlightened Church and the blindfolded Synagogue, along with a tympanum of the Death of the Virgin. Just indoors, in the northern transept, is a masterpiece of twentieth-century sculpture, the haunting *Monument to the Victims of World War I* by **Ernst Barlach**. It forms a surprisingly effective counterfoil to the idealised beauty of the late thirteenth-century *Madonna and Child* in the other transept, which was once believed to have miracle-working powers.

The rest of the interior

The most intriguing feature is the freestanding **sixteen-sided chapel** alongside the nave, whose original function is an enigma. It contains thirteenth-century statues of a seated royal couple, leading to speculation that it's another memorial to Otto the Great and Edith, though it's more likely to be an allegorical representation of Christ as ruler of the world, with the Church as his bride. Finally, under the tower is the **memorial chapel to Archbishop Ernst**, whose decision to honour himself in such a way has meant that the Dom's main entrance has been blocked up for the past five centuries, an act of megalomania partially mitigated by the sheer magnificence of the tomb, cast by the great bronze founder of Renaissance Nürnberg, Peter Vischer the Elder.

The rest of the city

While everything else in Magdeburg stands in the shadow of the Dom, there are a variety of other – somewhat scattered – sights well worth seeking out.

The Kulturhistorisches Museum

A couple of minutes' walk west of the Dom, at Otto-von-Guericke-Str. 68–73, is the **Kulturhistorisches Museum** (Tues–Sun 10am–6pm; DM1). The star exhibit here, housed right by the entrance, is the original of the **Magdeburg Rider** (*Magdeburger Reiter*), a secular product of the mid-thirteenth-century Dom workshop, which disputes with its Bamberg counterpart the right to be regarded as the first equestrian statue since Classical antiquity. This time, it's quite likely that the mounted figure is an idealised portrait of Otto the Great, accompanied by two maidens. The museum's other displays are pretty eclectic, ranging from an important archaeology section via local history, arts and crafts, minerals and stuffed animals to an array of paintings, including works by Cranach and Friedrich, which is sadly depleted as a result of losses in World War II. There's also a special display on the inventions of **Otto von Guericke**, inventor of the "Magdeburg hemispheres" that first demonstrated the power of the vacuum in the seventeenth century.

St Sebastian and the Kloster Unser Lieben Frauen

Immediately north of the museum is the former monastic church of **St Sebastian**, itself a cathedral nowadays (though never referred to as such), being the seat of the local Catholic bishop. Outwardly unprepossessing, it has a light late Gothic interior, with slender, twisting columns which put you in mind of English Tudor architecture.

Magdeburg's oldest surviving building, the **Kloster Unser Lieben Frauen** (Tues–Sun 10am–6pm; DM2), lies just beyond the northern end of Domplatz. Badly damaged during the war, this severe-looking former Premonstratensian monastery has been patiently restored to serve as a museum and cultural centre. The **church**, now the city's main concert hall, has a highly unusual interior, the original Romanesque forms having been clad with Gothic overlay and vaulting at around the same time as work began on the Dom. However, the most impressive part of the monastery is the **cloister**, and in particular its picturesque well chapel, nicknamed the *Tonsur*. Housed in the conventual buildings is a nationally owned collection of **small sculptures**, divided into a medieval section of mostly anonymous devotional works and a more extensive gallery of modern pieces, with examples of Rodin, Barlach and Lehmbruck, plus (for the time being, at least) examples of the socialist realism fostered by the GDR state. Good temporary exhibitions on a variety of artistic themes are also featured.

The Alter Markt

Ten minutes' walk to the north, the **Alter Markt** has regained since the fall of Communism its former role as the hub of day-to-day trading activity, with small-time hawkers using it and the streets nearby as a daily showcase for their wares. Sadly, the square itself is a shadow of its former self, with only the Baroque **Rathaus** restored to its prewar state. Fragments from burnt-out buildings have been stuck up on the side wall of the tourist office as a reminder of past splendours, while a bronze replica of the Magdeburg Rider has been set up under the Baroque canopy which once housed the original. There are also memorials to von Guericke and Till Eulenspiegel, while the Gothic hall church of **St Johannis** rears up behind. Burnt out in 1945, the shell was made into a war memorial, though the post-unification fever for overturning decisions made in the Communist epoch means that it's likely to be rebuilt. In the meantime, you can climb the southern **tower** (Tues–Sun 10am–6pm; DM1) for a view over the city.

Along the River Elbe

From 1680, when it was incorporated into Brandenburg-Prussia, until just before World War I, Magdeburg was one of the most strongly fortified cities in Germany. Fragments of the Prussian-built **Festungsanlagen** can be seen all along the banks of the Elbe; the most impressive bits are those incorporating parts of the medieval city walls, which include the two towers immediately to the rear of the Dom and the section north of St Johannis. The latter terminates at the **Lukasturm** (Tues–Sun 10am–6pm; DM1), a brick-built fifteenth-century tower now housing a collection of weapons, a restaurant and exhibition space for changing displays of contemporary art.

For a better perspective on these, it's well worth crossing over to the **Kulturpark Rotehorn**, a large park laid out in the 1920s between two branches of the Elbe, utilising a smaller central arm as a boating area. Overlooking the main course of the Elbe towards the southern end of the park, across from the striking **Pferdetor** (a row of columns topped by stylised sculptures of horses), is the Bauhaus-influenced **Aussichtsturm** (Tues–Sun 10am–6pm; DM1), which you can ascend by lift for a fine panoramic view. Moored in the river just outside is the **SS Württemberg** (Wed–Sun 10am–7pm; DM1.50), a paddle-steamer built in the 1900s, which has been preserved as a reminder of the sort of vessels used at the time Elbe shipping was at its peak; it also houses a decent restaurant. Immediately north is the city's most remarkable industrial monument, the **Hubbrücke**. This was built in the 1840s as a railway bridge on the line to Potsdam and was equipped with a turning central mechanism to allow ships to pass through; some fifty years later, it was converted into a lift bridge, before being transformed to its present appearance in the 1930s.

Eating, drinking and nightlife

Even if Magdeburg still lags well behind comparable western German cities in the gastronomic field, it's relatively well off by ex-GDR standards. It's also among the few eastern cities with much of a reputation left for beer-making – the *Diamant-Brauerei*, housed in splendid castellated mock-Gothic premises just north of the Neustadt S-Bahn station, was one of the few breweries allowed to maintain a diverse product line.

Restaurants

Bötelstube, Alter Markt 11. Basic but serviceable *Gaststätte* which offers the cheapest full meals available in the city centre.

Gastmahl des Meeres, Jacobstr. 20. Speciality fish restaurant.

Pliska, Breiter Weg 15. Offers the unfamiliar delights of Bulgarian cuisine.

Ratskeller, Alter Markt 13. Historic restaurant under the Rathaus, with similar standards and prices to its western counterparts.

Ristorante Roma, Erich-Weinert-Str. 27. Excellent Italian *trattoria* which has rapidly made a name for itself.

Savarin, Breiter Weg 226. At the time of writing, the best and most reliable eatery in town.

Stadt Prag, Breiter Weg 20. Large, old-fashioned restaurant and café with more than a hint of the ambience of *Mitteleuropa*. The food, however, seems predominantly German rather than Czech.

Weinkeller Buttergasse, Alter Markt 9. Classy wine bar-cum-restaurant in medieval cellars. Tues–Sat 8pm–3am.

Wildbretstübl, Breiter Weg 113. Theoretically the specialist in game dishes, though these are not always available. Also features live music.

Cafés

Café am Dom, Breiter Weg 214. Trendy café-bar and popular rendezvous point.

Café Lilliput, Breiter Weg 180. Small café-bar in one of the city's few remaining Baroque mansions.

Teestube Aserbaidjhan, Breiter Weg 18. As the name implies, this new venture is primarily a specialist in teas served from a samovar, but does Central Asian-style meals as well.

Nightlife

As yet, Magdeburg hasn't exactly developed a swinging nightlife, but if you're into **discos**, try the *Jugendklub Lokschuppen* in the Hauptbahnhof, or the aforementioned *Jugendtouristenhotel*, Leisterstr. 10. The main **theatre**, with a varied programme of drama, opera, operetta and ballet, is the *Maxim-Gorki-Theater* on Universitätsplatz: other venues include the cabaret *Kugelblitze* at Breiter Weg 200. Main **concert** venue is the Kloster Unser Lieben Frauen. It's named in honour of the most prolific composer of all time, the Magdeburg-born **Georg Philipp Telemann**, whose works are regularly featured. In Germany he's regarded as the near equal of his contemporaries Bach and Handel, though he's rather an underrated figure elsewhere, in spite of the genuine depth present in his finest music– and his rare talent for humorous effects.

Stendal

STENDAL, which lies 60km north of Magdeburg, is an important railway junction on the main route to the Baltic with the second-string line between Berlin and Hannover. It has maintained its historic role as the main town of the Altmark, and, despite its modest size, is positively cosmopolitan in comparison with the rest of this rural backwater. Curiously enough, its name has been made famous by a nineteenth-century Frenchman who had absolutely no connection with the place: Henri Beyle chose the Gallicised form of "Stendhal" as the pseudonym under which he published such seminal novels as *Scarlet and Black* and *The Charterhouse of Parma*. This was intended as a mark of his respect for the town's most famous son, Johann Joachim Winckelmann, whose researches mark the beginnings of modern approaches to archaeology and art history.

The southern Altstadt

The Hauptbahnhof is situated just beyond the southern edge of the Altstadt, which comprises a surprisingly large proportion of the present-day town. From here, follow Bahnhofstrasse in a northeasterly direction, and you come to the first of two surviving gateways, the **Tangermünder Tor**. Its lower storey of stone dates back to the town's thirteenth-century origins; the upper part, with its characteristically fancy brickwork, is from a hundred years later. Just across the street, occupying the former Katharinenkloster, is the **Altmärkisches Museum** (Tues–Fri 10am–noon & 2–5pm, Sat & Sun 1–5pm; DM3), which documents the history of Stendal and the Altmark region, and includes a collection of medieval religious art. The Gothic monastery buildings themselves are also atmospheric.

The Stiftskirche St Nikolaus

Set, in the manner of many an English cathedral, in splendid isolation in the spacious green to the west of here is the **Stiftskirche St Nikolaus**, popularly if inaccurately known as the **Dom** (May–Sept daily 10am–noon & 3–5pm; Oct–April Mon–Fri 1–2pm only). It's the largest of the town's medieval churches – which display a remarkable degree of similarity with one another, reducing the favoured North German format of the brick hall church to the barest essentials, with fortress-like towers and a minimum of surface decoration to relieve the huge, austere walls. A rare touch of extravagance, however, was allowed in the north transept, with its elaborate gable and bricks patterned into a false rose window and six-sided stars.

Pride of the interior is what's arguably the most impressive set of **stained glass windows** in Germany – 23 in all, each dating from the fifty-year period in the middle of the fifteenth century when the church itself was erected. The twelve windows in the choir use sombre colours in a deliberate attempt to create a mystical atmosphere in the holiest part of the building; those in the nave and transepts, in contrast, sparkle like jewels. Of similar vintage are the **choir stalls**, whose misericords are vivid illustrations of the humour of the day. Also of special note are the **reliefs** of the life of Christ on the back of the rood screen, masterly Romanesque carvings retained from the church which previously stood on the spot.

The Markt

From the north side of the Dom, follow Am Dom to the east, then turn right into Hallstrasse, which eventually leads to the central **Markt**. Guarding the picturesquely gabled Renaissance **Rathaus** is a weather-worn statue of Roland, almost as big as its celebrated counterpart in Bremen. However, it's only a replica of the sixteenth-century original, which was destroyed by a hurricane in 1972. Rising up behind the Rathaus is the main parish church, the **Marienkirche** (May–Oct daily 10am–noon & 3–5pm), whose similarities with the Dom even extend to having Romanesque carvings adorning the Gothic rood screen. However, the main treasure is the painstakingly reconstructed sixteenth-century **astronomical clock**. It's set underneath the organ gallery, whose frieze of paintings of the life of Christ, along with part of the instrument itself, are from the same epoch.

The northern Altstadt

Breitestrasse leads north from here to the oldest quarter of town, which is dominated by the **Jacobikirche** (if shut, get the key from the parish house at the back of the close). This church has another magnificent array of stained glass in the chancel; this time some of the windows date back to the fourteenth century. At the end of Breitestrasse, Altes Dorf leads west to the symbol of the city, the **Uenglinger Tor** (May–Sept Sat & Sun 10am–noon & 2–4pm; DM2). Incredible as it seems, this lovingly-crafted masterpiece of fifteenth-century patterned brickwork was built for a purely defensive role; nowadays it provides something of an obstacle for traffic – as well as the best view of the town.

Just south of here, at Winckelmannstr. 36, the **Winckelmann Museum** (Tues–Sun 10am–noon & 1–5pm; DM3) has been set up in the half-timbered house where Johann

Joachim Winckelmann, connoisseur and art historian, the son of the local shoemaker, was born in 1717. The rooms are devoted to displays on the life and work of the man whose writings, based on exhaustive research during a twelve-year stay in Rome, have been highly influential. Not only did they set the study of archaeology and art history on a rigorous scientific footing and provide the most potent stimulus for the great flowering of German Classicism in Weimar, they have shaped the way all subsequent generations have viewed the art of the ancients, in particular the superiority accorded Hellenistic art over the Roman derivatives hitherto more highly prized.

Practicalities

Stendal's **tourist office** (Mon–Wed & Fri 8.30am–4pm, Thurs 9am–5pm; ☎216186) is opposite the Rathaus at Kornmarkt 8. At the time of writing, there was a decided shortage of accommodation. There's no hostel; the nearest **campsite** (☎2249) is 10km to the northeast in the hamlet of WISCHER; while the only **private rooms** are at *Linder*, just south of the Hauptbahnhof at Jonasstr. 31 (☎214930). Otherwise, there are two **hotels** on Bahnhofstrasse: *Bahnhofshotel* at no. 30 (☎213200) and *Stadt Stendal* at no. 15 (☎212404), each charging DM35 for singles, around DM50 for doubles. Slightly lower rates were available at *Schwarzer Adler*, Kornmarkt 5–7 (☎212265), but prices are likely to double when a major refit is completed – and the patronising and unscrupulous management make this a place to avoid. The **restaurant** here is more worthy of a recommendation, though the *Ratskeller*, in the vaulted former merchants' hall under the Rathaus, is of similar quality and no more expensive, with the advantage of a highly atmospheric location.

Tangermünde

Towns languishing in centuries-long decay are a common enough feature of the Mediterranean lands, but are a rarity in Germany. TANGERMÜNDE, which lies at the confluence of the rivers Tanger and Havel 10km southeast of Stendal, is an exception – and a truly spectacular exception at that. When Charles IV, King of Bohemia and the most astute and successful Holy Roman Emperor of the later medieval period, acquired the Margravate of Brandenburg in 1373, he chose this prosperous market town, a midway point on the trade routes between the Baltic and Central Europe, as the second-string royal residence to Prague. Tangermünde's planned development into a national capital received a setback with the emperor's death five years later, though it continued to prosper for another hundred years, whereupon its star rapidly waned. At the beginning of the present century, it became the Altmark's only industrial centre other than Stendal; the GDR regime's ideology kept it in a time-warp, its skyline presenting an endearing juxtaposition of magnificent but crumbling medieval brick buildings and outdated factories. It's a picture which may not last much longer – it will no doubt be spruced up in a bid to exploit its undoubted tourist potential, though isolation from the well-trodden routes should spare it from too many harmful side-effects.

The fortifications

Tangermünde's **Stadtmauer** is one of the most complete and impressive municipal defences to have survived in Germany. The north side, the first you see if you arrive in town by public transport, has been laid out as a park and is relatively unforbidding, save for the bleak cylindrical **Schrotturm** which guards the northwestern corner. Altogether more arresting is the **Neustädter Tor**, which must have made an immediate impression on visitors arriving in town from the west. Its elaborately patterned tower is a stylistic twin of the Uenglinger Tor in Stendal and was clearly the work of the same builders; in addition, there's a sturdy barbican, adorned with coats of arms.

The defences were particularly strong along the harbour side, in case of attack from the river; to see them to best advantage, it's well worth crossing over to the rustic pathway laid out on the opposite bank. Towards the far end of this section is another fine gateway, the **Elbtor**; the part-brick, part-timber extension suspended above its archway on the side facing the town was the home of the watchman. Because of the subsequent expansion of the town, the eastern side of the walls is partially obscured, though the oldest of the gateways, the **Hünendorfer Tor**, which is at the opposite end of the axial Lange Strasse from the Neustädter Tor, survives as a marker.

Charles IV's **Burg** was built overlooking the Elbe just outside the confines of the Stadtmauer. It was successively occupied by the Danes and the Imperialists during the Thirty Years' War, and was all but destroyed in 1640 during an ultimately successful siege by the Swedes. At the beginning of the present century, the ruins were made into a shady public park, to which there's free access at all times. In addition to the main gateway and two very picturesque towers, the **Kanzlei**, which formerly served as a festive hall, survives, albeit in desperate need of restoration.

Inside the walls

Set in its own close just to the east of the Hünendorfer Tor is the fourteenth-century **Stephanskirche**, whose mighty westwork looks far more like a fortress than any of the far more decorative towers of the fortification system. Most of the rest of the exterior is equally austere, though there are occasional deft touches, such as the patterned double doorway. The hall interior, with its graceful pillars, is altogether lighter in feel. After its conversion to Protestant worship, it gained a number of intriguing adornments, including a Baroque altar which has an unusual depiction of Christ in the guise of the Lion of Judaea. The early seventeenth-century **organ** is by one of the greatest ever masters of the craft, the Hamburg builder Hans Scherer, and is especially valuable for being his only instrument to have survived relatively intact.

Tangermünde's other set-piece is the **Rathaus** (April–Nov Tues–Sun 10am–noon & 2–5pm; Dec–March Wed–Sun 10am–noon & 2–4pm; DM1), built on the central Markt in the 1430s, the period when the town was at its commercial peak. Its fantastical eastern facade, bristling with pinnacles and gables, and pierced by ornate open and false rose windows, is one of the great pieces of secular Gothic architecture, proving that brick is just as malleable as stone. The vaulted basement is given over to a small museum of local history; you can also see the two upstairs halls, the *Festsaal* and the *Standesamt*, on request.

Close to the harbour, the streets are cobblestoned and still medieval in aspect. In the centre, on the other hand, are large numbers of **half-timbered houses** from the seventeenth and eighteenth centuries, some with elaborate doorways. The reason for this new building activity was that much of Tangermünde was destroyed by fire in 1617; a woman by name of Grete Minde was made the scapegoat and burned as a witch. Over 250 years later, she became the eponymous heroine of a novel by Theodor Fontane, who used the incident to write one of his many powerful indictments of the moral injustices suffered by women.

Practicalities

Tangermünde is linked to Stendal by a branch railway and by buses, which alternate at approximately two-hourly intervals throughout the day; both arrive and depart from the **Bahnhof**, which is a couple of blocks north of the Altstadt. As yet, there's no **tourist office** as such, but maps and leaflets are available from the *Stadtverwaltung*, opposite the Rathaus at Lange Str. 60 (☎2971). There are two **hotels**: *Utescher*, Lange Str. 5 (☎2401), charges DM20 per person, while *Schwarzer Adler*, Lange Str. 52 (☎3642), has singles for DM26, doubles DM44. Slightly lower rates are available in two **private houses**: *Schmidt*, Albrechtstr. 15 (☎2502), and *Käsche*, Magdeburger Str. 68 (☎3826).

For **eating**, try the aforementioned *Schwarzer Adler*, *Zur Post*, Lange Str. 4, or the *Schiffsgaststätte*, which occupies a ship moored outside the Burg.

Jerichow

JERICHOW, which lies just 8km southeast of Tangermünde, is strictly speaking outside the Altmark, the Elbe having formed the natural eastern border of the old province. Its Biblical-sounding name seems a fitting reflection of its role as an important missionary centre in the early Middle Ages, though in fact this is pure coincidence, being a slight corruption of the title of the Slav settlement which preceded it. At the northern end of the village is the huge **Klosterkirche** (guided tours April–June, Sept & Oct Mon–Fri at 2pm, Sat & Sun at 11am & 2pm; July & Aug daily at 11am & 2pm; DM2). It's the oldest significant building in the area, its typically plain brick architecture Romanesque in style with a few later Gothic touches like the twin towers. Highlight of the interior is the **crypt** underneath the choir, whose columns bear immaculately carved stone capitals. The separately-run **Klostermuseum** (April–Oct daily 10am–5pm; Nov–March Tues–Fri 10am–noon & 1–4pm; DM2) occupies the attractive monastic buildings grouped round the cloister. Important archaeological finds from the cloister garden are on view, along with documentation on the history of the monastery and the Christianisation of the Elbe-Havel region.

Havelberg

HAVELBERG, which lies just shy of the confluence of the Havel with the Elbe some 45km north of Jerichow, is another medieval gem as yet barely touched by overzealous restoration, or by the invasion of foreign visitors. Founded in 968 by Otto the Great as a missionary bishopric, in what was then heathen Slav territory, it proved impossible to defend and was abandoned for nearly a century and a half before being re-settled by Premonstratensian monks. The town subsequently became a fishing port, even managing to establish a monopoly on fish sales on the Hamburg–Berlin trading route. When it fell to Brandenburg-Prussia after the Thirty Years' War, it was developed into a major ship-building centre, constructing ocean-going vessels of such repute that Tsar Peter the Great of Russia came to do business in 1716. All of which seems light years away from its present neglected toy-town appearance.

The Dom

Dominating the town from its hillside location above the north bank of the Havel, the **Dom** is no more than a Protestant parish church nowadays, with a gaunt, fortress-like **westwork** whose interior Gothic vaulting and false arcades were superimposed on a Romanesque framework. The most imposing work of art in the Dom is the **choir screen**, which ranks among the masterpieces of monumental German sculpture. In the manner of a poor man's Bible, it bears statues of saints and twenty large reliefs illustrating the Passion of Christ, carved by a workshop familiar with both the "Soft Style" of Prague and the more realistic Netherlandish masters. Each mason clearly gave free reign to his own artistic personality, rather than following the medieval practice of subsuming his individuality into that of the lodge – the refined, spiritual approach of the most accomplished of the sculptors contrasts sharply with the boisterous and patently anti-Semitic approach of one of his colleagues, who favoured an expressionistic approach, with exaggerated mannerisms and facial contortions.

Adjoining the south side of the Dom is a complex of part-Romanesque, part-Gothic brick monastic buildings, which bear more than a passing resemblance to their counterparts in Jerichow. The upper storeys now contain the **Prignitz-Museum** (Wed–Sun 10am–noon & 2–5pm; DM2), which details the history of Havelberg and the vicinity from prehistoric times to the nineteenth century. Clustered around the Dom's close are a number of formerly dependent buildings such as the school, the deanery and the houses of the canons; these are now put to an imaginative variety of uses, ranging from the local police headquarters to a small clothing factory.

The rest of the town

At the foot of the Dom's hill is the **Annenkapelle**, a small octagonal Gothic brick chapel with a strikingly pointed roof. From here, the Steintorbrücke leads to the compact little **Altstadt**, which occupies an island in the Havel; an alternative approach is by the Dombrücke, directly below the Dom. Crooked old houses once occupied by fisherfolk and farmers line the banks of the river; even today, smallholding and market gardening are clearly in evidence. The main attraction of the Altstadt is its constantly changing range of watery panoramic views. However, it's well worth walking all round the tightly packed little streets: look out for the late fourteenth-century **Beguinenhaus**, whose portal has a lintel of *The Crucifixion* carved in a similar style to the Dom's choir screen. Towering above the rest of the island is the Gothic **Stadtkirche St Laurentius**, whose vivid ceiling frescos were recently discovered when the wooden vaulting which had concealed them for over a century was removed.

Practicalities

Havelberg is no longer on a railway line: trains from Magdeburg and Brandenburg, via SCHÖNHAUSEN, now terminate at SANDAU, the next town to the south, from where you can pick up a **bus**, some of which come from Stendal via Tangermünde; the best place to alight or embark is at the stop by the Annenkapelle. Also near here, at Am Camps 5, is the sole **hotel**, *Stadt Havelberg* (☎377). The **campsite** (May–Sept only; ☎489) is on the Spülinsel, the island immediately to the west of the Altstadt; in addition to the usual facilities, there are a number of bungalows for rent. Otherwise, there are now some two dozen **private houses** (including one houseboat) offering bed and breakfast lodgings. Bookings can be made at the **tourist office** (Tues 9am–noon & 1–6pm, Wed–Fri 9am–noon & 1–3pm, Sat 9am–noon; ☎224) on Marktplatz. Best **restaurants** are *Güldene Pfanne*, Lehmkule 2, and *Harmonie*, Hinter der Kirche 3. Sailing **boats** can be hired at the quay on Uferstrasse.

On the first weekend in September, Havelberg takes on a wholly different appearance with the arrival of over 100,000 visitors – most of whom end up camping or sleeping in their cars – for the *Pferdemarkt*, one of the biggest **festivals** in the former GDR. As its name suggests, it was originally a horse market, but now spawns a flea market in which anything and everything is bought and sold, a handicrafts bazaar, a giant funfair, sports events, dancing and beer tents.

THE HARZ REGION

The **Harz** mountains were formerly divided right through the middle by the notorious barbed wire frontier separating the two German states. Uniquely, comparisons between the two were, the border itself apart, almost entirely in the east's favour – it inherited the best of the scenery, several gorgeous unspoiled old towns and an extensive network of narrow-gauge steam railways. Until the 1970s, it was almost impossible for westerners to stay, though it was one of the main holiday areas for East Germans themselves, with a vast provision of trade union holiday homes. Restrictions were subsequently relaxed, because the growing number of train buffs wanting to visit was seen a useful source of hard currency; since the fall of the Berlin Wall, the Harz has become one of the most desirable areas in the east in which to travel, not least because the tourist facilities are better and more extensive than almost anywhere else.

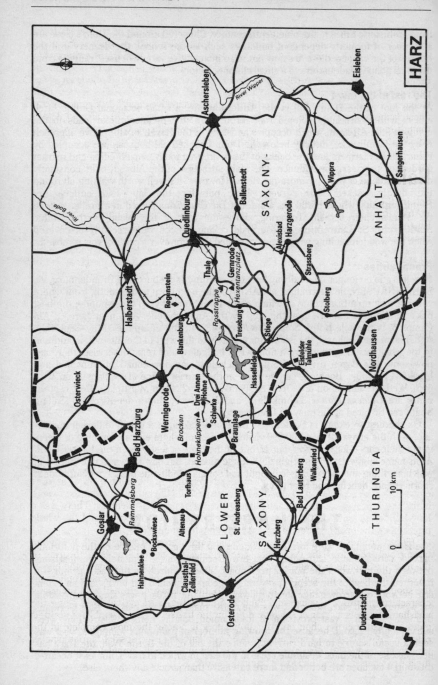

In the foothills of the Harz are the impressive old cathedral city of **Halberstadt** and the half-timbered towns of **Osterwieck** and **Quedlinburg**, both of which stand under comprehensive preservation orders. Similarly protected are **Blankenberg** and **Wernigerode** on the edge of the mountains, and **Stolberg** in the very heart of the range. Wernigerode is also the starting-point of the *Harzquerbahn*, the longest of the narrow-gauge railways; the other important line, the *Selketalbahn*, leaves from **Gernrode**, a village with one of Germany's most distinctive churches. Scenically, the finest landscapes are to be found in the **Bode valley**, particularly around **Thale**, though the legendary **Brocken**, rendezvous of the witches on *Walpurgisnacht*, is an equally irresistible destination.

Halberstadt

Set in the gentle foothills of the Harz, about 55km southwest of Magdeburg, **HALBERSTADT** is one of the oldest cities in eastern Germany, having been established as a bishopric by Charlemagne at the turn of the ninth century. It also used to be considered one of the most beautiful, but was devastated by an Anglo-American air-raid in the closing days of World War II, whereupon the Communists restored some of the showpieces but demolished the ruins of others which interfered with the creation of a new Stalinist-style commercial centre. Following unification, the city's appearance has begun to take on the beginnings of a pristine new aspect. This may herald a complete face-lift: since Halberstadt was chosen as one of five cities in the new Länder which will receive extensive government funds for restoration purposes, there's been excited talk of bulldozing much of the GDR legacy, replacing it with copies of old buildings lost in the war.

The Domplatz

Most of Halberstadt's prime attractions are grouped together on the spacious elliptical **Domplatz**. It suffered as much from bomb damage as the rest of the city, but monopolised the postwar restoration funds – though at least this was money well spent, as it still ranks among the country's most impressive squares.

The Dom

Halberstadt's **Dom** is the only one in Germany to conform to the pure Gothic forms established in the great French cathderals. The only exception to this is the facade: its lower storeys were built in the early thirteenth century by the same team of masons engaged on the archbishop's Dom in Magdeburg, while the current look of the towers is the result of a neo-Gothic remodelling at the very end of last century. There was a long lull before work on the main body of the building got underway, and the whole project took the better part of three hundred years to complete.

Placed proudly atop its rood screen is the Dom's greatest work of art, a wooden **triumphal cross** from the very end of the Romanesque period. The tragic bearing of the main participants is rivalled by the superb hierarchic characterisation of the highly stylised angels, and the supreme delicacy of the carvings of the busts of prophets on the supporting beam. Elsewhere in the church, the pillars are adorned with unusually characterful **statues** of saints and Biblical figures, the most eye-catching being the unashamedly sensual pair of Adam and Eve in the transept. The ensemble of **stained glass windows** in the choir and the ambulatory is among the most complete in the country; the earliest and finest are the five large lancets in the apsidal Marienkapelle, which date from 1330. Also of special note is that in the south ambulatory illustrating the life of Charlemagne, the Dom's original founder.

The Domschatz

One of the richest treasuries in Germany, the **Domschatz** (guided tours May–Oct Mon–Fri at 10am, 11.30am, 2pm & 3.30pm, Sat at 10am & 2pm, Sun at 11.30am & 2.30pm; Nov–April Mon–Sat at 10am & 2pm, Sun at 11.30am; donation expected) is housed in the cloister and its dependencies; entrance is via the doorway on the southeast side. The most valuable items are the textiles, and in particular three twelfth-century **tapestries** which are among the oldest in existence: one tells the story of the patriarch Abraham, another is dedicated to the Apostles, while the third shows Charlemagne with philosophers of Classical antiquity. From the same period are two outstanding pieces of **woodcarving** – *The Seated Madonna*, which was probably made in the same workshop as the great triumphal cross, and a cupboard painted with a depiction of *The Visitation*. The **treasury** items include the fourth-century *Consular Diptych* from Rome and the Byzantine *Weihbrotschale*, a magnificent gilded silver dish for consecrated bread which was brought here by a Crusader. Also included on the tour is a visit to the **Kapitelsaal**, the only surviving part of the Romanesque Dom.

The Kurien

The two long sides of Domplatz are lined with the **Kurien**, the houses of the members of the Dom chapter. Oldest of these is the **Dompropstei**, the elegant Renaissance mansion in the middle of the south side, which marries two very disparate styles in its Italianate arcaded lower storey and archetypally German half-timbered upperwork.

A similar architectural mix is found in the **Gleimhaus** (Mon & Wed–Sat 9am–noon & 1–4pm, Sun 9am–noon; DM1.50) at the far northeast corner of the square. It was the home of the eighteenth-century poet **Johann Wilhelm Ludwig Gleim**, who served as secretary to the Dom for 56 years, and has been preserved as one of the earliest – and best – literary museums in the country. Originally known for his lyric poetry in praise of love, wine and pastoral landscapes, Gleim later became, with his *Prussian War Songs of a Grenadier*, the great patriotic bard. A prolific letter-writer, he maintained contact with almost all the great and good in the German society of his day. To celebrate his range of contacts, he hit upon the idea of creating a **Freundschaftstempel** (Temple of Friendship), commissioning 150 portraits, which are hung densely throughout the first-floor rooms. While these are primarily of note for their documentary value, some are fine works of art in their own right, such as Graff's portrait of the balladeer Bürger, or Tischbein's of both himself and Gleim.

Next door, the stately Baroque **Domdechanei** is now a medical school. The slightly more modest palace next door houses the **Städtisches Museum** (Tues–Fri 9am–5pm, Sat & Sun 10am–5pm; DM2), which documents the history of the town, including material on the buildings lost in the bombings. However, the exhibits in the main building are overshadowed by those in the garden extension, the **Heineanum** (Tues–Fri 9am–4/5pm, Sat & Sun 10am–4pm; DM1.50). Greeting you on entry are two spectacular dinosaur skeletons, thought to be up to 220 million years old, found during excavations in the town. The rest of the collection is devoted to ornithology, with stuffed birds of the Harz region on the ground floor and an international display upstairs.

The Liebfrauenkirche

Forming a counterbalance to the Dom at the western end of Domplatz is the Romanesque **Liebfrauenkirche** (daily noon–3pm), formerly an Augustinian monastery. The main feature of the exterior is the roofline, with the two octagonal towers with pointed spires at the east end forming a contrast with the pair of "bishops' mitres" on the facade. Despite the dilapidated appearance of the interior, it's worth coming when it's open in order to see two more products of the school of sculptors active here in the early thirteenth century. Suspended on high is another **triumphal cross**, with a youthful-looking Christ in a strikingly classical pose. Even more impressive is the

choir screen, a rare work in stucco which still preserves its original polychromy; it features realistic portraits of Christ, the Virgin and the Apostles, plus decorative friezes carved with a gossamer sense of delicacy. Look out also for the Barbarakapelle, whose walls are covered with a cycle of late fourteenth-century frescos.

Set in an idiosyncratic position in front of the church, the Gothic **cloister** (Mon–Fri 9am–4pm; free) has been made into a small open-air museum, with decorative fragments from some of the many half-timbered houses destroyed in 1945. Adjoining it to the south is the **Petershof**, the massive former bishops' palace, entered via a handsome Renaissance portal.

The rest of the city centre

The **lower town** (*Unterstadt*) on the north side of Domplatz has a confusingly mazy layout, with some of the streets following quasi-circular routes. This quarter, which has most of the surviving **half-timbered houses**, fell into shocking disrepair in the 1970s, eventually taking on the appearance of a ghost town as the inhabitants were evacuated, to be rehoused in ugly new apartment blocks built nearby. Soon after the revolution, private citizens began buying up the properties, and some have already been turned into dream homes. A few showpieces had previously been restored by the GDR state; prominent among them being the mansion at Voigtei 48. Its courtyard wing, now the **Museum Bürgerliche Wohnkultur um 1900** (Museum of Middle-Class Living Conditions around 1900; Tues–Sat 9am–noon & 1–4pm, Sun 9am–noon; DM1), formerly the home of a wealthy burgher family, was bequeathed to the city as a time-capsule of life at the turn of the century.

Another half-timbered building well worth seeking out is the **Johanniskirche**, which lies in a peaceful garden just off Westendorf, the busy street immediately to the south of Domplatz. This rustic-looking church, built for a Protestant congregation at the end of the Thirty Years' War, has a disarmingly artless appearance from the outside, with its barn-like roof and stumpy detached belfry. Inside, however, it's surprisingly dapper, the coffered ceiling, galleries and pulpit all finely carved in late Renaissance style.

To the east of Domplatz lies the old market quarter. With the exception of the severe Gothic **Martinikirche**, what was left of its two old squares was bulldozed after the war in favour of a windswept piazza which had no apparent function until the recent return of open-air markets. The Martinikirche itself was the local rallying-point during the *Wende* of 1989 – an appropriate choice, as it had been built by the citizens as a deliberate statement of civic pride in opposition to the prince-bishops' Dom across the road. Indeed, the two towers, linked by a look-out gallery, were a key part of the city's defences, with the huge fifteenth-century **statue of Roland** underneath as a good luck charm. In the interior, which is open in summer for art exhibitions, look out for the elaborate Renaissance pulpit and the early fourteenth-century bronze **font**, resting on symbolic representations of the four rivers of Paradise and adorned with brightly-coloured scenes from the life of Jesus.

The Spiegelsberge

At the southern edge of the city, reached by tram #1 or #2, are the range of hills known as the **Spiegelsberge**. Following a visit to the famous gardens of Wörlitz, the poet Gleim had the idea of creating something similar in Halberstadt. The result was the construction here of a number of follies which, while falling short of their great model, nevertheless make for a pleasing diversion. Centrepiece of the complex is the **Jagdschloss**, now a restaurant (10am–6pm, closed Thurs). Ask to see inside the cellars, whose Renaissance doorway and great vat – the second largest in Germany – were brought here from the former country house of the defunct bishopric. Other attractions include a mausoleum, a grotto, a memorial column and the **Belvedere**, an observation tower (free access) built against a romanticised rocky backdrop, which commands a fine distant view of the city.

Practicalities

Halberstadt's **Hauptbahnhof** is situated well to the east of the centre; best take tram #1 or #2 (there's a booth for tickets by the stop) as the walk is boring. There are also a couple of suburban stations, including one for Spiegelsberge. The **bus station** is about midway between the Hauptbahnhof and the Markt; note that services to Goslar and the western parts of the Harz have been re-established, journeys which can only be made very circuitously by train.

Accommodation is still only at a fraction of the prewar level, with no hostel and just two (admittedly very enticing) **hotels**. *Haus St Florian*, Gerberstr. 10 (☎21033), which occupies a sixteenth-century half-timbered house just a couple of minutes' walk north of the Dom, has singles for DM58, doubles DM92. *Weisses Ross*, in a villa built according to the principles of the British Arts and Crafts movement, is ten minutes' walk south of the Markt at Johann-Sebastian-Bach-Str. 26 (☎21176) and charges upwards of DM40 per person. Otherwise, you should be able to find a **private room** via the very helpful **tourist office**, situated just north of Domplatz at Düsterngraben 3 (Mon–Fri 9am–1pm & 2–6pm, Sat 10am–1pm; ☎58316 or 24008). There's also a **campsite** (☎22037) on the right bank of the Halberstädter See at the northeastern edge of the city, and within easy walking distance of the Hauptbahnhof.

Despite the opening of a couple of cafés in the lower town, the **eating** and **drinking** scene in Halberstadt is fairly dire: other than the two hotels, it's impossible to get a meal after 7.30pm. Alternatives worth trying (all south of the centre) are the *Kulturhaus*, Spiegelstr. 21, *Am Kühlinger Tor*, Karl-Marx-Str. 24, and *Haus des Friedens*, corner of Thomas-Müntzer-Strasse and Otto-Grotewohl-Strasse.

Osterwieck

The entire town centre of **OSTERWIECK**, which lies between two arms of the River Ilm 25km northwest of Halberstadt, is under a protection order, and with good reason: it has some 400 historic **half-timbered houses**, many of them of outstanding quality. It's an archetypal example of a place stuck in a time-warp: the number of inhabitants has remained virtually unchanged for hundreds of years, despite extensive industrialisation last century, which saw the town become a leading centre for the manufacture of gloves. The GDR's penchant for outdated technology has left it as a wonderful period piece, but one consequence of this was that many of the houses were allowed to fall into a shocking state of decay – something which will need to be remedied quickly, as tourism looks to be its main hope for the future.

Around town

On the small central Markt, the **Altes Rathaus** (Tues–Thurs 10am–noon & 1–4pm, Sun 10am–2pm; DM1) has been converted into a museum of the town's history; it also serves as the nearest thing to a local tourist office and keeps the keys to the **Stephanikirche** (otherwise Sat & Sun 2–4pm only) in the close behind. The church's impressive fortress-like facade, crafted from rough stonework, dates from the first half of the twelfth century, with the tall steeples added four hundred years later. The main body of the church is built in a florid late Gothic style, its vault bearing elaborate keystones showing the crests of prosperous local families. Among the diverse furnishings are a Romanesque font, a Renaissance pulpit and many fine epitaphs.

Two of the finest half-timbered houses are on the L-shaped Schultenstrasse, which wends its way round the back of the Markt. The **Alte Voigtei** at no. 3 started a local trend for having a frieze of coloured rosettes for decoration, while the **Eulenspiegelhaus** at no. 8 is the best example of those favouring a richer decoration, with lots of small, symbolic carvings. Kapellenstrasse, the main street into town from the east, has another fine group; no. 4 here is the oldest in town, dating back to 1480. Following Hagen north from here, you come to one of the largest of the buildings, the **Hospital St Bartholmäus**. The other main set-piece is the **Bunter Hof**, a huge manor on Rössingstrasse at the southeastern end of the old town, but this is in a shocking state of disrepair.

Practicalities

Osterwieck – for the time being, at least – is on a **branch railway**; change at HEUDEBER if coming from Halberstadt. There are actually two stations, one to the east of the centre, the other (the terminus) to the north. Between the former and the Markt is the **bus station**, a halt on the Halberstadt–Goslar route, and with other services into the Harz. Accommodation options are limited to one **hotel**, *Deutsches Haus* on Schützenstrasse (☎208), whose rates begin at DM40 per person, and one **private house**, *Blum*, Birkenweg 15 (☎9443), at DM15. Best place to **eat** is the *Ratsweinstube* on the Markt.

Quedlinburg

QUEDLINBURG, 14km southeast of Halberstadt, is one of the most remarkable places in all of Germany – over 1600 of its buildings are listed as being of historic interest, and the entire town has been declared a World Heritage Site by UNESCO. The original medieval layout is preserved intact: the River Bode divides the Altstadt, the original merchants' quarter on the right bank, from the Neustadt, where the smallholders lived, while at the southern end of the former are the two hills where monastic life was centred. Although the big set-pieces are all hewn out of a whitish sandstone which has taken on a greyish patina, the town's character is defined by the **half-timbered houses** which line almost all its streets. The full diversity of this quintessentially German architectural form is on view, with examples ranging from the fourteenth to the nineteenth century; in artistry and ingenuity of design, they're surpassed only by the very depleted ensemble in Hildesheim. Thankfully, the GDR authorities saw Quedlinburg as a great national asset. Thus, although the factories the state's dogma deemed essential were built here, they were confined to the outskirts and have caused only a modest degree of pollution. For the time being, therefore, Quedlinburg is the ideal combination of a genuine, living community in a stunning visual setting. However, it's advisable to visit soon, as the likelihood is that it will become, within the next few years, the same sort of tourist trap as the comparably picturesque towns along the Romantic Road.

The Burgberg

Quedlinburg owes its distinctive silhouette to the buildings on the **Burgberg**, the larger of the two hills at the southern end of town. In the early part of the tenth century this became the headquarters of the German nation when the expansionist drive to the east was begun by the Saxon king, **Henry the Fowler** (*Heinrich der Vogler*). He built a palace here, which on several occasions hosted meetings of the Imperial Diet. On his death in 936, his widow **Mathilde** established a collegiate foundation for aristocratic women, which survived until the Napoleonic suppression. Its abbesses had the rank of princesses of the Holy Roman Empire, and were answerable on religious matters directly to the pope. They effectively controlled the town which grew up in the valley below; when it attempted to assert municipal independence by joining the Hanseatic League in the fifteenth century, the abbesses succeeded in re-establishing ecclesiastical dominance – hence the reason Quedlinburg never developed into a major city.

The Schloss

The present **Schloss** complex on the Burgberg is predominantly Renaissance, though the plain exterior walls below the frilly gables are evidence of the original defensive function. Access from the town is via the Torbau, a much-modified medieval gateway, beyond which are a number of half-timbered service buildings and a terrace commanding a sweeping view.

Apart from the the the Stiftskirche, the two main buildings on the courtyard are the **Residenzbau**, the palace of the abbesses, and the L-shaped **Wohntrakt**. which contained the apartments of the other canonesses, the kitchen, bakery, pharmacy and workshops. The former now contains the **Schlossmuseum** (May–Sept Tues–Sun 10am–6pm; Oct–April Tues–Sun 9am–5pm; DM2.50), a rambling, old-fashioned display which ranges through Ice Age fossils, a hoard of Bronze Age treasure and a comprehensive array of medieval instruments of torture, to regional costumes and sections on the history of the town. However, the main attraction is being able to wander through the building itself, whose rooms are surprisingly modest – even in the elegantly furnished Baroque extension which replaced a redundant part of the fortifications.

The Stiftskirche St Servatius

The **Stiftskirche St Servatius** (guided tours May–Oct Tues–Sat 10am–noon & 2–4pm, Sun 2–4pm; Nov–April Tues–Sat at 11am & 2pm, Sun at 2pm; DM2) is the eleventh- and twelfth-century successor to Mathilde's original church. Apart from the twin towers, which are nineteenth-century pastiches, and the Gothic apse, it's a very pure example of Romanesque architecture. Austere and regal, the nave adopts the characteristic regional format of alternating column and pillar supports in a ratio of two to one. The **capitals**, together with the friezes above, provide the only decoration; carved with supreme delicacy by Lombard craftsmen, they show animal, plant and geometric motifs. Another fine group can be seen in the **crypt**, the last resting-place of Henry and Mathilde. Their plain sarcophagi are overshadowed by those of the abbesses, which are placed upright against the south wall, a position which helps endow the life-size effigies with a Byzantine sense of hierarchy.

In the northern transept is the fabulous treasury known as the **Zitter**. The glittering twelfth-century reliquary of the church's patron Saint Servatius is outstanding, with its vibrant ivory carvings of the Apostles and its encrusted diamonds and enamels; the gilded casket dedicated to Saint Catherine, though more orthodox, is equally beautiful. Another highlight is an early thirteenth-century bridal chest, decorated with 31 different coats of arms, which rank as the earliest surviving heraldic symbols in Germany. Housed in the transept opposite, though not on view at the time of writing, is the church's most valuable treasure, the oldest tapestry north of the Alps; woven around 1200, it shows the marriage of Mercury to Philology, the Queen of Knowledge.

Three museums

At no. 12 on Schlossberg, the street of half-timbered houses below the Schloss, is the **Klopstockhaus** (Wed–Sun 9am–5pm; DM1), the boyhood home of the eighteenth-century poet **Friedrich Gottlieb Klopstock**. Founder of the Classicising tendency in German literature, Klopstock self-consciously regarded himself as a Christian Homer, devoting much of his life to the composition of a huge twenty-part epic, *The Messiah*; he also wrote odes on typical enlightenment themes such as man and nature, the fatherland, peace and liberty. Though his reputation is somewhat in eclipse, his verses have gained a wide audience through Mahler's settings, notably in the hugely popular *Resurrection Symphony*. The museum also contains memorabilia of two other influential Quedlinburgers of the same epoch: **Dorothea Christiana Erxleben**, the first German woman to gain the title of doctor, in 1754, and **Johann Christoph GuthsMuths**, the founding-father of school gymnastics – and thus the unwitting begetter of the somewhat sinister role sport has played in German society, from the days of Prussian militarism via the Nazis to the GDR.

To the rear of here, in a heavy turn-of-the-century building at Finkenherd 5a, is the **Lyonel-Feininger-Galerie** (Tues–Sun 10am–noon & 1–5/6pm; DM3), devoted to the German-American Cubist, a key member of staff of the Bauhaus during its Weimar and Dessau periods. A large selection of his woodcuts, engravings, lithographs, drawings and watercolours are on display in specially dimmed galleries; there are also a few oil paintings, including an early *Self-Portrait*.

A couple of minutes' walk northwest of here, on the bank of an arm of the Bode at Wordgasse 3, is the **Fachwerkmuseum Ständerbau** (May–Sept Mon–Wed & Fri–Sun 10am–2pm). The building itself, which probably dates from the early fourteenth century, is the earliest surviving timber-framed house in Germany and a good one hundred and fifty years older than any other in Quedlinburg. Inside, the displays illustrate how the different styles of half-timbering evolved from these rudimentary beginnings.

The Markt and around

Immediately north of the Ständerbau is the **Blasiikirche**, a strange combination of an octagonal Baroque church and a massive Romanesque tower. At the moment, it stands utterly neglected, though you can peer into the elegant interior, with its theatre-like box gallery, through an aperture which has thoughtfully been left open.

In contrast, the spacious triangular **Markt**, just a few paces to the east was the subject in the 1970s of the sort of thorough restoration programme characteristic of western Germany. The buildings are a varied mix – no. 5 and no. 13/14 were the sixteenth-century guild houses of the weavers and tanners respectively; the music school at no. 2 occupies a large Baroque palace, while the Neoclassical *Zum Bär* is a celebrated hotel whose reputation is tainted because of *Stasi* patronage. At the far end stands the **Rathaus**, most of which, including the graceful portal, is Renaissance. Outside the Rathaus is a puny-looking **statue of Roland**, erected as a symbol of municipal independence when Quedlinburg was a member of the Hansa – and removed as soon as the abbesses re-established full authority.

To the rear of the Rathaus, and set in an unusual semi circular close, is the **Marktkirche St Benedikti**. Its fortress-like facade shows the transition from Romanesque to early Gothic; the rest of the structure was rebuilt at the end of the Gothic period. Entrance is via the Kalandskapelle on the north side, whose walls are hung with Renaissance memorials to local dignitaries. The main body of the church is of much interest for the furnishings dating from after its conversion to Protestant worship, in particular the Mannerist wooden pulpit and the sober Baroque high altar. A more effusive form of Baroque was employed in the burial chapel of the Gebhardt family, which stands outside the church.

Breite Strasse, the long street leading north from here, has some superb half-timbered buildings, notably no. 33, which is Gothic, and no. 39, the Renaissance **Gildehaus zur Rose**; the latter, generally regarded as the most beautiful house in Quedlinburg, is currently a spit 'n' sawdust pub frequented by the town's most hardened boozers. East of here, at Klink 11, is the **Freihaus**, another outstanding Renaissance mansion of almost palatial dimensions.

The other historic quarters

Quedlinburg's other historic quarters stand very much in the shadow of the Burgberg and the Altstadt, but are well worth wandering round if you want to understand how life has gone on here down the centuries.

The Neustadt

Across the Bode from the Freihaus is Steinweg, the main east-west axis of the Neustadt, with the best examples of half-timbering to be found in the quarter. Particularly notable are the Baroque **Zur Goldenen Sonne** at no. 11 (which has recently been immaculately restored and returned to its historic role as an inn), and the late Renaissance **Zur Börse** at no. 23, which boasts an ingenious corner oriel. Due south of here, on Hinter der Mauer, are the best-preserved fragments of the **Stadtmauer**, including a couple of watchtowers.

The **Nikolaikirche** (Tues–Sat 10am–1pm & 1–3.30pm), the Gothic parish church of the Neustadt, is principally of note for its wonderful setting in the middle of a close of truly monumental grandeur. Outwardly, the two towers, one somewhat broader than the other, tend to overwhelm the rest of the building, an impression confirmed by the squat appearance of the hall interior, whose most notable furnishings are the elaborately Baroque high altar and pulpit and a touchingly naive statue of Saint Godehard.

The Münzenberg and the Wippertikirche

The **Münzenberg**, the hill just to the west of the Burgberg, was formerly crowned by a convent founded in Quedlinburg's tenth-century heyday. This was dissolved at the Reformation, whereupon a community of artisans, minstrels and travelling folk settled here, re-using its stones in the construction of their modest little houses. Even now, the quarter has an engagingly quiet, run-down feeling, and the view of the Burgberg from here alone justifies the trek up.

In the valley to the south, a large cemetery has grown up around the **Wippertikirche** (guided tours Tues & Thurs at 10.30pm; otherwise ask at the tourist office), a former monastic church whose simple architecture rather resembles that of a barn – which is exactly the function it performed throughout most of last century. Its crypt dates back to the tenth century and is the only surviving monument from Quedlinburg's period as the German capital, while the Romanesque north portal, with its exquisite columns and weather-worn carvings, was brought here from the destroyed convent on the Münzenberg.

Practicalities

Quedlinburg's **Bahnhof** and **bus station** are side by side to the east of town. The Neustadt lies just over the Bode, while the Altstadt is a ten-minute walk away straight ahead along Bahnhofstrasse, then left into August-Wolf-Strasse. However, the most atmospheric approach to the town is to follow the Bode upstream towards the Burgberg; many picturesque panoramic views open up en route.

The **tourist office** (April–Oct Mon–Fri 9am–5pm, Sat & Sun 10am–4pm; Nov–March Mon–Fri 9am–5pm only; ☎2633) is at Markt 12. They have a plentiful supply of **private rooms** on their books, though the town has no hostel or campsite. *Zur Goldenen Sonne*, Steinweg 10 (☎2318), is the most attractive of the **hotels**, and is very good value at DM30 for singles, DM50 for doubles. Of the former state-run hotels, *Zum Bär*, Markt 8 (☎2224), has a variety of rooms starting at DM32 for singles, DM62 for doubles, but rising much higher. The rather functional *Motel Quedlinburg* on Wippertistrasse (☎2855), charges DM46 per person, while *Quedlinburger Hof*, beside the Bahnhof at Harzweg 1 (☎2276), costs DM50 for a single, DM90 a double.

Choice of places to **eat** and **drink** is surprisingly wide by eastern German standards. Hearty German meals are available at the *Ratskeller* under the Rathaus, *Münzenberger Klause*, Pölle 22, *Zum Schloss*, Mühlenstr. 22, and the aforementioned hotels. There's also a restaurant, *Schlosskrug*, in the Schloss complex; this closes at 8pm, leaving late night drinking to the separate cellar bar, the *Schlosskeller. Buntes Lamm*, Schmale Str. 1a, is a pricey wine bar-cum-restaurant in one of the town's few ugly buildings. There are plenty of good traditional cafés, notably *Am Finkenherd*, Schlossberg 15, and *Boulevard-Café*, Markt 1.

Gernrode and the Selke valley

The recuperative health resort of **GERNRODE**, situated 9km south of Quedlinburg on the fringe of the Harz mountains, clusters round one of Germany's oldest and most remarkable churches. For the most part it's a somnolent little place – except around the Bahnhof to the north of the town proper, where the shed and freight yards of the *Selketalbahn*, the oldest **narrow-gauge steam railway** in the region, stand directly opposite the main line. The survival of this railway ensured a steady stream of foreign visitors in GDR days, but, as they were forced to lodge elsewhere, tourist facilities are underdeveloped in comparison with other parts of the Harz. If you want to stay here, a fair amount of private accommodation is now available; for more information, contact the **tourist office**, Marktstr. 20 (☎478).

The Stiftskirche St Cyriakus

Gernrode's history goes back to the mid-tenth century, when a women's collegiate church, the **Stiftskirche St Cyriakus** (guided tours daily at 3pm, otherwise only variably open) was founded. This is substantially the same building as the one which can be seen today, with the exception of the west choir and towers and the double-storey clois-

---

THE SELKETALBAHN

The **Selketalbahn**, the narrow-gauge railway which runs the 35km between Gernrode and STIEGE, is named after the peaceful valley of the **River Selke**, which defines part of its route. Gernrode itself does not lie in the valley, which is reached by the most atmospheric part of the journey, a steep climb past a couple of secluded lakes, then through wooded countryside unpenetrated by roads. Built in 1887, the line is plied by a number of antique locomotives, among them a *Mallet* of 1897, the oldest still-functioning train in Germany; unfortunately, (relatively) modern diesels have recently been introduced as well. Alone among eastern Germany's eight surviving narrow-gauge passenger lines, freight carriages are attached – proof that this is no tourist trap.

The River Selke is reached at MÄGDESPRUNG, 10km south of Gernrode. A couple of stops further on is **ALEXISBAD**, a curious, run-down little resort whose spa buildings are an illustration of the Romantic movement's infatuation with chinoisserie. From here there's a 3km-long branch line (served by six trains a day) to **HARZGERODE**. For several decades this small town was the capital of a minute principality of the House of Anhalt – hence the late Renaissance Schloss, which, with the half-timbered Rathaus and the slate-towered Marienkirche, gives the place an air of grandeur wholly inconsistent with its size.

Three trains a day go all the way to Stiege, where the link with the *Harzquerbahn* (see p.823), which fell into disuse after World War II, was reinstated in 1984. Here you can choose between continuing on the two through trains to the *Harzquerbahn*'s southern terminus at Nordhausen; going as far as EISFELDER TALMÜHLE, then changing to the service north to Wenigerode; taking the 5km-long branch line to HASSELFELDE; or returning with the train to its shed in Gernrode.

ter, all of which were added a couple of hundred years later. By far the best preserved of any church of its date, it exhibits most of the characteristics associated with Romanesque, the first original architectural style indigenous to Northern Europe. The nave's triforium gallery was the first ever built north of the Alps, and suggests a certain Byzantine influence – a connection explained by the fact that the dowager Empress Theophanu, a native of Greece, was then living in Quedlinburg. Curiously enough, this feature never caught on among later German builders, though it was to become obligatory in France. However, another innovation pioneered at Gernrode – alternating columns and pillars – became a hallmark of churches throughout the Saxon lands.

In the southern aisle stands a **Holy Sepulchre**, the oldest German reproduction of Christ's tomb in Jerusalem, which probably dates back to the late eleventh century. Unfortunately, it's somewhat mutilated, but the high quality of its carvings can still be seen on two of its sides, one showing Jesus appearing to Mary Magdalene after the Resurrection, the other with a wonderfully delicate frieze – a sort of carved version of an illuminated manuscript – featuring prophets, fantastic animals, foliage and a decorative border. Other highlights of the interior are the retouched frescos in the east choir, the twelfth-century font and the late Gothic monument in honour of Margrave Gero.

The Bode valley

Before reaching Quedlinburg, the **River Bode** travels a mazy route right through the Harz mountains. Not only is it, at 169km, the longest river in the range, it also offers by far the most beautiful scenery the region has to offer, seen at its best under the menacingly dramatic skies the uncertain climate so often brings – making it easy to understand why such a rich store of supernatural folklore has grown up in association. Because of the archetypally Germanic nature of both the landscape and the legends, the Bode has stirred the imagination of the literati to an extent unmatched by any other beauty spot in the country: Goethe, Herder, Klopstock, Eichendorff, Heine and Fontane all sang its praises.

Thale and around

German unification has meant that **THALE**, which lies right on the edge of the Harz 10km southwest of Quedlinburg, must look to tourism for its future, as its ironworks – the bedrock of the local economy for over five hundred years – was a casualty of the GDR's failure to invest in modern plant and machinery. The town itself is of scant interest, the only monument of note being the **Wendhusenturm**, a tower house (perhaps dating back as far as the tenth century) in the old quarter north of the Bode. However, the surroundings are marvellous; with 150km of marked trails in the vicinity, Thale is unquestionably one of the best **hiking** bases in eastern Germany. Nor should the unenergetic be put off: the best of the scenery starts to unfold just beyond the Friedenspark, the park across from the Bahnhof, terminus of a branch line from Quedlinburg.

Hexentanzplatz and Rosstrappe

Guarding the southern entrance to Thale are two rocky crags, both known to have been sites of pagan worship, and commanding superb views over the valley and beyond. On the right bank, 454 metres above the valley, is the vertiginous **Hexentanzplatz** (Witches' Dancing Place), so named because it was where the local witches supposedly had their initial rendezvous on *Walpurgisnacht* (see p.824), before flying off to the main celebration on the Brocken, a nearby mountain. The lazy way to reach it is by cable car; the station for this is on the opposite side of the Bode, just over the bridge at the end of Friedenspark. There's also a road up from the southeastern end of Thale, plus several pathways, quickest and most convenient being the steps of the *Hexenstiege*, which lead to the belvedere via the **Harzer Bergtheater**, a fine natural amphitheatre where plays are staged regularly during the summer months. Alongside is the **Walpurgishalle**, an exhibition hall with displays on the *Walpurgisnacht* legend.

Directly across the river, at a height of 437 metres, is the **Rosstrappe** (Horse's Clip-Clops). There were once plans to make a direct transport link with the Hexentanzplatz, but instead a chair lift was built just north of the valley terminus of the cable car. Alternative ways up are the looping main road from the centre of Thale, and a walking trail, the *Präsidentenweg*. From the plateau-like summit, you can descend to a curious group of rocks poised directly above the river; here can be seen a natural indentation closely resembling that of a horse's hoof. According to legend, this was made by the mighty steed being ridden by a princess called Brunnhilde, who was being chased through the Harz by a lustful knight by name of Bodo. Coming to this point, she spurred her mount on to make a succesful leap across to Hexentanzplatz. Bodo, however, plunged into the chasm, where he was turned into a hound, compelled forever to guard the crown of Brunnhilde which had fallen into the river in his wake.

Up the valley

The classic walk from Thale is the 10km route along a path (identified by signs marked with blue triangles) which closely follows the course of the Bode; contrary to what you'd expect, the views from the valley floor surpass those from the heights. If you don't want to walk the whole way, the best of the scenery can be seen in the first 3km, around the **Teufelsbrücke** (Devil's Bridge), from where you can make a detour up to the Rosstrappe via a belvedere-punctuated trail named the *Schurre*. Beyond the Teufelsbrücke, the main path climbs high above the river, affording wonderful views back to the Rosstrappe and of the spectacular **Bodekessel** below, a gorge in which steep granite cliffs rise directly from the foaming waters with their angry whirlpools. You then descend to a more placid landscape, which is chiefly notable for its richly varied flora and fauna. Orchids, daphnes, Turk's Cap lilies and hart's tongues are among the plants here; some of the trees are up to 3000 years old, while the large numbers of waterfowl make this stretch a magnet for birdwatchers.

TRESEBURG, the terminus of the walk, is a scattered village of grand houses pictu-resquely spaced out along the banks of the Bode, with a very ruinous castle crowning the hill above. It's beginning to develop its potential as a resort, with guest houses and holiday homes springing up, though it's being upstaged in this by **ALTENBRAK**, a somewhat larger village 4km upstream, which has taken to the new opportunities afforded by tourism like a duck to water.

Practicalities

Thale's **tourist office** (May–Aug Mon–Fri 9am–6pm, Sat & Sun 9.30am–1.30pm; Jan–April & Sept Mon–Fri 9am–5pm; Oct–Dec Mon–Fri 9am–4pm; ☎2597) is in the pavilion directly facing the Bahnhof. Here you can get a list of the fifty-odd **private houses** in the town with rooms to rent; prices begin at DM20 per person. **Hotels** include *Forelle*, Karl-Marx-Str. 84 (☎2757), and the half-timbered *Brauner Hirsch*, Rosstrappenstr. 1 (☎2504), which both charge in the region of DM30–35. On the summit of the Rosstrappe are the upmarket *Berghotel* (☎3011) and a privatised former trade union holiday home, the *Berghütte* (☎3346), the latter being good value at DM24 per person. The **youth hostel** (☎2881) occupies an ideal position for a hiking centre, on the right bank of the Bode just beyond the Hexenstiege. **Restaurants** can be found in the afore-mentioned hotels, as well as on Hexentanzplatz and around the Bode on the early stages of the path to Treseburg.

Rübeland and around

A few kilometres upstream from Altenbrak, the waters of the Bode and its tributaries have been harnessed to create an 8km-long reservoir, the **Rappbodetalsperre**, whose hilly eastern bank is another attractive walking area. The large dam at the northern end, built in the 1950s, was one of the GDR's proudest technological achievements, particularly as various prewar projects to build it had come to nought. A much smaller second reservoir, the **Talsperre Wendefurth**, was built in the 1960s, principally as a protection against flooding.

RÜBELAND, another old iron-smelting town, lies a couple of kilometres northwest of here, clustering round a remarkable group of stalactite caves. Oldest of these, formed some 600,000 years ago, is the **Baumannshöhle** (guided tours Feb & April–Oct Tues–Thurs, Sat & Sun 9.30–11.45am & 12.45–4.15pm, Mon & Fri same times, but alternate weeks only; Nov, Dec, Jan & March alternate days 9.30am–11.30am & 12.45–4.15pm; DM2). It was inhabited by prehistoric bears, some of whose skeletons, which are between 20,000 and 40,000 years old, are on display; much later, Stone Age peoples also made it their home. Discovered in the early sixteenth century, the Baumannshöhle already had the status of a famous tourist attraction when Goethe paid three visits there in the last quarter of the eighteenth century. In his honour, the superb natural auditorium at the heart of the complex has been named the *Goethesaal*, and is occasionally used as a theatre.

If anything, the stalactite formations are even finer in the only other cave open to the public, the triple-tiered **Hermannshöhle** (same times, though in winter only open on the days when the Baumannshöhle is closed). Although this lies directly opposite, its existence remained unknown until a workman engaged on the construction of the main road stumbled across it last century. A far more diverse range of skeletons of prehistoric mammals has been found here, while thirteen sorts of salamander still inhabit its underground lake. From the Hermannshöhle, you can walk up to Rübeland's only other attraction, the ruined **Burg Birkenfeld**, from where you get a fine panoramic view over the region.

Practicalities

Rübeland can be reached by regular **buses** from Thale and the other villages of the Bode valley. It also lies on a branch **railway** line from Halberstadt via Blankenburg; the Bahnhof is right beside the entrance to the Baumannshöhle. Several holiday homes have been converted into **hotels**; these include *Ferienhotel Hermannshöhle*, Blankenburger Str. 20 (☎9205), whose rates begin at DM37.50, and *Pension Zum Krockstein*, Kreuztal 68 (☎9161), which costs DM26 per person. The local **restaurants** are serviceable enough, but no more than that.

Blankenburg and around

BLANKENBURG, which lies on the edge of the Harz, 10km northeast of Rübeland and 13km west of Quedlinburg, is a quiet spa and residential town, which, at the turn of the seventeenth century, briefly found itself at the forefront of European power politics. In 1690, Ludwig Rudolf, a younger son of the Welf House of Braunschweig-Wolfenbüttel, made Blankenburg into the resplendent capital of a new principality. He also brought off an amazing double dynastic coup by marrying one of his daughters to the future Holy Roman Emperor Charles VI, and another to the son of Czar Peter the Great of Russia. Four decades later, he inherited his family's main duchy – and relegated the town he had himself built up to a second-string residence.

Around town

Despite the brevity of its period of glory, Blankenburg acquired two Baroque palaces. The smaller and prettier of these is the **Kleines Schloss** (Tues–Sat 10am–5pm, Sun 2–5pm; DM1.50) just east of the centre. Its curvaceous northern facade overlooks a fine French-style formal garden, in which stand an over-the-top grotto dedicated to Nepture and a copy of the celebrated Burglöwe (Lion Monument) of Braunschweig. At the time of writing, the interior housed a better-than-average local museum, though its future was under a question mark because the Welf family have staked a claim to both palaces.

From here, Marktstrasse leads west to the Renaissance **Rathaus**, above whose door are the coats of arms of both Blankenburg and Braunschweig. Steps lead up to the **Bartholomäuskirche**, a Gothic hall church recently restored through the munificence of the Welfs as a sweetener to their demand for the return of their property. East of here, Burgstrasse is lined with seventeenth-century **half-timbered houses**; others can be seen in the streets west of the Rathaus, though most are in a sadly dilapidated condition. At the very top of the town is the main **Schloss**: currently in use as a school, the building is likewise in a poor state of repair, though the monumental majesty of its courtyard is still evident.

Just to the north of the historic part of town is the **spa quarter**, centred on two large areas of greenery, the Kurpark and the Thiepark. At the edge of the latter is the **Teufelsbad**, which offers a wide range of facilities, the speciality of the house being mud baths.

The outskirts

Blankenburg, being set in particularly attractive surroundings, makes a good walking base. From a scenic point of view, the best excursion is the 4km circular path which leads southeast from the Kleines Schloss to the **Teufelsmauer** (Devil's Wall), a row of huge, heavily fissured sandstone boulders believed to have been formed some 90 million years ago. Near the beginning of the circuit are the Grossvaterfelsen (Grandfather Rocks), from where there's a wonderful view over Blankenburg and its surroundings.

Another walking trail leads 3km north from the Bahnhof to the fascinating labyrinthine ruins of **Burg Regenstein** (May–Oct daily 9am–6pm; Oct–March Wed–Sun 9am–4pm; DM1.50). The original twelfth-century Romanesque castle, partly carved out of the living rock, was the first seat of the local counts. It was badly damaged in feudal wars against the combined might of the Bishop of Halberstadt, the Count of Wernigerode and the burghers of Quedlinburg, who joined together to prevent Blankenburg establishing regional dominance. In 1670, the castle was taken over by the Prussians, although it actually lay outside the boundaries of their state; they converted it into a modern military stronghold, enlarging the old fortification system.

Practicalities

Blankenburg lies on the railway line from Halberstadt to Rübeland; the **Bahnhof** and **bus station** are both at the northern end of town. The **tourist office** (Mon–Fri 9am–1pm & 2–6pm; ☎2898) is right in the centre at Tränkestr. 1. There are dozens of **private rooms** for rent, mostly at around DM20 per person. Similar rates are available at a couple of larger **pensions** – *Becker*, Karl-Liebknecht-Str. 44 (☎3720), and *Wegener*, Friedrich-August-Str. 2 (☎3075). Even the posh three-star *Kurhotel*, Mauerstr. 9 (☎2683), is currently very reasonable, with prices in the DM37–48 range. Choice of **restaurants** is limited to *Am Markt*, Harzstr. 5, and *Am Rathaus*, Markt 5, in the town centre, and the *Gaststätte* at Burg Regenstein.

Wernigerode and around

Known as "the colourful town in the Harz" because of the kaleidoscopic paintwork on its half-timbered buildings, **WERNIGERODE** has by far the most animated atmosphere to be found in the region. In part, this is due to the fact that it's no stranger to international tourism – in GDR days, it was the only place in the Harz where westerners were encouraged to stay. This led to an influx of steam train buffs from all over the world, who came to ride the *Harzquerbahn*, the longest and most scenic **narrow-gauge railway** in the country. Wernigerode is its northern terminus, and the sight of antiquated locomotives puffing their way through the streets before beginning their ascent into the mountains remains the most enduring image of a town plentifully endowed with picturesque corners.

The Altstadt

The town clusters along the valleys of the Holtemme and Zillerbach, with the Altstadt lying just to the east of their confluence. Its pride and joy is the **Rathaus** on Marktplatz, a building of stridently pictorial qualities that could belong in no country but Germany. The bright orange facade, with sharply pointed lead steeples sprouting from resplendent double-storey oriels, represents the final phase of Gothic in the mid-sixteenth century. The exterior has painted corbels of saints and Carnival characters, which can be seen by walking down Klintgasse. On the western side of the Markt is the **Gothisches Haus**, another richly decorated building, originally the home of a wealthy fifteenth-century burgher family. Since the middle of last century, it has been a restaurant, and latterly a hotel as well; at the time of writing it was being refurbished with the aim of becoming the top place to stay in town. At no. 5 on Klintgasse is the **Teichmühle**, a seventeenth-century mill popularly known, for obvious reasons, as "The Leaning House of Wernigerode". The Neoclassical mansion at no. 10 on the same street houses the **Harzmuseum** (Mon–Fri 9am–4pm, Sat 9.30am–1pm; DM2), which features ho-hum displays on the town's half-timbered houses and their construction, as well as on the history, geology, flora, fauna and industries of the Harz region.

Just south of here is the **Silvestrikirche** the parish church of the Altstadt, but far more remarkable than the church itself is its peaceful close, the **Oberkirchhof**, which is lined with a beautiful and varied group of houses that range from two to four hundred years old. Particularly outstanding is no. 13, the **Gadenstedtsches Haus**, a late Gothic half-timbered construction to which was added a spectacularly protruding upper storey oriel in High Renaissance style.

On **Kochstrasse**, at the southernmost end of the Altstadt, can be seen the more modest dwellings of the local craftsmen. Notwithstanding its three storeys, no. 43 is the smallest house in town; sandwiched between the low-ceilinged kitchen and minute attic bedroom is the "main" level, consisting of a single room with a floor space of just ten square metres. Another street worth seeking out is **Hinterstrasse**, a block north of the Markt, which has the oldest houses in town, some of which date back to the 1400s.

Much the most imposing street, however, is **Breite Strasse**, the pedestrianised main shopping thoroughfare leading east from the Markt. Despite some losses in a 1944 air-raid, it preserves an almost uninterrupted array of high-quality vernacular architecture. Oldest house is the late sixteenth-century merchant's residence at no. 4, which was given an improbable but effective Jugendstil interior refit as a Viennese-style café. Even more eye-catching is the **Krummelsches Haus** at no. 72, whose half-timbering is all but obscured by the exuberant Baroque carvings which cover almost all its facade. Also of special note is the **Krellsche Schmiede** at no. 95, decorated with horseshoes and a horse's head to indicate its function as a smithy – which it remains today, an uninterrupted tradition dating back over three hundred years.

The rest of the town

From the streets of the Altstadt, the striking silhouette of the **Schloss** (Tues–Sun 9am–4.30pm; DM5), perched high on a hill at the southern end of town, can often be seen looming in the background. The original fortress was almost completely replaced by the present Romantic fantasy, the brainchild of Count Otto of Stolberg-Wernigerode, one of Bismarck's closest cronies. Although the architecture is pseudo-Gothic and Renaissance in style, there's nothing fake about the furnishings, which include valuable pieces ranging from the thirteenth to the nineteenth centuries, many of them brought from the former count's first-string residence of Stolberg. Especially notable are two works in the chapel – an embroidery dedicated to Saint Mary Magdalene woven around 1250 and the late fifteenth-century retable carved by Ulrich Mair. The other big attraction is the sweeping **view** over Wernigerode and the Harz from the ramparts.

Immediately beyond the Schloss, the thickly wooded slopes of the Harz mountains begin to unfold; even within the boundaries of the town there are marked walking trails which give a good idea of the characteristic scenery and vegetation of the range. In the **Wildpark Christianental**, set in a valley between two small lakes, examples of the

---

THE HARZQUERBAHN

The *Harzquerbahn*, undoubtedly one of Europe's most memorable railways, travels the 60.5km between Wernigerode and Nordhausen in Thuringia. Up to five trains per day make the complete trip; many others cover shorter stretches. Most of the locomotives used are steam trains built in the 1950s, but diesels, to the horror of purists, were introduced in 1988. A *Mallet* of 1898 – the same year as the line was inaugurated – is brought out of storage for occasional excursion trips, for which advance booking is necessary. Other than this, the *Harzquerbahn* functions as a normal part of the railway network; although it has been something of a tourist attraction since its inception, it has always been used for the movement of goods, as well as providing a genuine public transport service to the villages in the remotest part of the Harz. It accounts for nearly half the length of the surviving narrow-gauge network in the region; since the link with the *Selketalbahn* (see p.817) was re-established in 1984, it has been possible to travel along the whole system, apart from the short branch lines, in the course of a single day.

The first stop, *Westerntor*, a station designed by Fritz Höger, architect of notable Expressionist buildings in Hamburg and Hannover, is located just outside the eponymous medieval gateway at the western end of the Altstadt; it's a handy place to pick up the train if you don't want to trail down to the Hauptbahnhof. There are two more stations within Wernigerode itself, before the train passes through its only tunnel in the course of its exhilarating climb – maintaining an almost constant 1 in 30 gradient – to its highest point at **DREI ANNEN HOHNE**. Here is the junction with the *Brockenbahn* (see overleaf); it's also the place to alight if you want to follow the 10km trail up the other main mountain in the area, the Hohneklippen (908m).

The *Harzquerbahn* then descends to the villages of ELEND and SORGE, whose names ("Misery" and "Sorrow") seemed particularly appropriate in GDR days, as they found themselves right up against the notorious frontier between the two Germanys. Indeed, the train used to travel within a few metres of the electrified barbed wire on this stretch, and guards kept a wary eye on passengers' behaviour. Cold War thrills are now but a memory here, with only the markings on the trees to indicate where the border used to be. After climbing again to the little resort of BENNECKENSTEIN, the train begins its rapid descent to Nordhausen. The junction with the *Selketalbahn* is at EISFELDER TALMÜHLE, which is just over the boundary with Thuringia. At around 6.30pm each day, three passenger steam trains travelling in different directions have to wait for each other here, before proceeding in their separate directions – a sight which can no longer be seen anywhere else in the world.

region's indigenous wildlife, including many birds of prey, are kept in semi-captivity, and there are also comprehensive explanatory posters (German only) on all aspects of the natural history of the Harz.

Practicalities

Wernigerode's **Hauptbahnhof** – which, in addition to being the terminus of the *Harzquerbahn*, has mainline services to Magdeburg via Halberstadt – lies about fifteen minutes' walk north of the town centre. Alongside is the **bus station**, which now has a regular link over the former border to Bad Harzburg. The **tourist office** (Mon–Fri 9am–6pm, Sat 9.30am–1pm; ☎3035) is at Breite Str. 12. There's the usual **private room** booking service, though this has competition from an agency at Hinterstr. 24 (daily 10am–7.30pm; ☎33359). Although prices are low, the commission charged may mean that, for a short stay, you might pay even less in a **hotel**. Rates at *Schlossblick*, Burgstr. 58 (☎34049), begin at DM20; *Deutsches Eiche*, Mühlental 36 (☎32290), has doubles (only) from DM45; while *Zur Post*, Marktstr, 17 (☎32436), which has a long tradition as a rendezvous for foreign steam train buffs, now charges DM30 per person for the first night, DM25 thereafter. The **youth hostel** is at Leninstr. 53 (☎32061), but, at the time of writing, was due to close for refurbishment.

Almost inevitably, the best **restaurant** is the *Ratskeller* under the Rathaus. The strongest competition to it comes from *Weisser Hirsch* directly across the Markt, whose upper floors should by now have re-opened as a hotel; it's also worth checking on the bargain menus offered in *Zur Post*. The aforementioned *Café Wien*, Breite Str. 4, is the obvious place to go for ice-cream or coffee. Wernigerode's *Hasseröder* **beer** ranks fairly high by eastern standards; its premium product is called *Pilsator*. The town has a number of **festivals**, including the *Weintage* towards the end of May, the *Rathausfest* in late June and the *Schützenfest* in mid-July.

The Brocken

Southwest of Wernigerode is the celebrated peak of the **Brocken** (1142m), meeting place of the witches on *Walpurgisnacht* (30 April), an event vividly described in the first part of Goethe's *Faust*. The legend seems to have arisen at least partly as a result of the so-called "spectre of Brocken" – when the sun is low, it casts magnified silhouettes from the peak on to clouds hanging around the lower neighbouring mountains. *Walpurgisnacht* is somewhat oddly named after Saint Walburga, an eighth-century English-born missionary whose name is evoked as a protection against evil spirits; however, it seems she gained this role through her name having been confused with that of Waldborg, the pagan goddess of fertility.

Throughout the entire history of the GDR, the Brocken's mystique was increased by the fact that it was a restricted military area used for border surveillance activities, with westerners forbidden to come anywhere near it. Such is its impact on the German consciousness, however, that it was made accessible to walkers within a month of the fall of the Berlin Wall. There are also plans to restore the *Brockenbahn*, a narrow-gauge branch line of the *Harzquerbahn*, which followed a 19km route from Drei Annen Hohne to the summit of the mountain. Only the first 5km of this, to the resort of **SCHIERKE** (which can also be reached from Wernigerode in about forty minutes by bus), is currently in operation. The village is amply endowed with places to stay; a full list is available from the **tourist office** at Brockenstr. 5 (Mon–Fri 9am–noon & 1.30–4.30pm, Sat 10am–noon; ☎310). From here, there's a marked trail up the Brocken; allow at least five hours for the return journey. Of the many other paths up the mountain, the most atmospheric is that from Torfhaus (see *Chapter Six*), which has the benefit of offering the best views of the peak – and of crossing the long-forbidden border.

Stolberg

It's not without justification that **STOLBERG** styles itself as "the pearl of the southern Harz", as this former county capital occupies a secluded setting bestriding hills and valleys which is ready-made for picture-postcard photographs. Although a centre for silver, iron and copper mining for much of its history, it's had the status of a *Kurort* since 1945. Formerly it used this as a prefix to distinguish it from other towns of the same name, but, just before the *Wende* of 1989, this was replaced with the designation "Thomas-Müntzer-Stadt", in celebration of the five hundreth anniversary of the birth here of the most radical figure of the Reformation period. Müntzer's leadership of the Peasants' Revolt of 1525 was regarded by the GDR authorities as the first precursor of Communist rule, and he came close to rivalling Marx in the state's roll-call of heroes. However, this demagogic firebrand (see also Mühlhausen, *Chapter Eleven*) has generally been given a bad press by unbiased historians, and it remains a moot point as to whether or not Stolberg will want to continue to promote its link with him.

Around town

At first sight, the painted sundial seems to be the only remarkable feature of the half-timbered **Rathaus** on the Markt. A closer inspection shows that it's actually a real architectural curiosity – there are no interior stairways, access to each upper storey only being possible from the steps which serve as the public footpath up the hill. Formerly, there was a second peculiarity, in that the number of windows equalled the number of weeks in the year and the number of panes equalled the number of days in the year, but these tidy calculations have been spoiled by susequent remodelling.

At the top of the steps is the gaunt late Gothic church of **St Martini**, where, at the height of the Peasants' Revolt, Luther – who regarded Müntzer as a dangerous upstart liable to undo all the achievements of the Reformation – dared to come to preach against the town's famous son. At the top of the hill is the part-Renaissance, part-Baroque **Schloss**, which served as a restaurant and holiday home during the GDR period. However, it has been claimed by a descendant of the counts who once ruled from here, and seems certain to be made over to him – just one of many illustrations of the bitter irony that Germany's most recent popular revolution has led to the restoration of vast amounts of wealth and property to aristocrats. Müntzer must be turning in his grave.

The town's finest houses can be seen along Niedergasse, which leads south from the Markt. Best of all is the brightly-coloured **Alte Münze** (Tues–Sat 10am–12.30pm & 1–6pm, Sun 10am–12.30pm & 1.30–6pm; DM1.50) at no. 19. Inside, you can see a reconstruction, complete with original equipment, of the workshop of the mint formerly housed here; there are also sections on the other craft industries and on mining. The top floor is a memorial to Müntzer: the four sixteenth-century console figures are all that remain of the house on this street where he was born, which was destroyed by fire last century. Finally, while all the hills around which Stolberg is built offer fine views, the best of the town itself are from the belvedere known as the **Lutherbuche**, almost due west of the Markt.

Hikes and practicalities

Stolberg is an excellent hiking centre, with a wide variety of marked trails in the vicinity. The most popular destination is the **Josefshöhe** (Wed–Sun 10am–5pm; DM1.50) 6km to the northeast. This huge iron double cross, the largest in the world, was erected at the end of last century to replace its Schinkel-designed wooden predecessor, which had been destroyed by lightning. You can ascend the platform for a sweeping panoramic view stretching from the Brocken to the Kyffhäuser; there's also a bar-restaurant (same times) offering full meals or snacks.

Full information about walks is available from either of the **tourist offices** in Stolberg: the one at the eastern end of the Markt (Mon–Fri 9am–5pm; ☎542) is for the entire eastern Harz region; that at Niedergasse 31 (Mon–Fri 9am–12.30pm & 1–6pm; ☎298 or 316) is municipally-run. The latter will find you a room in a **private house**, of which there's an abundant supply, with DM15 and DM20 being the most common rates charged per person. By now, several **hotels**, including two on the Markt, should also be open for business. Best **restaurant** is the *Ratskeller* on the ground floor of the Rathaus. Note that trains from the **Bahnhof**, at the southern end of town, only go southwards into Thuringia, but that there are good bus connections from here – and from the stop on the Markt – to other towns in the Harz.

THE ELBE-SAALE REGION

As in the north of Saxony-Anhalt, the main tourist draws in the south of the province are found in the basin of the Elbe and one of its major tributaries, in this case the Saale. Of the old Anhalt princely capitals, **Bernburg** is particularly attractive, while **Köthen**, despite pollution, also has its points. **Dessau**, on the other hand, was devastated in the war, but is still worth a visit for its wonderful heritage of Bauhaus architecture; it's also the hub of an eighteenth-century scheme of landscaped gardens which reached its climax at nearby **Wörlitz**. Not far from here is **Wittenberg**, the unlikely-looking university town which, during its spell as the capital of Saxony, was the main setting for the Reformation. **Halle** is principally of note as a major city which still evokes the nation's vanished prewar existence; nearby **Merseburg** preserves reminders of its time as a missionary bishopric, though its Dom is overshadowed by that of **Naumburg** further up the Saale, which lies close to the river's most picturesque stretch around **Bad Kösen**.

Bernburg and Köthen

Until it was finally united in 1863, with Dessau as its capital, Anhalt had had an almost continuous history of political fragmentation, with each branch of the same family ruling a tinpot principality from its own *Residenzstadt*. Apart from Dessau itself (the only one which developed into a city), **Bernburg** and **Köthen** both served as courtly towns for extended periods and preserve reminders of their heady days – which contrast sharply with their present provincial status.

Bernburg

By far the most attractive of the Anhalt capitals is **BERNBURG**, which spreads across both banks of the River Saale, just east of the Harz range and about 30km south of Magdeburg. The town has been extraordinarily quick at shaking itself free from the decades of neglect in which it was plunged during the GDR epoch: shortly after unification, all the streets were renamed and glossy brochures were produced trumpeting its claims as an enticing tourist destination.

Around town

A curiosity of Berburg is that it's a place whose centre has shifted. The **Talstadt**, or lower town, on the north bank of the Saale is the oldest part: here are a couple of Gothic churches and a spacious but incongruously quiet Marktplatz lined with Renaissance and Baroque houses. Far more memorable than any of these, however, is the **waterfront**, where a lock and several museum-piece mills make a picturesque foreground to the wonderful view – an ideal front page illustration for the promotional leaflets – of the **Bergstadt**, or upper town, on the opposite bank.

Completely dominating the Bergstadt, which has become the modern commercial centre, is the **Schloss**, by origin a medieval fortress but converted into a magnificent Renaissance palace in the mid-sixteenth century. It has a richly varied skyline of towers, turrets and gables; a key factor in the success of this is the retention of the defensive features of the old castle, which were softened with decorative adornments so that they blend in with the new buildings. The courtyard is also impressive, particularly the showpiece northern facade with its two double-storey oriels adorned with colourful carvings, grotesque heads and heraldic emblems. A small part of the complex houses the **Schlossmuseum** (Tues–Fri 9am–1pm & 2–4.30pm, Sat & Sun 2–5pm; DM1.50), with the expected archaeology and local history displays, plus an extensive section on the local mills. There's also a surprisingly good lapidary department, with sculptures from the Romanesque period onwards: look out for the relief portraits, which formerly decorated the exterior of the Schloss, of seven princes of the Reformation period. On summer weekends, you can ascend the **Eulenspiegelturm** for a panorama over the town and the valley.

Practicalities

The **Bahnhof** is at the eastern end of the Bergstadt, while the **bus station** is right in the centre. Across from the latter, at Rheineplatz 1, is the **tourist office** (Mon–Fri 9am–6pm; ☎2031). In addition to the **private rooms** which can be booked here, there's a wide range of accommodation options. **Hotels** include *Wien*, Breite Str. 1 (☎3249), and *Bauernstube*, Karlstr. 3 (☎2751), whose rates both begin at DM30 per person, and *Goldene Kugel*, Wilhelmstr. 2 (☎2371), which charges DM39. There's a **youth hostel** at Krumbholzallee 2 (☎2967) and **campsites** at Dr-John-Rittermeister-Str. 21 (☎3876), and at Am Stadtbad (☎4234). Best **restaurants** are *Alter Markt* on the Markt in the Talstadt and the *Haus des Handwerks* on Karlsplatz. Between March and October, you can take a **cruise** on the Saale from the landing stage below the Schloss; the boats sail from here as far as Halle.

Köthen

KÖTHEN, which lies 20km east of Bernburg, is a blackened town standing at the northern end of the notorious industrial region centred on Halle. Despite its present sorry appearance, it's a place of considerable interest, holding an honoured place in musical history as a result of **Johann Sebastian Bach**'s period of service as court *Kappelmeister* from 1717 to 1723, and an equally distinguished position in the field of ornithology, as the home town of the German Audubon, **Johann Friedrich Naumann**, whose work is commemorated in a gem of a museum.

Around town

Like all the town's historic buildings, the outsized **Schloss** at the northern end of the town centre is hard to appreciate because of its thick coat of grime. Its southern wing, the **Ludwigsbau**, was built in Renaissance style at the turn of the seventeenth century, when the principality of Anhalt-Köthen was first established. It's undergoing a desperately-needed restoration programme at the moment, though the chapel, now the *Bachsaal*, and the throne room, the *Spiegelsaal*, are regularly used for concerts and can be viewed if you ask at the offices. There are plans to establish a Bach museum in due course, in recognition of the special place the Köthen period occupies in his career. Freed of the commitment he otherwise had to produce a continuous stream of church music, he wrote here a collection of instrumental masterpieces, including the *Brandenburg Concertos*, the first part of *The Well-Tempered Clavier*, and the extraordinary works for solo violin and cello which occupy unique places in the repertoire of their respective instruments.

Across the courtyard, the Neoclassical **Ferdinandsbau**, erected by the last ruler of Anhalt-Köthen, houses the **Naumann-Museum** (Tues–Fri 9am–4.30pm, Sun 10am–noon & 2–5pm; DM3). A series of Biedermeier display cabinets contain the collection of stuffed birds instituted by the great nineteenth-century ornithologist, one of the pioneers of taxidermy and author of a definitive thirteen-volume study of the birdlife of Germany. Naumann was a highly talented artist who made all the illustrations for his publications, and the highlight of the museum is a display of original watercolours which served as the basis for these.

On Springstrasse, to the west of the Schloss, is another Neoclassical building, the **Marienkirche**, which Duke Ferdinand erected to mark his conversion to Catholicism; it stands in the strongest possible contrast to the gaunt Gothic **Jacobskirche** used by the Protestants, which dominates the central Marktplatz. On Museumsgasse, a block south of here, is the **Historisches Museum** (Tues–Fri 9am–noon & 1–4.30pm, Sun 10am–noon & 2–5pm; DM3), a fusty array of local ephemera which includes, pending the restoration of the Schloss, a large collection of Bach memorabilia.

Practicalities

Köthen's **Bahnhof**, an important junction offering good connections to Magdeburg, Halle and Dessau, is about ten minutes' walk east of the centre. The **tourist office** (Mon 9am–3pm, Tues 9am–5.30pm, Wed 9am–4pm, Thurs 9am–5pm, Fri 9am–1pm; ☎3767) is in the Rathaus on Marktplatz. There's no real reason to stay overnight, which is just as well, as accommodation is limited to a few private rooms and one expensive **hotel**, *Stadt Köthen*, right by the Bahnhof at Friedrich-Ebert-Str. 22 (☎6106). **Eating** and **drinking** is similarly limited – try either *Troika*, Holzmarkt 8, or the *Ratskeller*.

Dessau

DESSAU, the former capital of Anhalt, lies 60km southeast of Magdeburg. These days, it's a bleak and soulless city which has suffered from all the worst aspects of modern Germany – with post-unification blight the latest sorry episode in a list which began with horrendous wartime damage followed by drab Stalinist rebuilding. All of which is a pity, as Dessau had previously maintained a highly distinguished cultural tradition. In the late eighteenth century, its pastoral-type setting between the Elbe and Mulde rivers was put to full use in its transformation into a garden city, with parks and palaces laid out all around its environs. Even more significantly, it was home to the **Bauhaus**, the most influential architecture and design movement of the twentieth century, during its most exciting and innovative period between 1925 and 1932. The survival of a large number of buildings from this time means that Dessau is a place no modern architecture buff should miss; for anyone else, there's little here to stop for.

The city

There are plenty of delights to be found amid the prefabricated concrete jungles – but this requires time and patience. Given that the sights are very scattered, it's worth investing in a book of five tickets on the public transportation system, costing DM2.50.

The Bauhausgebäude and around

The **Bauhausgebäude**, one of the classic buildings of modern times, stands just west of the Hauptbahnhof on Gropiusallee, and can be reached in about five minutes from the rear exit via Schwabestrasse and Bauhausstrasse. A striking-looking structure even today, it was a sensation when the Bauhaus director, **Walter Gropius**, designed it in 1925 as the new custom-built headquarters for the school on its move here from

Weimar (see *Chapter Eleven*). Built according to the very latest methods around a steel and concrete skeleton with much use of light-admitting glass, it was the forerunner of architectural styles that would not come into their own until the 1950s and 60s. There are actually three interconnected structures – one with the classrooms, a second with the workshops, the third the student residence. Following a comprehensive restoration programme in the 1970s (the Bauhausgebäude was damaged in World War II and not properly restored), an art and design college was re-established here, so there's unrestricted access to much of the building. The workshop wing – whose starkly Cubist appearance has inspired countless buildings around the world – also houses a **museum** (Wed–Fri 10am–5pm, Sat & Sun 10am–12.30pm & 2–5pm; DM2.10). This contains an enormous collection of furniture, ceramics, graphics and photographs detailing the work done here, with background information about the Germany of the 1920s. Special exhibitions are also featured, whereupon the entry price is doubled.

Ten minutes' walk north of the Bauhausgebäude itself, at the beginning of Ebertallee, are the **Meisterhäuser**, a collection of seven houses built for the senior staff of the school. Gropius, who was again responsible for the design, lived in the first house in the scheme, which was later occupied in turn by the subsequent directors, Hannes Meyer and Mies van der Rohe; the others were the homes of Moholy-Nagy, Feininger, Muche, Schlemmer, Kandinsky and Klee. These angular buildings were revolutionary for 1926, though the passing of years and familiarity with styles of architecture derived from Gropius and others lessens their impact today. About fifteen minutes' walk north of here, overlooking a horseshoe bend in the Elbe, is the **Kornhaus**, a restaurant-cum-dance hall by Carl Fieger, one of Gropius' assistants. With the fine views over the river from its terrace, it makes a good spot for a relaxing break from sightseeing.

The Georgium

Immediately to the northwest of the Hauptbahnhof is the **Georgium**, the most accessible of the eighteenth-century parks to be found in and around the city. At its heart stands the modest-sized and graceful Neoclassical **Schloss Georgium** (Wed–Sun 10am–6pm; DM3). The collection of old masters inside includes works by Cranach, Rubens, Hals and Dou; there are also a large number of official portraits of members of the ruling house, many by J. F. A. Tischbein. It's worth walking through the shady park itself, which is dotted with pools and artificial ruins. At its eastern end, just across Georgenallee, is the **Lehrpark**, planted with 125 different kinds of tree and home to numerous semi-captive small animals.

The city centre

Taking a stroll through the centre of Dessau, you could be forgiven for thinking that the bombing occurred only a few years ago, such is the desolate impression made by the concrete efforts of the rebuilders. The few surviving old buildings are the **Stadtbibliothek**, which lies just north of Schlossplatz, and, on the square itself, the turn-of-the-century **Rathaus** and the ruined **Marienkirche**. After unification, it was decided to rebuild the latter, the most southerly of the brick Gothic churches so characteristic of northern Germany, and work is now well underway. However, the **Schloss** itself is probably too far gone for any kind of meaningful restoration: the fragment known as the Johannbau is all that remains of what must once have been a splendid Renaissance palace.

A few minutes' walk west of here, on August-Bebel-Platz, is Gropius's **Arbeitsamt**, an employment office designed at the end of the 1920s, nowadays a health centre. The building consists of a semicircular hall, well-lit by glass skylights, joined to a two-storey administration building. It was built to achieve maximum efficiency, serving job-seekers as quickly as possible – something that was to become an urgent necessity after the start of the Depression in 1929.

Törten

A few kilometres south of town, reached by tram #1 from the Hauptbahnhof or the centre to Damaschkestrasse, is the suburb of **Törten**, a purpose-built settlement designed under the direction of Gropius to provide decent living conditions for Dessau's working-class population. The earliest buildings include the large **Konsumgebäude** in the middle of the scheme and the rows of houses along Klein Ring, Mittel Ring and Doppel Reihe; a second phase, constructed to designs by Hannes Meyer, added the **Laubenganghäuser**, the monumental blocks of flats on Peterholzstrasse. Unfortunately, the Bauhaus buildings are now somewhat engulfed by later apartment blocks which wouldn't look out of place on a public housing development in any big city. Nevertheless, fans of the school should definitely come out here to see two of its finest products – the austere, appropriately-named **Stahlhaus** (Steel House) by Georg Muche, and the futuristic **Haus Fieger**, built by Carl Fieger as his own home. Both are among the detached houses standing in their own gardens at the southern end of Südstrasse, occupying a privileged position vis-à-vis the rest of the estate.

Schloss Mosigkau and the Luisium

There are a couple of other worthwhile palace-garden complexes in the outer fringes of Dessau. The more important of the two is **Schloss Mosigkau** (guided tours Tues–Sun 10am–5pm; DM3), set in the western suburb of the same name, and reached by bus #D or #L or mainline train. Designed by Georg von Knobelsdorff, court architect to Frederick the Great, it contains a fine array of objets d'art and seventeenth-century Dutch and Flemish paintings, star piece being Van Dyck's *Portrait of Wilhelm II of Oranien-Nassau*. The **Luisium**, at the northeastern extremity of the city near the terminus of bus #G, is an English-style park with fake ruins, grottoes, sculptures and an Italianate villa – a pleasure to stroll through on summer afternoons.

Practicalities

Dessau's **tourist office** is at Friedrich-Naumann-Str. 12 (Mon & Wed–Fri 10am–noon & 2–6pm, Tues 10am–6pm; ☎4661). As ever, the best accommodation bet is a **private room** which can be arranged via the tourist office for DM25–35 plus a DM5 booking fee. There's also a **youth hostel** at Waldkaterweg 11 (☎3312); take bus #K from the Hauptbahnhof for four stops. Cheapest **hotels**, at around DM30 per person, are *Pension Claus*, Paul-König-Str. 34 (no phone), and *Neue Brücke*, Askanischer Str. 142 (☎2679). The only alternatives are both upmarket: *Central*, Albrechtplatz 6 (☎4863), has singles from DM53 and doubles from DM79, while *Stadt Dessau*, Kavalierstr. 35 (☎7285), has singles from DM63, doubles from DM104.

For **eating** and **drinking**, Dessau is relatively well off in comparison with most eastern German towns of its size. Top choice for a full sit-down meal is *Restaurant am Museum*, Franzstr. 90, with the *Ratskeller* in the Rathaus a more than acceptable alternative. If you're out visiting Törten, make a short detour south to *Jägerklause*, Alte Leipziger Str. 76, a restaurant specialising in game dishes which is open daily till late evening; the aforementioned *Kornhaus* on the eponymous street is the obvious destination if visiting the Bauhaus buildings at the opposite end of the city. In the Bauhausgebäude itself, there's a café serving coffee, cakes and snacks; another trendy hang-out is *An der Sieben Säulen*, Puschkinalle 57, a bookshop with art gallery and café, while the *Teehäuschen* in the Stadtpark at the western edge of the city centre is a tea-house which also serves full meals. The *Landestheater* on Fritz-Hesse-Platz offers a varied programme of **music** and **drama**.

Wörlitz

WÖRLITZ, which lies 18km east of Dessau, seems a world away in spirit: there's no sign of industrial blight here, just a quiet rural village destined to prosper as one of eastern Germany's greatest tourist magnets. For that, it can thank Leopold Friedrich Franz of Anhalt-Dessau, an enlightened despot who commissioned Friedrich Wilhlem von Erdmannsdorff, Anhalt's court architect, to upgrade his family's old hunting seat into the crowning showpiece of the principality's group of landscaped gardens.

The Schlosspark

Few places recall the spirit of the Age of Reason so evocatively as Worlitz's **Schlosspark**, whose layout, with its carefully planned axes and perspectives, was strongly influenced by the theoretical writings of Rousseau and Winckelmann. Not that there's anything remotely heavy-handed about it; on the contrary, it radiates a sense of sheer unbridled delight which remains as enjoyably heart-warming today as it ever did. It's a very conscious act of homage to England, then in the first throes of the Industrial Revolution, which had made a great impression on both Prince Leopold and Erdmannsdorff when they travelled there together. In particular, it copies the very English idea of a country house with a working estate, a concept then completely foreign to Germany, where the aristorcracy retained a far greater degree of feudalistic political power and hence generally resided in urban palaces, creating gardens for purely private recreational use.

The village and the Schloss

The park seems to grow seamlessly out of the **village**, which itself contains a number of buildings by Erdmannsdorff, including the central Markt with the Rathaus, a brewery and a farm. This embryonic relationship was inspired by the then-revolutionary intention that the public should be free to enjoy the park at all times – hence the lack of entrance barriers. To further emphasise the narrowing of the gap between rulers and ruled, the pristine white **Schloss** (guided tours April & Oct Mon 1–4pm, Tues–Sun 10am–4pm; May–Sept daily 10am–5pm; DM4) was built right beside the village, at the edge rather than the middle of the park. Strongly influenced by the neo-Palladian stately homes of England, it marked the German debut of Neoclassicism. Inside, there's none of the bombast normally found in German palaces; instead, everything is on an intimate scale. There are a number of impressive antique statues, the most important being the *Amazon of Wörlitz*, a Roman copy of a lost Greek original. Pick of a choice group of old master paintings is Rubens' *Alexander the Great Crowning Roxana*.

The gardens

To the rear of the Schloss is the elliptical **Wörlitzer See**, the largest of the park's four lakes, which are interconnected by means of canals. It's overlooked by the circular **Synagoge**, which, in a sad reversal of the original ideals of Wörlitz, had its interior burnt out on *Kristallnacht*. To reach the main gardens you have to take a ferry over the lake from here, but you can avoid the expense by making a detour east to the least visited but perhaps the most attractive part of the park. At the **Grotto der Egeria**, which stands opposite the **Stein**, an island with a number of fake Roman ruins, the path swings north, passing over a miniature version of the Industrial Revolution's symbol, the Iron Bridge in Shropshire, to the lakeside **Pantheon**, a mini-version of its great Roman counterpart.

West of here, on the northern shore of the Wörlitzer See, the central **Schochs Garten** is dotted with mock-Classical statues urns and sarcophagi, plus temples to

Flora and Venus. The wider historicist sympathies marking the beginnings of Romanticism are shown by the inexhaustible types of **bridges** – chain, swing, stepped, floating and arched being just some of the varieties. An even clearer indication of this trend comes with the second of the palaces, the **Gotisches Haus** (guided tours as for Schloss; DM3.50), which presents a somewhat squat, dream-like vision of the long-neglected Gothic style. The interior furnishings cunningly mix the genuine and the pastiche; among the former are a roomful of paintings by Cranach. At the southern-most end of the park are a number of islands. Largest of these is **Neumarks Garten**, which features a labyrinth, a pergola, a library and an exhibition building.

Practicalities

To see Wörlitz properly, you really need the best part of a day: it takes several hours just to walk round the entire length of the park – and there are surprises in even the most far-flung corners. If possible, avoid weekends and holidays, when an uncomfortably large number of people throng the immediate vicinity of the Schloss. Unfortunately, the most atmospheric way to approach the village – on the *Wörlitzer Eisenbahn*, a **train** which leaves from its own station just north of Dessau's Hauptbahnhof – is only possible on Wednesdays, Saturdays and Sundays between Easter and October; two return journeys are made each day, and historic locomotives are sometimes used. Otherwise, there's a very regular **bus** link with Dessau and a somewhat less frequent one with Wittenberg. The **tourist office** (May–Oct Mon–Wed & Fri 8am–5pm, Thurs 8am–6pm, Sat & Sun 9am–noon & 12.30–5pm; Nov–April Mon–Wed & Fri 8am–4pm, Thurs 8am–6pm; ☎216) is at the edge of the park. Should you want to stay, there's a handful of **private houses** in the village with rooms to rent, while the best place for a **meal** is *Gasthaus Zum Stein*, Thälmannstr. 7.

Wittenberg

Little land, little land,
You are but a heap of sand.
If I dig you, the soil is light,
If I reap you, the yield is slight.

Martin Luther.

It's seems hard to believe such a small and unassuming town as **WITTENBERG**, which lies 35km east of Dessau on the main Berlin–Halle railway line, played a pivotal role in the history of Europe. Built on a sandbank on the north bank of the Elbe, it stretched for no more than 1.5km end to end and had a population of just 2500 at the time when **Martin Luther** – the man whose impact on German society and culture has arguably been more profound and long-lasting than that of any other individual – formulated his 95 theses attacking the corrupt trade in indulgences and so launched the Protestant Reformation. Nowadays bearing the official designation of "Lutherstadt Wittenberg", the town retains its historic core and, though slightly run-down by western standards, is positively gleaming in comparison with most places in the former GDR, due to the comprehensive restoration programme carried out in 1983 to mark the 500th anniversary of Luther's birth. This had been preceded by a stealthy political rehabilitation of the reformer, hitherto regarded as a great historical villain for his opposition to the Peasants' Revolt of 1525. The appropriation of Luther for the Communist cause was one of the most absurdly illogical propaganda acts ever committed by the GDR authorities, whose irony was exposed six years later when the town's senior pastor, Friedrich Schorlemmer, took up the mantle of his illustrious predecessor and became a leading figure in the peaceful revolution which toppled the regime.

After Henry the Lion was divested of most of his territories by order of Emperor Frederick Barbarossa, two tiny duchies competed for the right to be regarded as the successor state of Saxony. The one centered on Wittenberg eventually gained the upper hand, and was awarded one of the seven Electorates of the Holy Roman Empire. In 1422, the House of Wettin won control of Saxony: when it divided into the rival Ernestine and Albertine lines in 1485, Wittenberg remained the capital of the former, the more senior of the two. The new Elector, **Frederick the Wise**, was both a pious and enlightened ruler who justified his sobriquet by his sure-footed political dealings. His greatest enthusiasm was for the **University** he founded here in 1502 as a rival to its hundred-year-old counterpart in Leipzig, which lay on Albertine territory. Luther, then an Augustinian monk, came to give philosophy lectures in 1508, settling permanently three years later, whereupon he was appointed to the chair of Biblical studies and quickly established a reputation as its star teacher.

Although Luther's attacks on Catholic dogma clashed with some of Frederick's most cherished beliefs, the Elector's unwavering support for his right to speak his mind was of fundamental importance to the success of the Reformation, whose impact on Germany was as profound in the political sense (in that it led to a new, highly decentralised order that was to last for centuries) as the religious. In as much as it was possible to do so, the course of the Reform movement was directed by Luther and his associates from Wittenberg, earning it the tongue-in-cheek nickname of "the Protestant Rome". The town's fortunes waned very quickly after Luther's death in 1546, though it was pure coincidence that just one year later it lost its status as capital of Electoral Saxony when the Albertines usurped the Ernestines and made Dresden the main seat of their court. Sacked in the Seven Years' War, Wittenberg sank into total insignificance in 1815, when it was absorbed by Prussia and the University was shut down and incorporated into that of Halle. However, unlike many of the other German cities which lost their universities around this time, it has managed a modest revival of academic life, regaining a theology faculty which functions once more as a leading centre of Protestant thought.

The Lutherhaus

Arriving at the Bahnhof, follow the tracks southwards, then go through the underpass. Immediately facing you is an oak known as the **Luthereiche**; it's planted on the exact spot where, in December 1520, Luther burned the papal bull threatening him with excommunication if he failed to retract his views. Collegienstrasse, Wittenberg's main street, leads west from here; at no. 54 is the **Augusteum**, the former medical faculty building of the University. On the southern side of its courtyard is the **Lutherhaus** (Tues–Sun 9am–5pm; DM4), which was originally the Augustinian monastery that Luther entered on arriving in Wittenberg. When this dissolved at the beginning of the Reformation, it was given to him as his home; he and his family occupied a few rooms, with the rest serving as a hall of residence for students. Entry is via the ornate **Katharinenportal**, a birthday gift to Luther from his wife, the former Cistercian nun Katherina von Bora, in 1540.

A display on the ground floor relates the history of the building itself, and in the former monks' refectory (now an occasional concert hall) an exhibition chronicles the career of one of Luther's immediate circle, **Lucas Cranach the Elder**. Court painter to the Electors of Saxony, Cranach had an astonishingly successful career, not only as an artist, but as a local businessman and politician, and was for several years mayor of the town. His role as chief pictorial propagandist for the Reformation is illustrated by his didactic depiction of *The Ten Commandments* which forms the centrepiece of the display. Eleven carefully laid out rooms on the first floor take the visitor through Luther's life and work, setting it in the social and political context of medieval Europe. His progress from early doubts as a young monk, through open criticism of the Roman

Catholic Church to confrontation with the Pope and Emperor, and eventual formulation of the principles of the Reformation, is detailed exhaustively, with the aid of contemporary paintings, excerpts from his writings and numerous items of Lutherabilia. Particularly intriguing is the **Lutherstube**, the part of the building Luther and his family lived in, complete with ornate Renaissance tiled oven and faded seventeenth-century wall decorations. The second floor is devoted to Luther's hugely influential role as a translator of the Bible, work which played an important role in the development of written German.

The Melanchthonhaus

A couple of doors down from the Lutherhaus at Collegienstr. 60 is the **Melanchthonhaus** (Mon–Thurs 9am–5pm, Sat & Sun 10am–noon & 2–5pm; DM1), a Renaissance residence with a gable that resembles fingers rising above an outstretched palm. It commemorates the career of Luther's closest lieutenant and the greatest scholar of the Reformation period, **Philipp Schwarzend**, who is generally known as **Melanchthon** (the Graecised form of his surname). He came to Wittenberg as Professor of Greek in 1519, when aged just 21, and soon found himself caught up in the dramatic events which had begun there two years previously. Though he lacked Luther's drive and self-assuredness, he possessed a sharper intellect and was primarily responsible for the precise articulation of the new Protestant doctrines: the Augsburg Confession, the definitive statement of the Lutheran faith, is chiefly his work.

Upstairs, Melanchthon's apartments have been recreated using cleverly aged furniture – even the woodworm is fake, reproduced by means of shotgun blasts. Along the ground-floor corridor is an exhibition devoted to the history of Wittenberg, including the mummified hand of a woman broken on a wheel before the Rathaus in 1728 for poisoning her four step-children.

The Marktplatz

Collegienstrasse terminates at the **Marktplatz**, which preserves a number of Renaissance mansions, among them the pharmacy owned by Cranach and the **Rathaus**, an august white gabled building with a red-tiled roof. Its richly decorated portal, adorned with allegorical figures, completes the picture of sixteenth-century grandeur, and provides a suitable backdrop for **monuments to Luther and Melanchthon**. That to Luther was erected in 1821, with a statue topped with a cage-like canopy designed by Schinkel. The similarly styled Melanchthon memorial was not added until 1860.

Rising high above the row of houses at the eastern end of Marktplatz is the **Stadtkirche St Marien** (daily 9am–noon & 2–4pm). This twin-towered Gothic church is Wittenberg's oldest surviving building; the choir dates back to around 1300, though work on the rest went on until 1470, while the distinctive octagonal turrets were only added after the Reformation. Luther often preached from its pulpit; he was married there in 1525, while each of his six children were baptised in the church's magnificent late Gothic **font**, which was made by Hermann Vischer, founder of the renowned Nürnberg dynasty of bronze casters. The church's walls are hung with a splendid series of carved and painted **epitaphs**, the finest being that to Lucas Cranach the Younger. However, the most eye-catching decorative feature is the large and complex **Reformation altar** by Cranach the Elder. In the central scene of *The Last Supper*, Luther is shown as the disciple receiving the cup; in the predella he preaches on the theme of the crucified Christ; while other leading figures of the Reformation, including Melanchthon and Frederick the Wise, are featured on the two wings.

The Schlosskirche and Residenzschloss

Schloss Strasse leads west from Marktplatz to the far end of the historic part of town, where stands the **Schlosskirche** (Tues–Sat 9am–noon & 2–4.45pm, Sun 10.30am–

noon & 2–4.45pm), late Gothic by origin, but extensively remodelled last century. The famous wooden **doors** where Luther nailed his theses on 31 October, 1517 were destroyed during the Seven Years' War; their heavy bronze replacements were installed in 1858 to commemorate the 375th anniversary of Luther's birth, and have the Latin texts of the 95 theses inscribed on them. On Christmas Day, 1521, when Luther was in hiding at the Wartburg near Eisenach, the church was the setting for the **first-ever** Protestant service, conducted by the most radical of the Wittenberg reformers, Andreas Carlstadt, in the presence of virtually the entire population of the town. Dressed in a plain black robe instead of the usual priestly vestments, he set the tenor of future public worship by addressing the congregation in the vernacular as well as Latin, and dispensing wine as well as bread during the Communion. More or less opposite the doorway of the church are the simple tombs of Luther and Melanchthon. The rest of the interior is a riot of statues, reliefs, portraits and epitaphs of local worthies. Look out for the bronze epitaph to Frederick the Wise, and the pair of large alabaster statues of the same Elector and his heir, John the Steadfast.

The Schlosskirche forms part of the **Residenzschloss**, though this once-resplendent Renaissance palace is but a shadow of its former self, having been repeatedly ravaged by fire and war. These days, it houses a youth hostel, reached via an unusual exterior staircase in the western wing. The same wing is also home to the **Stadtgeschichtliches Museum** (9–11.30am & 12.30–5pm; closed Fri; DM2), a local history museum which was closed indefinitely at the time of writing, and the **Museum für Natur- und Völkerkunde** (Tues–Fri 9am–5pm, Sat & Sun 9am–12.30pm & 2–4pm; DM2), which has natural history and ethnography collections.

Practicalities

Wittenberg's **tourist office** is at Collegienstr. 8 (April–Oct Mon–Fri 9am–6pm, Sat & Sun 10am–2pm; Nov–March Mon–Fri 9am–5pm; ☎2239 or 2537). They can fix you up with **private rooms**, though it's worth knowing that the **youth hostel**, with its enticing location in the Residenzschloss (☎3255), can accommodate you in doubles. There are only two **hotels** – *Goldener Adler*, Markt 7 (☎2053), and *Wittenberger Hof*, Collegienstr. 56 (☎3594); both charge around DM40 per person, though rates at the latter are likely to increase following refurbishment. For **eating** and **drinking**, the best bet is probably the *Haus des Handwerks*, Collegienstr. 53a, which offers tasty no-nonsense Teutonic cuisine at reasonable prices. Other options include the swanky *Schlosskeller*, Schlossplatz 1, the more downmarket *Ratschänke*, Markt 14, and the innovative if gimmicky *Schlossfreiheit* on Coswiger Strasse just off the Markt. For other **entertainments**, it's worth finding out what's on at the *Elbe-Elster-Theater*, Thomas-Müntzer-Str. 14, which features all kinds of dramatic offerings, including cabaret and puppet shows.

Halle

When the Land of Saxony-Anhalt was created in 1947, the old market and salt-producing city of **HALLE** was chosen as capital. It recommended itself to the Communists on account of its position at the heart of one of eastern Germany's largest industrial belts and its distinguished Socialist pedigree through its prominent role in the 1918 Revolution and the resistance to the 1920 Kapp Putsch. Communist favour, however, proved a severe disadvantage to its cause when it did battle with Magdeburg, capital of the other *Bezirk* into which Saxony-Anhalt had been divided, on the resurrection of the Land in 1990 – though its defeat seemed justified by the fact that it had actually belonged to its rival throughout most of the Middle Ages. In compensation, it has become the Land's largest city by incorporating the hitherto separately-governed Halle-

Neustadt (the most important new town built in the GDR epoch) on the opposite side of the Saale. Relatively little damaged in World War II, Halle ranks, along with Erfurt, as the German city most reminiscent of its prewar self. It has been horridly racked by pollution, but still contains enough of interest to warrant a visit of a day or two.

The city

A cross-section of Halle can be seen in the fifteen minutes it takes to walk to the central Marktplatz from the **Hauptbahnhof**. You're firstly confronted with a monumental Stalinist-style square-cum-highway intersection, complete with the one hotel westerners were allowed to stay in during GDR days. Crossing via the pedestrian underpass, you come to the **Leipziger Tor**, the sole surviving medieval gateway; this guards the inner ring road, whose course follows that of the fortifications, of which only fragments survive. Ahead is the pedestrianised Leipziger Strasse, lined with grandiose Wilhelmine buildings; since the *Wende*, this has adopted the character of a typical main shopping street.

The Marktplatz

Halle's **Marktplatz**, which is surveyed by a pensive statue of the city's favourite son, the composer **George Frederic Handel**, immediately impresses by virtue of its monumental dimensions and its many-towered skyline. Its aptness for large-scale political meetings was demonstrated during the *Wende* and the subsequent election campaigns, which featured a triumphant home-coming by the most famous contemporary native of Halle, West Germany's Foreign Minister (until his resignation in April 1992), **Hans-Dietrich Genscher**. Having defected from the GDR in 1952, Genscher had the perfect background for his key role in the unification process, and he played the part with aplomb, providing a pragmatic and steadying influence on the often over-emotional approach adopted by Chancellor Kohl.

Unfortunately, the Markplatz's beauty and its recently regained function as a market square are handicapped by the fact that it's the hub of the tram network. Doubtless the system will go underground in due course, but in the meantime there's an unsightly mass of rails and cables. A far less excusable eyesore is the gallery, now housing the tourist office, which was added in the 1970s to the **Roter Turm** (Red Tower), a free-standing late-Gothic belfry topped by an engagingly fantastical spire with little corner turrets. Outside is a **statue of Roland**, an eighteenth-century stone copy of the wooden original, which was erected during the days when Halle was a member of the Hansa as a visible symbol of the city's desire to assert its independence from its feudal overlords, the Magdeburg archbishops.

The **Marktkirche Unser Lieben Frauen** (Mon & Wed–Fri 3–6pm, Thurs 4–5pm, Sat 9am–noon, Sun 11am–noon) opposite is a real oddity. Both the Hausmannstürme to the east and the Blaue Türme (Blue Towers) to the west formerly belonged to two different Romanesque churches, which were demolished in 1529 by order of Cardinal Albrecht von Brandenburg, Archbishop of Magdeburg and Mainz, as part of his ambitious but ill-conceived programme to turn Halle into a showpiece Catholic city which would spearhead a counter-attack on the Wittenberg-led Reformation. The two pairs of towers were then linked up by a brand new hall church in the Flamboyant Gothic style. An unknown follower of Cranach, dubbed the Master of Annaberg, painted its **high altar**, which immodestly features a large portrait of Cardinal Albrecht flanked by Saints Mary Magdalene, John the Evangelist and Catherine; he also turns up at the far right of the predella in the group of saints adoring the Madonna and Child. A few years after the Marktkirche was completed, Halle adopted the Reformation; the church was then converted to Protestant use. A later adornment was the tiny Baroque **organ**, on which Handel received lessons; it can be heard on Tuesdays at 4.30pm, on Fridays at 5.30pm.

Further musical delights, this time of the visual variety, can be had at the **Marktschlösschen**, a small Renaissance palace at no. 13 on the square. Part of this houses a collection of historical instruments (Wed–Sun 1.30–5.30pm; DM1); the rest is a gallery featuring changing exhibitions of contemporary art.

The Händelhaus

Immediately north of Marktplatz is a maze of run-down but nonetheless evocative old streets. At Grosse Nikolaistr. 5 is the **Händelhaus** (Tues, Wed & Fri–Sun 9.30am–5.30pm, Thurs 9.30am–7pm; DM1.50), the large Baroque mansion where the great composer was born. It contains extensive documentation on his life and times, though at the time of writing this was still marred by being subject to tiresomely irrelevant Marxist interpretations. As compensation, you can listen to soundtracks of many of Handel's most famous works.

GEORGE FREDERIC HANDEL (1685–1759)

The career of the man born as Georg Friedrich Händel differs starkly from that of any previous German musician. Unattracted by the musician's normal, very provincial existence as *Kappelmeister* to a court, or *Kantor* in a large church (roles which occupied his close contemporary J.S. Bach throughout his entire life), Handel embarked on a dazzling peripatetic career as a virtuoso keyboard player and composer. Notwithstanding his devout Protestant faith, he was lionised during his long sojourn in Italy, and successfully blended the showy Italianate forms with solid German counterpoint into a unique musical language of his own. On his return to Germany, he had a spell as musical director to the court at Hannover. Anticipating the succession of his patron to the British throne, he moved to London, where he stayed for the rest of his life. There he found his true spiritual home – he abandoned his previously footloose existence altogether, changing both his name and nationality – and entered his most productive creative phase, in which his favoured format increasingly became oratorios set to English texts. Of these, the sublime *Messiah* has become one of the great set-pieces of Protestant culture, whose annual performance is a ritual performed by choirs, both amateur and professional, all round the world.

The rest of the northern Altstadt

A couple of minutes' walk west of the Händelhaus is the **Dom** (Mon–Sat 3–4pm, Sun 11.30am–12.30pm). Originally, this was part of a Dominican monastery, and the basic structure employs the simple, unadorned forms favoured by preaching orders of monks. Its present eccentric appearance, however, is largely due to a remodelling commissioned by Cardinal Albrecht, who took it over to serve as his court church. A curious gabled upper storey in brick, one of the earliest Renaissance constructions in central Germany, was tacked on to the old building; the entrance portal and interior staircase are also in this style. Most of the lavish interior decorations have been dispersed, though seventeen over-life-sized **statues of saints** remain *in situ*. A later Baroque transformation, carried out after the Dom became a Protestant parish church, brought the high altar and the organ, at which Handel presided as a teenager.

On the south side of the Dom is the **Neue Residenz**, a Tuscan-style *palazzo* which the Cardinal hoped to develop into the Catholic answer to Wittenberg University, but which, in a neat twist of fate, is used by the institution now known as the Martin-Luther-Universität Halle-Wittenberg. Part of the building is given over to the **Geiseltalmuseum** (Mon–Fri 9am–noon & 2.30–5pm; free), a collection of fossils, reckoned to be 50 million years old, found perfectly preserved in the brown coal region of the Geisel valley just south of the city. Don't be put off by the obtuse subject matter – it's a fascinating display.

A couple of blocks north of the Dom is the **Moritzburg**, constructed as a citadel against the rebellious burghers by Archbishop Ernst at the end of the fifteenth century, but converted into a palace a generation later under Cardinal Albrecht. It now contains the main student club and a satirical cabaret, while the south and west wings house the **Staatliche Galerie** (Tues 11am–8pm, Wed–Fri 10am–5pm, Sat & Sun 10am–5.30pm; DM1.50). In vaulted cellars is a good decorative arts section, the most notable pieces being statues from demolished buildings. Elsewhere, the emphasis is on painting and sculpture of the nineteenth and twentieth centuries: Klimt, Kirchner, Marc, Munch, Beckmann and Barlach are among those represented.

Following the ring road eastwards from here, you come to the main **University quarter**, which stretches along both sides of the divide. Predictably, it's a bustle of activity during term-time; it has already, to a certain extent, shaken off the shackles of Communism to become a centre of nightlife akin to its counterparts in western Germany. The main buildings are in the Altstadt section, attractive Neoclassical palaces erected in the early nineteenth century.

The southern Altstadt

From the Marktplatz, Schmeerstrasse leads to the **Alter Markt**, the elongated original square with the **Eselbrunnen** (Donkey Fountain) in the centre, which was used for markets until supplanted by its much larger successor. **Rannische Strasse**, which leads south from the intersection of Schmeerstrasse and Alter Markt, boasts a superb array of Renaissance, Baroque and Rococo mansions. Though thick with grime and in desperate need of restoration, the quality of nos. 10, 17, 20 and 21, in particular, is clear.

Beyond the western end of Alter Markt is the fifteenth-century **Moritzkirche**, the Catholic parish church. From outside, it presents an austere picture, an appearance accentuated by the fact that it's built directly on to one of the surviving sections of the medieval walls. The hall interior, in contrast, is light and spacious, with elaborate star and network vaults and limpid sculptures by Conrad von Einbeck.

Outside the Altstadt

Of the varied attractions outside the confines of the Altstadt, pride of place goes to the old saltworks, now the **Technisches Halloren- und Salinenmuseum** ((Tues–Sun 10am–4pm; DM1.50). It's set on an island formed by two arms of the Saale, and is about ten minutes' walk from either the Moritzkirche or the Neue Residenz, with the tall brick chimney which rises above the half-timbered buildings providing a useful pointer. If you come on a Sunday, you can see the last surviving salt pan being used to produce an excellent coarse-grained salt – which is on sale at the shop. At other times, you'll have to be content with seeing the machinery and the associated historical documentation.

On the fringes of the ring road are a couple of historical curiosities worth seeking out. East of the Moritzkirche is the **Franckesches Waisenhaus**, an immensely long Baroque structure erected at the turn of the eighteenth century by the pedagogue August Hermann Franck as an orphanage, school and charitable institution for the poor; in time, this spawned a number of other buildings behind, which formed a minia-ture town in their own right. Ten minutes' walk northeast of here, beyond the Leipziger Tor, is the **Stadtgottesacker**, a cemetery founded by the ubiquitous Cardinal Albrecht, which was converted by Nickel Hoffmann into an elaborate galleried necropolis in the manner of the Campo Santo in Pisa.

Well to the north of the city centre, at Richard-Wagner-Str. 9, is the **Landesmuseum für Vorgeschichte** (Tues, Thurs, Sat & Sun 10am–4pm, Wed 10am–5pm, Fri 10am–3pm; DM1.50), which contains an important collection of Stone, Bronze and Iron Age artefacts found in the Halle area. To get to the museum, it's best to take tram #7, which continues on to **Burg Giebichenstein** (also served by tram #8 from the centre). There are actually two castles here, both of which were destroyed in the Thirty Years' War.

The lower, or **Unterburg**, was first constructed in the tenth century under King Henry the Fowler, although the oldest surviving portions are mid-fifteenth-century. It was rebuilt in the Baroque period, and now serves as a school of arts and crafts. The fourteenth-century **Oberburg** (Tues–Sun 11am–6pm; DM1), perched on the cliff above, has been left in an appropriately ruinous and overgrown state, but it's well worth climbing for the sake of the sweeping view over the Saale valley. **Cruises** on the river depart daily in summer from the landing stage immediately below the castle.

Practicalities

The **tourist office** (Mon, Tues, Thurs & Fri 9am–6pm, Wed 10am–6pm, Sat 9am–1pm; ☎23340) is in the Roter Turm on Marktplatz. There's a separate number (☎28371) for their **room-finding** service; rates in private houses start at DM25. As in all large eastern cities, **hotels** are overpriced and generally fully booked during the week by businesspeople from the west. At the moment, the only promising possibility is the *Christliches Hospiz Marta-Haus*, Adam-Kuckhoff-Str. 5–8 (☎24411), which charges DM35 per person. However, a number of new pensions are beginning to appear; check with the tourist office for the latest details. There's also a **youth hostel** in the northern part of the University quarter at August-Bebel-Str. 48a (☎24716).

Halle looks like developing into one of the better places in the former GDR for **eating** and **drinking**; a whole string of new fast food joints, café-bars and bistros have opened up along Grosse Ulrichstrasse, which leads north from Marktplatz. Of the longer-established restaurants, best is probably that in the hotel *Rotes Ross*, Leipziger Str. 76, which also has a beer garden. Other options include *Zum Roland*, Markt 23, *Schellenmortiz*, An der Moritzkirche 1, and *Goldene Rose*, Rannische Str. 19. There are also a number of decent traditional cafés and ice-cream parlours on Leipziger Strasse, notably *Boulevard-Café* at no. 87 and *Café Fritze* at no. 12.

Trendiest **nightspot** is the *Studentenclub* in the Moritzburg (free admission with student ID); others include *Schorre*, Philipp-Müller-Str. 78 (south of the Franckesches Waisenhaus), and *Heinrich- und Thomas-Mann-Club* at no. 28 on the eponymous street in the north of the University quarter. The main **theatre** venue is the *Landestheater*, Universitätsring 24; there's also a *Puppentheater* at Mühlweg 12 and a satirical cabaret in the Moritzburg. **Concerts** are held in the Händelhaus and in the Ulrichkirche, a deconsecrated Gothic church just off Leipziger Strasse. **Festivals** include the *Händel-Festspiele* in June, featuring the music of Handel; the *Lanternenfest* on the last weekend of August; and the *Drachenfest* in October.

Merseburg

MERSEBURG, the most venerable of the towns in the region, was a favourite royal seat in the tenth century. Just 13km up the Saale from Halle, from which it can be reached by train or tram #5, it now has the decided misfortune to be sandwiched between two giant chemical plants, *Buna-Werke* and *Leuna-Werke*. The latter was the GDR's largest single enterprise – it's so vast that it has two train stations – and it remains as a shocking picture of the sort of technology which should now belong only in history books. As a result of the incessant burning of lignite by these two factories, the air in and around Merseburg is often suffocatingly heavy, and the city's historic monuments have been left appallingly scarred. There's no stronger evidence of the disastrous nature of the GDR's industrial policies than this – which is a terrible shame, as Merseburg must once have been among eastern Germany's prettiest towns, and still retains the arresting medieval skyline of its upper town, which completely overshadows the commercial quarter below.

The Dom

Set high above the Saale, the **Dom** (Mon–Sat 9am–noon & 1–4/6pm, Sun 1–5pm; DM1.50) was founded as a missionary bishopric in the early eleventh century, though only the crypt survives from this time. Of the thirteenth-century Transitional style rebuilding there remain the choir, transepts and westwork, whose pair of octagonal towers contrast well with their cylindrical counterparts at the east end. A Flamboyant Gothic hall nave was substituted in the sixteenth century.

The most eye-catching furnishings are the **funerary monuments**. Look out in particular for the hauntingly hierarchical bronze memorial in the choir to the eleventh-century royal pretender Rudolf of Swabia, and the Renaissance epitaph in the north transept, cast by Hermann Vischer of Nürnberg, to Bishop Thilo von Trotha. A chapel in the cloisters houses the mid-thirteenth-century memorial to the knight Hermann von Hagen, carved with a sense of characterisation clearly inspired by the famous workshop of nearby Naumburg.

The Schloss

Adjoining the north side of the Dom is the stately **Schloss**, originally the residence of the prince-bishops, later of the secular dukes. Its wings range in style from Flamboyant Gothic to Baroque, though Renaissance predominates, with the superb portal and oriel being the most distinguishing features. The peace of the courtyard is constantly disturbed by the squawkings of the caged **raven**, the latest in a line dating back to the late fifteenth century. Its presence is explained by the fact that, when Bishop Thilo von Trotha's most precious ring was stolen, an innocent man was charged with the crime, tried and executed. After his death, the missing ring was found in a raven's nest, whereupon the guilty bird was imprisoned in a cage for the rest of his life, with his sin ever after being visited on a member of the same species. Most of the Schloss is used as offices, but a small part contains the **Kreismuseum** (Tues–Sun 9am–5pm; DM1), with the standard archaeology and local history displays.

Naumburg

Before the war, **NAUMBURG**, which is set on heights overlooking the Saale valley 20km upstream from Merseburg, was considered one of Germany's most beautiful and distinctive towns, thanks mainly to its peerless Dom, which dominates the skyline and shows medieval architecture and sculpture at their highest peak. Although it suffered minimal bomb damage, Naumburg fell off tourist itineraries in the GDR period and became the headquarters of a large Soviet garrison, who still maintain an unusually visible presence. Despite this, the town has made giant steps in scraping off the grime which had smothered its buildings and is well on the way to reappearing at its best.

The Dom

In 1027, the prince-bishopric of Zeitz was transferred 29km northwest to Naumburg, which had been founded at the beginning of the century as a fortress by Margrave Ekkehardt I of Meissen. By the beginning of the thirteenth century, the town had prospered as a market centre, and it was decided to replace the original cathedral with a spectacular new structure – the present **Dom** (April–Sept Mon–Sat 8am–noon & 1–6pm, Sun noon–6pm; March & Oct Mon–Sat 9am–noon & 1–5pm, Sun noon–5pm; Nov–Feb Mon–Sat 9am–noon & 1–4pm, Sun noon–4pm; DM3.50). Yet, although it was built as one of Germany's showpiece cathedrals, with choirs at both ends of the building to emphasise its imperial status and a monastery-like range of ancillary buildings, it's no more than a Protestant parish church these days, the bishopric having been suppressed in 1564 following the reign of the first and last Lutheran incumbent.

The building

Because the Dom was built at a time of rapidly changing architectural tastes, it exhibits a variety of different yet compatible styles – despite having been substantially completed in the relatively short period of fifty years. Taking the national penchant for the picturesque to its limits, the original masons began by erecting the **east choir**, complete with its almost oriental-looking **towers**, according to florid late Romanesque principles; the cupolas added in the Baroque period further add to the exotic appearance. The transepts and the nave are Transitional in approach, whereas the superbly harmonious **west choir**, with its polygonal apse (a replica of which was added to the east choir the following century), adopts the pure High Gothic of the great French cathedrals. Nonetheless, its towers help give it a distinctively German accent, though only the northern one dates back to this time. Its stylistic twin was added, in accordance with the original plans, at the end of last century, as a result of the Romantic movement's frenzied enthusiasm for all things Gothic which inspired the belated completion of so many important German churches.

The west choir

Pride of the interior is the assemblage of sculptures in the west choir, which rank among the all-time masterpieces of the art; indeed, it's little exaggeration to say that they are to the medieval period what the Parthenon sculptures are to the Classical, or Michelangelo's Medici tombs to the High Renaissance. They were carved by a workshop led by the so-called **Master of Naumburg**, by far the most idiosyncratic and original of all the masons who created the great European cathedrals: his ideas and techniques were at least 150 years ahead of their time, anticipating both the Renaissance and the Reformation. Though it's reasonable to suppose that he was a German, he was trained in France, after which he worked at the Dom in Mainz, where a few fragmentary carvings by him can still be seen.

The polychrome **rood screen**, illustrating the Passion, is unlike anything previously found in religious art. Each of the life-sized figures of the crucified Christ, the Virgin and Saint John radiates an enormous sense of suffering and pathos – but recognisably human, not other-worldly. On the upper frieze, the small scenes unfold like a great drama, with plenty of anecdotal detail and a wonderfully rhythmic sense of movement imparted in the gestures and groupings of the figures. Sadly, the last two of these were destroyed by fire, and replaced by Baroque pastiches, whose feebleness serves to emphasise the Master's genius. As a bonus, plants, flowers and fruits are featured on a second frieze, and on the capitals and keystones; carved with a matchless sensitivity, these are the earliest botanically accurate depictions in western art.

Very different from the rood screen, but recognisably the product of the same humanistic mind, are the twelve large **statues of the founders**, again still preserving much of their original colouring, which are placed on pedestals within the west choir. The granting of such prominent positions of honour to lay personages was, to say the least, unusual, but what is even more remarkable is that each is given a highly distinctive and noble characterisation – no mean feat, given that the people depicted were all long dead and thus known to the sculptor from nothing more substantial than old chronicles. Particularly outstanding are the imperiously serene couple **Ekkehardt II and Uta**, who stand together on the first pillar on the north side of the apse; they've become the most famous statues in the country, symbolising the Germans' own romantic view of their chivalrous medieval past. The only other pair is of **Hermann and Reglindis** – he pensive, she smiling, as if to accentuate the contrast between the two and their counterparts opposite.

The east choir

Inevitably, the east choir is overshadowed by the west, though it's equally well preserved. It also has a **rood screen** – this is the only medieval church in Europe to have two – in this case a simple Romanesque structure adorned with a cycle of retouched frescos. Ascending to the intimate **high choir**, with its elaborate late Gothic stalls, its fourteenth-century high altar and its gleaming stained glass windows, is like eavesdropping on the past, as it can hardly have changed in centuries. Here also are two more works from the celebrated sculptural workshop – the statue of a deacon and the tomb of Bishop Dietrich II.

The rest of the town

Steinweg and its continuation Herrenstrasse – each of which has its fair share of fine houses, often complete with wrought-iron identification signs – lead eastwards from the Dom to the central **Markt**. Dominating the square is the **Rathaus**, late Gothic by origin but remodelled in Renaissance style in the sixteenth century, when it received the huge curved gables which clearly served as a model for other mansions in the city. The Mannerist portal, a later addition, strikes a supremely self-confident note, but the building's most endearing feature is the polychrome capital at the northeastern corner, showing two dogs fighting over a bone. Apparently this symbolises the conflict between the ruling prince-bishops and the increasingly self-confident burghers. Of the other houses on the Markt, the most imposing are the **Schlösschen** at no. 6, which was built for the one Protestant bishop, and the **Alte Residenz** at no.7, three houses knocked together to serve as the temporary palace for Duke Moritz of Saxony while he waited for Schloss Moritzburg outside Dresden to be completed.

Rising behind the south side of the Markt is the curiously elongated **Wenzelskirche** (May–Oct Mon–Sat 10am–noon & 2–4, Sun 11.30am–4pm) which was the burghers' answer to the prince-bishop's Dom. In the Baroque period, this late Gothic church was given an interior face-lift, including the provision of an organ, highly praised by Bach, built by Zacharias Hildebrand, a pupil of the great Silbermann. Also of note are two paintings by **Cranach** – *The Adoration of the Magi* and *Christ Blessing Children*. The single **tower** (April–Oct Wed–Sun 10am–6pm; DM2), which was deliberately built higher than those of the Dom, commands a magnificent panorama over the city and the Saale valley. A town watchman lived in the tower until quite recently, and this long tradition is maintained by the fact that the caretaker has her home there now.

More fine mansions can be seen on Jacobstrasse, which leads eastwards from the Markt. Continuing over Theaterplatz and down Grochlitzer Strasse, you come to the **Museum der Stadt Naumburg** (Tues–Fri 8am–1pm & 2–5pm, Sat & Sun 2–5pm; DM1), occupying a Neoclassical house at no. 49. The outstanding object is the *Ratstrinkhorn*, the elegant late fourteenth-century municipal drinking horn; there's also a complete eighteenth-century kitchen and the usual local history displays.

Also well worth seeing is the **Marientor** at the edge of the inner ring road due north of the Markt. This double gateway, one of the best preserved in the country, is the only significant reminder of the fifteenth-century fortifications which, on this evidence, must have presented a formidable obstacle to would-be invaders. In summer, the courtyard is used as a puppet theatre.

Practicalities

Naumburg's **Hauptbahnhof** is below and northwest of the historic centre, which is reached by heading along Bahnhofstrasse, then up Bergstrasse. It's fortunate that rail links, whether in the direction of Halle, Leipzig or Weimar, are so fast and frequent, as accommodation is very limited; if you want to stay in the immediate area, it's far better to look in Bad Kösen (see below). There are just two **hotels** in the town – *Haus des Handwerks*, Salzstr. 15 (☎2380), and *Deutscher Hof*, Raschstr. 10 (☎2712). Both charge around DM20–25 per person, but are almost invariably booked out. You might have more chance of getting into the similarly priced *Waldschloss*, way out on the edge of town at Neidschützer Str. 71 (☎2133). As the youth hostel seems to have closed for good, the only alternatives are a few noticeably overpriced **private rooms**, which can be booked at the none-too-helpful **tourist office** at Lindenring 39 (Mon–Fri 9am–6pm, Sat 9am–noon; ☎2514) between the Dom and the Markt.

There's a similar shortage of **restaurants**, though the *Ratskeller* in the Rathaus should have reopened by the time you read this. If not, best bets are *Drei Schwannen*, Jacobstr. 28, and *Domklause,* Herrenstr. 8, or, if you want to escape from the centre, *Hallescher Anger*, right by the Saale on Hallesche Strasse. The valley of the River Unstrut, which joins the Saale just north of Naumburg, is one of the northernmost **wine** areas in Europe; its products were featured in the inaugural *Weinfest* held at the end of August 1991 which it is hoped will become an annual event.

Bad Kösen

By far the best base for exploring the Saale region is the spa town of **BAD KÖSEN**, which lies in the most beautiful part of the valley, 7k upstream from Naumburg, and one stop away by train. It's a quiet and restful place to stay, with a wide choice of accommodation; it also has the advantage of having excellent transport connections into the neighbouring provinces of Saxony and Thuringia – Leipzig, Jena, Weimar and Erfurt can all be reached within an hour or so.

Around town

Bad Kösen presents a rare case of the GDR state's penchant for outdated technology being a cause for thanks rather than opprobrium. It's the only place in Europe which preserves apparatus for the extraction and production of **salt**, and the side of town on the southern bank of the Saale is dominated by an extraordinary set of very primitive-looking wooden structures erected in 1730, which survived in full working order until 1945, when they were electrified. There are four separate parts to the system. Right by the river is the **Wasserrad** or water wheel. From here, the **Kunstgestänge**, a double set of drill stems, travels to the **Soleschacht**, a well dug to a depth of 175 metres for the extraction of brine. The Kunstgestänge then continues up the hill to the **Gradierwerk**, where the salt was crystallised. This huge construction, which is some 320 metres long, looks decidedly flimsy and has lost its middle section, though it's now being restored. When the town became a spa in the middle of last century, the Gradierwerk doubled as part of the cure facilities, because of its unusually healthy air.

Overlooking the Wasserrad is the **Romanisches Haus** (Tues–Fri 9am–noon & 1–4pm, Sat & Sun 10am–4pm; DM1.20), which dates back to about 1140 and is thus the oldest surviving house in central Germany. It now contains a small museum, with displays on the history of local salt production, plus lapidary fragments from, and documentary material about Kloster Pforta (see below). Also on this side of the river is the **Loreleypromenade**, which is well worth walking along for the sake of the views over the town and the river. On the opposite bank is the shady **Kurpark**, in which you'll find exotic trees, floral gardens and the Neoclassical spa buildings.

Schulpforte

Now officially incorporated into Bad Kösen, the village of **SCHULPFORTE** lies 3km away, on the main road to Naumburg. It takes its name from the school which was founded in the secularised buildings of the Cistercian **Kloster Pforta** under the patronage of the Saxon dukes in 1543; still going strong today, it numbers among its old boys the poet Klopstock and the philosophers Fichte and Nietzsche (though the GDR authorities tried to suppress all mention of Nietzsche, one of their all-time bogeymen). You're free to wander around the complex at will, though it's necessary to be a bit circumspect in term-time. The magnificent thirteenth-century **church**, long in total disrepair, is currently being restored, with the aim of promoting it as a major tourist attraction. Modelled on the order's great monasteries in Burgundy, it looks far more French than German, with a pure early Gothic choir and a spacious High Gothic nave. However, the facade, which is unusually high and wide, is adorned with statues clearly influenced by those of Naumburg.

Rudelsburg and Burg Saaleck

From the landing pier by the Kurpark, you can take a DM2 motorboat cruise up the Saale to two feudal castles which both date back to the twelfth century. You're deposited below the first and larger of the two, the **Rudelsburg**, which was sacked by the citizens of Naumburg in 1348 and subsequently rebuilt. Although ruinous, a great deal of masonry survives, and the layout of the defensive *Vorburg* and residential *Kernburg* is still obvious. The latter now contains a restaurant (closed Mon), so there's free and unrestricted access to the castle, though you're expected to make a DM1 donation if you want to climb the keep, which commands a superb view over the valley.

It's only a few minutes' walk to **Burg Saaleck** (April–Oct Tues–Sun 9am–5pm; DM1), of which only the two keeps and the lower sections of the curtain wall remain. One of the keeps can be ascended for a view of the valley with the Rudelsburg in the picture. The other was the hiding place of the men who assassinated the German Foreign Minister Walther Rathenau in 1922. It now contains a display on the background to that event, which brought home the strength and determination of the anti-democratic forces ranged against the embryonic Weimar Republic.

Practicalities

Bad Kösen's **Bahnhof** is at the southern end of the Kurpark; the main bus stop lies slightly to the west. The **tourist office** (Mon–Fri 9am–5pm; May–Sept also Sat 9am–noon; ☎289) is just behind the Romanisches Haus on Rudolf-Breitscheid-Strasse. They have a long list of **private houses** with rooms to let in the range of DM20–35 per person. There's also a **campsite** (☎674) on the south bank of the Saale at the western edge of town, and a **youth hostel** at Bergstr. 3 (☎597). **Hotels** (which are also the best places to eat and drink) include *Zum Wehrdamm*, Loreleypromenade 3 (☎758), which charges from DM50; *Loreley*, Loreleypromenade 8 (☎538), at DM40; *Kaffeehaus Schoppe*, Naumburger Str. 1 (☎575), whose range is DM25–30; and the similarly priced *Schäfer* on Gerstenberg Kurpromenade (☎341).

travel details

Trains

From Magdeburg to Stendal (frequent; 1hr); Halberstadt (17 daily; 1hr 15min); Dessau (frequent; 1hr 45min); Köthen (33 daily; 1hr); Halle (30 daily; 1hr 30min).

From Halle to Dessau (frequent; 45min); Wittenberg (frequent; 45min); Halberstadt (8 daily; 1hr 45min); Merseburg (frequent; 15min); Naumburg (12 daily; 30min).

From Halberstadt to Quedlinburg (frequent; 30min); Thale (frequent; 45min); Blankenburg (frequent; 30min); Wenigerode (frequent; 40min).

From Dessau to Köthen (frequent; 30min); Bernburg (frequent; 1 hr); Wittenberg (frequent; 30min).

CHAPTER ELEVEN

THURINGIA

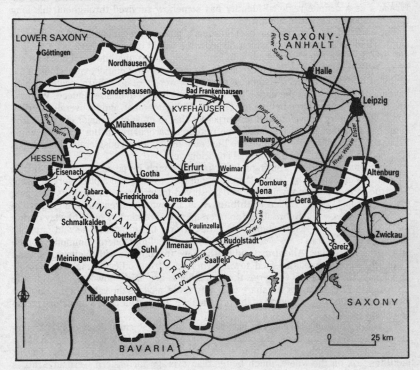

O f all the Länder, east or west, it's **Thuringia** (*Thüringen*) which comes nearest to encapsulating the nation's soul – and to providing an insight into the Germany of old, which elsewhere has largely been swept away by one or other of the dramatic events of the present century. In many ways, it stands apart from the other eastern provinces – for one thing, it has been German since the Dark Ages, rather than land won from Slavs; for another, it suffers relatively little from industrial blight, thanks to being predominantly rural in character, with a vast forest accounting for a considerable proportion of its area.

Despite having been one of the five original provinces of early medieval Germany, Thuringia became defunct as a political entity in the thirteenth century. Most of it fell to the powerful **House of Wettin**, who amalgamated it with their Saxon holdings; smaller tracts were held by the dynasties of **Schwarzburg** and **Reuss**. In the sixteenth century, the Wettin possessions began to fragment into a series of tiny duchies (identified in English by the prefix "Saxe-"), while Schwarzburg was divided in four and Reuss in two. Despite many subsequent amalgamations, there were still eight separate Thuringian principalities among the twenty-five states which came together to form the Second Reich in 1871. It took German defeat in World War I to bring this rather feuda-listic situation to an end: the aristocracy was forced to follow the Kaiser's lead in resign-ing political power and Thuringia made a phoenix-like return to the map, deprived only of Coburg, which elected to join Bavaria. It was abolished by the Communists in 1952, to be replaced by three *Bezirke*, but was an automatic choice for reinstatement after the *Wende* – as a definite regional identity has somehow survived throughout this long history of political fragmentation.

The most visible expression of Thuringia's past is the unparalleled number of **castles** and **palaces**, many of which turned what would otherwise have been villages into proud capital cities, and which should now help ensure that the Land has a secure future in the tourist stakes. Yet these are by no means always empty expressions of the vanity of Ruritanian princes – some of the courts were vibrant cultural centres which have made an impact on the nation out of all proportion to their size. Indeed, **Weimar** was the main driving force behind the German Enlightenment, and its overall contribu-tion to the country's development far surpasses that of most of its major cities. Nearby **Jena** has maintained a strong academic tradition, particularly in the sciences, while **Eisenach**, which likewise belonged to the same duchy for a considerable period, has also made a huge mark on the national consciousness.

The capital of modern Thuringia is **Erfurt**. Although its population is less than a quarter of a million, it's by far the largest city in the province and a place very different from the former courtly towns, the well-preserved historic core evoking its past as a major episcopal centre. Walled **Mühlhausen** is, if anything, even more suggestive of the Middle Ages, while **Schmalkalden** offers plenty of reminders of its heyday during the Renaissance and Reformation. In contrast, **Gera**, the province's second city, has shrugged off its past as a *Residenzstadt* to become a bustling modern community; of the other princely capitals, **Altenburg** and **Gotha** have (in common with Weimar, Jena and Eisenach) become medium-sized towns, whereas all the others remain engagingly provincial. In terms of scenery, the attractions are fairly low-key, though the **Thuringian Forest** has its fair share of beauty spots, as does the valley of the **Saale** at its far end, while at the far north of the province are the **Kyffhäuser**, a miniature moun-tain chain.

Travel in Thuringia is rendered particularly easy by the small distances separating most of the major attractions; at a pinch, it would even be possible to cover much of the province from a single centrally-sited base, such as Weimar, Erfurt or Gotha. Tourist **facilities** are, on the whole, much better than average for eastern Germany; this is particularly true of the Thuringian Forest, which has a glut of accommodation, though it also applies to the main towns, which are used to a heavy volume of visitors, albeit from the uncritical Communist bloc. Given its demographic make-up, it's no surprise that Thuringia leans **politically** to the right; in the 1990 elections, the CDU failed by just one seat to secure an outright majority over all the other parties.

CENTRAL THURINGIA

The central part of Thuringia is the part most tourists come to see. It's also the most easily assimilated – only 80km separates **Weimar**, which lies just beyond the Saxony-Anhalt border, with **Eisenach**, near the former East–West German border. The two are linked by one of eastern Germany's main express railways; en route are **Erfurt** and **Gotha**. From Gotha it's just a short hop down into the Thuringian Forest, which is equally accessible from **Arnstadt**, just south of Erfurt.

Weimar

If Heidelberg is the German city foreigners are most prone to drool over, then **WEIMAR** is the one the Germans themselves hold dearest: despite its modest size, its role in the development of national culture is unmatched. Above all, it was here that the German Enlightenment had its most brilliant flowering, when it was home to the writers Friedrich Schiller, Johann Gottfried Herder, Christoph-Martin Wieland, and, most significantly, **Johann Wolfgang von Goethe**, whose name is commemorated all over the town. Prior to this, Weimar's roll-call of famous citizens had included Lucas Cranach and J.S. Bach; it would later number Franz Liszt, Richard Strauss, Friedrich Nietzsche and the architects and designers of the Bauhaus school. Later, the name of Weimar became synonymous with the republic established after defeat in World War I, which marked the birth of German democracy by adopting the most liberal constitution the world had ever known. Its inglorious failure, culminating fifteen years later with the Nazis gaining power by largely legal means, brought a sad twist to the town's cultural reputation, as it was chosen as the site of one of the most notorious concentration camps. That this monument to the very depths of human depravity stands so close to reminders of some of the most noble outpourings of the human spirit starkly illustrates the double-edged nature of Germany's contribution to world civilisation.

Some history

Although Weimar is known to date back at least as far as the mid-thirteenth century, it was of small significance until 1547, when **Elector John Frederick the Magnanimous** of Saxony was defeated and captured by Emperor Charles V at the Battle of Mühlberg. Stripped of his Electorate and his capital of Wittenberg, he re-established control of the Thuringian territories remaining to him from a new base at Weimar. Gradually these splintered into a series of smaller duchies, of which Saxe-Weimar was but one. Its rise to the status of the "German Athens" was due mainly to the enlightened rule of the Regentess Anna Amalia, who brought the writer Christoph-Martin Wieland to the court. When her son, **Carl August**, reached his majority in 1775, Goethe was appointed as his advisor and senior minister. Goethe remained there for the rest of his life, describing the town as "paradise", and encouraging his friends Herder and Schiller to settle there as well. In 1815, Saxe-Weimar-Eisenach was raised to the status of a Grand Duchy, which lasted until the abolition of the monarchy in 1918.

The town was the meeting-place of the National Assembly in January 1919, and was where the democratic constitution was proclaimed in July of the same year, though thereafter the politicians moved back to Berlin, forgiving the city its tainted past which had inspired the original aim of establishing Weimar as the new seat of government. In compensation, the town was chosen as the capital of Thuringia, but was later dropped in favour of Erfurt.

Around town

If you aren't interested in its literary and artistic associations, Weimar can seem a dull and provincial sort of place. But its great merit is that it uncannily preserves both the appearance and atmosphere of its heyday as one of the hundreds of capitals of pint-sized independent states which once littered the map of Germany. Currently rather tatty, though not unattractively so, it was an automatic choice as the Thuringian town earmarked to receive large Federal grants for restoration projects, and will accordingly be spruced up considerably in the next few years.

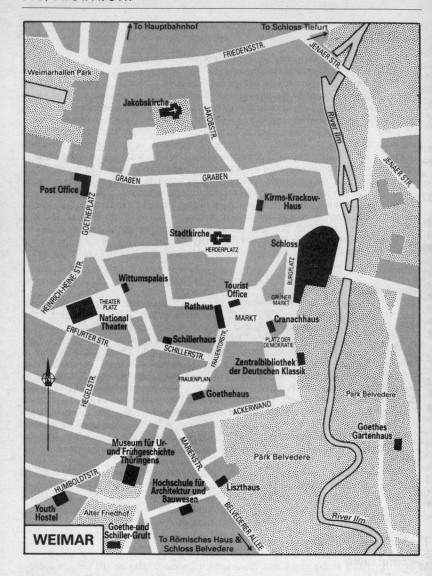

To Hauptbahnhof
To Schloss Tiefurt
FRIEDENSSTR.
JENAER STR.
River Ilm
JAKOBSTR.
Weimarhallen Park
Jakobskirche
JENAER STR.
GRABEN
GRABEN
Post Office
Kirms-Krackow-Haus
GOETHEPLATZ
Stadtkirche
Schloss
HERDERPLATZ
BURGPLATZ
HEINRICH-HEINE-STR.
Wittumspalais
Tourist Office
GRÜNER MARKT
THEATER PLATZ
Rathaus
National Theater
MARKT
Cranachhaus
ERFURTER STR.
PLATZ DER DEMOKRATIE
Schillerhaus
SCHILLERSTR.
FRAUENTORSTR.
Zentralbibliothek der Deutschen Klassik
FRAUENPLAN
Goethehaus
HEGELSTR.
ACKERWAND
Park Belvedere
Museum für Ur- und Frühgeschichte Thüringens
MARIENSTR.
Goethes Gartenhaus
Park Belvedere
HUMBOLDTSTR.
Hochschule für Architektur und Bauwesen
Liszthaus
Youth Hostel
BELVEDERER ALLEE
Alter Friedhof
River Ilm
WEIMAR
Goethe- und Schiller-Gruft
To Römisches Haus & Schloss Belvedere

The Schloss

Set by the River Ilm at the eastern edge of the town centre, Weimar's **Schloss** (Tues–Sun 9am–1pm & 2–6pm; DM4) is of a size more appropriate for ruling a great empire than a duchy whose population never rose much above 100,000. The complex is mostly in the Neoclassical style typical of the town: only the tall tower and the portal at the southwest corner remain of John Frederick's original Renaissance palace.

On the ground floor is a collection of old masters, dominated by important examples of the **Cranach** family, who followed the erstwhile Elector here from Wittenberg. Pick of the works by Lucas the Elder are *Luther as Junker Jörg* (showing him in the disguise he adopted when in hiding at the Wartburg), *John Frederick the Magnanimous and Sybille von Cleve* (a pair of official bridal portraits), *Samson and the Lion*, and the erotically suggestive *Age of Silver*, illustrating the favourite Renaissance theme of a battle between "wild men". Lucas the Younger's boisterous unsubtlety is seen at its best in the hilarious pair of *Hercules Asleep* and *Hercules Awake*, a pre-Swiftian vision of Lilliput painted for Dresden Residenzschloss. Other highlights are **Dürer's** *Hans and Elspeth Tucher* (a pair of portraits of a prominent Nuremberg patrician couple), and a typically idiosyncratic canvas by his pupil **Baldung**, *The Sacrifice of Marcus Civitius*.

Upstairs, some fine original interiors can be seen, of which the most distinctive is the **Falkengalerie** (Falcon Gallery). Also here are seventeenth-century Dutch school still-lifes and German painting from the Age of Enlightenment to the present day: look out for **Friedrich's** haunting *Tomb of Hutten* and **Moritz von Schwind's** colourful *Seven Ravens*, and for works by **Arnold Böcklin** and **Christian Rohlfs**, one of Germany's most accomplished Impressionists.

Herderplatz and Jakobstrasse

Just west of the Schloss on Herderplatz is the **Stadtkirche SS Peter und Paul** (Mon–Fri 10.30am–noon & 2–3.30pm, Sat & Sun 2–3pm), a much-remodelled Gothic church usually known as the **Herderkirche** in honour of the poet, folklorist and literary theorist who was its chief pastor for three decades. Inside, the eye is drawn to the large **triptych** at the high altar, which is usually described as the artistic swan-song of the elder Cranach, but was almost certainly painted as a memorial by his son. On the wings, John Frederick can be seen in the company of his wife and children. Also in the choir are a number of elaborate **tombstones**, including that of the elder Cranach and members of the ducal family; Herder is commemorated by a plain tablet under the organ loft.

Up Jakobsstrasse at the northeast corner of the square is the **Kirms-Krackow-Haus** (previously Wed–Sun 9am–noon & 1–5pm, but closed at the time of writing for de-Marxification of the displays), which contains souvenirs of Herder, who actually lived in the house beside the church which is still the parish residence. This mansion belonged to a rich bourgeois family and preserves a suite of rooms furnished according to early nineteenth-century taste. Its courtyard of wooden galleries is particularly characteristic of the domestic architecture favoured in Weimar's glory days.

Further up the street is the **Jakobskirche**, a plain Baroque church with a Neoclassical interior. In 1806, it was the scene of the wedding of Goethe to Christiane Vulpius, with whom he had been living for eighteen years in a relationship that had scandalised many influential figures in Weimar society; he gave as his reason for formalising the union that he wished to reward his companion for her fortitude earlier that year in the face of the French troops who occupied Weimar after their victory in the Battle of Jena. Christiane lies buried in the peaceful cemetery surrounding the church, as does Cranach, whose original tombstone has been replaced here by a copy.

The Markt and the Platz der Demokratie

South of Herderplatz is the **Markt**, lined by an unusually disparate jumble of buildings. Most eye-catching is the green and white gabled **Cranachhaus** on the eastern side, where the artist spent his final years; directly opposite is the neo-Gothic **Rathaus**. On the south side is the *Elephant*, a historic inn which features at the opening of Thomas Mann's novel about the town in Goethe's day, *Lotte in Weimar*. Much favoured by Hitler, it was just about the only place westerners were allowed to stay during the GDR period; it's now getting set to regain its former position as one of Germany's leading hotels. Adjoining it are two more old hostelries and the **Bachstube**, where the composer lived during his years as leader of the court orchestra and organist from 1708 to 1717. This ended with a month-long imprisonment, following his fury at being passed over for the musical directorship, whereupon he left for a new position at the much smaller court of Köthen.

Beyond is an even larger square, the **Platz der Demokratie**, lined by a colourful series of palaces, over which an equestrian statue of Grand Duke Carl August presides. On the north side is the **Rotes Schloss** (Red Palace), a Renaissance building with Neoclassical additions, while to the south is the grand Baroque **Fürstenhaus**, where Goethe was received on his arrival in Weimar; the latter now houses the Liszt-Hochschule, a prestigious academy of music. The east side of the square is closed by the **Grünes Schloss** (Green Palace), the finest of the group, containing three libraries – the national collection of German Classical Literature, the Thuringian State Library and the collection of the German Shakespeare Society. If you ask at the reception, you can see the exquisite central *Rokokosaal*. Beside it stands the more modest **Gelbes Schloss** (Yellow Palace), while further south is the **Haus Stein**, the former ducal stables, which the stablemaster, Baron Friedrich von Stein, converted into a house. His wife Charlotte was Goethe's first great Weimar love, notwithstanding the fact that she was seven years the poet's senior and the mother of seven children. He abandoned her after more than a decade's attention in favour of the much younger Christiane Vulpius.

Schillerstrasse and Theaterplatz

Schillerstrasse snakes away from the southwest corner of the Markt to the **Schillerhaus** (9am–noon & 1–5, closed Tues; DM3), the home of Friedrich Schiller for the last three years of his life, following his resignation of his academic chair at Jena. Here he wrote his last two dramas on great historical personalities, *The Maid of Orleans* (the story of Joan of Arc) and *William Tell*; the background to these works is extensively documented, as is his earlier career.

Beyond lies **Theaterplatz**, in the centre of which is a large monument to Goethe and Schiller. The **Nationaltheater** on the west side of the square was founded and directed by Goethe, though the present building, for all its stern Neoclassical appearance, is a pastiche, the facade from the beginning of the present century, the rest from a rebuilding necessitated by its almost complete destruction in World War II. Apart from having seen the premières of many of the greatest plays in the German language, the theatre was also the venue for the National Assembly's sittings in 1919 and saw the adoption of the constitution of the Weimar Republic.

Opposite is the **Wittumspalais** (Wed–Sun 9am–noon & 1–5pm; DM3), a large Baroque palace built as the retirement home of Regentess Anna Amalia. Even as a dowager duchess, she continued to play a leading role in the town's intellectual life, organising "Round Table" sessions here at which Goethe presided each Friday. The interiors are among the finest in Weimar, with the main *Festsaal* a design based on Goethe's ideas. There's also a large array of mementos of Christoph-Martin Wieland, now a rather neglected figure, but then regarded as the leading theoretician of the Enlightenment, as well as a major poet and philosopher.

The Goethe museums

On Frauenplan south of the Markt is the excellent **Goethewohnhaus und Nationalmuseum** (Tues–Sun 9am–1pm & 2–5pm; DM3). As its name suggests, it's in two parts. The more rewarding of these is the large Baroque mansion where the titan of German literature resided for some fifty years until his death in 1832. It's been preserved exactly as he knew it, and still has a lived-in feel to it, his private rooms in particular making a lasting impression, particularly the study with the desk where he sat dictating works to his secretary (he only composed poems with his own hand), and the little chamber where he died. In the adjoining museum, the full range and versatility of his achievement is chronicled with typically Teutonic attention to detail.

JOHANN WOLFGANG VON GOETHE (1749–1832)

Often regarded as the last of the great universal geniuses, **Johann Wolfgang von Goethe** produced a vast and diverse literary output – ranging from lyric to philosophic poetry, via comic and tragic dramas, to novels, short stories, travelogues, artistic criticism and scientific tracts – even though he was never truly a full-time writer. Despite his youth, he had already gained a European-wide literary reputation before his appointment to the Weimar court, thanks largely to the epistolary novel *The Sorrows of Young Werther*. His first decade in Weimar furnished him with a broad range of practical experience which he would later put to full use, but it left him little time for writing. By undertaking a long Italian sojourn in 1786, his creative spark was rekindled, though the play *Torquato Tasso* is a thinly veiled exposition of the frustration he felt at having to operate in the environment of a small court. His major prose work, *Wilhelm Meister*, is a cycle of six novels written over a period of five decades which, in common with much of his output, is a close reflection of his own personal development. A similarly protracted process attended the writing of his supreme masterpiece, the two-part drama *Faust*, completed just before his death, which symbolically examines the nature of western man, his errors and ultimate salvation. The reverence accorded Goethe in Germany, and the academic industry which has grown up around him, is almost as extensive as that surrounding Shakespeare.

The southern quarters

Most of the remaining sights are found in the southern part of town. From the Goethewhohnhaus, continue down Marienstrasse to the **Liszthaus** (Tues–Sun 9am–4pm & 2–5pm; DM1), the garden house of the great Austro-Hungarian composer Franz Liszt. His move to Weimar in 1848, where he spent eleven years as director of the local orchestra and opera company, marked a sea-change in his career away from his earlier preoccupation with barnstorming virtuoso piano playing towards richly-scored programmatic orchestral pieces – the most ambitious being the Goethe-inspired *Faust Symphony* – which in turn cast a strong spell over his son-in-law, Richard Wagner. Despite leaving in a huff over the town's narrow-minded tastes, he returned in 1869, staying at this house for each of the remaining seventeen summers of his life.

A couple of minutes' walk to the west down Geschwister-Scholl-Strasse is the **Hochschule für Architektur und Bauwesen**, designed in the early years of this century by the Belgian Art Nouveau architect Henry van de Velde. In 1919, Walter Gropius established the original **Bauhaus** – which was to have such a profound impact on the subsequent course of modern architecture and design throughout the world – in this college. However, it only remained here for six years before its move, prompted by hostility from reactionary elements in the town, to the more liberal climate at Dessau. The building is functioning once more as an art college, and isn't open to the public.

Further to the west, at Amalienstr. 6, is the **Museum für Ur- und Frühgeschichte Thüringens** (Museum of Ancient & Early Thuringian History; Tues–Fri 8am–5pm, Sat & Sun 10am–1pm & 2–5pm; DM2), the most important archaeological museum in the province. It charts the entire prehistory of the area from the Stone Age to the Thuringian tribes of the early medieval period; the star of the display is a rich horde of Neolithic pottery from Sondershausen. Immediately south of here is the **Alter Friedhof** (Old Cemetery), complete with a poignant array of carved tombstones and a Neoclassical **Mausoleum** (9am–1pm & 2–5pm, closed Tues; DM1). Originally, this was intended for the Grand Ducal family, but it now has the tombs of Goethe and Schiller as well, following Carl August's decision that he wanted to be buried beside the two brightest stars of his court – though this necessitated re-interring the latter's corpse. Behind the Mausoleum is the tiny **Russische Kapelle**, built for the Grand Duchess Maria Pavlova, daughter-in-law of Carl August, who insisted on remaining loyal to the Orthodox faith of the Russian royal family to which she belonged.

The Goethepark

The **Goethepark** is a large English-style park, complete with ruined follies, a statue of Shakespeare and a cemetery for Soviet soldiers killed in World War II, stretching south-wards on both sides of the Ilm from the Schloss to the southern edge of town. Almost due east of the Liszthaus, though on the opposite bank, is **Goethes Gartenhaus** (Tues-Sun 9am–noon & 1–5pm; DM3), where the writer stayed when he first came to Weimar; later, it served as his summer retreat. It now contains a selection of his original drawings along with other exhibits concentrating on his interest in the visual arts. Further south and back on the west side of the Ilm is the Neoclassical ducal summer house, known as the **Römisches Haus** (April–Oct Wed–Sun 9am–noon & 1–5pm; DM3).

Schloss Belvedere and Schloss Tiefurt

At the extreme south edge of town, in the suburb of Oberweimar, is the full-blown summer palace, **Schloss Belvedere** (April–Oct Wed–Sun 10am–1pm & 2–6pm; DM3), whose light and airy Rococo style forms a refreshing contrast to the Neoclassical solemnity of so much of the town. The **Orangerie** contains a collection of historic coaches, while the surroundings were transformed under Goethe's supervision into another park in the English manner.

A further fine palace, **Schloss Tiefurt** (Wed–Sun 9am–1pm & 2-5pm; DM3), situated northeast of the town centre, was created for the Dowager Duchess Anna Amalia, who transferred her "Round Table" meetings here during the summer months. Again, there's a fine park with plenty of small follies and retreats.

Buchenwald

For a complete change of emotion, the **Konzentratsionslager Buchenwald** (Tues-Sun 8.45am–4.30pm; free) is situated to the north of Weimar on the Ettersberg heights, and can be reached by buses which run regularly from the Hauptbahnhof. Over 240,000 prisoners were incarcerated in this concentration camp, with 56,000 dying here from starvation, torture and disease; but despite the high number of deaths – averaging 200 a day – Buchenwald was never an extermination camp. Among the prisoners killed here was the inter-war leader of the German Communist Party, **Ernst Thälmann**. This gave the place a special significance for the GDR authorities, but the official state prop-aganda was tarnished by the discovery in 1990 of mass graves in the nearby woods, which provided conclusive proof that the Soviets used the camp after the war to round up and eliminate former Nazis, their own political opponents. At the time of writing, the presentation still had a Marxist bias, highlighting the plight of imprisoned Communists and making no mention of the Jews, gypsies and homosexuals who suffered here. This is particularly true of the propagandist film, which is given regular showings in German and occasional ones in English.

Practicalities

Weimar's **Hauptbahnhof** is well to the north of the main sights. Begin by following Carl-August-Allee straight ahead; continue straight on if you want to go to Theaterplatz, but, to get to the Schloss, turn left at the first main junction into Friedenstrasse, then right into Jakobstrasse. The **tourist office** at Markstr. 4 (Mon 10am–6pm, Tues–Fri 9am–6pm, Sat 9am–4pm; ☎2173) can arrange accommodation in **private rooms**; a possibly cheaper alternative for this service is the agency *Werse & Reiseshop*, Kleine Kirchgasse 3 (☎3642). The only reasonably priced **hotels** are *International*, Am Bahnhof (☎2162), and *Pension Liszt*, Lisztstr. 3, which both charge from DM45 per person, though other rooms cost much more than this. There are two **youth hostels** – one at Carl-August-Allee 13 (☎2076), the other at Zum Wilden Graben 12 (☎3471).

Eating, drinking and nightlife

As elsewhere in the former GDR, the situation with regard to **eating** and **drinking** is in a state of flux. Best restaurants are the pricey *Weisser Schwan*, Frauentorstr. 23; the surprisingly affordable *Elephantenkeller* underneath the *Hotel Elephant*, Markt 19; and *Alt-Weimar*, Prellerstr. 3, which is open evenings only. Alternatives include the inevitable *Ratskeller*, Markt 10, and the fish restaurant, *Gastmahl des Meeres*, Herderplatz 16. If it has managed to survive, the *Galerie* at Markt 21 is a good place for a snack, while Café *Resi* on the adjoining Grüner Markt is recommended for coffee and cakes.

Liveliest **nightspot** is the *Studentenklub Kasseturm*, Goetheplatz 1, though it's normally necessary to have a student ID to gain admission. The main **theatre** venue is the aforementioned *Nationaltheater*, Theaterplatz 2 (☎7550), which regularly features plays by Goethe and Schiller, while **concerts** of all kinds are featured at the *Weimarhalle*, Karl-Liebknecht-Str. 3.

Erfurt

Of all Germany's large cities, it's the Thuringian capital of **ERFURT**, which lies 20km west of Weimar, that's most redolent of its prewar self. Although it lost several important monuments in the air-raids of 1944 and 1945, the damage to the overall historic fabric was relatively slight, while the many streets of stately turn-of-the-century shops were saved by the Communist interregnum from the developers who would have demolished them had the city lain on the other side of the Iron Curtain.

In 1970, Erfurt was the scene of the meeting between West German Chancellor Willy Brandt and East German Premier Willi Stoph which marked the beginning of the former's **Ostpolitik**, and the end of the GDR's status as an international pariah. During the *Wende*, the city again provided a national lead by being the first place where the *Stasi* offices were stormed, thus preventing the destruction of incriminating files. Suitably revived by the recent political and economic changes, 1992 sees Erfurt's 1250th birthday, which is being celebrated in style with a year-long programme of events. The culmination will be the re-establishment of the **University**, which was founded in 1392 as the first in Germany to have all four main faculties; it was once one of the largest and most prestigious in Northern Europe, numbering Martin Luther among its graduates, but has been dormant since the Prussian invasion in 1816.

The Domhügel and the Petersberg

Dominating the historic heart of Erfurt from its western side are two hills, the **Domhügel** and the **Petersberg**. The former is the city's episcopal centre, crowned by two highly distinctive churches. They're among the very few historically and artistically significant buildings in eastern Germany to remain in Catholic hands, this being a legacy of the decision taken in 1530 by the city's ruler, Cardinal Albrecht von Brandenburg, to divide Church property equally between the two different sides in the Reformation. A monumental flight of steps leads up to the Domhügel from **Domplatz**, a vast open space formed as the result of a fire in 1813 which destroyed most of the houses on this spot, though some fine buildings remain on the south side of the square, notably the sixteenth-century inn **Zur Hohen Lilie** and the eighteenth-century **Grüne Apotheke**. The military-minded Prussian authorities kept the area levelled to serve as a parade ground; having had no function other than as a viewpoint during the GDR period, it's now put to good use as a site for markets, fairs and other entertainments.

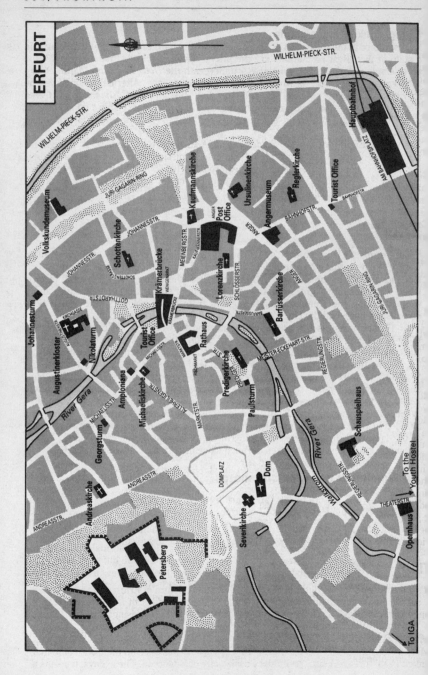

The Dom

On the southern side of Domhügel is the **Dom**, the larger of the two churches. The lower parts of its north and south **towers** are Romanesque and belonged to the previous church on the site, but otherwise it's a masterly Gothic construction which uses its sloping site to full advantage. From the first building period at the end of the thirteenth century are the central tower, whose *Gloriosa* is one of the world's largest bells, and the massive, fortress-like substructure known as the **Kavaten**. The choir and transepts, in a pure High Gothic style, were perched on top of the latter in the mid-fourteenth century, followed by the flamboyantly decorative **triangular porch**. A century later, the building was completed with the spacious hall nave, whose very German appearance is in marked contrast to the French influence manifested elsewhere.

Inside is one of the most impressive sets of **stained glass windows** to be found in Germany; but the Dom's most valuable treasures are the two mid-twelfth-century masterpieces in the south transept – a **candelabrum** in the shape of a man, popularly known as *Wolfram*, and the stucco **altar** of *The Enthroned Madonna with Saints*. Among the adornments of the nave are a small altar of *The Madonna and Child with SS Catherine and Barbara* by **Cranach**, and the tomb of the bigamous Count of Gleichen and his wives (for whose story see p.860).

The Severikirche

Alongside the Dom is the **Severikirche**, whose distinctive triple-towered east end, sheltering a disarmingly small choir, acts as a perfect foil to its neighbour. The five-aisled hall nave has an impressively lofty feeling considering its relatively modest size. It contains the monumental **tomb of St Severus**, carved out of a soft pink sandstone by a sensitive mid-fourteenth-century sculptor, now dubbed the Master of St Severus, who also made the statue of the saint over the entrance doorway. Both of the other important furnishings – **the alabaster relief** of *St Michael* on the south wall, and the font with its spectacular fifteen-metre-high canopy – date from the year 1467.

The Petersberg

Behind the Domhügel is a much larger hill, the **Petersberg**, which lies off the well-worn tourist trail. It was likewise once a centre of religious life, as the site of a Benedictine abbey, the **Peterskirche**, which five times hosted the Imperial Reichstag in the days of Emperor Frederick Barbarossa. This still stands, but what was once the outstanding creation of the Romanesque period in Thuringia is now a sorry sight, having been ruined by its change of status under Prussian rule to a gunpowder magazine. However, this wasn't the first use of the hill for military purposes: when in 1664 the Archbishops of Mainz re-asserted their authority over a city which had been functioning more or less independently for the previous two centuries, they turned it into a powerful **Zitadelle** (citadel). An outstanding example of Baroque military architecture, it proved its worth on many occasions up to the present century, by which time it had been strengthened on the standard Prussian model. As a bonus, there's a wonderful view over the city, with the spires on the Domhügel in the foreground.

The rest of the city

It's worth wandering through almost any street in the centre of Erfurt, which preserves a superb range of buildings evoking all the different periods of its past, and whose open, expansive layout offers the bonus of a whole range of surprising vistas.

Marktstrasse and the Fischmarkt

Marktstrasse, which leads eastwards from Domplatz, was once on the trade route that linked Frankfurt and Leipzig with the Russian city of Novgorod. These days, it seems a tad narrow for a major thoroughfare, particularly given the greatly increased volume of traffic since the *Wende*. It's worth making detours off it south down Grosse Arche, and north along Allerheiligenstrasse. At no. 11 on the latter is one of the city's finest houses, **Zum roten Stern**, the late Gothic home, complete with oriel window, of one of the city's many distinguished printers. The **Allerheiligenkirche**, at the corner with Marktstrasse, is a Gothic church with a late fifteenth-century tower and a fourteenth century tympanum showing the Crucifixion.

Given that it was trade and commerce which made Erfurt rich in the Middle Ages, the central **Fischmarkt** is of unassuming dimensions. The statue of Roland in the middle was built as a symbol of defiance against the feudal overlords of Mainz, though Erfurt never managed to gain the status of a Free Imperial City. On the north side of the square is a showy Renaissance mansion, **Zum breiten Herd**, which rivals the less demonstrative, more classically balanced **Zum roten Ochsen** on the west side for the title of best building on the square. The latter is now a gallery, often featuring good temporary exhibitions of modern art. The bulky **Rathaus** is nineteenth-century, and primarily of note for the heroically Romantic fresco cycles inside, depicting scenes from the lives of legendary and historical figures with a Thuringian connection.

The Krämerbrücke

Just east of Fischmarkt is Erfurt's most singular sight, the **Krämerbrücke**, which adds a welcome dash of colour to a city which, for all its grandeur, can appear rather mono-chromal. Walking along, you have the illusion of entering a narrow medieval alley; the fact that this is actually a bridge (the only one of its kind north of the Alps) lined with shops in the manner of the Ponte Vecchio in Florence is concealed at street level and only becomes obvious if you go down to the banks of the River Gera. The Krämerbrücke is known to have existed in the early twelfth century, but the history of the present structure begins with the stone rebuilding of 1325. In the Middle Ages, there were over sixty little shops on it, mostly associated with the trade in silk, spices, sugar and paper; their larger half-timbered replacements currently number thirty-two. A mixture of boutiques, antique dealers and commercial art galleries, these seemed wholly anomalous in GDR days, but are now very hot property indeed. The far end of the Krämerbrücke is terminated by the **Aegidienkirche**, a small upstairs Gothic church used by a German Methodist congregation.

Michaelisstrasse

Just before the western end of the Krämerbrücke, the **Michaelisstrasse** – the heart of the old University quarter, but now one of the quietest parts of the city – stretches northwards; just off it is Waagegasse, a picturesque alley lined with sixteenth- and seventeenth-century storehouses. At the junction with Allerheiligenstrasse is the **Michaeliskirche**, an early Gothic church which was the main place of worship of the academic community. Its Renaissance high altar doubles as a memorial to a local councillor, while the **Dreifaltigkeitskapelle**, added at the turn of the sixteenth century, boasts a prominent oriel window, an embellishment rarely found in ecclesiastical architecture. The galleried courtyard is one of the most peaceful spots in Erfurt.

Across the street is the imposing Flamboyant Gothic portal of the **Collegium Majus**; the rest of this, the main University building, was a casualty of World War II bombs. However, its outstanding collection of old manuscripts, the **Amploniana**, survived and is now kept in the nineteenth-century science library behind.

East of the River Gera

Across the river is the **Augustinerkloster** (guided tours Tues–Sat 10am–noon & 2–4pm, Sun at 10.30am; DM2), the monastery where Luther lived between 1505 and 1511,

rst as a novice, then as a monk and priest. The complex was badly damaged in the
ar and has only been partially restored. A visit to a reconstruction of Luther's cell
rms part of the tour, which also includes the cloister and the typically austere church,
w used by Protestants. It's enlivened by some of Erfurt's most beautiful stained glass
indows, including one depicting the life of the order's founder, Saint Augustine.

A few blocks to the south, not far from the eastern end of Krämerbrücke, is the
chottenkirche (Scottish Church), so called from the nationality of the monks who
ved here in the Middle Ages. The Baroque facade masks a simple pillar basilica which
one of the few Romanesque buildings left in Erfurt.

To the east is the north–south Johannesstrasse, the longest street in the Altstadt,
ed with some of its most impressive Renaissance mansions. Particularly striking is
e **Haus zum Stockfisch** (Wed–Sun 10am–6pm; DM1) at no. 169, which has a rusti-
ted facade reminiscent of an Italian *palazzo*, with a carving of a dried cod above the
or which gives the house its name. The interior now contains the local history
useum. Further east, the Juri-Gagarin-Ring marks the boundary of the medieval city.
cross it, at no. 140a, is the sixteenth-century **Hospital**, now housing the **Museum für
hüringer Volkskunde** (Wed–Sun 10am–6pm; DM2), a folklore collection focusing on
e province's traditional lifestyles (recreated in a number of interiors), festivals,
stumes, crafts and industries.

nger and around

hannesstrasse terminates at the **Kaufmannskirche** (Merchants' Church), with a
emorial to Luther outside. This also marks the beginning of **Anger**, which starts off
s a square but continues westwards as one of the main shopping streets, lined with
e most opulent mansions in the city. It's worth making a short detour down
ahnhofstrasse to see the **Reglerkirche**, another Augustinian collegiate church,
hose high altar is the best of the large carved and painted retables which were an
rfurt speciality in the fifteenth century.

Straddling Bahnhofstrasse and Anger is an ornate Baroque palace built as a weigh
ouse and repository. It's now the **Angermuseum** (Wed–Sun 10am-6pm; DM2), an
xcellent collection of fine and decorative arts. The highlight is the medieval section,
hich features the ceiling from the demolished fourteenth-century Rathaus, and
everal works – a *Crucifixion*, a *Pietá* and a *St Michael* – by the Master of St Severus.
rom the Renaissance period are paintings by Cranach and Baldung, while there's the
sual range of nineteenth- and twentieth-century German paintings.

Further down Anger, you pass the **Bartholomäusturm**,the only surviving part of
e court church of the Counts of Gleichen. At the far end of the street, there's a fork;
e northern branch, Reigierungsstrasse, leads to the **Statthalterei**, a magnificent
aroque palace built by Maximilian von Welsch, court architect to the Archbishops of
lainz, to serve as the headquarters of the city's government. A room on the first floor
as the scene in 1808 of one of history's most famous meetings of two great men – that
etween Goethe and Napoleon, who conversed knowledgeably about the former's
lays. The same year, the French dictator summoned Czar Alexander I to Erfurt, in a
ain attempt to win Russia over to his side.

he Barfüsserkirche and the Predigerkirche

ust north of here is the **Barfüsserkirche** (Wed–Sun 10am–6pm; DM1), a vast, austere
ranciscan monastery church which was the most serious casualty of World War II
ombs. Its nave has been left as a shell, but the choir has been restored to house a
mall branch of the Angermuseum's medieval collection. The stained glass windows,
hich include a depiction of the life of Saint Francis, have been restored to their origi-
al position; some of them date back to the early thirteenth century and show the influ-
nce of the Italo-Byzantine style.

On the other side of the river is the **Predigerkirche**, formerly the Dominican monastery but since the Reformation the city's main Protestant church. Its exterior takes plainness to an extreme, but the interior is a masterpiece of spacial harmony in the purest Gothic style, and has preserved its layout and furnishings intact. The church was constructed in the thirteenth century when Master Eckhart, Germany's most celebrated mystic, was a monk here; he later became prior and vicar for Thuringia, in spite of holding pantheistic beliefs which many regarded as heresy. On the **rood screen** which you can ascend for a rare aerial view, is a beautiful mid-fourteenth-century group of *The Annunciation*; the niches of the **choir screen** behind shelter a number of works of the same date. Elsewhere in the church are many elaborate epitaphs, a fifteenth-century carved and painted high altar and some lovely thirteenth-century stained glass made up of floral motifs.

Cyriaksburg

For the past three decades, the ample grounds of the **Cyriaksburg**, a castle southwest of the city centre, at the terminus of tram #2, have been given over to the **Internationale Gartenbauaustellung** (commonly known as *iga*), a vast garden show. Although open all year round, it's best visited in spring, when the eye-swimming plantations of flowers are in full bloom. However, there are plenty of other attractions, notably the **Gartenbaumuseum** (Easter–Oct daily 10am–5pm; DM1) in the Cyriaksburg itself, which traces the history of gardening. There are also several restaurants, exhibition halls, a look-out tower and hothouses displaying orchids, cacti and other tropical plants.

Practicalities

Erfurt's **Hauptbahnhof** is situated at the southeastern corner of the city centre. At no 37 on Bahnhofstrasse (which leads to the historic quarters) is one of the two **tourist offices** (Mon–Fri 9am–6pm, Sat 10am–3pm; ☎26267 or ☎26122); the other is a Krämerbrücke 3 (Mon–Fri 9am–12.30pm & 1.30–5pm, Sat & Sun 9–11am; ☎23436). The first of these is the place to go if you want a room in a **private house**. An alternative, seven days a week, round-the-clock telephone booking service is offered by *Zimmervermittlung Brigitte Scheel*, Paulinzeller Weg 23 (☎413838); a few rooms are available in the house itself, which lies close to the stop *Blücherstrasse* on the route of trams #3 and #6. **Hotels** are still thin on the ground and likely to be booked solid. *Bürgerhof*, Bahnhofstr. 35 (☎21307), is the cheapest with singles DM43, doubles DM83; the only other reasonably priced options are *Vilnius-Tourist*, Vilnius Str. 2 (☎721012) with singles DM46, doubles DM75, and *Thüringen*, Juri-Gagarin-Ring 154 (☎22214), with singles DM60, doubles DM82. There's also a **youth hostel** at Hochheimer Str. 12 (☎26705), southwest of the centre; take tram #5 or #51.

Eating, drinking and nightlife

Under Communism, Erfurt had a noticeable shortage of places to **eat** and **drink**, and the situation now, though better, is still well short of the ideal. Poshest restaurant used to be the aforementioned *Zur Hohen Lilie* on Domplatz, but its future was uncertain at the time of writing; at the moment the top choice is *Gildehaus*, Fischmarkt 13, though it's often difficult to get in because of its popularity with tour groups. Others to try are *Alter Schwan*, Gotthardtstr. 27, *Feuerkugel*, Michaelisstr. 3, and the *Museumsgaststätte*, Juri-Gagarin-Ring 140a. There's also a good wine bar-cum-restaurant, *Caponniere*, at Cyriaksburg, open evenings only, Friday to Tuesday. *Goldbroiler* on Anger is a down-market but acceptable establishment offering chicken as the main ingredient in everything, including the soup; across the street, the best selection of beers in town is found in *Restaurant Braugold* – a real drinkers' den in spite of its misleading name.

Liveliest **nightspots** are the *Studentenclub Engelsburg*, Allerheiligenstr. 20; the *Museumskeller*, Juri-Gagarin-Ring 140a, which features live music (Wed, Fri & Sat at 10.30pm); and *Café Rapunzel*, in the *Kunsthaus* at Michaelisstr. 34 (Thurs, Fri & Sat 8am–2am). Main **cultural** venues are the *Schauspielhaus* on Klostergang and the *Opernhaus* on Dalbergsweg, while the *Waidspecher* on Grosse Arche features cabaret and puppet shows. There's a **women's centre** at Espachstr. 3.

Arnstadt and around

First documented in 704, **ARNSTADT**, which lies just beyond the fringes of the Thuringian Forest, 18km southwest of Erfurt, has the best claim to be regarded as the oldest town in eastern Germany. It's well-preserved though rather run-down historic centre of narrow alleys and half-timbered houses evokes the sort of timeless provincial air that has all but vanished from the western Länder and may not last for much longer here; it also has the benefit of being surrounded by a typically Germanic landscape of woods and hills, with the most popular excursion goal being three castles steeped in a rich lore of legends.

Schloss Neideck and the Neue Palais

From the Hauptbahnhof, situated at the northern end of town, Bahnhofstrasse leads to the Stadtpark, where stand the tower and the few other scanty remains of the sixteenth-century **Schloss Neideck**. Before the old Schloss fell into disrepair a second palace, the **Neue Palais** (guided tours Tues–Sun 8.30am–noon & 1–4.30pm; DM2), was built to the south in the early eighteenth century. Its main attraction is *Mon Plaisir*, a collection of over 400 dolls arranged into 82 scenes, depicting scenes in the life of all social classes of the day. This is far more profound than it at first appears – far from being intended as playthings for children, these scenes were commissioned over half a century by Princess Augusta Dorothea as a serious artistic enterprise. As well as the figures, the clothes, utensils and furniture are all precisely crafted, and are a valuable documentary source on social conditions in the period. The palace is also renowned for its seventeenth- and eighteenth-century china, some of which is ingeniously displayed on gilded tables in the *Spiegelkabinett*.

The Markt and around

A few minutes' walk to the west is the Markt, where the Renaissance **Rathaus** springs a surprise in its uncompromising imitation of Dutch-style architecture. The church opposite was once known as the Neue Kirche. In 1703, the eighteen-year-old J.S. Bach gained his first major professional appointment as organist here; as a result, it's now officially called the **Bachkirche** (Mon–Fri 8am–noon & 2–4pm), and the organ on which he played still survives. Unfortunately, the Arnstadt congregation failed to appreciate his genius as either a composer or performer; stung by criticism of his revolutionary improvisatory style, he left four years later for Mühlhausen. The Bach theme is taken up in the Renaissance-Baroque **Haus zum Palmbaum** (Mon–Fri 8.30am–12.30pm & 1–5pm, last Sat in month 8am–1pm; DM1) at Markt 3, which contains the local history museum. Among the memorabilia of the composer, the most striking is the original console of his organ, which had to be removed when the instrument's action was modernised.

Beyond the far end of the Markt is the **Liebfrauenkirche** (Mon, Tues, Thurs & Fri 2–4pm, Wed & Sat 10am–noon), whose architecture, and in particular the two magnificent west towers, is loosely based on the Dom in Naumburg. The chapel on the north side of the choir served as the mausoleum of the Counts of Schwarzburg and contains the beautiful **tombs** of Günther XXV and his wife Elisabeth, thought to have been carved in the famous workshop of Peter Parler in Prague. Also of note is the **high altar** of *The Coronation of the Virgin*, a fine example of fifteenth-century Thuringian wood-carving. Alongside the church is one of the town's oldest half-timbered houses, the **Alte Mühle**, which began life as the corner mill of a convent..

Practicalities

The **tourist office** (Mon & Wed–Fri 9am–5pm, Tues 9am–6pm, last Sat in month 8am–noon; ☎2049) is in the aforementioned Haus zum Palmbaum. As well as the private rooms which can be booked here, there are three **hotels**, which have the merits of being both conveniently located and reasonably priced: the half-timbered *Zum Ritter*, Kohlenmarkt 20 (☎2224), and *Goldene Sonne*, Ried 3 (☎2776), both charge DM30 per person, while *Bahnhofshotel*, Am Bahnhof (☎2481), costs DM42. By far the best place to eat in the area is the *Wachsenburg* (see below): other **restaurants** include *Burgkeller*, Erfurter Str. 12, *Ratsklause*, Ledermarkt 3, and *Thüringer Hof* on Zimmerstrasse, while the best café is *Rokischkis* on the Markt. Arnstadt's **musical** tradition is maintained by the *Bachfest* at the end of March and the August *Orgelsommer*.

The Drei Gleichen

To the northwest of Arnstadt, in the direction of Gotha, stand three hill-top castles known as the **Drei Gleichen** ("Three Alike"). This nickname has its origins in a thirteenth-century legend, which maintains that all three were hit by a shot from a single cannon ball, whereupon they appeared on the skyline as three smouldering pyres. In reality, however, the three were and are totally dissimilar in appearance.

Closest to Arnstadt is the **Wachsenburg**, which is just outside HOLZHAUSEN, 5km away and reachable by bus. This Romanesque-Gothic fortress, barely visible from below because of its densely wooded slopes, was restored to an historicist approximation of its medieval form in the GDR period to serve as a luxury hotel; it was much favoured by Erich Honecker and his SED cronies as a base for their hunting jaunts in the region. Although the rooms are likely to remain very expensive, the restaurant is affordable and of high quality. From here, it's an easy half-hour walk northwest to the **Mühlburg**, which is known to have existed back in the eighth century. However, the present ruins, which are very scanty apart from the tower, are about five hundred years younger than this. The adjacent village of **MÜHLBERG** is also worth a quick look – its **Dorfkirche** is a Baroque period piece, with the original painted galleries, altar, organ and other furnishings all as they were when the church was first built.

The final castle, **Burg Gleichen** (Wed–Sun 9am–5pm; DM0.50), is a couple of kilometres further north, and a similar distance south of WANDERSLEBEN, where you can pick up a train back to Arnstadt, or on to Erfurt or Gotha. It's the most rewarding of the three to visit, preserving picturesque remains of the early medieval fortress plus its Renaissance residence. Associated with the castle is the true story of one of its counts, Ernst III. Taken prisoner during the Crusades, he became a slave of the Turkish sultan, but was saved from captivity by the latter's daughter, who fell in love with him and converted to Christianity. As he already had a wife, he had to obtain special dispensation from the Pope to enter into a bigamous marriage with her, to which his first wife, glad to have her husband released, readily consented. The two wives agreed to live together as sisters; the valley below the fortress has ever since been known as Freudenthal (Vale of Joy) in honour of this happy solution.

Paulinzella

From Arnstadt, there's a slow but scenic railway which travels along the eastern fringe of the Thuringian Forest to Saalfeld. If travelling this way, it's worth stopping off at the village of **PAULINZELLA**, about halfway along. Here you can see one of Germany's most imposing ruins, a large Romanesque **Kloster** of the reform movement initiated at Hirsau in the Black Forest, which in turn was influenced by that of Cluny in Burgundy, the most powerful monastery of the Middle Ages. Despite its roofless state, the church is a substantial torso, its massive portal, modelled on its vanished counterpart at Cluny, being especially impressive. To find out about the Kloster's history and former appearance, visit the **Zinsboden** (May–Sept daily 9am–noon & 1–5pm; DM1), a half-timbered medieval store resting on an older stone base, standing just to the west.

Gotha

GOTHA, which lies 25km west of Erfurt, is a handsome market town and main gateway to the popular holiday area of the Thuringian Forest. In the English-speaking world, it is indelibly associated with the **House of Saxe-Coburg-Gotha**, the name of the British royal family until they changed it to Windsor for patriotic reasons at the outbreak of World War I. The end of the war saw the dissolution of this united duchy, with the citizens of Coburg plumping for union with Bavaria rather than joining all the region's other petty states in the revived province of Thuringia. Ironically, Gotha also holds an honoured place in the pantheon of the German left, as it was here in 1875 that the Socialist Workers' Party of Germany – renamed the **Social Democratic Party** fifteen years later, and still one of the country's main political forces – was formed from the amalgamation of two rival working-class groups, the moderate General German Workers' Association and the more revolutionary Social Democratic Workers' Party of Bebel and Liebknecht.

The Schlosspark

Almost the whole of the southern half of central Gotha is taken up by the **Schlosspark**, whose spacious effect is slightly marred by being divided by two main thoroughfares – through the middle by Parkallee, and down the eastern fringe by Karl-Marx-Strasse. **Schloss Friedenstein**, which lies towards the northwestern end, is a U-shaped palace with massive square corner towers, built in sober early Baroque style.

The Schlossmuseum

The historical apartments and art collections of the Schloss are together designated the **Schlossmuseum** (Wed & Fri 9am–noon & 12.30–5pm, Thurs 10am–noon & 12.30–7pm, Sat & Sun 9am–noon & 1–5pm; DM2). Despite the plain exterior, it's highly elaborate inside, forming a visual encyclopaedia of changing tastes in interior design. In the **Dichter-Zimmer** (Poets' Chamber), adorned with Romantic landscapes, look out for **Friedrich**'s *Cross in the Mountains*, a variant of one of his favourite themes. The **Kunstkammer** is a typical princely curio cabinet, whose dazzling if slightly frivolous treasures include a gilded elephant by the great Dresden goldsmith Dinglinger.

The picture gallery's star attraction is the hauntingly enigmatic *Pair of Lovers*, the most important of the few surviving paintings by the great but mysterious Rhenish draughtsman dubbed the **Master of the Housebook**. No less striking are the little boxwood figures of *Adam and Eve* by **Conrad Meit**. In the same room hang a superb group of works by **Cranach**, including several known to be by the master's own hand, rather than the more usual products of his workshop. *The Adoration of the Magi* is the masterpiece of his middle period, while a rare self-portrait of the artist can be seen at the far left corner of *Judith at the Table of Holofernes*, a story continued in the companion *Death of Holofernes*. A diptych of *The Fall and Salvation of Man* is a complicated tract illustrating the theological teachings of Melanchthon. Another, albeit far less sophisticated work inspired by the new Protestant doctrines, is a folding altar painted by **Heinrich Füllmaurer** with 157 scenes full of anecdotal details on German life of the day. There's also a decent array of paintings from the Low Countries; look out for a brilliant pair of **Rubens**, sketches for the ceiling of the Jesuit church in Antwerp.

The rest of the Schloss

The southwest tower of the Schloss contains the **Ekhof-Theater** (guided tours Tues, Wed & Fri 9am–noon & 12.30–5pm, Thurs 10am–noon & 12.30–7pm, Sat 9am–noon & 1–5pm; DM1), a perfectly preserved Baroque gem, which is still in regular use. The same ticket also admits you to the local history displays of the **Regionalmuseum** upstairs.

At the northwestern end of the complex is the **Schlosskirche**, only open for services. The **Pagenhaus** (Pages' House) at the opposite end now contains the **Kartographisches Museum** (Mon–Wed & Fri 9am–noon & 12.30–5pm; Thurs 10am–noon & 12.30–7pm; DM1), which is claimed as the first and only map museum in the world. Its presence here is explained by Gotha's long tradition as a cartographic centre, with a still-functioning publishing house first established in 1785. If you're at all interested in the subject, it's a fascinating display, with examples ranging from Mercator's maps of Crete and Cyprus up to the prestige GDR world atlas of 1981.

Around the Schlosspark

Facing the Schloss across Parkallee is a heavy neo-Renaissance pile built to house the Kunstkammer, but now containing the **Museum für Natur** (Mon–Wed 9am–noon & 12.30–5pm, Thurs 10am–noon & 12.30–7pm, Fri 9am–noon & 1–5pm; DM1). Should you be intending to visit the Thuringian Forest, it's worth coming here to see the displays on its flora and fauna – including creatures such as the wolf and the lynx now extinct there. In addition, there's a section on the *Thüringer Waldbahn*, the forest tramway (see below). Elsewhere in the southern half of the Schlosspark, you'll find a large boating lake and the **Dorischer Tempel**, designed by Friedrich Wilhelm von Erdmannsdorff, creator of the gardens of Wörlitz. East of Schloss Friedenstein is the so-called **Teeschlösschen**, a folly, long used as a kindergarten, built in imitation of an English church. Beyond are the two pavilions of the **Orangerie**, one of which is a library, the other a café.

The rest of the town

After the Schlosspark, the rest of Gotha is for the most part an anti-climax, though the **Hauptmarkt** is a highly original square. Not only is it built on a pronounced incline, which sweeps majestically up to Schloss Friedenstein, but it also features the Renaissance **Rathaus** standing in spendid isolation in the middle, a positioning often found in central Europe but rarely in Germany. Also on the square are a Baroque fountain and a number of colourful houses, among them the **Lucas-Cranach-Haus** at the top end, which is known to have belonged to the painter, though the facade is much later. From here, Lucas-Cranach-Strasse leads to the Rococo **Frankenbergsches Gartenhaus**, which stands in its own pretty courtyard down a little alley.

A few minutes' walk southwest of the Hauptmarkt, at Cosmarstr. 10, is the **Haus Tivoli**, where the union of the two socialist parties took place in 1875. In the past, it has been open as a memorial, though it posed something of a problem for the Communist authorities, as Marx had bitterly opposed the new party, which he regarded as a sell-out; indeed, his scathing *Critique of the Gotha Programme* was rated by Lenin as one of his three seminal texts. At the time of writing, the building's future as a museum was uncertain.

Practicalities

Gotha's **Hauptbahnhof** is at the southern end of town. Trams #1, #2 and #4 will all take you in the direction of the centre; here also is the northern terminus of the *Thüringer Waldbahn*. To the east, at Mozartstr. 1 (☎54008), is the **youth hostel**. Also in the vicinity is one of the **hotels** – *Waldbahn*, Bahnhofstr. 16 (☎53252), which charges from DM43 per person. Other possibilities include the old SED hang-out, *Volkshaus Zum Mohren*, just to the east of the centre at Mohrenstr. 18a (☎52845), which charges from DM21; and *Pension Regina*, right in the heart of town at Schwabhäuser Str. 4 (☎53922), whose rates begin at DM29. As ever, **private rooms** can be booked at the **tourist office**, Marktstr. 2 (Mon 2–5pm, Tues–Fri 9am–5pm, Sat 9am–noon; ☎54036).

The top **restaurant** is the reasonably-priced *Tanne*, just west of the Augustinerkirche at Bürgeraue 7. Other options include the *Schlossgaststätte* in Schloss Friedenstein, and the Czech speciality restaurant in the expensive *Hotel Slovan*, Hauptmarkt 20. Best café is *Krivan* at the corner of Hauptmarkt and Jüdenstrasse, whose striking decor was something of a revelation in GDR days. Most of Gotha's festivals have a **musical** theme; the main event is the *Thüringer Bachtage* in late March and early April.

Friedrichroda and around

The **Thuringian Forest** (*Thüringer Wald*), a typical Central European highland land-scape of densely wooded hills and valleys, occupies most of the southern part of the province. In GDR days, it rivalled the Baltic coast as the main national holiday area, and its resorts had the advantage that they could function all year round, thanks to the suit-able conditions for skiing and other winter sports. Nowhere was more popular or devel-oped than the area centred on **FRIEDRICHRODA** in the very north of the forest, just 20km from Gotha. Thanks to the superabundance of cheap accommodation possibili-ties, this makes an excellent place for either a quiet break or some serious hiking – the only way to see the best of the forest.

Friedrichroda can be reached by the branch railway from FRÖTTSTÄDT, on the main line between Eisenach and Gotha. However, the best approach is by the **forest tramway**, the *Thüringer Waldbahn*, which runs from Gotha Hauptbahnhof to an inter-change at the small industrial town of WALTERSHAUSEN, whereupon it climbs steeply up to Friedrichroda before veering westwards to its terminus at the neighbour-ing resort of TABARZ. It's painfully slow – the timetable suggestion of an hour for the complete 23km journey is invariably an underestimate – but it's the easiest way to see the scenery in comfort. Before the war, rural tramways were a common feature of Germany: now the only other remaining is a much shorter one in Saxon Switzerland.

On leaving Friedrichroda, the *Waldbahn* stops outside the Thuringian Forest's most important natural curiosity, the **Marienglashöhle** (guided tours daily mid-April–Sept 9am–5pm; Oct–mid April 9am–4pm; DM2). This is the largest crystalline cave in Europe, complete with underwater lake; its name comes from the fact that, in times past, its products were used for making jewels to adorn statues of the Virgin Mary. The most pleasant part of Friedrichroda itself is the northern **REINHARDSBRUNN** suburb, which has its own station and *Waldbahn* stop. Here an English-style park has been laid out around the medieval monastery which was converted last century in grand neo-Gothic style into a **Schloss**, now the area's top hotel.

Hikes around Friedrichroda

By far the most popular hike in the area is the ascent of the Thuringian Forest's third highest and best-known peak, the **Grosser Inselberg** (916m), which lies just to the southwest of Tabarz. Unfortunately, the summit itself is disfigured by an ugly TV tower and a number of other buildings, including a couple of restaurants and a youth hostel (☎2551). In compensation, there's a truly sweeping view, which is often given added drama by fickle microclimatic conditions. It isn't necessary to expend much energy getting to the top – taking the Friedrichroda to Brotterode bus to the *Grenzwiese* stop leaves only a short walk up. The same place marks the convergence of several other trails; among these is the **Rennsteig** (see below), one of Germany's oldest and finest long-distance wilderness footpaths. It can now be walked in its entirety once more, westerners having been unable to cover more than short stretches of it during the GDR epoch because of travel restrictions.

Another recommended area for walks is the vicinity of **FINSTERBERGEN**, a small resort 4km southeast of Friedrichroda. Its name means "Dark Mountains", and the forest around here is unusually dense and seen at its best under lowering skies. The village itself is attractive, with an unassuming-looking **Dorfkirche** whose interior, complete with double galleries, painted ceiling and organ, is a perfectly preserved example of the rustic interpretation of the Baroque style.

THE RENNSTEIG

The 168km-long **Rennsteig** cuts right through the heart of the Thuringian Forest, from HÖRSCHEL near Eisenach (from where bus #351 or #352 will take you to close to the trail head) all the way to BLANKENSTEIN by the border with Czechoslovakia. In the Dark Ages, it served as the frontier between the Thuringians and the Franks; later, it was used to demarcate the limits of the province's petty principalities, and a number of boundary stones, some dating back as far as the sixteenth century, survive as a reminder of this. When hiking became a popular pastime last century, the Rennsteig was laid out as a marked footpath, identified by signs bearing a large R. Five or six days is the normal time needed for the complete walk: hostels, campsites and refuges lie directly on the trail, though there are also plenty of resorts on the way – BROTTERODE, OBERHOF, NEUSTADT, NEUHAUS and STEINBACH – which make obvious places for an overnight stop. If you don't want to do the complete route, plenty of small sections make for satisfying walks in their own right.

Practicalities

If you want help in finding accommodation, the **tourist office** is in the *Kurverwaltung*, Gartenstr. 9 (☎4461). There's a **youth hostel** at Waldstr. 25 (☎4410), while **hotels** include *Im Grund*, Im Grund 3 (☎4583), whose rates begin at DM25 per person, and *Pertheshöh*, Perthesweg 6 (☎4477), from DM38 per person.

Schmalkalden

Some of the buses which pass the Grosser Inselberg continue south to the lively market town of **SCHMALKALDEN**, 18km southwest of Friedrichroda. The town's name is associated above all with the Reformation, in which it played a key role; the Schmalkaldic League, formed here in 1531, was an alliance of Protestant princes and Free Imperial Cities determined to protect their independence against the renewed threat of a re-imposition of centralised political and religious authority posed by Emperor Charles V's attempts to guarantee the imperial succession for his brother Ferdinand. The Schmalkaldic Wars, which broke out just after Luther's death in 1546, led to a disastrous defeat for the Protestants and the occupation of Wittenberg, but they staged such a spirited recovery that by 1555 their aim of a decentralised Germany with each state free to choose its own religion had been enshrined in the Peace of Augsburg.

The town centre

The Altmarkt is dominated by the **Stadtkirche St Georg**, a late Gothic hall church whose clock-face shows Death claiming a young girl. Among the many notable old houses are the half-timbered **Lutherhaus** on Luthermarkt (formerly the potters' market), where the Reformer stayed during his visits to the town; the **Heiliggrabesbehausung**, a huge sixteenth-century tenement on Weidebrunner Gasse; and the **Hessenhof** on Neumarkt. Preserved under the last-named is a Romanesque cellar with some of the oldest secular frescos in Europe, depicting scenes from *The Iwein Saga* by the troubadour Hartmann von der Aue; unfortunately, these were not on public view at the time of writing.

Schloss Wilhelmsburg

Standing proudly on its hill at the eastern end of town is the whitewashed **Schloss Wilhelmsburg** (daily 9am–5pm; DM2), built in the 1580s as a summer residence and hunting seat for the Landgraves of Hessen-Kassel, who had recently won complete control of the town. One of the best-preserved Renaissance palaces in Germany, its interior now houses exhibits outlining the town's complicated history, but these are overshadowed by the reception rooms themselves, most of which have elaborate coffered ceilings and huge decorative wall paintings. Particularly outstanding is the **Riesensaal** (Hall of Giants), with Landgrave Wilhelm intruding among the portraits of Old Testament and mythological heroes.

However, the most striking and significant part of the building is the **Schlosskirche**, the earliest surviving church to adhere faithfully to the design tenets of Protestantism. Taking up most of one wing, the only clue to its presence from outside is the small tower. Inside, each of the three tiers has, grouped vertically one above the other, the three essential props of Protestant worship – the plain marble altar table, here resting on the four Evangelical symbols; the pulpit, whose basin is carved with a depiction of Pentecost; and the organ, which is adorned with painted shutters (and is still in fine working order, being regularly used during concerts). Otherwise, the rich stucco vault provides the only extravagant touch.

Practicalities

The **tourist office** (Mon–Fri 9am–noon & 1–5pm; ☎3182) can be found at Mohrengasse 2. Plenty of private rooms can be booked here, all at very low rates; the alternatives are an **hotel**, *Henneberger Haus*, on Notstrasse (☎2867), which charges DM35 per person, or two **pensions**, *Sengling*, Am Neuen Teich 13 (☎3861), and *Jägerklause*, Pffaffenbach 45 (☎2243), both at DM20. By far the best **restaurant** is the *Ratskeller*, Altmarkt 2.

Eisenach

EISENACH, 28km west of Gotha and 40km north of Schmalkalden, grew up as an appendage to the **Wartburg**, the original seat of the Landgraves of Thuringia, which overlooks it from the fringe of the Thuringian Forest to the south. Though foreigners may prefer the fantasy creations of King Ludwig II of Bavaria, the Wartburg's rich historical associations make it the castle the Germans themselves most treasure, and its proximity to the hated postwar border has made it something of a symbol of the newly united nation. Eisenach itself is currently suffering from post-unification blight, but, thanks to its geographical situation and a distinguished industrial tradition, it's reckoned to be one of the towns which will fit most comfortably into the changed economic framework.

Around town

For all its modest size, Eisenach is so rich in monuments and museums that it repays an unhurried visit. It's best to proceed systematically southwards, perhaps leaving the Wartburg, the undoubted climax, for a second day.

The fortifications

Arriving at the Hauptbahnhof, it's only a couple of minutes' walk along Bahnhofstrasse to the **Nikolaitor**, a massive gateway erected in the second half of the twelfth century. Above its arch are two sculptures, one presumed to be of Ludwig I, founder of the Ludowingian dynasty which first ruled Thuringia, the other the province's heraldic lion. A few decades later, the **Nikolaikirche** was built directly on to the Nikolaitor to serve both as a parish church and as a convent for Benedictine nuns. One other significant section of the **Stadtmauer**, including a couple of towers, survives; it can be seen at the northern end of town, just beyond Jakobsplan.

The Markt

Going diagonally across Karlsplatz brings you to Karlstrasse, leading to the bright orange **Rathaus**, many times rebuilt, which faces on to the Markt. On the north side of the square is the **Stadtschloss** (April–Oct Tues–Sun 10am–5pm; Nov–March Mon–Sat 10am–5pm; DM3), a compact Rococo palace begun in 1741 as the second residence of the newly united House of Saxe-Weimar-Eisenach, replacing the much grander Renaissance seat of the hitherto separate Eisenach duchy. The main attraction of the interior is the elegant decoration of the rooms themselves, which house a collection of Thuringian decorative arts from the eighteenth century to the present day.

In the middle of the Markt stands the **Georgenkirche**, the late Gothic successor to the church where Landgrave Ludwig IV married the Hungarian princess now known as Saint Elisabeth (see also Marburg, *Chapter Three*) in 1221, and where Luther, whose mother was a native of the town, sang as a choirboy. Soon after its construction, it was adapted to the needs of Protestant worship, notably by the erection of the tiered galleries. J.S. Bach was baptised here in 1685; and the church maintained its reputation as a place of destiny by being a key meeting place of opposition groups in the *Wende* of 1989. On the walls are a number of fourteenth-century carved epitaphs commemorating (in the case of Ludwig I, somewhat belatedly), the Ludowingian rulers. Outside the church is the mid-sixteenth-century **Martbrunnen**, showing its patron, Saint George, in his familiar dragon-slayer role .

The Thüringer Museum

Just off the eastern side of the Markt is the very run-down-looking **Predigerkirche**, built in the simple and austere Gothic style favoured by the Dominicans whose monastery church it was. For nearly a century it has been home to the **Thüringer Museum** (Tues–Fri 9am–12.30pm & 2–5pm, Sat & Sun 9am–4pm; DM2), an outstanding collection of wood sculpture, an art form in which Thuringia excelled throughout the Middle Ages. The earliest pieces are from the twelfth century, and include a *St John the Evangelist* of enormous tragic pathos, and range through a whole series of *Madonnas*, *Pietàs* and *Crucifixions* from the various phases of Gothic, to the large winged altars produced in Erfurt and Saalfeld in the years immediately before the Reformation. However, the most intriguing exhibit is the thirteenth-century **statue of Heinrich Raspe**, carved under the realist influence of the Naumburg school. As the crown on his head indicates, Raspe, the brother-in-law of Saint Elisabeth, usurped the German throne, though he was subsequently accorded the status of an "anti-king"; he was also the last Landgrave of Thuringia, his death without issue leading to a war which saw the end of the province as a unit.

The Lutherhaus and the Bachhaus

Off the southwestern corner of the Markt is Lutherplatz, on which stands the **Lutherhaus** (May–Sept 9am–1pm & 2–5pm; Oct–April Mon–Sat 9am–1pm & 2–5pm, Sun 2–5pm; DM3), in actual fact the home of the Cotta family, with whom Luther lodged as a schoolboy. The present house, predominantly a half-timbered structure of the sixteenth and eighteenth centuries, encloses the original, which preserves the two rooms used by the famous lodger. Inside are displays on his two periods in Eisenach, plus a large collection of Reformation books and other archive material.

A few minutes' walk south of the Lutherhaus is Frauenplan, with the **Bachhaus** (Mon 1.30–4.30pm, Tues–Fri 9am–4.30pm, Sat & Sun 9am–noon & 1.30–4.30pm; DM3), a large Baroque house presumed to be the birthplace of J.S. Bach. Inside, an attempt has been made at recreating the sort of bourgeois interiors typical of the composer's childhood; there's also extensive documention on his career and a valuable collection of historical musical instruments. To round off the visit, it's worth waiting for one of the demonstrations given by a member of staff, who puts a harpsichord, clavichord and chamber organ through their paces in performances of short pieces by Bach.

JOHANN SEBASTIAN BACH (1685–1750)

Despite the fact that popular imagination has turned Mozart into the supreme composer touched by a flawless genius, most practising musicians would, if pressed, be far more likely to accord this honour to **Johann Sebastian Bach**. The most remarkable feature of his career was its sheer provinciality: born into a long-standing Thuringian musical family, he followed their tradition of salaried employment, serving as a church organist in Arnstadt and Mühlhausen, and as a court musician in Weimar and Köthen, before spending the last 27 years of his life as *Kantor* in Leipzig. Bach's vast output, which includes well over 200 cantatas, the entire kernel of the organist's repertoire, and most of the greatest music written for solo violin, cello and harpsichord, is of a consistently high standard unmatched by any other composer. Although associated primarily with music of intense spirituality – of which the heart-rending *St Matthew Passion* is the supreme expression – Bach was a peerless practitioner of dance rhythms, as the *Orchestral Suites* show, and even adept at humorous effects, as in the *Coffee Cantata*. Strangely, his reputation during his lifetime was based primarily on his prowess as a virtuoso performer; few contemporaries appreciated the unique genius of his music, which, because it brought the Baroque age to a glorious climax rather than breaking new ground, was quickly forgotten after his death, not to be revived until Mendelssohn exhumed it a century later. Bach ensured the continuity of the family musical tradition by fathering twenty children, of whom at least two, the waywardly eccentric Carl Philipp Emmanuel and the elegantly refined Johann Christian, who brought the *galant* style to London, deserve to be considered as important composers in their own right.

Three more museums

Walking east from the Bachhaus, you come to the ring road, or Warburg-Allee. A bit further south is the **Automobil-Pavillon** (daily 9am–4pm; DM2), a collection of historic vehicles celebrating Eisenach's tradition, dating back to 1897, as a leading centre of the German car industry. One of the earliest exhibits, the *Dixi*, was capable of the then mind-boggling speed of 60km per hour; it initiated a reputation for quality products which continued with the flashy *BMW* sports cars of the 1930s. From the postwar period are examples of the different versions of the *Wartburg*, the flagship of GDR car production. Unlike the ridiculous *Trabant*, with which it was often unfairly bracketed, it was a respectable motor – and like the *Rolls-Royce*, one of very few which had the body fitted to the chassis by hand. To local dismay, the factory was closed down because of unprofitability in 1991, though many of the workers were able to find alternative employment with *BMW* and *Opel*, who have both set up plants here.

A place with a somewhat less certain future is the **Goldener Löwe** inn a block to the west at Marienstr. 45; this was where August Bebel and Wilhelm Liebknecht set up their revolutionary socialist party in 1869, only to amalgamate it with its more moderate rival six years later in Gotha. In the GDR period, it was, needless to say, a memorial museum, but this was closed indefinitely after the *Wende*. At the end of Marienstrasse, Reuterweg leads west to the **Reutervilla** (Tues–Sun 10am–5pm; DM3), home of the nineteenth-century Low German writer Fritz Reuter, and still furnished as he knew it. Of more general appeal is the huge array of Wagner memorabilia, including his death mask. These were bought to commemorate the composer's sojourn in Eisenach, where he came to find inspiration for his opera *Tannhäuser*, which is set in and around the Wartburg, fusing into an imaginary, romanticised whole two true episodes from the castle's history.

The Wartburg

From the Reutervilla, it's a steep thirty-minute ramble through the woods to the **Wartburg** (daily April–Oct 8.30am–6pm; Nov–March 9am–5pm; DM1) – a far more atmospheric approach than the circuitous main road. If at all possible, avoid visiting at weekends or holiday periods, and arrive first thing: tourism here has soared since the *Wende*, often stretching to bursting-point.

Given its richly varied history, it's perhaps appropriate that the Wartburg is a melange of several different epochs, unfolding like a great picture book of German architecture. The oldest and most imposing part is the late twelfth-century **Palas** at the left-hand end of the second courtyard, one of Europe's few surviving examples of a Romanesque palace. A number of structures – including the **Torhalle** between the courtyards, the cross-crowned **Bergfried** or keep and the **Neue Kemenate** adjoining the Palas – were added in Romantic style last century, when the whole castle was given a thorough, albeit over-enthusiastic, restoration. The basic entrance ticket entitles you to climb the **Südturm**, from where there's a good view over the complex – and of the dense tracts of the Thuringian Forest.

Some history

The Wartburg was founded by Count Ludwig I in 1067. His descendants, promoted to the status of Landgraves, presided over a cultured court, patronising some of the greatest **Minnesänger** (German troubadours), including Wolfram von Eschenbach, who wrote part of his epic *Parzifal* here, and Walter von der Vogelweide, the finest lyric poet of the day. The most significant event in the Wartburg's history began in May 1521 when **Martin Luther**, having been declared an outlaw by the Diet of Worms, was kidnapped by order of Elector Frederick the Wise and taken to this safe haven. During his ten-month stay, the hitherto tonsured and clean-shaven monk disguised himself under a head of hair and beard, passing as a minor landowner by name of *Junker Jörg* (Farmer George). In a frenzy of activity, he translated the New Testament from Erasmus' Greek into the vernacular language spoken by the people of his day, so creating the foundations of modern written German. In 1817 the Wartburg was the rallying-place of the **Burschenschaften**, idealistically-minded students protesting at the continued division of Germany, even after the Congress of Vienna, into a host of tinpot principalities.

The Palas

To see beyond the confines of the courtyard, you have to buy a ticket for a **guided tour** (April–Oct 9am–4.30pm; Nov–March 9.30am–3.30pm; DM5) of the Palas, at the end of which you're free to walk along the Wehrgang (sentry walk) and look round the museums at leisure. In all the Palas has around 200 carved **capitals**, a third of them original, highly stylised masterpieces of late Romanesque carving. The finest are those on the central columns which are a distinguishing feature of most of the rooms, including the fourteenth-century **Burgkapelle**. To the modern eye, it's a matter of regret that there are so many Romantic embellishments, though these are often beautiful works in their own right, notably the three fresco cycles by **Moritz von Schwind** illustrating the life of Saint Elisabeth, the Minnesänger contest and the history of the castle. Rather more over-the-top are the Jugendstil mosaics in the saint's bedroom, and the colossal coffered vault of the main **Festsaal**, where the Burschenschaften met.

The museums

The museum in the Neue Kemenate is largely devoted to artefacts from around the time of the Reformation, including paintings, sculptures, weapons, furniture and tapestries. Among several works by **Cranach**, look out for the pendants of *Hans and Margarete Luther*, the parents of the great reformer.

From here, you cross the courtyard to the beamed interior of the Wehrgang, which you follow round to the **Lutherstube**, the simple wood-panelled room where the German translation of the Bible was made. In the glass case is a copy of the original *Lutherbibel*, while on the walls hung portraits of Luther and Melanchton, plus an engraving of Luther as *Junker Jörg*, all by Cranach. There was once a blot on the wall by the stove which, according to tradition, was made when Luther threw an inkpot at an apparition of the Devil, but souvenir hunters chipped away at it so much that there's now nothing but a hole going right through to the bare masonry.

Practicalities

Eisenach's **tourist office** (Mon 10am–6pm, Tues–Fri 9am–6pm, Sat 9am–3pm; ☎76162) is at Bahnhofstr. 5; there's a separate number (☎4895) for the **room-finding** service in private houses, which operates until 6pm on Saturdays, 7pm otherwise. The **youth hostel** is at Mariental 24 (☎3613), on a road which branches off Wartburger Allee. Top **hotel**, in every sense, is *Auf der Wartburg* in the Wartburg itself (☎5111); rooms begin at DM65. Good alternatives in the town centre are *Thüringer Hof*, Karlsplatz 11 (☎3131), charging from DM45, and *Hospiz Glockenhof*, Grimmelsgasse 4 (☎3562), from DM40. There are also plenty of cheaper guest house-type establishments, predominantly in the wooded surroundings; the tourist office has a full list.

For **eating** and **drinking**, best bets are the hotels already mentioned. If visiting the Wartburg, the hotel has three separate eateries, plus a café in the castle itself and another restaurant, *Zum Parkhaus,* on the access road, Wartburgschleife. In the town centre, alternatives to the hotels include *Schlosskeller* on Auf der Esplanade, which has fish specialities, and *Marktschänke*, Markt 9. The main **festivals** are the folkloric *Sommergewinn* on the last Saturday in March, and the concerts of the *Thüringer Bachtage* around Easter.

NORTHERN THURINGIA

The northern part of Thuringia is, in comparison with the central belt, little touched by tourism. Here are two towns, **Mühlhausen** and **Nordhausen**, which went against the regional grain in the medieval period by functioning as city-states; though Nordhausen is now a shadow of its former self, the centre of Mühlhausen looks much as it has done for centuries. The other main draws in the north are the often-overlooked princely seat of **Sondershausen** and the hills of the **Kyffhäuser** range, whose historical connotations give it a special place in the nation's affections.

Mühlhausen

Even within Thuringia, there are few places which conjure up the past so vividly as **MÜHLHAUSEN**, which dates back at least as far as Charlemagne. Its historic core has almost completely intact medieval walls, inside which is a maze of alleys lined with half-timbered houses and six Gothic churches, with a further four standing just outside the fortifications. As a Free Imperial City througout the Middle Ages, Mühlhausen was a rare island of independence in this part of the country, which explains why it became the headquarters of the ill-fated Peasants' Revolt of 1525, led by the town's firebrand pastor, **Thomas Müntzer** (see below). To the GDR authorities, this was the first great social revolution in German history; accordingly, Müntzer became one of the state's supreme heroes, regarded as a Moses-like precursor of Marx. In 1975, to mark the 450th anniversary of the event, the town was officially renamed "Thomas-Müntzer-Stadt-Mühlhausen", and two of the churches were made over as memorials to him; it will be interesting to see whether or not all this will survive the latest re-evaluation of the country's past necessitated by the *Wende*.

THOMAS MÜNTZER AND THE PEASANTS' REVOLT

By far the most controversial, not to say sinister, figure of the Reformation, **Thomas Müntzer** has a significance far beyond the distorted one promoted by the GDR – he can be regarded as the father of all the myriad forms of sectarian Protestantism which retain such an influence to this day. As vitriolic about Luther (whom be dismissed as "Dr Pussyfoot" and "Dr Easychair") as about Catholicism, Müntzer believed that the Bible had to be reinterpreted by a second Daniel (needless to say, himself) who would lead the elect in a crusade against the ungodly. His electrifying preaching gained him a huge popular following, but his bloodthirsty message so alarmed the authorities of Electoral Saxony that he was expelled from the territory. On his appointment at Mühlhausen, he hitched his cause to that of the peasants, who were already in revolt against their feudal masters over their economic plight. In reality, Müntzer was primarily interested in them for religious reasons, though he was the only leading churchman of the day who understood that faith among the common people was not nourished by starvation. Incensed by Müntzer's actions, Luther was inspired to write a pamphlet condemning the peasants, and backed the princely armies which crushed his rival's untrained forces at Frankenhausen after the peasants had refused to hand over their leader in exchange for an offer of clemency. Müntzer was captured in the battle and brought back to Mühlhausen, where he was tried, tortured and executed.

Around town

The best introduction to Mühlhausen is to walk all the way round the outside of the 2.7km-long **Stadtmauer**, which still preserves six towers and two gateways. It's at its most impressive around the main western entrance, the **Inneres Frauentor**. Here a small section has been opened to the public, enabling you to go along part of the sentry walk and ascend the **Rabenturm** (July & Aug 10am–noon & 1–4.30pm, closed Fri; May, June & Sept Wed & Sat 2–5pm, Sun 10am–noon & 1–4.30pm; DM1.50).

On Holzstrasse, the northern of the two streets leading to the centre, you pass the thirteenth-century **Hospital** and a number of fine houses, of which the most notable is no. 1, which began life as the town house of Kloster Zella before becoming a post office in the period of the Thurn and Taxis monopoly. Herrenstrasse to the south also has fine buildings, though the parish house at the far end is a replacement of the one where Müntzer lived, which was destroyed by fire.

Both streets terminate at the **Marienkirche** (10am–noon & 2–4pm, closed Fri; DM2), where Müntzer served as pastor during the three fateful months he lived in

Mühlhausen. The church itself has a distinctive triple-towered **facade** in which the massive Flamboyant Gothic central tower, crowned with a bravura nineteenth-century steeple, is flanked by its two modest counterparts, one late Romanesque, the other early Gothic. No less idiosyncratic is the **south portal**: although some of its original statuary – carved by the Parler school of Prague – was destroyed as a result of the iconoclasm fomented by Müntzer, the balcony with the peering figures of Emperor Charles IV, Empress Elisabeth and two courtiers survives intact. Inside, the most impressive feature is the soaring architecture of the five-aisled hall nave with its elaborate vault. The **furnishings** include a number of fine retables (the high altar to the Virgin Mary was made during the brief return to Catholicism following Müntzer's demise), and the grand white *Ratsstuhl*, where councillors sat during services.

Following Ratsstrasse south from here brings you to the **Rathaus** complex, which dates back to about 1300 but which grew in size to such an extent down the centuries that it straddles the street, with the two parts linked by a covered passageway. In the **Ratsstube**, adorned with Gothic wall paintings, Müntzer held his daily *Ewig Rat* (Perpetual Council); the **Archiv**, with its complete set of Renaissance furniture and documents pertaining to Mühlhausen's period as a city-state, is also worth a look.

A couple of blocks south on Kornmarkt is the **Barfüsserkirche** (Tues–Sun 10am–4.30pm; DM1.50), a barn-like former Franciscan monastery church currently given over to a museum on the Peasants' Revolt interpreted from a Marxist standpoint.

Practicalities

Mühlhausen's **Bahnhof**, which has regular services to both Gotha and Erfurt, is three blocks beyond the easternmost part of the Stadtmauer. The **tourist office** (Mon–Fri 9am–noon & 1–5pm; ☎2912) is at the eastern end of the old town at Gömarstr. 57. In addition to the **private rooms** on offer here, there are three hotels – *Stadt Mühlhausen* on Untermarkt (☎5512) is top of the range, charging from DM40 per person; alternatives are *Grüne Linde*, Gömarstr. 49 (☎3385), and *Haus des Handwerks*, well to the southwest of the walled part of town at Goetheweg 52 (☎3377). There's a surprisingly good choice of **restaurants**; best is *Zum Nachbarn*, just east of the Marienkirche at Steinweg 65, which specialises in poultry dishes. Mühlhausen was one of the few places in the GDR which kept up much of a tradition in **festivals**, of which the most important is the *Kirmes*, a large fair held at the end of August.

Nordhausen

NORDHAUSEN lies just to the south of the Harz mountains, at the fringe of the fertile plain known as the "Golden Meadow" (*Goldene Aue*), about 45km northeast of Mühlhausen. It's predominantly an industrial town, best known for its production of spirits (a mouth-burning *Korn* has been made here since the early sixteenth century) and tobacco (especially *Kautabak*, or "chewing tobacco"). Unforunately, this rather overshadows its historical role as a former Free Imperial City, the more so as a large number of monuments were destroyed in 1945, during the severest bombing raid carried out on any Thuringian town. Nonetheless, there are a few sights well worth stopping to see if you happen to find yourself here – a not uncommon occurrence, as Nordhausen is the southern terminus of the narrow-gauge steam railway through the Harz, the *Harzquerbahn* (see *Chapter Ten*), and also has the only functioning train connection with the Lower Saxon side of the range.

The Altstadt

The **Stadtmauer** was among the monuments damaged in the war, though 1.5km of the circuit still remain, the most impressive section being the set of double fortifications around Jüdenstrasse, about halfway up the hill between the Hauptbahnhof and the Markt. Following the wall northwards, you can see the **Finkenburg**, one of the oldest and finest of the few half-timbered houses spared by the bombs, at An der Wassertreppe. East of here is the Markt, whose late Renaissance **Rathaus**, outside which stands the inevitable statue of Roland, was lovingly rebuilt from wartime ruins.

Further up, the skyline is dominated by the so-called **Dom**, more correctly the **Kloster zum Heiligen Kreuz**, the successor to a nunnery founded by Empress Mathilde in 963. The present church is an architectural jumble – the towers, the cloister and the crypt are Romanesque, the choir early Gothic, the lofty hall nave Flamboyant Gothic. Inside, the finest feature is the group of six late thirteenth-century statues in the choir, clearly modelled on their counterparts in Naumburg. Have a look, too, at the richly carved stalls.

The more modest **Blasiikirche** just to the east exhibits a remarkably similar architectural mix, though one of its two octagonal towers has had a truncated aspect since its damage in a seventeenth-century fire. Barfüsser Strasse, which leads north from here, is the least damaged of the Nordhausen's old streets, with a number of half-timbered houses, of which no. 6, now a children's library, was the town's first theatre.

The Konzentratsionslager Mittelbau-Dora

In 1943, a subsidiary concentration camp of Buchenwald, under the name of **Dora** was set up at the foot of the Kohnstein at the northernmost fringe of Nordhausen. The following year, renamed **Mittelbau**, it became a full-blown camp in its own right. 60,000 prisoners from 21 different countries were interned here, engaged on the secret production of V1 and V2 missiles, working underground in a network of tunnels and caverns. Nearly a third of them died here; in their honour, the site has been turned into a **memorial** (Tues–Sun 9am–3.15pm; free), with documentary displays on the conditions they suffered. The easiest way to get there is to take the *Harzquerbahn* to KRIMDERODE, then follow the main road round to the west.

Practicalities

Nordhausen's **Hauptbahnhof** lies south of the Altstadt, on the opposite side of the River Zorge; the *Harzquerbahn*'s terminus, misleadingly designated *Nordhausen-Nord*, is just across Bahnhofsplatz. At no. 2 on the same square is the only **hotel**, *Handelshof* (☎5121), which has singles for DM36, doubles from DM69. There's also a **youth hostel** at Johannes-Kleinspehn-Str. 1 (☎8587) in the suburb of SALZA, just behind the Bahnhof of the same name, the first stop on the mainline route north. Otherwise, you can book a **private room** for a DM5 fee at the **tourist office**, just off the Markt at Rautenstr. 42 (Mon, Thurs & Fri 9.30am–noon & 1.30–4.30pm, Tues 9.30am–noon & 1.30–5.30pm, Wed 9.30am–noon & 1.30–3.30pm; ☎4938). Nordhausen doesn't score highly for **eating** and **drinking**, but try *Café Altstadt*, Kranichstr. 19, or the fish restaurant *Gastmahl des Meeres*, Arnoldstr. 8. Main local **festival** is the *Rolandfest* on the second weekend in June.

Sondershausen

SONDERSHAUSEN, which lies 20km south of Nordhausen in a pretty setting in the valley cut by the River Wipper between two groups of wooded hills, the Hainleite and the Windleite, is a place which deserves to be far better known. Formerly the capital of the county of Schwarzburg, and later of the principality of Schwarzburg-Sondershausen, its main attraction is as one of the courtly towns so characteristic of Thuringia. However, it's far less sophorific than most of its counterparts. The huge winding tower (now preserved as a technical monument) which greets you on arrival at the Hauptbahnhof is a reminder that Sondershausen has for centuries been a major centre of potash production, while the historic heart of the town has regained its former role as a market and trading centre.

The Schloss

A typically oversized **Schloss** is Sondershausen's overwhelmingly dominant building; it can be approached from the west via its rustic park, or from the Markt by the monumental steps to the side of the Neoclassical guard house, the Alte Wache. The north wing dates back to the sixteenth century, when the scattered holdings of the ancient county of Schwarzburg were merged into a single unit and ruled from here. This was short-lived – the county was split among four sons, though only two lines, Rudolstadt and Sondershausen itself, lasted for more than a generation. At the end of the seventeenth century, the rulers of both were promoted to the rank of princes of the Holy Roman Empire. This inspired the beginning of a massive extension programme to the Schloss, including the addition of a Baroque tower and south wing; a late Rococo palace, subsequently modified in Neoclassical style, was then added at an angle of 45° to the original, creating an almost triangular courtyard.

The interior
Guided tours (Tues–Sun at 9am, 10am, 11am, 2pm, 3pm & 4pm; DM2) are run round the wonderfully eclectic interior, which graphically conjures up the real-life fantasy world of a petty German court. In the original palace is the most individual chamber, the Mannerist **Wendelstein**, which boasts a dazzlingly brilliant stucco vault showing the Elements, the Seasons, the Virtues, putti and mythological characters. The main reception room is the Baroque **Riesensaal** (Giants' Hall), so called from the sixteen over-life-sized statues of Classical deities; it boasts a superb coffered vault with ornate stucco trophies and paintings illustrating Ovid's *Metamorphoses*. If, as is probable, this is closed for repairs, there's the compensation of being able to see its recently restored Rococo counterpart, the turquoise **Festsaal**, whose vault continues the antique theme with the story of Jupiter and Calypso. Two other highlights are the **Liebhabertheater** (Conoisseurs' Theatre), a Biedermeier gem which is one of the smallest theatres in Germany, and the gilded **state coach**, which yields nothing in splendour to those used by any of the royal houses of Europe.

The Karussel
In the park west of the Schloss is the **Karussel** or **Achteckige Haus**, a tall, eccentric-looking octagon with interior galleries and a fresco of *The Triumph of Venus*. Built at the beginning of the eighteenth century to serve as the main venue for court entertainments, it's occasionally used for concerts by the *Loh-Orchester*.

The Hainleite

It's well worth taking a walk in the **Hainleite**, the hills to the south of Sondershausen; they're best reached by following Possenallee straight ahead from the town centre. From here, it's an easy ascent to the **Rondell**, a belvedere commanding a fine view of the valley. A couple of kilometres further south brings you to the **Jagdschloss Zum Possen**, the former hunting lodge of the court, which is now a hotel, restaurant and recuperative centre with a wildlife park alongside. There's also a tall half-timbered **Aussichtsturm** (daily 10am–6pm; DM1) dating from the very end of the eighteenth century, which you can climb for the most extensive panorama of the whole region.

Practicalities

Sondershausen's **Hauptbahnhof** is about fifteen minutes' walk west of the centre; the *Haltepunkt Sondershausen-Süd* below the Hainleite is actually slightly nearer the Markt and the Schloss. The **tourist office** (Mon–Fri 9am–12.30pm & 1.30–5pm, Sat 9–11am; ☎8111) is a couple of blocks south of the Schlosspark at Ferdinand-Schlufter-Str. 20. There are plenty of **private rooms** for rent here, many for just DM15 per person. Alternatively, rates at the main **hotel**, *Thüringer Hof*, Wilhelm-Pieck-Str. 30 (☎2474), start at DM29, while the *Gasthaus Zum Possen* (☎2884) and the *Erholungszentrum* (☎2665) in the Hainleite are incredible bargains for a rustic break at DM20 or less. Best **restaurants** are those in the hotels, plus the *Ratskeller*, Markt 7.

The Kyffhäuser

The **Kyffhäuser**, a small group of wooded sandstone mountains, form a virtual southern continuation of the Harz, which they closely resemble – except for the fact that they're virtually uninhabited. Despite their modest dimensions – they occupy less than 60 square kilometres, while the peaks are all under 500m – they have a grandeur that belies their actual size. In addition, they hold a special place in the national consciousness, being the seat of one of the great imperial castles of early medieval Germany and the place where, according to legend, Emperor Frederick Barbarossa (the country's real-life counterpart of King Arthur) lies slumbering, awaking his second coming. For the GDR state, the Kyffhäuser had the additional allure of being where the first German revolution, the Peasants' Revolt of 1525, came to its untimely end.

Bad Frankenhausen

The gateway to the Kyffhäuser, and the obvious base for a visit, is the small spa town of **BAD FRANKENHAUSEN**, which lies at their southern edge, 20km east of Sondershausen, just below the **Schlachtberg** (Battle Hill) where Thomas Müntzer's peasant army was routed by vastly superior forces loyal to the nation's rulers.

In the late sixteenth century, Frankenhausen became the capital of one of the four counties into which Schwarzburg was divided, an event which necessitated the building of the modest little **Schloss** (Tues–Sun 10am–noon & 2–5pm; DM2) at the southern end of the old quarter, about five minutes' walk from the Bahnhof. After a generation, Frankenhausen's territories were incorporated into those of Rudolstadt, so this was thereafter never more than a second residence. It's now a museum devoted to the Kyffhäuser region, with displays on its flora, fauna, archaeology, history, arts and crafts, with the highlight being a diorama of the battle of 1525.

Just north of the Schloss is the Markt, with a Neoclassical Rathaus; from here, Kräme, a pedestrianised shopping street, leads to **Anger**, the spacious main square, which boasts a few half-timbered houses. Uphill lies the best preserved section of the thirteenth-century fortification system, centred on the impressive **Hausmannsturm**.

Much further up, crowning the top of the Schlachtberg and visible for miles around, is the white rotunda housing one of Germany's newest yet already somewhat anachronistic tourist attractions, the **Bauernkriegs-Panorama** (guided tours, lasting 1hr, daily April–Sept 9am–5pm; Oct–March 10am–4pm; DM10). Claimed as the largest painting in the world, this huge, vividly coloured panoramic picture of the battle was unveiled in 1989 to celebrate Müntzer's 500th anniversary, and the 40th birthday of the GDR. Begun twelve years previously, it was commissioned as a co-operative work by a team of artists, on the model of the many nineteenth-century panoramic battle pictures, a once-popular art form which, until then, seemed to have been killed off by the cinema.

As work progressed, the Leipzig professor **Werner Tübke** took an increasingly dominant role, eventually taking over the project completely: over seventy percent of the
painting is by him, with much of the rest being detail provided by specialists. Both
politically and artistically the end result is controversial, though neither critical derision nor the inflated entrance fee deters the crowds who flock here, often queuing for
hours during the main holiday periods because of the restricted admissions policy.

Practicalities

The **tourist office** (Mon–Fri 9am–5pm; ☎3037) is at Anger 14, the oldest half-timbered
house in town. You can book a **private room** here, though they're easy enough to find
on your own if you look for the *Zimmer frei* signs; there are over a hundred in all,
charging from as little as DM10. For a bit more luxury, there are three **hotels** –
Thüringer Hof, Anger 15 (☎2079), is top of the range, charging from DM48 per person;
rates at *Bellevue*, Goethestr. 13 (☎2726), begin at DM40, while *Stolberg*, Bahnhofstr. 15
(☎2577), has singles for DM32, doubles DM48. There's also a **youth hostel** at
Bahnhofstr. 6 (☎2018).

The mountains

The Kyffhäuser are combed with marked walking trails, and it's easy enough to devise
your own circular routes. Easiest hike is to the **Barbarossahöhle** (daily May–Sept
9am–6pm; Oct–April 9am–5pm; DM3), 5km to the west and just north of ROTTLEBEN,
the next stop on the rail line to Sondershausen. Discovered during mining operations
last century – whereupon it immediately became coupled to the Barbarossa legend –
this is, with a total length of 800 metres, one of Europe's largest gypsum caves, featuring some amazing vaults and tiny lakes with crystal clear waters.

For the more energetic, there's a 10km path from Bad Frankenhausen which travels
right through the heart of the Kyffhäuser to its highest summit, the **Kulpenberg**
(477m). If you want a yet more extensive view, you can go up its **Fernsehturm** (television tower; daily April–Sept 10am–5pm; Oct–March 10am–4pm) to the café and observation platform.

A few kilometres east of here, and linked by a direct trail to Bad Frankenhausen, is
the **Kyffhäuserdenkmal** (daily May–Sept 9am–7pm; Oct–March 9am–5pm; DM4).
This historicist monstrosity, which commands another sweeping view over the region,
was erected at the end of nintenth century in honour of the recently-deceased Kaiser
Wilhelm I, the first emperor of the Second Reich and thus the man seen as something
of a reincarnation of Frederick Barbarossa, an early champion of German unity. In
order to build it, a substantial portion of the surviving fragments of the upper fortress
of the famous Romanesque **Reichsburg**, one of the strongholds of the Hohenstaufen
emperors, had to be demolished – an act of vandalism uncharacteristic of the time.
Thankfully, the ruins of the lower fortress, including a well some 176 metres deep,
survive to give an idea of the scale and appearance of the original.

EASTERN THURINGIA

The easternmost part of Thuringia has a natural border in the form of the middle
reaches of the valley of the River Saale, on whose banks lie the university city of **Jena**,
and the two former courtly towns of **Rudolstadt** and **Saalfeld**. Further east lie the two
old principalities of Reuss, with their capitals at **Gera** and **Greiz**, while jutting into
Saxony, and only recently returned to its traditional Thuringian homeland, is a strip of
land centred on **Altenburg**.

Jena

JENA, which is just 20km southeast of Weimar, lies at the point where the Saale valley is at its grandest, surrounded by red sandstone and chalk hills, which give the appearance of being much higher than they actually are, and which have a climate mild enough for the growing of vines. The **University** is among the most famous in Germany; founded in 1558 with the help of Melanchthon, it was closely associated with the great flowering of Classicism in Weimar, to which Jena then belonged, following its own short-lived period as capital of an independent duchy. In the nineteenth century, it played a leading role in scientific research, and was closely associated with the world-renowned optics company, the Carl-Zeiss-Stiftung, whose works are still a prominent feature of the skyline. Sadly, the city was exceptionally badly bombed in World War II and still bears the scars of this. Nevertheless, there's still plenty to see – particularly if you are at all of a scientific bent – while the atmosphere is the liveliest, and the choice in eating, drinking and nightlife by far the best in Thuringia.

Arrival and practicalities

Jena has two main stations – the **Westbahnhof** to the southwest of the centre has services to Erfurt, Weimar and Gera, while the **Saalbahnhof** to the north is for the line along the Saale betwen Saalfeld and Halle. Slow trains on the latter route also stop at the **Paradiesbahnhof**, which is at the southern fringe of the centre; slightly to the north of here is the **bus station**. The **tourist office** (Mon–Fri 9am–6pm, Sat 9am–2pm; ☎24671) is in a pavilion just south of Eichplatz at Löbderstr. 9. **Private rooms** can be booked here for an average of DM25, plus DM2 booking fee; this is by far the best accommodation option, particularly as there's no hostel or campsite. **Hotels** include *Pension Kerzel*, Lutherstr. 38 (☎25760), charging from DM30 per person; *Schwarzer Bär*, Lutherplatz 2 (☎22543), whose rates begin at DM50; and *Zur Goldenen Traube*, Fritz-Ritter-Str. 44 (☎31592), with singles for DM52, doubles DM80. There are a number of privatised holiday homes, mostly in the hillside suburbs, where it's also easy enough to find rooms in private houses under your own steam.

The city

Given its size, Jena's attractions are fairly spread out. However, most of what you're likely to want to see is concentrated in a few easily assimilated areas and, with the exception of the hillside suburbs, can be covered comfortably on foot.

Eichplatz

Dominating the centre of Jena from the middle of the spacious Eichplatz, dwarfing even the Carl Zeiss buildings just to the west (of which it was originally intended to be a part), is the **Universitätshochhaus**, a 120-metre-high cylindrical tower inaugurated in 1972. Though by no means the worst example of the GDR school of Brutalist architecture, it's distinctly unloved locally: irreverent students were quick to dub it *Phallus Jenensis*, and this has since passed into the cruder vernacular form of *Jenaer Pimmel* ("Jena's Willie"). If the building has a saving grace, it's the view from the café at the top – just walk in and take the lift up.

In order to build the tower, many of the surviving historical buildings on Eichplatz and the streets around had to be razed, and it was only as a result of a protest campaign that the original University, the **Collegium Jenense**, which stands just to the south on Collegienstrasse, was spared. Originally a Dominican monastery, it's a marvellously ramshackle array of bits and pieces from various epochs, which evoke the cloistered tranquillity of academe. The most arresting feature is the bravura Renaissance carving in the courtyard of the coat of arms of the Ernestine line of the House of Wettin, the University's original patrons. Just east of the Collegium is the ruined **Anatometurm**, one of the three towers surviving from the fourteenth-century fortifications system.

The Markt and around

Separating Eichplatz from the much smaller Markt is the **Rathaus**, a simple Gothic structure crowned with a miniature Baroque belfry housing the *Schnapphans*, a mechanism which strikes the hours. In the middle of the square stands the **statue of Hannfried**, this being the nickname given locally to the University's founder, John Frederick the Magnanimous, who here created a new institution to make up for his loss of Wittenberg.

Such few old houses as Jena possesses can be found mostly on the Markt itself and in the two alleys, Oberlauengasse and Unterlauengasse, immediately to the east. The finest of these, at Markt 7, is now the **Stadtmuseum Göhre** (Tues & Thurs–Sun 10am–1pm & 2–5pm, Wed 10am–1pm & 2–6pm; DM2). It contains displays on local arts and crafts, wine-making, religious art, the so-called "Seven Wonders of Jena" and the history of the University (including a reproduction of the Studentenkarzer or prison with its characteristic grafitti). There's also a reconstruction of a nineteenth-century café if you need a bit of light refreshment.

Despite its name, Unterem Markt, which stretches to the west, is a street rather than a square. At no. 12a is the large Baroque mansion which was formerly the home of Johann Gottlieb Fichte, one of a host of renowned philosophers (Hegel, Schelling, the Schlegels and the Humboldts were others) based in Jena during the Romantic period. Now designated the **Gedenkstätte der deutschen Frühromantik** (Tues & Thurs–Sat 10am–1pm & 2–5pm, Wed 10am–1pm & 2–6pm; DM1), it's decked out with period furnishings, and also has a small art gallery. Just to the east is the **Roter Turm**, a handsome round tower from the former city walls; unfortunately, it's too blackened by pollution for its designation as the "Red Tower" to make much sense anymore.

The Stadtkirche and around

Behind the Markt rises another building in need of a clean, the Gothic **Stadtkirche St Michael** (May–Sept Mon–Fri 10am–5.30pm, Sat 10am–2pm). Outside the main features are the *Brautportal* (Bridal Doorway) on the south side, and the remarkable street passageway under the chancel, the best-known of the "Seven Wonders", the more so as there's not the slightest hint of its presence in the brightly painted hall interior, whose light and lofty feel is achieved by means of slender pillars which shoot directly up to the vault. The church's most celebrated treasure is the original bronze **tombstone of Luther** – with a full-length portrait cast from designs provided by Cranach – on the north wall; it was brought here for safekeeping because of the threat of desecration from the Imperial forces occupying Wittenberg, but was never returned.

From the Stadtkirche, Johanniskirche leads west along the northern side of Eichplatz; no. 12, the **Haus Zur Rosen**, is a Baroque mansion whose cellars contain a renowned student club. At the end of the street is the **Johannistor**, the only gateway remaining from the city's fortifications; just to the north is the most impressive of the surviving towers, the battlemented **Pulverturm**.

The Botanical Gardens

Across Goetheallee are the **Botanical Gardens** (Tues–Sun 9am–4/5pm; free), which were first created for growing medicinal herbs; they were then turned into a pleasure park before assuming their current function, which is primarily scientific research. The **Inspektorhaus** on the street side was designed by Goethe and was his favourite residence during his many sojourns in Jena, which he found to be a more amenable working environment than Weimar. Here he completed many of his literary projects; he also undertook a great deal of scientific research and produced the rather odd work he himself considered his masterpiece, *The Theory of Colours*. Part of the building is now designated the **Goethe Gedenkstätte** (Tues–Sun 9am–1pm; free) and contains memorabilia of his stays here.

On the eastern fringe of the gardens is the domed **Planetarium**, which, when it was built in 1925, was the first such structure in the world. Now as then, it utilises the technology of the Carl Zeiss works; there are several sessions each day, except Mondays, though the times differ. There are occasional showings in English for groups, so it would also be worth checking here or at the tourist office if any are scheduled during the course of your stay.

The Carl-Zeiss-Stiftung

The factory buildings of the Carl-Zeiss-Stiftung, mostly dating from the first two decades of this century, stand immediately to the west of Eichplatz; among them is a tower which is claimed as Germany's earliest skyscraper. **Carl Zeiss** was a mechanic who established himself in Jena in 1846, and attempted to develop microscopes of improved optical performance. Having failed to make the desired progress within twenty years, he realised his own very practical skills needed to be joined to a more theoretical approach; accordingly he formed what proved to be a spectacularly fruitful partnership with the physicist **Ernst Abbe**. Their company soon became the world leader in the field of optics, and has maintained this position ever since, though its post-1945 history was sullied by the existence of rival companies in the two Germanys, which have recently come together again.

The **Optisches Museum** (Tues–Fri 9am–5.30pm, Sat 9am–4pm; DM3) on Carl-Zeiss-Platz is in two parts. In the first, there's a recreation of the 1866 workshop of Zeiss and Abbe; the second contains a huge collection of historic spectacles, microscopes, telescopes and other instruments. Outside stands the imposing **memorial** to Abbe, a shrine-like construction by Henry van de Velde, inside which are four bronze reliefs of working-class life by Constantin Meunier.

Three more museums

A few minutes' walk to the south is Ernst-Haeckel-Strasse, where, at the corner with Berggasse is the **Ernst-Haeckel-Haus** (guided tours Mon–Fri at 8.30am, 10am, 11.30am, 2pm & 3.30pm, Sat at 8.30am, 10am, 11am & 2pm; DM2). Haeckel, the leading Continental protagonist of Darwin's theories of evolution, dominated intellectual life at Jena around the turn of the century. He was also a talented artist, and his watercolour landscapes are the highlight of the displays in the villa where he lived. Just to the south, at Am Paradiesbahnhof, is the **Phyletisches Museum** (Mon–Fri 9am–4pm, Sat & Sun 9am–2pm), which Haeckel founded in 1907. It's a natural history collection with a difference, concentrating on how each species developed.

For a time Haeckel lived in the house at Schillergässchen 2, which is now the **Schiller-Gedenkstätte** (Tues–Fri 10am–noon & 1-4pm, Sat 11am–4pm; DM1) in honour of a previous occupant, the poet and dramatist **Friedrich Schiller**, after whom the University is now named. As Professor of History, he lived in Jena for ten years, the longest he spent in any place in his life. The conditions in which he worked have been lovingly recreated; particularly evocative is the upstairs room in the garden pavilion, his favourite work place.

The hills

If you want more than a superficial impression of Jena, it's well worth taking time to explore the hills around the city, many of them crowned with country *Gaststätten* (see below). One good afternoon's outing would be to take bus #16 west to the end of Erfurter Strasse, then climb up via Cospedaer Grund to the village of **COSPEDA**, site of the Battle of Jena, in which Napoleon gained victory over the Prussians, an event documented in the **Gedenkstätte 1806** (Tues–Sun 9am–noon & 1–5pm; DM1).

Eating, drinking and nightlife

Undoubtedly one of the prime attractions of Jena is its wide variety of places to eat, drink and socialise; indeed, within the former GDR it offers a better choice than almost anywhere outside the three largest cities.

Restaurants

Forelle, Am Holzmarkt 14. Fish restaurant, whose main line, as its name suggests, is trout.

Fuchsturm, Auf dem Hausberg. Traditional *Gaststätte* in a tower on top of the Hausberg, a hill on the west side of the Saale. Closes 10pm during the week, midnight on Sat, 7pm on Sun.

Grüner Baum zur Nachtigall, Cospeda. Historic *Gaststätte* right next door to the Gedenkstätte 1806. Wed–Fri & Sun Sun 4–11pm, Sat 11am–midnight.

Marienlust, Carolinerstr. 4. Candle-lit wine bar offering good if somewhat pricey meals to the accompaniment of soft music. Evenings only.

Roter Hirsch, Holzmarkt 10. Serves cheap but decent food, with a fast lunchtime service.

Saaltor, Saalstr. 8. Thuringia's first ever Chinese restaurant; the food is reasonably authentic, and the set lunches are exceptional value.

Bars and cafés

Jenaer Kaffeehaus, Am Markt 1. The best of the traditional cafés; also has a first-floor bar.

Modern Art Club, Johannisstr. 11. Trendy cocktail bar-cum-disco. Mon–Sat 9pm–4am.

Rosenkeller, Johannisstr. 13. By far the most popular student club, set in cavernous cellars. Often features live music; even out of term, it has an animated atmosphere. Free admission with student ID, otherwise you'll have to pay DM2–4 to get in.

Weinhaus Tanne, Jenergasse 13. Historic pub whose pipe-smoking landlady is one of the city's best-known characters; also does basic meals. Mon–Thurs 4pm–midnight, Fri 11am–2pm.

Zur Noll, Oberlauengasse 19. Jazz and piano bar open daily until midnight or 1am; also does low-cost meals.

Zwei Linden, Naumburger Str. 82. Student and working men's pub, with very cheap food and drink. Mon–Fri 3–11pm.

Dornburg

The one unmissable excursion from Jena is to **DORNBURG**, 15km down the Saale. From the Bahnhof, it's a steep twenty-minute climb up to the three palaces lining the terrace which has been laid out on a precipitous 90-metre-high rock perched directly above the valley, of which there's a stunning view. Entry to the park is by the **Renaissanceschloss** (Tues–Sun 10am–noon & 1–4pm; combined ticket DM4), at the southern end, a grand country house with frilly gables and prominent stair turret. Built at the turn of the seventeenth century by a high official of the Duchy of Saxe-Weimar, this was one of Goethe's favourite retreats. The three rooms he used are furnished and decorated according to the tastes of Weimar Classicism, and contrast strongly with the splendours of the *Kaminzimmer*, the one chamber to have survived in something like its original form. The **Rokokoschloss** in the middle of the terrace was commissioned as a summer retreat for the Weimar dukes; it's decorated with stucco-work, porcelain and period furniture, though the show is stolen by the garden, which combines formal elements with a blaze of well-tended floral displays. Beyond it is the **Altes Schloss**, by origin an Imperial fortress of the Romanesque period, though most of what you see today dates from the mid-fifteenth century, when it belonged to the Electors of Saxony. At the moment, it's used as an old folks' home, so you have to be satisfied with seeing it from the outside.

Rudolstadt

Some 40km upstream from Jena is **RUDOLSTADT**, set in a picturesque stretch of wooded and hilly countryside, near the point where the Saale is joined by the Schwarza, which cuts a particularly beautiful valley to the southwest. For three and a half centuries it was the capital of the county, later principality, of Schwarzburg-Rudolstadt, then, for the decade before its abolition after World War I, of the united province of Schwarzburg, and it still preserves both the authentic appearance and the languid atmosphere of a rural county town.

Schloss Heidecksburg

Perched high on a hill above Rudolstadt is the vast bulk of **Schloss Heidecksburg**. The previous Renaissance Schloss was so badly damaged by fire in 1735 that Friedrich Anton, who also wanted to celebrate his earlier promotion from count to a fully-fledged prince of the Holy Roman Empire, decided to a commission an extravagant new building in the Dresden Rococo style. In lieu of the great Pöppelmann, who was too ill to accept, the plans were drawn up by the most talented Dresden architect of the next generation, Johann Christoph Knöffel, while the work was completed by another native of that city, Gottfried Heinrich Krohne.

The former chapel in the west wing has been stripped of all religious connotations and now houses a collection of porcelain, much of it of local manufacture. This is the departure point for the **guided tours** (Tues–Sun 9am–5pm; DM2.50) round the state apartments, which are ornate without ever seeming over-the-top. Highlights are the galleried main *Festsaal*, with its huge ceiling fresco of Mount Olympus, the gorgeous *Spiegelkabinett*, with its striking inlaid floor and mock oriental touches, and the highly original *Bänderzimmer*, whose medallion portraits give a foretaste of the forthcoming Neoclassical style. At the end of the tour, you're free to wander round the art gallery at leisure; the star piece is Friedrich's brooding *Morning Mist in the Mountains*. The north wing of the Schloss, which still preserves the brightly painted double Renaissance portal with statues of the Virtues, now houses the **Schlossmuseum** (9am–5pm, closed Fri; DM2.50 or DM4 for combined ticket). On the ground floor is a particularly outstanding arsenal, containing weapons from the fifteenth to the nineteenth centuries. The upstairs displays on local history are more prosaic, but include the *Schwarzenburger Willkomm*, a fine piece of late sixteenth-century goldsmithery.

The rest of the town

In the town itself, the main building is the **Stadtkirche St Andreas** at its eastern end, which in its own way evokes the local courtly tradition as vividly as the Schloss itself. By origin an unexceptional Gothic hall church, it was progressively beautified down the years to create the present sumptuous effect. From the Renaissance period are the fantastical portal with its fake door knockers and resplendent coat of arms, and the monumental marble and alabaster epitaph to the Schönefeld family on the end wall of the nave. A burst of creative activity after the Thirty Years' War brought a host of Baroque embellishments including the eccentric sculptures of angels suspended from the vault, plus the princes' loft and burial chamber, the pulpit and the organ.

Rudolstadt's only other attraction is the **Volkskundemuseum Thüringer Bauernhäuser** (Wed–Sun 9–11.30am & 1–4.30pm; DM2) in the Stadtpark to the rear of the Bahnhof. One of Germany's oldest open-air museums, this brings together two redundant farmhouses from the region, complete with their furnishings. The larger, standing alongside its original barn, dates back to the 1660s; the other, which is a few decades younger, houses a complete village apothecary.

Practicalities

Rudolstadt's **tourist office** (Mon 1.30–5pm, Tues & Fri 9am–12.30pm & 1.30–5pm, Wed 9am–12.30pm & 1.30–4pm, Thurs 9am–12.30pm & 1.30–6pm, Sat 10am–1pm; ☎23633) is just off the central Markt at Ernst-Thälmann-Str. 32a. There's the usual booking service for **private rooms**; the only current accommodation alternative is the **hotel**, *Zum Löwen*, Markt 5 (☎2059), which has singles for DM40, doubles from DM60. Choice in eating is also very restricted, the main choice being between the hotel and two other **restaurants** on the Markt, the *Ratskeller* and the *Adler*.

Saalfeld

The old mining town of **SAALFELD**, 10km south of Rudolstadt, marks the transition between the middle and upper parts of the Saale valley; beyond lie the Schiefergebirge (Slate Mountains), now a popular recreational area of wooded hills and artificial lakes with watersports facilities. Saalfeld itself seems all set to reclaim its former status as a tourist resort – apart from its value as an excursion base, it possesses one of Germany's most strangely beautiful natural wonders and has a historic centre which will look very striking once it has been tidied up.

The town centre

The Hauptbahnhof lies on the east bank of the Saale; Bahnhofstrasse leads over the two arms of the river to the **Saaltor**, one of three surviving medieval gateways. From here, there's a choice of routes. The right-hand fork, Puschkinstrasse, follows the former course of the fortifications past two more gates, beyond which lies the largest remaining stretch of the walls. Saalstrasse, to the left, leads straight to the Markt, but it's worth making a small detour to the south up Am Hügel to see the Renaissance **Schlösschen Kitzerstein** (now the music school), with its stylised, Dutch-looking gable, and the ruins of the **Hoher Schwarm**, a feudal castle of the type characteristic of the Saale, though the effect is somewhat spoilt by the modern hotel built alongside.

At the southeastern corner of the Markt, returned once more to its original function, is the pristine white **Rathaus**. It's a quintessential building of the German Renaissance with its lingering Gothic feel, its protruding stairwell, its prominent gables and its two strongly contrasted oriel windows. Across is the partially Romanesque **Markapotheke**, which dates back to the town's twelfth-century origins, though it's been repeatedly altered down the centuries.

Towering above the northern side of the Markt, and fronting Blankenburger Strasse, the pedestrianised main shopping street, is the Gothic **Johanneskirche**. Its exterior is richly decorated with late fourteenth-century sculptures of the Parler school; the west portal tympanum of *The Last Judgment* is particularly good. The most startling feature of the hall interior is the bright red colouring of the vault – a symbolical reference to the blood of Christ. It reaches its climax in the elaborate network design in the chancel, which is painted with a recently uncovered vision of the path to Heaven.

Up Brudergasse is the former Franciscan monastery, now housing the **Thüringer Heimatmuseum** (Tues–Fri 8am–noon & 1–4pm, Sat & Sun 9.30am–noon & 1–5pm; DM1), a good quality regional collection featuring displays on mining, folklore and arts and crafts, the highlight being examples of the local Gothic school of woodcarvers.

Between 1680 and 1735, Saalfeld was capital of the duchy of Saxe-Saalfeld, which was then assumed into Saxe-Coburg. The inevitable legacy of this period is a large Baroque **Schloss**, situated a few minutes' walk north of the confines of the Altstadt along Schloss Strasse, then right into Schlossberg. It's now used by the municipality as offices, but you can wander in and have a look round, particularly at the showpiece staircase; ask to see the ornate chapel, which is regularly used for concerts in summer.

The Feengrotten

The **Feengrotten** (Fairy Grottoes; guided tours Feb–early Nov daily 9am–5pm; DM4)), Saalfeld's chief attraction, lie about twenty minutes' walk southwest of the town centre; from the Markt follow Obere Strasse straight ahead, then turn right into Sonnenberger Strasse – the way is then well signposted. Geologically formed 400 million years ago, the present astonishing appearance of this site is the result of a fluke caused by the interaction of natural and human forces. From the mid-sixteenth century, there was a mine here, which was exploited for its alum slate and vitriol; this functioned until the 1840s, when it was run down and closed as stocks moved towards exhaustion and demand from the chemical industry slumped. In 1910, waters rich in mineral resources were found pouring out of the abandoned mine; an investigation of its interior revealed that an oxidisation process had turned the galleries into something resembing a natural drip-water cave, with stalactites and stalagmites formed from iron phosphate – and the walls cloaked in an astonishing kaleidoscope of colours. Artificial lighting, which can be varied to give widely differing pictures, further enhances the effect, seen at its best in the *Märchendom* (Fairy-tale cathedral), also known as the *Gralburg* (Holy Grail Castle) because of its uncanny resemblance to a Wagnerian theatre set.

Practicalities

Saalfeld's **tourist office** (Mon & Sat 9am–1pm, Tues–Fri 9am–1pm & 2–5pm; ☎3950) is at Blankenburger Str. 4. There are plenty of **private rooms** available for as little as DM10–15 per person, but the youth hostel has recently closed and may not reopen. The cheapest **hotel** is the *Quellenhaus* (☎2351), right at the Feengrotten, which charges DM16–18 according to length of stay, but these prices will rise once a refurbishment has been carried out. Of the old state-run establishments, *Zum Anker*, Markt 26 (☎2963), has rooms from DM30, while *Tanne*, Saalstr. 37 (☎2670), charges DM19, though both it and another hotel on the same street were closed at the time of writing. If **camping**, you'll find three sites on the Saaletalsperre Hohenwarte 10km south. **Restaurants** include *Zum Roten Hirsch*, Markt 6, and *Klosterstübel*, Barfüssergasse 1; best place for ice-cream or *Kaffee und Kuchen* is the *Marktcafé* on the Markt.

Gera

Thuringia's second largest city is **GERA**, which lies 45km east of Jena in the hilly countryside of the Weisse Elster valley. For nearly four centuries it was the capital of one of Germany's smallest states, the junior of the two Reuss principalities. However, it's totally different from the province's other courtly residences, being predominantly an industrial town, with a long tradition in the production of textiles and musical instruments, to which mechanical and metallurgical manufacturing were added last century. Despite this background, and heavy wartime damage, it's a surprisingly agreeable place, generally recognised as being the one and only town in the GDR where postwar planning was carried out with sensitivity and good taste. The result is a lively city which offers a balanced mixture of old and new; though it lacks much in the way of major sights, it well warrants a day's exploration.

The Altstadt

Gera's compact historical centre lies on a gentle incline about fifteen minutes' walk southeast of the Hauptbahnhof. At its heart is the **Markt**, whose good looks compensate for its modest dimensions. In the centre burbles the **Simsonbrunnen**, showing the Old Testament hero Samson wrestling with the lion; this is a modern replica of the water-worn late seventeenth-century original. The whitewashed Renaissance **Rathaus**, the town's finest building, stands proudly to the northeastern corner. Designed by

Nicol Gromann, the Saxon court architect, it boasts a dignified off-centre octagonal tower and a riotously decorative portal with busts, grotesque figures, inscriptions and brightly painted coats of arms. A similar style can be seen on the oriel of the **Stadt-Apotheke** at the opposite end of the square; apart from heraldic motifs, its carvings show the Apostles and the Four Seasons.

Going down Kleine Kirchstrasse you come to a vast open square, recently renamed Zentraler Platz, which is the best place to observe the cunning way the tramway system, the second oldest in Germany, was adapted in line with the postwar planning to become a modern light railway on the western German model. The handsome red Baroque palace standing in splendid isolation was once the town orphanage; nowadays it houses the local history displays of the **Stadtmuseum** (Sat–Thurs 10am–5pm; DM1).

Uphill from the Markt, Grosse Kirchstrasse – which is lined with a number of fine mansions, now mostly used as shops – leads to the **Salvatorkirche**, a large Baroque church with Jugendstil furnishings perched at the top of a monumental stairway. On its northern side stands the **Schreiberhaus** (Tues–Sun 10am–5pm; DM1), the late seventeenth-century mansion of a rich merchant; it now contains a dull museum of the natural history and geology of the region centred on Gera, though the interior itself is at least as good a reason for a visit. At the back of the house is the entrance to the town's most unusual attraction, the **Geraer Höhle** (guided tours Mon–Thurs at 11am & 3pm, Sat at 2pm & 3pm, Sun at 10am, 11am, 2pm & 3pm; DM1), a network of caverns and tunnels used in the seventeenth and eighteenth centuries as workshops, and as a place where home-brewed beer could mature in cool conditions.

The western quarters

To the rear of the Hauptbahnhof is the **Bühnen der Stadt**, the Jugendstil municipal theatre. It overlooks the Küchengarten, a pleasant park at whose far end stands the Rococo **Orangerie** (Tues, Wed & Fri–Sun 10am–6pm, Thurs noon–8pm; DM1). A curiosity of this is that the central pavilion was an afterthought to the original twin structures, each consisting of an angular and a semicircular section. Inside is a collection of paintings and sculptures from the Middle Ages to the present day. **Otto Dix**, one of the most highly regarded German artists of the present century, was born on Mohrenplatz, just to the west over the Weisse Elster. By the time you read this, the house should be open and contain a significant collection of his works. Apart from the Markt, this is the finest square in Gera, dominated by the Romanesque-Gothic **Marienkirche**.

Schlossberg Strasse leads up from here to **Schloss Osterstein**, where a café-restaurant has been set up in the ruins of the Romanesque Burg; giving a good view over the town and the valley. Until 1945, the large Baroque palace of the Reuss princes also stood here, but it was so badly damaged by bombs that the Communist authorities had no qualms about razing it completely – a sad loss which has obliterated from the face of the town a key part of its historical heritage and cast a blot on its otherwise excellent conservation record.

Practicalities

Gera has two **tourist offices** – the main one is just off Zentraler Platz at Breitscheidstr. 1 (Mon–Fri 10am–5pm, Sat 9am–noon; ☎26432), and a branch in the front hall of the Hauptbahnhof (Mon–Fri noon–7pm) also serves as a Mitfahrzentrale agency. **Private rooms** on offer start at DM20, but all the **hotels** are currently charging fancy rates, with the exception of the huge *Pension Wasserrose*, Liselotte-Herrmann-Str. 82 (☎32085), which has singles from DM30, doubles from DM50. For **eating** and **drinking**, try the *Ratskeller* in the Rathaus, the Bulgarian restaurant *Sliven*, Kornmarkt 4, or the *Haus der Kultur* at the corner of Schloss Strasse and Sorge. The main **theatre** venue is the aforementioned *Bühnen der Stadt*; there's also a *Puppentheater* on Gustav-Henning-Platz, and a satirical cabaret, *Fettnäppchen*, in the cellars of the Rathaus.

Greiz

A scenic railway line follows the course of the Weisse Elster 32km south to **GREIZ**, the former capital of the senior line of the Reuss princes. In contrast to Gera, it never developed into a city, and remains today an archetypal Thuringian town lost in a more peaceful age. Dominating the town is the **Oberes Schloss**, medieval by origin but many times remodelled; it now houses the local archives and is not open to the public. However, you can wander in its pretty English-style park, and visit the **Sommerpalais** (Tues–Fri 10am–4pm, Sat & Sun 10am–1pm; DM1), an early Neoclassical edifice with displays on printing and the graphic arts drawn from the old court library. The biggest surprise is provided by a large collection of eighteenth-century English caricatures which is claimed as the best on the continent. In the town centre is the **Unteres Schloss** (9am–12.30pm & 2–5pm, closed Sat; DM1), a later, more sober Neoclassical palace, now serving as the local history museum.

Altenburg

ALTENBURG, 40km northeast of Gera, dubs itself *Skatstadt* in honour of the fact that *skat*, Germany's most popular card game, has both its main production centre and governing headquarters here. As this is very much a national enthusiasm, the town's name is relatively little-known abroad, though it's one of the most characteristic and worthwhile of Thuringia's old courtly towns. Lying in the easternmost part of the *Land*, close to the borders with both Saxony and Saxony-Anhalt, Altenburg makes an excellent base for forays into three provinces; alternatively, it can be used as a stopover if travelling on the main rail route south from Leipzig.

The Lindenau-Museum

From the Hauptbahnhof at the northern end of town, the rusticated neo-Renaissance *palazzo* containing the **Lindenau-Museum** (Tues–Sun 10am–6pm; DM2) can be seen facing you from the Schlosspark at the far end of Wettiner Strasse. Its cosmopolitan displays, originating in the private collections of Bernhard von Lindenau, a nineteenth-century statesman and Italophile, are a world away from those normally found in small German towns. On the ground floor, an important group of Greek and Roman vases are kept in one wing, changing selections of modern art in the other. Upstairs, the old masters department includes choice examples of Gothic and Renaissance paintings from Florence and Siena. Small panels from dispersed polyptychs predominate – look out for a rare pair by **Masaccio** of *The Agony in the Garden* and *St Jerome in the Desert*, and for **Fra Angelico**'s exquisite *Three Dominican Monks* and *St Francis' Trial by Fire*.

The Schloss

The vast hill-top **Schloss** complex, which features just about every European architectural style, has to be entered from the southern end of its park. Despite its long spell as a ducal residence, it still preserves part of its medieval defences, among which the round tower known as the **Flasche**, built into the northern walls, dates back as far as the eleventh century. Nearby is a freestanding tower of uncertain vintage, the **Hausmannsturm** (Tues–Sun 10am–4pm; DM1), which can be ascended for a fine view over the Schloss and the town. Across the courtyard, in the centre of which is a Mannerist fountain to Neptune, lies the main palace block, now designated the **Schloss- und Spielkarten Museum** (Tues–Sun 9am–5pm; DM2). Predictably, the main emphasis is on the history of playing cards throughout the last five centuries, and in particular of *skat*; other highlights are a display of medieval weapons, and Bernhard von Lindenau's collections of oriental and Meissen porcelain.

From the museum, **guided tours** (Tues–Sun 10am–4pm; DM1.50) are run round the state apartments of the Schloss, which are slowly being restored. They're a surprising mixture: the *Goldsaal* is elegantly Baroque, while the main *Festsaal* is a nineteenth-century historicist extravaganza in red, white and gold, with frothy ceiling frescos by the Munich Romantic artist Karl Mossdorf depicting stories from Apuleius' *The Golden Ass*. It's occasionally used for concerts, as is the more intimate *Bachsaal*, an early twentieth-century pastiche of its fire-destroyed Renaissance predecessor.

Included in the tour is a visit to the sumptuous **Schlosskirche**. This is otherwise only open for services and for the summer weekend recitals on the eighteenth-century **organ**; its silvery tone won the plaudits of J.S. Bach, while its ornate case also gives it visual appeal. The church itself is predominantly late Gothic, with a superb star vault. However, the general appearance owes much to a mid-seventeenth-century interior transformation, which added the ducal loft at the west end, the galleries with their statues of saints and Old Testament figures, and the theatrical high altar.

The rest of the town

The townscape south of the Schloss is dominated by the **Rote Spitze** (Red Points), the two brick towers of a twelfth-century Augustinian collegiate church. In the recent past, a museum of medieval sculpture has been housed here, but this was closed at the time of writing. To the west, across the busy Wallstrasse, lies the old merchant quarter, centred on two squares. Much the larger of these, the Weibermarkt, has become the modern commercial heart of town; it's overlooked by the handsome Renaissance **Rathaus**, with its dignified portal and showpiece corner oriel. Further north is the Alter Markt, with the Baroque **Seckendorff'sche Palais** and a turn-of-the-century fountain that honours the game of *skat*. Just off the square is the main parish church, the **Bartholmäikirche**, whose kernel is Gothic, but whose most notable features are the tapering octagonal Renaissance tower and the graceful little Romanesque crypt.

Practicalities

The **tourist office** (Mon, Thurs & Fri 9am–4pm, Tues 9am–5pm, Wed 9am–6pm; ☎311145) is at Weibermarkt 17. You can ask here for a **private room**, though it would be cheaper to go directly to Frau Melitta Engert, Stauffenbergstr. 29 (☎82293, or ask for her at the Schloss), who also has a summer house for rent. There are also a couple of now rather pricey **hotels** – *Zum Wenzel*, Wettiner Str. 21 (☎311171) and, *Altenburg-Nord*, Eli-Wiesel-Str. 51 (☎81156 or 81190). The town's **restaurant** situation was in total chaos in 1991: the *Ratskeller* in the Rathaus is the only safe bet. Altenburg does, on the other hand, manage to maintain an ambitious **cultural** programme centred on the *Landestheater* on Theaterplatz below the Schloss.

travel details

Trains

From Erfurt to Weimar (frequent; 15min); Arnstadt (frequent; 25min); Gotha (frequent; 30min); Eisenach (frequent; 1hr); Mühlhausen (11 daily; 1hr); Nordhausen/Sondershausen (10 daily; 1hr 30min/2hr); Jena (frequent; 45min), Gera (11 daily; 2hr).

From Gotha to Friedrichroda (frequent; 35min); Mühlhausen (frequent; 1hr).

From Jena to Weimar (frequent; 30min); Rudolstadt/Saalfeld (frequent; 1hr/1hr 20min); Gera (frequent; 1hr).

From Gera to Saalfeld (frequent; 1hr 15min/2hr); Greiz (9 daily; 1 hr).

CHAPTER TWELVE

SAXONY

Saxony (*Sachsen*) is the most enigmatic of Germany's Länder. Its identity appears very secure and well defined, yet it has only the most nebulous connection with the tribes and territories after which it's named. Seemingly so archetypally German, it occupies land which originally belonged to the Slavs, while much of its scenery has more in common with neighbouring Czechoslovakia than anywhere in Germany and not a few of the towns bear the distinctive Central European hallmark of a diversity of cultural influences. Other than Berlin, all three of the ex-GDR's largest cities are here, yet the Land, judged by the 1990 election results, is politically by far the most right-wing in all of Germany. Whereas at least two of the major cities should slot into the new economic framework without too much disruption, other parts of Saxony seem to belong to a bygone age, trying to maintain the same industries that have supported them for centuries. The list of contradictions seems endless.

Like Thuringia, Saxony's history is closely tied to that of the **Wettin** family, whose original early medieval power base was as **Margraves of Meissen**, charged with securing the Holy Roman Empire's eastern frontier and pushing it deeper into Slav territory to the east and south. The name of "Saxony" only came to be associated with the territory when it became the heartland of the **Albertine** line of the dynasty, which gained the prized Electorate in the Holy Roman Empire in 1547 and thereafter built up a strong, centralised state, confining the rival Ernestines to the ever-fragmenting principalities of Thuringia. They also gained the crown of Poland on three separate occasions, but failed to make it a hereditary possession. Compensation came in 1806, when Napoleon proclaimed Saxony a **kingdom** in its own right; a heavy price had to be paid for this nine years later, when Prussia made huge territorial annexations, although the royal status was retained until 1918.

Dresden, the capital since the foundation of the Albertine line in 1485, is nowadays chiefly associated with the terrible Anglo-American bomb raid of 1945 which obliterated one of Europe's greatest artistic and cultural centres. Its remarkable comeback has gathered pace since the *Wende*, the ultimate aim being to return it to its former appearance. The marginally larger city of **Leipzig** is currently basking in the glory of having provided the leadership of the revolution which overthrew totalitarian rule. **Chemnitz**, wallowing in industrial filth, is a place only the most dedicated of travellers will include on their itinerary, but is of special interest for the remarkable insights it offers into the preoccupations of the GDR period. The one other place large enough to be regarded as a city is **Zwickau**, whose attraction of a well-preserved centre is overshadowed by a reputation as home of the appalling but now world-famous *Trabi* car.

Of the smaller towns, the undoubted star is **Meissen**, the original political heart of the region, and the place where the first European porcelain was manufactured. **Freiberg** and **Annaberg-Buchholz** are the most notable of the mining towns which reached the height of their prosperity in the sixteenth century, a period commemorated in the dazzlingly rich interiors of their churches. **Bautzen** is the main cultural centre of the Sorbs, the Slav peoples who have remained in the area throughout a millennium of German rule, while **Görlitz** is another place with a richly diverse historical tradition. **Torgau** is best-known to English-speaking people for its wartime connections, though it's the litte town of **Colditz** which brings back the most vivid memories of that era. **Saxon Switzerland**, the rocky and wooded countryside round the Elbe

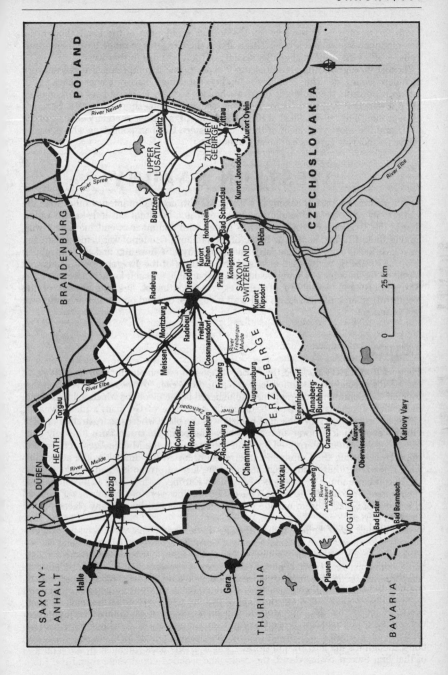

south of Dresden, is deservedly the best-known scenic part of the Land, though the raw mountain landscapes around **Zittau** and in the **Erzgebirge** range have their attractions, as does the somewhat gentler scenery of the **Vogtland** further west.

Travel throughout the area presents few problems; a comprehensive rail network includes four of the country's eight surviving narrow-gauge lines. For **accommodation**, the multitude of private houses recently opened up for tourism often offer a valuable lifeline as several towns are noticeably short of hotels. Saxony's high-profile Minister-President is **Kurt Biedenkopf**, a former secretary-general of the CDU and the most prominent of the many western German politicians who chose to revive floundering careers by moving to the east.

WESTERN SAXONY

The northwestern part of Saxony is a flat plain, with nothing of interest other than the vibrant city of **Leipzig**. Bounding it on the east is a beautiful but little-known valley, that of the **Zwickauer Mulde**, which is dotted with a number of enticing little towns, among them **Colditz**, sometime home of the famous prisoner-of-war camp. Upstream, **Zwickau** itself, along with the large industrial city of **Chemnitz** and the old mining town of **Freiberg** to the east, stands in the foothills of the **Erzgebirge**, a windswept highland region whose mineral wealth was responsible for such former boom towns as **Schneeberg** and **Annaberg**. To the extreme southwest lies the plateau of the **Vogtland**, an area of spa resorts and craft industries centred on the lace-making town of **Plauen**.

Leipzig

Pictures from **LEIPZIG** filled the world's television screens in the autumn of 1989, as the GDR's second city assumed leadership of the *Wende*, the peaceful revolution that toppled the Communist dictatorship and ushered in the elections which led to national unification a year later. Having traditionally been one of Germany's most dynamic cities, it was perhaps inevitable that Leipzig was the place where the frustration of GDR citizens about their postwar lot reached breaking point. Its **trade fairs** (the only ones in Europe with an uninterrupted tradition dating back to the Middle Ages) remained of importance during the Communist interregnum: for all the difficulties the authorities had in squaring these with their ideology, the lure of promoting and developing the GDR as the economic success story of Eastern Europe, with Leipzig as its commercial heart, proved too difficult to resist. This did mean, however, that the city never suffered the sense of isolation from outside influences experienced by so many places behind the Iron Curtain.

In Goethe's *Faust*, Leipzig is described as "Little Paris". That was always an exaggeration – it has never been considered one of Germany's more visually appealing cities – and seems even less so now. Not only did Leipzig suffer horrendous wartime damage; the Communist years have bequeathed a legacy of eyesores and pollution, added to an inappropriate economic infrastructure which will now be even more dependent on trade fair business for a secure future. Nonetheless, the city remains an important cultural centre, particularly in the field of **music**, where the great tradition of Bach, Mendelssohn, Schumann and Wagner is jealously maintained. Indeed, the conductors of the city's two orchestras, Kurt Masur and Horst Neumann, were such respected figures that they were able to play mediating roles at a time when the revolution looked in danger of spilling into a bloodbath, ensuring that it remained both peaceful and successful.

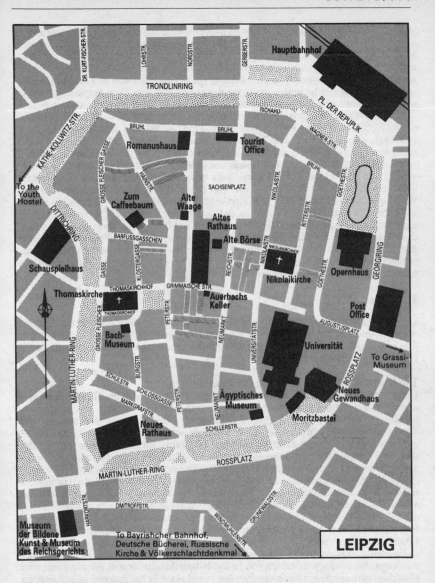

LEIPZIG

Arrival and practicalities

The vast **Hauptbahnhof** is at the northeastern end of the Ring (ring road), which encircles the Altstadt; a few local services, particularly from Zwickau, use the **Bayrischer Bahnhof**, which is a few minutes' walk south of the Ring. By the Hauptbahnhof's western upstairs exit is a **Zimmerver-Mittlung** (Mon–Fri 9am–9pm, Sat 9.30am–2pm; ☎275319). The same room-finding service is also available in the **tourist office** a short walk to the south on Sachsenplatz (Mon–Fri 9am–6pm, Sat 9.30am–2pm; ☎79590). This also has a branch at the **airport** (daily 8am–10pm; ☎313103), the most important in the former GDR, and linked to the Hauptbahnhof by buses which run approximately every 30 minutes. One point to note about all these agencies is that the trade fair business means that prices are high – upwards of DM40 for a single, DM60 a double, of which nearly half is commission. If you're planning on an extended stay and aren't offered a special rate, it would be best to book for a night or two only, then negotiate privately with the landlord, or find a room yourself by using one of the national directories.

Alternative accommodation options include the **youth hostels** at Käthe-Kollwitz-Str. 62 (☎470530), west of the centre (take trams #1, #2 or #8), and at Gustav-Esche-Str. 4 (☎57189), way to the northwest (reached by trams #10 or #28). Near the latter is the **campsite** (☎52648), which also has bungalows to rent – by far the cheapest option if you're travelling in a group. Most **hotels** are prohibitively priced and heavily oversubscribed, though the next few years are likely to see the opening of a host of new establishments at all price levels. In the medium range, the best bets are *Bayrischer Hof*, Wintergartenstr. 13 (☎209251), and *Parkhotel*, Richard-Wagner-Str. 7 (☎7821), whose rates are each around DM65 for singles, DM100 for doubles. Two of the current cheaper options, both charging around DM30 per person and lying just a short walk west from the Hauptbahnhof, are *Haus-Ingeborg*, Nordstr. 58 (☎294816), and *Pension am Zoo*, Dr-Kurt-Fischer-Str. 23 (☎291838); within the former building is one of the many houses registered with the agency (a card will notify if there's a vacancy). **Mitfahrzentrale** have an office at Rudolf-Breitscheid-Str. 39 (☎200671).

The city

Leipzig is easy to get to grips with: the historic buildings lie mostly within the Altstadt, whose boundaries are defined by the Ring, with the main museums lying just outside. The only sights beyond immediate walking distance are conveniently grouped near to each other southwest of the centre.

The Hauptbahnhof, the Ring and the Nikolaikirche

Despite its current decrepit condition, complete with leaky roof, the **Hauptbahnhof** is a masterpiece of early twentieth-century railway architecture that deserves to be considered one of the main sights of Leipzig. It's claimed as the largest passenger station in the world and occupies a site formerly occupied by four small terminals. A curiosity is that it has two entrance halls and two levels, this being a legacy of the fact that, until centralisation was introduced under the Third Reich, the Prussian and Saxon authorities each ran their own half of the station as a separate concern.

The **Ring**, now busy with a far heavier volume of traffic than it had in GDR days, is familiar from news footage as the place where the famous Monday demonstrations against totalitarian abuses of power took place. At about 3pm, the city centre began to clear; by 5pm people had congregated in large numbers around the Ring; a couple of hours later the road was a seething mass of bodies marching in defiance against their Communist government.

Following Nikolaistrasse (the street immediately facing the Hauptbahnhof's entrance) due southwards brings you to the **Nikolaikirche**, one of the two main civic churches, and one which has gained an honoured place in the national consciousness. Not only was it the local key rallying-point during the *Wende*, but the Monday meetings and prayers which had been held there since 1982 entitle it to be considered as the true fountainhead of the revolution. Although a sombre medieval structure from outside, the church's interior is a real eye-grabber, thanks to an audacious late eighteenth-century transformation which flirts between Rococo and Neoclassical. The double galleried nave is particularly striking: its coffered vault is supported by fluted Corinthian columns with capitals sprouting out in the shape of palm trees.

The Altes Rathaus

A couple of blocks to the west of the Nikolaikirche is the open space of the Markt, whose eastern side is entirely occupied by the city's finest building, the **Altes Rathaus** (Tues–Fri 10am–6pm, Sat & Sun 10am–4pm; DM1). Designed by **Hieronymous Lotter**, it's in the grandest German Renaissance style, with elaborate gables, an assymmetrical clock tower – and the longest inscription to be found on any building in the world. The ground floor retains its traditional function as a covered walkway with shops; the upper storeys, long abandoned as the town hall, now house the local history museum. However, the main reason for going in is to see the 53-metre-long **Festsaal** on the first floor, with its ornate chimneypieces and haughty full-length portraits of the local mayors and Saxon Electors. Upstairs, there's a room of memorabilia of **Felix Mendelssohn-Bartholdy**, who spent the last twelve years of his life in the city. In addition to his compositional activities, he directed the *Gewandhausorchester*, founded the Conservatory, and was responsible for reviving the long forgotten music of his great predecessor J.S. Bach.

The historic trade fair buildings

On the north side of the square is another handsome public building by Lotter, the old weigh house or **Alte Waage**; only its sundial-crowned facade was restored following its destruction in the war. A survivor of the Baroque period is **Barthels Hof**, just off the west side of the square. This is the only extant example of the courtyards where trading used to take place; a distinctive feature is that it also opens out on to Kleine Fischergasse behind, in order that carriages bearing goods for sale did not have to turn. As the trade fair grew in the early years of this century, many historic buildings nearby were demolished to make way for the functional modern structures which now predominate; the Altes Rathaus only escaped this fate through the casting vote of the mayor. Thus, although the fair grounds have now been moved to the suburbs, the heart of the city still bears evidence of the way it sold itself to commerce.

Auerbachs Keller and Zum Kaffeebaum

Tucked underneath the Mädler-Passage, one of the covered shopping malls off Grimmaische Strasse at the southeastern end of the Markt, is **Auerbachs Keller**, setting for the famous scene in Goethe's *Faust* when Mephistopheles tricked the local boozers with optical illusions before vanishing into the air on a barrel. This, along with other scenes from the play, is depicted in the murals now adorning the cellar.

Following Barfussgässchen off the western side of the Markt brings you to Kleine Fleischergasse and Leipzig's other celebrated eatery, the cheerful Baroque **Zum Kaffeebaum**. Leipzig was one of the main centres of the craze for coffee which followed the Turkish invasion of Central Europe in the late seventeenth century, a theme satirised by Bach in the *Coffee Cantata*. In this café, the only one from the period to survive, look out for the carving above the doorway, which shows a Turk reclining under a coffee tree, proffering a cup of the beverage to a small cherub.

The Thomaskirche and around

Klostergasse leads southwards from here to the **Thomaskirche**, the senior of the two big civic churches, and the place where **Johann Sebastian Bach** (see also Eisenach, *Chapter Eleven*) served as *Kantor* for the last 27 years of his life, composing a vast body of choral works for use in its services. Originally part of an Augustinian monastery, the church is predominantly Gothic but has been repeatedly altered down the centuries. However, the most remarkable feature of the church is its musical tradition: its **choir**, the *Thomanerchor*, which Bach once directed, can usually be heard on Fridays at 6pm and Saturdays at 1.30pm, and at the Sunday service at 9.30am.

Outside the church is a **monument to Bach**, commissioned and paid for by Mendelssohn. Across from it, at Thomaskirchhof 16, is the **Bosehaus**, which contains a concert hall, a satirical cabaret and the **Bachmuseum** (Tues–Sun 9am–6pm; DM1), which has an extensive show of mementos of the great composer plus a collection of musical instruments of his time.

Augustusplatz and the University quarter

East of the Markt is a vast square, recently returned to its old name of Augustusplatz, which serves as the main focus of both academic and music life in the city. On its northern side is the **Opernhaus**, whose sombre pseudo-Neoclassical form recalls the architecture of the Third Reich, though it was actually built under Communism. Very different is the **Neue Gewandhaus** opposite, an avant-garde building inaugurated in 1981 as the new home of the famous *Gewandhausorchester*, the oldest and largest orchestra in the world – and still one of the best, the tradition of Felix Mendelssohn, Arthur Mikisch, Wilhelm Fürtwängler and Bruno Walter having been maintained over the last two decades by Kurt Masur.

Rising high up from the centre of the square is the 34-storey **Universitätshochhaus**, begun in 1968 as a prestige project of the then dictator of the GDR, Walter Ulbricht, a native of Leipzig. In order to build this new home for the University, which was founded back in 1409, a number of historic buildings were demolished, including the Universitätskirche. Only a Schinkel-designed gateway on the west side remains, looking hopelessly forlorn against the skyscraper, which is shaped to resemble an open book. By far the best thing about the latter is the view from the café at the top, which can only be reached by lift, at a cost of DM1.50. The **Moritzbastei** to the rear, another Lotter creation, is the only surviving part of the fortifications, and has found a new lease of life as the focal point of the student social scene.

To the west, at Schillerstr. 6, is the **Ägyptisches Museum** (Tues–Fri 2–6pm, Sun 10am–1pm; DM1), a surprisingly good collection of Egyptian antiquities from nineteenth-century excavations by University archaeologists. At the end of Schillerstrasse is Burgplatz, on which stands the **Neues Rathaus**, a turn-of-the-century monstrosity, which uses elements of just about every European architectural style, even incorporating a "Bridge of Sighs" to link the main building to its extension.

The Reichsgerichts and the Museum für bildene Kunst

South across the Ring is Georgi-Dimitroff-Platz and the supreme court of prewar Germany, the **Reichsgerichts**, a bulky neo-Renaissance palace. The upper floor of this, centred on the opulent main courtroom, contains a **museum** (Tues–Fri & Sun 10am–4pm, DM2) devoted to the famous trial on the Reichstag fire – the event which served as a pretext for the Nazis' clampdown on the activities of their political opponents. During the trial, one of those accused of starting the fire, Georgi Dimitroff, the Bulgarian head of the Communist International, completely outwitted Hermann Göring, the chief prosecutor. This was celebrated with relish in GDR days, but, in the current political climate, the future of the museum is uncertain.

No such doubts concern the **Museum für bildene Kunst** (Museum of Fine Arts; Tues & Thurs 10am–6pm, Wed 2–8pm, Fri 10am–1pm, Sat & Sun 10am–5pm; DM1.50) downstairs, an eclectic collection of paintings from the Middle Ages to the present century. This kicks off with some fine early German works, the most notable being a *Man of Sorrows* by Hamburg's **Master Francke** and an erotic allegory, *The Magic of Love*, by an unknown Lower Rhenish painter. There are also a few outstanding Netherlandish panels of the same period, among which *The Visitation* by **Rogier van der Weyden** and *The Institution of the Rosary*, attributed to the very rare **Geertgen tot Sint Jans**, stand out. German painting of the Renaissance is dominated by several examples of **Cranach**, among which *Nymph at the Well* is outstanding, and **Baldung**, whose *Seven Ages of Woman* is one of his most inspired compositions. From a strong display of Romantic painting, *The Steps of Life* by **Friedrich** and the celebrated *Isle of the Dead* by **Böcklin** stand out. Finally, there are a large number of works by the versatile Leipzig artist **Max Klinger**, who was equally proficient at painting, engraving and sculpture, and who is increasingly coming to be seen as a figure of some stature.

The Grassi-Museum

From Augustusplatz, crossing the Ring and following Grimmaisch Steinweg eastwards brings you to Johannisplatz and the **Grassi-Museum**, a vast complex of separate displays which was once one of the most important municipally owned museum complexes in Europe, but which still has a long way to go to recover from extensive war damage. In the meantime, two reasonably complete and one fragmentary section can be visited. The **Musikinstrumentenmuseum** (Tues–Thurs 2–5pm, Fri & Sun 10am–1pm, Sat 10am–3pm; DM1), entered from Täubschenweg to the north, houses the University's collection of historical musical instruments; the keyboards are particularly notable, and sometimes used for recitals. On the left side of the interior courtyard is the **Museum für Völkerkunde** (Tues–Fri 9.30am–5.30pm, Sat 10am–4pm, Sun 9am–1pm; DM1), whose ethnology displays range across Russia and the other states of the former Soviet Union, China, India, Australia and the South Seas. Across from it the **Museum für Kunsthandwerk** (Tues–Thurs 9.30am–6pm, Fri 9.30am–1pm, Sat & Sun 10am–5pm; DM1) hosts temporary exhibitions but has on view only a tiny fraction of what is said to be one of Europe's finest collections of decorative art.

South of the centre

Railway buffs should make the trek south of the Altstadt to see the **Bayrischer Bahnhof**, the oldest still-functioning train station in Europe. The grand Neoclassical structure erected in the 1840s was virtually flattened during the last war, and only the facade has been restored. Just a handful of services still run from here, suggesting it's kept open principally for the sake of preserving its record.

A few other worthwhile sights lie south of here on the route of tram #21; they can also be reached by trams #15 and #20 from elsewhere. On Deutscher Platz is the **Deutsche Bücherei**, the largest German-language library in the world. Part of it is given over to the **Deutsches Buch- und Schriftmuseum** (Mon–Sat 9am–4pm; free), which traces the history of books throughout the past 5000 years. Just to the east is the **Russische Kirche**, a striking pastiche of the churches of Novgorod, decorated inside with original eighteenth-century icons. It was built in 1913 to commemorate the 22,000 Russian soldiers who died in the **Battle of the Nations** a hundred years previously.

The actual site of this conflict, in which the Russians combined with the Prussians, Austrians and Swedes to defeat Napoleon, lies just to the south, on the opposite side of the trade fair site. The French dictator was thereafter banished to exile in Elba; another consequence was the confirmation of the elimination of Poland from the map of Europe, a situation which prevailed for the next century. A colossal and tasteless monument, known as the **Völkerschlachtdenkmal** (daily 9am–4pm; DM2), was erected to commemorate the centenary of the victory; it can be ascended for an extensive if unexciting view over the city and the flat countryside around.

Eating and drinking

Leipzig offers a choice between traditional German taverns and an esoteric range of ethnic restaurants which are a hangover from the recent Communist past; most of the best places are close to the Markt.

German restaurants

Auerbachs Keller, Mädlerpassage. This restaurant's fame makes it a must; the quality of the food served has improved recognisably since the *Wende* and, except when there's a fair on, there's seldom any problem getting a table.

Burgkeller, Naschmarkt 1. Leipzig's oldest tavern, an archetypal German *Bierkeller*.

Falstaff, Georgiring 9. Excellent wine bar-cum-restaurant.

Gastmahl des Meeres, Dr-Kurt-Fischer-Str. 1. Speciality fish restaurant.

Ratskeller, Im Neuen Rathaus, Burgplatz. Typically reliable cellar restaurant; because of its situation well away from the Markt, it's less than usually prone to be full of tourists.

Thüringer Hof, Burgstr. 19. Old *Gaststätte* with rambling layout of rooms that's the safest and best value choice for a hearty German meal.

Zill's Tunnel, Barfussgässchen 9. Self-consciously smart restaurant, with a beer hall downstairs, a wine bar upstairs. Food relatively pricey and often erratic.

Ethnic restaurants

Kubanische Speisebar Varadero, Barfussgässchen 8. Popular and genuine Cuban restaurant specialising in grills and cocktails.

Ostasiatishes Restaurant, Grosse Fleischergasse 4. Serves a variety of oriental cuisines, though predominantly Vietnamese.

Plovdiv, Katharinenstr. 17. Top-class but very expensive Bulgarian restaurant; best visited in a group, as the speciality dishes are for two or more people.

Stadt Kiev, Messehaus am Markt. Laid-back, old-fashioned Ukrainian restaurant.

Cafés

Café am Brühl, Richard-Wagner-Platz 1. Olde-worlde café housed in an elegant Rococo mansion.

Café de Saxe, Markt 11. New and very trendy café which also does full meals.

Café Vis à Vis, Rudolf-Breitscheid-Str. 33. Café-bar with a predominantly youthful clientele; open round the clock.

Zum Kaffeebaum, Kleine Fleishchergasse 4. One of the unmissable addresses in Leipzig, whether for *Kaffee und Kuchen* or a full meal.

Nightlife, culture and festivals

A comprehensive programme of monthly listings of **what's on** in Leipzig is available free from the tourist office. As yet, the city's **nightlife** is still rather moribund, the exception being the *Moritzbastei* on Universitätstrasse, a complex of student clubs, bars and a disco which offers a choice of live entertainments most evenings. The other main venue for live music is *Anker*, Knopstr. 1. Though you'll need to have a good command of German to understand what's being said, the city's **cabaret** tradition is worth catching; choice lies between *Academixer*, Kupfergasse 6, *Pfeffermühle*, Thomaskirchhof 16, and *Funzel* on Nelkenweg. There's a **women's centre** at Löbauer Str. 149.

Culture

The highbrow cultural scene is one of the city's great strengths. In the field of **music**, the Thomaskirche continues its role with regular organ recitals and choral concerts (by the *Thomanerchor* and others), to which there's often free admission. The *Gewandhausorchester* is renowned for the clean, beautifully balanced sound it produces; the *Rundfunkorchester* is also of good standing, while the *Rundfunkchor* is one of Europe's best large mixed-voiced choirs. Main venue for major **concerts** is the *Neues Gewandhaus*, Augustusplatz 8 (☎71320); performances by small ensembles are held at the *Bosehaus*, Thomaskirchhof 16 (☎7866). **Operas** are staged at the

Opernhaus, Augustusplatz 12 (☎71680), operettas and musical comedy at *Musikalische Komödie*, Dreilindenstr. 30. Leading **theatre** is the *Schauspielhaus* on Bosestrasse (☎7521), which concentrates on dramatic classics, while *Neue Szene*, Gottschedstr. 16 (☎7651), focus on modern plays and other contemporary art forms.

Festivals

Most of Leipzig's **festivals** maintain the cultural theme. The *Gewandhaus Festage* at the beginning of October alternate each year between concerts by international orchestras, and the promotion of new young artists. In late November and early December, there's the *Dokfestival*, featuring documentaries and short films. Every four years (1993, 1997), the *Internationales Bachfest* celebrates the music of J.S. Bach, featuring prize-winners from the competitions held the previous year. The *Lachmesse*, a festival of humour and satire centred on the three cabaret venues, was inaugurated in late June 1991.

Torgau

As a major railway junction, Leipzig makes an excellent base for excursions, with many towns in three different Länder within comfortable range of day trips. One place within Saxony itself well worth an afternoon is **TORGAU**, a former residence of the province's Electors, which stands on the banks of the Elbe 50km to the northeast; it can be reached in an hour or less by the regular trains on the fast line to Cottbus. Beside the road bridge is a memorial commemorating the fact that it was at this spot, in the closing days of World War II, that the advancing Soviet and American armies finally met up.

From here, you can ascend to the town centre, built on a cliff high above the river, and centred on a typically spacious Markt with a handsome **Rathaus**. Directly overlooking the river is the **Marienkirche**, a Gothic church containing a panel of *The Fourteen Helpers in Need* by Cranach. This was part of his early masterpiece, *The Holy Kinship*, now in the Städel in Frankfurt.

Schloss Hartenfels

Frederick the Wise, the man of power who made the Reformation possible, was born in **Schloss Hartenfels**, the large castle which dominates the town. It dates back to the tenth century, but in its present form is predominantly a residential palace; entry is over a moat with a bear pit, into which brown bears have recently been reintroduced. The **Albrechtsbau** at the southeastern corner is one of the earliest Renaissance buildings in Germany; its **tower** (May–Sept Tues–Sun 10am–noon & 1–3.30pm; DM1) can be ascended for a fine view over the town and the complex. An altogether grander style is present in the **Johann-Friedrich-Bau** which forms the east wing of the courtyard; its exterior spiral staircase, the *Grosse Wendelstein*, is the Schloss's most arresting feature.

Part of the north wing is given over to the **Kreismuseum** (May–Oct Tues–Fri 9am–5pm, Sat & Sun 9am–noon & 1–5pm; Nov–April Tues–Fri 9am–4pm, Sat & Sun 10am–noon & 1–4pm; DM1), which houses a collection of medieval arms and armour, together with displays on the history of the town. Far more intriguing is the **Schlosskapelle** alongside, which was consecrated by Luther in 1544 and thus has the best claim to be regarded as the first building ever built specifically for Protestant worship, though this is disputed with its counterpart in Stuttgart. In line with the ideals of the Reformation, the architecture is plain and simple, adopting a rectangular format with no apse. The galleries introduced here were to become a standard feature of Protestant buildings, while the elaborate vaulting was also much favoured in early Lutheran churches.

Colditz and the Zwickauer Mulde valley

Mention the name of **COLDITZ** to most Germans and you're likely to be met with a blank stare: this is the one place in the country that, because of **Oflag IVC**, the wartime maximum security camp for prisoners-of-war, is far better known abroad than at home. The main reason for this is that the GDR regime, embarrassed about the fact that the camp had been on their territory and unable to make any pro-Communist propaganda out of it (as they could with the concentration camps, where many of their own number had been incarcerated), chose to suppress its very existence. No references to it could be found in the official English-language guide to the country, while the 64-page German booklet on the town gave it just one sentence. Although a fair number of English-speaking visitors used to travel the 48km south from Leipzig out of curiosity, they were unable to visit the site of the camp, which reverted to its prewar status as a psychiatric hospital, while Colditz itself went back to being a sleepy rural community engaged in the production of ceramics and beer. While this situation to a large extent persists, it has already changed since the *Wende* because of the positive encouragement of visitors, helped by a willingness to make a dispassionate examination of the past.

The town

On its own merits, Colditz is a suprisingly pretty town in attractive surroundings: add in the wartime connection and it's easy to see why the potential for tourism is very real. The streets, laid out on a ramshackle old pattern, are full of historic half-timbered houses, while the main **Markt** is a highly distinctive sloping cobblestoned square, complete with the local brewery. At the top stands a handsome gabled **Rathaus** in the ebullient style of the German Renaissance.

The Schloss

From the foot of Marktplatz, there's a great view of the huge **Schloss** (guided tours Tues–Sun 10am–4pm; DM3), the former Oflag IVC, which completely dominates the town from its cliff-top site. There's been a fortress here since the eleventh century, which came into the possession of the Wettins, the Saxon ruling house, in 1404. In the middle of the following century, Elector August rebuilt it as a Renaissance palace, though retaining its medieval format of defensive *Vorburg* protecting the main *Hauptburg*; the magnificent armorial decoration above the second gateway show his own coat of arms, alongside those of his wife.

Under Augustus the Strong (see p.915), the Schloss was used as a hunting lodge, but it was abandoned by later Saxon rulers in favour of more modern palaces. In 1800, it became the local poorhouse, later becoming one of Germany's first psychiatric hospitals. It was specially chosen in World War II as the place to house men who had escaped from less secure confinements and subsequently been recaptured, and for *Prominenten*, prisoners who were specially prized because of their high rank or important connections. In due course, it's planned to restore the Schloss as a major museum; there's also talk of a hotel. For the time being, you have to be content with seeing inside the galleried chapel and descending to the 44-metres-long **tunnel** which the French prisoners dug over an eight-month period. They intended this to be the means of a mass escape, but it was discovered before it could be used.

The Städtisches Museum

To join one of the tours, go first to the **Städtisches Museum** (same times; DM2), Tiergartenstr. 1, just uphill from the church near the entrance to the Schloss. Occupying a fine Baroque house, this makes an essential supplement to a visit, as it includes a large number of photographs taken during World War II plus a fascinating

---

OFLAG IVC

Schloss Colditz was chosen as the site of **Oflag IVC**, the Third Reich's most secure prisoner-of-war camp, principally because of its geographical position – it was 700km to any
border not controlled by the Nazis. The nature of the castle itself, with its secure medieval defences and situation above a small, isolated town, was another factor: **Major Pat
Reid**, who wrote a trilogy of books about his Colditz experiences, recorded his initial
impression of it as "beautiful, serene, majestic and yet forbidding enough to make our
hearts sink into our boots". According to the Nazi authorities, Colditz castle was impossible to escape from, but that proved to be another of their empty boasts – in all, thirty-one
men performed the feat, aided by the fact that the main qualification for being sentenced
to the castle – that of having attempted to escape before – was at the same time the
camp's main weakness, as the prisoners had among them a rich fund of experience and
ingenuity, which they gladly pooled.

In 1941, **Peter Allan** became the first Briton to escape, by hiding in a sack which was
taken away in a delivery van; however, on reaching Vienna, he was recaptured and sent
back. Following a number of successful getaways by French prisoners, **Airey Neave**
(who later led the campaign to make Margaret Thatcher the Conservative Party leader,
five years before he was blown up the IRA) made the first of the eleven British "home-
runs" early in 1942, dressed in the uniform of a German officer; Reid was among the
others who accomplished the feat that same year. The latter's books are the best source
for an insight into life in the camp; for a completely different perspective, see *Colditz – the
German Story* by Reinhold Eggers, the official in charge of security.

---

display of some of the ingenious devices the prisoners used in planning their escapes,
including a typewriter which could be taken to pieces to prevent its discovery, a razor
transformed into a saw and a home-made sewing-machine, along with false identification papers and German bank notes.

Practicalities

The easiest way to reach Colditz is by the direct train service between Leipzig and
Rochlitz (see below). There's a **youth hostel** just below the Schloss at Haingasse 42
(☎335), while at the edge of town are a **campsite** (☎590) and a **hotel**, *Waldhaus*,
Lausicker Str. 60 (☎371). In the village of ZSCHADRASS a couple of kilometres to the
northeast is another hotel – *Gildehof Zschadrass*, Hauptstr. 4 (☎2070 or ☎2170). For
information about private rooms, ask in the Rathaus during normal working hours. The
best places to **eat** and **drink** are the *Schloss-Café* (a traditional *Gaststätte*, in spite of its
name) and the *Marktstübl*, both on the Markt. Be sure to sample the full-bodied
Colditzer Pils, one of the two or three best **beers** made in eastern Germany.

The Zwickauer Mulde valley

Colditz lies towards the end of the valley of the **Zwickauer Mulde**, just before its confluence with the Freiberger Mulde, whereupon the combined river, thereafter known
simply as the Mulde, flows north to its confluence with the Elbe near Dessau. Upstream
from Colditz lies a really lovely secluded valley, which is often surprisingly deep, considering the modest scale of the river itself. Along its banks are several outstandingly picturesque towns and villages: they're all linked by a scenic railway line, though its days may
be numbered as a result of the impending rationalisation of the DR network.

Rochlitz

ROCHLITZ, 11km upstream from Colditz, is a junction of three railways. From the
Bahnhof at the northern end, the line along the Zwickauer Mulde departs from the
river's snaking course at this point to run right down the length of the town, passing

over a viaduct before traversing the river. At this point, there's briefly a dramatic view of the large fifteenth- and sixteenth-century **Schloss** (April–Oct Tues–Sun 8–11.30am & 1–4.30pm; Nov–March Mon–Fri 8–11.30am & 1–4.30pm; DM1), the former headquarters of the local counts, with its picturesque silhouette of church-like towers and palace blocks with huge sloping roofs. It's in a poor state of repair and is currently the subject of a long-term restoration project. However, you can visit the small museum of local history and climb one of the towers for a view over the valley.

The town centre, with its two market squares, has recaptured its old county town atmosphere and is worth a quick stroll. Varied perspectives on the Schloss can be had from the pedestrian footbridge, and from the hills above, which are dotted with marked trails. Sassnitzer Weg leads up from the footbridge to the **youth hostel** (☎2131); other accommodation possibilities include two reasonably priced **hotels**, *Bayrische Bierstube*, Markt 23 (☎2220), and *Gerichtsschänke*, Mühlplatz 2 (☎2054), plus a plentiful number of private rooms.

Wechselburg

Set high above the valley a further 9km south is **WECHSELBURG**, formerly one of the seats of another aristocratic dynasty, the Counts of Schönburg. In contrast to Rochlitz, it's a quiet village sleeping in rural obscurity, with its Renaissance **Schloss** now functioning as a children's home.

The other dominant monument is the Romanesque **Stiftskirche**, which, in line with the faith of the former aristocratic masters, is Catholic – one of the few such historic churches in eastern Germany. Its extraordinary **rood screen**, made around 1235, is a masterpiece of both architecture and sculpture. Not the least remarkable feature about it is that it was reassembled a couple of decades ago; for the previous three hundred years, its constituent parts were scattered throughout the building, with the section above the archway, with its relief of Christ in Majesty, serving as the pulpit. The six niche figures of Old Testament characters, particularly the large statue of Melchiseadek to the far right and the triumphal cross group at the summit, are brilliant bits of carving. Look out also for the **tomb** of the founders, Count Dedo and his wife Mechthila.

Rochsburg

Another 8km upstream is **ROCHSBURG**, entered via a spectacular double viaduct over the river. The village is, if anything, even more soporific than Wechselburg, and is similarly set on lofty heights. It takes its name from the **Rochsburg** (Tues–Sun 9am–noon & 1–4/5pm; DM1) whose silhouette rears up proudly above the wooded slopes. Originally built as a feudal castle by an offshoot of the Counts of Rochlitz, it was acquired by the Schönburgs in the sixteenth century and skilfully transformed, after a fire, into the present Renaissance palace, which has the best of both worlds by retaining many of the old defensive features. The interiors, though fairly low-key, have some impressive doorways and Renaissance furniture. One wing is now a **youth hostel** (☎503).

Zwickau

ZWICKAU, Saxony's fourth largest city, is a major rail junction and gateway to both the rural areas in the south of the province, the Vogtland and the Erzgebirge. It's about 90km south of Leipzig, and can be reached directly by express services via the Thuringian town of Altenburg, or more picturesquely by the line along the Zwickauer Muhle, which at this point (in sharp contrast to the stretch downstream) cuts so unassuming a valley that you're hardly aware of its presence. For the foreseeable future, Zwickau's name will be irrevocably associated with the *Trabant* (*Trabi* in popular parlance), the wretched but now rather celebrated "people's car" of the GDR, which was manufactured here. However, in spite of its industrial tradition, it's an agreeable city of broad parks with a historic centre which came through World War II almost entirely unscathed.

The Altstadt

The medieval core of Zwickau, which grew up as a market town trading in minerals mined in the Erzgebirge, occupies a roughly circular area inside the busy inner ring road, Dr-Friedrichs-Ring, with the Zwickauer Mulde forming a second boundary to the east. Because of earlier wars, only a few monuments from the Middle Ages remain; instead, there's a varied assemblage, with plenty of grand nineteenth- and early twentieth-century offices and stores. Largely pedestrianised, it's quickly developing into a modern commerical city centre on the western German model.

The Hauptmarkt

Prior to the fame of the *Trabi*, Zwickau was best-known as the birthplace of the composer **Robert Schumann**, German music's purest Romantic spirit. He was born in the large house at the southwestern corner of the Hauptmarkt, which is now a **museum** (Tues–Fri 10am–5pm, Sat & Sun 10am–noon; DM2). It documents all phases of his career, from his early days as a virtuoso pianist in Leipzig (which were brought to an end after his fingers were damaged in a hand-stretching machine), to his sad final years, during which he was racked by mental instability. There's similarly extensive material on his devoted wife, **Clara Schumann**, who inspired his vast outpourings of passionate, heart-on-sleeve piano pieces and songs. As the leading pianist of her day and an accomplished composer in a style derived from her husband's, she was herself a substantial figure – arguably the most talented-ever woman musician.

In the middle of the south side of the square is the **Rathaus**, whose showy facade masks a medieval structure. Further along is the Renaissance **Gewandhaus**, built in the early sixteenth century as the market hall and guild house of the drapers. Now serving as the town's main theatre, its most notable feature is the amazing five-tiered gable.

The Marienkirche

Just off the western side of Hauptmarkt is the main civic church, the **Marienkirche** (now designated as the **Dom**, though it's never been a cathedral). Its decorative late Gothic hall church format, and the profusion of furnishings from the same period, are typical of the Erzgebirge region; the irony is that the Reformation, which emphasised artistic and architectural simplicity, was adopted here just after the building's completion. Many of the present sumptuous exterior adornments, including the large south porch with its depiction of the Wise and Foolish Virgins, and the now very blackened figures on the buttresses, were only added a century ago in a flush of Romantic over-enthusiasm. The **tower**, whose lead helmet with double cupola is a Baroque embellishment, can be ascended for a view over the Hauptmarkt and the city (entry from inside the church; Mon–Fri at 3.30pm; DM1.50).

Inside, the main adornment is the magnificent **high altar**, made in the Nürnberg workshop of **Michael Wolgemut**, the teacher of Dürer. It can be opened to reveal any of three sections, though only one of these is visible at a time: normally the carved part, with life-size gilded figures of the Madonna and Child surrounded by eight female saints, is on view, but the cycles of paintings illustrating the Nativity and the Passion are shown during their respective seasons. Also in the chancel is a **Holy Sepulchre**, carved in filigree style in the manner of a Flamboyant Gothic chapel, and adorned with figures of sleeping knights. The other work of art of special note is the *Pietà* in a north aisle chapel, the masterpiece of **Peter Breuer**, a local man who is one of the brilliant group of German sculptors straddling the late Gothic and early Renaissance eras.

The rest of the Altstadt

Just south of the Marienkirche, on the triangular site formed by the pointed intersection of Domhof and Münzstrasse, is Zwickau's most eccentric building, the **Schiffchen-Haus**, a late fifteenth-century house shaped like the prow of a ship. The Altstadt's remaining sights are all north of the Hauptmarkt. The semicircular Otto-Grotewohl-Strasse loops round via the back of the **Pulverturm** (Powder Tower), the only remaining part of the city walls, to the **Katharinenkirche**, another late Gothic hall church, which formerly belonged to a Benedictine monastery; inside are a high altar made in Cranach's workshop and a statue of *The Risen Christ* by Breuer. Opposite is the Renaissance **Posthalterei**, which was built as the home of a wealthy cloth manufacturer and merchant, later becoming a coaching house, before acquiring its present function as a top-class restaurant. At the extreme northern end of the Altstadt is an even grander Renaissance structure, **Schloss Osterstein**. Formerly a residence of the Electors of Saxony, it's currently under restoration with the aim of converting into a luxury hotel and conference centre. Alongside is the late fifteenth-century **Kornhaus**, one of the largest and oldest grain stores in the country.

The rest of the city

Between the Altstadt and the Hauptbahnhof to the west is the extensive **Stadtpark**, which provides welcome peace in the middle of the city. It's centred on a huge artificial boating lake; other attractions are an open-air theatre, a music pavilion and an aviary, though it's fun enough just to wander through and watch the locals at play.

About ten minutes' walk north along Crimmitschauer Strasse is Lessingstrasse, on which stands the **Städtisches Museum** (Tues–Fri 9am–5pm, Sat & Sun 10am–5pm; 1st Thurs in month 10am–7pm; DM1), a rambling, old-fashioned collection in a specially designed domed building from the end of the Jugendstil epoch. Its exhibits range from medieval sculpture, including a triptych and a *Crucifixion* by Beuer, via displays of locally produced porcelain and official portraits of the Saxon Electors, to the minerals and mining history of the Erzgebirge.

From here, it's just a short walk north to the **Automobilmuseum** at Walter-Rathenau-Str. 51 (Tues & Wed 9am–4pm, Thurs 9am–6pm, Fri 9am–2pm, Sat & Sun 10am–2pm; DM1), which celebrates Zwickau's role as a leading centre of car production. As the exhibits show, the *Trabi* was the unworthy and improbable inheritor of a distinguished tradition dating back via the prewar *Audi* to the Horch factory of 1904. Another ten minutes' walk to the northeast brings you to Leipziger Strasse, the city's north–south arterial road. At no. 182, set in a small park by the Zwickauer Mulde, is **Neue Welt** (New World), a Jugendstil complex built for concerts and dances. Part of it now houses a restaurant; a door on the north side is usually kept open, allowing you to peek in at the ornate main hall.

Practicalities

Zwickau's **Hauptbahnhof** is about fifteen minutes' walk west of the Hauptmarkt. On Bahnhofstrasse, which leads to the centre, are most of the city's few **hotels** – *Stadt Zwickau* at no. 67 (☎24781) is the best, with singles DM59, doubles DM99; *Am Hauptbahnhof* at no. 62 (☎24781) has singles for DM40, doubles DM70; while *Merkur* at no. 58 (☎25433) has singles from DM57, doubles from DM78. The restaurant *Zum Uhu* at no. 51 (☎22875) also offers accommodation, but the only other hotel in the city is *Zur Tanne*, way in the western outskirts at Karl-Keil-Str. 42 (☎73240); it charges DM60 per person without breakfast and is best reached by tram #4. The best accommodation bets are **private rooms**, which can be arranged for a DM3 booking fee at the **tourist office** (Mon–Fri 9am–6pm, Sat 9am–noon; ☎26007) in the heart of town at Hauptstr. 6.

Because it is now a common sight on western German streets (from which it was previously banned on environmental grounds), the *Trabi* has, perversely, become the most potent symbol of the unification of Germany – though it's also a very visible expression of the vast gap in living standards which existed, and to a great extent still exists, between the two parts of the nation. The first version of the Communist answer to the *Volkswagen* was first built in 1955 in the former *Horch* and *Audi* works; two years later, it was put into mass production under the name of *Trabant*. Three million vehicles were subsequently manufactured, repeating the original formula almost exactly, apart from a few changes introduced in 1964. With its plastic bodywork and two-cylinder, two-stroke engine, the *Trabi* was hopelessly antiquated even in its early days: it was also a major contributor to the GDR's pollution, belching out five times as much carbon monoxide and nine times as much hydrocarbon as the average western car. Though it was the cheapest and most readily available car in the GDR, it wasn't easy to obtain – twelve years was about the normal waiting time. Its lawnmower-like noise was and is an omnipresent feature on GDR streets, while it's the only car ever built capable of coming off the worse in a collision with a pedestrian. The most popular of the many *Trabi* jokes – the suggestion that you could double its value by filling it up with petrol – suddenly came true in the summer of 1989, when East Germans escaping to the west via Hungary gladly exchanged their *Trabis* for the price of the petrol in its tank. On unification, the West German ban on the car was lifted for sound practical reasons; production ended in 1990, when *Volkswagen* moved back to Zwickau, but the *Trabi* will be a familiar sight for a while yet, as its one strong point was its remarkable longevity.

Among a surprisingly good range of centrally-sited places to eat and drink are a couple of excellent **restaurants** – the aforementioned *Posthalterei*, Wilhelm-Pieck-Str. 27, and *Goldener Anker*, Hauptmarkt 6; both are very good value, considering their quality. The *Ringkaffee*, Dr-Friedrichs-Ring 21a, is also recommended; in spite of its name, it's a traditional *Gaststätte*. There are, however, plenty of traditional **cafés** if it's coffee and cake or ice-cream you're after; *Villa Wolf*, Humboldstr. 14, occupies an engaging little building from the early years of this century, while *Engelmann* on Hauptstrasse is particularly popular with local people.

The Vogtland

The southwesternmost part of Saxony is known as the **Vogtland**, a name which has lingered on from the Middle Ages, when it was governed on behalf of the Holy Roman Emperor by administrators known as Vogts. For the most part, the Vogtland is a high plateau, but the scenery is far from being monotonous – it's cut by many rivers and streams which often cleave surprisingly deep valleys. Since medieval times, it has been one of Germany's main centres of textile production; a strong handicrafts tradition, and in particular the making of musical instruments, has also been maintained in the villages. The Vogtland has long been a popular holiday destination, with a couple of spas at the very southern tip of the region and a clutch of resorts offering both winter and summer facilities further east.

Plauen

PLAUEN is the only major town in the Vogtland, lying 48km southwest of Zwickau. The journey there via a stretch of the Leipzig–Nürnberg railway is one of Germany's most spectacular train rides – the viaducts, and in particular the triple-tiered

Göltzschtalbrücke just beyond MYLAU, are a triumph of mid-nineteenth-century engineering; the only pity is that they aren't seen to best effect from the train itself. Although Plauen itself was devastated in World War II, with much of its centre rebuilt in an uncompromisingly modern style, it has many attractive features, not least its imposing setting in the hills above the Weisse Elster and Syra rivers, and the profusion of Jugendstil houses scattered all over the town.

Around town

At the heart of Plauen is the Alter Markt, recently revived as an outdoor market. On its northern side is the **Altes Rathaus**, now dwarfed by its monstrous early twentieth-century replacement behind. The facade facing the square is a handsome building, complete with curly gables, a resplendent clock and a balcony with a double stairway. The ground floor still preserves an elegant Gothic hallway, which, together with the adjoining rooms, is home to the **Museale Abteilung Plauener Spitze** (Tues–Fri 10am–4.30pm, Sat 9am–12.30pm; June–Sept also Sun 10am–1pm; DM1.50), which traces the history and production methods of **Plauen lace**, with plenty of examples of the town's most celebrated product.

Southeast of Alter Markt is the **Johanniskirche**, fronted by the twin Romanesque towers of the original building, which are now capped with Baroque cupolas. The rest of the structure is a hall church of the 1550s, one of the last major buildings in Germany to be built in the Gothic style. By this time the Reformation had been adopted in Plauen, so the church was constructed with the Renaissance galleries characteristic of Lutheran churches. In the choir stands a late Gothic winged altar, with expressive carvings of John the Baptist, Mary Magdalene and the Madonna and Child.

East across the broad expanse of Syrastrasse is the **Schloss** of the Vogts; apart from the Rote Turm (Red Tower), which survives intact, the rest has been left as a ruin following its destruction in World War II. From here, you can descend to the Weisse Elster, which can be crossed on foot via the **Alte Elsterbrücke**, a bridge known to date back at least as far as the thirteenth century. Uphill from the Schloss is the **Nonnenturm** (Nuns' Tower), the only remaining part of the medieval fortifications, now standing forlorn in the large open square created during postwar reconstruction of the town. Just to the west is the **Lutherkirche**, which has a superb late fifteenth-century retable from Erfurt with emotional carvings of scenes from the Passion.

Plauen's most imposing street is **Nobelstrasse**, a block west of the Markt. Here three adjacent merchants' houses of the late eighteenth century have been converted to contain the **Vogtland Museum** (Tues–Fri 9am–12.30pm & 1–4.30pm, Sun 10am–4pm; DM1.50), which documents the folklore, arts, crafts and history of the region, but is mainly of interest for a captivating series of period interiors, some recreated, others original to the buildings themselves. Among the latter are the very French-looking **Festsaal**, decorated in the full-blown Louis XVI style, whose rich stuccowork includes wall panels symbolising the months of the year.

West of here is the **Friedensbrücke** over the Syra, which was the world's largest arched stone bridge at the time of its construction at the beginning of the century, a distinction it kept until 1945. An equally impressive technical monument is the **Syratalbrücke** further to the west, which the Upper Vogtland railway crosses on its journey south towards the Czech frontier.

Practicalities

Plauen has two train stations, each for separate lines – the **Obere Bahnhof** at the top of the town, reached from the centre straight along Bahnhofstrasse, is on the Leipzig–Nürnberg route, and is the start of the line to PLZEN via the Upper Vogtland; the

Untere Bahnhof, on the south bank of the Weisse Elster, has services along that valley to the Thuringian towns of Greiz and Gera. The **tourist office** (Mon–Fri 9am–noon & 1–6pm, Sat 9–11am; ☎24945) at the corner of Bahnhofstrasse and Rädelstrasse has the usual range of **private rooms** on its books. There's a **youth hostel** in the Syra valley at Wolfsbergweg 30 (☎22125), but the few hotels are all heavily overpriced, particularly given the plentiful supply of good cheap accommodation in the nearby resort towns. Best **restaurants** are the *Ratskeller*, Herrenstr. 1, and *Hammerklause*, Nobelstr. 18, which offers Italian food and wines. Just south of the latter on Pfarrgasse is the *Malzhaus*, an eighteenth-century maltings which is now a lively bar and arts centre. Each June, Plauen hosts a major **popular festival**, the *Spitzenfest*.

The Upper Vogtland spas

BAD ELSTER, 35km south of Plauen via the main Upper Vogtland railway (the town itself is 2km west of its Bahnhof), was the GDR's largest spa, noted for its highly carbonated springs. It's been plunged into crisis by the collapse of its captive market, but is well placed to make a comeback – it's an archetypal Central European health resort, with attractive spa buildings, well-manicured gardens and pleasant wooded surroundings, all of which must have seemed like a different world to the GDR city-dwellers who used to frequent it.

Right by the Czech frontier, a further 13km south, is **BAD BRAMBACH**, whose waters have a high radioactive content. Both these Vogtland towns have ample accommodation facilities, but are rather overshadowed by the famous triangle of Bohemian spas, which are still best-known under their former German names of FRANZENSBAD, MARIENBAD and KARLSBAD. Now just a short train ride away, and no longer requiring a visa to visit, they make an unmissable excursion if you're in the area. Full details about them can be found in our *Czechoslovakia* guide.

The Musikwinkel

During the Counter-Reformation, large numbers of Bohemian Protestants escaped into Saxony, settling in a cluster of villages now collectively known as the **Musikwinkel** (Music Corner), because of their long tradition, introduced by these Czechs, for handmade musical instruments. The main centre for this is **MARKNEUKIRCHEN**, where around 200 different kinds of instruments are made. A huge array of historical examples – not only from here, but also from around the world – are on display in a small Baroque palace, the **Paulusschlössel** (Tues–Sun 10am–noon & 2–5pm; DM2). Markneukirchen can be reached by bus; it also lies 3km west of SIEBENBRUNN, the first stop on a branch railway running west from ADORF, the first station north of Bad Elster. This line terminates at **KLINGENTHAL**, itself one of the instrument-producing towns, albeit now much better known as a major winter sports resort.

The Erzgebirge

The **Erzgebirge** (Iron Ore Mountains) occupy most of southern Saxony, stretching from the Vogtland to just before the Elbe. They take their name from the rich mineral deposits found there in the Middle Ages; these were of crucial importance to the wealth of the Saxon state and in turn to its high-profile political role within the Holy Roman Empire. As the mines became exhausted, the inhabitants turned to cottage industries, notably lace-making, woodcarving and the production of children's toys, of which the last-named is especially significant.

The landscapes of the Erzgebirge are stark and often bleak, while the climate is decidedly raw – and both these conditions are exacerbated by the fact that much of the range is an environmental disaster area. In particular, a huge percentage of its trees are suffering from *Waldsterben* as a result of smog blown here from lignite-burning factories in Czechoslovakia. Despite this, the Erzgebirge is a popular tourist area, both in summer and winter – this being a rare part of Germany where snow is virtually guaranteed. Another plus is that it's one of the few parts of eastern Germany which has retained much of a tradition in **popular festivals**; it also has a couple of historic towns which are well worth a detour in their own right.

Schneeberg

The old silver-mining town of **SCHNEEBERG** lies on a ridge high above the valley of the Zwickauer Mulde, 18km southeast of Zwickau. It's rich in old traditions and is particularly worth visiting during the run-up to Christmas, when there are a whole series of events, including the *Fest des Lichtes und der Freude* (Festival of Light and Joy) in the second week of Advent. At this time, the town (in common with others in the region) is decorated with huge illuminated wooden pyramids adorned with figures of miners. Another big annual event is the *Streittag* on 22 July, featuring a costumed procession of mining guilds.

Focal point of most of Schneeberg's festivities is the sixteenth-century **Stadtkirche St Wolfgang** (Mon–Thurs 8am–5pm, Sat & Sun 2–3pm) at the top of the town. Outwardly plain, it has a highly original hall interior whose galleries, most unusually, go all the way round the church, including the chancel; equally unusual is the fact that you're allowed to climb up and walk round. The suspiciously fresh look the church has is due to the fact that its restoration following destruction in the closing days of World War II has only just been completed. It may be a year or two yet, however, before the huge *Passion Altar*, a mature masterpiece by Cranach, is returned, as it's currently undergoing conservation treatment.

Down on the **Markt** is an assemblage of handsome Baroque, Rococo and Neoclassical mansions. Just off the western side, on Obere Zobelgasse, is the **Museum für Bergmannische Volkskunst** (Tues–Thurs, Sat & Sun 9am–12.30pm & 1–5pm, Fri 1–5pm; DM1), which illustrates the crafts and costumes of the local miners.

Practicalities

Schneeberg is one of the few places of any size in the former GDR to have lost its rail link – the nearest station is in the adjacent town of AUE, which lies just across the valley, but there are regular **bus** connections with Zwickau, departing from just off the Markt. The **tourist office** (Mon & Wed 9am–4pm, Tues 9am–6pm, Thurs 9am–5pm, Fri 9am–2pm, Sat 9am–1pm; ☎2251) is in the Rathaus on the Markt. Here you can book **private rooms**, which cost in the range of DM15–20 per person. There are also a couple of **hotels**; *Karlsbader Haus*, Karlsbader Str. 56 (☎8734), and *Fortschritt*, Zwickauer Str. 2 (☎2510). As ever, the best place to **eat** is the *Ratskeller* in the Rathaus.

Annaberg-Buchholz

In the early sixteenth century, the largest town in Saxony was neither Leipzig nor Dresden, but **ANNABERG**, which grew up alongside the range's richest silver mines. It's now the northern half of a double town set high above both sides of the Sehma valley and in the lee of the commanding heights of the Pöhlberg, 35km east of Schneeberg and 30km south of Chemnitz. Although nowadays very provincial in feel, it remains the undoubted star of the Erzgebirge, possessing the finest artistic and technical monuments in the region.

The Stadtkirche St Annen

From the outside, there's little remarkable, other than its dominant position, about the **Stadtkirche St Annen** (May–Oct Mon–Fri 10.30–11.30am & 2.30–3.30pm, Sat 10.30–1.30am & 2–4.30pm, Sun 2–4.30pm; Nov–April Mon–Sat 10.30–11.30am & 2.30–3pm, Sun 2.30–3.30pm), which was erected during the town's short-lived heyday in the first quarter of the sixteenth century. Crafted from rough masonry, the exterior's only feature of note is the tower, shaped like the keep of a castle with an octagonal super-structure; the rest is little more than a shell covering one of Germany's most dazzlingly brilliant interiors. Ribs spring in all directions from the slender columns, forming an intricate star vault adorned with fancy keystones and elaborate little carved figures.

The rich and colourful furnishings are contemporary with the architecture. There are two masterpieces by **Hans Witten**, who was the equal of the far more famous Riemenschneider and Stoss, but whose reputation has suffered from the fact that most of his work is found in the relative obscurity of the Erzgebirge region. The **Schöne Pforte** (Beautiful Doorway) at the facade end of the northern aisle shows the Holy Trinity adored by the angelic host, with Saints Francis and Clare looking on. Witten's **font** is another extraordinary creation, which looks strangely anticipatory of the productions of Fabergé. Both the **pulpit** and the **gallery** were carved by his colleague Franz Maidburg; the latter forms a complete illustrated Bible in 100 scenes. The **high altar**, by the Augsburg sculptor Adolf Daucher, shows the Tree of Jesse, its cool Renaissance poise standing in marked contrast to the late Gothic sumptuousness of the other works.

The museums

Just across from the Stadtkirche, at Grosse Kirchgasse 16, is the **Erzgebirgsmuseum** (9am–4pm, closed Fri; DM1), which is mainly of note for some fine displays on the folk art of the region. There's also a roomful of medieval sculptures, plus sections on mining and the guilds.

In the valley below the town is the **Frohnauer Hammer** (guided tours Feb–May, Oct & Nov Tues–Sun 9–11.45am & 1–4pm; June–Sept daily 9am–noon & 1–4.30pm; Dec & Jan Tues–Sun 9–11.45am & 1–3pm; DM3). The visit has three separate parts, beginning with the hammer mill itself, the only one of its kind left in Europe. In the fifteenth century it was a grain mill with four millstones, but was rebuilt at the turn of the seventeenth century for iron and copper production, worked by three huge hammers which each weigh nearly six hundredweight. After this has been demon-strated, you cross over the road to see another collection of local crafts, before touring the Baroque **Herrenhaus**, the half-timbered mansion of the millowner.

Arrival and practicalities

Annaberg-Buchholz has three train stations, the most useful being the **Untere Bahnhof**, which lies about ten minutes' walk east of the Frohnauer Hammer, and immediately below the town centre. The **bus station** is at the western end of the upper part of town. Just across from it is one of the town's few **hotels**, *Goldene Sonne*, Adam-Ries-Str. 11 (☎2183), which charges around DM30 per person. At the time of writing, *Wilder Mann* on Markt (☎2122), hitherto the best hotel, was closed and its future uncertain, leaving *Berggaststätte Pöhlberg* (☎2081), way up on the eponymous moun-tain, as the only alternative. As usual, there are plenty of **private rooms**, though these are often inconveniently situated; they can be booked for a DM2 fee at the **tourist office** (Mon–Fri 9am–6pm, Sat 10am–noon; ☎3697), which is situated at the corner of Grosse Kirchgasse and Mittelgasse.

The **restaurants** in the town centre aren't a patch on those down in the valley – try either the *Frohnauer Hammer* (in the Herrenhaus) or *Waldschlösschen*, which has a secluded setting on the street of the same name, running between the Untere Bahnhof and Buchholz; the way is clearly signposted. Annaberg is host to the biggest **festival** in the Erzgebirge, the *Rät*, which has been going since 1520, and begins on the Saturday after Trinity Sunday (May–June).

Kurort Oberwiesenthal

The main resort in the Erzgebirge is **KURORT OBERWIESENTHAL**, which lies hard by the Czech border, 27km south of Annaberg. It's most easily reached by bus, but it's far more fun to take a mainline train to CRANZAHL, then transfer to the **narrow-gauge steam railway** which puffs its way along a roundabout 17km route to terminate at the very centre of the town. If you want to stay, there should be no problem in finding accommodation: in addition to the big Alpine-style hotels, geared mainly to the skiing market, practically every other house seems to have rooms to let.

Oberwiesenthal, itself the highest village in the former GDR, stands at the foot of its highest mountain, the **Fichtelberg** (1214m). A fairly straight hiking path leads to the summit, or you can ascend in five minutes by cable car, which costs DM5 single, DM6 return. Even by the standards of the Erzgebirge, the Fichtelberg has a depressing climate – it's said to have fog on an average of 270 days each year and storms on 150 days; small wonder that it has a meteorological station at the top. On the rare clear days, the view is extensive, but, because the whole range is so high above sea-level, the individual peaks have little sense of grandeur.

Chemnitz

When the GDR authorities looked for a place to be renamed in honour of Karl Marx, their choice fell on **CHEMNITZ** (pronounced "Kemnitz"), their fourth largest city, set in the northern foothills of the Erzgebirge, at a pivotal point on the main communications network between Zwickau and Dresden. Thus, between 1953 and 1990, the city became "Karl-Marx-Stadt", with its real name expunged altogether – though the West Germans insisted on retaining it as a suffix. The irony was that Marx had absolutely no connection with Chemnitz whatsoever, though the vast majority of the city's population did belong to the urban proletariat, it being one of the first and leading centres of the German Industrial Revolution. This spawned an uncompromisingly left-wing political tradition – even in the wake of the Nazi terror campaign before the 1933 elections, 50,000 votes were cast here for the Communists. Now the wheel has turned full circle – a plebiscite in 1990 voted to reinstate the old name, while in the general elections the same year the CDU-led coalition scored a landslide victory.

The local tourist office, in marked contrast to its counterparts in equally industrialised parts of western Germany, seems to consider its task a lost cause. That's rather a pity, because Chemnitz, as a city which was deliberately rebuilt after the war in a Soviet-influenced style, has a special curiosity value. In GDR days, its broad boulevards, with their creaking trams and Stalinist-style high-rise offices and tenements, looked and felt quite unnervingly like Russia rather than Germany; the illusion to some extent persists, though the heavy volume of traffic rather changes the effect.

The city centre

Chemnitz's main north–south axis is Strasse der Nationen; the bus station lies just off its western side, while the Hauptbahnhof is a block to the east. Walking south, you past the **Steinerner Wald**, the remains of a petrified forest, with tree stumps reckoned to be 250 million years old. Behind stands the **Museum am Theaterplatz** (Tues–Sun

9am–6pm; DM2.50), which is currently in the process of a long-term reparations project, with whole departments closed indefinitely. At the time of writing, the sections which could be seen were: two rooms of works by the local painter Karl Schmidt-Rottluff, the most abstract member of the *Die Brücke* group of Expressionists; the natural history collection, including explanatory material (in German) on the Steinerner Wald; the furnishings from a Jugendstil villa, Haus Esche, designed by Henry van de Velde (it's aimed to restore the original house as a museum in due course); and several galleries of twentieth-century art.

Turning right at the next junction, previously Karl-Marx-Allee, now Brückenstrasse, you come to the huge forty-ton Soviet-made **bronze head of Karl Marx**, behind which stands a plaque bearing his famous dictum, "Working men of all countries, unite!" in several languages. After the *Wende*, there were plans to tear these monuments down, but it's been decided to retain them as a reminder of the "culture" of the GDR years. Across the road is a park with the Stadthalle and the **Roter Turm** (Red Tower), a survivor from the medieval city wall.

Further south is the Markt, the only olde-worlde corner of Chemnitz, and the scene once more of market stalls. The whitewashed **Altes Rathaus** is entered via a portal bearing statues of Judith and Lucretia. Behind is the **Hoher Turm** (High Tower) and the turn-of-the-century Neues Rathaus. This incorporates a few Jugendstil features, but a better example of the style is the facade which was added to the Gothic **Jakobikirche** alongside. The house at no. 20, with its frilly Rococo facade, seems something of an anomaly in this city, though all the more welcome for that.

At the far northern end of town is a park centred on a large artificial lake, the Schlossteich. On the hill above is the **Schlosskirche**, a late Gothic hall church with a stumpy neo-Gothic tower, which incorporates some of the masonry of its predecessor, the twelfth-century monastery from which the town of Chemnitz itself derives. Inside are two masterpieces by **Hans Witten** – a typically idiosyncratic carved group of *Christ at the Column* at the high altar, and the church's original north portal, carved with the help of Franz Maidburg, which now stands against the south wall. This has a tympanum showing the Holy Trinity, along with carvings of the church's founders, Emperor Lothar and Empress Richenza, in the company of saints.

A Renaissance **Schloss** for the Electors of Saxony supplanted the former monastic buildings; this used to be a museum, but has been closed for many years for restoration. It's due to reopen in 1994 to mark the 500th anniversary of the birth of Georgius Agricola, Chemnitz's favourite son and four times burgomaster, and an early pioneer in the sciences of mineralogy and metallurgy.

Outside the centre

In the far north of Chemnitz, standing in a disarmingly rustic setting in open fields quite close to the route of bus #40, is the **Stiftskirche Eb'ersdorf** (if shut, get the key from the parish house at the back of the close). This was a popular pilgrimage spot in the late Middle Ages, the goal being the beautiful Marienkapelle, the star-vaulted chapel on the south side. The whole interior bristles with works of art, notably of the late Gothic period, including several by Witten – a *Crucifixion*, statues of an angel and a deacon, and the tomb of Dietrich von Harras, which bears a startlingly realistic effigy of the dead knight.

At the western extremity of the city, reached by tram #3 or bus #38, is the **Schaubergwerk Felsendome Rabenstein** (guided tours 9am–4pm, closed Tues; DM3), an underground limestone quarry where the atmospheric conditions since the cessation of mining have caused the walls to take on subtly luminous effects. Alongside is the former lime-kiln, a half-timbered eighteenth-century structure which you can visit at leisure; it has an exhibition outlining the history of the works. About twenty minutes, walk west of here, connected to the city centre by bus #47, is **Burg Rabenstein** (Tues–Sun 9am–noon & 1–5.30pm; DM1), the tower and residential block of a large feudal castle, the rest of which has disappeared. Inside are a few Renaissance murals, and a display of *objets d'art*.

Practicalities

The **tourist office** (Mon–Fri 9am–6pm, Sat 9am–noon; ☎62051) is at Strasse der Nationen 3. You can book **private rooms** here, though the two privately-run bureaux at the Hauptbahnhof are handier and more co-operative – the one opposite the entrance to platforms 11–16 (Mon–Fri 8am–10pm, Sat 8am–2pm) charges less commission; its competitor by the taxi rank outside the main entrance (daily 1–9pm) is of most use at weekends. Most of the few **hotels** are in the immediate vicinity; the only one with reasonable rates is *Carola*, Otto-Grotewohl-Str. 10, which charges DM50 for singles, DM85 doubles. There are two **youth hostels**, both out in the southeastern suburbs – at Augustusburger Str. 369 (☎71331; take bus ☎35, or tram #1 or #6 to the terminus and then walk) and at Kleinolbersdorfer Str. 61 (☎643027; take bus #33). The **campsite** is at Thomas-Müntzer-Höhe 10, just north of Burg Rabenstein.

Places to **eat** and **drink** in the centre include the usual *Ratskeller* in the Rathaus, the *Theaterrestaurant*, Theaterplatz 2, and *Weinstube Bodega*, Strasse der Nationen 12; there are homely *Gaststätten* outside both Burg Rabenstein and the Schaubergwerk Felsendome. Chemnitz maintains a lively **cultural** scene, with concerts at the *Luxorpalast*, Hartmannstr. 11, operas at the *Opernhaus*, Theaterplatz 2, plays at the *Schauspielhaus* in the Park der Opfer des Faschismus, and puppet shows at the *Puppentheater* on Schillerplatz.

Augustusburg

The first thing you'll probably want to do when you get to Chemnitz is to get out of it, and the most obvious excursion from the city is to the village of **AUGUSTUSBURG** 14km to the east. Augustusburg clusters below the eponymous cliff-top Renaissance **Schloss**, built as the hunting lodge of the Saxon Electors by the Leipzig architect, Hieronymous Lotter, though its colossal dimensions suggest an altogether grander function. To get there, alight at ERDMANNSDORF, on the main railway line between Chemnitz and Annaberg-Buchholz; from here a funicular railway, the *Drahtseilbahn*, ascends directly to the Schloss, part of which is now a **youth hostel** (☎256).

Much of the complex can only be visited on a **guided tour** (daily 9am–5pm; DM2). This takes in the **Brunnenhaus**, a deep well still preserving its original wooden machinery; the **Marstall**, which has a collection of historic coaches; and the **Schlosskapelle**, a beautiful galleried Renaissance chapel, which is among the earliest buildings designed specifically for Lutheran worship. The last-named features a tiny historic organ on which recitals are occasionally given; an altarpiece by Cranach the Younger showing the Elector Augustus and his wife with fourteen children; and a pulpit adorned with paintings of scenes from the life of Christ by the same artist.

Two other parts of the Schloss can be visited independently. The **Hasenhaus** (same times; DM0.50) has a museum on the fauna of the Erzgebirge region, but is mainly of note for the rooms themselves, adorned with monumental *trompe l'oeil* murals, including the humorous depictions of hares in the guise of humans which give the wing its name. Opposite is the **Küchenhaus** (same times; DM1), formerly the kitchens, now a museum of bicycles and motorbikes, ranging from a *Laurin-Klement* from the end of last century, through the many productions of *NSU* to the latest roadsters.

Freiberg

Exactly halfway along the 80km-long railway line between Chemnitz and Dresden is **FREIBERG**, whose town centre looks, by eastern German standards, startlingly immaculate. Somehow the town came through World War II completely undamaged and thereafter its long history as a mining community so endeared it to the GDR authorities that they had all the historic buildings cleaned and spruced up a few years back. The mining tradition is enshrined in the town's name, "Free Mountain", which is a reference to a twelfth-century Imperial decree allowing anyone to come to the area to prospect for minerals and keep all the proceeds. In 1765, the Bergakademie, the world's first college of mining, was founded here, and it survives as a centre of metal-lurgical training and research of international repute, imparting a degree of sophistica-tion to what might otherwise now be a very provincial town indeed.

The Dom

The **Dom** (guided tours May–Oct Mon–Sat at 10am, 11am, 2.30pm & 3.30pm, Sun at 11am, 2.30pm & 3.30pm; Nov–April daily at 11am & 2.30pm; DM2), as the Marienkirche is officially designated despite never having been a bishop's seat, is outwardly unas-suming and doesn't even have a prominent position, being stuck at the back of the lower of the two main squares, the Untermarkt. However, in sheer richness and variety of interior decoration (a legacy of the patronage of the Saxon Electors, and of the wealth brought by the mines), it's unsurpassed by any of the country's cathedrals.

Two important survivors of the original building, destroyed by fire in the late fifteenth century, were incorporated in the airily light hall church that replaced it. One is the **Goldene Pforte** ("Golden Doorway" – a reference to its original gilding), which formed the main entrance, but is now placed on the south side. Dating from the 1230s, it's one of the few German counterparts of the great figure portals characteristic of the Gothic cathedrals of France; it's a symbolical vision of a heavenly paradise, centred on a tympanum showing *The Adoration of the Magi*. Similar in date, though still Romanesque in spirit, is the anguished **triumphal cross** group placed high up on a beam above the entrance to the choir. Below it is an early example of a Protestant **high altar**; painted by a follower of Cranach, it incorporates suitably modest-sized figures of a host of local burghers as spectators at the Last Supper.

In the nave, your eye is drawn to the extraordinary writhing, twisting forms of the most precious adornment from the time of the church's construction, the **Tulpenkanzel** (Tulip Pulpit) by **Hans Witten**. Even judged against his own prodigious originality, it's a singular work, being an allegory of the Church as the flower in the garden of God. Resting at the foot is the figure of a local miner in the guise of Daniel in the lion's den, a theme developed in the second pulpit alongside, accordingly known as the **Bergmannskanzel** (Miners' Pulpit), which was made just over a century later. The chancel was transformed to serve as the **mausoleum** of the Albertine line of the House of Wettin; the huge tomb of the Elector Moritz occupies centre stage, though the double memorial to two princesses by Balthasar Permoser, the Baroque sculptor of Dresden, is no less imposing. Another addition from this period is the **ducal loft** on the north side of the nave, designed by the Dresden architect Pöppelmann.

However, the church's most significant Baroque adornments are the two **organs**, both the work of **Gottfried Silbermann**, a friend of Bach and one of the first manufac-turers of pianos. The ringing, silvery tones of the larger of these, which many organists regard as the greatest instrument ever made, can be heard at the recitals held each Thursday from May to October at 8pm. This is also the best time to visit the Dom, as you're then able to look round at leisure, though it's to be hoped that the compulsory guided tours, a relic of the Communist years, will soon be scrapped.

The rest of the town

At the corner of Am Dom and Untermarkt, a number of late Gothic houses have been knocked together to contain the **Stadt und Bergbaumuseum** (Tues–Sun 9am–4pm; DM1), which explains the history of mining in the area in a surprisingly illuminating way, with plenty of large-scale models. Untermarkt itself has a fine assemblage of mansions, including examples of Gothic, Renaissance and Baroque, as does Kirchgasse, the western continuation of Am Dom. If you want to pursue the mineralogical connection, visit the **Mineralogische Sammlung der Bergakademie** (April–Sept Wed & Thurs 8–11am & 2–4pm, Fri 8–11am; Nov–March Wed & Thurs 10am–noon & 2–4pm, Fri 10am–noon; free), just off the northwestern corner of Untermarkt at Brenhausgasse 14, which has a valuable collection drawn from all round the world.

A block to the north, at the edge of the historic part of town, is **Schloss Freudenstein**, a much-restored Renaissance palace of the Saxon Electors; there's free access to the courtyard, but otherwise nothing much to see. From here Ringstrasse, which is lined with a number of superb Renaissance and Baroque houses, leads to the harmonious-looking main square, the **Obermarkt**, where local youths loll around the central fountain with its statue of Emperor Otto the Rich, the town's founder. The late Gothic **Rathaus** stands on the east side, with the (for once) separate **Ratskeller**, entered via a handsome Renaissance portal, to the north. Just to the west of Obermarkt, set in its own peaceful close, is the Gothic **Petrikirche**, proud possessor of another Silbermann organ.

Practicalities

Freiburg's **Hauptbahnhof** is located about fifteen minutes' walk south of Obermarkt, while the **bus station** is about halfway between the two, just before the inner ring road. Directly opposite the Hauptbahnhof, at the corner of Am Bahnhof and Buchstrasse, is one of the **hotels**, *Freiberger Hof* (☎2029), which charges DM46 for singles, DM66 for doubles. A reliable alternative is *Motel Saxonia*, a huge converted *Gastarbeiter* hostel, located at the eastern edge of town at Schachtweg 4 (☎59589), and costing DM30 per person without breakfast. A full list of **private rooms** and various other accommodation options can be had from the **tourist office** (Mon 9am–1pm, Tues–Fri 9am–1pm & 2–6pm, last Sat in month 8–11am; ☎3602) at Wallstr. 24. Much the best **restaurant** is the aforementioned *Ratskeller*, Obermarkt 16; the *Schlosskeller* in Schloss Freudenstein is among the few alternatives. Also recommended is a long-established **café**, *Hartmann*, at the corner of Obermarkt and Korngasse.

EASTERN SAXONY

In GDR days, the eastern part of Saxony was jokingly referred to as the "Valley of the Clueless", on the grounds that most of the area, unlike everywhere else in the country, was unable to receive West German television and hence unable to hear a non-Communist view of the outside world; whether by cause or effect, it also had the highest ratio of applicants seeking to emigrate. The real-life valley of the **River Elbe**, which marks the end of the Erzgebirge range, is one of the most beautiful parts of Germany, particularly the area immediately beyond the Czech border known as **Saxon Switzerland**. Upstream lies the state capital of **Dresden** which, despite its wartime losses, still has some of Europe's greatest buildings, museums and theatres. The former capital of **Meissen**, a short distance beyond, is also one of eastern Germany's most attractive towns, preserving its medieval appearance almost intact. All of these places are worth seeing: reckon on a day at least in each.

To the east is **Upper Lusatia** (*Oberlausitz*), one of the two main homelands of the Sorbs, the original Slav inhabitants of the region (see p.792). It's had a turbulent history, having frequently changed hands, though the two finest towns, **Bautzen** and **Görlitz**, along with **Zittau**, the gateway to the mountain region to the south, all came through the last war with relatively little damage.

Dresden

The name of **DRESDEN** stands alongside Hiroshima as a symbol of the horrendously destructive consequences of modern warfare. What was generally regarded as Germany's most beautiful large city – the "Baroque Florence" – survived World War II largely unscathed until the night of 13 and 14 February, 1945. Then, in a matter of hours, it was reduced to a smouldering heap of ruins in the most savage case of **saturation bombing** against civilian targets ever mounted by the British and American air forces. At least 35,000 people died – though the total was probably much higher (perhaps by as much as 100,000), as the city was packed with refugees fleeing from the advancing Red Army. With this background, it's all the more remarkable that Dresden is the one city in the former GDR which seems capable of slotting into the economic framework of the re-united Germany with minimal problems. Like Berlin, it's an exciting place to be in at the moment: be prepared for striking visual changes as the post-Communist authorities put into effect their new policy of restoring all the historic buildings left as ruins.

By origin a Slav fishing village, Dresden stood in the shadow of nearby Meissen until it was made capital of the Albertine line of the House of Wettin in 1485. Its glory period came in the early eighteenth century, when the Elector **Augustus the Strong**, gathered round him a brilliant group of artists and architects who transformed the city into a great European capital built in a distinctive, highly decorative Baroque style. At the same time, the court collections were organised into public **museums** which, as a

THE BOMBING OF DRESDEN

The **bombing of Dresden** has attracted far more criticism of British and American methods during World War II than any other event – even though it was in reality merely the culmination of a deliberately destructive bombing policy, operational since 1940, in which civilian targets and historic buildings were regarded as fair game. However, the sheer extent of the damage, and the fact that thousands of innocent people who were themselves victims of Nazism perished in the raids, put it in a different class from all previous such attacks.

The greatest tragedy of Dresden is that it remains unclear exactly why the raids were carried out at all: the genesis seems to have been a nebulous decision taken in 1944 to carry out a saturation raid on some city (none was specified) which had hitherto not been bombed, as a means of breaking the German resolve once and for all. Although the Soviets specifically requested this tactic, they later distanced themselves from it completely, using it during the Cold War period as a useful propaganda tool against the West. Paradoxically, they were also primarily responsible for establishing the "official" total of casualties as 35,000; it has been alleged that they reduced this by a round 100,000 in order to play down the "effectiveness" of the Anglo-American action. Winston Churchill, who certainly authorised the attack, also tried to feign ignorance almost immediately afterwards, leaving most of the opprobrium to fall on **Sir Arthur Harris**, the controversial head of Bomber Command. After the war, Harris was denied the peerage which all other service chiefs received, and was shunned by the British establishment, while his forces, who had suffered appalling casualties throughout the war, were refused a campaign medal. The posthumous reassessment of his reputation, culminating in the decision to honour him with a statue in central London, has drawn widespread official protests from Dresden and other bombed cities.

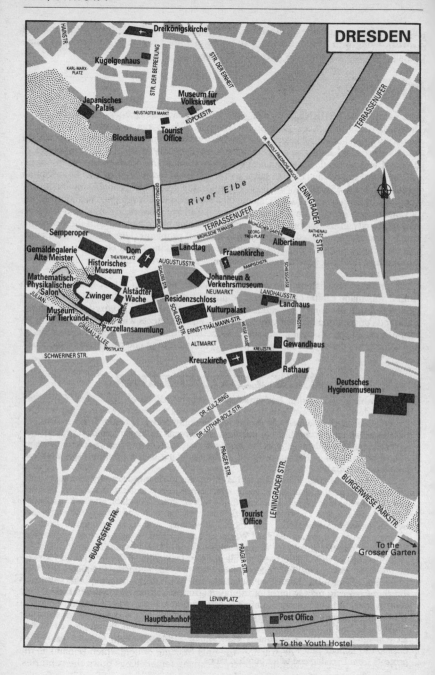

group, remain among the finest anywhere in the world. The city built on its already distinguished musical tradition during the Romantic period, becoming one of Europe's leading performance centres, a position it has retained to this day.

Arrival and practicalities

Dresden has two main train stations – the **Hauptbahnhof** is south of the Altstadt, while **Neustadt** is at the northwestern corner of the "new city" (which in fact is eight-eenth-century) on the opposite bank of the Elbe, and only slightly further away from the main sights, which are grouped close to the river. Between the two, located beside an old cigarette factory built in the shape of a mosque, is the unmanned **Mitte** station, but, in spite of its name, it's no more convenient than the others. Undoubtedly the most atmospheric way to arrive is by **boat**: all *Weisse Flotte* services, whether from Saxon Switzerland downstream or Meissen upstream, dock at the landing stage at Terrassenufer 2 (☎437241 for information) in the very heart of the city. The main **tourist office** is just a couple of minutes' walk from the Hauptbahnhof at Prager Str. 10/11 (April–Sept Mon–Sat 9am–8pm, Sun 9am–1pm; Oct–March Mon–Fri 9am–8pm, Sat 9am–2pm, Sun 9am–1pm; ☎495 5205); there's also a branch in Neustadt in the underground passageway at the southern side of the Markt (Mon–Wed 9am–6pm, Thurs 9am–6.30pm, Fri 9am–7pm, Sat & Sun 9am–3pm; ☎53539).

Accommodation

Both tourist offices can book **private rooms** for a DM3 fee; rates are surprisingly reasonable, at DM25–30 per person. For late arrivals, there's a special service offered by *Zimmervermittlung Vera Zwerg*, Zschonergrundstr. 1 (☎432 6475), on the route of tram #1. **Hotels** are typically overpriced: the only centrally-sited budget options are *Stadt Rendsburg*, Kamenzer Str. 1 (☎51551), at upwards of DM40, and *Rothenburger Hof*, Rothenburger Str. 17 (☎572143), at DM55 per head. Much more capacious than these, and charging DM50, is *Parkhotel*, Bautzener Landstr. 17 (☎36852), which can be reached by tram #11. Of the more expensive options, *Gewandhaus*, Ringstr. 1 (☎4956180), is the best value, with singles from DM54, doubles from DM84; it also has the benefit of an excellent location.

One of the two **youth hostels** is just south of the Hauptbahnhof at Hübnerstr. 11 (☎470667); the other is well to the east of the centre at Sierksstr. 33 (☎36672) on the route of bus #84 and within walking distance of the terminus of tram #11. Among many **campsites** in the area, two are within the city boundaries and both have bungalows to rent as an alternative to pitching a tent: *Mockritz*, Boderitzer Str. 8 (☎478226), reached by trams #15 or #16 or bus #76, and *Wostra*, at Triekestrasse (☎223 1903) on the banks of the Elbe, south of the terminus of trams #9 and #14.

The southern Altstadt

If you arrive at the Hauptbahnhof, you see the worst of modern Dresden first, as the **Prager Strasse**, which leads to the historic part of the city, is an example of Stalinist town planning on the grand scale – a spacious pedestrian precinct containing the standard cocktail of high-rise luxury hotels, public offices, box-like flats, soulless cafés and restaurants catering mainly for organised tour groups, with a few fountains and statues thrown in for relief. As if in retaliation, it was here that masses of people congregated in October 1989, hoping to be able to jump aboard the special trains laid on for the East Germans who had sought refuge in the West German embassy in Prague.

At the far end, beyond the inner ring road, is the **Altmarkt**, which was much extended after its wartime destruction; the only building of note which remains is the **Kreuzkirche**, a church which has undergone many remodellings down the centuries.

The present structure mixes a Baroque body with a Neoclassical tower and a modernised interior impressive in its starkness and loftiness. On Saturdays at 6pm and at the 9.30am Sunday service you can usually hear the *Kreuzchor*, one of the world's leading church choirs, which specialises in performances of the seventeenth-century Dresden composer Heinrich Schütz, father-figure of Germany's rich musical tradition.

Behind stands the heavy bulk of the **Rathaus**, built early this century in a lumbering historicist style complete with a belfry which rises well above that of the church. Further east is the late eighteenth-century **Gewandhaus**, the old cloth hall, which has been transformed into a hotel. Across the wide Ernst-Thälmann-Strasse from here is the contemporaneous **Landhaus** (10am-6pm, closed Fri; DM2), containing an unusually interesting museum devoted to the history of the city. Extensive changes to the displays are underway in order to eliminate the Marxist bias.

The Zwinger

North of Ernst-Thälmann-Strasse lies the palace quarter. At its western end is the great glory of Baroque Dresden, the joyous pleasure-palace known as the **Zwinger**, which was built for festivals and tournaments at the western end of the city centre; it was badly damaged in the war, but quickly rebuilt and is now once more the subject of a major restoration programme. It was designed by **Matthaeus Daniel Pöppelmann**, one of the most original architects Germany ever produced, and the plan he chose here is appropriately daring: a vast open space with fountains surrounded by a single-storey gallery linking two-storey pavilions, and entered from exuberantly grandiose gateways. The effect is further enhanced by the superbly expressive decoration by the sculptor **Balthasar Permoser**, though much of this has had to be replaced by copies. Unfortunately, the northern wing was never built because funds ran out, the space being filled the following century by a gallery built by **Gottfried Semper**, the city's leading nineteenth-century architect.

The main entry to the courtyard is via the **Kronentor**, which guards the moat on the western side; shaped like a triumphal arch, it takes its name from the huge carving of the Polish royal crown which stands on top. An alternative way in is via the **Glockenspielpavillion** at the southwest corner, which has a carillon of forty bells crafted out of Meissen porcelain. At the opposite end of the courtyard is the most beautiful pavilion, the lantern-shaped **Wallpavillion**, astride which rises a heroic figure of Hercules carrying the world on his shoulders. Behind it is the **Nymphenbad**, an elaborate sculptured fountain which ranks as Permoser's most ornate creation.

The museums

The Zwinger contains several museums. Beautifully displayed in the southeastern pavilion, entered from Sophienstrasse, is the **Porzellansammlung** (Sat–Thurs 9am–5pm; DM3); products from the famous Meissen factory are extensively featured, making a fascinating comparison with examples drawn from the 2000-year-old history of Chinese porcelain manufacture. A small natural history display, the **Tierkundemuseum** (Sat–Wed 9am–4pm; DM1), is housed in the southern gallery. The southwestern pavilion is known as the **Mathematisch-physikalischer Salon** (Fri–Wed 9.30am–5pm; DM3), which is a good deal more interesting than it sounds, offering a fascinating array of old globes, clocks and scientific instruments. In the northeastern part of Semper's extension is the **Historisches Museum** (9am–5pm, closed Wed; DM3), though it will not re-open until autumn 1992. This is in reality the Saxon armoury, with a superb collection of historic arms and armour from around the world; highlights include the sword of Elector Frederick the Valiant, a glittering set of harnesses and the coronation robes of Augustus the Strong (see box).

The irony behind Dresden's magnificent Baroque heritage is that it was commissioned by, and for the greater glory of, **Augustus the Strong** (*August der Starke*), who, even by the standards of the Age of Absolutism, was an exceptionally loathsome character. He came to power in 1694 as Elector Friedrich August I of Saxony, and three years later won the contest to become King of Poland, assuming the title Augustus II. As if to disprove the false maxim that religion and politics do not mix, Augustus converted to Catholicism in order to qualify for the latter election, thus reversing the stance of his ancestors who had backed Luther against the papacy and the empire, in the process strengthening their own political position. His nickname derives partly from his great physical strength – he could allegedly break a horseshoe with his bare hands – but mainly from his sexual prowess, which is said to have included the siring of a child for each day of the year. This may have been a scurrilous exaggeration put about by his estranged wife, a member of the Hohenzollern family, but he certainly did keep a bevy of regular mistresses, many of them prominent figures in their own right, such as Countess Aurora of Königsmark, abbess of the Imperial convent in Quedlinburg. But if he was popular in bed, Augustus was an inept political operator, whose reign was an unmitigated disaster for Poland, which plummeted from its position as Europe's premier military power to being a client state of Russia, a position from which, it could be argued, it has only recently managed to escape. Deposed by the Poles in 1706, he was reinstated with Russian help four years later, but was no more than a puppet ruler for the remaining 23 years of his reign. Saxony also suffered financially by being tied to an old nation in terminal decline – but in compensation gained a gloriously beautiful capital.

The Gemäldegalerie Alte Meister

The Semper building also contains the **Gemäldegalerie Alte Meister** (Tues & Thurs–Sun 9am–5pm, Wed 9am–6pm; DM5). Although it has had almost no additions made to it in the past century, the collection of old masters built up by the Saxon Electors still ranks among the dozen best in the world – and is arguably the choicest of all, with a quite amazingly high general standard. Note that this building is also likely to be closed until autumn 1992, though the main works, including all those mentioned here, are temporarily on display in the Albertinum (see p.918).

ITALIAN PAINTINGS

The Gemäldegalerie contains some of the most familiar of all Italian Renaissance paintings, of which the star is **Raphael's** *Sistine Madonna*, a wondrous vision of the Virgin and Child among the clouds, adored by Saints Sixtus (who bears the features of the warrior pope Julius II) and Barbara. Almost equally celebrated is the *Holy Night* by **Correggio**, which interprets one of the most ubiquitous artistic subjects in a completely fresh manner, stressing the nocturnal element ignored by so many other painters. The *Sleeping Venus* by **Giorgione** is one of the most sensual nudes of western art, and among the few paintings almost universally accepted as being by this short-lived father-figure of the Venetian Renaissance. It's documented as having been unfinished at the time of his death by plague and was completed by his friend **Titian**, who is represented here by several of his own finest works, including *Young Woman with a Fan* and the deeply psychological *Christ and the Pharisees*. Among several typically resplendent works by **Veronese** is one of his famous banquet scenes, *The Marriage at Cana*, while **Tintoretto** is represented with a diverse group of works, the most memorable being the vividly sketched *St Michael*.

Antonello da Messina's *St Sebastian* is a composition of startling audacity, using an unorthodox low vantage point and incorporating plenty of anecdotal detail in the background, to which the eye is irresistibly drawn. Other Renaissance works to look out for are the sumptuous depiction of *The Annunciation* by the rare Ferrarese painter **Francesco del Cossa**; the disarmingly simple *Portrait of a Boy* by **Pinturicchio**, and the consciously theatrical *Scenes from the Life of St Zenobius* by **Botticelli**. A distinguished group of seventeenth-century Italian pictures includes **Carracci**'s famous *The Genius of Fame* and **Guercino**'s arresting *Ecstasy of St Francis*. However, the gems are the series of the Parables – including many rarely depicted scenes – which rank as the masterpieces of **Domenico Feti**; the wonderfully simple *Parable of the Lost Coin* is particularly memorable. From the eighteenth century, the brilliantly detailed views of Dresden, then at its most resplendent, by the court painter **Bernardo Bellotto** (often known as Canaletto, after his more celebrated uncle) particularly merit attention, not least for the poignance they have acquired since the wartime destruction of the city.

GERMAN PAINTING

Among the German pictures are two masterpieces by **Holbein the Younger** – *Thomas and John Godsalve* presents, in its unusual diagonal poses, a successful solution to the particularly tricky art of the double portrait, while *Le Sieur de Morette* is executed with stunning virtuosity of technique. Very different is the almost abstract style apparent in the pendants *Duke Henry the Pious* and *Duchess Anna of Mecklenburg* by **Cranach**, which are among the earliest full-length portraits ever painted. The same artist's *Martyrdom of St Catherine* was painted for the Schlosskirche in Wittenberg, as was the so-called *Dresden Altarpiece* by **Dürer**, who is also represented by *Portrait of a Young Man*, traditionally assumed to be a likeness of the Flemish painter Barent van Orley. Among later paintings, there's a striking *Rape of Proserpine* by **Josef Heintz**, a Swiss Mannerist who worked at the Imperial court in Prague, and a large number of works by the highly influential Neoclassicist **Anton Raffael Mengs** and other painters of the Dresden school.

PAINTINGS OF OTHER SCHOOLS

The Gemäldegalerie has few early Netherlandish works, but the *Madonna and Child* triptych by **van Eyck**, executed with a miniature-like precision, is unquestionably one of its supreme treasures. Pick of the many works by **Rubens** is *Bathsheba Receiving King David's Letter*, a subject which provided him with an excuse to paint a suggestive portrait of his youthful second wife. **Van Dyck** is represented by one of the variants of his *The Three Children of King Charles I*, and by a superbly characterised *Man in Armour*. The most famous of the **Rembrandt** canvases here is *Self-Portrait with Saskia*, in which he somewhat enigmatically shows himself with his new and clearly not overjoyous wife in the guise of the Prodigal Son carousing in an inn. His interpretation of *The Rape of Ganymede* is also highly unconventional – instead of the handsome young boy carried off to become the cupbearer to the gods by the jealous Jupiter disguised as an eagle, he chose to depict an infant being dragged by his shirt tail, stricken with fear and peeing in desperation. There are two canvases by **Vermeer** – *Girl Reading a Letter* is a typical work, set by a window, and concentrating on the subtle play of light and shade, while the painting known as *The Procuress* is a mysterious composition whose exact meaning is unclear.

Among the French paintings, **Poussin**'s vivacious mythological scenes, such as *The Kingdom of Flora* and *Pan and Syrinx*, make a fascinating contrast with the cooly Classical approach favoured by **Claude** in works like *Landscape with Acis and Galatea*. In the eighteenth-century section, **Watteau**'s frilly *Conversation in a Park* stands out, though the canvases of the Swiss painter **Liotard**, and in particular *The Chocolate Girl*, are among the most popular with visitors to the gallery. The Spanish section is modest, but shows no fall-off in quality, with **El Greco**'s *Christ Healing the Blind* (which actually dates from his Venetian years), **Ribera**'s *St Agnes in Prison* and **Zurbarán**'s *St Bonaventure Kneeling before the Papal Crown* being particularly outstanding.

The Residenzschloss and around

Across from the Zwinger is the colossal main palace of the Electors and Mings of Saxony, the predominantly Renaissance **Residenzschloss**. This was horribly destroyed in the war, and although the GDR authorities paid lip-service to the ideal of restoring it, in practice they did little more than employ two or three workmen to ensure that the ruins, which were kept fenced off, remained upright. The rebuilding programme now underway is a massive task, which will cost an estimated DM500 million: even the projected completion date of 2006 (the city's 800th anniversary) seems optimistic. In the meantime, the **Spiegelzimmern** (Mirror Rooms; Mon, Tues & Fri–Sun 9am–5pm, Thurs 9am–6pm; DM5), which miraculously survived the bombing, have been reopened; the entrance is on Sophienstrasse. Until autumn 1992, they will house a selection of items from the Historisches Museum (see above), though the intention is to return the famous Grünes Gewölbe treasures (see below) to their original location here.

The Hofkirche

At the end of this street is the **Hofkirche** (now the **Dom**), the largest church in Saxony. It was commissioned by Friedrich August II, the only legitimate son of Augustus the Strong, who succeeded him as Elector of Saxony and, after a short interregnum, as King of Poland as well. To emphasise its Catholic allegiance in what was otherwise a staunchly Protestant province, an Italian architect was imported to draw up plans. He responded with a highly original design, featuring advancing and receding walls topped by numerous theatrical statues, the whole rounded off with a flourish by an elegant campanile. The gleaming white interior has an elliptical central space surrounded by large chapels. Some of these are normally fenced off; to see them, and the crypt with its tombs of members of the Wettin dynasty, you have to take a **guided tour** (Mon–Thurs at 10am, 11am, noon, 2pm & 3pm, Fri & Sat at 1pm & 2pm, Sun at 11.45am; donation expected).

At the **high altar** is a large canvas of *The Ascension* by Anton Raffael Mengs, who had been appointed court artist in Madrid by the time he finished the work; the side altar of *The Immaculate Conception* and *The Dream of Joseph* are by the same artist. Balthasar Permoser made the wonderfully frilly limewood **pulpit**, which was later given an extravagant canopy; he also made the marble font, and the huge statues of Saints Ambrose and Augustine under the gallery. The immaculately voiced **organ** (on which recitals are given on summer Saturdays at 4pm) is the last work by the doyen of the craft, Gottfried Silbermann.

Theaterplatz

Facing the Hofkirche across Theaterplatz is the **Italienisches Dörfchen** (Italian Village), whose name recalls that it was the site of the huts of the Italian masons who built the church. The handsome building with a fine terrace view of the Elbe which currently stands here deserves rather better than the present tacky café it now holds. Opposite is the plush **Staatsoper**, now named in honour of its architect, Gottfried Semper. Its tradition is second to none, having seen the first performances of Wagner's *The Flying Dutchman* and *Tannhäuser* and Richard Strauss's *Elektra*, *Salome* and *Der Rosenkavalier*. Guided tours of the interior take place throughout the year, except for two months in mid-summer; check the noticeboard for details. Tickets for performances are hard to come by; the box office for this and other musical events is in the **Altstädter Wache**, a sternly Neoclassical guard house which lies just to the south.

The Johanneum and Neumarkt

Augustus Strasse snakes southeast from the Hofkirche between the **Landtag**, the parliament building, and the back of the **Johanneum**, the former stables. Along the wall of the latter can be seen a huge turn-of-the-century Meissen porcelain frieze, the *Fürstenzug*, showing a procession of all the ruling members of the Wettin dynasty. On the other side of the complex is the **Lange Gang** (Long Walk), an arcaded late sixteenth-century courtyard in Florentine Renaissance style, and the **Schöne Pforte** (Beautiful Gateway). Part of the building is given over to the **Verkehrsmuseum** (Transport Museum; April–Sept Tues–Sun 9am–5pm; Oct–March 10am–5pm; DM4), with exhibits ranging from trams to aeroplanes.

The entrance to the museum is on Neumarkt, which was formerly dominated by the **Frauenkirche**. Since it was reduced to a heap of rubble in the war with only a fragment of wall left standing, the Communists decided to leave it in this condition as a permanent war memorial. It became the focus for annual peace meetings to mark the anniversary of the wartime bomb raids, and was an important rallying-point during the *Wende*. After a fierce controversy, the decision was taken in 1991 to rebuild it completely.

The Albertinum

North of here, overlooking the spacious Brühl' sche Terrasse on the Elbe, is the **Albertinum**, which houses many of Dresden's most celebrated art treasures, grouped in several collections. Until autumn 1992, there will be two entrances here, each requiring a separate ticket, or the purchase of a combined one for DM8.

The Gemäldegalerie Neue Meister

The **Gemäldegalerie Neue Meister** (Tues & Thurs–Sun 9am–5pm, Wed 9am–6pm; DM5) normally contains only nineteenth- and twentieth-century paintings and sculpture, but at the time of writing temporarily had on show a selection from the collection of old masters housed in the Zwinger (see above). It begins with German Romantic paintings, among which the dozen canvases by **Friedrich** stand out. These include one of his most famous and haunting works, *The Cross in the Mountains*, a purely secular subject framed to resemble an altarpiece and originally used as such in a private chapel. The Saxon **Ludwig Richter**, better known as a book illustrator, is well represented, while the Biedermeier style is seen at its best in the humorous compositions of **Spitzweg**. Realist masterpieces include several striking works by **Menzel**, but the portraits – including **Lenbach**'s *Paul Heyse* (the Nobel Prize-winning writer) and *Wilhelm Busch* (the cartoonist), and **Leibl**'s *Baron von Stauffenberg* – steal the show. Works by most of the French Impressionists and their German contemporaries, including Liebermann and Corinth, precede a section devoted to the Expressionist artists of the *Die Brücke* group, which was founded in Dresden. Of the later pictures, look out for two pacifist works in an anachronistic triptych format: *War* by **Otto Dix** and the Bosch-like *The Thousand Year Reich* by **Hans Grundig**, a local artist who spent four years in a concentration camp.

The Grünes Gewölbe

The Albertinum's other museums are centred on the famous **Grünes Gewölbe** or Green Vault (Mon, Tues & Fri–Sun 9am–5pm, Wed 9am–6pm; DM5). This dazzling array of treasury items, one of the richest in the world, was formerly shown in the Spiegelzimmern of the Residenzschloss, and it's intended to return them there in due course, although the display cabinets here make a good stab at recreating the original effect. After a few medieval works, the collection really gets into its stride with the elaborate creations by sixteenth-century Nürnberg goldsmiths. However, the most fetching works are the Rococo fancies specially created by Augustus the Strong's court jeweller, **Johann Melchior Dinglinger**. His *Court of Delhi on the Birthday of the Great Moghul* is a real tour de force, featuring 137 gilded and enamelled figures studded with 3000 diamonds, emeralds, rubies and pearls. He and his brothers, together with a host of apprentices, worked on this for seven years; its glorification of an absolute monarch is a thinly veiled allegory praising the Saxon Electors themselves. Many of Dinglinger's smaller pieces were made in collaboration with Balthasar Permoser: the pick of these are the riotously ornate *Bath of Diana* and the *Moor with a Basket of Emeralds*. By Permoser are a number of dainty little ivories, notably the *Hottentot Couple*.

With the same entry ticket you also get to see the **Münzkabinett** with its displays of coins and medallions, and the **Skulpturensammlung**, which is particularly strong on the Classical period, with Roman copies of lost Greek originals.

The Neustadt

The Neustadt across the Elbe was a planned Baroque town, and its layout is still obvious, even if few of the original buildings survive. In the centre of the Markt rises the **Goldener Reiter**, a gilded equestrian statue of Augustus the Strong; the only Baroque building to have been rebuilt here is the **Blockhaus**, a guard house designed by Zacharias Longuelune, a Frenchman who worked closely with Pöppelmann. Just to the east of the square, on Köpckestrasse, is the seventeenth-century **Jägerhaus**, now housing the **Museum für Volkskunst** (Tues–Sun 10am–5pm; DM2), a collection of folklore objects from throughout Saxony.

The Neustadt's central axis, currently still known by the Communist name, Strasse der Befreiung, is a pedestrian precinct lined with a host of restaurants and cafés. It's something of a compromise between the old and the new: though it in some ways resembles Prager Strasse, a number of Baroque houses have been preserved, among them the **Kügelgenhaus** at no. 13, now decked out with early nineteenth-century furnishings as the **Museum zur Dresdner Frühromantik** (Wed–Sat 10am–5pm, Sun 10am–4pm; DM2). Beyond stands the Neustadt's parish church, the **Dreikönigskirche**, which was designed by Pöppelmann and built by Georg Bähr; it's at long last nearing the end of its restoration following war damage.

In the park overlooking the Elbe is the most esoteric creation of Dresden Baroque, the **Japanisches Palais**, in which most of the city's leading architects had a hand. It now contains a turgid archaeological museum (Mon–Thurs 9am–5pm, Sun 10am–4pm; DM3), but you don't have to pay to see the courtyard, a fantasy inspired by the eighteenth-century infatuation with chinoiserie.

Schloss Pillnitz and Schloss Moritzburg

Two authentic, undamaged examples of the work of the great Baroque architects of Dresden survive in the outskirts of the city, and are, along with Meissen and Saxon Switzerland, the most obvious destinations for a half or full day excursion from the city. As a bonus, the journey to each can be an enjoyable experience in itself.

Schloss Pillnitz

Schloss Pillnitz, which lies up the Elbe at the extreme edge of the city boundary, is another Pöppelmann creation inspired by the mystique of the orient. He built two separate summer palaces: the **Wasserpalais** (9.30am–5pm, closed Tues; DM3) directly above the river contains a museum of applied arts; the **Bergpalais** (Tues–Sun 9.30am–5pm; DM3) across the courtyard is an almost exact replica, although this time you get to see round the apartments. However, what you can see inside is of small account in comparison with the exteriors, whose main inspiration seems to have been the palaces of Moghul India, despite the painted Chinese scenes under the eaves. Between the two palaces is a formal garden, while the **Neues Schloss** at the far end is a Neoclassical replacement for its burnt-out Renaissance predecessor, which Pöppelmann retained as

---

THE LÖSSNITZTALBAHN AND THE OSTERZGEBIRGSBAHN

Within easy reach of Dresden are two of eastern Germany's eight remaining **narrow-gauge steam railways**. They're the least known of the group (largely because the locomotives used are relatively modern and hence not so highly prized by enthusiasts), but are every bit as enticing as the others. The *Lössnitztalbahn* starts from the Ostbahnhof at RADEBEUL, which is on the S-Bahn line between Dresden-Neustadt and Meissen; it takes about an hour to cover the 17km to its terminus at RADEBURG. En route is mostly rustic scenery of fields, meadows and lakes; Moritzburg is almost exactly halfway along. The *Osterzgebirgsbahn* begins at FREITAL-HAINSBERG, 10km west of Dresden on the main line to Freiberg. From there, it skirts the western edge of the Erzgebirge all the way to its terminus at KURORT KIPSDORF, 26km away. This unassuming little health resort has by far the largest narrow-gauge station in Germany, a sight in itself with its eight running lines. However, the highlight of the journey comes 5km before at SCHMIEDEBURG, where the train passes high above the village on a stone viaduct.

---

the focus of his design. In addition, there's a fine park laid out according to the aristocratic tastes of the time, with sections in both the English and Chinese styles.

Pillnitz can be reached by taking tram #9 or #14 to the terminus, then crossing the Elbe by ferry. More enjoyably, it's a stop on the route of the *Weisse Flotte* cruise ships which sail from the Terrassenufer in the heart of the city down into Saxon Switzerland. From the landing stage nearby, it's just a short walk to Körnerplatz, from where a **funicular** ascends to the *Luisenhof* restaurant, which commands a wonderful view over Dresden and the Elbe.

Schloss Moritzburg

Schloss Moritzburg (March–Dec Tues–Sun 10am–5pm; DM3) lies about 15km north of Dresden, beyond the nondescript village named after it. It was founded as a hunting lodge in 1542 by Duke Moritz of Saxony, but little remains of his Schloss: it was almost completely rebuilt in the 1720s for Augustus the Strong using designs provided by Pöppelmann: only the chapel (an addition of the 1660s), the corner towers and the foundations were retained. A large artifical lake, fashioned out of several small ponds, was created round the Schloss, giving it an appearance akin to the great French châteaux of the Loire. Like them, the interior doesn't quite match the exterior, though there are some fine rooms, notably the *Audienzsaal* with its grand mythological paintings, the *Zimmer mit Damenbildnissen*, featuring portraits of court beauties (including some of Augustus' mistresses) and the *Spiesesaal*, which was used both as a dining room and a theatre and is adorned with a large number of hunting trophies.

It's also worth taking a stroll in the vast English-style **Schlosspark**. Towards its western end is the **Fasanenschlösschen** (mid-March–Oct Tues–Sun 9am–4pm; DM2), a small gaming lodge of the 1780s, which is now given over to a collection of stuffed birds. The quickest and easiest way to reach Moritzburg is by bus from Dresden Hauptbahnhof; but it's far more fun to travel by *Lössnitztalbahn*, a narrow-gauge railway (see above).

Eating, drinking and nightlife

When looking for somewhere to eat or drink in Dresden, it's worth bearing in mind that places in Neustadt generally offer better value than the more tourist-oriented establishments close to the main sights. The city has one of the most adventurous nightlife scenes in the former GDR, though it's still very much in the shadow of the more highbrow cultural offerings.

Restaurants and cafés in the Altstadt

Am Zwinger, Ernst-Thälmann-Str. 24. Large complex of different eateries: the cellar restaurant is best, the self-service to be avoided unless time is of the essence.

Gaststätte am Gewandhaus, Am Gewandhaus. Non-smoking restaurant serving hearty food; it's tucked away on a quiet square and therefore less prone than others in this quarter to being packed out.

Haus Altmarkt, Corner of Altmarkt and Ernst-Thälmann-Strasse. This huge complex, with the typically German cellar restaurant plus four separate cafés and bars, remains the city's most frequented venue.

International, Prager Str. 15. Another complex including two cafés and a Polish restaurant, *Wrocław*.

Kulturpalast, Altmarkt. Classy second-floor restaurant in the main arts centre.

Pirnaisches Tor, Grunaer Str. 5. Non-smoking restaurant incorporating a fish grill bar.

Semperoper, Theaterplatz 2. Modern and expensive restaurant and bar right beside the opera house.

Szeged, Ernst-Thälmann-Str. 4. The local Hungarian restaurant.

Restaurants and cafés in the Neustadt

Äberlausitzer Töppl, Str. der Befreiung 14. Specialises in dishes from Upper Lusatia.

Am Thor, corner of Str. der Befreiung and Platz der Einheit. *The* place in Dresden for good beer; also serves excellent food, with changing daily specials.

Blockhaus, Neustädter Markt 19. Russian dishes are the speciality of of this restaurant housed in a famous Baroque building commanding a fine view over the Elbe.

Kügelgenhaus, Str. der Befreiung 13. Probably Dresden's best and most atmospheric café-cum-restaurant, housed in a Baroque building with a beer cellar.

Meissner Weinkeller, Str. der Befreiung 1b. Expensive wine bar and restaurant; open evenings only.

Piccolo, corner of Str. der Befreiung and Platz der Einheit. Has an unusually varied menu of international dishes.

Winzerstuben Alt-Dresden, Antonstr. 19. Historic wine bar; open evenings only.

Nightlife

Bärenzwinger, Brühlscher Garten. Student club with a varied nightly programme of discos, films, folk music, jazz and dancing.

Club Müllerbrunnen, F.-C.Weiskopf-Str. 96. Theatre and music are featured in this club, which is open nightly except Mondays.

Jazzclub Tonne, Tzschimerplatz 3. The main year-long jazz venue in a city which has a Dixieland festival every May; features live music on Fridays, Saturdays and Sundays at 8.30pm.

Culture

Dresden has three main **theatres**, each conforming to the highest international standards – the *Staatsoper*, Theaterplatz 2 (☎48420) for opera, the *Schauspielhaus* on Ostrallee for drama, and the *Staatsoperette*, Pirnaer Landstr. 131 for operetta. Tickets for all three are available from the booking office in the Altstädter Wache on Theaterplatz (☎48420); unsold tickets can be bought at the venue immediately before each performance.

The *Staatskapelle Dresden*, long famed for its silky-toned string sound, is one of the world's top **orchestras**; the *Dresdner Philharmonie* is also an international-class body. Concerts are held in either the *Staatsoper* or the *Kulturpalast*, a large arts centre at the northern end of Altmarkt; it's also well worth checking up on the regular musical events in the city's churches. Other venues include *Dresdner Brettl*, Maternistr. 17, for **cabaret**, the *Puppentheater*, Leipziger Str. 220, for puppet shows, and *theater 50*, Clara-Zetkin-Str. 44, for avant-garde shows.

Listings

Festivals In mid-March there's a film festival, centred on the celebrated *Rundkino* on Prager Strasse. A big jazz event, the *International Dixieland Festival*, is held each May/June; around the same time, there's a classical music event, the *Dresdner Musikfestspiele*.

Mitfahrzentralen Friedrich-Engels-Str. 10 (☎51216), Bischofsweg 66 (☎53439), Wormser Str. 15 (☎35259).

Parks The *Grosser Garten* on the east side of the city centre contains a miniature steam railway, a zoo and botanical gardens. There's a third Baroque park to add to those at Pillnitz and Moritzburg, south of the former at Grosser Sedlitz, a stop on the S-Bahn to Saxon Switzerland.

Petrol stations A round-the-clock service, along with lead-free petrol, is available at the corner of Wienerstrasse and Gerhart-Hauptmann-Strasse.

Sports *FC Dynamo Dresden* were one of only two ex-GDR teams admitted to the *Bundesliga*; their stadium is in the Blüher Park, just northeast of the Hauptbahnhof.

Meissen

Reachable from Dresden by a cruise down the Elbe or (more prosaically but much more quickly) by the regular S-Bahn trains, which take around 45 minutes to cover the 25km, **MEISSEN** is associated in most peoples' minds with "Dresden china". Yet the famous porcelain factory is only one of the attractions of what ranks among the most photogenic and least spoiled old cities in Germany. In total contrast to Dresden, it came through World War II almost unscathed; it suffered quite badly from pollution under the GDR, but is already been cleaned up, having been one of five cities selected to receive special Federal restoration grants.

Around town

Never having grown into a major city, Meissen is compact and ideal for exploration on foot. Even from afar, its feudal layout is apparent, with the houses of the **Bürgerstadt** clustered in the valley under the **Burgberg**, which itself is crowned by the buildings – each of them among the greatest of their kind in the country – of the joint rulers, the Margrave and the bishop. Arriving at the Hauptbahnhof, which lies on the right bank of the Elbe, it's well worth beginning your tour by following the promenade a short distance downstream, rather than crossing directly over to the centre: that way, you can appreciate the strategic significance of the site more easily; you're also rewarded with the best of the many breathtaking panoramas the town has to offer.

The Albrechtsburg

Centrepiece of all the views is the commandingly sited **Albrechtsburg** (Feb–Dec daily 10am–6pm; DM3). This isn't the original castle of the Margraves of Meissen, but a late fifteenth-century replacement commissioned by Elector Ernst of Saxony and his brother Duke Albrecht, who jointly ruled the combined Wettin territories. It retains the medieval requirement for a military fortress, but combines this, for the first time in Germany, with the new demands of Renaissance princes for a residential palace. It's the masterpiece of one of the most prolific and accomplished builders of the time, **Arnold von Westfalen**. To appreciate the ingenuity of his design, it really needs to be viewed from afar: that way, you can see how the architect was forced to use the contours of the rocky, sloping site, solving the problem by building in huge blocks of six storeys, the first two being essentially to support the superstructure. While work was underway, the heirs of the two brothers split into two hostile factions, with Meissen becoming the seat of the Albertines, the junior of the two lines. Soon after completion, the court decamped to Dresden, leaving the Albrechtsburg as something of a white elephant. In 1710, it was given a wholly new function as the headquarters of the original porcelain factory, the first in Europe.

As it stands directly above the valley, the Albrechtsburg has to be approached via the rear, where it's guarded by a bridge and gateway; you then pass through a vast courtyard, in which stand a number of other historic buildings. The under-use of the palace largely explains the somewhat bare feeling of most of its **interior**, which over-enthusiastic nineteenth-century Romantic painters tried to liven up by adding cycles of heroic historical frescos, with decidedly dubious consequences. Nonetheless, it's worth paying to go inside just to see the truly spectacular, almost crazy, **vaulting**, which was something of a speciality of Arnold von Westfalen. There's a seemingly inexhaustible range of variations from one room to another, those with deep pyramidal niches between their ribs being the most original. The other highlight of the visit is the ascent of the beautiful **external staircase**, the *Grosse Wendelstein*, the main feature of the castle's courtyard exterior. Housed in the last few rooms on the visitors' circuit is the medieval section of the state sculptural collection, the rest of which is in Dresden.

The Dom

Cocooned within the Albrechtsburg courtyard is the **Dom** (daily May–Sept 9am–4.30pm; Oct–April 9am–3.30pm; DM2.50), along with its subsidiary buildings, such as the bishop's palace and the houses of the canons, most of which have been repeatedly altered down the years. For the most part, the Dom iself is a pure High Gothic structure, begun in the mid-thirteenth century by the same masonic workshop that had built the famous west choir in Naumburg, though the relative decline in quality suggests that its director, the so-called Master of Naumburg, had died in the interim. However, the somewhat eccentric facade for long remained unfinished: Arnold von Westfalen added the third storey in Flamboyant Gothic style, but the florid openwork spires, which soar above the rest of Meissen's skyline, only date from the early 1900s.

Entry is via the **Fürstenkapelle**, which was tacked on to the facade in the fifteenth century to serve as a mausoleum for members of the Wettin family. It contains a number of superb bronze memorials, sometimes using designs by Dürer and Cranach. The richly sculptured **portal** behind was made the previous century as the main entrance to the Dom; its archway is cleverly used as a frame for the depiction of Christ in Majesty. Just to the right of here is the **Georgenkapelle**, the private memorial chapel of Duke George the Bearded, entered via a strikingly Italianate Renaissance doorway. At the far end of the south nave aisle is the **Achteckbau** (Octagon); it opens directly outside, and contains three fine statues by the Naumburg carvers.

The same men were also responsible for the **rood screen**, except for its Flamboyant upper storey, added in the sixteenth century as a choir gallery; and for the statues of the founders and patron saints in the choir. The central **stained glass window**, showing Old and New Testament scenes in pairs, dates back to the thirteenth century, while the *Adoration of the Magi* **triptych** is by an unknown Netherlandish painter of the turn of the sixteenth century. From here you can exit via the **cloister**, off which is the **Magdalenenkapelle**, where the original statues of the south portal have been brought for conservation reasons.

The Bürgerstadt

The Bürgerstadt is laid out as a series of twisting and meandering streets between the Burgberg and the Elbe. More impressive as an ensemble than for any outstanding highlights, it's ideal for an aimless stroll. Centrepiece is the Markt, dominated by the **Rathaus**, in which the dying flickers of Flamboyant Gothic are fused with the new spirit of the Renaissance. At no. 8 on the square is the *Fachgeschaft*, the porcelain factory's shop, which is well worth a visit even if you aren't intending to buy; no. 9, the *Küfertheke*, is one of the places where the local wines can be sampled.

On its own small square to the side is the Flamboyant Gothic **Frauenkirche** (May–Sept Tues–Thurs 10am–12.30pm & 1–5pm), whose carillon, with the first bells in the world to be fashioned from porcelain, can be heard six times daily. The **tower** (May–Sept Tues–Thurs 1–4pm; DM1) commands a superb view over the city and the Elbe; pride of the interior is the retable of *The Coronation of the Virgin*, made around 1500. At the back of the church is the **Tuchmachertor**, a pretty Renaissance gateway, while on the terrace above is the celebrated **Gasthaus Vinzenz Richter**, an old half-timbered tavern which preserves an early eighteenth-century wine press. The wines served here have the reputation of being the best in eastern Germany, though that's less of a claim than it might appear, as the area around is the only significant part of the former GDR with a climate mild enough for growing grapes. Further north, on Freiheit, another Gothic church, the **Afrakirche**, boasts a fine mid-seventeenth-century altar, while its parish house is adorned with an impressive Renaissance oriel.

The Staatliche Porzellan-Manufaktur Meissen

The **Staatliche Porzellan-Manufaktur Meissen** lies about 1.5km south of the Markt, and is easiest reached by going down Fleischer Gasse, then continuing straight along Neu Gasse; it also lies close to the S-Bahn terminus, *Meissen–Triebischtal*. This is the latest factory to manufacture "Dresden china", whose invention had unusual origins. Augustus the Strong imprisoned the alchemist **Johann Friedrich Böttger** in Festung Königstein in Saxon Switzerland, charging him with what was then believed to be a feasible task, the producion of gold. Instead, he invented the first true European porcelain, according to a formula which remains a jealously guarded secret; its products are identified by the trademark of crossed blue swords.

Guided tours (Tues–Sun 8.30am–noon & 1–3.45pm; DM4) are run round the workshops, enabling you to see all the different stages of the production process. Be aware that this is on the itinerary of just about every tour group visiting eastern Germany; in summer you can be faced with a horrendous wait unless you arrive early. No such problems beset the **Schauhalle** (Tues–Sun 8.30am–4.30pm; DM4), which in any event is of far more immediate appeal, showing how the style of the factory has developed from the beginning to the present day. Highlight is the display of the gloriously over-the-top Rococo fripperies created by the most talented artist ever employed here, **Joachim Kaendler**.

If walking between the town centre and the factory, it's worth stopping off at the **Nikolaikirche** (May–Sept Tues–Thurs & Sun 2–4pm, Sat 10am–noon), a little Romanesque church set in the Stadtpark. Inside, forming a poignant memorial to the fallen of World War I, are the largest porcelain figures ever made, two groups of mothers with children, each of which is 2.5 metres high and 300kg in weight.

Practicalities

Meissen's **tourist office** (Mon–Fri 10am–6pm; April–Sept also Sat 10.30am–4.30pm; ☎4470) is at An der Frauenkirche 3. In pre-*Wende* days, the city was well worth considering as an alternative accommodation base to Dresden on the grounds of price, but that is now much less of a factor than it was. If you do want to stay, the tourist office can book **private rooms**; a rival service is offered by *Zimmervermittlung Stadtblick*, in the southern suburbs at Stadtblick 8 (Mon–Fri 4–10pm, Sat & Sun 10am–10pm). There are also several **hotels**, which are invariably far better value than their Dresden counterparts. Handy for the Hauptbahnhof are *Hamburger Hof*, Dresdener Str. 9 (☎2118), whose rates begin at DM30, and *Mitropa-Hotel*, Grosenhainer Str. 2 (☎558), which charges around DM50 per person. *Goldener Löwe*, Heinrichsplatz 6 (☎3304), offers an unbeatable central location; its rates vary widely, starting at DM35. A newcomer is *Pension Goldgrund*, facing the Stadtpark at Goldgrund 14 (☎4286); here singles cost

DM30, doubles DM50. There's a **youth hostel** at Wildsruffer Str. 28 (☎3065) and a **campsite** (☎2680) south of town on the left bank of the Elbe.

Food and drink

For **eating** and **drinking**, the one unmissable place is the aforementioned *Gasthaus Vinzenz Richter*, An der Frauenkirche 12; the menu is short, but the food excellent. Note that it opens at 4pm and is closed on Mondays, a pattern followed by most of the other wine restaurants, best of which is the historic *Bauernhäusl*, on the right bank of the Elbe at Oberspaarer Str. 20. The alternatives in the town centre are *Sächsischer Hof*, Hahnemannsplatz 17 (which closes on Thursdays instead of Mondays), and *Winkelkrug*, Schlossberg 13. Pick of the other restaurants is *Parkrestaurant*, Elbegasse 1; other possibilities include the *Ratskeller* and *Am Tuchmachertor* below the Frauenkirche, and, in the castle precinct, the *Domkeller* and *Burgkeller*. The main **wine-tasting** venue is the *Probierenstube der Sächsischen Winzergerossenschaft* (daily 5pm–1am), located in the northeast of town at Bennoweg 9.

Saxon Switzerland

The area between Dresden and the Czech border 50km south is popularly known as **Saxon Switzerland** (*Sächsische Schweiz*), though this nickname, first coined by artists of the Romantic movement, is misleading: the landscape, far from looking Swiss, is archetypally Middle European, with the meandering **River Elbe** cutting a grand valley through dense forests interrupted by outcrops of rock wielded into truly fantastic shapes. There's no better **hiking** country in all of Germany, and some walking is essential if you want to see the best of the scenery. Experienced rock climbers will relish the challenge of the cliffs; the marked trails, which require no special precautions other than the wearing of sensible footwear, cater for everyone else. If pressed for time, the S-Bahn line down the left bank offers a good (and cheap) overview of the region; even on a day trip from Dresden, it should be possible to combine this with a visit to a couple of the main set-piece attractions. An enticing alternative is to take a **cruise** with the *Weisse Flotte* ships: there are two or three departures daily from Dresden throughout the season. However, given that there's now abundant and inexpensive **accommodation** in all the resorts mentioned below (a stark contrast with the situation a few years ago, when just one hotel was open to westerners), it would be a pity not to stay for a few days.

Pirna

PIRNA, 17km south of Dresden Hauptbahnhof, is the gateway to Saxon Switzerland. Untouched in the last war, this old market town, hitherto rather scruffy, is currently being spruced up in preparation for its development as a major tourist centre. Set on a hill overlooking the town is **Schloss Sonnenstein**, now mainly used as offices, though it does have a terrace-restaurant. The central **Markt** is lined with a variety of handsome mansions, several with picturesque identification signs; the Rathaus stands on its own in the middle of the square.

Between the Schloss and the Markt is the **Stadtkirche St Marien** (daily 10am–noon & 2–3.30pm), a Flamboyant Gothic hall church similar to those in the Erzgebirge region, with all interest concentrated inside. Here, it's the stupendous star and network **vaulting** that steals the show; at times the ribs erupt into audacious flights of fancy, notably in the chancel, where they take on the form of a tree trunk. A curiosity of the church's building history is that it was begun at the turn of the sixteenth century as a Catholic parish church, but was appropriated for Protestant use before its completion. This change was immediately given visible expression in the painted decoration which was added to the vault: two of the Evangelists are depicted with the features of Luther and Melanchthon. Also marked with the theology of the new faith are two Renaissance adornments – the **font**, which rests on a base with sweet depictions of babies at play, and the sandstone **high altar**, with its paired Old and New Testament scenes.

Practicalities

The **tourist office** (Mon–Thurs 9am–6pm, Fri 9am–3pm; ☎2897) is north of the Markt at no. 31 on the main shopping street, Dohnaische Strasse. Here you can book **private rooms** in the town, and in other places in Saxon Switzerland; prices start at as little as DM10. A recommendable **hotel** is *Deutsches Haus*, occupying one of the town's most picturesque old mansions at Niedere Burgstr. 1 (☎2854), and charging DM28 for singles, DM46 for doubles. There's also a **youth hostel**, situated on the opposite side of the Elbe from the centre at Birkwitzer Str. 51 (☎2388).

Kurort Rathen and Hohnstein

If you're visiting Saxon Switzerland on a day trip, one place you should definitely make for is **KURORT RATHEN**, a small health resort on the east bank of the Elbe, linked by regular ferries to its Bahnhof, which is 12km and three stops on from Pirna. Should you want to stay, there are ample accommodation possibilities on both sides of the river, including a **youth hostel** at Niederrathen 3 (☎425).

High above the village, about thirty minutes' walk away, is the **Bastei**. Even the unfortunate siting of a new luxury hotel cannot detract from the grandeur of this natural belvedere of strangely shaped rocks, which is not only astonishing in itself – seemingly fashioned by some great divine sculptor – but also commands really stunning views, both over the Elbe and into the forest. As a bonus, there are the ruins of **Felsenburg Neurathen**, a thirteenth-century castle ingeniously juxtaposed among the rocks. Lower down, the setting has been put to a more peaceful use in modern times by the creation of a spectacular open-air theatre.

Another walk well worth making is the hour-long trail along the *Knotenweg* to **HOHNSTEIN**, the most picturesque of the villages set away from the riverside, with a hilly site which affords a wide range of perspectives, The **Schloss** (daily 9am–5pm; free), itself a fine vantage point, houses a particularly enticing **youth hostel** (☎202), and there are a number of fine Baroque buildings on and around the Markt.

Königstein

From Rathen, the train follows the loops of the Elbe round to the small country town of **KÖNIGSTEIN**, 6km away. It's of no interest in itself, but the colossal fortress above, **Festung Königstein** (May–Sept 8am–8pm; Oct–April 9am–5pm; DM5), rivals the Bastei as the most impressive sight in Saxon Switzerland. It takes a steep climb of thirty or forty minutes to reach it, though a tourist "train" has recently been introduced for the benefit of the better-heeled visitors who now visit the region. Once a virtually impregnable frontier post of the Saxon state, the fortress was continually strengthened right up until the Napoleonic period, so that it forms a virtual encyclopaedia of changing defensive techniques. Long before this, it had ceased to have much strategic value, and its main function was as Saxony's most secure prison. Johann Friedrich Böttger, the inventor of Meissen porcelain, was incarcerated here by Augustus the Strong; the same fate later befell the nineteenth-century Socialist leader August Bebel, and a number of prominent anti-Nazis. It also proved a secure home in World War II for the movable art treasures of Dresden. The most remarkable structure is the sixteenth-century **Tiefer Brunnen** (Deep Well), which is dug to a depth of 152 metres, a task which kept a group of miners from Freiberg occupied for six years. Also of note are the cellars, the barracks and the two arsenals, both containing an array of historic weapons. However, there's no doubt that the view – even finer than that from the Bastei – is the prime draw.

To see Königstein itself at reasonably close range, there's a choice of vantage points – the **Pfaffenstein** to the south, or the **Lilienstein** on the opposite side of the Elbe. Ferries run across to the latter from Königstein; it's then a walk of about an hour to the summit. The local **youth hostel** is on this side of the riverbank, at Halbestadt 13 (☎2432); directly across from it is a **campsite**.

Bad Schandau and around

Next stop, a further 5km on, is the spa of **BAD SCHANDAU**, the chief resort of the area and a wonderful base for hikes. It's also the border post, having swallowed up all the villages before the frontier. The best view over the area is from the tall platform tower of the iron lift or **Personenaufzug** (daily dawn–dusk; DM1) which was built at the southern end of town in 1904. Also worth a quick look is the **Johanniskirche** just off the Markt, a Gothic church remodelled in the Baroque period which contains two notable Renaissance furnishings in the pulpit and the high altar.

From the park in the centre of Bad Schandau, the *Kirnitzschtalbahn*, one of only two surviving examples of the once-ubiquitous **rural tramways**, creaks along the banks of the River Kirnitzsch to the **Lichtenhainer Wasserfall** 7km northeast. (If driving along this stretch, take extra care, as the tram travels on the main road most of the time, making overtaking extremely hazardous.) From the terminus, where there's a restaurant, it's a gentle uphill signposted walk to the **Kuhstall** (Cow Stall), one of Saxon Switzerland's most picturesque rock groupings and a fine vantage point over the wooded countryside away from the Elbe. Overlooking the river, a couple of hours' walk from here or Bad Schandau, are the **Schrammsteine**, the most extended group of rock formations in the area and a favourite haunt of daredevil climbing enthusiasts.

Practicalities

Bad Schandau's **tourist office** at Markt 8 (April–Sept Mon–Fri 9am–6pm, Sat 9am–noon; Oct–March Mon–Fri 9am–noon & 1–5pm; ☎2355 or 2412) will find you a room for a DM1 booking fee. If you prefer to look yourself, there's a large **hotel**, *Elbeterrasse* at Markt 11, which charges DM24 per person, while the little *Braustübl*, Kirchstr. 10 (☎2566), has singles for DM20, doubles DM35. There's a **campsite** at Ostrauer Mühle on the Kirnitzsch (☎2742) and a **youth hostel** at Rudi-Hempel-Str. 14 (☎2408) in the village of OSTRAU to the south.

Bautzen (Budyšin)

Some 60km east of Dresden is **BAUTZEN**, the cultural capital of the Sorbs, Germany's only indigenous Slav minority, whose homeland is divided between Upper Lusatia in Saxony and Lower Lusatia in Brandenburg (see the Spreewald, *Chapter Nine*). They settled in this area as far back as the sixth century, and have remained ever since; the bilingual signs, and the two official forms of the town's name, impart a touch of exoticism, though in Bautzen itself (as opposed to some of the outlying villages), you're unlikely to hear the language spoken in the streets, especially since all Sorbs are bilingual. Bautzen is potentially a really beautiful town: it occupies a compact site high above the still young River Spree, which here looks relatively wild and untamed, although it's harnessed to form a reservoir immediately beyond the northern suburbs. The town's silhouette, dotted with towers of all shapes and sizes, looks magnificent when seen from a distance. Closer up, it's not quite so impressive, the GDR period having bequeathed a legacy of pollution and tattiness which will take years to clean up.

The central streets

A good way to begin your tour is by climbing the **Reichenturm** (May–Sept daily 9am–5pm; DM1), which lies at the top end of Kornmarkt at the eastern edge of the Altstadt and is reached in about fifteen minutes from the Hauptbahnhof via streets still named Ernst-Thälmann-Strasse and Karl-Marx-Strasse. The original defensive tower dates back to the late fifteenth century, and was subsequently adorned with a relief portrait of Bautzen's then overlord, Emperor Rudolf II, ruler of the famously degenerate court at Prague. When an over-large Baroque lantern was added in the early eighteenth century, a pronounced tilt immediately occurred – hence the nickname of "the leaning tower of Bautzen". After World War II there were plans to demolish it for saftey reasons, but thankfully it was decided to secure the foundations instead. From the top, you get a good overview of the layout of the town.

The busy pedestrianised **Reichenstrasse**, lined with Baroque houses built after one of the many fires that have ravaged the town throughout its history, leads from the Reichenturm to the Hauptmarkt. This is separated from a second market square, Fleischmarkt, by the **Rathaus**, a Classically-inspired Baroque building whose most pleasing feature is the tall tower, Gothic by origin, but neatly remodelled to harmonise with the rest of the structure. Opposite is the **Gewandhaus**, a neo-Renaissance replacement of the old trading hall and weigh house, whose handsome vaulted cellars, now the *Ratskeller* restaurant, survive underneath.

Fleishmarkt's top end is closed by the very parochial-looking **Dom**, whose late Gothic architecture reduces the hall church to its simplest format. It's chiefly of note for two peculiarities. Firstly, as can be seen from the outside, but is far more noticeable within, the body of the church is built with a very pronounced curve. One theory is that this is a symbolical reference to the body of Christ on the cross (in which case, it's an audacious feat of design quite brilliantly executed); more prosaically but more plausibly, it may have been forced on the builders by the restricted nature of the site. The second curiosity is that this is a *Simultankirche*, one used by Protestants and Catholics alike. Immediately the Reformation was introduced, it was divided in two, the Catholics taking the choir and the Protestants the nave, a situation that persists to this day, with only a small iron barrier separating the two congregations. The very different set of furnishings immediately betray which part you're in; the Catholics have the star piece in the large *Crucifixion* by Balthasar Permoser, a donation from the sculptor himself.

To the rear of the Dom is the **Domstift**, a triple-winged Baroque palace entered via a cheerful gateway adorned with statues inspired by Counter-Reformation theology. It was the residence of a Catholic bishop until a few years ago, when Bautzen was demoted to the status of a co-cathedral in favour of Dresden. All around this area are twisting little alleys of peeling houses which are marvellously evocative of days gone by, but desperately in need of restoration.

Along the fortifications

The Reichenturm also makes a good jumping-off point for a walk round the fortifications, of which many portions survive. Immediately to the north is the **Wendischer Turm**, whose name signifies that it presided over the quarter where the Wends (the alternative name for the Sorbs) lived. For long used as a prison, it was saved from demolition through the ingenuity of Gottfried Semper, who incorporated it into the castellated **Kaserne** (barracks) he was commissioned to build on the site. This rather wonderful neo-Gothic fantasy itself became redundant, but has found a new lease of life as municipal offices.

The L-shaped alley known as Gickelsberg leads from here to the **Schülerturm**, beyond which is Am Zwinger, a rustic looking potholed road which leads west past the

Gerberbastei (now the youth hostel) to the **Nikolaiturm**. Alongside the latter is the **Nikolaikirche**, once the church of the Catholic Sorbs, but a ruin since its destruction in the Thirty Years' War. It's a peaceful spot, now used as a cemetery, commanding a fine view over the Spree.

An even better vantage point is the terrace of **Schloss Ortenburg** further west. The present castle, replacing a much earlier stronghold of the Margraves of Meissen, was erected in the late fifteenth century by order of Matthis Corvinus, King of Hungary and Bohemia, who is depicted seated between crown-bearing angels in the nine-metres-high memorial on the entrance gateway. Later additions include the playful Renaissance gables and the plain Baroque wing now housing the **Sorbisches Museum** (Mon, Wed & Fri–Sun 9.30am–12.30pm & 1.30–4pm, Tues & Thurs 9.30am–12.30pm & 1.30–5pm; DM1), documenting the festivals, costumes and literature of the Sorbs. If you've got time to spare, it's well worth descending to the Spree and crossing the footbridge to a belvedere offering a view of the Schloss and the town.

Following Osterweg southwards, you pass the **Mühlenturm** en route to the **Michaeliskirche**, the parish church of the Sorb Protestants, which forms a picturesque corner in conjunction with the **Alte Wasserkunst** (May–Sept daily 9am–5pm; DM1), a mid-sixteenth-century water tower which was operational until 1963. Inside is a small museum outlining the technical particulars of its machinery, while the viewing platform at the top offers yet another outlook on the valley. On the bank of the Spree below is the **Hexenhäuschen** (Witches' House), the only old fisherman's house to have withstood all the fires which destroyed its counterparts – the belief that the inhabitants must therefore have been possessed of magical powers led to its present nickname. Finally, the wonderful full-frontal view of Bautzen that appears in all the tourist brochures can be seen for real by walking a short distance south to **Friedensbrücke**.

Practicalities

Bautzen's **tourist office** is at Fleischmarkt 2 (Mon 9am–1pm, Tues–Fri 9am–5pm; May–Sept also Sat 9am–noon; ☎42016). They should be able to find you a **private room**, though the provision in the town itself is relatively meagre. Other possibilities are the aforementioned **youth hostel**, Am Zwinger 1 (☎44045), and a couple of **hotels** – *Weisses Ross*, Äussere Lauenstr. 11, whose rates start at DM30, and *Lubin*, Wendischer Graben 20 (☎511114), which costs upwards of DM50 per person. There's also a **campiste** (☎41113) by the reservoir to the north of town. As so often in eastern Germany, the best reasonably priced place to **eat** and **drink** is the *Ratskeller*, Innere Lauenstr. 1. However, it's worth trying the *Sorbisches Café*, Postplatz 2, for local specialities (it serves full meals), while a real oddity is *Kaniga*, just east of the Reichenturm at Kurt-Pchalek-Str. 1, whose entire menu consists of different sorts of rabbit dishes. The *Deutsch–Sorbisches Volkstheater*, Seminarstr. 12, is the only bilingual **theatre** in the country, with performances in Sorb alternating with those in German.

Zittau and around

Some 65km from Bautzen, near the meeting point of the frontiers with Czechoslovakia and Poland at the extreme southeastern corner of Saxony, is the town of ZITTAU. Despite its industrial infrastructure, it's a well-preserved historic town, but is best-known as the gateway to a wooded upland area, the **Zittau mountains** (*Zittauer Gebirge*). The wild scenery, characterised by dramatic rock formations, is of the type more associated with Germany than Czechoslovakia, a reminder that the region was once part of the old kingdom of Bohemia, with Zittau itself having been founded in the early thirteenth century by one of its monarchs, Otakar I.

Around town

Zittau's Altstadt is a circular area bounded by the green boulevards which have replaced the dismantled fortifications. With its spacious squares and innumerable fountains, it has a vaguely Mediterranean look to it, which seems more than a little incongruous, given its volatile Central European climate, though at least it has lost the ghost town feel it had after closing time in GDR days. Coming from the Hauptbahnhof, which lies due north of the centre, Strasse der Einheit and Bautzener Strasse lead to the **Johanniskirche**, whose present sombre Neoclassical aspect, with a grand facade and a high, flat-ceilinged interior, is due to plans provided by Schinkel. In summer months (no set times), it's often possible to climb the tower for a view over the town. Across from the church stands the oldest of the town's surviving houses, the sixteenth-century **Dornspachhaus**, named after the burgomaster who lived there.

Just to the south is the Platz der Jugend, which features a fountain dedicated to Mars, an old pharmacy, and a number of Baroque and Rococo mansions. To the east, it merges seamlessly with Rathausplatz, dominated by the **Rathaus** itself, a Schinkel-designed reinterpretation of an Italian Renaissance *palazzo*. Beyond lies August-Bebel-Platz, an enormous elongated open space. It has no fewer than three fountains: from south to north these respectively depict the Good Samaritan, Hercules and a group of swans. The **Marstall** in the middle of the square was originally a sixteenth-century warehouse for storing salt, but was transformed into stables a couple of centuries later, when the colossal mansard roof was added.

Off the northwestern end of August-Bebel-Platz is Klosterplatz, named after the Franciscan monastery that now houses the **Stadtmuseum** (Mon, Tues & Thurs–Sat 10am–noon & 2–4pm, Wed 10am–noon & 2–6pm, Sun 10am–noon; DM1). The cellars, with an intact drinking well and a frightening display of torture instruments, are the highlight of the displays. On the same square are the town's finest fountain, the **Grüner Born**, which shelters under a superb wrought-iron canopy, and a gabled Renaissance mansion, the **Heffterhaus**.

Practicalities

The **tourist office** (Mon & Wed 9am–5pm, Tues & Thurs 9am–6pm, Fri 9am–3pm; ☎3986) is at Rathausplatz 6. They can find you a **private room** here or in one of the nearby villages. Alternatively, there are several **hotels** – *Volkshaus*, Äussere Weberstr. 6 (☎3044), *Stadt Rumberg*, Äussere Weberstr. 23 (☎5547), *Schwarzer Bär*, Karl-Marx-Platz 12 (☎2366), and *Weisses Ross*, Oststr. 2 (☎2859); all currently cost around DM30 per person, but prices are liable to increase. **Restaurants** include *Klosterstübel*, Johannisstr. 4, *Dreiländereck*, Bautzener Str. 9, and *Gewandhauskeller*, Rathausplatz 14.

Into the Zittau mountains by steam train

Most visitors to Zittau come to ride the *Bimmelbahn*, a **narrow-gauge steam railway** which travels from the Hauptbahnhof into the mountains to the south. This was earmarked for closure a few months before the *Wende*, as a seam of lignite, the GDR's favourite but most environmentally damaging fuel, was discovered in the area; national unification has won it a reprieve, thanks to the nostalgia of West Germans for something they had destroyed in their own country.

Kurort Oybin and Kurort Jonsdorf

After 9km, there's a fork in the *Bimmelbahn* at BERTSDORF; one part of the train continues a further 3km south to **KURORT OYBIN**, a quiet little health resort centred on the **Bergkirche**, a perfectly preserved example of Baroque at its most rustic. Towering above the village is **Berg Oybin**, on which stand a ruined castle and monastery founded by Emperor Charles IV in his capacity as King of Bohemia, and built by masons of the great Parler workshop of Prague, but destroyed by lightning in the sixteenth century. A great deal of the monastic church still survives; given its semi-overgrown appearance and theatrical backdrop, it's hardly surprising that it was a favourite subject with painters of the Romantic movement.

The other section of the *Bimmelbahn* branches 4km southwest from Bertsdorf to **KURORT JONSDORF**. It's far less attractive than its neighbour but has an attractive open-air theatre, and is an equally good base for **hiking** in the range, which is peppered with marked trails, some of them closely hugging the frontier. Westerners were unable to stay in either resort during GDR days; now there's a wide choice of accommodation, ranging from a luxury hotel in each via plenty of private rooms to Jonsdorf's **youth hostel** at Hainstr. 14 (✆220).

Gross Schönau

The postcard-pretty town of **GROSS SCHÖNAU** lies in the valley of the River Mandau immediately below the Zittau Mountains; it's about 9km northwest of Jonsdorf and can be reached by mainline train from Zittau. For centuries, weaving was the foundation of the local economy, with the production of damask a speciality. A surprisingly entertaining **Damask- und Heimatmuseum** (guided tours Mon–Sat 9–11am & 2–4pm, 1st Sun in month 2–4pm; DM2) has been set up in the early nineteenth-century mansion of a factory owner overlooking the river at Schenaustr. 3. In addition to demonstrations of the old looms (with explanations in English on request), you are also shown displays on the folklore of the region.

Gross Schönau has a fine ensemble of historic houses, including the best examples of a vernacular style of building peculiar to Upper Lusatia, a hybrid between half-timbering and wood panelling known as an *Umgebindehaus*. The *Gaststätte* next to the museum is a recommendable place to **eat**, while the only **campsite** in the Zittau Mountains is located by an artificial lake a couple of kilometres out of town on the road to Jonsdorf.

Görlitz

GÖRLITZ, the largest town of Upper Lusatia and Germany's easternmost point, lies 45km east of Bautzen and 34km north of Zittau. Travelling by train from the latter has a certain curiosity value (though it's no longer the bureaucratic comic opera it was during the Communist era): the line threads its way along the Neisse valley, skipping from one bank to the other and therefore in and out of Poland, as the river, along with the Oder, was designated as the limit of German territory by the victorious Allies in 1945. One of the consequences of the Oder–Neisse border was that Görlitz found itself divided between two countries – the historic part of the city lies on the west bank and therefore remained German, while the suburbs opposite became the Polish town of ZGORZELEC.

Perhaps that's an appropriate fate for a true Central European city which doesn't easily fit into any nationalist framework. Slav by origin, Görlitz has been dominated by Germans since the thirteenth century, but belonged to Bohemia for much of its history; it fell to Saxony in the Thirty Years' War, but following its annexation by Prussia in 1815, was incorporated into Silesia. It now stands as one of the few reminders of a province that the Germans have finally accepted is lost to them forever.

Around town

Wartime damage to Görlitz, whose ensemble of Renaissance and Baroque houses is unsurpassed in Germany, was minimal. The Communist authorities put the entire city centre under a preservation order; thus, though it has suffered badly from pollution, it will no doubt soon assume its rightful place as one of the most beautiful medium-sized towns in the country.

Marienplatz and Demianiplatz

From the Hauptbahnhof, which lies southwest of the Altstadt, it's about a ten-minute walk straight ahead to Marienplatz, dominated by the very blackened **Frauenkirche**, the late Gothic church of the now disappeared hospital and poorhouse, whose most notable feature is the double portal topped by an Annunciation group. Close by is the **Centrum Warenhaus**, a large Jugendstil department store which has miraculously defied the retail trade's mania for perpetual modification, surviving as an intact period-piece, both in its statue-lined exterior, and in its steel-framed galleried interior. Just to the north is the **Dicker Turm** (Fat Tower), a cylindrical structure of the early four-teenth century, adorned with a prominent sandstone relief of Görlitz's coat of arms and crowned by a graceful Renaissance cupola.

Following either of the alleys to the left, you come to Demianiplatz, the first in a row of three squares at the heart of the town. On the south side is the Neoclassical **Theater**, now named in honour of Gerhard Hauptmann, the Nobel Prize-winning Realist writer whose attachment to his native Silesia was such that he continued to live there even after it was incorporated into Poland. His intense early drama *The Weavers*, set against the background of a heroic but inevitably futile mid-nineteenth-century uprising by the Silesian weavers against the mill-owners, was a theatrical sensation, gaining its reputa-tion as the first "Socialist" play by having a collective rather than a single hero.

The west side of the square is framed by the **Kaisertrutz** (Tues & Wed 10am–1pm & 2–6pm, Thurs–Sun 10am–1pm & 2–4pm; DM2), a circular double bastion from the middle of last century, encasing its fifteenth-century predecessor. Inside is part of the local museum, including sections on medieval religious art, Upper Lusatian painters of the last two centuries and the history of the city, though the curious building is itself the main attraction. The original formed a defensive pair with the tall **Reichenbacher Turm** (same times, May–Oct only; DM1) opposite, whose lower storey, culminating in the sentry gallery, dates back to the fourteenth century; the cylindrical upper section was added a hundred years later, and the whole finally topped off with a Baroque turret. A collection of arms and armour is housed inside; you can also climb to the summit for a fine view over the city.

Obermarkt and Untermarkt

Demianiplatz opens out to the east into the long oblong **Obermarkt**, the main market square, which is aligned with a colourful array of Baroque houses. At the northeastern corner stands the **Dreifaltigkeitskirche**, formerly the church of a Franciscan monas-tery. Its somewhat gloomy exterior appearance is redeemed by a splendidly musty interior with several fine late Gothic furnishings, including a set of richly carved choir stalls, a touching *Holy Sepulchre* and a carved retable to the Virgin. Underneath the **Mönch** (Monk), as the church's tall, curiously thin-looking tower is popularly known, is the **Kunstbrunnen**, a Renaissance figure bearing the arms of Electoral Saxony. Bruderstrasse, which prolongs the Obermarkt to the east, is lined with some of the town's finest mansions, including the **Schönhof** at no. 8, the work of Wendel Roskopf, leading local architect of the Renaissance period.

Downhill is the **Unter Markt**, one of Germany's most imposing squares, which is built up in the middle, on the normal Central European model. Best of the many mansions are nos. 2–5 along the south side, which spawn the late Gothic and early Renaissance and are collectively known as the **Lange Laube**; they belonged to the richest merchants and officials, and characteristically have bright vaulted entrance halls. It's particularly worth peeking into no. 5, whose original murals have survived. Also of special note are the Renaissance **Ratsapotheke** at no. 24, with its elaborate sundial; the **Flüsterbogen** (Whispering Arch) at no. 22; the large **Waage** (Weigh House) in the central block; and the early Baroque **Alte Börse**, the merchant's hall.

The **Städtisches Museum** (same times as the Kaisertrutz; DM2) occupies a Baroque mansion just off the east side of Untermarkt at Neissestr. 30; it displays fine and decorative arts from the Renaissance to Biedermeier, along with material on Upper Lusatian folklore, and documentation on **Jakob Böhme**, the city's most distinguished son, the man regarded as both the first true German philosopher and the last of the medieval mystics and alchemists. Alongside at no. 29 is one of Görlitz's most unusual buildings, the **Biblisches Haus**; it dates from about 1570 and is adorned with little reliefs of scenes from the Old and New Testaments – a sure sign that the Reformation had taken root here, as religious depictions had hitherto been banned from secular buildings. Peterstrasse, which leads north from Untermarkt, is another impressive street; take a look inside no. 14, whose amazing stairway seems to defy gravity.

The northern quarters

At the end of Peterstrasse is the **Peterskirche**, a five-aisled Flamboyant Gothic hall church with whitewashed exterior walls, a sturdy pair of towers crowned by fantastical nineteenth-century steeples, and a crypt which is itself of church-like dimensions. To the south side is the thirteenth-century **Renthaus**, the oldest house in the city; the terrace beyond preserves remnants of the former walls and commands a view over the Neisse to Poland. A few minutes' walk to the northeast lies the **Nikolaifriedhof**, a hillside cemetery with many elaborate tombstones, including that of Jakob Böhme.

East along Steinweg, you come to Görlitz's most intriguing sight, the **Heiliges Grab** (Tues–Sun 11am–1pm; DM0.50). The only complete (and reasonably authentic) medieval reproduction of the Holy Places of Jerusalem, it has its origins in a true German version of the tale of Romeo and Juliet. Georg Emmerich, a rich young citizen, was prevented from marrying his beloved, as her parents belonged to the opposing political party. Accordingly, he went on pilgrimage to the Holy Land, where he made plans of the Biblical sites which he commissioned Conrad Pflüger, the architect of the Peterskirche, to build on a site meant to resemble the Garden of Gethsemane. You first visit the **Kapelle zum Heiligen Kreuz**, a two-storey chapel whose crypt is named in honour of Adam, the upper part after Golgotha, symbolising the tradition that Christ was crucified on the site of Adam's grave. Alongside is the tiny **Salbhaus**, behind whose wrought-iron gates is a sculpture of the Virgin Mary lamenting over Jesus's dead body. Finally comes the **Grabkapelle**, which is of special interest as being a far more accurate, if miniaturised, version of the original, than its much-altered counterpart in Jerusalem. It's an elegant building in its own right; particularly outstanding is the turret, a skilful fusion of European and Middle Eastern architecture. Incidentally, in case you're still wondering, Georg didn't get the girl – but did become Burgomaster of Görlitz, and thus powerful and rich enough to build the Heiliges Grab.

Practicalities

Görlitz's **tourist office** (Mon–Fri 9am–5pm; April–Sept also Sat 9am–noon; ☎5391) occupies a handsome Baroque mansion at Obermarkt 29. They have plenty of **private rooms** on offer, generally at around DM20–25. Cheapest **hotel** is *Görlitzer Hof*, Berliner Str. 43 (☎4690), with singles from DM30, doubles from DM46; there are several others directly across from the Hauptbahnhof, but their future is uncertain. Somewhat more upmarket are *Monopol*, Postplatz 9 (☎5667), with singles DM45, doubles from DM75; and *Stadt Dresden*, Berliner Str. 37 (☎5263), with singles DM52, doubles DM94. Top of the range is *Goldener Baum*, in one of the city's most beautiful houses at Untermarkt 4 (6268), whose rates begin at DM55 per person. The **youth hostel**, which has a good central location at Goethestr. 17 (☎5510), also has rooms which can be let as doubles or triples. By far the best place to **eat** and **drink** in the city centre is the vaulted cellar restaurant in the aforementioned *Goldener Baum*; other possibilities include *Café Schwibbogen*, Briderstr. 17, and the fish specialist *Gastmahl des Meeres*, Struvestr. 2.

travel details

Trains

From Dresden to Meissen (every 30min; 45min); Pirna/Bad Schandau (every 30min; 30min/1hr); Bautzen (hourly; 1hr); Zittau (10; 2hr), Görlitz (hourly; 2hr); Freiberg (every 30min; 50min); Chemnitz (hourly; 1 hr 30min); Leipzig (hourly; 2hr).

From Leipzig to Colditz/Rochlitz (10 daily; 1hr 20min/1hr 40min); Torgau (frequent; 1hr); Zwickau (hourly; 1hr 30min); Chemnitz (15 daily; 1hr 30min/2hr); Plauen (15; 2hr).

From Chemnitz to Freiberg (every 30min; 50min); Zwickau (hourly; 1hr); Annaberg-Buchholz (10 daily; 2hr); Rochlitz (5 daily; 1hr 15min).

From Zwickau to Plauen (hourly; 1hr).

From Görlitz to Bautzen (hourly; 1hr), Zittau (10; 1hr).

PART THREE

THE

CONTEXTS

THE HISTORICAL FRAMEWORK

To think of a continuous German history is impossible, since there was no single nation called Germany until 1871, and even then it was not strictly speaking a country, but an empire made up of a number of sovereign states. Nevertheless, a recognisable German culture can be traced through the history of a large and disparate group of territories and traditions.

THE BEGINNINGS

From around the eighth century BC, the bulk of present-day Germany was inhabited by **Celtic peoples**, who established the first permanent settlements. Warlike, nomadic Germanic tribes gradually appeared further north and began pushing their way into the Celtic lands. Their loose structure later made them awkward opponents to the expanding **Roman Empire**, which decided to use the natural boundaries of the Rivers Rhine and Danube as the limit of their territory: attempts to push eastwards were finally abandoned after a crushing defeat in the Teutoburger Wald in 9 AD.

A number of towns founded by the Romans – Trier, Regensburg, Augsburg, Mainz and Cologne – were to be the main bases of urban settlement for the next millennium. **Christianity** was introduced under Emperor Constantine, and a bishopric (the first north of the Alps) was established in Trier in 314.

At the beginning of the fifth century Germany was overrun by the Huns, an action which precipitated the indigenous Saxons to invade England. Gradually the **Franks**, who had been based in what is now Belgium, began to assert themselves over the other Germanic peoples, particularly towards the end of the fifth century under King Clovis, who established the **Merovingian** dynasty and built up a powerful Rhenish state. In time, the Merovingians were supplanted by their former henchmen, the **Carolingians**, with the help of papal support. The new dynasty was bent on expansion, and saw the benefits of involving the Church in its plans. Missionaries – the most influential of whom was the English-born St Boniface – were recruited to undertake mass conversion campaigns among rival tribes.

Under **Charlemagne**, who succeeded to the throne in 768, the fortunes of the Franks went from strength to strength. A series of campaigns saw them stretch their power base from the North Sea to Rome, and from the Pyrenees to the River Elbe. In the context of western Europe, only Britain plus the southern parts of Spain and Italy lay beyond their control. A power-sharing structure for Europe, in which the pope and the king of the Germans would be the dominant forces, was agreed. On Christmas Day 800, Charlemagne was anointed Emperor in Rome, giving him the official status of heir to the Caesars. Though the name was only coined much later, this brought into existence the concept of the **Holy Roman Empire**, which was to last for the next thousand years. This gave the German king considerable power over Italian internal affairs, while the Church's influence in matters of state was similarly assured.

When Charlemagne died, however, the empire began to crack because of its very size. In 843, by the **Treaty of Verdun**, it was split into a Germanic Eastern Europe and a Latin Western Europe, thus sharply delineating the French and Germans for the first time. The first king of the newly formed German eastern empire was **Ludwig the German**. Under his rule the Germanic people became more closely defined, with a specific culture of their own – still with many disparate regions but recognisably made up of the same peoples. When the last of Charlemagne's descendants died in 911, rulership passed to the Saxon King Henry, bringing the Carolingian era to an end.

THE BUILDING OF A NEW EMPIRE

In the mid-tenth century the second Saxon monarch, **Otto the Great**, was faced with the problem of the growing power of the hereditary duchies which posed a threat to the unity of the empire. In order to curb this, he strengthened his alliance with the papacy. The Church was given grants of land, coupled with temporal powers of jurisdiction over them, thus creating the basis for subsequent ecclesiastical dominance over much of the country by a series of prince-bishoprics. In 962, he was crowned **Holy Roman Emperor**, firmly establishing himself as the main ruler in the Christian world. In many respects, this marks a second foundation of the curious dichotomy that characterised the Holy Roman Empire; from then on, only kings of Germany could gain the title of Roman Emperor, and it was only the pope who could grant this title.

Imperial interference in Church affairs from then on was severely curtailed, as was the centralised power of the emperor, as the nobility were released by the pope from their vows of allegiance to any secular authority. They soon made their own demands, the most important of which was that emperors should no longer be hereditary rulers, but elected by a council of princes.

By the twelfth century, most of the powerful **dynasties** which were to dominate German politics at both local and national level for hundreds of years to come had appeared. There was an intense feud between the two most powerful, the **Hohenstaufens** and **Welfs**, which was to continue for centuries, particularly in Italy. The Hohenstaufens, until they died out, managed to keep the upper hand, holding on to the office of Holy Roman Emperor for well over a century. **Frederick Barbarossa**, best known as an enthusiastic Crusader in the Holy Land, was their most successful ruler.

By the mid-thirteenth century the nation's boundaries began to be pushed increasingly eastwards, following a policy begun by Otto the Great. Impetus for this came from many sources; it's particularly associated with the **Knights of the Teutonic Order**, which turned its attentions towards the Christianisation of

Eastern Europe. By the early fourteenth century, they had conquered much of the Baltic (notably the area known as Prussia) and repopulated the land with German peasants. Subsequently, they grew rich on their control of the highly profitable grain trade.

THE MIDDLE AGES

In the fourteenth century, a number of significant changes were made to the structure of the Holy Roman Empire. The **Golden Bull** of 1356 finally established the method for choosing the monarch. This fixed the electoral college at the traditional number of seven, with three **Electors** drawn from the ecclesiastical sphere (the Archbishops of Cologne, Mainz and Trier) and four from different ranks of the nobility (the King of Bohemia, the Duke of Saxony, the Margrave of Brandenburg and the Count Palatine of the Rhine).

From then on, these seven princes were tremendously powerful grandees – they had the right to construct castles, mint their own coinage, impose tolls and act as judges in all disputes, with no right of appeal. Oddly enough, the title of emperor almost invariably went to a candidate outside this group. Increasingly, it was conferred on a member of the **Habsburg** dynasty who had built up Austria into the most powerful of the German states.

The Church's residual power over internal German affairs was killed off by the **Great Schism** of 1378–1417, when rival popes held court in Rome and Avignon. By this time, the social structure was undergoing changes that had far-reaching effects. The most important was the growth of **towns** at strategic points and along important trading routes. Initially, these were under patrician control. However, merchants and craftsmen organised themselves into guilds which gradually wrested control of civic life and laid the foundations for a capitalist economy.

Most important towns gained the status of **Free Imperial City**, which meant they were independent city-states, responsible only to the emperor. Their prosperity was greatly enhanced by the ruinous Hundred Years' War between France and England, which enabled them to snap up diverted trade to and from the Mediterranean. Though in many ways in competition with each other, the leadership of the towns realised they also had common cause. This led to the foundation of various trading and defence leagues. Of particular importance was the north German **Hanseatic League**, founded in Lübeck, which successfully combated piracy, and led not only to German economic domination of the Baltic and North Sea, but to increased political power as well, with the establishment of German communities in Scandinavia and all along the opposite coast as far as Estonia.

The **bubonic plague** swept Europe in the fourteenth century, wiping out a quarter of the German population. In all probability, the plague was introduced by merchants returning from Asia, but a different scapegoat had to be found, and the **Jews**, who lived in segregated settlements around the towns, readily fitted the bill. Jews had lived in Europe since the tenth century, but their place had never been an easy one, with their close-knit and separate communities giving rise to popular suspicion and prejudice. Excluded from guilds and trades, they took up the only occupation forbidden to Christians: money-lending — a necessary but hated service that did nothing to endear them to the locals. **Pogroms** therefore frequently occurred.

The fifteenth century saw the Habsburgs establish themselves firmly as the driving force in high politics, holding on to the office of Holy Roman Emperor from 1432 until its abolition nearly four hundred years later. **Maximilian I** acceded to the title in 1493, and embarked on a policy of making his family the most powerful not just in Germany, but in all of Europe. His own wedding to Mary of Burgundy gained him the Netherlands; a series of astute dynastic marriages involving his relatives led to Spain, Hungary and Bohemia all coming under Habsburg control. However, he antagonised the members of the Swiss Confederation, which broke away from the empire to become a separate state in 1499.

THE REFORMATION AND AFTER

In order to cash in on popular fear, the Church demanded money from the faithful to ensure salvation of their souls, and a lucrative trade in **indulgences** was established, whereby people could buy absolution of their sins. Bishops across the land acted as agents, and the papal coffers filled up to finance the build-

ing of St Peter's and many other great sacred buildings.

Discontent with the Church was particularly widespread within Germany, given the Church's dual role within society and the fact that territories under the control of religious office-holders tended to be particularly harshly run. Thus it was hardly surprising that it was here that the full-frontal assault on the Church's traditional powers began.

The attack was led by a man of burning religious convictions, the Augustinian monk **Martin Luther**, who had been appointed to the influential position of Professor of Theology at the University of Wittenberg. Believing that the Church was corrupt and had totally lost its way, Luther focused his attentions on the problem of **salvation**, finding in the Bible that Man justifies himself by faith alone. This meant that he could play no part in his own salvation; therefore the trade in indulgences was a total fraud. On the eve of All Saints' Day, 1517, he nailed his **95 theses** to the door of the court church in Wittenberg. This was in fact the normal way of inviting academic discussion, but it was seen as a deliberately provocative act and is now considered the official **beginning of the Reformation**.

In time Luther widened his attack, denouncing the centralised power of the Pope, the privileged position of priests as intercessors between God and the faithful, and the doctrine of transubstantiation, which maintained that the bread and wine used in the sacrament of the Eucharist physically turned into Christ's body and blood.

However, Luther's arguments might have had as little impact as any other scholarly dispute, or led to his immediate execution as a heretic, had not the curious power structure in Germany dealt him an amazing piece of good fortune. The death of Maximilian I in 1519 led to a bizarre **European-wide power struggle** for the crown of the Holy Roman Empire. Francis I of France decided to stake a claim for the title, in order to stop the unhealthy concentration of power which would ensue if victory went to the Habsburg candidate, Charles I of Spain. In order to stop this interference from abroad, the Pope had to keep the electors sweet, even suggesting one of their number, Luther's patron Elector Frederick the Wise of Saxony, as a compromise candidate.

After much bribery by the two main contenders, the Spanish king duly won the election unanimously and took office as Emperor Charles V. However, he immediately became embroiled in a war with France. As a result, the powerful princes of the Holy Roman Empire seized this chance to establish a far greater degree of independence. Many of them saw the religious struggle as a convenient cloak for their ambitions. Luther was excommunicated in 1520, but still had the right, as a citizen of the empire, to have a hearing before an Imperial Diet. This was hastily convened at Worms the following year, and, though Luther was branded an outlaw and his books were ordered to be burned, he was given a safe haven at the Wartburg castle in Thuringia, under the protection of Duke Frederick. There he **tarnslated the Bible into German**, thus making it accessible to the common man for the first time; this work is also seen as the foundation stone of the modern German language.

Luther's ideas spread like wildfire throughout society, greatly aided by the fact that books could now be produced cheaply and quickly, thanks to the printing revolution launched by the German inventor **Johannes Gutenberg** during the previous century. They found a ready market among the oppressed classes, who took the attacks on Church authority as invitations to attack authority in general.

This formed one of the causes of the **Peasants' Revolt** of 1524–25, which brought wholesale destruction of monasteries and castles. Poorly armed, organised and led, it was brutally crushed by the princely armies. To the dismay of the rebels, Luther aligned himself on the side of worldly authority, arguing that it was God's will that there should be different strata in society; equality was only for the hereafter. Thus, the Reformation progressed as a revolution controlled from above, setting the tone for German history for centuries to come.

In 1529, the representatives of six principalities and fourteen Free Imperial Cities which supported Luther met at Speyer, where the name **Protestant** came to be used for the first time. The following year, Charles V convened a Diet at Augsburg in an attempt to defuse the growing crisis. However, he was confronted by a closely argued definition of the Reformers' position, thereafter known as the **Confession of Augsburg**, which was drawn up by Luther's indispensible sidekick, the brilliant scholar Philipp Melanchthon. This set the seal not only on the division of the Western Church, but also on the effective division of Germany into a plethora of small states.

So many states had joined the Protestant cause by 1555 that Charles V had to admit defeat, abdicating in order to retire to a Spanish monastery. He was succeeded by his brother Ferdinand, who almost immediately signed the **Peace of Augsburg**, an historic agreement that institutionalised religious tolerance, leaving the decision as to the form of religion practised in each state firmly in the hands of its secular rulers. Though a measure of considerable significance, it was in effect a carve-up between the Catholics and Lutherans at the expense of more radical Protestant groups.

THE STRUGGLE FOR RELIGIOUS SUPREMACY

After Luther's death in 1546, the Catholics began to make something of a comeback after the reforms thrashed out at the Council of Trent launched the **Counter-Reformation**. Radical Protestantism was also given a fillip by Melanchthon's shift away from central Lutheran doctrines to more extreme solutions.

A Catholic attack on the Protestant Bavarian town of Donauwörth in 1608 led to the formation of the **Protestant Union**, an armed alliance under the leadership of the Palatinate. The **Catholic League** was set up in opposition by the Bavarians the following year, meaning that there was now a straight division of the country into two hostile camps. Meanwhile, the way central authority in Germany had collapsed was cruelly exposed by the weak 36-year reign of Rudolf II, who chose to govern from the very fringe of the empire. His court in Prague is chiefly remembered for its bizarre erotic practices, and he himself eventually became insane.

As it happened, this same city was to see the beginning of the great trial of strength between the two faiths. In 1618, the youthful Count Palatine Friedrich V usurped the crown of Bohemia, which itself was an elected office, thus seemingly ensuring a Protestant majority in the next imperial election. Unfortunately for him, he lost both his titles a year later, and had by then set in train the complicated series of religious and dynastic conflicts commonly known as the **Thirty Years' War**.

Much of the German countryside was laid waste, towns were pillaged, and there was mass rape and slaughter, at the end of which the total population of the country may have been reduced by as much as a third. Initially, the Catholic League, commanded by the brutal Johann Tilly, held the upper hand, but first Denmark, then Sweden intervened, fearing for both their independence and their Protestant faith. The Swedes, led by King Gustavus II Adolphus, had their greatest moment of triumph on the European stage, defeating Tilly and overrunning the country, thus briefly rising to the rank of a major power. Spain intervened on behalf of its Habsburg cousins, while Catholic France supported the Protestants, on the grounds that their faith was a lesser evil than the threatened Habsburg hegemony over Europe.

From 1643, concerted attempts were made to end the war, with the Catholics meeting in Münster, the Protestants in Osnabrück. The negotiations are generally seen as the beginnings of modern diplomacy; they culminated five years later in the signing of the **Peace of Westphalia**. While the ending of the messy conflicts was a major achievement in itself, for Germany the peace treaty was as disastrous as the war itself; the Holy Roman Empire was killed off in all but name, with the emperor reduced to a figurehead.

Real power was concentrated in a **plethora of states**, numbering some 300 principalities, plus over 1000 other territories, some of them minute – a system which could hardly have been better designed to waste resources and stunt economic and political development. Germany ceased to be a factor of importance on the European stage.

THE RISE OF PRUSSIA

In the course of the late seventeenth century and eighteenth century, almost all the petty German princes adopted an **absolutist** system of government, based on the divine right of rulers. Only a few managed to rise above the general level of mediocrity; one of these was the House of Welf, which made an astonishing comeback after centuries of confinement to their Lower Saxon heartlands. As a result of clever politicking, the **Hanoverian** branch of the family gained the British crown in 1714 and maintained a royal union until 1837.

Within the Holy Roman Empire itself, **Austria** at first maintained her dominance, with the Habsburgs holding on to the imperial title, for what it was worth. The country received a severe jolt when the Turks reached the gates of Vienna in 1683, but after the enemy was beaten back, the way was cleared for Austria to build up an empire in the Balkans. As German-speaking influence spread eastwards, so the western flank become vulnerable. The **French**, like the Romans before them, saw the Rhine as the natural limit of their territory. They formally annexed Alsace and Strasbourg in 1681, then laid claim to the Palatinate in a series of bloody campaigns between 1688 and 1697.

By then, a new power had arisen in north-eastern Germany in the shape of **Brandenburg-Prussia**. In 1415, the old frontier district of Brandenburg was given to the ambitious **Hohenzollern** family, whose attempts to gain power at the heart of the empire had met with no success. Since 1525, the family had also held the Baltic territory known as Prussia, which lay outside the Holy Roman Empire and thus was not subject to any of its rules. One of these forbade princes from promoting themselves to royal titles: in 1701, Friedrich III defied this with impunity by having himself crowned as King of Prussia. The Habsburgs duly turned a blind eye to this in order to gain Hohenzollern support in the **War of the Spanish Succession**, which broke out as a result of rival Austrian and French claimants for the throne of Spain.

Throughout the eighteenth century, Prussia was built up as a strongly centralised state, based in Berlin. There was a tight administrative structure, but it became associated above all with **militarism**. It was a second Sparta, described with some justification as not a state with an army, but an army with a state: at times, an amazing two-thirds of national revenue was spent on the military. The other dominant force in society was the **Junker** class, landowners who ran huge estates in which the labourers were treated as little more than serfs.

Prussia's rise to the rank of a major European power was achieved under **Frederick the Great**, who came to the throne in 1740. A Francophile and epitome of the enlightened despot, Frederick softened his country's rough-hewn image by introducing a few liberal reforms at home, and developed a cultured courtly life. However, his main concern was expansion by military force, and he used an old Prussian claim on Silesia to extract that territory from Austria. In revenge, the Habsburgs launched the Seven Years' War in 1756, thereby hoping to annihilate Prussia as a potential rival; in this, they had the full military backing of the two other great continental powers, France and Russia, whereas Frederick had only the tacit support of Britain and Hannover to fall back on.

Within three years, the highly rated Prussian troops seemed to have overreached themselves. They were given an unexpected reprieve when the Austrians and Russians fell out; new recruits were thrown into the conflict, eventually achieving an incredible turn-around in fortunes, in the process establishing Prussia as a force of the first rank.

THE NAPOLEONIC PERIOD AND ITS AFTERMATH

Ironically, the first steps towards unifying Germany came as a result of the expansionist aims of revolutionary France. By the War of the First Coalition of 1792–97, the left bank of the Rhine fell under French control. However, it was only with the advent of the dictator **Napoleon Bonaparte** that radical changes were made. Following the defeat of Austria in 1802 in the War of the Second Coalition (in which Prussia tactfully remained aloof), he decided to completely re-order the German map, which he rightly saw as anachronistic.

Napoleon created a series of buffer states; Bavaria, Württemberg and Saxony were raised to the rank of kingdoms, while Baden and Hessen-Darmstadt became Grand Duchies. In 1806, during the War of the Third Coalition, the Holy Roman Empire was officially abolished and the German satellite states gradually began to remove economic, religious and servile restrictions, developing into societies which were liberal by German standards .

The same year, Prussia suffered a series of humiliating defeats; Berlin was occupied and the country forced to sign away half its territory and population. Thereafter, it was forced to mend its ways: serfdom was abolished, and its cities were allowed to develop their own municipal government. In the event, Prussia's

humiliation was short-lived, and it soared in international prestige as a result of its key role at the **Battle of Waterloo** in 1815, when Napoleon's over-ambitious plans for the total subjugation of Europe were finally put to rest.

The **Congress of Vienna**, which met the same year to determine the structure of post-Napoleonic Europe, established Prussian dominance in German affairs. Westphalia and the Rhineland were added to its territories, meaning that it now stretched all the way from the French border to the River Memel, interrupted only by a few enclaves. Otherwise, much of the Napoleonic re-organisation of the Holy Roman Empire was ratified, leaving 39 independent states: still far too many, but a major step forward nonetheless. A German Confederation was established, with each state represented in the Frankfurt-based Diet, which, however, had no effective power.

TOWARDS GERMAN UNIFICATION

Whereas the main political forces in German society in the aftermath of the Congress of Vienna were still staunchly conservative, the accelerating **Industrial Revolution** was resulting in radical economic and social changes. This closely followed the British lead, but profited by learning from the pioneering country's mistakes. The first German railway was established in 1835, and industrial production advanced in leaps and bounds. Thanks to its rich mineral deposits, the dominant centre for industry was the Rhine-Ruhr area, which had recently been allocated to Prussia. In 1834, Prussia's increasingly dominant role within the German nation was underlined by the establishment of a customs union, known as the **Zollverein**.

The Industrial Revolution led to a whole **new social order**, with wage-earning workers and an emergent bourgeoisie. Both groups were quick to agitate for their interests – the workers for better working conditions and the bourgeoisie for political representation. Meanwhile the large peasantry was still living in abject poverty and under almost feudal conditions, which pressed hard during the failed harvests of the late 1840s. Social unrest was inevitable, and violence erupted both in the countryside and the cities, causing ever more reactionary policies from the land-owning elite with the political power.

In 1848, there were uprisings all over Europe. This forced the Prussian king to allow elections to the **National Assembly** in Frankfurt, thereby hoping to nip republican and socialist aspirations in the bud. For the first time, an opportunity was presented to found a liberal tradition in the country, but it was completely muffed. The bourgeois members of the Assembly were much too keen to establish the new-found status of their own social groups to attempt any far-reaching political reforms, and they certainly posed no threat to the existing order. Thus, when armed rebellions broke out in 1849, the National Assembly was exposed as an ineffective talking shop, easily disbanded in the face of the revolutionary emergency. Any steps towards constitutional rule were wiped out by the combined forces of the Prussian army and battalions from other German kingdoms and principalities.

The 1850s saw political stagnation, but the increasing success of the Industrial Revolution meant that the creation of a single internal German market, preferably accompanied by a political union, was of paramount importance. By now, Prussia had manoeuvred herself into a position of such power that she was the only possible agent for enforcing such a change.

In 1862, **King Wilhelm I** chose as Chancellor the career diplomat **Otto von Bismarck**, a member of the Junker class who had already gained a reputation as an operator of a rare sharpness. In order to win over the Prussian liberals, Bismarck backed the concept of universal male suffrage. He also played the nationalist card immediately: seeing that the Chancellor was bent on creating a united Germany, the liberals muted their opposition and backed his plans for a thorough modernisation of the army.

In 1864, Bismarck lured Austria into supporting him in a war against Denmark to recapture the lost duchies of Schleswig and Holstein. Having achieved an easy victory, he then provoked a disagreement over the spoils: the result was the **Seven Weeks' War** of 1866, in which the superior Prussian weapons and organisation achieved a crushing victory. Not only was Austria forced out of Germany's affairs, but those states which had remained neutral, including Hannover and Hessen-Kassel, were incorporated into Prussia. The German Confederation was dissolved, to be replaced by one covering the north of the country only, which was totally under Prussian domination.

To complete the jigsaw, Bismarck still needed to woo the southern states. His tactic was an original one: to provoke a war against the old enemy, France. In 1870, having carefully prepared the diplomatic ground to ensure that no other power would intervene to support the French, he goaded them by proposing that a Hohenzollern should succeed to the vacant throne of Spain. The French Emperor, Napoleon III, managed to force the Prussians to withdraw, but foolishly sent a telegram asking for an apology. Bismarck doctored this to make it seem worse than it was, giving the excuse to begin the **Franco-Prussian War**.

By January 1871, the Prussian field guns had helped chalk up yet another easy victory. A united German Empire, which once more included the long-disputed provinces of Alsace and Lorraine, was proclaimed in Versailles. King Wilhelm I of Prussia was the inevitable choice as Kaiser; four other monarchs were among the rulers who were henceforth subjugated to him. The new empire became known as the Second Reich, in honour of the fact that it had revived the German imperial tradition after a gap of 65 years.

THE SECOND REICH

In his domestic policy for the united Germany, Bismarck indulged in a series of **liberal reforms**. Uniform systems of law, administration and currency were introduced, an imperial bank was set up, restrictions on trade and movement of labour were lifted, and cities were given municipal autonomy.

By such measures, Bismarck aimed to control the opposition parties in the Reichstag, and to keep power in the hands of the élite. The darker side of his nature came out in the *Kulturkampf*, which aimed at curbing the power of the Catholic church, whose power and influence was anathema to the Protestant aristocracy of Prussia. However, this met with spirited opposition, which led to Bismarck making a rare retreat, though not until he had exacted his price: the Catholics were forced to support protectionist agricultural measures, designed to subsidise the large, outdated Junker estates. By then, a formidable new opposition had arisen in the shape of the **Social Democratic**

Party (SPD), founded in 1875. In order to take the wind out of its sails, Bismarck introduced a system of welfare benefits for workers, a system belatedly copied in many other industrialised countries.

Bismarck's **foreign policy** involved a complicated set of jugglings. He set up the *Dreikaiserbund*, an alliance of the three great imperial powers of Germany, Austria and Russia; indulged in a Mediterranean naval alliance with Britain in order to check Russian designs on the Balkans; yet initiated a bit of colonial rivalry with the British.

Bismarck's awesome reputation for political sure-footedness meant that Germany's internal and external stability seemed completely safe in his hands. However, Friedrich III, who succeeded his father Wilhelm I in 1888, died after only a few months on the throne. His son, **Wilhelm II**, was a firm believer in the divine right of kings. He was of a generation which did not feel beholden to Bismarck, and strongly disliked the veteran politician. Two years later, he removed the Chancellor from office – a move compared to dropping the pilot from a ship – and thereafter relied on a series of ineffective kowtowers to lead his government.

Britain, which had hitherto been a natural ally of Germany as a result of dynastic ties and mutual suspicion of France, was increasingly seen as the main rival. A notorious telegram sent by the Kaiser in support of the Boers in 1896 signalled the beginning of a severe deterioration in relations between the two countries. This was fuelled by an **arms race**, affecting all of Europe, in which the Krupp armaments factory played a crucial role. Nowhere was the attempt to establish supremacy more evident than in the naval sphere, where the Germans set out to usurp Britain's long period of supremacy, achieving parity by 1909.

By this time, the major powers of Europe were divided into **two nervous alliances**. Bismarck's successors failed to maintain his two-faced foreign policy. As a result, Germany was bound up once more with Austria, whose eastern empire was tottering under the nationalist aspirations of the many ethnic groups contained within it; Italy was a somewhat reluctant partner. Ranged against them were France and Russia, drawn together by mutual fear of the ever-increasing power of the German-speaking countries. Britain, maintaining her time-honoured policy of trying to preserve an effective balance of power in Europe, was increasingly drawn towards the latter alliance.

WORLD WAR I

Everybody expected that war would come sooner or later, and master strategies were carefully planned. The Germans developed the **first-strike theory**, which envisaged a quick knock-out blow against both France and Russia, as a prelude to a tougher struggle against the more formidable British. Public opinion in the country was easily won over by the bogus theory that the Fatherland was under threat from the "iron ring" which surrounded it. Even the Social Democrats were persuaded of the necessity and desirability of a war.

The spark which lit the inferno happened to come in **Austria's unwieldy empire**. In 1914, the Crown Prince, Archduke Franz Ferdinand, was assassinated in Sarajevo by a Bosnian nationalist. A military force was sent to crush the independent neighbouring state of Serbia, although no connection between its government and the conspirators who planned the assassination was ever proved. This inevitably provoked the Russians, who had an agreement to protect their fellow Slavs from any threat. The German generals saw this as a golden opportunity to put their first-strike theory into operation. As soon as the Russians mobilised, German troops were sent to attack France. The quickest route was through Belgium, thus violating its neutrality, which was guaranteed by Britain. So fast did events move that the Kaiser sent a telegram ordering withdrawal, but this was ignored. **World War I** was thus underway.

The German High Command believed the French would capitulate within six weeks, the Russians within six months. They were soon proved hopelessly wrong, and found themselves with what they had been most anxious to avoid – a war on two fronts. Even then, they could hardly have anticipated the Armageddon which was unleashed. After the first Battle of the Marne in September, they were forced to retreat and dig **trenches** all across northern France and Belgium, which led to a wholly new form of warfare, with casualties quite unlike any that had previously been known. In 1916, an attempt to exhaust the French at the four-month-long Battle of Verdun proved to be self-defeating, while the same year saw the British prove their continued mastery of the seas at the Battle of Jutland.

As a result of these setbacks, the Kaiser handed over effective military and political power to the dual leadership of the Field Marshal, **Paul von Hindenburg**, and his Quartermaster-General, **Erich Ludendorff**; though the latter was nominally the junior partner, he became the effective dictator of the country. In January 1917, it was decided to introduce unrestricted submarine warfare. This was a complete disaster, its barbarity prompting the United States to enter the war. Later the same year, an all-out offensive on the western front was routed. A reprieve was gained as a result of the revolution in Russia that autumn; this not only closed the eastern front but allowed the Germans to enforce a draconian peace settlement by the Treaty of Brest-Litovsk, which included vast annexations of territory. However, the euphoria of this triumph was tempered by the knowledge that defeat in the west was now seemingly inevitable.

THE END OF WORLD WAR I AND THE FAILURE OF THE GERMAN REVOLUTION

The Allied penetration of the German lines on 8 August 1918 finally convinced Ludendorff that the war was irretrievably lost. Looking for ways to minimise the High Command's loss of face, he seized on the idea of letting a parliamentary government handle the peace negotiations; it would be likely to secure more lenient terms, and would also be a useful scapegoat in the event of a harsh treaty. Furthermore, it would help counteract the far more horrifying alternative of a Bolshevik-style revolution, an only too real prospect once the German people realised the extent to which their leaders had been deceiving them.

Accordingly, he persuaded the Kaiser to appoint the liberal monarchist **Prince Max von Baden** as Chancellor. A full parliamentary democracy was proclaimed; the cabinet was drawn from the ranks of the Reichstag, with Social Democrats included for the first time. On 3 October, Prince Max sued for peace. Ludendorff, sensing that the Allies were going to drive a hard bargain, subsequently resigned; Hindenburg offered to do likewise, but was allowed to remain at his post.

Towards the end of the month, Admiral Scheer decided to mount a futile last-ditch offensive; his crews mutinied, refusing to lay down their lives so unnecessarily. This revolt spread throughout northern Germany and might well have developed into the full-scale revolution Ludendorff had been conniving to avert, had it not been for the bitter **division of the political left-wing** into three factions.

The SPD had previously split into two separate parties over the war; the pacifist group, the USPD, were now frustrated by the tepid nature of their erstwhile colleagues' socialism, which embraced constitutional monarchy and a bourgeois social order. In turn, their politics were seen as too tame by the Spartakist League, a Marxist group who aimed to follow the example of their Russian mentors by seizing power in Berlin. **Friedrich Ebert**, leader of the SPD, decided to forestall them by calling a general strike to demand the Kaiser's abdication. Prince Max took matters into his own hands by announcing this without the monarch's consent, and then himself resigned in favour of Ebert. Matters were still delicately poised with the news that **Karl Liebknecht** of the Spartakists intended to proclaim the establishment of a socialist republic on 9 November.

In order to wrest the initiative, Ebert's lieutenant **Philipp Scheidemann** made an impromptu declaration of a free German Republic from the Reichstag balcony, thus bringing the regime of the Kaisers to an abrupt end. Two days later, an armistice was signed, as Ebert realised that either a collapse of military discipline, or the spread of Bolshevism, would lead to an Allied invasion. As part of his plans, he made a pact with the High Command, which provided him with an army to protect the state against internal left-wing opponents, but at the price of allowing it almost complete autonomy.

This policy paid immediate dividends for him, as the military was used to crush an attempted revolution by the Spartakists in January, a last-ditch attempt at a Communist seizure of power before the elections for the new National Assembly later in the month. The brutal behaviour of the army – Liebknecht and his co-leader Rosa Luxemburg were among those murdered – exacerbated the already deep divisions on the left. However, it did not signal military acceptance of the democratic ideal; indeed, the unholy alliance into which Ebert had entered was to have disastrous long-term consequences for the fledgling republic, which should have made a purging of the anti-democratic and war-crazed officer class one of its most urgent priorities.

THE WEIMAR REPUBLIC

The elections confirmed the SPD as the new political leaders of the country, with 38 percent of the vote; as a result, Ebert was made President, with Scheidemann as Chancellor. **Weimar**, the small country town which had seen the most glorious flowering of the German Enlightenment, was chosen as the seat of government in preference to Berlin, which was tinged by its monarchical and militaristic associations.

A **new constitution** was drawn up, hailed as the most liberal and progressive in the world. While on the surface an admirable document, this constitution was hopelessly idealistic for a people so unfamiliar with democratic practice and responsibilities. No attempt was made to outlaw parties hostile to the system; this opened the way for savage attacks on the republic by extremists at both ends of the political spectrum. The use of proportional representation, without any qualifying minimum percentage of the total vote, favoured a plethora of parties promoting sectional interests. This meant that the Weimar governments were all unwieldy coalitions, whose average life was about eight months and which often pursued contradictory policies in different ministries.

Two months before the constitution was ratified in July 1919, Germany had been forced to accede to the **Treaty of Versailles**. In contrast to the Habsburg Empire, which was broken up into a series of successor states, German territorial integrity was largely preserved, but the losses were painful ones – the industrially productive Saarland and Alsace-Lorraine went to France, while the resurrected country of Poland was given Upper Silesia plus a corridor to the sea, which left East Prussia cut off from the rest of the country. All overseas colonies were confiscated, the Rhineland was declared a demilitarised zone, the navy limited to six light battleships, and the army to 100,000 men with conscription prohibited. Germany and her allies were found guilty of having started the war, and, as a result,

were landed with an enormous **reparations bill**, which would have taken over half a century to pay.

In all, this amounted to a pretty stiff settlement, albeit one considerably less harsh than the Germans had recently enforced on the Russians at Brest-Litovsk. So incensed were the military leaders with this humiliating diktat that they toyed with the idea of resuming hostilities. As this was not a feasible option, they contented themselves with inventing the **"stab in the back" legend**, maintaining that the army, undefeated in the field, had been betrayed by unscrupulous politicians – a preposterous distortion accepted all too easily by gullible sections of the public.

The treaty spelled the beginning of the end for the Social Democratic republic. Scheidemann immediately resigned as Chancellor, and, following gains by the two political extremes in the 1920 elections under the new constitution, the party, though still the largest in the Reichstag, withdrew from government altogether, leaving power in the hands of minority administrations drawn from liberal and moderate conservative parties. Right-wing extremism flourished in a series of political murders and attempted putsches, which were barely punished by a judiciary which rivalled the army in its contempt for the republic.

The reparations bill crippled the economy, to the extent that payments began to be withheld. This gave the French the excuse to occupy the Ruhr in 1923; they were met by a policy of passive resistance. As no work was done, galloping **inflation** – the most catastrophic ever known in world history – quickly ensued, causing the ruin of the entire middle class as the currency became utterly worthless. The Weimar Republic seemed irretrievably doomed, but it made an astonishing comeback, largely due to the political skills of the new Chancellor, **Gustav Stresemann**. He was an unlikely saviour, an old-fashioned conservative who had begun his career as Ludendorff's mouthpiece in the Reichstag, and whose precise commitment to the republic is still disputed. A supreme pragmatist, he realised the danger of economic collapse and the futility of confrontation with the Allies. Therefore he ended passive resistance and negotiated huge American loans to rebuild the economy; this was so successful that by October 1924 money had regained its former value; (nearly) full employment and general prosperity soon followed.

Although Stresemann's government broke up long before these effects were felt, he subsequently served as Foreign Minister for six years in a variety of coalitions, achieving **Germany's rehabilitation on the world stage**. By the 1925 Locarno Pact, he gained rapprochement with France and guarantees that there could be no further threat of foreign occupation. Reparation payments were scaled down, and further American aid given. It seemed that the republic was set for a secure future, even if the political immaturity of the German people was still apparent, most notably in the Presidential election of 1925. This was won by the 78-year-old Hindenburg, a wily operator basking in an undeserved military reputation, vocal exponent of the "stab in the back" legend, and an embarrassing reminder of times past.

THE RISE OF NAZISM

The **National Socialist German Workers' Party** was founded in 1918 by a locksmith by the name of Anton Drexler, but only gained momentum when he was ousted three years later by **Adolf Hitler**, a failed artist and ex-corporal from Austria. It was a rag-bag group of fanatics and misfits whose views, as the party name suggests, were an odd mixture of the extreme right and left. They modelled their organisation on the Communists and the Italian *Fascisti*, adopting their own uniform and slogans, and developing a private army, the brown-shirted **SA** (*Sturmabteilung*, or "Storm Troopers"). Such limited success as the party enjoyed was at first confined to Bavaria, where a botched attempt at a putsch was made in 1923; following this, Hitler was arrested and convicted of high treason.

The leniency shown by the judiciary to right-wing opponents of the republic – aided by the fact that he had involved Ludendorff in the plot – meant that Hitler only served nine months in prison, during which he set out his ideology and political programme in his autobiography, *Mein Kampf*. This consists of verbose rantings and ravings, drawing from all the nastiest and most reactionary theories of the day, but is an important source, as it sets out unequivocally what Hitler genuinely believed, and was to serve as his blueprint for power.

Sales of the book – in spite of its ready captive market in the ranks of the party faithful – failed to reach 10,000 in the first year, and declined steadily for the next five. Nazi representation in the Reichstag also decreased from 25 in 1924 to just twelve after the 1928 elections, making it the ninth and smallest party, and one widely regarded as something of a joke. Only the extraordinarily mesmeric personality of Hitler held it together; having learnt from past mistakes, he was now determined to gain power by strictly legal means.

Stresemann died in October 1929, exhausted by over-work and by persecution from his former right-wing allies. Three weeks later came the **Wall Street crash** in America, whose repercussions swiftly destroyed the new German order he had created. Wholesale withdrawal of credit – on which the economy was totally dependent – led to another bout of escalating employment and inflation, to which there was no ready-made solution, as there had been in 1923. The coalition partners quarrelled over what measures to take; as a result, the SPD, who had only recently returned to government following eight years voluntarily out of office, once more abdicated the responsibility of leadership. A minority government was set up under the Centrist **Heinrich Brüning**; frustrated by having to rely on rule by Presidential decree, he took a gamble by asking Hindenburg to dissolve the Reichstag.

The elections, held in September 1930, offered a golden opportunity for the political extremes, with their formulas for righting all wrongs. The Nazi rise was meteoric, taking even Hitler by surprise – they gained 6.4 million votes and became the second largest party. This support was overwhelmingly from the disaffected ranks of the unemployed (particularly the young) and the ruined petty bourgeoisie.

Though a significant breakthrough, it was far from being a decisive one, and there was still no inevitability about the Nazi triumph, which was only achieved because of the short-sightedness and greed of the traditional right wing.

In Hitler, they at last found their Kaiser-substitute, a man who could give them the broad mass of support they could not otherwise muster and who would return Germany to its traditions of hierarchical authoritarian rule at home and military glory abroad. Leading figures in industry and politics latched on to Hitler and gave him respectability; by acting as his financiers and power brokers, they believed they would be able to control his excesses. Nazi coffers were swelled by contributions from many of the giant corporations, following a lead given some years before by the steel magnate Fritz Thyssen. The army began to abandon its role above party politics, overlooking its earlier aversion to the paramilitary SA.

Hitler offered a clue as to the naivety of these hopes by standing against the revered Hindenburg in the 1932 Presidential election, only just managing to secure German citizenship in time to be eligible. The desperate straits into which the republic had fallen was shown by the fact that the ancient soldier, teetering on the verge of senility, was supported by the SPD and all the other democratic parties, who abstained from fielding a candidate of their own in the belief that there was no other way of beating Hitler.

In the event, Hindenburg only just failed to obtain an outright majority on the first ballot, and comfortably won the second, with the Communists trailing a very poor third. Fresh hope was provided by the remarkable success of Chancellor Brüning, still dependent on Presidential decree, who was developing into a worthy successor to Stresemann. His sensible economic programme alleviated the worst hardships, and he was on the verge of pulling off a tremendous double success in foreign affairs, with the end of reparations and the return of Germany's right to equality of armaments in sight. An attempt at reforming the outdated pattern of land ownership proved to be Brüning's undoing; the aristocracy howled with rage at this alleged crypto-Bolshevism, and Hindenburg was left with no alternative but to ditch him.

That marked the last attempt to make the republic work; power passed to a small coterie of traditional conservatives close to the President, who bear the final responsibility for Hitler's assumption of power. The next two Chancellors – the bumbling intriguer **Franz von Papen** and the far more astute fixer **General Kurt von Schleicher**, who had elaborate plans for using Hitler and then destroying him – had no taste for democracy, and were content to play courtier-style politics.

Two elections held in 1932 were inconclusive; in the first, following a campaign of mass terror by the SA, the Nazis gained nearly 14 million votes and became the largest party, but were still well short of a majority. As Hindenburg's hand-picked cabinet failed to secure the support of the Reichstag, new elections had to be called; these saw the Nazis lose two million votes, as the party's true aims and methods became clearer. However, having been toppled by von Schleicher, it was von Papen – a figure seemingly escaped from a comic opera, now at centre-stage in one of the world's greatest-ever tragedies – who entered into a disastrous plot with Hitler which brought the end of the republic.

Von Papen persuaded Hindenburg to make Hitler Chancellor, with himself as deputy, of a coalition able to command a Reichstag majority. As the Nazis would only be given two other cabinet seats, von Papen assumed that he would retain the real control for himself. Hitler was therefore sworn in on 30 January 1933, having achieved with incredible ease his objective of coming to power by constitutional means.

THE THIRD REICH

Once in power, **Hitler acted swiftly to make his position absolute**; he had no intention of being beholden to anyone, least of all a fool and political amateur such as von Papen. New elections were arranged for March; this time, the Nazis had the advantage of being able to use the full apparatus of the state to back up their campaign of terror. In this, they were greatly aided by the fact that **Hermann Göring**, one of the Nazis in the cabinet, was Prussian Minister of the Interior and thus in control of the police.

On the night of 27 February, the **Reichstag** was burned down; a simple-minded Dutch Communist was arrested for this, though the fire was almost certainly the work of the Nazis themselves. At any rate, it gave them the excuse to force Hindenburg into declaring a state of emergency. Thereafter, opponents could be gagged legally, and Communists persecuted. The Nazis were duly elected with over 17 million votes, just short of an absolute majority.

An **Enabling Bill** was laid before the Reichstag, which was effectively asked to vote itself out of existence. By the arrest of the Communist deputies and some of the SPD, and the support of the traditional right, Hitler was only just short of the two-thirds majority he needed to abolish the Weimar Republic quite legally. The SPD salvaged some self-respect by refusing to accede to this, but the Catholic Centrists failed to repeat their act of defiance against Bismarck, meekly supporting the measure in return for minor concessions.

Now officially the country's dictator, Hitler immediately put into effect the remainder of his **policy of co-ordination** (*Gleichschaltung*), by which society was completely Nazified. With breathtaking speed, every institution surrendered. The Länder were stripped of their powers, making Germany a centralised state for the first time. All political parties except the Nazis were forced to dissolve, and free trade unions were banned. Purges were carried out in the police, judiciary and professions, to ensure that each was in the control of party loyalists.

Many of the vicious features for which Nazism became notorious soon made their appearance. **Jews were ostracised and persecuted**; their businesses were boycotted and they were banned from the professions; two years later, they were stripped of citizenship and forbidden to marry Germans. Fifty or so **concentration camps** were set up for political opponents, who were sadistically tortured and often cold-bloodedly murdered. Conformity was ensured by networks of informers under the control of the secret police, the **Gestapo**. The educational system was perverted in order to indoctrinate the great "truths" of Nazi ideology.

Recognising the importance of controlling young minds at all times, membership of the Hitler Youth and League of Young German Women was made compulsory. Cultural life virtually collapsed, as "degenerate" forms of expression were suppressed. These ranged from virtually all modern art to books and plays with a liberal or socialist slant; it even affected music, as the performance of works by composers with Jewish blood was outlawed. Soon the main threat to the regime lay within the Nazi Party itself, with the original socialist wing, backed by the SA, pressing for a second revolution.

On 30 June 1934, the **"Night of the Long Knives"**, hundreds of potential Nazi opponents were assassinated, notably the leading left-winger Gregor Strasser and the SA chief Ernst Röhm. The SA was stripped of its powers and put under the control of **Heinrich Himmler**'s black-shirted **SS** (*Schutzstaffel*), originally no more than Hitler's bodyguard. This measure also had the benefit of laying to rest the one remaining threat, that of intervention by the army; with their potential usurpers out of the way, they quickly came to terms with Nazism. When Hindenburg died a few weeks later, Hitler combined the offices of President and Chancellor into that of an all-powerful *Führer*, a measure he had ratified by a plebiscite in which he was endorsed by 90 percent of those eligible to vote.

The genuine **popular support** Hitler enjoyed is one of the most striking and disturbing features of what became known as the Third Reich, the successor to the empires of Charlemagne and Bismarck. Although many of the most talented people, especially in the arts and sciences, fled the country, and many others tenaciously defied it from within, the level of opposition was negligible.

However, there's no doubt that the economic policies Hitler pursued were popular on both sides of industry. Full employment was restored, and, although industrial and agricultural workers were effectively reduced to the status of serfs, there was no question of starvation or total financial ruin. Business leaders were pleased for a different reason – when it came to profits, the totalitarian state stopped short of its normal all-embracing function.

One by one, the terms of Versailles were breached – reparation payments were stopped, the formerly secret rearmament was stepped up and made open, with conscription reintroduced; the Rhineland was re-occupied; and Austria was forced into becoming part of the Reich. The German-speaking people in the Sudetenland part of Czechoslovakia, who had never previously been a source of discontent, were used as an excuse to begin the policy of *Lebensraum*; the matter escalated into an international crisis in 1938, in which the British and French made a humiliating climb-down by an agreement signed at Munich, in which they sacrificed Czech territorial integrity – a despicable and self-interested act – for what they believed would be world peace.

Hitler was encouraged by this show of weakness to launch one of his most cherished ambitions the following year – the elimination of Poland. It's probable he believed there would be a similar collapse of will by the western powers, the more so as he first pulled off the spectacular coup of signing a non-aggression pact with his ultimate enemy, the Soviet Union, thus ensuring there would not be a war on two fronts. However, this was a miscalculation; two days after the invasion began on 1 September, Britain and France, realising that the earlier promises of an end to German expansion in Eastern Europe were a sham, decided to honour their treaty obligations; thus **World War II** began.

WORLD WAR II

At first, the war went well for the Nazis, aided by the fact that Germany was the only country properly prepared, by reason of the massive arms build-up that it had semi-secretly been preparing since 1930. Poland was routed and the Low Countries soon fell, leading to the British evacuation from Dunkirk in May 1940. Within a month, France had signed an armistice, and a puppet government was installed. A quick invasion would then have probably accounted for Britain, but Hitler delayed in favour of an aerial bombardment in which the *Luftwaffe* were repulsed by the RAF. Rather than prolong this approach, German sights turned eastwards again. The Balkans were subdued, and in June 1941 plans were hatched for the largest military operation in history – the invasion of the Soviet Union. This period also marks the beginnings of the worst **concentration camps**, in which Nazi racial theories were put fully into practice. Inmates from the conquered territories were used as slave labour, and horrendous experiments in the name of Nazi "science" were carried out, followed by an attempt at the "final solution" of the Jewish "problem". Over 6 million (about a third of the population of world Jewry) perished as a result; a similar number of other "undesirable" peoples were massacred in addition.

On 7 December, 1941 Hitler's Japanese allies attacked Pearl Harbour, an action which almost immediately **brought the USA into the war**, the very reverse of German intentions. In any event, Nazi Germany had hopelessly overreached itself; defeats in North Africa in 1942 were followed by **the turning-point at Stalingrad** (today's Volgograd/Tsaritsyn) the following year when the Russian winter and the vast size of the country combined, not for the first time, to repulse a foreign invader. German losses rivalled those sustained in World War I, and a crushing blow was dealt to morale, as this ranked as the most disastrous defeat in the country's military history.

THE DEFEAT OF NAZISM

From then onwards, the story is one of Nazi retreat on all fronts. A **German resistance movement** sprang up under the leadership of senior army officers. Various attempts were made to assassinate Hitler, and he had several extraordinary escapes, most notably in the carefully hatched plot of 20 July, 1944, when a planted bomb killed several people sitting alongside him. Yet, bad luck apart, the conspiratorial groups were handicapped by their excessive concern to secure in advance lenient terms for a defeated but democratic Germany; they also had no firm base of popular support, nor a detailed plan of campaign for what to do once Hitler had been killed.

As it turned out, the country's ultimate collapse was drawn out, and did not occur before all major German cities and innumerable small towns had been ruthlessly bombed. Eventually, the Allies occupied the entire country; on 30 April, 1945, marooned in his Berlin bunker, Hitler committed suicide, so bringing the "thousand year Reich" to an inglorious end.

THE DIVISION OF GERMANY

The Allied powers, determined not to repeat the mistakes of Versailles, now had to decide **what to do with Germany**. At Potsdam in August, the country was partitioned into four zones of occupation, corresponding to an agreement made earlier in the year at Yalta when the war was still in progress; Berlin was similarly divided. The eastern frontier of Germany was redrawn at the Oder-Neisse line, meaning that East Prussia and most of Pomerania and Silesia passed to Poland, in compensation for territory annexed by the Soviet Union.

Initially, there was a great deal of co-operation amongst the Allies. All the leading Nazis who had survived were brought to **trial in Nürnberg** for war crimes or crimes against humanity, and the civil service was purged of the movement's sympathisers. Relief measures were taken against the terrible famine sweeping the country, refugees from the former Eastern Territories were given help to begin a new life, and the first steps were made towards rebuilding destroyed cities and the shattered economy.

Germany's internal **political life** was relaunched under the leadership of prominent anti-Nazis. The right of the spectrum was occupied by a new and moderate party, the **Christian Democrats** (CDU). Left-wing politics were still marred by the legacy of bad blood between the SPD and the Communists. In the Russian zone, the SPD took the lead in forming a new group, the **Socialist Unity Party** (SED), which was intended to be Marxist but not Marxist-Leninist; the Communists only tagged along under Russian pressure after the poor showing of the party in the Austrian elections. This new grouping was not repeated in the other zones.

Inevitably, **strains developed among the Allies**; the zones began to develop in different ways, mirroring the societies of their conquerors. Frustrated by Russian stalling, the western powers began a currency reform in their zones in 1948, soon extended to West Berlin. This gesture was regarded as highly provocative by the Soviets, who retaliated by cutting off western access to the divided city in the **Berlin Blockade**. Another world war could have ensued, but the beleaguered western zones were saved by the success of **air lifts** bringing essential supplies, forcing the Russians to abandon the blockade within a year.

By this time, two different societies were emerging on German soil; the Russians enforced massive nationalisation and collectivisation; in contrast, the western powers allowed even those industrialists most associated with the Nazis, such as Thyssen and the Krupps, to return to their businesses with minimal punishment. Rocked by the independent line taken by Tito in Yugoslavia, the Russians transformed the SED into a Soviet-style party led by a Politburo into which the erstwhile SPD members were trapped, while a Parliamentary Council was set up in the west to draft a new constitution. The logical conclusion of these events – the creation of two rival states – soon followed. In May 1949, the three western zones amalgamated to form the **German Federal Republic**; four months later, the Russians launched their territory as the **German Democratic Republic**.

THE FEDERAL REPUBLIC

Like the Weimar Republic, the new West German state was founded on **liberal democratic principles**, only this time the constitution was much tighter. The power of the President was sharply reduced, giving him a role not unlike that of the British monarch. A true federal structure was created, in which the Länder were given considerable powers over all areas of policy except defence, foreign affairs and currency control. Proportional representation was retained, but with a 5 percent qualifying minimum, and elections were fixed for every four years. A constitutional court was established to guarantee civil and political liberties, and anti-democratic parties were outlawed.

Konrad Adenauer became the first Chancellor following elections in which his Christian Democrats emerged as the largest party, though far short of a majority. Aged 73 and with no experience of national politics – he had been mayor of Cologne until removed by the Nazis – he bore the look of a temporary leader, though as an elder statesman with an untainted past he fitted the precise needs of the time exactly.

In the event, the evening of his career was a prolonged one; he remained in power for fourteen years, during which time he developed an aura of indispensability at home and appeared as a figure of substance abroad. Much of this success was due to the **"Economic Miracle"** masterminded by **Ludwig Erhard**, in which the wrecked economy made a spectacular recovery, with high-quality products fuelling an export boom. An annual growth rate of 8 percent was achieved; within a decade West Germany ranked as the most prosperous major European country. In many ways, this was due simply to disciplined hard work by the bulk of the population, but it was also aided by the fact that a fresh start had to be made. Industry was re-launched with the most modern equipment, and in a sensible atmosphere of partnership between management and just seventeen large trade unions which eliminated the class-based fear and inter-union rivalry which continued to dog other countries.

In foreign affairs, priority was given to **ending the long era of enmity with France**; the two countries formed the European Coal and Steel Pact in 1951, serving as a prelude to the creation of the European Economic Community six years later. The Federal Republic's integration into the western alliance was cemented by admission to **NATO**, and the adoption of a hard-nosed attitude towards the Soviet Union and her satellites.

By the **Hallstein Doctrine**, the Federal Republic claimed to be the legitimate voice of all Germany, arguing that it was the only part properly constituted. Not only did it fail to recognise the GDR, it successfully ostracised its neighbour by refusing to establish diplomatic relations with any country who did.

THE GERMAN DEMOCRATIC REPUBLIC

Meanwhile the inappropriately-styled German Democratic Republic rapidly evolved a **centralised system of government on the Soviet model**. The Christian Democratic and Liberal parties were forcibly subordinated to the SED, and two further bourgeois groups were created from above. Elections were still held, but a single list of candidates was drawn up which the voters had to accept _en bloc_. The only method of protest was to reject it outright, which had to be done publicly, making it a dangerous as well as a futile gesture. Police, education and management of the economy were all put under SED control. Real power was centralised in the hands of party secretary **Walter Ulbricht**, a hard-line Stalinist who had spent almost the entire Nazi period ensconced in the Soviet Union.

At first, the Russians were ambivalent about their rump state. They administered punitive reparations, stripping it of much of its industry and shipping valuable plant and machinery to the Soviet Union; they were worried about the GDR's long-term viability and may even have been prepared to sacrifice it altogether in their own defensive interests. Stalin was on record as saying in 1944, "Communism fits Germany as a saddle fits a cow", and it's doubtful if he was ever particularly keen on a separate GDR. In 1952, he made **an offer to establish a unified and neutral Germany on a democratic basis**, which was rejected out of hand in the west as mere bluff.

The **GDR began life unpromisingly**, exploited by its parent, having no historical or economic rationale, unloved by the vast majority of its populace, thousands of whom emigrated to the west, and seemingly wanted only by its leaders who had power handed to them on a plate. A second industrial revolution had to be launched, simply to meet reparation commitments; the existing infrastructure included very little heavy industry (which was now developed apace, though more for ideological reasons than out of necessity), and was now deprived of access to its commercial hinterland. The pressure of this caused the first revolt in the Soviet satellite states, a series of **workers' strikes** in 1953, put down by Russian tanks. The following year, reparations were ended and the country began to develop as a key member of the bloc, becoming one of the founder members of the **Warsaw Pact**.

In spite of many problems – access to western markets was hindered by the lack of a convertible currency, trade with the Soviet Union was conducted on unfavourable terms, and imbalances were caused by the ideological imperative to give massive subsidies to basic necessities – the 1950s saw an **economic recovery** which in its own way was as extraordinary as West Germany's. Once again, the people showed their legendary ability to adapt to any kind of regime; they were in any event now well attuned to totalitarian life. If West Germans felt a sense of superiority in their far more advanced lifestyle, the comparison was hardly a fair one – they had received munificence from their conquerors, not retribution; they had also started with the enormous benefit of being in possession of the Ruhr and other areas of rich natural resources and advanced industry. At the 1958 Party Congress, Ulbricht was rash enough to predict that, within a few years, the country would have overtaken its neighbour in terms of per capita income, thus proving the inherent superiority of the Communist system.

THE BERLIN WALL

This optimism proved short lived, as the late 1950s saw the beginning of a period of **unprecedented West German prosperity and expansion**. A shortage of labour meant that workers had to be imported; the unskilled labourers tended to come from Turkey, Greece,

Yugoslavia, Italy and Spain. For the better-qualified positions, industry looked to East Germany and a flood of **emigration** started.

Quickly realising that he could not afford to lose so many professionals, engineers, intellectuals and craftsmen, Ulbricht was forced into drastic action. The loophole was the western sector of Berlin; if it could be sealed off, the problem would disappear. Having failed at a second attempt to make the allies evacuate the city, Ulbricht persuaded the Soviets of the necessity of constructing the **Berlin Wall**, erected on 13 August, 1961. It was immediately patrolled by armed guards under instructions to shoot to kill, and the main boundaries of the country were also greatly strengthened. A visual and moral affront to humanity, it was justified as the "Anti-Fascist Protection Wall", a label it retained until its demolition.

In the Federal Republic Adenauer was finally forced into retirement in 1963, to be succeeded by Erhard, who proved far less successful as the country's leader than he had been as economic guru. The liberal Free Democrats (FDP), who had served as the CDU's junior coalition partners for all but a short period of the Federal Republic's history, went into opposition in 1966. A **"Grand Coalition"** was established with the SPD, who thus returned to government for the first time since 1930. To rid itself of its tarnished image, the party had undergone a substantial reform (or sell-out, according to many) at its 1959 conference, disavowing its roots in Marxism and class conflict and its traditional anti-clericalism, embracing instead the CDU's "social market economy", but with a stronger emphasis on the social side of the equation.

The Chancellor, the CDU's Kurt Georg Kiesinger, was remarkable mainly for being a reformed Nazi – a rather uncomfortable indicator as to how far West Germans were prepared to forget the past. It was hardly surprising that the period of the Grand Coalition saw the first simmerings of disenchantment with the cosy form of consensus politics which had dominated the country's postwar history, with the Communists re-formed as a counterweight to the neo-Nazi NPD; neither party, however, gained much of a following. More serious were the beginnings of what has since become a persistent feature of West German life, **extra-parliamentary opposition**. This first came to the fore with the 1968 student revolt under Rudi Dutschke. Grievances initially centred on unsatisfactory conditions in the universities – then, as now, one of the worst-run sectors in the Federal Republic – but spread to wider discontent with society and the new materialistic culture.

OSTPOLITIK

A more positive feature of the Grand Coalition was the rise of **Willi Brandt**, the dynamic leader of the SPD, who assumed the foreign affairs portfolio. A former Resistance journalist, he had been mayor of West Berlin throughout the period of crisis leading up to the building of the Wall, and was determined to take a new tack on the problem. His **Ostpolitik** began in earnest, helped by a general thawing of the Cold War, when he became Chancellor in 1969, at the head of a SPD-FDP coalition, itself something of a mould-breaker. Treaties were signed with the Soviet Union and Poland in 1970, recognising the validity of the Oder-Neisse line; West Berlin's special status was guaranteed by the Four Power Agreement the following year; and in 1972 a Basic Treaty was signed between the two Germanys which at last normalised relations.

This stopped short of full diplomatic recognition of the GDR, but the Federal Republic recognised its frontiers and separate existence, abandoning the Hallstein Doctrine. In return, West Germans were allowed to visit family and friends over the border, though movement the other way was confined to pensioners and the disabled. One consequence of *Ostpolitik* was the **fall of Ulbricht** in 1971; he wanted to drive a harder bargain than suited the Soviets, who were in any case tired of his constant lectures to them on ideological purity. His replacement was **Erich Honecker**, who, although regarded as a comparative liberal, had first come to prominence as construction supremo of the Berlin Wall.

With the mirage of re-unification now cleared, the two German societies were able to continue developing in their separate ways. **The GDR began to clarify and modify its image**; in 1974, the country was given yet another new constitution, which omitted previous references to overcoming the division of Germany, and stated the country was "forever and irrevocably" allied with the USSR. The GDR was characterised as a "developed socialist society", in which different divisions existed. This had the twin benefits of justifying both the inequality which was still clearly manifest (though less extreme than in the west) and the continued leadership role of the SED – along with all the attendant privileges for its élite.

To counterbalance this, a **"social contract"** was made with the population, which curbed arbitrary use of police powers, effectively meaning that only active dissidents were persecuted. Honecker cultivated an avuncular image for himself which came as a refreshing change after the austere authoritarianism of his predecessor. **Sports** – or at least those with a high profile in the Olympic Games, such as athletics, swimming and skiing – were increasingly used as the chief means of gaining international prestige, and the results proved stunningly successful, catapulting the country to the dizzy heights of the improbable third "super-power" in these events. **Economic performance** became ever more impressive, and was easily the best in the Soviet bloc; full employment was preserved as much out of necessity as principle. However, in comparison with West Germany the economic mix looked hopelessly outdated, and the average earner was little more than half as well off in real terms, with the gap widening rather than narrowing. As well as all the old problems, there were frequent shortages (often caused by sudden opportunities to sell stocks to gain hard currency) and a lack of worthwhile consumer goods for which the demand was growing apace.

Boosted by the success of both his *Ostpolitik* and his welfare programmes, Brandt led his coalition to victory in 1972, with the SPD winning more votes than the CDU for the first (and, as yet, only) time. In view of the reconciliatory nature of his approach to the GDR, it was ironical that Brandt's downfall occurred two years later as a result of the unmasking of one of his closest aides as an East German spy.

Staying on in the influential role as SPD chairman (until 1987, when another scandal, this time over a bizarre choice of a young CDU-sympathising Greek woman as party spokesperson, caused his retirement), Brandt was succeeded by **Helmut Schmidt**, an able pragmatist who increasingly came to be seen as

something of a right-winger, though this was in part due to the nature of the problems he faced. The quadrupling of OPEC oil prices in 1974, and the stagnation in world trade which ensued, posed particular difficulties for the export-led and growth-geared German economy. These were tackled more successfully than in most countries, but **unemployment** became an issue for the first time since Hitler.

Extra-parliamentary opposition had by now taken on a fearsome and anarchic character. In the early 1970s, there had been a spate of kidnappings and armed bank robberies by the Baader-Meinhof gang. These had no sooner been quelled than there arose a far more organised and ruthless offshoot, the **Red Army Faction**, who assassinated a number of public figures. The turning-point in the government's campaign against them came with the hijacking of a Lufthansa plane in 1977, and a threat to kill the hostages if the remaining members of the gang were not released from prison.

On personal instructions from Schmidt – on which he was prepared to stake his Chancellorship – the aircraft was successfully stormed; within three years, most of the terrorist leaders had been arrested and imprisoned. Peaceful extra-parliamentary opposition proved to have a far more potent significance. This was inspired above all by fears that divided Germany would serve as the stage for a future nuclear war. NATO's 1979 decision to install medium-range American nuclear missiles in West Germany was a particular source of protest, but there was also **increased general concern about the environment**, especially pollution of the beloved forests.

These issues then served as a focus for the many who were dissatisfied with a society which had become over-competitive and too obsessed with consumerism, and out of an amorphous collection of pressure groups active in these areas the **Green Party** was born. Schmidt's backing of the bases alienated the SPD's left wing, but he was still able to lead his coalition to victory in 1980. In this he was aided by the CDU's recurrent leadership problem, which reached its nadir at this point with the fielding of **Franz Josef Strauss**, who had last held federal office under Adenauer, as Chancellor-candidate. Long-standing leader of the CSU, the separate and exclusively Bavarian counterpart of the CDU, this blatant careerist and strident right-winger unsurprisingly proved to be a major electoral liability.

THE 1980s

Despite this lifeline, the long period of SPD domination was coming to an end. Schmidt's tough economic policies under the influence of another round of drastic oil price increases further widened the party's divisions, leading the FDP to lose confidence and withdraw from the government in September 1982. The CDU, now revived under **Helmut Kohl**, gambled on a "constructive vote of no confidence" – the only way round the fixed-term parliaments enshrined in the constitution. Having won this, they formed a new government with the FDP and called for fresh elections. Fears that the FDP would fail to surmount the 5 percent threshold (having damaged themselves by their rather dubious stance) proved unfounded, and Kohl was able to continue as before.

Kohl was something of a departure, the first German leader drawn from a generation too young to have Nazi associations of any kind. He has remained in power ever since, unexpectedly seeing Germany through its biggest upheaval since the Second World War.

Initially, his government was rather unexciting, cutting back on the state's very modest role in economic intervention, but making **further strides in Ostpolitik**. Since Brandt, this had become low-key, and depended very much on the climate of super-power relations. The new developments were in many cases cynical – massive **interest-free loans** were given to the GDR in return for allowing greater numbers of its citizens to emigrate, and football-style transfer fees were paid for its political prisoners.

Honecker was keen to **set the seal of legitimacy on the GDR** by paying an official visit to the Federal Republic; two attempts were abandoned in the face of Soviet pressure before he finally made it in September 1987. It was the highpoint of his career and seemed to provide its justification as, amid much publicity, he was received in a way just below that for a head of state.

As the nineteen-eighties drew to a close the **West German political scene** settled down into a straight left/right division with the well-entrenched CDU/FDP ruling coalition lined up against the SPD and Greens. The Greens however demonstrated an unexpected staying power, and a new generation of SPD leaders, most notably Oskar Fontaine, seemed to be advocating the creation of an effective red-green alliance as the left's only way forward. At the other end of the political scale was the emergence of a new far-right group, the **Republicans**, who made worrying advances at local level, notably in West Berlin.

In **East Germany** things remained static, much to the dismay of large sections of the populace who had hoped that the reformist policies promoted by **Mikhail Gorbachev** in the Soviet Union might eventually filter down to their own leadership. The ageing SED hierarchy remained solidly in place and despite some easing of travel restrictions, public dissent was not tolerated. Typical of the regime's attitude to would-be reformers was the arrest and expulsion to the West of a group of protesters who called for greater freedom at an official demonstration in memory of Karl Liebknecht and Rosa Luxemburg in January 1988.

As Gorbachev's *glasnost* and *perestroika* transformed Soviet political life, the GDR regime found it necessary to **insulate its citizens from the mood of reform in the east**; the Soviet magazine Sputnik was banned, and a number of Russian-language films examining the Stalin and Brezhnev periods were accused of "distorting history" and withdrawn from circulation. An implacable Erich Honecker declared that the Berlin Wall, that most potent symbol of the SED's increasingly isolated stance, would stand for another fifty or a hundred years if necessary, "to protect our republic from robbers".

For many individuals in the GDR, **leaving the country** seemed to be the only way forward. One option sought by increasing numbers of people was legal emigration, a soul-destroying process dogged by bureaucratic obstruction. Others, more desperate, attempted to **escape to the West** across the country's heavily guarded borders. When Chris Gueffroy, a young East Berliner was shot dead while trying to cross the border in Berlin on February 6, 1989, no one could know that he would be the last person to be killed making such an attempt. Things were about to change in a way that would have a colossal effect on not only the GDR, but also on West Germany and the rest of Europe.

1989 – DIE WENDE

1989 ranks as the most significant year in German history since 1945. In the space of twelve months a complete and unforeseeable transformation (what Germans call *Die Wende*) occurred. The unification of Germany went from being a remote possibility to reality, forcing everyone to reassess the postwar world order.

It was reform in another country that provided the initial impetus for the incredible events of 1989. On May 2, 1989, the Hungarian authorities began taking down the barbed wire along their border with Austria, creating **a hole in the Iron Curtain**. Many East Germans, aware that visa laws making travel to Hungary more difficult would come into force in the autumn, headed south for their summer holidays.

By August about 200 East Germans were **crossing into Austria every night**, and on August 19, 700 people surged across the frontier in broad daylight unhindered by the Hungarian border guards. By this stage about 20,000 refugee East Germans were being housed in the West German embassy in Budapest and in Hungarian holiday camps, awaiting their chance to leave for the West. On September 10 the Hungarian government finally **gave the East Germans leave to depart**. Forbidden to travel to Hungary, would-be refugees now made for Prague, swamping the West German embassy. On September 30 they too were allowed to leave, the result of a special deal announced by West German foreign minister Hans-Dietrich Genscher.

In the GDR **opposition groups** such as *Neues Forum* were starting to emerge. Popular unrest came to a head at the **October 7** celebration of the fortieth anniversary of the GDR. Guest Mikhail Gorbachev stressed the need for dialogue and openness to new ideas, while Erich Honecker responded with a clichéd speech praising the status quo. A vainglorious official parade of military hardware was followed by angry **demonstrations** which were brutally suppressed by the police. There were also demonstrations in Leipzig and Dresden, and open popular unrest spread across the country over the following weeks despite widespread fears of an armed crackdown by the authorities. The expected violence never materialised and on October 18 Erich Honecker was suddenly replaced by **Egon Krenz**, his long-time heir apparent, a man widely regarded as a neo-Stalinist hardliner.

To everyone's surprise Krenz **expressed a desire for dialogue** with opposition groups. The exodus of GDR citizens continued but there was now a feeling that change might be possible. On November 4 one million people gathered in the centre of East Berlin, in **the biggest anti-Communist demonstration** since the workers' uprising of 1953. Three days later most of the old government resigned and **Hans Modrow**, the former Dresden SED chief and a man widely regarded as a liberal, was appointed Prime Minister. By now 200,000 East Germans had left the GDR since the start of the year.

The **opening of the Berlin Wall** was announced almost casually. On the evening of Thursday, November 9, Berlin party boss Günter Schabowski told a press conference that East German citizens were free to leave the GDR with valid exit visas which were henceforth to be issued without delay. Events immediately took on a momentum of their own. TV stations broadcast the announcement and citizens began heading for the nearest border crossings. All along the frontier border guards began letting through the masses, and people on both sides of the city flocked to the Wall. Huge crowds converged on the Brandenburg Gate where an impromptu street party broke out celebrating an event that many Germans had never imagined they would see. Over the days that followed **East Germans poured across the border**: 2,700,000 exit visas were issued in the first weekend after the Wall was opened, and the two Germanys, separated for so long, rediscovered each other at breakneck speed.

The writing was now on the wall for the Communists and the GDR. On December 1 the East German parliament passed a motion ending the leading role of the SED and **free elections were promised** for the following May. The SED changed their name, becoming the supposedly voter-friendly PDS - *Partei Demokratische Sozialismus* or "Democratic Socialist Party". A more significant event for the future of Germany was Chancellor Helmut Kohl's visit to Dresden on December 19 when he declared to cheering crowds that his ultimate goal was a **united Germany**.

THE 1990s

With the new decade things progressed rapidly. The GDR elections, brought forward to March 18, resulted in a **victory for a right-wing alliance dominated by the CDU** under Lothar de Mazière. This really represented a victory for Chancellor Helmut Kohl, the self-proclaimed champion of reunification.

Almost immediately the new East German government set about dissolving the GDR. An agreement with the West Germans about **economic union** was hammered out and put into effect on July 1. The next step was to work out a formula for political reunification. This was effectively left to Helmut Kohl and Mikhail Gorbachev (who at this stage still had the final say); between them during a July summit in the Caucasus, they worked out a mutually acceptable agreement which was quickly rubber-stamped by the GDR parliament.

October 3, 1990 was the date of **German reunification**, an event which did not see a repeat of earlier celebrations. For many ordinary people in the East, dazed by the rapid economic collapse of the GDR and subsequent social dislocation, reunification seemed to offer little, other than the prospect of unemployment and uncertainty. Nevertheless Kohl's audacious and opportunistic masterminding of events paid off, when, in December 1990, the first united German elections resulted in triumph for the CDU.

However, 1991 brought vastly unpopular **tax increases in western Germany** to pay for reunification, and a sharp rise in unemployment in the east meant an end to the Chancellor's wide public popularity. On April 1 Red Army Faction terrorists **assassinated Detlev Rohwedder**, the head of the *Treuhandgesellschaft*, the body responsible for the privatisation of the ex-GDR's industry. This was an isolated incident but did little to bolster public confidence in the way the domestic political situation was being handled. Shortly afterwards the CDU were defeated in local elections in Rhineland-Palatinate, an area widely regarded as Helmut Kohl's powerbase.

On June 20 an unexpected *Bundestag* decision to **relocate the seat of government to Berlin** (all key functions to be transferred by 2003 at the latest) provided brief distraction, but by September attention was once more focussed on the darker side of reunification.

Attacks on foreigners, commonplace in the GDR even before the *Wende*, had been increasing steadily since the fall of the Wall. In September they mounted in intensity with one of the worst outbreaks taking place in the small Saxon town of **Hoyerswerda**, where a mob stormed a hostel housing asylum seekers, necessitating the removal of the residents under police escort.

Hoyerswerda became a symbol for a wave of anti-foreigner violence that extended into western Germany, and which the government seemed unable to deal with. Rather than condemning the attacks in a forthright manner, the political establishment concentrated on calling for reform of Germany's liberal asylum laws. Electorally this made sense — the far-right was gaining ground as shown by the **Republicans gaining 10.5 percent of the vote in Baden-Württemberg's local elections** in April 1992 — but many observers felt that such moral haziness only served to offer encouragement to the extremists.

TOWARDS THE TWENTY-FIRST CENTURY

Unsurprisingly the German political agenda for the remainder of the century seems likely to be dominated by the **problems thrown up by reunification**.

Foremost among these is the continuing **economic gap between western and eastern Germany**. Despite steady investment from the west and other European countries, the east still lags badly and pessimists predict that it may well continue to do so indefinitely in much the same way that southern Italy trails the more prosperous north. Another pressing problem is the social gulf that separates the two parts of the country, a result of forty years of separate development. This is exacerbated by western anger at higher taxes to subsidise the east, and eastern resentment of what are seen as patronising and neo-colonialist western attitudes to the people of the former GDR.

At the beginning of 1992 it had become apparent that the ever-increasing cost of reunification had pushed the German economy into **recession**. Unemployment in the east and popular fear that it could spread to the west have proved to be a boon for the far-right and there are fears that if economic problems intensify their significant gains in Baden-

Württemberg could be repeated on a nation-wide scale.

There can be no doubt that the united Germany will dominate Europe politically and economically, and the prospect of internal instability is one that causes much trepidation in other countries. Both within Germany and in neighbouring countries it is hoped that the **European Community** will exert a stabilising influence, enabling Germany to play a responsible and constructive role in the shaping of the new Europe.

PAINTING AND GRAPHICS

Germany's artistic history is marked more by solid and sustained achievement than by the more usual pattern of pre-eminence followed by decline. As in Italy, the fragmentation of the nation into a multitude of tiny states led to the development of many important centres of art, often of a very distinctive character.

The country's geographical position has meant that it has been a melting-pot for influences from Italy, France and the Low Countries, although, with several notable exceptions, the work of German painters never managed to gain the same international esteem. This, however, is mainly because the vast majority of German paintings have remained within the German-speaking countries, a consequence of the fact that many of the petty princes were great art collectors, and also because of the Romantic movement, which fostered a sense of awareness of the national heritage. As a result, important **museums** existed all over the country by the mid-nineteenth century.

German **graphic work**, being by its nature for dissemination, is perhaps more immediately familiar; the stark contrasts enforced by the media of woodcut, engraving and etching obviously proved temperamentally ideal for the country's artists, whose legacy in these fields far surpasses that of anywhere else in Europe.

BEGINNINGS

German painting has its roots in the ninth-century Carolingian epoch. **Illuminated manuscripts** were created in the scriptoria of the court and the monasteries; these typically featured vibrant figures in flowing draperies, charged with movement and set in elaborate architectural surrounds. This art form was refined and developed in the subsequent Ottonian period, most notably in Trier, which in the late tenth century boasted the first great German artist in an illuminator now dubbed **Master of the Registrum Gregorii**. A number of manuscripts by him have been identified; they show a new, more plastic style based on an understanding of Classical antiquity solving the problems of space and form which baffled all the other illuminators of the time. He built up a highly influential fund of forms which was imitated in the other great places of book production – Fulda, Hildesheim and Bavaria – although there were also more conservative centres, particularly those on the island of the Reichenau, which favoured an expressive linear form.

Fresco cycles were the other chief form of painting, and were often more closely related to the art of the book than might be supposed from the contrasting nature of the two forms. One of the best early examples to have survived is again from Trier; probably dating from the end of the ninth century, it originally adorned the crypt of St Maximin, but has been removed to the museum. From the following century, there is an important cycle still *in situ* at St Georg in Oberzell on the Reichenau, along with one in the Andreaskirche am Neuenberg, just outside Fulda. Belonging more obviously to international Romanesque currents are the later fresco cycles of the Lower Rhineland and Regensburg. The former – St Gereon in Cologne, Schwarzrheindorf and Knechtsteden – are all influenced by Byzantine concepts of form, style and iconography; regrettably, their quality has been impaired by over-enthusiastic nineteenth-century restorers who indulged in far too much speculative re-touching.

Later Romanesque illuminated manuscripts tend to follow rather than develop the Ottonian forms, although there was something of a revival in the late twelfth century, with such deluxe products as the *Gospels of Henry the Lion*, now in Wolfenbüttel. Roughly contemporary is a survival which is unique of its kind, the painted **wooden ceiling** illustrating the *Tree of Jesse* which adorns the vault of St Michael in Hildesheim.

THE EARLY GOTHIC PERIOD

The earliest Gothic **panel paintings** to have survived in Germany date from around 1300. Throughout the fourteenth century, religious themes retained their monopoly, and the most active workshops were in Cologne and Westphalia. The former was the dominant city of medieval Germany, and maintained its own strong and characteristic traditions right up until the early sixteenth century, assimilating varied foreign influences yet remaining rooted in tradition. Painting there was based on a strict **guild system**, which imposed stiff tests of skill on would-be applicants and even stipulated the quality of materials which had to be employed. Among the most important productions of this school in the fourteenth century were the monumental paintings on the backs of the Dom's stalls, the *Clares Altar*, again in the Dom, and some very ruinous frescos for the Rathaus which have been attributed to a somewhat legendary figure named **Master Wilhelm**.

The first German artist about whom much information has survived is **Master Bertram** (c.1345–1415), a Westphalian who worked in Hamburg. He seems to have been influenced by the art of Bohemia, which was part of the Holy Roman Empire, and was far in advance of fourteenth-century Germany in terms of the achievements of its painters. Bertram favoured narrative cycles of little panels grouped round pieces of sculpture; his major work is the *Grabow Altar* of 1379 in Hamburg, which displays prodigious and original imaginative powers, particularly in the charming scenes of the Creation. From about a decade later is the *Passion Altar* in Hannover, while the *Buxtehude Altar*, again in Hamburg, is from ten years later; both are remarkably consistent in style.

Another Westphalian was the **Master of the Berswordt Altar** (active late fourteenth century), named after a triptych still *in situ* in the Marienkirche in Dortmund; he also painted a polyptych for the Neustädterkirche in Bielefeld. The influence of French and Burgundian manuscripts is apparent, and he was an early representative of the courtly and idealised International Gothic style which was

to spread all over Europe. In Germany, this is usually referred to as the **Soft Style**, and is found in sculpture as well as painting. Its greatest exponent was **Conrad von Soest** (active c.1394–1422), one of the most immediately appealing of all German painters, who may even have been the son of the previous artist. His panels are refined and beautiful, executed in glowing colours and including a fair amount of amusing anecdotal detail. The late high altar triptych of the Marienkirche in his native Dortmund shows his art at its peak, but is sadly truncated. Another major painter in this style was **Master Francke** (active c.1405–25), who succeeded Bertram in Hamburg and could conceivably have been his pupil; his reputation rests largely on the *St Thomas à Becket Altar* which was commissioned by the local merchants who traded with England. Also active at this time were the **Master of the Virgin of Benediktbeuern** in Bavaria and various artists in Lower Saxony, most of whose works are now in Hannover.

THE FIFTEENTH-CENTURY COLOGNE SCHOOL

The entire fifteenth century was an outstandingly brilliant artistic period for Cologne. Although the artists still mostly remain anonymous, their styles became far more contrasted than in former times, and art historians have been able to group bodies of work under pseudonyms based on the names of their major masterpieces, which are now mostly housed in the city's Wallraf-Richartz Museum, or in the Alte Pinakothek in Munich. As well as large-scale commissions to adorn the plethora of churches and monasteries, there's increasing evidence of the burgeoning of the merchant class in the number of small altarpieces (obviously intended for private devotion) which have survived. The symbolical depiction of the Madonna and Child in the Garden of Paradise was enduringly popular; another vogue subject (the two were sometimes combined) was the Holy Kinship, depicting the extended family of Christ. First to develop a distinctive style was the **Master of St Veronica** (active c.1400–20), named after *St Veronica with the Sudarium*, now in Munich. The monumental faces in this work, mirrored elsewhere in his output, give evidence of influence from Bohemia, but that he had also understood the lessons of Burgundian miniatures is proved by the crowded *Calvary* in Cologne. His workshop may have been taken over after his death by the **Master of St Lawrence** (active c.1415–30), whose main work is a retable made for the demolished church of St Lorenz, parts of which survive in the museums of Cologne and Nürnberg.

These artists were surpassed by **Stefan Lochner** (c.1400–51), a Swabian who settled in the city and perfectly assimilated its traditions, along with innovations from Flanders. His soft, gentle and painstakingly detailed panels are among the peaks of the entire International Gothic movement, and he appears to have been something of a celebrity, which accounts for his name surviving the oblivion into which his rivals have plunged. His masterpiece is the *Epiphany* triptych now in Cologne's Dom, originally painted for the Rathaus, a far more monumental work than was usual in Cologne. It has been criticised for a failure to characterise the figures, but that is to miss the point – Lochner's art is quite consciously ethereal in spirit. If anything, the later *Presentation in the Temple*, now in Darmstadt, is even more sumptuous, while his last work, *Madonna of the Rose Bower* in Cologne, takes the art of the small altar to a level beyond which it could not progress. Even with gruesome subjects, such as *Last Judgment* in Cologne and its reverse, *Martyrdoms of the Apostles*, now in Frankfurt, Lochner did not depart from his essential gentleness, always drawing the optimistic lesson from the subject; if that can be counted as a failing, his extraordinary inventive powers amply compensate.

The following generation moved away from static and decorative effects to a lively narrative style, clearly modelled on the great contemporary Netherlanders. Rogier van der Weyden's late *St Columba* triptych (now in Munich) was painted for a church in Cologne, and must have made an enormous impact, although the more rounded and less emotional style of Dieric Bouts is the obvious source for the leading artist of the group, the **Master of the Life of the Virgin** (active c.1460–85), so named from a cycle of eight panels, seven of which are also now in Munich. He displays all the qualities of a great story-teller, the figures strongly drawn and richly clad, standing out in sharp relief from the background, with plenty of subsidiary anecdotal detail including exquisite still-lifes. This artist's later work includes portraits of merchants, which mark the end of the ecclesiastical monopoly over art. Three other painters closely associated with him are the **Master of the Lyversberg Passion**, the **Master of the St George Legend** and the **Master of the Bonn Diptych**; they may even have shared the same studio. Slightly later is the **Master of the Glorification of the Virgin** (active c.1475–95) who is less overtly Flemish in spirit; his backgrounds include accurate depictions of Cologne and its surrounding countryside.

Among the final generation of Cologne painters, the **Master of the Holy Kinship** (c.1450–1515) takes his name from the most spectacular version ever painted of the favourite Cologne subject, which shows acquaintance with the very latest Flemish innovations; otherwise, he seems to have been more adept on a smaller scale, his larger canvases betraying the use of inexperienced assistants. His contemporary, the **Master of the St Ursula Legend** (active c.1490–1505), developed the narrative tradition in a now dispersed series, partly preserved in the museums of Cologne, Bonn and Nürnberg. This artist displays far more interest in integrating the backgrounds with the action, and his handling of space and perspective show a sizeable advance, while his technique of rapid brushstrokes is quite different from the smooth layered approach of his predecessors. He strongly influenced the **Master of St Severin** (active c.1490–1510) a prolific and uneven painter, with whom he probably shared a studio.

Ultimately, the Cologne School simply burned itself out, but it did come to a fitting climax with the **Master of the St Bartholomew Altar** (active c.1470–1510) whose highly idiosyncratic compositions display all the sense of freedom and mannerism which so often characterise the final fling of an artistic style. He was trained in Utrecht and may have been Dutch; at first he worked as a manuscript illuminator. His earlier panels are rather hesitant, but by about 1495 he was painting with ever-increasing confidence, using bright, enamel-type colours. Invariably his figures are executed as if in imitation of sculpture, and some of his paintings, such as the eponymous work in Munich and the *Crucifixion* triptych in Cologne, appear as *trompe l'oeil* versions of carved retables. Even more bizarre are canvases such as the *St Thomas Altar* in Cologne, where the highly realistic figures are made to float quite illogically in space.

GOTHIC ELSEWHERE IN GERMANY

In the early fifteenth century, Cologne unquestionably held the artistic lead in Germany; a gorgeous *Garden of Paradise* preserved in Frankfurt by an unknown Upper Rhenish master from about 1420 is a clear case of the hegemony this style enjoyed. As the century wore on, however, it was Swabian painters who pioneered moves towards more realistic forms, and thus paved the way to the Renaissance. First of these was **Lucas Moser**, probably a stained glass designer by training, whose sole known work is the outside of the triptych still *in situ* in Tiefenbronn, dated 1431. Although the execution is still very soft and beautiful, an attempt is made at diminishing perspectives, while the water in the sea has both ripples and reflections. Very different is the *Wurzach Altar* of six years later, now in Berlin, which was made in the workshop of the great Ulm sculptor **Hans Multscher** (c.1400–67), though it's unresolved as to whether it was executed by the master himself, or by an unknown assistant who specialised in the painting side of the business. The figures in these Passion scenes are made deliberately crude, with exaggerated theatrical gestures, and seem to have been modelled on real-life peasants; they are about as far away from the contemporary work of Lochner as it is possible to get.

A far more refined painter of the realist tendency was **Konrad Witz** (c.1400–46) of Rottweil, who spent all his working life in Switzerland. His surviving legacy consists of about twenty panels taken from three separate retables; Basel and Geneva have the best examples, but others are in Berlin and Nürnberg. In them, he successfully resolved the new realism with traditional forms and grappled with such problems as perspective and movement. His figures have a sculptural quality and are treated as masses, not as means of portrayal; the rich and luminous colours employed are also an important feature. Most enduring of all was his contribution to landscape painting, being the first to introduce topographically accurate views of scenery, as opposed to cities, into his pictures. Witz's influence is discernible in the few surviving works of the **Master of the Darmstadt Passion**, who was active mid-century in the Middle Rhine region. **Friedrich Herlin** (c.1435–1499) of Nördlingen, who painted grave, severe figures, was another to follow his example; he in turn was succeeded by **Bartholomäus Zeitblom** (c.1455–1520) of Ulm.

Among Bavarian painters of this period, **Master of the Tegernsee Altar** (active c.1430–50) was somewhat archaic in style but capable of highly dramatic effects, notably the curious *Crucifixion* in his native Munich, which is set within elaborate Gothic architecture. Also working in this city was the **Master of the Polling Panels** (active c.1434–50) who retained the International Gothic style, whilst injecting it with a dose of realism. In the same period, Nürnberg boasted the **Master of the Imhoff Altar** and the **Master of the Tucher Altar**; the latter's work is characterised by strongly-drawn thick-set figures, prominent still lifes, and attempts at perspective. They were succeeded by **Hans Pleydenwurff** (c.1420–72), who showed a thorough knowledge of Netherlandish artists such as Bouts in colour, figure modelling and background cityscapes, often with small subsidiary scenes; he was also a notable portraitist. After his death, his workshop was taken over by **Michael Wolgemut** (1434–1519). **Rueland Frueauf** (c.1440–1507) founded the Danube School of painting in Passau and Salzburg; although few works by him survive, the *Man of Sorrows* in Munich is an arresting masterpiece, achieved by great economy of means. His son of the same name (c.1470–1545) carried on his style.

The late Gothic period also saw something of a revival in Westphalia. In Münster, **Johann Koerbecke** (active 1446–90) gave a more forceful treatment to facial expression than his Cologne contemporaries. A delicate, sensitive touch is revealed in the work of the **Master of Liesborn** (active late fifteenth century); in contrast, **Derick Baegert** (c.1440–1515) imbued his paintings with a rugged dramatic quality.

Jan Joest of Kalkar (c.1455–1519) submerged himself in the art of the nearby Netherlands; he appears to have had a remarkable career, travelling as far afield as Spain, where he painted a retable for Palencia Cathedral which remains *in situ*. Lübeck's

Hermen Rode (active 1485–1504) was another practitioner of the new realism.

THE RISE OF GRAPHIC ARTS

Gutenberg's printing revolution sounded the death knell for illuminated manuscripts and gave an enormous stimulus to the black-and-white arts, with the traditional woodcut being followed by the new techniques of line engraving and drypoint, which appeared in the 1440s. At first, the forms were dominated by obscure figures from the Mainz area – the two pioneers were the so-called **Master of the Playing Cards**, whose reputation rests on an elaborate card deck, and **Master ES**, among whose creations is a fantastic alphabet. Another engraver known only by his initials is **Master LCZ** of Bamberg, by whom some expressive panels also survive.

A more rounded personality appears in **Master of the Housebook** (active c.1470–1500), around whom a sizeable body of work has been gathered; many attempts have been made to equate him with **Erhard Reuwich**, who executed a series of woodcuts for a book on a journey to the Holy Land. His pseudonym derives from an extraordinary book of drawings in a private collection; it was the manual of a master of munitions at a princely court, and contains elaborate astrological groupings as well as scenes of warfare. Even finer are his delicate drypoints, which depict with both humanity and humour the everyday life of the time, from the fashions and fantasies of the small courts to the earthy pastimes of the peasantry. The draughtsman's technique is also evident in the linear form of his few paintings, which include two retables, one in Mainz, the other dispersed in the museums of Freiburg, Berlin and Frankfurt.

An equally great but very different graphic artist was **Martin Schongauer** (c.1450–91) of Colmar, which was then very much a German city. He has always been a revered figure, as he marks the transition from the late Gothic to the Renaissance, and is thus the founding father of the short but glorious period when the German visual arts reached the highest peaks of their achievement. Over a hundred surviving engravings show his successful fusion of realism and expressionism from Northern artists with the exotic interests and technical innovations of space, form and perspective which characterise the Italian Renaissance. They were to serve as a model and an inspiration to the succeeding generation, who increasingly came to realise that the print was an important new democratic art form closely in tune with the spirit of the age, with potential for reaching a far wider public than had ever been possible before. Schongauer's surviving paintings are tantalisingly few but always of very high quality – they include the large *Madonna of the Rose Bush* in his native city, some damaged frescos of *The Last Judgment* in nearby Breisach, and several highly finished little panels of *The Nativity*, the finest of which is in Berlin.

THE TRIUMPH OF THE RENAISSANCE

The most dominant personality in the history of German art was **Albrecht Dürer** (1471–1528), who trained under Wolgemut in his native Nürnberg. Dürer was a true man of the Renaissance, gaining a broad range of experiences in antithesis to the painstaking workshop traditions which were the lot of the medieval artist. He undertook travels to Italy, Switzerland, Alsace and the Low Countries, assimilating their traditions and gained mastery in all artistic media, yet also found time to write and engage in mathematical and scientific research as well as to be involved in the Reformation, ending up excommunicated for Lutheran sympathies. Surprisingly, canvas painting does not always show Dürer at his best – he was at times rather conservative in his earlier religious panels, but increased in confidence with time, as can be seen in his valedictory *Four Apostles* in Munich. His portraits from life, however, are almost uniformly superb, laying bare the soul of the subject in penetrating psychological observations, as in *Jacob Muffel* and *Hieronymus Holzschuher*, both now in Berlin. With the woodcut, Dürer was in a class of his own; while still in his twenties he created an *Apocalypse* series of quite menacing power and profound imagination, which he printed and published himself. This was followed by two *Passion* series, a lovely *Life of the Virgin* and the stupendous *Triumphal Arch* commissioned by the Emperor Maximilian; he also made many memorable engravings, often deeply overlaid with symbolic meaning. Dürer was also the first artist to realize the possibilities of watercolour, making beautiful landscapes, plant and animal studies for his own edification. The originals of these are now rarely exhibited for conservation reasons, yet such works as *Young Hare* and *Blade of Grass* rank among the most familiar images in Renaissance art.

In Munich, the Polish-born **Jan Polack** (active c.1480–1519) painted mannered altarpieces featuring emotional figures clad in swirling draperies, along with portraits more obviously imbued with the new Renaissance outlook. A far more significant artistic centre was Augsburg, seat of the Habsburg court. **Hans Holbein the Elder** (c.1465–1524) showed increasing Renaissance influence in his prolific output of retables, although he was never entirely able to free himself from the old forms. His brother-in-law **Hans Burgkmair** was more successful, benefiting from a spell as Schongauer's assistant; he particularly delighted in the most luxuriant Italianate features, which he skilfully synthesised into his altars. This decorative talent was given full rein by Emperor Maximilian I, who commissioned him to supervise the overall programme of the huge series of woodcuts of his *Triumphal Procession*; many of the leading German artists, including Dürer, contributed, although the success of the project was due to the relish shown by Burgkmair. **Jörg Breu** (c.1475–1537) was another fine retable painter resident in the city, while **Bernhardin Strigel** (c.1460–1528) served as court portraitist. The latter's linear approach is distinctive, and he developed family groups as an independent art form.

By far the greatest painter Augsburg produced was **Hans Holbein the Younger** (1497/8–1543), but he left while still in his teens, and spent the rest of his career in Switzerland and England. He first settled in Basel (which retains by far the best collection of his art), where he was enormously productive in all kinds of media – portraits, altarpieces, decorative schemes of many types (now mostly lost) and woodcuts, including the celebrated *Dance of Death*. One of his masterpieces from this period, and one of few works by him actually in Germany, is the *Madonna of Burgomaster Mayer* in Darmstadt Schloss, which combines sharply characterised portraits and a devotional theme. He subsequently concentrated almost exclusively on portraiture,

developing a cool, detached style based on absolute technical mastery, and frequently incorporating amazingly precise still-lifes based on the paraphernalia of the sitter's occupation; *The Danzig Merchant Georg Gisze*, now in Berlin, is an outstanding example. On his second visit to England, he became court painter to Henry VIII, and left a haunting series of drawings of that magnificent but tragic circle, though sadly few of the finished paintings have been preserved.

Lucas Cranach the Elder (1472–1553) was the earliest great Saxon painter. The first thirty years of his life are obscure; he is first known as a mature artist playing a dominant role in the Danube School, painting portraits and religious scenes set in lush and suggestively beautiful verdant landscapes. His masterpiece of this period is *The Three Crosses* in Munich, which uses a blatantly eccentric vantage point in order to emphasise the artist's technical control. Whereas these works have consistently been admired, Cranach's long second phase at Wittenberg in the service of the Electors of Saxony is far more controversial. He ran the equivalent of a picture factory, often repeating the same subjects *ad infinitum* with only minor variations; the style is mannered with imperfections in drawing and subjects placed in wholly unrealistic relationships. Yet these were surely deliberate traits by a great humorist and individualist, whose sinuous nudes and erotic mythological scenes added a dimension to German painting which had previously been lacking. He seems to have invented the full-length portrait as a genre, and excelled at characterisation. As a personal friend of Luther and Melanchthon, he created the definitive images of the leaders of the Reformation and made propaganda woodcuts on their behalf, but was not averse to accepting traditional commissions from the Catholics as well. His son **Lucas Cranach the Younger** (1515–86) took over the workshop and continued its tradition very faithfully, although at times he was prone to overdo the bucolic effect.

Albrecht Altdorfer (c.1480–1538) of Regensburg became the leading master of the Danube School; his luxuriant landscape backgrounds assume even greater significance than with Cranach, and at times the ostensible subject is quite unimportant, as with *St George* *and the Dragon* in Munich. Fantastic buildings also feature in several of his works, reflecting the fact that he was also a practising architect. When the figures do matter, they are integrated with their surroundings and given highly expressive tendencies, achieved by deliberate anatomical imprecisions and exaggerated gestures. Light is often an important feature, with unnaturally colourful effects; unorthodox aerial perspectives further distinguish his paintings. The largest group of Altdorfer's work, in which all these features appear, is still mostly *in situ* in the Austrian monastery of St Florian. However, his masterpiece is the *Battle of Darius and Alexander* in Munich; commissioned as part of a war series, each by different artists, it makes all the others look like the work of bumbling amateurs. The actual battle is depicted with all the skill of a miniaturist, yet it is set within a spectacular cosmic perspective in what ranks as one of the most formidable displays of sheer pyrotechnics in the history of painting. His chief follower was **Wolf Huber** (c.1490–1553) of Passau, who was rather more restrained in his effects.

The extreme tendency towards expression in German painting is found in the work of the painter known as **Grünewald**, although his real name was **Mathis Gothardt-Neithardt** (c.1470/5–1528), who is almost a direct opposite of Dürer. Fully proficient in the new Renaissance developments of space and perspective, he used them as mere adjuncts to his sense of drama; he was also the only great German artist of his time who seems to have had no interest in the print. Even in an early work such as *The Mocking of Christ* in Munich, Grünewald's emotional power is evident. No artist ever painted Passion scenes with anything like the same harrowing intensity; in the words of the nineteenth-century French novelist Huysmans, "he promptly strikes you dumb with the fearsome nightmare of a Calvary". His huge folding polyptych, the *Isenheim Altar*, represents the majority of his surviving work. Though its panels are of uneven quality, its moods – ranging from a tender *Madonna and Child* to the blazing triumphant glory of *The Resurrection* are of such variety that it deserves its reputation as the ultimate masterpiece of German painting; ironically, its Colmar home is now French territory. Its *Crucifixion* manages to radiate hope through

the darkness, whereas the later version in Karlsruhe is of a forbidding bleakness.

Grünewald's art is so individual and overpowering that he had no successors. However, **Jerg Ratgeb** (c.1480–1526) must have come under his influence as his few works – fresco cycles in Frankfurt and Maulbronn, and the *Herrenberg Altar* in Stuttgart – have an even rawer expressiveness, which might have developed had he not been quartered for his leading role in the Peasants' Revolt.

Of the younger generation of Renaissance artists, by far the most interesting is **Hans Baldung Grien** (1484/5–1545), a flawed genius who studied under Dürer and eventually settled in Strasbourg. Colour and volume play a large part in his pictures, but his fascination with the bizarre is the most obvious recurring element, with moralistic fantasies being among his finest works. Baldung's main religious works are two altars for the Freiburg Münster, but there is no concentration of his output, which is now spread among many museums. The late engravings such as *Wild Horses* and *Bewitched Stable Boy* are quite unlike the work of any other artist, and arguably rank as his greatest achievements.

Hans Süss von Kulmbach (c.1480–1522) and **Hans Leonard Schäuffelein** (c.1483–1539/40) were loyal followers of Dürer's example, but their productions ultimately lack his inspired touch; the specialist engravers, the brothers **Hans Sebald Beham** (1500–50) and **Barthel Beham** (1502–40), and the Westphalian **Heinrich Aldegraver** (1502–60) were arguably more successful at capturing his spirit. The **Master of Messkirch** (active c.1430–45) added a personal expressive sense to the Düreresque idiom.

The early sixteenth century also saw a mushrooming of talented provincial portraitists who were able to satisfy the ever-increasing demand from the rising middle-classes; they often painted religious and mythological subjects as well, but with less success. In Nürnberg, **Georg Pencz** (c.1500–50), possibly another pupil of Dürer, was strongly influenced by Venetian models. Augsburg at this time had **Cristoph Amberger** (c.1500–61/2), who was more associated with the court, and **Ulrich Apt** (c.1460–1532). The works of Frankfurt's **Conrad Faber von Creuznach** (c.1500–53) are particularly felicitous, with the sitters placed against landscapes reminiscent of the Danube School; he also executed a magnificent woodcut of the siege of his home city. **Barthel Bruyn** (1492/3–1555) was the first Cologne painter to break away from two centuries of tradition; in spite of several diverse influences, the city's great heritage seems to have made little impression on his art. In Münster, **Ludger tom Ring the Elder** (1496–1547) founded a dynasty which specialized in slightly crude portraits and altars for both Protestant and Catholic use. His style was continued by his sons **Hermann tom Ring** (1521–96) and **Ludger tom Ring the Younger** (1522–84); the latter seems to have been the first German artist to treat still-life as an independent form.

MANNERISM AND BAROQUE

Mannerism is already evident in the work of the generation after Dürer, but only appears in a full-blooded way with **Hans von Aachen** (1552–1616), who particularly excelled at sensual mythological subjects, and who played a leading role in the highly distinctive erotic style fostered at the court of Emperor Rudolph II in Prague. **Johann Rottenhammer** (1564–1625) travelled extensively in Italy, before returning to his native Augsburg. He came under the spell of Paolo Veronese's huge decorative works filled with figures; his response was to reduce such compositions on to little copper panels, adding an extra degree of luminosity into the landscapes.

This highly skilled technique was developed by his pupil, **Adam Elsheimer** (1578–1610), who settled in Rome and achieved a remarkable synthesis of diverse influences which gives his works a stature that belies their small size. Elsheimer drew on Altdorfer's heritage in creating a union between the subjects and nature, which Rottenhammer left as rather disparate features. He also seemed to share the earlier master's genius for light effects, and was particularly adept at night scenes and at strong contrasts of brightness and shadow derived from Caravaggio. A slow and deliberate worker, his early death meant that his legacy is numerically modest, but it was to influence such contrasting great successors as Rubens, Rembrandt and Claude. The largest assemblage of his work is *Altar of the Holy Cross* whose panels have been painstakingly reassembled over the years in his native Frankfurt;

many of his best paintings are in Britain, due to the esteem in which he was held by the aristocrats of the Grand Tour. Unfortunately, there was no great German successor, although his style was continued with varying success long after his death by **Johann König** (1586–1642).

The other main German painter of the early seventeenth century, **Johann Liss** (1597–1629), was constantly on the move, leaving his native Holstein for the Low Countries and then Italy, absorbing their diverse traditions. One vein of his work, the small arcadian landscapes, reveals the impact of Elsheimer or at least his Roman followers, but his best canvases are far more monumental in scale, swaggering in the full pomp characteristic of the new Baroque age. These religious and mythological scenes, sometimes featuring sumptuous banquets, are executed with fluid brushwork in luminous and daringly unorthodox colours.

Liss was also to occupy a premature grave, and it seems as if German painting in the seventeenth century was to be jinxed, in contrast to its richness and diversity in this period over the rest of Europe. The Thirty Years' War, which so exhausted and preoccupied the country, acted as a massive restraint on artistic activity at the time, but was to fuel a long-standing vogue for depictions of battles and genre scenes of military life evidenced in the work of **Matthias Scheits** (c.1630–1700) and **Georg Philip Rugendas** (1666–1742), though these tend to follow the decorative Dutch manner, rather than convey the true horrors the country suffered. An increased religious fervour as a result of the war is mirrored in the emotional cycles of canvases and frescos by the Catholic convert **Michael Willmann** (1630–1706), the best of which are in the monasteries in Silesia (now part of Poland).

Specialist painters of the period include **Wolfgang Heimbach** (c.1613–78), a deaf-mute who created small scenes of middle-class life and used nocturnal lighting to good effect; the animal artist **Karl Andreas Ruthard** (c.1630–1703); and **Abraham Mignon** (1640–79), whose cool and precise still-lifes typically show ripe fruit and flowers in full bloom. Far more versatile than any of these was **Johann Friedrich Schönfeld** (1609–84), whose output is rather uneven due to an excessive number of changes of style in response to the diversity he encountered on his Italian travels. His best paintings are colourful history scenes with elaborate backgrounds, painted under the influence of the classically derived compositions of Poussin which held sway in Rome, but tempered by the more light-hearted Neapolitan approach.

However, the most significant art works produced in mid-seventeenth-century Germany were the detailed engravings of towns, known as *Topographia Germaniae*, started by **Matthäus Merian** (1593–1650), and continued by his sons. In due course, the appearances of some 2000 German communities – a unique pictorial record – were preserved for posterity.

LATE BAROQUE, ROCOCO AND NEOCLASSICISM

The best late Baroque German painting is not to be found in any museum, but on the walls of the ornate pilgrimage churches of Bavaria and Baden-Württemberg. These buildings, which aimed at fusing all the visual arts into a coherent synthesis, are among the most original creations in the country. Their rich interior decoration formed an intrinsic part of the architecture from the outset, and was often the work of the same masters.

One of the most accomplished of these was **Cosmas Damian Asam** (1686–1739), who formed a team with his sculptor brother, Egid Quirin Asam. At first they decorated existing churches, such as the Dom in Freising, but later moved on to the logical conclusion of undertaking the entire programme themselves. They trained in Rome and remained loyal to its dignified High Baroque, rather than to the more frivolous Rococo derivatives favoured by their fellow countrymen. C.D. Asam's ceiling frescos fall into two separate categories – the trick device of diminishing perspective in the manner of the Italian Jesuit Andrea Pozzo, and a more conventional spatial format of open heavens. **Johann Baptist Zimmerman** (1680–1758), in contrast, is fully Rococo; he did not design buildings himself, but enjoyed a particularly close relationship with two of the leading architects of the time, François Cuvilliés, with whom he collaborated on the Munich Residenz and Schloss Nymphenburg; and his own younger brother Dominikus, with whom he worked on the Wieskirche near Munich.

By this time, Prussia had arisen as a major power in European affairs, and was by far the dominant German state. Frederick the Great was a major patron of the arts, but he was also a Francophile whose court painter was the Parisian-born **Antoine Pesne** (1683–1757). This artist was commissioned to paint allegorical and mythological decorative schemes for the royal palaces, but his realistic portraits, very much in the French manner of the time with rich colours and subtle lighting effects, were more successful and ultimately highly influential, serving as the model for later Berlin artists. His most important pupil was **Bernhard Rode** (1725–97), who was also involved in the work on the palaces, but who is seen at his best in quietly observed genre scenes. For the last period of his life, he directed the Berlin Academy, one of several founded in the major cities in order to foster a theoretical approach to painting. Another of this circle was **Daniel Nikolaus Chodowiecki** (1726–1801), although his talent was best suited to vignette etchings, mostly to illustrate books. A later Berlin artist, the Danish-born **Asmus Jakob Carstens** (1754–98) was also at his finest in black and white media, executing large chalk cartoons of classically inspired subjects.

One of the guiding lights of the movement was **Anton Raffael Mengs** (1728–79), son of the court painter in Dresden, who had ruthlessly prepared him for artistic fame from a very early age. Mengs was to have an amazingly successful career in Germany, Italy and particularly Spain. He was a key theorist and guru of the new Neoclassicism; his works are enormously skillful technically, but emotionally cold. The Swiss-born **Anton Graff** (1736–1835) was also a leading academic portraitist in Dresden. This same city was home to a succession of landscape painters throughout the century, whose work foreshadows the far more arresting compositions of the Romantics; **Johann Alexander Thiele** (1685–1752) was the first and most accomplished of these.

A strict Neoclassical style was adopted at the Kassel Academy under **Johann Heinrich Tischbein** (1722–89). This was modified by his nephews **Johann Friedrich August Tischbein** (1750–1812) and **Johann Heinrich Wilhelm Tischbein** (1751–1829) who introduced the greater warmth found in English and

French works of the time, though both remained loyal academicians. The latter's *Goethe in the Campagna* in Frankfurt is the most celebrated work of the dynasty.

Another family of painters had as by far its most accomplished member **Januarius Zick** (1730–97), who turned his back on his academic training. He was a theatrical but effective frescoist in the grand manner, as can be seen in the cycles in Wiblingen and Bruchsal. In contrast, his canvases are often of modest size, achieving an original synthesis of the light effects often found in Rembrandt's deeply intimate small-scale works with the airy Rococo grace of Watteau.

ROMANTICISM

The Romantic movement, a reaction against the rigidity of Neoclassicism but with the same Roman roots, was particularly strong in Germany; the rich outpourings of music and literature make it one of the supreme high-points in the country's cultural history. Although there was not the same depth of talent in painting, the haunting and highly original landscapes of **Caspar David Friedrich** (1774–1840) form a fitting visual counterpart to the works of the great poets and composers of the time. Friedrich created a new spiritual way of looking at the scenery: it was always the immensity and majesty of Nature that he sought to convey, often using the technique of enormously long perspectives. Unlike his great predecessor Altdorfer, he did not stress the unity of man and landscape, but rather the unconquerable power of the latter. Where figures are introduced, they are typically seen from the back, contemplating the wonders before them; in the more common absence of humans, the evidence of Man's presence tends to stress his fragility and ephemeral status – as in the famous *Eismeer* in Hamburg, or the many scenes with Classical temples and Gothic abbeys – in comparison with the omnipotent changelessness of the surroundings.

The influence of Friedrich's way of looking can sometimes be detected in the canvases of **Karl Friedrich Schinkel** (1781–1841), who was forced by financial considerations to turn to painting, where he abandoned the Neoclassicism of his buildings in favour of vast panoramas, architectural fantasies and theatrical spectaculars. **Philipp Otto Runge** (1777–

1810) might have developed into Friedrich's figurative counterpart had he lived longer. He had enormously grandiose ideas, aiming to recover the lost harmony of the universe through the symbolism of colours and numbers, and began a project called *The Times of Day*, of four panels over eight metres in height, which he aimed to instal in a specially-designed building in which poetry and music would be performed. That he managed to persuade no less than Goethe to co-operate in this suggests that there was genuine substance to this apparently utopian dream, but it was never executed and only studies survive, leaving Runge's reputation to rest largely on his portraits, particularly the over-sized ones of children.

Johann Friedrich Overbeck (1789–1869) was another Romantic with original convictions, settling in Rome where he founded the **Nazarene Brotherhood** of painters who lived like monks in a deconsecrated monastery. They produced two large co-operative fresco cycles: *The Story of Joseph*, which is currently in store in east Berlin, and another, still *in situ*, of scenes taken from Italian Renaissance literature. These very detailed works emphasised theme and content at the expense of form. The figures are ideal types, not taken from nature, the aim being to return to the soft otherworldly beauty found in quattrocento painting, an ideal followed soon afterwards by the English Pre-Raphaelites.

Whereas Overbeck remained in Italy, his collaborators **Peter von Cornelius** (1783–1867), **Julius Schnorr von Carolsfeld** (1794–1872) and **Wilhelm Schadow** (1788–1862) returned to Germany where they pursued careers in the academies. Cornelius had spells in charge of the two most dominant, Düsseldorf and Munich, and aimed to establish a tradition of monumental historical painting to rival the great frescos of Italy. Although both influential and genuinely popular in its day, this style of painting has, since the turn of the present century, attracted nothing but critical scorn, appearing as an empty display of bombastics. It can still be seen all over the country, often desecrating the walls of great medieval buildings; among the better efforts are the cycles by **Alfred Rethel** (1816–59) in the Aachen Rathaus and by the Austrian-born **Moritz von Schwind** (1804–71) in Karlsruhe's Kunsthalle, and the Wartburg near Eisenach. **Ferdinand Olivier** (1785–1841) painted narrative canvases in the Nazarene style, as well as more conventional Romantic landscapes. Standing somewhat apart are the expansive, open-ended fresco views painted in Munich by Ludwig I's court artist **Carl Rottmann** (1797–1850).

Romanticism in one form or another flourished throughout the nineteenth century. The brothers **Andreas Achenbach** (1815–1910) and **Oswald Achenbach** (1827–1905) continued in Friedrich's manner; the former was particularly successful at evocative northern scenery, whereas the latter added popular scenes to his pictures. **Karl Blechen** (1798–1840) also began in this style, but his later works, following a visit to Paris, became more consciously realist. **Anselm Feuerbach** (1829–80) pursued a heavily Italianate form of Romanticism in his portraits and densely crowded mythological scenes. There is a highly personal mixture of the Neoclassical and Romantic in **Hans von Marées** (1837–87), who achieved his masterpiece in his one commission for monumental frescos, the Aquarium in Naples. For long out of critical favour, his canvases have recently begun to attract a great deal of interest, even if the technical execution falls short of the artist's challenging intellect. The inconsistent **Hans Thoma** (1839–1924) tried many styles in his time; the Romantic views of the Black Forest are by far the most successful.

OTHER NINETEENTH-CENTURY STYLES

Although many different trends were current in nineteenth-century German painting, none of them can match the vitality of the best Romantic work. A style which was largely confined to the country and its immediate neighbours from about 1815–48 was Biedermeierstil, a bourgeois-inspired Classicism which drew on the pleasant aspects of living. **Carl Spitzweg** (1808–85) was its principal exponent; his homely pictures of the middle-classes are injected with a touch of humour mocking the complacency that was all too apparent. **Franz Krüger** (1797–1857) chronicled Berlin life of the time in a more straightlaced vein, particularly in his ceremonial scenes and architectural views; **Eduard Gärtner** (1801–77) is another painter of this type. Though he sometimes worked in the Düsseldorf academic manner, **Georg Friedrich Kersting** (1785–1847) was at his best in small-scale interiors, in which he showed his interest in everyday objects and activities as matters of beauty in their own right. Another Düsseldorf painter was **Ludwig Richter** (1804–83), but again his true métier lay in a quite different field, in this case illustrations of legends for children's books.

In contrast to this movement, there was a continued demand for official portraitists; one of the most accomplished was **Franz von Lenbach** (1836–1904), who painted Bismarck no less than eighty times. **Franz Xaver Winterhalter** (1805–73) had the most dazzling career of all, progressing round all the main European courts, leaving behind unremittingly flattering portrayals of smug monarchs and their pampered retinues whose psychological penetration is non-existent and artistic value small.

In the Realist tradition, Germany lagged behind France, although the versatile **Adolf Menzel** (1815–1905), who also executed portraits and history scenes in the grand manner, was one of the first to portray the Industrial Revolution and its effects. **Wilhelm Trübner** (1851–1917) was another to undertake this mix of subjects. The best examples of this style were to come from **Wilhelm Leibl** (1844–1900), who aimed to recreate the technical skill of the old masters. To this end he conducted such experiments as reviving tempera to create an enamel-like surface, and painting with the attention to detail of a miniaturist, as in *Three Women in Church* in Hamburg. Much of his finest work was done in the 1870s, when he lived in rural Bavaria, and used peasants as real-life models.

Impressionism was very slow to catch on, and never seems to have suited the German temperament, but three artists who adopted it at some point in their careers were **Max Liebermann** (1847–1935), who originally favoured the sombre colours of the French Barbizon School and the Realists; **Lovis Corinth** (1858–1925), whose best works are the late landscapes executed in cold colours; and **Max Slevogt** (1868–1932), who was also a book illustrator and, late in life, a painter of monumental frescos. Liebermann was the leading figure in the Berlin section of the

Secession movement which began in the 1890s; this was a reaction by the avant-garde against the stultifying power wielded by the academies. The earlier Munich group was dominated by **Franz von Stuck** (1863–1928), an artist of violent mythological scenes, humorous drawings and large-scale decorative work.

EXPRESSIONISM

Much as the early part of the nineteenth century saw the dominance of Romanticism in German painting, so the first decades of this century came under the sway of Expressionism, a new and largely indigenous style, which aimed to root modern painting firmly in the tradition of the old German masters, and to establish it on an equal footing with France, for some time the dominant force in world art. Because of the entrenched power of existing interests, artists found they had to bind themselves into **groups** in order to make an impact; the early history of Expressionism is particularly associated with two of these.

Although its members were younger, *Die Brücke* (The Bridge) was first to be founded, in 1905. Its initial personnel, **Ernst Ludwig Kirchner** (1880–1938), **Erich Heckel** (1883–1970) and **Karl Schmidt-Rottluff** (1884–1976) were architectural students in Dresden who felt constrained by the inability of their subject to capture the immediate freshness of inspiration. Consequently, they turned to painting, in which none had much experience; they were shortly joined by **Max Pechstein** (1881–1955) and **Otto Müller** (1874–1930). They valued colour as a component in its own right, and later strove to enhance its surface effect as well. Their devotion to the country's artistic heritage was shown in the emphasis they placed on feeling, and on their revival of the woodcut as a valid alternative to oils.

The group moved to Berlin, where they turned away from their original preoccupation with landscapes to the depiction of city life. Kirchner developed into the leader and best artist of the group. *Three Women in the Street*, now in Essen, is a key work; its strong sense of line shows the impact made by the arts of primitive peoples, then being appreciated in Europe for the first time. The group broke up in 1913, and thereafter each artist pursued an independent career. Kirchner turned to decorative design in the 1920s, working on embroideries

and tapestries; his later paintings show a stronger sense of abstraction. Heckel's work is closest to Kirchner's, though he was later to add a greater sense of realism to his pictures. Pechstein, at the time regarded as the most important Expressionist of all, has since suffered a slump in reputation; he was the most loyal to naturalistic representation and thus stands furthest removed from the path followed by Schmidt-Rottluff. Gipsy culture features strongly in Müller's work; he seems to have felt a genuine affinity with it, and spent much of the 1920s travelling among Balkan communities.

The second group of artists was *Der Blaue Reiter* (The Blue Rider), a strongly intellectual movement originating in Munich which aimed at uniting all the arts. Its name is taken from its magazine, which appeared only once (in 1912); it was very loosely structured and far more diverse than *Die Brücke*, with the lead being taken by two contrasting artistic personalities. The Russian-born **Wassily Kandinsky** (1866–1944) was a pioneer of pure abstraction, using fluid and soft forms, but strong and vibrant colours; he was also a noted writer and used words as the starting points for his images. **Franz Marc** (1880–1916), on the other hand, always retained at least a partial form of representation in his compositions. He was devoted to nature, and animals are a recurrent theme in his art; he regarded them as noble and uncorrupted, the complete antithesis to Man. At first they appear detached in the foreground; from 1913, when he adopted more abstract methods, they are more closely integrated with their surroundings. Geometry was always important to Marc, and he favoured prismatic colours, to which he attached a mystical significance. His development was cut short by the outbreak of war, and he was to die in combat.

This fate also befell an even younger member of the group, **August Macke** (1887–1914). Although Macke was clearly influenced by the new Cubist movement, his works are always representational, and he ranks as the most poetic and gentle of all the Expressionists. The figures are unmistakeable; slim and column-like, as though from a medieval cathedral, they glide across the picture surface, taking their Sunday stroll in the park, or indulging in a bit of window-shopping. More often than not, they wear a hat, which serves to distinguish them, as their facial features are never included. Strong colours are used, but they are never strident; they rather add to the happy and relaxed atmosphere.

Paul Klee (1879–1940), born in Switzerland but having German nationality as well, was the fourth main member of the group. He never concerned himself with any of the social, political or psychological problems of the age, but preferred to construct his own abstract language in which he aimed to recapture the mystery and magic of the universe. To this end, he developed a series of fractured and fragmented forms – arcs, forks and bars – which were usually painted black against a coloured background. In the 1920s, when they worked at the Bauhaus, he and Kandinsky formed *Die Blauen Vier* (The Blue Four) as a successor to *Der Blaue Reiter*.

The other members were **Alexej Jawlensky** (1864–1941), also of Russian birth, who specialised in characterful portrait heads; and **Lyonel Feininger** (1871–1956), who was born and died in New York, but who can be regarded as the most loyal German Cubist, being most notable for his architectural and marine scenes. Russian influence is apparent in the paintings of **Heinrich Campendonk** (1889–1957), the youngest member of *Der Blaue Reiter*, although his preferred medium was the woodcut.

A number of Expressionists unattached to either group were active in the Rhine-Ruhr area, where Macke also spent much of his life. Throughout a very long career, **Christian Rohlfs** (1849–1938) tried many different styles; he clearly came under the influence of the Impressionists but never fully adopted their manner. His true artistic personality did not emerge until his Expressionist phase, particularly the architectural paintings he made in Soest and Erfurt, and the very late flower pieces. Rohlfs clearly inspired **Wilhelm Morgner** (1891–1917), another war casualty. **Heinrich Nauen** (1880–1940) was one of several Expressionists who were quite overt about following French leads, in his case Matisse and the Fauves, whose bright colours form an important feature of his hybrid style.

Fauvism, particularly the Classically-inspired works of Derain, was also important to **Carl Hofer** (1878–1955). Primitive art as filtered through Gauguin made a strong impression on

Paula Becker-Modersohn (1876–1907), the most talented artist of the colony at Worpswede near Bremen. Whether or not she is really an Expressionist is debatable, as she did not concern herself with drama or emotions, though her favourite *Mother and Child* theme has achieved a certain poignancy in that she was to die during childbirth.

The most individualistic Expressionist of all, even though he had a spell as a member of *Die Brücke*, was **Emil Hansen** (1867–1956), generally called **Nolde** after his birthplace. In his depictions of the rugged Baltic coastline that was his home, he can be regarded as the successor to Friedrich. However, there's no sense of romance in Nolde's landscapes, which convey the harsh and forbidding nature of the terrain and its climate, emphasised in the way he captured its special colours and light effects by means of rich, strong and violently contrasting tones. Flowers and garden scenes provide a lighter note, but he also revived the somewhat lost art of religious painting, in which he aimed to recreate something of the intensity of Grünewald, along with the simple devotion he found in primitive art.

Ludwig Meidner (1884–1966) was dubbed the most Expressionist of the Expressionists, as a result of the powerful apocalyptic visions he painted before the war, which stand at the opposite extreme to the primitive trends in the movement. The union of all the arts sought by so many found its best individual manifestation in the work of **Ernst Barlach** (1870–1938). Primarily a sculptor, he was also a talented graphic artist, illustrating his own plays and travel writings. Another sculptor, **Käthe Kollwitz** (1867–1945) achieved great emotional power in her pacifist woodcuts, engravings and lithographs of wartime horrors.

OTHER TWENTIETH-CENTURY MOVEMENTS

Expressionism, in spite of its dominance, does not by any means cover the entire richness of German art in the early part of this century. The nihilistic Dada movement, which grew up during the war, included **Kurt Schwitters** (1887–1948), who took the concept of non-art to its extreme, experimenting with collages incorporating pieces of torn-up paper before moving on to using rubbish as his basic component. He dubbed his art *Merz* after the letters from one of the pieces of paper he used, and intended his life's work to be a huge composition which would fill a house, but the first two completed versions were destroyed, and his last attempt, in exile in England, was unfinished at his death. **Hannah Höch** (1889–1978) and the Austrian-born **Raoul Hausmann** (1886–1944) were two rather milder Dadaists. **George Grosz** (1893–1959) also began in this style, but his later works were more representational. A committed Communist, he was a savage satirist, particularly in his humorous drawings, ruthlessly attacking the corrupt and decadent vested interests of the Weimar Republic. Ironically, he was entranced by America and emigrated there just before the Nazi accession.

Inevitably, there grew a tendency which stood in polar opposition to Expressionism: **Neue Sachlichkeit** (New Objectivity), a term first used in 1923 to describe trends already apparent. This can be thought of as an updated form of realism, which aimed at depicting subjects in a straightforward and detailed way. Some of Grosz's work belongs to this style, but its finest practitioner was **Otto Dix** (1891–1969), who had been profoundly affected by the war, which thereafter formed a persistent subject of his work, although he used it to depict Man's suffering as opposed to any directly political overtone. He aimed to recapture the actual technique of the old masters, and his portraits show larger-than-life characters under a rich sheen of paint. In spite of the overt eroticism of many of his canvases, he was also drawn to the Passion, on which he placed a humanitarian and allegorical interpretation. The former Dadaist **Christian Schad** (1894–1982) represents a more extreme form of Dix's style, with many explicit scenes drawn from the bohemian world he himself inhabited; **Rudolf Schlichter** (1890–1955) had similar preoccupations. In contrast, there was a romantically-inclined wing of this movement, exemplified by **Georg Schrimpf** (1898–1938).

Max Beckmann (1884–1950) defies classification, lying somewhere between Expressionism and **Neue Sachlichkeit**. He believed it was the artist's duty to express Man's spiritual condition. To this end, he used the self-portrait as a means of expressing his changing reaction to world events, making himself appear in different guises, whether as clown, convict, king or hero. The symbolism associated with Carnival and the circus is a recurring theme in his work, as are the use of gesture to reveal character and the manipulation of space. To express opposition to the Nazis, he took to the anachronistic format of the triptych.

Max Ernst (1891–1976) was another who began as a Dadaist, producing first collages and then frottages. However, he is best known as one of the leading Surrealist painters, a style he turned to on its foundation in 1924, and for which his early interest in psychology and the creative works of the mentally ill made him most suitable. His scenes are less suggestive than those of Dalí and Magritte, but at their best they present a gnawingly haunting imagery. To what extent he can be considered a German artist is debatable, as he left his native country in 1922, taking first American then French nationality.

Oskar Schlemmer (1888–1943) was one of the most varied German painters of the century, touched by seemingly every style; he also practised both decorative and functional art. Among the practitioners of abstraction following Kandinsky and Klee, **Willi Baumeister** (1889–1955), **Ernst Wilhelm Nay** (1902–68) and **Alfred Wolfgang Schulze** (1913–51), better known as **Wols**, acquired the largest reputations.

POSTSCRIPT: THE PRESENT DAY

In the postwar Federal Republic, avant-garde artistic activity has flourished, thanks to generous subsidy levels by all tiers of government. How many of the painters whose work currently lines the walls of the country's many museums of modern art will prove to be of lasting significance remains a moot point. Among those who have gained international standing, **Georg Baselitz** (b.1940) paints figuratively but groups the different components of his works in a deliberately arbitrary way. **Sigmar Polke** (b.1941) can be seen as something of a disciple of Dadaism in the objects he tacks on to his canvases, mirroring his interest in West German society's obsession with kitsch. **Anselm Kiefer** (b.1945) has been concerned with the German psyche in its historical context, focusing on gestures, symbols and myths. **Jörg Immendorff** (b.1945) and **Bernd Koberling** (b.1938) have taken an overtly left-wing political stance in their work, with ecological themes also being associated with the latter.

The GDR fostered a particularly sterile form of Socialist realism as the only officially acceptable form of artistic activity: artists who rebelled against this, such as **Roger Loewig** (b.1930), faced persecution and eventual expul-

sion. Few products of the state-sponsored style are likely to survive much longer on public display unless as mere historical curiosities. An exception, however, is the most spectacular commission granted by the regime, the controversial *Panorama* in Bad Frankenhausen in honour of the Peasants' Revolt, painted by Leipzig professor **Werner Tübke**.

BOOKS

Publishers are detailed below in the form of British publisher/American publisher, where both exist. Where books are published in one country only, UK or US precedes the publisher's name.

TRAVEL

Heinrich Heine *Deutschland: A Winter's Tale* (Angel, £4.95/$12.95; also in the *Complete Poems*). This superb verse travelogue describes Heine's journey from exile in Paris to his family home in Hamburg; it's full of insight into the places he passed through, and contains devastating exposés of mid-nineteenth-century German society. It's also worth looking in libraries or second-hand shops for Heine's *Travel Pictures* (in prose, with inserted poems), which describe his wanderings in the Harz and his sojourn in Norderney.

Mark Twain *A Tramp Abroad* (Century Hutchinson, £5.95/Hippocrene, $11.95). The early, German-based part of this book, particularly the descriptions of Heidelberg, show Twain on top form, by turns humorous and evocative. There's an hilariously over-the-top appendix entitled "The Awful German Language", which mercilessly pillories the over-complexity of "this fearsome tongue".

Patrick Leigh Fermor *A Time of Gifts* (Penguin, £6.99/$6.95). The author set out to walk from Rotterdam to Constantinople in 1933, travelling along the Rhine and Danube valleys en route. Written up forty years later in luscious, hyper-refined prose, it presents the fresh sense of youthful discovery distilled through considerable subsequent learning and reflection. Prewar Germany is shown suffering from all the schizophrenic influences of the era,

yet the country's enduring beauty is also captured.

Bernard Levin *To the End of the Rhine* (UK: Sceptre, £6.99). "The Rhine is the hero of my book, as he has been the hero of my life", declares Levin. However, the journey undertaken is really an excuse for yet another self-satisfied portrait of this journalist and his familiar "enthusiasms", tied in to a TV series. Deeply unenlightening.

Claudio Magris *Danube* (Collins Harvill, £7.99/$14.99). Absorbing, searching exploration of the great river and the places along it from the Black Forest to the Black Sea, mixing travelogue with all manner of scholary diversions; not the easiest of reads, but rewards the effort.

Michael Farr *Vanishing Borders* (UK: Viking Penguin, £15.99). The *Daily Telegraphs*'s former German correspondent here recounts his travels, particularly in the GDR, before and after the *Wende*; mildly diverting, but bears the hallmarks of a rushed publication.

HISTORY

Tacitus *The Germania* (Penguin, £5.99/$4.99). Brilliant series of concise analyses of each of the warlike Germanic tribes, which are often compared favourably with the author's native Rome; some of the observations about German character are quite startling prophetic.

Einhard and Notker the Stammerer *Two Lives of Charlemagne* (Penguin, £5.99/$6.95). Einhard was a leading courtier in the service of the founder of the Holy Roman Empire, and provided a beautifully written, all-too-short biography of his master. Written a century later, Notker's book is a series of monkish anecdotes, many no doubt apocryphal, which help flesh out the overall portrait of Charlemagne.

Mary Fulbrook *A Concise History of Germany* (Cambridge University Press, £6.95/$10.95). "Concise" is the key word for this post-unification history, whose brevity is simultaneously its strength and its weakness. Nevertheless, a useful basic history.

Geoffrey Barraclough *Origins of Modern Germany* (Blackwell, £10.95/Norton, $13.95). The most easily digestible general introduction to the country's history, tackling the medieval period better than any more specialised book.

Ronald Bainton *Here I Stand* (Lion, £6.95/ NAL, $3.95). The best and liveliest biography of Martin Luther, one of the undisputed titans of European history.

Owen Chadwick *The Reformation* (Pelican, £7.99/$6.95). Traces the German origins of the biggest-ever rupture in the fabric of the Church, and follows their impact on the rest of Europe.

Veronica (C.V.) Wedgwood *The Thirty Years War* (Methuen, £10.99/Routledge, Chapman & Hall, $15.95). Easily the most accomplished book on the series of conflicts which devastated the country and divided the continent in the first half of the seventeenth century.

Walter Hubatsch *Frederick the Great: Absolutism and Administration* (Thames & Hudson, £15/US: o/p); **Christopher Duffy** *Frederick the Great: A Military Life* (RKP, £9.95/ Routledge, Chapman & Hall, $16.95). Two contrasting biographies on different aspects of the man who brought Prussia to the forefront of German affairs, and to a place among the great powers of Europe.

Golo Mann *The History of Germany Since 1787* (Peregrine, £10.99/Praeger, o/p). Written by the son of Thomas Mann, this comprehensive study traces not only the politics but also the intellectual and cultural currents of the period. Another recommendable general study, this time by a British author, is **William Carr** *A History of Germany 1815–1985* (Edward Arnold, £12.99/St Martin's Press, $25).

A.J.P. Taylor *Bismarck: The Man and the Statesman* (Hamish Hamilton, £8.99/Random House, $7.95). Britain's most controversial historian here provides a typically stirring portrait of the ruthless schemer who forged (reluctantly, in the author's view) the nineteenth-century unification of Germany.

Volker Berghahn *Germany and the Approach of War in 1914* (Macmillan, £10.50/St Martin's Press $17.35). Fundamentally a history book, but also presenting an instructive general picture of Germany before World War I. It chronicles the political, economic and social pressures that were current at the time, and succeeds in giving plausible explanations for the apparently inevitable.

Alexander Reissner *Berlin 1675–1945* (UK: Oswald Wolff, £8.95). Subjective and often highly opinionated history of the city. A stimulating read nevertheless.

Ebehard Kolb *The Weimar Republic* (Unwin & Hyman, £10.99/US o/p). The most recent study of the endlessly fascinating but fundamentally flawed state – until recently the only experiment at a united and democratic German nation – which survived for just fourteen years.

John Willett *Weimar Years* (Thames & Hudson, £9.95/Abbeville Press, o/p). The man who has brilliantly translated Brecht's works into English here turns his attentions to the wider culture of the Weimar Republic.

NAZISM AND WORLD WAR II

Alan Bullock *Hitler: A Study in Tyranny* (Pelican, £8.99/Harper & Collins, $12.95). Ever since it was published, this scholarly yet highly readable tome has ranked as the classic biography of the failed Austrian artist and discharged army corporal whose evil genius fooled a nation and caused the deaths of millions.

William Shirer *The Rise and Fall of the Third Reich* (Mandarin, £9.99/Simon and Schuster, $14.95). This makes a perfect compliment to Bullock's book: Shirer was an American journalist stationed in Germany during the Nazi period. Notwithstanding the inordinate length and excessive journalese, this book is full of insights and is ideal for dipping into, with the help of its exhaustive index.

Hugh Trevor-Roper *The Last Days of Hitler* (Macmillan, £10.99/US o/p). A brilliant reconstruction of the closing chapter of the Third Reich, set in the Berlin Bunker. Trevor-Roper subsequently marred his reputation as the doyen of British historians by authenticating the forged *Hitler Diaries*, which have themselves been the subject of several books.

Joachim Fest *The Face of the Third Reich* (Pelican, £8.99/Pantheon $7.95). Mainly of interest for its biographies of the men surrounding the Führer – Göring, Goebbels, Hess, Himmler, Speer et al.

Claudia Koonz *Mothers in the Fatherland* (Methuen, £8.50/St Martin's Press, $16.95). Recent and brilliantly perceptive study of the role of women in Nazi German. Includes a rare and revealing interview with the chief of Hitler's Women's Bureau, Gertrud Scholtz-Klink.

James Taylor and Warren Shaw *A Dictionary of the Third Reich* (Grafton, £4.99/ Pharos $24.95). The handiest reference book of the period.

Adolf Hitler *Table Talk* (OUP, o/p/AMS Press, $49.50). Hitler in his own words: Martin Bormann, one of his inner circle, recorded the dictator's pronouncements at meetings between 1941 and 1944. The early *Mein Kampf* (Pimlico, £15/Noontide, $8), a series of rambling, irrational and hysterical outbursts on every subject under the sun is also of interest, as it genuinely constituted Hitler's blueprint for power.

Rebecca West *A Train of Powder* (Virago, o/p/ Viking o/p) The author's celebrated writings on the Nürnberg Trials, which she covered on behalf of the *Daily Telegraph*, as well as a number of other inspired articles on postwar Germany.

SOCIETY AND POLITICS

John Ardagh *Germany and the Germans* (Penguin, £7.99/Harper & Collins, $12.95). The latest and most up-to-date English-language characterisation of the country and its people, taking into account its history, politics and psyche, and covering almost every aspect of national life, newly revised after unification. Its approach is always lively, yet remains scrupulously unbiased

Günther Wallraff *Lowest of the Low* (Methuen, o/p/Freundlich, $16.95). In 1983, Wallraff put an ad in the papers saying: "Foreigner, strong, seeks work of any kind, including heavy and dirty jobs, even for little money." Then he spent two years labouring among Turkish and other immigrant workers, finding out about the underside of German affluence. The book was a political bombshell when it came out, painting a picture of exploitation and malpractice rarely discussed in Germany. Unfortunately, it now seems that the author was guilty of fabricating some of the evidence, thus diminishing its long-term impact.

Werner Hülsberg *The German Greens* (Verso, o/p/Routledge, Chapman & Hall, $15.95) An in-depth analysis of Germany's most exciting political phenomenon, this book traces the movement's intellectual and political origins, chronicles the internal disputes, introduces the main characters and analyses its shortcomings.

W. A. Coupe *Germany Through the Looking-Glass* (Berg, £8.50). The author presents the period 1945–1986 via a collection of German political cartoons, adding his own analysis of the issues in each case. Opinionated and subjective, the book introduces German humour and a German view of the country's postwar development.

Julia Becker *Hitler's Children* (UK: Michael Joseph, o/p). An analysis by a British writer of the political terrorism which rocked the complacent society of 1970s Germany to its very foundations.

Ralf Dahrendorf *Society and Democracy in Germany* (Weidenfeld and Nicholson, o/p/ Norton, $10.95). An in-depth sociological analysis of the German psyche, prompted by the awful question, "How was Auschwitz possible?"

Ian Derbyshire *Politics in Germany* (UK Chambers, £5.99). Bang up-to-date survey on the German political scene, with the *Wende* and the subsequent elections fully documented.

David Childs *The GDR - Moscow's German Ally* (Unwin Hyman, £6.50/$17.95). The best book on the GDR period, fully revised the year before the *Wende*, when the regime still seemed fully secure. Obviously now dated, but still of considerable interest for its detailed descriptions and explanations.

GERMANY IN ENGLISH FICTION

Rudolph Erich Raspe *The Adventures of Baron Münchausen* (Dedalus, £6.99/ Hippocrene, $8.95). The outrageously exaggerated humorous exploits of the real-life Baron Münchausen were embroidered yet further by Raspe and first published in English. Copies with the classic nineteenth-century engravings of Gustav Doré can often be found in remainder and second-hand shops.

Jerome K. Jerome *Three Men on the Bummel* (Penguin, £3.50/$3.95). Sequel to the (deservedly) more famous *Three Men in a Boat*, this features the same trio of feckless English travellers taking a cycling holiday through Germany at the turn of the century. The second half of the book features plenty of entertaining anecdotes, with opinions bandied about on every conceivable subject. *Diary of a Pilgrimage* (Alan Sutton, £2.50/$8) is an account of the same author's visit to see the Oberammergau Passion Play.

Katherine Mansfield *In a German Pension* (Penguin £4.99/$6.95). One of the author's earliest works, this is a collection of short stories set in early twentieth-century Bavaria. Funny but often acerbic too.

Elizabeth von Arnim *Elizabeth and her German Garden* and *Elizabeth in Rügen* (UK: Virago, £4.99 each). Although billed as novels, these are effectively autobiographical works by Katherine Mansfield's cousin, an Australian who married a German aristocrat and went to live in his Pomeranian estates.

Peter Schneider *The Wall Jumper* (Allison and Busby, £3.95/Pantheon, $6.95). A series of fascinating cameos which describe life under the Wall, and the intrigue, characters and tragedy it caused. His most recent book, *The German Comedy*, (I.B. Taurus, £9.95/Farrar, Strauss & Giroux, $19.95) reveals the paradoxes and absurdities that have occurred now that the Wall has been removed.

Christopher Isherwood *Mr Norris Changes Trains, Goodbye to Berlin* (Methuen, £3.50/New Directions, $8.95). Set in the decadent atmosphere of the Weimar Republic, these short stories brilliantly evoke the period and bring to life some classic German characters. They subsequently formed the basis of the films *I Am a Camera* and the later remake *Cabaret*.

Ian Walker *Zoo Station* (Abacus, £3.99/Atlantic Monthly, $7.95). Not really fiction but a personal recollection of time spent on Berlin in the late 1980s by a British journalist. Perceptive, engaging and well informed, it is the most enjoyable account of contemporary life in that city available.

CLASSICAL PROSE

Johann Jacob Christoffel von Grimmelshausen *Simplicius Simplicissimus* (Dedalus, £7.25/University Press of America, $26). This massive semi-autobiographical novel is one of the highpoints of seventeenth-century European literature. Set against the uncertainties of the Thirty Years' War, it charts the story of its hero from boyhood to middle-age.

Johann Wolfgang von Goethe *The Sorrows of Young Werther* (Penguin, £4.99/Random House, $7.95). An early epistolary novella, treating the theme of suicide for the first time ever. *Wilhelm Meister: The Years of Apprenticeship* (John Calder, 3 vols, £4.99 each/Riverrun Press, 3 vols, $7.95 each) and *Wilhelm Meister: The Years of Travel* (John Calder, 3 vols, £4.99 each/Riverrun Press, 3 vols, $7.95 each) is a huge, episodic and partly autobiographical cycle of novels. *Tales for Transformation* (City Lights, £5.95/$5.95) is a wide-ranging series of short stories, showing Goethe's interest in alchemy and the supernatural.

Ernst Theodor Amadeus Hoffmann *Tales of Hoffmann* (Penguin, £7.99/$5.95), *The Best Tales of Hoffmann* (Dover, £6.75/$8.95). These selections of work by the schizophrenic master of fantasy and the macabre overlap slightly, but each features only one of his two greatest masterpieces; Penguin has *Mademoiselle de Scudéry*, the world's first detective story, while *Dover* includes the nightmarish allegory, *The Golden Pot*, in Thomas Carlyle's inspired translation.

Gehart Hauptmann *Lineman Thiel and Other Stories* (Angel, £4.95/Ungar, $8.95). These three remarkable stories, written towards the end of last century, anticipate Freud in their psychological penetration, and the techniques of the cinema in their use of strong visual symbols.

Heinrich von Kleist *The Marquise of O and Other Stories* (Penguin, £5.50/$5.95). Like Hoffmann, who was only one year older, Kleist was one of the all-time greats of short story writing. His eight tales range in length from 3 to 100 pages, but they're all equally compelling.

Joseph von Eichendorff *Memoirs of a Good-For-Nothing* (John Calder, o/p/Riverrun Press $8.95). A beautifully poetic little novel in the most optimistic Romantic vein.

Annette von Droste-Hülshoff *The Jew's Beech* (John Calder, o/p/Basil Blackwell, $15.95). The great nineteenth-century poetess' mastery of small-scale descriptions of nature is blended with a sense of the supernatural in this exquisite prose idyll.

Theodor Storm *Immensee* (John Calder, £3.95/Irvington, $7.95). This Romantic tale about an old man reminiscing over his lost youth can be found in an anthology which also includes **Georg Büchner**'s only prose work, *Lenz*.

Theodor Fontane *Before the Storm* (OUP, £6.95/$6.95). Set in Prussia during the period of the Napoleonic Wars, this is by some way the greatest German novel of the second half of the nineteenth century, dealing with the conflict between patriotism and liberty. The much shorter *Effi Briest* (Penguin, £5.99/$5.95) focuses on adultery in the context of the social mores of the age.

TWENTIETH-CENTURY NOVELS

Thomas Mann *The Magic Mountain* (Penguin, £8.99/Random House $10.95). Generally considered the author's masterpiece, this is a weighty novel of ideas discussing love, death, politics and war through a collection of characters in a Swiss sanatorium, whose sickness mirrors that of European society as a whole. The earlier *Buddenbrooks* (Penguin, £8.99/Random House, $12.95) is the story of a merchant dynasty in the author's native Lübeck, while *Doctor Faustus* (Penguin, £7.99/Random House, $9.95) updates the Faust legend through the story of a twentieth-century German composer.

Heinrich Mann *Man of Straw* (Penguin, o/p). The best book by Thomas Mann's more politically committed elder brother, here analysing the authoritarian nature of life under the Second Reich.

Klaus Mann *Mephisto* (Penguin, £5.99/$7.95), *The Pious Dance* (UK: Gay Men's Press, £4.95). The erotic novels of Thomas Mann's son were long banned; he now appears as a remarkable individual voice in his own right, particularly in his vivid descriptions of the Berlin underworld. *Mephisto* is a striking allegory of a wartime actor who sells his soul to the Nazi party.

Hermann Hesse *Narziss and Goldmund* (Penguin, £3.99/Bantam, $4.50). A beautifully polished novel, set in medieval Germany and narrated in the picaresque vein, about two monks, one a dedicated scholar, the other a wanderer, artist and lover. *Steppenwolf* (Penguin, £5.99/Bantam, $4.50) is a bizarre fantasy about schizophrenia, while *The Glass Bead Game* (Picador, £6.99/Henry Holb, $12.95) is a monumental Utopian novel, set in a future where an élite group develops a game which resolves the world's conflicts into a state of order.

Erich Maria Remarque *All Quiet on the Western Front* (Picador, £4.99/Fawcett, $5.95). The classic German novel of World War I, focusing on the traumatic impact of the conflict on the life of an ordinary soldier.

Arnold Zweig, *The Case of Sergeant Grischa* (Penguin, o/p/$7.95). Another World War I classic, focusing on the conflict between individual justice and the demands of military discipline.

Bertolt Brecht *The Threepenny Novel* (Penguin, £6.99/o/p). Brecht's only novel, a much-expanded version of the "Opera", is a disaster. The joke underpinning the book has worn thin after about three chapters, but the author plows on relentlessly through a further 300 pages.

Alfred Döblin *Berlin-Alexanderplatz* (Penguin, o/p/Ungar, $12.95). A prominent socialist intellectual during the Weimar period, Döblin went into exile shortly after the banning of his books in 1933. *Berlin-Alexanderplatz* is his weightiest and most durable achievement, an unrelenting epic of the city's proletariat.

Günter Grass *From the Diary of a Snail* (Picador, £4.95/Harcourt Brace, $6.95); *The Flounder* (Picador, £5.95/Harcourt Brace, $11.95); *The Tin Drum* (Picador, £7.99/Random House, $9.95). Grass is one of Germany's best-known postwar novelists, concerned to analyse and come to terms with his country's awful recent heritage. His highly political novels are all studies of the German character, concentrating on how Nazism found a foothold among ordinary Germans, on postwar guilt, but also on postwar materialism and spiritual poverty.

Heinrich Böll *The Lost Honour of Katharina Blum* (Penguin, £3.99/McGraw Hill, $6.95). Winner of the Nobel Prize for Literature in 1972, Heinrich Böll is the most popular postwar German novelist – at least with non-Germans. Certainly his books are accessible and always on contentious topics: this is the harrowing story of a young woman whose life is ruined by the combined effects of a gutter press campaign and her accidental involvement with a wanted terrorist. *The Clown* (Marion Boyars, £5.95/McGraw Hill, $6.95) again uses the backdrop of the city of Cologne for a more detailed critique of modern German society. *And Where Were You, Adam?* (Penguin, £4.99/McGraw Hill, $7.95) is set in 1944, chronicling the effect of war and Nazism on ordinary German people.

Gisela Elsner *Offside* (UK: Virago, £3.95). Feminist novel about women's life in middle-class postwar Germany.

Gert Hofmann *The Parable of the Blind* (Minerva, £3.99/Fromm $7.95); *Balzac's Horse* (UK: Minerva, £4.99). Hofmann was a late-comer to fiction, but quickly established himself among the most original contemporary German writers. The first of these is an imaginative rendering of the story behind Breugel's enigmatic painting; the other is a richly varied crop of short stories.

Stefan Heym *The King David Report* (UK: Abacus, o/p). Heym was one of the many Marxist writers who settled in the former GDR, but he quickly became disillusioned and for decades functioned as the most effective opposition to the regime. Many of his novels were translated into English, but are now out of print; this is the best, a devastatingly witty send-up of modern totalitarianism by means of a Biblical allegory.

Christa Wolf *A Model Childhood* (Virago, £5.99/Farrar, Strauss & Giroux $9.95). The author gained a reputation for literary integrity, despite her loyalty to the GDR; this book is a fictionalised account of her own youth in Bavaria in the 1930s, providing an excellent portrait of a child's confrontation with Nazi ideas and the shattering disillusionment that came from facing the truth as an adult.

Ulrich Plenzdorff *The New Sufferings of Young W* (Ungar, £3.85/$7.95). Spoof reworking of Goethe's celebrated *Werther* story in 1970s East Berlin.

POETRY

Leonard Forster (ed.) *The Penguin Book of German Verse* (£6.99/$7.95). Best of the anthologies, representing all the big names (and many more) from the eighth century to the present day, with folk songs, ballads and chorales added for good measure.

Anon *Carmina Burana* (Penguin, £4.50/Focus Information Group, $15.95). A wonderful collection of (originally) dog-Latin songs and poems from thirteenth-century Bavaria; in spite of their monastic origin, the texts are often bawdy and erotic. Many were used by Carl Orff in his choral showpiece named after the manuscript.

Johann Wolfgang von Goethe *Selected Poems* (John Calder, £9.95/AMS Press, £18.50), *Selected Verse* (Penguin, £6.99/Richard West, $45), *Epigrams and Poems* (UK: Anvil, £6.95), *Roman Elegies and Other Poems* (Libris £9.95: Black Swan, $7.95). Varied anthologies drawn from Goethe's prodigious output.

Heinrich Heine *Complete Poems* (OUP, £14.95/Gordon Press, $75), *Selected Verse* (Penguin, £6.99/$7.95). Heine's works, with their strong rhythms and dramatic, acerbic thrusts, translate far better into English than those of any of his contemporaries; he was also the favourite composer of the great Romantic composers.

Friedrich Hölderlin *Selected Verse* (UK: Anvil, £6.95). Hölderlin's poetry, with its classical metres and vivid imagery, is notoriously difficult to translate, but this anthology makes a successful stab at the thankless task. Another selection (US: University of Chicago Press, £3.95) also includes some of the very different lyric poetry of **Eduard Mörike**.

Bertolt Brecht *Poems* (Eyre Methuen, £7.50/Routledge, Chapman and Hall, $14.95). Brecht's poems sound even more inspired when heard in the musical settings provided by Kurt Weill and the more ideologically-inspired Paul Dessau and Hans Eisler; plenty of recordings are available of these.

DRAMA

Johann Wolfgang von Goethe *Faust Part One* (Penguin, £4.50/Oxford University Press, $3.95), *Faust Part Two* (Penguin, £4.50/Oxford University Press, $3.95). Goethe made the completion of this vast drama – which examines the entire gamut of preoccupations of European civilisation – the major task of his life, and he duly finished it just before his death, having worked at it for around sixty years. Other Goethe plays include the historical dramas *Egmont* (Barron, £2.95/Ungar, $5.95) and *Torquato Tasso* (Angel, £5.95/Ungar, $6.95).

Friedrich Schiller *The Robbers, Wallenstein* (Penguin, £7.99/$6.95). It's even harder to find translations of Schiller than Goethe. This pairs an early *Sturm und Drang* drama (which established him as the leader of that movement) with one of his later historical plays, set against the background of the Thirty Years' War. *William Tell* (University of Chicago Press, £7.25/ $9.95) is the playwright's last work.

Heinrich von Kleist *Five Plays* (Yale University Press, £14.95/$22.95). Ranges over Kleist's varied output, from German theatre's finest comedy, *The Broken Jug*, to the patriotic drama, *Prince Frederick of Homburg*.

Gotthold Ephraim Lessing *Minna von Barnhelm* (US: University of Chicago Press, $10). One of German theatre's earliest examples of middle-class comedy, using contemporary eighteenth-century events as a backdrop.

Georg Büchner *Complete Plays* (Methuen, £5.99/Oxford University Press, $5.95). Büchner died in 1837 at the age of 23. Two of his three plays are masterpieces – *Danton's Death* is a political statement about the French Revolution, while the astonishing unfinished *Woyzeck*, a tragedy based on the life of an insignificant soldier, must be the tersest drama ever written, with not a word wasted in the telling.

Georg Kaiser *Plays Vol. 1, Plays Vol. 2* (John Calder, £5.99 each/Riverrun, $9.95 each). These contain a selection of the vast output of the leading dramatist of the Expressionist movement, typically using very stark language and stressing ideas at the expense of characterisation – the players are typically denoted by their worldly function, rather than their name. Another piece by Kaiser features in *Seven Expressionist Plays* (John Calder, £4.95/ Riverrun, $9.95) which also contains works by two dramatists better known as artists – Ernst Barlach and Oskar Kokoschka.

Bertolt Brecht *Plays* (Eyre Methuen, around £4.99 each/Random House, from $3.96 to $7.95). Brecht's short but fruitful collaboration during the Weimar Republic with the composer Kurt Weill – *The Threepenny Opera, The Rise and Fall of the City of Mahogany* and *The Seven Deadly Sins* – show him on top form, though the music is an essential component in these works. Of his other plays, the "parables" – *The Caucasian Chalk Circle* and *The Good Woman of Sezuan* – are generally more successful than those with a more overtly polit-

ical tone. On the other hand, many of the collected *Short Stories* (Methuen, £3.95/ Routledge $14.95) are highly entertaining, proving that this side of his output has been unfairly neglected.

Martin Walser *Rabbit Race Detour* (UK: Marion Boyars, £4.95). Walser is a writer critical of postwar German society and its ambivalent attitude to Nazism.

LEGENDS AND FOLKLORE

Jakob and Wilhelm Grimm *Complete Grimm's Tales* (Penguin, £6.99/Doubleday, $15.95). The world's most famous collection of folk-tales, meticulously researched by the Brothers Grimm, has stories to appeal to all age ranges. A selection of the tales (Penguin, £6.99/$5.95) has the ingenious idea of rendering some of them in Scots and Irish, thus capturing something of the dialect flavour of the originals, which is otherwise lost in translation.

Anon *The Nibelungenlied* (Penguin, £5.99/ $4.95). Germany's greatest epic was written around 1200 by an unknown Danubian poet; the story varies greatly from Wagner's *Ring*, which draws equally heavily on Nordic sources of the legend. It's here given a highly entertaining prose translation.

Gottfried von Strassburg *Tristan* (Penguin, £5.99/$4.95), **Wolfram von Eschenbach** *Parzifal* (Penguin, £5.95/Random House, $6.95) are two more epic masterpieces from early thirteenth-century Germany, both based on the Grail and associated legends.

Friedrich Heinrich Karl de la Motte-Fouqué *Undine* (Dedalus, £5.99/Marboro, $8.95). Although an original novel – which had a huge influence on the Romantic movement – this is primarily of note for encapsulating, in its world of water sprites and chivalric knights, the entire German folklore tradition.

Wilhelm Ruhland *Legends of the Rhine* (o/p in UK and US, but available in Germany). Narrates all the rich store of myths associated with the great river.

Jennifer Russ *German Festivals* (Oswald Wolff, £7.95/Ungar, $12.95). Rather a pity it's not a bit longer, but this book provides useful background information on all the main annual folklore celebrations.

THE ARTS

Amazingly, there's no good general book in English specifically on Germany's art and architecture. Standard academic monographs are, of course, available on the work of most of the great German painters, though these are usually very expensive and prone to go out of print quickly. Many of the Pelican *History of Art* series are partly devoted to Germany; coverage is always very sound, with good black and white photographs, but essentially scholarly and very dry.

Albrecht Dürer *The Complete Woodcuts* (Dover, £10.95/$10.95), *The Complete Etchings, Engravings and Drypoints* (Dover, £10.95/$10.95). These two books enable you to own, at minimal cost, a complete set of the graphic work of one of the world's greatest-ever masters of the art. The book of woodcuts is particularly recommended.

Jost Amman *The Book of Trades* (Dover, £5.35/$6.95). As much a work of history and literature as of art, the 114 woodcuts illustrate the trades and crafts practised in early sixteenth-century Germany; each is accompanied by a poem by the most famous of the *Meistersinger* Hans Sachs.

Michael Baxendall *The Limewood Sculptors of Renaissance Germany* (Yale University Press, £17.95/$25). One of the best art history books published in recent years, this examines the work of Tilman Riemenschneider, Veit Stoss, and many other lesser-known artists, in their social and political context. A lavish series of photographs accompanies the text.

William Vaughan *German Romantic Painting* (Yale University Press, £25/$25). A good introduction to many of Germany's best nineteenth century artists, though the price is high for a book mostly illustrated in black and white.

Wolf-Dieter Dube *The Expressionists* (Thames & Hudson, £6.95/$11.95). A general introduction to Germany's most distinctive contribution to twentieth-century art.

Julius Baum *German Cathedrals* (Thames & Hudson, o/p), **Ernst Gall** *Cathedrals and Abbeys of the Rhineland* (Thames & Hudson, o/p). It's well worth seeking these out in a library, particularly for their outstanding black and white photographs of architectural and sculptural details.

Frank Whiteford *Bauhaus* (Thames & Hudson £6.95/$16.95). Introduction to the twentieth century's most influential art and design movement, tracing its development during its early years in Weimar, Dessau and Berlin.

John Sandford *The New German Cinema* (Oswald Wolff, £14.50/Da Capo Press, £13.95. Now somewhat out-of-date, but gives good coverage for the period up to 1980.

Peter Adam *The Arts of the Third Reich* (Thames & Hudson, £24.95/$49.95). Engrossing and well-written account of the officially approved state art of Nazi Germany – a subject that for many years has been ignored or deliberately made inaccessible. Includes over three hundred illustrations, many reproduced for the first time since the war.

GUIDE BOOKS

Jack Holland *Berlin: The Rough Guide* (Rough Guides, £6.99), published in the US as *The Real Guide Berlin* (Prentice Hall, $11.95). Companion volume to the book you're holding, this gives the full lowdown on the sights, culture and nightlife of one of Europe's most exciting cities. Essential reading for those bound for the city.

Karl Baedeker *The Rhineland, Northern Germany, Southern Germany, Berlin* (all o/p, but staple fare at second-hand bookshops). The old Baedekers are still indispensible classics. They covered a Germany which was considerably more extensive than today, stretching well into what is now the Soviet Union. Look out for the editions dating from the early years of the present century, immensely learned and full of now-untenable opinions. The glossy successors to these (published in Britain by the AA) are not in the same class.

Bob Larson *Your Swabian Neighbours* (available only in Germany). Written by a US Army liaison officer and long-time resident of the semi-mythical part of southern Germany known as Swabia, this book is very American and error-prone in places, but is nonetheless a highly entertaining and remarkably candid account of a fascinating part of the country.

George Wood *The Visitor's Guide to the Black Forest* (Moorland, £9.99/Hunter Publishing,

New York, $12.95). A specific guide for hiking or motoring round one of Germany's most beautiful – and touristed – areas; unfortunately, a bit short on detail.

Fleur and Colin Speakman *Walking in the Black Forest* (UK: Cicerone, £5.95), *King Ludwig Way* (UK: Cicerone, £3.95). Two guides for specific hikes in southern Germany.

LANGUAGE

German is a very complex language and you can't hope to master it in a short time. As English was a compulsory subject in the West German school curriculum, most people who have grown up in the West since the war have some familiarity with it, which eases communication a great deal.

Nonetheless, a smattering of German does help, especially in out-of-the-way rural areas, or in the former East, where Russian was more commonly taught in schools. Also, given the long-standing and continued presence of American and British forces who make little effort to integrate into local communities or learn German, people are particularly sensitive to presumptious English-speakers. On the other hand, most will be delighted to practise their English on you once you've stumbled through your German introduction.

In the former East Germany, few people learned English during the Communist period; hence a phrase-book knowledge of German is essential.

Should you be interested in studying the language during your stay, the best places to enrol in are the *Goethe-Instituten*, which can be found in most major cities. The German Tourist Board or local information offices have all relevant addresses. Of the many teach-yourself courses available, best is the BBC course, *Deutsch Direkt* (£6.95 plus tapes). The most useful dictionary is the pocket-sized *Mini Dictionary* (Harrap, £1.95). For a phrase book, look no further than Harrap's *German Phrase Book* (£1.95).

PRONUNCIATION

English speakers find the complexities of German grammar hard to handle, but pronunciation isn't as daunting as it might first appear. Individual syllables are generally pronounced as they're printed – the trick is learning how to place the stresses in the notoriously lengthy German words.

VOWELS AND UMLAUTS

a as in f**a**ther, but can also be used as in h**u**t

e as in d**ay**

i as in l**ee**k

o as in b**o**ttom

u as in b**oo**t

ä is a combination of a and e, sometimes pronounced like **e** in b**e**t (eg Länder) and sometimes like **ai** in p**ai**d (eg spät).

ö is a combination of o and e, like the French *eu*

ü is a combination of u and e, like tr**ue**

VOWEL COMBINATIONS

ai as in l**ie**

au as in h**ou**se

ie as in fr**ee**

ei as in tr**ia**l

eu as in **oi**l

CONSONANTS

Consonants are pronounced as they are written, with no silent letters. The differences from English are:

r is given a dry throaty sound, similar to French

s pronounced similar to, but slightly softer than an English z

v pronounced somewhere between f and v

w pronounced same way as English v

z pronounced ts

GENDER

German words can be one of three genders: masculine, feminine or neuter. Each has its own ending and corresponding ending for attached adjectives. If you don't know any German grammar, it's safest to use either neuter or male forms.

The German letter ß, the *Scharfes S*, usually replaces *ss* in a word: pronunciation is identical.

GERMAN WORDS AND PHRASES

BASICS

Ja, Nein	Yes, No	*Dieses*	This one
Bitte	Please/ You're welcome	*Jenes*	That one
Bitte Schön	A more polite form of *Bitte*	*Gross, Klein*	Large, Small
Danke, Danke Schön	Thank you, Thank you very much	*Mehr, Weniger*	More, less
Wo, Wann, Warum ?	Where, When, Why ?	*Wenig*	A little
		Viel	A lot
Wieviel ?	How much ?	*Billig, Teuer*	Cheap, expensive
Hier, Da	Here, There	*Gut, Schlecht*	Good, Bad
Jetzt, Später	Now, Later	*Heiss, Kalt*	Hot, Cold
Geöffnet, offen, auf	All mean "open"	*Mit, Ohne*	With, Without
		Wo ist . . . ?	Where is . . . ?
Geschlossen, zu	Both mean "closed"	*Wie komme ich nach . . . ?*	How do I get to (a town)?
Früher	Earlier		
Da drüben	Over there	*Wie komme ich zur/ zum . . . ?*	How do I get to (a building, place)?

GREETINGS AND TIMES

Guten Morgen	Good morning	*Vorgestern*	The day before yesterday
Guten Abend	Good evening		
Guten Tag	Good day	*Übermorgen*	The day after tomorrow
Grüss Gott	Good day (in southern Germany)	*Tag*	Day
		Nacht	Night
Wie geht es Ihnen ?	How are you? (polite)	*Woche*	Week
Wie geht es Dir ?	How are you? (informal)	*Wochenende*	Weekend
Lass mich in Ruhe	Leave me alone	*Monat*	Month
Hau ab	Get lost	*Jahr*	Year
Geh weg	Go away	*Am Vormittag/ vormittags*	In the morning
Heute	Today		
Gestern	Yesterday	*Am Nachmittag/ nachmittags*	In the afternoon
Morgen	Tomorrow		
Auf Wiedersehen	Goodbye	*Am Abend*	In the evening
Tschüs	Goodbye (informal)		

DAYS, MONTHS AND DATES

Montag	Monday	*Januar*	January	*Frühling*	Spring
Dienstag	Tuesday	*Februar*	February	*Sommer*	Summer
Mittwoch	Wednesday	*März*	March	*Herbst*	Autumn
Donnerstag	Thursday	*April*	April	*Winter*	Winter
Freitag	Friday	*Mai*	May		
Samstag	Saturday	*Juni*	June	*Ferien*	Holidays
Sonnabend	Saturday (in northern Germany)	*Juli*	July	*Feiertag*	Bank holiday
		August	August	*Montag, der erste April*	Monday, the first of April
Sonntag	Sunday	*September*	September		
		Oktober	October	*Der zweite April*	the second of April
		November	November		
		Dezember	December	*Der dritte April*	the third of April

QUESTIONS AND REQUESTS

All enquiries should be prefaced with the phrase *Entschuldigen Sie bitte* (excuse me, please). Note that *Sie* is the polite form of address to be used with everyone except close friends, though young people and students often don't bother with it. The older generation will certainly be offended if you address them with the familiar *Du*, as will all officials.

Sprechen Sie Englisch ?	Do you speak English ?	*Die Rechnung bitte*	The bill please
Ich spreche kein Deutsch	I don't speak German	*Ist der Tisch frei ?*	Is that table free?
		Die Speisekarte bitte	The menu please
Sprechen sie bitte langsamer	Please speak more slowly	*Fräulein . . . !*	Waitress . . . ! (for attention)
Ich verstehe nicht	I don't understand	*Herr Ober . . . !*	Waiter . . . ! (for attention)
Ich verstehe	I understand		
Wie sagt mann das auf Deutsch ?	How do you say that in German ?	*Haben Sie etwas billigeres ?*	Have you got something cheaper ?
Können Sie mir sagen wo . . . ist ?	Can you tell me where . . . is ?	*Haben Sie Zimmer frei ?*	Are there rooms available ?
Wieviel kostet das ?	How much does that cost ?	*Wo sind die Toiletten bitte ?*	Where are the toilets ?
Wann fährt der nächste Zug ?	When does the next train leave ?	*Ich hätte gern dieses*	I'd like that one
Um wieviel Uhr ?	At what time ?	*Ich hätte gern ein Zimmer für zwei*	I'd like a room for two
Wieviel Uhr ist es ?	What time is it ?	*Ich hätte gern ein Einzelzimmer*	I'd like a single room
Sind die Plätze noch frei ?	Are these seats taken ?	*Hat es Dusche, Bad, Toilette . . . ?*	Does it have a shower, bath, toilet . . . ?

SOME SIGNS

Damen/Frauen	Women's toilets	*Autobahn*	Motorway
Herren/Männer	Men's toilets	*Geschwindigkeitsbegrenzung*	Speed limit
Eingang	Entrance		
Ausgang	Exit	*Baustelle*	Building works
Ankunft	Arrival	*Ampel*	Traffic light
Abfahrt	Departure	*Krankenhaus*	Hospital
Ausstellung	Exhibition	*Polizei*	Police
Auffahrt	Motorway entrance	*Nicht rauchen*	No smoking
Ausfahrt	Motorway exit	*Kein Eingang*	No entrance
Umleitung	Diversion	*Verboten*	Prohibited
Vorsicht !	Attention	*Zoll*	Customs
Notausgang	Emergency exit	*Grenzübergang*	Border crossing

NUMBERS

1	*eins*	10	*zehn*	19	*neunzehn*	80	*achtzig*
2	*zwei, zwo*	11	*elf*	20	*zwanzig*	90	*neunzig*
3	*drei*	12	*zwölf*	21	*ein-und-zwanzig*	100	*hundert*
4	*vier*	13	*dreizehn*	22	*zwei-und-zwanzig*	1992	*neunzehn-hundert-zwei-und-neunzig*
5	*fünf*	14	*vierzehn*	30	*dreissig*		
6	*sechs*	15	*fünfzehn*	40	*vierzig*		
7	*sieben*	16	*sechzehn*	50	*fünfzig*		
8	*acht*	17	*siebzehn*	60	*sechzig*		
9	*neun*	18	*achtzehn*	70	*siebzig*		

GLOSSARIES

ART AND ARCHITECTURE

AISLE part of church to the side of the nave.

AMBULATORY passage round the back of the altar, in continuation of the aisles.

APSE vaulted termination of the east (altar) end of a church.

ART DECO geometrical style of art and architecture prevalent in 1930s.

ART NOUVEAU sinuous, highly stylised form of architecture and interior design; in Germany, mostly dates from period 1900–15 and is known as *Jugendstil*.

BALDACHIN canopy over an altar or tomb.

BAROQUE expansive, exuberant architectural style of the seventeenth and early eighteenth centuries, characterised by ornate decoration, complex spatial arrangements and grand vistas. The term is also applied to the sumptuous style of painting of the same period.

BASILICA church in which nave is higher than the aisles.

BAUHAUS plain, functional style of architecture and design, originating in early twentieth-century Germany.

BIEDERMEIERSTIL simple, bourgeois style of painting and decoration practised throughout first half of the nineteenth century.

CAPITAL top of a column, usually sculpted.

CHANCEL part of the church in which altar is placed; normally at east end, though some German churches have one at the west end as well.

CHOIR part of church in which service is sung, usually beside the altar.

CRYPT underground part of a church.

EXPRESSIONISM emotional style of painting, concentrating on line and colour, extensively practised in early twentieth-century Germany; term is also used for related architecture of the same period.

FRESCO mural painting applied to wet plaster, so that colours immediately soak into the wall.

GOTHIC architectural style with an emphasis on verticality, characterised by pointed arch, ribbed vault and flying buttress; introduced to Germany around 1235, surviving in an increasingly decorative form until well into the sixteenth century. The term is also used for paintings of this period.

GRISAILLE painting executed entirely in monochrome.

HALF-TIMBERED, TIMBER-FRAMED style of building in which the walls have a framework of timber interspersed with either bricks or plaster.

HALL CHURCH (*Hallenkirche*) church design much favoured in Germany, in which all vaults are of approximately equal height.

LAVABO well-house in a cloister.

MANNERISM deliberately mannered style of late Renaissance art and architecture.

MODELLO small version of a large picture, usually painted for the patron's approval.

NAVE main body of a church, generally forming the western part.

NEOCLASSICAL late eighteenth- and early nineteenth-century style of art and architecture returning to Classical models as a reaction against Baroque and Rococo excesses.

ORIEL projecting bay window.

POLYPTYCH carved or painted altarpiece on several joined panels.

PREDELLA lowest part of an altarpiece, with scenes much smaller than in main sections.

RENAISSANCE Italian-originated movement in art and architecture, inspired by the rediscovery of Classical ideals.

RETABLE altarpiece.

ROCOCO highly florid, light and graceful eighteenth-century style of architecture, painting and interior design, forming the last phase of Baroque.

ROMANESQUE solid architectural style of late tenth to mid-thirteenth centuries, characterised by round-headed arches and a penchant for horizontality and geometrical precision. The term is also used for paintings of this period.

ROMANTICISM late eighteenth- and early nineteenth-century movement, particularly strong in Germany, rooted in adulation of the natural world and rediscovery of the achievements of the Middle Ages.

ROOD SCREEN screen dividing nave from chancel (thus separating laity and clergy), originally bearing a rood (crucifix).

SOFT STYLE (*Weicher Stil*) delicate style of painting and sculpture pioneered in fourteenth-century Bohemia, which dominated German art to the mid-fifteenth century.

STUCCO plaster used for decorative effects.

TABERNACLE a free-standing canopy or ornamental recess designed to contain the Holy Sacrament.

TRANSEPT arm of a cross-shaped church, placed at ninety degrees to nave and chancel.

TRANSITIONAL architectural style between Romanesque and Gothic in which the basic shapes of the older style were modified by the use of such new forms as the pointed arch and ribbed vault.

TRIPTYCH carved or painted altarpiece on three panels.

TROMPE L'OEIL painting designed to fool the viewer into believing it is three-dimensional.

TYMPANUM sculptured panel above a doorway.

WESER RENAISSANCE archaic, highly elaborate style of secular Renaissance architecture cultivated in and around the Weser valley in Hessen, Lower Saxony and Westphalia.

WESTWORK (*Westwerk*) grandiose frontage found on many German medieval churches, traditionally reserved for the use of the Emperor and his retinue.

GERMAN TERMS

ABTEI abbey.

ALTSTADT old part of a city.

AUSKUNFT information.

BAD spa (before the name of a town), bath.

BAHNHOF station.

BAU building.

BERG mountain, hill.

BERGBAHN funicular.

BIBLIOTHEK library.

BRÜCKE bridge.

BRUNNEN fountain, well.

BUNDESKANZLER Federal Chancellor (Prime Minister).

BUNDESRAT Upper House of German Parliament.

BUNDESTAG Lower House of German Parliament.

BURG castle, fortress.

BURGERMEISTER Mayor.

CAROLINGIAN dynasty founded by Charles Martel in the early eighth century which ruled Germany until last quarter of ninth century. The term is particularly associated with the reign of Charlemagne (768–814).

DENKMAL memorial.

DIET Parliament of Holy Roman Empire.

DOM cathedral.

DONAU River Danube.

DORF village.

EASTERN TERRITORIES lands to the east of the Oder-Neisse line, occupied by German-speaking peoples since the Middle Ages, but forcibly evacuated, and allocated to Poland and the Soviet Union after the Second World War.

EINBAHNSTRASSE one-way street.

ELECTOR (*Kurfürst*) sacred or secular prince with a vote in the elections to choose the Holy Roman Emperor. There were seven for most of the medieval period, with three more added later.

EVANGELISCHE KIRCHE federation of Protestant churches, both Lutheran and Reformed.

FACHWERKHAUS half-timbered house.

FASCHING name given to Carnival, especially in Bavaria.

FASTNET name given to Carnival, especially in Baden-Württemberg.

FEIERTAG holiday.

FEST festival.

FESTUNG fortress.

FLUGHAFEN airport.

FLUSS river.

FRANCONIA (*Franken*) historical province of central Germany, stretching as far west as Mainz; name later became associated only with the eastern portion of this territory, most of which is now incorporated in Bavaria.

FREE IMPERIAL CITY (*Freiereichstadt*) independent city state within the Holy Roman Empire.

FREMDENZIMMER room for short-term let.

FÜRST prince.

FUSSGÄNGERZONE pedestrian area.

GASSE alley.

GASTARBEITER ("guest worker") anyone who comes to Germany to do menial work.

GASTHAUS, GASTHOF guest house, inn.

GEMÄLDE painting.

GRAF count.

GRÜNEN, DIE ("The Greens") political party formed from environmental and anti-nuclear groups.

HABSBURG the most powerful family in medieval Germany, operating from a power base in Austria. They held the office of Holy Roman Emperor 1452–1806, and by marriage, war and diplomacy acquired territories all over Europe.

HAFEN harbour, port.

HANSEATIC LEAGUE medieval trading alliance of Baltic and Rhineland cities, numbering about 100 at its fifteenth-century peak. Slowly died out in the seventeenth century with competition from Baltic nation-states and rise of Brandenburg-Prussia.

HAUPTBAHNHOF main railway station in a city.

HAUPTBURG central, residential part of a castle.

HAUPTSTRASSE main street.

HEIDE heath.

HEIMAT homeland; often given a mystical significance and used emotively in connection with Germans displaced from the Eastern Territories.

HERZOG duke.

HÖHLE cave.

HOF court, courtyard, mansion.

HOHENSTAUFEN Swabian dynasty who held office of Holy Roman Emperor 1138–1254.

HOHENZOLLERN dynasty of Swabian origin, who became Margrave-Electors of Brandenburg in 1415, and slowly built up their territorial base. In nineteenth century they ousted the Habsburgs from pre-eminent place in German affairs, forging the Second Reich in 1871 and serving as its Emperors until 1918.

HOLY ROMAN EMPIRE title used to describe the First German Reich, established in 800. Despite its weak structure, it survived until 1806, when the ruling Habsburgs, in response to the Napoleonic threat, began building up a more solid empire from their Austrian base.

INSEL island.

JAGDSCHLOSS hunting lodge.

JUGENDHERBERGE youth hostel.

JUGENDSTIL German version of Art Nouveau.

JUNKER Prussian landowning class.

KAISER emperor.

KAMMER room, chamber.

KAPELLE chapel.

KARNEVAL term used for Carnival, especially in Rhineland.

KAUFHAUS department store.

KINO cinema

KIRCHE church.

KLOSTER monastery, convent.

KÖNIG king.

KREUZGANG cloister.

KUNST art.

KURHAUS assembly rooms (in a spa).

KURORT health resort.

LAND (pl. **LÄNDER**) name given to the constituent states of the Federal Republic; first introduced in Weimar Republic.

LANDGRAVE (*Landgraf*) count in charge of a large province.

MARGRAVE (*Markgraf*) count in charge of a *Mark* ("March"; later "Margraviate"), a frontier district established at the time of Charlemagne.

MARKT market, market square.

MEER sea.

MEROVINGIAN Frankish dynasty established by Clovis in 481; ruled until the early eighth century.

MIKWE Jewish ritual bath.

MÜNSTER minster, large church.

NATURPARK area of protected countyside.

NEUES FORUM umbrella group for political opposition organisations within the former GDR

ODER-NEISSE LINE eastern limit of German territory set by victorious Allies in 1945.

OSTPOLITIK West German policy of detente towards the GDR.

OTTONIAN epoch of Otto I and his two eponymous successors. Term is used in connection with the early Romanesque art forms pioneered in this and the subsequent Salian epoch (midtenth to mid-eleventh century).

PALAS, PALAST residential part of a castle.

PALATINATE (*Pfalz*) territory ruled by the Count Palatine, a high-ranking imperial official. The present Land is only the western part of the historical province, whose original centre is now part of Baden-Württemberg.

PFARRKIRCHE parish church.

PLATZ square.

PRINZ prince; since 1918, used in a less grandiose way as a courtesy title for aristocrats in place of the plethora of now-defunct titles.

PROPSTEIKIRCHE former monastic church transferred to parish use.

PRUSSIA originally, an Eastern Baltic territory (now divided between Poland and the Soviet Union). It was acquired in 1525 by the Hohenzollerns who merged it with their own possessions to form Brandenburg-Prussia (later shortened to Prussia); this took the lead in forging the unity of Germany, and was thereafter its overwhelmingly dominant province. The name was abolished after World War II because of its monarchical and militaristic connotations.

RASTPLATZ picnic area.

RATHAUS town hall.

RATSKELLER cellars below the Rathaus, invariably used as a restaurant serving *burgerlich* cuisine.

REICH empire.

REISEBÜRO travel agency.

RESIDENZ palace.

RITTER knight.

ROMANTISCHE STRASSE ("Romantic Road") scenic road in Bavaria and Baden-Württemberg, running between Würzburg and Füssen.

RUNDGANG way round.

SAAL hall.

SALIAN dynasty of Holy Roman Emperors 1024–1125.

SAMMLUNG collection.

S-BAHN commuter railway network operating in and around conurbations.

SCHATZKAMMER treasury.

SCHICKIE or "Schickie-Mickie": yuppie.

SCHLOSS castle, palace (equivalent of French *château*).

SEE lake.

SEILBAHN cable car.

SESSELBAHN chairlift.

STADT town, city.

STAMMTISCH table in a pub or restaurant reserved for regular customers.

STASI (Staatssicherheitsdienst) former "State Security Service" or secret police of the GDR.

STAUFIAN pertaining to the epoch of the Hohenstaufen.

STIFT collegiate church.

STIFTUNG foundation.

STRAND beach.

STRASSENBAHN tram.

SWABIA (*Schwaben*) name used for the south-western part of Germany from the eleventh century onwards; after the ruling Hohenstaufen dynasty died out, became politically fragmented.

TAL valley.

TALSPERRE reservoir, artificial lake.

TANKSTELLE petrol station.

TOR gate, gateway.

TRABI conversational shorthand for the now-famous *Trabant*, East Germany's two-cylinder, two-stroke car.

TURM tower.

U-BAHN network of underground trains or trams.

VERKEHRSAMT, **VERKEHRSVEREIN** tourist office.

VIERTEL quarter, district.

VOLK people, folk; given mystical associations by Hitler.

VORBURG outer, defensive part of a castle.

WALD forest.

WALDSTERBEN ("dying forest syndrome" term used to describe the environmental pollution which has decimated Germany's forests.

WALLFAHRT pilgrimage.

WASSERBURG castle surrounded by a moat.

WECHSEL exchange.

WEIMAR REPUBLIC parliamentary democracy established in 1918 which collapsed with Hitler's assumption of power in 1933.

WELF dynastic rivals of Hohenstaufens in Germany and Italy. Descendants became Electors of Hannover, and subsequently Kings of Great Britain.

WENDE, literally "turning point" – the term used to describe the events of November 1989 and after.

WETTIN dynasty chiefly responsible for pushing Germany's frontiers eastwards from the tenth century, becoming Electors of Saxony in 1423 and ruling the province and the Thuringian principalities until 1918. The Saxe-Coburg line provided monarchs for several countries; renamed as Windsor, it is the current Brittish royal family.

WIES field, meadow.

WILHELMINE pertaining to the epoch of the Second Reich (1871–1918).

WITTELSBACH dynasty which ruled Bavaria from 1180 to 1918; a branch held the Palatinate Electorate, while the family often held several bishoprics, notably the Archbishop-Electorate of Cologne.

ZEUGHAUS arsenal.

ZIMMER room.

ACRONYMS

BRD (*Bundesrepublik Deutschlands*) official name of West German state (1949–90) and of the unified Germany since 1990.

CDU (*Christlich Demokratische Union*) ruling Christian Democratic (Conservative) Party.

CSU (*Christlich Soziale Union*) Bavarian-only counterpart of CDU, generally more right-wing in outlook.

DB (*Deutsche Bundesbahn*) West German railway company.

DDR (*Deutsche Demokratische Republik*) the Communist East German state, 1949–90.

DR (*Deutsche Reichsbahn*) East German railway company.

GDR (*German Democratic Republic*) English version of DDR.

FDP (*Freie Demokratische Partei*) Free Democratic (Liberal) Party.

NSDAP (*National Sozialistische Deutsche Arbeiterpartei*, "National Socialist German Workers' Party") official name for the Nazis, totalitarian rulers of Germany in the Third Reich 1933–45.

SED (*Sozialistische Einheitspartei Deutschlands*) Socialist Unity Party of Germany, the permanent governing party of the GDR, formed in 1946 as a union of the SPD and Communists in the Russian zone of occupation.

SPD (*Sozialdemokratische Partei Deutschlands*) Social Democratic (Labour) Party.